THE GOOD, THE BAD
—AND THE AWFUL

This is the complete, up-to-date insider's guide to TV movies. It tells you what not to miss—and what to miss. It describes films so bad they're good, and so good they're bad. It identifies the all-time Greats and Classics—and the unforgettable Duds.

They're all listed here in alphabetical order, complete with all the essential information: director, stars, plot, date, color or black and white, original length (so you'll know how much they've been cut), key songs (for musicals)—and a concise capsule summary and review of each film.

THE EDITOR: At the ripe old age of 18, Leonard Maltin has gained a reputation as an authority on the cinema. Editor of *Film Fan Monthly*, he has written for *Esquire, Books and Films in Review*, and has been written about in *Saturday Review* and *Variety*. He is currently writing a book about famous comedy teams, also to be published by The New American Library.

Other SIGNET Books
of Special Interest

☐ **TV '70 by Dave Kaufman.** Here's the big TV line-up for the 1970 season. (#N4004—$1.00)

☐ **DRAT! W. C. Fields' Picture Book. Edited by Richard J. Anobile—Introduction by Ed McMahon.** DRAT is the encapsulate view, and what a view! of the greatest comedian of the century. Here, in happy juxtaposition of photos and quotes is the irreverent irrelevancy of W. C. Fields, the man and the actor. (#Q3933—95¢)

☐ **W. C. FIELDS: His Follies and Fortunes, by Robert Lewis Taylor.** A Pulitzer Prize-winning author chronicles the life of one of our century's funniest men, a man whose private adventures were no less hilarious than his masterful performances. Illustrated with photographs. (#Q3064—95¢)

☐ **BOGIE, by Joe Hyams.** The biography of Humphrey Bogart, a great star in his lifetime and now a cult hero for a whole generation who never saw his films while he was alive, written by a close friend of the star, with the authorization and cooperation of Bogart's widow. Introduction by Lauren Bacall. Thirty-two pages of photographs. (#T3071—75¢)

THE NEW AMERICAN LIBRARY, INC., P.O. Box 2310, Grand Central Station, New York, New York 10017

Please send me the SIGNET BOOKS I have checked above. I am enclosing $_____ (check or money order—no currency or C.O.D.'s). Please include the list price plus 10¢ a copy to cover mailing costs. (New York City residents add 6% Sales Tax. Other New York State residents add 3% plus any local sales or use taxes.)

Name_____

Address_____

City_____ State_____ Zip Code_____
Allow at least 3 weeks for delivery

TV MOVIES

Edited by Leonard Maltin

**Associate Editors:
James Robert Parish and Florence Solomon**

A SIGNET BOOK
Published by The New American Library

Copyright © 1969 by Leonard Maltin

All rights reserved

PHOTOGRAPH CREDITS AND ACKNOWLEDGEMENTS: *Film Fan Monthly*, Al Marill, Doug McClelland, Peter Miglierini, James Robert Parish, Jeff Satkin, Jerry Vermilye, John Willis; Walter Reade-Sterling, Paramount Pictures, Warner Brothers-Seven Arts, Embassy Pictures, Universal Pictures, Metro-Goldwyn-Mayer, American-International Pictures, Filmersa Productions, Columbia Pictures, RKO Radio Pictures, Screen Gems, 20th Century-Fox.

SIGNET TRADEMARK REG. U.S. PAT. OFF. AND FOREIGN COUNTRIES
REGISTERED TRADEMARK—MARCA REGISTRADA
HECHO EN CHICAGO, U.S.A.

SIGNET BOOKS are published by
The New American Library, Inc.,
1301 Avenue of the Americas, New York, New York 10019

FIRST PRINTING, SEPTEMBER, 1969

PRINTED IN THE UNITED STATES OF AMERICA

PREFACE

There are some fourteen thousand movies currently available for television, enough to keep any film buff glued to the set for weeks on end. For this book we have selected approximately eight thousand films that are most likely to turn up in your TV listings every day. The films we have omitted include several hundred "B" Westerns starring everyone from Whip Wilson to Buster Crabbe, many lesser foreign films, scores of low-grade cheapies ground out by Hollywood, and many early talkies which are seldom shown these days.

For each of the eight thousand films we have supplied a concise description and star-rating to help you decide whether or not the film is worth watching. Admittedly, movies, like everything else in this world, are a matter of personal taste, and a film that appeals to Mr. X might bore Mr. Y. (There are, however, some diehard film buffs who will watch *anything*.) Therefore, in addition to our subjective ratings, we have provided vital facts about each film—facts you might want to know regardless of whether the movie is great or dreadful: the director, the year of release, the country of production, the cast, whether it is in color or black and white, and the original running time. We have set up a standard one-to-four-star rating system with one difference: if the film is a total disaster, we have simply labeled it a BOMB.

In our thirty-two pages of photos we have tried to give a good cross-section of films and stars most familiar to TV-moviegoers, and we apologize in advance if we didn't include one of your favorites.

We have not rated individual entries in the series films, from **Andy Hardy** to **The Whistler.** Instead, we have written summaries of each series, giving some background and noting some of the more interesting episodes.

Assembling a book like this, one encounters many problems and questions along the way. Many people have been generous with their time and talent, and I would like to thank

Gordon Berkow, John Cocchi, Ed Connor (whose articles in *Films in Review* and *Screen Facts* were invaluable), Denis Gifford, Robert Seipp, Drew Simels, and Jerry Vermilye. Special thanks must go to my father, Aaron I. Maltin, for living the book with me from start to finish, and most of all my editor, Patrick O'Connor, who had faith in me in the first place.

LEONARD MALTIN

KEY
TO THIS BOOK

Film titles are given in boldface, followed by the year of release. Country of origin, unless it is the United States, is listed with the release date. Running times (in minutes) are also in boldface; these are the original theatrical times except in certain cases (such as the silent film classics) where films have been especially edited for television. "C" before a running time denotes a color film. Star-ratings are followed by "D:" and the name of the film's director.

Aaron Slick From Punkin Crick (1952) C-95m. ** D: Claude Binyon. Alan Young, Dinah Shore, Adele Jergens, Veda Ann Borg. Innocuous musical satire of city slicker trying to fleece innocent widow Shore. Unmemorable score.

Abandon Ship! (1957) 100m. *** D: Richard Sale. Tyrone Power, Mai Zetterling, Lloyd Nolan, Stephen Boyd, Moira Lister. Tyrone is naval officer suddenly in command of small boat holding survivors from sunken ship. Tense study of people fighting to stay alive, exposed to savage seas and each other.

Abandoned (1949) 79m. *½ D: Joe Newman. Gale Storm, Dennis O'Keefe, Raymond Burr, Marjorie Rambeau, Jeff Chandler. Lukewarm tale of newspaperman O'Keefe helping Storm find her sister's illegitimate baby, and becoming involved with adoption racket.

Abbott and Costello Go to Mars (1953) 77m. ** D: Charles Lamont. Robert Paige, Mari Blanchard, Martha Hyer, Horace McMahon, Jack Tebler, Hal Forrest, Harold Goodwin. Unimaginative vehicle has Bud and Lou sailing through space with escaped gangster, landing on most earthlike planet.

Abbott and Costello In Hollywood (1945) 83m. ** D: S. Sylvan Simon. Frances Rafferty, Robert Stanton, Jean Porter, Warner Anderson. Uneven comedy with A&C as barber and porter in cinemaland.

Abbott and Costello In the Foreign Legion (1950) 80m. ** D: Charles Lamont. Patricia Medina, Walter Slezak, Douglass Dumbrille. Unexceptional A&C vehicle pitting them against nasty sergeant Slezak. Best scene involves mirages in the desert.

Abbott and Costello in the Navy SEE: **In the Navy**

Abbott and Costello Meet Captain Kidd (1952) C-70m. ** D: Charles Lamont. Charles Laughton, Hillary Brooke, Fran Warren, Bill Shirley, Leif Erickson. OK A&C, but poor Charles Laughton!

Abbott and Costello Meet Dr. Jekyll and Mr. Hyde (1953) 77m. ** D: Charles Lamont. Boris Karloff, Craig Stevens, Reginald Denny, Helen Westcott, John Dierkes. Disappointing attempt to mix A&C with Jekyll and Hyde (Karloff), with too few funny scenes. Special effects are film's main assets.

Abbott and Costello Meet Frankenstein (1948) 92m. *** D: Charles Barton. Lon Chaney, Bela Lugosi, Glenn Strange, Lenore Aubert, Jane Randolph, Frank Ferguson. And Dracula and the Wolfman too, in this superb blend of comedy and horror, never duplicated by A&C or anyone else. Lugosi is in especially fine form as the Count.

Abbott and Costello Meet the Invisible Man (1951) 82m. *** D: Charles Lamont. Nancy Guild, Arthur Franz, Adele Jergens, Sheldon Leonard. One of the team's best vehicles, with Bud and Lou as detectives helping boxer (Franz) who's been framed to trap mobster Leonard, with aid of invisibility formula. Special effects are top-notch.

Abbott and Costello Meet the Keystone Kops (1955) 79m. ** D: Charles Lamont. Fred Clark, Lynn Bari, Mack Sennett, Maxie Rosenbloom, Frank Wilcox, Henry Kulky, Sam Flint. Low-budget comedy could have been better. Clark is fine as conniving producer in this synthetic period-piece of silent-movie days.

Abbott and Costello Meet the Killer (1949) 94m. **½ D: Charles Barton. Boris Karloff, Alan Mowbray, Roland Winters. Pretty good blend of comedy and whodunit with bodies hanging in closets, phony mystic Karloff trying to do away with Costello, etc.

Abbott a ' Costello Meet the Mummy (1955) 79m. **½ D: Charles Lamont. Marie Windsor, Michael Ansara, Dan Seymour, Kurt Katch, Richard Deacon. Amusing adventure with A&C getting mixed up with villainess Windsor, a valuable tomb, and a mummy who's still alive.

Abductors, The (1957) 80m. *½ D: Andrew McLaglen. Victor McLaglen, George Macready, Fay Spain, Gavin Muir. Boring account of men attempting to rob Lincoln's grave.

Abe Lincoln In Illinois (1940) 110m. **** D: John Cromwell. Raymond Massey, Gene Lockhart, Ruth Gordon, Mary Howard, Dorothy Tree. Firstrate Americana; sincere story of Lincoln's life and career is beautifully acted by Massey, with top support by Gordon as Mary Todd.

Abie's Irish Rose (1946) 96m. Bomb D: A. Edward Sutherland. Joanne Dru, Richard Norris, Michael Chekov, Eric Blore, Art Baker. Outdated when written in 1920's, even worse now. Irish girl marries Jewish boy, families clash.

Abilene Town (1946) 89m. *** D: Edwin L. Marin. Randolph Scott, Ann Dvorak, Edgar Buchanan, Rhonda Fleming, Lloyd Bridges. Aboveaverage Scott vehicle as patient sheriff tries to straighten out homesteader conflict out West after the Civil War.

Abominable Snowman (1957) 85m. **½ D: Val Guest. Forrest Tucker, Peter Cushing, Richard Wattis, Maureen Connell. Low-budget but exciting tale of Himalayan expedition searching for title monster. Good cast lends credibility.

About Face (1952) C-94m. *½ D: Roy Del Ruth. Gordon MacRae, Eddie Bracken, Dick Wesson, Phyllis Kirk, Joel Grey. Dull comedy-musical remake of BROTHER RAT about three friends in military academy, one of them secretly married.

About Mrs. Leslie (1954) 104m. *** D: Daniel Mann. Shirley Booth, Robert Ryan, Marjie Millar, Alex Nicol. Flashbacks reveal romance between rooming-house owner (Booth) and business magnate (Ryan). Finely acted soaper; forgivable illogical coupling of stars.

Above and Beyond (1952) 122m. *** D: Melvin Frank, Norman Panama. Robert Taylor, Eleanor Parker, James Whitmore, Jim Backus. Meaningful account of U.S. pilot who flew over Hiroshima with first atomic bomb; film focuses on his training and its effect on his personal life.

Above Suspicion (1943) 90m. *** D: Richard Thorpe. Joan Crawford, Fred MacMurray, Conrad Veidt, Basil Rathbone, Reginald Owen, Richard Ainley. Crawford and MacMurray asked to do spy mission during European honeymoon in midst of WW2. Pure escapism, with Joan more than a match for the Nazis.

Above Us the Waves (1956-British) 92m. *** D: Ralph Thomas. John Mills, John Gregson, Donald Sinden, James Robertson Justice. Utilizing documentary style, film relates account of unrelenting British attempt to destroy Nazi warship.

Abraham Lincoln (1930) 97m. **½ D: D. W. Griffith. Walter Huston, Una Merkel, Edgar Dearing, Russell Simpson, Cameron Prud'homme, Oscar Apfel, Henry B. Walthall. Huston is excellent in this sincere but static biography of Lincoln; cannot match Griffith's silent masterpieces.

Abroad With Two Yanks (1944) 80m. **½ D: Allan Dwan. William Bendix, Helen Walker, Dennis O'Keefe, John Loder, John Abbott. Bendix and O'Keefe are marines on the loose in Australia, both chasing Walker; breezy comedy.

Accent On Youth (1935) 77m. *** D: Wesley Ruggles. Sylvia Sidney, Herbert Marshall, Phillip Reed, Holmes Herbert, Catherine Doucet. Entertaining film of Samson Raphaelson play about young girl Sidney in love with older man Marshall. Remade as MR. MUSIC and BUT NOT FOR ME.

Accident (1967-British) C-105m. ***½ D: Joseph Losey. Dirk Bogarde, Stanley Baker, Jacqueline Sassard, Michael York. Pensive study of intellectual set in England, with sideswipes at their human nonclassroom behavior; thoughtfully handled by all.

Accidental Death (1963-British) 57m.

**½ D: Geoffrey Nethercott. John Carson, Jacqueline Ellis, Derrick Sherwin, Richard Vernon. Edgar Wallace suspenser with gimmick of letting the viewer guess the identity of the murderer in question.

Accomplices, The (1959-Italian, dubbed) 93m. *½ D: Gianni Vernuccio. Sandro Luporini, Sandro Fizzotro, Annabella Incontrera, Jeannie. Lurid, minor film of love triangle, with resulting murder; unconvincing and pat.

Accursed, The (1958-British) 78m. *½ D: Michael McCarthy. Donald Wolfit, Robert Bray, Jane Griffiths, Anton Diffring. Tepid whodunit involving the extinction of veterans of British military unit, and survivors' attempt to find killer.

Accused, The (1948) 101m. *** D: William Dieterle. Loretta Young, Robert Cummings, Wendell Corey, Sam Jaffe. Loretta accidentally becomes a murderess in this taut thriller of a woman on the run; good support from Cummings.

Accused of Murder (1956) C-74m. ** D: Joseph Kane. David Brian, Vera Ralston, Sidney Blackmer, Virginia Grey. Bland handling of police detective Brian, entranced with singer Ralston, involved in underworld killing.

Ace in the Hole SEE: Big Carnival, The

Across the Bridge (1957-British) 103m. **½ D: Ken Annakin. Rod Steiger, David Knight, Bernard Lee, Eric Pohlmann. Agreeable study of panicky businessman Steiger on the run from authorities for stealing a fortune; taut performances.

Across the Pacific (1942) 97m. **½ D: John Huston. Humphrey Bogart, Mary Astor, Sydney Greenstreet, Keye Luke, Richard Loo, Monte Blue. Three MALTESE FALCON leads re-teamed for enjoyable WW2 adventure. Bogart trails spies in Panama, has running battle of wits with Greenstreet, all the while romancing enticing Astor.

Across the Wide Missouri (1951) C-78m. **½ D: William Wellman. Clark Gable, Ricardo Montalban, John Hodiak, Adolphe Menjou. On-location filming in Rockies and star cast don't bolster pedestrian Western about pathfinders moving westward in 19th century.

Act of Love (1953) 108m. *** D: Anatole Litvak. Kirk Douglas, Dany Robin, Barbara Laage, Robert Strauss. Sharply portrayed story of U.S. soldier (Douglas) romancing girl (Robin) in WW2 Paris, eventually deserting her, despite good intentions.

Act of Murder, An (1948) 91m. *** D: Michael Gordon. Fredric March, Florence Eldridge, Edmond O'Brien, Geraldine Brooks. March is excellent as strict judge who must judge himself for saving his wife the anguish of illness by killing her; absorbing drama.

Act of Violence (1948) 82m. *** D: Fred Zinnemann. Van Heflin, Robert Ryan, Janet Leigh, Mary Astor. Stark melodrama of disturbed man (Ryan) trying to kill old army nemesis (Heflin). Fine vignette by Astor as sympathetic call-girl.

Act One (1963) 110m. **½ D: Dore Schary. George Hamilton, Jason Robards, George Segal, Eli Wallach, Sam Levene, Ruth Ford, Jack Klugman. Interesting for oddball cast, this fabrication of writer Moss Hart's autobiography lacks finesse or any sense of reality.

Action in Arabia (1944) 72m. **½ D: Leonide Moguy. George Sanders, Virginia Bruce, Gene Lockhart, Robert Armstrong, Michael Ansara. OK low-budgeter, with reporter Sanders uncovering Nazi plot to gain Arab support in WW2.

Action in the North Atlantic (1943) 127m. *** D: Lloyd Bacon. Humphrey Bogart, Raymond Massey, Alan Hale, Julie Bishop, Ruth Gordon, Sam Levene, Dane Clark. Rousing tribute to WW2 merchant marines with officers Bogart and Massey, seamen Hale and Levene, usual hothead Clark, and Gordon as Massey's wife.

Action of the Tiger (1957) C-94m. **½ D: Terence Young. Van Johnson, Martine Carol, Herbert Lom, Sean Connery, Helen Goss. Adequate actioner suffers from contra-casting of Johnson as virile American who rescues pro-Western refugees from Albania.

Actors and Sin (1952) 82m. **½ D: Ben Hecht. Edward G. Robinson, Marsha Hunt, Dan O'Herlihy, Eddie Albert, John Crawford. Interesting two-part film: "Actor's Blood," has-been actor is overconcerned about daughter's stage career; "Woman of Sin," literary agent's hottest client is a child of 9.

Actress, The (1953) 91m. **½ D: George Cukor. Spencer Tracy, Jean Simmons, Teresa Wright, Anthony Perkins, Mary Wickes. Flavorful account based on Ruth Gordon's experiences as a teen-ager in early 20th-century Massachusetts, determined to become an acting star; Tracy is the irascible father.

Ada (1961) C-109m. *** D: Daniel Mann. Susan Hayward, Dean Martin, Wilfrid Hyde-White, Martin Balsam. Rags-to-riches soaper of poor gal (Hayward) maneuvering easygoing Martin to governor's mansion, using hellbent stamina to overcome political corruption. Hayward vs. Hyde-White in state senate is film's highlight.

Adam and Evalyn (1949-British) 92m. **½ D: Harold French. Jean Simmons, Stewart Granger, Wilfrid Hyde-White, Raymond Young. Satisfactory account of gambler Granger and his love match with Simmons.

Adam Had Four Sons (1941) 81m. *** D: Gregory Ratoff. Ingrid Bergman, Warner Baxter, Susan Hayward, Fay Wray, Richard Denning. Good cast in story of governess Bergman watching over Baxter's family when his wife dies. Hayward is a bit extravagant in this one.

Adam's Rib (1949) 101m. **** D: George Cukor. Spencer Tracy, Katharine Hepburn, Judy Holliday, Tom Ewell, Jean Hagen, Polly Moran, David Wayne. Top comedy of husband-wife lawyers on opposing sides of same case. Star duet ably supported by newcomers Holliday, Ewell, Hagen, Wayne.

Address Unknown (1944) 72m. *** D: William Cameron Menzies. Paul Lukas, Peter Van Eyck, Mady Christians, Emory Parnell. Allies vs. Nazis boiled down to focus on American-German business partners on opposite sides of fence.

Admirable Crichton, The (1957-British) C-94m. ** D: Lewis Gilbert. Kenneth More, Diane Cilento, Cecil Parker, Sally Ann Howes, Martita Hunt. Oft-filmed James Barrie classic wears thin; impeccable servant proves to be most resourceful when he and his aristocratic employers are shipwrecked on an island. Retitled: PARADISE LAGOON.

Admiral Was a Lady, The (1950) 87m. ** D: Sidney Salkow. Edmond O'Brien, Wanda Hendrix, Rudy Vallee, Steve Brodie. Ex-Wave Hendrix encounters quartet of fun-loving, work-hating men, all interested in courting her; weak.

Adorable Creatures (1956-French, dubbed) 108m. ** D: Christian-Jaque. Daniel Gelin, Martine Carol, Edwige Feuillère, Danielle Darrieux, Marilyn Buferd, Louis Seigner. Saucy, inconsequential study of life and love in Gallic country, focusing on bedroom romances.

Adorable Julia (1964-French, dubbed) 94m. *** D: Alfred Weidenmann. Lilli Palmer, Charles Boyer, Jean Sorel, Thomas Fritsch. Charming rendering of Somerset Maugham's novel THEATRE. Middle-aged actress dabbles in romances but allows nothing to interfere with career. Palmer and Boyer are admirable as wife-husband acting team.

Advance to the Rear (1964) 97m. **½ D: George Marshall. Glenn Ford, Stella Stevens, Melvyn Douglas, Joan Blondell, Jim Backus, Andrew Prine. During Civil War, Northern soldier rejects are sent to Western territory. Stevens as Reb spy and Blondell as saucy worldly woman add only spice to predictable happenings.

Adventure (1945) 125m. ** D: Victor Fleming. Clark Gable, Greer Garson, Joan Blondell, Thomas Mitchell, Tom Tully, John Qualen, Richard Haydn. Gable's back, Garson's got him; they both sink in cumbersome comedy of seagoing roustabout and meek librarian. Not even breezy Blondell can save it.

Adventure in Baltimore (1949) 89m. ** D: Richard Wallace. Shirley Temple, John Agar, Robert Young, Josephine Hutchinson. Mild romancer of 1900's with Temple full of new-fangled notions, yet seeking old-fashioned romance.

Adventure in Diamonds (1940) 76m. ** D: George Fitzmaurice. George Brent, Isa Miranda, John Loder, Nigel Bruce. Tepid formula programmer dealing with jewel robberies in Africa.

Adventure in Manhattan (1936) 73m. **½ D: Edward Ludwig. Jean Arthur, Joel McCrea, Reginald Owen, Thomas Mitchell, Herman Bing. Bizarre blend of comedy and melodrama with the stars foiling planned bank robbery. Doesn't always work, but interesting.

Adventure in Washington (1941) 84m. ** D: Alfred E. Green. Herbert Marshall, Virginia Bruce, Gene Reynolds, Samuel S. Hinds, Ralph Morgan. Misleading title for tame account of delinquent youth reformed by Senator Marshall.

Adventure Island (1947) C-66m. ** D: Peter Stewart. Rory Calhoun, Rhonda Fleming, Paul Kelly, John Abbott. Weak remake of EBB TIDE with innocents marooned on island with self-made ruler, who is a maniac. Colorful scenery can't save this.

Adventurers, The SEE: Fortune in Diamonds.

Adventures at Rugby SEE: Tom Brown's School Days.

Adventures of Captain Fabian (1951) 100m. *½ D: William Marshall. Errol Flynn, Micheline Prelle, Agnes Moorehead, Vincent Price. Soggy sea yarn has Flynn involved with gal accused of murder; lackluster costumer.

Adventures of Casanova (1948) 83m. ** D: Roberto Galvaldon. Arturo de Cordova, Lucille Bremer, Turhan Bey, John Sutton. Very ordinary swashbuckler of Casanova de Cordova leading the oppressed people of Sicily against tyrannical rule; this one cries for color.

Adventures of Don Juan (1948) C-110m. *** D: Vincent Sherman. Errol Flynn, Viveca Lindfors, Robert Douglas, Alan Hale, Ann Rutherford, Raymond Burr. Handsome tongue-in-cheek swashbuckler has Errol stringing along countless maidens and even enticing the Queen (Lindfors).

Adventures of Gallant Bess (1948) C-73m. ** D: Lew Landers. Cameron Mitchell, Audrey Long, Fuzzy Knight, James Millican. Mitchell is torn between his girl and his horse in this colorful but routine equestrian drama.

Adventures of Hajji Baba, The (1954) 94m. **½ D: Don Weis. John Derek, Elaine Stewart, Thomas Gomez, Amanda Blake. Derek gives spark to title role, in OK desert tale of his romancing sheik's daughter, who's out to marry heir of rival kingdom.

Adventures of Huckleberry Finn, The (1939) 90m. *** D: Richard Thorpe. Mickey Rooney, Walter Connolly, William Frawley, Rex Ingram, Lynne Carver. Subdued Rooney fine, Ingram excellent as Huck and Jim in classic Mark Twain tale of early 19th-century America; Connolly and Frawley are amusing as riverboat con-artists.

Adventures of Huckleberry Finn, The (1960) C-107m. *** D: Michael Curtiz. Tony Randall, Eddie Hodges, Archie Moore, Patty McCormack, Neville Brand. Good version of Twain's story with an appealing Hodges (Huck) and excellent Archie Moore (Jim). Assorted characters played by veterans Buster Keaton, Andy Devine, Judy Canova, John Carradine, Mickey Shaughnessy, and Sterling Holloway.

Adventures of Marco Polo, The (1938) 100m. **½ D: Archie Mayo. Gary Cooper, Sigrid Gurie, Basil Rathbone, George Barbier, Binnie Barnes, Ernest Truex, Alan Hale. Lighthearted approach to famed explorer's life doesn't always work, but Cooper is pleasant and Rathbone's a good villain; sumptuous production. Look for Lana Turner as one of the handmaidens.

Adventures of Mark Twain, The (1944) 130m. *** D: Irving Rapper. Fredric March, Alexis Smith, Donald Crisp, Alan Hale, C. Aubrey Smith, John Carradine, Percy Kilbride. Life story of great writer-humorist is well-acted and interesting but not in the same league with PASTEUR, ZOLA, etc.

Adventures of Martin Eden, The (1942) 87m. *** D: Sidney Salkow. Glenn Ford, Claire Trevor, Evelyn Keyes, Stuart Erwin, Dickie Moore. Sturdy Jack London tale of seaman aboard terror of a ship, writing account of sailing, fighting for literary recognition.

Adventures of Robin Hood, The (1938) C-105m. ***½ D: Michael Curtiz, William Keighley. Errol Flynn, Olivia de Havilland, Basil Rathbone, Claude Rains, Patric Knowles, Eugene Pallette, Alan Hale. Dashing Flynn in the definitive swashbuckler, winning hand of De Havilland, foiling evil prince Rains, dueling wicked Rathbone. Beautiful color, production, music score (by Erich Wolfgang Korngold).

Adventures of Robinson Crusoe (1954) C-90m. *** D: Luis Buñuel. Dan O'Herlihy, James Fernandez, Felipe De Alba, Chel Lopez. Faithful enactment of Defoe book with fine work by O'Herlihy, well-directed and photographed in color.

Adventures of Sadie, The (1955-British) C-88m. **½ D: Noel Langley. Joan Collins, Kenneth More, Hermione Gingold, Robertson Hare. Obvious sex satire relying on premise of Collins stuck on desert isle with love-hungry men.

Adventures of Scaramouche, The (1964-French, dubbed) C-98m. ** D: Antonio Isamendi. Gerard Barray, Gianna Maria Canale, Michele Girardon, Yvette Lebon. Gallic rendering of Sabatini cloak-and-sword tale has action and wit, but not on grand scale.

Adventures of Sherlock Holmes (1939) 85m. D: Alfred L. Werker. Basil Rathbone, Nigel Bruce, Ida Lupino, Alan Marshal, Terry Kilburn, George Zucco, E. E. Clive, Mary Gordon. SEE: Sherlock Holmes series.

Adventures of Tartu (1943-British) 103m. **½ D: Harold S. Bucquet. Robert Donat, Valerie Hobson, Walter Rilla, Phyllis Morris, Glynis Johns. Improbable but well-acted account of British spy (Donat) trying to help Czech partisans destroy a poison gas factory manned by Nazis. Retitled: TARTU

Adventures of Tom Sawyer, The (1938) C-93m. ***½ D: Norman Taurog. Tommy Kelly, Jackie Moran, Ann Gillis, May Robson, Walter Brennan, Victor Jory. Excellent children's story from Mark Twain is excitingly filmed, with Injun Joe (Jory) sequences the highlights.

Adventuress, The (1947-British) 98m. ***½ D: Frank Launder. Deborah Kerr, Trevor Howard, Raymond Huntley, Norman Shelley. Kerr is a joy in this change-of-pace espionage tale of young Irish girl who unwittingly aids the Nazis during WW2. Splendid British gem.

Advise and Consent (1962) 139m. *** D: Otto Preminger. Henry Fonda, Don Murray, Charles Laughton, Walter Pidgeon, Peter Lawford, Gene Tierney, Franchot Tone, Lew Ayres, Burgess Meredith, Paul Ford, George Grizzard. Long but engrossing drama of Washington wheeling and dealing, from Allen Drury novel. Cast is fine, with effective underplaying by Ayres and Tone standing out among more flamboyant performances by Laughton and Grizzard.

Affair in Havana (1957) 71m. *½ D: Laslo Benedek. John Cassavetes, Raymond Burr, Sara Shane, Lila Lazo. Unexciting tale of songwriter in love with crippled man's wife.

Affair in Monte Carlo (1953-British) C-75m. ** D: Victor Saville. Merle Oberon, Richard Todd, Leo Genn, Peter Illing. Rich widow tries to convince gambler that romance is more rewarding than roulette. Monte Carlo backgrounds don't spark this trifle.

Affair in Reno (1957) 75m. *½ D: R. G. Springsteen. John Lund, John Archer, Doris Singleton, Alan Hale. Inoffensive little film about detective Singleton falling in love with p.r.-man Lund while in Arizona.

Affair in Trinidad (1952) 98m. **½ D: Vincent Sherman. Rita Hayworth, Glenn Ford, Alexander Scourby, Torin Thatcher, Juanita Moore, Steven Geray. Hayworth and Ford sparkle as cafe singer and boyfriend seeking her husband's murder. Hayworth is most enticing.

Affair to Remember, An (1957) C-115m. **½ D: Leo McCarey. Cary Grant, Deborah Kerr, Cathleen Nesbitt, Neva Patterson, Richard Denning. Middling remake of McCarey's LOVE AFFAIR (Charles Boyer-Irene Dunne). Bubbling shipboard comedy in first half, overshadowed by draggy soap-opera clichés and unnecessary musical numbers in N.Y. finale.

Affair With a Stranger (1953) 89m. **½ D: Roy Rowland. Victor Mature, Jean Simmons, Jane Darwell, Dabbs Greer, Olive Carey. Title figure is child adopted by couple on brink of divorce. Formula plot of marital seesaw; stars work well together.

Affairs in Versailles SEE: Royal Affairs in Versailles.

Affairs of Cellini (1934) 80m. *** D: Gregory La Cava. Constance Bennett, Fredric March, Frank Morgan, Fay Wray, Jessie Ralph. March is excellent as roguish Renaissance painter who falls in love with Duchess. Lavish production, fine cast make this most entertaining.

Affairs of Dobie Gillis, The (1953) 74m. *** D: Don Weis. Debbie Reynolds, Bobby Van, Hans Conried, Lurene Tuttle, Bob Fosse. Entertaining musicomedy based on Max Shulman's book of college kids. Debbie and Van a cute couple; Conried the dour prof.

Affairs of Susan, The (1945) 110m. **½ D: William A. Seiter. Joan Fon-

Laine, George Brent, Dennis O'Keefe, Don DeFore, Rita Johnson, Walter Abel. Fairly entertaining comedy of actress Fontaine who does more acting for her beaus than she does onstage.

Affectionately Yours (1941) 90m. ** D: Lloyd Bacon. Merle Oberon, Dennis Morgan, Rita Hayworth, Ralph Bellamy, George Tobias. Attractive triangle flounders in weak comedy of Morgan trying to win back wife Oberon, with interference from Hayworth. Bellamy is the poor sap again.

Africa Addio (1966-Italian) C-122m. *** D: Gualtiero Jacopetti, Franco Prosperi. Intriguing survey of contemporary Africa focusing on racial differences and variant tribal customs on the continent; overly gruesome at times.

Africa Screams (1949) 79m. ** D: Charles Barton. Bud Abbott, Lou Costello, Hillary Brooke, Max Baer, Clyde Beatty, Frank Buck, Shemp Howard. Tame A&C slapstick with duo on safari seeking buried treasure.

Africa—Texas Style! (1967) C-106m. **½ D: Andrew Marton. Hugh O'Brian, John Mills, Nigel Green, Tom Nardini, Adrienne Corri. Feature (which served as TV pilot) doesn't offer much excitement, with O'Brian helping Mills preserve wild game in the dark continent.

African Queen, The (1951) C-105m. **** D: John Huston. Katharine Hepburn, Humphrey Bogart, Robert Morley, Peter Hull, Theodore Bikel. Superb combination of souse Bogart (who won an Oscar) and spinster Hepburn traveling up the Congo during WW1, combating the elements and the Germans.

African Treasure (1952) 70m. D: Ford Beebe. Johnny Sheffield, Laurette Luez, Lyle Talbot, Arthur Space, Smoki Whitfield. SEE: Bomba, the Jungle Boy series.

After Midnight With Boston Blackie (1943) D: Lew Landers. Chester Morris, Ann Savage, George E. Stone, Richard Lane, Cy Kendall, George McKay. SEE: Boston Blackie series.

After Office Hours (1935) 75m. **½ D: Robert Z. Leonard. Constance Bennett, Clark Gable, Stuart Erwin, Billie Burke. OK romantic comedy with good cast in story of newspaper editor and reporter who join forces to expose murderer.

After the Fox (1966) C-103m. **½ D: Vittorio De Sica. Peter Sellers, Victor Mature, Britt Ekland, Martin Balsam. Not always successful comedy of Italian movie director (Sellers) is a must for Mature's performance as a fading romantic star with tremendous ego.

After the Thin Man (1936) 110m. D: W. S. Van Dyke II. William Powell, Myrna Loy, James Stewart, Elissa Landi, Joseph Calleia. SEE: Thin Man series.

Against All Flags (1952) C-83m. **½ D: George Sherman. Errol Flynn, Maureen O'Hara, Anthony Quinn, Mildred Natwick. Flynn found his forte again as dashing British soldier who maneuvers way into pirate fortress, while managing to flirt with O'Hara.

Agent 8¾ (1965-British) C-77m. *** D: Ralph Thomas. Dirk Bogarde, Sylva Koscina, Leo McKern, Robert Morley, Roger Delgado, John Le Mesurier. Released at height of James Bond craze, this spoof features Bogarde as a bumbling secret agent working in Czechoslovakia. Sometimes witty, bright comedy.

Agony and the Ecstasy, The (1965) C-140m. **½ D: Carol Reed. Charlton Heston, Rex Harrison, Diane Cilento, Harry Andrews, Adolfo Celi. Huge spectacle of Michelangelo's artistic conflicts with Pope Julius II has adequate acting overshadowed by meticulous production. Short documentary on artist's work precedes fragmentary drama based on bits of Irving Stone's novel.

A-Haunting We Will Go (1942) 68m. *½ D: Alfred L. Werker. Stan Laurel, Oliver Hardy, Sheila Ryan, Elisha Cook, Jr., Willie Best. Later Laurel and Hardy comedy-mystery is poor, not up to their former standard. Dante the Magician provides most interesting scenes.

Ah, Wilderness (1935) 101m. *** D: Clarence Brown. Wallace Beery, Mickey Rooney, Lionel Barrymore, Aline MacMahon, Eric Linden, Cecilia Parker. Good cast in atmospheric film of Eugene O'Neill play of boy tackling adolescence in turn-of-the-century Connecticut. Rooney, playing younger brother, took lead role in musical remake SUMMER HOLIDAY.

Ain't Misbehavin (1955) C-82m. **½
D: Edward Buzzell. Rory Calhoun, Piper Laurie, Jack Carson, Mamie Van Doren, Reginald Gardiner. Harmless musical; lively Laurie marries tycoon Calhoun; he tries to refine her personality.

Air Cadet (1951) 94m. ** D: Joseph Pevney. Stephen McNally, Gail Russell, Alex Nicol, Richard Long, Rock Hudson. Standard training-recruit story, with McNally looking bored as head instructor.

Air Force (1943) 124m. *** D: Howard Hawks. John Garfield, John Ridgely, Gig Young, Arthur Kennedy, Charles Drake, Harry Carey, George Tobias, Faye Emerson. Taut, exciting WW2 combat film of army air force men in Pacific during earliest stage of war.

Air Mail (1932) 83m. *** D: John Ford. Pat O'Brien, Ralph Bellamy, Russell Hopton, Slim Summerville, Frank Albertson, Gloria Stuart. Routine story of pioneer airmail pilots supercharged by fine aerial scenes and good cast. First-rate all the way.

Air Raid Wardens (1943) 67m. ** D: Edward Sedgwick. Stan Laurel, Oliver Hardy, Edgar Kennedy, Jacqueline White, Horace McNally, Donald Meek. Weak, later Laurel and Hardy comedy. One potentially good scene with slowburn Kennedy doesn't meet expectations.

Aku Aku (1961) 60m. **½ Documentary of anthropologist Thor Heyerdahl's trip to Easter Island and his encounters with the natives.

Al Capone (1959) 105m. **½ D: Richard Wilson. Rod Steiger, Fay Spain, James Gregory, Martin Balsam, Nehemiah Persoff, Murvyn Vye. Good latter-day gangster biography with Steiger tirading as scarfaced Capone: good supporting cast, bringing back memories of Cagney-Robinson-Bogart films of the '30s.

Al Jennings of Oklahoma (1951) C-79m. ** D: Ray Nazarro. Dan Duryea, Gale Storm, Dick Foran, Gloria Henry. Modest Western enhanced by Duryea in title role of gangster who serves his time and goes straight; sporadic action.

Aladdin and His Lamp (1952) C-67m. *½ D: Lew Landers. Patricia Medina, Richard Erdman, John Sands, Noreen Nash. Poppycock made by adults based on juvenile fable.

Alakazam the Great (1961) C-84m. Bomb Voices of: Frankie Avalon, Dodie Stevens, Jonathan Winters, Arnold Stang. Japanese cartoon with American actors doing voices might have been more appealing in Japanese. Bad excuse for children's entertainment: dull.

Alaska Seas (1954) 78m. ** D: Jerry Hopper. Robert Ryan, Jan Sterling, Brian Keith, Gene Barry, Ross Bagdasarian. Crooks will be crooks, in insipid tale of north-country salmon canner who regrets rehiring former partner, now an ex-con.

Albuquerque (1948) C-89m. ** D: Ray Enright. Randolph Scott, Barbara Britton, Gabby Hayes, Lon Chaney, Russell Hayden. Good Western for Scott fans, with young man finally rebelling against overly strict uncle.

Alexander Hamilton (1931) 73m. ** D: John Adolfi. George Arliss, Doris Kenyon, Montagu Love, Dudley Digges, June Collyer, Alan Mowbray, Charles Middleton. Episodic American historical drama of country's earliest financial whiz is interesting but quite stagy.

Alexander the Great (1956) C-141m. *** D: Robert Rossen. Richard Burton, Fredric March, Claire Bloom, Danielle Darrieux. Remarkable cast, intelligent acting, but a static epic, lacking essential sweep to make tale of Greek conqueror moving.

Alexander's Ragtime Band (1938) 105m. *** D: Henry King. Tyrone Power, Alice Faye, Don Ameche, Ethel Merman, Jack Haley, Jean Hersholt. Large-scale musical with stale plot but good stars and a flock of Irving Berlin songs. "Now It Can Be Told," "My Walking Stick," "I'm Marching Along with Time."

Alfie (1966-British) C-114m. ***½ D: Lewis Gilbert. Michael Caine, Shelley Winters, Millicent Martin, Shirley Anne Field, Vivien Merchant, Denholm Elliot. Well-turned version of Bill Naughton play. Caine is superb as philandering Cockney playboy who can't decide if carefree bachelor life is so bloody marvelous.

Algiers (1938) 95m. *** D: John Cromwell. Charles Boyer, Sigrid Gurie, Hedy Lamarr, Joseph Calleia, Alan Hale, Gene Lockhart, Johnny

Downs. Boyer as Pepe LeMoko, falls in love with alluring Lamarr visiting Casbah district of Algiers; Calleia as police official, Lockhart as informer, stand out in well-cast romance. Remake of French PEPE LE MOKO, remade as CASBAH.

Ali Baba and the Forty Thieves (1944) C-87m. **½ D: Arthur Lubin. Maria Montez, Jon Hall, Scotty Beckett, Turhan Bey, Andy Devine, Frank Puglia. Colorful escapism with rightful-prince Hall battling evil man who put him out of the way years ago; much footage reused in recent SWORD OF ALI BABA.

Ali Baba Goes to Town (1937) 81m. **½ D: David Butler. Eddie Cantor, Tony Martin, Roland Young, June Lang, John Carradine, Virginia Field, Warren Hymer. Eddie and Arabian Nights is premise for Cantor's antics and Martin's romancing and singing.

Alias a Gentleman (1948) 76m. ** D: Harry Beaumont. Wallace Beery, Tom Drake, Dorothy Patrick, Gladys George, Leon Ames. Minor saga of an aging jailbird (Beery) who doesn't want to see his daughter involved with shady characters like himself.

Alias Bulldog Drummond (1935-British) 62m. D: Walter Forde. Jack Hulbert, Fay Wray, Claude Hulbert, Ralph Richardson, Paul Graetz. SEE: Bulldog Drummond series.

Alias Jesse James (1959) C-92m. *** D: Norman McLeod. Bob Hope, Rhonda Fleming, Wendell Corey, Jim Davis, Gloria Talbott. One of Hope's funniest has him an insurance salesman out West, mistaken for sharpshooter. Miss Fleming is a lovely Western belle; the two do a cute song together. Many guests appear at the climax.

Alias Nick Beal (1949) 93m. *** D: John Farrow. Ray Milland, Audrey Totter, Thomas Mitchell, George Macready, Fred Clark. Allegory of Devil (Milland) corrupting honest politician Mitchell with help of trollop Totter. Interesting drama with unusually sinister Milland.

Alibi Ike (1935) 73m. *** D: Ray Enright. Joe E. Brown, Olivia de Havilland, Eddie Schubert, Ruth Haviland. Another Ring Lardner baseball comedy with Brown a tall-tale spinner in baseball, mixed up with mobsters. This one has distinction of young De Havilland as leading lady.

Alice Adams (1935) 99m. ***½ D: George Stevens. Katharine Hepburn, Fred MacMurray, Fred Stone, Evelyn Venable, Frank Albertson. Excellent small-town Americana with social-climbing girl finally finding love in person of unpretentious MacMurray. Booth Tarkington book becomes fine film.

Alice in Wonderland (1933) 90m. **½ D: Norman Z. McLeod. Charlotte Henry, Richard Arlen, Gary Cooper, W. C. Fields, Edward Everett Horton, Baby LeRoy, Mae Marsh, Edna May Oliver, Jack Oakie, many others. Noteworthy only as curio; unsuccessful adaptation of Lewis Carroll boasts incredible cast, but they're disguised as various fantasy characters.

Alice in Wonderland (1950-British) C-83m. ** D: Dallas Bower. Carol Marsh, Stephen Murray, Pamela Brown, Felix Aylmer, Ernest Milton. Static adaptation of Lewis Carroll classic with gimmick of mixing live action and puppets; most of the wit and charm are missing.

All About Eve (1950) 138m. **** D: Joseph L. Mankiewicz. Bette Davis, Anne Baxter, George Sanders, Celeste Holm, Gary Merrill, Thelma Ritter, Marilyn Monroe, Hugh Marlowe. Cynical view of theater life, filled with epigrammatic gems. Davis glows as aging star, Merrill her young beau, Baxter a grasping actress, Sanders a poison-pen critic, Marlowe a playwright, and Holm his sugary wife.

All American, The (1953) 83m. ** D: Jesse Hibbs. Tony Curtis, Lori Nelson, Richard Long, Mamie Van Doren, Gregg Palmer, Stuart Whitman. Football is secondary aspect of typical romance story between two wholesome young people (Curtis-Nelson).

All Ashore (1953) C-80m. *½ D: Richard Quine. Mickey Rooney, Dick Haymes, Peggy Ryan, Ray MacDonald. Yarn of three gobs on shore leave finding gals, sinks despite Rooney's sprite spirit.

All at Sea (1958-British) 87m. *** D: Charles Frend. Alec Guinness, Irene Browne, Percy Herbert, Harold Goodwin. Robust comedy that holds its own throughout. Guinness is admirable as seaman who can't bear sight of water but buys rundown house-laden pier, turning it into an amusement palace.

All Fall Down (1962) 110m. *** D: John Frankenheimer. Warren Beatty, Eva Marie Saint, Karl Malden, Angela Lansbury, Brandon de Wilde. Improbable William Inge script about narcissistic young man (Beatty), his admiring younger brother (De Wilde), indulgent parents (Lansbury and Malden), and the older woman (Saint) who suffers tragic results from loving him. Fine performances.

All Hands on Deck (1961) C-98m. ** D: Norman Taurog. Pat Boone, Buddy Hackett, Dennis O'Keefe, Barbara Eden. Innocuous musical comedy of free-wheeling sailors, Boone and Hackett, is lightweight entertainment.

All I Desire (1953) 70m. **½ D: Douglas Sirk. Barbara Stanwyck, Richard Carlson, Lyle Bettger, Lori Nelson, Maureen O'Sullivan. Family togetherness and home-town approval is answer to title, in period-piece uplifted by Stanwyck's valiant performance as erring mother of three who returns to her husband.

All in a Night's Work (1961) C-94m. **½ D: Joseph Anthony. Dean Martin, Shirley MacLaine, Charles Ruggles, Cliff Robertson. Pleasant formula comedy-mystery. MacLaine and Martin get into spirit of things well, the latter in an offbeat role.

All Mine to Give (1957) C-102m. **½ D: Allen Reisner. Cameron Mitchell, Glynis Johns, Patty McCormack, Hope Emerson. Often touching story of pioneer family in Wisconsin determined to overcome all obstacles.

All My Sons (1948) 94m. *** D: Irving Reis. Edward G. Robinson, Burt Lancaster, Mady Christians, Louisa Horton, Howard Duff. Arthur Miller's compelling drama of family discovering their father's unsavory business ethics during WW2 is well-acted, but quite verbose.

All Night Long (1961-British) 95m. ** D: Michael Relph, Basil Dearden. Patrick McGoohan, Marti Stevens, Betsy Blair, Keith Michell, Richard Attenborough. Bland mixture of jazz music with modern parable on Othello love triangle. Guest appearances by Dave Brubeck, Tubby Hayes, et al.

All of Me (1934) 75m. ** D: James Flood. Fredric March, Miriam Hopkins, George Raft, Helen Mack, Blanche Frederici. Ineffectual melodrama of professor March yearning for open spaces and lover Hopkins learning about true devotion from gun moll Mack.

All Quiet on the Western Front (1930) 105m. **** D: Lewis Milestone. Lew Ayres, Louis Wolheim, Russell Gleason, Beryl Mercer, Ben Alexander, Slim Summerville. Brilliant version of Erich Maria Remarque's pacifist WW1 novel; beautifully acted and directed. A must-see classic.

All That Heaven Allows (1955) C-89m. *** D: Douglas Sirk. Jane Wyman, Rock Hudson, Agnes Moorehead, Virginia Grey, Conrad Nagel. When widow Wyman allows younger man Hudson to romance her, she faces the ire of friends and society. Nicely mounted production.

All That Money Can Buy (1941) 112m. ***½ D: William Dieterle. Edward Arnold, Walter Huston, James Craig, Anne Shirley, Jane Darwell, Simone Simon, Gene Lockhart. Stephen Vincent Benét's THE DEVIL AND DANIEL WEBSTER is visual delight with Huston's sparkling performance as "Mr. Scratch," the Devil, matched by Arnold as Daniel Webster. Considerably cut for TV, but still a must.

All the Brothers Were Valiant (1953) C-101m. **½ D: Richard Thorpe. Robert Taylor, Stewart Granger, Ann Blyth, Keenan Wynn, James Whitmore, Lewis Stone. Water-logged adventurer based on Ben Ames Williams' novel. Taylor and Granger lack conviction as New Bedford whalers having career and romantic conflicts.

All the Fine Young Cannibals (1960) C-112m. *½ D: Michael Anderson. Robert Wagner, Natalie Wood, Susan Kohner, George Hamilton, Pearl Bailey, Anne Seymour. Trio of young lovers in a soaper with clichés galore; Pearl Bailey is paired with Robert Wagner.

All the King's Men (1949) 109m. **** D: Robert Rossen. Broderick Crawford, Joanne Dru, John Ireland, Mercedes McCambridge, John Derek. Top-notch study of political corruption in Southern state, based on Robert Penn Warren novel. Crawford and McCambridge won Oscars for their incisive portrayals.

All the Way Home (1963) 103m. ***½ D: Alex Segal. Jean Simmons, Robert Preston, Aline MacMahon, Pat Hingle, John Cullum, Thomas Chalmers. Outstanding film of James Agee's A DEATH IN THE FAMILY. Preston is subdued in pivotal role (set in rural 1910 America) of father who is accidentally killed, leaving family to interpret meaning of their lives before and after his death. Beautifully done.

All the Young Men (1960) 87m. **½ D: Hall Bartlett. Alan Ladd, Sidney Poitier, James Darren, Glenn Corbett, Mort Sahl. Hackneyed war story with all the stereotypes present, mouthing the same old platitudes.

All These Women (1964-Swedish, dubbed) C-80m. **½ D: Ingmar Bergman. Jarl Kulle, Harriet Andersson, Bibi Andersson, Allan Edwall. Satirical frolic involving woman-chasing cellist. He bargains with music critic to have biography written by agreeing to play writer's composition.

All This and Heaven Too (1940) 143m. *** D: Anatole Litvak. Bette Davis, Charles Boyer, Jeffrey Lynn, Barbara O'Neil, Virginia Weidler, Helen Westley, Walter Hampden. Nobleman Boyer falls in love with governess Davis, causing scandal and death; stars do very well in elaborate filmization of Rachel Field book set in 19th-century France.

All Through the Night (1942) 107m. *** D: Vincent Sherman. Humphrey Bogart, Conrad Veidt, Kaaren Verne, Jane Darwell, Frank McHugh, Peter Lorre, Judith Anderson, Jackie Gleason, Phil Silvers. Bogart's gang tracks down Fifth Columnists (Veidt, Lorre, Anderson) in WW2 N.Y.C. Interesting blend of spy, gangster, and comedy genres, with memorable double-talk scene.

Allegheny Uprising (1939) 81m. *** D: William Seiter. John Wayne, Claire Trevor, George Sanders, Brian Donlevy, Robert Barrat, Moroni Olsen, Chill Wills. Good saga of Revolutionary days with pioneer Americans fighting the redcoats; fine cast, plenty of action.

Alligator Named Daisy, An (1957-British) C-88m. **½ D: J. Lee Thompson. Diana Dors, Donald Sinden, Stanley Holloway, Roland Culver, Margaret Rutherford, Stephen Boyd. Dors reveals pleasing comic talent in fabricated account of salesman who mistakenly picks up someone else's alligator suitcase, leading to complications.

Alligator People, The (1959) 74m. **½ D: Roy Del Ruth. Beverly Garland, George Macready, Lon Chaney, Richard Crane, Frieda Inescort, Bruce Bennett. Above-par horror entry details transformation of a man into part-reptile; makeup artist is star of production.

Allotment Wives (1945) 83m. ** D: William Nigh. Kay Francis, Paul Kelly, Otto Kruger, Gertrude Michael, Teala Loring. Mild sensationalism involving women who marry servicemen to collect their military pay; not one of Francis' better films.

Almost a Bride SEE: **Kiss For Corliss, A**

Aloma of the South Seas (1941) C-77m. ** D: Alfred Santell. Dorothy Lamour, Jon Hall, Lynne Overman, Philip Reed, Katherine DeMille. Still another sarong saga with native Hall sent to U.S. for education, returning when father dies to stop revolution on once peaceful island.

Along Came Jones (1945) 90m. *** D: Stuart Heisler. Gary Cooper, Loretta Young, William Demarest, Dan Duryea, Frank Sully, Russell Simpson. Cooper is delightful as timid young man thought to be famous gunfighter.

Along the Great Divide (1951) 88m. **½ D: Raoul Walsh. Kirk Douglas, Virginia Mayo, John Agar, Walter Brennan. Douglas is appropriately tight-lipped as lawman determined to bring in his man, despite desert storm; some spectacular scenery.

Alphabet Murders, The (1966-British) 90m. **½ D: Frank Tashlin. Tony Randall, Anita Ekberg, Robert Morley, Guy Rolfe. Flat spy spoof with Randall as Hercule Poirot in England, confounding British Intelligence while trying to find missing Ekberg.

Alphaville (1965-French, dubbed) 100m. ** D: Jean-Luc Godard. Eddie Constantine, Anna Karina, Akim Tamiroff, Howard Vernon. Constantine, as super private eye Lemmy Caution, is sent to futuristic city run by electronic brain to rescue scientist trapped there. Jumbled Godard epic, recommended for new-wave disciples only.

Alvarez Kelly (1966) C-116m. **½ D: Edward Dmytryk. William Holden, Richard Widmark, Janice Rule, Victoria Shaw, Patrick O'Neal. Slow-moving Civil War tale. Holden is cattle driver who sells herd to Yankees, then is kidnapped by Reb Widmark who wants him to steal cattle for the South; incongruous love scenes thrown in.

Always a Bride (1954-British) 83m. ** D: Ralph Smart. Peggy Cummins, Terence Morgan, Ronald Squire, James Hayter. Mild comedy of treasury officer romancing girl, aiding her dad to fleece others.

Always Goodbye (1938) 75m. **½ D: Sidney Lanfield. Barbara Stanwyck, Herbert Marshall, Ian Hunter, Cesar Romero, Lynn Bari, Binnie Barnes. Still another sacrificing mother tale as Stanwyck is forced to give up her illicit child; nicely done, but the same story.

Always In My Heart (1942) 92m. *½ D: Joe Graham. Kay Francis, Walter Huston, Gloria Warren, Una O'Connor, Sidney Blackmer. Soaper of convict Huston returning to find wife Francis about to marry Blackmer and a daughter (Warren) who doesn't know him.

Always Leave Them Laughing (1949) 116m. **½ D: Roy Del Ruth. Milton Berle, Virginia Mayo, Ruth Roman, Bert Lahr, Alan Hale. Berle is at home in tale of stage comedian, his ups and downs; script is clichéd.

Always Together (1948) 78m. **½ D: Frederick de Cordova. Robert Hutton, Joyce Reynolds, Cecil Kellaway, Ernest Truex; guests Humphrey Bogart, Jack Carson, Errol Flynn, Dennis Morgan, Janis Paige, Eleanor Parker, Alexis Smith. Innocuous fluff of dying millionaire Kellaway giving money to young Reynolds, then discovering he's quite healthy. Worthwhile only for amusing cameos by many Warner Brothers stars throughout film.

Amazing Colossal Man, The (1957) 80m. **½ D: Bert I. Gordon. Glenn Langan, Cathy Downs, James Seay, Larry Thor. Thought-provoking sci-fi detailing the mental turmoil army officer undergoes when radioactive explosion causes him to grow to mammoth proportions.

Amazing Doctor Clitterhouse, The (1938) 87m. *** D: Anatole Litvak. Edward G. Robinson, Claire Trevor, Humphrey Bogart, Allen Jenkins, Donald Crisp, Gale Page. Amusing film of "method doctor" Robinson trying to discover what makes a crook tick; he joins Bogart's gang and becomes addicted.

Amazing Mr. Williams (1939) 80m. **½ D: Alexander Hall. Melvyn Douglas, Joan Blondell, Clarence Kolb, Ruth Donnelly. Douglas holds up his marriage to investigate murder in this satisfying comedy-mystery.

Amazing Mr. X, The (1948) 78m. ** D: Bernard Vorhaus. Turhan Bey, Lynn Bari, Cathy O'Donnell, Richard Carlson. Low-budget nonsense involving Bey utilizing Bari for his fraudulent mystical con schemes. Retitled: THE SPIRITUALIST.

Amazing Mrs. Halliday, The (1943) 96m. **½ D: Bruce Manning. Deanna Durbin, Edmond O'Brien, Barry Fitzgerald, Arthur Treacher, Frieda Inescort. Well-meant but unexciting drama of devoted missionary Durbin protecting a group of Chinese orphans; undistinguished songs.

Amazing Transparent Man, The (1960) 58m. Bomb D: Edgar G. Ulmer. Marguerite Chapman, Douglas Kennedy, James Griffith, Ivan Triesault. Tawdry sci-fi of stereotyped mad scientist inventing formula to make an invisible man his accomplice in bank robberies.

Ambassador's Daughter, The (1956) C-102m. **½ D: Norman Krasna. Olivia de Havilland, John Forsythe, Myrna Loy, Adolphe Menjou. Oomph is missing even though stars give all to uplift sagging comedy of De Havilland out for a fling in Paris, romanced by soldier Forsythe.

Ambush (1949) 89m. **½ D: Sam Wood. Robert Taylor, John Hodiak, Arlene Dahl, Jean Hagen, Chief Thundercloud. Pat Western with Apaches vs. Cavalry, salvaged by star cast.

Ambush at Cimarron Pass (1958) 73m. ** D: Jodie Copelan. Scott Brady, Margia Dean, Baynes Barron, William Vaughn. Title tells all.

Ambush at Tomahawk Gap (1953) C-73m. *½ D: Fred F. Sears. John Hodiak, John Derek, David Brian, Percy Helton, Maria Elena Marques. Standard oater has quartet of ex-convicts caught by Indian attack. One is left alive; he rides into sunset with newly-found squaw.

Ambush Bay (1966) C-109. **½ D: Ron Winston. Hugh O'Brian, Mickey Rooney, James Mitchum, Harry Lauter. Lackluster adventures of marine group on Jap-held island during WW2 trying to help partisans—good cast wasted.

Ambush in Leopard Street (1961-British) 60m. *½ D: J. Henry Piperno. James Kenney, Michael Brennan, Bruce Seton, Norman Rodway. Listless crime tale involving heist of diamond shipment.

Ambushers, The (1967) C-102m. **½ D: Henry Levin. Dean Martin, Senta Berger, Janice Rule, James Gregory, Albert Salmi, Kurt Kasznar, Beverly Adams. Usual Matt Helm nonsense; if you liked the others in this series, this will probably suit your taste. As usual, there are plenty of gorgeous girls to hold male viewers' attention.

American Dream, An (1966) C-103m. **½ D: Robert Gist. Stuart Whitman, Eleanor Parker, Janet Leigh, Barry Sullivan, Lloyd Nolan. Distorted, watered-down Norman Mailer novel, superficially dealing with TV commentator who's wanted by underworld and police for murdering his wife; nightmarish sequences are sterile.

American Empire (1942) 82m. **½ D: William McGann. Richard Dix, Leo Carrillo, Preston Foster, Frances Gifford, Guinn Williams. Dix and Foster join forces to develop cattle empire in Texas after Civil War, but not without problems. Pretty good outdoor actioner.

American Guerrilla in the Philippines (1950) C-105m. **½ D: Fritz Lang. Tyrone Power, Micheline Prelle, Tom Ewell, Jack Elam. If one ignores flaws in over-patriotic script, film is agreeable account of naval officer Power left behind enemy lines on WW2 Pacific island, helping natives combat Japanese.

American Romance, An (1944) C-122m. **½ D: King Vidor. Brian Donlevy, Ann Richards, Walter Abel, John Qualen, Stephen McNally. Long flavorful story of immigrant couple Americanized over the years.

Americanization of Emily, The (1964) 117m. ***½ D: Arthur Hiller. James Garner, Julie Andrews, Melvyn Douglas, James Coburn, Joyce Redman, Keenan Wynn, Judy Carne. Garner is fall guy for U.S. admiral's master plan to have American naval officer first Normandy invasion victim, with predictable results. Cynical Garner-Andrews romance blends well with realistic view of life among U.S. military brass.

Americano, The (1955) C-85m. **½ D: William Castle. Glenn Ford, Cesar Romero, Frank Lovejoy, Ursula Thiess, Abbe Lane. Routine good-guy (Ford) vs. bad-guy Western has change of scenery, set in South America, but otherwise it's strictly standard.

Among the Living (1941) 68m. **½ D: Stuart Heisler. Albert Dekker, Susan Hayward, Harry Carey, Frances Farmer, Gordon Jones. Twin brother murderer causes trouble for innocent Dekker in tense drama.

Amorous Adventures of Moll Flanders, The (1965) C-126m. **½ D: Terence Young. Kim Novak, Richard Johnson, Angela Lansbury, George Sanders, Vittorio DeSica, Lilli Palmer, Leo McKern, Cecil Parker. Billed as female Tom Jones, Moll is far from thrilling. Fine cast romps through 18th-century England from bedroom to boudoir, but film needs more spice than Novak can muster.

Amorous Mr. Prawn, The (1962-British) 89m. **½ D: Anthony Kimmins. Joan Greenwood, Cecil Parker, Ian Carmichael, Robert Beatty. Diverting fluff of general Parker and wife Greenwood planning to retire in style, devising a scheme to obtain badly needed money.

Anastasia (1956) C-105m. **** D: Anatole Litvak. Ingrid Bergman, Yul Brynner, Helen Hayes, Akim Tamiroff. Inspired casting makes this film exceptional. Bergman won Oscar as amnesiac refugee selected by Brynner to impersonate surviving daughter of Russia's last czar. Confrontation scene in which Hayes as grand duchess must determine if girl is her relative is grand.

Anatomist, The (1961-British) 73m. ** D: Leonard William. Alastair Sim, George Cole, Jill Bennett, Margaret Gordon. Respected surgeon encourages corpse-stealing for experiments, causing rash of murders. Sim is wry in tame spooker.

Anatomy of a Marriage (1964-French, dubbed) 193m. **½ D: André Cayatte. Comprised of: MY DAYS WITH JEAN-MARC — MY NIGHTS WITH FRANCOISE. Jacques Charrier, Marie-Jose Nat, Georges Riviere, Macha Meril. Well-intentioned film which through its two parts attempts to analyze problems of young married couple from each one's point of view; becomes repetitious.

Anatomy of a Murder (1959) 160m. *** D: Otto Preminger. James Stewart, Lee Remick, Ben Gazzara, Arthur O'Connell, Eve Arden, Kathryn Grant, George C. Scott, Orson Bean. Long, exciting courtroom drama; daring when released, tamer now. Large cast is fine—O'Connell outstanding as drunken lawyer aroused by Stewart, Joseph M. Welch as a judge, Scott as prosecuting attorney. Duke Ellington score gives it added boost.

Anatomy of a Syndicate SEE: Big Operator, The

Anchors Aweigh (1945) C-140m. **½ D: George Sidney. Frank Sinatra, Kathryn Grayson, Gene Kelly, Jose Iturbi, Dean Stockwell, Pamela Britton. Popular musical of two sailors on leave doesn't hold up well; musical numbers still good: "I Fall In Love Too Easily," and Kelly's famous dance with cartoon mouse.

And Baby Makes Three (1949) 84m. ** D: Henry Levin. Robert Young, Barbara Hale, Robert Hutton, Billie Burke, Melville Cooper. OK comedy has Hale about to marry for second time, only to discover she's pregnant, and she really does want to stay married to Hubby #1 (Young).

. . . And Now Miguel (1966) C-95m. *** D: James Clark. Pat Cardi, Michael Ansara, Guy Stockwell, Joe De Santis. Flavorful, leisurely paced account of young boy who wants to join his father on their summer mountain trip to graze sheep; set in Southwest.

And Now Tomorrow (1944) 85m. **½ D: Irving Pichel. Alan Ladd, Loretta Young, Susan Hayward, Barry Sullivan, Beulah Bondi, Cecil Kellaway. Poor doctor Ladd falls in love with deaf socialite patient Young in this Rachel Field romance; sticky going at times.

And Quiet Flows the Don (1960-Russian, dubbed) C-107m. *** D: Sergi Gerasimov. Ellina Bystritskaya, Pyotr Glebov, Zinaida Kirienko, Danilo Ilchenko. Faithful realization of Mikhail Sholokhov novel revolving around life of small village family during WW1 and postwar period. Absorbing study of social upheavals caused by revolution and war.

And So They Were Married (1936) 74m. **½ D: Elliott Nugent. Melvyn Douglas, Mary Astor, Edith Fellows, Jackie Morgan, Donald Meek. Predictable but amusing little comedy with good co-stars.

And So They Were Married (1944) SEE: Johnny Doesn't Live Here Any More.

And Suddenly It's Murder! (1964-Italian, dubbed) 90m. **½ D: Mario Camerini. Alberto Sordi, Vittorio Gassman, Silvana Mangano. Frail but frantic minor comedy satire revolving around trip of couples on the Riviera, each suspected of murder.

And the Angels Sing (1944) 96m. **½ D: Claude Binyon. Dorothy Lamour, Fred MacMurray, Betty Hutton, Diana Lynn, Raymond Walburn, Eddie Foy, Jr. Agreeable musical of singing sister act trying to make it big; MacMurray gives them their break. Brassy Hutton tries to steal the show.

And Then There Were None (1945) 98m. ***½ D: Rene Clair. Barry Fitzgerald, Walter Huston, Louis Hayward, Roland Young, June Duprez, C. Aubrey Smith, Judith Anderson, Mischa Auer, Richard Haydn. High-grade Agatha Christie yarn of ten people converging on a deserted island, with the eventual murder of most of the group. Highly suspenseful. Remade as TEN LITTLE INDIANS.

Androcles and the Lion (1952) 98m. *** D: Chester Erskine. Jean Simmons, Alan Young, Victor Mature, Maurice Evans, Elsa Lanchester. Shaw's amusing satire of ancient Rome can't be dampened by dull production retelling fable of Christian and the lion he has befriended.

Andy (1965) 86m. *** D: Richard C. Sarafian. Norman Alden, Tamara Daykarhonova, Svee Scooler, Murvyn Vye. Touching insight into existence of retarded middle-aged man and his unique problems in N.Y.C. slum life.

Andy Hardy One of the most popular series of all time, the Hardy family first appeared in A Family Affair (1937) with Lionel Barrymore and Mickey Rooney as father and son. 1938's You're Only Young Once began the official series in the town of Carvel, with Rooney as Andy Hardy, typical American teen-ager, interested in cars and girls, Lewis Stone as Judge James Hardy, a stern but understanding father, Fay Holden as his "swell" mother, Cecilia Parker as Marian, his older sister striving to be a young lady, Sara Haden as Aunt Millie, and Ann Rutherford as Polly, the girlfriend who was often neglected for other prospects but to whom Andy always returned; George B. Seitz directed most entries in the series. MGM used the films to springboard young starlets such as Judy Garland, Lana Turner, Esther Williams, Kathryn Grayson, and Donna Reed. The Andy Hardy films do not always wear well, with typical Rooney mugging and a plethora of 1940's slang dating them rather badly. In one film Andy tells his dad "You can say that again!" and the Judge replies, "Why should I say it again? Didn't you understand me the first time?" The sentimental nature of much of the series also doesn't fit into today's way of thinking, and in general the Hardy films serve mainly as reminders of an era in Hollywood and in America that is long gone. Indeed, when the cast, except Stone, was reunited in 1958 for Andy Hardy Comes Home, the formula just didn't jell. What survives in the Hardy films is the very real talent that went into them.

Andy Hardy Comes Home (1958) 81m. D: Howard W. Koch. Mickey Rooney, Patricia Breslin, Fay Holden, Cecilia Parker, Sara Haden, Joey Forman, Jerry Colonna, Vaughn Taylor, Frank Ferguson.

Andy Hardy Gets Spring Fever (1939) 85m. D: W. S. Van Dyke II. Lewis Stone, Mickey Rooney, Cecilia Parker, Fay Holden, Ann Rutherford, Sara Haden, Addison Richards.

Andy Hardy Meets Debutante (1940) 86m. D: George B. Seitz. Mickey Rooney, Lewis Stone, Judy Garland, Cecilia Parker, Ann Rutherford, Fay Holden, Diana Lewis, Sara Haden.

Andy Hardy's Blonde Trouble (1944) 107m. D: George B. Seitz. Lewis Stone, Mickey Rooney, Fay Holden, Sara Haden, Herbert Marshall, Bonita Granville, Jean Porter, Keye Luke.

Andy Hardy's Double Life (1942) 92m. D: George B. Seitz. Mickey Rooney, Lewis Stone, Cecilia Parker, Fay Holden, Ann Rutherford, Sara Haden, Bobby Blake, William Lundigan, Susan Peters.

Andy Hardy's Private Secretary (1941) 101m. D: George B. Seitz. Mickey Rooney, Lewis Stone, Fay Holden, Ann Rutherford, Sara Haden, Kathryn Grayson, Ian Hunter, Gene Reynolds.

Angel (1937) 98m. ** D: Ernst Lubitsch. Marlene Dietrich, Herbert Marshall, Melvyn Douglas, Edward Everett Horton, Laura Hope Crews. Disappointing film for Dietrich-Lubitsch team about Marlene leaving husband Marshall for vacation, falling in love with Douglas. Not worthy of star trio.

Angel and the Badman (1947) 100m. *** D: James Edward Grant. John Wayne, Gail Russell, Harry Carey, Irene Rich, Bruce Cabot. First-rate Western with Russell humanizing gunfighter Wayne; predictable plot is extremely well handled.

Angel Baby (1961) 97m. *** D: Paul Wendkos, Hubert Cornfield. George Hamilton, Salome Jens, Mercedes McCambridge, Joan Blondell, Henry Jones. Penetrating expose of evangelistic circuit plying backwood country; Jens in title role, Hamilton the promoter, McCambridge his shrewish wife—marvelous cameos by Blondell and Jones.

Angel Face (1953) 90m. **½ D: Otto Preminger. Robert Mitchum, Jean Simmons, Herbert Marshall, Mona Freeman, Leon Ames, Barbara O'Neil, Jim Backus. Title figure (Simmons) in slowly-paced film revealed as angel of death causing demise of those who love her.

Angel on My Shoulder (1946) 101m. *** D: Archie Mayo. Paul Muni, Anne Baxter, Claude Rains, George Cleveland, Onslow Stevens. Entertaining fantasy of murderer Muni sent to earth by Devil as respected judge, who outwits Satan while in mortal form.

Angel on the Amazon (1948) 86m. *½ D: John H. Auer. George Brent, Vera Ralston, Constance Bennett, Brian Aherne, Fortunio Bonanova. Ludicrous "romance" with Vera in a state of eternal youth; good cast can't rescue clumsy story.

Angel Wore Red, The (1960) 99m. **½ D: Nunnally Johnson. Ava Gardner, Dirk Bogarde, Joseph Cotten, Vittorio DeSica. Sometimes engrossing tale of clergyman who joins the Spanish loyalist cause and his romance with a good-natured entertainer.

Angel's Alley (1948) 67m. D: William Beaudine. Leo Gorcey, Huntz Hall, Billy Benedict, David Gorcey. SEE: Bowery Boys series.

Angels in Disguise (1940) 63m. D: Jean Yarbrough. Leo Gorcey, Huntz Hall, Gabriel Dell, Mickey Knox, Jean Dean, Bernard Gorcey. SEE: Bowery Boys series.

Angels in the Outfield (1951) 102m. *** D: Clarence Brown. Paul Douglas, Janet Leigh, Keenan Wynn, Donna Corcoran. Engaging fantasy as heavenly forces help Pittsburgh Pirates go on a winning streak.

Angels of Darkness (1956-Italian, dubbed) 84m. ** D: Giuseppe Amato. Linda Darnell, Anthony Quinn, Valentina Cortesa, Lea Padovani. Aimless account of life and love among unhappy inhabitants of Rome—waste of stars' abilities.

Angels One Five (1954-British) 98m. ** D. George O'Ferrall. Jack Hawkins, Michael Denison, Dulcie Gray, John Gregson. Grounded for accidental plane mishap, British war pilot (Hawkins) rebels against officers and friends, seeking to fly again.

Angels Over Broadway (1940) 80m. ***½ D: Ben Hecht, Lee Garmes. Douglas Fairbanks, Jr., Rita Hayworth, Thomas Mitchell, John Qualen, George Watts. Strange Hecht script of sharpster Fairbanks enlisting hard-luck Hayworth in embezzling plot; fine support from Mitchell and Qualen.

Angels Wash Their Faces (1939) 76m. **½ D: Ray Enright. Ann Sheridan, Dead End Kids, Frankie Thomas, Bonita Granville, Ronald Reagan, Margaret Hamilton, Marjorie Main. Protective sister Sheridan tries to clear brother Thomas' police record, but he joins Dead End Kids for more trouble. OK juvenile-delinquent drama.

Angels With Dirty Faces (1938) 97m. *** D: Michael Curtiz. James Cagney, Pat O'Brien, Humphrey Bogart, Ann Sheridan, George Bancroft, Billy Halop. Superior cast in tale of two playmates; one (Cagney) becomes a gangster, the other (O'Brien) a priest. The Dead End Kids come to idolize Cagney, much to O'Brien's chagrin.

Angry Hills, The (1959) 105m. **½ D: Robert Aldrich. Robert Mitchum, Elisabeth Mueller, Stanley Baker, Gia Scala, Theodore Bikel, Sebastian Cabot. Mitchum shows vim in WW2 actioner as war correspondent plotting escape from Greece with valuable data for Allies.

Angry Silence, The (1960-British) 95m. *** D: Guy Green. Richard Attenborough, Pier Angeli, Michael Craig, Bernard Lee. Rewarding, unheralded film about courageous stand by a simple Britisher who refuses to join a wildcat strike, the repercussions he endures.

Animal Farm (1955-British) C-75m. *** D: John Halas, Joy Batchelor. Admirable cartoon version of George Orwell's political satire, intelligently conceived and well-drawn.

Anna (1951-Italian, dubbed) 95m. **½ D: Alberto Lattuada. Silvana Mangano, Raf Vallone, Vittorio Gassman, Gaby Morlay. Thoughtful study of confused young woman who enters convent to avoid deciding which man she really loves, with fates forcing decision upon her.

Anna and the King of Siam (1946) 128m. ***½ D: John Cromwell. Irene Dunne, Rex Harrison, Linda Darnell, Lee J. Cobb, Gale Sondergaard, Mikhail Rasumny. Sumptuous production of 19th-century British governess who journeys to Thailand, engaging in battle of wits with strong-willed ruler. Dunne and Harrison are superb. Remade as musical THE KING AND I.

Anna Christie (1930) 74m. *** D: Clarence Brown. Greta Garbo, Charles Bickford, Marie Dressler, Lee Phelps, George Marion. Garbo is effective in her first talkie as girl with shady past finding love with seaman Bickford, from O'Neill play. Film itself is rather static.

Anna Karenina (1935) 95m. **** D: Clarence Brown. Greta Garbo, Fredric March, Freddie Bartholomew, Maureen O'Sullivan, May Robson, Basil Rathbone. Tolstoy's tragic love chronicle makes excellent Garbo vehicle, with fine support from March as her lover, Rathbone her husband, and Bartholomew, her adoring son.

Anna Karenina (1948-British) 110m. **½ D: Julien Duvivier. Vivien Leigh, Ralph Richardson, Kieron Moore, Hugh Dempster. Despite excellent cast, strictly turgid adaptation of Tolstoy classic about a woman blindly in love with officer.

Anna Lucasta (1958) 97m. ** D: Arnold Laven. Eartha Kitt, Sammy Davis, Jr., Frederick O'Neal, Henry Scott, Rex Ingram. Tepid melodrama about promiscuous Kitt who leaves home when boyfriend learns her true morality. Based on Philip Yordan play.

Annapolis Story, An (1955) C-81m. ** D: Don Siegel. John Derek. Diana Lynn, Kevin McCarthy, Pat Conway. Uninspired reuse of old service-school formula with Derek and McCarthy undergoing rigid training, both romancing Lynn.

Anne of Green Gables (1934) 79m. *** D: George Nicholls, Jr. Anne Shirley, Tom Brown, O. P. Heggie, Helen Westley. Well-handled story of orphan accepted in household, trying to forget past experiences.

Anne of the Indies (1951) C-81m. **½ D: Jacques Tourneur. Jean Peters, Louis Jourdan, Debra Paget, Herbert Marshall. Peters isn't always believable as swaggering pirate, but surrounded by professionals and good production, actioner moves along.

Anne of Windy Poplars (1940) 88m. ** D: Jack Hively. Anne Shirley, James Ellison, Henry Travers, Patric Knowles. Fair acting in tired story of teacher overcoming small-town prejudices. Follow-up to ANNE OF GREEN GABLES.

Annie Get Your Gun (1950) C-107m. *** D: George Sidney. Betty Hutton, Howard Keel, Louis Calhern, Edward Arnold, Keenan Wynn. Lively filming of Irving Berlin's Wild West show musical of Annie Oakley getting her man. Songs include "Anything You Can Do," "Doin' What Comes Naturally."

Annie Oakley (1935) 88m. *** D: George Stevens. Barbara Stanwyck, Preston Foster, Melvyn Douglas, Pert Kelton, Andy Clyde. Lively biography of female sharpshooter Stanwyck and her on-again off-again romance with fellow-performer Foster. Tight direction within episodic scenes, gives believeable flavor of late 19th-century America.

Another Dawn (1937) 73m. **½ D: William Dieterle. Kay Francis, Errol Flynn, Ian Hunter, Frieda Inescort, Mary Forbes. Francis is torn between devotion to husband Hunter and officer Flynn in well-paced adventure story set at British army post in African desert.

Another Man's Poison (1952-British) 89m. ** D: Irving Rapper. Bette Davis, Gary Merrill, Emlyn Williams, Anthony Steel. Hazy melodrama with a tame Davis performance as authoress who kills her escaped convict husband and is blackmailed by another con (Merrill) on the loose.

Another Part of the Forest (1948) 107m. *** D: Michael Gordon. Fredric March, Dan Duryea, Edmond O'Brien, Ann Blyth, Florence Eldridge, John Dall. Lillian Hellman's story predates THE LITTLE FOXES by tracing the Hubbard family's ruthlessness; unpleasant but well-acted movie.

Another Thin Man (1939) 105m. D: W. S. Van Dyke II. William Powell, Myrna Loy, Virginia Grey, Otto Kruger, C. Aubrey Smith, Ruth Hussey, Nat Pendleton, Tom Neal, Sheldon Leonard, Marjorie Main. SEE: Thin Man Series.

Another Time, Another Place (1958) 98m. **½ D: Lewis Allen. Lana Turner, Barry Sullivan, Glynis Johns, Sean Connery. Unconvincing melodrama; Turner suffers nervous breakdown when her lover is killed during WW2.

Anthony Adverse (1936) 136m. ***½ D: Mervyn LeRoy. Fredric March, Olivia de Havilland, Donald Woods, Anita Louise, Edmund Gwenn, Claude Rains, Louis Hayward. Blockbuster filmization of Hervey Allen book of young man gaining maturity through adventures in various parts of early 19th-century America, Mexico, et al. Gale Sondergaard won Oscar as Best Supporting Actress; rousing musical score by Erich Wolfgang Korngold.

Any Number Can Play (1949) 112m. ** D: Mervyn LeRoy. Clark Gable, Alexis Smith, Wendell Corey, Audrey Totter, Mary Astor, Lewis Stone, Marjorie Rambeau. Low-key drama of gambling house owner Gable, estranged from wife Smith and son Darryl Hickman. Good character roles breathe life into film.

Any Number Can Win (1963-French, dubbed) **½ D: Henri Verneuil. Jean Gabin, Alain Delon, Viviane Romance, Carla Marlier. Gabin leads bank robbery in Riviera resort. Comedy and suspense blend in "perfect crime" attempt.

Any Wednesday (1966) C-109m. *** D: Robert Miller. Jane Fonda, Jason Robards, Dean Jones, Rosemary Murphy. Bedroom farce of N.Y.C. executive using his mistress' apartment for business deductions. Fonda is appropriately addled in unstagy sex comedy.

Anything Can Happen (1952) 107m. ** D: George Seaton. Jose Ferrer, Kim Hunter, Kurt Kasznar, Eugenie Leontovich. Ferrer is overly flavorful as immigrant Russian adapting to American life and courting pert Hunter.

Anything Goes (1936) 92m. **½ D: Lewis Milestone. Bing Crosby, Ethel Merman, Charlie Ruggles, Ida Lupino, Grace Bradley, Arthur Treacher. Pleasant Crosby shipboard musical with stunning Cole Porter songs: title tune, "You're The Top," "I Get A Kick Out of You." Mild distortion of Broadway original. Retitled: TOPS IS THE LIMIT.

Anything Goes (1956) C-106m. ** D: Robert Lewis. Bing Crosby, Jeanmaire, Donald O'Connor, Mitzi Gaynor, Phil Harris. Flat musical involving show business partners Crosby and O'Connor each signing a performer for the leading role in their show. Songs likewise aren't memorable.

Apache (1954) C-91m. ** D: Robert Aldrich. Burt Lancaster, Jean Peters, John McIntire, Charles (Bronson) Buchinsky. Pacifist Indian (Lancaster) learns might makes right from U.S. cavalry; turns to fighting one man crusade for his tribe's rights. Overacted and improbable.

Apache Ambush (1955) 68m. ** D: Fred R. Sears. Bill Williams, Richard Jaeckel, Movita, Tex Ritter. So what else is new?

Apache Drums (1951) C-75m. *½ D: Hugo Fregonese. Stephen McNally, Coleen Gray, Willard Parker, Arthur Shields. Humdrum Western with gambler McNally coming to town's rescue when attacked by Indians.

Apache Gold (1965-German) C-91m. **½ D: Harald Reinl. Lex Barker, Mario Adorf, Pierre Brice, Marie Versini. A sort of Eastern-Western has good Indian atmosphere, plenty of action.

Apache Rifles (1964) C-92m. **½ D: William Witney. Audie Murphy, Michael Dante, Linda Lawson, John Archer, J. Pat O'Malley. Audie is stalwart cavalry captain assigned to corral renegading Apaches. Stock footage and plot mar potentials of actioner.

Apache Territory (1958) C-75m. *½ D: Ray Nazarro. Rory Calhoun, Barbara Bates, John Dehner, Carolyn Craig. Calhoun almost singlehandedly routs rampaging Apaches and rescues defenseless Bates.

Apache War Smoke (1952) 67m. *½ D: Harold F. Kress. Gilbert Roland, Robert Horton, Glenda Farrell, Gene Lockhart, Bobby Blake. Pat Western involving stagecoach robbery and Indian attack on stage-line station. Good supporting cast wasted.

Apache Warrior (1957) 74m. ** D: Elmo Williams. Keith Larsen, Jim Davis, Michael Carr, Eddie Little. When an Indian leader's brother is killed, redskins go on the warpath. Nothing new.

Apartment, The (1960) 125m. **** D: Billy Wilder. Jack Lemmon, Shirley MacLaine, Fred MacMurray, Ray Walston, Jack Kruschen, Edie Adams. Superb comedy-drama which won Best Picture Award of 1960. Wilder is in top form with a great cast. Lemmon loans his apartment key to friends, and complications ensue involving his boss (MacMurray) and a girl (MacLaine). Don't miss it.

Apartment For Peggy (1948) 99m. *** D: George Seaton. Jeanne Crain, William Holden, Edmund Gwenn, Gene Lockhart. Breezy story of newlyweds trying to live on college campus; old pros Gwenn and Lockhart steal film from young lovers.

Ape, The (1940) 62m. ** D: William Nigh. Boris Karloff, Gertrude W. Hoffman, Henry Hall, Maris Wrixon. Low-budget shocker with mad doctor Karloff killing and experimenting with title character in order to save girl's life.

Ape Man, The (1943) 64m. ** D: William Beaudine. Bela Lugosi, Louise Currie, Wallace Ford, Henry Hall, Minerva Urecal. Minor horror effort with Lugosi and cast overacting in story of scientist injecting himself to attain power of simian relatives.

Appaloosa, The (1966) C-98m. **½ D: Sidney J. Furie. Marlon Brando, Anjanette Comer, John Saxon, Alex Montoya, Frank Silvera. Brooding Western set in 1870's with Brando trying to recover horse stolen from him by Mexican bandit; slowly-paced, well photographed.

Applause (1929) 78m. **½ D: Rouben Mamoulian. Helen Morgan, Joan Peers, Henry Wadsworth, Dorothy Cummings. Revolutionary early talkie with many advanced techniques dates badly because of trite dialogue, but Morgan is fine in seedy N.Y.C. burlesque atmosphere.

Appointment For Love (1941) 89m. **½ D: William Seiter. Charles Boyer, Margaret Sullavan, Rita Johnson, Reginald Denny, Ruth Terry, Eugene Pallette. Frothy comedy showcasing delightful stars: husband and wife with careers find happy marriage almost impossible.

Appointment In Berlin (1943) 77m. **½ D: Alfred E. Green. George Sanders, Marguerite Chapman, Onslow Stevens, Gale Sondergaard, Alan Napier. Another WW2 intrigue film, better than most, with Sanders joining Nazi radio staff to learn secret plans.

Appointment in Honduras (1953) C-79m. **½ D: Jacques Tourneur. Ann Sheridan, Glenn Ford, Zachary Scott, Jack Elam. Idealistic American (Ford) out to save Latin-American country, corrals villainous companions into helping crusade. Sheridan is not focal point, and a pity.

Appointment With a Shadow (1958) 73m. ** D: Joseph Pevney. Richard Carlson, George Nader, Joanna Moore, Brian Keith, Virginia Field. Former ace reporter swears off alcohol and scoops big story.

Appointment With Danger (1951) 89m. *** D: Lewis Allen. Alan Ladd, Phyllis Calvert, Paul Stewart, Jan Sterling, Jack Webb. Ladd's rugged performance as crusading postal aviator combatting robbery scheme is aided by good aerial shots.

Appointment With Murder (1948) 67m. D: Jack Bernhard. John Calvert, Catherine Craig, Lyle Talbot, Jack Reitzen, Peter Brocco. SEE: The Falcon series.

April in Paris (1952) C-101m. **½ D: David Butler. Doris Day, Ray Bolger, Claude Dauphin, Eve Miller, George Givot. Drab musical pegged on diplomat Bolger and showgirl Day having uninspired shipboard problems before reaching Paris.

April Love (1957) C-97m. **½ D: Henry Levin. Pat Boone, Shirley Jones, Dolores Michaels, Arthur O'Connell, Matt Crowley. Engaging musical with wholesome Boone visiting relatives' Kentucky farm, falling in love with neighbor Jones.

April Showers (1948) 94m. ** D: James V. Kern. Jack Carson, Ann Sothern, Robert Alda, S. Z. Sakall, Robert Ellis. Hackneyed backstage vaudeville yarn with Carson-Sothern teaming, splitting, reteaming, etc.

Arabesque (1966) C-105m. *** D: Stanley Donen. Sophia Loren, Gregory Peck, Alan Badel, Kieron Moore, George Coulouris. Modern secret-agent escapism as Peck is drawn into espionage with Sophia, who was never more beautiful. Exciting, beautifully photographed, minus any message or deep thought.

Arabian Nights (1942) C-86m. ** D: John Rawlins. Jon Hall, Maria Montez, Sabu, Leif Erickson, Turhan Bey, Billy Gilbert, Shemp Howard, John Qualen, Thomas Gomez. Good production values evident in average desert meller. Hall again leads movement to depose evil caliph. Corny dialogue.

Arch of Triumph (1948) 120m. **½ D: Lewis Milestone. Ingrid Bergman, Charles Boyer, Charles Laughton, Louis Calhern. Sluggish drama of refugee Boyer falling in love with Bergman in WW2 France, based on Erich Maria Remarque's novel.

Are Husbands Necessary? (1942) 79m. ** D: Norman Taurog. Ray Milland, Betty Field, Patricia Morison, Eugene Pallette, Cecil Kellaway. — And what about this film?

Are Parents People? (1925) 60m. **½ D: Malcolm St. Clair. Betty Bronson, Adolph Menjou, Florence Vidor, Lawrence Gray. Enjoyable vintage silent with good cast; innocuous story of young Bronson bringing her estranged parents together again. No great shakes, but fun.

Are You With It? (1948) 90m. **½ D: Jack Hively. Donald O'Connor, Olga San Juan, Martha Stewart, Lew Parker. Bright little musical of math-whiz O'Connor joining a carnival.

Arena (1953) C-83m. ** D: Richard Fleischer. Gig Young, Jean Hagen, Polly Bergen, Henry Morgan, Robert Horton. Flat rodeo tale with Tucson location traces rise of cowboy performer (Young) who nearly lets success mis-steer his future.

Arise, My Love (1940) 113m. *** D: Mitchell Leisen. Claudette Colbert, Ray Milland, Walter Abel, Dennis O'Keefe, Dick Purcell. News correspondent Colbert loves flyer-of-fortune Milland, who is working in war-torn Spain. Bright stars make script seem better than it is.

Arizona (1940) 127m. **½ D: Wesley Ruggles. Jean Arthur, William Holden, Warren William, Porter Hall, Paul Harvey. Arthur is always charming, and she has fine supporting cast, but this standard Western seems endless.

Arizona Mission SEE: **Gun the Man Down**.

Arizona Raiders (1965) C-88m. **½ D: William Witney. Audie Murphy, Michael Dante, Ben Cooper, Buster Crabbe, Gloria Talbott. Murphy is confederate army officer heading Arizona rangers after Civil War, involved in battling Quantrill's raiders.

Armored Attack SEE: **North Star**.

Armored Car Robbery (1950) 68m. *½ D: Richard Fleischer. Charles McGraw, Adele Jergens, William Talman, Steve Brodie. Inoffensive study of attempted large theft and the repercussions on those involved.

Armored Command (1961) 99m. ** D: Byron Haskin. Howard Keel, Tina Louise, Warner Anderson, Burt Reynolds. Bland war film with stars merely going through their paces.

Arnelo Affair, The (1947) 86m. ** D: Arch Oboler. John Hodiak, George Murphy, Frances Gifford, Dean Stockwell, Eve Arden. Neglected wife drawn hypnotically to client of husband finally learns of his involvement in girl's murder.

Around the World Under the Sea (1966) C-117m. ** D: Andrew Marton. Lloyd Bridges, Shirley Eaton, David McCallum, Brian Kelly, Keenan Wynn, Marshall Thompson. Several TV personalities appear together in this undistinguished underwater tour about testing earthquake warnings. Eaton adds femininity to otherwise all-male cast.

Arrest Bulldog Drummond (1939) 57m. D: James Hogan. John Howard, Heather Angel, H. B. Warner, George Zucco, E. E. Clive, Reginald Denny, John Sutton. SEE: **Bulldog Drummond** series.

Arrow in the Dust (1954) 80m. ** D: Lesley Selander. Sterling Hayden, Coleen Gray, Keith Larsen, Tom Tully. Deserting horse soldier (Hayden) learns sterling virtues when he assumes identity of dead commanding officer, warding off Indian attack on passing wagon train.

Arrowhead (1953) 105m. **½ D: Charles Marquis Warren. Charlton Heston, Jack Palance, Katy Jurado, Brian Keith, Milburn Stone. Apaches prefer war to peace, with many Indian vs. cavalry skirmishes; Heston and Palance are intense.

Arsene Lupin (1932) 84m. *** D: Jack Conway. John Barrymore, Lionel Barrymore, Karen Morley, John Miljan, Henry Armetta, Tully Marshall. Ripe detective yarn set in Paris: John is dapper jewel thief—Lionel the harried detective. They make a marvelous team.

Arsenic and Old Lace (1944) 118m. *** D: Frank Capra. Cary Grant, Priscilla Lane, Raymond Massey,

Peter Lorre, Jack Carson, Josephine Hull, Jean Adair, James Gleason, Grant Mitchell, John Ridgely, Edward Everett Horton. Hilarious adaptation of play about two seemingly harmless old ladies who murder gentlemen callers; frantic cast is excellent in bizarre comedy, especially Lorre and Massey as unsuspecting murderers holed up in the Brooklyn household.

Art of Love, The (1965) C-99m. ** D: Norman Jewison. James Garner, Dick Van Dyke, Elke Sommer, Angie Dickinson, Ethel Merman, Carl Reiner. Ordinary comedy set in France with a bemused cast headed by Van Dyke as a struggling artist and Sommer as his virtuous girl. Boisterous Merman is a local madam with a yen for singing.

Artists & Models (1937) 97m. **½ D: Raoul Walsh. Jack Benny, Ida Lupino, Judy Canova, Gail Patrick, Richard Arlen, Martha Raye, Connee Boswell, Ethel Clayton. Lupino pretends to be a socialite in flimsy plot with uncharacteristic Benny and songs "Stop You're Breaking My Heart," "Whispers in the Dark." Vintage fun.

Artists and Models (1955) C-109m. *** D: Frank Tashlin. Dean Martin, Jerry Lewis, Shirley MacLaine, Dorothy Malone, Eva Gabor, Anita Ekberg. Overblown daffy-duo shenanigans spiced by feminine beauty and a few wacky sequences, with cartoonist Martin utilizing Lewis' far-out dreams for his strips.

Artists and Models Abroad (1938) 90m. *** D: Mitchell Leisen. Jack Benny, Joan Bennett, Mary Boland, Charley Grapewin, Yacht Club Boys, Joyce Compton. Breezy, entertaining froth of musical troupe stranded in Paris, perennially saved by conniving boss Benny. Yacht Club Boys sing incredible song, "You're Broke, You Dope."

As If It Were Raining (1963-French, dubbed) 85m. ** D: Jose Monter. Eddie Constantine, Henri Cogan, Elisa Montes, Jose Nieto, Sylvia Solar. Constantine is at liberty in Spain, enmeshed in an embezzlement scheme; wooden yarn.

As Long As They're Happy (1957-British) C-76m. *½ D: J. Lee Thompson. Janette Scott, Jean Carson, Diana Dors, Hugh McDermott, Jack Buchanan. Mini-musical involving daughter of staid British stockholder who falls for visiting song-and-dance man.

As the Sea Rages (1960) 74m. **½ D: Horst Haechler. Maria Schell, Cliff Robertson, Cameron Mitchell. Seaman Robertson arrives in Greece planning a sponge-diving business, meeting resistance from townfolk and the elements; muddled script.

As You Desire Me (1932) 71m. *** D: George Fitzmaurice. Greta Garbo, Melvyn Douglas, Erich von Stroheim, Hedda Hopper, Owen Moore. Garbo enhances this far-fetched tale of amnesiac allied with three families.

As Young As You Feel (1951) 77m. *** D: Harmon Jones. Monty Woolley, Thelma Ritter, David Wayne, Jean Peters, Constance Bennett, Marilyn Monroe. Marvelous cast enhances timely story of Woolley resenting retirement at age 65 and determined to alter corporate policy.

Ashes and Diamonds (1958-Polish, dubbed) 104m. *** D: Andrezej Wajda. Zbigniew Cybulski, Ewa Krzyzanowska, Adam Pawlikowski, Bogumil Kobiela, Waclaw Zastrzezynski. Intelligent, penetrating account of resistance movement during closing days of WW2 with anti-Communist partisans engaged in ambushing the new Communist commandant; slowly-paced.

Ask Any Girl (1959) C-101m. *** D: Charles Walters. David Niven, Shirley MacLaine, Gig Young, Rod Taylor, Jim Backus, Elisabeth Fraser. Effervescent gloss of naive MacLaine coming to New York, discovering most men have lecherous designs on girls; she wants a husband, however.

Asphalt Jungle, The (1950) 112m. ***½ D: John Huston. Sterling Hayden, Louis Calhern, Jean Hagen, Marilyn Monroe, Sam Jaffe, James Whitmore. Powerful crime drama, realistically done. Monroe shines in brief bit, with sturdy work by Hayden as thief and Hagen his devoted girl.

Assassin, The (1953-British) 90m. ** D: Ralph Thomas. Richard Todd, Eva Bartok, George Coulouris, Margot Grahame. Todd is detective on manhunt in postwar Venice; usual murders and romance result.

Assassin, The (1961-Italian, dubbed) 105m. **½ D: Elio Petri. Marcello Mastroianni, Salvo Randone, Micheline Presle, Cristina Gajoni. Engaging study of scoundrel Mastroianni implicated in a murder, broken by the police, proven innocent, with a wry ending.

Assault on a Queen (1966) C-106m. **½ D: Jack Donohue. Frank Sinatra, Virna Lisi, Tony Franciosa, Richard Conte, Reginald Denny. Sloppy Sinatra vehicle about big heist of H.M.S. Queen Elizabeth's vault.

Assignment in Brittany (1943) 96m. ** D: Jack Conway. Jean-Pierre Aumont, Susan Peters, Richard Whorf, Margaret Wycherly, Signe Hasso, Reginald Owen. Aumont is lookalike for Nazi leader, uses this to his advantage working for French underground; patriotic WW2 melodrama.

Assignment—Paris (1952) 85m. ** D: Robert Parrish. Dana Andrews, Marta Toren, George Sanders, Audrey Totter. Fitfully entertaining drama of reporter Andrews trying to link together threads of plot between Communist countries against the West. Filmed in Paris.

Astonished Heart, The (1950-British) 92m. **½ D: Terence Fisher, Anthony Darnborough. Noel Coward, Celia Johnson, Margaret Leighton, Joyce Carey. Drawing-room melodrama involving a psychiatrist who prefers a tawdry girl to his well-bred wife; not the perky production one would expect with Coward in cast.

At Gunpoint (1955) C-81m. **½ D: Alfred L. Werker. Fred MacMurray, Dorothy Malone, Walter Brennan, Tommy Rettig, Jack Lambert. MacMurray is well suited to role of peaceloving man drawn into gunplay by taunting outlaws.

At Sword's Point (1952) C-81m. **½ D: Lewis Allen. Cornel Wilde, Maureen O'Hara, Robert Douglas, Dan O'Herlihy, Blanche Yurka, Lucien Littlefield. Vaguely drawing upon Dumas' THREE MUSKETEERS characters, this actioner is filled with usual French court intrigue and abundance of swordplay.

At the Circus (1939) 87m. **½ D: Edward Buzzell. Groucho, Chico and Harpo Marx, Margaret Dumont, Eve Arden, Nat Pendleton, Kenny Baker, Fritz Feld, Florence Rice. Not topgrade Marx Brothers, but some good scenes as they save circus from bankruptcy; highlight, Groucho singing "Lydia The Tattooed Lady."

At War With the Army (1950) 93m. **½ D: Hal Walker. Dean Martin, Jerry Lewis, Polly Bergen, Angela Greene. Dean and Jerry in the service, with some funny sequences, including memorable soda machine gag.

Athena (1954) 96m. **½ D: Richard Thorpe. Jane Powell, Debbie Reynolds, Edmund Purdom, Vic Damone, Louis Calhern, Evelyn Varden, Linda Christian. Back Bay lawyer (Purdom) and singer (Damone) romance two sisters living with eccentric grandparents. Wispy plot, average tunes.

Atlantis, the Lost Continent (1961) C-90m. *½ D: George Pal. Anthony Hall, Joyce Taylor, John Dall, Frank de Kova. Unintentionally funny fantasy, occasionally diverting. Good special effects, but basically corny.

Atoll K SEE: Utopia.

Atomic Brain, The SEE: Monstrosity.

Atomic City, The (1952) 85m. **½ D: Jerry Hopper. Gene Barry, Nancy Gates, Lydia Clarke, Lee Aaker. Tightly-knit caper involving kidnapping of atomic scientist's son, well played by young Aaker.

Atomic Kid, The (1954) 86m. *½ D: Leslie Martinson. Mickey Rooney, Robert Strauss, Elaine Davis, Bill Goodwin. Rooney survives desert atomic blast, discovering he's radioactive. Slight spy-comedy.

Atomic Man, The (1956-British) 78m. ** D: Ken Hughes. Gene Nelson, Faith Domergue, Joseph Tomelty, Peter Arne. Bland narrative of reporter and girlfriend encountering scientists who have experimented with nuclear materials and suffered dire consequences.

Atomic Submarine, The (1959) 72m. ** D: Spencer Bennet. Arthur Franz, Dick Foran, Brett Halsey, Tom Conway, Bob Steele, Victor Varconi, Joi Lansing. Programmer sci-fi involving flying saucers lodged in underwater headquarters.

Attack! (1956) 107m. *** D: Robert Aldrich. Jack Palance, Eddie Albert, Lee Marvin, Robert Strauss. Reenactment of the Battle of the Bulge, emphasizing a group of American soldiers; tightly directed, avoids warflick clichés.

Attack and Retreat SEE: Italiano Brava Gente.

Attack of the Crab Monsters (1957) 64m. *½ D: Roger Corman. Richard Garland, Pamela Duncan, Russell Johnson, Leslie Bradley. Poor fools trapped on remote island with ferocious giant crabs. Few thrills.

Attack of the 50 Ft. Woman (1958) 66m. Bomb D: Nathan Juran. Allison Hayes, William Hudson, Yvette Vickers, Roy Gordon. Visitor from outer space creates title monster and predictable results occur.

Attack of the Puppet People (1958) 78m. *½ D: Bert I. Gordon. John Agar, John Hoyt, June Kenney, Scott Peters. Low-class shocker involving transformation of people into robot dolls; predictable and amateurish.

Attempt to Kill (1961-British) 57m. ** D: Royston Morley. Derek Farr, Tony Wright, Richard Pearson, Freda Jackson. Mild Edgar Wallace entry, salvaged by superior cast in predictable Scotland Yard manhunt caper.

Attila (1958-Italian, dubbed) C-83m. *½ D: Pietro Francisci. Anthony Quinn, Sophia Loren, Henri Vidal, Irene Papas. Inept spectacle with ridiculous script of Attila readying to conquer Rome.

Auntie Mame (1958) C-143m. **½ D: Morton DaCosta. Rosalind Russell, Forrest Tucker, Coral Browne, Fred Clark. Roz Russell's film all the way, based on Patrick Dennis' book and play, elaborately staged but disjointed. Tucker and Peggy Cass lend excellent support to elegantly gowned and coiffed Russell.

Autumn Leaves (1956) 108m. **½ D: Robert Aldrich. Joan Crawford, Cliff Robertson, Vera Miles, Lorne Greene. Middle-aged typist marries younger man (Robertson), only to discover he is mentally disturbed and already married. Stalwart performance by Crawford as troubled woman.

Avalanche (1946) 70m. *½ D: Irving Allen. Bruce Cabot, Roscoe Karns, Helen Mowery, Veda Ann Borg. Programmer tale of murder and suspense at an isolated ski lodge; shoddy production.

Avenger, The (1960-German, dubbed) 102m. **½ D: Karl Anton. Ingrid Van Bergen, Heinz Drache, Ina Duscha, Maria Litto. Above-par shocker based on Edgar Wallace tale of bestial villain beheading several people, mailing them to appropriate recipients.

Away All Boats (1956) C-114m. **½ D: Joseph Pevney. Jeff Chandler, George Nader, Julie Adams, Lex Barker. Improbably heroic and overpartial slanting of America's participation in naval engagements during WW2 mar the movie's total effect.

Awful Dr. Orloff, The (1961-Spanish, dubbed) 95m. ** D: Jess Franco. Howard Vernon, Conrado Sanmartin, Diana Lorys, Ricardo Valle, Perla Cristal. Medium spooker about deranged surgeon operating on a series of women, trying to find spare parts to revitalize his disfigured daughter.

Awful Truth, The (1937) 92m. ***½ D: Leo McCarey. Irene Dunne, Cary Grant, Ralph Bellamy, Cecil Cunningham, Mary Forbes, Alex D'Arcy. Smash-bang social comedy as Cary and Irene divorce, she to marry hayseed Bellamy, he to wed aristocratic Molly Lamont. Each does his best to spoil the other's plans. Remade as musical: LET'S DO IT AGAIN.

B. F.'s Daughter (1948) 108m. *½ D: Robert Z. Leonard. Barbara Stanwyck, Van Heflin, Charles Coburn, Richard Hart, Keenan Wynn, Margaret Lindsay. Disastrous film of J. P. Marquand novel, with Stanwyck the domineering girl ruining marriage to professor Heflin.

Babbitt (1934) 74m. *** D: William Keighley. Guy Kibbee, Aline MacMahon, Claire Dodd, Nan Grey, Mary Treen. Fine Sinclair Lewis Americana of pettiness, ambition, and social life in small Midwestern town; Kibbee is fine in lead role.

Babe Ruth Story, The (1948) 106m. ** D: Roy Del Ruth. William Bendix, Claire Trevor, Charles Bickford, Sam Levene, William Frawley. "Biography" is insult to famed baseball star; inept.

Babes in Arms (1939) 96m. *** D: Busby Berkeley. Mickey Rooney, Judy Garland, Charles Winninger, Guy Kibbee, June Preisser, John Sheffield, Henry Hull, Margaret Hamilton. Rodgers-Hart musical becomes Rooney-Garland vehicle, one of their best, with "Where or When," "Lady Is A Tramp," and other great songs.

Babes In Bagdad (1952) 79m. Bomb

D: Edgar G. Ulmer. Paulette Goddard, Gypsy Rose Lee, John Boles, Sebastian Cabot. Embarrassing, hokey costumer made even seedier by miscast veteran performers.

Babes in Toyland (1934) 73m. *** D: Gus Meins, Charles R. Rogers. Stan Laurel, Oliver Hardy, Charlotte Henry, Johnny Downs, Jean Darling, Henry Brandon, Felix Knight. L&H version of Victor Herbert operetta is solid children's entertainment with enough good music and horseplay by duo to keep adults amused. Retitled: MARCH OF THE WOODEN SOLDIERS.

Babes on Broadway (1941) 118m. **½ D: Busby Berkeley. Mickey Rooney, Judy Garland, Fay Bainter, Virginia Weidler, Richard Quine. Showcase vehicle for Mickey and Judy's talents, with duo doing everything from imitations of Carmen Miranda and Bernhardt to minstrel numbers. Standout is Judy's "F.D.R. Jones."

Babette Goes to War (1960-French, dubbed) C-103m. **½ D: Christian-Jaque. Brigitte Bardot, Jacques Charrier, Francis Blanche, Ronald Howard. Bardot is not at her forte playing lighthearted comedy. Flimsy WW2 account of French agent Bardot working for British, being sent back to France to help underground.

Baby and the Battleship, The (1957-British) C-96m. **½ D: Jay Lewis. John Mills, Richard Attenborough, Bryan Forbes, Michael Hordern. Diverting if not hilarious account of gobs who smuggle infant aboard ship, and their antics to keep the child hidden from top brass.

Baby Face Nelson (1957) 85m. ** D: Don Siegel. Mickey Rooney, Carolyn Jones, Cedric Hardwicke, Jack Elam, Ted De Corsia. Rooney gives flavorful performance in title role of gunhappy gangster in Prohibition-Depression days; low-budget product, but action-filled.

Baby, the Rain Must Fall (1965) 100m. *** D: Robert Mulligan. Steve McQueen, Lee Remick, Don Murray, Paul Fix, Josephine Hutchinson, Ruth White. Much underrated account of ex-convict McQueen returning to his wife and daughter, but unable to change his restless ways. Murray is sincere sheriff who tries to help.

Bachelor and the Bobby-Soxer, The (1947) 95m. *** D: Irving Reis. Cary Grant, Myrna Loy, Shirley Temple, Rudy Vallee, Ray Collins, Harry Davenport. Judge Loy orders playboy Grant to wine and dine her niece Temple, so the teen-ager will forget her infatuation for him. Breezy entertainment.

Bachelor Apartment (1931) 83m. **½ D: Lowell Sherman. Lowell Sherman, Irene Dunne, Mae Murray, Claudia Dell, Noel Francis, Bess Flowers. Sophisticated comedy about gay-blade Sherman shuffling his various girls back and forth; ancestor of COME BLOW YOUR HORN, etc.

Bachelor Father (1931) 90m. **½ D: Robert Z. Leonard. Marion Davies, Ralph Forbes, C. Aubrey Smith, Doris Lloyd, Halliwell Hobbes, Ray Milland. Oft-married Smith visits his grown children in amusing comedy spotlighting the fine British character actor.

Bachelor Flat (1961) C-91m. ** D: Frank Tashlin. Tuesday Weld, Richard Beymer, Celeste Holm, Terry-Thomas. Weld visits her mother's beach house and finds scientist Thomas at work; she moves in anyway and creates eventual havoc. Thomas has had better material; film's entertainment is all in his lap.

Bachelor in Paradise (1961) C-109m. ** D: Jack Arnold. Bob Hope, Lana Turner, Janis Paige, Jim Hutton, Paula Prentiss, Don Porter, Agnes Moorehead. Hope vehicle about the only bachelor in a community of married couples. Amusing, but not great. Hope has done better; Paige is fun as always.

Bachelor Mother (1939) 81m. ***½ D: Garson Kanin. Ginger Rogers, David Niven, Charles Coburn, Frank Albertson, Ernest Truex. Rogers unwittingly become guardian for abandoned baby in this delightful comedy; remade as BUNDLE OF JOY.

Bachelor Party, The (1957) 93m. *** D: Delbert Mann. Don Murray, E. G. Marshall, Jack Warden, Patricia Smith, Carolyn Jones, Nancy Marchand. Low-key film version of Paddy Chayefsky teleplay vividly depicts anguish of single life among middle-aged men, focusing on their reaction to one of the group's approaching marriage.

Back at the Front (1952) 87m. **½

Back Door to Heaven D: George Sherman. Tom Ewell, Harvey Lembeck, Mari Blanchard, Richard Long. Follow-up adventures of Bill Mauldin's army goof-offs Willie and Joe scampering around post-WW2 Tokyo. Retitled: WILLIE AND JOE BACK AT THE FRONT.

Back Door to Heaven (1939) 85m. ** D: William K. Howard. Van Heflin, Aline MacMahon, Wallace Ford, Stuart Erwin, Patricia Ellis, Kent Smith, Iris Adrian, William Harrigan. Sentimental drama of poor children struggling to escape from drudgery of home and work-weary parents.

Back From Eternity (1956) 97m. **½ D: John Farrow. Robert Ryan, Anita Ekberg, Rod Steiger, Phyllis Kirk. Moderately engrossing account of victims of plane crash, stranded in South American jungle, and their various reactions to the situation. Poor remake of FIVE CAME BACK.

Back From the Dead (1957) 79m. Bomb D: Charles Marquis Warren. Peggie Castle, Arthur Franz, Marsha Hunt, Evelyn Scott, James Bell. Castle is earnest as wife possessed by will of husband's dead first spouse, but cliché-ridden production makes everything ridiculous.

Back Street (1941) 89m. *** D: Robert Stevenson. Charles Boyer, Margaret Sullavan, Richard Carlson, Frank McHugh, Tim Holt. Fine team of Boyer and Sullavan breathes life into Fannie Hurst perennial soaper of woman whose love for man doesn't die when he marries another.

Back Street (1961) C-107m. **½ D: David Miller. Susan Hayward, John Gavin, Vera Miles, Virginia Grey. Updated, lavish, unbelievable third version of Fannie Hurst's story of a woman's love for married man. Doesn't play as well as Irene Dunne or Margaret Sullavan versions.

Back to Bataan (1945) 95m. *** D: Edward Dmytryk. John Wayne, Anthony Quinn, Beulah Bondi, Fely Franquelli, Philip Ahn, Lawrence Tierney. Good sturdy WW2 action film with officer Wayne leading Yank soldiers to victory in the Philippines.

Back to God's Country (1953) 78m. **½ D: Joseph Pevney. Rock Hudson, Marcia Henderson, Steve Cochran, Hugh O'Brian. Sea captain Hudson and wife Henderson undergo rigors of nature and villainy of Cochran et al before settling, moving onward in the north country for their dream existence.

Back to the Wall (1959-French, dubbed) 94m. ** D: Edouard Molinaro. Gerard Oury, Jeanne Moreau, Philippe Nicaud, Claire Maurier, Jean Lefebvre. As the adulterous wife, Moreau spins entertaining web of extortion and murder; satisfactory suspenser.

Backfire (1950) 91m. ** D: Vincent Sherman. Virginia Mayo, Gordon MacRae, Edmond O'Brien, Viveca Lindfors, Dane Clark, Ed Begley. OK mystery tale has MacRae search for missing friend through maze of murder and romance.

Backfire (1961-British) 59m. ** D: Paul Almond. Alfred Burke, Zena Marshall, Oliver Johnston, Noel Trevarthen is insurance investigator solving arson and murder at a cosmetics firm; adequate programmer based on Edgar Wallace yarn.

Background to Danger (1943) 80m. **½ D: Raoul Walsh. George Raft, Brenda Marshall, Sydney Greenstreet, Peter Lorre, Osa Massen, Kurt Katch. Middling WW2 mystery of intrigue, only asset being peerless Lorre and Greenstreet team.

Backlash (1947) 66m. ** D: Eugene Forde. Jean Rogers, Richard Travis, Larry Blake, John Eldredge, Leonard Strong, Robert Shayne, Louise Currie, Douglas Fowley. Standard programmer of man trying to frame his wife for murder he committed.

Backlash (1956) C-84m. **½ D: John Sturges. Richard Widmark, Donna Reed, William Campbell, John McIntire, Barton MacLane. Widmark is only survivor of Indian massacre; knowing the whereabouts of buried treasure, he is object of outlaw manhunt.

Bad and the Beautiful, The (1952) 118m. *** D: Vincente Minnelli. Lana Turner, Walter Pidgeon, Kirk Douglas, Gloria Grahame, Dick Powell, Barry Sullivan, Gilbert Roland. At times penetrating look at Hollywood, involving various strata of cinema society, displaying ambitions and romances. This multi-Oscar-winning film now seems contrived MGM gloss.

Bad Bascomb (1946) 110m. *½ D: S. Sylvan Simon. Wallace Beery,

Margaret O'Brien, Marjorie Main, J. Carrol Naish, Marshall Thompson. Overlong Western with fine action scenes, overshadowed by incredibly syrupy scenes with Beery and O'Brien.

Bad Boy (1949) 86m. **½ D: Kurt Neumann. Lloyd Nolan, Jane Wyatt, Audie Murphy, James Gleason, Martha Vickers. Juvenile delinquent rehabilitated by being sent to boys' ranch, where Nolan befriends him. Young Murphy is belligerently effective.

Bad Day at Black Rock (1954) C-81m. ***½ D: John Sturges. Spencer Tracy, Robert Ryan, Anne Francis, Dean Jagger, Walter Brennan, John Ericson, Ernest Borgnine, Lee Marvin. Powerhouse cast in yarn of one-armed man (Tracy) uncovering skeleton in Western town's closet. Borgnine memorable as a slimy heavy.

Bad For Each Other (1953) 83m. **½ D: Irving Rapper. Charlton Heston, Lizabeth Scott, Dianne Foster, Mildred Dunnock, Marjorie Rambeau. Idealistic doctor Heston finds Pennsylvania mining town has more worthy patients than idle social set. Pouty Scott and wise Rambeau are good cast assets.

Bad Girl (1959-British) 100m. *½ D: Herbert Wilcox. Anna Neagle, Sylvia Syms, Norman Wooland, Wilfrid Hyde-White, Kenneth Haigh, Julia Lockwood. Modest trivia enhanced by good cast involving teenager who becomes involved with sordid side of life. Retitled: TEENAGE BAD GIRL.

Bad Lord Byron (1951-British) 85m. **½ D: David Macdonald. Dennis Price, Joan Greenwood, Mai Zetterling, Sonia Holm. Potentially exciting but static retelling of the life of 19th-century poet and lover, focusing on his many romances.

Bad Man, The (1941) 70m. **½ D: Richard Thorpe. Wallace Beery, Lionel Barrymore, Laraine Day, Ronald Reagan, Henry Travers. Fairly good co-starring vehicle for Beery, as Western outlaw, and Barrymore, as former friend who depends on the bad man's loyalty.

Bad Man of Brimstone (1938) 90m. ** D: J. Walter Ruben. Wallace Beery, Virginia Bruce, Dennis O'Keefe, Joseph Calleia, Lewis Stone, Guy Kibbee, Bruce Cabot. Low-grade Western vehicle is for Beery fans, with star as outlaw who is reformed by family revelation.

Bad Men of Missouri (1941) 74m. *** D: Ray Enright. Dennis Morgan, Jane Wyman, Wayne Morris, Arthur Kennedy, Victor Jory, Alan Baxter. Younger brothers, enraged by Southern carpetbaggers, turn to lawless life in fictional Western, with good cast.

Bad Seed, The (1956) 129m. *** D: Mervyn LeRoy. Nancy Kelly, Patty McCormack, Henry Jones, Eileen Heckart, Evelyn Varden. Stagy but spellbinding account of malicious child McCormack whose inherited evil causes death of several people.

Badge of Marshal Brennan, The (1957) 76m. *½ D: Albert C. Gannaway. Jim Davis, Arleen Whelan, Lee Van Cleef, Louis Jean Heydt. Uninspired account of criminal Davis mistaken as law enforcer, who redeems himself by corraling rustling gang.

Badlanders, The (1958) C-83m. *** D: Delmer Daves. Alan Ladd, Ernest Borgnine, Katy Jurado, Claire Kelly. Turn-of-the-century Western set in Arizona with Ladd and Borgnine planning gold robbery, each trying to outsmart the other; nicely handled by all.

Badlands of Dakota (1941) 74m. **½ D: Alfred E. Green. Robert Stack, Ann Rutherford, Richard Dix, Frances Farmer, Broderick Crawford, Hugh Herbert. Brothers Crawford and Stack fight over Rutherford, while Wild Bill Hickok (Dix) does fighting of another kind.

Badlands of Montana (1957) 75m. *½ D: Daniel B. Ullman. Rex Reason, Beverly Garland, Keith Larsen, Jack Kruschen. Unimaginative oater leading up to inevitable climax of former buddies, sheriff and gunslinger, having shoot-out.

Badman's Country (1958) 68m. **½ D: Fred F. Sears. George Montgomery, Buster Crabbe, Neville Brand, Malcolm Atterbury. Fictionalised Western history with name-dropping cast of characters. Sheriff Pat Garrett (Montgomery) joins with Wyatt Earp (Crabbe) and Buffalo Bill (Atterbury) for showdown with outlaw Butch Cassidy (Brand).

Badman's Territory (1946) 97m. ***

D: Tim Whelan. Randolph Scott, Ann Richards, Gabby Hayes, Ray Collins, Chief Thundercloud. Sheriff Scott is helpless when bandits flee across border into territory uncontrolled by government; good Western.

Bagdad (1949) C-82m. ** D: Charles Lamont. Maureen O'Hara, Paul Christian, Vincent Price, John Sutton. Costume hijinks with O'Hara fetching if not believable as native chieftain's daughter seeking revenge for father's death in old Turkey.

Bahama Passage (1941) C-83m. **½ D: Edward Griffith. Madeleine Carroll, Sterling Hayden, Flora Robson, Leo G. Carroll, Mary Anderson. Scenery is chief asset of routine tale of lovely Madeleine meeting handsome Sterling in beautiful Bahama, with much hamming by Carroll and Robson.

Bailout at 43,000 (1957) 78m. ** D: Francis D. Lyon. John Payne, Karen Steele, Paul Kelly, Richard Eyer, Constance Ford. Dilemma of air force pilot Payne whose relief at not having to test new safety device is outweighed by coward-guilt complex. Routine material is not enhanced by flight sequences or romantic relief.

Bait (1954) 79m. *½ D: Hugo Haas. Cleo Moore, Hugo Haas, John Agar, Emmett Lynn. Plodding melodrama; old geezer Haas connives to get rid of his prospector partner.

Balalaika (1939) 102m. ** D: Reinhold Schunzel. Nelson Eddy, Ilona Massey, Charles Ruggles, Frank Morgan, Lionel Atwill, George Tobias. Plodding operetta of Russian revolution with little to recommend it.

Ball of Fire (1941) 111m. ***½ D: Howard Hawks. Gary Cooper, Barbara Stanwyck, Oscar Homolka, Dana Andrews, Dan Duryea, S. Z. Sakall, Richard Haydn, Gene Krupa. Delightful reworking of Snow White and Seven Dwarfs; burlesque dancer Stanwyck moves in with seven prissy professors, headed by Cooper, studying slang for encyclopedia. Remade as A SONG IS BORN.

Ballad of a Soldier (1960-Russian, dubbed) 89m. *** D: Grigori Chukhrai. Vladimir Ivashov, Shanna Prokhorenko, Antonina Maximova, Nikolai Kruchkov. Effectively simple love story of Russian soldier on leave during WW2, who meets and falls in love with unaffected country girl.

Ballad of Josie, The (1967) C-102m. **½ D: Andrew McLaglen. Doris Day, Peter Graves, George Kennedy, Andy Devine, William Talman. Uninspired Western spoof with widow Day running a ranch and trying to lead the good life.

Bamboole! (1965-Italian) 111m. ** D: Dino Risi, Luigi Comencini, Franco Rossi, Mauro Bolognini. Virna Lisi, Nino Manfredi, Elke Sommer, Monica Vitti, Gina Lollobrigida, Akim Tamiroff, Jean Sorel. Quartet of stories on Italian life that never sparkles. THE PHONE CALL, TREATISE ON EUGENICS, THE SOUP, MONSIGNOR CUPID. Retitled: FOUR KINDS OF LOVE.

Bamboo Prison, The (1954) 80m. ** D: Lewis Seiler. Robert Francis, Dianne Foster, Brian Keith, Jerome Courtland, E. G. Marshall, Earle Hyman. Superficial handling of loyal American soldier Francis posing as informer in North Korean P.O.W. camp to outwit enemy.

Band of Angels (1957) C-127m. **½ D: Raoul Walsh. Clark Gable, Yvonne De Carlo, Sidney Poitier, Efrem Zimbalist, Jr., Patric Knowles. Flat attempt to make costume epic of Robert Penn Warren's civil war novel; Gable is Southern gentleman with shady past, in love with high-toned De Carlo who discovers she has Negro ancestors. Poitier is resolute educated slave.

Band Wagon, The (1953) C-112m. ***½ D: Vincente Minnelli. Fred Astaire, Cyd Charisse, Oscar Levant, Nanette Fabray, Jack Buchanan. Top musical of Broadway show biz. Songs: "That's Entertainment," "By Myself," "Triplets." Astaire's "Shine on Your Shoes" number is one of his all-time best.

Bandido (1956) C-92m. **½ D: Richard Fleischer. Robert Mitchum, Ursula Thiess, Gilbert Roland, Zachary Scott. Mitchum as profiteering munitions seller is chief interest in tale of love and bandit-fighting, set in Mexico in 1916.

Bandit of Sherwood Forest, The (1946) C-86m. **½ D: George Sherman, Henry Levin. Cornel Wilde, Anita Louise, Jill Esmond, Edgar Buchanan. Colorful but standard swashbuckler with Wilde as son of

35

Robin Hood carrying on in faithful tradition with the Merry Men.

Bandit of Zhobe, The (1959-British) C-80m. **½ D: John Gilling. Victor Mature, Anthony Newley, Norman Wooland, Anne Aubrey, Walter Gotell, Sean Kelly. Moderate actioner set in 19th-century India with Mature as native chief turned outlaw combatting the British.

Bandits of Corsica, The (1953) 81m. ** D: Ray Nazarro. Richard Greene, Paula Raymond, Raymond Burr, Lee Van Cleef. Pat costumer with Greene championing cause of the righteous.

Bang, Bang, You're Dead! (1966-British) C-92m. **½ D: Don Sharp. Tony Randall, Senta Berger, Terry-Thomas, Herbert Lom, Wilfrid Hyde-White. Unsuspecting Randall gets involved with Moroccan gangsters in OK spoof; good location shooting. Shown on TV as BANG BANG!

Bang You're Dead SEE: Game of Danger.

Banjo on My Knee (1936) 80m. *** D: John Cromwell. Barbara Stanwyck, Joel McCrea, Walter Brennan, Buddy Ebsen, Helen Westley, Walter Catlett, Tony Martin. Stanwyck's the whole show in riverboat saga, singing with Martin, dancing with Ebsen, scrapping with Katherine DeMille.

Bank Dick, The (1940) 74m. **** D: Eddie Cline. W. C. Fields, Cora Witherspoon, Una Merkel, Evelyn Del Rio, Jessie Ralph, Grady Sutton, Franklin Pangborn. Classic of insane humor loosely wound about a no-account who becomes a bank guard; Sutton as nitwit son-in-law, Pangborn as bookkeeper match the shenanigans of Fields.

Bannerline (1951) 88m. ** D: Don Weis. Keefe Brasselle, Sally Forrest, Lionel Barrymore, Lewis Stone. Brasselle is optimistic fledgling reporter who sparks civic pride into town fighting corruption; film marred by typecasting and clichéd plotline.

Banning (1967) C-102m. *** D: Ron Winston. Robert Wagner, Anjanette Comer, Jill St. John, Guy Stockwell, James Farentino. Pleasing study of corruption in and about a swank L.A. golf club. Wagner, the pro with a past; St. John, the love-hungry gal.

Bar Sinister SEE: It's a Dog's Life.

Barabbas (1962) C-134m. *** D: Richard Fleischer. Anthony Quinn, Silvana Mangano, Arthur Kennedy, Jack Palance, Ernest Borgnine, Katy Jurado. Lavish production, coupled with good script (based on Lagerkvist's novel) and generally fine acting by large cast make for engrossing, literate experience. Overly long.

Barbados Quest SEE: Murder on Approval.

Barbarian and the Geisha, The (1958) C-105m. **½ D: John Huston. John Wayne, Eiko Ando, Sam Jaffe, So Yamamura. Twisting of 19th-century history allows Wayne as Ambassador Harris to romance Japanese beauty (Ando). Miscasting of Wayne is ludicrous, throwing costumer amuck.

Barbary Coast (1935) 97m. ***½ D: Howard Hawks. Miriam Hopkins, Edward G. Robinson, Joel McCrea, Walter Brennan, Frank Craven, Brian Donlevy. Lusty tale of San Francisco in the late 19th century with dancehall queen Hopkins running head-on into big-shot Robinson.

Barbary Coast Gent (1944) 87m. ** D: Roy Del Ruth. Wallace Beery, Binnie Barnes, John Carradine, Noah Beery, Sr., Frances Rafferty, Chill Wills, Donald Meek. Typical Beery vehicle, with good supporting cast, about smooth-talking bandit who goes straight.

Barefoot Contessa, The (1954) C-128m. *** D: Joseph L. Mankiewicz. Humphrey Bogart, Ava Gardner, Edmond O'Brien, Marius Goring, Rossano Brazzi. Cynical tale of beautiful Ava promoted into Hollywood star by mentor-director Bogart. O'Brien won an Oscar as press agent.

Barefoot Mailman, The (1951) C-83m. ** D: Earl McEvoy. Robert Cummings, Terry Moore, Jerome Courtland, Will Geer. Potentially engaging story of a first postal route in Florida bogs down in tale of former con-man (Cummings) tempted to fleece citizens of Miami with phony railroad stock; Moore is pert leading lady.

Barefoot Savage SEE: Sensualita.

Barkleys of Broadway, The (1949) C-109m. *** D: Charles Walters. Fred Astaire, Ginger Rogers, Oscar Levant, Billie Burke. After a decade apart, Astaire-Rogers reteamed on screen as show biz couple who split and then make up. Songs: "You'd Be Hard to Replace," "My One And Only Highland Fling." Ginger reading "La Marseillaise" is one of movie's unforgettable low points.

Barnacle Bill (1941) 98m. ** D: Richard Thorpe. Wallace Beery, Marjorie Main. Leo Carrillo, Virginia Weidler, Donald Meek, Barton MacLane. Beery and Main support basically run-of-the-mill material as old salt and woman trying to snare him into marriage.

Baron of Arizona, The (1950) 90m. **½ D: Samuel Fuller. Vincent Price, Ellen Drew, Beulah Bondi, Reed Hadley. Price has field day as land-grabbing scoundrel who almost gains control of Arizona in the 19th century.

Baroness and the Butler, The (1938) 75m. ** D: Walter Lang. William Powell, Annabella, Helen Westley, Henry Stephenson, Joseph Schildkraut, J. Edward Bromberg. Powell leads double life as Annabella's butler and member of parliament. He's fine as usual but script is rather thin.

Baron's African War, The (1943) 100m. **½ D: Spencer Bennet. Rod Cameron, Joan Marsh, Duncan Renaldo, Lionel Royce. Flavorful Republic serial set in WW2 Africa, with Cameron tackling sinister Nazis and Arabs with equal relish; quite well paced. Re-edited movie serial: SECRET SERVICE IN DARKEST AFRICA.

Barretts of Wimpole Street, The (1957) C-105m. **½ D: Sidney Franklin. Jennifer Jones, John Gielgud, Bill Travers, Virginia McKenna. Tame interpretation of the lilting romance between poets Browning-Barrett, with actors bogged down in prettified fluff.

Barricade (1939) 71m. ** D: Gregory Ratoff. Alice Faye, Warner Baxter, Charles Winninger, Arthur Treacher, Keye Luke, Moroni Olsen. Faye and Baxter are trapped in Chinese embassy and fall in love; rather tame.

Barricade (1950) C-75m. ** D: Peter Godfrey. Dane Clark, Ruth Roman, Raymond Massey, Robert Douglas. Clark pitted against Massey in gold-mining-camp Western lends a spark to usual battle of good vs. evil.

Bashful Elephant, The (1962-German, dubbed) 82m. Bomb D: Dorrell McGowan, Stuart E. McGowan. Molly Mack, Helmut Schmid, Kai Fischer, Buddy Baer. Supposedly a family film, this import spends more time on an elephant trainer's divorce than anything else. Not worth your time.

Bat, The (1959) 80m. **½ D: Crane Wilbur. Vincent Price, Agnes Moorehead, Gavin Gordon, John Sutton, Lenita Lane, Darla Hood. Nothing like Mary Roberts Rinehart's novel, but fairly exciting yarn of masked killer using bats as his gimmick, terrorizing Moorehead's mansion.

Bataan (1943) 114m. *** D: Tay Garnett. Robert Taylor, George Murphy, Thomas Mitchell, Lloyd Nolan, Lee Bowman, Robert Walker, Desi Arnaz, Barry Nelson. Realistically made drama of famous WW2 incident on Pacific Island; good combat scenes.

Bathing Beauty (1944) C-101m. **½ D: George Sidney. Red Skelton, Esther Williams, Basil Rathbone, Ethel Smith, Xavier Cugat, Bill Goodwin. Attractive cast in lavish MGM musical bogged down with silly comedy interludes. One of Rathbone's most thankless roles.

Batman (1966) C-105m. ** D: Leslie Martinson. Adam West, Burt Ward, Burgess Meredith, Cesar Romero, Lee Meriwether, Neil Hamilton, Madge Blake, Reginald Denny. Quickly made feature to cash in on then-hot TV series pulls out all stops, features the Joker, Riddler, Penguin, and Catwoman trying to undo the caped crusader. Unfortunately they don't. For younger minds only.

Batmen of Africa (1936) 100m. ** D: B. Reeves Eason, Joseph Kane. Clyde Beatty, Manuel King, Elaine Shepard, Lucien Prival. Diverting cliff-hanger (Republic Pictures' first serial) of Beatty leading expedition to jungle city to rescue captured white girl; good special effects, primitive acting. Re-edited movie serial: DARKEST AFRICA.

Battle at Apache Pass, The (1952) C-85m. **½ D: George Sherman. Jeff Chandler, John Lund, Beverly Tyler, Richard Egan, Hugh O'Brian, Jay Silverheels. Chandler is Cochise (again) trying to prevent further Indian warring, but for sake of action-hungry viewers he doesn't succeed.

Battle at Bloody Beach (1961) 83m. **½ D: Herbert Coleman. Audie

Murphy, Gary Crosby, Dolores Michaels, Alejandro Rey. Sporadically exciting WW2 action with soldier Murphy locating his wife on a Pacific Island, involved with partisan cause and its leader.

Battle Circus (1953) 90m. ** D: Richard Brooks. Humphrey Bogart, June Allyson, Keenan Wynn, Robert Keith, Philip Ahn. Soaper of doctor under fire during Korean war; Bogie saddled with bad script and syrupy June.

Battle Cry (1955) C-149m. *** D: Raoul Walsh. Van Heflin, Tab Hunter, Dorothy Malone, Anne Francis, Raymond Massey, Mona Freeman, Aldo Ray. Watered-down version of Leon Uris WW2 marine novel, focusing on service men in training, action, and in love. Hunter as wholesome soldier and Malone a love-hungry dame stand out in episodic actioner, which now seems less than daring.

Battle Flame (1959) 78m. *½ D: R. G. Springsteen. Scott Brady, Elaine Edwards, Robert Blake, Gordon Jones, Wayne Heffley, Richard Harrison. Programmer about Korean War and soldier Brady's romance with nurse Edwards.

Battle Hymn (1956) C-108m. *** D: Douglas Sirk. Rock Hudson, Martha Hyer, Anna Kashfi, Dan Duryea, Don DeFore. Hudson turns in convincing performance as clergyman who returns to military duty in Korean War to train fighter pilots; expansive production values.

Battle in Outer Space (1960-Japanese, dubbed) C-74m. *½ D: Inoshiro Honda. Ryo Ikebe, Kyoko Anzai, Leonard Stanford, Harold Conway. Unexciting sci-fi, lacking sufficient special effects, action, or story.

Battle of Rogue River (1954) C-71m. ** D: William Castle. George Montgomery, Richard Denning, Martha Hyer, John Crawford. Much needed action sequence never comes in lopsided Western of Montgomery negotiating Indian truce as settlers seek statehood for Oregon in 1850's.

Battle of the Coral Sea (1959) 80m. **½ D: Paul Wendkos. Cliff Robertson, Gia Scala, Teru Shimada, Patricia Cutts, Gene Blakely, Gordon Jones. Staunch Robertson is submarine captain on Jap-held island during WW2, seeking to send vital data to U.S. fleet.

Battle of the Sexes, The (1960-British) 88m. *** D: Charles Crichton. Peter Sellers, Robert Morley, Constance Cummings, Jameson Clark. Sparkling British comedy with macabre overtones; Sellers is elderly Scotsman contemplating murder. Supporting cast keeps this moving.

Battle of the Villa Florita, The (1965-British) C-111m. **½ D: Delmer Daves. Maureen O'Hara, Rossano Brazzi, Richard Todd, Phyllis Calvert, Martin Stephens. Unconvincing soaper with O'Hara running off to Italy to carry on with widower Brazzi; predictable interference from each's children.

Battle Stations (1956) 81m. *½ D: Lewis Seiler. John Lund, William Bendix, Keefe Brasselle, Richard Boone. Rehash about crew in WW2 Pacific and their preparation for fighting the Japs.

Battle Stripe SEE: **Men, The**

Battle Taxi (1955) 82m. ** D: Herbert L. Strock. Sterling Hayden, Arthur Franz, Marshall Thompson, Joel Marston, Leo Needham. Ordinary tale of Korean War missions; strictly pedestrian.

Battle Zone (1952) 82m. ** D: Lesley Selander. John Hodiak, Linda Christian, Stephen McNally, Philip Ahn. Hodiak vies with McNally for Christian, with brief time out to fight Commies in static Korean War film.

Battleaxe, The (1962-British) 66m. ** D: Godfrey Grayson. Jill Ireland, Francis Matthews, Joan Haythorne, Michael Beint. Obvious sex farce with Matthews suing Ireland for breach of promise, Haythorne in title role supplying expected gags.

Battleground (1949) 118m. *** D: William Wellman. Van Johnson, John Hodiak, Ricardo Montalban, George Murphy, Marshall Thompson. Star-studded replay of Battle of the Bulge: division of American troops, their problems and reactions to war. Slick script, which was awarded Oscar, lacks genuine insight into characterization.

Battling Bellhop SEE: **Kid Galahad.**

Bay of Saint Michel, The (1963-British) 73m. ** D: John Ainsworth. Keenan Wynn, Mai Zetterling, Ronald Howard, Rona Anderson. Adequate actioner concerning trio of ex-commandos hunting for Nazi buried treasure, with expected conflicts and murders. Retitled: OPERATION MERMAID.

Be Beautiful But Shut Up (1957-French, dubbed) 94m. ** D: Henri Verneuil. Mylene Demongeot, Henri Vidal, Isabelle Miranda. Unremarkable study of young hoods involved with smuggling and carefree living.

Beach Ball (1965) C-83m. ** D: Lennie Weinrib. Edd Byrnes, Chris Noel, Robert Logan, Gale Gilmore, Aron Kincald. Different group tries a beach picture, but it's essentially the same. Pretty girls, rock groups, surfing, pretty girls.

Beach Blanket Bingo (1965) C-98m. ** D: William Asher. Frankie Avalon, Annette Funicello, Deborah Walley, Harvey Lembeck, John Ashley, Jody McCrea, Donna Loren, Don Rickles, Paul Lynde, Buster Keaton. Sole attraction is the guest cast of Keaton, Rickles, and Lynde. Otherwise, same surfing and bikini routine. If you've seen one . . .

Beach Party (1963) C-101m. ** D: William Asher. Dorothy Malone, Bob Cummings, Frankie Avalon, Annette Funicello, Morey Amsterdam. First in long line of beach epics, this boasts a good adult cast, mostly wasting their time. Moves swiftly to pie-throwing climax with little rhyme or reason.

Beachcomber, The (1938-British) 80m. *** D: Erich Pommer. Charles Laughton, Elsa Lanchester, Tyrone Guthrie, Robert Newton, Dolly Mollinger. Disheveled bum Laughton, living on island paradise, reformed by missionary Lanchester. Two stars delightful in filmization of Maugham story originally titled VESSEL OF WRATH.

Beachcomber, The (1955-British) C-82m. *** D: Muriel Box. Glynis Johns, Robert Newton, Donald Sinden, Michael Hordern, Donald Pleasence. Remake of Somerset Maugham tale of South Sea island bum entangled with strait-laced sister of missionary is still flavorful.

Beachhead (1954) C-89m. *** D: Stuart Heisler. Tony Curtis, Frank Lovejoy, Mary Murphy, Eduard Franz, Skip Homeier. Nicely handled action of marine quartet on dangerous mission in WW2.

Beast From 20,000 Fathoms, The (1953) 80m. ** D: Eugene Lourie. Paul Christian, Paula Raymond, Cecil Kellaway, Donald Woods, Lee Van Cleef, Ross Elliott. Rampaging monster tale with good special effects.

Beast of Budapest, The (1958) 72m. *1/2 D: Harmon Jones. Gerald Milton, John Hoyt, Greta Thyssen, Michael Mills. Trite rendering of father vs. son conflict over politics, resolved when elder's death awakens son to truth about life in Communist Hungary.

Beast of Hollow Mountain, The (1956) C-80m. **1/2 D: Edward Nassour, Ismael Rodriquez. Guy Madison, Patricia Medina, Eduardo Noriega, Carlos Rivas. Unusual combination of Western and monster-on-the-loose formula works well, with clever ending.

Beast With Five Fingers, The (1946) 88m. *1/2 D: Robert Florey. Robert Alda, Andrea King, Peter Lorre, J. Carrol Naish. Poor story of pianist's severed hands running wild saved by good cast.

Beat Generation, The (1959) 95m. *1/2 D: Charles Haas. Steve Cochran, Mamie Van Doren, Ray Danton, Fay Spain, Louis Armstrong, Maggie Hayes, Jackie Coogan, Ray Anthony, Maxie Rosenbloom. Exploitation-type story of detective Cochran tracking down insane sexual assaulter; vivid sequences marred by hokey script. Retitled: THIS REBEL AGE.

Beat Girl SEE: **Wild For Kicks**.

Beat the Devil (1954) 92m. *** D: John Huston. Humphrey Bogart, Jennifer Jones, Gina Lollobrigida, Robert Morley, Peter Lorre, Edward Underdown. Huston-Truman Capote (scriptwriter) in-joke emerges as hilarious satire on MALTESE FALCON-ish films, with cast having a ball in Italy. Gina gives beautiful, if unwitting, comedy performance. Humor is subtle, not for all tastes.

Beau Brummel (1954) C-113m. **1/2 D: Curtis Bernhardt. Stewart Granger, Elizabeth Taylor, Peter Ustinov, Robert Morley. Handsome cast in lavish production from Granger's rash of costume epics. Here, he's the famous British Casanova-fop.

Beau Geste (1939) 120m. ***½ D: William Wellman. Gary Cooper, Ray Milland, Robert Preston, Brian Donlevy, Susan Hayward, J. Carrol Naish, Albert Dekker, Broderick Crawford, Donald O'Connor. Exciting actioner with Geste brothers (Cooper, Milland, Preston) pitted against tyrannical officer Donlevy in noble tale of Foreign Legion fighting desert hordes. Elaborate remake of Ronald Colman silent is fine entertainment.

Beau Geste (1966) C-103m. **½ D: Douglas Heyes. Telly Savalas, Guy Stockwell, Doug McClure, Leslie Nielsen. Programmer-like version of Christopher Wren adventure tale dealing with honor among brothers in French Foreign Legion, their battle with sadistic commander and rampaging Arabs.

Beau James (1957) C-105m. *** D: Melville Shavelson. Bob Hope, Vera Miles, Paul Douglas, Alexis Smith, Darren McGavin, narrated by Walter Winchell. Flavorful recreation of 1920's N.Y.C. and the political career of Mayor Jimmy Walker. Smith and Miles are two women in his life, with Hope fine as colorful title figure. Based on Gene Fowler book; guest appearances by George Jessel, Jack Benny.

Beauties of the Night (1954-French, dubbed) 84m. **½ D: René Clair. Gerard Philippe, Martine Carol, Gina Lollobrigida, Magali Vendeuil. Diverting fantasy involving aspiring composer Philippe with a penchant for dreaming and wandering through various eras of history.

Beautiful Blonde From Bashful Bend, The (1949) C-77m. **½ D: Preston Sturges. Betty Grable, Cesar Romero, Rudy Vallee, Olga San Juan, Sterling Holloway, El Brendel. High-budget satirical fizzle of Grable, a gun-toting saloon gal in the old West. Disappointing film for writer-director Sturges.

Bebo's Girl (1964-Italian, dubbed) 106m. **½ D: Luigi Comencini. Claudia Cardinale, George Chakiris, Mario Lupi, Dany Paris. At times memorable love story spotlighting Cardinale's decision to leave her new lover in order to reaffirm her attachment with first love, now serving a prison term.

Because of Him (1946) 88m. *** D: Richard Wallace. Deanna Durbin, Franchot Tone, Charles Laughton, Helen Broderick, Donald Meek. Entertaining Durbin vehicle with Deanna becoming protegee of outrageous ham Laughton, convincing playwright Tone that she's star material.

Because of You (1952) 95m. *** D: Joseph Pevney. Loretta Young, Jeff Chandler, Alex Nicol, Frances Dee, Mae Clarke. Nifty tear-jerker has Young a parolee whose marriage is threatened by her past.

Because They're Young (1960) 102m. **½ D: Robert Peterson. Dick Clark, Michael Callan, Tuesday Weld, Victoria Shaw. Screen version of John Farris' HARRISON HIGH becomes predictable account of do-gooder teacher Clark trying to help his wayward students.

Becket (1964) C-148m. *** D: Peter Glenville. Richard Burton, Peter O'Toole, John Gielgud, Donald Wolfit, Martita Hunt, Pamela Brown, Felix Aylmer. Beautifully photographed medieval pageantry based on the historical story of Archbishop of Canterbury Thomas à Becket benefits from very good acting but suffers from over-talky script.

Becky Sharp (1935) C-83m. **½ D: Rouben Mamoulian. Miriam Hopkins, Frances Dee, Cedric Hardwicke, Billie Burke, Alison Skipworth, Nigel Bruce. First full-Technicolor feature, from Thackeray's VANITY FAIR, is more interesting as curio than as entertainment. Episodic costumer with Hopkins as self-centered heroine in Napoleonic England.

Bedevilled (1955) C-85m. ** D: Mitchell Leisen. Anne Baxter, Steve Forrest, Simone Renant, Victor Francen. Bizarre yarn of chanteuse Baxter fleeing from murder scene, protected by Forrest, who's studying for priesthood; filmed in Paris.

Bedford Incident, The (1965) 102m. *** D: James B. Harris. Richard Widmark, Sidney Poitier, James MacArthur, Martin Balsam, Wally Cox, Eric Portman. Strong Cold War story of authoritarian submarine commander (Widmark) scouting Russian subs near Greenland, mental conflicts that develop on his ship.

Poitier is reporter too good to be true, Balsam is disliked doctor. Cast excels in intriguing battle of wits.

Bedlam (1946) 79m. *** D: Mark Robson. Boris Karloff, Anna Lee, Ian Wolfe, Richard Fraser, Billy House, Jason Robards, Sr. Atmospheric Val Lewton chiller of courageous Lee trying to expose inadequate conditions at insane asylum, committed to one by institution head Karloff.

Bedtime for Bonzo (1951) 82m. ** D: Frederick de Cordova. Ronald Reagan, Diana Lynn, Walter Slezak, Lucille Barkley. Reagan plays professor who treats a chimp as his child for a heredity experiment, allowing for monkey-shenanigans. Sequel: BONZO GOES TO COLLEGE.

Bedtime Story, A (1933) 87m. **½ D: Norman Taurog. Maurice Chevalier, Helen Twelvetrees, Baby LeRoy, Adrienne Ames, Edward Everett Horton. Breezy Chevalier musical vehicle with Parisian playboy playing father to abandoned baby who interferes with his romancing.

Bedtime Story (1941) 85m. *** D: Alexander Hall. Fredric March, Loretta Young, Robert Benchley, Allyn Joslyn, Eve Arden. Fine cast in sparkling comedy of playwright March trying to stop wife Young from retiring so she can star in his next play.

Bedtime Story (1964) C-99m. **½ D: Ralph Levy. Marlon Brando, David Niven, Shirley Jones, Dody Goodman, Marie Windsor. Offbeat casting of stars provides chief interest in lackluster comedy of Brando and Niven competing for Jones' affection.

Before I Hang (1940) 71m. **½ D: Nick Grinde. Boris Karloff, Evelyn Keyes, Bruce Bennett, Pedro de Cordoba, Edward Van Sloan. Contrived but intriguing tale of mad-scientist Karloff having unusual serum backfire on him.

Beginning of the End (1957) 73m. ** D: Bert I. Gordon. Peggie Castle, Peter Graves, Morris Ankrum, Richard Benedict. Oversized grasshoppers are true stars of this passable sci-fi with giant insects destroying anything in their path.

Beginning or the End, The (1947) 112m. *** D: Norman Taurog. Brian Donlevy, Robert Walker, Beverly Tyler, Audrey Totter, Hume Cronyn. Engrossing account of atomic bomb development, depicting both human and spectacular aspects.

Behave Yourself! (1951) 81m. ** D: George Beck. Farley Granger, Shelley Winters, William Demarest, Francis L. Sullivan. Strange casting of Granger-Winters as couple with dog wanted by criminal gang detracts from comic potential of this comedy.

Behind Locked Doors (1948) 62m. ** D: Budd Boetticher. Lucille Bremer, Richard Carlson, Douglas Fowley, Tom Henry. Mishmash of judge on the lam seeking refuge in an insane asylum, and the reporter who tracks him down for the story.

Behind the Front (1926) 60m. **½ D: A. Edward Sutherland. Wallace Beery, Mary Brian, Raymond Hatton, Richard Arlen, Tom Kennedy, Chester Conklin, Gertrude Astor. Entertaining silent army comedy, broadly played by buddies Beery and Hatton, supported by fine cast. Many devices have been reused countless times, but they're handled smoothly here.

Behind the High Wall (1956) 85m. ** D: Abner Biberman. Tom Tully, Sylvia Sidney, Betty Lynn, John Gavin. Intertwining yarn of grasping prison warden, his crippled wife (nicely played by Sidney), hidden money, and convict escape plan.

Behind the Iron Curtain SEE: **Iron Curtain, The**

Behind the Mask (1932) 70m. ** D: John Francis Dillon. Boris Karloff, Jack Holt, Constance Cummings, Edward Van Sloan. Karloff heads notorious dope ring, tracked down by Holt in this bland thriller.

Behind the Rising Sun (1943) 89m. **½ D: Edward Dmytryk. Margo, Tom Neal, J. Carrol Naish, Robert Ryan, Gloria Holden, Don Douglas, George Givot. Naish plays Japanese-American who favors the Jap cause during WW2; propaganda holds up thanks to fine acting.

Behold a Pale Horse (1964) 118m. **½ D: Fred Zinnemann. Gregory Peck, Anthony Quinn, Omar Sharif, Mildred Dunnock, Christian Marquand, Raymond Pellegrin. Peck and Quinn wage an ideological battle in post-Spanish Civil War story of politics and violence that loses its focus and becomes confused talky film. Valiant try by all.

Behold My Wife (1935) 78m. ** D: Mitchell Leisen. Sylvia Sidney, Gene Raymond, Juliette Compton, Laura Hope Crews, Ann Sheridan. Raymond's snobbish family objects to his love for Indian maiden Sidney. Predictable wrong-side-of-the-reservation romance.

Bell' Antonio (1962-Italian, dubbed) 101m. **1/2 D: Mauro Bolognini. Marcello Mastroianni, Claudia Cardinale, Pierre Brasseur, Rina Morelli. OK Italian import of man ridiculed for his sexual impotence, saved by village girl who names him her lover.

Bell, Book and Candle (1958) C-103m. **1/2 D: Richard Quine. James Stewart, Kim Novak, Jack Lemmon, Ernie Kovacs, Hermione Gingold. John Van Druten play becomes so-so vehicle to showcase Novak as fetching witch who charms about-to-be-married publisher Stewart. Kovacs and Gingold supply their brand of humor.

Bell for Adano, A (1945) 103m. ***1/2 D: Henry King. John Hodiak, Gene Tierney, William Bendix, Glenn Langan, Richard Conte, Stanley Prager, Henry Morgan. John Hersey's moving narrative of American WW2 occupation of small Italian village; Hodiak is sincere commander, Bendix his aide, blonde Tierney the local girl he is attracted to.

Bellboy, The (1960) 72m. *** D: Jerry Lewis. Jerry Lewis, Alex Gerry, Bob Clayton, Sonny Sands, Milton Berle, Walter Winchell. Amusing series of blackouts with Jerry as a bellboy at Fountainbleau in Miami Beach. No plot but a lot of funny gags. Berle and Winchell have guest appearances.

Belle le Grand (1951) 90m. *1/2 D: Allan Dwan. Vera Ralston, John Carroll, William Ching, Muriel Lawrence. Weak Ralston vehicle has her a Western lady gambler willing to play any stakes to win back rambunctious Carroll.

Belle of New York, The (1952) C-82m. **1/2 D: Charles Walters. Fred Astaire, Vera-Ellen, Marjorie Main, Keenan Wynn, Alice Pearce. Uninspired musical set in gay 90's N.Y.C. with Astaire a rich playboy chasing mission gal Vera-Ellen; Pearce adds comic touches. Songs include "Let A Little Love Come In."

Belle of the Nineties (1934) *** D: Leo McCarey. Mae West, Roger Pryor, Johnny Mack Brown, Warren Hymer, Duke Ellington orchestra. Mae struts and sings "My Old Flame" and heats up a gallery of admirers in amusing example of West-ern humor.

Belle of the Yukon (1944) C-84m. **1/2 D: William Seiter. Randolph Scott, Gypsy Rose Lee, Dinah Shore, Charles Winninger, William Marshall, Florence Bates. Minor musical of saloon-owner Scott going straight at insistence of his girl (Lee); fast-moving, forgettable.

Belle Starr (1941) 87m. **1/2 D: Irving Cummings. Randolph Scott, Gene Tierney, Dana Andrews, John Shepperd, Elizabeth Patterson. Sophisticated Tierney miscast as notorious female outlaw in slowly paced account of her criminal career.

Belle Starr's Daughter (1948) 86m. ** D: Lesley Selander. George Montgomery, Rod Cameron, Ruth Roman, Wallace Ford, Isabel Jewell. Roman is title character, coming to rough Western town to avenge her mother's murder; fair Western.

Belles of St. Trinian's, The (1955-British) 90m. **1/2 D: Frank Launder. Alastair Sim, Joyce Grenfell, George Cole, Hermione Baddeley, Beryl Reid. Amusing romp with Sim and Grenfell in charge of girls' school filled with madcap pupils, ever ready for pranks.

Belles on Their Toes (1952) C-89m. *** D: Henry Levin. Myrna Loy, Jeanne Crain, Debra Paget, Jeffrey Hunter, Edward Arnold, Hoagy Carmichael. Pleasing sequel to CHEAPER BY THE DOZEN focuses on Loy's lecture career and her ability to find romance while tending to her maturing brood. Twentieth Century-Fox backlot seen at its best recapturing 1900's America.

Bellissima (1951-Italian, dubbed) 95m. **1/2 D: Luchino Visconti. Anna Magnani, Walter Chiari, Tina Apicella, Gastone Renzelli, Alessandro Blasetti. Lackluster tale of ambitious mother entering her child in talent contest, focusing on repercussion of her pushing child into the limelight.

Bells Are Ringing (1960) C-127m. *** D: Vincente Minnelli. Judy Holliday, Dean Martin, Fred Clark, Eddie Foy, Jr. Sprightly musical comedy by Jule Styne, Betty Comden, and Adolph Green. Holliday, in her last film, is fine as answering-service operator; Martin makes a good leading man. Songs include "Just in Time," "The Party's Over."

Bells of St. Mary's, The (1954) 126m. *** D: Leo McCarey. Bing Crosby, Ingrid Bergman, Henry Travers, William Gargan, Ruth Donnelly, John Carroll, Martha Sleeper. Not the total success of GOING MY WAY, but highly entertaining story of priest Crosby and nun Bergman raising money for new church school.

Beloved Enemy (1936) 90m. *** D: H. C. Potter. Merle Oberon, Brian Aherne, Karen Morley, Henry Stephenson, Jerome Cowan, David Niven, Donald Crisp. High-class love story set during Irish Rebellion with Britisher Oberon in love with rebel leader Aherne.

Beloved Infidel (1959) C-123m. ** D: Henry King. Gregory Peck, Deborah Kerr, Eddie Albert, Philip Ober, Herbert Rudley, John Sutton, Karin Booth, Ken Scott. Ill-conceived casting of Peck as F. Scott Fitzgerald makes romance with Hollywood columnist Sheilah Graham (Kerr) in late 1930's more ludicrous than real; lush photography is only virtue of blunt look at cinema capital.

Bend of the River (1952) C-91m. *** D: Anthony Mann. James Stewart, Julia Adams, Rock Hudson, Arthur Kennedy, Stepin Fetchit. Expansive Western set in 1840's Oregon with right ingredients for adventure-seekers. Stewart and Kennedy are spry adversaries.

Beneath the 12 Mile Reef (1953) C-102m. **1/2 D: Robert Webb. Robert Wagner, Terry Moore, Gilbert Roland, J. Carrol Naish, Richard Boone, Peter Graves. Romeo-Juliet-ish tale of sponge-diving families on Key West, Florida. Scenery outshines all.

Benefit of the Doubt, The (1967-British) C-70m. **1/2 D: Peter Whitehead. Eric Allan, Mary Allen, Jeremy Anthony, Noel Collins. Documentary shows British view of Vietnam War, featuring scenes from Peter Brook play US (Royal Shakespeare Company); thought-provoking at times. Retitled US.

Bengal Brigade (1954) C-87m. ** D: Laslo Benedek. Rock Hudson, Arlene Dahl, Ursula Thiess, Torin Thatcher. Stilted costumer with process shots and stock footage, as Hudson stands off natives in 1850's India.

Bengazi (1955) 78m. *1/2 D: John Brahm. Richard Conte, Victor McLaglen, Richard Carlson, Mala Powers. Lackluster adventure of Powers and trio of men entrapped in desert shrine by marauding natives.

Benny Goodman Story, The (1955) C-116m. **1/2 D: Valentine Davies. Steve Allen, Donna Reed, Sammy Davis, Sr., Gene Krupa, Harry James, Martha Tilton. Cinematic fiction about life of swing bandleader, focusing on his romance with Reed and rise in musical world. Guest performers spice up Allen's clarinet-playing and band-leading.

Berkeley Square (1933) 84m. *** D: Frank Lloyd. Leslie Howard, Heather Angel, Irene Browne, Beryl Mercer, Samuel S. Hinds. Intriguing fantasy of young American Howard finding himself in 18th-century London, living completely different life. Remade as I'LL NEVER FORGET YOU.

Berlin Correspondent (1942) 70m. **1/2 D: Eugene Forde. Virginia Gilmore, Dana Andrews, Mona Maris, Martin Kosleck, Sig Ruman. Reporter Andrews flees Germany with professor and young girl, amid much patriotic talk.

Berlin Express (1948) 86m. *** D: Jacques Tourneur. Merle Oberon, Robert Ryan, Charles Korvin, Paul Lukas, Robert Coote. Taut tale of underground movement during WW2 with Ryan and Oberon working to save German scientist in danger.

Bermuda Mystery (1944) 65m. ** D: Benjamin Stoloff. Preston Foster, Ann Rutherford, Charles Butterworth, Helene Reynolds. Mild account of strange murder and dead man's heirs' search to track down criminal.

Bernadette of Lourdes (1961-French; dubbed) 90m. **1/2 D: Robert Darene. Daniele Ajoret, Nadine Alari, Robert Arnoux, Blanchette Brunoy. Straightforward account of the peasant girl who saw a vision and was elevated to sainthood; unpretentious.

Bernardine (1957) **C-95m. **** D: Henry Levin. Pat Boone, Terry Moore, Janet Gaynor, Dean Jagger, Walter Abel. Very weak look at teen-age life (all different now) marked return of Janet Gaynor to films after twenty years. Wholesome Pat Boone sings and sings and sings. Eh!

Berserk (1967-British) **C-96m. **1/2** D: Jim O'Connolly. Joan Crawford, Ty Hardin, Diana Dors, Michael Gough, Judy Geeson. Mild shocker with Crawford the shapely owner of a British circus, haunted by series of brutal murders. Supporting cast lacks verve.

Best Foot Forward (1943) **C-95m. ***** D: Edward Buzzell. Lucille Ball, William Gaxton, Virginia Weidler, Tommy Dix, Nancy Walker, Gloria DeHaven, June Allyson. Entertaining film of Broadway musical about movie-star Ball visiting small-town school for a lark; score includes "Buckle Down Winsockie." Walker is dynamic plain Jane.

Best Man, The (1964) **102m. ***** D: Franklin Schaffner. Henry Fonda, Cliff Robertson, Edie Adams, Margaret Leighton, Shelley Berman, Lee Tracy, Ann Sothern, Gene Raymond, Richard Arlen, Mahalia Jackson. Sharp filmization of Gore Vidal's play about political conventioning with several determined presidential candidates seeking important endorsement; brittle, engrossing drama.

Best of Enemies, The (1962) **104m. ***** D: Guy Hamilton. David Niven, Michael Wilding, Harry Andrews, Alberto Sordi, Noel Harrison. Nice counterplay between Niven and Sordi, who point out the futility of warfare in this study of WW2.

Best of Everything, The (1959) **C-121m. ***** D: Jean Negulesco. Hope Lange, Stephen Boyd, Suzy Parker, Martha Hyer, Joan Crawford, Brian Aherne, Robert Evans, Louis Jourdan. Multifaceted fabrication about women seeking success and love in the publishing jungles of N.Y.C., highlighted by Crawford's performance as tough executive with empty heart of gold; from superficial Rona Jaffe novel.

Best of the Badmen (1951) **C-84m. **1/2** D: William D. Russell. Robert Ryan, Claire Trevor, Jack Buetel, Robert Preston. Ryan is grimly effective in actioner of Union officer who joins Confederate renegades to form outlaw gang, but eventually gives up to the law.

Best Things in Life Are Free, The (1956) **C-104m. **1/2** D: Michael Curtiz. Gordon MacRae, Dan Dailey, Ernest Borgnine, Sheree North. Typical of the antiseptic 1950's musicals, this film "recreates" the careers of Tin Pan Alley writers DeSylva, Brown, and Henderson.

Best Years of Our Lives, The (1946) **172m. ****** D: William Wyler. Fredric March, Myrna Loy, Teresa Wright, Dana Andrews, Virginia Mayo, Harold Russell, Hoagy Carmichael, Gladys George, Steve Cochran. American classic of three veterans returning home after WW2, readjusting to civilian life. Robert Sherwood's script from MacKinlay Cantor's book perfectly captured mood of postwar U.S., still powerful today.

Betrayal from the East (1945) **82m. **** D: William Berke. Lee Tracy, Nancy Kelly, Richard Loo, Abner Biberman, Regis Toomey, Philip Ahn. Americans vs. Japanese in usual flag-waving espionage film, no better or worse than most.

Betrayed (1954) **C-108m. **** D: Gottfried Reinhardt. Clark Gable, Lana Turner, Victor Mature, Louis Calhern. Unconvincing WW2 espionage melodrama of Dutch underground.

Betrayed Women (1955) **70m. *1/2** D: Edward L. Cahn. Carole Mathews, Beverly Michaels, Peggy Knudsen, Tom Drake, Sara Haden. Low-key filming of potentially volatile subject, sadistic treatment of inmates in women's prison.

Between Heaven and Hell (1956) **C-94m. ***** D: Richard Fleischer. Robert Wagner, Terry Moore, Broderick Crawford, Buddy Ebsen. Lightweight cast does extremely well by conventional story of thoughtless Southern boy who matures during army experience.

Between Midnight and Dawn (1950) **89m. **** D: Gordon Douglas. Edmond O'Brien, Gale Storm, Mark Stevens, Roland Winters, Madge Blake. Passable crimeland caper with cops battling escaped crooks.

Between Time and Eternity (1960-

German, dubbed) C-98m. **½ D: Arthur Maria Rabenalt. Lilli Palmer, Willy Birgel, Ellen Schwiers, Carlos Thompson. Palmer makes tear-jerker believable in story of middle-aged woman dying of rare disease, seeking romance and fun while she can.

Between Two Women (1944) 83m. D: Willis Goldbeck. Van Johnson, Lionel Barrymore, Gloria DeHaven, Keenan Wynn, Marilyn Maxwell, Keye Luke, Alma Kruger. SEE Dr. Kildare series.

Between Two Worlds (1944) 112m. **½ D: Edward A. Blatt. John Garfield, Eleanor Parker, Sydney Greenstreet, Faye Emerson, Paul Henreid, Sara Allgood, Isobel Elsom, George Tobias, Edmund Gwenn. Updated remake of OUTWARD BOUND has flaws, but good acting by Warner Bros. star stock company makes it worthwhile.

Between Us Girls (1942) 89m. ** D: Henry Koster. Ida Lupino, Diana Barrymore, Robert Cummings, Andy Devine, John Boles, Scotty Beckett, Ethel Griffies. Chic Francis and daughter Barrymore both have romances at the same time in this OK comedy. Boles and Cummings are respective leads.

Beware, My Lovely (1952) 77m. **½ D: Harry Horner. Ida Lupino, Robert Ryan, Taylor Holmes, O. Z. Whitehead, Barbara Whiting. Widow Lupino hires Ryan as handyman, discovers he is psychopath; brooding and atmospheric.

Beware of Blondie (1950) 66m. D: Edward Bernds. Penny Singleton, Arthur Lake, Larry Simms, Adele Jergens, Dick Wessel. SEE: Blondie series.

Beware of Children (1961-British) 80m. *½ D: Gerald Thomas. Leslie Phillips, Geraldine McEwan, Julia Lockwood, Noel Purcell. Tedious attempt at lighthearted romp; young married couple transforms an inheritance of land into summer camp for all sorts of children, focusing on predictable pranks of youngsters.

Beware of Pity (1946-British) 102m. **½ Maurice Elvey. Lilli Palmer, Albert Lieven, Cedric Hardwicke, Gladys Cooper. Maudlin but effective yarn of crippled young woman who finds romance and meaning to life.

Beware, Spooks! (1939) 68m. ** D: Edward Sedgwick. Joe E. Brown, Mary Carlisle, Clarence Kolb, Marc Lawrence. Good fun as Brown solves mystery and becomes hero in Coney Island fun house.

Bewitched (1945) 65m. **½ D: Arch Oboler. Edmund Gwenn, Phyllis Thaxter, Henry Daniels, Jr., Addison Richards, Kathleen Lockhart. Interesting story of schizophrenic Thaxter who commits murder as one girl, doesn't recall it as the other.

Beyond a Reasonable Doubt (1956) 80m. *** D: Fritz Lang. Dana Andrews, Joan Fontaine, Sidney Blackmer, Philip Bourneuf, Barbara Nichols. Low production values detract from engaging story of writer Andrews framed for real murder when he participates in experiment to test how just the law is.

Beyond Glory (1948) 82m. **½ D: John Farrow. Alan Ladd, Donna Reed, George Macready, George Coulouris. Predictable account of West Point captain Ladd, a WW2 veteran, on trial for misconduct; nicely done trivia. Also Audie Murphy's first film.

Beyond Mombasa (1957) C-90m. ** D: George Marshall. Cornel Wilde, Donna Reed, Leo Genn, Ron Randell, Christopher Lee. Tame African adventure tale with Wilde seeking mysterious killers of his brother and clues to hidden uranium mine.

Beyond the Blue Horizon (1942) C-76m. ** D: Alfred Santell. Dorothy Lamour, Richard Denning, Jack Haley, Walter Abel, Elizabeth Patterson, Abner Biberman, Patricia Morison. Sarong queen Lamour turns out to be heiress to great fortune; witless film wastes more talent than usual.

Beyond the Forest (1949) 96m. ** D: King Vidor. Bette Davis, Joseph Cotten, David Brian, Ruth Roman, Dona Drake, Regis Toomey. Muddled murder story of grasping Davis, her small-town doctor husband (Cotten), and wealthy neighbor (Brian). Davis' overly mannered performance doesn't help.

Beyond the Time Barrier (1960) 75m. ** D: Edgar G. Ulmer. Robert Clarke, Darlene Tompkins, Arianne Arden, Vladimir Sokoloff. Military pilot is thrust into 21st century, seeing tragic results of worldwide epidemic of 1970.

Beyond Tomorrow (1940) 84m. **½ D: A. Edward Sutherland. Richard Carlson, Jean Parker, Harry Carey, C. Aubrey Smith, Charles Winninger, Maria Ouspenskaya, Rod LaRocque. Sensitive little drama of three wealthy men sharing Christmas with down-and-out Carlson and Parker, who fall in love.

Bhowani Junction (1956) C-110m. *** D: George Cukor. Ava Gardner, Stewart Granger, Bill Travers, Abraham Sofaer. At times overblown dramatics as half-caste Gardner wanders between romance with Britisher and duty to her Indian relatives. Based on John Masters novel of post-WW2 Pakistan.

Bicycle Thief, The (1949-Italian, dubbed) 90m. **** D: Vittorio DeSica. Lamberto Maggiorani, Lianella Carell, Enzo Staiola, Elena Altieri. Stark, realistic account of Italian worker and the shattering loss of his bicycle vital to obtaining jobs in post-WW2 Rome.

Big Bluff, The (1955) 70m. ** D: W. Lee Wilder. John Bromfield, Martha Vickers, Robert Hutton, Rosemarie Bowe. Interesting premise poorly executed. Vickers is fatally ill girl married to fortune-hunter who seeks to murder her when he recovers from illness.

Big Boodle, The (1957) 83m. *½ D: Richard Wilson. Errol Flynn, Pedro Armendariz, Rossana Rory, Jacques Aubuchon. Seedy programmer emphasizing Flynn's career decline. Tame caper of gangsters and counterfeit money, set in Havana.

Big Broadcast, The (1932) 78m. *** D: Frank Tuttle. Bing Crosby, Kate Smith, George Burns, Gracie Allen, Stuart Erwin, Leila Hyams, Cab Calloway, Mills Brothers, Boswell Sisters. Failing radio station owned by Burns is saved by all-star show featuring Bing and many radio stars. Many offbeat, bizarre touches in standard love-triangle story make this a delight. Bing sings "Please," "Here Lies Love."

Big Broadcast of 1936, The (1935) 97m. *** D: Norman Taurog. Jack Oakie, George Burns, Gracie Allen, Lyda Roberti, Wendy Barrie, Bing Crosby. No real plot, just enjoyable star-filled routines, including Amos and Andy, Bojangles Robinson, Ethel Merman; such songs as: "Crooner's Lullaby," "Why Stars Come Out At Night."

Big Broadcast of 1937, The (1936) 102m. *** D: Mitchell Leisen. Jack Benny, George Burns, Gracie Allen, Bob Burns, Martha Raye, Shirley Ross, Ray Milland. Another plotless but enjoyable variety romp with many stars, plus guests Benny Goodman, Leopold Stokowski, Larry Adler, etc. Songs such as: "Here's Love In Your Eye," "La Bomba," "Night In Manhattan."

Big Broadcast of 1938, The (1938) 90m. ** D: Mitchell Leisen. W. C. Fields, Martha Raye, Dorothy Lamour, Shirley Ross, Lynne Overman, Bob Hope, Ben Blue, Leif Erickson. Hodgepodge of bad musical numbers from Tito Guizar to Kirsten Flagstad, notable only for Fields' few scenes, Hope's "Thanks For The Memory."

Big Brown Eyes (1936) 77m. **½ D: Raoul Walsh. Joan Bennett, Cary Grant, Walter Pidgeon, Isabel Jewell, Lloyd Nolan. Bennett helps detective Grant trap a gang of notorious thieves in pleasing romantic mystery.

Big Cage, The (1933) 76m. **½ D: Kurt Neumann. Clyde Beatty, Anita Page, Wallace Ford, Andy Devine, Raymond Hatton, Mickey Rooney. Good actioner with animal-trainer Beatty and young sidekick Rooney; designed for family-juvenile audiences.

Big Caper, The (1957) 84m. **½ D: Robert Stevens. Rory Calhoun, Mary Costa, James Gregory, Robert Harris. Well-done account of Calhoun and Costa posing as married couple in small town in order to set up gang caper; realities of life reform them.

Big Carnival, The (1951) 112m. *** D: Billy Wilder. Kirk Douglas, Jan Sterling, Bob Arthur, Porter Hall. Unrelenting cynicism is theme of hard-hitting Wilder drama of reporter Douglas, who capitalizes on Albuquerque tragedy. Not for all tastes, but biting and extremely well-acted. Retitled: ACE IN THE HOLE.

Big Circus, The (1959) C-108m. **½ D: Joseph M. Newman. Victor Mature, Red Buttons, Rhonda Fleming, Kathryn Grant, Vincent Price, Peter

Lorre, David Nelson, Gilbert Roland, Howard McNear, Steve Allen. Familiar but well-done circus story with exceptional cast (Lorre as a clown is worth the price of admission). Big-top action and intrigue is entertaining.

Big City, The (1937) 80m. **½ D: Frank Borzage. Spencer Tracy, Luise Rainer, Eddie Quillan, William Demarest, Regis Toomey, Charley Grapewin, Victor Varconi. Cabdriver Tracy and wife Rainer are pitted against crooked taxi bosses in well-acted but average film. Retitled: SKYSCRAPER WILDERNESS.

Big City, The (1948) C-103m. **½ D: Norman Taurog. Margaret O'Brien, Robert Preston, Danny Thomas, George Murphy, Betty Garrett. Priest Preston, cantor Thomas, and cop Murphy "adopt" little O'Brien in this maudlin drama.

Big City Blues (1932) 65m. **½ D: Mervyn LeRoy. Joan Blondell, Eric Linden, Inez Courtney, Evalyn Knapp, Guy Kibbee, Humphrey Bogart, Ned Sparks. Polished Warner Bros. programmer of hayseed Linden encountering disillusionment and love in N.Y.C.

Big Clock, The (1948) 95m. *** D: John Farrow. Ray Milland, Charles Laughton, Maureen O'Sullivan, Rita Johnson. Tyrannical editor of crime magazine (Laughton) commits murder; his ace reporter (Milland) tries to solve case. Vibrant melodrama; Elsa Lanchester has hilarious vignette as eccentric artist.

Big Combo, The (1955) 89m. **½ D: Joseph H. Lewis. Cornel Wilde, Jean Wallace, Brian Donlevy, Richard Conte, Lee Van Cleef. Wilde, as police detective relentlessly hunting down leader of gangster syndicate, Wallace as the gal, make an effective team in above-average caper.

Big Country, The (1958) C-166m. *** D: William Wyler. Gregory Peck, Burl Ives, Jean Simmons, Carroll Baker, Charlton Heston, Chuck Connors. Overblown Western has ex-seacaptain Peck arrive to marry Simmons, but forced to take sides in battle against Ives and sons over water rights. Heston as quick-tempered ranch foreman and Ives (who won an Oscar) as burly patriarch stand out in energetic cast.

Big Deal on Madonna Street (1956-Italian, dubbed) 91m. ***½ D: Mario Monicelli. Vittorio Gassman, Marcello Mastroianni, Renato Salvatori, Rossana Rory, Carla Gravina, Toto. Classic account of misadventures of amateurish crooks attempting to rob a store; hilarious satire on all burglary capers. Retitled: BIG DEAL.

Big Gamble, The (1961) C-100m. **½ D: Richard Fleischer. Stephen Boyd, Juliette Greco, David Wayne, Sybil Thorndike. Not-too-convincing account of Irish adventurer and bride Greco who dally on the African Ivory Coast seeking to build their future the easy way.

Big Gusher, The (1951) 68m. *½ D: Lew Landers. Wayne Morris, Preston Foster, Dorothy Patrick, Paul Burns. Unshiny account of oil workers involved in hackneyed deadline to strike oil or lose all their savings.

Big Guy, The (1940) 78m. ** D: Arthur Lubin. Jackie Cooper, Victor McLaglen, Ona Munson, Peggy Moran, Edward Brophy. Fairly interesting story of warden McLaglen given choice between wealth and saving innocent man from death penalty.

Big Hand for the Little Lady, A (1966) C-95m. *** D: Fielder Cook. Henry Fonda, Joanne Woodward, Jason Robards, Charles Bickford, Burgess Meredith. Excellent comedy centering on poker game in old West. Outstanding cast includes John Qualen, Paul Ford, and Robert Middleton. There's a neat surprise ending, too.

Big Hangover, The (1950) 82m. **½ D: Norman Krasna. Van Johnson, Elizabeth Taylor, Leon Ames, Edgar Buchanan, Rosemary DeCamp. Goofy premise of Johnson allergic to liquor but wanting to get ahead in social swing and romance Taylor.

Big Heat, The (1953) 90m. ***½ D: Fritz Lang. Glenn Ford, Gloria Grahame, Jocelyn Brando, Lee Marvin, Carolyn Jones. Gripping melodrama of Ford determined to bust city crime ring, with bad-girl Grahame's help. First-rate.

Big House, The (1930) 80m. *** D: George Hill. Wallace Beery, Chester Morris, Robert Montgomery, Lewis Stone, Karl Dane, Leila Hyams. The original prison drama, this set the pattern for all later copies; it's still good, hard-bitten stuff with one of Beery's best tough-guy roles.

Big House, U.S.A. (1955) 82m. **½ D: Howard W. Koch. Broderick Crawford, Ralph Meeker, Reed Hadley, Charles Bronson, Lon Chaney, Jr. Brutal account of kidnappers and extortion, and the FBI agents sent to track them down.

Big Jack (1949) 85m. ** D: Richard Thorpe. Wallace Beery, Marjorie Main, Edward Arnold, Richard Conte, Vanessa Brown. Beery's last film, rather flat; he and Main are vagabond thieves in colonial America, Conte a moralistic doctor they meet on the road.

Big Jim McLain (1952) 90m. **½ D: Edward Ludwig. John Wayne, James Arness, Nancy Olson, Veda Ann Borg, Hans Conried. One of the few dull Wayne films: story filmed in Hawaii tells of zealous government agent Wayne tracking down gangster syndicate.

Big Knife, The (1955) 111m. *** D: Robert Aldrich. Jack Palance, Ida Lupino, Shelley Winters, Rod Steiger, Ilka Chase, Wendell Corey. Clifford Odets' cynical view of Hollywood comes across well in hard-punching film, with fine portrayals that almost overcome stereotypes.

Big Land, The (1957) C-92m. **½ D: Gordon Douglas. Alan Ladd, Virginia Mayo, Edmond O'Brien, Julie Bishop. Cattle owners and grain farmers join together to bring railroad link to Texas; easygoing, familiar.

Big Leaguer, The (1953) 70m. ** D: Robert Aldrich. Edward G. Robinson, Vera-Ellen, Jeff Richards, Richard Jaeckel. Baseball programmer for college-bound boy being scouted for the big diamond. Robinson wasted.

Big Lift, The (1950) 120m. **½ D: George Seaton. Paul Douglas, Montgomery Clift, Cornell Borchers, O. E. Hasse. GI pilots involved in post-WW2 airlift and romance with German girls.

Big Mouth, The (1967) C-107m. **½ D: Jerry Lewis. Jerry Lewis, Harold Stone, Susan Bay, Buddy Lester, Del Moore, Paul Lambert. Typical Lewis effort, with Jerry involved in murder and search for missing treasure; set in Southern California.

Big Night, The (1951) 75m. **½

D: Joseph Losey. John Barrymore, Jr., Preston Foster, Howland Chamberlain, Joan Lorring, Dorothy Comingore, Howard St. John. Brooding account of rebellious teen-ager Barrymore's emotional flare-up with humanity at large; well done.

Big Noise, The (1944) 74m. Bomb D: Malcolm St. Clair. Stan Laurel, Oliver Hardy, Arthur Space, Veda Ann Borg, Bobby Blake, Jack Norton. L&H's worst film, about them delivering a bomb . . . and they do.

Big Operator, The (1959) 91m. ** D: Charles Haas. Mickey Rooney, Steve Cochran, Mamie Van Doren, Mel Torme, Ray Danton, Jim Backus. Ray Anthony, Jackie Coogan. Rooney tries to add vim and vigor to title role as tough hood who goes on violent rampage when federal agents investigate his business activities. Retitled: ANATOMY OF A SYNDICATE.

Big Pond, The (1930) 75m. **½ D: Hobart Henley. Maurice Chevalier, Claudette Colbert, George Barbier, Nat Pendleton. Claudette brings Maurice to America, where to make good he works in chewing gum factory. Chevalier charm overcomes trivia; song: "You Brought A New Kind Of Love To Me."

Big Risk, The (1960-French, dubbed) 111m. ** D: C. Sautet. Jean-Paul Belmondo, Lino Ventura, Marcel Dalio, Sandra Milo. Too-leisurely-paced account of criminal on the lam, who for sake of his family gives himself up to police.

Big Shakedown, The (1934) 64m. ** D: John Francis Dillon. Bette Davis, Ricardo Cortez, Glenda Farrell, Charles Farrell, Adrian Morris. Inconsequential tale. Davis rejects husband Farrell when he joins forces with mobster Cortez in cosmetic fraud.

Big Shot, The (1942) 82m. **½ D: Lewis Seiler. Humphrey Bogart, Irene Manning, Susan Peters, Minor Watson, Richard Travis. Bogart's sworn off crime, since one more rap will mean life imprisonment. Unfortunately, he lives dangerously.

Big Show, The (1961) C-113m. **½ D: James B. Clark. Esther Williams, Cliff Robertson, Nehemiah Persoff, Robert Vaughn. Drama of family conflict, similar to 1949's HOUSE OF STRANGERS, somehow set in a circus with swimmer Williams in a dramatic role. Glug!

Big Sky, The (1952) 140m. ** D: Howard Hawks. Kirk Douglas, Dewey Martin, Arthur Hunnicutt, Jim Davis. Douglas leads fur-trappers up Missouri River into Indian lands, finding more conflicts with companions than redskins.

Big Sleep, The (1946) 114m. *** D: Howard Hawks. Humphrey Bogart, Lauren Bacall, Dorothy Malone, Martha Vickers, Elisha Cook, Jr., Peggy Knudsen, Bob Steele. Bogie is Raymond Chandler's detective Philip Marlowe in exciting, more often confusing mystery. Still fun to watch Bogie and Bacall together.

Big Steal, The (1949) 71m. **½ D: Don Siegel. Robert Mitchum, Jane Greer, William Bendix, Patric Knowles, Ramon Novarro. Well-made robbery caper set in Southwest and Mexico with Mitchum hustling after heisters, getting involved with enticing Greer.

Big Store, The (1941) 80m. ** D: Charles Riesner. Groucho, Chico and Harpo Marx, Tony Martin, Virginia Grey, Margaret Dumont, Douglass Dumbrille. Big comedown for Marxes in weak film of detective Groucho investigating crooked Dumbrille's department store. Low spot is Martin's crooning "Tenement Symphony."

Big Street, The (1942) 88m. **½ D: Irving Reis. Henry Fonda, Lucille Ball, Barton MacLane, Eugene Pallette, Agnes Moorehead. Damon Runyon fable of timid busboy Fonda who devotes himself to disinterested nightclub singer Ball wavers from good to too-sticky.

Big T.N.T. Show, The (1966) 93m. ** D: Larry Peerce. David McCallum, Roger Miller, Ray Charles, Joan Baez, The Lovin' Spoonful. Unexciting taping of a "live" youth show, with guest musical artists doing routine numbers; poorly photographed.

Big Town (1947) 60m. ** D: William C. Thomas. Philip Reed, Hillary Brooke, Robert Lowery, Byron Barr. Standard story of newspaper reporter working with police to rid town of dangerous mob.

Big Town After Dark (1947) 69m. ** D: William C. Thomas. Philip Reed, Hillary Brooke, Richard Travis, Anne Gillis. OK drama of daring reporters walking into danger while trying to get lowdown on criminal gang. Retitled: UNDERWORLD AFTER DARK.

Big Trees, The (1952) C-89m. **½ D: Felix Feist. Kirk Douglas, Eve Miller, Patrice Wymore, Edgar Buchanan. Douglas is staunch in so-so logging saga of lumbermen vs. homesteaders.

Big Wave, The (1960-Japanese, dubbed) 60m. *½ D: Tad Danielewski. Sessue Hayakawa, Ichizo Itami, Mickey Curtis, Koji Shitara. Slowly paced account from Pearl Buck novel involving two boys who are childhood friends but later in life clash over their love for a local girl.

Big Wheel, The (1949) 92m. **½ D: Edward Ludwig. Mickey Rooney, Thomas Mitchell, Spring Byington, Allen Jenkins, Michael O'Shea. Rooney is determined race-car driver following in father's footsteps despite dad's death on track; familiar plot well done.

Bigamist, The (1953) 80m. **½ D: Ida Lupino. Edmond O'Brien, Joan Fontaine, Ida Lupino, Edmund Gwenn. Mildly sensational account of O'Brien married to two women, torn between his love for both of them.

Bigger Than Life (1956) C-95m. *** D: Nicholas Ray. James Mason, Barbara Rush, Walter Matthau, Robert Simon. Compelling drama of teacher Mason who becomes hooked on drugs, and its devastating effects on him and his family.

Bikini Beach (1964) C-100m. ** D: William Asher. Frankie Avalon, Annette Funicello, Martha Hyer, Harvey Lembeck, Don Rickles. Frankie and Annette are at it again; you know all about it. Same formula casts yet another surfing spectacle.

Bill and Coo (1947) 61m. *** D: Dean Riesner. Produced and narrated by Ken Murray. Charming, unique animated feature of two birds fighting it out against their enemy, the crow. 1947 Oscar winner.

Bill of Divorcement, A (1932) 75m. ***½ D: George Cukor. John Barrymore, Katharine Hepburn, Billie Burke, David Manners, Bramwell Fletcher, Henry Stephenson. Barrymore gives a sensitive portrayal as man released from mental institution who returns to wife Burke and gets to know daughter Hepburn (in her first film).

Bill of Divorcement, A (1940) 74m. **½ D: John Farrow. Maureen O'Hara, Adolphe Menjou, Fay Bainter, Herbert Marshall, Dame May Whitty. Refilming of '32 drama follows it closely, but cast can't match the original's class. Retitled: NEVER TO LOVE or NOT FOR EACH OTHER.

Billie (1965) C-87m. **½ D: Don Weis. Patty Duke, Warren Berlinger, Jim Backus, Jane Greer, Billy DeWolfe, Charles Lane, Dick Sargent. Airy comedy of tomboyish Billie (Duke) and her athletic aspirations. Backus and Greer are her perplexed parents, Berlinger her boyfriend. Duke sings, runs, prances.

Billy Budd (1962) 112m. **** D: Peter Ustinov. Robert Ryan, Terence Stamp, Peter Ustinov, Melvyn Douglas, John Neville. Melville's moralist good vs. evil novella of a sailor entirely too pure, going to sea and confronting unyielding evil, results in an ironic climax. Ryan, evil ship officer, and Ustinov, sympathetic captain, are excellent.

Billy Liar (1963-British) 96m. ***½ D: John Schlesinger. Tom Courtenay, Julie Christie, Mona Washbourne, Ethel Griffies, Finlay Currie. Cast excels in story of ambitious but lazy young man caught in dull job routine who escapes into fantasy world, offering some poignant vignettes of middle-class life. Based on Keith Waterhouse novel and play.

Billy Rose's Diamond Horseshoe SEE: Diamond Horseshoe.

Billy Rose's Jumbo (1962) C-125m. *** D: Charles Walters. Doris Day, Stephen Boyd, Jimmy Durante, Martha Raye, Dean Jagger. OK circus picture, at best during Rodgers and Hart songs, well-staged by Busby Berkeley. Durante and Raye are marvelous. Songs include "The Most Beautiful Girl in the World," "My Romance," "This Can't Be Love."

Billy the Kid (1930) 90m. **½ D: King Vidor. Johnny Mack Brown, Wallace Beery, Kay Johnson, Karl Dane, Roscoe Ates. Realistic early talkie Western with marshal Beery trying to capture outlaw Brown.

Billy the Kid (1941) C-95m. **½ D: David Miller. Robert Taylor, Brian Donlevy, Ian Hunter, Mary Howard, Gene Lockhart, Lon Chaney, Jr. Cast looks uncomfortable in remake of 1930 Western, but plot is sturdy enough for OK viewing, with Taylor in title role and Donlevy as mashal.

Bimbo the Great (1961-German, dubbed) C-96m. *½ D: Harold Philipp. Claus Holm, Germaine Damar, Elma Karlowa, Marina Orschel. Hackneyed circus yarn of high-wire performer discovering wife's death was caused by his step-brother, with inevitable confession scene slightly spiced by potential big-top blaze.

Biography of a Bachelor Girl (1935) 82m. **½ D: Edward Griffith. Ann Harding, Robert Montgomery, Edward Everett Horton, Edward Arnold, Una Merkel. Actress Harding publishes autobiography, unwittingly causing trouble for many people involved. Intriguing story, well acted.

Bird of Paradise (1951) C-100m. ** D: Delmer Daves. Louis Jourdan, Debra Paget, Jeff Chandler, Everett Sloane. Jourdan's marriage to South Sea isle chief's daughter causes native uprising in grandly filmed but vapid tale. Remake of King Vidor's 1932 film with Joel McCrea and Dolores Del Rio.

Birdman of Alcatraz (1962) 143m. *** D: John Frankenheimer. Burt Lancaster, Karl Malden, Thelma Ritter, Betty Field, Neville Brand, Edmond O'Brien, Hugh Marlowe. Pensive study of prisoner Robert Stroud who during his many years in jail became a world-renowned bird authority. Film becomes static despite imaginative sidelights to enlarge scope of action.

Birds, The (1963) C-120m. ***½ D: Alfred Hitchcock. Rod Taylor, Tippi Hedren, Suzanne Pleshette, Jessica Tandy, Ethel Griffies, Charles McGraw. Hitchcock's story of a girl (Hedren) and mass bird attacks that follow her around in isolated California community. Not for the squeamish; a delight for those who are game. Hold on to something and watch.

Birds and the Bees, The (1956) C-94m. ** D: Norman Taurog. George Gobel, Mitzi Gaynor, David Niven, Reginald Gardiner. Bland remake of THE LADY EVE about rich playboy who breaks off romance with cardshark girlfriend, but later decides he still loves her.

Birds Do It (1966) C-95m. ** D: Andrew Marton. Soupy Sales, Tab Hunter, Arthur O'Connell, Edward Andrews. Soupy's first starring vehicle has him under the spell of serum that enables him to fly. Fairly entertaining for kids.

Birth of the Blues (1941) 85m. *** D: Victor Schertzinger. Bing Crosby, Brian Donlevy, Carolyn Lee, Eddie (Rochester) Anderson, Mary Martin, Johnny Mercer. Fiction about Crosby organizing jazz band in New Orleans has great music like "St. Louis Blues," "St. James Infirmary," "Melancholy Baby" and title tune to uplift fair story.

Bishop's Wife, The (1947) 108m. *** D: Henry Koster. Cary Grant, Loretta Young, David Niven, Monty Woolley, James Gleason, Gladys Cooper, Elsa Lanchester. Christmas fantasy of suave angel (Grant) coming to earth to help Bishop Niven and wife Young raise money for new church. Engaging performances by all.

Bitter Creek (1954) 74m. *½ D: Thomas Carr. Bill Elliott, Carleton Young, Beverly Garland, Claude Akins, Jim Hayward. Tame happenings as Elliott seeks revenge for his brother's untimely death in the old West.

Bitter Rice (1950-Italian, dubbed) 107m. *** D: Giuseppe De Santis. Silvana Mangano, Vittorio Gassman, Raf Vallone, Doris Dowling, Lia Corelli. Somber account of dank existence of women working the rice fields of Po Valley.

Bitter Sweet (1940) C-92m. **½ D: W. S. Van Dyke, II. Jeanette MacDonald, Nelson Eddy, George Sanders, Felix Bressart, Lynne Carver, Ian Hunter. Noel Coward operetta of love, honor and song is fluffy basis for duo to sing "I'll See You Again" et al.

Bitter Tea of General Yen, The (1933) 89m. **½ D: Frank Capra. Barbara Stanwyck, Nils Asther, Walter Connolly, Lucien Littlefield, Richard Loo. Dated but interesting yarn of American girl held captive by Chinese general and her gradual attraction to him.

Bitter Victory (1958-French, dubbed) 82m. **½ D: Nicholas Ray. Richard Burton, Curt Jurgens, Ruth Roman, Raymond Pellegrin. Jurgens does well as unfit commander who receives undeserved citation for mission against Rommel's desert headquarters; Roman is his wife who's had prior affair with officer Burton.

Black Abbot, The (1963-German, dubbed) 95m. ** D: Franz Gottlieb. Joachim Fuchsberger, Dieter Borsche, Grit Bottcher, Eva Scholtz. Unearthly "Abbot" is on a killing rampage warding off those who approach country house with buried treasure underneath.

Black Angel (1946) 80m. **½ D: Roy William Neill. Dan Duryea, June Vincent, Peter Lorre, Broderick Crawford, Wallace Ford. Innocent man is convicted of murdering Duryea's wife, but he and Crawford seek out real killer; plenty of red herrings in this OK melodrama.

Black Arrow, The (1948) 76m. *** D: Gordon Douglas. Louis Hayward, Janet Blair, George Macready, Edgar Buchanan, Paul Cavanagh. Superior swashbuckler with dashing knight Hayward, lovely heroine Blair, and villain Macready. Truly exciting finale with hero vs. villain in jousting tournament.

Black Bart (1948) C-80m. **½ D: George Sherman. Yvonne De Carlo, Dan Duryea, Jeffrey Lynn, Percy Kilbride. Enticing De Carlo steps between outlaws Duryea and Lynn, foiling their attempt to overthrow Wells Fargo company.

Black Beauty (1946) 74m. **½ D: Max Nosseck. Mona Freeman, Richard Denning, Evelyn Ankers, Terry Kilburn, Arthur Space. Another animal film from famous story of girl's love for her horse; as good as most of others but not in color.

Black Book SEE: **Reign of Terror**

Black Camel (1931) 71m. D: Hamilton MacFadden. Warner Oland, Sally Eilers, Bela Lugosi, Victor Varconi, Robert Young, Dwight Frye, Mary Gordon. SEE: **Charlie Chan** series.

Black Castle, The (1952) 81m. ** D: Nathan Juran. Richard Greene, Boris Karloff, Lon Chaney, Jr., Stephen McNally. Horror flick has Greene seeking fate of two pals who disappeared, almost getting himself killed; Karloff is more lordly than menacing.

Black Cat, The (1934) 65m. *** D:

Edgar G. Ulmer. Boris Karloff, Bela Lugosi, David Manners, Herman Bing, Jacqueline Wells (Julie Bishop). Royal treat for horror fans; Karloff is cultist-Devil worshipper, Lugosi a mad scientist; together they work wonders in adaptation of Poe tale.

Black Cat, The (1941) 70m. **½ D: Albert S. Rogell. Basil Rathbone, Hugh Herbert, Broderick Crawford, Bela Lugosi, Gale Sondergaard. Herbert and Crawford provide laughs, the others provide chills, in lively comedy-mystery not to be confused with earlier horror film. Look for Alan Ladd in a small role.

Black Cross (1960-Polish, dubbed) C-175m. ** D: Aleksander Ford. Urszula Modrzynska, Grazyna Staniszewska, Andrzej Szalawski, Henryk Borowski. Unremarkable account of Teutonic knights raiding Poland; notable only for detailed medieval settings; sterile presentation.

Black Dakotas, The (1954) C-65m. ** D: Ray Nazarro. Gary Merrill, Wanda Hendrix, John Bromfield, Noah Beery, Jr. Bland oater of greedy men who try to outwit the redskins and incite a war.

Black Devils of Call, The SEE: Mystery of the Black Jungle.

Black Dragon of Manzanar (1943) 100m. **½ D: William Witney. Rod Cameron, Roland Got, Constance Worth, Nino Pipitone, Noel Cravat. Sufficiently action-packed Republic cliff-hanger with Cameron the dynamic federal agent outdoing Oriental Axis agents during WW2. Re-edited movie serial: G-MEN VS. THE BLACK DRAGON.

Black Fox, The (1962) 89m. ***½ D: Louis Clyde Stoumen. Narrated by Marlene Dietrich. Exceedingly taut, grim documentary tracing the rise and fall of Adolph Hitler, focusing on his use of power during Third Reich. Academy Award winner as best documentary feature of the year.

Black Friday (1940) 70m. ** D: Arthur Lubin. Boris Karloff, Bela Lugosi, Stanley Ridges, Anne Nagel, Anne Gwynne, Virginia Brissac. Another mad-scientist yarn with Karloff transplanting brain, turning respectable man into mad killer.

Black Fury (1935) 92m. ***½ D: Michael Curtiz. Paul Muni, Karen Morley, William Gargan, Barton MacLane, Mae Marsh. Tough social drama of coal-miners plagued by unsafe conditions, labor strikes, and corruption, is top drama. Muni memorable as usual in lead role.

Black Gold (1963) 98m. **½ D: Leslie Martinson. Philip Carey, Diane McBain, James Best, Claude Akins, Iron-Eyes Cody. Predictable search for oil set in Oklahoma, with standard villain and supposedly ironic outcome.

Black Hand (1950) 93m. ** D: Richard Thorpe. Gene Kelly, J. Carrol Naish, Teresa Celli, Marc Lawrence, Frank Puglia. 1900's N.Y.C. with Kelly battling Mafia; uninspired.

Black Horse Canyon (1954) C-81m. **½ D: Jesse Hibbs. Joel McCrea, Mari Blanchard, Race Gentry, Murvyn Vye. Diverting, gentle Western about rebellious black stallion and those who recapture him.

Black Knight, The (1954) C-85m. **½ D: Tay Garnett. Alan Ladd, Patricia Medina, Andre Morell, Harry Andrews, Peter Cushing. Ladd lends some bounce to small budgeter about mysterious horseman championing King Arthur's cause in merry old England.

Black Legion (1936) 83m. *** D: Archie Mayo. Humphrey Bogart, Erin O'Brien-Moore, Dick Foran, Ann Sheridan. Factory worker Bogart becomes involved with Ku Klux Klan-ish group in powerful social drama, compactly told.

Black Like Me (1964) 107m. **½ D: Carl Lerner. James Whitmore, Roscoe Lee Browne, Sorrell Booke, Will Geer, Al Freeman, Jr., Dan Priest. Exploitation feature pegged on premise of reporter taking medication that allows him to pass for Negro, thus experiencing racial problems first-hand.

Black Magic (1944) 67m. D: Phil Rosen. Sidney Toler, Mantan Moreland, Frances Chan, Jacqueline DeWit, Claudia Dell, Edward Earle, Joseph Crehan. SEE Charlie Chan series.

Black Magic (1949) 105m. **½ D: Gregory Ratoff. Orson Welles, Akim Tamiroff, Nancy Guild, Raymond Burr, Frank Latimore. Welles gives overenthusiastic performance in chronicle of charlatan Cagliostro who seeks to rise to power in 18th century Italy.

Black Narcissus (1947) C-99m. ***½ D: Michael Powell, Emeric Pressburger. Deborah Kerr, Flora Robson, Kathleen Byron, Sabu, Jean Simmons, David Farrar, Jenny Laird, Judith Furse. Unique film based on Godden novel of missionaries finding temptation in Himalayas. Successful movie with Kerr in great form.

Black Orchid, The (1959) 96m. **½ D: Martin Ritt. Sophia Loren, Anthony Quinn, Ina Balin, Jimmie Baird, Mark Richman, Naomi Stevens, Frank Puglia. Fabricated soaper of bumbling businessman (Quinn) romancing criminal's widow (Loren) and the problem of convincing their children that marriage will make all their lives better.

Black Orpheus (1960-Brazil, dubbed) C-98m. ***½ D: Marcel Camus. Breno Mello, Marpessa Dawn, Lourdes De Oliveira, Lea Garcia. Lyrical Brazilian film has achieved near-classic status for its acting, a memorable score, excellent carnival scenes. Worth watching.

Black Patch (1957) 83m. Bomb D: Allen H. Miner. George Montgomery, Diana Brewster, Leo Gordon, Sebastian Cabot. Inconsequential trivia with Montgomery as gun-toting sheriff out to clear his name.

Black Pirates, The (1954-Mexican, dubbed) C-72m. **½ D: Allen H. Miner. Anthony Dexter, Martha Roth, Lon Chaney, Robert Clarke. Uninspired account of pirates searching for gold.

Black Room, The (1935) 67m. **½ D: Roy William Neill. Boris Karloff, Marian Marsh, Robert Allen, Katherine DeMille, John Buckler. First-rate horror with menace Karloff (in a dual role) enticing innocent Marsh into his dastardly clutches.

Black Rose, The (1950) C-120m. **½ D: Henry Hathaway. Tyrone Power, Orson Welles, Jack Hawkins, Michael Rennie, Herbert Lom, Laurence Harvey, Cecile Aubry. Sweeping pageantry follows Saxon Power on Oriental adventures during 1200's; dynamic action scenes.

Black Sabbath (1964-Italian, dubbed) C-99m. **½ D: Mario Bava. Boris Karloff, Mark Damon, Suzy Anderson, Jacqueline Pierreux. Italian three-part film hosted by Karloff, who appears in final episode about a vampire controlling an entire family. Other sequences are good, atmospheric.

Black Scorpion, The (1957) 88m. *½ D: Edward Ludwig. Richard Denning, Carlos Rivas, Mara Corday, Mario Navarro. Giant-size title insects run rampant in Mexico ; lower-case thriller.

Black Shield of Falworth, The (1954) C-99m. **½ D: Rudolph Maté. Tony Curtis, Janet Leigh, David Farrar, Barbara Rush, Herbert Marshall. Juvenile version of Howard Pyle novel, MEN OF IRON; Curtis unconvincing as nobility rising through ranks to knighthood in medieval England. Settings, supporting cast bolster production.

Black Sleep, The (1956) 81m. *½ D: Reginald LeBorg. Basil Rathbone, Akim Tamiroff, Lon Chaney, John Carradine, Bela Lugosi. Big horror cast cannot save dull, unatmospheric tale of doctor performing brain transplants in remote castle. Laughable.

Black Spurs (1965) C-81m. *½ D: R. G. Springsteen. Rory Calhoun, Terry Moore, Linda Darnell, Scott Brady, Lon Chaney, Bruce Cabot, Richard Arlen. Ordinary Western with attraction of one-time movie stars including Darnell (her last film). Standard horse opera.

Black Sunday (1961-Italian, dubbed) 83m. **½ D: Mario Bava. Barbara Steele, John Richardson, Ivo Garrani, Andrea Checchi. Intriguing story of the one day each century when Satan roams the earth. Steele is a witch who swears vengeance on the descendants of those who killed her hundreds of years ago. Beautifully atmospheric.

Black Swan, The (1942) C-85m. *** D: Henry King. Tyrone Power, Maureen O'Hara, Laird Cregar, Thomas Mitchell, George Sanders, Anthony Quinn. Power makes a dashing pirate in this colorful swashbuckler, fighting Sanders and Quinn, rescuing O'Hara from their clutches.

Black Tent, The (1957-British) C-93m. ** D: Brian Hurst. Anthony Steel, Donald Sinden, Anna Maria Sandri, Donald Pleasence. Passable mixture of romance and action in the African desert as British soldier Steel romances native chief's daughters and helps tribe fight off Nazi attack.

Black Tuesday (1954) 80m. *** D: Hugo Fregonese. Edward G. Robinson, Peter Graves, Jean Parker, Milburn Stone. Throwback to 1930-ish gangster films, with Robinson and Graves as escaped convicts being hunted by cops—nice gunplay, with Parker good as the moll.

Black Whip, The (1957) 77m. *½ D: Charles Marquis Warren. Hugh Marlowe, Coleen Gray, Angie Dickenson, Sheb Wooley. Only spice to this oater is bevy of beautiful girls who are rescued by Marlowe.

Black Widow, The SEE: Somba, The Spider Woman.

Black Widow (1954) C-95m. **½ D: Nunnally Johnson. Ginger Rogers, Van Heflin, Gene Tierney, George Raft, Peggy Ann Garner, Reginald Gardiner, Otto Kruger. Detective Raft investigates murder among show biz folk. Slick whodunit, twist finis.

Black Zoo (1963) 88m. Bomb D: Robert Gordon. Michael Gough, Virginia Grey, Jerome Cowan, Elisha Cook, Jeanne Cooper. Good cast flounders in silly story of killer loose in zoo; from the man who gave you I WAS A TEEN-AGE WEREWOLF.

Blackbeard, The Pirate (1952) C-99m. ** D: Raoul Walsh. Robert Newton, Linda Darnell, William Bendix, Keith Andes, Richard Egan, Irene Ryan. Newton is rambunctious as 17th-century buccaneer, with lovely Darnell his captive; fun for a while, but Newton's hamming soon grows tiresome.

Blackboard Jungle, The (1955) 101m. ***½ D: Richard Brooks. Glenn Ford, Anne Francis, Louis Calhern, Sidney Poitier, Richard Kiley, Warner Anderson. Excellent adaptation of Evan Hunter's novel of a teacher's (Ford) harrowing experiences in N.Y. school system with Poitier memorable as a troublemaker. Hard-hitting entertainment.

Blackjack Ketchum, Desperado (1956) 76m. *½ D: Earl Bellamy. Howard Duff, Victor Jory, Maggie Mahoney, Angela Stevens. Former gunslinger must endure another shoot-out before returning to a peaceful way of life.

Blackmail (1939) 81m. **½ D: H. C. Potter. Edward G. Robinson, Gene Lockhart, Guinn Williams, Ruth Hussey, Esther Dale. Robinson is freed after serving stretch for crime he didn't commit; guilty Lockhart blackmails him in taut drama.

Blackout (1954-British) 87m. ** D: Terence Fisher. Dane Clark, Belinda Lee, Betty Ann Davies, Eleanor Summerfield. Programmer: down-and-out Clark accepts good-paying job, which leads him into life of crime.

Blackwell's Island (1939) 71m. **½ D: William McGann. John Garfield, Rosemary Lane, Dick Purcell, Victor Jory, Stanley Fields, Peggy Shannon. Peppy little gangster comedy with Garfield a crusading reporter getting the rap on thick-witted thug Fields.

Blanche Fury (1948-British) C-93m. **½ D: Marc Allegret. Valerie Hobson, Stewart Granger, Michael Gough, Walter Fitzgerald. Heavy-handed, complicated period drama has fine actors trying to bolster story of bizarre girl involved in illicit romance and murder.

Blast-Off (1967) C-95m. ** D: Don Sharp. Burl Ives, Troy Donahue, Gert Frobe, Hermione Gingold, Lionel Jeffries, Daliah Lavi. Wooden attempt at spicing up Jules Verne tale about space trip set in Victorian times. Retitled THOSE FANTASTIC FLYING FOOLS.

Blaze of Noon (1947) 91m. **½ D: John Farrow. Anne Baxter, William Holden, Sonny Tufts, William Bendix, Sterling Hayden. Hokey story of Holden torn between his wife (Baxter) and true love, flying.

Blazing Forest, The (1952) C-90m. *½ D: Edward Ludwig. John Payne, Agnes Moorehead, Richard Arlen, William Demarest, Susan Morrow. Felling trees and romancing Moorehead's niece (Morrow) occupies Payne till big fire diverts him, but not the bored viewer.

Blind Spot (1947) 73m. *** D: Robert Gordon. Chester Morris, Constance Dowling, Steven Geray, Sid Tomack. Mystery writer Morris has to extricate himself from charge of murdering his publisher in this tight little mystery.

Blindfold (1966) C-102m. **½ D: Philip Dunne. Rock Hudson, Claudia Cardinale, Jack Warden, Guy Stockwell, Anne Seymour. Attractive cast falters in film that wavers from comedy to mystery. Slapstick scenes seem incongruous as Hudson engages in international espionage with a noted scientist. Shot partly in N.Y.C.

Blob, The (1958) C-86m. ** D: Irvin S. Yeaworth, Jr. Steve McQueen, Aneta Corseaut, Earl Rowe, Olin Howlin. OK sci-fi has McQueen accidentally involved in trying to rid humanity of insatiable formless creature from outer space.

Block Busters (1944) 60m. D: Wallace Fox. Leo Gorcey, Huntz Hall, Gabriel Dell, Minerva Urecal, Noah Beery, Sr., Billy Benedict, Harry Langdon. SEE: Bowery Boys series.

Block-Heads (1938) 55m. *** D: John G. Blystone. Stan Laurel, Oliver Hardy, Patricia Ellis, Minna Gombell, Billy Gilbert, James Finlayson. Stan's been marching in a trench for twenty years—nobody told him WW1 was over! Ollie brings him home to find he hasn't changed. Top L&H.

Blockade (1938) 85m. *** D: William Dieterle. Madeleine Carroll, Henry Fonda, Leo Carrillo, John Halliday, Vladimir Sokoloff, Reginald Denny. Vivid romance drama of Spanish Civil War with globe-trotting Carroll falling in love with fighting Fonda.

Blonde Blackmailer (1958-British) 58m. Bomb D: Charles Deane. Richard Arlen, Susan Shaw, Constance Leigh, Vincent Ball. Hackneyed plot of innocent ex-con (Arlen) determined to prove innocence and find real killers.

Blonde Bombshell SEE: Bombshell.

Blonde Crazy (1931) 73m. **½ D: Roy Del Ruth. James Cagney, Joan Blondell, Louis Calhern, Ray Milland, Polly Walters, Nat Pendleton. Cagney's a delight as smooth con-artist who falls for snappy Blondell; young Milland plays harried lawyer.

Blonde Dynamite (1950) 66m. D: William Beaudine. Leo Gorcey, Huntz Hall, Gabriel Dell, Adele Jergens, Jody Gilbert. SEE: Bowery Boys.

Blonde Fever (1944) 69m. ** D: Richard Whorf. Philip Dorn, Mary Astor, Felix Bressart, Gloria Grahame, Marshall Thompson. Astor lends class to this mild account of widow on the loose in Europe finding love with Dorn, with Grahame as sultry competition.

Blonde In a White Car SEE: Nude In a White Car.

Blonde Venus (1932) 80m. *** D: Josef von Sternberg. Marlene Dietrich, Herbert Marshall, Cary Grant, Dickie Moore, Sidney Toler. Episodic story of notorious Dietrich leading unsavory life to support herself and child. Good cast, unusual direction. Marlene sings "Hot Voodoo" in an ape suit!

Blondie With a vast audience already familiar with the Chic Young comic strip, a Blondie series seemed like a shoo-in in 1938—and it was. The series, with Arthur Lake as Dagwood, Penny Singleton as Blondie, Larry Simms as Baby Dumpling (later Alexander), Marjorie Kent as Cookie, Jonathan Hale as Mr. Dithers (later Jerome Cowan as Mr. Radcliffe), and Daisy as Daisy, prospered for 13 years, spanning 28 episodes. As with most series, the first ones were the best—fresh, and original, with many clever touches belying the fact that they were low-budget films. By the mid-1940's, however, with less capable directors and a fairly standard formula, the films became even more predictable, and the humor more contrived. Nevertheless, Blondie carried on with the same cast until 1951. Unlike some series, the Blondie films actually continued from one to the next, with Baby Dumpling growing up, starting school in the fourth film, taking the name of Alexander in the eleventh. Cookie is also born in the eleventh film, and Daisy has pups in the following one. Many interesting people pop up in the Blondie casts, such as Rita Hayworth in BLONDIE ON A BUDGET, Glenn Ford in BLONDIE PLAYS CUPID, Larry Parks and Janet Blair in BLONDIE GOES TO COLLEGE, Anita Louise in BLONDIE'S BIG MOMENT, and Adele Jergens in BLONDIE'S ANNIVERSARY. Many character actors appeared as well, with Irving Bacon usually playing the harried Bumstead mailman, Mr. Beasley. After twenty years of TV situation comedies, Blondie has lost some of its punch, but generally still stands out as an enjoyable, smoothly made series of comedies.

Blondie (1938) 69m. D: Frank Strayer. Penny Singleton, Arthur Lake, Larry Simms, Gene Lockhart, Ann Doran, Jonathan Hale, Gordon Oliver, Stanley Andrews.

Blondie Brings Up Baby (1939) 67m. D: Frank Strayer. Penny Singleton, Arthur Lake, Larry Simms, Danny Mummert, Jonathan Hale, Fay Helm, Peggy Ann Garner, Helen Jerome Eddy, Irving Bacon.

Blondie Goes Latin (1941) 69m. D: Frank Strayer. Penny Singleton, Arthur Lake, Larry Simms, Tito Guizar, Ruth Terry, Danny Mummert, Irving Bacon, Janet Buston.

Blondie Goes to College (1942) 74m. D: Frank Strayer. Penny Singleton, Arthur Lake, Larry Simms, Jonathan Hale, Larry Parks, Janet Blair, Lloyd Bridges, Esther Dale, Adele Mara.

Blondie Has Servant Trouble (1940) 70m. D: Frank Strayer. Penny Singleton, Arthur Lake, Larry Simms, Daisy, Danny Mummert, Jonathan Hale, Arthur Hohl, Esther Dale, Irving Bacon.

Blondie Hits the Jackpot (1949) 66m. D: Edward Bernds. Penny Singleton, Arthur Lake, Larry Simms, Jerome Cowan, Lloyd Corrigan.

Blondie in Society (1941) 75m. D: Frank Strayer. Penny Singleton, Arthur Lake, Larry Simms, Jonathan Hale, Danny Mummert, William Frawley, Edgar Kennedy, Chick Chandler.

Blondie in the Dough (1947) 69m. D: Abby Berlin. Penny Singleton, Arthur Lake, Larry Simms, Marjorie Kent, Jerome Cowan, Hugh Herbert, Clarence Kolb, Danny Mummert.

Blondie Knows Best (1946) 69m. D: Abby Berlin. Penny Singleton, Arthur Lake, Larry Simms, Marjorie Kent, Shemp Howard, Ludwig Donath, Jerome Cowan.

Blondie Meets the Boss (1939) 58m. D: Frank Strayer. Penny Singleton, Arthur Lake, Larry Simms, Dorothy Moore, Jonathan Hale, Stanley Brown, Inez Courtney, Don Beddoe.

Blondie of the Follies (1932) 90m. **½ D: Edmund Goulding. Marion Davies, Robert Montgomery, Billie Dove, Jimmy Durante, Zasu Pitts, Sidney Toler, Louise Carter. Rival girls in love with Montgomery both become Follies stars—better as musical than as drama. James Gleason fine as Marion's father. Best scene has Davies and Durante spoofing Garbo and Barrymore in Grand Hotel.

Blondie on a Budget (1940) 73m. D: Frank Strayer. Penny Singleton, Arthur Lake, Larry Simms, Danny Mummert, Rita Hayworth, Don Beddoe, John Qualen, Fay Helm.

Blondie Plays Cupid (1940) 68m. D: Frank Strayer. Penny Singleton, Arthur Lake, Larry Simms, Daisy, Jonathan Hale, Danny Mummert, Irving Bacon, Glenn Ford.

Blondie Takes a Vacation (1939) 61m. D: Frank Strayer. Penny Singleton, Arthur Lake, Larry Simms, Danny Mummert, Donald Meek, Elizabeth Dunne, Robert Wilcox, Irving Bacon.

Blondie's Anniversary (1947) 75m. D: Abby Berlin. Penny Singleton, Arthur Lake, Larry Simms, Marjorie Kent, Adele Jergens, Jerome Cowan, Grant Mitchell, William Frawley.

Blondie's Big Deal (1949) 66m. D: Edward Bernds. Penny Singleton, Arthur Lake, Larry Simms, Jerome Cowan, Marjorie Kent, Collette Lyons, Ray Walker, Stanley Andrews, Alan Dinehart III.

Blondie's Big Moment (1947) 69m. D: Abby Berlin. Penny Singleton, Arthur Lake, Larry Simms, Marjorie Kent, Jerome Cowan, Anita Louise, Danny Mummert, Jack Rice, Jack Davis.

Blondie's Hero (1950) 67m. D: Edward Bernds. Penny Singleton, Arthur Lake, Larry Simms, William Frawley, Iris Adrian, Edward Earle.

Blondie's Holiday (1947) 67m. D: Abby Berlin. Arthur Lake, Penny Singleton, Larry Simms, Marjorie Kent, Jerome Cowan, Grant Mitchell, Sid Tomack, Jeff York, Mary Young.

Blondie's Lucky Day (1946) 75m. D: Abby Berlin. Penny Singleton, Arthur Lake, Larry Simms, Marjorie Kent, Frank Jenks, Paul Harvey, Charles Arnt.

Blondie's Reward (1948) 67m. D: Abby Berlin. Penny Singleton, Arthur Lake, Larry Simms, Marjorie Kent, Jerome Cowan, Gay Nelson, Danny Mummert, Paul Harvey, Frank Jenks.

Blondie's Secret (1948) 68m. D: Edward Bernds. Penny Singleton, Arthur Lake, Larry Simms, Marjorie Kent, Jerome Cowan, Thurston Hall, Jack Rice, Danny Mummert, Frank Orth.

Blood Alley (1955) C-115m. **½ D: William Wellman. John Wayne, Lauren Bacall, Paul Fix, Mike Mazurki, Anita Ekberg. Enjoyable escapism with Wayne, Bacall, and assorted Chinese escaping down river to Hong Kong pursued by Communists.

Blood and Black Lace (1965-Italian, dubbed) C-88m. *½ D: Mario Bava. Cameron Mitchell, Eva Bartok, Mary Arden. Sex-killer stalking the streets isn't enough to enliven this film with wooden performances and script.

Blood and Roses (1961-Italian) C-74m. **½ D: Roger Vadim. Mel Ferrer, Elsa Martinelli, Annette Vadim, Marc Allegret. Trivia disguised by colorful production; vampire-possessed girl is incited to blood-seeking; Ferrer wanders bewildered through costumer.

Blood and Sand (1941) C-123m. *** D: Rouben Mamoulian. Tyrone Power, Linda Darnell, Rita Hayworth, Nazimova, Anthony Quinn, J. Carrol Naish, John Carradine, George Reeves. Pastel remake of Valentino's silent film about naive bullfighter who ignores true-love Darnell for temptress Hayworth. Slow-paced romance, uplifted by Nazimova's knowing performance as Power's mother, beautiful color production.

Blood and Steel (1959) 63m. *½ D: Bernard Kowalski. John Lupton, James Edwards, Brett Halsey, John Brinkley. Routine study of U.S. navy men landing on Jap-held island, and their assistance of the partisan cause to free the villagers from bondage.

Blood Arrow (1958) 75m. *½ D: Charles Marquis Warren. Scott Brady, Paul Richards, Phyllis Coates, Don Haggerty. Uninspired tale of Mormon girl Coates trudging through Indian territory to obtain needed medicine, with usual Indian attacks.

Blood of Dracula (1957) 68m. *½ D: Herbert L. Strock. Sandra Harrison, Gail Ganley, Jerry Blaine, Louise Lewis. Inoffensive programmer about girl being hypnotized into a life of vampirism.

Blood of the Vampire (1958-British) C-87m. ** D: Henry Cass. Donald Wolfit, Barbara Shelley, Vincent Ball, Victor Maddern. Potentially vivid horror film weakened by slack production: doctor sent to prison becomes involved with inmate vampire in blood-seeking experiments.

Blood on the Arrow (1964) C-91m. *½ D: Sidney Salkow. Dale Robertson, Martha Hyer, Wendell Corey, Elisha Cook, Ted de Corsia. Humdrum Western dealing with Apache massacre and survivors' attempt to rescue their son held captive by redskins.

Blood on the Moon (1948) 88m. *** D: Robert Wise. Robert Mitchum, Barbara Bel Geddes, Robert Preston, Walter Brennan. Tough Western with rivals Mitchum and Preston becoming bitter enemies because of scheme to undo ranchers Bel Geddes-Brennan.

Blood on the Sun (1945) 98m. *** D: Frank Lloyd. James Cagney, Sylvia Sidney, Wallace Ford, Rosemary DeCamp, Robert Armstrong. Cagney, in Japan during the 1930's, smells trouble coming but is virtually helpless; good melodrama.

Bloodhounds of Broadway (1952) C-90m. **½ D: Harmon Jones. Mitzi Gaynor, Scott Brady, Mitzi Green, Michael O'Shea, Marguerite Chapman. Hick Gaynor becomes slick gal in N.Y.C. involved with pseudo-Damon Runyon folk; funny Green has too small a role. Songs include "I Wish I Knew."

Blossoms in the Dust (1941) C-100m. *** D: Mervyn LeRoy. Greer Garson, Walter Pidgeon, Felix Bressart, Marsha Hunt, Fay Holden, Samuel S. Hinds. Slick tear-jerker of Texas orphanage founded by Garson when she loses her own child; tastefully acted.

Blowing Wild (1953) 90m. ** D: Hugo Fregonese. Gary Cooper, Barbara Stanwyck, Ruth Roman, Anthony Quinn, Ward Bond. Cooper and Stanwyck don't click as oil driller and vital wife who leads him on to bringing in big gusher.

Blue Angel, The (1959) C-107m. *½ D: Edward Dmytryk. Curt Jurgens, May Britt, Theodore Bikel, John Banner, Ludwig Stossel, Fabrizio Mioni. Disastrous remake of Josef von Sternberg-Marlene Dietrich classic, from Heinrich Mann's novel of precise professor won over by tawdry nightclub singer.

Blue Bird, The (1940) C-88m. **½ D: Walter Lang. Shirley Temple, Spring Byington, Nigel Bruce, Gale Sondergaard, Eddie Collins, Sybil

Jason. Overblown Temple vehicle based on classic story of girl seeking true happiness; slowly paced, but beautifully filmed. Forest-fire sequence is highlight.

Blue Blood (1951) C-72m. *½ D: Lew Landers. Bill Williams, Jane Nigh, Arthur Shields, Audrey Long. Lackluster racehorse story with a few good moments by Shields as elderly trainer seeking comeback.

Blue Dahlia, The (1946) 96m. *** D: George Marshall. Alan Ladd, Veronica Lake, William Bendix, Howard da Silva, Hugh Beaumont, Doris Dowling. Exciting Raymond Chandler melodrama has Ladd returning from military service to find wife unfaithful. She's murdered, he's suspected in well-turned film.

Blue Denim (1959) 89m. *** D: Philip Dunne. Carol Lynley, Brandon de Wilde, Macdonald Carey, Marsha Hunt, Warren Berlinger, Roberta Shore. De Wilde and Lynley are striking as teen-agers faced with Carol's pregnancy. Generation gap problem and youths' naïveté date story, but believable performances make it worthwhile.

Blue Gardenia, The (1953) 90m. **½ D: Fritz Lang. Anne Baxter, Richard Conte, Ann Sothern, Raymond Burr, Jeff Donnell, George Reeves, Nat King Cole. Engaging murder caper with 1940's flavor. Baxter seeks Conte's help to find real killer of her artist-friend.

Blue Grass of Kentucky (1950) C-71m. ** D: William Beaudine. Bill Williams, Jane Nigh, Ralph Morgan. Routine account of horse-breeding families, their rivalry and eventual healing of old wounds when romance blooms between the younger generations.

Blue Hawaii (1961) C-101m. **½ D: Norman Taurog. Elvis Presley, Joan Blackman, Angela Lansbury, Iris Adrian. Agreeable Presley vehicle bolstered by Lansbury's presence as mother of soldier (Presley) returning to islands and working with tourist agency.

Blue Lagoon, The (1949-British) C-101m. *** D: Frank Launder. Jean Simmons, Donald Houston, Noel Purcell, Cyril Cusack, Maurice Denham. Idyllic romance of Simmons and Houston, shipwrecked on tropic isle, falling in love as they grow to maturity; slowly paced but refreshing.

Blue Lamp, The (1950-British) 84m. *** D: Basil Dearden. Jack Warner, Peggy Evans, Dirk Bogarde, Tessie O'Shea, Jimmy Hanley. Unpretentious, relentless manhunt for murderer by Scotland Yard investigator.

Blue Murder at St. Trinian's (1958-British) 86m. *** D: Frank Launder. Joyce Grenfell, Terry-Thomas, George Cole, Alastair Sim. Uncontrollable pupils at madcap school make a robber on the lam wish he'd never hidden out there; deft comedy.

Blue Skies (1946) C-104m. *** D: Stuart Heisler. Fred Astaire, Bing Crosby, Joan Caulfield, Billy DeWolfe, Olga San Juan. Sticky plot salvaged by DeWolfe specialties, dancing by Astaire, songs: title tune, "Puttin' On The Ritz," "A Couple of Song and Dance Men."

Blue Veil, The (1951) 113m. *** D: Curtis Bernhardt. Jane Wyman, Charles Laughton, Joan Blondell, Richard Carlson, Agnes Moorehead. Wyman is self-sacrificing nursemaid whose life story is chronicled with intertwined episodes of her charges and their families.

Bluebeard (1944) 73m. *** D: Edgar G. Ulmer. Jean Parker, John Carradine, Nils Asther, Ludwig Stossel, Iris Adrian, Emmett Lynn. Surprisingly effective story of incurable strangler Carradine, who falls for smart-girl Parker who senses that something is wrong.

Bluebeard (1963-French, dubbed) C-114m. **½ D: Claude Chabrol. Charles Denner, Michele Morgan, Danielle Darrieux, Hildegarde Neff, Françoise Lugagne. Retelling of life of French wife-killer, far less witty than Chaplin's MONSIEUR VERDOUX. Retitled: LANDRU.

Bluebeard's Ten Honeymoons (1960) 93m. ** D: W. Lee Wilder. George Sanders, Corinne Calvet, Jean Kent, Patricia Roc. Sanders enlivens OK chronicle of fortune-hunter who decides that marrying and murdering a series of women is the key to financial success.

Blueprint for Murder, A (1953) 76m. **½ D: Andrew L. Stone. Joseph Cotten, Jean Peters, Gary Merrill, Jack Kruschen, Mae Marsh. Whodunit has Peters as prime suspect of poison killings, with Cotten seeking the truth.

Blues Busters (1950) 67m. D: William Beaudine. Leo Gorcey, Huntz Hall, Adele Jergens, Gabriel Dell, Craig Stevens, William Benedict. SEE: Bowery Boys series.

Blues in the Night (1941) 88m. *** D: Anatole Litvak. Priscilla Lane, Richard Whorf, Betty Field, Lloyd Nolan, Jack Carson, Elia Kazan, Wallace Ford. Original, taut musical drama of band splitting up, each member finding tragedy and disappointment on his own. Fine score includes title song, "This Time The Dream's On Me."

Bob Mathias Story, The (1954) 80m. *** D: Francis D. Lyon. Bob Mathias, Ward Bond, Melba Mathias, Paul Bryar, Ann Doran. Agreeable biography of star track athlete, his sports career, military duty, family life. Mathias turns in an engaging portrayal of himself.

Bobbikins (1960-British) 89m. ** D: Robert Day. Max Bygraves, Shirley Jones, Steven Stocker, Billie Whitelaw. Gimmicky comedy with British singer Bygraves and Jones the parents of an infant who talks like an adult. Not bad . . . but that awful title!

Bobby Ware Is Missing (1955) 67m. *1/2 D: Thomas Carr. Neville Brand, Arthur Franz, Jean Willes, Walter Reed. Tedious boy-hunt as his parents and sheriff track down kidnappers.

Boccaccio '70 (1962-Italian, dubbed) C-165m. *** D: Federico Fellini, Luchino Visconti, Vittorio De Sica. Anita Ekberg, Sophia Loren, Romy Schneider, Peppino De Filippo, Dante Maggio, Thomas Milian. Trio of episodes: THE RAFFLE—timid soul wins a liaison with a girl as prize; THE BET—aristocrat's wife takes a job as her husband's mistress; THE TEMPTATION OF DR. ANTONIO—fantasy of puritanical fanatic and a voluptuous poster picture which comes alive.

Body and Soul (1947) 104m. **** D: Robert Rossen. John Garfield, Lilli Palmer, Hazel Brooks, Anne Revere, William Conrad, Joseph Pevney, Canada Lee. Most boxing films pale next to this classic of Garfield working his way up by devious means, becoming famous champ. Superb photography.

Body Disappears, The (1941) 72m. ** D: Ross Lederman. Jeffrey Lynn, Jane Wyman, Edward Everett Horton, Marguerite Chapman. Not a very inspired mixture of comedy, suspense, and sci-fi, as Lynn is involved in invisible-making formula causing havoc with the police.

Body Snatcher, The (1945) 77m. ***1/2 D: Robert Wise. Boris Karloff, Bela Lugosi, Henry Daniell, Edith Atwater, Russell Wade, Rita Corday. Fine, atmospheric adaptation of Robert Louis Stevenson story. Notorious Burke and Hare provide bodies for doctor's experiments in 19th-century Scotland.

Bodyguard (1948) 62m. ** D: Richard Fleischer. Lawrence Tierney, Priscilla Lane, Philip Reed, June Clayworth. Routine story of man accused of murder trying to clear himself.

Bodyhold (1949) 63m. *1/2 D: Seymour Friedman. Willard Parker, Lola Albright, Hillary Brooke, Allen Jenkins, Gordon Jones. Programmer of wrestler and girlfriend seeking to clean up corruption in the fight game.

Boeing Boeing (1965) 102m. *** D: John Rich. Jerry Lewis, Tony Curtis, Dany Saval, Christine Schmidtmer, Suzanna Leigh, Thelma Ritter. Surprisingly subdued Lewis paired with Curtis as two airline pilots who run a swinging pad in Paris, constantly stocked with stewardesses, to the chagrin of housekeeper Ritter. Amusing, offbeat for Lewis.

Bohemian Girl, The (1936) 70m. *** D: James Horne, Charles R. Rogers. Stan Laurel, Oliver Hardy, Thelma Todd, Antonio Moreno, Darla Hood, Jacqueline Wells, Mae Busch. Nifty comic opera with Stan and Ollie part of gypsy caravan. They adopt abandoned girl who turns out to be princess.

Bold and the Brave, The (1956) 87m. *** D: Lewis R. Foster. Wendell Corey, Mickey Rooney, Don Taylor, Nicole Maurey. Routine WW2 study of soldiers fighting in Italy, greatly uplifted by unstereotyped performances; Rooney is outstanding.

Bolero (1934) 83m. **1/2 D: Wesley Ruggles. George Raft, Carole Lombard, Sally Rand, Gertrude Michael, William Frawley, Ray Milland. Peppy story of dancer Raft's rise to fame, stepping on anyone and everyone along the way. He and Lombard are enticing team.

Bomb at 10:10 (1966-Yugoslavian, dubbed) C-86m. ** D: Charles Damic. George Montgomery, Rada Popovic, Peter Banicevic, Branko Plesa. Thrown-together mishmash with Montgomery escaping from Nazi P.O.W. camp, plotting to help partisans and destroy prison leaders.

Bomb in the High Street (1964-British) 60m. **½ D: Terence Bishop. Ronald Howard, Terry Palmer, Suzanna Leigh. Unpretentious robbery caper involving phony bomb scare to divert authorities from site of crime.

Bomba the Jungle Boy In 1949 producer Walter Mirisch, who has gone on to far greater things, decided to produce a series of low-budget adventure films based on a series of popular juvenile books about a boy who has grown up in the jungle. For this road-company Tarzan series he got Johnny Sheffield, who had played Boy in the Tarzan films, and director Ford Beebe, an expert at making something out of nothing. With a small studio backlot and plenty of footage of wild animals, BOMBA THE JUNGLE BOY emerged, a notbad little adventure. The subsequent eleven films in the series, however, worked their way into a standard formula that by the last episodes was all too familiar. BOMBA was made for younger audiences, and the films will probably still please the kids. As for adults, well, there have been worse films than the BOMBA series.

Bomba and the Elephant Stampede SEE: **Elephant Stampede**.

Bomba and the Hidden City (1950) 71m. D: Ford Beebe. Johnny Sheffield, Sue England, Paul Guilfoyle, Leon Belasco, Smoki Whitfield.

Bomba and the Jungle Girl (1952) 70m. D: Ford Beebe. Johnny Sheffield, Karen Sharpe, Walter Sande, Martin Wilkins.

Bomba on Panther Island (1949) 76m. D: Ford Beebe. Johnny Sheffield, Allene Roberts, Lita Baron, Smoki Whitfield.

Bomba, The Jungle Boy (1949) 70m. D: Ford Beebe. Johnny Sheffield, Peggy Ann Garner, Smoki Whitfield, Onslow Stevens.

Bombardier (1943) 99m. *** D: Richard Wallace. Pat O'Brien, Randolph Scott, Anne Shirley, Eddie Albert, Walter Reed, Robert Ryan, Barton MacLane. Familiar framework of fliers being trained during WW2 comes off well with fast-moving script.

Bombers B-52 (1957) C-106m. **½ D: Gordon Douglas. Natalie Wood, Karl Malden, Marsha Hunt, Efrem Zimbalist, Jr., Dean Jagger. Ordinary love story between army pilot Zimbalist and Wood, with latter's officer father (Malden) objecting, intertwined with good aerial footage of jet plane maneuvers.

Bombs Over Burma (1942) 62m. ** D: Joseph H. Lewis. Anna May Wong, Noel Madison, Dan Seymour, Richard Loo, Dennis Moore. Grade-B wartime saga of devoted Wong risking life for sake of China on espionage mission.

Bombshell (1933) 91m. ***½ D: Victor Fleming. Jean Harlow, Lee Tracy, Frank Morgan, Franchot Tone, Una Merkel, Pat O'Brien. Still amusing satire of Hollywood with Harlow as movie glamour queen with romantic problems. Retitled: BLONDE BOMBSHELL.

Bonjour Tristesse (1958) C-94m. *** D: Otto Preminger. Deborah Kerr, David Niven, Jean Seberg, Mylene Demongeot. Teen-ager does her best to break up romance between playboy widowed father and his mistress, with tragic results. Françoise Sagan's philosophy seeps through glossy production; Kerr exceptionally fine in soaper set on French Riviera.

Bonnie Parker Story, The (1958) 81m. **½ D: William Witney. Dorothy Provine, Jack Hogan, Richard Bakalyan, Joseph Turkel. With the success of BONNIE AND CLYDE, this film takes on added luster, recounting the lurid criminal life of the female crook (Provine); low-budget production.

Bonnie Scotland (1935) 80m. **½ D: James Horne. Stan Laurel, Oliver Hardy, June Lang, William Janney, Anne Grey, Vernon Steel, James Finlayson. Stan and Ollie accidentally end up in the desert with Scottish regiment, making a shambles of their unit. Disjointed, with occasional bright spots.

Bonzo Goes to College (1952) 80m. ** D: Frederick de Cordova. Maureen O'Sullivan, Edmund Gwenn, Gigi Perreau, Gene Lockhart, Irene Ryan, David Janssen. Follow-up to BEDTIME FOR BONZO has brainy chimp lead college football team to victory; good cast takes back seat to monkeyshines.

Boom Town (1940) 116m. *** D: Jack Conway. Clark Gable, Spencer Tracy, Claudette Colbert, Hedy Lamarr, Frank Morgan, Lionel Atwill, Chill Wills. No surprises in tale of get-rich-quick drilling for oil, but star-studded cast gives it life.

Boomerang (1947) 88m. **** D: Elia Kazan. Dana Andrews, Jane Wyatt, Lee J. Cobb, Arthur Kennedy, Sam Levene. Priest's murder brings a rapid conviction of an innocent man; prosecuting attorney determines to hunt out real facts. Brilliant drama in all respects.

Boots Malone (1952) 103m. *** D: William Dieterle. William Holden, Johnny Stewart, Ed Begley, Henry Morgan, Whit Bissell. Holden comes alive in role of shady character who reforms when he trains Stewart to become a jockey.

Border Incident (1949) 92m. ** D: Anthony Mann. Ricardo Montalban, George Murphy, Howard da Silva, Teresa Celli, Charles McGraw. Interesting cast in pedestrian account of U.S. agents cracking down on wetback smuggling on Mexican-Texas line.

Border River (1954) C-80m. ** D: George Sherman. Joel McCrea, Yvonne De Carlo, Pedro Armendariz, Howard Petrie. Mildly intriguing Western about Rebel officer McCrea's mission to buy much-needed weapons from Mexicans to continue fight against Yankees.

Borderline (1950) 88m. **½ D: William Seiter. Fred MacMurray, Claire Trevor, Raymond Burr, Roy Roberts. Trevor and MacMurray work well together as law enforcers each tracking down dope smugglers on Mexican border, neither knowing the other isn't a crook.

Bordertown (1935) 90m. *** D: Archie Mayo. Paul Muni, Bette Davis, Eugene Pallette, Margaret Lindsay. Fine drama of unusual triangle in bordertown cafe, with Davis as flirtatious wife of Pallette with designs on lawyer Muni. Used as basis for later THEY DRIVE BY NIGHT, but more serious in tone.

Borgia Stick, The (1967) C-120m. *** D: David Lowell Rich. Don Murray, Inger Stevens, Barry Nelson, Sorrell Booke, Marc Donnelly. Intense dramatic telefeature with Murray and Stevens posing as suburban married couple while working for crime syndicate, trying to break loose but unable to.

Born Free (1966) C-96m. ***½ D: James Hill. Virginia McKenna, Bill Travers, Geoffrey Keen, Peter Lukoye, Omar Chambati. Exceptional adaptation of Joy Adamson's book about Elsa the lioness, who was raised as a tame pet by African game wardens McKenna and Travers. Sincere, engrossing film, a must for family viewing.

Born Reckless (1959) 79m. ** D: Howard W. Koch. Mamie Van Doren, Jeff Richards, Arthur Hunnicutt, Carol Ohmart, Tom Dugan. Fitfully promising romp with Van Doren-Richards romancing while seeking success as rodeo performers.

Born To Be Bad (1934) 61m. ** D: Lowell Sherman. Loretta Young, Cary Grant, Henry Travers, Howard Lang, Matt Briggs. Pat soaper with poor Young trying to reclaim her illegitimate child from couple who have adopted him.

Born To Be Bad (1950) 94m. *** D: Nicholas Ray. Joan Fontaine, Robert Ryan, Joan Leslie, Mel Ferrer, Zachary Scott. Fontaine at her best as waspish female taking anything she wants.

Born To Be Loved (1959) 82m. ** D: Hugo Haas. Carol Morris, Vera Vague, Hugo Haas, Dick Kallman, Jacqueline Fontaine. Low-key yarn of poor-but-honest Morris and rich Widow Vague seeking romance, helped by elderly music instructor Haas.

Born To Dance (1936) 105m. *** D: Roy Del Ruth. Eleanor Powell, James Stewart, Virginia Bruce, Una Merkel, Sid Silvers, Frances Langford, Raymond Walburn, Buddy Ebsen. Powell bears out title in good Cole Porter musical with sensational footwork and fine songs: "Easy To Love," "I've Got You Under My Skin."

Born To Kill (1947) 92m. ** D: Robert Wise. Claire Trevor, Lawrence Tierney, Walter Slezak, Philip Terry, Elisha Cook, Jr. Unattractive melodrama of bad-guy Tierney marrying Trevor but continuing his philandering.

Born Yesterday (1950) 103m. ***½ D: George Cukor. Judy Holliday, William Holden, Broderick Crawford, Howard St. John. Hood-made-good Crawford wants his gal (Holliday) culturfied, hires Holden to teach her in hilarious Garson Kanin comedy set in Washington, D. C. Priceless Judy won Oscar for her Pygmalion performance.

Boss, The (1956) 89m. *** D: Byron Haskin. John Payne, William Bishop, Gloria McGhee, Doe Avedon, Joe Flynn. Effective study of WW1 veteran returning to St. Louis and combatting corruption and crime; one of Payne's best performances as the city's underworld boss.

Boston Blackie Over a span of nine years, Chester Morris starred in thirteen films as Boston Blackie, a former thief now on the right side of the law but preferring to work for himself than for the police. He brought to the role a delightful offhand manner and sense of humor that kept the films fresh even when the scripts weren't. From MEET BOSTON BLACKIE (1941) to BOSTON BLACKIE'S CHINESE VENTURE (1949), Morris was Blackie. Regulars included Richard Lane as a frustrated police detective convinced that Blackie was up to no good, but always one step behind him; George E. Stone as Blackie's talkative dimwitted buddy; and Lloyd Corrigan as a dizzy millionaire pal who'd do anything for a lark. Top-flight directors Robert Florey and Edward Dmytryk got the series started, and when the films fell into less capable hands, Morris and company came to the rescue with consistently ingratiating performances. While no classics, the Boston Blackie films offer a great deal of fun.

Boston Blackie and the Law (1946) 69m. D: D. Ross Lederman. Chester Morris, Trudy Marshall, Constance Dowling, Richard Lane.

Boston Blackie Booked on Suspicion (1945) 66m. D: Arthur Dreifuss. Chester Morris, Lynn Merrick, Richard Lane, Frank Sully, Steve Cochran.

Boston Blackie's Chinese Venture (1949) 59m. D: Seymour Friedman. Chester Morris, Joan Woodbury, Philip Ahn, Benson Fong.

Boston Blackie's Rendezvous (1945) 64m. D: Arthur Dreifuss. Chester Morris, Nina Foch, Steve Cochran, Richard Lane, George E. Stone, Frank Sully.

Botany Bay (1953) C-94m. **½ D: John Farrow. Alan Ladd, James Mason, Patricia Medina, Cedric Hardwicke. Based on Charles Nordhoff novel set in 1790's, picturesque yarn tells of convict ship bound for Australia, focusing on conflict between prisoner Ladd and sadistic skipper Mason, with Medina as Ladd's love interest.

Both Sides of the Law (1954-British) 94m. *** D: Muriel Box. Peggy Cummins, Terence Morgan, Anne Crawford, Rosamund John. Documentary-style account of London policewomen and their daily activity. Unpretentious production allows for good natural performances.

Bottom of the Bottle, The (1956) C-88m. **½ D: Henry Hathaway. Van Johnson, Joseph Cotten, Ruth Roman, Jack Carson. Overblown melodramatics south of the border involving a seemingly respectable attorney, his alcoholic younger brother, and assorted seedy townfolk.

Bounty Hunter, The (1954) C-79m. **½ D: Andre de Toth. Randolph Scott, Dolores Dorn, Marie Windsor, Howard Petrie. Scott is on his horse again, this time tracking down three murderers.

Bounty Killer, The (1965) C-92m. **½ D: Spencer G. Bennet. Dan Duryea, Rod Cameron, Audrey Dalton, Richard Arlen, Buster Crabbe, Fuzzy Knight, Johnny Mack Brown, Bob Steele, Bronco Billy Anderson. Western's chief interest is cast of old-timers from Hollywood oaters of years gone by. Unlike their previous vehicles, this is an adult, low-key Western minus happy ending. Interesting on both counts.

Bowery, The (1933) 90m. *** D: Raoul Walsh. Wallace Beery, George Raft, Jackie Cooper, Fay Wray, Pert Kelton, Herman Bing. Raft is Steve Brodie, Beery a notorious saloon owner, Cooper his young nemesis in rowdy story of N.Y.C.'s Bowery during the gay 90's. Pert Kelton is marvelous as Beery's saloon soubrette.

Bowery at Midnight (1942) 63m. ** D: Wallace Fox. Bela Lugosi, John Archer, Wanda McKay, Tom Neal, Dave O'Brien. Cheap melodrama of mad killer terrorizing Bowery neighborhood.

Bowery Boys, The Sidney Kingsley's serious, dramatic indictment of tenement slums, DEAD END, came to the screen in 1937; unfortunately, it did little to change the slum problem of our cities. What it did do was introduce the Dead End Kids, a group of fun-loving hoodlums headed by Leo Gorcey and Huntz Hall; Warner Bros. used various members of the gang in seven subsequent films of high caliber with such co-stars as Humphrey Bogart and John Garfield. Between 1939 and 1943 various studios used different Dead End Kids in films like LITTLE TOUGH GUYS and serials such as JUNIOR G-MEN. Finally in 1940 most of the separate factions joined at Monogram Studios to begin a low-budget series called THE EAST SIDE KIDS. In 1946 the name changed to the BOWERY BOYS, which remained until 1957. With the exception of early titles like ANGELS WITH DIRTY FACES, not part of the actual series, the Bowery Boys comedies were very-low-budget action comedies with an abundance of silly jokes and primitive sight gags that got worse as the series progressed. Even guests like Bela Lugosi couldn't save them, and one Lugosi effort, SPOOKS RUN WILD, is embarrassing. Budgets on some films were so low one could see actors' shadows on the process-screen sequences. Nevertheless, the films were popular, and are shown constantly on TV. Some offer lightweight entertainment, such as JALOPY, MASTER MINDS, NO HOLDS BARRED, and BOWERY BOYS MEET THE MONSTER. Most of the others are juvenile comedies meant for a juvenile audience. Longest-lasting players in the series were Huntz Hall, Leo Gorcey, Billy Benedict, Bennie Bartlett, David Gorcey, and Bernard Gorcey as the so-called adult Louie Dumbrowski. Others who floated in and out include Gabriel Dell, Bernard Punsley, Billy Halop, Bobby Jordan, and Stanley Clements.

Bowery Battalion (1951) 69m. D: William Beaudine. Leo Gorcey, Huntz Hall, Donald MacBride, Virginia Hewitt, Russell Hicks.

Bowery Blitzkrieg (1941) 62m. D: Wallace Fox. Leo Gorcey, Bobby Jordan, Huntz Hall, Warren Hull, Charlotte Henry, Keye Luke, Bobby Stone.

Bowery Bombshell (1946) 65m. D: Phil Karlson. Leo Gorcey, Huntz Hall, Bobby Jordan, Billy Benedict, Sheldon Leonard, Emmett Vogan.

Bowery Boys Meet the Monsters, The (1954) 65m. D: Edward Bernds. Leo Gorcey, Huntz Hall, Bernard Gorcey, Lloyd Corrigan, Ellen Corby.

Bowery Buckaroos (1947) 66m. D: William Beaudine. Leo Gorcey, Huntz Hall, Bobby Jordan, Gabriel Dell, Billy Benedict.

Bowery Champs (1944) 62m. D: William Beaudine. Leo Gorcey, Huntz Hall, Billy Benedict, Bobby Jordan, Gabriel Dell, Anne Sterling, Evelyn Brent, Ian Keith.

Bowery to Bagdad (1955) 64m. D: Edward Bernds. Huntz Hall, Leo Gorcey, Joan Shawlee, Eric Blore.

Bowery to Broadway (1944) 94m. **½ D: Charles Lamont. Jack Oakie, Donald Cook, Maria Montez, Louise Allbritton, Susanna Foster, Turhan Bey, Andy Devine, Rosemary DeCamp, Frank McHugh, Ann Blyth, Leo Carrillo, Evelyn Ankers, Peggy Ryan, Donald O'Connor. Film depends solely on its many guest stars for what entertainment it has; limp story of Montez becoming Hollywood star doesn't make it.

Boy and the Pirates, The (1960) C-82m. **½ D: Bert I. Gordon. Charles Herbert, Susan Gordon, Murvyn Vye, Paul Guilfoyle. Good fantasy-adventure for kids moves along well, has Murvyn Vye giving his all as a pirate.

Boy Cried Murder, The (1966) C-86m. **½ D: George Breakston. Veronica Hurst, Phil Brown, Beba Loncar,

Frazer MacIntosh, Tim Barrett. A reworking of THE WINDOW set in Adriatic resort town. Youngster noted for his fabrications witnesses a murder; no one but the killer believes him.

Boy, Did I Get a Wrong Number! (1966) C-99m. Bomb D: George Marshall. Bob Hope, Elke Sommer, Phyllis Diller, Cesare Danova, Marjorie Lord. They sure did; result is worthless film not worth watching. Absolutely painful.

Boy From Indiana (1950) 66m. ** D: John Rawlins. Lon McCallister, Lois Butler, Billie Burke, George Cleveland. Modest horseracing yarn, with McCallister grooming his beloved horse while romancing Butler.

Boy From Oklahoma, The (1954) C-88m. **½ D: Michael Curtiz. Will Rogers, Jr., Nancy Olson, Lon Chaney, Anthony Caruso, Wallace Ford, Merv Griffin. Quiet Western film with Rogers as pacifist sheriff who manages to keep the town intact and romance Olson; good production values.

Boy Meets Girl (1938) 80m. *** D: Lloyd Bacon. James Cagney, Pat O'Brien, Marie Wilson, Ralph Bellamy, Frank McHugh, Dick Foran, Ronald Reagan, Penny Singleton. Screenwriters Cagney and O'Brien provide quick-paced gag lines in this screwball spoof of Hollywood.

Boy on a Dolphin (1957) C-111m. **½ D: Jean Negulesco. Alan Ladd, Clifton Webb, Sophia Loren, Laurence Naismith. Grecian isles are backdrop to pedestrian sunken-treasure yarn. Loren, in U.S. film debut, cast as skindiver helping Ladd.

Boy Ten Feet Tall, A (1965-British) C-88m. *** D: Alexander Mackendrick. Edward G. Robinson, Fergus McClelland, Constance Cummings, Harry H. Corbett. Very effective narrative of youth traveling down continent (Africa) encountering such flavorful characters as freebooter Robinson.

Boy Who Caught a Crook (1961) 72m. ** D: Edward L. Cahn. Wanda Hendrix, Roger Mobley, Don Beddoe, Richard Crane. Title is self-explanatory for this passable programmer.

Boy Who Stole a Million, The (1960-British) 64m. ** D: Charles Crichton. Maurice Reyna, Virgilio Texera, Marianne Benet, Harold Kasket. Family-type film of youth who gets involved in bank theft to help father with oppressive debts.

Boy With Green Hair, The (1948) C-82m. *** D: Joseph Losey. Dean Stockwell, Pat O'Brien, Robert Ryan, Barbara Hale. Thought-provoking fable of war orphan who becomes social outcast when hair changes color. Competent acting.

Boys, The (1961-British) 123m. *** D: Sidney J. Furie. Richard Todd, Robert Morley, Felix Aylmer, Wilfred Brambell. Thoughtful study of Todd, an attorney who seeks to uncover the motives behind alleged crimes committed by a group of boys; well-handled study of human nature.

Boys From Syracuse, The (1940) 73m. *** D: A. Edward Sutherland. Allan Jones, Joe Penner, Martha Raye, Rosemary Lane, Irene Hervey, Eric Blore. Pleasing film of Rodgers-Hart musical comedy of errors set in ancient Greece. Songs: "This Can't Be Love," "Falling In Love With Love."

Boys' Night Out (1962) C-115m. *** D: Michael Gordon. Kim Novak, James Garner, Tony Randall, Howard Duff, Janet Blair, Patti Page, Zsa Zsa Gabor, Howard Morris. Trio of married men and bachelor Garner decide to set up an apartment equipped with Novak. Script manages some interesting innuendos, with comic relief coming from Blair, Page, and Gabor.

Boys of the City (1940) 65m. D: Joe Lewis. Bobby Jordan, Leo Gorcey, Dave O'Brien, Vince Barnett, George Humbert, Hally Chester. SEE: Bowery Boys series.

Boys Town (1938) 96m. *** D: Norman Taurog. Spencer Tracy, Mickey Rooney, Henry Hull, Leslie Fenton, Addison Richards, Edward Norris, Gene Reynolds. Tracy won Oscar as Father Flanagan, who develops school for juvenile delinquents; Rooney is his toughest enrolee. On the syrupy side, but well done. Sequel: MEN OF BOYS TOWN.

Brain From Planet Arous (1958) 70m. ** D: Nathan Juran. John Agar, Joyce Meader, Robert Fuller, Henry Travis. Lack of imagination in production mars tale of alien force which takes possession of scientist's mind, trying to conquer the world.

Brain Machine, The (1956-British) 72m. ** D: Ken Hughes. Patrick Barr, Elizabeth Allan, Maxwell Reed, Vanda Godsell. Average yarn about drug smuggling and those involved, one of them as the result of mind-shattering machine.

Brain That Wouldn't Die, The (1963) 81m. *½ D: Jason Evers. Virginia Leith, Adele Lamont, Herb Evers. Poorly produced tale of surgeon trying to find body to attach to fiancee's head (she was decapitated but still lives).

Brainstorm (1965) 114m. ** D: William Conrad. Jeff Hunter, Anne Francis, Dana Andrews, Viveca Lindfors, Stacy Harris, Kathie Brown. Fair thriller about a determined man (Hunter) who attempts the perfect crime in order to eliminate Andrews and marry Francis. Contrived.

Brainwashed (1961-French, dubbed) 102m. ** D: Gerd Oswald. Curt Jurgens, Claire Bloom, Hansjorg Felmy, Albert Lieven. Austrian Jurgen's struggle to retain his sanity while undergoing intense Nazi interrogation is basis of this psychological drama, with flashbacks.

Bramble Bush, The (1960) C-105m. **½ D: Daniel Petrie. Richard Burton, Barbara Rush, Jack Carson, Angie Dickinson. Charles Mergendahl's potboiler becomes superficial gloss with Burton totally ill at ease playing New England doctor returning to Cape Cod, where he falls in love with his dying friend's wife.

Branded (1950) C-95m. **½ D: Rudolph Mate. Alan Ladd, Mona Freeman, Charles Bickford, Joseph Calleia, Milburn Stone. Outlaws use carefree Ladd to impersonate rancher Bickford's long-missing son, leading to much different outcome than anticipated; action and love scenes balanced OK.

Brasher Doubloon, The (1947) 72m. ** D: John Brahm. George Montgomery, Nancy Guild, Conrad Janis, Roy Roberts, Fritz Kortner. Rare coin seems to be object of several murders in very uneven Phillip Marlowe detective mystery.

Brass Bottle, The (1964) C-89m. *½ D: Harry Keller. Tony Randall, Burl Ives, Barbara Eden, Edward Andrews, Ann Doran. Juvenile comedy-fantasy about genie Ives coming out of magic bottle to serve Randall. Leading lady Eden fared better when she went into a lamp herself on TV.

Brass Legend, The (1956) 79m. *½ D: Gerd Oswald. Hugh O'Brian, Nancy Gates, Raymond Burr, Reba Tassell. Routine Western uplifted by Burr's villain role.

Bravados, The (1958) C-98m. *** D: Henry King. Gregory Peck, Joan Collins, Stephen Boyd, Albert Salmi. Compelling Western starring Peck, seeking four men who raped and killed his wife, discovering that he has become no better than those he hunts.

Brave Bulls, The (1951) 108m. *** D: Robert Rossen. Mel Ferrer, Miroslava, Anthony Quinn, Eugene Iglesias. Flavorful account of public and private life of a matador, based on Tom Lea book. Film admirably captures atmosphere of bullfighting.

Brave Warrior (1952) C-73m. *½ D: Spencer G. Bennet. Jon Hall, Jay Silverheels, Michael Ansara, Christine Larson. Inept yarn, set in 1800's Indiana, has Hall preventing Indian hostilities.

Bread, Love and Dreams (1954-Italian, dubbed) 90m. *** D: Luigi Comencini. Vittorio DeSica, Gina Lollobrigida, Marisa Merlini, Roberto Risso. Peppery comedy with spicy Gina vying for attention of town official DeSica.

Break in the Circle (1957-British) 69m. *½ D: Val Guest. Forrest Tucker, Eva Bartok, Marius Goring, Guy Middleton. Unexciting chase tale has Tucker a boat owner thrust into helping to get scientist out of Communist Germany.

Break of Hearts (1935) 80m. **½ D: Philip Moeller. Katharine Hepburn, Charles Boyer, John Beal, Sam Hardy, Anne Grey. Slow-moving but well-acted study of musicians Hepburn and Boyer who fall in love but conflict over their occupational differences.

Break to Freedom (1955-British) 88m. ** D: Lewis Gilbert. Anthony Steel, Jack Warner, Robert Beatty, William Sylvester, Michael Balfour. Typical P.O.W.'s escape-from-German-camp, uplifted by restrained acting.

Breakfast at Tiffany's (1961) C-115m. ***½ D: Blake Edwards. Audrey Hepburn, George Peppard, Patricia Neal, Buddy Ebsen, Mickey Rooney.

Charming film with Audrey as Holly Golightly, a small-town girl who goes mod in New York. Cast is good, but Rooney as a Japanese neighbor is a must. Award-winning "Moon River" is sung by Miss Hepburn.

Breakfast for Two (1937) 65m. **½ D: Alfred Santell. Barbara Stanwyck, Herbert Marshall, Glenda Farrell, Eric Blore, Frank Thomas, Donald Meek. Energetic Stanwyck helps Marshall's business career and falls in love with him; pleasant.

Breakfast in Hollywood (1946) 100m. *½ D: Harold Schuster. Tom Breneman, Bonita Granville, Beulah Bondi, Edward Ryan, Spike Jones and band. Uninspired film derived from radio series, focusing on romance of G.I. and his sweetheart, with predictable quarrels and eventual happy ending.

Breaking Point, The (1950) 97m. ***½ D: Michael Curtiz. John Garfield, Patricia Neal, Phyllis Thaxter, Wallace Ford, Sherry Jackson. High-voltage refilming of Hemingway's TO HAVE AND HAVE NOT, with Garfield as skipper so desperate for money he takes on illegal cargo. Garfield and mate Juano Hernandez give superb interpretations.

Breaking the Sound Barrier (1952-British) 109m. ***½ D: David Lean. Ralph Richardson, Ann Todd, Nigel Patrick, John Austin. Grade-A documentary-style story of early days of jet planes, and men who tested them; Richardson particularly good.

Breakout (1959-British) 99m. **½ D: Don Chaffey. Richard Todd, Richard Attenborough, Michael Wilding, Dennis Price, Bernard Lee. Although format is familiar, cast gives good interpretation of story of British P.O.W.'s escaping from Axis prison camp. Retitled: DANGER WITHIN.

Breakthrough (1950) 91m. **½ D: Lewis Seiler. David Brian, John Agar, Frank Lovejoy, Paul Picerni, William Self. Saga of men training for combat, their days of fighting and romancing; stark and satisfactory.

Breath of Scandal, A (1960) C-98m. ** D: Michael Curtiz. Sophia Loren, John Gavin, Maurice Chevalier, Isabel Jeans, Angela Lansbury. Molnar's play OLYMPIA is limp costume vehicle for Loren, playing a princess romanced by American Gavin. Chevalier and Lansbury vainly try to pump some life into proceedings.

Breathless (1961-French, dubbed) 89m. *** D: Jean-Luc Godard. Jean Seberg, Jean-Paul Belmondo, Daniel Boulanger, Liliane David. Belmondo is ideally suited to the carefree crook who has an affair with American Seberg, with tragic result. Good candid shots of Paris life.

Brewster's Millions (1945) 79m. **½ D: Allan Dwan. Dennis O'Keefe, Helen Walker, Eddie "Rochester" Anderson, June Havoc, Gail Patrick, Mischa Auer. Bright comedy with fine cast; O'Keefe has to spend a million dollars quickly if he is to receive major inheritance.

Bribe, The (1949) 98m. ** D: Robert Z. Leonard. Robert Taylor, Ava Gardner, Charles Laughton, Vincent Price, John Hodiak. Taylor looks uncomfortable playing federal man who almost sacrifices all for sultry singer Gardner.

Bridal Path, The (1959-Scottish) C-95m. **½ D: Frank Launder. Bill Travers, Bernadette O'Farrell, Alex MacKenzie, Eric Woodburn, Jack Lambert, John Rae. Travers is naive Scotsman in search of a wife: his unsubtle courting methods provide sufficient humor.

Bride and the Beast, The (1958) 78m. Bomb D: Adrian Weiss. Charlotte Austin, Lance Fuller, Johnny Roth, Steve Calvert. Set in the African jungle, title tells all about explorer's wife and the gorilla who fancies her.

Bride Came C.O.D., The (1941) 92m. **½ D: William Keighley. James Cagney, Bette Davis, Stuart Erwin, Eugene Pallette, Jack Carson, George Tobias. Unlikely comedy team in vehicle made enjoyable only by their terrific personalities; he's a flier, she's a runaway bride.

Bride Comes Home, The (1935) 82m. **½ D: Wesley Ruggles. Claudette Colbert, Fred MacMurray, Robert Young, William Collier, Sr., Edgar Kennedy. Breezy fluff with wealthy Young competing against roughneck MacMurray for Claudette's affections in vintage comedy.

Bride for Sale (1949) 87m. **½ D: William D. Russell. Claudette Colbert, Robert Young, George Brent, Max Baer. Veteran star trio carries on despite thin story of female tax ex-

pert (Colbert) seeking wealthy spouse.
Bride Goes Wild, The (1948) 98m. **½ D: Norman Taurog. Van Johnson, June Allyson, Butch Jenkins, Hume Cronyn, Una Merkel, Arlene Dahl. Silly, sometimes funny tale of Johnson pretending to be Jenkins' father in order to woo Allyson; nice cast does its best.

Bride Is Much Too Beautiful, The (1958-French, dubbed) 90m. **½ D: Fred Surin. Brigitte Bardot, Micheline Presle, Louis Jourdan, Marcel Amont. Gallic sex romp with BB a farm girl who becomes famous magazine model.

Bride of Frankenstein (1935) 80m. *** D: James Whale. Boris Karloff, Colin Clive, Valerie Hobson, Elsa Lanchester, Ernest Thesiger, Una O'Connor. Better than FRANKENSTEIN, chilling sequel is highlighted by monster's visit with blind man and creation of female monster-mate (Lanchester) for Karloff.

Bride of Vengeance (1949) 91m. ** D: Mitchell Leisen. Paulette Goddard, John Lund, Macdonald Carey, Raymond Burr, Albert Dekker, Rose Hobart. Medium-warm costumer of medieval Italy with Goddard as the Borgia sent to do mischief but instead falling in love.

Bride Walks Out, The (1936) 75m. ** D: Leigh Jason. Barbara Stanwyck, Gene Raymond, Robert Young, Ned Sparks, Helen Broderick. Flimsy comedy; stars do their best with Stanwyck and Raymond trying to survive on his meager salary.

Bride Wore Boots, The (1946) 86m. ** D: Irving Pichel. Barbara Stanwyck, Robert Cummings, Diana Lynn, Peggy Wood, Robert Benchley, Natalie Wood, Willie Best. Witless comedy of horse-loving Stanwyck saddled by Cummings, who does his best to win her total affection; they all try but script is weak.

Bride Wore Red, The (1937) 103m. ** D: Dorothy Arzner. Joan Crawford, Franchot Tone, Robert Young, Billie Burke, Reginald Owen. More fashion show than plot in this typical glossy Crawford soaper of girl who works her way up society ladder.

Brides of Dracula, The (1960-British) C-85m. **½ D: Terence Fisher. Peter Cushing, Martita Hunt, Yvonne Monlaur, Freda Jackson. Above-average entry in Hammer horror series, with the famed vampire's disciple seeking female victims.

Brides of Fu Manchu, The (1966-British) C-94m. **½ D: Don Sharp. Christopher Lee, Douglas Wilner, Marie Versini, Tsai Chin. Fu doesn't give up easily, still bent on conquering the world by forcing scientists to develop powerful ray gun. Sequel to FACE OF FU MANCHU, not as good, still diverting.

Bridge, The (1960-German, dubbed) 100 m. *** D: Bernhard Wicki. Folker Bohnet, Fritz Wepper, Michael Hinz, Frank Glaubrecht. Unrelenting account of teen-age boys drafted into the German army in 1945, as last resort effort to stem Allied invasion.

Bridge of San Luis Rey, The (1944) 85m. ** D: Rowland V. Lee. Lynn Bari, Nazimova, Louis Calhern, Akim Tamiroff, Francis Lederer, Blanche Yurka, Donald Woods. Thornton Wilder's moody, unusual story of five people meeting doom on a rickety bridge makes a slow-moving film.

Bridge on the River Kwai, The (1957) C-161m. **** D: David Lean. William Holden, Alec Guinness, Jack Hawkins, Sessue Hayakawa, Geoffrey Horne, James Donald. High-powered excitement set in WW2 Ceylon. Holden assigned to destroy an important bridge under the nose of Japanese commander Hayakawa, who is also holding British officer Guinness prisoner. Taut action sequences.

Bridge to the Sun (1961) 113m. *** D: Etienne Perier. Carroll Baker, James Shigeta, James Yagi. Well-intentioned telling of Southern girl Baker who marries Japanese diplomat Shigeta and moves to Japan at outbreak of WW2.

Bridges at Toko-Ri, The (1954) C-103m. ***½ D: Mark Robson. William Holden, Grace Kelly, Fredric March, Mickey Rooney, Robert Strauss. Top-flight adventure based on James Michener's book of American flier and family in Korean conflict.

Brief Encounter (1946-British) 85m. **** D: David Lean. Celia Johnson, Trevor Howard, Stanley Holloway, Cyril Raymond, Joyce Carey. Touching interlude of two married people meeting in a train station cafe and their short but poignant romance; effective use of Rachmaninoff's piano concerto highlights believable love affair.

Brigand, The (1952) C-94m. ** D: Phil Karlson. Anthony Dexter, Anthony Quinn, Gale Robbins, Jody Lawrance. Dexter is lookalike for king and becomes involved with court intrigue; flat costumer.

Brigand of Kandahar, The (1965-British) C-81m. **½ D: John Gilling. Ronald Lewis, Oliver Reed, Duncan Lamont, Yvonne Romain, Catherine Woodville. Mostly nonsense set on British outpost in 1850's India with rampaging natives; good cast tries hard.

Brigham Young—Frontiersman (1940) 114m. ** D: Henry Hathaway. Tyrone Power, Linda Darnell, Dean Jagger, Brian Donlevy, John Carradine, Jane Darwell, Jean Rogers, Mary Astor, Vincent Price. Well-intentioned but ludicrous depiction of Mormon leader with Jagger nominally in the lead, focus shifting to tepid romance between Power and Darnell; Astor all wrong as homespun wife.

Bright Eyes (1934) 83m. **½ D: David Butler. Shirley Temple, James Dunn, Judith Allen, Jane Withers, Lois Wilson. Early Shirley, and pretty good, with juvenile villainy from Withers and the unforgettable "On the Good Ship Lollypop."

Bright Leaf (1950) 110m. **½ D: Michael Curtiz. Gary Cooper, Lauren Bacall, Patricia Neal, Jack Carson, Donald Crisp. Loose chronicle of 19th-century tobacco farmer (Cooper) building successful cigarette empire, seeking revenge on old enemies and finding romance.

Bright Lights (1935) 83m. ** D: Busby Berkeley. Joe E. Brown, Ann Dvorak, Patricia Ellis, William Gargan, Joseph Cawthorn, Arthur Treacher. Rags-to-riches show business tale of husband and wife separating while trying to hit it big. Entertaining, but full of clichés.

Bright Road (1953) 69m. ** D: Gerald Mayer. Dorothy Dandridge, Harry Belafonte, Robert Horton, Philip Hepburn. Well-intentioned but labored tale of Negro teacher in small Southern town who tries to solve her young pupils' problems.

Bright Victory (1951) 97m. *** D: Mark Robson. Arthur Kennedy, Peggy Dow, Julia Adams, James Edwards. Touching account of blinded ex-soldier who slowly readjusts to civilian life, even finding love. Potentially sticky subject handled well, with Kennedy excellent in lead role.

Brighton Strangler, The (1945) 67m. ** D: Max Nosseck. John Loder, June Duprez, Michael St. Angel, Miles Mander, Rose Hobart, Gilbert Emery. Strained thriller of demented stage actor Loder with a strangling complex, set in England.

Brimstone (1949) C-90m. ** D: Joseph Kane. Rod Cameron, Walter Brennan, Adrian Booth, Forrest Tucker, Jack Holt. Usual account of cattle-rustling and law enforcer who brings outlaws to justice.

Bringing Up Baby (1938) 102m. *** D: Howard Hawks. Katharine Hepburn, Cary Grant, Charlie Ruggles, Barry Fitzgerald, May Robson. Anthropologist Grant gets mixed up with dizzy Hepburn and pet leopard. Fast-moving screwball comedy shows stars in peak form.

British Agent (1934) 81m. **½ D: Michael Curtiz. Kay Francis, Leslie Howard, William Gargan, Philip Reed. Howard is lead character in peril while in 1910's Russia, falling in love with slinky spy Francis. Good stars in plush blend of spying and romance.

British Intelligence (1940) 62m. ** D: Terry Morse. Boris Karloff, Margaret Lindsay, Maris Wrixon, Holmes Herbert, Leonard Mudie, Bruce Lester. American nonsense about double-agent Lindsay encountering butler-spy Karloff in British official's home; far-fetched story.

Broad-Minded (1931) 72m. **½ D: Mervyn LeRoy. Joe E. Brown, William Collier, Jr., Margaret Livingston, Thelma Todd, Bela Lugosi, Ona Munson, Holmes Herbert. Pleasant Brown comedy with added spice of lovely Todd and hilarious cameo by Lugosi as man whose hot-dog was stolen.

Broadway (1942) 91m. *** D: William A. Seiter. George Raft, Pat O'Brien, Janet Blair, Broderick Crawford, Marjorie Rambeau, S. Z. Sakall. Engaging Prohibition period tale of rival gangsters Raft and O'Brien with Raft dancing, doing prototype of his own life even better than GEORGE RAFT STORY.

Broadway Gondolier (1935) 98m. **½

D: Lloyd Bacon. Dick Powell, Joan Blondell, Adolphe Menjou, Louise Fazenda, William Gargan, Grant Mitchell. Powell goes globe-trotting so he'll be discovered by famous producer. Songs include: "Lulu's Back in Town."

Broadway Limited (1941) 74m. ** D: Gordon Douglas. Dennis O'Keefe, Victor McLaglen, Zasu Pitts, Patsy Kelly, George E. Stone. Strange little film of scatterbrained events occurring on a train trip, with expected nutty characters all aboard.

Broadway Melody (1929) 104m. **½ D: Harry Beaumont. Bessie Love, Anita Page, Charles King, Jed Prouty, Kenneth Thomson, Edward Dillon, Mary Doran. Early talkie musical of putting-on-the-show is basis of curio with good score by Arthur Freed and Nacio Herb Brown: "You Were Meant For Me," "Wedding of the Painted Doll," etc., and Cohan's "Give My Regards to Broadway."

Broadway Melody of 1936 (1935) 110m. *** D: Roy Del Ruth. Jack Benny, Eleanor Powell, Robert Taylor, Una Merkel, Sid Silvers, Buddy Ebsen. Pleasant musicomedy with Winchell-like columnist Benny trying to frame producer Taylor via dancer Powell, whose solo spots are pure delight. Arthur Freed-Nacio Herb Brown songs: "You Are My Lucky Star," "Broadway Rhythm," "I've Got A Feelin' You're Foolin'."

Broadway Melody of 1938 (1937) 110m. **½ D: Roy Del Ruth. Robert Taylor, Eleanor Powell, Judy Garland, Sophie Tucker, Binnie Barnes, Buddy Ebsen, Billy Gilbert, Raymond Walburn. Not up to 1936 MELODY, with tuneful but forgettable songs, overbearing Tucker, and elephantine finale. Powell's dancing is great and Garland sings "Dear Mr. Gable."

Broadway Melody of 1940 (1940) 102m. *** D: Norman Taurog. Fred Astaire, Eleanor Powell, George Murphy, Frank Morgan, Ian Hunter, Florence Rice. Standard backstage story of dance team trying to make good, with great dancing. Cole Porter songs: "I Concentrate On You," "Begin The Beguine."

Broadway Rhythm (1941) C-114m. **½ D: Roy Del Ruth. George Murphy, Ginny Simms, Charles Winninger, Gloria De Haven. Typical MGM Broadway musical yarn of putting on the show, allowing for several solo spots, including brief bit by Lena Horne.

Broadway Serenade (1939) 114m. ** D: Robert Z. Leonard. Jeanette MacDonald, Lew Ayres, Ian Hunter, Frank Morgan, Rita Johnson, Virginia Grey, William Gargan, Katharine Alexander. Mediocre musical of songwriter Ayres and wife, singer MacDonald, having careers split up their marriage.

Broken Arrow (1950) C-93m. *** D: Delmer Daves. James Stewart, Jeff Chandler, Debra Paget, Will Geer, Jay Silverheels. Authentic study of 1870's Apache Indian chief (Chandler) and ex-army man (Stewart) trying to seek accord between feuding redskins and whites. Flavorful and effectively understated; good action sequences.

Broken Lance (1954) C-96m. ***½ D: Edward Dmytryk. Spencer Tracy, Robert Wagner, Jean Peters, Richard Widmark. Tracy is superlative in tight-knit script about patriarchal rancher who finds he's losing control of his cattle empire and his family is fragmenting into warring factions; sharply photographed. Remake of HOUSE OF STRANGERS with Tracy in the Edward G. Robinson role.

Broken Lullaby (1932) 77m. *** D: Ernst Lubitsch. Lionel Barrymore, Nancy Carroll, Phillips Holmes, Zasu Pitts, Lucien Littlefield, Emma Dunn. Retitled: THE MAN I KILLED. Excellent drama of French soldier who feels guilty for killing German during war, then falls in love with dead man's sweetheart.

Bronco Buster (1952) C-81m. *½ D: Budd Boetticher. John Lund, Scott Brady, Joyce Holden, Chill Wills, Casey Tibbs. Minor story of rodeo star Lund helping Brady learn the ropes, but forced to fight him for Holden's love.

Broth of a Boy (1959-Irish) 77m. **½ D: George Pollock. Barry Fitzgerald, Harry Brogan, Tony Wright, June Thorburn, Eddie Golden. British TV producer hits upon scheme of filming birthday celebration of oldest man in the world, Irish villager Fitzgerald. The latter's battle to get cut of the pie is vehicle for study of human nature; quietly effective.

Brother Orchid (1940) 91m. ***½ D: Lloyd Bacon. Edward G. Robinson, Ann Sothern, Humphrey Bogart, Ralph Bellamy, Donald Crisp, Allen Jenkins. Robinson is delightful in tale of gangster who hides out in monastery and finds "real class" there.

Brother Rat (1938) 90m. *** D: William Keighley. Priscilla Lane, Wayne Morris, Johnnie Davis, Jane Bryan, Eddie Albert, Ronald Reagan, Jane Wyman, William Tracy. Comedy of three pals at Virginia Military Institute isn't as fresh as it was thirty years ago, but still remains entertaining, with enthusiastic performances by all. Remade as ABOUT FACE.

Brother Rat and a Baby (1940) 87m. **½ D: Ray Enright. Priscilla Lane, Wayne Morris, Eddie Albert, Jane Bryan, Ronald Reagan, Jane Wyman. Sassy follow-up to BROTHER RAT is not the same success, but still fun with three comrades graduating military school.

Brothers Karamazov, The (1958) C-146m. *** D: Richard Brooks. Yul Brynner, Maria Schell, Claire Bloom, Lee J. Cobb, Richard Basehart, William Shatner, Albert Salmi. Set in 19th-century Russia, film version of Dostoyevsky's tragedy revolving about death of a dominating father (Cobb) and effect on his sons: fun-seeking Brynner, scholarly Basehart, religious Shatner, and epileptic Salmi. Exceptionally well-scripted by Brooks.

Brothers Rico, The (1957) 92m. **½ D: Phil Karlson. Richard Conte, Dianne Foster, Kathryn Grant, Larry Gates, James Darren. Incisive gangster yarn; Conte comes to N.Y.C. to counteract nationwide criminal gang's plot to eliminate his two brothers.

Browning Version, The (1951-British) 90m. *** D: Anthony Asquith. Michael Redgrave, Jean Kent, Nigel Patrick, Wilfrid Hyde-White. Middle-aged teacher is faced with several crises: unfaithful wife, forced retirement, no future. Cast does full justice to Rattigan's play.

Brute Force (1947) 98m. ***½ D: Jules Dassin. Burt Lancaster, Hume Cronyn, Charles Bickford, Yvonne de Carlo, Ann Blyth, Ella Raines. By now prison-break facet of film is hackneyed, but subplot concerning sadistic treatment of prisoners is still gripping.

Brute Man (1946) 60m. *½ D: Jean Yarbrough. Tom Neal, Rondo Hatton, Jane Adams, Peter Whitney, Jan Wiley. Programmer trivia about manhunt to capture an insane man running rampant.

Buccaneer, The (1958) C-121m. *** D: Anthony Quinn. Yul Brynner, Charlton Heston, Claire Bloom, Charles Boyer. Starchy swashbuckler retelling events during War of 1812 when Andrew Jackson (Heston) is forced to rely on buccaneer Lafitte (Brynner) to stem the British invasion; action is spotty but splashy.

Buccaneer's Girl (1950) C-77m. ** D: Frederick de Cordova. Yvonne de Carlo, Philip Friend, Elsa Lanchester, Andrea King, Henry Daniell. Pure escapism with De Carlo cavorting as New Orleans singer and later leading forces to free pirate-friend from prison.

Buchanan Rides Alone (1958) C-78m. **½ D: Budd Boetticher. Randolph Scott, Craig Stevens, Barry Kelley, Tol Avery. Compact oater with Scott grappling with townsfolk because he defends outcast Mexican.

Buck Benny Rides Again (1940) 82m. ** D: Mark Sandrich. Jack Benny, Ellen Drew, Andy Devine, Phil Harris, Virginia Dale, Lillian Cornell, Dennis Day. Weak Western spoof with Benny and most of his radio gang: disappointing for Benny, whose films never matched his radio-TV programs.

Buck Privates (1941) 84m. **½ D: Arthur Lubin. Lee Bowman, Alan Curtis, Bud Abbott, Lou Costello, Andrews Sisters, Jane Frazee, Nat Pendleton. Bud and Lou wind up in the army through mishap, resulting in above average fling for duo; guest stars and lively music. This was their first starring film.

Buck Privates Come Home (1947) 77m. *** D: Charles Barton. Bud Abbott, Lou Costello, Tom Brown, Joan Fulton, Nat Pendleton, Beverly Simmons, Don Beddoe. One of A&C's most enjoyable romps has duo returning to civilian life and finding their tough sergeant (Pendleton) is now cop on their beat. Climactic chase a highlight.

Bucket of Blood, A (1959) 66m. *½ D: Roger Corman. Dick Miller, Barboura Morris, Anthony Carbone, Ed Nelson. Low-budget hokum of sculptor killing people and using them for his clay forms.

Buffalo Bill (1944) C-90m. **½ D: William Wellman. Joel McCrea, Maureen O'Hara, Linda Darnell, Thomas Mitchell, Anthony Quinn, Edgar Buchanan, Chief Thundercloud, Sidney Blackmer. Colorful biography of legendary Westerner should have been much better, but still provides some fun and has good cast.

Bugle Sounds, The (1941) 110m. ** D: S. Sylvan Simon. Wallace Beery, Marjorie Main, Lewis Stone, George Bancroft, Henry O'Neill, Donna Reed. Old-time officer Beery objects to progress in the army, bails cavalry out of trouble in finale. The usual.

Bugles in the Afternoon (1952) C-85m. **½ D: Roy Rowland. Ray Milland, Forrest Tucker, George Reeves, Helena Carter, Gertrude Michael. Standard tale of man branded coward (Milland) during Civil War, with Little Big Horn finale.

Bull Fighters, The (1945) 61m. ** D: Mal St. Clair. Stan Laurel, Oliver Hardy, Margo Woode, Richard Lane, Carol Andrews, Diosa Costello. One of better L&H later works, involving mistaken identity (Stan is lookalike for famous matador), subsequent nonsense in bull ring.

Bulldog Drummond Hugh "Bulldog" Drummond, an ex-British army officer who yearned for adventure, was created in 1919 by "Sapper" (Herman Cyril McNeile); the character's film possibilities were realized and Drummond was the subject of several silent films. The definitive BULLDOG DRUMMOND was made in 1929 with Ronald Colman in the lead and Claude Allister as his constant companion Algy; Colman also starred in a sequel, BULLDOG DRUMMOND STRIKES BACK, but unfortunately neither of these is on TV. The major series was made in the late 1930's by Paramount, with John Howard as Drummond, John Barrymore as Inspector Neilson of Scotland Yard, Reginald Denny as Algy, E. E. Clive as the butler Tenny, and a variety of girls as love interest for Howard. These were brief (around one hour), entertaining mysteries with such formidable villains as J. Carrol Naish, Anthony Quinn, George Zucco, and Eduardo Ciannelli. In the late 1940's Ron Randell and Tom Conway did two Drummonds each, which weren't bad but didn't catch on. The last one was CALLING BULLDOG DRUMMOND, a 1951 film with Walter Pidgeon in the lead and David Tomlinson as Algy; it was an enjoyable, slickly made film; it was only unfortunate that no one saw fit to continue the series beyond this point. Other older films that still pop up include such Drummonds as John Lodge and Ray Milland doing their bit in unremarkable but entertaining vehicles.

Bulldog Drummond at Bay (1937-British) 62m. D: Norman Lee. John Lodge, Dorothy Mackaill, Victor Jory, Claude Allister, Hugh Miller, Maire O'Neill, Brian Buchel.

Bulldog Drummond at Bay (1947) 70m. D: Sidney Salkow. Ron Randell, Anita Louise, Pat O'Moore, Terry Kilburn, Holmes Herbert.

Bulldog Drummond Comes Back (1937) 64m. D: Louis King. John Barrymore, John Howard, Louise Campbell, Reginald Denny, E. E. Clive, J. Carrol Naish, John Sutton.

Bulldog Drummond Escapes (1937) 65m. D: James Hogan. Ray Milland, Guy Standing, Heather Angel, Porter Hall, Reginald Denny, E. E. Clive, Fay Holden, Clyde Cook, Walter Kingsford.

Bulldog Drummond in Africa (1938) 60m. D: Louis King. John Howard, Heather Angel, H. B. Warner, J. Carrol Naish, Reginald Denny, Anthony Quinn, Michael Brooke.

Bulldog Drummond Strikes Back (1947) 65m. D: Frank McDonald. Ron Randell, Gloria Henry, Pat O'Moore, Anabel Shaw, Terry Kilburn.

Bulldog Drummond's Bride (1939) 55m. D: James Hogan. John Howard, Heather Angel, H. B. Warner, Reginald Denny, Elizabeth Patterson, Eduardo Ciannelli.

Bulldog Drummond's Peril (1938) 66m. D: James Hogan. John Barrymore, John Howard, Louise Campbell, Reginald Denny, E. E. Clive, Porter Hall, Elizabeth Patterson, Nydia Westman.

Bulldog Drummond's Revenge (1937) 60m. D: Louis King. John Barrymore,

John Howard, Louise Campbell, Reginald Denny, E. E. Clive, Nydia Westman, Lucien Littlefield, John Sutton.

Bulldog Drummond's Secret Police (1939) 56m. D: James Hogan. John Howard, Heather Angel, H. B. Warner, Reginald Denny, Leo G. Carroll, Elizabeth Patterson.

Bullet for a Badman (1964) C-80m. **½ D: R. G. Springsteen. Audie Murphy, Darren McGavin, Ruta Lee, Skip Homeier, George Tobias, Bob Steele. Another revenge tale involving outlaw, his ex-wife, and a friend who married her.

Bullet for Joey, A (1955) 85m. **½ D: Lewis Allen. Edward G. Robinson, George Raft, Audrey Totter, Peter Van Eyck. Veteran cast improves caper about Communist agent attempting to kidnap U.S. nuclear scientist.

Bullet for Stefano (1950-Italian, dubbed) 96m. ** D: Duilio Coletti. Rossano Brazzi, Valentina Cortesa, Carlo Campanini, Lillian Laine. Carefree young man (Brazzi) falls into life of crime and finds it pleasant; cast is engaging.

Bullet is Waiting, A (1954) C-82m. **½ D: John Farrow. Jean Simmons, Rory Calhoun, Stephen McNally, Brian Aherne. Interesting human nature study hinging on sheriff's discovery that his prisoner is really innocent; nice desert locale.

Bullets or Ballots (1936) 77m. *** D: William Keighley. Edward G. Robinson, Joan Blondell, Barton MacLane, Humphrey Bogart, Frank McHugh. Cop Robinson pretends to leave police force to crack citywide mob ring run by MacLane. Good, tough gangster film.

Bullfighter and the Lady, The (1951) 87m. *** D: Budd Boetticher. Robert Stack, Joy Page, Gilbert Roland, Virginia Grey. Atmospheric account of American Stack coming to Mexico where he learns the true art of bullfighting.

Bullwhip (1958) C-80m. ** D: Harmon Jones. Guy Madison, Rhonda Fleming, James Griffith, Don Beddoe. Madison is offered the choice of marrying Fleming or being hanged on phony murder charge; expected results.

Bundle of Joy (1956) C-98m. ** D: Norman Taurog. Eddie Fisher, Debbie Reynolds, Adolphe Menjou, Tommy Noonan. Labored musical remake of BACHELOR MOTHER has Reynolds as salesgirl who takes custody of a baby, causing scandal that boyfriend Fisher is child's father.

Bunny Lake is Missing (1965) 107m. ** D: Otto Preminger. Laurence Olivier, Carol Lynley, Keir Dullea, Noel Coward, Martita Hunt, The Zombies. Aimless story of Lynley's child being kidnapped, subsequent investigation among several homosexual characters and other oddballs. Pretty dreary going.

Bureau of Missing Persons (1933) 79m. **½ D: Roy Del Ruth. Bette Davis, Lewis Stone, Pat O'Brien, Glenda Farrell. Snappy drama with O'Brien aiding Davis to find missing hubby, falling in love with her himself.

Burglar, The (1957) 90m. *½ D: Paul Wendkos. Dan Duryea, Jayne Mansfield, Martha Vickers, Mickey Shaughnessy. Cast is defeated by weak material in robbery caper about theft of big diamond.

Burma Convoy (1941) 72m. **½ D: Noel Smith. Charles Bickford, Evelyn Ankers, Frank Albertson, Cecil Kellaway, Keye Luke, Turhan Bey. Neat little actioner of conflicting trucking interests involved in carrying needed supplies over the Burma Road during hectic days of WW2.

Burn Witch Burn (1962-British) 90m. *** D: Sidney Hayers. Janet Blair, Peter Wyngarde, Margaret Johnston, Anthony Nicholls. Filmed before as WEIRD WOMAN, excellent tale of supernatural set in England has Blair under spell of witch because of some innocent charms. Good acting, scripting, direction in this suspenseful film.

Burning Hills, The (1956) C-94m. ** D: Stuart Heisler. Tab Hunter, Natalie Wood, Skip Homeier, Eduard Franz. Passive Hunter can't spark much life into tired script of man on the run from cattle thieves who is sheltered by miscast Wood (as half-breed Mexican gal).

Bus Riley's Back in Town (1965) C-93m. **½ D: Harvey Hart. Ann-Margret, Michael Parks, Janet Margolin, Brad Dexter, Kim Darby, Jocelyn Brando, Larry Storch. Muddled William Inge script of folksy people in the Midwest. Parks, ex-sailor, returns home, torn by faltering ambitions and taunted by wealthy ex-girlfriend Ann-Margret. Character cameos make the film worthwhile.

Bus Stop (1956) C-96m. ***½ D: Joshua Logan. Marilyn Monroe, Don Murray, Arthur O'Connell, Betty Field, Eileen Heckart. Excellent comedy-drama proves Monroe knows about acting, playing a chanteuse sensitively. Murray is rowdy cowboy who tries to rope her; Field fine as cafe waitress.

Bushwackers, The (1952) 70m. *½ D: Rod Amateau. Dorothy Malone, John Ireland, Wayne Morris, Lawrence Tierney, Lon Chaney. Confederate army veteran forced into becoming gunman again; Malone wasted here.

Buster Keaton Story, The (1957) 91m. *½. D: Sidney Sheldon. Donald O'Connor, Ann Blyth, Rhonda Fleming, Peter Lorre. Weak fiction ignores the facts about silent-star Keaton, making up its own. More private life than on-screen moments are detailed with Blyth as his true love and Fleming as a siren. Little comedy in this tale of a great comedian.

Busy Body, The (1967) C-90m. **½ D: William Castle. Sid Caesar, Robert Ryan, Anne Baxter, Kay Medford, Jan Murray, Richard Pryor, Dom DeLuise, Godfrey Cambridge, Marty Ingels, Bill Dana, George Jessel. Broad, forced comedy involving gangsters and corpses, with Caesar as the patsy for Ryan's underworld gang. Supporting comics give film its funniest moments.

But Not For Me (1959) 105m. *** D: Walter Lang. Clark Gable, Carroll Baker, Lilli Palmer, Barry Coe, Lee J. Cobb, Thomas Gomez. Chic remake of ACCENT ON YOUTH dealing with theatrical producer Gable thwarting advances of young secretary Baker, deciding sophisticated Palmer is more logically suitable.

Bwana Devil (1952) C-79m. *½ D: Arch Oboler. Robert Stack, Barbara Britton, Nigel Bruce, Paul McVey. Dud actioner was sparked theatrically as first commercial 3-D feature: man-eating lions set their teeth on railway workers in Africa.

By Love Possessed (1961) C-115m. *** D: John Sturges. Lana Turner, Efrem Zimbalist, Jr., Jason Robards, Jr., George Hamilton, Thomas Mitchell. Not true to James Gould Cozzens novel; ultra-glossy romantic vehicle for Turner, whose lover is prominent New England attorney Zimbalist—personable cast.

By the Light of the Silvery Moon (1953) C-102m. **½ D: David Butler. Doris Day, Gordon MacRae, Leon Ames, Rosemary DeCamp, Mary Wickes. Sentimental Americana; Ames causes family crisis when it's thought he's romancing French actress; Day-MacRae provide wholesome love duo. Wickes is her delightful self as family maid.

Bye Bye Birdie (1953) C-112m. **½ D: George Sidney. Janet Leigh, Dick Van Dyke, Ann-Margret, Maureen Stapleton, Paul Lynde, Ed Sullivan. Entertaining version of Broadway musical about rock 'n' roll idol and his adoring fans. Lynde stands out as Ann-Margret's father. Songs include "Put on a Happy Face."

C-Man (1949) 75m. ** D: Joseph Lerner. Dean Jagger, John Carradine, Harry Landers, Rene Paul. Acceptable programmer with Jagger as customs agent involved in murder and theft case.

Cabin in the Cotton (1932) 77m. **½ D: Michael Curtiz. Bette Davis, Richard Barthelmess, Dorothy Jordan, Henry B. Walthall, Tully Marshall, Dorothy Peterson. Dated melodrama of sharecroppers with earnest Barthelmess almost led to ruin by Southern belle Davis; exaggerated, but interesting.

Cabinet of Caligari (1962) 104m. **½ D: Roger Kay. Dan O'Herlihy, Glynis Johns, Richard Davalos, Lawrence Dobkin, Estelle Winwood, J. Pat O'Malley. Unimaginative remake of the 1919 German classic, removing all the mystery-exotic appeal; Johns tries hard as lady with bizarre nightmares in a mental institution.

Caddy, The (1953) 95m. ** D: Norman Taurog. Dean Martin, Jerry Lewis, Donna Reed, Fred Clark, Clinton Sundberg, Marshall Thompson. Not up to duo's usual daffy vehicles, but still engaging antics with Lewis cutting up as Martin's golf instructor on the links.

Caesar and Cleopatra (1946-British) C-127m. ***½ D: Gabriel Pascal.

Claude Rains, Vivien Leigh, Stewart Granger, Flora Robson, Francis L. Sullivan, Cecil Parker. Acid, witty film of George Bernard Shaw's play, not for all tastes; fine performances and unforgettable dialogue, lavishly produced.

Cafe Society (1939) 83m. **½ D: Edward H. Griffith. Madeleine Carroll, Fred MacMurray, Shirley Ross, Jessie Ralph, Claude Gillingwater. This time around Carroll chases MacMurray to win husband on a bet; chic fluff.

Caged (1950) 96m. *** D: John Cromwell. Eleanor Parker, Agnes Moorehead, Ellen Corby, Hope Emerson, Jan Sterling, Jane Darwell, Gertrude Michael. Remarkable performances by entire cast in stark record of Parker going to prison and becoming hardened criminal after exposure to brutal jail life. Both Parker and Emerson were nominated for Academy Awards.

Caged Fury (1948) 60m. ** D: William Berke. Richard Denning, Sheila Ryan, Mary Beth Hughes, Buster Crabbe. Not bad low-budgeter about mad-killer on the loose in a circus.

Cain and Mabel (1936) 90m. ** D: Lloyd Bacon. Marion Davies, Clark Gable, Allen Jenkins, Roscoe Karns, Walter Catlett. Musical romance of prizefighter and showgirl has gargantuan production numbers to overcome stale plot.

Caine Mutiny, The (1954) C-125m. **** D: Edward Dmytryk. Humphrey Bogart, Jose Ferrer, Van Johnson, Fred MacMurray, E. G. Marshall, Lee Marvin. Bogie goes psycho as the court-martialed Captain Queeg in this exciting adaptation of Herman Wouk's novel.

Cairo (1941) 101m. ** D: W. S. Van Dyke II. Jeanette MacDonald, Robert Young, Ethel Waters, Reginald Owen, Lionel Atwill, Dooley Wilson. Musicomedy spoof of WW2 spy films is strained, although stars are pleasant and production is well-mounted.

Calamity Jane (1953) C-101m. *** D: David Butler. Doris Day, Howard Keel, Allyn McLerie, Philip Carey, Gale Robbins. Musical Western with Doris at her bounciest as tomboyish Calamity Jane who changes her ways for Keel. Includes Oscar-winning song: "Secret Love."

Calamity Jane and Sam Bass (1949) 85m. *½ D: George Sherman. Yvonne de Carlo, Howard Duff, Dorothy Hart, Lloyd Bridges, Milburn Stone. Tattered retelling of 19th-century cowgirl and Texas outlaw, with De Carlo and Duff a disinterested duo.

Calcutta (1947) 83m. **½ D: John Farrow. Alan Ladd, Gail Russell, William Bendix, June Duprez, Lowell Gilmore. Standard actioner with pilot Ladd avenging friend's murder.

California (1946) C-97m. **½ D: John Farrow. Barbara Stanwyck, Ray Milland, Barry Fitzgerald, Albert Dekker, Anthony Quinn, Julia Faye, George Coulouris. Ray is a wagonmaster with a past, Stanwyck a shady gal who makes good in this elaborately ordinary Western.

California Conquest (1952) C-79m. **½ D: Lew Landers. Cornel Wilde, Teresa Wright, John Dehner, Hank Patterson. Film deals with sidelight of American history. Californian Wilde et al under Spanish control help their ally against Russian attempt to confiscate the territory.

California Straight Ahead (1937) 67m. ** D: Arthur Lubin. John Wayne, Louise Latimer, Robert McWade, Theodore Von Eltz, Tully Marshall. Good little actioner with Wayne competing in cross-country truck race.

Call a Messenger (1939) 65m. D: Arthur Lubin. Billy Halop, Huntz Hall, William Benedict, David Gorcey, Robert Armstrong, Buster Crabbe, Victor Jory, El Brendel, Mary Carlisle. SEE: Bowery Boys series.

Call It a Day (1937) 89m. ** D: Archie Mayo. Olivia de Havilland, Ian Hunter, Alice Brady, Anita Louise, Peggy Wood, Frieda Inescort, Roland Young, Bonita Granville. Mild fluff of wacky British family's various problems during a normal day.

Call Me Bwana (1963) 103m. ** D: Gordon Douglas. Bob Hope, Anita Ekberg, Edie Adams, Lionel Jeffries, Arnold Palmer. Hope and Adams on an African jungle safari encounter Ekberg and Jeffries—nothing much happens—the ladies are lovely.

Call Me Madam (1953) C-117m. *** D: Walter Lang. Ethel Merman,

Donald O'Connor, George Sanders, Vera-Ellen, Billy DeWolfe, Walter Slezak, Lilia Skala. Often stagy musical from Irving Berlin tuner based on Perle Mesta's life as Washington, D. C. hostess and Lichtenburg ambassadress. Merman is blowsy delight.

Call Me Mister (1951) C-95m. **½ D: Lloyd Bacon. Betty Grable, Dan Dailey, Danny Thomas, Dale Robertson. Acceptable plot-line helps buoy this musical. Soldier Dailey, based in Japan, goes AWOL to patch up marriage with Grable traveling with USO troupe.

Call Northside 777 (1948) 111m. ***½ D: Henry Hathaway. James Stewart, Richard Conte, Lee J. Cobb, Helen Walker, Moroni Olsen, E. G. Marshall. Absorbing drama of reporter Stewart convinced that convicted killer is innocent, trying to prove it; handled in semi-documentary style. Retitled: CALLING NORTHSIDE 777.

Call of the Wild (1935) 95m. *** D: William Wellman. Clark Gable, Loretta Young, Jack Oakie, Reginald Owen. Not really Jack London, but good Northern romp with Gable, Young, and Oakie prospecting in Klondike country, at odds with villain Owen.

Callaway Went Thataway (1951) 81m. **½ D: Norman Panama, Melvin Frank. Fred MacMurray, Dorothy McGuire, Howard Keel, Jesse White, guests Clark Gable, Elizabeth Taylor. Neat spoof of HOPALONG CASSIDY craze has Keel a lookalike for former Western star whose films are hot on TV. MacMurray and McGuire use promotion to make him a hot item; several stars appear in cameo roles.

Calling Bulldog Drummond (1951) 80m. D: Victor Saville. Walter Pidgeon, Margaret Leighton, Robert Beatty, David Tomlinson. SEE: **Bulldog Drummond** series.

Calling Dr. Death (1943) 63m. **½ D: Reginald LeBorg. Lon Chaney, Ramsay Ames, Patricia Morison, J. Carrol Naish, David Bruce, Fay Helm. Tight B-melodrama with doctor Chaney's unfaithful wife found murdered.

Calling Dr. Gillespie (1942) 82m. D: Harold S. Bucquet. Lionel Barrymore, Donna Reed, Phil Brown, Nat Pendleton, Alma Kruger, Mary Nash, Charles Dingle. SEE: **Dr. Kildare** series.

Calling Dr. Kildare (1939) 86m. D: Harold S. Bucquet. Lew Ayres, Lionel Barrymore, Laraine Day, Nat Pendleton, Lana Turner, Samuel S. Hinds, Emma Dunn, Alma Kruger, Marie Blake, Phillip Terry, Donald Barry. SEE: **Dr. Kildare** series.

Calling Homicide (1956) 61m. *½ D: Edward Bernds. Bill Elliott, Don Haggerty, Kathleen Case, Myron Healey. Low-keyed detective yarn following detective Elliott's search for cop-killer.

Calling Northside 777 SEE: **Call Northside 777**.

Calling Philo Vance (1940) 62m. D: William Clemens. James Stephenson, Margot Stevenson, Henry O'Neill, Edward Brophy, Ralph Forbes. SEE: **Philo Vance** series.

Caltiki, the Immortal Monster (1960-Italian, dubbed) 76m. ** D: Robert Hampton. John Merivale, Didi Sullivan, Gerald Haerter, Daniela Rocca. Sci-fi highlighting conflict between Mayan archaeologists and messy title figure.

Camille (1936) 85m. ***½ D: George Cukor. Greta Garbo, Robert Taylor, Lionel Barrymore, Elizabeth Allan, Laura Hope Crews, Henry Daniell. Garbo is most alluring as Dumas' tragic heroine in 19th-century Paris, but the film lacks punch. Large burden falls on Taylor as Armand, but he's unconvincing. Daniell steals film in a superbly subtle villainous role.

Camp on Blood Island, The (1958-British) 81m. ** D: Val Guest. Andre Morell, Carl Mohner, Walter Fitzgerald, Edward Underdown. So-so gore as inhabitants rebel against brutal commander of prison compound.

Campbell's Kingdom (1958-British) C-102m. ** D: Ralph Thomas. Dirk Bogarde, Stanley Baker, Michael Craig, Barbara Murray. Set in Canadian Rockies, big-budget adventure film focuses on landowner Bogarde's conflict with Baker et al, when latter seeks to build large dam near his property.

Canadian Mounties vs. Atomic Invaders SEE: **Missile Base at Taniak**

Canadian Pacific (1949) C-95m. **½ D: Edwin L. Marin. Randolph Scott,

Jane Wyatt, J. Carrol Naish, Victor Jory, Nancy Olson. Scott is railroad surveyer helping with construction of train link, fighting Indians while romancing Wyatt and Olson.

Canadians, The (1961) C-85m. **½ D: Burt Kennedy. Robert Ryan, John Dehner, Torin Thatcher, John Sutton, Teresa Stratas. Cornball nonsense about Mounties who pacify warhappy Sioux. Film features Brooklyn opera singer Stratas to no advantage.

Canaris Master Spy (1954-German, dubbed) 92m. ** D: Alfred Weidenmann. O. E. Hasse, Martin Held, Barbara Rutting, Adrian Hoven. Potentially interesting account of German Intelligence leader during 1930's who tried to depose Hitler; meandering film.

Canary Murder Case (1929) 81m. D: Malcolm St. Clair. William Powell, Louise Brooks, James Hall, Jean Arthur, Charles Lane. SEE: Philo Vance series.

Can-Can (1960) C-131m. **½ D: Walter Lang. Frank Sinatra, Shirley MacLaine, Maurice Chevalier, Louis Jourdan, Juliet Prowse. Lackluster version of Cole Porter musical of 1890's Paris involving lawyer Sinatra defending MacLaine's right to perform "daring" dance in her nightclub. Chevalier and Jourdan try to inject charm, but Sinatra is blasé and MacLaine shrill. Songs: "C'est Magnifique," "I Love Paris," "Let's Do It," "Just One of Those Things."

Candidate for Murder (1962-British) 60m. **½ D: David Villiers. Michael Gough, Erika Remberg, Hans Barsody, John Justin. Gough is deranged husband of actress Remberg, out to kill her; nicely told Edgar Wallace suspenser.

Cannibal Attack (1954) 69m. D: Lee Sholem. Johnny Weissmuller, Judy Walsh, David Bruce, Bruce Cowling. SEE: Jungle Jim series.

Can't Help Singing (1944) 89m. **½ D: Frank Ryan. Deanna Durbin, Robert Paige, Akim Tamiroff, Ray Collins, Thomas Gomez. Durbin goes West to find her roaming lover; despite good cast and Jerome Kern songs, it's nothing much.

Canterville Ghost, The (1944) 96m. *** D: Jules Dassin. Charles Laughton, Margaret O'Brien, William Gargan, Rags Ragland, Una O'Connor, Robert Young, Peter Lawford, Mike Mazurki. Enjoyable fantasy of 17th-century ghost Laughton, spellbound until descendant Young performs heroic deed.

Canyon Crossroads (1955) 83m. **½ D: Alfred L. Werker. Richard Basehart, Russell Collins, Phyllis Kirk, Stephen Elliott. On-location filming in Colorado highlights this tale of uranium hunt, with Basehart quite convincing.

Canyon Passage (1946) C-90m. *** D: Jacques Tourneur. Dana Andrews, Brian Donlevy, Susan Hayward, Ward Bond, Andy Devine, Lloyd Bridges. Fast-moving Western of pals Andrews and Donlevy both in love with Hayward.

Canyon River (1956) C-80m. *½ D: Harmon Jones. George Montgomery, Marcia Henderson, Peter Graves, Richard Eyer. Trite Western of Indian and rustler attacks on cattle drive.

Cape Fear (1962) 105m. *** D: J. Lee Thompson. Gregory Peck, Polly Bergen, Robert Mitchum, Martin Balsam, Lori Martin, Jack Kruschen, Telly Savalas. Well-laced suspenser as sadistic Mitchum seeks revenge on Peck and wife Bergen, highlighted by cat-and-mouse chase in Southern bayous.

Captain Blood (1935) 119m. ***½ D: Michael Curtiz. Errol Flynn, Olivia de Havilland, Lionel Atwill, Basil Rathbone, Ross Alexander, Guy Kibbee. Flynn's first swashbuckler is fine; he plays doctor forced into becoming pirate, teaming for short spell with French cutthroat Rathbone, but paying more attention to proper young lady De Havilland.

Captain Blood (1960-French, dubbed) C-95m. ** D: Andre Hunebelle. Jean Marais, Elsa Martinelli, Arnold Foa, Bourvil, Pierrette Bruno. Set in 17th-century France, this juvenile costumer deals with plot to overthrow throne of Louis XIII.

Captain Boycott (1947-British) 92m. ***½ D: Frank Launder. Stewart Granger, Kathleen Ryan, Cecil Parker, Mervyn Johns, Alistair Sim, Robert Donat. Excellent historical drama of Irish farmers going on strike to protest mistreatment by landowners; Donat appears briefly as Charles Parnell.

Captain Carey, U.S.A. (1950) 83m. *** D: Mitchell Leisen. Alan Ladd, Wanda Hendrix, Francis Lederer, Russ Tamblyn. Nicely-turned account of ex-military officer Ladd returning to Italy to uncover informer who cost lives of villagers. Theme song "Mona Lisa" won an Oscar.

Captain Caution (1940) 85m. ** D: Richard Wallace. Victor Mature, Louise Platt, Leo Carrillo, Bruce Cabot, Vivienne Osborne, Robert Barrat. OK action film of spunky Platt commandeering her father's ship into war; no messages, just fast-moving narrative.

Captain China (1949) 97m. ** D: Lewis R. Foster. John Payne, Gail Russell, Jeffrey Lynn, Lon Chaney, Edgar Bergen. Often listless sea yarn of Payne, seeking out persons responsible for his losing his ship's command.

Captain Eddie (1945) 107m. **½ D: Lloyd Bacon. Fred MacMurray, Lynn Bari, Charles Bickford, Thomas Mitchell, Lloyd Nolan, James Gleason. Routine aviation film doesn't do justice to exciting life of Eddie Rickenbacker; it's standard stuff.

Captain Falcon (1958-Italian, dubbed) C-97m. *½ D: Carlo Campogalliani. Lex Barker, Rossana Rory, Anna Maria Ferrero, Carla Calo, Massimo Serato. Juvenile account of Barker (Captain Falcon) saving Rory and her principality from clutches of Serato.

Captain From Castille (1947) C-140m. **½ D: Henry King. Tyrone Power, Jean Peters, Cesar Romero, Lee J. Cobb, John Sutton. Spaniard longs for adventure, seeks fame and fortune in New World expedition. Lots of action, but sparse on intelligent script.

Captain Fury (1939) 91m. *** D: Hal Roach. Brian Aherne, Victor McLaglen, Paul Lukas, June Lang, John Carradine. Australia serves as background in story of illustrious adventurer fighting evil head of penal colony.

Captain Hates the Sea (1934) 92m. ** D: Lewis Milestone. Victor McLaglen, John Gilbert, Walter Connolly, Alison Skipworth, Wynne Gibson. In his last film, Gilbert is teamed with McLaglen on ocean voyage filled with vague intrigue and hazy plot-line.

Captain Horatio Hornblower (1951) C-117m. *** D: Raoul Walsh. Gregory Peck, Virginia Mayo, Robert Beatty, Denis O'Dea. Well-produced sea epic based on C. M. Forester hero of Napoleonic era. Peck in title role strains to seem adventuresome.

Captain is a Lady, The (1940) 63m. ** D: Robert B. Sinclair. Charles Coburn, Beulah Bondi, Virginia Grey, Helen Broderick, Billie Burke, Dan Dailey. Thin little comedy of Coburn pretending to be a woman to accompany wife Bondi to old ladies' home.

Captain January (1936) 75m. **½ D: David Butler. Shirley Temple, Guy Kibbee, Slim Summerville, Buddy Ebsen. Sentimental family film with Shirley at her best, attaching herself to lighthouse-keeper Kibbee.

Captain John Smith and Pocahontas (1953) C-75m. *½ D: Lew Landers. Anthony Dexter, Jody Lawrance, Alan Hale, Jr., Douglass Dumbrille. Title tells all in pedestrian tale set in colonial America.

Captain Kidd (1945) 89m. ** D: Rowland V. Lee. Charles Laughton, Randolph Scott, Barbara Britton, Reginald Owen, John Carradine, Gilbert Roland, Sheldon Leonard. Even with Laughton, this is slow-going low-budget stuff.

Captain Kidd and the Slave Girl (1954) 83m. ** D: Lew Landers. Anthony Dexter, Eva Gabor, Alan Hale, Jr., James Seay. Modest costumer has Dexter and Gabor in title roles romping the seas to find treasure for their benefactor.

Captain Lightfoot (1955) C-91m. **½ D: Douglas Sirk. Rock Hudson, Barbara Rush, Jeff Morrow, Finlay Currie. Nineteenth-century Irish rebellion is subject of lightweight costumer with Hudson romancing Rush in between sword fights.

Captain Mephisto and the Transformation Machine (1945) 100m. ** D: Spencer Bennet. William Forrest, Louise Currie, Johnny Arthur, Rod Bacon, Richard Clarke, Roy Barcroft. Diverting Republic cliff-hanger with veteran villain Barcroft in rare form as Mephisto seeking ore deposits from his underground hideout. Re-edited movie serial: MANHUNT OF MYSTERY ISLAND

Captain Newman, M.D. (1963)

C-126m. *** D: David Miller. Gregory Peck, Angie Dickinson, Tony Curtis, Eddie Albert, Jane Withers, Bobby Darin, Larry Storch. Alternately dramatic and comic film of army psychiatrist doesn't always work but is generally entertaining. Darin is surprising in a melodramatic role, but the whole cast is good.

Captain Scarlett (1953) C-75m. *½ D: Thomas Carr. Richard Greene, Leonora Amar, Nedrick Young, Edourado Noriega. Acceptable costumer with Greene properly dashing.

Captain Sindbad (1963) C-85m. **½ D: Byron Haskin. Guy Williams, Heidi Bruhl, Pedro Armendariz, Abraham Sofaer, Bernie Hamilton. Above average costumer involving Williams capering about as Sindbad.

Captain Sirocco SEE: Pirates of Capri, The

Captain Tugboat Annie (1945) 60m. ** D: Phil Rosen. Jane Darwell, Edgar Kennedy, Charles Gordon, Mantan Moreland, Pamela Blake, Hardie Albright, H. B. Warner. Annie sails again in low-budget epic which depends entirely on its stars, Darwell and Kennedy, for its flavor.

Captains Courageous (1937) 116m. **** D: Victor Fleming. Spencer Tracy, Freddie Bartholomew, Melvyn Douglas, Lionel Barrymore, Mickey Rooney, John Carradine, Walter Kingsford. Spoiled rich-boy Bartholomew falls off cruise ship, rescued by Portuguese fisherman Tracy (who won Oscar for role). Boy learns to love seafaring on crusty Barrymore's fishing ship. Enthusiastic cast; top-notch production of Kipling's story.

Captains of the Clouds (1942) C-113m. *** D: Michael Curtiz. James Cagney, Dennis Morgan, Alan Hale, Brenda Marshall, George Tobias. Cagney and company join Canadian air force as a lark, but prove their worth under fire. Colorful wartime drama.

Captain's Paradise, The (1953-British) 80m. *** D: Anthony Kimmins. Alec Guinness, Yvonne de Carlo, Celia Johnson, Bill Fraser. Guinness has field-day as carefree skipper who shuttles back and forth between wives in opposite ports. De Carlo and Johnson make good contrasts as the two women.

Captain's Table, The (1960-British) C-90m. ** D: Jack Lee. John Gregson, Peggy Cummins, Donald Sinden, Nadia Gray. Satisfactory comedy involving skipper of cargo vessel (Gregson) who is given trial command of luxury liner, and the chaos ensuing trying to keep order among crew and passengers.

Capture, The (1950) 81m. **½ D: John Sturges. Lew Ayres, Teresa Wright, Victor Jory, Duncan Renaldo. Straightforward account climaxing in Mexico: Detective reinvestigates robbery to learn if he might have shot an innocent man.

Captured (1933) 72m. **½ D: Roy Del Ruth. Leslie Howard, Douglas Fairbanks, Jr., Paul Lukas, Margaret Lindsay. Fair story of honor and love, switching WW1 story from German prison camp, to warfront, to society England. Good cast major asset of production.

Caravan (1934) 101m. **½ D: Erik Charrell. Loretta Young, Charles Boyer, Jean Parker, Phillips Holmes, Louise Fazenda. Offbeat musical of royal Loretta forced to marry vagabond Boyer; main interest is curiosity in this not-altogether successful film.

Carbine Williams (1952) 91m. *** D: Richard Thorpe. James Stewart, Jean Hagen, Wendell Corey, Paul Stewart, James Arness. Sturdy history of the inventor of famed gun, his problems with the law, and his simple family life. Stewart is most convincing in title role.

Cardinal Richelieu (1935) 83m. **½ D: Rowland V. Lee. George Arliss, Maureen O'Sullivan, Edward Arnold, Cesar Romero. Arliss etches another historical portrayal of France's unscrupulous cardinal who controlled Louis XIII (Arnold). Good cast supports star.

Cardinal, The (1964) C-175m. **½ D: Otto Preminger. Tom Tryon, Romy Schneider, Carol Lynley, Maggie McNamara, John Saxon, John Huston, Robert Morse, Cecil Kellaway, Dorothy Gish, Burgess Meredith. Long, long story of an Irish-American's rise from priesthood to the college of Cardinals. Has some outstanding vignettes by old pros like Meredith, but emerges as an uneven, occasionally worthwhile film.

Career (1959) 105m. *** D: Joseph

Anthony. Dean Martin, Anthony Franciosa, Shirley MacLaine, Carolyn Jones, Joan Blackman, Robert Middleton, Donna Douglas. Occasionally shrill, generally forceful presentation of an actor's (Franciosa's), tribulations in seeking Broadway fame; Jones is exceptional as lonely talent agent.

Career Girl (1959) C-61m. *½ D: Harold David. June Wilkinson, Charles Robert Keane, Lisa Barrie, Joe Sullivan. Sloppy account of Wilkinson going to Hollywood, seeking screen career; sleazy production values.

Carefree (1938) 80m. *** D: Mark Sandrich. Fred Astaire, Ginger Rogers, Ralph Bellamy, Luella Gear, Jack Carson. Madcap Rogers goes to psychiatrist Fred is wacky musicomedy with outstanding Irving Berlin numbers: "Change Partners," "I Used To Be Color Blind."

Caretakers, The (1963) 97m. *** D: Hall Bartlett. Robert Stack, Joan Crawford, Polly Bergen, Susan Oliver, Janis Paige, Constance Ford, Barbara Barrie, Herbert Marshall. At times incisive view of a West Coast mental hospital, marred by flimsy script and poor editing. Good characterizations by Crawford and Ford as nurses, Bergen and Paige as patients.

Cargo to Capetown (1950) 80m. *½ D: Earl McEvoy. Broderick Crawford, John Ireland, Ellen Drew, Edgar Buchanan. Tramp steamer is setting for mild love triangle as Crawford and Ireland vie for Drew.

Caribbean (1952) C-97m. ** D: Edward Ludwig. John Payne, Arlene Dahl, Cedric Hardwicke, Francis L. Sullivan, Woody Strode. Costume vehicle set in 18th century allows Payne to battle pirates and flirt with Dahl.

Cariboo Trail (1950) C-81m. **½ D: Edwin L. Marin. Randolph Scott, George "Gabby" Hayes, Bill Williams, Karin Booth, Victor Jory. Standard telling of conflict between cattlemen and settlers bringing civilization obliterating the grazing lands.

Carnival in Costa Rica (1947) C-95m. ** D: Gregory Ratoff. Dick Haymes, Vera-Ellen, Cesar Romero, Celeste Holm, Anne Revere, J. Carrol Naish. Despite fair cast, boring musical of trip to Costa Rica and the shenanigans of newlyweds and their quarreling parents.

Carnival Story (1954) C-95m. ** D: Kurt Neumann. Anne Baxter, Steve Cochran, Lyle Bettger, George Nader, Jay C. Flippen. Sluggish romantic triangle set in Germany, involving high-wire star and two of the circus men in love with her; Baxter sparks some life into show with her performance.

Carolina Cannonball (1955) 74m. *½ D: Charles Lamont. Judy Canova, Andy Clyde, Jack Kruschen, Ross Elliott. Hicksville hokum with Canova involved with enemy agents and a missile that lands in her backyard.

Carpetbaggers, The (1964) C-150m. **½ D: Edward Dmytryk. George Peppard, Alan Ladd, Carroll Baker, Bob Cummings, Martha Hyer, Lew Ayres, Martin Balsam, Audrey Totter, Archie Moore. Blowsy claptrap based on Harold Robbins' novel of millionaire plane manufacturer (Peppard) dabbling in movies and lovemaking. Set in 1920's-30's; Sexploitational values are tame.

Carrie (1952) 118m. **½ D: William Wyler. Jennifer Jones, Laurence Olivier, Miriam Hopkins, Eddie Albert, Mary Murphy. Jones is passive in title role in turn-of-the-century account of farm girl who becomes famed actress, tossing aside those who loved and used her; based on Theodore Dreiser novel.

Carry on Admiral SEE: Ship Was Loaded, The

Carry on Cleo (1965-British) C-92m. **½ D: Gerald Thomas. Amanda Barrie, Sidney James, Kenneth Williams, Joan Sims, Kenneth Connor, Charles Hawtrey. Diverting reworking of ancient history to serve as amusing satire on CLEOPATRA epic, sufficiently laced with hijinks by perennial misfits.

Carry on Nurse (1960-British) 90m. *** D: Gerald Thomas. Kenneth Connor, Kenneth Williams, Charles Hawtrey, Terence Longdon. Quite hilarious madcaps with series stock company involved in patients-vs.-hospital-staff battle of authority.

Carry on Sergeant (1959-British) 88m. ** D: Gerald Thomas. William

Hartnell, Bob Monkhouse, Shirley Eaton, Eric Barker, Dora Bryan, Bill Owen, Kenneth Connor. This time around prankish misfits are the bane of army officer's existence, who swears he'll make these recruits spiffy soldiers or bust.

Carry on Spying (1965-British) 88m. **½ D: Gerald Thomas. Kenneth Williams, Barbara Windsor, Bernard Cribbins, Charles Hawtrey, Eric Barker, Victor Maddern. Acceptable James Bond spoof with daffy novice spy-catchers on the hunt for enemy agents who stole secret formula.

Carson City (1952) C-87m. ** D: Andre de Toth. Randolph Scott, Raymond Massey, Lucille Norman, George Cleveland. OK railroad story in 1870's West as construction engineer Scott battles to get the track down.

Carthage in Flames (1959-Italian, dubbed) 96m. ** D: Carmine Gallone. Jose Suarez, Pierre Brasseur, Anne Heywood, Illaria Occhini. Unremarkable mixture of love and intrigue set against backdrop of Rome-Carthage war of 2nd century B.C.; spirited action scenes.

Casa Ricordi SEE: **House of Ricordi**

Casablanca (1942) 102m. **** D: Michael Curtiz. Humphrey Bogart, Ingrid Bergman, Paul Henreid, Claude Rains, Peter Lorre, Sydney Greenstreet, Conrad Veidt, Dooley Wilson, S. Z. Sakall, Joy Page. Everything is right in this WW2 classic of war-torn Casablanca with elusive nightclub owner Rick (Bogart) finding old flame (Bergman) and her husband, underground leader Henreid, among skeletons in his closet. Rains is marvelous as dapper police chief, and nobody sings "As Time Goes By" like Dooley Wilson.

Casanova Brown (1944) 94m. **½ D: Sam Wood. Gary Cooper, Teresa Wright, Frank Morgan, Anita Louise, Isabel Elsom. Cooper has divorced Wright, but now she's pregnant; entertaining little comedy with stars outshining material.

Casanova in Burlesque (1944) 74m. ** D: Leslie Goodwins. Joe E. Brown, June Havoc, Dale Evans, Lucien Littlefield, Ian Keith. Brown's a clown during the summer but a professor for the rest of the year; fair comedy.

Casanova's Big Night (1954) C-86m. **½ D: Norman Z. McLeod. Bob Hope, Joan Fontaine, Audrey Dalton, Basil Rathbone, Raymond Burr, Vincent Price. Lavish costumed fun with Bob masquerading as Casanova (Price) in Venice and wooing lovely Fontaine.

Casbah (1948) 94m. **½ D: John Berry. Yvonne de Carlo, Tony Martin, Peter Lorre, Marta Toren, Hugo Haas. Musical remake of ALGIERS isn't bad, with Martin coming off surprisingly well amid good tunes and colorful production; Lorre fine as determined police detective after Martin in the Casbah.

Case Against Brooklyn, The (1958) 82m. *½ D: Paul Wendkos. Darren McGavin, Maggie Hayes, Warren Stevens, Peggy McCay. Unexciting little exposé yarn involves fledgling cop McGavin combatting gambling syndicate in title borough.

Case Against Mrs. Ames, The (1936) 85m. **½ D: William Seiter. Madeleine Carroll, George Brent, Arthur Treacher, Alan Baxter, Beulah Bondi. D. A. Brent finds himself falling in love with beautiful Carroll, suspected of murdering her husband.

Case of Dr. Laurent, The (1958-French, dubbed) 91m. ** D: Jean-Paul le Chanois. Jean Gabin, Nicole Courcel, Sylvia Monfort, Michel Barbey. Film was exploited theatrically for its frank birth sequence, only small logical sequence in recounting life of country doctor Gabin who advocates natural childbirth.

Case of Mrs. Loring, The SEE: **Question of Adultery, A**

Case of the Red Monkey (1955-British) 73m. ** D: Ken Hughes. Richard Conte, Rona Anderson, Colin Gordon, Russell Napier. Acceptable police-on-the-case fare, tracking down murderers of atomic scientists.

Cash McCall (1959) C-102m. **½ D: Joseph Pevney. James Garner, Natalie Wood, Nina Foch, Dean Jagger, E. G. Marshall, Henry Jones, Otto Kruger, Roland Winters. Garner is just right as business tycoon who adopts new set of values as he romances daughter (Wood) of failing businessman Jagger. Superficial film from Cameron Hawley novel.

Cash on Delivery (1956-British) 82m. ** D: Muriel Box. Shelley Winters, John Gregson, Peggy Cummins, Wilfrid Hyde-White. Story with a twist suffers from sloppy execution. Winters seeks to earn inheritance by preventing ex-husband's wife from having a child.

Casino Murder Case (1935) 85m. D: Edwin L. Marin. Paul Lukas, Alison Skipworth, Donald Cook, Rosalind Russell, Arthur Byron. SEE: Philo Vance series

Casino Royale (1967) C-100m. **½ D: John Huston, Ken Hughes, Robert Parrish, Joe McGrath, Val Guest. Peter Sellers, Ursula Andress, David Niven, Orson Welles, Joanna Pettet, Daliah Lavi, Woody Allen, Deborah Kerr, William Holden, Charles Boyer, John Huston, Kurt Kasznar, George Raft, Jean-Paul Belmondo. Gigantic, overdone spoof of James Bond films with Niven as the aging secret agent who relinquishes his position to nephew Allen and host of others. Money, money everywhere, but film is most uneven—sometimes funny, often not.

Cass Timberlane (1947) 119m. **½ D: George Sidney. Spencer Tracy, Lana Turner, Zachary Scott, Tom Drake, Mary Astor, Albert Dekker. Overblown adaptation of Sinclair Lewis novel of esteemed judge trying to keep pace with new young wife; not Tracy's cup of tea.

Cast a Dark Shadow (1957-British) 84m. *** D: Lewis Gilbert. Dirk Bogarde, Margaret Lockwood, Kay Walsh, Mona Washbourne. Bogarde is well cast as money-grasping wife-killer who is out to do in his latest wife, Lockwood; exciting throughout.

Cast a Long Shadow (1959) 82m. *½ D: Thomas Carr. Audie Murphy, Terry Moore, John Dehner, James Best, Rita Lynn, Denver Pyle, Ann Doran. Murphy, troubled by shady past, is reformed by being given a ranch and building a new future; plodding oater.

Castilian, The (1963-Spanish, dubbed) C-129m. **½ D: Javier Seto. Cesar Romero, Alida Valli, Frankie Avalon, Broderick Crawford. Strange grouping of actors are given little support by sticky script in costumer of nobleman Avalon leading his people against invaders.

Castle of Terror, The (1963-Italian, dubbed) C-77m. **½ D: Anthony Dawson. Rossana Podesta, George Riviere, Christopher Lee, Jim Nolan. Above-par chiller with Lee the demented WW2 victim running rampant in a Rhine castle; sufficient gore and suspense.

Castle on the Hudson (1940) 77m. *** D: Anatole Litvak. John Garfield, Pat O'Brien, Ann Sheridan, Burgess Meredith, Jerome Cowan, Henry O'Neill. Faithful remake of 20,000 YEARS IN SING SING is by-now-familiar prisoner vs. warden battle, but an outstanding cast helps elevate it.

Cat, The (1966) C-87m. Bomb D: Ellis Kadison. Peggy Ann Garner, Barry Coe, Roger Perry, Dwayne Redlin. Humdrum account of boy separated from parents on camping trip, saved from rustler's wrath by wildcat he befriended.

Cat and the Canary, The (1927) 60m. *** D: Paul Leni. Laura LaPlante, Tully Marshall, Flora Finch, Creighton Hale, Gertrude Astor, Lucien Littlefield. Delightful silent classic, the forerunner of all "old dark house" mysteries, with nice touch of humor throughout as heiress LaPlante and nervous group spend night in haunted house.

Cat and the Fiddle, The (1934) 90m. **½ D: William K. Howard. Jeanette MacDonald, Ramon Novarro, Frank Morgan, Jean Hersholt. Backstage musical sets scene for Parisian romance of singer MacDonald and composer Novarro in Jerome Kern-Otto Harbach musical. Songs: "She Didn't Say Yes," "The Night Was Made For Love."

Cat Ballou (1965) C-96m. ***½ D: Elliott Silverstein. Jane Fonda, Lee Marvin, Michael Callan, Dwayne Hickman, Reginald Denny, Jay C. Flippen. Funny Western spoof with Fonda as Cat Ballou, notorious female outlaw, Marvin in an Oscar performance as a drunken gunman. Nat King Cole and Stubby Kaye add to film as strolling minstrels.

Cat Creeps, The (1946) 58m. Bomb D: Erle C. Kenton. Noah Beery, Jr., Lois Collier, Paul Kelly, Douglass

Dumbrille, Rose Hobart. Lowest of low-grade horrors, with cat possessing dead girl's soul.

Cat Girl (1957-British) 69m. *½ D: Alfred Shaughnessy. Barbara Shelley, Robert Ayres, Kay Callard, Paddy Webster. Shelley is possessed by family curse which transforms her into blood-seeking animal, with rash of murders; pacing and low production values spoil total effect.

Cat on a Hot Tin Roof (1958) C-108m. ***½ D: Richard Brooks. Elizabeth Taylor, Paul Newman, Burl Ives, Jack Carson, Judith Anderson. Entire cast is excellent in this tour de force Tennessee Williams story of mendacity uprooting a patriarchal Southern family.

Cat People (1942) 73m. ***½ D: Jacques Tourneur. Simone Simon, Kent Smith, Tom Conway, Jack Holt, Jane Randolph. Classic horror tale for its suspense and intelligence. Smith's bride, Simon, believes she possesses ancient curse of panther.

Catered Affair, The (1956) 93m. *** D: Richard Brooks. Bette Davis, Ernest Borgnine, Debbie Reynolds, Barry Fitzgerald, Rod Taylor. Davis sheds all glamour as Bronx taxi-driver's wife wanting to give daughter ritzy wedding. Based on Paddy Chayefsky TV play.

Catherine the Great (1934-British) 92m. **½ D: Paul Czinner. Douglas Fairbanks, Jr., Elizabeth Bergner, Flora Robson, Joan Garner. Lavish historical drama of Russian czarina whose life is spoiled by rigidly planned marriage. Slow-moving but good.

Cattle Drive (1951) C-77m. **½ D: Kurt Neumann. Joel McCrea, Dean Stockwell, Leon Ames, Chill Wills. Stockwell does well in role of bratty teen-ager who learns a sense of values from veteran cowhand McCrea on arduous cow drive.

Cattle Empire (1958) C-83m. ** D: Charles Marquis Warren. Joel McCrea, Gloria Talbott, Don Haggerty, Phyllis Coates. McCrea agrees to lead cattle drive, planning revenge on cattle owners who sent him to jail; OK Western.

Cattle Queen of Montana (1954) C-88m. **½ D: Allan Dwan. Barbara Stanwyck, Ronald Reagan, Gene Evans, Lance Fuller. Staunch Stanwyck is determined to keep lands her father left her, despite townfolk and Indians. More talk than real action.

Cattle Town (1952) 71m. ** D: Noel Smith. Dennis Morgan, Philip Carey, Amanda Blake, Rita Moreno, Sheb Wooley, Merv Griffin. Both Warner Bros. and Morgan were at low points when this sad echo of a slick Western was churned out.

Caught (1949) 88m. *** D: Max Ophuls. James Mason, Barbara Bel Geddes, Robert Ryan, Natalie Schafer. Bel Geddes-Mason teaming heightens suspense tale of innocent girl who discovers that her husband is an insane murderer.

Caught in the Draft (1941) 82m. *** D: David Butler. Bob Hope, Dorothy Lamour, Lynne Overman, Eddie Bracken. The last thing movie-star Hope wants is to get drafted, but he accidentally enlists himself. Very funny WW2 service comedy.

Cause for Alarm (1951) 74m. **½ D: Tay Garnett. Loretta Young, Barry Sullivan, Bruce Cowling, Margalo Gillmore. Young registers most convincing as panic-stricken woman being framed for murder by her insane husband Sullivan.

Cavalcade (1933) 110m. *** D: Frank Lloyd. Diana Wynyard, Herbert Mundin, Ursula Jeans, Margaret Lindsay, Clive Brook, Beryl Mercer, Una O'Connor, Billy Bevan. Lavish adaptation of Noel Coward episodic play of British family surviving through war, scandal, depression, etc. Witty Coward songs included.

Cavalry Scout (1951) C-78m. ** D: Lesley Selander. Rod Cameron, Audrey Long, Jim Davis, James Millican. Routine Western of scout Cameron tracking down stolen army goods and romancing Long.

Cave of Outlaws (1951) C-75m. ** D: William Castle. Macdonald Carey, Alexis Smith, Edgar Buchanan, Victor Jory. Search for stolen gold leads ex-con, lawman, miner, et al to title situation; Smith is wasted.

Ceiling Zero (1935) 95m. *** D: Howard Hawks. James Cagney, Pat O'Brien, June Travis, Stuart Erwin, Barton MacLane. Rival fliers working for same company risk lives, also risk friendship when woman comes between them. Better than most Cagney-

O'Brien films. Good aerial photography.

Cell 2455, Death Row (1955) 77m. **
D: Fred F. Sears. William Campbell, Kathryn Grant, Vince Edwards, Marian Carr. Unsensational retracing of life of sex-offender Caryl Chessman and his bouts, while in prison, for retrials.

Centennial Summer (1946) C-102m. **½ D: Otto Preminger. Jeanne Crain, Cornell Wilde, Linda Darnell, Dorothy Gish, Constance Bennett, Walter Brennan. Leisurely, plush musical of Philadelphia Exposition of 1876, with sisters Crain and Darnell both after handsome Wilde; nice Jerome Kern score helps.

Ceremony, The (1963) 105m. **½ D: Laurence Harvey. Laurence Harvey, Sarah Miles, Robert Walker, Jr., John Ireland, Ross Martin, Lee Patterson, Noel Purcell. Mishmash about convicted killer rescued by brother who demands liaison with sister-in-law as reward.

Certain Smile, A (1958) C-106m. **½ D: Jean Negulesco. Rossano Brazzi, Joan Fontaine, Bradford Dillman, Christine Carere. Françoise Sagan's novella becomes overblown soap opera in romantic trivia between Parisian students Carere and Dillman, interrupted when she is beguiled by roué Brazzi; chic Fontaine is wasted.

Chad Hanna (1940) C-86m. ** D: Henry King. Henry Fonda, Dorothy Lamour, Linda Darnell, Guy Kibbee, Jane Darwell, John Carradine. Rather flat circus drama set in 19th-century Pennsylvania; colorful but empty.

Chain Lightning (1950) 94m. ** D: Stuart Heisler. Humphrey Bogart, Eleanor Parker, Raymond Massey, Richard Whorf. Static account of jet pilot Bogart who reforms in an effort to win back Parker; flight scenes uninspired.

Chain of Evidence (1957) 64m. *½ D: Paul Landres. Bill Elliott, Don Haggerty, James Lydon, Claudia Barrett. Programmer has dedicated cop Elliot track down real killer of businessman.

Chained (1934) 71m. **½ D: Clarence Brown. Joan Crawford, Clark Gable, Otto Kruger, Stuart Erwin, Una O'Connor, Akim Tamiroff. Chic formula MGM love triangle with Crawford torn between love for Gable and honorable husband Kruger.

Chalk Garden, The (1964) C-106m. *** D: Ronald Neame. Deborah Kerr, Hayley Mills, John Mills, Edith Evans, Felix Aylmer, Elizabeth Sellars. Very high-class soap opera with good cast supporting story of teenager set on right path by governess Kerr; colorful production, quite entertaining.

Challenge, The SEE: **It Takes a Thief.**

Challenge to Lassie (1949) C-76m. ** D: Richard Thorpe. Edmund Gwenn. Geraldine Brooks, Reginald Owen, Sara Allgood, Arthur Shields. Pleasant trivia, with Lassie's ownership in dispute; solid performances by character-actor cast.

Chamber of Horrors (1941-British) 80m. **½ D: Norman Lee. Leslie Banks, Lilli Palmer, Romill Lange, Gina Malo, Richard Bird, R. Montgomery, David Horne. Low-budget horror comes over fairly well with dastardly Banks making his emporium a mass morgue, menacing lovely Palmer.

Chamber of Horrors (1966) C-99m. *½ D: Hy Averback. Patrick O'Neal, Cesare Danova, Wilfrid Hyde-White, Patrice Wymore, Suzy Parker, Marie Windsor, Tony Curtis. Wax museum provides setting for uneven mystery about mad killer on the loose. Intended for TV, it has mark of low-budget film. Uses gimmick of horn sounding before each murder.

Champ, The (1931) 87m. *** D: King Vidor. Wallace Beery, Jackie Cooper, Roscoe Ates, Irene Rich, Marcia Mae Jones, Ed Brophy. Sentimental tale of washed-up boxer Beery and child (Cooper) who idolizes him; the two are memorable team. Remade as THE CLOWN.

Champ for a Day (1953) 90m. ** D: William Seiter. Alex Nicol, Audrey Totter, Charles Winninger, Hope Emerson, Henry Morgan. Brooklyn boxer tracks down friend's murderers; average.

Champagne for Caesar (1950) 99m. *** D: Richard Whorf. Ronald Colman, Celeste Holm, Vincent Price, Barbara Britton, Art Linkletter. Genius Colman becomes national celebrity on TV quiz show; sponsor

Price sends temptress Holm to distract big winner. Enjoyable spoof, with Price hilarious as neurotic soap manufacturer.

Champagne Murders, The (1968) 98m. **½ D: Claude Chabrol. Anthony Perkins, Maurice Ronet, Stéphane Audran, Yvonne Furneaux, Suzanne Lloyd. Brooding, muddled murder tale with Perkins married to rich girl who owns vineyards, Ronet the third part of unusual love triangle; ending is quite good, but story is sterile.

Champagne Waltz (1937) 85m. **½ D: A. Edward Sutherland. Gladys Swarthout, Fred MacMurray, Jack Oakie, Herman Bing, Benny Baker. Operatic Swarthout doing schmaltzy songs in Vienna with publicity-hustler MacMurray. Songs: "Could I Be In Love," "When Is A Kiss Not A Kiss?"

Champion (1949) 90m. ***½ D: Mark Robson. Kirk Douglas, Marilyn Maxwell, Arthur Kennedy, Ruth Roman, Lola Albright. Unscrupulous boxer punches his way to the top, thrusting aside everybody and everything only to discover gangster element in fight game is stronger than he. Douglas perfectly cast in title role; gripping film.

Chance Meeting (1960-British) 96m. **½ D: Joseph Losey. Hardy Kruger, Stanley Baker, Micheline Presle, John Van Eyssen. Actors are more convincing than weak murder mystery script about artist Kruger accused of killing his girlfriend.

Chapman Report, The (1962) C-125m. **½ D: George Cukor. Efrem Zimbalist, Jr., Jane Fonda, Shelley Winters, Claire Bloom, Glynis Johns, Ray Danton, Ty Hardin. Slick, empty yarn about Kinsey-like sex researchers coming to suburban community to get statistical survey, with repercussions on assorted females.

Charade (1963) C-114m. ***½ D: Stanley Donen. Cary Grant, Audrey Hepburn, Walter Matthau, James Coburn, George Kennedy. Suave mystery with Grant aiding widow Hepburn to recover fortune secreted by late husband, being sought by quartet of sinister crooks; set in chic Paris.

Charge at Feather River, The (1953) C-96m. **½ D: Gordon Douglas. Guy Madison, Vera Miles, Frank Lovejoy, Helen Westcott, Ron Hagerthy. One of many Westerns which literally threw action at viewers to utilize 3-D used for original release; now, just standard.

Charge of the Black Lancers (1961-Italian, dubbed) C-97m. **½ D: Giacomo Gentilomo. Mel Ferrer, Yvonne Furneaux, Jean Claudio, Leticia Roman. Effective costumer, well-mounted and fast-paced. Claudio is traitor to country with his brother (Ferrer) leading patriots in defense of homeland.

Charge of the Lancers (1954) C-74m. ** D: William Castle. Paulette Goddard, Jean-Pierre Aumont, Richard Stapley. Stilted affair of gypsy Goddard and British officer Aumont finding romance in midst of Crimean War.

Charge of the Light Brigade, The (1936) 116m. *** D: Michael Curtiz. Errol Flynn, Olivia de Havilland, Patric Knowles, Henry Stephenson, Nigel Bruce, Donald Crisp, David Niven. Thundering action based on Tennyson's poem, with climactic charge into certain death by British army. Lavish production values accent romantic tale of Flynn and De Havilland at army post in India.

Charlie Chan Earl Derr Biggers' character of an Oriental detective on the Honolulu police force first appeared on the screen in 1926, but did not make an impression upon moviegoers until Warner Oland took over the role in 1931 with CHARLIE CHAN CARRIES ON. He essayed the part until his death in 1937, when he was replaced by Sidney Toler. Toler carried on for nine years, and upon his death was replaced in turn by Roland Winters, who starred for the last two years of the fading series. The early entries with Oland are the best, with CHARLIE CHAN AT THE OPERA and ON BROADWAY standing out; Toler's first attempts are quite good, especially CHARLIE CHAN AT TREASURE ISLAND (one of the best in the whole series) and IN PANAMA. But in the 1940's, with less interest and a change of studios, the series declined, and so did Toler. His last efforts, like DANGEROUS MONEY, were pretty bad, and Mr. Toler had aged considerably. The series gave out a dying gasp with Roland Winters, who was totally unsuited for the role. The last Chan film, SKY DRAGON, is unbearable. Despite their age, the early efforts remain fresh and entertaining today, with Charlie constantly at odds with his #1 or #2 son (Keye Luke and Sen Yung, respectively) and mouthing his famous words of wisdom: "Insignificant molehill sometimes more important than conspicuous mountain," etc. Today the Charlie Chan films offer a delightful change of pace and for the most part are highly recommended.

Charlie Chan at Monte Carlo (1937) 71m. D: Eugene Forde. Warner Oland, Keye Luke, Virginia Field, Sidney Blackmer, Harold Huber, Louis Mercier, Robert Kent.

Charlie Chan at the Circus (1936) 72m. D: Harry Lachman. Warner Oland, Keye Luke, George and Olive Brasno, Francis Ford, Maxine Reiner, John McGuire, Shirley Deane, J. Carrol Naish.

Charlie Chan at the Olympics (1937) 71m. D: H. Bruce Humberstone. Warner Oland, Keye Luke, Katherine DeMille, Pauline Moore, C. Henry Gordon, Jonathan Hale, Allan Lane, John Eldredge.

Charlie Chan at the Opera (1936) 66m. D: H. Bruce Humberstone. Warner Oland, Boris Karloff, Keye Luke, Charlotte Henry, Thomas Beck, Gregory Gaye, Nedda Harrigan, William Demarest.

Charlie Chan at the Race Track (1936) 70m. D: H. Bruce Humberstone. Warner Oland, Keye Luke, Helen Wood, Thomas Beck, Alan Dinehart, Gavin Muir, Gloria Roy, Jonathan Hale.

Charlie Chan at the Wax Museum (1940) 63m. D: Lynn Shores. Sidney Toler, Sen Yung, C. Henry Gordon, Marc Lawrence, Joan Valerie, Marguerite Chapman, Ted Osborne, Michael Visaroff.

Charlie Chan at Treasure Island (1939) 59m. D: Norman Foster. Sidney Toler, Cesar Romero, Pauline Moore, Douglass Dumbrille, Billie Deward, Louis Jean Heydt, Charles Halton.

Charlie Chan in City of Darkness (1939) 75m. D: Herbert I. Leeds, Sidney Toler, Lynn Bari, Richard Clarke, Pedro de Cordoba, Douglass Dumbrille, Lon Chaney, Jr., Leo G. Carroll.

Charlie Chan in Egypt (1935) 65m. D: Louis King. Warner Oland, "Pat" Paterson, Thomas Beck, Rita Hayworth, Jameson Thomas, Frank Conroy, Nigel de Brulier, Paul Porcasi, Stepin Fetchit.

Charlie Chan in Honolulu (1938) 65m. D: H. Bruce Humberstone. Sidney Toler, Phyllis Brooks, Sen Yung, Eddie Collins, John King, Claire Dodd, George Zucco, Robert Barrat.

Charlie Chan in London (1934) 79m. D: Eugene Forde. Warner Oland, Ray Milland, Mona Barrie, Drue Leyton, Alan Mowbray, David Torrence, Madge Bellamy.

Charlie Chan in Panama (1940) 67m. D: Norman Foster. Sidney Toler, Jean Rogers, Kane Richmond, Lionel Atwill, Mary Nash, Sen Yung, Chris-Pin Martin.

Charlie Chan in Reno (1939) 70m. D: Norman Foster. Sidney Toler, Ricardo Cortez, Phyllis Brooks, Slim Summerville, Kane Richmond, Robert Lowery, Morgan Conway, Sen Yung.

Charlie Chan in Rio (1941) 60m. D: Harry Lachman. Sidney Toler, Mary Beth Hughes, Cobina Wright, Jr., Ted North, Victor Jory, Harold Huber, Sen Yung.

Charlie Chan in Shanghai (1935) 70m. D: James Tinling. Warner Oland, Irene Hervey, Russell Hicks, Keye Luke, Halliwell Hobbes, Charles Locher (Jon Hall).

Charlie Chan in the Secret Service (1944) 63m. D: Phil Rosen. Sidney Toler, Mantan Moreland, Gwen Kenyon, Benson Fong, Eddie Chandler.

Charlie Chan on Broadway (1937) 68m. D: Eugene Ford. Warner Oland, Keye Luke, Joan Marsh, J. Edward Bromberg, Leon Ames, Joan Woodbury, Douglas Fowley, Louise Henry, Donald Woods, Harold Huber.

Charlie Chan's Murder Cruise (1940) 75m. D: Eugene Ford. Sidney Toler, Sen Yung, Marjorie Weaver, Lionel Atwill, Robert Lowery, Don Beddoe, Leo G. Carroll.

Charlie Chan's Secret (1936) 71m. D: Gordon Wiles. Warner Oland, Rosina Lawrence, Charley Quigley,

Henrietta Crossman, Edward Trevor, Astrid Allwyn.

Charlie Chaplin Carnival (1938) 75m. **** Four vintage comedies from Chaplin's 1916-17 peak period: BEHIND THE SCREEN, THE COUNT, THE FIREMAN, THE VAGABOND. First one is best, with leading lady Edna Purviance and oversized villain Eric Campbell.

Charlie Chaplin Cavalcade (1938) 75m. **** More priceless gems from 1916-17 period: ONE A.M. (Chaplin's famous solo film), THE RINK, THE PAWNSHOP, THE FLOORWALKER. All great.

Charlie Chaplin Festival (1938) 75m. **** Best of the Chaplin compilations, which all suffer from obtrusive sound effects and music: THE ADVENTURER, THE CURE, EASY STREET, THE IMMIGRANT. Four of the greatest comedies ever made—don't miss them.

Chartroose Caboose (1960) C-75m. ** D: William "Red" Reynolds. Molly Bee, Ben Cooper, Edgar Buchanan, Mike McGreevey. Buchanan, an eccentric retired train conductor, shelters a young couple in his strange house, a converted caboose.

Chase, The (1946) 86m. ** D: Arthur Ripley. Robert Cummings, Michele Morgan, Steve Cochran, Peter Lorre. Slow-moving second-rate story set in Cuba with Morgan running off from her husband.

Chase a Crooked Shadow (1958) 87m. **½ D: Michael Anderson. Richard Todd, Anne Baxter, Herbert Lom, Alexander Knox. Rich heiress Baxter doubts her sanity when allegedly dead brother Todd appears to claim inheritance; acting better than contrived script.

Chase Me Charlie (1932) 61m. ** Narrated by Teddy Bergman. Edna Purviance, Ben Turpin. Inept attempt to string early Chaplin shorts into story line—1914 material used is often weak.

Chatterbox (1943) 76m. **½ D: Joseph Santley. Joe E. Brown, Judy Canova, Rosemary Lane, John Hubbard, Gus Schilling, Chester Clute, Anne Jeffreys. Entertaining comedy of radio-cowboy Brown (not much of a hero in real life) visiting dude ranch for publicity purposes.

Cheaper by the Dozen (1950) C-85m. *** D: Walter Lang. Clifton Webb, Myrna Loy, Jeanne Crain, Mildred Natwick, Edgar Buchanan. Charming turn-of-the-century story of the Gilbraith children, twelve strong, their exacting father (well-played by Webb) and mother (Loy).

Cheaters, The (1945) 87m. *** D: Joseph Kane. Joseph Schildkraut, Billie Burke, Eugene Pallette, Ona Munson, Raymond Walburn, Ruth Terry. Excellent cast in enjoyable tale of wealthy family of snobs humanized by downtrodden actor they invite for Christmas dinner.

Cheers for Miss Bishop (1941) 95m. *** D: Tay Garnett. Martha Scott, William Gargan, Edmund Gwenn, Sterling Holloway, Sidney Blackmer, Mary Anderson, Dorothy Peterson. Sentimental story of schoolteacher Scott, devoting her life to teaching in small Midwestern town. Nicely done.

Cheyenne (1947) 100m. ** D: Raoul Walsh. Dennis Morgan, Jane Wyman, Janis Paige, Bruce Bennett, Alan Hale, Arthur Kennedy, Barton MacLane. Standard Western as gambler attempts to capture outlaw—instead spends time with outlaw's wife.

Cheyenne Autumn (1964) C-160m. **½ D: John Ford. Carroll Baker, Richard Widmark, Edward G. Robinson, Dolores Del Rio, Ricardo Montalban, Gilbert Roland, Sal Mineo, Victor Jory. Sprawling, tedious account of American Indians' ill treatment at hands of whites; methodically filmed but generally sterile.

Chicago Calling (1951) 74m. ** D: John Reinhardt. Dan Duryea, Mary Anderson, Gordon Gebert, Ross Elliot. Slim premise has Duryea sitting by telephone awaiting news of estranged family, injured in car accident; mild tour de force.

Chicago Confidential (1957) 73m. **½ D: Sidney Salkow. Brian Keith, Beverly Garland, Dick Foran, Beverly Tyler, Elisha Cook. Keith and Garland make good protagonists in their crusade to clean up corruption and crime amid the labor unions of the Windy City.

Chicago Deadline (1949) 87m. **½ D: Lewis Allen. Alan Ladd, Donna Reed, June Havoc, Irene Hervey, Arthur Kennedy, Shepperd Strudwick.

Potentially top-notch actioner bogs down in clichés, with Ladd as crusading reporter in corruption-filled city; Reed is very tame love interest.

Chicago Syndicate (1955) 83m. ** D: Fred F. Sears. Dennis O'Keefe, Abbe Lane, Paul Stewart, Xavier Cugat. Passable exposé film involving clean-up of Windy City rackets.

Chicken Every Sunday (1948) 91m. **½ D: George Seaton. Dan Dailey, Celeste Holm, Colleen Townsend, Alan Young, Natalie Wood. Easy-going turn-of-the-century Americana about get-rich-quick schemer Dailey and understanding wife Holm.

Chief Crazy Horse (1955) C-86m. **½ D: George Sherman. Victor Mature, Suzan Ball, John Lund, Ray Danton, Keith Larsen. Clichéd nonsense focusing on Mature in title role as idealistic tough redskin.

Child is Born, A (1940) 79m. *** D: Lloyd Bacon. Geraldine Fitzgerald, Jeffrey Lynn, Gladys George, Gale Page, Spring Byington, Eve Arden. Smooth, touching remake of LIFE BEGINS about everyday life in maternity ward, involving prisoner Fitzgerald sent to hospital to have her child.

Child is Waiting, A (1963) 102m. *** D: John Cassavetes. Burt Lancaster, Judy Garland, Gena Rowlands, Steven Hill, Bruce Ritchey. Poignant story of Lancaster's attempts to treat retarded children with the help of overly sympathetic Garland. Sensitive subject handled with honesty and candor.

Children of Paradise (1945-French, dubbed) 161m. ***½ D: Marcel Carné. Jean-Louis Barrault, Arletty, Pierre Brasseur, Albert Remay, Maria Cesarès, Leon Larive. Story of love affair between pantomimist and beautiful woman is touching, well-acted, a French classic.

Children of the Damned (1964-British) 81m. **½ D: Antone Leader. Ian Hendry, Alan Badel, Barbara Ferris, Patrick White, Bessie Love. Follow-up to VILLAGE OF THE DAMNED suffers from unimaginative account of precocious deadly children and their quest for power.

Children's Hour, The (1962) 107m. **½ D: William Wyler. Audrey Hepburn, Shirley MacLaine, James Garner, Miriam Hopkins, Fay Bainter, Veronica Cartwright. Updated version of Lillian Hellman's play is more explicit in its various themes, including lesbianism, than original THESE THREE, but not half as good. Impact is missing, despite MacLaine and Hepburn as two teachers, Hopkins as meddling aunt, Bainter as questioning grandmother.

China (1943) 79m. ** D: John Farrow. Loretta Young, Alan Ladd, William Bendix, Philip Ahn, Iris Wong, Sen Yung. Pat wartime tale of mercenary Ladd who suddenly realizes his true allegiance while helping enemy.

China Clipper (1936) 85m. **½ D: Ray Enright. Pat O'Brien, Beverly Roberts, Ross Alexander, Humphrey Bogart, Marie Wilson, Henry B. Walthall. O'Brien stars as man determined to develop trans-Pacific flights; usual plot of initial failure, grim determination, and neglected wife; fairly well done.

China Corsair (1951) 67m. *½ D: Ray Nazzaro. Jon Hall, Lisa Ferraday, Ron Randell, Douglas Kennedy, Ernest Borgnine. Tinsel-like adventurn of Hall's romancing, combatting crooks aboard title ship.

China Doll (1958) 88m. *½ D: Frank Borzage. Victor Mature, Li Li Hua, Bob Mathias, Stuart Whitman. Bizarre story-line can't boost dull film of Mature accidentally buying Oriental wife whom he grows to love. When they are killed, daughter comes to U.S.A.

China Gate (1957) C-97m. ** D: Samuel Fuller. Gene Barry, Angie Dickinson, Nat King Cole, Lee Van Cleef. French legionnaires tackle Communist munition dumps in this OK actioner set in Indochina.

China Girl (1942) 95m. ** D: Henry Hathaway. Gene Tierney, George Montgomery, Lynn Bari, Victor McLaglen, Sig Ruman, Bobby Blake, Ann Pennington, Philip Ahn. American photographer in mysterious Orient during WW2 is background for unbelievable adventure yarn; Bari best item in film.

China Seas (1935) 90m. *** D: Tay Garnett. Clark Gable, Jean Harlow, Wallace Beery, Lewis Stone, Rosalind Russell, Dudley Digges, Robert

Benchley, C. Aubrey Smith. Luxury ship involved in piracy; powerhouse cast complements interesting tale.

China Sky (1945) 78m. ** D: Ray Enright. Randolph Scott, Ruth Warrick, Ellen Drew, Anthony Quinn, Carol Thurston, Richard Loo. Slow-moving Pearl Buck story of dedicated doctor Scott fighting Japanese with Chinese comrades during WW2.

China Venture (1953) 83m. *1/2 D: Don Siegel. Edmond O'Brien, Barry Sullivan, Jocelyn Brando, Richard Loo, Philip Ahn. Often sleazy WW2 adventure film of marine group on mission to capture Japanese naval commander wanted by U. S. interrogation department.

China's Little Devils (1945) 74m. ** D: Monta Bell. Harry Carey, Paul Kelly, Ducky Louie, Hayward Soo Hoo, Gloria Ann Chew. Patriotic yarn of Chinese waifs helping downed American pilots get going again.

Chinese Cat, The (1944) 65m. D: Phil Rosen. Sidney Toler, Benson Fong, Joan Woodbury, Mantan Moreland, Sam Flint, John Davidson, Betty Blythe, Jack Norton, Ian Keith. SEE: Charlie Chan series.

Chinese Ring, The (1947) 67m. D: William Beaudine. Roland Winters, Warren Douglas, Victor Sen Yung, Mantan Moreland, Philip Ahn. SEE: Charlie Chan series.

Chip Off the Old Block (1944) 82m. ** D: Charles Lamont. Donald O'Connor, Peggy Ryan, Ann Blyth, Helen Vinson, Helen Broderick, Arthur Treacher, Patric Knowles, Ernest Truex. Innocuous wartime musical of misunderstandings climaxing in teenage romance and musical show, of course.

Chocolate Soldier, The (1941) 102m. ** D: Roy Del Ruth. Nelson Eddy, Rise Stevens, Nigel Bruce, Florence Bates, Dorothy Gilmore, Nydia Westman. Don't expect Oscar Straus' operetta—this is from play THE GUARDSMAN, about married couple performing operettas; too talky, not enough music.

Christmas Carol, A (1938) 69m. *** D: Edwin L. Marin. Reginald Owen, Gene Lockhart, Kathleen Lockhart, Terry Kilburn, Barry McKay, Lynne Carver, Leo G. Carroll. Nicely done adaptation of Dickens' classic with Owen a well-modulated Scrooge, surrounded by good MGM players and period settings.

Christmas Carol, A (1951-British) 86m. *** D: Brian Desmond Hurst. Alastair Sim, Kathleen Harrison, Jack Warner, Michael Hordern. Effective retelling of Dickens' holiday classic, with Sim restrained as Scrooge, supported by nice characterizations.

Christmas Eve (1947) 90m. *1/2 D: Edwin L. Marin. George Brent, George Raft, Randolph Scott, Joan Blondell, Virginia Field, Ann Harding, Reginald Denny. Slow-moving mixture of comedy and drama as foster sons discover evil intentions of relations to victimize Harding. Retitled: SINNER'S HOLIDAY.

Christmas Holiday (1944) 92m. *** D: Robert Siodmak. Deanna Durbin, Gene Kelly, Gale Sondergaard, Gladys George, Richard Whorf. Somerset Maugham novel reset in America. Crime story with Durbin gone wrong to help killer-hubby Kelly; songs include "Spring Will Be A Little Late this Year."

Christmas in Connecticut (1945) 101m. **1/2 D: Peter Godfrey. Barbara Stanwyck, Dennis Morgan, Sydney Greenstreet, Reginald Gardiner, S. Z. Sakall, Robert Shayne, Una O'Connor. Airy fluff of recipe-writer (Stanwyck) having soldier Morgan for dinner to impress boss Greenstreet.

Christmas in July (1940) 70m. ***1/2 D: Preston Sturges. Dick Powell, Ellen Drew, Raymond Walburn, William Demarest, Ernest Truex, Franklin Pangborn. Top Sturges film of hopeful contest-winner Powell going on shopping spree on anticipated winnings. Walburn and Demarest are at their best.

Christopher Columbus (1949-British) C-104m. *** D: David Macdonald. Fredric March, Florence Eldridge, Francis L. Sullivan, Nora Swinburne, James Robertson Justice. Stark, slowly-paced biography of 15th-century explorer, with earnest portrayal by March in title role; good period setting.

Christopher Strong (1933) 77m. **1/2 D: Dorothy Arzner. Katharine Hepburn, Colin Clive, Billie Burke, Helen Chandler, Jack LaRue. Hepburn's an aviatrix in love with married Clive. Dated but smoothly produced film.

Chump at Oxford, A (1940) 63m. **½ D: Alfred Goulding. Stan Laurel, Oliver Hardy, James Finlayson, Forrester Harvey, Wilfred Lucas, Anita Garvin, Peter Cushing. Concussion changes Stan from usual self to aristocratic genius at Oxford; lots of fun.

Cimarron (1960) C-140m. **½ D: Anthony Mann. Glenn Ford, Maria Schell, Anne Baxter, Arthur O'Connell. Edna Ferber's chronicle of frontier life in Oklahoma between 1890-1915 becomes an indifferent sprawling soap opera unsalvaged by a few spectacular scenes. What's worse, this remake keeps the 1930 original off TV.

Cimarron Kid, The (1951) C-84m. ** D: Budd Boetticher. Audie Murphy, Beverly Tyler, James Best, Yvette Dugay. Uninspired formula Western with Murphy in title role, persuaded to give up his criminal life by his sweetheart.

Cincinnati Kid, The (1965) 113m. **½ D: Norman Jewison. Steve McQueen, Ann-Margret, Edward G. Robinson, Karl Malden, Tuesday Weld, Joan Blondell, Rip Torn, Jack Weston, Cab Calloway. Focus of film is on roving card-sharks who get together for big game; side episodes of meaningless romance. Robinson, Blondell, and Malden come off best as vivid members of the playing profession.

Cinderella Jones (1946) 88m. ** D: Busby Berkeley. Joan Leslie, Robert Alda, S. Z. Sakall, Edward Everett Horton, Ruth Donnelly, Elisha Cook. Silly comedy of girl who must marry brainy husband to collect inheritance; good cast defeated by trivial script.

Cinderfella (1960) C-91m. **½ D: Frank Tashlin. Jerry Lewis, Ed Wynn, Judith Anderson, Anna Maria Alberghetti, Count Basie. Fairy tale classic revamped as a Lewis romp; talky interludes and ineffectual musical sequences featuring Alberghetti.

Circle, The (1959-British) 84m. **½ D: Gerald Thomas. John Mills, Derek Farr, Roland Culver, Wilfrid Hyde-White. Well-acted, neatly paced murder yarn involving London medico. Retitled: THE VICIOUS CIRCLE.

Circle of Danger (1951) 86m. **½ D: Jacques Tourneur. Ray Milland, Patricia Roc, Marius Goring, Hugh Sinclair. Straightforward account of Milland returning to England to ferret out brother's killers.

Circle of Deception (1961) 100m. **½ D: Jack Lee. Bradford Dillman, Suzy Parker, Harry Andrews, Paul Rogers. At times engaging psychological yarn of WW2 espionage agent Dillman who breaks under Axis torture; ironic climax.

Circumstantial Evidence (1945) 68m. **½ D: John Larkin. Michael O'Shea, Lloyd Nolan, Trudy Marshall, Billy Cummings. Engaging programmer about efforts to save an innocent man from going to the electric chair.

Circus Clown (1934) 63m. ** D: Ray Enright. Joe E. Brown, Dorothy Burgess, Patricia Ellis, Lee Moran, Tom Dugan, William Demarest. Brown mixes comedy and drama in account of circus star whose father objects to his work.

Circus of Horrors (1960-British) C-89m. **½ D: Sidney Hayers. Anton Diffring, Erika Remberg, Yvonne Monlaur, Donald Pleasence. A most unethical plastic surgeon and nurse join bizarre circus to escape deformed patient threatening their lives; rousing horror film.

Circus World (1964) C-135m. **½ D: Henry Hathaway. John Wayne, Rita Hayworth, Claudia Cardinale, Lloyd Nolan, Richard Conte. Made in Spain, film has nothing new to offer, but rehashes usual circus formula quite nicely. Climactic fire sequence is truly spectacular.

Citadel, The (1938-British) 110m. ***½ D: King Vidor. Robert Donat, Rosalind Russell, Ralph Richardson, Rex Harrison, Emlyn Williams, Penelope Dudley-Ward, Francis L. Sullivan. Superb adaptation of A. J. Cronin novel of impoverished doctor Donat eschewing ideals for wealthy life of treating rich hypochondriacs, neglecting wife and friends in the process; tragedy opens his eyes. Weak ending, but fine acting makes up for it.

Citizen Kane (1941) 120m. **** D: Orson Welles. Orson Welles, Joseph Cotten, Harry Shannon, Everett Sloane, Agnes Moorehead, Dorothy Comingore, Ray Collins, George Coulouris. Welles' first and best, a film that broke all the rules and invented some new ones, with fascinating story of Hearst-like publisher's rise to power. Direction is sometimes over-elaborate, but overall effect is staggering.

City Across the River (1949) 90m. **½ D: Maxwell Shane. Stephen McNally, Thelma Ritter, Luis Van Rooten, Jeff Corey. Watered-down version of Irving Shulman's novel THE AMBOY DUKES, involving tough life in Brooklyn slums, with predictable hoods et al.

City After Midnight (1959-British) 84m. *½ D: Compton Bennett. Phyllis Kirk, Dan O'Herlihy, Petula Clark, Wilfrid Hyde-White, Jack Watling. Tame detective film of private eye O'Herlihy investigating death of antique dealer.

City Beneath the Sea (1953) C-87m. **½ D: Budd Boetticher. Robert Ryan, Mala Powers, Anthony Quinn, Suzan Ball. Inconsequential underwater yarn invigorated by Ryan and Quinn as deep-sea divers hunting treasure off Jamaican coast.

City for Conquest (1940) 101m. *** D: Anatole Litvak. James Cagney, Ann Sheridan, Frank Craven, Arthur Kennedy, Donald Crisp, Frank McHugh, George Tobias, Elia Kazan, Anthony Quinn. Cagney makes this a must as boxer devoted to younger brother Kennedy (his film debut). Beautiful production overshadows film's pretentious faults.

City in Darkness SEE: **Charlie Chan in City of Darkness**

City of Bad Men (1953) C-82m. ** D: Harmon Jones. Jeanne Crain, Dale Robertson, Richard Boone, Lloyd Bridges, Carl Betz. Robbers attempt to steal prizefight proceeds in 1890's Nevada; film combines Western with recreation of Jim Corbett-Bob Fitzsimmons fight bout.

City of Fear (1959) 81m. *½ D: Irving Lerner. Vince Edwards, Lyle Talbot, John Archer, Steven Ritch, Patricia Blair. Programmer involving escaped convict Edwards sought by police and health officials; container he stole is filled with radioactive material, not money.

City of Fear (1965) 90m. *½ D: Peter Bezencenet. Paul Maxwell, Terry Moore, Marisa Mell, Albert Lieven, Pinkas Braun. Tedious caper involving news reporter and refugee going to Hungary to smuggle out pro-Westerners.

City of Shadows (1955) 70m. *½ D: William Witney. Victor McLaglen, John Baer, Kathleen Crowley, Anthony Caruso. Mild happenings about crafty newsboys involved with derelict racketeer McLaglen.

City on a Hunt SEE: **No Escape**

City Streets (1931) 70m. *** D: Rouben Mamoulian. Gary Cooper, Sylvia Sidney, Paul Lukas, Wynne Gibson, Guy Kibbee, Stanley Fields. Sidney is pulled into unsavory underworld when lover Cooper is involved in a crime. Kibbee in offbeat casting in sinister role. First-rate drama.

City That Never Sleeps, The (1953) 90m. ** D: John H. Auer. Gig Young, Mala Powers, Edward Arnold, Marie Windsor. Average melodrama of married patrolman Young who almost gives up all for sake of Windsor, tawdry cafe singer; set in Chicago.

Clancy Street Boys (1943) 66m. D: William Beaudine. Leo Gorcey, Huntz Hall, Bobby Jordan, Noah Beery, Sr., Lita Ward, Bennie Bartlett, Ric Vallin, Billy Benedict. SEE: **Bowery Boys series**

Clarence, The Cross-Eyed Lion (1965) C-98m. **½ D: Andrew Marton. Marshall Thompson, Betsy Drake, Cheryl Miller, Richard Haydn, Alan Caillou. Basis for DAKTARI TV show is good family entertainment set in Africa with adventure and wholesome comedy well blended.

Clash by Night (1952) 105m. **½ D: Fritz Lang. Barbara Stanwyck, Paul Douglas, Robert Ryan, Marilyn Monroe, Keith Andes. Lurid Clifford Odets melodrama about frustrated Stanwyck marrying fisher captain Douglas, having an affair with friend Ryan. Monroe-Andes provide secondary love plot.

Clash of Steel (1962-French, dubbed) C-79m. **½ D: Bernard Borderie. Gerard Barray, Gianna Maria Canale, Michele Grellier, Jean Topart. Thin plot involving overthrow of French king, Henry of Navarre, boosted by lively production and zesty swordplay.

Claudelle Inglish (1961) 99m. **½ D: Gordon Douglas. Diane McBain, Arthur Kennedy, Constance Ford, Chad Everett. Trite soaper derived from Erskine Caldwell tale of Southern farm gal who gives all to find excitement, with predictable tragedy to all.

Claudia (1943) 91m. *** D: Edmund Goulding. Dorothy McGuire, Robert Young, Ina Claire, Reginald Gardiner, Olga Baclanova, Jean Howard. Warm comedy of young Claudia (McGuire) suddenly marrying, facing adult problems, learning a lot about life in short period; beautifully acted.

Claudia and David (1946) 78m. *** D: Walter Lang. Dorothy McGuire, Robert Young, Mary Astor, John Sutton, Gail Patrick, Florence Bates. Enjoyable follow-up to CLAUDIA with McGuire and Young having a baby, adjusting to suburban life; engaging, well-acted.

Claw Monsters, The (1955) 100m. *½ D: Franklin Adreon. Phyllis Coates, Myron Healey, Arthur Space, John Day, Mike Ragan. Latter-day Republic cliff-hanger is short on action, long on stock footage, in account of out-of-whack scientist guarding his diamond mines via superstitions and animal-skin-covered henchmen. Re-edited movie serial: PANTHER GIRL OF THE KONGO

Cleo from 5 to 7 (1962-French, dubbed) 90m. *** D: Agnes Varda. Corinne Marchand, Antoine Bourseiller, Dorothée Blanck, Michel Legrand, Anna Karina, Eddie Constantine, Jean-Luc Godard. Intelligent, fluid account of Parisian songstress forced to reevaluate her life while awaiting vital medical report on her physical condition.

Cleopatra (1934) 95m. ***½ D: Cecil B. DeMille. Claudette Colbert, Warren William, Henry Wilcoxon, Gertrude Michael, Joseph Schildkraut, C. Aubrey Smith, Claudia Dell, Robert Warwick. Opulent De Mille version of Cleopatra doesn't date badly, stands out as one of his most intelligent films, thanks in large part to fine performances by all. Top entertainment.

Cleopatra (1963) C-243m. ** D: Joseph L. Mankiewicz. Elizabeth Taylor, Richard Burton, Rex Harrison, Roddy McDowall, Pamela Brown, Martin Landau, Michael Hordern, Kenneth Haigh, Andrew Keir, Hume Cronyn. Saga of the Nile goes on and on and on; definitely a curiosity item, but you'll be satisfied after an hour. Good acting, especially by Harrison and McDowall, but they are lost in this flat, four-hour misfire.

Cleopatra's Daughter (1960-Italian, dubbed) C-102m. ** D: Richard McNamara. Debra Paget, Ettore Manni, Erno Crisa, Robert Alda, Corrado Panni. American actors are lost in this costumer, more intent on playing up sadistic sequences; intrigue at Egyptian court the highlight.

Climax, The (1944) C-86m. *** D: George Waggner. Boris Karloff, Gale Sondergaard, Susanna Foster, Turhan Bey, Thomas Gomez, Scotty Beckett. Tense Karloff vehicle of seemingly polished opera physician who is really a murderer; Foster gets to sing, too.

Clipped Wings (1953) 65m. D: Edward Bernds. Leo Gorcey, Huntz Hall, Bernard Gorcey, Mary Treen, Philip Van Zandt, Lyle Talbot. SEE: Bowery Boys series.

Clive of India (1935) 90m. **½ D: Richard Boleslawski. Ronald Colman, Loretta Young, Colin Clive, Francis Lister, C. Aubrey Smith, Cesar Romero. Average adventure of British-in-India variety. Colman plays man of destiny, puts down Indian rebellions, defeats tyrant.

Cloak and Dagger (1946) 106m. *** D: Fritz Lang. Gary Cooper, Lilli Palmer, Robert Alda, Vladimir Sokoloff, Ludwig Stossel. Professor Cooper becomes a secret agent on his trip to Germany; Lang intrigue is not among his best, but still slick.

Cloak Without Dagger SEE: Operation Conspiracy

Clock, The (1945) 90m. ***½ D: Vincente Minnelli. Judy Garland, Robert Walker, James Gleason, Keenan Wynn, Marshall Thompson, Lucille Gleason. Soldier Walker has one day leave in N.Y.C., meets office worker Judy; they spend the day falling in love, encountering friendly milkman Gleason, drunk Wynn; charming little love story with beguiling Garland.

Close Call for Boston Blackie, A (1946) 60m. D: Lew Landers. Chester Morris, Lynn Merrick, Richard Lane, Frank Sully, George E. Stone, Russell Hicks. SEE: Boston Blackie series

Close Call for Ellery Queen (1942) 67m. D: James Hogan. William Gargan, Margaret Lindsay, Ralph Morgan, Edward Norris. SEE: Ellery Queen series.

Close to My Heart (1951) 90m. *** D: William Keighley. Ray Milland, Gene Tierney, Fay Bainter, Howard St. John. Superior soaper; Tierney attaches herself to waif in Bainter's orphanage, but husband Milland won't allow adoption until child's background is traced.

Cloudburst (1951-British) C-83m. **½ D: Francis Searle. Robert Preston, Elizabeth Sellars, Harold Lang, Noel Howlett. Impressive little film of Preston, WW2 veteran working in British Foreign Office, seeking his wife's murderers.

Clouded Yellow, The (1951-British) 85m. *** D: Ralph Thomas. Jean Simmons, Trevor Howard, Barry Jones, Maxwell Reed, Kenneth More. Cast is exceptional in unpretentious murder-hunt film with Simmons seeking to prove her innocence.

Clouds Over Europe (1939-British) 78m. *** D: Tim Whelan. Laurence Olivier, Ralph Richardson, Valerie Hobson, George Curzon, David Tree. Fine British account of pilot Olivier and detective Richardson nabbing spies of British aircraft secrets. Retitled: Q PLANES.

Clown, The (1953) 92m. **½ D: Robert Z. Leonard. Red Skelton, Jane Greer, Tim Considine, Steve Forrest. Sentimental remake of Wallace Beery-Jackie Cooper THE CHAMP about down-and-out comic losing his family's love. Skelton OK in rare dramatic role.

Club Havana (1945) 62m. ** D: Edgar G. Ulmer. Tom Neal, Margaret Lindsay, Don Douglas, Gertrude Michael, Isabelita, Dorothy Morris, Ernest Truex. Road-show GRAND HOTEL is very cheap production with little of interest.

Clue of the New Pin (1960-British) 58m. *½ D: Allan Davis. Paul Daneman, Bernard Archard, James Villiers, Catherine Woodville, Clive Morton. Old-fashioned Edgar Wallace yarn about "perfect crime," with Villiers a TV interviewer who tangles with murderer; ponderous.

Clue of the Silver Key (1961-British) 59m. **½ D: Gerald Glaister. Bernard Lee, Lyndon Brook, Finlay Currie, Jennifer Danie. Above-par Edgar Wallace yarn, highlighted by Lee's performance as determined Scotland Yard inspector unraveling series of murders.

Cluny Brown (1946) 100m. ***½ D: Ernst Lubitsch. Charles Boyer, Jennifer Jones, Peter Lawford, Helen Walker, Reginald Gardiner, C. Aubrey Smith, Reginald Owen, Una O'Connor. Delightful Lubitsch comedy of romance between plumber Jones and refugee Boyer in pre-WW2 England. Beautiful character performances help out.

Coast of Skeletons (1964) C-84m. **½ D: Robert Lynn. Richard Todd, Marianne Koch, Vivi Bach, Albert Lieven. Based on Edgar Wallace tale, film deals with diamond-smuggling doctor now on deathbed; set in Africa. Remake of SANDERS OF THE RIVER.

Cobra Strikes, The (1948) 62m. ** D: Charles F. Riesner. Sheila Ryan, Richard Fraser, Leslie Brooks, Herbert Heyes. Weak low-budgeter about thief who meddles in inventor's workshop, complications ensue.

Cobra Woman (1944) C-70m. ** D: Robert Siodmak. Maria Montez, Jon Hall, Sabu, Edgar Barrier, Lois Collier, Lon Chaney, Jr., Mary Nash. Montez plays twins, one of whom is a dreaded killer; tame island yarn.

Cobweb, The (1955) C-124m. **½ D: Vincente Minnelli. Richard Widmark, Lauren Bacall, Gloria Grahame, Charles Boyer, Lillian Gish, John Kerr, Susan Strasberg, Oscar Levant. Muddled hokum involving patients and staff of mental clinic, boosted by varied casting.

Cockeyed Miracle, The (1946) 81m. ** D: S. Sylvan Simon. Frank Morgan, Keenan Wynn, Cecil Kellaway, Audrey Totter, Marshall Thompson. Good cast carries weak material. Morgan returns from heaven to make up for financial error he made involving family.

Cockleshell Heroes, The (1956-British) C-97m. ** D: Jose Ferrer. Jose Ferrer, Trevor Howard, Dora Bryan, Anthony Newley, Victor Maddern. Training of special task force troops during WW2 never jells into excitement.

Cocoanut Grove (1938) 85m. ** D:

Alfred Santell. Fred MacMurray, Harriet Hilliard, Yacht Club Boys, Ben Blue, Rufe Davis, Billy Lee, Eve Arden. MacMurray's band just has to make good at the Cocoanut Grove audition in this flimsy musical, with nine songs you'll never hear again.

Cocoanuts (1929) 96m. *** D: Joseph Santley, Robert Florey. Groucho, Harpo, Chico, Zeppo Marx, Kay Francis, Oscar Shaw, Mary Eaton, Margaret Dumont. The Marxes' first film suffers from stagy filming and stale musical subplot, but when the brothers have scenes to themselves it's a riot; best scene comes when Groucho tries to tell Chico about a viaduct.

Code of Scotland Yard (1948-British) 60m. ** D: George Kign. Oscar Homolka, Muriel Pavlow, Derek Farr, Kenneth Griffith. Man escapes from Devil's Island and takes up unassuming front for underhanded activities. OK low-grade mystery.

Code 7 Victim 5 (1964-British) C-88m. **½ D: Robert Lynn. Lex Barker, Ronald Fraser, Walter Rilla, Dietmar Schonberr. Moderate actioner with Barker investigating murder in South Africa; nicely paced.

Code 645 (1948) 100m. ** D: Fred Brannon, Yakima Canutt. Clayton Moore, Roy Barcroft, Ramsay Ames, Drew Allen, Tom Steele. Tame Republic cliff-hanger relying on too much stock footage and pat situations in contest between federal agents and escaped arch-criminal with his own master plan of destruction and success. Re-edited movie serial: G-MEN NEVER FORGET.

Code Two (1953) 69m. ** D: Fred Wilcox. Ralph Meeker, Sally Forrest, Keenan Wynn, Robert Horton, Jeff Richards. Three recruits on L. A. motorcycle police force face occupational hazards; when Richards is killed, Meeker et al seek to capture those responsible.

Cold Wind In August, A (1961) 80m. **½ D: Alexander Singer. Lola Albright, Scott Marlowe, Herschel Bernardi, Joe De Santis. Offbeat account of tenement boy Marlowe having affair with stripper Albright; frank, flavorful tale.

Colditz Story, The (1957-British) 97m. **½ D: Guy Hamilton. Eric Portman, John Mills, Ian Carmichael, Bryan Forbes, Frederick Valk. Well-executed film depicting group of British soldiers and their escape maneuvers from prison stronghold.

Cole Younger, Gunfighter (1958) C-78m. ** D: R. G. Springsteen. Frank Lovejoy, James Best, Abby Dalton, Jan Merlin. Modest actioner has gunfights to perk up trite account of 1870's Texas.

Colleen (1936) 89m. **½ D: Alfred E. Green. Dick Powell, Ruby Keeler, Joan Blondell, Hugh Herbert, Jack Oakie, Louise Fazenda, Paul Draper. Formula Warner Bros. stock company musical arranges for Powell to meet Keeler, allowing them to go into their numbers: "An Evening With You," "Boulevardier from the Bronx."

College Coach (1933) 75m. **½ D: William Wellman. Dick Powell, Ann Dvorak, Pat O'Brien, Hugh Herbert, Herman Bing, Lyle Talbot. Well-paced tale of ruthless football coach O'-Brien, neglected wife Dvorak, star player Powell who also likes chemistry. Look for John Wayne in a bit part.

College Confidential (1960) 91m. *½ D: Albert Zugsmith. Steve Allen, Jayne Meadows, Mamie Van Doren, Walter Winchell. Hanky-panky involving college professor (Allen) and the shenanigans of his sexually precocious brood of students; a few violent scenes thrown in for good measure.

College Holiday (1936) 88m. **½ D: Frank Tuttle. Jack Benny, George Burns, Gracie Allen, Mary Boland, Martha Raye, Marsha Hunt, Eleanore Whitney. Benny's hotel needs business, so he induces the college crowd to come; spiffy musical with first-rate cast.

College Humor (1933) 80m. *** D: Wesley Ruggles. Bing Crosby, Jack Oakie, Richard Arlen, Mary Carlisle, George Burns, Gracie Allen, Grady Sutton. Spirited collegiate musical with Crosby singing "Learn To Croon," "Down The Old Ox Road." Burns & Allen as wacky caterers and Oakie the perennial student provide laughs.

College Swing (1938) 86m. *** D: Raoul Walsh. George Burns, Gracie Allen, Martha Raye, Bob Hope, Edward Everett Horton, Florence

George, Ben Blue, Betty Grable, John Payne. Gracie hasn't been able to graduate from school in this entertaining collegiate musicomedy with top cast, forgettable songs like "What Did Romeo Say to Juliet?"

Colonel Blimp (1943-British) C-93m. *** D: Michael Powell, Emeric Pressburger. Roger Livesey, Deborah Kerr, Anton Walbrook, James McKechnie, Neville Mapp, Vincent Holman, David Hutchinson. Fine British satire set during the early 20th century, digging at stolid British soldiers involved in Boer War and WW1. Edited down from original version, LIFE AND DEATH OF COLONEL BLIMP.

Colonel Effingham's Raid (1945) 70m. **½ D: Irving Pichel. Charles Coburn, Joan Bennett, William Eythe, Allyn Joslyn, Elizabeth Patterson, Donald Meek. Entertaining little comedy of ex-officer Coburn fighting to save town's historical landmark; cast supports fair material.

Colorado Territory (1949) 94m. **½ D: Raoul Walsh. Joel McCrea, Virginia Mayo, Dorothy Malone, Henry Hull, John Archer, Frank Puglia. Fitful-action Western dealing with McCrea on the lam from the law, involved in inevitable shoot-out.

Colossus of New York, The (1958) 70m. ** D: Eugene Lourie. John Baragrey, Mala Powers, Otto Kruger, Robert Hutton. Doctor implants dead son's brain into oversized robot with predictable chaos.

Colt .45 (1950) C-74m. **½ D: Edwin L. Marin. Randolph Scott, Zachary Scott, Ruth Roman, Lloyd Bridges, Chief Thundercloud. The renowned title gun is star of this sometimes actionful Western. Retitled: THUNDER CLOUD.

Column South (1953) C-85m. ** D: Frederick de Cordova. Audie Murphy, Joan Evans, Robert Sterling, Ray Collins. OK mixture of Civil War and Indian fighting, as Union officer Murphy champions underdog redskins to prevent hostilities.

Comanche (1956) C-87m. ** D: George Sherman. Dana Andrews, Kent Smith, Linda Cristal, Nestor Paiva, Henry Brandon. Andrews is staunch as Indian scout seeking to patch redskin-cavalry hostilities. Film is pat Western.

Comanche Station (1960) C-74m. **½ D: Budd Boetticher. Randolph Scott, Nancy Gates, Claude Akins, Skip Homeier. Better-than-usual actioner with Scott leading a group through Indian lands, hoping to find his wife who has been kidnapped by redskins.

Comanche Territory (1950) C-76m. **½ D: George Sherman. Maureen O'Hara, Macdonald Carey, Will Geer, James Best, Edmund Cobb. Fictional bio of Western scout Jim Bowie (Carey) who helps Comanches save their lands from whiteskins.

Comancheros, The (1961) C-107m. *** D: Michael Curtiz. John Wayne, Stuart Whitman, Lee Marvin, Ina Balin, Bruce Cabot. Well-paced Wayne actioner with Big John a Texas Ranger out to bring in gang supplying firearms to warring Indians.

Combat Squad (1953) 72m. *½ D: Cy Roth. John Ireland, Lon McCallister, Hal March, Tris Coffin. Weak study of men in war; this time Korea.

Come and Get It (1936) 105m. ***½ D: Howard Hawks, William Wyler. Edward Arnold, Joel McCrea, Frances Farmer, Walter Brennan, Andrea Leeds, Frank Shields. Elaborate filming of Edna Ferber book about life in the lumber country of Wisconsin, with Arnold playing the great American capitalist and Brennan winning Best Supporting Actor Oscar for his fine work.

Come Back, Little Sheba (1952) 99m. ***½ D: Daniel Mann. Burt Lancaster, Shirley Booth, Terry Moore, Richard Jaeckel. William Inge play is emotional tour de force for Booth (who won an Oscar) as slovenly housewife coping with drunken ex-veterinarian husband (Lancaster) and boarder Moore, whose curiosity about her landlords sets drama in motion.

Come Blow Your Horn (1963) C-112m. *** D: Bud Yorkin. Frank Sinatra, Lee J. Cobb, Molly Picon, Barbara Rush, Jill St. John, Tony Bill. Sinatra is good as a free-swinging bachelor with wall-to-wall girls and a nagging father (Cobb). He also sings the title song, and takes on a protege (Bill) to teach him the ropes.

Come Dance with Me! (1960-French, dubbed) C-91m. **½ D: Michel Boisrond. Brigitte Bardot, Henri Vidal, Dawn Addams, Noel Roquevert. Fairly well-blended mixture of mystery-comedy involving dentist accused of murdering a barroom pickup and his wife Bardot finding the real killer.

Come Fill the Cup (1951) 113m. **½ D: Gordon Douglas. James Cagney, Phyllis Thaxter, Raymond Massey, James Gleason, Gig Young. Cagney is quite restrained as ex-newspaperman seeking to conquer alcoholism. Fine performance by Gleason as helpful ex-drunk and by Young as drunken playboy.

Come Fly with Me (1963) C-109m. **½ D: Henry Levin. Hugh O'Brian, Pamela Tiffin, Dolores Hart, Karl Boehm, Lois Nettleton, Karl Malden. Flighty fluff of three stewardesses trying to catch husbands, becoming involved with three men on a trans-Atlantic flight. Glossy, easy to take.

Come Live with Me (1941) 86m. ** D: Clarence Brown. James Stewart, Hedy Lamarr, Ian Hunter, Verree Teasdale, Donald Meek, Barton MacLane, Edward Ashley. Stewart helps wealthy European Lamarr stay in the U.S. by marrying her. Occasionally amusing comedy.

Come Next Spring (1956) C-92m. *** D: R. G. Springsteen. Ann Sheridan, Steve Cochran, Walter Brennan, Sherry Jackson. Arkansas Americana beautifully interpreted by intelligent acting, with Sheridan and Cochran overcoming nature and townfolks to make their farm go.

Come-On, The (1956) 83m. ** D: Russell Birdwell. Anne Baxter, Sterling Hayden, John Hoyt, Jesse White. Baxter is dramatically fine as unscrupulous con-gal involved with murder, but the story is hackneyed.

Come Out Fighting (1945) 62m. D: William Beaudine. Leo Gorcey, Huntz Hall, Billy Benedict, Gabriel Dell, June Carlson. SEE: Bowery Boys series

Come September (1961) C-112m. *** D: Robert Mulligan. Rock Hudson, Gina Lollobrigida, Sandra Dee, Bobby Darin, Walter Slezak. Frothy comedy about the younger generation (Darin and Dee) vs. the "older" folks (Hudson and Lollobrigida) at an Italian villa. Bobby sings, but the rest of the film is good fun.

Come Spy With Me (1967) C-85m. *½ D: Marshall Stone. Troy Donahue, Andrea Dromm, Albert Dekker, Mart Hulswit, Valerie Allen. Amateurish spy spoof set in Bahamas, involving stock ingredients of senseless killings and secret agents.

Come to the Stable (1949) 94m. *** D: Henry Koster. Loretta Young, Celeste Holm, Hugh Marlowe, Elsa Lanchester, Regis Toomey, Mike Mazurki. Young and Holm register well as French nuns living in New England, seeking aid from a variety of local characters in building a children's dispensary.

Comin' Round the Mountain (1951) 107m. ** D: Charles Lamont. Bud Abbott, Lou Costello, Dorothy Shay, Kirby Grant, Joe Sawyer, Glenn Strange. Bud and Lou invade hillbilly country and soon tame the feuding townfolk with their pranks; standard A&C.

Coming-Out Party, A (1962-British) 90m. **½ D: Ken Annakin. James Robertson Justice, Leslie Phillips, Stanley Baxter, Eric Sykes, Richard Wattis. Wry comedy with Justice chomping through role as indolent scientist who had contempt for all during WW2 and still has no use for mankind.

Command, The (1954) C-88m. ** D: David Butler. Guy Madison, Joan Weldon, James Whitmore, Carl Benton Reid. Madison unflinchingly copes with smallpox epidemic and rampaging redskins as he leads troops and civilians through Wyoming Indian lands.

Command Decision (1948) 112m. ***½ D: Sam Wood. Clark Gable, Walter Pidgeon, Van Johnson, Brian Donlevy, Charles Bickford, John Hodiak, Edward Arnold. All-star cast in taut WW2 drama. Commander Gable faced with dilemma of doing what is right or what looks good to public.

Commando (1964-Italian, dubbed) 90m. **½ D: Frank Wisbar. Stewart Granger, Dorian Gray, Fausto Tozzi, Carlos Casarvilla. Granger leads mission to rescue Algerian rebel leader, later learning ironic political significance. Satisfactory actioner.

Company She Keeps, The (1950) 81m. **½ D: John Cromwell. Lizabeth Scott, Jane Greer, Dennis O'Keefe, Fay Baker, John Hoyt, Don Beddoe. Actors and unique love triangle spice this story of parole officer Greer and ex-con Scott both in love with O'Keefe.

Compulsion (1959) 103m. ***½ D:

Richard Fleischer. Orson Welles, Diane Varsi, Dean Stockwell, Bradford Dillman, E. G. Marshall, Martin Milner. Hard-hitting version of Leopold-Loeb thrill murder case of 1920's Chicago. Good characterizations, period decor, and well-edited courtroom scenes highlight picture.

Comrade X (1940) 90m. **½ D: King Vidor. Clark Gable, Hedy Lamarr, Felix Bressart, Oscar Homolka, Eve Arden, Sig Ruman. NINOTCHKA-esque plot with American Gable warming up icy Russian Lamarr (a streetcar conductor). Synthetic romance tale never convinces.

Concrete Jungle, The (1962-British) 86m. **½ D: Joseph Losey. Stanley Baker, Margit Saad, Sam Wanamaker, Gregoire Aslan, Jill Bennett, Laurence Naismith, Edward Judd. Thoughtful filming of prison life focusing on convict who escapes and double-crosses pal. Baker is exceptionally able.

Condemned (1929) 86m. ** D: Wesley Ruggles. Ronald Colman, Ann Harding, Louis Wolheim, Dudley Digges, William Elmer. Attempt to depict social evils of Devil's Island with interspersed romantic plot, in stiff early talkie.

Condemned of Altona, The (1963) 114m. **½ D: Vittorio DeSica. Sophia Loren, Fredric March, Robert Wagner, Maximilian Schell. Sluggish pseudo-intellectual version of Jean-Paul Sartre play about post-WW2 Germany involving dying magnate (March), his two sons—one a playboy (Wagner) with an actress wife (Loren); the other an insane Nazi war criminal (Schell).

Coney Island (1943) 96m. *** D: Walter Lang. Betty Grable, George Montgomery, Cesar Romero, Charles Winninger, Phil Silvers, Matt Briggs. Breezy, enjoyable turn-of-the-century musical of saloon entertainer Grable turned into famous musical star by hustling Montgomery. Remade as WABASH AVENUE.

Confess, Dr. Corda (1958-German, dubbed) 81m. ** D: Josef von Baky. Hardy Kruger, Elisabeth Muller, Lucie Mannheim, Hans Nielsen. Tedious handling of story of Kruger circumstantially involved in death of his mistress, with his attempt to prove innocence at trial.

Confession (1937) 86m. **½ D: Joe May. Kay Francis, Basil Rathbone, Jane Bryan, Ian Hunter, Donald Crisp, Laura Hope Crews, Veda Ann Borg, Robert Barrat. Well-mounted. MADAME X-ish soaper. Francis on trial details her murder of pianist Rathbone. Francis registers good range of emotions; Crews is fine as empty-headed partygoer.

Confessions of a Nazi Spy (1939) 102m. *** D: Anatole Litvak. Edward G. Robinson, Francis Lederer, George Sanders, Paul Lukas, Henry O'Neill, James Stephenson, Sig Ruman. Bristling drama of G-man Robinson investigating Nazi underground in U.S. Patriotic zest is forgivable.

Confessions of an Opium Eater (1962) 85m. *½ D: Albert Zugsmith. Vincent Price, Linda Ho, Richard Loo, June Kim, Philip Ahn, Victor Sen Yung. Bizarre low-budgeter. Price is hammy in weak tale of slave girls brought to San Francisco and the adventurer who aids them.

Confessions of Boston Blackie (1941) 65m. D: Edward Dmytryk. Chester Morris, Harriet Hilliard, Richard Lane, George E. Stone, Lloyd Corrigan, Joan Woodbury. SEE: **Boston Blackie** series.

Confessions of Felix Krull, The (1958-German, dubbed) 107m. **½ D: Kurt Hoffman. Horst Buchholz, Lisa Pulver, Ingrid Andree, Susi Nicoletti. Waggish chronicle of charming rascal Buchholz rising in rank as Parisian hotel employee; based on Thomas Mann novel.

Confidential Agent (1945) 118m. *** D: Herman Shumlin. Charles Boyer, Lauren Bacall, Peter Lorre, Katina Paxinou, Victor Francen, Wanda Hendrix. Boyer is Graham Greene's hero in engrossing spy yarn of Spanish Civil War; he meets Bacall along the way, they battle enemy agents Lorre and Paxinou.

Confidential Report SEE: **Mr. Arkadin**

Confidentially Connie (1953) 74m. **½ D: Edward Buzzell. Van Johnson, Janet Leigh, Louis Calhern, Walter Slezak, Gene Lockhart. Mild chuckles as pregnant wife Leigh schemes to get underpaid professor hubby (Johnson) to leave academic circles. Calhern as Van's rich Texan father is amusing.

Confirm or Deny (1941) 73m. **½ D: Archie Mayo. Don Ameche, Joan Bennett, Roddy McDowall, John Loder, Raymond Walburn, Arthur Shields. Love in an air-raid shelter with Ameche and Bennett as reporter and wireless operator; pleasant romance.

Conflict (1945) 86m. **½ D: Curtis Bernhardt. Humphrey Bogart, Alexis Smith, Sydney Greenstreet, Rose Hobart, Charles Drake, Grant Mitchell. Far-fetched story of husband (Bogart) plotting to murder wife (Hobart) to marry her sister (Smith). Unconvincing plot not salvaged by good cast.

Congo Crossing (1956) C-87m. ** D: Joseph Pevney. Virginia Mayo, George Nader, Peter Lorre, Michael Pate, Rex Ingram. OK adventure yarn set in Africa, involving wanted criminals and construction engineer's attempt to civilize the Congo territory.

Congo Maisie (1940) 70m. D: H. C. Potter. Ann Sothern, John Carroll, Rita Johnson, Shepperd Strudwick, J. M. Kerrigan, E. E. Clive, Everett Brown. SEE: Maisie series

Conjugal Bed, The (1963-Italian, dubbed) 90m. *** D: Marco Ferreri. Ugo Tognazzi, Marina Vlady, Walter Giller, Linda Sini. Tognazzi is admirably suited to role of roué whose marriage to young beauty results in ironic twist of events.

Connecticut Yankee in King Arthur's Court (1949) C-107m. **½ D: Tay Garnett. Bing Crosby, Rhonda Fleming, William Bendix, Cedric Hardwicke, Henry Wilcoxon. Mark Twain's story becomes carefree Crosby musical, with Bing transported into past, branded a wizard. No great songs, but colorful production.

Conquered City (1965 - Italian, dubbed) 91m. ** D: Joseph Anthony. David Niven, Ben Gazzara, Michael Craig, Martin Balsam, Lea Massari. Tawdry WW2 story set in Athens, with diverse group of people holed up in hotel under Axis attack.

Conquest (1937) 112m. *** D: Clarence Brown. Greta Garbo, Charles Boyer, Reginald Owen, Alan Marshall, Henry Stephenson, Leif Erikson, Dame May Whitty. Boyer as Napoleon and Garbo as Polish countess Walewska in fairly interesting costumer with fine performances making up for not-always-thrilling script.

Conquest of Cochise (1953) C-70m. ** D: William Castle. John Hodiak, Robert Stack, Joy Page, John Crawford. Unspectacular Indian vs. cavalry, set in 1850's Southwest, as Stack and troops try to calm Cochise's (Hodiak) rampaging braves.

Conquest of Space (1955) C-80m. **½ D: Byron Haskin. Eric Fleming, William Hopper, Ross Martin, Walter Brooke, Joan Shawlee. George Pal's special effects bolster this account of space satellite and men who man it.

Conspiracy of Hearts (1960-British) 116m. *** D: Ralph Thomas. Lilli Palmer, Sylvia Syms, Yvonne Mitchell, Ronald Lewis. Despite familiar situation of nuns sheltering refugee Jewish youths in Northern Italy, this film manages to be suspenseful and moving.

Conspirator (1950) 85m. **½ D: Victor Saville. Robert Taylor, Elizabeth Taylor, Honor Blackman, Wilfrid Hyde-White. Elizabeth is confronted by the fact that British husband Taylor is a Communist agent; story often better than stars.

Conspirators, The (1944) 101m. **½ D: Jean Negulesco. Hedy Lamarr, Paul Henreid, Sydney Greenstreet, Peter Lorre, Victor Francen, Vladimir Sokoloff, George Macready, Monte Blue, Joseph Calleia. WW2 intrigue in Lisbon, with echoes of CASABLANCA. Opulently done, with fine cast headed by gorgeous Lamarr.

Constant Nymph, The (1943) 112m. ***½ D: Edmund Goulding. Charles Boyer, Joan Fontaine, Alexis Smith, Brenda Marshall, Charles Coburn, Dame May Whitty, Peter Lorre. Impeccable performances in story of young girl (Fontaine) infatuated with suave musician Boyer. Fontaine has never been better.

Constantine and the Cross (1962-Italian, dubbed) C-120m. *** D: Lionello de Felice. Cornel Wilde, Christine Kaufman, Belinda Lee, Elisa Cegani, Massimo Serato. Intelligent interpretation of 4th century B.C. Emperor (Wilde) battling Romans for Christianity. Good action.

Contempt (1964-Italian, dubbed) C-103m. **½ D: Jean-Luc Godard. Brigitte Bardot, Jack Palance, Fritz

Lang, Giorgia Moll. Pretentious slop about moviemaking set in Rome with veteran director Lang taking role.

Contest Girl (1966-British) C-82m. **½ D: Val Guest. Ian Hendry, Janette Scott, Ronald Fraser, Edmund Purdom, Linda Christian. Film well conveys glamorous and seamy sides of beauty-contest world. Purdom gives effective performance.

Convicted (1950) 91m. **½ D: Henry Levin. Glenn Ford, Broderick Crawford, Dorothy Malone, Roland Winters, Ed Begley. Sincere account of prison warden's efforts to help unjustly convicted man, and those on the outside seeking actual killer.

Convicts Four (1962) 105m. *** D: Millard Kaufman. Ben Gazzara, Stuart Whitman, Ray Walston, Vincent Price, Rod Steiger, Broderick Crawford, Sammy Davis, Jr., Jack Kruschen. Gazzara gives sincere portrayal as long-term prisoner who becomes professional artist. Oddball supporting cast. Retitled: REPRIEVE

Cool and the Crazy, The (1958) 78m. *½ D: William Witney. Scott Marlowe, Gigi Perreau, Dick Bakalyan, Dick Jones. Exploitation value of this low-budgeter has lost novelty; dope addict becomes high school gang leader in order to push dope.

Copacabana (1947) 92m. ** D: Alfred E. Green. Groucho Marx, Carmen Miranda, Andy Russell, Steve Cochran, Gloria Jean, Louis Sobol, Abel Green, Earl Wilson. Unengrossing musical comedy about wild complications when same girl applies for two jobs at nightclub; cast can't save it.

Copper Canyon (1950) C-83m. **½ D: John Farrow. Ray Milland, Hedy Lamarr, Macdonald Carey, Mona Freeman. Milland-Lamarr occasionally sparkle in this Western of post-Civil War days and movement West to find riches.

Corn Is Green, The (1945) 114-m. ***½ D: Irving Rapper. Bette Davis, Nigel Bruce, John Dall, Joan Lorring, Rhys Williams, Rosalind Ivan, Mildred Dunnock. Thoughtful acting in this story of devoted middle-aged teacher Davis in Welsh mining town, coming to terms with her prize pupil; from Emlyn Williams play.

Cornered (1945) 102m. *** D: Edward Dmytryk. Dick Powell, Walter Slezak, Micheline Cheirel, Nina Vale, Morris Carnovsky. High-tension drama with tough-guy Powell in Buenos Aires tracking down the man who killed his wife during WW2; Powell in peak form.

Coroner Creek (1948) C-93m. ** D: Ray Enright. Randolph Scott, Marguerite Chapman, George Macready, Sally Eilers, Edgar Buchanan. Good little Western: Scott seeks revenge on his fiancee's killer.

Corpse Came C.O.D., The (1947) 87m. ** D: Henry Levin. George Brent, Joan Blondell, Adele Jergens, Jim Bannon, Leslie Brooks, Grant Mitchell, Una O'Connor. Two rival reporters attempt to solve mystery of dead body showing up at actress' residence. Strictly B material.

Corpse Vanishes, The (1942) 64m. *½ D: Wallace Fox. Bela Lugosi, Luana Walters, Tristram Coffin, Minerva Urecal, Vince Barnett. Grade-B horror movie with poor-to-adequate cast; has Lugosi performing experiments to restore wife's youth. Hardly scary.

Corregidor (1943) 73m. ** D: William Nigh. Otto Kruger, Elissa Landi, Donald Woods, Frank Jenks, Rick Vallin, Wanda McKay, Ian Keith. Not a battle-action film but a routine love triangle set against wartime background, rather cheaply done.

Corridors of Blood (1963-British) 87m. **½ D: Robert Day. Boris Karloff, Betta St. John, Christopher Lee, Finlay Currie. At times engaging account of 19th-century British doctor experimenting with anesthetics, creating havoc when he accidentally becomes a dope addict.

Corsican Brothers, The (1941) C-112m. **½ D: Gregory Ratoff. Douglas Fairbanks, Jr., Ruth Warrick, Akim Tamiroff, J. Carrol Naish, H. B. Warner, Henry Wilcoxon. Fairbanks plays twin brothers who join forces to avenge parents' death; Warrick comes between them. Based on Alexander Dumas novel; entertaining swashbuckler.

Corvette K-225 (1943) 99m. *** D: Richard Rossen. Randolph Scott, James Brown, Ella Raines, Barry Fitzgerald, Andy Devine, Walter Sande, Richard Lane. First-rate war film with Canadian officer Scott fighting to save prominent navy destroyer from enemy attack; realistic film.

Cosmic Man, The (1959) 72m. *½ D: Herbert Greene. Bruce Bennett, John Carradine, Angela Greene, Paul Langton, Scotty Morrow. Mediocre sci-fi with now-you-see-me, now-you-don't title figure on a mission to earth.

Cossacks, The (1959-Italian, dubbed) C-113m. ** D: Giorgio Rivalta. Edmund Purdom, John Drew Barrymore, Giorgia Moll, Massimo Girotti. Heavy-handed historical tale set in 1850's Russia; Cossack Purdom and son Barrymore clash in loyalties to Czar Alexander II.

Couch, The (1962) 100m. **½ D: Owen Crump. Shirley Knight, Grant Williams, Onslow Stevens, William Leslie. Bizarre yarn of psychopathic killer on the prowl while under analysis.

Count Five and Die (1958) 92m. **½ D: Victor Vicas. Jeffrey Hunter, Nigel Patrick, Ann-Marie Duringer, David Kossoff. WW2 espionage flick has Hunter an American agent working with British to mislead Nazis about Allied landing site.

Count of Bragelonne, The SEE: Last Musketeer, The

Count of Monte Cristo, The (1954-French, dubbed) C-97m. **½ D: Robert Vernay. Jean Marais, Lia Amanda, Roger Piguar. Serviceable rendition of Alexander Dumas costume classic.

Count of Monte Cristo, The (1961-French, dubbed). C-90m. **½ D: Claude Autant-Lara. Louis Jourdan, Yvonne Furneaux, Pierre Mondy, Bernard Dheran. Faithful adaptation of Dumas novel, but Jourdan hasn't the zest that Robert Donat gave the role in 1934.

Count the Hours (1953) 76m. ** D: Don Siegel. Teresa Wright, Macdonald Carey, Dolores Moran, Adele Mara. Trim but implausible story of ranch hand and pregnant wife. When police accuse them of murdering their employers, he takes blame so she can have their child.

Count Three and Pray (1955) C-102m. **½ D: George Sherman. Van Heflin, Joanne Woodward, Raymond Burr, Nancy Kulp. Atmospheric rural Americana in post-Civil War days, with Heflin exerting influence on townfolk as new pastor with reckless past. Woodward as strong-willed orphan lass and Burr the perennial villain are fine.

Count Your Blessings (1959) C-102m. ** D: Jean Negulesco. Deborah Kerr, Rossano Brazzi, Maurice Chevalier, Martin Stephens, Tom Helmore, Patricia Medina. Unfunny comedy that even Chevalier's smile can't help. Kerr marries French playboy Brazzi during WW2; he goes off philandering for years. Their child conspires to bring them together again.

Counter-Attack (1945) 90m. **½ D: Zoltan Korda. Paul Muni, Marguerite Chapman, Larry Parks, Philip Van Zandt, George Macready, Roman Bohnen. Satisfactory WW2 movie of Allied fighters going behind enemy lines to sabotage German positions; no classic, but good.

Counter Tenors, The SEE: White Voices, The

Counterfeit Killer, The (1968) C-95m. ** D: Josef Leytes. Jack Lord, Shirley Knight, Jack Weston, Charles Drake, Joseph Wiseman, Don Hanmer. Adapted from TV film THE FACELESS MAN, meandering actioner has Lord a secret service man infiltrating a counterfeit syndicate, with predictable results.

Counterfeit Plan, The (1957) 80m. ** D: Montgomery Tully. Zachary Scott, Peggie Castle, Mervyn Johns, Sydney Tafler. Scott is appropriately nasty as escaped murderer who sets up international counterfeit syndicate.

Counterfeit Traitor, The (1962) C-140m. ***½ D: George Seaton. William Holden, Lilli Palmer, Hugh Griffith, Erica Beer, Werner Peters, Eva Dahlbeck. Holden runs around Europe as a double agent during WW2, falls in love with Palmer between various dangerous missions. Authentic backgrounds and fine cast.

Counterplot (1959) 76m. ** D: Kurt Neumann. Forrest Tucker, Allison Hayes, Gerald Milton, Edmundo Rivera Alvarez, Jackie Wayne. Mundane hide-and-seeker set in Puerto Rico where Tucker is hiding out from police and his double-dealing attorney.

Counterpoint (1967) C-107m. **½ D: Ralph Nelson. Charlton Heston, Maximilian Schell, Kathryn Hays, Leslie Nielsen. Flabby tale of orchestra leader Heston caught behind

German lines in WW2 with his symphonic orchestra; battle of wits against Nazi commander Schell.

Countess of Monte Cristo, The (1948) 77m. ** D: Frederick de Cordova. Sonja Henie, Olga San Juan, Dorothy Hart, Michael Kirby, Arthur Treacher. Sonja and Olga pretend to be royal visitors in this limp costume comedy.

Country Girl, The (1954) 104m. ***½ D: George Seaton. Bing Crosby, Grace Kelly, William Holden, Anthony Ross. Kelly won an Oscar as wife of alcoholic singer (Crosby) trying for comeback via help of director (Holden). Crosby excels in one of his finest roles.

Courage of Black Beauty (1957) C-77m. ** D: Harold Schuster. John Crawford, Diane Brewster, J. Pat O'Malley, John Bryant. Wholesome programmer of Crawford and colt he is given.

Courage of Lassie (1946) C-92m. **½ D: Fred Wilcox. Elizabeth Taylor, Frank Morgan, Tom Drake, Selena Royle, George Cleveland. Tasteful, folksy tale of Lassie used in WW2 as a killer dog, Taylor his mistress who reforms him into kindly animal once again.

Courageous Dr. Christian, The (1940) 67m. ** D: Bernard Vorhaus. Jean Hersholt, Dorothy Lovett, Robert Baldwin, Tom Neal, Maude Eburne, Vera Lewis. If you can sit through this you're pretty brave yourself; this time the good doctor is battling a local epidemic.

Court Jester, The (1956) C-101m. ***½ D: Norman Panama, Melvin Frank. Danny Kaye, Glynis Johns, Basil Rathbone, Angela Lansbury, Robert Middleton. One of Danny's best: swashbuckler-spoof with elaborate sets, costumes, and hilarious gags as Kaye, a jester, is forced into a jousting match with villain Middleton.

Court Martial (1955-British) 105m. **½ D: Anthony Asquith. David Niven, Margaret Leighton, Victor Maddern, Maurice Denham. Diverting courtroom story of officer Niven accused of stealing military funds; trial reveals provocations of grasping wife Leighton, etc.

Court-Martial of Billy Mitchell, The (1955) C-100m. *** D: Otto Preminger. Gary Cooper, Charles Bickford, Ralph Bellamy, Rod Steiger, Elizabeth Montgomery. Honest adaptation of true story of military pioneer on trial for predicting Japanese attack on U. S. in 1930's. Slowly paced film saves powerful Steiger for closing reels as clever attorney.

Courtship of Andy Hardy, The (1942) 93m. D: George B. Seitz. Lewis Stone, Mickey Rooney, Cecilia Parker, Fay Holden, Ann Rutherford, Sara Haden, Donna Reed, William Lundigan, Frieda Inescort. SEE: **Andy Hardy** series.

Courtship of Eddie's Father, The (1963) C-117m. *** D: Vincente Minnelli. Glenn Ford, Shirley Jones, Stella Stevens, Dina Merrill, Roberta Sherwood. Cute family comedy with Ronny Howard trying to find wife for widower father Ford.

Cousins, The (1959-French, dubbed) 112m. ** D: Claude Chabrol. Jean-Claude Brialy, Gerard Blain, Juliette Mayniel. Uneven drama concerning competition between cousins Brialy-Blain for affection of Meyniel.

Cover Girl (1944) C-107m. *** D: Charles Vidor. Rita Hayworth, Gene Kelly, Lee Bowman, Phil Silvers, Jinx Falkenburg, Eve Arden, Otto Kruger, Anita Colby. Incredibly clichéd plot is overcome by loveliness of Rita, fine musical score including "Long Ago And Far Away," and especially Kelly's solo numbers. Silvers gets some laughs, but Eve Arden steals the film as Kruger's wisecracking assistant.

Covered Wagon, The (1923) 60m. **½ D: James Cruze. J. Warren Kerrigan, Lois Wilson, Alan Hale, Ernest Torrence. Slow-paced silent forerunner of Western epics, following a wagon train as it combats Indians and the elements; beautifully photographed, but rather tame today.

Cow and I (1961-French, dubbed) 98m. *** D: Henri Verneuil. Fernandel, Rene Havard, Albert Remy, Bernard Musson. Country-style humor bolstered by Fernandel as peasant escaped from German farm prison, assisted by loyal cow.

Cow Country (1953) 82m. ** D: Lesley Selander, Curtis Bishop. Edmond O'Brien, Helen Westcott, Peggie Castle, Raymond Hatton. Earnest Western of 1880's Texas, with debt-ridden ranchers overcoming all.

Cowboy (1958) C-92m. *** D: Delmer

100

Daves. Glenn Ford, Jack Lemmon, Anna Kashfi, Brian Donlevy, Dick York. Intelligent, atmospheric Western based on Frank Harris' reminiscences as a tenderfoot. Lemmon is Harris, with Ford as his stern boss on eventful cattle roundup.

Cowboy and the Lady, The (1938) 91m. **½ D: H. C. Potter. Gary Cooper, Merle Oberon, Patsy Kelly, Walter Brennan, Fuzzy Knight, Harry Davenport. Aristocratic Oberon falls in love with rodeo star Cooper in mild comedy uplifted by stars.

Cowboy From Brooklyn, The (1938) 80m. **½ D: Lloyd Bacon. Dick Powell, Pat O'Brien, Priscilla Lane, Dick Foran, Ann Sheridan, Johnnie Davis, Ronald Reagan, Emma Dunn. Powell can only get radio job if he proves he's an authentic cowhand. Silly musicomedy includes songs "Ride Tenderfoot Ride," title tune.

Crack in the Mirror (1960) 97m. *** D: Richard Fleischer. Orson Welles, Juliette Greco, Bradford Dillman, Alexander Knox. Welles, Greco, and Dillman enact contrasting dual roles in intertwining love triangles set in contemporary Paris, involving murder, courtroom trial, and illicit love; novelty eventually wears thin, marring Grade-A effort.

Crack in the World (1965) C-96m. **½ D: Andrew Marton. Dana Andrews, Janette Scott, Kieron Moore, Alexander Knox, Peter Damon. Believable sci-fi about scientists trying to harness earth's inner energy but almost causing destruction of the world; realistic special effects.

Crack-Up (1946) 93m. *** D: Irving Reis. Pat O'Brien, Claire Trevor, Herbert Marshall, Wallace Ford. Swindler takes advantage of O'Brien's amnesia to further his art-forging racket. Fine cast in suspenseful mystery.

Craig's Wife (1936) 75m. *** D: Dorothy Arzner. Rosalind Russell, John Boles, Billie Burke, Jane Darwell, Dorothy Wilson, Alma Kruger, Thomas Mitchell. Russell scored first big success as domineering wife who thinks more of material objects than of her husband. Based on George Kelly play, remade as HARRIET CRAIG.

Cranes are Flying, The (1959-Russian, dubbed) 94m. ***½ D: Mikhail Kalatozov. Tatyana Samoilova, Alexei Batalov, Vasily Merkuryev, A. Shvorin. Lilting love story set in WW2 Russia. Doctor's son (Batalov) leaves his sweetheart (Samoilova) to join the army. She is seduced by his cousin, marries him, and from subsequent tragedies tries to rebuild her life.

Crash Dive (1943) 105m. **½ D: Archie Mayo. Tyrone Power, Anne Baxter, Dana Andrews, James Gleason, Dame May Whitty, Henry Morgan. Submarine battleground just backdrop for love story; Power and Andrews both love young Baxter. Oscar-winner for special effects, film's main asset.

Crash Landing (1958) 76m. *½ D: Fred F. Sears. Gary Merrill, Nancy Davis, Irene Hervey, Roger Smith. Insipid revelations of passengers aboard plane facing possible crash landing into the ocean.

Crash of Silence (1953-British) 93m. *** D: Alexander Mackendrick. Phyllis Calvert, Jack Hawkins, Terence Morgan, Mandy Miller. Honest drama of young deaf girl (Miller) and her mother's dilemma: keep her at home or send her to special school. Sensibly acted.

Crashing Las Vegas (1956) 62m. D: Jean Yarbrough. Leo Gorcey, Huntz Hall, Jimmy Murphy, David Condon. SEE: Bowery Boys series.

Crashout (1955) 90m. **½ D: Lewis R. Foster. William Bendix, Arthur Kennedy, Luther Adler, William Talman. Low-budget but interesting story of prison break headed by Bendix. Kennedy as humane gang member is fine.

Crazy Desire (1964-Italian, dubbed) 108m. ***½ D: Luciano Salce. Ugo Tognazzi, Catherine Spaak, Gianni Garko, Beatrice Altariba. Disarming fluff of Tognazzi enamoured of young fun-seekers, and Spaak in particular.

Crazy House (1943) 80m. *** D: Edward F. Cline. Ole Olsen, Chic Johnson, Martha O'Driscoll, Patric Knowles, Cass Daley, Percy Kilbride, Leighton Noble. Olsen & Johnson take over film studio to make epic in frantic musicomedy with guests galore: Basil Rathbone, Count Basie, Allan Jones, Edgar Kennedy, Billy Gilbert, Andy Devine, etc.

Crazy Over Horses (1951) 65m. D: William Beaudine. Huntz Hall, Leo

Gorcey, David Gorcey, William Benedict, Bernard Punsley SEE: Bowery Boys series.

Crazylegs (1953) 87m. *½ D: Francis D. Lyon. Elroy Hirsch, Lloyd Nolan, Joan Vohs, Louise Lorimer. Inconclusive fiction based on the football escapades of Elroy Crazylegs Hirsch with gridiron star playing himself.

Creature from the Black Lagoon (1954) 79m. ** D: Jack Arnold. Richard Carlson, Julia Adams, Richard Denning, Antonio Moreno. Unsuspenseful sci-fi as expedition travels up Amazon River, encountering the Gillman, who hankers for Adams. When released theatrically, shown 3-D. Follow-ups: RETURN OF THE CREATURE, THE CREATURE WALKS AMONG US.

Creature Walks Among Us, The (1956) 78m. ** D: John Sherwood. Jeff Morrow, Rex Reason, Leigh Snowden, Gregg Palmer. Follow-up to CREATURE FROM BLACK LAGOON has Gill-man caged by humans, returning to ocean after few mild tantrums.

Creature with the Atom Brain (1955) 70m. ** D: Edward L. Cahn. Richard Denning, Angela Stevens, Gregory Gaye, Tristram Coffin. Passable hokum: scientist revives the dead via high-charged brain tissue, and these robots are used by gangster seeking revenge.

Creeper, The (1948) 64m. ** D: Jean Yarbrough. Eduardo Ciannelli, Onslow Stevens, June Vincent, Ralph Morgan, Janis Wilson. Ciannelli is mad doctor whose serum turns man into catlike killer.

Creeping Unknown, The (1956-British) 78m. ** D: Val Guest. Brian Donlevy, Margia Dean, Jack Warner, Richard Wordsworth. Ordinary sci-fi with space craft returning to earth with title beast seeking to wreak havoc on all.

Crest of the Wave (1954-British) 90m. **½ D: John Boulting, Roy Boulting. Gene Kelly, John Justin, Bernard Lee, Jeff Richards. Static account of navy officer Kelly joining British research group to supervise demolition experiments.

Crime and Punishment (1935) 88m. *** D: Josef von Sternberg. Edward Arnold, Peter Lorre, Marian Marsh, Tala Birell, Elisabeth Risdon. Lorre is outstanding in smooth filming of Dostoyevsky's novel about man haunted by murder he committed.

Crime and Punishment (1958-French, dubbed) 108m. *** D: Georges Lampin. Jean Gabin, Marina Vlady, Ulla Jacobsson, Bernard Blier. Perceptive updating of Dostoyevsky novel set in Paris. Retitled: THE MOST DANGEROUS SIN.

Crime & Punishment, USA (1959) 79m. **½ D: Denis Sanders. George Hamilton, Mary Murphy, Frank Silvera, Marian Seldes, John Harding, Wayne Heffley. Trim, updated version of Dostoyevsky novel has Hamilton (film debut) a law student who becomes involved in robbery and murder.

Crime Against Joe (1956) 69m. ** D: Lee Sholem. John Bromfield, Julie London, Henry Calvin, Patricia Blake. Standard find-the-actual-murderer fare.

Crime by Night (1944) 72m. **½ D: Geoffrey Homes. Jane Wyman, Jerome Cowan, Faye Emerson, Eleanor Parker, Creighton Hale. Good little murder mystery with detective Cowan unwittingly walking into murder case.

Crime Doctor In 1943 Columbia Pictures took Max Marcin's successful radio show CRIME DOCTOR and initiated a film series of that name with Warner Baxter in the lead. The first film set the premise of an amnesia victim named Dr. Ordway becoming the country's leading criminal psychologist, later discovering that he was a gang-leader himself before a blow clouded his memory. This idea served as the basis for ten fairly respectable, enjoyable mysteries, all starring Baxter as Ordway. Most of the films followed a standard whodunit formula, but were well-acted and directed (by such people as William Castle and George Archainbaud), with competent players rounded up from Columbia's contract list. The films moved along briskly, most of them running barely over an hour. CRIME DOCTOR (1943) is interesting for its depiction of the origin of the character; CRIME DOCTOR'S GAMBLE takes him to Europe for an above-average murder hunt; and SHADOWS IN THE NIGHT has the distinction of refined George Zucco as an arch-fiend. Unremarkable but interesting, the Crime Doctor films held their own among the many mystery series of the day.

Crime Doctor (1943) 66m. D: Michael Gordon. Warner Baxter, Margaret Lindsay, John Litel, Ray Collins, Harold Huber, Don Costello, Leon Ames.

Crime Doctor's Courage, The (1945) 70m. D: George Sherman. Warner Baxter, Hillary Brooke, Jerome Cowan, Robert Scott, Lloyd Corrigan, Emory Parnell, Stephen Crane.

Crime Doctor's Diary (1949) 61m. D: Seymour Friedman. Warner Baxter, Lois Maxwell, Adele Jergens, Robert Armstrong.

Crime Doctor's Gamble, The (1947) 66m. D: William Castle. Warner Baxter, Micheline Cheirel, Roger Dann, Steven Geray, Marcel Journet.

Crime Doctor's Manhunt (1946) 61m. D: William Castle. Warner Baxter, Ellen Drew, William Frawley, Frank Sully, Claire Carleton, Bernard Nedell.

Crime Doctor's Strangest Case (1943) 68m. D: Eugene J. Forde. Warner Baxter, Lynn Merrick, Reginald Denny, Barton MacLane, Jerome Cowan, Rose Hobart, Gloria Dickson.

Crime Doctor's Warning, The (1945) 69m. D: William Castle. Warner Baxter, John Litel, Dusty Anderson, Coulter Irwin, Miles Mander, John Abbott.

Crime Does Not Pay (1962-French, dubbed) 159m. **½ D: Gerard Oury. Pierre Brasseur, Gino Cervi, Danielle Darrieux, Gabriele Ferzetti, Annie Girardot, Michele Morgan, Richard Todd. Interesting gimmick for threepart film—would-be-wife-killer goes to cinema showing trio of stories on murder: THE SPIDER'S WEB, THE FENYROU CASE, and THE MASK. Retitled: GENTLE ART OF MURDER.

Crime in the Streets (1956) 91m. ** D: Don Siegel. James Whitmore, John Cassavetes, Sal Mineo, Mark Rydell. Cassavetes and Mineo do justice by script as juvenile delinquents planning gang murder, conflicting with socialworker Whitmore.

Crime of Dr. Crespi, The (1935) 63m. ** D: John A. Auer, Erich von Stroheim, Dwight Frye, Paul Guilfoyle, Harriett Russell, John Bohn. Von Stroheim gets even with man who loves his girl by planning unspeakable torture for him. Low-grade chiller.

Crime of Passion (1957) 84m. ** D: Gerd Oswald. Barbara Stanwyck, Sterling Hayden, Raymond Burr, Fay Wray, Virginia Grey. Stanwyck is rough and tough as grasping wife who'll do anything to forward hubby's career.

Crime School (1938) 86m. ** D: Lewis Seiler. Humphrey Bogart, Billy Halop, Bobby Jordan, Huntz Hall, Leo Gorcey, Gale Page. If you can see Bogart as a reform school warden, you're already one up on the writers; not bad, but predictable.

Crime Wave (1954) 74m. ** D: Andre de Toth. Sterling Hayden, Gene Nelson, Phyllis Kirk, Charles Bronson, Ted de Corsia. Low-keyed telling of ex-con Nelson's attempt to go straight, despite insistence of crooks that he help on bank robbery; Hayden is toothpick-chewing cop.

Crime Without Passion (1934) 72m. *** D: Ben Hecht, Charles MacArthur. Claude Rains, Margo, Whitney Bourne, Stanley Ridges, Esther Dale, Leslie Adams. Bizarre, fascinating melodrama of callous lawyer Rains, jealous of Margo's escorts. Helen Hayes and Fannie Brice have brief cameos in hotel lobby scene.

Criminal Lawyer (1951) 74m. *½ D: Seymour Friedman. Pat O'Brien, Jane Wyatt, Carl Benton Reid, Mary Castle. Alcoholic attorney O'Brien sobers up to defend friend saddled with homicide charge.

Crimson Ghost, The SEE: Cyclotrode "X"

Crimson Kimono (1959) 82m. ** D: Samuel Fuller. Victoria Shaw, Glenn Corbett, James Shigeta, Anna Lee, Paul Dubov, Jaclynne Greene. Corbett and Shigeta are tight-lipped L. A. detectives investigating a stripper's murder; mutual admiration for Shaw causes discord.

Crimson Pirate, The (1952) 104m. **½ D: Robert Siodmak. Burt Lancaster, Nick Cravat, Eva Bartok, Torin Thatcher, Christopher Lee. Lancaster has athletic romp as 1750's buccaneer with a thirst for adventure often satisfied in this well-paced movie.

Cripple Creek (1952) C-78m. **½ D: Ray Nazarro. George Montgomery, Karin Booth, Jerome Courtland, Richard Egan. Government agents Montgomery and Courtland track down mining crooks by joining gang in this average oater.

Crisis (1950) 95m. **½ D: Richard Brooks. Cary Grant, Jose Ferrer, Paula Raymond, Signe Hasso, Ramon Novarro, Antonio Moreno, Leon Ames, Gilbert Roland. Melodrama of American doctor (Grant) held in South American country to treat ailing dictator (Ferrer); intriguing but slow.

Criss Cross (1949) 87m. **½ D: Robert Siodmak. Burt Lancaster, Yvonne de Carlo, Dan Duryea, Stephen McNally. Low-keyed robbery yarn sparked by Lancaster and Duryea each trying to do the other in.

Critic's Choice (1963) C-100m. **½ D: Don Weis. Bob Hope, Lucille Ball, Marilyn Maxwell, Rip Torn, Jessie Royce Landis, Marie Windsor, John Dehner. An in-joke Broadway play diluted for movie audience consumption. Lucy as a novice playwright outshines Hope who plays her drama critic hubby. Film emerges as tired, predictable comedy, with best moments contributed by supporting players.

Crooked Road, The (1965-British) 86m. **½ D: Don Chaffey. Robert Ryan, Stewart Granger, Nadia Gray, Marius Goring, George Coulouris. OK battle of wits between dictator Granger and newspaperman Ryan, who's got the goods on him.

Crooked Web, The (1955) 77m. *½ D: Nathan Juran. Frank Lovejoy, Mari Blanchard, Richard Denning, Richard Emory. Ponderous unspinning of government officer's ensnaring prime suspect to return to Germany, scene of the crime.

Crooked Way, The (1949) 90m. ** D: Robert Florey. John Payne, Sonny Tufts, Ellen Drew, Rhys Williams. Military hero Payne recovers from shellshock to be confronted by criminal past and his old gang seeking to eliminate him.

Cross of Lorraine, The (1943) 90m. ***½ D: Tay Garnett. Jean-Pierre Aumont, Gene Kelly, Cedric Hardwicke, Richard Whorf, Joseph Calleia, Peter Lorre, Hume Cronyn. High-grade propaganda of WW2 POW camp with hero Aumont rousing defeated Kelly to battle; Whorf is dedicated doctor, Lorre a despicable Nazi, Cronyn a fickle informer.

Crossed Swords (1954-Italian, dubbed) C-86m. *½ D: Nato de Angelis, Arthur Villiesid, Milton Krims. Errol Flynn, Gina Lollobrigida, Cesare Danova, Nadia Grey. Unsuccessful attempt to recapture flavor of swashbucklers of 1930's; set in 16th-century Italy with Flynn out to save Gina and her father's kingdom.

Crossfire (1947) 86m. ***½ D: Edward Dmytryk. Robert Young, Robert Mitchum, Robert Ryan, Gloria Grahame, Paul Kelly, Richard Benedict, Sam Levene. Engrossing film of insane ex-soldier leading city police in murderous chase. Anti-Semitic question handled with taste, intelligence.

Crossroads (1942) 84m. ** D: Jack Conway. William Powell, Hedy Lamarr, Claire Trevor, Basil Rathbone, Margaret Wycherly, Felix Bressart, Sig Ruman. Improbable story of French diplomat Powell discovered to be notorious criminal suffering from amnesia. Story doesn't jell.

Crosstrap (1961-British) 62m. *½ D: Robert Hartford-Davis. Laurence Payne, Jill Adams, Gary Cockrell, Zena Marshall. Juvenile thriller involving rival gangs of jewel thieves and murder.

Crosswinds (1951) C-93m. ** D: Lewis R. Foster. John Payne, Rhonda Fleming, Forrest Tucker, Robert Lowery. Payne tries to retrieve cargo of gold from plane that crashed in New Guinea, encountering headhunters, crooks, and gorgeous Fleming.

Crowd Roars, The (1932) 85m. **½ D: Howard Hawks. James Cagney, Joan Blondell, Ann Dvorak, Eric Linden, Guy Kibbee, Frank McHugh. Exciting racing-driver tale with Cagney in typically cocky role, familiar plot devices, but well done by Warner Bros. stock company. Remade as INDIANAPOLIS SPEEDWAY.

Crowd Roars, The (1938) 92m. **½ D: Richard Thorpe. Robert Taylor, Edward Arnold, Frank Morgan, Maureen O'Sullivan, William Gargan, Lionel Stander, Jane Wyman. Tippling Morgan gets son Taylor into fighting game, and involved with underworld chief Arnold in well-handled yarn.

Crowded Sky, The (1960) C-105m. **½ D: Joseph Pevney. Dana Andrews, Rhonda Fleming, Efrem Zimbalist, Jr., John Kerr, Troy Donahue, Patsy Kelly. Slick film focusing on emotional problems aboard jet liner and navy plane bound for fateful collision; superficial but diverting.

Crucible, The (1958-French, dubbed) 120m. *** D: Raymond Rouleau. Simone Signoret, Yves Montand, Mylene Demongeot, Raymond Rouleau. If anything, Jean-Paul Sartre's version improves upon Arthur Miller parable of Salem witch trials in 17th-century New England; Signoret is outstanding.

Cruel Sea, The (1953-British) 121m. ***½ D: Charles Frend. Jack Hawkins, Donald Sinden, Stanley Baker, Virginia McKenna. Well-conceived documentary-style account of British warship during WW2 and its crew.

Cruel Swamp SEE: Swamp Women.

Crusades, The (1935) 123m. *** D: Cecil B. de Mille. Loretta Young, Henry Wilcoxon, Ian Keith, Katherine de Mille, C. Aubrey Smith. Love, action, and orgies galore in typical De Mille medieval spectacle that's good for fun, with Young a glamorous heroine.

Cry Danger (1951) 79m. *** D: Richard Parrish. Dick Powell, Rhonda Fleming, Richard Erdman, Regis Toomey. Effective revenge yarn as ex-con Powell hunts down those responsible for his prison term.

Cry For Happy (1961) C-110m. **½ D: George Marshall. Glenn Ford, Donald O'Connor, Miiko Taka, Myoshi Umeki. Poor man's TEAHOUSE OF AUGUST MOON, involving Navy photography team in Tokyo using a geisha house for their home.

Cry From the Streets, A (1959-British) 99m. *** D: Lewis Gilbert. Max Bygraves, Barbara Murray, Colin Peterson, Dana Wilson, Kathleen Harrison. Poignant handling of story about homeless London children and social workers who attempt to rehabilitate them; plot is forgivably diffuse and episodic.

Cry Havoc (1943) 97m. **½ D: Richard Thorpe. Margaret Sullavan, Ann Sothern, Joan Blondell, Fay Bainter, Marsha Hunt, Ella Raines, Frances Gifford. Sincere story of nurses in Philippines. Like similar SO PROUDLY WE HAIL, it doesn't have impact it had when first released but performances are still good.

Cry in the Night (1956) 75m. **½ D: Frank Tuttle. Edmond O'Brien, Brian Donlevy, Natalie Wood, Raymond Burr. Capable cast enhances this tale of deranged man kidnapping girl from lover, with suspenseful police hunt ensuing.

Cry of Battle (1963) 99m. **½ D: Irving Lerner. Van Heflin, Rita Moreno, James MacArthur, Leopoldo Salcedo. Uneven actioner set in Philippines with MacArthur as son of wealthy businessman who joins partisan cause, finding romance and sense of maturity.

Cry of the City (1948) 95m. **½ D: Robert Siodmak. Victor Mature, Richard Conte, Fred Clark, Shelley Winters, Betty Garde, Debra Paget. Rehash of MANHATTAN MELODRAMA about childhood pals, one who becomes a cop, the other a criminal—slick but predictable.

Cry of the Hunted (1953) 80m. ** D: Joseph H. Lewis. Vittorio Gassman, Barry Sullivan, Polly Bergen, William Conrad. Unnoteworthy chase film involving escaped convict Gassman being sought by lawman Sullivan, with a few atmospheric sequences set in Louisiana marshland.

Cry of the Werewolf (1944) 63m. ** D: Harold Levin. Nina Foch, Stephen Crane, Osa Massen, Blanche Yurka, Fritz Lieber. Gypsy girl hears the cry when it's proved her mother was a werewolf; OK low-grade thriller.

Cry Terror (1958) 96m. *** D: Andrew L. Stone. James Mason, Rod Steiger, Inger Stevens, Neville Brand, Angie Dickinson. Tight pacing conceals implausibilities in caper of psychopath Steiger forcing Mason to aid him in master extortion plot, set in N.Y.C. Stevens registers well as Mason's frightened but resourceful wife.

Cry the Beloved Country (1951-British) 105m. ***½ D: Zoltan Korda. Canada Lee, Charles Carson, Sidney Poitier, Geoffrey Keen, Reginald Ngeabo. Vivid filmization of Alan Paton's book on Negro's plight in cities of South Africa and temperaments separating whites and blacks.

Cry Tough (1959) 83m. ** D: Paul Stanley. John Saxon, Linda Cristal, Joseph Calleia, Arthur Batanides, Joe De Santis, Barbara Luna, Frank Puglia. Saxon emotes well as Puerto Rican ex-con tempted back into criminal life by environment and his old gang. Torrid Saxon-Cristal love scenes shot for foreign markets gave film initial publicity.

Cry Vengeance (1954) 83m. **½ D: Mark Stevens. Mark Stevens, Martha Hyer, Skip Homeier, Joan Vohs. Stevens lives up to title as innocent ex-con seeking gangsters who sent him to prison.

Cry Wolf (1947) 83m. ** D: Peter Godfrey. Barbara Stanwyck, Errol Flynn, Geraldine Brooks, Richard Basehart, Jerome Cowan. Static adventure-mystery of Stanwyck attempting to untangle family secrets at late husband's estate.

Crystal Ball, The (1943) 81m. ** D: Elliott Nugent. Paulette Goddard, Ray Milland, Virginia Field, Gladys George, William Bendix, Ernest Truex. Weak comedy of beauty-contest loser who becomes fortune-teller; good players left stranded by stale material.

Cult of the Cobra (1955) 82m. **½ D: Francis D. Lyon. Faith Domergue, Richard Long, Marshall Thompson, Jack Kelly, David Janssen. Minor camp masterpiece involves ex-servicemen being killed by exotic serpent lady Domergue.

Curley (1947) C-53m. ** D: Bernard Carr. Larry Olsen, Frances Rafferty, Eilene Janssen, Walter Abel, Marie Wilson, Donald Meek, Sheldon Leonard. Inconsequential juvenile nonsense about youngsters playing pranks on their schoolteacher. Original title: HAL ROACH COMEDY CARNIVAL.

Curly Top (1935) 75m. **½ D: Irving Cummings. Shirley Temple, John Boles, Rochelle Hudson, Jane Darwell, Rafaela Ottiano, Arthur Treacher. Shirley sings "Animal Crackers In My Soup" as she plays Cupid again, this time for sister Hudson and handsome Boles.

Curse of the Cat People, The (1944) 70m. *** D: Gunther Fritsch and Robert Wise. Simone Simon, Kent Smith, Jane Randolph, Elizabeth Russell, Julia Dean, Sir Lancelot. Despite title, sensitive fantasy of child's vision of dead mother guiding her to various adventures, produced by Val Lewton.

Curse of the Demon (1958-British) 83m. **½ D: Jacques Tourneur. Dana Andrews, Peggy Cummins, Niall MacGinnis, Maurice Denham. Andrews unleashes unspeakable horror when he discovers ancient magic stone. Good cast helps this suspenseful science-fiction tale set in England.

Curse of the Faceless Man (1958) 66m. Bomb D: Edward L. Cahn. Richard Anderson, Elaine Edwards, Adele Mara, Luis Van Rooten. Laughable attempt at horror yarn, with ridiculous title monster aroused from sleep by excavation on site of ancient Pompeii.

Curse of the Fly, The (1965-British) 86m. ** D: Don Sharp. Brian Donlevy, Carole Gray, George Baker, Michael Graham, Jeremy Wilkins, Charles Carson. When will they ever learn? Same family involved in previous Fly adventures gets involved with the same human-insect transformation all over again. Not up to previous efforts in series.

Curse of the Mummy's Tomb, The (1965-British) C-81m. ** D: Michael Carreras. Terence Morgan, Ronald Howard, Fred Clark, Jeanne Roland, George Pastell. Programmer horror attempt involving mummy seeking revenge on people who unearthed him.

Curse of the Undead (1959) 79m. ** D: Edward Dein. Eric Fleming, Michael Pate, Kathleen Crowley, John Hoyt, Bruce Gordon, Edward Binns. Once-novel mixture of horror-Western tale hasn't much zing. Mysterious stranger has vampirish designs on Crowley.

Curse of the Voodoo (1965-British) 77m. *½ D: Lindsay Shonteff. Bryant Halliday, Dennis Price, Lisa Daniely, Mary Kerridge. Modest film promises some exotic native black magic hijinks, but nothing worthwhile occurs.

Curse of the Werewolf, The (1961-British) C-91m. **½ D: Terence Fisher. Clifford Evans, Oliver Reed, Yvonne Romain, Anthony Dawson. Reed has wolf's blood and struggles to control the monster within him; it finally erupts when he is denied his girl's love. Eerie atmosphere pervades this good chiller.

Curse of the Yellow Snake, The (1963-German, dubbed) 98m. **½ D: Franz Gottlieb. Joachim Fuchsberger, Eddi Arent, Brigitte Grothum, Charles Regnier, Werner Peters, Claus Holm. Edgar Wallace yarn dealing with anti-Western uprising by fanatic Oriental cult; eerie and atmospheric.

Curtain Call at Cactus Creek (1950) 86m. **½ D: Charles Lamont. Donald O'Connor, Gale Storm, Vincent Price, Walter Brennan, Eve Arden. Sometimes foolish slapstick as O'Connor, touring with road show, gets involved with bank robbers and irate citizens of Arizona.

Curtain Up (1953-British) 81m. **½ D: Ralph Smart. Robert Morley, Margaret Rutherford, Kay Kendall, Joan Rice. Droll little film of rural repertory company battling among themselves as they prepare for their dramatic season.

Curucu, Beast of the Amazon (1956) C-76m. *½ D: Curt Siodmak. John Bromfield, Beverly Garland, Tom Payne, Harvey Chalk. Bromfield and Garland set out on African hunt to find title monster. Pure cornball.

Cyclops (1957) 75m. ** D: Bert I. Gordon. James Craig, Gloria Talbott, Lon Chaney, Jr., Tom Drake. Sci-fi is set in Mexico with Talbott seeking boyfriend Craig but finding one-eyed giant beast instead.

Cyclotrode "X" (1946) 100m. **½ D: William Witney, Fred Brannon. Charles Quigley, Linda Stirling, Clayton Moore, I. Stanford Jolley. Well-paced Republic cliff-hanger, with bouncy action as sinister Crimson Ghost tries to gain control of supernuclear device. Re-edited movie serial: THE CRIMSON GHOST.

Cynara (1932) 75m. ** D: King Vidor. Ronald Colman, Kay Francis, Henry Stephenson, Phyllis Barry, Paul Porcasi, Viva Tattersall. Colman is good as British lawyer who has interlude with working-girl while wife is gone, but film dates badly, is stiff today.

Cynthia (1947) 98m. *½ D: Robert Z. Leonard. Elizabeth Taylor, George Murphy, S. Z. Sakall, Mary Astor, Gene Lockhart, Spring Byington, Jimmy Lydon. Sugary film of sickly girl Taylor finding outlet in music; good cast wasted.

Cyrano de Bergerac (1950) 112m. **** D: Michael Gordon. Jose Ferrer, Mala Powers, William Prince, Morris Carnovsky, Elena Verdugo. Ferrer received an Oscar for portraying the tragic wit, renowned for his nose but longing for love of a beautiful lady. Based on Edmond Rostand play of 17th-century Paris.

D-Day on Mars (1945) 100m. ** D: Spencer Bennet, Fred Brannon. Dennis Moore, Linda Stirling, Roy Barcroft, James Craven, Bud Geary, Mary Moore. Average Republic nonsense keyed on action of dynamic Purple Monster fighting against alien forces bent on taking over earth; Stirling is the fetching heroine. Re-edited movie serial: THE PURPLE MONSTER STRIKES.

D-Day the Sixth of June (1956) C-106m. *** D: Henry Koster. Robert Taylor, Richard Todd, Dana Wynter, Edmond O'Brien. Well executed study of the Normandy invasion during WW2, with massive action shots; film focuses on American officer Taylor and British leader Todd, their professional and personal problems.

D. I., The (1957) 106m. ** D: Jack Webb. Jack Webb, Don Dubbins, Lin McCarthy, Barbara Pepper. Potentially intriguing narrative of marine drill instructor pushing his men to breaking point, becomes typical bootcamp account of life at Parris Island.

D.O.A. (1949) 83m. *** D: Rudolph Mate. Edmond O'Brien, Pamela Britton, Luther Adler, Neville Brand, Henry Hart, Virginia Lee, Beverly (Garland) Campbell. Surprisingly well-done suspenser involving O'Brien, almost murdered, setting out to find out who made the attempt and why.

Daddy Long Legs (1955) C-126m. **½ D: Jean Negulesco. Fred Astaire, Leslie Caron, Terry Moore, Thelma Ritter, Fred Clark. Overly long adaptation of Jean Webster novel about playboy (Astaire) anonymously sponsoring waif's (Caron) school education, falling in love; some imaginative dance numbers.

Daffodil Killer SEE: **Devil's Daffodil**.

Daggers of Blood SEE: **With Fire and Sword**.

Daisy Kenyon (1947) 99m. **½ D: Otto Preminger. Joan Crawford, Dana

Andrews, Henry Fonda, Ruth Warrick, Martha Stewart, Peggy Ann Garner. Talky love triangle with Crawford torn between Fonda and married man Andrews.

Dakota (1945) 82m. ** D: Joseph Kane. John Wayne, Vera Ralston, Walter Brennan, Ward Bond, Ona Munson, Hugo Haas. Sprawling Wayne vehicle with Duke involved in pioneer railroad territory dispute; Vera is his lovely wife!

Dakota Incident (1956) C-88m. **½ D: Lewis R. Foster. Linda Darnell, Dale Robertson, John Lund, Ward Bond. Indians attack stagecoach, leading to fight to the finish.

Dakota Lil (1950) C-88m. ** D: Lesley Selander. George Montgomery, Marie Windsor, Rod Cameron, Marion Martin, Wallace Ford. Pedestrian Western saved by Windsor's vitality in title role as crook who helps lawmen trap railroad thieves.

Daleks-Invasion Earth 2150 A.D. (1966-British) C-84m. **½ D: Gordon Flemyng. Peter Cushing, Bernard Cribbins, Andrew Keir, Ray Brooks. Futuristic sci-fi deals with Daleks' conquest of earth, turning people into robots; moves along at nice clip. Retitled: INVASION EARTH 2150 A.D.

Dallas (1950) C-94m. **½ D: Stuart Heisler. Gary Cooper, Ruth Roman, Steve Cochran, Raymond Massey, Antonio Moreno. Cooper returns to Big D of post-Civil War days seeking revenge; finds love with Roman and gunplay from Cochran and other intended victims.

Dalton Girls, The (1957) 71m. *½ D: Reginald LeBorg. Merry Anders, Penny Edwards, Sue George, John Russell, Lisa Davis. Gimmick of female bandits wears thin in mild Western of Dalton Brothers' relatives carrying on in family tradition.

Dam Busters, The (1954-British) C-102m. **½ D: Michael Anderson. Richard Todd, Michael Redgrave, Ursula Jeans, Basil Sydney. During WW2, British devise a plan to blow up the Germans' Ruhr dam; film intelligently recounts the episode.

Dames (1934) 90m. *** D: Ray Enright. Joan Blondell, Dick Powell, Ruby Keeler, Zasu Pitts, Hugh Herbert, Guy Kibbee, Phil Regan. Short on plot (let's-back-a-Broadway-musical) but top Busby Berkeley production ensembles like "I Only Have Eyes For You" and incredible "When you were a Smile on your Mother's Lips and a Twinkle in your Daddy's Eye."

Damn Citizen (1958) 88m. **½ D: Robert Gordon. Keith Andes, Maggie Hayes, Gene Evans, Lynn Bari. Realistically told account of WW2 veteran (Andes) hired to wipe out corruption in state police.

Damn the Defiant! (1962-British) C-101m. *** D: Lewis Gilbert. Alec Guinness, Dirk Bogarde, Maurice Denham, Nigel Stock, Richard Carpenter, Anthony Quayle. Bogarde vs. Guinness in stalwart tale of British warship during Napoleonic campaign. Production shows great attention to historic detail.

Damn Yankees (1958) C-110m. *** D: George Abbott, Stanley Donen. Tab Hunter, Gwen Verdon, Ray Walston, Russ Brown. Broadway musical expanded to lively film. Hunter nifty as rejuvenated baseball fan, now star player; Verdon is Lola, temptress helper of Devil Walston. Songs: "You've Got To Have Heart," "Whatever Lola Wants."

Damned Don't Cry, The (1950) 103m. **½ D: Vincent Sherman. Joan Crawford, David Brian, Steve Cochran, Kent Smith, Richard Egan. Follow-up to FLAMINGO ROAD formula; Crawford is well cast as lower-class gal rising to wealth via wit and looks, discovering too late that a gangster's moll has no right to love and happiness.

Damon and Pythias (1962-Italian, dubbed) C-99m. ** D: Curtis Bernhardt. Guy Williams, Don Burnett, Ilaria Occhini, Liana Orfei, Arnoldo Foa. Title reveals all in this routine costumer making legendary figures juvenile cardboard heroes.

Damsel in Distress, A (1937) 98m. *** D: George Stevens. Fred Astaire, George Burns, Gracie Allen, Joan Fontaine, Constance Collier, Reginald Gardiner, Montagu Love. Bright Gershwin musical set in London; Fontaine is heiress whom Astaire thinks is a chorus girl. Burns & Allen have never been better, even get to sing and dance. Songs include "Foggy Day in London Town," "Nice Work if You Can Get It."

Dance, Fools, Dance (1931) 81m.

**½ D: Harry Beaumont. Joan Crawford, Cliff Edwards, Clark Gable, Earl Foxe, Natalie Moorhead. Crawford, alone in the world, becomes reporter out to expose mobster Gable by winning him over. Interesting for early Gable-Crawford teaming; brisk drama.

Dance, Girl, Dance (1940) 90m. **½ D: Dorothy Arzner. Maureen O'Hara, Louis Hayward, Lucille Ball, Virginia Field, Ralph Bellamy, Maria Ouspenskaya, Mary Carlisle. O'Hara and Ball both have their eye on Hayward in good romantic drama. Ouspenskaya is fine as dancing coach.

Dance Hall (1941) 74m. *½ D: Irving Pichel. Carole Landis, Cesar Romero, William Henry, June Storey. Mild romantic musical with Romero, who runs a dance hall, falling in love with worker Landis.

Dance With Me Henry (1956) 79m. ** D: Charles Barton. Lou Costello, Bud Abbott, Gigi Perreau, Rusty Hamer. Low-grade Abbott and Costello involving the duo's ownership of rundown amusement park and two kids they've adopted; their last film together.

Dancers in the Dark (1932) 60m. **½ D: David Burton. Miriam Hopkins, Jack Oakie, George Raft, William Collier, Jr., Eugene Pallette, Lyda Roberti. Hopkins is in love with Oakie, but gangster Raft comes out of her past to cause trouble. Interesting triangle.

Dancing in the Dark (1949) C-92m. **½ D: Irving Reis. William Powell, Betsy Drake, Mark Stevens, Adolphe Menjou, Walter Catlett. Occasionally bubbly musical comedy with Powell hoping to cement good relations with film company by signing Broadway star; he becomes intrigued with talents of unknown girl, who turns out to be his daughter.

Dancing Lady (1933) 82m. **½ D: Robert Z. Leonard. Joan Crawford, Clark Gable, Franchot Tone, May Robson, Winnie Lightner, Fred Astaire, Robert Benchley, Ted Healy, Three Stooges. Crawford sings and dances in this glossy musicomedy of her romance with stage manager Gable and playboy Tone. Astaire's first film. Songs: "Everything I Have Is Yours," title tune.

Dancing Masters, The (1943) 63m. *½ D: Mal St. Clair. Oliver Hardy, Stan Laurel, Trudy Marshall, Robert Bailey, Matt Briggs, Margaret Dumont. L&H overcome by routine material, special effects that look phony. Robert Mitchum has bit as a hood.

Dancing Mothers (1927) 60m. **½ D: Herbert Brenon. Clara Bow, Alice Joyce, Dorothy Cummings, Norman Trevor. Sprightly account of Flapper Bow defying conventions as prototype of the Jazz Age. Silent film has simple plot but enthusiastic performances.

Dancing on a Dime (1941) 74m. **½ D: Joseph Santley. Grace McDonald, Robert Paige, Virginia Dale, Peter Lind Hayes. Programmer musical with wispy plot allowing for McDonald et al to do some dancing and vocalizing, such as "I Hear Music." Not bad.

Danger by My Side (1962-British) 63m. ** D: Charles Saunders. Anthony Oliver, Maureen Connell, Alan Tilvern, Bill Nagy. Connell hunts her brother's murderer by taking a job in a strip club; standard detective caper.

Danger—Love at Work (1937) 81m. **½ D: Otto Preminger. Ann Sothern, Jack Haley, Mary Boland, John Carradine, Edward Everett Horton, E. E. Clive, Stanley Fields. Wacky comedy of family headed by nutty Boland involved in shotgun wedding of Sothern and Haley.

Danger Signal (1945) 78m. ** D: Robert Florey. Faye Emerson, Zachary Scott, Rosemary DeCamp, Bruce Bennett, Mona Freeman. No-account Scott comes between Emerson and her family in this routine drama; Scott is a most convincing heel.

Danger Within SEE: **Breakout**

Dangerous (1935) 72m. **½ D: Alfred E. Green. Bette Davis, Franchot Tone, Margaret Lindsay, Alison Skipworth, John Eldredge. Former star Davis, on the skids, rehabilitated by Tone in good but syrupy tale, with Oscar-winning performance by Davis.

Dangerous Crossing (1953) 75m. **½ D: Joseph M. Newman. Jeanne Crain, Michael Rennie, Carl Betz, Casey Adams. Well-acted suspenser has Crain a new bride on ocean liner whose husband mysteriously disappears.

Dangerous Days of Kiowa Jones, The (1966) C-120m. **½ D: Alex March. Robert Horton, Diane Baker, Sal Mineo, Nehemiah Persoff, Gary Merrill. Routine telefeature Western with Horton, a drifter, deputized to take two escaped killers to jail.

Dangerous Exile (1958-British) C-90m. ** D: Brian Desmond Hurst. Louis Jourdan, Belinda Lee, Keith Mitchell, Richard O'Sullivan. Jourdan is properly dashing in OK adventurer in which he saves royalty from execution during French revolution, aided by English lass (Lee).

Dangerous Female (1931) 80m. ** D: Roy Del Ruth. Bebe Daniels, Ricardo Cortez, Dudley Digges, Robert Elliott, Thelma Todd. Good first version of Dashiell Hammett's THE MALTESE FALCON, involving murder over a priceless artifact. Remade as SATAN WAS A LADY; THE MALTESE FALCON.

Dangerous Mission (1954) C-75m. ** D: Louis King. Victor Mature, Piper Laurie, Vincent Price, William Bendix, Betta St. John. Laurie, witness to gang murder, flees N.Y.C. to Glacier National Park, where girlhunt climaxes.

Dangerous Money (1947) 64m. D: Terry Morse. Sidney Toler, Gloria Warren, Victor Sen Yung, Rick Vallin, Joseph Crehan. SEE: Charlie Chan series.

Dangerous Moonlight (1941-British) 83m. *** D: Brian Desmond Hurst. Anton Walbrook, Sally Gray, Derrick de Marney, Kenneth Kent. Intelligently presented account of concert pianist who becomes a member of the British bomber squadron during WW2; musical interludes well handled. Retitled: SUICIDE SQUADRON.

Dangerous Partners (1945) 74m. **½ D: Edward L. Cahn. James Craig, Signe Hasso, Edmund Gwenn, Audrey Totter, Mabel Paige. Craig and Hasso stumble into fortune in airplane accident; ensuing complications and chase are exciting.

Dangerous Profession, A (1949) 79m. ** D: Ted Tetzlaff. George Raft, Pat O'Brien, Ella Raines, Jim Backus, Roland Winters. Mystery yarn involving ex-bondsman, blackmail, and murder; not bad but standard.

Dangerous to Know (1938) 70m. **½ D: Robert Florey. Akim Tamiroff, Anna May Wong, Gail Patrick, Lloyd Nolan, Harvey Stephens, Anthony Quinn. Neat little B about mobster Tamiroff fixing things so he can marry high-class Patrick; everything backfires.

Dangerous When Wet (1953) C-95m. ** D: Charles Walters. Esther Williams, Fernando Lamas, Jack Carson, Charlotte Greenwood, Denise Darcel. Williams is Midwestern lass hankering to win fame and fortune by swimming English Channel; Lamas romances her in between laps, Greenwood supplies brief comic moments.

Dangerously They Live (1941) 71m. **½ D: Robert Florey. John Garfield, Nancy Coleman, Raymond Massey, Moroni Olsen, Lee Patrick. When spy Coleman is captured by Nazis, doctor Garfield comes to her aid. Tried-and-true WW2 spy melodrama.

Dangers of the Canadian Mounted SEE: R.C.M.P. and the Treasure of Genghis Khan

Daniel Boone, Trail Blazer (1956) C-76m. **½ D: Albert C. Gannaway, Ismael Rodriguez. Bruce Bennett, Lon Chaney, Faron Young, Ken Dibbs. Generally well-acted low-budget version of life of famous frontier scout, with various skirmishes with the redskins.

Dante's Inferno (1935) 88m. **½ D: Harry Lachman. Spencer Tracy, Claire Trevor, Henry B. Walthall, Alan Dinehart, Scotty Beckett. No Milton in this yarn of carnival owner who gets too big for his own good; just one scene showing Satan's paradise in good Tracy vehicle. Young Rita Hayworth dances in one scene.

Darby's Rangers (1958) 121m. **½ D: William Wellman. James Garner, Etchika Choureau, Jack Warden, Edward Byrnes, David Janssen. Garner does well in WW2 actioner as leader of assault troops in North Africa and Italy, focusing on relationship among his command and their shore romances.

Daring Young Man (1942) 73m. ** D: Frank Strayer. Joe E. Brown, Marguerite Chapman, William Wright, Roger Clark. Brown is able to make this formula Nazi spy chase film of passable interest; set in N.Y.C.

Dark Alibi (1946) 61m. D: Phil Karlson. Sidney Toler, Mantan Moreland, Ben Carter, Benson Fong, Russell Hicks, Joyce Compton, Edward Earle. SEE: Charlie Chan series.

Dark Angel, The (1935) 110m. *** D: Sidney Franklin. Fredric March,

Merle Oberon, Herbert Marshall, Janet Beecher, John Halliday. Well-acted soaper of two men in love with same woman; fighting in WW1, one of them going blind.

Dark at the Top of the Stairs, The (1960) C-123m. *** D: Delbert Mann. Robert Preston, Dorothy McGuire, Eve Arden, Angela Lansbury, Shirley Knight. Superficial handling of William Inge play set in 1920's Oklahoma, revolving around Preston's family and neighbors, their problems and frustrations; still good. Arden and Lansbury come off best.

Dark City (1950) 88m. **½ D: William Dieterle. Charlton Heston, Lizabeth Scott, Viveca Lindfors, Dean Jagger, Jack Webb. In first major film role, Heston portrays jilted WW2 veteran-turned-gambler who becomes object of gangster manhunt. Scott and Webb uplift predictable casino-club-naked-city proceedings.

Dark Command (1940) 94m. *** D: Raoul Walsh. Claire Trevor, John Wayne, Walter Pidgeon, Roy Rogers, George Hayes, Porter Hall, Marjorie Main. Elaborate production of roaming cutthroat Quantrill who reigns supreme after Civil War until he meets his match; large-scale Western.

Dark Corner, The (1946) 99m. *** D: Henry Hathaway. Lucille Ball, Clifton Webb, William Bendix, Mark Stevens, Reed Hadley, Constance Collier. Top-notch mystery with secretary Ball helping boss Stevens escape from phony murder charge. Well-acted, exciting film.

Dark Delusion (1947) 90m. D: Willis Goldbeck. Lionel Barrymore, James Craig, Lucille Bremer, Jayne Meadows, Warner Anderson. SEE: **Dr. Kildare** series.

Dark Hazard (1934) 72m. ** D: Alfred E. Green. Edward G. Robinson, Genevieve Tobin, Glenda Farrell, Henry B. Walthall, Sidney Toler. Robinson is bright spot of programmer about his precarious married life to Tobin, endangered by girlfriend Farrell and urge to gamble.

Dark Horse (1932) 75m. **½ D: Alfred E. Green. Warren William, Bette Davis, Guy Kibbee, Vivienne Osborne, Frank McHugh. Lively political spoof with nitwit Kibbee running for governor with help from campaign manager William and co-worker Davis.

Dark Intruder (1965) 59m. ** D: Harvey Hart. Leslie Nielsen, Gilbert Green, Charles Bolender, Mark Richman, Judi Meredith. Passable turn-of-the-century yarn about San Francisco strangler.

Dark Mirror, The (1946) 85m. ***½ D: Robert Siodmak. Olivia de Havilland, Lew Ayres, Thomas Mitchell, Garry Owen. Fine work by De Havilland as twin sisters, one good, one disturbed, and Ayres as doctor trying to straighten things out.

Dark Passage (1947) 106m. *** D: Delmer Daves. Humphrey Bogart, Lauren Bacall, Bruce Bennett, Agnes Moorehead. Engrossing caper of escaped convict (Bogart) undergoing plastic surgery, hiding out at Bacall's apartment till his face heals. Stars outshine far-fetched happenings.

Dark Past, The (1948) 75m. *** D: Rudolph Mate. William Holden, Nina Foch, Lee J. Cobb, Adele Jergens, Stephen Dunne. Absorbing narrative of mad-killer holding psychologist prisoner and latter's attempts to talk sense into the maniac. Remake of **BLIND ALLEY**.

Dark Victory (1939) 106m. ***½ D: Edmund Goulding. Bette Davis, George Brent, Humphrey Bogart, Geraldine Fitzgerald, Ronald Reagan, Cora Witherspoon, Henry Travers. Definitive Davis performance as spoiled socialite whose life is ending; Brent as brain surgeon husband, Fitzgerald as devoted friend register in good soaper. Bogart as Irish stablemaster seems out of place. Remade as **STOLEN HOURS**.

Dark Waters (1944) 90m. ** D: Andre de Toth. Merle Oberon, Franchot Tone, Thomas Mitchell, Fay Bainter, Rex Ingram, John Qualen, Elisha Cook, Jr. Cast sinks into the bog (some literally) in confused film of innocent girl staying with peculiar family.

Darkest Africa SEE: **Batmen of Africa**

Darling (1965-British) 122m. ***½ D: John Schlesinger. Julie Christie, Dirk Bogarde, Laurence Harvey, Roland Curram, Jose Luis de Villalonga, Alex Scott, Basil Henson. Christie won Oscar as girl who rises from commonplace life to marry an Italian noble, with several unsatisfactory love affairs in between. Film's cynical approach and flowing style improve the proceedings.

Darling, How Could You (1951) 96m. ****½ D**: Mitchell Leisen. Joan Fontaine, John Lund, Mona Freeman, Peter Hanson. Chic stars brighten old-fashioned James Barrie play about teen-ager who thinks her mother (Fontaine) is having an affair.

Date With Judy, A (1948) C-113m. ****½ D**: Richard Thorpe. Wallace Beery, Jane Powell, Elizabeth Taylor, Carmen Miranda, Xavier Cugat, Robert Stack. Weak musicomedy of two teen-agers involved in family shenanigans; highlight is Beery dancing with Miranda.

Date with the Falcon, A (1941) 63m. **D**: Irving Reis. George Sanders, Wendy Barrie, Allen Jenkins, James Gleason, Mona Maris, Frank Moran. SEE: Falcon series

Daughter of Dr. Jekyll (1957) 71m. ***½ D**: Edgar G. Ulmer. John Agar, Gloria Talbott, Arthur Shields, John Dierkes. Silly spinoff on Robert Louis Stevenson's novel. Talbott thinks she is cursed with inheritance of part human, part monster.

Daughter of Mata Hari SEE: **Mata Hari's Daughter**

Daughter of Rosie O'Grady, The (1950) C-104m. ****½ D**: David Butler. June Haver, Gordon MacRae, Debbie Reynolds, S. Z. Sakall, Jane Darwell. Formula period musical: Haver in title role, singing turn-of-the-century song favorites; talented MacRae her love interest; Sakall forced to give another cuddly stereotype.

Daughter of Shanghai (1937) 63m. **** D**: Robert Florey. Anna May Wong, Charles Bickford, Buster Crabbe, Cecil Cunningham, J. Carrol Naish, Anthony Quinn, Philip Ahn. Good-girl Wong seeks to expose Shanghai thievery in tight-knit B actioner.

Daughters Courageous (1939) 107m. ***** D**: Michael Curtiz. John Garfield, Claude Rains, Fay Bainter, Priscilla Lane, Rosemary Lane, Lola Lane, Gale Page, May Robson, Donald Crisp, Frank McHugh. Rehash of FOUR DAUGHTERS with same cast, made enjoyable by natural performances of Lane sisters, fine work by Garfield.

Daughters of Destiny (1954-French, dubbed) 94m. **** D**: Marcel Pagliero. Claudette Colbert, Michele Morgan, Andree Clement, Daniel Ivernel. Overblown, sluggish trio of tales telling of three famous women of history: Elizabeth I, Lysistrata, Joan of Arc.

David and Bathsheba (1951) C-116m. **** D**: Henry King. Gregory Peck, Susan Hayward, Raymond Massey, Kieron Moore, James Robertson Justice. Biblical epic with good production values but generally boring script; only fair performances.

David and Goliath (1961-Italian, dubbed) C-95m. **** D**: Richard Pottier, Ferdinando Baldi. Orson Welles, Ivo Payer, Edward Hilton, Eleonora Rossi-Drago, Massimo Serato. Juvenile spectacle based on biblical tale, with wooden script, bad acting, Welles as hefty King Saul.

David and Lisa (1963) 94m. ***** D**: Frank Perry. Keir Dullea, Janet Margolin, Howard Da Silva, Neva Patterson, Clifton James. Independently made film about two disturbed teen-agers is excellent, sensitively played by newcomers Dullea and Margolin. Da Silva is fine as an understanding doctor.

David Copperfield (1935) 133m. ****** D**: George Cukor. W. C. Fields, Lionel Barrymore, Madge Evans, Maureen O'Sullivan, Edna May Oliver, Lewis Stone, Basil Rathbone, Roland Young. Another expensive MGM Dickens classic well mounted with unforgettable characterizations by Fields (Micawber), Rathbone (Murdstone), Young (Uriah Heep), Oliver (Aunt Betsy), helping to bring story of British youth in old England to life. A must. Freddie Bartholomew is David as a boy, Frank Lawton plays him as an adult.

David Harum (1934) 83m. ****½ D**: James Cruze. Will Rogers, Louise Dresser, Evelyn Venable, Kent Taylor, Stepin Fetchit, Noah Beery, Charles Middleton. Foxy rancher Rogers plays matchmaker for Venable and Taylor, while spinning his own brand of folksy humor.

Davy Crockett, Indian Scout (1950) 71m. **** D**: Ford Beebe. George Montgomery, Ellen Drew, Philip Reed, Chief Thundercloud. Montgomery in title role is contrast to Fess Parker's portrayal of historical figure in minor

Western dealing with Indian attacks on wagon trains.

Dawn at Socorro (1954) C-80m. **½ D: George Sherman. Rory Calhoun, Piper Laurie, David Brian, Kathleen Hughes, Edgar Buchanan, Alex Nicol. Calhoun is gunslinger wishing to reform, but fate forces inevitable shootout.

Dawn Patrol, The (1938) 103m. ***½ D: Edmund Goulding. Errol Flynn, Basil Rathbone, David Niven, Donald Crisp, Melville Cooper, Barry Fitzgerald. Remake of 1930 classic is fine actioner of WW1 flyers in France; Rathbone as stern officer forced to send up green recruits, Flynn and Niven as pilot buddies, all excellent.

Day at the Races, A (1937) 111m. ***½ D: Sam Wood. Groucho, Harpo and Chico Marx, Allan Jones, Maureen O'Sullivan, Margaret Dumont, Douglass Dumbrille. Groucho is Dr. Hackenbush, treating hypochondriac Dumont; many classic scenes (Chico selling Groucho race tips, etc.) but not the success A NIGHT AT THE OPERA was, due to less exciting music and subplot.

Day of Fury, A (1956) C-78m. *** D: Harmon Jones. Dale Robertson, Mara Corday, Jock Mahoney, Carl Benton Reid. Offbeat study of rebellious Robertson who can't cope with conventions of Western town he lives in.

Day of the Bad Man (1958) C-81m. ** D: Harry Keller. Fred MacMurray, Joan Weldon, John Ericson, Robert Middleton. MacMurray is appropriately stiff in tame account of country judge holding off condemned man's brothers so scheduled hanging can occur.

Day of the Evil Gun (1968) 95m. ** D: Jerry Thorpe. Glenn Ford, Arthur Kennedy, Dean Jagger, Paul Fix, Royal Dano. Tedious Western with Ford tracking down redskins who stole his wife, Kennedy also in love with her.

Day of the Outlaw (1959) 90m. ** D: Andre de Toth. Robert Ryan, Burl Ives, Tina Louise, Alan Marshal, Nehemiah Persoff, Venetia Stevenson. When their leader is wounded, outlaw group seeks refuge in small town, faces showdown with pursuing cavalry. Bristling Ryan and Ives, and snowstorm, only highlights.

Day of the Triffids, The (1963) C-93m. **½ D: Steve Sekely. Howard Keel, Nicole Maurey, Janette Scott, Kieron Moore, Mervyn Johns. Meteor showers blind local populace, also drop strange pods about countryside which grow into man-eating plants. Good special effects.

Day the Earth Caught Fire, The (1962-British) 90m. *** D: Val Guest. Janet Munro, Leo McKern, Edward Judd, Michael Goodliffe, Bernard Braden. Intelligent sci-fi of atomic explosions drawing earth toward sun and sure doom. Focuses on human aspect of world coming to an end.

Day the Earth Stood Still, The (1951) 92m. ***½ D: Robert Wise. Michael Rennie, Patricia Neal, Hugh Marlowe, Sam Jaffe. Superior science-fiction with Rennie as a visitor from another planet on an exploratory mission to earth. Klaktu biranankto!

Day the Sky Exploded, The (1958-Italian, dubbed) 80m. **½ D: Paolo Heusch. Paul Hubschmid, Madeleine Fischer, Fiorella Mari, Ivo Garrani. Film doesn't live up to potential excitement as exploding missile in outer space sends debris to earth, causing chaos.

Day the World Ended, The (1956) 82m. ** D: Roger Corman. Richard Denning, Lori Nelson, Adele Jergens, Touch Connors. Modest sci-fi involving survivors of radiation blast and interplay of human nature that causes friction among the group.

Day-Time Wife (1939) 71m. ** D: Gregory Ratoff. Tyrone Power, Linda Darnell, Warren William, Binnie Barnes, Wendy Barrie. Power and Darnell make an engaging couple, even in lightweight fare such as this: wife gets office job to see if work is really all play.

Daybreak (1946-British) 88m. ** D: Compton Bennett. Eric Portman, Ann Todd, Maxwell Reed, Bill Owen, Jane Hylton. Murky tale of young couple living on houseboat, with infidelity causing traumatic repercussion to all.

Days of Glory (1944) 86m. **½ D: Jacques Tourneur. Gregory Peck, Alan Reed, Maria Palmer, Lowell Gilmore, Tamara Toumanova. Sincere but plodding WW2 action drama with the Russians combatting Nazi enemies.

Days of Thrills and Laughter (1961)

93m. **** Compiled by Robert Youngson. The third Youngson compilation of old movie clips is as funny and exciting as his first two. Scenes with Laurel and Hardy, Chaplin, the Keystone Kops, and others are hilarious, and action scenes with Doug Fairbanks and Pearl White are still fun. Nostalgic and thoroughly enjoyable.

Days of Wine and Roses (1962) 117m. ***1/2 D: Blake Edwards. Jack Lemmon, Lee Remick, Charles Bickford, Jack Klugman, Alan Hewitt, Tom Palmer, Jack Albertson. Modern LOST WEEKEND set in San Francisco, with Lemmon marrying Remick and pulling her into state of alcoholism. Realistic direction and uncompromising writing combine for excellent results; poignant score by Henry Mancini.

Dead End (1937) 93m. ***1/2 D: William Wyler. Sylvia Sidney, Joel McCrea, Humphrey Bogart, Wendy Barrie, Claire Trevor, Marjorie Main, Huntz Hall, Leo Gorcey, Gabriel Dell, Ward Bond, Billy Halop, Bernard Punsley, Allen Jenkins. Grim Sidney Kingsley play of slum life shows vignettes of humanity at breaking point in N.Y.C. tenement slums; extremely well directed, engrossing: Film introduced Dead End Kids.

Dead Heat on a Merry-Go-Round (1966) C-104m. *** D: Bernard Girard. James Coburn, Camilla Sparv, Aldo Ray, Ross Martin, Severn Darden, Robert Webber. Involved crime movie about intricate plan to rob airport bank (with surprise ending). All-round very good film with excellent cast.

Dead of Night (1946-British) 77m. **** D: Cavalcanti, Basil Deardon, Robert Hammer. Mervyn Johns, Roland Culver, Frederick Valk, Anthony Baird, Michael Redgrave, Sally Ann Howes. Exceedingly fine chiller involving a gathering of people who have experienced dreams which seem to repeat themselves in reality; admirable cast.

Dead Man's Eyes (1944) 64m. ** D: Reginald Le Borg. Lon Chaney, Jr., Jean Parker, Paul Kelly, Thomas Gomez, Acquanetta. Mad-doctor Chaney is doing eye transplants this time; usual low-budget chills.

Dead Reckoning (1947) 100m. *** D: John Cromwell. Humphrey Bogart, Lizabeth Scott, Morris Carnovsky, William Prince, Wallace Ford, Charles Crane. Bogart's fine as tough WW2 veteran solving soldier-buddy's murder. Well-acted drama.

Dead Ringer (1964) 115m. **1/2 D: Paul Henreid. Bette Davis, Karl Malden, Peter Lawford, Jean Hagen, George Macready, Estelle Winwood. A double dose of Davis, playing twin sisters bearing a long-time grudge over a man, the sinister one trying to get even. Far-fetched but fun; Bette's vehicle all the way.

Deadlier Than the Male (1957-French, dubbed) 104m. ** D: Julien Duvivier. Jean Gabin, Daniele Delorme, Lucienne Bogaert, Gerard Blain. Delorme encamps in ex-stepfather's home, planning to marry and then murder him; Gabin is stodgy as girl's intended victim.

Deadliest Sin, The (1956-British) 77m. *1/2 D: Ken Hughes. Sydney Chaplin, Audrey Dalton, John Bentley, Peter Hammond. Good triumphing over evil is moral of this slight story of thief involved in murder.

Deadline at Dawn (1946) 83m. **1/2 D: Harold Clurman. Susan Hayward, Paul Lukas, Bill Williams, Osa Massen, Lola Lane. Fairly interesting murder mystery by Clifford Odets with suspected sailor Williams and singer Hayward helping to clear him.

Deadline U.S.A. (1952) 87m. *** D: Richard Brooks. Humphrey Bogart, Ethel Barrymore, Kim Hunter, Ed Begley, Paul Stewart, Jim Backus. Biting account of newspaper's struggle to survive and maintain civic duty. Bogie is editor, Begley his assistant, Stewart a sports reporter who brings in wanted man; most enjoyable.

Deadly Affair, The (1967) C-107m. *** D: Sidney Lumet. James Mason, Simone Signoret, Maximilian Schell, Harriet Andersson, Harry Andrews, Kenneth Haigh, Lynn Redgrave, Roy Kinnear, Max Adrian. Top-notch suspense tale with British agent Mason trying to unravel complicated mystery behind an agency official's suicide. From John LeCarre's book.

Deadly Bees, The (1967-British) C-85m. ** D: Freddie Francis. Suzanna Leigh, Guy Doleman, Catherine Finn, Katy Wild, Frank Finlay.

High-powered shock scenes involving swarming bees are only worthwhile attraction in horror film marred by dull script.

Deadly Companions, The (1961) C-90m. **½ D: Sam Peckinpah. Maureen O'Hara, Brian Keith, Steve Cochran, Chill Wills. Ex-army officer accidentally kills O'Hara's son and he makes amends by escorting the funeral procession through Indian country.

Deadly Mantis, The (1957) 78m. ** D: Nathan Juran. Craig Stevens, William Hopper, Alix Talton, Donald Randolph. N.Y.C. is threatened again, here by giant insect heading south after Arctic tour de force; obligatory love story interrupts special effects.

Dear Brat (1951) 82m. **½ D: William A. Seiter. Mona Freeman, Billy DeWolfe, Edward Arnold, Lyle Bettger. Another follow-up to DEAR RUTH has Freeman in title role involved with a crook trying to reform.

Dear Brigitte (1965) C-100m. **½ D: Henry Koster. James Stewart, Glynis Johns, Fabian, Billy Mumy, John Williams, Jack Kruschen, Ed Wynn. Guest: Brigitte Bardot. Good cast in OK family farce about an 8-year-old genius (Stewart's son, Mumy) with a crush on Brigitte Bardot. Bardot makes a brief appearance at the end. Film tries hard to be whimsical but is contrived instead.

Dear Heart (1964) 114m. *** D: Delbert Mann. Glenn Ford, Geraldine Page, Michael Anderson, Jr., Barbara Nichols, Angela Lansbury, Alice Pearce, Mary Wickes. Winning romance story with Ford and Page visiting N.Y.C. for conventions, falling in love; excellent characterizations with fine comedy supporting players.

Dear Ruth (1947) 95m. **½ D: William D. Russell. Joan Caulfield, William Holden, Mona Freeman, Edward Arnold, Billy DeWolfe. Bouncy, naive comedy of errors with young girl pretending to be her older sister to impress soldier she corresponds with.

Dear Wife (1949) 88m. **½ D: Richard Haydn. Joan Caulfield, William Holden, Edward Arnold, Billy DeWolfe, Mona Freeman. Follow-up to DEAR RUTH focuses on Freeman's antics to get Holden elected to the state senate, although her politician father Arnold is seeking same position.

Death In Small Doses (1957) 79m. *½ D: Joseph M. Newman. Peter Graves, Mala Powers, Chuck Connors, Merry Anders. Low-budget drama of narcotics use among truck drivers; dull presentation.

Death of a Salesman (1951) 115m. ***½ D: Laslo Benedek. Fredric March, Mildred Dunnock, Kevin McCarthy, Cameron Mitchell. Arthur Miller social drama of middle-aged man at end of emotional rope is transformed to the screen intact, with stagy flashbacks. March in title role can't fathom why business and family life failed; Dunnock is patient wife, McCarthy and Mitchell are disillusioned sons. Superb.

Death of a Scoundrel (1956) 119m. **½ D: Charles Martin. George Sanders, Yvonne de Carlo, Zsa Zsa Gabor, Victor Jory. Episodic chronicle of foreigner coming to U.S., ingratiating himself with an assortment of women whom he cons into helping him get ahead. Low-budget but fascinating.

Death Takes a Holiday (1934) 78m. ***½ D: Mitchell Leisen. Fredric March, Evelyn Venable, Guy Standing, Gail Patrick, Helen Westley. Fascinating allegory about Death (March) entering the human world to discover what makes us tick, and falling in love.

Decameron (1953) C-87m. ** D: Hugo Fregonese. Joan Fontaine, Louis Jourdan, Binnie Barnes, Joan Collins, Marjorie Rhodes. Distillation of robust medieval tales with Jourdan the story-spinning Boccaccio seeking fair Fontaine's love.

Deception (1946) 112m. ***½ D: Irving Rapper. Bette Davis, Claude Rains, Paul Henreid, John Abbott, Benson Fong. Acting duel de force by Davis and Rains as pianist and her jealous benefactor, with Henreid overshadowed by star duo.

Decision Against Time (1957-British) 87m. **½ D: Charles Crichton. Jack Hawkins, Elizabeth Sellars, Eddie Byrne, Lionel Jeffries, Donald Pleasence. Hawkins is effective as test pilot giving all to save troubled craft for boss and to protect job future.

Decision at Sundown (1957) C-95m. ** D: Budd Boetticher. Randolph Scott, John Carroll, Karen Steele,

115

Noah Beery, John Litel. Scott tracks wife's assaulter to title town, discovering she provoked the attack.

Decision Before Dawn (1951) 119m. *** D: Anatole Litvak. Richard Basehart, Gary Merrill, Oskar Werner, Hildegarde Neff. Werner is exceptional in realistic WW2 thriller of Nazi POW returning to Germany as American spy.

Decision of Christopher Blake, The (1948) 75m. **1/2 D: Peter Godfrey. Alexis Smith, Robert Douglas, Cecil Kellaway, Ted Donaldson, John Hoyt. Insipid drama of child suffering from his parents' divorce. Not slickly done, with sugary ending.

Decks Ran Red, The (1958) 84m. **1/2 D: Andrew L. Stone. James Mason, Dorothy Dandridge, Broderick Crawford, Stuart Whitman. Bizarre sea yarn with strange casting, involves sailors' attempt to murder freighter captain and use vessel for salvage.

Deep Blue Sea, The (1955-British) C-99m. **1/2 D: Anatole Litvak. Vivien Leigh, Kenneth More, Eric Portman, Emlyn Williams. Terence Rattigan play of marital infidelity and the repercussions on Leigh, frustrated well-married woman; slow-moving, but thoughtfully presented.

Deep In My Heart (1954) C-132m. **1/2 D: Stanley Donen. Jose Ferrer, Merle Oberon, Helen Traubel, Doe Avedon, Walter Pidgeon, Paul Henreid. Sigmund Romberg's life bad excuse for horde of guest stars, but musical numbers are satisfying. Guests include Ann Miller, Gene Kelly, Tony Martin, Rosemary Clooney.

Deep Six, The (1958) C-105m. **1/2 D: Rudolph Mate. Alan Ladd, Dianne Foster, William Bendix, Keenan Wynn, James Whitmore, Joey Bishop. Ladd is Quaker naval officer during WW2 who compensates for past inaction by heading dangerous shore mission; Bendix gives able support.

Deep Valley (1947) 104m. *** D: Jean Negulesco. Ida Lupino, Dane Clark, Wayne Morris, Fay Bainter, Henry Hull. Into Lupino's humdrum farm life comes a gangster from nearby prison camp; first rate cast in excellent drama.

Deep Waters (1948) 85m. ** D: Henry King. Dana Andrews, Jean Peters, Cesar Romero, Dean Stockwell, Anne Revere, Ed Begley. Slick, empty tale of fisherman Andrews and landlubber Peters brought together by cute little Stockwell.

Deerslayer, The (1957) C-78m. *1/2 D: Kurt Neumann. Lex Barker, Forrest Tucker, Rita Moreno, Jay C. Flippen. James Fenimore Cooper's leatherstocking novel of white man (Barker) raised by Indians is given pedestrian treatment, virtually all indoor sets and rear-screen projection.

Defector, The (1966) C-106m. **1/2 D: Raoul Levy. Montgomery Clift, Hardy Kruger, Roddy McDowall, David Opatoshu. Hackneyed Cold War spy trivia filmed in Europe, interesting only as Clift's last film; good cameo by McDowall.

Defiant Ones, The (1958) 97m. **** D: Stanley Kramer. Tony Curtis, Sidney Poitier, Theodore Bikel, Charles McGraw, Cara Williams, Lon Chaney, Jr. Engrossing story of two escaped convicts (Curtis and Poitier) shackled together as they flee from police in the South. Fine performances by Williams and Chaney as people they meet along the way.

Delicate Delinquent, The (1957) 100m. *** D: Don McGuire. Jerry Lewis, Martha Hyer, Darren McGavin, Horace McMahon. Jerry's first solo effort after Dean Martin split-up has him as delinquent who becomes a cop with McGavin's help. Not as wacky as later vehicles, this one hits the right note.

Delightfully Dangerous (1945) 93m. **1/2 D: Arthur Lubin. Jane Powell, Ralph Bellamy, Constance Moore, Morton Gould Orchestra, Arthur Treacher, Louise Beavers. Pleasant froth of sisters Powell (sedate) and Moore (stripper) competing for Bellamy's love.

Demetrius and the Gladiators (1954) C-101m. **1/2 D: Delmer Daves. Victor Mature, Susan Hayward, Michael Rennie, Debra Paget, Anne Bancroft, Richard Egan, Ernest Borgnine. Hokey sequel to THE ROBE has Emperor Caligula (Jay Robinson) searching for magic robe of Christ; Mature dallies with royal Hayward.

Demoniaque (1958-French, dubbed) 97m. **1/2 D: Luis Saslavsky. François Perier, Micheline Presle, Jeanne Moreau, Madeleine Robinson. Perky yarn of French P.O.W. escaping and seeking refuge with girl his dead

buddy romanced via the mails; girl believes him to be the letter-writer.
Den of Doom SEE: Glass Cage
Dentist in the Chair (1961-British) 84m. ** D: Don Chaffey. Peggy Cummins, Bob Monkhouse, Kenneth Connor, Eric Barker. Occasionally amusing shenanigans of dentists involved in crooked dealings, trying to undo their mischievious thefts.
Denver and Rio Grande, The (1952) C-89m. **½ D: Byron Haskin. Edmond O'Brien, Sterling Hayden, Dean Jagger, Zasu Pitts, J. Carrol Naish. Another railroad rivalry Western as two competing companies battle elements and each other to complete tie-line through title area.
Deported (1950) 80m. **½ D: Robert Siodmak. Marta Toren, Jeff Chandler, Claude Dauphin, Carlo Rizzo. Engaging gangster yarn with Chandler deported to Italy, involved in the black market, but going straight to win Toren's love.
Derby Day (1951-British) 84m. **½ D: Herbert Wilcox. Anna Neagle, Michael Wilding, John McCallum, Googie Withers. Diverting study of human nature, as an assortment of people intermingle at Epson Downs race track. Retitled: FOUR AGAINST FATE.
Desert Attack (1960-British) 80m. *** D: J. Lee Thompson. John Mills, Sylvia Syms, Anthony Quayle, Harry Andrews, Diane Clare. Well-handled psychological drama of British ambulance officer, two nurses, and a German soldier brought together in African desert. Original title: ICE COLD IN ALEX.
Desert Desperadoes (1959) 81m. * D: Steve Sekely. Ruth Roman, Akim Tamiroff, Othelo Toso, Gianni Glori. Unsuccessful mishmash of romance and unconvincing intrigue set in the Egyptian desert, wasting Roman's most capable talents. Retitled: THE SINNER.
Desert Fox, The (1951) 88m. *** D: Henry Hathaway. James Mason, Cedric Hardwicke, Jessica Tandy, Luther Adler. Mason standout as Field Marshal Rommel in sensitive account of his military defeat in WW2 Africa and disillusioned return to Hitler Germany. Mason repeated role in later DESERT RATS.
Desert Fury (1947) C-95m. **½ D: Lewis Allen. John Hodiak, Lizabeth Scott, Burt Lancaster, Mary Astor, Wendell Corey. Mild drama of love and mystery among gamblers, stolen by Astor in bristling character portrayal.
Desert Hawk, The (1950) C-77m. ** D: Frederick de Cordova. Yvonne de Carlo, Richard Greene, Jackie Gleason, Rock Hudson, George Macready. Pat Arabian desert tale, interesting for Gleason and Hudson in secondary roles.
Desert Hell (1958) 82m. ** D: Charles Marquis Warren. Brian Keith, Barbara Hale, Richard Denning, Johnny Desmond. French Foreign Legion battles warring Arabs to save peace; very little of promised action given to viewer.
Desert Legion (1953) C-86m. ** D: Joseph Pevney. Alan Ladd, Richard Conte, Arlene Dahl, Akim Tamiroff. Mild Ladd entry of battling French Foreign Legion.
Desert Patrol (1958-British) 78m. **½ D: Guy Green. Richard Attenborough, John Gregson, Michael Craig, Vincent Ball. Staunch account of British patrol attempting to blow up Axis fuel dump before pending WW2 battle of El Alamein. Retitled: SEA OF SAND.
Desert Rats, The (1953) 88m. *** D: Robert Wise. Richard Burton, James Mason, Robert Newton, Chips Rafferty. Fine WW2 actioner with Mason convincing as Field Marshal Rommel (played same role in earlier DESERT FOX); Burton is British commando trying to ward off Germans in North Africa.
Desert Song, The (1953) C-110m. **½ D: H. Bruce Humberstone. Kathryn Grayson, Gordon MacRae, Steve Cochran, Raymond Massey. Third filming of Sigmund Romberg operetta set in Africa creaks along on thin plot. American MacRae is secret leader of good natives (Riffs) in battle against evil Arabs. Songs: "The Riff Song," "One Alone."
Design for Living (1933) 90m. ***½ D: Ernst Lubitsch. Gary Cooper, Fredric March, Miriam Hopkins, Edward Everett Horton, Franklin Pangborn. Hopkins leaves starving suitors Cooper and March to marry wealthy Horton in chic fluff by Noel Coward,

with most of the witty innuendos left intact. Delightful.

Design for Scandal (1941) 85m. **½ D: Norman Taurog. Rosalind Russell, Walter Pidgeon, Edward Arnold, Lee Bowman, Jean Rogers, Mary Beth Hughes, Guy Kibbee. Deft performances by stars in comedy of reporter Pidgeon doing sensational story involving prominent female judge Russell.

Designing Woman (1957) C-118m. *** D: Vincente Minnelli. Gregory Peck, Lauren Bacall, Dolores Gray, Sam Levene, Chuck Connors. Sportswriter and fashion designer run head-on in this chic comedy reminiscent of the great Hepburn-Tracy comedies. Bacall and Peck do their best.

Desire (1936) 89m. *** D: Frank Borzage. Marlene Dietrich, Gary Cooper, John Halliday, William Frawley, Ernest Cossart, Akim Tamiroff. American car-designer Cooper falls in love with jewel thief Dietrich. Sophisticated romancer set in Spain; Marlene sings "Awake In A Dream."

Desire in the Dust (1960) 102m. **½ D: William F. Claxton. Raymond Burr, Martha Hyer, Joan Bennett, Ken Scott. Good casting carries this turgid soaper of a Southern aristocrat with a yen for politics, who tries to hide the shady past of some family members.

Desire Me (1947) 91m. ** D: George Cukor, Mervyn LeRoy. Greer Garson, Robert Mitchum, Richard Hart, George Zucco, Morris Ankrum. Weak melodramatic romance with poor Garson caught between new love and old husband, presumed dead, who returns to make problems. Familiar story not helped by limp script.

Desire Under the Elms (1958) 114m. **½ D: Delbert Mann. Sophia Loren, Anthony Perkins, Burl Ives, Frank Overton. Eugene O'Neill stage piece about family hatred and greed for land. Loren miscast as Ives' young wife in love with step-son Perkins, but she sparks some life into brooding account of 19th-century New England farm story.

Desiree (1954) C-110m. **½ D: Henry Koster. Marlon Brando, Jean Simmons, Merle Oberon, Michael Rennie, Cameron Mitchell, Elizabeth Sellars. Tepid, elaborate costumer: Brando plays a confused Napoleon, Simmons his seamstress love who marries another man; Oberon, Empress Josephine (quite lovely). Fiction and fact are muddled backdrop for rise and fall of the Emperor; few action scenes.

Desk Set (1957) C-103m. ***½ D: Walter Lang. Spencer Tracy, Katharine Hepburn, Joan Blondell, Gig Young, Dina Merrill. Broadway play becomes a vehicle for Hepburn and Tracy, a guarantee for top entertainment. He's an efficiency expert automating her research department at a TV network; they clash, argue, and fall in love. Great fun.

Desperadoes, The (1943) C-85m. *** D: Charles Vidor. Randolph Scott, Glenn Ford, Claire Trevor, Evelyn Keyes, Edgar Buchanan, Raymond Walburn, Guinn Williams. Pretty good Western; bandit Ford goes straight, joins forces with marshal Scott to clean up town.

Desperados are in Town, The (1956) 73m. **½ D: Kurt Neumann. Robert Arthur, Kathy Nolan, Rhys Williams, Rhodes Reason. Bland oater of young man proving his worth by killing outlaws who murdered his friend.

Desperate Hours, The (1955) 112m. ***½ D: William Wyler. Humphrey Bogart, Fredric March, Arthur Kennedy, Martha Scott, Dewey Martin, Gig Young, Robert Middleton, Richard Eyer. Excellently acted account of escaped convicts terrorizing family household, allowing for interplay of emotional clashes. Based on Broadway play and actual events.

Desperate Journey (1942) 107m. *** D: Raoul Walsh. Errol Flynn, Raymond Massey, Ronald Reagan, Nancy Coleman, Alan Hale, Arthur Kennedy, Albert Basserman. Spirited WW2 drama of American pilots stranded in Germany, struggling to cross border; propaganda interludes are forgivable.

Desperate Man, The (1959-British) 57m. *½ D: Peter Maxwell. Jill Ireland, Conrad Phillips, William Hartnell, Charles Gray. Dull yarn of reporter Phillips and gal (Ireland) involved in tracking down a Sussex crook; photography only virtue.

Desperate Moment (1953-British) 88m. **½ D: Compton Bennett. Dirk Bogarde, Mai Zetterling, Philip Friend, Gerald Heinz. Taut melodrama involving displaced person in post-WW2 Berlin falsely accused of homicide; sensibly acted.

Desperate Search (1952) 73m. **½ D: Joseph H. Lewis. Howard Keel, Jane Greer, Patricia Medina, Keenan Wynn. Trim film of two kids stranded in Canadian wastelands after plane crash, and their father's efforts to find them.

Desperate Siege SEE: Rawhide

Destination Fury (1961-French, dubbed) 85m. ** D: Giorgio Bianchi. Eddie Constantine, Renato Rascel, Dorian Gray, Pierre Grasset. Silly spy spoof with Constantine a double-agent involved with Interpol.

Destination Gobi (1953) C-89m. **½ D: Robert Wise. Richard Widmark, Don Taylor, Darryl Hickman, Martin Milner. Unusual WW2 actioner involving U.S. naval men joining forces with natives against Japanese assaults; nice action sequences.

Destination Inner Space (1966) C-92m. ** D: Francis D. Lyon. Sheree North, Scott Brady, Gary Merrill, John Howard. Programmer sci-fi set on ocean's bottom with a most unterrifying monster on the prowl.

Destination Moon (1950) C-90m. **½ D: Irving Pichel. John Archer, Warner Anderson, Tom Powers, Dick Wesson, Erin O'Brien-Moore. One of the pioneer sci-fi films, modestly produced but still effective.

Destination 60,000 (1957) 65m. Bomb D: George Waggner. Preston Foster, Pat Conway, Jeff Donnell, Coleen Gray. Worn-out premise of test pilots zooming through space, families waiting nervously on the ground.

Destination Tokyo (1943) 135m. *** D: Delmer Daves. Cary Grant, John Garfield, Alan Hale, John Ridgely, Dane Clark, Warner Anderson, William Prince. Suspenseful WW2 account of U.S. submarine sent into Japanese waters and interaction among crew. Commander Grant, seamen Garfield and Clark ring true.

Destiny (1944) 65m. ** D: Reginald LeBorg. Gloria Jean, Alan Curtis, Frank Craven, Grace McDonald. Routine study of man sent to prison on homicide charge, and snowballing effects on his life.

Destroyer (1943) 99m. **½ D: William Seiter. Edward G. Robinson, Glenn Ford, Marguerite Chapman, Edgar Buchanan, Leo Gorcey, Regis Toomey, Ed Brophy. Predictable wartime drama of aging seaman Robinson shown up by novice Ford; of course Eddie comes through in the end.

Destructors, The (1968) C-97m. ** D: Francis D. Lyon. Richard Egan, Patricia Owens, John Ericson, Michael Ansara, Joan Blackman. Programmer nonsense with Egan a federal agent hunting international thieves who stole laser rubies.

Destry (1954) C-95m. **½ D: George Marshall. Audie Murphy, Mari Blanchard, Lyle Bettger, Lori Nelson, Thomas Mitchell, Edgar Buchanan, Wallace Ford. Audie is gun-shy sheriff who tames town and dance-hall girl without violence. Earlier version still unsurpassed.

Destry Rides Again (1939) 94m. ***½ D: George Marshall. James Stewart, Marlene Dietrich, Charles Winninger, Brian Donlevy, Una Merkel, Irene Hervey, Jack Carson, Billy Gilbert, Samuel S. Hinds. Slam-bang, action-filled Western satire with Stewart taming rowdy town without violence and becalming boisterous dance-hall gal Dietrich as well. Marlene sings "See What The Boys In The Back Room Will Have." Remade as DESTRY.

Detective, The (1954-British) 91m. *** D: Robert Hamer. Alec Guinness, Joan Greenwood, Peter Finch, Cecil Parker, Bernard Lee, Sidney James. Guinness in rare form as G. K. Chesterton's sleuth after stolen art treasures. Remake of Walter Connolly's 1934 FATHER BROWN, DETECTIVE.

Detective Kitty O'Day (1944) 63m. ** D: William Beaudine. Jean Parker, Peter Cookson, Tim Ryan, Veda Ann Borg. Parker adds bubbly zest as amateur sleuth who sets out to solve a crime; pleasant fluff on low-budget scale.

Detective Story (1951) 103m. ***½ D: William Wyler. Kirk Douglas, Eleanor Parker, William Bendix, Lee Grant. Sidney Kingsley's once-forceful play of life at N.Y.C. police precinct has lost much of its punch but is still fine film; Douglas is hard-hitting detective, Parker his ignored wife, Bendix in one of his best roles as sympathetic sergeant.

Devil, The SEE: **To Bed . . . Or Not To Bed**

Devil and Miss Jones, The (1941) 92m. *** D: Sam Wood. Jean Arthur, Robert Cummings, Charles Coburn, Spring Byington, S. Z. Sakall, William Demarest. Delightful cast pulls off tale of gruff Coburn secretly taking job in his own store. Arthur is unwitting salesgirl.

Devil and the Deep (1932) 78m. **½ D: Marion Gering. Tallulah Bankhead, Gary Cooper, Charles Laughton, Cary Grant, Paul Porcasi. Overplayed but lush melodrama of Bankhead, her suitors Grant and Cooper, and jealous husband, submarine commander Laughton.

Devil and the Ten Commandments, The (1962-French, dubbed) 143m. **½ D: Julien Duvivier. Michel Simon, Lucien Baroux, Claude Nollier, Dany Saval, Charles Aznavour. Episodic film in ten parts illustrating each of the commandments—too often superficial instead of cynical.

Devil at 4 O'clock, The (1961) C-126m. **½ D: Mervyn LeRoy. Spencer Tracy, Frank Sinatra, Jean-Pierre Aumont, Kerwin Matthews, Barbara Luna. Static production, not saved by volcanic eruption climax, involving priest Tracy helping to evacuate children's hospital in midst of lava flow. Stars are lost in weak film.

Devil Bat (1941) 69m. ** D: Jean Yarbrough. Bela Lugosi, Suzanne Kaaren, Dave O'Brien, Guy Usher, Yolande Mallot, Donald Kerr. Lugosi raises bats and trains them to suck victim's blood on cue.

Devil Bat's Daughter (1946) 66m. ** D: Frank Wisbar. Rosemary La Planche, Molly Lamont, Ed Cassidy, Michael Hale. OK mystery with La Planche going crazy while her strange father fools around with killer-bats.

Devil Commands, The (1941) 65m. ** D: Edward Dmytryk. Boris Karloff, Amanda Duff, Richard Fiske, Anne Revere, Ralph Penney, Dorothy Adams, Walter Baldwin. Fairly interesting Karloff vehicle about man trying to communicate with his deceased wife, causing death and other complications.

Devil-Doll, The (1936) 79m. *** D: Tod Browning. Lionel Barrymore, Maureen O'Sullivan, Frank Lawton, Robert Grieg, Lucy Beaumont, Henry B. Walthall, Grace Ford, Rafaela Ottiano. Barrymore is impressive as escapee from Devil's Island who practices body-shrinking (literally) for revenge.

Devil Doll (1964-British) 80m. *** D: Lindsay Shonteff. Bryant Halliday, William Sylvester, Yvonne Romain, Philip Ray. Underrated British macabre mystery features very good Halliday performance as hypnotist-ventriloquist trying to transfer soul into dummy. Atmospheric, with countless subplots.

Devil in the Flesh (1946-French, dubbed) 110m. ***½ D: Claude Autant-Lara. Gerard Philippe, Micheline Presle, Denise Grey. Beautiful, sensual love tale set in 1940's France, with Philippe and Presle ideal as passionate lovers.

Devil Is a Sissy (1936) 92m. **½ D: W. S. Van Dyke, II. Freddie Bartholomew, Jackie Cooper, Mickey Rooney, Ian Hunter, Peggy Conklin. Undemanding vehicle for three child stars of the 30's is pegged on tale of son's problems when parents divorce.

Devil Is a Woman, The (1935) 85m. **½ D: Josef von Sternberg. Marlene Dietrich, Lionel Atwill, Cesar Romero, Edward Everett Horton, Alison Skipworth. Beautifully photographed but dull film of a revolutionist, destroyed by woman's hold over him. Set in Spain.

Devil Makes Three, The (1953) 96m. ** D: Andrew Marton. Gene Kelly, Pier Angeli, Richard Egan, Claus Benton. Kelly always seems pretentious in straight roles: here he's a soldier returning to Munich to thank family who helped him during WW2; he becomes involved with daughter Angeli and black market gangs.

Devil Pays Off (1941) 56m. ** D: John H. Auer. J. Edward Bromberg, Osa Massen, William Wright, Margaret Tallichet. Meager account of one-time navy man trying to redeem his honor by tracking down espionage agents within the naval service.

Devil-Ship Pirates (1964-British) C-89m. **½ D: Don Sharp. Christopher Lee, Andrew Kier, Michael Ripper, John Cairney. Good little movie of stray Spanish ships conquering English countryside, unaware that the Armada has been defeated.

Devil to Pay, The (1931) 65m. **½

D: George Fitzmaurice. Ronald Colman, Loretta Young, David Torrence, Myrna Loy, Mary Forbes, Paul Cavanaugh. Early talkie shows its age, but Colman is fine in this drawing-room comedy.

Devil's Bait (1959-British) 58m. *½ D: Peter Graham Scott. Geoffrey Keen, Jane Hylton, Gordon Jackson, Dermot Kelly. Intriguing if leisurely paced B-film, about baker and his wife who accidentally put poison in their wares, trying to find purchasers.

Devil's Brother, The (1933) 88m. *** D: Hal Roach, Charles R. Rogers. Stan Laurel, Oliver Hardy, Dennis King, Thelma Todd, James Finlayson, Henry Armetta. L&H adaptation of operetta with King as romantic lead, a famous bandit, the boys as would-be assistants. One of their best. Originally titled: FRA DIAVOLO.

Devil's Canyon (1953) C-92m. ** D: Alfred L. Werker. Virginia Mayo, Dale Robertson, Stephen McNally, Arthur Hunnicutt. Former marshal put in prison for shoot-outs, where he's entangled in prison riot.

Devil's Cargo (1948) 61m. D: John F. Link. John Calvert, Rochelle Hudson, Roscoe Karns, Lyle Talbot, Tom Kennedy, Theodore Von Eltz. SEE: The Falcon series.

Devil's Daffodil, The (1961-British) 86m. ** D: Akos Rathony. William Lucas, Penelope Horner, Christopher Lee, Ingrid van Bergen, Albert Lieven. Flabby entry in Edgar Wallace series, involving rash of murders linked with dope smuggling into England. Retitled: DAFFODIL KILLER.

Devil's Disciple, The (1959-British) 82m. **½ D: Guy Hamilton. Burt Lancaster, Kirk Douglas, Laurence Olivier, Janette Scott, Eva LeGallienne, Harry Andrews, Basil Sydney. George Bernard Shaw's witty observation on the American Revolution becomes modest costumer, highlighted by Olivier's dashing British General Burgoyne.

Devil's Doorway (1950) 84m. *** D: Anthony Mann. Robert Taylor, Louis Calhern, Paula Raymond, Marshall Thompson. Well-turned Western with offbeat casting of Taylor as Indian who served in Civil War, returning home to find that he must fight to right the injustices done against his people.

Devil's Eye, The (1960-Swedish, dubbed) 90m. **½ D: Ingmar Bergman. Jarl Kulle, Bibi Andersson, Nils Poppe, Sture Lagerwall. Confused account of the demon sending envoy Kulle to rob Andersson of her virginity; long morality dialogue uplifted by cast.

Devil's Hairpin, The (1957) C-82m. **½ D: Cornel Wilde. Cornel Wilde, Jean Wallace, Mary Astor, Arthur Franz. Wilde is reckless sports car champion who learns fair play on the track; obligatory racing scenes above average.

Devil's Henchman, The (1949) 69m. ** D: Seymour Friedman. Warner Baxter, Mary Beth Hughes, Mike Mazurki, Harry Shannon. In this programmer, Baxter sets out to capture waterfront gang and becomes involved in murder.

Devil's Island (1940) 62m. **½ D: William Clemens. Boris Karloff, Nedda Harrigan, James Stephenson, Adia Kuznetzoff, Will Stanton, Edward Keane. Above-average Karloff vehicle of innocent doctor exiled to Devil's Island, mistreated by supervisor Stephenson, saved in twist finish.

Devil's Mask, The (1946) 66m. ** D: Henry Levin. Anita Louise, Jim Bannon, Michael Duane, Mona Barrie, Ludwig Donath. Beautiful Louise turns detective to solve mysterious series of circumstances involving voodoo. Fairly good whodunit.

Devil's Messenger (1961-Swedish, dubbed) 72m. *½ D: Curt Siodmak. Lon Chaney, Karen Kadler, John Crawford. Sultry girl is sent to earth to help Satan carry out master plan to envelop the world; hazy plot, poor production values.

Devil's Playground (1937) 74m. **½ D: Erle C. Kenton. Richard Dix, Dolores Del Rio, Chester Morris, Pierre Watkin, Ward Bond, Stanley Andrews. Good combination of action and romance with diver Dix discovering wife Del Rio in love with Morris; exciting underwater climax.

Devil's Wanton, The (1962-Swedish, dubbed) 72m. **½ D: Ingmar Bergman. Doris Svenlund, Birger Malmsten, Eva Henning, Hasse Ekman. Sober account of desperate girl finding romance with another equally unhappy soul, reaffirming their faith in humanity.

Devotion (1946) 107m. **½ D: Curtis Bernhardt. Olivia de Havilland, Ida Lupino, Paul Henreid, Sydney Greenstreet, Nancy Coleman, Arthur Kennedy, Dame May Whitty. Powerful real-life story of Brontë sisters becomes routine love triangle with Henreid in the middle—dramatic, intense performances make it worthwhile.

Diabolical Dr. Mabuse, The SEE: Secret of Dr. Mabuse, The

Dial M for Murder (1954) C-105m. *** D: Alfred Hitchcock. Ray Milland, Grace Kelly, Robert Cummings, John Williams, Anthony Dawson. Frederick Knott's suspense play of man plotting wife's murder and subsequent police investigation; intriguing but not top Hitchcock.

Dial 1119 (1950) 75m. ** D: Gerald Mayer. Marshall Thompson, Virginia Field, Andrea King, Sam Levene, Keefe Brasselle. Modest suspenser hinged on plot of killer holding a group of bar patrons hostages.

Diamond Earrings SEE: Earrings of Madame De

Diamond Head (1962) C-107m. **½ D: Guy Green. Charlton Heston, Yvette Mimieux, George Chakiris, France Nuyen, James Darren, Aline MacMahon, Elizabeth Allen. Soap opera set in Hawaii with Heston the domineering head of his family, whose dictates almost ruin their lives.

Diamond Horseshoe (1945) C-104m. *** D: George Seaton. Betty Grable, Dick Haymes, Phil Silvers, William Gaxton, Beatrice Kay, Carmen Cavallaro. Colorful musical set in Billy Rose's famous cabaret, with Grable giving up luxury for medical student Haymes. Song "The More I See You." Original title: BILLY ROSE'S DIAMOND HORSESHOE.

Diamond Jim (1935) 93m. *** D: A. Edward Sutherland. Edward Arnold, Jean Arthur, Binnie Barnes, Cesar Romero, Eric Blore. Big-budget biography of eccentric millionaire of 19th century whose appetite for money only matched by love of food and Lillian Russell; Arthur has dual role in re-creation of gay 90's era. Most entertaining.

Diamond Queen, The (1953) C-80m. ** D: John Brahm. Fernando Lamas, Arlene Dahl, Gilbert Roland, Michael Ansara. Dahl is dazzling title figure over whom Lamas and Roland fight in costumer set in India.

Diamond Wizard, The (1954-British) 83m. ** D: Dennis O'Keefe. Dennis O'Keefe, Margaret Sheridan, Philip Friend, Allan Wheatley. OK caper of U.S. and British agents tracking down diamond counterfeiters.

Diane (1956) C-110m. **½ D: David Miller. Lana Turner, Pedro Armendariz, Roger Moore, Marisa Pavan, Sir Cedric Hardwicke, Henry Daniell. Although predictable, medieval romance has good cast, gorgeous sets and costumes, and comes off surprisingly well. Lana looks lovely, and Miklos Rozsa's score helps set the mood.

Diary of a Bachelor (1964) 88m. *½ D: Sandy Howard. William Traylor, Dagne Crane, Joe Silver, Chris Noel, Paula Stewart. Meager pickings. Fiancee reads boyfriend's daily ledger and decides he'd better mend his ways; time passes and he has, but she's changed her way of life.

Diary of a Chambermaid, The (1946) 86m. **½ D: Jean Renoir. Paulette Goddard, Burgess Meredith, Hurd Hatfield, Florence Bates, Irene Ryan, Francis Lederer, Judith Anderson, Almira Sessions. Attempt to make foreign-style film in Hollywood doesn't work. Nineteenth-century chambermaid Goddard is hired by Meredith's mother.

Diary of a Madman (1963) C-96m. **½ D: Reginald Le Borg. Vincent Price, Nancy Kovack, Chris Warfield, Ian Wolfe, Nelson Olmstead. Bizarre yarn with Price in title role of law official possessed with homicidal urge; incredible yet entertaining.

Diary of Anne Frank, The (1959) 180m. ***½ D: George Stevens. Millie Perkins, Joseph Schildkraut, Shelley Winters, Richard Beymer, Lou Jacobi, Diane Baker, Ed Wynn. Meticulously produced version of Broadway drama dealing with Jewish refugees hiding in WW2 Amsterdam. Perkins never captures pivotal charm of title character; Winters won Supporting Actress Oscar as shrill Mrs. Van Daan, ever fearful of Nazi arrest; Schildkraut fine as Father Frank, the lone survivor. Moving Alfred Newman score.

Dick Tracy, Detective (1945) 62m. ** D: William Berke. Morgan Conway, Anne Jeffreys, Mike Mazurki, Jane Greer. Programmer entry about Chester Gould's square-jawed detective combatting crime; needed production values are lacking. Retitled: DICK TRACY.

Dick Tracy Meets Gruesome (1947) 65m. ** D: John Rawlins. Boris Karloff, Ralph Byrd, Anne Gwynne, Edward Ashley, June Clayworth. Karloff as the nemesis of Tracy adds some spice to this series' entry; predictable but enjoyable.

Dick Tracy Versus Cueball (1946) 62m. ** D: Gordon Douglas. Morgan Conway, Anne Jeffreys, Lyle Latell, Rita Corday. Ralph Byrd is definitive screen Tracy, but he isn't in this one; Conway does his best in OK entry in the Tracy series.

Dick Tracy's Dilemma (1947) 60m. ** D: John Rawlins. Ralph Byrd, Lyle Latell, Kay Christopher, Jack Lambert, Ian Keith. RKO contract players abound in this Tracy series entry; fast pacing makes predictable crime-solving satisfactory.

Did You Hear the One About the Traveling Saleslady? (1968) C-97m. ** D: Don Weis. Phyllis Diller, Bob Denver, Joe Flynn, Eileen Wesson, Jeanette Nolan, Bob Hastings. You've all heard it, so why bother watching this dud. For only the most fervent fans of Miss Diller.

Die! Die! My Darling! (1965-British) C-97m. **½ D: Silvio Narizzano. Tallulah Bankhead, Stefanie Powers, Maurice Kaufman, Peter Vaughan, Yootha Joyce, Donald Sutherland. Tallulah has a field day as Mrs. Trefoil, a weirdo who keeps Powers under lock and key for personal vengeance against the death of her son. Engaging fun, especially for Bankhead devotees.

Die, Monster, Die (1965) C-80m. ** D: Daniel Haller. Boris Karloff, Nick Adams, Freda Jackson, Suzan Farmer, Terence de Marney, Patrick Magee. Based on H. P. Lovecraft story, this thriller has Karloff a recluse who discovers a meteor which gives him strange powers. Good premise is not carried out well.

Dig That Uranium (1956) 61m. D: Edward Bernds. Leo Gorcey, Huntz Hall, Bernard Gorcey, Mary Beth Hughes. SEE: Bowery Boys series

Dillinger (1945) 89m. *** D: Max Nosseck. Edmund Lowe, Anne Jeffreys, Lawrence Tierney, Eduardo Ciannelli, Elisha Cook, Jr., Marc Lawrence. Tierney is well cast as famed criminal Dillinger; the film zips along retracing his gunslinging career. Quite good.

Dimples (1936) 78m. **½ D: William Seiter. Shirley Temple, Frank Morgan, Helen Westley, Robert Kent, Stepin Fetchit, Astrid Allwyn. Prime Shirley Temple, with our heroine doing her best to save her destitute father, played by marvelous Morgan. Songs: "Oh Mister Man Up In The Moon," "What Did The Bluebird Say."

Dingaka (1965-South African) C-98m. **½ D: Jamie Uys. Stanley Baker, Juliet Prowse, Ken Gampu, Siegfried Mynhardt, Bob Courtney. Film focuses on contrasting white-Negro ways of life and the clashes of the two cultures; production bogs down in stereotypes.

Dinky (1935) 65m. ** D: D. Ross Lederman, Howard Bretherton. Jackie Cooper, Mary Astor, Roger Pryor, Henry Armetta. Astor is framed, accused of fraud. She tries to keep it from hurting son Cooper in military school. Fairly interesting tale offers nothing special.

Dinner at Eight (1933) 113m. **** D: George Cukor. Marie Dressler, John Barrymore, Wallace Beery, Jean Harlow, Lionel Barrymore, Lee Tracy, Billie Burke, Jean Hersholt, May Robson, Madge Evans, Phillips Holmes, Edmund Lowe. Vintage MGM constellation of stars portray various strata of society in N.Y.C., invited to dine and shine; Harlow in fine comedy form, but Dressler as dowager steals focus in filmization of George Kaufman-Edna Ferber play. Don't miss this one.

Dinner at the Ritz (1937) C-77m. **½ D: Harold Schuster. Annabella, Paul Lukas, David Niven, Romney Brent. Diverting murder whodunit with Annabella seeking the killer of her father; classy settings spice film.

Dino (1957) 94m. **½ D: Thomas Carr. Sal Mineo, Brian Keith, Susan Kohner, Joe De Santis, Mineo at his rebellious best playing juvenile delinquent befriended by social-worker Keith and gal Kohner.

Dinosaurus! (1960) C-85m. **½ D: Irvin S. Yeaworth, Jr. Ward Ramsey, Paul Lukather, Kristina Hanson, Alan Roberts. Scandinavian-made prehistoric monster on the loose, reborn in West Indies, has plenty of excitement, competent acting.

Diplomatic Courier (1952) 97m. *** D: Henry Hathaway. Tyrone Power, Patricia Neal, Hildegarde Neff, Karl Malden. Power seeks to avenge friend's death in Trieste, becomes involved in international espionage. Cold War film is exciting, well acted.

Dirty Game, The (1966-Italian, dubbed) 91m. **½ D: Terence Young, Christian-Jaque, Carlo Lizzani. Henry Fonda, Vittorio Gassman, Annie Girardot, Robert Ryan, Peter Van Eyck. Hodgepodge of stories dealing with espionage in post-WW2 era; none of episodes is convincing, stars don't help much.

Disembodied, The (1957) 65m. *½ D: Walter Grauman. Paul Burke, Allison Hayes, Eugenia Paul, Robert Christopher. Standard voodoo chiller situated in dark jungle; usual results.

Dishonorable Discharge (1958-French, dubbed) 105m. ** D: Bernard Borderie. Eddie Constantine, Pascale Roberts, Lino Ventura, Lise Bourdin. Variation on Hemingway's TO HAVE AND TO HAVE NOT, with Constantine skippering luxury ship loaded with hidden dope; flabby film.

Dishonored (1931) 91m. **½ D: Josef von Sternberg. Marlene Dietrich, Victor McLaglen, Lew Cody, Warner Oland, Gustav von Seyffertitz. Alluring Dietrich makes the most of a creaky script with Marlene as secret agent X-27 during WW1. Worth seeing for Dietrich's masquerade as peasant girl.

Dishonored Lady (1947) 85m. *½ D: Robert Stevenson. Hedy Lamarr, Dennis O'Keefe, John Loder, William Lundigan, Natalie Schafer, Paul Cavanagh. Limp Lamarr vehicle of glamorous magazine art director accused of murder; ponderous.

Disorderly Orderly, The (1964) 90m. **½ D: Frank Tashlin. Jerry Lewis, Glenda Farrell, Susan Oliver, Everett Sloane, Jack E. Leonard, Alice Pearce, Kathleen Freeman, Barbara Nichols, Milton Frome. Jerry runs amuck in a hospital with hilarious results, thanks to a terrific chase finish and a large cast of pros like Farrell, Freeman, Nichols, Benny Rubin, and Frome.

Dispatch From Reuters, A (1940) 89m. **½ D: William Dieterle. Edward G. Robinson, Edna Best, Eddie Albert, Albert Basserman, Gene Lockhart, Nigel Bruce, Otto Kruger. Warner Bros. biography series slipped a notch in this retelling of first news service in Europe. Good production values but emotional impact needed to tag episodes is missing.

Disputed Passage (1939) 87m. **½ D: Frank Borzage. Dorothy Lamour, Akim Tamiroff, John Howard, Victor Varconi, Keye Luke, Elizabeth Risdon, Philip Ahn. Average drama of conflict between two scientists in their ideals. One believes that there's no place for marriage in business.

Disraeli (1929) 89m. **½ D: Alfred E. Green. Joan Bennett, George Arliss, Florence Arliss, Anthony Bushell. Arliss won an Oscar for his portrayal of the British politician who maneuvered much legislation for colonial-minded England during later part of Queen Victoria's reign; production suffers from stagy, episodic quality.

Distant Drums (1951) C-101m. ** D: Raoul Walsh. Gary Cooper, Mari Aldon, Richard Webb, Ray Teal. Tame actioner of Seminole Indians on warpath in early 19th-century Florida, with Cooper as stalwart swamp fighter.

Distant Trumpet, A (1964) C-117m. **½ D: Raoul Walsh. Troy Donahue, Suzanne Pleshette, Kent Smith, Claude Akins, James Gregory. Paul Horgan's novel gets short-circuited in stock presentation of army men in the old West combatting warring Indians while romancing women on the post; good supporting cast.

Dive Bomber (1941) C-133m. *** D: Michael Curtiz. Errol Flynn, Fred MacMurray, Ralph Bellamy, Alexis Smith, Robert Armstrong, Regis Toomey, Craig Stevens. Exciting, well-paced aviation film of experiments to eliminate pilot-blackout. Flynn, MacMurray, and Smith perform well in formula war story.

Divided Heart (1953-British) 89m. *** D: Charles Crichton. Cornell

Borchers, Yvonne Mitchell, Armin Dahlen, Alexander Knox. Intelligent study of dilemma parents face when their adopted child's real mother shows up, demanding her son back.

Divorce (1945) 71m. ** D: William Nigh. Kay Francis, Bruce Cabot, Helen Mack, Craig Reynolds, Larry Olsen, Mary Gordon. Francis is city girl who returns to home town, enticing Cabot away from Mack and family; satisfactory programmer.

Divorce, American Style (1967) C-109m. *** D: Bud Yorkin. Dick Van Dyke, Debbie Reynolds, Jason Robards, Jean Simmons, Van Johnson, Joe Flynn, Shelley Berman, Martin Gabel, Lee Grant, Pat Collins, Tom Bosley. Highly entertaining comedy of Van Dyke and Reynolds finding more problems than they expected when they get divorced. Stars are unusually good in offbeat roles.

Divorce—Italian Style (1962-Italian, dubbed) 104m. ***½ D: Pietro Germi. Marcello Mastroianni, Daniela Rocca, Stefania Sandrelli, Leopoldo Trieste. Marcello can't stomach his wife and schemes to marry another girl. Flavorful Italian film provides hilarious comedy with ironic ending.

Divorce of Lady X, The (1938-British) 90m. *** D: Tim Whelan. Merle Oberon, Laurence Olivier, Binnie Barnes, Ralph Richardson, Morton Selten, J. H. Roberts. Frothy British comedy with fine cast; Olivier is innocently implicated in Oberon's divorce.

Dixie (1943) C-89m. *** D: A. Edward Sutherland. Bing Crosby, Dorothy Lamour, Billy De Wolfe, Marjorie Reynolds, Lynne Overman, Raymond Walburn, Eddie Foy, Jr., Grant Mitchell. Atmosphere overshadows plot in this biography of pioneer minstrel Dan Emmett, who wrote title song; Bing also sings "Sunday, Monday or Always."

Do Not Disturb (1965) C-102m. **½ D: Ralph Levy. Doris Day, Rod Taylor, Hermione Baddeley, Sergio Fantoni, Reginald Gardiner, Mike Romanoff, Leon Askin. Mild Day vehicle with Taylor as executive husband who brings her to suburban England. She meets suave Fantoni, enraging jealous hubby. Not up to her earlier fashion romps.

Do You Love Me? (1946) C-91m. **½ D: Gregory Ratoff. Maureen O'Hara, Dick Haymes, Harry James, Reginald Gardiner, Alma Kruger. Lightweight musical of band-singer Haymes romancing college dean O'Hara.

Dock Brief, The (1962-British) 88m. **½ D: James Hill. Peter Sellers, Richard Attenborough, Beryl Reid, David Lodge. Sellers is aging barrister who incompetently represents accused killer Attenborough with strange results; pleasant comic satire.

Docks of New Orleans (1948) 64m. D: Darwin Abrahams. Roland Winters, Victor Sen Young, Mantan Moreland, John Gallaudet, Virginia Dale. SEE: Charlie Chan series.

Docks of New York (1945) 61m. D: Wallace Fox. Leo Gorcey, Huntz Hall, Billy Benedict, Gloria Pope, Carlyle Blackwell, Jr., Bud Gorman, George Meeker. SEE: Bowery Boys series.

Doctor and the Girl, The (1949) 98m. **½ D: Curtis Bernhardt. Glenn Ford, Charles Coburn, Gloria De Haven, Janet Leigh, Warner Anderson. Ford is appropriately sterile as idealistic young doctor who marries poor girl and practices medicine in slum area of N.Y.C.

Doctor at Large (1957-British) C-98m. **½ D: Ralph Thomas. Dirk Bogarde, James Robertson Justice, Shirley Eaton, George Coulouris, Anne Heywood, Lionel Jeffries. Another entry in pleasing series, with novice doctor Bogarde seeking staff position in wealthy hospital.

Doctor at Sea (1956-British) C-92m. **½ D: Ralph Thomas. Dirk Bogarde, Brigitte Bardot, Brenda De Banzie, James Robertson Justice. Bogarde prefers bachelor life and signs on a freight boat as ship's doctor, becoming involved with BB.

Doctor Blood's Coffin (1961-British) 92m. **½ D: Sidney Furie. Kieron Moore, Hazel Court, Ian Hunter, Fred Johnson. Capable cast in well-paced chiller set in lonely village where people are being used for mysterious scientific experiments.

Dr. Christian Meets the Women (1940) 68m. ** D: William McGann. Jean Hersholt, Dorothy Lovett, Edgar Kennedy, Rod La Roque, Frank Albertson, Marilyn Merrick. Film deals with crooked medico who comes into contact with the good doctor. Typical series entry.

Dr. Cyclops (1940) C-75m. **½ D: Ernest Schoedsack. Albert Dekker, Thomas Coley, Janice Logan, Victor Kilian, Charles Halton. Title character (Dekker) shrinks humans to doll-size; plot is average, but special effects always intrigue.

Dr. Ehrlich's Magic Bullet (1940) 103m. **** D: William Dieterle. Edward G. Robinson, Ruth Gordon, Otto Kruger, Donald Crisp, Maria Ouspenskaya, Montagu Love, Sig Ruman, Donald Meek. Outstanding chronicle of 19th-century German scientist who developed cure for venereal disease. Robinson earnest in interpreting superior script; surprisingly compelling.

Dr. Gillespie's Criminal Case (1943) 89m. D: Willis Goldbeck. Lionel Barrymore, Van Johnson, Donna Reed, Keye Luke, John Craven, Nat Pendleton, Marilyn Maxwell. SEE: Dr. Kildare series.

Dr. Gillespie's New Assistant (1942) 87m. D: Willis Goldbeck. Lionel Barrymore, Van Johnson, Susan Peters, Keye Luke, Richard Quine, Alma Kruger, Rose Hobart, Nat Pendleton, Stephen McNally, Marie Blake, Ann Richards. SEE: **Dr. Kildare** series.

Doctor In Love (1962-British) C-93m. ** D: Ralph Thomas. Michael Craig, Virginia Maskell, Leslie Phillips, Carole Lesley, James Robertson Justice. Craig inherited Bogarde's role in DOCTOR series. This entry centers on young medic's inability to avoid romantic attachments.

Doctor In the House (1953-British) C-92m. *** D: Ralph Thomas. Dirk Bogarde, Muriel Pavlow, Kenneth More, Donald Sinden, Kay Kendall. Droll British comedy beginning series of humorous accounts of young doctors intent on love and adventure as well as becoming wealthy physicians.

Dr. Jekyll and Mr. Hyde (1941) 127m. *** D: Victor Fleming. Spencer Tracy, Ingrid Bergman, Lana Turner, Donald Crisp, Barton MacLane, C. Aubrey Smith, Sara Allgood. Tracy and Bergman are excellent in thoughtful, lush remake of Robert Louis Stevenson's classic, which stresses Hyde's emotion rather than physical horror.

Dr. Kildare From 1939 to 1947, this series, set in Blair General Hospital, was one of the most successful and entertaining of all. INTERNES CAN'T TAKE MONEY (1938, Paramount) was the first film based on Max Brand's characters, with Joel McCrea as Kildare, but it was not part of the series and did not use any of the later familiar roles. The first official entry, YOUNG DR. KILDARE, starred Lew Ayres as Kildare, Lionel Barrymore as Dr. Gillespie, Laraine Day (Mary Lamont), Alma Kruger (Nurse Molly Bird), Walter Kingsford (Dr. Carewe, head of the hospital), Nat Pendleton (Joe Wayman, ambulance driver), Emma Dunn and Samuel S. Hinds (Dr. Kildare's benevolent parents), Nell Craig (Nurse Parker), Marie Blake (Sally, switchboard operator), Frank Orth (Mike), and George Reed (Conover). Indeed, the Kildare series had more running characters than most others. Laraine Day left the series after DR. KILDARE'S WEDDING DAY, and the parents left along with Lew Ayres after DR. KILDARE'S VICTORY. Van Johnson and Keye Luke spent several films trying to become Dr. Gillespie's assistant, with Marilyn Maxwell as love interest for Van. Philip Dorn tried out in CALLING DR. GILLESPIE, and James Craig finished the series with DARK DELUSION. Lionel Barrymore appeared in all of them as the crusty Dr. Gillespie, and supported those entries with lesser plots and casts, often by himself. Each film had at least three plots going at once, with a stress on comedy as well as non-gory hospital drama. None of the Kildare films is bad; a few are mediocre, but most of the films are quite enjoyable, with such interesting names as Lana Turner, Ava Gardner, Robert Young, and Red Skelton turning up from time to time.

Dr. Kildare Goes Home (1940) 78m. D: Harold S. Bucquet. Lew Ayres, Lionel Barrymore, Laraine Day, Samuel S. Hinds, Gene Lockhart, Nat Pendleton.

Dr. Kildare's Crisis (1940) 75m. D: Harold S. Bucquet. Lew Ayres, Lionel Barrymore, Laraine Day, Robert Young, Nat Pendleton, Walter Kingsford, Alma Kruger.

Dr. Kildare's Strange Case (1940) 76m. D: Harold S. Bucquet. Lew

Ayres, Lionel Barrymore, Laraine Day, Shepperd Strudwick, Samuel S. Hinds, Emma Dunn, Nat Pendleton.

Dr. Kildare's Victory (1941) 92m. D: W. S. Van Dyke, II. Lew Ayres, Lionel Barrymore, Ann Ayars, Robert Sterling, Jean Rogers, Alma Kruger.

Dr. Kildare's Wedding Day (1941) 82m. D: Harold S. Bucquet. Lew Ayres, Lionel Barrymore, Laraine Day, Red Skelton, Alma Kruger, Samuel S. Hinds, Nils Asther.

Dr. No (1963) C-111m. ***½ D: Terence Young. Sean Connery, Ursula Andress, Joseph Wiseman, Jack Lord, Bernard Lee, Lois Maxwell. First James Bond film is least pretentious, with meatier story, better all-around production of Ian Fleming caper. Bond investigates strange occurences in Jamaica; encounters master-fiend Dr. No (Wiseman).

Dr. Rhythm (1938) 80m. **½ D: Frank Tuttle. Bing Crosby, Mary Carlisle, Beatrice Lillie, Andy Devine, Laura Hope Crews, Rufe Davis. Bing battles another silly script playing bodyguard for Carlisle in Lillie's house. Bea isn't allowed to let go, which might have perked up film.

Doctor Satan's Robot (1940) 100m. **½ D: William Witney, John English. Eduardo Ciannelli, Robert Wilcox, William Newell, Ella Neal, C. Montague Shaw. Ciannelli as mad Dr. Satan gives this Republic cliff-hanger a zingy flair, with Wilcox et al battling the seemingly invincible robot who can even do a double-take. Re-edited movie serial: MYSTERIOUS DR. SATAN.

Dr. Socrates (1935) 70m. **½ D: William Dieterle. Paul Muni, Ann Dvorak, Barton MacLane, Raymond Brown, Mayo Methot. Enjoyable, offbeat film about small-town doctor Muni who unwillingly becomes official doctor for wounded mobsters. Fine performances by all. Remade as KING OF THE UNDERWORLD with Kay Francis in the Muni role!

Dr. Strangelove or: How I Learned to Stop Worrying and Love the Bomb (1964) 93m. ***½ D: Stanley Kubrick. Peter Sellers, George C. Scott, Sterling Hayden, Slim Pickens, Keenan Wynn, Peter Bull. Biting satire on the bomb and government, with Sellers in three roles, one being the President of the U.S. His phone conversation with the Soviet Premier is classic.

Doctor Takes a Wife, The (1940) 89m. *** D: Alexander Hall. Ray Milland, Loretta Young, Reginald Gardiner, Gail Patrick, Edmund Gwenn, Frank Sully, Gordon Jones. Milland is mistaken for Young's husband, then forced to pretend he is. Stars and material spark each other at a lively pace.

Dr. Terror's House of Horrors (1965-British) C-98m. **½ D: Freddie Francis. Peter Cushing, Christopher Lee, Roy Castle, Donald Sutherland, Neil McCallum, Max Adrian, Edward Underdown. Don't let title steer you from this intelligent episodic thriller about a strange doctor (Cushing) who tells five men's fortunes on a train. Enjoyable horror-fantasy.

Dr. Who and the Daleks (1966-British) C-85m. **½ D: Gordon Flemyng. Peter Cushing, Roy Castle, Jennie Linden, Geoffrey Toone. U.S. release of BBC serial has good acting, nice suspense in imaginative invasion-Earth story.

Doctor X (1932) 80m. ***½ D: Michael Curtiz. Lionel Atwill, Fay Wray, Lee Tracy, Preston Foster, Robert Warwick, Mae Busch. Beautifully handled old-style thriller of full-moon strangler traced by police to laboratory. Comedy relief is only weakness. RETURN OF DR. X is no credit to original.

Doctor's Dilemma (1958-British) C-99m. *** D: Anthony Asquith. Leslie Caron, Dirk Bogarde, Alastair Sim, Robert Morley. Bubbly Shaw period play of young wife Caron conniving to convince medical specialists that her scoundrel husband is worth saving.

Dodge City (1939) C-105m. *** D: Michael Curtiz. Errol Flynn, Olivia de Havilland, Ann Sheridan, Bruce Cabot, Frank McHugh, Alan Hale, John Litel, Victor Jory, Ward Bond, Cora Witherspoon. Errol tames the West and De Havilland, in entertaining large-scale Western, with Warner Bros. stock company giving good vignettes. As dance-hall gal, Sheridan sings one number, has even less dialogue.

Dodsworth (1936) 90m. ***½ D: William Wyler. Walter Huston, Ruth

Chatterton, Paul Lukas, Mary Astor, David Niven. Fine adaptation of Sinclair Lewis novel about man who returns to Midwest having found new set of values in Europe; stylish production, with John Payne's screen debut in small role.

Dog, a Mouse and a Sputnik, A SEE: Sputnik.

Dog of Flanders, A (1959) C-96m. ** D: James B. Clark. David Ladd, Donald Crisp, Theodore Bikel, Max Croiset, Monique Ahrens. Tear-jerker for children about a boy, his dog, and friends they make. Crisp and Bikel have good character roles.

Doll Face (1945) 80m. **½ D: Lewis Seiler. Vivian Blaine, Dennis O'Keefe, Perry Como, Carmen Miranda, Martha Stewart, Michael Dunne. Burlesque dancer Blaine makes good in the big time; pleasant musical with Como's hit "Hubba Hubba Hubba."

Dolwyn (1949-British) 90m. **½ D: Emlyn Williams. Dame Edith Evans, Richard Burton, Anthony James, Emlyn Williams. Well-acted study of Evans, who, out of desire for revenge, comes to aid of her town; good character delineation. Retitled: LAST DAYS OF DOLWYN, THE; WOMAN OF DOLWYN.

Dolly Sisters, The (1945) C-114m. **½ D: Irving Cummings. Betty Grable, John Payne, June Haver, S. Z. Sakall, Reginald Gardiner. Sassy hokum with two lovely stars and a bevy of old song favorites from vaudeville's golden age.

Domino Kid, The (1957) 73m. *½ D: Ray Nazarro. Rory Calhoun, Kristine Miller, Andrew Duggan, Roy Barcroft. Revenge-oater with Calhoun returning to Lone Star State to seek killers of his family.

Don Juan Quilligan (1945) 75m. **½ D: Frank Tuttle. William Bendix, Joan Blondell, Phil Silvers, Anne Revere, B. S. Pully, Mary Treen. Through mishap Bendix is married to two girls at same time; lightweight comedy.

Dondi (1961) 100m. Bomb D: Albert Zugsmith. David Janssen, Patti Page, David Kory, Walter Winchell, Gale Gordon. Watch this film and you'll know why Janssen became a fugitive!

Donovan's Brain (1953) 83m. **½ D: Felix Feist. Lew Ayres, Gene Evans, Nancy Olson, Steve Brodie. Modest presentation of eerie experimentation with dead man's brain and subsequent chaos. Previously filmed as THE LADY AND THE MONSTER. Siodmak story refilmed several times.

Donovan's Reef (1963) C-109m. *** D: John Ford. John Wayne, Lee Marvin, Elizabeth Allen, Cesar Romero, Dorothy Lamour. Action-comedy bounces along with a good cast. Wayne and his free-wheeling friends on a Pacific island are disrupted by Duke's grown daughter (Allen) who comes to visit. Lots of fun.

Don't Bother to Knock (1952) 76m. **½ D: Roy Baker. Richard Widmark, Marilyn Monroe, Anne Bancroft, Jeanne Cagney, Elisha Cook, Jr., Gloria Blondell. Title has more punch than improbable yarn of mentally disturbed Monroe hired as babysitter in large hotel, saved from killing herself and charge by tough-but-good Widmark.

Don't Give Up the Ship (1959) 89m. *** D: Norman Taurog. Jerry Lewis, Dina Merrill, Diana Spencer, Mickey Shaughnessy, Robert Middleton, Gale Gordon, Claude Akins. Top comedy with Jerry as an ensign who lost a battleship during war and doesn't remember how. Shaughnessy is pal who helps look for it underwater. One of Lewis' all-time best.

Don't Go Near the Water (1957) C-102m. *½ D: Charles Walters. Glenn Ford, Gia Scala, Anne Francis, Fred Clark, Eva Gabor. Submerged comedy of sailors in the South Pacific of WW2 building a recreation hall. Clark as a frustrated officer, is best thing in slow film.

Don't Just Stand There (1968) C-100m. **½ D: Ron Winston. Robert Wagner, Mary Tyler Moore, Harvey Korman, Glynis Johns, Barbara Rhoades. Frantic comedy with perky stars; Wagner and Moore try to unravel mystery of disappearance of authoress Johns after writing the first half of a new book. Players' vivacity makes script seem better than it is.

Don't Take It to Heart (1945-British)

89m. *** D: Jeffrey Dell. Richard Greene, Patricia Medina, Richard Bird, Wylie Watson, Ernest Thesiger, Ronald Squire. Pleasant romantic comedy of ghost-ridden castle; Greene helps Medina and her townfolk overcome avaricious landowner.

Don't Touch the Loot SEE: **Grisbi**

Don't Trust Your Husband SEE: **Innocent Affair, An.**

Don't Worry, We'll Think of a Title (1966) 83m. Bomb D: Harmon Jones. Morey Amsterdam, Rose Marie, Joey Adams, Danny Thomas, Milton Berle, Nick Adams. Grade-Z shambles, despite many guest cameos by big TV and movie stars. Start worrying when you turn it on.

Doolins of Oklahoma, The (1949) 90m. **½ D: Gordon Douglas. Randolph Scott, George Macready, Louise Allbritton, John Ireland. Actionpacked western with Scott as head of the Doolin gang, who decides to give up his life of crime.

Doomsday Flight, The (1966) C-120m. **½ D: William Graham. Jack Lord, Edmond O'Brien, Katherine Crawford, John Saxon, Van Johnson, Michael Sarrazin. Smooth but clichéd telefeature yarn about passenger plane with time bomb aboard; Lord is FBI agent on the case. Disappointing Rod Serling script.

Door With Seven Locks, The (1962-German, dubbed) 96m. **½ D: Alfred Vohrer. Eddie Arent, Heinz Drache, Klaus Kinski, Adi Berber, Sabina Sesselman. Bizarre account of man who leaves in his will seven keys to treasure vault, with expected friction and murder; from Edgar Wallace story.

Double, The (1963-British) 56m. ** D: Lionel Harris. Jeannette Sterke, Alan MacNaughton, Robert Brown, Jane Griffiths. Meandering Edgar Wallace yarn. MacNaughton, suffering from amnesia, seeks to unravel his life, revealing espionage plot.

Double Bunk (1960-British) 92m. *½ D: C. M. Pennington-Richards. Ian Carmichael, Janette Scott, Sidney James, Liz Fraser. Slapstick account of Carmichael-Scott navigating their houseboat down the Thames, with predictable sight gags.

Double Confession (1951-British) 86m. ** D: Harry Reynolds. Derek Farr, Joan Hopkins, Peter Lorre. Potentially exciting study of human nature given pedestrian treatment: film centers on various people who happen to be at seaside resort beach.

Double Cross (1941) 66m. *½ D: Albert Kelley. Kane Richmond, Pauline Moore, Wynne Gibson. Mild account of cop seeking to get the goods on criminal gang; nothing unusual.

Double Cross (1949-Italian, dubbed) 77m. **½ D: Riccardo Freda. Vittorio Gassman, Amedeo Nazzari, Gianna Maria Canale. Acceptable account of two crooks who double-cross each other, with the victim seeking revenge years later.

Double Cross (1956-British) 71m. ** D: Anthony Squire. Donald Houston, Fay Compton, Anton Diffring, Delphi Lawrence. Mild account of foreign agents involved in typical espionage plot to steal government secrets.

Double Crossbones (1950) C-75m. ** D: Charles Barton. Donald O'Connor, Helena Carter, Will Geer, Hope Emerson, Glenn Strange. Flimsy costumer satire with O'Connor turned buccaneer, finally winning his sweetheart and exposing crooked city magistrate.

Double Dynamite (1951) 80m. ** D: Irving Cummings, Jr., Frank Sinatra, Jane Russell, Groucho Marx, Don McGuire. Star trio were at career lowpoints when flat comedy was made; Sinatra is bank clerk accused of theft.

Double Exposure (1944) 63m. ** D: William Berke. Chester Morris, Nancy Kelly, Jane Farrar, Richard Gaines. Fairly entertaining saga of girl who unwittingly takes photograph of murder.

Double Indemnity (1944) 106m. **** D: Billy Wilder. Barbara Stanwyck, Fred MacMurray, Edward G. Robinson, Porter Hall, Fortunio Bonanova, Jean Heather. Raymond Chandler-James Cain script packs fireworks in account of insurance salesman MacMurray coerced into murder plot by alluring Stanwyck and subsequent investigation by Fred's boss Robinson.

Double Life, A (1948) 104m. **** D:

George Cukor. Ronald Colman, Signe Hasso, Edmond O'Brien, Shelley Winters, Ray Collins. Colman gives a bravura Oscar-winning performance as actor whose stage roles affect his real-life actions; brilliant melodrama by Ruth Gordon-Garson Kanin.

Double or Nothing (1937) 95m. **½ D: Theodore Reed. Bing Crosby, Martha Raye, Andy Devine, Mary Carlisle, Benny Baker, John Gallaudet, Samuel S. Hinds. Contrived plot about Bing searching for get-rich-quick scheme helped by wonderful Raye and songs: "Don't Look Now," "The Moon Got In My Eyes."

Double Wedding (1937) 87m. *** D: Richard Thorpe. William Powell, Myrna Loy, Florence Rice, Edgar Kennedy, Sidney Toler, Mary Gordon. Wackier than usual for Powell and Loy, as avant-garde painter and dress designer who want Loy's sister Rice to marry, but do it themselves.

Doughgirls, The (1944) 102m. **½ D: James V. Kern. Ann Sheridan, Alexis Smith, Jane Wyman, Eve Arden, Jack Carson, Charlie Ruggles, Alan Mowbray, Craig Stevens, Regis Toomey. Brittle comedy, still another variation on crowded-situation-in-wartime-Washington, with newlyweds Carson and Wyman on hectic honeymoon. Arden standout as Russian hotel maid.

Down Among the Sheltering Palms (1953) C-87m. ** D: Edmund Goulding. William Lundigan, Jane Greer, Mitzi Gaynor, David Wayne, Gloria De Haven, Billy Gilbert, Jack Paar. Poor man's SOUTH PACIFIC recounts love problems of two U.S. army officers stationed in Pacific after WW2.

Down Argentine Way (1940) C-94m. **½ D: Irving Cummings. Don Ameche, Betty Grable, Carmen Miranda, Charlotte Greenwood, J. Carrol Naish, Henry Stephenson. Flimsy, entertaining musical; Grable's first solo film hit as wealthy American in love with horsebreeder Ameche.

Down Memory Lane (1949) 72m. **½ D: Phil Karlson. Steve Allen, Franklin Pangborn, Mack Sennett; scenes of W. C. Fields, Bing Crosby, etc. Allen is TV host who invites Sennett to show some of his representative comedies, the peg for this compilation film, interspersed with Allenisms. Crosby sequences are vintage enjoyment.

Down Three Dark Streets (1954) 85m. **½ D: Arnold Laven. Broderick Crawford, Ruth Roman, Martha Hyer, Marisa Pavan. Smoothly done interweaving episodes, pegged on FBI agent following through on trio of dead buddy's cases; Roman quite effective.

Down to Earth (1947) C-101m. *** D: Alexander Hall. Rita Hayworth, Larry Parks, Marc Platt, Roland Culver, James Gleason. Terpsichore, the Goddess of Dance (Hayworth) comes earthward to add life to director Parks' musical play. Engaging musical with Rita at her loveliest.

Down to the Sea in Ships (1949) 120m. *** D: Henry Hathaway. Richard Widmark, Lionel Barrymore, Dean Stockwell, Cecil Kellaway, Gene Lockhart. Young Stockwell fulfills seafaring goal on crusty Barrymore's whaling ship, under guidance of sailor Widmark. Good atmospheric yarn.

Dracula (1931) 85m. ***½ D: Tod Browning. Bela Lugosi, David Manners, Helen Chandler, Dwight Frye, Edward Van Sloan, Herbert Munston, Frances Dade. Classic horror film of Transylvanian vampire working his evil spell on perplexed group of Londoners. Lugosi's most famous role with his definitive interpretation of the Count.

Dracula—Prince of Darkness (1966-British) C-90m. ** D: Terence Fisher. Christopher Lee, Barbara Shelley, Andrew Keir, Suzan Farmer. Sequel to HORROR OF DRACULA doesn't measure up. Lee is reincarnated as the evil Count who wreaks terror on a group of tourists in a secluded castle.

Dacula's Daughter (1936) 72m. *** D: Lambert Hillyer. Otto Kruger, Marguerite Churchill, Gloria Holden, Irving Pichel, Edward Van Sloan, Nan Gray. Daughter is quite a match for poor boy she falls in love with. Holden is fine in title role, making the vampirish proceedings believable.

Dragon Murder Case (1934) 68m. D:

H. Bruce Humberstone. Warren William, Margaret Lindsay, Lyle Talbot, Eugene Pallette, Dorothy Tree. SEE: Philo Vance series.

Dragon Seed (1944) 145m. **½ D: Jack Conway, Harold S. Bucquet. Katharine Hepburn, Walter Huston, Aline MacMahon, Turhan Bey, Hurd Hatfield, Agnes Moorehead, Frances Rafferty, J. Carrol Naish, Akim Tamiroff, Henry Travers. Well-meant but overlong film of Pearl Buck's tale of Chinese town torn asunder by Japanese occupation; fascinating attempts at Oriental characterization.

Dragonfly Squadron (1954) 82m. ** D: Lesley Selander. John Hodiak, Barbara Britton, Bruce Bennett, Jess Barker. Usual Korean War story, alternating between pilots in the air and their romantic problems on ground.

Dragonwyck (1946) 103m. **½ D: Joseph L. Mankiewicz. Gene Tierney, Walter Huston, Vincent Price, Anne Revere, Spring Byington, Henry Morgan, Jessica Tandy, Trudy Marshall. Period chiller set at a gloomy mansion on the Hudson, with good cast but episodic presentation.

Dragoon Wells Massacre (1957) C-88m. ** D: Harold Schuster. Barry Sullivan, Dennis O'Keefe, Mona Freeman, Katy Jurado, Sebastian Cabot. Marauding Apaches force lawmen and renegades to join forces for self-protection; some action-packed scenes.

Dramatic School (1938) 80m. **½ D: Robert B. Sinclair. Luise Rainer, Paulette Goddard, Alan Marshal, Lana Turner, Anthony Allan (John Hubbard), Henry Stephenson, Genevieve Tobin. Carbon-copy STAGE DOOR with Rainer the center of attraction as fanciful girl who makes good in both marriage and career; look for Ann Rutherford, Dick Haymes, Hans Conried in early bit roles.

Drango (1957) 92m. ** D: Hall Bartlett, Jules Bricken. Jeff Chandler, Joanne Dru, Julie London, Donald Crisp. Chandler is Yankee Civil War veteran assigned to restore order to Southern town his command plundered. OK Western.

Dream Girl (1948) 85m. ** D: Mitchell Leisen. Betty Hutton, Macdonald Carey, Virginia Field, Patric Knowles, Walter Abel, Peggy Wood. Hutton stars as female Walter Mitty with constant daydreams; low-brow version of Elmer Rice play.

Dream Wife (1953) 101m. *½ D: Sidney Sheldon. Cary Grant, Deborah Kerr, Walter Pidgeon, Buddy Baer, Movita, Steve Forrest. Silly bedroom comedy about Grant "marrying" an Eastern princess for good-will reasons. Cast is wasted.

Dreamboat (1952) 83m. *** D: Claude Binyon. Ginger Rogers, Clifton Webb, Jeffrey Hunter, Anne Francis, Elsa Lanchester. Clever romp: silent-star Rogers cashes in on old movies now on TV, to chagrin of co-star Webb, now a distinguished professor. Scenes showing their old silent films are most enjoyable.

Dressed to Kill (1946) 72m. D: Roy William Neill. Basil Rathbone, Nigel Bruce, Patricia Morison, Edmond Breon, Carl Harbord, Patricia Cameron, Tom Dillon. SEE: Sherlock Holmes series.

Drive a Crooked Road (1954) 82m. ** D: Richard Quine. Mickey Rooney, Dianne Foster, Kevin McCarthy, Jack Kelly, Harry Landers. Quietly paced film of auto mechanic Rooney dreaming of being racing-car champ; instead becomes chump for gangsters, due to girlfriend.

Drum Beat (1954) C-111m. ** D: Delmer Daves. Alan Ladd, Audrey Dalton, Marisa Pavan, Robert Keith. Post-Civil War tale has Ladd as Indian fighter assigned to negotiate peacefully with warring Indian group.

Drums (1938) C-99m. *** D: Zoltan Korda. Sabu, Raymond Massey, Valerie Hobson, David Tree, Desmond Tester. Fine, colorful adventure with precocious Sabu rescuing the British cavalry in 19th-century India; atmospheric and actionful.

Drums Across the River (1954) C-78m. ** D: Nathan Juran. Audie Murphy, Lisa Gaye, Walter Brennan, Lyle Bettger. Murphy ties in with gold-jumpers overrunning Indian land, redeems himself by joining forces against these men to achieve peace.

Drums Along the Mohawk (1939) C-103m. *** D: John Ford, Claudette Colbert, Henry Fonda, Edna May

Oliver, John Carradine, Jessie Ralph, Arthur Shields, Robert Lowery, Ward Bond. Stirring tale of colonists in upstate N.Y. during Revolutionary War; not always engrossing, but Oliver's scene-stealing and repeated Indian attacks help.

Drums In the Deep South (1951) C-87m. ** D: William Cameron Menzies. James Craig, Barbara Payton, Guy Madison, Barton MacLane, Craig Stevens. Stagnant Civil War yarn of West Pointers who find themselves fighting for opposite causes.

Drums of Tahiti (1954) C-73m. Bomb D: William Castle. Dennis O'Keefe, Patricia Medina, Francis L. Sullivan, George Keymas. Three-D process only redeeming virtue of trite costumer (lost to viewer of course). O'Keefe is footloose American who aids revolt against French annexation attempt of Tahiti.

DuBarry Was a Lady (1943) C-101m. *** D: Roy Del Ruth. Red Skelton, Lucille Ball, Gene Kelly, Virginia O'Brien, Zero Mostel, Donald Meek, George Givot, Louise Beavers, Tommy Dorsey and Orchestra. Minus most of Cole Porter's score (except "Friendship") this changed DUBARRY is still fun with Skelton imagining himself in Madame DuBarry's French court; slow moving in spots.

Duchess of Idaho (1950) C-98m. **½ D: Robert Z. Leonard. Esther Williams, Van Johnson, John Lund, Paula Raymond, Amanda Blake, Eleanor Powell, Lena Horne. Williams' vehicle takes her to Sun Valley, where she's trying to help patch up roommate's romance but falls in love herself. MGM guest stars pep up the formula production.

Duck Soup (1933) 70m. **** D: Leo McCarey. Groucho, Harpo, Chico, Zeppo Marx, Margaret Dumont, Louis Calhern, Raquel Torres, Edmund Breese, Edgar Kennedy. Groucho is Rufus T. Firefly, King of Freedonia, in matchless comedy satire on toy kingdoms, with more zany routines than a circus. Don't miss it.

Dude Goes West, The (1948) 87m. ** D: Kurt Neumann. Eddie Albert, Gale Storm, James Gleason, Binnie Barnes, Gilbert Roland, Barton MacLane. Innocuous little comedy of Easterner Albert becoming a Western hero.

Duel at Apache Wells (1957) 70m. *½ D: Joe Kane. Anna Maria Alberghetti, Ben Cooper, Jim Davis, Bob Steele, Frank Puglia. Title tells more than all in standard oater.

Duel at Diablo (1966) C-103m. *** D: Ralph Nelson. James Garner, Sidney Poitier, Bibi Andersson, Dennis Weaver, Bill Travers. Aging Indians vs. cavalry formula comes alive in this exciting Western; offbeat casting with tight direction. Some may find it too violent, but a must for action and Western fans.

Duel at Silver Creek, The (1952) C-77m. *½ D: Don Siegel. Audie Murphy, Stephen McNally, Faith Domergue, Susan Cabot, Gerald Mohr. Ponderous oater has Murphy as the "Silver Kid" helping marshal fight town criminals.

Duel at the Rio Grande (1962-Italian, dubbed) C-93m. ** D: Mario Caiano. Sean Flynn, Danielle de Metz, Folco Lulli, Armando Calvo. Bland reworking of THE MARK OF ZORRO, with Flynn uneasy in lead role.

Duel in Durango SEE: **Gun Duel in Durango**

Duel in the Jungle (1954) C-102m. **½ D: George Marshall. Dana Andrews, Jeanne Crain, David Farrar, Patrick Barr. Actioner of insurance investigator tracking allegedly dead man to Africa, battle of survival that ensues.

Duel in the Sun (1946) C-138m. *** D: King Vidor. Jennifer Jones, Joseph Cotten, Gregory Peck, Lionel Barrymore, Lillian Gish, Herbert Marshall, Walter Huston, Butterfly McQueen, Charles Bickford, Harry Carey. Producer Selznick tried to duplicate success of GONE WITH THE WIND; this one's big but nowhere near GWTW. Essentially it's a colorful, sexy Western, elaborate but empty-headed . . . and, of course, long.

Duel of Champions (1961-Italian, dubbed) C-105m. ** D: Ferdinando Baldi. Alan Ladd, Franca Bettoja, Franco Fabrizi, Robert Keith, Luciano Marin. Stodgy epic set in ancient Rome with bored-looking Ladd the Roman leader who challenges forces of Alba.

Duel of the Titans (1961-Italian, dubbed) 88m. ** D: Sergio Corbucci.

Steve Reeves, Gordon Scott, Virna Lisi, Massimo Girotti. Reeves is Romulus and Scott is Remus in this fictional account of justice overcoming tyranny in ancient Rome.

Duffy of San Quentin (1954) 78m. **½ D: Walter Doniger. Louis Hayward, Joanne Dru, Paul Kelly, Maureen O'Sullivan, George Macready. Low-keyed account of Warden Duffy's reforms within the famed prison.

Duffy's Tavern (1945) 97m. Bomb D: Hal Walker. Barry Sullivan, Marjorie Reynolds, Bing Crosby, Dorothy Lamour, Alan Ladd, Betty Hutton, Eddie Bracken, Veronica Lake, Robert Benchley, Paulette Goddard, Brian Donlevy. Disastrous "comedy" of radio character Ed Gardner trying to save Duffy's Tavern, Victor Moore trying to save his record company. No redeeming values despite guest appearances by several dozen Paramount stars.

Duke of West Point, The (1938) 96m. **½ D: Alfred E. Green. Louis Hayward, Joan Fontaine, Tom Brown, Richard Carlson, Alan Curtis, Donald Barry. Predictable West Point saga of honor and love at the Academy is trite but entertaining, with Fontaine winning as the ingenue.

Dulcimer Street (1948-British) 112m. **½ D: Sidney Gilliat. Richard Attenborough, Alastair Sim, Stephen Murray, Fay Compton. Atmospheric account of a slum area of London and its inhabitants who champion one of their own accused of murder. Retitled: LONDON BELONGS TO ME.

Dulcy (1940) 64m. *½ D: S. Sylvan Simon. Ann Sothern, Ian Hunter, Roland Young, Reginald Gardiner, Billie Burke, Lynne Carver, Dan Dailey, Jr. Pretty bad comedy of Chinese orphan mending new family's problems. Good cast with inferior material.

Dunkirk (1958-British) 113m. **½ D: Leslie Norman. John Mills, Robert Urquhart, Ray Jackson, Meredith Edwards. Documentary-style drama recounting 1940 evacuation of Allied troops, relying too much on newsreel footage.

Durant Affair, The (1962-British) 73m. *½ D: Godfrey Grayson. Jane Griffiths, Conrad Phillips, Nigel Green, Simon Lack. Flabby courtroom melodrama.

Dust Be My Destiny (1939) 88m. **½ D: Lewis Seiler. John Garfield, Priscilla Lane, Alan Hale, Frank McHugh, John Litel, Billy Halop, Henry Armetta, Stanley Ridges. Garfield ideally cast as young misfit trying to find himself, with Lane a good partner in his search.

Dynamite (1929) 129m. *½ D: Cecil B. de Mille. Conrad Nagel, Kay Johnson, Charles Bickford, Julia Faye, Muriel McCormack, Joel McCrea. Tame De Mille nonspectacle detailing stale plot of girl who must find a husband in order to obtain a legacy. Archaic fun.

Each Dawn I Die (1939) 92m. *** D: William Keighley. James Cagney, George Raft, George Bancroft, Jane Bryan, Maxie Rosenbloom, Thurston Hall. Reporter Cagney is innocently sent to jail, where he encounters tough-guy Raft. Rugged prison film, well done.

Eagle and the Hawk (1933) 68m. ***½ D: Stuart Walker. Fredric March, Cary Grant, Jack Oakie, Carole Lombard, Guy Standing, Douglas Scott. Well-produced antiwar film with reluctant hero March, copilot Grant, everyone's friend Oakie, society girl Lombard. Still timely.

Eagle and the Hawk (1950) C-104m. **½ D: Lewis R. Foster. John Payne, Rhonda Fleming, Dennis O'Keefe, Thomas Gomez, Fred Clark. Contrived actioner set in 1860's Mexico-Texas with O'Keefe and Payne U.S. law enforcers stifling coup to make Maximilian ruler of Mexico; Fleming is fetching love interest.

Eagle Squadron (1942) 109m. **½ D: Arthur Lubin. Robert Stack, Eddie Albert, Diana Barrymore, Nigel Bruce, Jon Hall, Evelyn Ankers, Gladys Cooper, Mary Carr. Usual WW2 action and romance as young American fliers fought the war in the RAF. Good action scenes help average script.

Earl Carroll Vanities (1945) 91m. **½ D: Joseph Santley. Dennis O'Keefe, Constance Moore, Eve Arden, Otto Kruger. Republic Pictures tried hard to give this musical class, but zest and production values are lacking; Arden adds her usual quips.

Earl of Chicago, The (1940) 85m. *** D: Richard Thorpe. Robert Montgomery, Edward Arnold, Reginald Owen, Edmund Gwenn. Far-out film of prohibition racketeer who turns out to be titled Englishman, goes to London to claim inheritance. Montgomery handles difficult role admirably.

Early to Bed (1936) 75m. **½ D: Norman Z. McLeod. Mary Boland, Charlie Ruggles, George Barbier, Gail Patrick, Robert McWade, Lucien Littlefield. Ruggles' sleepwalking involves him in shady adventure with gangsters. Boland-Ruggles make sparkling team.

Earrings of Madame De, The (1954-French, dubbed) 105m. ** D: Max Ophuls. Charles Boyer, Danielle Darrieux, Vittorio DeSica. Continental froufrou involving Boyer, flirtatious wife Darrieux, and roué DeSica; thin and airy.

Earth Dies Screaming, The (1964-British) 62m. **½ D: Terence Fisher. Willard Parker, Virginia Field, Dennis Price, Vanda Godsell. Grim British thriller with invaders taking over remote village; packs great initial suspense but labors.

Earth vs. the Flying Saucers (1956) 83m. ** D: Fred F. Sears. Hugh Marlowe, Joan Taylor, Donald Curtis, Morris Ankrum. Unremarkable sci-fi records efforts of scientists on earth to combat inhabitants from outer space.

Earthworm Tractors (1936) 63m. **½ D: Ray Enright. Joe E. Brown, June Travis, Guy Kibbee, Dick Foran, Carol Hughes, Gene Lockhart, Olin Howland. Fair cast with Brown as Saturday Evening Post character Alexander Botts, salesman extraordinaire.

East End Chant SEE: **Limehouse Blues**

East of Eden (1955) C-115m. ***½ D: Elia Kazan. Julie Harris, James Dean, Raymond Massey, Burl Ives, Jo Van Fleet, Richard Davalos, Albert Dekker. Sprawling version of John Steinbeck novel of dominating father (Massey), romance between his rebellious son (Dean) and strange local girl (Harris). Good acting, but continuity doesn't ring true.

East of Sumatra (1953) C-82m. **½ D: Budd Boetticher. Jeff Chandler, Marilyn Maxwell, Anthony Quinn, Suzan Ball, Peter Graves. Satisfactory actioner set on Pacific island. Chandler is mining engineer trying to prevent native uprising while romancing Maxwell; Quinn effective as villain.

East of the River (1940) 73m. **½ D: Alfred E. Green. John Garfield, Brenda Marshall, Marjorie Rambeau, William Lundigan. Another variation of MANHATTAN MELODRAMA, with two childhood pals growing up on opposite sides of the law. Rambeau gives a fine performance.

East Side of Heaven (1939) 90m. **½ D: David Butler. Bing Crosby, Joan Blondell, Mischa Auer, Irene Hervey, C. Aubrey Smith. Cute Crosby comedy with songs; Bing becomes guardian of abandoned baby, croons title tune, "Sing A Song Of Moonbeams."

East Side, West Side (1949) 108m. **½ D: Mervyn LeRoy. Barbara Stanwyck, James Mason, Ava Gardner, Van Heflin, Cyd Charisse, Gale Sondergaard, William Frawley. Stanwyck-Mason have pivotal roles as chic N.Y.C. society couple with abundant marital woes, stirred up by alluring Gardner and understanding Heflin. Static MGM version of Marcia Davenport's superficial novel.

Easter Parade (1948) C-103m. ***½ D: Charles Walters. Judy Garland, Fred Astaire, Peter Lawford, Ann Miller, Jules Munshin. Delightful Irving Berlin musical with Astaire trying to forget ex-dance partner Miller as he rises to stardom with Judy. One good song after another, Astaire and Garland in top form.

Easy Come, Easy Go (1947) 77m. **½ D: John Farrow. Barry Fitzgerald, Diana Lynn, Sonny Tufts, Dick Foran, Frank McHugh, Allen Jenkins. Fitzgerald is his usual self as a horseplayer who refuses to let daughter Lynn get married.

Easy Go SEE: **Free and Easy**.

Easy Life, The (1963-Italian, dubbed) 105m. *** D: Dino Risi. Vittorio Gassman, Catherine Spaak, Jean-Louis Trintignant, Luciana Angiolilio. Gassman has proper joie de vivre for playing middle-aged playboy who introduces student Trintignant to life of frolic with tragic results; well-paced and haunting.

Easy Living (1937) 66m. *** D: Mitchell Leisen. Jean Arthur, Edward Arnold, Ray Milland, Franklin Pangborn, William Demarest, Mary Nash, Luis Alberni. Millionaire Arnold throws spoiled wife's mink out the window; it drops on unsuspecting working-girl Arthur. Arnold's son Milland, off making his career, falls in love, the girl—Jean Arthur. Delightful comedy written by Preston Sturges.

Easy Living (1949) 77m. ** D: Jacques Tourneur. Victor Mature, Lucille Ball, Lizabeth Scott, Sonny Tufts. Gridiron life is no picnic for pro football player Mature when he has to please grasping wife; Scott sulks effectively.

Easy to Love (1953) C-96m. **½ D: Charles Walters. Esther Williams, Van Johnson, Tony Martin, Carroll Baker. Pleasant Williams aquatic vehicle set at Cypress Gardens, with Johnson and Martin vying for her love.

Easy to Wed (1946) C-110m. **½ D: Edward Buzzell. Van Johnson, Esther Williams, Lucille Ball, Keenan Wynn, Cecil Kellaway. Routine comedy with good cast about newspaper libel suit. Typically confusing but fairly engrossing. Remake of LIBELED LADY.

Easy Way, The SEE: Room For One More.

Ebb Tide (1937) C-94m. **½ D: James Hogan. Frances Farmer, Ray Milland, Oscar Homolka, Lloyd Nolan, Barry Fitzgerald, David Torrence. Hokey but entertaining outdoors picture in color with Homolka a madman on strange island. Remade as ADVENTURE ISLAND.

Eddie Cantor Story, The (1953) C-116m. *½ D: Alfred E. Green. Keefe Brasselle, Marilyn Erskine, Aline MacMahon, Marie Windsor. If Brasselle doesn't turn you off as Cantor, MacMahon's Grandma Esther or a putty-nosed young actor playing Jimmy Durante certainly will.

Eddy Duchin Story, The (1956) C-123m. ** D: George Sidney. Tyrone Power, Kim Novak, Victoria Shaw, James Whitmore. Glossy Hollywood biography of pianist-bandleader of 30's-40's; Power tries hard (Carmen Cavallaro dubs at keyboard). Tearjerker ending and theme song memorable.

Edge of Darkness (1943) 120m. *** D: Lewis Milestone. Errol Flynn, Ann Sheridan, Walter Huston, Nancy Coleman, Helmut Dantine, Judith Anderson, Ruth Gordon. Skillfully acted drama of Norway rebelling against Nazi takeover during WW2; Warner Bros. troupe at its peak.

Edge of Doom (1950) 99m. ** D: Mark Robson. Dana Andrews, Farley Granger, Joan Evans, Mala Powers, Adele Jergens. Granger reaches peak of histrionic despair in moody piece about young man baffled by poverty, religion, murder, and assorted other problems.

Edge of Eternity (1959) C-80m. ** D: Don Siegel. Cornel Wilde, Victoria Shaw, Mickey Shaughnessy, Edgar Buchanan, Rian Garrick, Jack Elam. Deputy sheriff Wilde tracks killers to Grand Canyon, leading to shoot-out on mining buckets suspended on cables way above canyon.

Edge of Hell (1956) 76m. *½ D: Hugo Haas. Hugo Haas, Francesca de Scaffa, Ken Carlton, June Hammerstein. Offbeat, minor film of pauper Haas, his beloved dog, and small boy who enters on the scene.

Elge of the City (1957) 85m. **** D: Martin Ritt. John Cassavetes, Sidney Poitier, Jack Warden, Ruby Dee, Kathleen Maguire, Ruth White. Somber, realistic account of N.Y.C. waterfront life and corruption. Friendship of army deserter Cassavetes and dock worker Poitier, both conflicting with union racketeer Warden, provides focus for reflections on integration and integrity in lower-class society. Masterfully acted by all.

Edison, The Man (1940) 107m. *** D: Clarence Brown. Spencer Tracy, Rita Johnson, Lynne Overman, Charles Coburn, Gene Lockhart, Henry Travers, Felix Bressart. Sequel to YOUNG TOM EDISON perfectly casts Tracy as earnest inventor with passion for mechanical ingenuity. Facts and MGM fantasy combine well in sentimental treatment.

Edward, My Son (1949-British) 112m. *** D: George Cukor. Spencer Tracy, Deborah Kerr, Ian Hunter, James Donald, Mervyn Johns, Felix Aylmer,

Leueen McGrath. Film recounts rocky marriage of British couple Tracy and Kerr who discover they drove their son to suicide. Gimmicks of Tracy talking to viewer, title character never being shown, come off as forced.

Egg and I, The (1947) 108m. *** D: Chester Erskine. Claudette Colbert, Fred MacMurray, Marjorie Main, Louise Allbritton, Percy Kilbride. Colbert is delightful as city girl who marries chicken farmer MacMurray and struggles to survive on his farm; first appearance of Ma and Pa Kettle.

Egyptian, The (1954) C-140m. **½ D: Michael Curtiz. Edmund Purdom, Jean Simmons, Victor Mature, Gene Tierney, Michael Wilding, Peter Ustinov. Beautiful scenery and sets make for great atmosphere in otherwise uneven biblical spectacle. Some good acting by Purdom, others wasted.

8½ (1963-Italian, dubbed) 135m. *** D: Federico Fellini. Marcello Mastroianni, Claudia Cardinale, Anouk Aimee, Sandra Milo, Barbara Steele. Either you'll love or you'll hate this overlong flight of fantasy from disturbed mind of Fellini. Cast is excellent but dwarfed by filmic techniques of director-writer; Mastroianni plays filmmaker trying to develop new project amid frequent visions and countless subplots. Will leave you either exultant, confused, or asleep.

Eight Iron Men (1952) 80m. **½ D: Edward Dmytryk. Lee Marvin, Richard Kiley, Nick Dennis, Arthur Franz, Mary Castle. WW2 actioner focusing on a group of soldiers, strain they undergo during continued enemy attack.

Eight O'clock Walk (1952-British) 87m. **½ D: Lance Comfort. Richard Attenborough, Cathy O'Donnell, Derek Farr, Ian Hunter. Courtroom drama manages to create pace and tension, involving murder trial; nicely played by Attenborough.

Eighteen and Anxious (1957) 93m. ** D: Joe Parker. Martha Scott, Jim Backus, Mary Webster, William Campbell, Jackie Coogan. Oddball cast atones for amateurish muck about pregnant teen-ager forced to face life's realities.

80,000 Suspects (1963-British) 113m. ** D: Val Guest. Claire Bloom, Richard Johnson, Yolande Donlan, Cyril Cusack. Capable cast saddled with yarn of doctor (Johnson) and wife (Bloom) finding new love together while combating local smallpox outbreak.

El Alamein (1953) 67m. ** D: Fred R. Sears. Scott Brady, Edward Ashley, Rita Moreno, Michael Pate. No surprises in WW2 desert actioner with Brady heading group being attacked by Germans.

El Cid (1961) C-184m. *** D: Anthony Mann. Charlton Heston, Sophia Loren, Raf Vallone, Genevieve Page, Hurd Hatfield. Mammoth spectacle with above-average script and acting in film of legendary Cid (Heston) who drove Moors from Spain.

El Paso (1949) C-92m. ** D: Lewis R. Foster. John Payne, Gail Russell, Sterling Hayden, Gabby Hayes. Routine Western of post-Civil War Texas, with Payne an attorney who discovers gunplay more than words will rid town of crooks.

Eleanor Roosevelt Story, The (1965) 91m. ***½ D: Richard Kaplan. Narrated by Archibald Macleish, Eric Severeid, Francis Cole. Intelligently handled account of the great American citizen, who overcomes personal obstacles to become a beacon of human kindness.

Electronic Monster, The (1960-British) 72m. *½ D: Montgomery Tully. Rod Cameron, Mary Murphy, Meredith Edwards, Peter Illing. Cameron investigates actress' death, revealing strange experiments at a clinic; scientific gadgetry has its moments.

Elephant Boy (1937-British) 80m. *** D: Robert Flaherty. Sabu, W. E. Holloway, Walter Hudd, Allan Jeayes, Bruce Gordon, D. J. Williams. Successful adaptation of Rudyard Kipling story. Native boy Sabu (in film debut) claims he knows location of elephant burying ground. Atmospheric direction.

Elephant Gun (1959-British) C-84m. ** D: Ken Annakin. Belinda Lee, Michael Craig, Patrick McGoohan, Anna Gaylor, Eric Pohlmann, Pamela Stirling. Jungle love triangle has virtue of on-location shooting in Africa.

Elephant Stampede (1951) 71m. D: Ford Beebe. Johnny Sheffield, Donna Martell, Edith Evanson, Martin Wilkins, Myron Healey, Leonard Mudie,

Guy Kingsford. SEE: **Bomba the Jungle Boy** series.

Elephant Walk (1954) C-103m. ** D: William Dieterle. Elizabeth Taylor, Dana Andrews, Peter Finch, Abraham Sofaer. Overblown melodrama set on Ceylon tea plantation, with Taylor as Finch's new bride who must cope with environment and his father complex. Pachyderm stampede climax comes none too soon.

El Greco (1966-Italian-French, dubbed) C-95m. ** D: Luciano Salce. Mel Ferrer, Rosanna Schiaffino, Franco Giacobini, Renzo Giovampietro, Adolfo Celi. Despite lavish trappings, story of painter reduced to soap-opera terms falls flat. Beautiful color, but no plot of any distinction.

Ella Cinders (1926) 60m. *** D: Alfred E. Green. Colleen Moore, Lloyd Hughes, Jed Prouty, Harry Langdon. Excellent Colleen Moore silent vehicle about small-town girl going to Hollywood to make good; bright and peppy, with amusing guest appearance by Langdon.

Ellery Queen Perhaps the most successful series of detective stories ever written, the Ellery Queen mysteries rank as one of the least successful film series. A few scattered attempts to film Queen stories in the 1930's with Donald Cook and Eddie Quillan were justifiably ignored; then in 1940 Columbia began a series starring Ralph Bellamy as Ellery Queen, Charley Grapewin as his Inspector father, Margaret Lindsay as his girl Friday Nikki, and James Burke as Inspector Queen's dim-witted aide. The first entry, ELLERY QUEEN, MASTER DETECTIVE, was fast-paced and enjoyable; the subsequent three films with Bellamy were variable, distinguished mainly by excellent casts. With a switch to William Gargan in the title role in 1942, the series went downhill, the mysteries becoming more obvious and the original conception of the character well obscured by original screenplays unrelated to published stories. Gargan's three efforts as Queen were undistinguished, and his last film, ENEMY AGENTS MEET ELLERY QUEEN, was also the last in the short-lived series. The first film, ELLERY QUEEN, MASTER DETECTIVE, and the third, ELLERY QUEEN AND THE MURDER RING, are probably the best in the series, the others ranging from entertaining to rather weak, a vast disappointment to the mystery fans who have come to regard the stories of the clever sleuth as top-grade in the mystery genre.

Ellery Queen and the Murder Ring (1941) 65m. D: James Hogan. Ralph Bellamy, Margaret Lindsay, Charley Grapewin, Mona Barrie, Paul Hurst, James Burke, Blanche Yurka.

Ellery Queen and the Perfect Crime (1941) 68m. D: James Hogan. Ralph Bellamy, Margaret Lindsay, Charley Grapewin, Spring Byington, H. B. Warner, James Burke.

Ellery Queen, Master Detective (1940) 66m. D: Kurt Neumann. Ralph Bellamy, Margaret Lindsay, Charley Grapewin, James Burke, Michael Whalen, Marsha Hunt.

Ellery Queen's Penthouse Mystery (1941) 69m. D: James Hogan. Ralph Bellamy, Charley Grapewin, Margaret Lindsay, James Burke, Anna May Wong, Eduardo Ciannelli, Frank Albertson.

Elmer Gantry (1960) C-145m. ***½ D: Richard Brooks. Burt Lancaster, Jean Simmons, Dean Jagger, Arthur Kennedy, Shirley Jones. Charlatan Lancaster joins evangelist Simmons, exploiting her touring show; newspaperman Kennedy tries to expose their hypocrisy. Lancaster won Oscar in title role, as did Jones, playing jilted-girlfriend-turned-prostitute. Vibrant handling of Sinclair Lewis story of 1920's Midwest is a must-see film.

Elmer the Great (1933) 74m. *** D: Mervyn LeRoy. Joe E. Brown, Patricia Ellis, Claire Dodd, Sterling Holloway, Jessie Ralph. Excellent Ring Lardner baseball comedy, filmed before as FAST COMPANY, of naive country boy who becomes ball star, gets involved with crooks at the same time.

Elopement (1951) 82m. ** D: Henry Koster. Clifton Webb, Anne Francis, Charles Bickford, William Lundigan, Reginald Gardiner. Tame proceedings despite Webb's arch performance as Francis' father, who disapproves of her marriage to Lundigan.

Elusive Corporal, The (1963-French, dubbed) 108m. **½ D: Jean Renoir. Jean-Pierre Cassel, Claude Brasseur, Claude Rich, O. E. Hasse. Flavorful if predictable account of Frenchmen in German prison camp during WW2, determined to escape.

Embraceable You (1948) 80m. ** D: Felix Jacoves. Dane Clark, Geraldine Brooks, S. Z. Sakall, Wallace Ford. Tough-guy Clark injures young girl, then falls in love with her, in this sentimental romance.

Emergency (1962-British) 63m. ** D: Francis Searle. Glyn Houston, Zena Walker, Dermont Walsh, Colin Tapley. Adequate programmer dealing with Walker-Walsh reaffirming their marriage while waiting for blood donor to save their daughter's life.

Emergency Wedding (1950) 78m. ** D: Edward Buzzell. Barbara Hale, Larry Parks, Una Merkel, Jim Backus, Queenie Smith. Sterile remake of YOU BELONG TO ME detailing jealous Parks who thinks new wife, doctor Hale, spends too much time with her male patients.

Emma (1931) 73m. ** D: Clarence Brown. Marie Dressler, Richard Cromwell, Jean Hersholt, Myrna Loy, John Miljan, Leila Bennett. OK Dressler hokum about family servant becoming actual member of family through marriage.

Emperor Waltz, The (1948) C-106m. **½ D: Billy Wilder. Bing Crosby, Joan Fontaine, Roland Culver, Lucile Watson, Richard Hayden, Sig Ruman. Lavish but standard Crosby musical set in Franz Joseph Austria (on Hollywood's backlots) with Bing selling record-players to royalty. Awfully schmaltzy material for writer-director Wilder.

Emperor's Candlesticks, The (1937) 89m. **½ D: George Fitzmaurice. William Powell, Luise Rainer, Robert Young, Maureen O'Sullivan, Frank Morgan, Emma Dunn, Douglass Dumbrille. Romance and intrigue in Russia between Powell and Rainer, spies on opposite sides of the fence; lavish frou-frou.

Enchanted April (1935) 66m. ** D: Harry Beaumont. Ann Harding, Frank Morgan, Katherine Alexander, Reginald Owen, Jane Baxter. Slightly overworn drama of four different women spending their vacation at same Italian villa; Harding is staunch.

Enchanted Cottage, The (1945) 91m. **½ D: John Cromwell. Dorothy McGuire, Robert Young, Herbert Marshall, Mildred Natwick, Spring Byington, Hillary Brooke. Fantasy set in New England cottage where two misfits find love; sensitively handled, from Arthur Pinero play.

Enchanted Forest (1945) C-78m. **½ D: Lew Landers. Edmund Lowe, Brenda Joyce, Billy Severn, Harry Davenport, John Litel. Nicely done story of young boy who learns about life from old man who lives amid nature in the forest.

Enchanted Island (1958) C-94m. *½ D: Allan Dwan. Dana Andrews, Jane Powell, Don Dubbins, Arthur Shields. Miscast, low-budget version of Herman Melville's TYPEE. Andrews is deserter from American whaling ship who finds love with native girl Powell on South Sea island; some minor uprisings by local cannibals for good measure.

Enchantment (1948) 102m. *** D: Irving Reis. David Niven, Teresa Wright, Evelyn Keyes, Farley Granger, Jayne Meadows, Leo G. Carroll. Weepy romancer with elderly Niven recalling his tragic love as he watches grandson Granger embark upon his own love life.

Encore (1952-British) 89m. *** D: Pat Jackson, Anthony Pelissier, Harold French. Nigel Patrick, Roland Culver, Kay Walsh, Glynis Johns, Terence Morgan. Entertaining trilogy of Somerset Maugham stories: brothers try to outdo one another over money; grouchy matron almost ruins ship cruise; apprehensive circus performer faces a crisis.

End of Desire (1962-French, dubbed) C-86m. ** D: Alexandre Astruc. Maria Schell, Christian Marquand, Pascale Petit, Ivan Desny. Schell is only bright light in De Maupassant tale of wife who discovers her husband loves her money and prefers to romance servant (Antonella Lualdi).

End of the Affair, The (1955-British) 106m. **½ D: Edward Dmytryk. Deborah Kerr, Van Johnson, John Mills, Peter Cushing, Michael Goodliffe. Graham Greene's mystic-religious novel about a wartime love affair in London loses much in screen version, especially from bad Johnson portrayal; Kerr is earnest.

End of the River, The (1948-British) 80m. ** D: Derek Twist. Sabu, Bibi Ferreira, Esmond Knight, Torin

Thatcher, Robert Douglas. Native boy Sabu fights for acceptance in white world; ambitious drama suffers from mediocre casting.

Endless Summer, The (1966) C-95m. *** D: Bruce Brown. Mike Hynson, Robert August. Superior documentary on surfing, filmed on location around the world, with a most diverting tongue-in-cheek narrative.

Enemy Agents Meet Ellery Queen (1942) 65m. D: James Hogan. William Gargan, Gale Sondergaard, Margaret Lindsay, Charley Grapewin, Gilbert Roland. SEE: Ellery Queen series.

Enemy Below, The (1957) C-98m. *** D: Dick Powell. Robert Mitchum, Curt Jurgens, Theodore Bikel, Doug McClure, Russell Collins, David Hedison. Select WW2 submarine chase tale, which manages to garner interest from usual crew interaction of U.S. vs. Germany in underwater action; special effects notable.

Enemy From Space (1957-British) 84m. ** D: Val Guest. Brian Donlevy, Michael Ripper, Sidney James, Bryan Forbes. Undistinguished sci-fi which leaves mandatory monster from outer space to one's imagination but spells out dreary plot in detail.

Enemy General, The (1960) 74m. **½ D: George Sherman. Van Johnson, Jean-Pierre Aumont, Dany Carrel, John Van Dreelen. OSS officer (Johnson) and French resistance leader Aumont join forces to rescue Nazi general (Van Dreelen) who wants to defect to Allies; satisfactory handling of middling material.

Enforcer, The (1951) 87m. *** D: Bretaigne Windust. Humphrey Bogart, Zero Mostel, Ted de Corsia, Everett Sloane, Roy Roberts. Bogie is D.A. cracking down on crime ring led by Sloane in this raw drama, realistically done.

Ensign Pulver (1964) C-104m. ** D: Joshua Logan. Robert Walker, Jr., Burl Ives, Walter Matthau, Tommy Sands, James Farentino, Diana Sands, Kay Medford, Millie Perkins. Flat sequel to MR. ROBERTS has Walker sinking in Jack Lemmon role amid synthetic seaboard and coral isle shenanigans.

Enter Arsene Lupin (1944) 72m. ** D: Ford Beebe. Charles Korvin, Ella Raines, J. Carrol Naish, George Dolenz, Gale Sondergaard. Good supporting cast of villains gives zest to tame tale of naive heroine possessing a wealth of jewels.

Enter Laughing (1967) C-112m. *** D: Carl Reiner. Jose Ferrer, Shelley Winters, Elaine May, Jack Gilford, Reni Santoni, Janet Margolin, David Opatoshu, Michael J. Pollard, Don Rickles, Richard Deacon, Nancy Kovack. Reiner's adaptation of his autobiographical play provides a steady stream of laughs as a young would-be actor tries to break into show business despite a nagging family and endless catastrophes. Enthusiastic cast puts this over quite nicely.

Enter Madame (1935) 83m. **½ D: Elliott Nugent. Elissa Landi, Cary Grant, Lynne Overman, Sharon Lynne, Frank Albertson. Grant marries opera star Landi and winds up taking back seat to her career; pleasant romantic comedy.

Entertainer, The (1960-British) 97m. ***½ D: Tony Richardson. Laurence Olivier, Brenda De Banzie, Albert Finney, Alan Bates, Joan Plowright, Roger Livesey, Shirley Ann Field. Seedy vaudevillian (Olivier) ruins everyone's life and won't catch on. Film captures flavor of chintzy seaside resort, complementing Olivier's brilliance as egotistical song-and-dance man.

Erik the Conqueror (1963-Italian, dubbed) C-81m. ** D: Mario Bava. Cameron Mitchell, Alice Kessler, Ellen Kessler, Françoise Cristophe. Unexceptional account of 10th-century Viking life, with Mitchell fighting for virtue and love.

Errand Boy, The (1962) 92m. **½ D: Jerry Lewis. Jerry Lewis, Brian Donlevy, Howard McNear, Sig Ruman, Fritz Field, Iris Adrian, Kathleen Freeman, Doodles Weaver. Jerry on the loose in a movie studio has its moments. Long string of gags provide the laughter; veteran character actors produce the sparkle.

Escapade (1957-British) 87m. ** D: Philip Leacock. John Mills, Yvonne Mitchell, Alastair Sim, Jeremy Spenser. Authoritarian headmaster must cope with rebellious trio of students, leading to pacifist philosophy talkathon between Mills, Sims, et al.

Escapade in Japan (1957) C-92m. ** D: Arthur Lubin. Teresa Wright,

Cameron Mitchell, Jon Provost, Philip Ober. Premise of American boy and Japanese friend seeking former's parents is acceptable excuse for nice scenic tour of Japan.

Escape (1940) 104m. *** D: Mervyn LeRoy. Norma Shearer, Robert Taylor, Conrad Veidt, Nazimova, Felix Bressart. Countess Shearer helps Taylor get his mother (Nazimova) out of German concentration camp before WW2; polished, with sterling cast.

Escape (1948-British) 78m. *** D: Joseph L. Mankiewicz. Rex Harrison, Peggy Cummins, William Hartnell, Norman Wooland, Jill Esmond. Compelling account of man sent to prison, unjustly in his opinion; his attempted escape climaxes narrative.

Escape From East Berlin (1962) 94m. ** D: Robert Siodmak. Don Murray, Christine Kaufmann, Werner Klemperer, Ingrid van Bergen, Karl Schell. At least Murray is earnest.

Escape From Fort Bravo (1953) C-98m. *** D: John Sturges. William Holden, Eleanor Parker, John Forsythe, Polly Bergen, William Demarest. Well-executed Western set in 1860's Arizona, balancing North-South conflict with whites vs. Indians, climaxed by tense redskin ambush.

Escape From Red Rock (1958) 75m. *1/2 D: Edward Bernds. Brian Donlevy, Jay C. Flippen, Eilene Janssen, Gary Murray. Modest oater of rancher and gal involved in theft, being chased into Indian country by pursuing posse; film has virtue of Donlevy's presence.

Escape From San Quentin (1957) 81m. Bomb D: Fred F. Sears. Johnny Desmond, Merry Anders, Richard Devon, Roy Engel. Drab film has Desmond as runaway convict who decides to give himself and buddy up to police.

Escape From Zahrain (1962) C-93m. *1/2 D: Ronald Neame. Yul Brynner, Sal Mineo, Madlyn Rhue, Jack Warden, James Mason, Jay Novello. Plodding film of five prisoners escaping from jail in Mideastern country, being chased across desert. Nice photography at least.

Escape in the Desert (1945) 81m. ** D: Edward A. Blatt. Philip Dorn, Helmut Dantine, Jean Sullivan, Alan Hale. Tame remake of THE PETRIFIED FOREST involving American flyer encountering Nazi at desert hotel.

Escape in the Fog (1945) 65m. ** D: Budd Boetticher. Nina Foch, William Wright, Otto Kruger, Konstantin Shayne. Eerie programmer of girl who has strange dream of murder being committed and encounters the dream victim in real life.

Escape Me Never (1947) 104m. ** D: Peter Godfrey. Ida Lupino, Errol Flynn, Gig Young, Eleanor Parker, Reginald Denny. Everybody is having an illicit affair with someone else's wife, husband, or fiancee in this muddled drama.

Escape to Glory (1940) 74m. **1/2 D: John Brahm. Constance Bennett, Pat O'Brien, John Halliday. Hokey WW2 yarn of Nazi scientist destroying Allies' ships via secret ray device; Bennett makes it worthwhile.

Escort for Hire (1960-British) 66m. ** D: Godfrey Grayson. June Thorburn, Noel Trevarthan, Pete Murray, Jill Melford, Guy Middleton. Clichéd murder yarn, enhanced by Technicolor, with Trevarthan an out-of-work actor joining escort service, becoming involved in murder.

Espionage Agent (1939) 83m. ** D: Lloyd Bacon. Joel McCrea, Brenda Marshall, George Bancroft, Jeffrey Lynn, James Stephenson, Martin Kosleck. Formula spy caper with McCrea and Marshall tracking down the head of notorious spy ring.

Esther and the King (1960) C-109m. **1/2 D: Raoul Walsh. Joan Collins, Richard Egan, Denis O'Dea, Sergio Fantoni. Cardboard costumer pretends to recreate 4th-century B.C. Persia, with stony performances by Collins and Egan in title roles; non-epic battle scenes.

Esther Waters (1947-British) 108m. **1/2 D: Peter Proud. Dirk Bogarde, Fay Compton, Kathleen Ryan, Cyril Cusack, Mary Clare. Well-appointed account of rogue Bogarde involved with lovely damsels frequenting the racetracks; set in 19th-century England. Film bogs down into soaper of gloomy married life, marring initial zest.

Eternal Sea, The (1955) 103m. **1/2 D: John H. Auer. Sterling Hayden, Alexis Smith, Dean Jagger, Virginia Grey. Well-played biography of Admiral John Hoskins' efforts to retain active command despite WW2 injury. Hayden is restrained in lead role; modest production values.

Eternally Yours (1939) 95m. **½ D: Tay Garnett. Loretta Young, David Niven, Hugh Herbert, C. Aubrey Smith, Billie Burke, Broderick Crawford, Zasu Pitts, Eve Arden. Wayout idea comes off fairly well; Young is married to magician Niven, thinks his tricks are taking precedence to their married life.

Europa '51 SEE: **Greatest Love, The**

Eva (1965) 115m. *** D: Joseph Losey. Jeanne Moreau, Stanley Baker, Virna Lisi, Nona Medici, Francesco Rissone, James Villiers. Brooding account of writer Baker whose continued attraction for Eva (Moreau) causes wife (Lisi) to have tragic death. Premise isn't always workable, but Moreau is well cast as personification of evil.

Eve Knew Her Apples (1945) 64m. **½ D: Will Jason. Ann Miller, William Wright, Robert Williams, Ray Walker. Sprightly musical variation of IT HAPPENED ONE NIGHT, with Miller on the lam from her marriage-minded fiance.

Eve of St. Mark, The (1944) 96m. *** D: John M. Stahl. Anne Baxter, William Eythe, Michael O'Shea, Vincent Price, Dickie Moore. Human focus on WW2 in tale of soldier Eythe and girl friend Baxter at outset of war; not always successful Maxwell Anderson story.

Evelyn Prentice (1934) 80m. *** D: William K. Howard. William Powell, Myrna Loy, Una Merkel, Rosalind Russell, Isabel Jewell. Sturdy courtroom drama with lawyer Powell defending his own wife Loy. Remade as STRONGER THAN DESIRE.

Ever Since Eve (1937) 79m. **½ D: Lloyd Bacon. Marion Davies, Robert Montgomery, Frank McHugh, Patsy Kelly, Allen Jenkins, Louise Fazenda, Barton MacLane, Mary Treen. Cute idea; perennially pursued Davies makes herself homely in order to find decent job. Davies and cast at home in witty repartee.

Every Day's a Holiday (1937) 80m. **½ D: A. Edward Sutherland. Mae West, Edmund Lowe, Charles Butterworth, Charles Winninger, Walter Catlett, Lloyd Nolan, Louis Armstrong, Herman Bing. Gay 90's again with lavish production and good cast supporting Mae; not top-drawer West, but entertaining account of politics.

Every Girl Should Be Married (1948) 85m. **½ D: Don Hartman. Cary Grant, Franchot Tone, Diana Lynn, Betsy Drake, Alan Mowbray. Airy comedy of girl (Drake) setting out to trap bachelor (Grant) into marriage; Tone has thankless "other man" role.

Everybody Does It (1949) 98m. ***½ D: Edmund Goulding. Paul Douglas, Linda Darnell, Celeste Holm, Charles Coburn, Millard Mitchell. Exceptionally amusing yarn of aspiring singer Holm, harried husband Douglas, and prima donna Darnell. Celeste wants vocal career, Douglas gets one instead. Remake of WIFE, HUSBAND, AND FRIEND.

Everybody Sing (1938) 80m. **½ D: Edwin L. Marin. Allan Jones, Fannie Brice, Judy Garland, Reginald Owen, Billie Burke, Reginald Gardiner. Pleasant little musical of family putting on a show, with listenable tunes and fine work by Brice.

Everything But the Truth (1956) C-83m. ** D: Jerry Hopper. Maureen O'Hara, John Forsythe, Tim Hovey, Frank Faylen. When youngster Hovey joins truth pledge crusade at school, repercussions to his family and townfolk grow; cutesy.

Everything Happens at Night (1939) 77m. *** D: Irving Cummings. Sonja Henie, Ray Milland, Robert Cummings, Alan Dinehart, Fritz Feld, Jody Gilbert, Victor Varconi. One of Henie's best romantic skating vehicles, with Milland and Cummings as rival writers vying for girl's attention.

Everything I Have Is Yours (1952) C-92m. ** D: Robert Z. Leonard. Marge and Gower Champion, Dennis O'Keefe, Eduard Franz. Champions play dance team who finally get Broadway break, only to discover she's pregnant. Mild musical helped by stars' multitalents.

Everything's Ducky (1961) 81m. ** D: Don Taylor. Mickey Rooney, Buddy Hackett, Jackie Cooper, Roland Winters. Nonsense of Rooney-Hackett teaming up with talking duck, with trio ending up on navy missile orbiting earth; strictly for kids.

Evil Eye, The (1962-Italian, dubbed)

92m. **½ D: Mario Bava. Leticia Roman, John Saxon, Valentina Cortesa, Dante Di Paolo. Incredible but enjoyable chiller set in Rome, with Roman involved in a series of unsolved brutal murders.

Evil of Frankenstein, The (1964-British) C-87m. ** D: Freddie Francis. Peter Cushing, Duncan Lamont, Peter Woodthorpe, James Maxwell. Tepid entry in the famed monster series, with Cushing unfreezing his namesake who inevitably goes on the rampage.

Ex-Champ (1939) 64m. ** D: Phil Rosen. Victor McLaglen, Tom Brown, Nan Gray, Constance Moore. Routine programmer of old salty boxer trying to do good deed for his son, in dutch with the gambling syndicate.

Ex-Lady (1933) 65m. ** D: Robert Florey. Bette Davis, Gene Raymond, Frank McHugh, Claire Dodd, Ferdinand Gottschalk. Davis is a gorgeous man-trap in this programmer, wanting love, not marriage.

Ex-Mrs. Bradford, The (1936) 80m. *** D: Stephen Roberts. William Powell, Jean Arthur, James Gleason, Eric Blore, Robert Armstrong. Chic à la THIN MAN comedy-mystery, with Powell teaming with ex-wife Arthur to crack a case.

Exclusive (1937) 85m. **½ D: Alexander Hall. Fred MacMurray, Frances Farmer, Charlie Ruggles, Lloyd Nolan, Fay Holden, Ralph Morgan, Horace MacMahon. Lively newspaper story; Farmer joins tabloid over objections of father, rival editor Ruggles. She meets fellow reporter MacMurray, and romance results.

Excuse My Dust (1951) C-82m. **½ D: Roy Rowland. Red Skelton, Sally Forrest, Macdonald Carey, Monica Lewis, William Demarest. Amiable Skelton musicomedy. Red invents automobile which almost costs him his sweetheart; her father owns town livery stable.

Executive Suite (1954) 104m. *** D: Robert Wise. William Holden, June Allyson, Barbara Stanwyck, Fredric March, Walter Pidgeon, Louis Calhern, Shelley Winters, Paul Douglas, Nina Foch, Dean Jagger. Slick, multifaceted story of company power struggle with top cast, from Cameron Hawley novel. Similar film PATTERNS is much better.

Exile, The (1947) 95m. **½ D: Max Ophuls. Douglas Fairbanks, Jr., Maria Montez, Paule Croset, Henry Daniell, Nigel Bruce, Robert Coote. OK swashbuckler with exiled King Fairbanks falling in love with common girl; guest appearance by Montez, fine support by Bruce.

Exodus (1960) C-213m. *** D: Otto Preminger. Paul Newman, Eva Marie Saint, Ralph Richardson, Peter Lawford, Lee J. Cobb, Sal Mineo, Hugh Griffith, Felix Aylmer, John Derek, Jill Haworth. Leon Uris' sprawling history of Palestinian war for liberation becomes sporadic action epic. Newman as Israeli resistance leader, Saint as non-Jewish army nurse aren't a convincing duo; supporting roles offer stereotypes. Best scene shows refugees escaping Cyprus detention center, running British blockade into homeland.

Experiment in Terror (1962) 123m. *** D: Blake Edwards. Glenn Ford, Lee Remick, Stefanie Powers, Ross Martin, Roy Poole, Ned Glass. Taut suspenser as FBI agent Ford tracks down killer (Martin) who has kidnapped bank teller Remick's sister (Powers). Remick and Martin are extremely convincing.

Experiment Perilous (1944) 91m. **½ D: Jacques Tourneur. Hedy Lamarr, George Brent, Paul Lukas, Albert Dekker, Margaret Wycherly, Julia Dean. Lamarr's wealthy husband is killed and detective wonders if she was involved or not. Good whodunit.

Explosive Generation, The (1961) 89m. ** D: Buzz Kulik. William Shatner, Patty McCormack, Billy Gray, Steve Dunne. Film fails to be exploitational: Shatner is high school teacher expelled for conducting sex talks in class; school board and parent group eventually reach compromise.

Expresso Bongo (1960-British) 108m. *** D: Val Guest. Laurence Harvey, Sylvia Syms, Yolande Donlan, Cliff Richard. Harvey is ideally cast as opportunist talent agent who almost makes the big time with bongo-playing discovery Richard, but bluffs himself back into small time.

Eye for an Eye, An (1966) C-92m. ** D: Michael Moore. Robert Lansing, Pat Wayne, Slim Pickens, Gloria Talbott. Oater with twist: two physically disabled men, who can function via teamwork as one sharpshooter, hunt down killers of older man's family.

Eye Witness (1950-British) 104m. **½ D: Robert Montgomery. Robert Montgomery, Felix Aylmer, Leslie Banks, Michael Ripper. Unpretentious yarn of American attorney Montgomery in London to defend friend accused of homicide, coping with contrasting British legal system while hunting title figure.

Eyes in the Night (1942) 80m. ** D: Fred Zinnemann. Ann Harding, Edward Arnold, Donna Reed, Stephen McNally, Reginald Denny, Rosemary DeCamp, Mantan Moreland. Abovepar mystery with Arnold as blind detective helping Reed and Harding. Director Zinnemann's feature film debut.

Eyes of the Underworld (1943) 61m. **½ D: Roy William Neill. Richard Dix, Wendy Barrie, Lon Chaney, Lloyd Corrigan, Don Porter, Billy Lee, Marc Lawrence. Police chief Dix is on the spot when mobster uncovers his old prison record; good crime story.

FBI Girl (1951) 74m. ** D: William Berke. Cesar Romero, George Brent, Audrey Totter, Tom Drake, Raymond Burr. Title tells all in standard fare about federal agency tracking down extortion gang.

FBI 99 (1945) 100m. ** D: Spencer Bennet, Wallace Grissell, Yakima Canutt. Marten Lamont, Helen Talbot, George J. Lewis, Lorna Gray, Hal Taliaferro. Satisfactory Republic cliffhanger involving federal agents' persistent attempts to overcome criminal syndicate planning robbery capers et al. Re-edited movie serial: FEDERAL OPERATOR 99.

FBI Story, The (1959) C-149m. *** D: Mervyn LeRoy. James Stewart, Vera Miles, Murray Hamilton, Larry Pennell, Nick Adams, Diane Jergens, Joyce Taylor. Well-mounted fabrication of history of FBI as seen through career of agent Stewart, allowing for episodic sidelights into action-packed capers and view of his personal life.

Fabiola (1951-Italian, dubbed) 96m. **** D: Alessandro Blasetti. Michele Morgan, Henri Vidal, Michel Simon, Gino Cervi. Excellently produced and acted spectacle. Roman aristocracy plots massive Christian massacre before Constantine reaches Rome. Best of Italian spectacles, although cut quite a bit.

Fabulous Dorseys, The (1947) 88m. ** D: Alfred E. Green. Tommy Dorsey, Jimmy Dorsey, Janet Blair, Paul Whiteman, William Lundigan. Limp "biography" of band-leading brothers, constantly arguing in between "Marie," "Green Eyes," and other hit songs.

Fabulous Joe, The (1947) C-60m. ** D: Bernard Carr, Harve Foster. Marie Wilson, Walter Abel, Margot Grahame, Donald Meek. Abel is typecast in this featurized segment from THE HAL ROACH COMEDY CARNIVAL (1947). He's harassed husband who gains moral support from talking dog.

Fabulous Suzanne, The (1946) 71m. ** D: Steve Sekely. Barbara Britton, Rudy Vallee, Otto Kruger, Richard Denning, Veda Ann Borg. Fair potential of romantic story of woman who has more luck at horses than with men doesn't come across, due to script and indifferent acting.

Fabulous World of Jules Verne, The (1961-German, dubbed) 83m. *** D: Karel Zeman. Louis Tock, Ernest Navara, Milo Holl, Francis Sherr. Inventive Czech compilation of various Verne stories features combination live-action and animation.

Face Behind the Mask, The (1941) 69m. **½ D: Robert Florey. Peter Lorre, Evelyn Keyes, Don Beddoe, George E. Stone, John Tyrell. Good horror tale with Lorre as badly scarred man seeking refuge behind mask, turning to life of crime.

Face in the Crowd, A (1957) 125m. ***½ D: Elia Kazan. Andy Griffith, Patricia Neal, Anthony Franciosa, Walter Matthau, Lee Remick, Kay Medford. Perceptive script by Budd Schulberg about homespun hobo (Griffith) discovered by Neal and promoted into successful TV star. Cast gives life to fascinating story.

Face in the Rain, A (1963) 91m. **½ D: Irvin Kershner. Rory Calhoun, Marina Berti, Niall McGinnis, Massimo Giuliani. At times tense melodrama of Calhoun, U.S. spy, being hidden in Italy by partisan whose wife has been associating with Axis.

Face of a Fugitive (1959) C-81m. ** D: Paul Wendkos. Fred MacMurray, Lin McCarthy, Dorothy Green, James Coburn, Alan Baxter, Myrna Fahey. OK Western about MacMurray forced to start over again in a new town when he's falsely accused of murder; his past still haunts him.

Face of Fire (1959) 83m. *** D: Albert Band. Cameron Mitchell, James Whitmore, Bettye Ackerman, Royal Dano, Robert Simon, Richard Erdman. Unique adaptation of Stephen Crane short story THE MONSTER about man disfigured while saving child from fire. Uneven cast, good direction.

Face of Fu Manchu, The (1965-British) C-96m. *** D: Don Sharp. Christopher Lee, Nigel Green, James Robertson Justice, Howard Marion-Crawford, Tsai Chin, Walter Rilla. First of wild new series with Emperor Fu bent on conquering West. Great 1920's atmosphere, good international cast.

Face of Marble (1946) 70m. ** D: William Beaudine. John Carradine, Claudia Drake, Robert Shayne, Maris Wrixon. Another mad doctor with new technique for bringing dead back to life. Carradine is good, others less impressive.

Face of the Frog. (1959-German, dubbed) 92m. ** D: Harold Reinl. Joachim Fuchsberger, Fritz Rasp, Siegfled Lowitz, Joachen Brochmann. Lowitz is Inspector Elk tracking down the "Frog" in this routine Edgar Wallace actioner; serial-like techniques utilized. Retitled: FELLOWSHIP OF THE FROG.

Face That Launched a Thousand Ships, The SEE: Loves of Three Queens

Face to Face (1952) 92m. **½ D: John Brahm, Bretaigne Windust. James Mason, Michael Pate, Robert Preston, Marjorie Steele. Quiet two-part film: Joseph Conrad's SECRET SHARER faithfully filmed with Mason as captain, Pate as fugitive; Stephen Crane's BRIDE COMES TO YELLOW SKY bland with Preston bringing bride Steele out West.

Facts of Life, The (1960) 103m. *** D: Melvin Frank. Bob Hope, Lucille Ball, Ruth Hussey, Don DeFore. Sophisticated comedy with Bob and Lucy leaving their spouses for an interlude together. The two stars make a good team worth watching.

Fahrenheit 451 (1966-British) C-111m. ** D: François Truffaut. Julie Christie, Oskar Werner, Cyril Cusack, Anton Diffring. Stolid adaptation of Ray Bradbury futuristic novel of society where reading books is forbidden; Werner is book-burner who rebels; Christie plays dual role as his wife and a liberal teacher.

Fail-Safe (1964) 111m. *** D: Sidney Lumet. Henry Fonda, Walter Matthau, Fritz Weaver, Dan O'Herlihy, Sorrell Booke, Larry Hagman, Frank Overton. Lost in the shuffle of DR. STRANGELOVE's wake, this grim account tells of U.S.'s accidental bombing of USSR and retaliation on America. Based on Eugene Burdick-Harvey Wheeler book.

Fair Wind to Java (1953) C-92m. **½ D: Joseph Kane. Fred MacMurray, Vera Ralston, Victor McLaglen, Robert Douglas, Philip Ahn. MacMurray is out of place in period sea yarn of of skipper seeking jewels. Ralston is exotic love interest.

Faithful in My Fashion (1946) 81m. ** D: Sidney Salkow. Donna Reed, Tom Drake, Edward Everett Horton, Spring Byington, Sig Ruman. Stale comedy-romance as soldier on leave discovers his girl engaged to someone else. Good cast in familiar settings.

Faithless (1932) 76m. **½ D: Harry Beaumont. Tallulah Bankhead, Robert Montgomery, Hugh Herbert, Louise Closser Hale, Henry Kolker. Impoverished Bankhead tries to start life fresh after dismal past; polished soaper.

Fake, The (1953-British) 80m. ** D: Godfrey Grayson. Dennis O'Keefe, Coleen Gray, Guy Middleton, John Laurie. Famous painting is stolen, starting a police hunt; OK crime drama.

The Falcon Michael Arlen's debonaire trouble-shooter, The Falcon, served as the basis for sixteen above-average mysteries in the 1940's, and while the series cannot be called unusual, one of its entries presented a perhaps-unique situation. George Sanders had played the character in three films when, in 1942, he decided to leave the series. In THE FALCON'S BROTHER it was arranged to put him out of the way so his brother could take over for him. What made the transition unique was that Sanders' real-life brother, Tom Conway, was the replacement; he carried on for nine subsequent films. John Calvert played the character in three final low-budget films which aren't really part of the main series. Various character actors came in and out of the series playing cronies of the Falcon, such as Allen Jenkins, Ed Brophy, Eddie Dunn, and Ed Gargan. James Gleason played a thick-witted inspector in the first few films, and Cliff Clark took over for the rest. In fact, some of the films had so much comedy relief, one yearned for some mystery relief from the comedy! One interesting gimmick in several films had a beautiful girl enter near the end of the picture to alert the Falcon to danger in a new location; this would lead into the next film in which the Falcon and the girl would embark upon the new mystery. One entry, THE FALCON TAKES OVER, was from a Raymond Chandler novel FAREWELL MY LOVELY which was remade as MURDER MY SWEET with Dick Powell as Philip Marlowe. Such young hopefuls as Wendy Barrie, Barbara Hale, Lynn Bari, Jane Greer, Harriet Hilliard, and Rita Corday appeared in the series from time to time; and to the everlasting glory of that great neurotic-character actor Elisha Cook, Jr., THE FALCON'S ALIBI cast him as a homicidal disk jockey!

Falcon and the Co-eds, The (1943) 68m. D: William Clemens. Tom Conway, Jean Brooks, Rita Corday, Amelita Ward, Isabel Jewell, George Givot, Cliff Clark, Dorothy Malone (in a bit).

Falcon in Danger, The (1943) 73m. D: William Clemens. Tom Conway, Jean Brooks, Elaine Shepard, Amelita Ward, Cliff Clark, Ed Gargan.

Falcon in Hollywood, The (1944) 67m. D: Gordon Douglas. Tom Conway, Barbara Hale, Veda Ann Borg, Sheldon Leonard, Frank Jenks, Rita Corday, John Abbott.

Falcon in Mexico, The (1944) 70m. D: William Berke. Tom Conway, Mona Maris, Nestor Paiva, Bryant Washburn, Emory Parnell.

Falcon in San Francisco, The (1945) 66m. D: Joseph H. Lewis. Tom Conway, Rita Corday, Edward Brophy, Sharyn Moffett, Fay Helm, Robert Armstrong.

Falcon Out West, The (1944) 64m. D: William Clemens. Tom Conway, Barbara Hale, Ed Gargan, Lyle Talbot, Chief Thundercloud, Joan Barclay, Minor Watson.

Falcon Strikes Back, The (1943) 66m. D: Edward Dmytryk. Tom Conway, Harriet Hilliard, Jane Randolph, Edgar Kennedy, Cliff Edwards, Rita Corday, Wynne Gibson.

Falcon Takes Over, The (1942) 63m. D: Irving Reis. George Sanders, Lynn Bari, James Gleason, Allen Jenkins, Helen Gilbert, Ward Bond, Anne Revere, Hans Conried.

Falcon's Adventure, The (1946) 61m. D: William Berke. Tom Conway, Madge Meredith, Edward S. Brophy, Robert Warwick, Myrna Dell, Ian Wolfe.

Falcon's Alibi, The (1946) 62m. D: Ray McCarey. Tom Conway, Rita Corday, Vince Barnett, Jane Greer, Elisha Cook, Jr., Al Bridge, Jason Robards, Sr.

Falcon's Brother, The (1942) 63m. D: Stanley Logan. George Sanders, Tom Conway, Jane Randolph, Keye Luke, Charles Arnt, Ed Brophy.

Fall of the Roman Empire, The (1964) C-149m. ***½ D: Anthony Mann. Sophia Loren, Stephen Boyd, James Mason, Alec Guinness, Christopher Plummer, Anthony Quayle, John Ireland, Mel Ferrer, Omar Sharif, Eric Porter. Intelligent scripting, good direction, and fine acting place this far above the usual empty-headed spectacle. Mason and Guinness are superb; several action sequences are outstanding. A winner all the way.

Fallen Angel (1945) 97m. **½ D: Otto Preminger. Alice Faye, Dana Andrews, Linda Darnell, Charles Bickford, Anne Revere, Bruce Cabot, John Carradine. Andrews plans to dump wife Faye for Darnell, when latter is murdered; offbeat production.

Fallen Idol, The (1949-British) 94m. ***½ D: Carol Reed. Ralph Richardson, Michele Morgan, Bobby Henrey, Sonia Dresdel. Incisive study of human relations based on Graham Greene story of young boy who idolizes the household servant suspected of murdering his wife. Highly professional production.

Fallen Sparrow, The (1943) 94m. *** D: Richard Wallace. John Garfield, Maureen O'Hara, Walter Slezak, Patricia Morison, Martha O'Driscoll, Bruce Edwards, John Banner. Puzzling WW2 thriller with Garfield returning from Spanish Civil War to find American-based Nazis after him for artifact he's supposed to have.

Fame is the Name of the Game (1966) C-120m. **½ D: Stuart Rosenberg. Tony Franciosa, Jill St. John, Jack Klugman, Susan Saint James, Lee Bowman, George Macready. Flashy, nonsensical telefeature with Franciosa a magazine writer seeking clues to death of a girl, meeting assorted types. Very similar to CHICAGO DEADLINE (1949). Film pilot for new TV series.

Fame is the Spur (1946-British) 116m. **½ D: John and Roy Boulting. Michael Redgrave, Rosamund John, Anthony Wager, Brian Weske. Thoughtful if slow-moving chronicle of Redgrave portraying a noted politician-diplomat who rises from poverty to fame.

Family Affair, A (1937) 69m. D: George B. Seitz. Lionel Barrymore, Mickey Rooney, Spring Byington, Cecilia Parker, Eric Linden, Julie Haydon, Sara Haden, Charley Grapewin. SEE: Andy Hardy series.

Family Honeymoon (1948) 80m. **½ D: Claude Binyon. Claudette Colbert, Fred MacMurray, Rita Johnson, William Daniels. What could have been fine comedy turns out to be uneven farce as widow takes children on second honeymoon. Very good cast does its best.

Family Secret, The (1951) 85m. **½ D: Henry Levin. John Derek, Lee J. Cobb, Erin O'Brien-Moore, Jody Lawrance. Good drama involving Cobb who defends man accused for crime which son committed.

Fan, The (1949) 89m. ** D: Otto Preminger. Jeanne Crain, Madeleine Carroll, George Sanders, Richard Greene. Oscar Wilde's comedy of manners LADY WINDEMERE'S FAN, involving marital indiscretion and social-climbing in Victorian England, loses much of its wit in film version. Remake of 1925 silent.

Fan-Fan the Tulip (1951-French, dubbed) 96m. *** D: Christian-Jaque. Gerard Philippe, Gina Lollobrigida, Noel Roquevert, Olivier Hussenot, Marcel Herrard, Sylvie Pelayo. Most delightful satire of swashbuckling epics, with Philippe ideally cast as the sword-wielding, love-hungry 18th-century Frenchman joining Louis XV's army. Retitled: SOLDIER IN LOVE.

Fanatics, The (1957-French, dubbed) 85m. ** D: Alex Joffe. Pierre Fresnay, Michel Auclair, Gregoire Aslan, Betty Schneider. Occasionally taut tale of assassination plot on South American dictator, efforts of one rebel member to stop bomb explosion.

Fancy Pants (1950) C-92m. *** D: George Marshall. Lucille Ball, Bob Hope, Bruce Cabot, Eric Blore. Generally amusing comedy remake of RUGGLES OF RED GAP, has Hope as valet who brings couth to Western town.

Fanny (1961) C-133m. *** D: Joshua Logan. Leslie Caron, Maurice Chevalier, Charles Boyer, Horst Buchholz, Baccaloni, Lionel Jeffries. Gorgeously photographed and beautifully scored dramatic version of Marcel Pagnol's trilogy involving young girl left with child by adventure-seeking sailor. Chevalier and Boyer give flavorful performances.

Fantastic Voyage (1966) C-100m. ***½ D: Richard Fleischer. Stephen Boyd, Raquel Welch, Edmond O'Brien, Donald Pleasence, Arthur O'Connell, William Redfield, Arthur Kennedy. Tremendously entertaining science fiction story of medical team reduced to microscopic size, injected inside human body. Film's great effects will be lost on TV screen, but story and action will keep you glued to your seat nevertheless.

Fantomas Against Scotland Yard (1966-French, dubbed) C-104m. **½ D: Andre Hunebelle. Jean Marais, Louis De Funes, Mylene Demongeot, Henri Serre. Satirical cliff-hanger-type adventure yarn, with Marais as supercriminal engaged in a number of athletic escapades. Retitled: FANTOMAS.

Far Country, The (1955) C-97m. *** D: Anthony Mann. James Stewart, Ruth Roman, Corinne Calvet, Walter Brennan, Jay C. Flippen. Sturdy cast, plausible story of cattle drive to

Alaska make this Western agreeable; Stewart leads fight for justice.

Far Horizons, The (1955) C-108m. **½ D: Rudolph Mate. Fred MacMurray, Charlton Heston, Donna Reed, Barbara Hale, William Demarest. Movie fiction about Lewis and Clark expedition, beautifully photographed; sporadic action; implausible love interest.

Farewell Again (1937-British) 81m. **½ D: Tim Whelan. Leslie Banks, Flora Robson, Sebastian Shaw, Patricia Hilliard. Neatly handled minor film detailing events in the lives of British soldiers on short leave before embarking for the front again.

Farewell to Arms, A (1957) C-152m. **½ D: Charles Vidor. Rock Hudson, Jennifer Jones, Vittorio DeSica, Alberto Sordi, Mercedes McCambridge, Elaine Stritch, Oscar Homolka. Overblown, padded remake has unconvincing leads, static treatment of WW1 story so romantically told in Hemingway novel. Hudson is American ambulance driver wounded in WW1 Italy who falls in love with nurse Jones. Earlier 1932 version starred Gary Cooper and Helen Hayes.

Farmer Takes a Wife, The (1935) **½ D: Victor Fleming. Janet Gaynor, Henry Fonda, Charles Bickford, Slim Summerville, Jane Withers. Vintage romance of farmers living by the Erie Canal in 1800's; Fonda's first film, and he's still enjoyable as Gaynor's suitor.

Farmer Takes a Wife, The (1953) 81m. ** D: Henry Levin. Betty Grable, Dale Robertson, Thelma Ritter, John Carroll, Eddie Foy, Jr. Musical remake of 1935 film is slow-paced account of life in 1800's along the Erie Canal.

Farmer's Daughter, The (1940) 60m. ** D: James Hogan. Martha Raye, Charlie Ruggles, Richard Denning, Gertrude Michael, William Frawley. Not to be confused with later film, this one is about show business on the farm circuit, worthwhile only for Raye.

Farmer's Daughter, The (1947) 97m. ***½ D: H. C. Potter. Loretta Young, Joseph Cotten, Ethel Barrymore, Charles Bickford, Rose Hobart, Harry Davenport. Young won an Oscar for her performance as headstrong Swedish girl who fights her way into Congress; delightful comedy with uniformly excellent cast. Basis for later TV series.

Fashions (1934) 78m. *** D: William Dieterle. William Powell, Bette Davis, Verree Teasdale, Reginald Owen, Frank McHugh, Phillip Reed, Hugh Herbert. Trivial but enjoyable romp of con-man Powell and designer Davis conquering the Paris fashion world. Fine cast glides along with dapper Powell; Busby Berkeley's "Spin a Little Web of Dreams" number is great fun. Original title: FASHIONS OF 1934.

Fast and Loose (1930) 75m. *½ D: Fred Newmeyer. Miriam Hopkins, Carole Lombard, Frank Morgan, Ilka Chase, Charles Starrett. Attempt at witty comedy doesn't come through; Hopkins' first film; Lombard has small role.

Fast and Loose (1939) 80m. **½ D: Edwin L. Marin. Robert Montgomery, Rosalind Russell, Reginald Owen, Ralph Morgan, Sidney Blackmer. Average mystery about theft of Shakespearean manuscript during weekend stay at owner's estate.

Fast and Sexy (1960-Italian, dubbed) C-98m. **½ D: Vittorio DeSica. Gina Lollobrigida, Dale Robertson, Vittorio DeSica, Carla Macelloni. Lollobrigida is fun-loving widow who returns to her village seeking new husband.

Fast and the Furious, The (1954) 73m. ** D: Edwards Sampson. John Ireland, Dorothy Malone, Iris Adrian, Bruce Carlisle, Jean Howell, Larry Thor. Ireland is fugitive on the lam from murder frame-up who jockeys Malone's sports car, with uninspired romantic interludes and cops-on-the-chase sequences.

Fast Company (1953) 67m. ** D: John Sturges. Polly Bergen, Howard Keel, Marjorie Main, Nina Foch, Iron Eyes Cody. Not very exciting musical comedy about horse who prances to music, owned by racing enthusiast Bergen.

Fastest Gun Alive, The (1956) 92m. *** D: Russell Rouse. Glenn Ford, Jeanne Crain, Broderick Crawford, Russ Tamblyn. Sincere Western with a moral. Ford is a peace-loving storekeeper trying to live down renown as fast gunslinger, but there's always someone wanting to challenge him.

Fat Man, The (1951) 77m. **½ D: William Castle. J. Scott Smart, Julie London, Rock Hudson, Jayne Meadows. Heavyweight detective investigates dentist's murder, leading him to criminal at the circus; offbeat.

Fatal Desire (1963-Italian, dubbed) 80m. ** D: Carmine Gallone. Anthony Quinn, Kerima, Mai Britt, Ettore Manni. Nonmusical version of Verdi's opera CAVALLERIA RUSTICANA, dealing with military man (Quinn) rekindling romance with former girlfriend, now married.

Fatal Witness, The (1945) 59m. *½ D: Lesley Selander. Evelyn Ankers, Richard Fraser, George Leigh, Barbara Everest, Frederick Worlock. Quickie mystery yarn with obvious plot about wealthy matron's murder, capture of culprit.

Fate Takes a Hand (1961-British) 72m. **½ D: Max Varnel. Ronald Howard, Christina Gregg, Basil Dignam, Sheila Whittingham. Agreeable format about bag of mail recovered fifteen years after a robbery; effect of letters on recipients allows for five trim little tales.

Father Goose (1964) C-115m. *** D: Ralph Nelson. Cary Grant, Leslie Caron, Trevor Howard, Jack Good, Nicole Felsette. Grant goes native as shiftless bum on a South Seas island during WW2. Caron is schoolteacher who, with her girls in tow, tames Grant. Lightweight and enjoyable.

Father Is a Bachelor (1950) 84m. ** D: Norman Foster, Abby Berlin. William Holden, Coleen Gray, Mary Jane Saunders, Stuart Erwin, Sig Ruman. Vagabond Holden with five "adopted" kids meets Gray who wants to marry him; "cute" comedy.

Father Makes Good (1950) 61m. *½ D: Jean Yarbrough. Raymond Walburn, Walter Catlett, Barbara Brown, Gertrude Astor. Mild little film in Walburn series of small-town man who purchases a cow to show his contempt for new milk tax.

Father of the Bride (1950) 93m. **** D: Vincente Minnelli. Spencer Tracy, Elizabeth Taylor, Joan Bennett, Billie Burke, Leo G. Carroll, Russ Tamblyn, Moroni Olsen. Liz is marrying Don Taylor, but dad (Tracy) has all the aggravation. Perceptive view of American life, witty script, and peerless Tracy performance.

Father Takes a Wife (1941) 79m. ** D: Jack Hively. Adolphe Menjou, Gloria Swanson, John Howard, Desi Arnaz, Helen Broderick, Florence Rice, Neil Hamilton. Suave Menjou is Father, Gloria is the wife; frothy comedy worth seeing for fine stars.

Father Takes the Air (1951) 61m. *½ D: Frank McDonald. Raymond Walburn, Walter Catlett, Florence Bates, Gary Gray. Walburn is involved with local flying school, and accidentally captures a crook.

Father Was a Fullback (1949) 84m. **½ D: John M. Stahl. Fred MacMurray, Maureen O'Hara, Betty Lynn, Rudy Vallee, Thelma Ritter, Natalie Wood. Wholesome comedy with most engaging cast. MacMurray is football coach with as many household problems as on the gridiron.

Father's Little Dividend (1951) 82m. **** D: Vincente Minnelli. Spencer Tracy, Joan Bennett, Elizabeth Taylor, Don Taylor, Billie Burke. Delightful sequel to FATHER OF THE BRIDE with same cast. Now Spencer is going to be a grandfather; he doesn't look forward to it.

Father's Wild Game (1950) 61m. *½ D: Herbert I. Leeds. Raymond Walburn, Walter Catlett, Jane Darwell, Roscoe Ates, Ann Tyrrell. In this entry, Walburn is protesting inflation at the meat market and decides to hunt wild game himself.

Fathom (1967) C-99m. *** D: Leslie H. Martinson. Raquel Welch, Tony Franciosa, Ronald Fraser, Greta Chi, Richard Briers, Clive Revill. Fastpaced, tongue-in-cheek spy caper with sky-diver Welch getting mixed up with dubious good-guy Franciosa. Great fun, with Revill's performance as eccentric millionaire stealing the show.

Fear (1946) 68m. *½ D: Alfred Zeisler. Peter Cookson, Warren William, Anne Gwynne, James Cardwell, Nestor Paiva. Rather tepid remake of Dostoyevsky's CRIME AND PUNISHMENT, suffering from low-budget production values.

Fear in the Night (1947) 72m. ** D: Maxwell Shane. Paul Kelly, Ann Doran, Kay Scott, DeForest Kelley, Robert Emmett Keane. Nifty chiller involving man who commits murder while under hypopsis.

Fear Strikes Out (1957) 100m *** D: Robert Mulligan. Anthony Perkins, Karl Malden, Norma Moore, Adam Williams, Perry Wilson. Stark account of baseball star Jimmy Piersall and his bout with mental illness. Perkins properly intense in star role.

Fearmakers, The (1958) 83m. **½ D: Jacques Tourneur. Dana Andrews, Dick Foran, Mel Torme, Marilee Earle. Well-done Communist witchhunt theme as returning war veteran Andrews discovers subversives in his Washington, D. C. ad agency.

Feathered Serpent, The (1948) 61m. D: William Beaudine. Roland Winters, Keye Luke, Victor Sen Yung, Mantan Moreland, Carol Forman, Robert Livingston, Nils Asther. SEE: Charlie Chan series.

Federal Agents vs. Underworld Inc. SEE: Golden Hands of Kurigal

Federal Operator 99 SEE: FBI 99

Fellowship of the Frog SEE: Face of the Frog

Female and the Flesh SEE: Light Across the Street

Female Animal, The (1958) 84m. **½ D: Harry Keller. Hedy Lamarr, Jane Powell, Jan Sterling, George Nader. Sad waste of Lamarr as mature Hollywood star who grapples with adopted daughter Powell over Nader.

Female Jungle (1956) 56m. ** D: Bruno De Sota. Jayne Mansfield, Lawrence Tierney, John Carradine, Kathleen Crowley, Rex Thorsen, Burt Carlisle, Bruno De Sota. Attempt at sensationalism in this murder yarn fails to catch on; Tierney is cop seeking killer of cinema lovely.

Female on the Beach (1955) 97m. *** D: Joseph Pevney. Joan Crawford, Jeff Chandler, Jan Sterling, Cecil Kellaway, Judith Evelyn, Natalie Schafer. Crawford makes this mystery believable as woman who suspects her husband (Chandler) may want to do her in. Sterling offers contrasting performance and fine support.

Feminine Touch, The (1941) 97m. **½ D: W. S. Van Dyke, II. Rosalind Russell, Don Ameche, Kay Francis, Van Heflin, Donald Meek, Gordon Jones. Brittle comedy of author Ameche writing book on jealousy, finding himself a victim when he brings wife Russell to N.Y.C.; she suspects he's carrying on with glamorous Francis.

Fernandel the Dressmaker (1957-French, dubbed) 84m. **½ D: Jean Boyer. Fernandel, Suzy Delair, Fabian, Georges Chamarat. Undemanding plot has Fernandel wanting to be high-fashion designer rather than drab man's tailor.

Ferry to Hong Kong (1961) C-103m. **½ D: Lewis Gilbert. Orson Welles, Curt Jurgens, Sylvia Syms, Jeremy Spenser. Jurgens and Welles have field day romp as straitlaced skipper of ferry boat and drunken Aussie on trip to Macao. Film is otherwise just routine.

Feudin' Fool (1952) 63m. D: William Beaudine. Leo Gorcey, Huntz Hall, Dorothy Ford, Lyle Talbot, Benny Baker, Russell Simpson. SEE: Bowery Boys series.

Feudin', Fussin' and A-Fightin' (1948) 78m. ** D: George Sherman. Donald O'Connor, Marjorie Main, Percy Kilbride, Penny Edwards. Title and cast names tell all; loud and brassy.

Fever in the Blood, A (1961) 117m. **½ D: Vincent Sherman. Efrem Zimbalist, Jr., Angie Dickinson, Herbert Marshall, Don Ameche, Jack Kelly, Carroll O'Connor. Turgid dramatics focusing on murder trial which various candidates for governorship utilize to further political ambitions; film lacks verve.

Fiend Who Walked the West, The (1958) 101m. *** D: Gordon Douglas. Hugh O'Brian, Robert Evans, Dolores Michaels, Linda Cristal. Variation of film KISS OF DEATH involves psychopathic killer on rampage and the law's ingenious trap to capture him. Adult Western.

Fiend Without a Face (1958-British) 74m. *½ D: Arthur Crabtree. Marshall Thompson, Kim Parker, Terence Kilburn, Michael Balfour, Gil Winfield. Title monsters seek to wreak havoc and nothing seems to stop them.

Fiercest Heart, The (1961) C-91m. ** D: George Sherman. Stuart Whitman, Juliet Prowse, Ken Scott, Raymond Massey, Geraldine Fitzgerald.

Good cast and action-packed skirmishes with Zulus can't raise this programmer to any heights. Set in Africa.

Fiesta (1947) C-104m. ** D: Richard Thorpe. Esther Williams, Akim Tamiroff, Ricardo Montalban, John Carroll, Mary Astor, Cyd Charisse. Williams trades in her bathing suit for a toreador outfit in this weak musical opus.

15 Maiden Lane (1936) 65m. ** D: Allan Dwan. Claire Trevor, Cesar Romero, Douglas Fowley, Lloyd Nolan, Lester Matthews. Trevor lures Romero in order to crack his underworld gang in this satisfactory programmer.

Fifth Avenue Girl (1939) 83m. **½ D: Gregory La Cava. Ginger Rogers, Walter Connolly, Kathryn Adams, Verree Teasdale, Tim Holt, James Hamilton, Franklin Pangborn. Peppy comedy with one exception: sociological comments sprinkled in ridiculing the rich.

55 Days at Peking (1963) C-150m. *** D: Nicholas Ray. Charlton Heston, Ava Gardner, David Niven, Flora Robson, John Ireland, Paul Lukas, Jacques Sernas. Stars provide most of the interest in this confusing historical account of Boxer Rebellion in 1900's China.

Fifty Roads to Town (1937) 81m. ** D: Norman Taurog. Don Ameche, Ann Sothern, Slim Summerville, Jane Darwell, John Qualen, Stepin Fetchit, Oscar Apfel, Russell Hicks. Above-par comedy of Ameche and Sothern, both on the lam for different reasons, snowbound together in small inn.

52 Miles to Midnight SEE: Hot Rods to Hell

Fighter, The (1952) 78m. **½ D: Herbert Kline. Richard Conte, Vanessa Brown, Lee J. Cobb, Roberta Haynes. Absorbing tale set in Mexico with Conte a boxer who uses winnings to buy arms to seek revenge for family's murder.

Fighter Attack (1953) C-80m. ** D: Lesley Selander. Sterling Hayden, J. Carrol Naish, Joy Page, Paul Fierro. Modest film uses flashback to recount Hayden's last important mission in Italy during WW2.

Fighter Squadron (1948) C-96m. ** D: Raoul Walsh. Edmond O'Brien, Robert Stack, John Rodney, Tom D'Andrea, Henry Hull. OK WW2 drama of dedicated flier O'Brien, has abundance of clichés weighing against good action sequences. Rock Hudson's first film.

Fighting Chance, The (1955) 70m. ** D: William Witney. Rod Cameron, Julie London, Ben Cooper, Taylor Holmes, Bob Steele. Standard fare. Horse trainer and jockey friend both fall in love with London and come to odds with each other.

Fighting Coast Guard (1951) 86m. **½ D: Joseph Kane. Brian Donlevy, Forrest Tucker, Ella Raines, John Russell. Better than usual entry in training-for-war film, mixing romance with military action during WW2.

Fighting Devil Dogs SEE: Torpedo of Doom

Fighting Father Dunne (1948) 93m. **½ D: Ted Tetzlaff. Pat O'Brien, Darryl Hickman, Charles Kemper, Una O'Connor. Road company BOYS TOWN with O'Brien doing his usual competent work.

Fighting Fools (1949) 69m. D: Reginald Le Borg. Leo Gorcey, Huntz Hall, Gabriel Dell, Frankie Darro, Lyle Talbot, Evelynne Eaton, Benny Bartlett, Bernard Gorcey. SEE: Bowery Boys series

Fighting Guardsman (1945) 84m. ** D: Henry Levin. Williard Parker, Anita Louise, Janis Carter, John Loder, Edgar Buchanan, George Macready, Lloyd Corrigan. OK costumer of oppressed Frenchmen rising against tyranny in days before French Revolution.

Fighting Kentuckian, The (1949) 100m. **½ D: George Waggner. John Wayne, Vera Ralston, Philip Dorn, Oliver Hardy, Marie Windsor. Frontierland around 1810 is setting for two-fisted saga of Kentuckian (Wayne) combating land-grabbing criminals and courting Ralston, French General's daughter.

Fighting Lawman, The (1953) 71m. *½ D: Thomas Carr. Wayne Morris, Virginia Grey, Harry Lauter, John Kellogg, Myron Healey, Dick Rich. Grey tries to work with flimsy script as gal out to grab loot from robbers, pursued by sheriff.

Fighting Man of the Plains (1949) 94m. **½ D: Edwin L. Marin. Randolph Scott, Bill Williams, Victor Jory, Jane Nigh. Another version of the Jesse James saga, with Scott as Frank James seeking to avenge his brother's death. Dale Robertson's first important part.

Fighting O'Flynn, The (1949) 94m. **½ D: Arthur Pierson. Douglas Fairbanks, Jr., Richard Greene, Helen Carter, Patricia Medina. Enjoyable swashbuckler set in 1800's Ireland with Fairbanks-Greene vying in love and intrigue.

Fighting Seabees, The (1944) 100m. *** D: Edward Ludwig. John Wayne, Susan Hayward, Dennis O'Keefe, William Frawley, Duncan Renaldo. Spirited WW2 saga of valiant seabees Wayne and O'Keefe stationed in China, fighting for Hayward.

Fighting 69th, The (1940) 90m. *** D: William Keighley. James Cagney, Pat O'Brien, George Brent, Jeffrey Lynn, Alan Hale, Frank McHugh, Dennis Morgan. Excellent WW1 saga of rough-and-tumble American battalion with priest O'Brien, upstart Cagney, and fighting hero Brent.

Fighting Trouble (1956) 61m. D: George Blair. Huntz Hall, Stanley Clements, Adele Jergens, Joseph Downing. SEE: Bowery Boys series

Fighting Wildcats, The (1957-British) 74m. *½ D: Keefe Brasselle. Keefe Brasselle, Kay Callard, Karel Stepanek, Ursula Howells. Innocuous intrigue in the Middle East involving gangsters.

File on Thelma Jordan, The (1949) 100m. **½ D: Robert Siodmak. Barbara Stanwyck, Wendell Corey, Joan Tetzel, Paul Kelly. Murky drama, focusing largely on romance between D.A. Corey and shady lady Stanwyck. Retitled: THELMA JORDAN.

Final Test, The (1953-British) 84m. **½ D: Anthony Asquith. Jack Warner, Robert Morley, George Relph, Adrianne Allen. Droll, minor comedy of father-son rivalry over charming Allen.

Finders Keepers (1951) 74m. **½ D: Frederick de Cordova. Tom Ewell, Julia Adams, Evelyn Varden, Dusty Henley. Scatterbrained comedy that chugs down at end. Ewell and Varden enliven proceedings about a little boy who comes home with a cartful of money.

Fine Madness, A (1966) C-104m. *** D: Irvin Kershner. Sean Connery, Joanne Woodward, Jean Seberg, Patrick O'Neal, Colleen Dewhurst, Renee Taylor. Sturdy adaptation of Elliott Baker novel about individualist, rebellious novelist and his capers in N.Y.C.

Finger Man (1955) 82m. ** D: Harold Schuster. Frank Lovejoy, Forrest Tucker, Peggie Castle, Glenn Gordon, Evelynne Eaton. Convincing performances uplift account of federal agents capturing liquor gang.

Finger of Guilt (1956-British) 84m. ** D: Alec Snowden (Joseph Losey). Richard Basehart, Mary Murphy, Constance Cummings, Roger Livesey. Uneven drama about mysterious woman spouting incredible story of intimate affair with movie producer, causing him to lose job.

Finger on the Trigger (1965) C-87m. Bomb D: Sidney Pink. Rory Calhoun, James Philbrook, Todd Martin, Silvia Solar, Brad Talbot. Reb and Yankee veterans join forces to secure buried treasure while holding off hostile Indians.

Fingers at the Window (1942) 80m. **½ D: Charles Lederer. Lew Ayres, Laraine Day, Basil Rathbone, Walter Kingsford. Miles Mander, James Flavin. Entertaining mystery of Ayres-Day tracking down maniac killer masterminding repeated axe murders.

Fire Down Below (1957) C-116m. **½ D: Robert Parrish. Rita Hayworth, Robert Mitchum, Jack Lemmon, Herbert Lom. Contrived melodrama of Mitchum-Lemmon, owners of tramp boat, falling in love with shady girl Hayworth on voyage between islands.

Fire Over Africa (1954) C-84m. ** D: Richard Sale. Maureen O'Hara, Macdonald Carey, Binnie Barnes, Guy Middleton, Hugh McDermott. O'Hara makes a pretty law enforcer traveling to Africa to track down dope-smuggling syndicate. Filmed on location.

Fire Over England (1937-British) 89m. *** D: William K. Howard. Laurence Olivier, Flora Robson, Vivien Leigh, Raymond Massey, Leslie Banks, Cecil Mainwaring. Nice historical drama of British-Spanish conflict in 1500's with flawless performance by Robson (Queen Elizabeth), fine villainy by Massey, romantic support by Olivier and Leigh.

Fireball, The (1950) 84m. *** D: Tay Garnett. Mickey Rooney, Pat O'Brien, Beverly Tyler, Marilyn Monroe, Milburn Stone, Glenn Corbett. Rooney's energetic performance carries this film. Orphan boy devotes himself to becoming big-time rollerskating champ.

Firefly, The (1937) 131m. **½ D: Robert Z. Leonard. Jeanette MacDonald, Allan Jones, Warren William, Billy Gilbert, Henry Daniell, Douglass Dumbrille, George Zucco. Tried-and-true operetta moves slowly and goes on too long, but Jones' "Donkey Serenade" and Jeanette's vivacity remain enjoyable.

Fireman Save My Child (1932) 67m. ** D: Lloyd Bacon. Joe E. Brown, Evalyn Knapp, Guy Kibbee, Virginia Sale. Amusing Brown romp with Joe dividing his time between fire-fighting and baseball.

Fireman Save My Child (1954) 80m. *½ D: Leslie Goodwins. Spike Jones, The City Slickers, Buddy Hackett, Hugh O'Brian, Adele Jergens. Sloppy slapstick with Spike Jones et al manning fire station in 1900's San Francisco, running amuck when they receive a new fire engine.

First Comes Courage (1943) 88m. **½ D: Dorothy Arzner. Merle Oberon, Brian Aherne, Carl Esmond, Fritz Leiber, Erik Rolf. Fairly good wartime film of Norwegian Oberon using her feminine wiles to extract secrets from Nazi officer.

First Legion, The (1951) 86m. *** D: Douglas Sirk. Charles Boyer, William Demarest, Lyle Bettger, Barbara Rush. Engrossing low-key account of Jesuit priest who is dubious about an alleged miracle occurring in his town. Boyer gives one of his best performances.

First Love (1939) 84m. *** D: Henry Koster. Deanna Durbin, Robert Stack, Helen Parrish, Eugene Pallette, Leatrice Joy, Marcia Mae Jones, Frank Jenks. Charming love story of orphaned girl (Durbin) going to live with uncle and finding romance with Stack. Durbin sings: "Amapola" and other songs.

First Love (1958-Italian, dubbed) 103m. ** D: Mario Camerini. Carla Gravina, Raf Mattioli, Lorella De Luca, Luciano Marin. Simple, unengrossing account of the pangs of adolescent love.

First Man Into Space (1959-British) 77m. *½ D: Robert Day. Marshall Thompson, Marla Landi, Robert Ayres, Bill Nagy, Carl Jaffe, Bill Edwards. Uninspired account of test pilot who is exposed to radioactivity, causing severe repercussions to all.

First Men In the Moon (1964-British) C-103m. *** D: Nathan Juran. Edward Judd, Martha Hyer, Lionel Jeffries, Erik Chitty. Lavish British adaptation of H. G. Wells novel inserts much comic relief but is still imaginative sci-fi fantasy adventure. Great cast and special effects.

First Spaceship on Venus (1960-German, dubbed) C-78m. *½ D: Kurt Maetzig. Yoko Tani, Oldrich Lukes, Ignacy Machowski, Julius Ongewe. Few special effects can't salvage this wooden account of international group trekking to Venus to save the world; set in 1980's.

First Texan, The (1956) 82m. **½ D: Byron Haskin. Joel McCrea, Felicia Farr, Jeff Morrow, Wallace Ford. McCrea is forceful as Sam Houston, leading Texans in fight against Mexico for independence; good action sequences.

First Time, The (1952) 89m. ** D: Frank Tashlin. Robert Cummings, Barbara Hale, Jeff Donnell, Mona Barrie, Cora Witherspoon. Predictable comedy pegged on young couple's many problems with raising a young baby.

First To Fight (1967) C-97m. **½ D: Christian Nyby. Chad Everett, Marilyn Devlin, Dean Jagger, Bobby Troup, Claude Akins, Gene Hackman. Conventional WW2 yarn with Everett the one-time hero who almost loses his courage on the battlefield.

First Traveling Saleslady, The (1956) C-92m. ** D: Arthur Lubin. Ginger Rogers, Barry Nelson, Carol Channing, David Brian. Rogers and Channing try to elevate plodding comedy of girdle-sellers in the old West.

First Yank Into Tokyo (1945) 82m. ** D: Gordon Douglas. Tom Neal, Barbara Hale, Marc Cramer, Richard Loo, Keye Luke, Leonard Strong, Benson Fong. Low-budget quickie made to be topical isn't so any more, and it's not too good either; Neal undergoes plastic surgery to obtain Japanese secrets.

Five (1951) 93m. **½ D: Arch Oboler. William Phipps, Susan Douglas, James Anderson, Charles Lampkin, Earl Lee. Interesting study of five people, sole survivors of radiation attack which destroyed remainder of earth's population.

Five Against the House (1955) 84m. *** D: Phil Karlson. Guy Madison, Kim Novak, Brian Keith, Kerwin Matthews, William Conrad, Alvy Moore. "Perfect crime" caper has five friends set out to rob a Reno, Nevada casino. Execution of the robbery along with gorgeous Novak, keep this film rolling along.

Five Angles on Murder SEE: **Woman In Question**

Five Branded Women (1960) 106m. ** D: Martin Ritt. Van Heflin, Silvana Mangano, Jeanne Moreau, Vera Miles, Barbara Bel Geddes, Carla Gravina. Overambitious production, badly miscast, set in WW2 Middle Europe. Five girls scorned by partisans for consorting with Nazis prove their patriotism.

Five Came Back (1939) 75m. ** D: John Farrow. Chester Morris, Lucille Ball, Wendy Barrie, John Carradine, Allen Jenkins, Joseph Calleia, C. Aubrey Smith, Patric Knowles. Typical study of human interaction among survivors of plane crash in Amazon jungle. Remade as BACK FROM ETERNITY.

Five Day Lover SEE: **Time Out for Love**

Five Finger Exercise (1962) 109m. **½ D: Daniel Mann. Rosalind Russell, Jack Hawkins, Maximilian Schell, Richard Beymer, Lana Wood, Annette Gorman. Peter Shaffer's play suffers from change of locale and alteration of original ideas; now it becomes embarrassing soap opera of possessive mother in love with daughter's tutor. Stars are miscast but try their best.

Five Fingers (1952) 108m. *** D: Joseph L. Mankiewicz. James Mason, Danielle Darrieux, Michael Rennie, Richard Loo. Polished espionage film is endowed with fine Mason performance as unsuspected spy working for Germans during WW2.

Five Gates to Hell (1959) 98m. *½ D: James Clavell. Neville Brand, Benson Fong, Shirley Knight, Ken Scott, John Morley, Dolores Michaels, Nancy Kulp. Overly melodramatic plot of American nurses captured by Chinese mercenaries and the various ordeals they undergo.

Five Golden Dragons (1967-British) C-93m. ** D: Jeremy Summers. Bob Cummings, Margaret Lee, Maria Perschy, Brian Donlevy, Christopher Lee, George Raft, Dan Duryea. Cummings is naive American caught up in international crime in Hong Kong; a most conventional actioner, not saved by veteran guest stars.

Five Golden Hours (1961-British) 90m. **½ D: Mario Zampi. Ernie Kovacs, Cyd Charisse, George Sanders, Kay Hammond, Dennis Price. Comedy mishmash wavering between satire and slapstick as con man plots to utilize a witch to bedevil rich victims.

Five Graves to Cairo (1943) 96m. ***½ D: Billy Wilder. Franchot Tone, Anne Baxter, Akim Tamiroff, Erich von Stroheim, Peter Van Eyck. WW2 intrigue situated in Sahara oasis hotel run by Tamiroff and Baxter; Tone attempts to obtain secrets from visiting Field Marshal Rommel (Von Stroheim). Fine cast in convincing drama.

Five Guns West (1955) C-78m. ** D: Roger Corman. John Lund, Dorothy Malone, Mike Connors, Jack Ingram. Rebel soldiers, ex-convicts, hold up a Yankee stagecoach to obtain cache of money.

Five Miles To Midnight (1963) 110m. **½ D: Anatole Litvak. Tony Perkins, Sophia Loren, Gig Young, Jean-Pierre Aumont, Pascale Roberts. Jumbled murder mystery with Perkins convincing wife Loren to collect insurance money when it's thought he's been killed, with ironic results.

Five Pennies, The (1959) C-117m. **½ D: Melville Shavelson. Danny Kaye, Barbara Bel Geddes, Tuesday Weld, Louis Armstrong, Bob Crosby, Harry Guardino, Ray Anthony, Shelley Manne, Bobby Troup. Danny plays jazz trumpeter Red Nichols in this sentimental biography. Only bright spots are musical numbers, especially duets with Kaye and Armstrong.

Five Star Final (1931) 89m. *** D: Mervyn LeRoy. Edward G. Robinson, H. B. Warner, Marian Marsh, George E. Stone, Ona Munson, Boris Karloff, Aline MacMahon. Powerful drama of sensationalist newspaper sometimes falls apart with bad acting by second leads, but editor Robinson and unscrupulous reporter Karloff make it a must.

Five Steps to Danger (1957) 80m. ** D: Henry S. Kesler. Ruth Roman, Sterling Hayden, Werner Klemperer, Richard Gaines. By-now clichéd spy drama, enhanced by Roman and Hayden.

5,000 Fingers of Dr. T., The (1953) C-88m. ***½ D: Roy Rowland. Peter Lind Hayes, Mary Healy, Tommy Rettig, Hans Conried. Largely ignored, this is one of Hollywood's most imaginative fantasies: boy's nightmare of cruel piano teacher and life in which he must practice every minute.

Fixed Bayonets (1951) 92m. **½ D: Samuel Fuller. Richard Basehart, Gene Evans, Michael O'Shea, Richard Hylton, Craig Hill. Korean War film that does have some stimulating action fighting.

Flame, The (1947) 97m. ** D: John H. Auer. Vera Ralston, John Carroll, Robert Paige, Broderick Crawford, Henry Travers, Constance Dowling. Innocuous drama of woman searching for new husband; complications arise when scandal unfolds. Good cast in routine script.

Flame and the Arrow, The (1950) C-88m. *** D: Jacques Tourneur. Burt Lancaster, Virginia Mayo, Robert Douglas, Aline MacMahon. Bouncy, colorful action with Lancaster romping through his gymnastics as rebel leader in medieval Italy leading his people on to victory. Mayo is gorgeous heroine.

Flame and the Flesh (1954) C-104m. ** D: Richard Thorpe. Lana Turner, Pier Angeli, Carlos Thompson, Bonar Colleano, Charles Goldner, Peter Illing. Pointless Turner romance vehicle filmed in Europe, involving brunette Lana being romanced by continental Thompson, causing a lot of misery.

Flame Barrier, The (1958) 70m. *½ D: Paul Landres. Arthur Franz, Kathleen Crowley, Robert Brown, Vincent Padula. Ineffective jungle trek story. Fair cast tries hard in story of search for missing scientist in Central America.

Flame of Araby (1951) C-77m. **½ D: Charles Lamont. Maureen O'Hara, Jeff Chandler, Maxwell Reed, Susan Cabot. O'Hara, looking fetching as ever, rides through this costumer of the Far East, involving battle over a prize horse.

Flame of Calcutta (1953) C-70m. *½ D: Seymour Friedman. Denise Darcel, Patric Knowles, Paul Cavanagh. Darcel champions her people's cause in this costumer set in India in 1750. Low-grade nonsense.

Flame of New Orleans, The (1941) 78m. *** D: René Clair. Marlene Dietrich, Bruce Cabot, Roland Young, Laura Hope Crews, Mischa Auer, Andy Devine. Dietrich turns up in New Orleans and can have her pick of any man in town, can't decide between wealthy Young or hard-working Cabot. Picturesque, entertaining.

Flame of Stamboul (1951) 68m. *½ D: Ray Nazarro. Richard Denning, Lisa Ferraday, Norman Lloyd, Nestor Paiva. Programmer about espionage in ancient title city.

Flame of the Barbary Coast (1945) 91m. **½ D: Joseph Kane. John Wayne, Ann Dvorak, Joseph Schildkraut, William Frawley, Virginia Grey. Above-average Wayne Western with John becoming a gambling-house entrepreneur, romancing dance-hall queen Dvorak. Standard, but well done.

Flame of the Islands (1955) C-90m. ** D: Edward Ludwig. Yvonne de Carlo, Howard Duff, Zachary Scott, Kurt Kasznar, Barbara O'Neil. Caribbean scenery and sultry De Carlo provide most of the spice in this tale of a cafe singer and the men who fall in love with her.

Flame Over India (1960-British) C-130m. *** D: J. Lee Thompson. Lauren Bacall, Kenneth More, Herbert Lom, Wilfrid Hyde-White. Fast-paced actioner set on northern frontier of India as British soldiers accompanied by governess Bacall seek to speed an Indian prince to safety aboard a run-down train.

Flame Within, The (1935) 71m. ** D: Edmund Goulding. Ann Harding, Herbert Marshall, Maureen O'Sullivan, Louis Hayward. Tired story of unrequited love. Young woman psychologist falls in love with patient, despite fact that she knows that it could never succeed.

Flaming Feather (1951) C-77m. *** D: Ray Enright. Sterling Hayden, Forrest Tucker, Barbara Rush, Arleen Whelan. Rousing Western as vigilantes rescue white woman from renegade Indians.

Flaming Frontier (1958) 70m. *½ D: Sam Newfeld. Paisley Maxwell, Cecil Linder, Peter Humphreys, Ben Lennick. Indian war is averted by half-breed army officer; very cheap Western.

Flaming Star (1960) C-101m. **½ D: Don Siegel. Elvis Presley, Barbara Eden, Steve Forrest, Dolores Del Rio. Film's major interest is Presley's dramatic debut as half-breed Indian who must choose sides when redskins go on warpath. Del Rio good as Presley's Indian mother.

Flamingo Road (1949) 94m. *** D: Michael Curtiz. Joan Crawford, Zachary Scott, Sydney Greenstreet, David Brian, Gertrude Michael, Gladys George. Crawford is excellent as tough carnival dancer ditched in small town where she soon is loving Scott and Brian and matching wits with corrupt politician Greenstreet.

Flat Top (1952) C-83m. **½ D: Lesley Selander. Sterling Hayden, Richard Carlson, Bill Phipps, Keith Larsen. Well-paced WW2 film of training of aircraft-carrier fighter pilots. Film integrates news footage successfully.

Flaxy Martin (1949) 86m. **½ D: Richard Bare. Virginia Mayo, Zachary Scott, Dorothy Malone, Tom D'Andrea, Helen Westcott, Elisha Cook, Jr. Smooth melodrama of lawyer framed by client on a murder charge.

Fleet's In, The (1942) 93m. **½ D: Victor Schertzinger. Dorothy Lamour, William Holden, Betty Hutton, Eddie Bracken, Cass Daley, Rod Cameron, Jimmy Dorsey. Loud wartime musical of two sailors (Holden and Bracken) going after uppity Lamour and frantic Hutton on shore leave. Songs: "I Remember You," "Tangerine."

Flesh (1932) 95m. *** D: John Ford. Wallace Beery, Karen Morley, Ricardo Cortez, Jean Hersholt, Herman Bing. Lame-brain German fighter Beery brought to U.S. by Cortez, who falls in love with innocent Morley. Offbeat characterization by Beery in taut drama.

Flesh and Blood (1949-British) 102m. ** D: Anthony Kimmins. Richard Todd, Glynis Johns, Joan Greenwood. Turbulent study of generations of family life, focusing on clashes and romances of parents and children.

Flesh and Desire (1955-French, dubbed) 94m. ** D: Jean Josipovici. Rossano Brazzi, Viviane Romance, Peter Van Eyck, Jean-Paul Roussillon. Turgid farm romance tale of virile Brazzi's appearance setting into motion jealousy and murder.

Flesh and Fantasy (1943) 93m. *** D: Julien Duvivier. Charles Boyer, Edward G. Robinson, Barbara Stanwyck, Robert Benchley, Betty Field, Robert Cummings, Thomas Mitchell, Charles Winninger. Three-part film of supernatural linked by Benchley; Field is ugly girl turned beauty by Cummings' love; Robinson's life is changed by fortune-teller Mitchell; Boyer is psychic circus star haunted by Stanwyck. Robinson episode most interesting.

Flesh and Flame SEE: **Night of the Quarter Moon**

Flesh and Fury (1952) 82m. **½ D: Joseph Pevney, Tony Curtis, Jan Sterling, Mona Freeman, Wallace Ford, Harry Guardino. Curtis gives presentable performance as deaf prizefighter who seeks to regain hearing and love of decent girl.

Flesh and the Woman (1958-French, dubbed) C-102m. ** D: Robert Siodmak. Gina Lollobrigida, Jean-Claude Pascal, Arletty, Raymond Pellegrin. Whole film is Lollobrigida, who plays dual roles; a Parisian whose corrupt ways cause her husband to join the Foreign Legion, and a lookalike prostitute in Algiers.

Flight Command (1940) 110m. ** D: Frank Borzage. Robert Taylor, Ruth Hussey, Walter Pidgeon, Paul Kelly, Nat Pendleton, Shepperd Strudwick, Red Skelton, Dick Purcell. Hackneyed story with good cast as upstart Taylor tries to make the grade in naval flight squadron.

Flight for Freedom (1943) 99m. **½ D: Lothar Mendes. Rosalind Russell, Fred MacMurray, Herbert Marshall,

Eduardo Ciannelli, Walter Kingsford. Pseudo-biography of Amelia Earhart has dynamic Russell as aviatrix whose devotion to flying alienates her from MacMurray.

Flight from Ashiya (1964) C-100m. ** D: Michael Anderson. Yul Brynner, Richard Widmark, George Chakiris, Suzy Parker, Shirley Knight. Slow movie dealing with three aviators in rescue attempt over Pacific. "Big name" cast will attract; stiff script.

Flight from Destiny (1941) 73m. *** D: Vincent Sherman. Geraldine Fitzgerald, Thomas Mitchell, Jeffrey Lynn, James Stephenson, Mona Maris, Jonathan Hale. Well-acted tale of Mitchell, with short time to live, helping young couple by clearing young Lynn of charges brought against him; Fitzgerald a joy as Lynn's wife.

Flight Lieutenant (1942) 80m. *1/2 Sidney Salkow. Pat O'Brien, Glenn Ford, Evelyn Keyes, Minor Watson, Larry Parks, Lloyd Bridges, Hugh Beaumont. Contrived plot of airman Ford's romance with Keyes bringing back sore memories for commander O'Brien . . . sore is right.

Flight Nurse (1953) 90m. ** D: Allan Dwan. Joan Leslie, Forrest Tucker, Jeff Donnell, Arthur Franz. Leslie elevates this tame production of army nurse in Korean War who finds a new romance.

Flight of the Phoenix (1966) C-147m. ***1/2 D: Robert Aldrich. James Stewart, Richard Attenborough, Peter Finch, Hardy Kruger, Ernest Borgnine, Ian Bannen, Ronald Fraser, Christian Marquand, Dan Duryea, George Kennedy. A plane crash leaves a group of men stranded in the Arabian desert; film avoids clichés as tension mounts among the men. Stewart as the captain, Attenborough as the navigator stand out in uniformly fine cast.

Flight of the Lost Balloon (1961) C-91m. *1/2 D: Bernard Woolner. Marshall Thompson, Mala Powers, James Lanphier, Douglas Kennedy. Potentially interesting mixture of sci-fi and adventure drowns in low-budget telling of Thompson using balloon transport to travel across African wasteland to find missing explorer.

Flight to Hong Kong (1956) 88m. ** D: Joseph M. Newman. Rory Calhoun, Barbara Rush, Dolores Donlon, Soo Yong. Standard fare of gangster in Far East preferring Rush to his smuggler friends; it almost costs him his life.

Flight to Mars (1951) 72m. ** D: Lesley Selander. Marguerite Chapman, Cameron Mitchell, Virginia Houston, Arthur Franz. Adequate sci-fi about trip in outer space. Special effects hampered by modest budget production.

Flight to Nowhere (1946) 75m. Bomb D: William Rowland. Evelyn Ankers, Alan Curtis, Jack Holt, Jerome Cowan, Micheline Cheirel. Dismal cheapie about international spies maneuvering to grab nuclear secrets.

Flight to Tangier (1953) C-90m. **1/2 D: Charles Marquis Warren. Joan Fontaine, Jack Palance, Corinne Calvet, Robert Douglas. Fast-paced drama involving a cache of money aboard plane that has crashed, and the assorted people chasing after the loot.

Flim Flam Man, The (1967) C-115m. *** D: Irvin Kershner. George C. Scott, Sue Lyon, Michael Sarrazin, Harry Morgan, Jack Albertson, Alice Ghostley, Albert Salmi, Slim Pickens. Scott is engaging as a veteran Southern con-man who takes on young Sarrazin as apprentice in his travels, but finds the novice a bit too honest. Entertaining comedy.

Flipper (1963) 90m. **1/2 D: James Clark. Chuck Connors, Luke Halpin, Kathleen Maguire, Connie Scott. Pilot for later TV series is typical family fare as the bright dolphin helps Connors' family in many ways.

Flirtation Walk (1934) 97m. **1/2 D: Frank Borzage. Dick Powell, Ruby Keeler, Pat O'Brien, Ross Alexander, Guinn Williams, Henry O'Neill. West Point plot is clichéd and trivial as usual as cadet Powell falls in love with officer's daughter Keeler; some fairly good numbers highlighted by "Mr. and Mrs. Is The Name."

Flirting With Fate (1938) 69m. **1/2 D: Frank McDonald. Joe E. Brown, Leo Carrillo, Beverly Roberts, Wynne Gibson, Steffi Duna, Stanley Fields. Slapstick comedy about traveling vaudeville troupe down in South America; good for Brown fans.

Flood Tide (1958) 82m. **1/2 D: Abner Biberman. George Nader, Cornell Borchers, Michel Ray, Judson Pratt. Soapy mystery of an innocent man being convicted of murder on the say-so of a lame child, reputed to be a first-class liar.

Floods of Fear (1959-British) 82m. ** D: Charles Crichton. Howard Keel, Anne Heywood, Cyril Cusack, Harry H. Corbett, John Crawford. Adequate drama about prisoner Keel on the lam, who performs heroic deeds during flood, later proving innocence and winning girl's love.

Florida Special (1936) 70m. ** D: Ralph Murphy. Jack Oakie, Sally Eilers, Kent Taylor, Frances Drake, J. Farrell MacDonald, Sam (Schlepperman) Hearn, Claude Gillingwater, Sidney Blackmer. Romance, mystery, and murder aboard southbound train. Song: "It's You I'm Talking About." Fun, but nothing special.

Florian (1940) 91m. ** D: Edwin L. Marin. Robert Young, Helen Gilbert, Charles Coburn, Lee Bowman, Reginald Owen, Lucile Watson. Young and Gilbert, poor man and rich girl, marry, united by their love of horses.

Flower Drum Song (1961) C-133m. ** D: Henry Koster. Nancy Kwan, James Shigeta, Miyoshi Umeki, Juanita Hall, Benson Fong. Pleasant enough Rodgers and Hammerstein musical. No great songs, but listenable score and good choreography stringing together story of San Francisco's Chinatown. Major problem: it goes on too long.

Flowing Gold (1940) 82m. **½ D: Alfred E. Green. John Garfield, Frances Farmer, Pat O'Brien, Raymond Walburn, Cliff Edwards, Tom Kennedy. Dynamic Garfield in story that doesn't flow; standard fare of men trying to succeed with oil well.

Fluffy (1965) C-92m. ** D: Earl Bellamy. Tony Randall, Shirley Jones, Edward Andrews, Ernest Truex, Howard Morris, Dick Sargent. Silly film dealing with professor Randall experimenting with a lion; he can't shake the beast, causing all sorts of repercussions, even winning Jones' affection.

Fly, The (1958) C-94m. *** D: Kurt Neumann. David Hedison, Patricia Owens, Vincent Price, Herbert Marshall. Improbable but diverting sci-fi of scientist experimenting with disintegration machine, only to become victim of same and change into insect.

Flying Deuces, The (1939) **½ D: A. Edward Sutherland. Stan Laurel, Oliver Hardy, Jean Parker, Reginald Gardiner, Charles Middleton, James Finlayson. Stan and Ollie join the Foreign Legion so Ollie can forget sad love affair; usual complications result. Duo do song and dance to "Shine on Harvest Moon."

Flying Down to Rio (1933) 89m. *** D: Thornton Freeland. Dolores Del Rio, Gene Raymond, Raul Roulien, Ginger Rogers, Fred Astaire, Blanche Frederici, Eric Blore. Slim vehicle memorable for its scene of dancing girls cavorting on the plane's wing, plus Astaire and Rogers doing "The Carioca" in their first screen teaming.

Flying Fontaines, The (1959) C-84m. **½ D: George Sherman. Michael Callan, Evy Norlund, Joan Evans, Joe De Santis, Roger Perry, Rian Garrick. Circus yarn involving egocentric high-wire artist Callan who covets one of the showgirls, and the repercussions involved.

Flying Irishman, The (1939) 72m. ** D: Leigh Jason. Douglas Corrigan, Paul Kelly, Robert Armstrong, Gene Reynolds. Routine biog, largely fictional, dealing with life of Douglas "Wrong Way" Corrigan.

Flying Leathernecks (1951) C-102m. *** D: Nicholas Ray. John Wayne, Robert Ryan, Don Taylor, Janis Carter. Rugged WW2 actioner with Wayne stauncher than usual. Good fighting scenes.

Flying Missile, The (1950) 93m. ** D: Henry Levin. Glenn Ford, Viveca Lindfors, Henry O'Neill, Jerry Paris, Richard Quine. Clichéd WW2 story of commander Ford's attempt to modernize his fighting ship, with predictable results.

Flying Saucer, The (1950) 69m. *½ D: Mikel Conrad. Mikel Conrad, Pat Garrison, Russell Hicks, Denver Pyle. Sci-fi set in Alaska will leave you cold.

Flying Serpent, The (1946) 59m. ** D: Sherman Scott. George Zucco, Ralph Lewis, Hope Kramer, Eddie Acuff, Milton Kibbee. Zucco sole interest in B movie, reminiscent of serials. Doctor protects Aztec treasure with prehistoric bird. Bad script.

Flying Tigers (1942) 102m. **½ D: David Miller. John Wayne, John Carroll, Anna Lee, Paul Kelly, Mae Clarke, Gordon Jones. Good Wayne vehicle of famous Flying Tigers stationed in WW2 China. Exciting dogfight scenes top fair production values.

Flying Wild (1941) 62m. D: Wallace Fox. Leo Gorcey, Bobby Jordan, Donald Haines, Joan Barclay, David Gorcey, Bobby Stone, Sunshine Sammy Morrison. SEE: Bowery Boys series

Fog Island (1945) 72m. *½ D: Terry Morse. George Zucco, Lionel Atwill, Veda Ann Borg, Jerome Cowan, Sharon Douglas. Grade-B chiller situated at eerie mansion with usual gathering of people suspecting one another of murder and intrigue; Zucco and Atwill are potentially terrific team.

Fog Over Frisco (1934) 68m. ** D: William Dieterle. Bette Davis, Lyle Talbot, Margaret Lindsay, Donald Woods, Henry O'Neill. Quick-paced Warner Bros. programmer enhanced by Davis as reckless young girl who gets involved with mobsters; sister Lindsay tries to help.

Folies Bergère (1935) 84m. **½ D: Roy Del Ruth. Maurice Chevalier, Ann Sothern, Merle Oberon, Eric Blore, Ferdinand Munier. Entertainer Chevalier is asked to impersonate lookalike nobleman in this dated musical, with several Busby Berkeley-ish numbers that won Oscar in '35. Remade as ON THE RIVIERA.

Folies Bergère (1958-French, dubbed) C-90m. ** D: Henri Decoin. Jeanmaire, Eddie Constantine, Nadia Gray, Ives Robert. Slim plot allows for expansive cafe production numbers in tale of American crooner in Paris who almost loses wife when she becomes more successful in show biz than he.

Follow a Star (1960-British) 93m. *½ D: Robert Asher. Norman Wisdom, Jerry Desmonde, June Laverick. Flabby slapstick musical involving zany Wisdom as a cleaning store worker who is stagestruck.

Follow That Dream (1962) C-110m. **½ D: Gordon Douglas. Elvis Presley, Arthur O'Connell, Anne Helm, Joanna Moore, Jack Kruschen, Simon Oakland. Presley and family move to southern Florida where they intend to homestead, despite all opposition. Based on Richard Powell's PIONEER GO HOME.

Follow That Woman (1945) 69m. ** D: Lew Landers. Nancy Kelly, William Gargan, Regis Toomey, Ed Gargan, Byron Barr, Pierre Watkin. Predictable murder yarn, heightened by Kelly's sincerity as woman implicated in murder; Gargan her husband trying to solve case.

Follow the Boys (1944) 122m. *** D: A. Edward Sutherland. Marlene Dietrich, George Raft, Orson Welles, Vera Zorina, Dinah Shore, W. C. Fields, Jeanette MacDonald, Maria Montez, Andrews Sisters, Sophie Tucker, Nigel Bruce, Gale Sondergaard. Universal Pictures' entry in all-star WW2 series with Welles sawing Dietrich in half, MacDonald singing "Beyond The Blue Horizon," Fields doing classic pool-table routine, etc. Lots of fun.

Follow the Boys (1963) C-95m. ** D: Richard Thorpe. Connie Francis, Paula Prentiss, Randolph Scott, Janis Paige, Russ Tamblyn. Dumb comedy unspiked by Francis' singing or antics as quartet of girls chase around the French Riviera seeking husbands.

Follow the Fleet (1936) 110m. **** D: Mark Sandrich. Fred Astaire, Ginger Rogers, Randolph Scott, Harriet Hilliard, Astrid Allwyn, Harry Beresford, Betty Grable. Delightful musical with sailors Astaire and Scott romancing singers Rogers and Hilliard. Irving Berlin songs: "Let's Face The Music and Dance," "Let Yourself Go," "We Saw The Sea."

Follow the Leader (1944) 64m. D: William Beaudine. Leo Gorcey, Huntz Hall, Gabriel Dell, Joan Marsh, Mary Gordon, J. Farrell MacDonald, Billy Benedict. SEE: Bowery Boys series.

Follow the Sun (1951) 93m. **½ D: Sidney Lanfield. Glenn Ford, Anne Baxter, Dennis O'Keefe, June Havoc. Fictionalized sports biography of golfer Ben Hogan with hokey dramatics to fill in lean spots.

Fool Killer, The (1965) 103m. *** D: Servando Gonzalez. Anthony Perkins, Dana Elcar, Henry Hull, Salome Jens, Charlotte Albert, Arnold Moss. Set in post-Civil War

South, brooding film relates strange adventures of runaway boy, focusing on encounter with pensive Perkins, all of which gives the youth maturer sense of values.

Fools for Scandal (1938) 81m. **½ D: Mervyn LeRoy. Carole Lombard, Fernand Gravet, Ralph Bellamy, Allen Jenkins, Isabel Jeans, Marie Wilson. Generally a misfire, despite lovely Lombard as movie star who meets impoverished nobleman Gravet in Paris; Bellamy plays the sap again.

Folly to be Wise (1952-British) 91m. *** D: Frank Launder. Alastair Sim, Elizabeth Allan, Roland Culver, Martita Hunt. Generally amusing nonsense with Sim an army chaplain trying to enliven service life with various unique entertainment programs.

Footlight Parade (1933) 100m. ***½ D: Lloyd Bacon. James Cagney, Joan Blondell, Ruby Keeler, Dick Powell, Guy Kibbee, Ruth Donnelly, Hugh Herbert, Herman Bing, Frank McHugh. Warner Bros. stock company has a romp in this fast-paced, almost believable N.Y.C. show biz tale, highlighted by Busby Berkeley production numbers, including fabulous "By A Waterfall," infectious "Honeymoon Hotel."

Footlight Serenade (1942) 80m. **½ D: Gregory Ratoff. Betty Grable, Victor Mature, John Payne, Jane Wyman, Phil Silvers, James Gleason, Mantan Moreland, Cobina Wright, Jr. Standard backstage musical with boxer Mature turning to Broadway for change, meeting Grable. No memorable songs.

Footsteps in the Dark (1941) 96m. **½ D: Lloyd Bacon. Errol Flynn, Brenda Marshall, Ralph Bellamy, Alan Hale, Lee Patrick, Allen Jenkins. Flashy comedy-mystery with Flynn as playboy doubling as independent detective.

Footsteps in the Fog (1955-British) C-90m. ** D: Arthur Lubin. Jean Simmons, Stewart Granger, Finlay Currie, Bill Travers, Ronald Squire. Cat-and-mouse battle involving servant girl who blackmails her employer for having murdered his wife, their efforts to do away with each other.

Footsteps in the Night (1957) 62m. *½ D: Jean Yarbrough. Bill Elliott, Don Haggerty, Eleanore Tanin, Zena Marshall. Programmer detective tale with Elliott solving the murder of a friend, occurring at a motel.

For Better For Worse (1954-British) C-83m. **½ D: J. Lee Thompson. Dirk Bogarde, Susan Stephen, Cecil Parker, Eileen Herlie. Intelligently handled account of young married couple harrassed by bills, in-laws, and marital adjustment.

For Heaven's Sake (1950) 92m. **½ D: George Seaton. Clifton Webb, Joan Bennett, Robert Cummings, Edmund Gwenn, Joan Blondell. Droll fantasy with Webb and Gwenn two angels sent to earth to speed along the arrival of Bennett and Cummings' heavenly baby.

For Love or Money (1963) C-108m. **½ D: Michael Gordon. Kirk Douglas, Mitzi Gaynor, Gig Young, Thelma Ritter, William Bendix, Julie Newmar. Comedy strains to be funnier than it is. Widow Ritter hires lawyer Douglas to find spouses for her three daughters. Inevitably he marries one of them.

For Me and My Gal (1942) 104m. **½ D: Busby Berkeley. Judy Garland, Gene Kelly, George Murphy, Horace McNally, Marta Eggerth, Keenan Wynn, Richard Quine, Ben Blue. Music sustains old-hat plot of vaudeville couple determined to play Palace, circa WW1. Kelly's film debut enhanced by Garland-Kelly singing favorite songs.

For Men Only (1952) 93m. ** D: Paul Henreid. Paul Henreid, Kathleen Hughes, Russell Johnson, James Dobson, Margaret Field, Vera Miles, Douglas Kennedy, O. Z. Whitehead. Sincere if obvious study of fraternity hazing that gets out of hand on a college campus. Retitled: THE TALL LIE.

For the Love of Mary (1948) 90m. **½ D: Frederick de Cordova. Deanna Durbin, Edmond O'Brien, Don Taylor, Jeffrey Lynn. Airy fluff with Durbin a White House switchboard operator getting political figures and her own romance tangled up.

For the Love of Mike (1960) C-84m. **½ D: George Sherman. Richard Basehart, Stuart Erwin, Arthur Shields, Armando Silvestre. Mild happenings as Indian boy trains a horse, hoping to use prize money for a village shrine.

For Those Who Think Young (1964) C-96m. ** D: Leslie Martinson. James Darren, Pamela Tiffin, Tina Louise, Paul Lynde, Woody Woodbury. Witless plug for Pepsi is about low-jinks at college, undistinguished by Nancy Sinatra and Claudia Martin's presence, or cameos by George Raft, Robert Armstrong, Allen Jenkins et al.

For Whom the Bell Tolls (1943) C-170m. ***½ D: Sam Wood. Gary Cooper, Ingrid Bergman, Akim Tamiroff, Arturo de Cordova, Joseph Calleia, Katina Paxinou, Vladimir Sokoloff, Mikhail Rasumny, Fortunio Bonanova. Hemingway story of U.S. mercenary Cooper fighting for Spain with motley crew of peasants, including Bergman; tense action, beautiful color, marvelous Victor Young score. Paxinou won Best Supporting Actress Oscar.

Forbidden (1953) 85m. **½ D: Rudolph Mate. Tony Curtis, Joanne Dru, Lyle Bettger, Marvin Miller, Victor Sen Yung. Curtis and Dru are engaging in story of gangland chief seeking the whereabouts of girlfriend (Dru), hiring Curtis to find her.

Forbidden Cargo (1956-British) 83m. ** D: Harold French. Nigel Patrick, Elizabeth Sellars, Terence Morgan, Jack Warner. Modest drama about customs agents clashing with dope-smuggling syndicate.

Forbidden Fruit (1959-French, dubbed) 97m. **½ D: Henri Verneuil. Fernandel, Françoise Arnoul, Claude Nollier, Sylvie, Jacques Castelot. Unpretentious little film of Fernandel's touching love affair with a young maiden.

Forbidden Games (1951-French, dubbed) 87m. *** D: René Clement. Brigitte Fossey, Georges Poujouly, Louis Herbert. Sensitive study of orphaned girl in 1940's France who is sheltered by kindly family, focusing on touching relationship between her and their son.

Forbidden Island (1959) C-66m. *½ D: Charles B. Griffith. Jon Hall, Nan Adams, John Farrow, Jonathan Haze, Greigh Phillips. Sleazy film with Hall a skindiver seeking to find sunken treasure before a gang of crooks uncovers the loot.

Forbidden Planet (1956) C-98m. *** D: Fred McLeod Wilcox. Walter Pidgeon, Anne Francis, Leslie Nielsen, Warren Stevens. Elaborate, intelligent science-fiction fantasy of travelers to lost planet where Pidgeon, daughter Francis, and Robby the Robot reign supreme. Elaborate production values.

Forbidden Street, The (1949) 91m. ** D: Jean Negulesco. Dana Andrews, Maureen O'Hara, Sybil Thorndike, Fay Compton. Fanciful melodrama of wealthy O'Hara defying her family by marrying down-and-out artist Andrews. Set in 1870's England.

Force of Arms (1951) 100m. **½ D: Michael Curtiz. William Holden, Nancy Olson, Frank Lovejoy, Gene Evans. Updating of Hemingway's A FAREWELL TO ARMS to WW2 Italy, with Holden-Olson teaming acceptable.

Force of Evil (1948) 78m. *** D: Abraham Polonsky. John Garfield, Beatrice Pearson, Thomas Gomez, Roy Roberts, Marie Windsor. Excellent study of the numbers racket, with Garfield inexorably involved, battling to break loose.

Foreign Affair, A (1948) 116m. ***½ D: Billy Wilder. Jean Arthur, Marlene Dietrich, John Lund, Millard Mitchell. Staid Arthur is sent to Berlin to investigate post-WW2 morals, but finds romance instead, with hot competition from chic Dietrich. Marlene's third "comeback" vehicle.

Foreign Correspondent (1940) 119m. **** D: Alfred Hitchcock. Joel McCrea, Laraine Day, Herbert Marshall, George Sanders, Albert Basserman, Robert Benchley, Eduardo Ciannelli, Edmund Gwenn. McCrea in title role caught in middle of spy ring with reporters Sanders and Benchley, innocent Day, suspicious father Marshall. Pace and atmosphere are a tribute to the director in tremendously entertaining film.

Foreign Intrigue (1956) C-100m. **½ D: Sheldon Reynolds. Robert Mitchum, Genevieve Page, Ingrid Thulin, Frederick O'Brady. Based on TV series, film has virtue of on-location shooting in Europe as unemotional Mitchum checks out the cause of his employer's death.

Foreman Went to France, The (1942-British) 88m. **½ D: Charles Frend. Clifford Evans, Constance Cummings, Robert Morley, Mervyn Johns, Gordon Jackson, Ernest Milton. Documentary-style tale of industrial engineer who journeys to France during WW2 to help save secret machinery from being confiscated by the Axis.

Forest Rangers, The (1942) C-87m. **½ D: George Marshall. Fred MacMurray, Paulette Goddard, Susan Hayward, Albert Dekker, Rod Cameron, Lynne Overman, Eugene Pallette. Goddard tries to show ranger MacMurray that he's made a mistake marrying wealthy Hayward in this OK romance with good action scenes.

Forever Amber (1947) C-140m. **½ D: Otto Preminger. Linda Darnell, Cornel Wilde, Richard Greene, George Sanders, Jessica Tandy, Anne Revere, Leo G. Carroll. Standard costume drama of 17th-century England, with Darnell forfeiting love for success in court of Charles II. Plush production from Kathleen Windsor novel.

Forever and a Day (1943) 104m. **** D: René Clair, Edmund Goulding, Cedric Hardwicke, Frank Lloyd, Victor Saville, Robert Stevenson, Herbert Wilcox. Brian Aherne, Robert Cummings, Ida Lupino, Charles Laughton, Herbert Marshall, Ray Milland, Anna Neagle, Merle Oberon, Claude Rains, Victor McLaglen, Roland Young, C. Aubrey Smith, Edward Everett Horton, Elsa Lanchester, Edmund Gwenn. Eighty-odd British stars appear in episodic film of British house, its inhabitants over the years. Fine entertainment, once-in-a-lifetime cast.

Forever Darling (1956) C-96m. **½ D: Alexander Hall. Lucille Ball, Desi Arnaz, James Mason, Louis Calhern. Ball's madcap antics nearly drive husband Arnaz to divorce, but guardian angel Mason saves the day. Contrived but enjoyable.

Forever Female (1953) 93m. ***½ D: Irving Rapper. Ginger Rogers, William Holden, Paul Douglas, Pat Crowley, James Gleason. Top-notch show business comedy, with Rogers the star who finally realizes she is too old for the ingenue role, allowing writer Holden to cast Crowley in the part. Film captures flavor of the Broadway, summer stock scene.

Forever My Love (1962-German, dubbed) C-147m. **½ D: Ernst Marischka. Romy Schneider, Karl Boehm, Magda Schneider, Vilma Degischer. Typical German confection dealing with 19th-century Austrian Emperor Franz Josef and Empress Elizabeth.

Forger of London (1961-German, dubbed) 91m. ** D: Harald Reinl. Eddi Arent, Viktor de Kowa, Karin Dor, Hellmut Lange, Robert Graf. Scotland Yard investigates counterfeit gang tied in with prime suspect, an amnesiac playboy; from Edgar Wallace tale.

Forgiven Sinner, The (1961-French, dubbed) 101m. **½ D: Jean-Pierre Melville. Jean Paul Belmondo, Emmanuele Riva, Patricia Gozzi, Irene Tunc. Belmondo gives subdued, offbeat performance as clergyman trying to set shady woman onto the path of righteousness.

Forgotten Woman (1939) 63m. **½ D: Harold Young. Sigrid Gurie, William Lundigan, Eve Arden, Elizabeth Risdon, Virginia Brissac. Overnight star (and overnight fadeout) Gurie is helpless woman, framed by influential gangsters, suffering on trial.

Forsaking All Others (1935) 84m. **½ D: W. S. Van Dyke, II. Joan Crawford, Clark Gable, Robert Montgomery, Charles Butterworth, Billie Burke. When Montgomery stands up Crawford for wedding date, she thinks again and sees the light. Pat, but smooth.

Fort Algiers (1953) 78m. ** D: Lesley Selander. Yvonne de Carlo, Carlos Thompson, Raymond Burr, Leif Erickson. De Carlo romps through this adventure set in Algiers, dealing with villainous Arab leader inciting the natives to rebel.

Fort Apache (1948) 127m. *** D: John Ford. John Wayne, Henry Fonda, Shirley Temple, Pedro Armendariz, John Agar, Anna Lee, Ward Bond. First of Ford's three large-scale historical Westerns, this one a sturdy drama of Indian attacks and conflict among army officers.

Fort Defiance (1951) C-81m. **½ D: John Rawlins. Dane Clark, Ben Johnson, Peter Graves, Tracey Roberts. Film focuses on human relations in between preparations for threatened Indian attacks.

Fort Dobbs (1958) 90m. ** D: Gordon Douglas. Clint Walker, Virginia Mayo, Brian Keith, Richard Eyer. Rugged Walker is believable as hero who fights all obstacles in the old West to make decent life for himself and Mayo.

Fort Massacre (1958) C-80m. ** D:

Joseph M. Newman. Joel McCrea, Forrest Tucker, Susan Cabot, John Russell. McCrea is leader of troop platoon which constantly is entangled with redskin skirmishes.

Fort Osage (1952) C-72m. Bomb D: Lesley Selander. Rod Cameron, Jane Nigh, Douglas Kennedy, Iron Eyes Cody. Inept Grade-D Western involving perennial Indian uprisings.

Fort Ti (1953) C-73m. ** D: William Castle. George Montgomery, Joan Vohs, Irving Bacon, James Seay. Best facet of this oater set during French-Indian war of 1760's was 3-D effects, lost to TV viewers.

Fort Vengeance (1953) 75m. *1/2 D: Lesley Selander. James Craig, Rita Moreno, Keith Larsen, Reginald Denny, Emory Parnell. Film lacks much-needed action in its account of Pacific Northwest and mounties chasing fur thieves, quelling Indian uprisings.

Fort Worth (1951) C-80m. ** D: Edwin L. Marin. Randolph Scott, David Brian, Phyllis Thaxter, Helena Carter. Scott learns that pen is not mightier than the sword; he's a gunslinger who becomes newspaper editor but can only rid town of outlaws via six-shooter.

Fort Yuma (1955) C-78m. ** D: Lesley Selander. Peter Graves, Joan Taylor, Addison Richards, Joan Vohs. Indians go on warpath when their chief is killed. Occasionally good combat sequences.

Fortune Cookie, The (1966) 125m. *** D: Billy Wilder. Jack Lemmon, Walter Matthau, Ron Rich, Cliff Osmond, Judi West, Lurene Tuttle. Biting Wilder comedy about TV cameraman (Lemmon) injured during football game and shyster lawyer (Matthau) who exaggerates damages for insurance purposes. Matthau's Oscar-winning performance hits home.

Fortune in Diamonds (1952-British) 74m. ** D: David MacDonald. Dennis Price, Jack Hawkins, Siobhan McKenna. Good cast of disparate types all thirsting for cache of gems hidden in the heart of African jungle. Retitled: THE ADVENTURERS.

Fortunes of Captain Blood (1950) 91m. ** D: Gordon Douglas. Louis Hayward, Patricia Medina, George Macready, Terry Kilburn. This filming of Sabatini novel lacks flair and scope of the Flynn version. Costumer recounts tale of Irish doctor who becomes notorious pirate to revenge wrongdoings.

Forty Guns (1957) 80m. **1/2 D: Samuel Fuller. Barbara Stanwyck, Barry Sullivan, Dean Jagger, John Ericson, Gene Barry. Stanwyck is chief virtue of pedestrian Western involving lady outlaw leader in old Arizona being pursued by the law.

Forty Little Mothers (1940) 90m. **1/2 D: Busby Berkeley. Eddie Cantor, Judith Anderson, Ralph Morgan, Rita Johnson, Bonita Granville, Diana Lewis. Second-rate Cantor, as reluctant schoolteacher. Veronica Lake is one of the mothers.

49th Man, The (1953) 73m. ** D: Fred F. Sears. John Ireland, Richard Denning, Mike Connors, Suzanne Dalbert. Suspenseful account of federal agents tracing down foreign agents smuggling atomic bombs piecemeal into the U.S.

Forty Ninth Parallel (1942-British) 105m. ***1/2 D: Michael Powell. Anton Walbrook, Eric Portman, Leslie Howard, Raymond Massey, Laurence Olivier, Finlay Currie, Glynis Johns, Niall Macginnis. Taut WW2 yarn of Nazi servicemen seeking to reach Canadian land when their U-boat is sunk; top-notch cast; admirably played for suspense and characterizations. Retitled: THE INVADERS.

Forty Pounds of Trouble (1962) C-106m. **1/2 D: Norman Jewison. Tony Curtis, Phil Silvers, Suzanne Pleshette, Larry Storch, Howard Morris, Stubby Kaye, Claire Wilcox, Jack LaRue. "Cute" Curtis comedy has Tony a casino manager who "adopts" little girl and endless number of complications. Film depends mostly on Disneyland location scenes, fine character actors to pep it up.

Forty-Second Street (1933) 85m. ***1/2 D: Lloyd Bacon. Warner Baxter, Ruby Keeler, George Brent, Bebe Daniels, Dick Powell, Guy Kibbee, Una Merkel, Ginger Rogers, Ned Sparks, Henry B. Walthall, George E. Stone. Engaging pioneer backstage musical with ingenious Busby Berkeley numbers strung to wispy plot of star (Daniels) breaking leg, chorus gal Keeler replacing her. Highlights: title tune, "Shuffle Off To Buffalo," "You're Getting To Be A Habit With Me."

Fountain, The (1934) 83m. **½ D: John Cromwell. Ann Harding, Paul Lukas, Brian Aherne, Jean Hersholt, Ian Wolfe. WW1 romance with Harding in love with Lukas and Aherne at the same time; respectable film.

Fountainhead, The (1949) 114m. **½ D: King Vidor. Gary Cooper, Patricia Neal, Raymond Massey, Kent Smith, Robert Douglas, Henry Hull, Ray Collins, Jerome Cowan. Ambitious but confused version of Ayn Rand philosophic novel, spotlighting an idealistic architect's clash with compromises of big business; cast does what it can with the script.

Four Against Fate SEE: Derby Day.

Four Bags Full (1956-French, dubbed) 84m. **½ D: Claude Autant-Lara. Jean Gabin, Bourvil, Jeanette Batti, Louis de Funes. Slender comedy vehicle for two top stars, involving duo who smuggle meat across French border during WW2.

4D Man (1959) C-85m. **½ D: Irvin S. Yeaworth, Jr. Robert Lansing, Lee Meriwether, James Congdon, Guy Raymond, Robert Strauss, Patty Duke. Well-handled sci-fi of scientist who learns art of transposing matter, thus giving him power to pass through any substance.

Four Daughters (1938) 90m. ***½ D: Michael Curtiz. Claude Rains, Rosemary Lane, Lola Lane, Priscilla Lane, Gale Page, John Garfield, Jeffrey Lynn, Frank McHugh, May Robson, Dick Foran. Believable, beautifully acted soaper of small-town life; four young women with musical father Rains have lives altered by four young men. Garfield is superb in first film break, matched by fine cast. Remade as YOUNG AT HEART.

Four Days Leave (1950) 98m. ** D: Leopold Lindtberg. Cornel Wilde, Josette Day, Simone Signoret, Alan Hale, Jr. Rather tame account of GI Wilde finding romance while on leave in Switzerland.

Four Desperate Men (1960-Australian) 104m. **½ D: Harry Watt. Aldo Ray, Heather Sears. Stark study of human nature as quartet of hardened thugs decide whether or not to set off huge bomb attack that would destroy Southern hemisphere.

Four Faces West (1948) 90m. **½ D: Alfred E. Green. Joel McCrea, Frances Dee, Charles Bickford, Joseph Calleia. Quiet Western of fugitive pursued by determined sheriff, with cast giving intelligent interpretation to standard formula.

Four Fast Guns (1959) 72m. *½ D: William J. Hole, Jr. James Craig, Martha Vickers, Edgar Buchanan, Brett Halsey, Paul Richards. Shootout of good vs. bad pits brother against brother.

Four Feathers (1939-British) C-115m. ***½ D: Zoltan Korda. Ralph Richardson, C. Aubrey Smith, June Duprez, Clive Baxter, John Clements, Jack Allen, Donald Gray. Impressive actioner of British nobleman who must prove he's not a coward by helping army comrades combat Sudan uprising. Smith steals much of film as tale-spinning army veteran. Remade as STORM OVER THE NILE.

Four for Texas (1963) C-124m. *** D: Robert Aldrich. Frank Sinatra, Dean Martin, Anita Ekberg, Ursula Andress, Victor Buono, Charles Bronson, Three Stooges, Mike Mazurki. Nonsensical Sinatra-Martin romp set in the old West, with their antics only outdone by Buono as villainous banker. Ekberg and Andress both outstanding scenery attractions.

Four Frightened People (1934) 78m. **½ D: Cecil B. DeMille. Claudette Colbert, Herbert Marshall, Mary Boland, Leo Carrillo, William Gargan. Unspectacular De Mille vehicle of four disparate types lost in dense jungle. Colbert is plain Jane who gets prettier scene by scene; wry Boland steals the show.

Four Girls in Town (1956) C-85m. *** D: Jack Sher. George Nader, Julie Adams, Gia Scala, Marianne Cook, Elsa Martinelli. Clichéd but absorbing account of four contrasting would-be stars coming to Hollywood seeking fame and romance; excellent musical score.

Four Guns to the Border (1954) C-82m. **½ D: Richard Carlson. Rory Calhoun, Colleen Miller, George Nader, Walter Brennan, Nina Foch. Better than usual handling of outlaws vs. Indians, with slight morality lesson for finale.

Four Horsemen of the Apocalypse (1962) C-153m. **½ D: Vincente Minnelli. Glenn Ford, Ingrid Thulin,

Charles Boyer, Lee J. Cobb, Paul Henreid, Paul Lukas, Yvette Mimieux, Karl Boehm. Compared to silent version, this is glossy, padded trash, losing all sense of reality in its telling of a family whose members fight on opposite sides during WW2. Allegedly Angela Lansbury dubbed in Thulin's lines.

400 Blows, The (1959-French, dubbed) 99m. **** D: François Truffaut. Jean-Pierre Leaud, Patrick Auffray, Claire Maurier, Albert Remy. Captivating study of Parisian youth who turns to life of small-time crime as a reaction to derelict parents. Film captures viewpoint of young people.

Four in a Jeep (1951) 97m. **1/2 D: Leopold Lindtberg. Viveca Lindfors, Ralph Meeker, Joseph Yadin, Michael Medwin. On-location shooting in Vienna, Lindfors' creditable performance as refugee seeking international MP's help makes this a diverting film.

Four Jills in a Jeep (1944) 89m. ** D: William Seiter. Kay Francis, Martha Raye, Carole Landis, Mitzi Mayfair, Phil Silvers, Alice Faye, Betty Grable, Carmen Miranda. Fictionalized account of female entertainers working for USO overseas; pat film despite several guest stars.

Four Kinds of Love SEE: Bamboie!

Four Men and a Prayer (1938) 85m. ***1/2 D: John Ford. Loretta Young, Richard Greene, George Sanders, David Niven, C. Aubrey Smith, J. Edward Bromberg, John Carradine, Peter Lorre. Exciting story of four sons avenging father's murder by crooked factory officials. Fine cast under Ford's sure direction.

Four Mothers (1941) 86m. **1/2 D: William Keighley. Priscilla Lane, Rosemary Lane, Lola Lane, Gale Page, Claude Rains, Jeffrey Lynn, May Robson, Eddie Albert. FOUR DAUGHTERS formula wearing thin in soapy tale of Albert going bankrupt, whole family helping out.

Fourposter, The (1952) 103m. ***1/2 D: Irving Reis. Rex Harrison, Lilli Palmer. Jan de Hartog play is tour de force for stars who enact the various phases of married life, with its joys and sorrows. Story musicalized as I DO, I DO on Broadway stage.

Four Skulls of Jonathan Drake, The (1959) 70m. ** D: Edward L. Cahn. Eduard Franz, Valerie French, Henry Daniell, Grant Richards, Paul Cavanagh, Howard Wendell. Acceptable horror fare involving centuries-old voodoo curse upon family and contemporary scientist who puts an end to the weird goings-on.

Four Sons (1940) 89m. **1/2 D: Archie Mayo. Don Ameche, Eugenie Leontovich, Mary Beth Hughes, Alan Curtis, George Ernest, Robert Lowery. Czech family affected by Nazi rise to power; not unlike MORTAL STORM, with sons choosing different allegiances.

Four Ways Out (1954-Italian, dubbed) 77m. **1/2 D: Pietro Germi. Gina Lollobrigida, Renato Baldini, Cosetta Greco, Paul Muller, Enzio Maggio. Drama points up futility of a robbery by quartet who individually plan their own escapes, all to no avail.

Four Wives (1939) 110m. **1/2 D: Michael Curtiz. Claude Rains, Eddie Albert, Priscilla Lane, Rosemary Lane, Lola Lane, Gale Page, John Garfield, May Robson, Frank McHugh, Jeffrey Lynn. Rains' daughters are all married, but life isn't easy for them. Garfield appears briefly in flashback.

Four's a Crowd (1938) 91m. **1/2 D: Michael Curtiz. Errol Flynn, Olivia de Havilland, Rosalind Russell, Patric Knowles, Hugh Herbert. Light-headed romance in which everyone loves another; straight comedy's a switch for Flynn, who proves he can handle genre well.

14 Hours (1951) 92m. *** D: Henry Hathaway. Paul Douglas, Richard Basehart, Barbara Bel Geddes, Debra Paget. Well-done suspenser of man threatening to throw himself off ledge. Grace Kelly's film debut.

Foxes of Harrow, The (1947) 117m. **1/2 D: John M. Stahl. Rex Harrison, Maureen O'Hara, Richard Haydn, Victor McLaglen, Vanessa Brown, Patricia Medina, Gene Lockhart. Lavish but lumbering tale of philanderer breaking up his marriage to seek affluence and fame in New Orleans in 1820. It's pretty stale despite the trimmings.

Foxfire (1955) C-92m. *** D: Joseph Pevney. Jane Russell, Jeff Chandler,

Dan Duryea, Mara Corday, Barton MacLane. Russell and Chandler work well together as married couple who almost divorce because of his obsessive working habits as mining engineer.

Foxhole in Cairo (1961-British) 79m. ****½** D: John Moxey. James Robertson Justice, Adrian Hoven, Peter Van Eyck, Neil McCallum. Sensibly told account of counterintelligence at work in Egypt during WW2 with British vs. Rommel's Nazis.

Foxiest Girl in Paris (1956-French, dubbed) 100m. ****½** D: Roger De Broin. Martine Carol, Michel Piccoli, Mischa Auer. Sultry Carol, a fashion model, becomes amateur sleuth to solve a robbery and a murder.

Fra Diavolo SEE: Devil's Brother.

Framed (1947) 82m. ****** D: Richard Wallace. Glenn Ford, Janis Carter, Barry Sullivan, Edgar Buchanan, Karen Morley. Title almost self-explanatory. Innocent man mistaken for robber is brought in, enabling real thief to escape.

Francis (the Talking Mule) Never hailed as an artistic triumph, the Francis series made up for that in box-office receipts from 1950 to 1956. Based on a book by David Stern, each of the seven films dealt with a sincere but stupid young man (at West Point he is 647th in a class of 647) led into and out of trouble by a canny talking mule. The off-screen voice was Chill Wills, the on-screen bumbler was Donald O'Connor in all but the last film, which starred Mickey Rooney. O'Connor recently explained, "When you've made six pictures and the mule still gets more fan mail than you do . . ." Universal worked their contract starlets (Piper Laurie, Martha Hyer, Julia Adams, etc.) into the series as love interests, but the center of attraction was always the mule. The films, except the last one, were all about on a par: silly but amusing. The first six films were directed by Arthur Lubin, who went on to create a similar TV series called MR. ED, about a talking horse.

Francis (1950) 91m. D: Arthur Lubin. Donald O'Connor, Patricia Medina, Zasu Pitts, Ray Collins.

Francis Covers the Big Town (1953) 86m. D: Arthur Lubin. Donald O'Connor, Gene Lockhart, Nancy Guild, Gale Gordon.

Francis Goes to the Races (1951) 88m. D: Arthur Lubin. Donald O'Connor, Piper Laurie, Cecil Kellaway, Jesse White.

Francis Goes to West Point (1952) 81m. D: Arthur Lubin. Donald O'Connor, Lori Nelson, William Reynolds, James Best, Les Tremayne, David Janssen.

Francis in the Haunted House (1956) 80m. D: Charles Lamont. Mickey Rooney, Virginia Welles, Paul Cavanagh, David Janssen.

Francis in the Navy (1955) 80m. D: Arthur Lubin. Donald O'Connor, Martha Hyer, Jim Backus, Paul Burke, David Janssen, Clint Eastwood, Martin Milner.

Francis Joins the Wacs (1954) 94m. D: Arthur Lubin. Donald O'Connor, Julia Adams, Mamie Van Doren, Chill Wills, Lynn Bari, Zasu Pitts.

Francis of Assisi (1961) C-111m. ****½** D: Michael Curtiz. Bradford Dillman, Dolores Hart, Stuart Whitman, Cecil Kellaway, Finlay Currie, Pedro Armendariz. Lavish religious epic dealing with story of founder of school of monks with sympathetic performance by Dillman. Good cast and atmosphere. Script tends to sag at wrong moments.

Frankenstein (1931) 71m. ******* D: James Whale. Colin Clive, Mae Clarke, Boris Karloff, John Boles, Edward Van Sloan, Lionel Belmore, Dwight Frye. Definitive monster movie of mad scientist Clive creating being (Karloff), accidentally using criminal brain. Impressive production, although creaky in plot development of Mary Shelley tale.

Frankenstein Conquers the World (1966-Japanese, dubbed) C-87m. ****** D: Inoshiro Honda. Nick Adams, Tadao Takashima, Kumi Mizuno. Grade-C horror film, with Adams a scientist in Tokyo trying to combat overgrown human monster terrorizing the countryside; poor special effects.

Frankenstein Meets the Space Monster (1965) 78m. ***½** D: Robert Gaffney. James Karen, David Kerman, Nancy Marshall, Marilyn Hanold. Low-grade horror entry dealing with interplanetary robot whose mechanism runs amuck as he goes berserk.

Frankenstein Meets the Wolf Man (1943) 72m. **½ D: Roy William Neill. Lon Chaney, Bela Lugosi, Patric Knowles, Ilona Massey, Dennis Hoey, Maria Ouspenskaya, Lionel Atwill. Impressive duo in atmospheric horror film about determined scientist tampering with unknown.

Frankenstein — 1970 (1958) 83m. Bomb D: Howard W. Koch. Boris Karloff, Tom Dugan, Jana Lund, Donald Barry. Poor science fiction almost sacrilegious to the name of Frankstein; no monster, just talk. Karloff is lost in this jumble.

Frankenstein's Daughter (1959) 85m. *½ D: Richard Cunha. John Ashley, Sandra Knight, Donald Murphy, Sally Todd, Harold Lloyd, Jr. Low-grade descendant of famed monster series with a new female horror-robot being created with typical results; tinsel sets.

Frankie and Johnny (1966) C-87m. **½ D: Frederick de Cordova. Elvis Presley, Donna Douglas, Harry Morgan, Sue Ann Langdon, Nancy Kovack. Saloon song expanded into feature film story for Elvis. Riverboat setting, cohort Morgan, several pretty starlets, and tuneful songs make this a satisfactory time-filler.

Frantic (1964-French, dubbed) 94m. *½ D: Serge Friedman. Jacques Riberolles, Ellen Kessler, Alice Kessler, Ginette Leclerc. Misfire; muddled murder account of Riberolles in love with circus performer E. Kessler; pursued by her jealous twin sister A. Kessler.

Fraulein (1958) C-98m. ** D: Henry Koster. Dana Wynter, Mel Ferrer, Dolores Michaels, Maggie Hayes. Bizarre tale of German girl in post-WW2 Berlin helping American soldier, then being held by the Communists. Wynter miscast.

Freckles (1960) C-84m. *½ D: Andrew V. McLaglen. Martin West, Carol Christensen, Jack Lambert, Roy Barcroft, Ken Curtis, Steven Peck. Bland study of crippled youth who manages to be accepted as normal working member of lumber camp.

Free and Easy (1930) 75m. **½ D: Edward Sedgwick. Buster Keaton, Anita Page, Robert Montgomery, Edgar Dearing, Lionel Barrymore, Dorothy Sebastian, Trixie Friganza. Interesting early talkie musicomedy of Keaton becoming movie star; many guest appearances by Cecil B. DeMille, William Haines et al to boost uneven film. Retitled: EASY GO.

Free, Blonde and Twenty One (1940) 67m. *½ D: Ricardo Cortez. Lynn Bari, Mary Beth Hughes, Joan Davis, Henry Wilcoxon. Low-grade hokum about gold-digging gals on the make for wealthy men.

Free for All (1949) 83m. ** D: Charles Barton. Robert Cummings, Ann Blyth, Percy Kilbride, Ray Collins. Mild froth about Cummings inventing instant gasoline.

Free Soul, A (1931) 91m. *** D: Clarence Brown. Norma Shearer, Lionel Barrymore, Clark Gable, Leslie Howard, James Gleason, George Irving. Outstanding acting makes dated story worthwhile, as Shearer supports drunken father Barrymore by working as reporter, luring gangster Gable to get the goods on him. Film won Barrymore an Oscar, gave big boost to Gable's budding career.

French Can Can SEE: Only the French Can.

French Key, The (1946) 64m. **½ D: Walter Colmes. Albert Dekker, Mike Mazurki, Evelyn Ankers, John Eldredge, Frank Fenton, Richard Arlen, Byron Foulger. Dekker gives mystery drama some class in this murder yarn.

French Line, The (1954) C-102m. ** D: Lloyd Bacon. Jane Russell, Gilbert Roland, Arthur Hunnicutt, Mary McCarty. Russell's bust in 3-D was the gimmick to sell this dull musical. All that's left is flat tale of wealthy girl in Paris being romanced by Parisian. McCarty's wisecracking is a blessing.

French They are a Funny Race, The (1957-British) 83m. ** D: Preston Sturges. Jack Buchanan, Martine Carol, Noel-Noel, Catherine Boyl. Slim premise of married couple Buchanan and Carol fighting over virtues of their nations. Stars try hard.

French Without Tears (1940-British) 67m. **½ D: Anthony Asquith. Ray Milland, Ellen Drew, Janine Darcey, David Tree, Roland Culver. Chipper British cast in sophisticated, talky comedy of manners that never quite makes it.

Frenchie (1950) C-81m. **½ D: Louis

King. Joel McCrea, Shelley Winters, John Russell, John Emery, George Cleveland, Elsa Lanchester, Marie Windsor. When her father is murdered, Winters returns to Western home town and opens a saloon, planning revenge. Shelley makes the nonsense enjoyable.

Frenchman's Creek (1944) C-113m. *** D: Mitchell Leisen. Joan Fontaine, Arturo de Cordova, Basil Rathbone, Nigel Bruce, Cecil Kellaway, Ralph Forbes, George Kirby. Colorful escapism of Fontaine romanced by dashing pirate De Cordova; good supporting cast.

Fresh From Paris (1955) C-70m. *½ D: Leslie Goodwins. Forrest Tucker, Margaret Whiting, Martha Hyer. Grade-C musical filmed at Moulin Rouge cafe in Hollywood, with tiresome musical interludes. Original title: PARIS FOLLIES OF 1956.

Freud (1962) 139m. ***½ D: John Huston. Montgomery Clift, Susannah York, Larry Parks, David McCallum, Susan Kohner, Eileen Herlie. Intelligent, unglamorous account of events in life of Sigmund Freud, focusing on his psychiatric treatments. Clift gives sincere performance.

Frieda (1947-British) 97m. *** D: Basil Dearden. David Farrar, Glynis Johns, Mai Zetterling, Flora Robson, Albert Lieven. Interesting study of Farrar bringing German wife Zetterling back home to England, and bigotry they encounter.

Friendly Enemies (1942) 95m. **½ D: Allan Dwan. Charles Winninger, Charlie Ruggles, James Craig, Nancy Kelly. Thoughtful minor film of conflicts between lifelong friends when WW1 breaks out and their German heritage leads to friction.

Friendly Persuasion (1956) C-140m. *** D: William Wyler. Gary Cooper, Dorothy McGuire, Marjorie Main, Anthony Perkins, Robert Middleton, Walter Catlett. Charming account of Quaker family struggling to maintain its identity amid confusion and heartbreak of Civil War. McGuire is strong-willed mother, Cooper an easygoing father, Perkins a naive son; memorable score.

Frightened Bride, The (1953-British) 75m. ** D: Terence Young. Andre Morell, Flora Robson, Mai Zetterling, Michael Denison, Mervyn Johns. Murder haunts a family when the youngest son becomes involved in homicide.

Frightened City, The (1962-British) 97m. **½ D: John Lemont. Herbert Lom, John Gregson, Sean Connery, Alfred Marks, Yvonne Romain. Interesting inside look at a London racketeer amalgamating various city gangs for master plan syndicate.

Frisco Kid (1935) 77m. ** D: Lloyd Bacon. James Cagney, Margaret Lindsay, Ricardo Cortez, Lili Damita, Fred Kohler, George E. Stone, Donald Woods. Routine drama of Barbary Coast with Cagney fighting his way to the top, almost dethroned by local gangs but saved by blueblood Lindsay.

Frisco Sal (1945) 63m. ** D: George Waggner. Susanna Foster, Turhan Bey, Alan Curtis, Andy Devine, Thomas Gomez, Samuel S. Hinds. Tepid costume drama of Foster out West in California, determined to find her brother's killer.

Frisky (1955-Italian, dubbed) 98m. **½ D: Luigi Comencini. Gina Lollobrigida, Vittorio DeSica, Roberto Risso, Marisa Merlini. Lollobrigida provides sufficient sex appeal to carry simple tale of flirtatious village girl who beats out competition in winning heart of police official DeSica.

Frogmen, The (1951) 96m. *** D: Lloyd Bacon. Richard Widmark, Dana Andrews, Gary Merrill, Jeffrey Hunter. Intriguing look at underwater demolition squads in action in the Pacific during WW2.

From Hell It Came (1957) 71m. *½ D: Dan Miller. Tod Andrew, Linda Watkins, Gregg Palmer, Robert Swan. Monstrous limb rises from grave of native chief's son, causing terror in African village.

From Hell to Borneo (1964) C-96m. ** D: George Montgomery. George Montgomery, Julie Gregg, Torin Thatcher, Lisa Moreno. Filmed in the Philippines, tale recounts Montgomery's efforts to maintain sanctity of his private island against aggressive crooks and smugglers.

From Hell to Texas (1958) C-100m. **½ D: Henry Hathaway. Don Murray, Diane Varsi, Chill Wills, Dennis Hopper. Sincere Western with Murray on the run with posse on his trail for accidentally killing a man.

From Here to Eternity (1953) 118m. **** D: Fred Zinnemann. Burt Lancaster, Montgomery Clift, Deborah Kerr, Frank Sinatra, Donna Reed, Ernest Borgnine, George Reeves. Excellent film of army life in Hawaii at start of WW2. Sinatra and Reed won Oscars in this tight version of James Jones' novel; powerful and engrossing.

From Russia With Love (1964) C-118m. ***½ D: Terence Young. Sean Connery, Daniela Bianchi, Lotte Lenya, Pedro Armendariz, Robert Shaw, Lois Maxwell. Second James Bond film is one of the best; plenty of suspense and action, and one of the longest, most exciting fight scenes ever staged. Lenya makes a very sinister spy.

From the Earth to the Moon (1958) C-100m. **½ D: Byron Haskin. Joseph Cotten, George Sanders, Debra Paget, Don Dubbins. Jules Verne's fiction doesn't float well in contrived sci-fi of early rocket flight to the moon. Veteran cast looks most uncomfortable.

From the Terrace (1960) 144m. *** D: Mark Robson. Paul Newman, Joanne Woodward, Myrna Loy. Ina Balin. John O'Hara's ironic chronicle of poor boy's rise to financial and social success becomes superficial film. Woodward is chic and Newman wooden; Loy is superb as drunken mother.

From This Day Forward (1946) 95m. *** D: John Barry. Joan Fontaine, Mark Stevens, Rosemary DeCamp, Henry Morgan, Arline Judge, Bobby Driscoll, Mary Treen. Agreeable soaper of Fontaine and Stevens readjusting their lives when he returns from war, their struggle to get on in the world.

Front Page Story (1955-British) 95m. **½ D: Gordon Parry. Jack Hawkins, Elizabeth Allan, Eva Bartok, Martin Miller. Hawkins' restrained acting makes believable the massive problems confronting newspaper editor; pending divorce, murder, lost children, and rebellious staff members.

Front Page Woman (1935) 82m. **½ D: Michael Curtiz. Bette Davis, George Brent, Winifred Shaw, Roscoe Karns, Joseph Crehan. Breezy yarn of rival reporters Davis and Brent trying to outdo each other covering unusual fire story; prime ingenue-Davis fare.

Frontier Gal (1945) C-84m. **½ D: Charles Lamont. Yvonne de Carlo, Rod Cameron, Andy Devine, Fuzzy Knight, Andrew Tombes, Sheldon Leonard, Clara Blandick. Sex in the West as saloon queen De Carlo falls in love with outlaw Cameron; no sympathy from villain Leonard in OK Western-comedy.

Frontier Gun (1958) 70m. ** D: Paul Landres. John Agar, Robert Strauss, Barton MacLane, Morris Ankrum. Agar is honest sheriff who discovers that gunplay is only solution to town's crooks.

Frontier Hellcat (1966-German, dubbed) C-98m. **½ D: Alfred Vohrer. Stewart Granger, Elke Sommer, Pierre Brice, Gotz George. Another Karl May WINNETOU story, which captures flavor of old West, recounting adventure of pioneers passing through Rockies.

Frontier Uprising (1961) 68m. *½ D: Edward L. Cahn. James Davis, Nancy Hadley, Ken Mayer, Nestor Paiva. Scout leading pioneers to West Coast in 1840's discovers that Mexico and U.S. are at war.

Frozen Dead, The (1967-British) 95m. **½ D: Herbert J. Leder. Dana Andrews, Anna Palk, Philip Girlbert, Kathleen Breck, Karel Stepanek. Bizarre account of scientist Andrews who froze group of Nazi leaders, now trying to revive them and the Third Reich; sloppy production values mar tale.

Frozen Ghost, The (1945) 61m. ** D: Harold Young. Lon Chaney, Evelyn Ankers, Milburn Stone, Douglass Dumbrille, Martin Kosleck, Elena Verdugo. Typical 1940's Chaney nonsense about tormented hypnotist who stumbles into murder plot.

Fugitive, The (1947) 104m. ***½ D: John Ford. Henry Fonda, Dolores Del Rio, Pedro Armendariz, J. Carrol Naish, Leo Carrillo. Brooding drama set in Mexico with revolutionist priest turned in by man who once sheltered him. Good cast works well.

Fugitive Kind, The (1959) 135m. **½ D: Sidney Lumet. Marlon Brando, Anna Magnani, Joanne Woodward, Maureen Stapleton, Victor Jory, R.

G. Armstrong. Uneven filming of Tennessee Williams' ORPHEUS DESCENDING, with strange casting. Wandering bum (Brando) arrives in Southern town, sparking romances with middle-aged married woman (Magnani) and spunky Woodward. Movie gets nowhere.

Full Confession (1939) 73m. ** D: John Farrow. Victor McLaglen, Sally Eilers, Joseph Calleia, Barry Fitzgerald. Mild yet effective yarn of clergyman who listens to a criminal's confessions and convinces him that he should go to the police to save innocent man accused of crime.

Full of Life (1956) 91m. *** D: Richard Quine. Judy Holliday, Richard Conte, Salvatore Baccaloni, Esther Minciotti. Holliday's antics as pregnant wife are almost matched by Baccaloni as excitable father-in-law with his own way of running things.

Fuller Brush Girl, The (1950) 85m. ** D: Lloyd Bacon. Lucille Ball, Eddie Albert, Jeff Donnell, Jerome Cowan, Lee Patrick. Acceptable slapstick with energetic Lucy as door-to-door salesgirl, mixed up with thieves.

Fuller Brush Man, The (1948) 93m. **1/2 D: S. Sylvan Simon. Red Skelton, Janet Blair, Don McGuire, Adele Jergens, Ross Ford. Usual Skelton slapstick, with Red involved in murder while valiantly trying to succeed as a door-to-door salesman.

Fun in Acapulco (1963) C-97m. **1/2 D: Richard Thorpe. Elvis Presley, Ursula Andress, Paul Lukas, Alejandro Rey. Scenery outshines story of Presley working as lifeguard and entertainer in Mexican resort city. Lukas is amusing as temperamental chef; lush scenery.

Fun on a Weekend (1947) 93m. ** D: Andrew L. Stone. Eddie Bracken, Priscilla Lane, Tom Conway, Allen Jenkins, Arthur Treacher, Alma Kruger. Scatterbrain fluff as Bracken and Lane maneuver their way from penniless fortune to love and riches, all in the course of a day.

Funny Face (1957) C-103m. ***1/2 D: Stanley Donen. Audrey Hepburn, Fred Astaire, Kay Thompson, Michel Auclair, Suzy Parker, Ruta Lee. Chic musical with lilting score and gorgeous shots of Paris. Astaire is fashion photographer who makes drab Hepburn into glamorous model. Thompson is wisecracking fashion editor.

Furies, The (1950) 109m. *** D: Anthony Mann. Barbara Stanwyck, Walter Huston, Wendell Corey, Gilbert Roland, Judith Anderson, Beulah Bondi. Western centering on the conflict between strong-minded Stanwyck and her dogmatic cattle-rancher father Huston; quite talky.

Fury (1936) 94m. ***1/2 D: Fritz Lang. Sylvia Sidney, Spencer Tracy, Walter Abel, Bruce Cabot, Edward Ellis, Walter Brennan, Frank Albertson. Still timely drama of lynch mobs and mob role in small town, making hardened criminal of innocent Tracy, spoiling his love for sweetheart Sidney.

Fury at Furnace Creek (1948) 88m. ** D: H. Bruce Humberstone. Victor Mature, Coleen Gray, Glenn Langan, Reginald Gardiner, Albert Dekker. Ordinary Western tale of Mature erasing mar on father's career against formidable opposition.

Fury at Gunsight Pass (1956) 68m. ** D: Fred F. Sears. David Brian, Neville Brand, Richard Long, Lisa Davis. Occasionally actionful Western, in which outlaw gang takes over a town.

Fury at Showdown (1957) 75m. *1/2 D: Gerd Oswald. John Derek, John Smith, Carolyn Craig, Nick Adams. Peace-loving man branded a coward, must shoot it out to rescue his girl.

Fury at Smugglers Bay (1963-British) 92m. ** D: John Gilling. Peter Cushing, Michele Mercier, Bernard Lee, George Coulouris, Liz Fraser. Sea yarn of pirates scavenging passing ships and reaping rewards off the English coastline.

Fury of Hercules, The (1961-Italian, dubbed) C-95m. ** D: V. Scega. Brad Harris, Brigitte Corey, Mara Berni, Carlo Tamberlani, Serge Gainsbourg. Harris is musclebound hero who helps Corey and her followers overcome evil ruler of their land; standard production.

Fury of the Congo (1951) 69m. D: William Berke. Johnny Weissmuller, Sherry Moreland, William Henry, Lyle Talbot. SEE: Jungle Jim series.

Fury of the Pagans (1963-Italian, dubbed) 86m. ** D: Guido Malatesta.

Edmund Purdom, Rossana Podesta, Livio Lorenzon, Carlo Calo. Routine adventure set in ancient Rome, with Purdom leading his tribe to victory and rescuing his true love.

Fuzzy Pink Nightgown, The (1957) 87m. ** D: Norman Taurog. Jane Russell, Ralph Meeker, Adolphe Menjou, Keenan Wynn, Fred Clark, Una Merkel. Outside of Russell's appearance, film is boring satire. When movie star is kidnapped, everyone thinks it's a publicity gag.

GI Blues (1960) C-104m. *** D: Norman Taurog. Elvis Presley, Juliet Prowse, Robert Ivers, Leticia Roman. Prowse's versatile performance uplifts standard Presley fare of GI trio in Germany forming a music group.

G-Men, The (1935) 85m. *** D: William Keighley. James Cagney, Robert Armstrong, William Harrigan, Regis Toomey, Ann Dvorak, Margaret Lindsay. Cagney switches sides and becomes an FBI man after early life of crime. Good cops-and-robbers tale, plenty of action.

G-Men Never Forget SEE: Code 645

G-Men vs the Black Dragon SEE: Black Dragon on Manzanar

Gabriel Over the White House (1933) 87m. **½ D: Gregory La Cava. Walter Huston, Karen Morley, C. Henry Gordon, Franchot Tone, Samuel S. Hinds, Jean Parker, Dickie Moore. Offbeat film of President Huston facing up to gangster community; one-of-a-kind.

Gaby (1956) C-97m. **½ D: Curtis Bernhardt. Leslie Caron, John Kerr, Sir Cedric Hardwicke, Taina Elg. Remake of WATERLOO BRIDGE, telling of ballerina Caron and her romance with soldier Kerr in WW2 England; not up to original.

Gal Who Took the West, The (1949) C-84m. ** D: Frederick de Cordova. Yvonne de Carlo, Charles Coburn, Scott Brady, John Russell. De Carlo is attractive as opera singer in 1890's Arizona who allows Brady and Russell to court her.

Gallant Bess (1946) C-101m. ** D: Andrew Marton. Marshall Thompson, George Tobias, Jim Davis, Chill Wills. Confusing yarn of horse and its master is acceptably acted but will bore most viewers.

Gallant Blade, The (1948) C-81m. ** D: Henry Levin. Larry Parks, Marguerite Chapman, Victor Jory, George Macready. Colorful, standard swashbuckler with dashing Parks protecting French general from villainous plot.

Gallant Hours, The (1960) 111m. *** D: Robert Montgomery. James Cagney, Dennis Weaver, Ward Costello, Richard Jaeckel. Sincere, low-key biog of Admiral Halsey played documentary-style. Cagney is reserved and effective, but production needs livening.

Gallant Journey (1946) 85m. **½ D: William Wellman. Glenn Ford, Janet Blair, Charles Ruggles, Henry Travers, Arthur Shields, Selena Royle. Ford pioneers glider plane development in 19th century. OK, but not as stirring as it's meant to be.

Galloping Major (1950-British) 82m. ** D: Henry Cornelius. Basil Radford, Jimmy Hanley, Janette Scott, A. E. Matthews. Uninspired comedy about horseracing, with slow-running nag winning the day.

Gambit (1966) C-109m. *** D: Ronald Neame. Michael Caine, Shirley MacLaine, Herbert Lom, Roger C. Carmel, John Abbott. Gimmicky robbery yarn with scoundrel Caine hiring Eurasian MacLaine to carry out perfect heist of invaluable piece of sculpture; great fun.

Gambler and the Lady, The (1952-British) 71m. *½ D: Patrick Jenkins, Sam Newfield. Dane Clark, Kathleen Byron, Naomi Chance, Meredith Edwards, Anthony Forwood, Eric Pohlmann. Tepid little drama of gambling man Clark who falls in love, altering his unorthodox way of life.

Gambler From Natchez, The (1954) C-88m. ** D: Henry Levin. Dale Robertson, Debra Paget, Thomas Gomez, Lisa Daniels. Set in 1840's, film focuses on Robertson's plot to eliminate trio of men who shot his father, a gambler caught cheating.

Gambler's Choice (1944) 66m. ** D: Frank McDonald. Chester Morris, Nancy Kelly, Russell Hayden, Lee Patrick, Lyle Talbot, Sheldon Leonard. Another variation of MANHATTAN MELODRAMA—three kids grow up; one becomes a lawman, another a shady gambler, the third the nice girl they both love.

Gambling House (1950) 80m. ** D: Ted Tetzlaff. Victor Mature, Terry Moore, William Bendix, Cleo Moore, Ann Doran. At times overly melodramatic account of man acquitted for murder, facing deportation as undesirable alien.

Gambling Lady (1934) 66m. **½ D: Archie Mayo. Barbara Stanwyck, Pat O'Brien, Claire Dodd, Joel McCrea, C. Aubrey Smith, Arthur Treacher. Family disapproves when wealthy McCrea marries gambler's daughter Stanwyck, but she proves her worth when McCrea encounters trouble.

Game of Danger (1954-British) 88m. **½ D: Lance Comfort. Jack Warner, Veronica Hurst, Derek Farr. Offbeat study of two youngsters involved in homicide, with strange effects on their lives. Original title: BANG YOU'RE DEAD.

Game of Death, A (1946) 72m. *½ D: Robert Wise. John Loder, Audrey Long, Edgar Barrier, Russell Wade. Potentially interesting tale about crazed island inhabitant who hunts down shipwrecked victims for amusement; poorly produced film. Rehash of MOST DANGEROUS GAME, refilmed as RUN FOR THE SUN.

Games (1967) C-100m. *** D: Curtis Harrington. Simone Signoret, James Caan, Katharine Ross, Don Stroud, Kent Smith. Signoret is the focal point in this rehash of DIABOLIQUE, with Simone the strange guest involved in homicide with Caan and Ross; set in N.Y.C.

Gamma People, The (1956-British) 79m. ** D: John Gilling. Paul Douglas, Eva Bartok, Leslie Phillips, Walter Rilla. Minor horror entry involving Communist scientist with a device to turn people into robot creatures.

Gang War (1958) 75m. **½ D: Gene Fowler, Jr. Charles Bronson, Kent Taylor, Jennifer Holden, John Doucette. Grade-B film tracing the savage events resulting from a teacher testifying against gang brutality.

Gang War (1962-British) 65m. ** D: Frank Marshall. Sean Kelly, Eira Heath, David Davies, Sean Sullivan. Tame account of life among London gangsters.

Gangbusters (1955) 78m. ** D: Bill Karan. Myron Healy, Don C. Harvey, Sam Edwards, Frank Gerstle. Standard prison-life drama, focusing on the breakout plan.

Gang's All Here, The (1943) C-103m. **½ D: Busby Berkeley. Alice Faye, Carmen Miranda, Phil Baker, Benny Goodman and Orchestra, Eugene Pallette, Charlotte Greenwood, Edward Everett Horton. Loud, lighthearted musical doesn't equal Faye's other vehicles, with no top songs and very thin plot; Miranda comes off best.

Gangster, The (1947) 84m. *** D: Gordon Wiles. Barry Sullivan, Belita, Joan Lorring, Akim Tamiroff, Henry Morgan, John Ireland, Fifi Dorsay, Shelley Winters. Sullivan gives strong performance as man who falls victim to his slum environment and ends up a vengeful crook.

Gangster Boss (1959-French, dubbed) 100m. ** D: Henri Verneuil. Fernandel, Papouf, Gino Cervi. Buffoon Fernandel becomes involved with criminal gang when he accidentally snatches parcel containing stolen loot.

Gangster Story (1960) 65m. **½ D: Walter Matthau. Walter Matthau, Carol Grace, Bruce McFarlan, Garrett Wallberg. Straightforward, tight little gangster chronicle, focusing on the crook's gal who tries to reform him.

Garden of Allah, The (1936) C-85m. *** D: Richard Boleslawski. Marlene Dietrich, Charles Boyer, Tilly Losch, Basil Rathbone, Joseph Schildkraut, Henry (Brandon) Kleinbach, John Carradine. Sensitive, well-played romance in the Algerian desert, with sultry Dietrich meeting her match in ascetic Boyer; Technicolor shares credit for lavish production.

Garden of Evil (1954) C-100m. **½ D: Henry Hathaway. Gary Cooper, Susan Hayward, Richard Widmark, Hugh Marlowe, Cameron Mitchell, Rita Moreno. Meandering adventure story set in 1850's Mexico, with trio escorting Hayward through bandit territory to save her husband.

Garden of the Moon (1938) 94m. **½ D: Busby Berkeley. Pat O'Brien, Margaret Lindsay, John Payne, Johnnie Davis, Melville Cooper, Isabel Jeans, Penny Singleton. Nightclub owner O'Brien and bandleader Payne have running feud; plot is pleasant excuse to work in many Berkeley numbers: "Girlfriend Of The Whirling Dervish," "Love Is Where You Find It," title tune.

Garment Jungle, The (1957) 88m. **½ D: Vincent Sherman. Lee J. Cobb, Kerwin Matthews, Gia Scala, Richard Boone. Well-handled account of union-gangster corruption in dressmaking industry, with romantic interludes slowing down violent pace.

Gaslight (1944) 114m. ***½ D: George Cukor. Ingrid Bergman, Charles Boyer, Joseph Cotten, Dame May Whitty, Angela Lansbury, Terry Moore, Halliwell Hobbes. Highbrow drama of husband (Boyer) trying to drive wife (Bergman) insane; classy production, fine acting.

Gaslight Follies (1955) 110m. *½ D: Joseph E. Levine. Charlie Chaplin, Douglas Fairbanks, Mary Pickford, Will Rogers. If it's possible to take priceless footage of Chaplin and his silent contemporaries and end up with a horrible hodgepodge, this film has done it. A mess.

Gate of Hell (1954-Japanese, dubbed) C-89m. ***½ D: Teinosuke Kinugasa. Machiko Kyo, Kazuo Hasegawa, Isao Yamagata, Koreya Senda. Stark historical film set in 12th-century Japan of young woman who prefers death to submitting to conqueror of her homeland. Lavishly produced.

Gates of Paris (1958-French, dubbed) 103m. **½ D: René Clair. Pierre Brasseur, Georges Brassens, Henri Vidal, Dany Carrel. Offbeat story of souse who gains a sense of importance when a criminal seeks refuge in his home.

Gateway (1938) 73m. ** D: Alfred L. Werker. Don Ameche, Arleen Whelan, Gregory Ratoff, Binnie Barnes, Gilbert Roland, Raymond Walburn, John Carradine. On a luxury ship Whelan is pursued by every man aboard, including racketeer, reporter, and city mayor; usual stuff and nonsense.

Gathering of Eagles, A (1963) C-115m. ***½ D: Delbert Mann. Rock Hudson, Rod Taylor, Mary Peach, Robert Lansing, Barry Sullivan, Henry Silva. Film uses formula of men in training and their off-duty activities to focus on the Strategic Air Command, with Hudson giving very creditable performance.

Gay Adventure, The (1953-British) 87m. *** D: Gordon Parry. Burgess Meredith, Jean-Pierre Aumont, Paul Valenska, Kathleen Harrison. Interestingly done yarn of trio of men on a train theorizing about pretty girl sitting across from them.

Gay Bride, The (1934) 80m. *½ D: Jack Conway. Carole Lombard, Chester Morris, Zasu Pitts. Leo Carrillo, Nat Pendleton. Flat script, listless performances in story of chorus girl involved with mobsters. Even Lombard can't help it.

Gay Desperado, The (1936) 85m. *** D: Rouben Mamoulian. Nino Martini, Ida Lupino, Leo Carrillo, Harold Huber, Mischa Auer, James Blakely, Stanley Fields. Entertaining musical spoof, with Martini's cutthroats holding heiress Lupino prisoner. Song: "The World Is Mine Tonight."

Gay Divorcee, The (1934) 107m. ***½ D: Mark Sandrich. Fred Astaire, Ginger Rogers, Alice Brady, Edward Everett Horton, Erik Rhodes, Betty Grable. Top Astaire-Rogers froth with usual needless plot and unusual musical numbers, including Oscar-winning "Continental," "Night and Day." Rhodes is memorable as would-be gigolo.

Gay Falcon, The (1941) 67m. D: Irving Reis. George Sanders, Wendy Barrie, Allen Jenkins, Anne Hunter, Gladys Cooper. SEE: Falcon series.

Gay Purr-ee (1962) C-86m. **½ D: Abe Levitow. Animated cartoon with the voices of Judy Garland, Robert Goulet, Red Buttons, Hermione Gingold, Paul Frees, Morey Amsterdam. Stylish cartoon from UPA studio, too sophisticated in many ways for kiddies. Adults will enjoy Garland and Goulet singing fairly good songs; broader characters played by others will attract youngsters.

Gay Lady, The (1949-British) C-91m. **½ D: Brian Desmond Hurst. Jean Kent, James Donald, Hugh Sinclair, Bill Owen. Well-produced period drama of theater girl who marries nobility and becomes a celebrity; saucy presentation. Retitled: TROTTIE TRUE.

Gay Sisters, The (1942) 108m. ** D: Irving Rapper. Barbara Stanwyck, George Brent, Geraldine Fitzgerald, Gig Young, Nancy Coleman, Donald Crisp, Gene Lockhart, Anne Revere.

Stanwyck secretly marries Brent to gain inheritance money in thin soaper, immensely aided by Fitzgerald and Coleman as her two sisters.

Gazebo, The (1959) 100m. *** D: George Marshall. Glenn Ford, Debbie Reynolds, Carl Reiner, Doro Merande, John McGiver, Mabel Albertson. Offbeat comedy involving murder and a backyard gazebo that covers up crime. Character actors McGiver and Merande wrap this up, but stars are competent.

Geisha Boy, The (1958) C-98m. **½ D: Frank Tashlin. Jerry Lewis, Marie McDonald, Sessue Hayakawa, Nobu McCarthy. Jerry, an inept magician, travels to the Far East, with disastrous consequences. Imaginative visual gags highspot this comedy.

Gene Krupa Story, The (1959) 101m. **½ D: Don Weis. Sal Mineo, Susan Kohner, James Darren, Susan Oliver, Yvonne Craig, Lawrence Dobkin, Red Nichols, Buddy Lester. Hackneyed version of great drummer's life, his ups and downs, and his siege of dope addiction.

General Della Rovere (1960-Italian, dubbed) 129m. ***½ D: Roberto Rossellini. Vittorio DeSica, Hannes Messemer, Sandra Milo, Giovanna Ralli, Mary Greco, Linda Veras, Anne Vernon. Brilliantly acted account of DeSica forced to impersonate Axis general, with the role and situation going to his head; slowly paced but well-executed study.

General Died at Dawn, The (1936) 97m. ***½ D: Lewis Milestone. Gary Cooper, Madeleine Carroll, Akim Tamiroff, Dudley Digges, Porter Hall, William Frawley. Fine, atmospheric drama of Oriental intrigue, with mercenary Cooper falling in love with spy Carroll while battling evil warlord Tamiroff. Author John O'Hara has cameo as reporter on train.

Genevieve (1954-British) C-86m. ***½ D: Henry Cornelius. John Gregson, Dinah Sheridan, Kenneth More, Kay Kendall. High-grade comedy rising above slapstick in tale of cross-country race between two couples in old-roadster cars.

Genghis Khan (1965) C-124m. **½ D: Henry Levin. Omar Sharif, Stephen Boyd, James Mason, Eli Wallach, Françoise Dorleac, Telly Savalas, Robert Morley, Yvonne Mitchell, Woody Strode. Laughable epic with gross miscasting and juvenile script, loosely based on legend of Chinese leader. No sweep or spectacle, but radiant Dorleac and earnest Sharif.

Gentle Annie (1944) 80m. ** D: Andrew Marton. Donna Reed, Marjorie Main, Henry Morgan, James Craig, Barton MacLane. Main vehicle about female outlaw with heart of gold.

Gentle Art of Murder SEE: **Crime Does Not Pay**

Gentle Gunman, The (1952-British) 86m. *** D: Basil Dearden. Dirk Bogarde, John Mills, Elizabeth Sellars, Robert Beatty. Unpretentious actioner of Irish revolution and enthusiast whose attempt to prove his patriotism backfires.

Gentle Touch, The (1955-British) C-86m. ** D: Pat Jackson. George Baker, Belinda Lee. Delphi Lawrence, Adrienne Corri, Diana Wynyard. Good cast, tame script—narrative of nurses' workday problems.

Gentleman After Dark (1942) 77m. ** D: Edwin L. Marin. Brian Donlevy, Miriam Hopkins, Preston Foster, Harold Huber. Hodgepodge yarn of man escaping prison to redeem honor of his daughter by killing his shady wife; good cast stifled by sloppy script. Remake of FORGOTTEN FACES.

Gentleman at Heart (1942) 66m. ** D: Ray McCarey. Cesar Romero, Carole Landis, Milton Berle, J. Carrol Naish. Occasionally amusing trivia concerning con-men Berle and Romero who become involved in cultural undertakings, changing their outlook on life. Remade as LOVE THAT BRUTE.

Gentleman Jim (1942) 104m. ***½ D: Raoul Walsh. Erroll Flynn, Alexis Smith, Jack Carson, Alan Hale, Minor Watson, Ward Bond, Arthur Shields. Sassy biography of polished boxer Jim Corbett in fight game's early days. Flynn is athletic in title role.

Gentleman's Agreement (1947) 118m. *** D: Elia Kazan. Gregory Peck, Dorothy McGuire, John Garfield, Celeste Holm, Anne Revere, June Havoc, Albert Dekker, Jane Wyatt, Dean Stockwell. Sincere adaptation of Laura Z. Hobson's novel of writer

(Peck) pretending to be Jewish, discovering rampant anti-Semitism. Holm won supporting actress Oscar as chic but lonely fashion editor. Then-daring approach to subject matter is tame now.

Gentlemen Marry Brunettes (1955) C-97m. ** D: Richard Sale. Jane Russell, Jeanne Crain, Alan Young, Rudy Vallee, Scott Brady. Anita Loos' follow-up to GENTLEMEN PREFER BLONDES, has Russell and Crain two sisters in show biz in Paris, trying to avoid romances. Not up to original.

Gentlemen Prefer Blondes (1953) C-91m. **½ D: Howard Hawks. Jane Russell, Marilyn Monroe, Charles Coburn, Tommy Noonan, George Winslow. Pleasant musicomedy from Anita Loos' tale of two girls from Little Rock making good in Paris. Gals are knockouts, but plot drags. Song: "Diamonds are a Girl's Best Friend."

George Raft Story, The (1961) 106m. **½ D: Joseph M. Newman. Ray Danton, Jayne Mansfield, Barbara Nichols, Julie London, Neville Brand, Frank Gorshin. Danton is good in title role of fast-moving account of Raft's rise from Broadway dancer to top Hollywood star. How much is true, who can say?

George Washington Slept Here (1942) 93m. **½ D: William Keighley. Jack Benny, Ann Sheridan, Charles Coburn, Hattie McDaniel, Percy Kilbride, Franklin Pangborn. Brittle but dated comedy of N.Y.C. couple moving to the country and a dilapidated house. Benny plays himself smoothly, Sheridan is great straight gal to the wacky, predictable turmoil.

George White's Scandals (1945) 95m. ** D: Felix E. Feist. Joan Davis, Jack Haley, Phillip Terry, Martha Holliday, Jane Greer. Mild musical heightened by Davis' zany antics, involving the usual show-biz clichés. Slapstick saves hackneyed plot.

Georgy Girl (1966-British) 100m. ***½ D: Silvio Narizzano. Lynn Redgrave, James Mason, Alan Bates, Charlotte Rampling, Bill Owen, Claire Kelly. Delightful, adult British comedy of modern-day morals, with Redgrave as ugly-duckling Georgy, Mason as the wealthy, aging married man who wants her for his mistress. Entire cast is excellent, with Rampling scoring as Georgy's bitchy roommate.

Geronimo (1939) 89m. ** D: Paul H. Sloane. Preston Foster, Ellen Drew, Andy Devine, Gene Lockhart, Ralph Morgan, Marjorie Gateson, Chief Thundercloud. Run-of-the-mill Western marred by overuse of stock footage and bad process shots to simulate outdoor scenes. Lockhart getting just desserts is best item in trivial Indian vs. cavalry contest.

Geronimo (1962) C-101m. **½ D: Arnold Laven. Chuck Connors, Kamala Devi, Ross Martin, Adam West, Pat Conway, Larry Dobkin. Exciting Indians-on-the-warpath, with Connors satisfactory in title role.

Gervaise (1956-French, dubbed) 116. *** D: Rene Clement. Maria Schell, François Perier, Suzy Delair, Armand Mestral. Spendidly acted version of Emile Zola tale of Schell struggling to keep her family going but finally succumbing to tawdry life of her drunken husband.

Get Hep to Love (1944) 71m. *½ D: Charles Lamont. Gloria Jean, Donald O'Connor, Jane Frazee, Robert Paige. Weak musical with precocious musical personality Jean running away to find happier home and singing career.

Get Out of Town (1962) 62m. ** D: Charles Davis. Douglas Wilson, Jeanne Baird, Marilyn O'Connor, Tony Louis. Contrived account of ex-gangster returned home to locate his brother's killer.

Getting Gertie's Garter (1945) 72m. **½ D: Allan Dwan. Dennis O'Keefe, Marie McDonald, Barry Sullivan, Binnie Barnes, Sheila Ryan, J. Carrol Naish, Jerome Cowan. Similar to UP IN MABEL'S ROOM, a funny little comedy of O'Keefe trying to retrieve embarrassing memento without wife's knowledge.

Ghidrah, the Three-Headed Monster (1965-Japanese, dubbed) C-85m. **½ D: Inoshiro Honda. Yosuke Natsuki, Uuriko Hoshi, Hiroshi Koizumi, Emi Ito. Ingenious scripter works three favorites into plot (Mothra, Rodan, Godzilla). Trio champions people of Tokyo against rampaging title fiend.

Ghost and Mr. Chicken, The (1966) C-90m. **½ D: Alan Rafkin. Don Knotts, Joan Staley, Skip Homeier, Dick Sargent, Reta Shaw. Featherweight comedy with Knotts a would-be reporter seeking the big scoop.

Ghost and Mrs. Muir, The (1947)

104m. ***½ D: Joseph L. Mankiewicz. Gene Tierney, Rex Harrison, George Sanders, Edna Best, Vanessa Brown, Anna Lee, Robert Coote, Natalie Wood. Bubbly comedy of woman who has "romance" with ghost of old sea captain. Beautifully mounted; basis for recent TV series.

Ghost Breakers, The (1940) 82m. ***** D:** George Marshall. Bob Hope, Paulette Goddard, Richard Carlson, Paul Lukas, Anthony Quinn, Willie Best. Follow-up to Hope's CAT AND THE CANARY also mixes horror and comedy, as Bob and Paulette visit spooky castle.

Ghost Catchers (1943) 67m. ****½ D:** Edward Cline. Ole Olsen, Chic Johnson, Gloria Jean, Martha O'Driscoll, Leo Carrillo, Andy Devine, Lon Chaney, Walter Catlett. Usual frantic O&J insanity, with duo involved with a haunted house.

Ghost Chasers (1951) 69m. **D:** William Beaudine. Leo Gorcey, Huntz Hall, Jan Kayne, Bernard Gorcey, Lloyd Corrigan, Billy Benedict. SEE: Bowery Boys series.

Ghost Comes Home, The (1940) 79m. **** D:** William Thiele. Frank Morgan, Billie Burke, Ann Rutherford, John Shelton, Reginald Owen, Donald Meek. Morgan, thought dead, returns to family which has been doing fine without him; cast does its best with fair material.

Ghost Diver (1957) 76m. ***½ D:** Richard Einfeld, Merrill G. White. James Craig, Audrey Totter, Nico Minardos, Lowell Brown. Programmer of underwater search for treasure city.

Ghost Goes West, The (1936-British) 78m. ***** D:** René Clair. Robert Donat, Eugene Pallette, Jean Parker, Elsa Lanchester. Pallette purchases castle haunted by ghost of fast-living ancestor of hero Donat in amusing fantasy-comedy penned by Robert Sherwood.

Ghost in the Invisible Bikini (1966) C-82m. **** D:** Don Weis. Tommy Kirk, Aron Kincaid, Nancy Sinatra, Harvey Lembeck, Claudia Martin, Francis X. Bushman, Boris Karloff, Patsy Kelly, Basil Rathbone, Benny Rubin. Sluggish blend of macabre and beach boys provides uneven mixture; veteran greats like Rathbone wasting their time.

Ghost of Dragstrip Hollow, The (1959) 65m. Bomb **D:** William Hole, Jr. Jody Fair, Martin Braddock, Russ Bender, Leon Tyler, Elaine DuPont. Trite mixture of hot rod gangs and haunted house formulas, with most uneven results.

Ghost of Frankenstein, The (1942) 68m. ****½ D:** Erle C. Kenton. Sir Cedric Hardwicke, Lon Chaney, Lionel Atwill, Ralph Bellamy, Bela Lugosi, Evelyn Ankers. Sequel to SON OF FRANKENSTEIN. Igor returns to foul professor's plan to replace monster's brain with that of educated man. Good cast manages to save stale plot.

Ghost of the China Sea (1958) 79m. **** D:** Fred F. Sears. David Brian, Lynn Bernay, Jonathan Haze, Norman Wright. Brian et al flee Japanese invasion of Philippines; nothing new here.

Ghost of Zorro (1959) 69m. **** D:** Fred C. Brannon. Clayton Moore, Pamela Blake, Roy Barcroft, George J. Lewis, Eugene Roth. Feature version of 1949 serial is a confusingly edited account of descendant of Zorro adopting same guise to combat outlaws destroying telegraph lines.

Ghost Ship (1952-British) 69m. **** D:** Vernon Sewell. Dermot Walsh, Hazel Court, Hugh Burden, John Robinson, Joss Ambler. Small-budget yarn about young couple purchasing a haunted yacht.

Ghosts of Rome (1961-Italian, dubbed) C-105m. ****½ D:** Antonio Pietrangeli. Marcello Mastroianni, Belinda Lee, Sandra Milo, Vittorio Gassman, Franca Marzi. Scatterbrain antics of oddball characters inhabiting rundown house soon to be demolished, with prospects of finding new quarters frightening them all.

Ghosts on the Loose (1943) 65m. **D:** William Beaudine. Leo Gorcey, Huntz Hall, Bobby Jordan, Bela Lugosi, Ava Gardner, Rick Vallin, Minerva Urecal. SEE: Bowery Boys series.

Giant Behemoth, The (1959-British) 80m. **** D:** Eugene Lourie. Gene Evans, Andre Morell, John Turner, Leigh Madison, Jack MacGowran. Title monster on the rampage; OK, no more.

Giant Claw, The (1957) 76m. ***½ D:** Fred F. Sears, Jeff Morrow, Mara Corday, Morris Ankrum, Edgar Barrier. Lack of decent special effects ruins the running battle between colossal bird and fighter jets. Big bird is laughable.

Giant Gila Monster, The (1959) 74m. ** D: Ray Kellogg. Don Sullivan, Lisa Simone, Shug Fisher, Jerry Cortwright, Beverly Thurman, Don Flourney, Pat Simmons. Typical horror drama of lurking creature causing series of strange murders.

Giant of the Metropolis, The (1962-Italian, dubbed) C-82m. ** D: Umberto Scarpelli. Mitchell Gordon, Roldano Lupi, Bella Cortez, Liana Orfei. Uneven mixture of costumer and sci-fi with a dash of sadism, set in 10,000 B.C.

Giants of Thessaly, The (1960-Italian, dubbed) C-86m. ** D: Riccardo Freda. Roland Carey, Ziva Rodann, Massimo Girotti, Alberto Farnese. Episodic sword-and-sandal account of Jason (Carey) and Orpheus (Girotti) seeking golden fleece, with expected clashes with monsters, evil women, etc.

Gideon of Scotland Yard (1959-British) 91m. **½ D: John Ford. Jack Hawkins, Anna Massey, Anna Lee, Dianne Foster, Ronald Howard, Laurence Naismith, John Loder, Hermione Bell. Narrative of the various problems confronting a detective inspector during an average day. Nicely handled.

Gidget (1959) C-95m. **½ D: Paul Wendkos. Sandra Dee, James Darren, Cliff Robertson, Arthur O'Connell, Joby Baker, Yvonne Craig, Doug McClure. First and best of series has spirited Dee in title role, with Robertson most engaging as beach bum who almost wins her away from surfer Darren.

Gidget Goes Hawaiian (1961) C-102m. ** D: Paul Wendkos. James Darren, Michael Callan, Deborah Walley, Carl Reiner, Peggy Cass, Eddie Foy, Jr. Inane follow-up has teen-ager off to the Islands, with embarrassing results for all.

Gidget Goes to Rome (1963) C-101m. ** D: Paul Wendkos. Cindy Carol, James Darren, Jesse Royce Landis, Cesare Danova, Jeff Donnell. Mild follow-up has fetching teen-ager off to Italy involved in predictable romancing.

Gift of Love, The (1958) C-105m. **½ D: Jean Negulesco. Lauren Bacall, Robert Stack, Evelyn Rudie, Lorne Greene, Anne Seymour. If you could put up with SENTIMENTAL JOURNEY you might bear this remake, which isn't even as good. Bacall dies but returns to earth as guiding spirit for her husband and daughter.

Gigantis, the Fire Monster (1959-Japanese, dubbed) 78m. ** D: Motoyoshi, Hugo Grimaldi. Hiroshi Koizumi, Setsuko Makayama, Mindru Chiaki. There he is!

Gigi (1958) C-116m. **** D: Vincente Minnelli. Leslie Caron, Maurice Chevalier, Louis Jourdan, Hermione Gingold, Jacques Bergerac, Eva Gabor. Charming turn-of-the-century Parisian musical based on Colette's story of a French girl who becomes a lady. Entire cast is fine; Chevalier and Gingold memorable in their duet, "I Remember It Well." Songs include: "Thank Heaven For Little Girls," "Gigi." Winner of many Academy Awards; a must.

Gigot (1962) C-104m. *** D: Gene Kelly. Jackie Gleason, Katherine Kath, Gabrielle Dorziat, Albert Remy, Yvonne Constant. Sentimental, well-acted tale of a deaf mute (Gleason) and a young girl in Paris. Simple film, well done; Gleason is excellent.

Gilda (1946) 110m. *** D: Charles Vidor. Rita Hayworth, Glenn Ford, George Macready, Joseph Calleia, Steven Geray. Colorful combination romance and drama in story of South American owner of cafe hiring American as lieutenant, ignorant that wife loves him; Hayworth most alluring, sings "Put The Blame On Mame" in classic scene.

Gilded Lily, The (1935) 80m. *** D: Wesley Ruggles. Claudette Colbert, Fred MacMurray, Ray Milland, C. Aubrey Smith, Edward Craven. Colbert has to choose between aristocratic Milland and down-to-earth MacMurray. Fine romantic fluff.

Gildersleeve's Ghost (1944) 64m. ** D: Gordon Douglas. Harold Peary, Marion Martin, Richard LeGrand, Amelita Ward. Programmer entry in the Great Gildersleeve series, involving mixture of spooks and gangsters, with predictable results.

Girl, a Guy, and a Gob, A (1941) 91m. ** D: Richard Jones. George Murphy, Lucille Ball, Edmond O'-

Brien, Henry Travers, Franklin Pangborn, George Cleveland. Not very original triangle love story, with Ball undecided between Murphy and O'Brien.

Girl Can't Help It, The (1956) C-99m. *** D: Frank Tashlin. Tom Ewell, Jayne Mansfield, Edmond O'Brien, Julie London. Out-of-work press agent Ewell is glad to help make O'Brien's moll a movie star, but he falls in love with her; quite funny.

Girl Crazy (1943) 99m. ***½ D: Norman Taurog. Mickey Rooney, Judy Garland, Gil Stratton, Robert E. Strickland, "Rags" Ragland, June Allyson, Nancy Walker, Guy Kibbee. Rooney sent to small Southwestern school to forget girls, but he meets Garland and that's that. Great Gershwin score! Remade as WHEN THE BOYS MEET THE GIRLS.

Girl From Jones Beach, The (1949) 78m. ** D: Peter Godfrey. Ronald Reagan, Virginia Mayo, Eddie Bracken, Dona Drake, Henry Travers, Jerome Cowan. Nice little film of Reagan meeting his dream girl at the beach.

Girl From Manhattan, The (1948) 81m. ** D: Alfred E. Green. Dorothy Lamour, George Montgomery, Charles Laughton, Hugh Herbert, Constance Collier, Ernest Truex. Weary tale of big-city gal (Lamour) returning home, finding love there.

Girl From Missouri (1934) 75m. **½ D: Jack Conway. Jean Harlow, Lionel Barrymore, Franchot Tone, Lewis Stone, Patsy Kelly, Alan Mowbray. Cast is fine in potboiler story of small-town girl hunting a rich bachelor, doing pretty well in the end.

Girl From 10th Avenue (1935) 69m. ** D: Alfred E. Green. Bette Davis, Ian Hunter, Colin Clive, Alison Skipworth, John Eldredge. Old soap rehashed nicely with Hunter marrying Davis during drunken spree, regretting it when ex-wife wants him back. Acting saves it.

Girl-Getters, The (1966-British) 79m. *** D: Michael Winner. Oliver Reed, Jane Merrow, Barbara Ferris, Julia Foster. Realistic study of hoodlum youths at British seaside resort, their prankish games and romances; intelligently portrayed. Retitled: THE SYSTEM.

Girl Happy (1965) C-96m. **½ D: Boris Sagal. Elvis Presley, Shelley Fabares, Harold J. Stone, Gary Crosby, Joby Baker, Nita Talbot, Mary Ann Mobley, Chris Noel, Jackie Coogan. Formula Presley musical with tiresome plot of Elvis in Fort Lauderdale chaperoning Fabares, daughter of Chicago mobster.

Girl He Left Behind, The (1956) 103m. **½ D: David Butler. Tab Hunter, Natalie Wood, Jessie Royce Landis, Jim Backus. Reminiscent of SEE HERE PRIVATE HARGROVE, without any of the warmth or humor. Hunter is new recruit in army.

Girl Hunters, The (1963) 103m. **½ D: Roy Rowland. Mickey Spillane, Lloyd Nolan, Shirley Eaton, Hy Gardner. Spillane plays his own fictional detective Mike Hammer in this rugged murder mystery, filmed in England.

Girl In a Million, A (1945-British) 81m. ** D: Francis Searle. Joan Greenwood, Hugh Williams, Yvonne Owen, Edward Lexy, Jane Hylton, Michael Hordern. Sometimes wacky comedy focusing on deaf mute who uses her charm to reform several cantankerous gentlemen.

Girl In Black Stockings, The (1957) 73m. ** D: Howard W. Koch. Lex Barker, Anne Bancroft, Mamie Van Doren, Ron Randell, Marie Windsor. Minor murder mystery with some nice touches and good performances; set at chic Utah resort.

Girl In Every Port, A (1952) 86m. ** D: Chester Erskine. Groucho Marx, William Bendix, Marie Wilson, Don DeFore, Gene Lockhart. Nonsense of two gobs who hide a racehorse aboard ship. Great grouping of comedians wasted.

Girl in His Pocket (1957-French, dubbed) 82m. **½ D: Pierre Kast. Jean Marais, Agnes Laurent, Genevieve Page. Strange tale of scientist who invents shrinking formula, changing his romantic life with unforetold complications.

Girl in Room 13 (1961) C-97m. *½ D: Richard Cunha. Brian Donlevy, Andrea Bayard, Elizabeth Howard, Victor Merinow, John Herbert. Lowgrade private eye story set in Brazil, with Donlevy tracking down a murder and counterfeit gang.

Girl In the Kremlin, The (1957) 81m. ** D: Russell Birdwell. Lex Barker,

Zsa Zsa Gabor, Jeffrey Stone, William Schallert. Espionage hokum involving Gabor in dual role as twins, one of whom is Stalin's mistress.

Girl in the Painting (1948-British) 89m. *** D: Terence Fisher. Mai Zetterling, Robert Beatty, Guy Rolfe, Herbert Lom, Patrick Holt. Intriguing drama of serviceman involved in strange case of amnesiac girl seeking her lost past in Germany. Retitled: PORTRAIT FROM LIFE.

Girl in the Red Velvet Swing, The (1955) C-109m. **½ D: Richard Fleischer. Ray Milland, Joan Collins, Farley Granger, Cornelia Otis Skinner, Glenda Farrell, Luther Adler. Glossy, fictionalized account of Evelyn Nesbit-Stanford White-Harry Thaw escapade of early 20th-century N.Y.C. Showgirl falls in love with prominent architect, which upsets mentally disturbed millionaire. Fanmagazine pulp, smoothly done.

Girl in the Woods (1958) 71m. *½ D: Tom Gries. Forrest Tucker, Maggie Hayes, Barton MacLane, Diana Francis. Tale of lumbermen, their work and their loves. Little excitement.

Girl in White, The (1952) 93m. ** D: John Sturges. June Allyson, Arthur Kennedy, Gary Merrill, Mildred Dunnock, James Arness. Clichéd account of first female doctor in N.Y.C. Allyson tries to perk up lifeless script.

Girl Most Likely, The (1957) C-98m. *** D: Mitchell Leisen. Jane Powell, Cliff Robertson, Keith Andes, Tommy Noonan, Una Merkel. Musical remake of TOM, DICK AND HARRY comes off as bright, cheerful entertainment. A girl must decide which one of trio she'll wed; Kaye Ballard does very well in supporting role.

Girl Named Tamiko, A (1962) C-110m. **½ D: John Sturges. Laurence Harvey, France Nuyen, Martha Hyer, Gary Merrill, Michael Wilding, Myoshi Umeki, Lee Patrick. Overblown soaper set in Tokyo. Harvey charms Hyer into proposing marriage so he can get U.S. citizenship. Nuyen is sweet Oriental whom Harvey really loves.

Girl Next Door, The (1953) C-92m. **½ D: Richard Sale. Dan Dailey, June Haver, Dennis Day, Cara Williams, Natalie Schafer. Pleasing musical of singing star Haver moving to new home and falling in love with neighbor Dailey, a cartoonist.

Girl of the Golden West, The (1938) 120m. **½ D: Robert Z. Leonard. Jeanette MacDonald, Nelson Eddy, Walter Pidgeon, Leo Carrillo, Buddy Ebsen, Leonard Penn. Oft-produced tale of love affair of good-girl MacDonald and bandit Eddy, with tuneful Gus Kahn-Sigmund Romberg score that didn't produce any hits.

Girl of the Night (1960) 93m. **½ D: Joseph Cates. Anne Francis, Lloyd Nolan, Kay Medford, John Kerr. Francis gives a vivid performance as prostitute undergoing psychoanalysis.

Girl on the Bridge (1951) 77m. Bomb D: Hugo Haas. Hugo Haas, Beverly Michaels, Robert Dane, Johnny Close, Anthony Jochim. Trashy study of Michaels as a so-called femme fatale and her effect on the men in her life.

Girl Rush, The (1955) C-85m. **½ D: Robert Pirosh. Rosalind Russell, Fernando Lamas, Eddie Albert, Gloria De Haven, Marion Lorne. Russell inherits a Las Vegas casino and determines to make it go, romanced by Lamas. Minor musical numbers and forced gaiety are all too evident.

Girl Trouble (1942) 82m. ** D: Harold Schuster. Don Ameche, Joan Bennett, Billie Burke, Frank Craven, Vivian Blaine. Pleasant frou-frou with Ameche and Bennett involved in business and romancing, with fine support from the adept scatterbrain Burke.

Girl Who Had Everything, The (1953) 69m. **½ D: Richard Thorpe. Elizabeth Taylor, Fernando Lamas, William Powell, Gig Young. Murky melodrama with top cast. Girl falls in love with criminal client of her attorney father.

Girl With a Suitcase (1960-Italian, dubbed) 96m. ***½ D: Valerio Zurlini. Claudia Cardinale, Jacques Perrin, Luciana Angelillo, Corrado Pani. Impressive Italian film of devoted but shady girl Cardinale following her ex-lover to Parma, only to fall in love with his adolescent brother. Confusing at times, but extremely well acted, worth seeing.

Girls' Dormitory (1936) 66m. **½ D: Irving Cummings. Herbert Marshall, Ruth Chatterton, Simone Simon, Constance Collier, J. Edward Bromberg, Dixie Dunbar, Tyrone

Power. Fairly standard tale of girl's infatuation for school head Marshall spotlights newcomer Simon, who does quite well, and young leading man Power in featured role.

Girls! Girls! Girls! (1962) C-106m. **½ D: Norman Taurog. Elvis Presley, Stella Stevens, Laurel Goodwin, Jeremy Slate, Benson Fong, Robert Strauss, Ginny Tiu. Presley is chased by a mass of girls and can't decide which one he prefers.

Girls in Prison (1956) 87m. *½ D: Edward L. Cahn. Richard Denning, Joan Taylor, Adele Jergens, Helen Gilbert, Lance Fuller, Jane Darwell, Raymond Hatton, Mae Marsh. Tawdry study of prison life with usual female stereotype prisoners.

Girls in the Night (1953) 83m. ** D: Jack Arnold. Joyce Holden, Glenda Farrell, Harvey Lembeck, Patricia Hardy, Jaclynne Greene. Compact account of young people seeking to better their lives, blighted by N.Y.C. tenement existence.

Girls of Pleasure Island, The (1953) C-95m. **½ D: F. Hugh Herbert, Alvin Ganzer. Leo Genn, Don Taylor, Gene Barry, Elsa Lanchester, Audrey Dalton. Unfunny comedy involving Genn and brood of daughters combating swarm of GI's who establish a base on their island.

Girls of the Night (1959-French, dubbed) 114m. **½ D: Maurice Cloche. Georges Marchal, Nicole Berger, Claus Holm, Kay Fischer, Gil Vidal. Sensible telling of plight of group of prostitutes, and clergyman who tries to help them.

Girls on the Loose (1958) 78m. ** D: Paul Henreid. Mara Corday, Lita Milan, Barbara Bostock, Mark Richman. Drama unfolds account of Corday heading robbery gang, and eventual downfall.

Girls Town (1959) 92m. *½ D: Charles Haas. Mamie Van Doren, Mel Torme, Paul Anka, Ray Anthony, Maggie Hayes, Cathy Crosby, Gigi Perreau, Gloria Talbott, Jim Mitchum. Bad girl accused of crime sent to correctional institution, finds real culprit. Fails at being a sensational-type film. Retitled: INNOCENT AND THE DAMNED.

Give a Girl a Break (1953) 82m. **½ D: Stanley Donen. Marge and Gower Champion, Debbie Reynolds, Kurt Kasznar, Larry Keating. Bland musical of a show producer, his emotional star, and the girl seeking the lead role.

Give 'Em Hell (1954-French, dubbed) 90m. **½ D: John Berry. Eddie Constantine, Mai Britt, Jean Danet, Jean Carmet. If not taken seriously, amusing gangster yarn of Johnny Jordan (Constantine), with usual amount of fisticuffs and gunplay.

Give Me a Sailor (1938) 80m. **½ D: Elliott Nugent. Martha Raye, Bob Hope, Betty Grable, Jack Whiting, Clarence Kolb, J. C. Nugent. Fast-moving musicomedy of sailor Hope's complicated love affairs. Raye is always worth watching; undistinguished score.

Give Me Your Heart (1936) 87m. **½ D: Archie Mayo. Kay Francis, George Brent, Roland Young, Patric Knowles, Henry Stephenson, Frieda Inescort, Helen Flint. Involved romance of Francis, the English lord she loves, his crippled wife, Kay's baby, and her protector. All is peg for chic Francis-Brent repartee and glamorous wardrobe changes.

Give My Regards to Broadway (1948) C-89m. ** D: Lloyd Bacon. Dan Dailey, Charles Winninger, Nancy Guild, Charles Ruggles, Fay Bainter. Blah musical of old-time vaudevillian Winninger refusing to admit that the family act should break up.

Give Us Wings (1940) 62m. D: Charles Lamont. Billy Halop, Huntz Hall, Gabriel Dell, Anne Gwynne, Bernard Punsley, Bobby Jordan, Wallace Ford, Victor Jory. SEE: Bowery Boys series.

Gladiator, The (1938) 70m. **½ D: Edward Sedgwick. Joe E. Brown, Man Mountain Dean, June Travis, Dickie Moore, Lucien Littlefield. Timid boy (Brown) takes serum, becomes all-star hero at college. Simple, sincere, enjoyable.

Glass Alibi, The (1940) 70m. ** D: W. Lee Wilder. Paul Kelly, Douglas Fowley, Anne Gwynne, Maris Wrixon, Jack Conrad. Satisfactory drama involving con-man who thinks marrying a dying heiress is a sure bet, till he discovers she's recovering.

Glass Bottom Boat, The (1966) C-110m. *** D: Frank Tashlin. Doris Day, Rod Taylor, Arthur Godfrey, Paul Lynde, Eric Fleming, Alice

Pearce, Ellen Corby. Better-paced-than-usual Day nonsense with Doris trying to steal Taylor's business secrets. Godfrey is Day's father, skipper of title vehicle. Lots of slapstick in this one.

Glass Cage, The (1964) 78m. *½ D: Antonio Santean. John Hoyt, Elisha Cook, Arline Sax, Robert Keljan. Programmer of burglar shot in self-defense and romance developing between police investigator and suspect. Retitled: DEN OF DOOM.

Glass Key, The (1942) 85m. ***½ D: Stuart Heisler. Veronica Lake, Alan Ladd, Brian Donlevy, William Bendix, Bonita Granville, Richard Denning. Fast-moving remake of 1935 film with politician Donlevy accused of murder, detective Ladd bailing him out. Lake fine as mysterious love interest, Bendix effective as brutal bodyguard.

Glass Menagerie, The (1950) 107m. *** D: Irving Rapper. Jane Wyman, Kirk Douglas, Gertrude Lawrence, Arthur Kennedy. More notable for its cast and intention than results. Slow-moving version of Tennessee Williams's drama of lame girl, her faded Southern belle mother, and idealistic brother, all living in their own fragile dream worlds.

Glass Mountain, The (1950-British) 94m. *** D: Henry Cass. Valentina Cortesa, Michael Denison, Dulcie Gray, Sebastian Shaw. Beautifully-made film of a British composer who writes an opera, inspired by majestic Italian Alps. A treat for music-lovers, with many singers from La Scala appearing in opera sequence.

Glass Slipper, The (1955) C-94m. **½ D: Charles Walters. Leslie Caron, Michael Wilding, Keenan Wynn, Estelle Winwood, Elsa Lanchester, Amanda Blake. Silky musical of Cinderella story with talky plot bogging down lilting fantasy dance and song sequences.

Glass Tomb, The (1955-British) 59m. ** D: Montgomery Tully. John Ireland, Honor Blackman, Geoffrey Keen, Eric Pohlmann, Sydney Tafler, Liam Redmond, Sam Kydd. Bizarre carnival backgrounds give this typical murder tale some spice.

Glass Tower, The (1957-German, dubbed) 92m. **½ D: Harold Braun. Lilli Palmer, O. E. Hasse, Peter Van Eyck, Brigitte Horney, Hannes Messemer. Interesting study of overly jealous husband keeping beautiful wife Palmer a prisoner so she won't be tempted by other men; well acted.

Glass Wall, The (1953) 80m. ** D: Maxwell Shane. Vittorio Gassman, Gloria Grahame, Ann Robinson, Jerry Paris, Kathleen Freeman. Drama of refugee Gassman who illegally came to N.Y.C. and, rather than accept deportation, goes on the lam.

Glass Web, The (1953) 81m. *** D: Jack Arnold. Edward G. Robinson, John Forsythe, Marcia Henderson, Richard Denning. Robinson is fine as criminal research authority for TV mystery show, who commits murder utilized as basis for one of the programs.

Glenn Miller Story, The (1954) C-116m. *** D: Anthony Mann. James Stewart, June Allyson, Charles Drake, George Tobias, Henry Morgan, Frances Langford, Louis Armstrong, Gene Krupa. Marvelous music is most of this film, sentimental story the rest. All of Miller's hits played, many guest performers. Stewart most convincing as popular bandleader.

Global Affair, A (1964) 84m. **½ D: Jack Arnold. Bob Hope, Yvonne de Carlo, Robert Sterling, John McGiver, Lilo Pulver. Unwitty Hope vehicle has Bob in charge of a baby found at U.N., with female representative from each nation demanding the child.

Glory (1956) C-100m. ** D: David Butler. Margaret O'Brien, Walter Brennan, Charlotte Greenwood, John Lupton. Bland horseracing story, with grown-up O'Brien as gal who owns champion horse.

Glory Alley (1952) 79m. **½ D: Raoul Walsh. Ralph Meeker, Leslie Caron, Gilbert Roland, Louis Armstrong, John McIntire. Just before the championship bout, boxer Meeker quits the fight game. Series of flashbacks tells his intriguing story. New Orleans backgrounds allow for some good musical interludes.

Glory Brigade, The (1953) 82m. ** D: Robert D. Webb. Victor Mature, Alexander Scourby, Lee Marvin, Richard Egan, Alvy Moore. Passable Korean War actioner with good cast.

Glory Guys, The (1965) C-112m. ** D: Arnold Laven. Tom Tryon, Harve

Presnell, Michael Anderson, Jr., Senta Berger, James Caan, Slim Pickens. Lumbering Western of life and love in the old West; cliché-ridden instead of bullet-packing action.

Go For Broke! (1951) 92m. *** D: Robert Pirosh. Van Johnson, Gianna Maria Canale, Warner Anderson, Lane Nakona, George Miki. WW2 story with a twist. Johnson is commander of special U.S. squad made up of American-Japanese team.

Go Into Your Dance (1935) 89m. **½ D: Archie Mayo. Al Jolson, Ruby Keeler, Glenda Farrell, Helen Morgan, Patsy Kelly, Benny Rubin, Phil Regan, Barton MacLane. Flimsy plot allows Jolson and Keeler to sing and dance through seven listenable tunes in OK musical; highlight: "About A Quarter To Nine."

Go, Man, Go (1954) 82m. **½ D: James Wong Howe. Dane Clark, Pat Breslin, Sidney Poitier, Edmond Ryan. Imaginative telling of the formation of Harlem Globetrotters and their rise as famed basketball team.

Go Naked In the World (1961) C-103m. ** D: Ranald MacDougall. Gina Lollobrigida, Anthony Franciosa, Ernest Borgnine, Luana Patten. Turgid melodrama badly cast. Easyloving Lollobrigida hooks Franciosa, much to his father's (Borgnine's) dismay.

Go West (1940) 81m. ** D: Edward Buzzell. Groucho, Chico, and Harpo Marx, John Carroll, Diana Lewis, Walter Woolf King, Robert Barrat. Big letdown from Marxes, until hilarious train-ride climax. Occasional bits sparkle through humdrum script.

Go West, Young Man (1936) 82m. **½ D: Henry Hathaway. Mae West, Warren William, Randolph Scott, Alice Brady, Elizabeth Patterson, Lyle Talbot, Isabel Jewell. Disappointing tale of movie-queen West stuck in the sticks, finding amusement with brainy farmhand Scott. Supporting cast is fine, but Mae's character has lost its sting.

God Is My Co-Pilot (1945) 90m. **½ D: Robert Florey. Dennis Morgan, Raymond Massey, Andrea King, Alan Hale, Dane Clark, John Ridgely, Stanley Ridges, Donald Woods. Well-intentioned drama of WW2 pilots bogs down in clichés, still has many good scenes.

God Is My Partner (1957) 80m. ** D: William F. Claxton. Walter Brennan, John Hoyt, Marion Ross, Jesse White, Nancy Kulp. Sincere but hokey little film of old-timer who feels he owes a spiritual obligation which he can redeem by giving away his money.

Goddess, The (1958) 105m. *** D: John Cromwell. Kim Stanley, Lloyd Bridges, Steven Hill, Betty Lou Holland, Patty Duke. Absorbing biography of an ambitious girl seeking Hollywood fame. Author Paddy Chayefsky based his story somewhat on Marilyn Monroe; the film captures tragedy of the real-life Monroe with fine acting by Stanley and Bridges, among others.

Goddess of Love (1960-Italian, dubbed) C-68m. *½ D: W. Tourjansky. Belinda Lee, Jacques Sernas, Massimo Girotti, Maria Frau. Drivel concerning country girl who becomes prostitute when her lover is killed. Set in ancient times.

God's Country (1946) C-62m. ** D: Robert E. Tansey. Buster Keaton, Robert Lowery, Helen Gilbert, William Farnum. Chief virtue of this flabby Western is Keaton prancing around trying to recreate some of his better pantomine skits.

God's Country and the Woman (1936) C-80m. ** D: William Keighley. George Brent, Beverly Roberts, Barton MacLane, Robert Barrat, Alan Hale, Joseph King. Routine tale of Brent and Roberts running rival lumber companies; color is only asset.

God's Little Acre (1958) 110m. *** D: Anthony Mann. Robert Ryan, Tina Louise, Aldo Ray, Buddy Hackett, Jack Lord, Fay Spain, Michael Landon. Effective Americana of Georgia farmers as seen by Erskine Caldwell, focusing on amusing as well as lusty, violent aspects of their existence.

Godzilla SEE: Godzilla, King of the Monsters

Godzilla, King of the Monsters (1956-Japanese, dubbed) 80m. **½ D: Terry Morse, Inoshiro Honda. Raymond Burr, Takashi Shimura, Momoko Kochi, Akira Takarada, Akihiko Hirata. Special effects are the star of this film. Retitled: GODZILLA.

Godzilla vs. the Thing (1964-Japanese, dubbed) C-90m. **½ D: Inoshiro Honda. Akira Takarada, Yuriko

Hoshi, Hiroshi Koizumi, Yu Fujiki. Vivid special effects highlight battle between reptile Godzilla and Mothra, giant moth.

Gog (1954) C-85m. ** D: Herbert L. Strock. Richard Egan, Constance Dowling, Herbert Marshall, John Wengraf. Machine-made brain is utilized to sabotage missile station; OK sci-fi.

Goin' to Town (1935) 74m. *** D: Alexander Hall. Mae West, Paul Cavanaugh, Ivan Lebedeff, Marjorie Gateson, Tito Coral. Good West vehicle of dance-hall girl trying to crash society, highlight: Mae doing "Samson and Delilah" scenes.

Going My Way (1944) 130m. ***1/2 D: Leo McCarey. Bing Crosby, Barry Fitzgerald, Rise Stevens, Gene Lockhart, Frank McHugh, James Brown, Jean Heather, Stanley Clements, Carl Switzer, Porter Hall. Multiple-award-winning story of down-to-earth priest (Crosby) winning over aging superior (Fitzgerald) and sidewalk gang of kids. Holds up quite well. Songs: title tune, "Swinging On A Star," "Too-ra-Loo-ra-Loo-ra."

Going Places (1939) 84m. ** D: Ray Enright. Dick Powell, Anita Louise, Allen Jenkins, Ronald Reagan. Nonsensical musical with a variety of songs, steeplechase riding, and obligatory romantic interludes.

Going Steady (1958) 79m. *1/2 D: Fred F. Sears. Molly Bee, Bill Goodwin, Alan Reed, Jr., Irene Hervey. Uninspired happenings involving secretly married teen-agers and the repercussions when in-laws discover fact.

Gold Diggers of 1933 (1933) 96m. ***1/2 D: Mervyn LeRoy. Joan Blondell, Ruby Keeler, Aline MacMahon, Dick Powell, Guy Kibbee, Warren William, Ned Sparks, Ginger Rogers, Sterling Holloway. Another spectacular Busby Berkeley dance outing in familiar let's-produce-a-Broadway-show plot. Highlights: Blondell's "Forgotten Man," Rogers' "We're In The Money," chorus gals' "Shadow Waltz."

Gold Diggers of 1935 (1935) 95m. *** D: Busby Berkeley. Dick Powell, Adolphe Menjou, Gloria Stuart, Alice Brady, Glenda Farrell, Frank McHugh, Winifred Shaw. Big-scale Berkeley musical with stereotypes providing plot-line and laughs between fantastic precision production numbers, including "The Words Are In My Heart," and film classic "Lullaby Of Broadway," sung by Wini Shaw.

Gold Diggers of 1937 (1936) 100m. **1/2 D: Lloyd Bacon. Dick Powell, Joan Blondell, Glenda Farrell, Victor Moore, Lee Dixon, Osgood Perkins. Those gold-diggers won't give up; this time it's a group of insurance salesmen backing a show. Top song: "With Plenty of Money and You."

Gold Is Where You Find It (1938) 90m. **1/2 D: Michael Curtiz. George Brent, Olivia de Havilland, Claude Rains, Margaret Lindsay, John Litel, Barton MacLane. And gold-rush miners find it on California farmland, starting bitter feud in brisk film, perked by good cast.

Gold of Naples (1957-Italian, dubbed) 107m. ** D: Vittorio DeSica. Toto, Sophia Loren, Vittorio DeSica, Silvana Mangano. Four episodes detailing surprising facets of human nature: THE GAMBLER, THE RACKETEERS, PIZZA ON CREDIT, THERESA.

Gold Raiders (1951) 56m. *1/2 D: Edward Bernds. George O'Brien, Three Stooges, Sheila Ryan, Clem Bevans, Lyle Talbot. Three Stooges add the only life to this flabby Western, with their usual shenanigans foiling the crooks and saving the day.

Gold Rush Maisie (1940) 82m. D: Edwin L. Marin. Ann Sothern, Lee Bowman, Slim Summerville, Virginia Weidler, Mary Nash, John F. Hamilton. SEE: Maisie series.

Goldbergs, The (1950) 83m. **1/2 D: Walter Hart. Gertrude Berg, Philip Loeb, Eli Mintz, Betty Walker, David Opatoshu, Barbara Rush. Warm, human story of famous radio-TV Bronx family and their everyday problems. Retitled: MOLLY

Golden Age of Comedy, The (1958) 78m. **** D: Compiled by Robert Youngson. Laurel and Hardy, Carole Lombard, Ben Turpin, Will Rogers, Harry Langdon. Peerless grouping of some of silent comedy's greatest moments, including Rogers' classic spoofs of silent stars, and ending with Laurel and Hardy's legendary pie fight from BATTLE OF THE CENTURY.

Golden Arrow, The (1936) 68m. **½ D: Alfred E. Green. Bette Davis, George Brent, Eugene Pallette, Dick Foran, Carol Hughes, Catherine Doucet, Craig Reynolds. Davis and Brent in flighty comedy of phony heiress and the reporter doing her story; fun.

Golden Blade, The (1953) C-81m. **½ D: Nathan Juran. Rock Hudson, Piper Laurie, Gene Evans, Kathleen Hughes. OK swashbuckler with Hudson going through gymnastics in Bagdad to save Laurie and help virtue triumph; strictly formula production.

Golden Boy (1939) 99m. **½ D: Rouben Mamoulian. Barbara Stanwyck, Adolphe Menjou, William Holden, Lee J. Cobb, Joseph Calleia, Sam Levene, Don Beddoe. Clifford Odets' narrative of music-minded boy who becomes prizefighter dates badly; Holden, in film debut, still good, but Cobb blows the works with his Henry Armetta imitation.

Golden Coach, The (1952-Italian, dubbed) C-105m. ** D: Jean Renoir. Anna Magnani, Odoardo Spadaro, Nada Fiorelli, Dante, Duncan Lamont. Puzzling yarn set in 18th-century South America, revolving around fiery actress Magnani and her assorted love affairs.

Golden Earrings (1947) 95m. **½ D: Mitchell Leisen. Ray Milland, Marlene Dietrich, Murvyn Vye, Dennis Hoey, Quentin Reynolds. Incredible yet enjoyable escapism set in WW2 Europe has Milland joining gypsy Dietrich for espionage work; Dietrich most convincing. Gypsy Vye sings title song.

Golden Eye, The (1948) 69m. D: William Beaudine. Roland Winters, Victor Sen Yung, Tim Ryan, Wanda McKay, Bruce Kellogg, Evelyn Brent. SEE: **Charlie Chan** series.

Golden Girl (1951) C-108m. **½ D: Lloyd Bacon. Mitzi Gaynor, Dale Robertson, Dennis Day, Una Merkel. Undistinguished musical set in California in Civil War days, with Gaynor a fun-loving girl intrigued by Reb officer Robertson.

Golden Gloves Story, The (1950) 76m. *½ D: Felix E. Feist. James Dunn, Dewey Martin, Kay Westfall, Kevin O'Morrison. Ordinary fare dealing with two boxers and the effect of the pending championship bout on their lives.

Golden Hands of Kurigal (1949) 100m. *½ D: Fred C. Brannon. Kirk Alyn, Rosemary La Planche, Roy Barcroft, Carol Forman, James Dale, Bruce Edwards. Spotty Republic cliffhanger of federal agent (Alyn) rescuing missing archaeologist held by arch-criminal. Re-edited movie serial: FEDERAL AGENTS VS. UNDERWORLD INC.

Golden Hawk, The (1952) C-83m. ** D: Sidney Salkow. Rhonda Fleming, Sterling Hayden, John Sutton, Raymond Hatton. Frank Yerby's novel of Spanish-English fight against France in 17th century, set in Caribbean seas.

Golden Horde, The (1951) C-77m. ** D: George Sherman. Ann Blyth, David Farrar, George Macready, Henry Brandon, Richard Egan. Typical Arabian adventure set in 13th century, with Blyth using her brains to outwit invaders of her people's city.

Golden Idol, The (1954) 71m. D: Ford Beebe. Johnny Sheffield, Anne Kimbell, Paul Guilfoyle, Smoki Whitfield. SEE: **Bomba the Jungle Boy** series.

Golden Madonna, The (1949-British) 88m. **½ D: Ladislas Vajda. Phyllis Calvert, Michael Rennie, Tullio Carminati. Lively romantic yarn of Yankee lass inheriting an Italian villa and, aided by Rennie, seeking to retrieve a holy painting.

Golden Mask, The (1954-British) C-88m. **½ D: Jack Lee. Van Heflin, Wanda Hendrix, Eric Portman, Charles Goldner. Intelligent adventure yarn of people seeking fabulous treasure mask in Egyptian desert.

Golden Mistress, The (1954) C-82m. ** D: Joel Judge. John Agar, Rosemarie Bowe, Abner Biberman, Andre Narcisse. Agar comes to Bowe's rescue in hunting out alleged voodoo killers of her father.

Golden Salamander, The (1951-British) 96m. *** D: Ronald Neame. Trevor Howard, Anouk Aimee, Walter Rilla, Herbert Lom, Wilfrid Hyde-White. Courting a Tunisian girl, Howard becomes involved in gun smuggling; taut actioner.

Goldfinger (1964) C-108m. ***½ D: Guy Hamilton. Sean Connery, Gert Frobe, Honor Blackman, Shirley

Eaton, Bernard Lee, Lois Maxwell, Harold Sakata. Entertaining James Bond adventure, the third in the series. Full of ingenious gadgets and nefarious villains, with hair-raising climax. Frobe (Goldfinger) and Sakata (Oddjob) are villains in the classic tradition.

Goldwyn Follies, The (1938) C-120m. **½ D: George Marshall. Adolphe Menjou, The Ritz Brothers, Zorina, Kenny Baker, Andrea Leeds, Helen Jepson, Bobby Clark. Fragmentary all-star revue has nice color and good solo spots, but is very uneven film. Gershwin songs like "Our Love Is Here To Stay" do help.

Goliath Against the Giants (1961-Italian, dubbed) C-90m. *½ D: Guido Malatesta. Brad Harris, Gloria Milland, Fernando Ray, Barbara Carrol. Juvenile cartoon characterizations in this sword-and-sandal, with Harris overcoming sea creatures, Amazons, and his people's enemies.

Goliath and the Barbarians (1960-Italian, dubbed) C-86m. ** D: Carlo Campogalliani. Steve Reeves, Bruce Cabot, Giulia Rubini, Chelo Alonso, Arturo Dominici, Gino Scotti. Muscleman Reeves comes to the rescue of Italy by holding off rampaging hordes pressing down from the Alps.

Goliath and the Dragon (1960-Italian, dubbed) C-87m. Bomb D: Vittorio Cottafavi. Mark Forest, Broderick Crawford, Gaby Andre, Leonora Ruffo. Baby-style fantasy costumer with embarrassing performances by all; poor special effects, with Forest challenging villainous Crawford.

Goliath and the Vampires (1964-Italian, dubbed) C-91m. *½ D: Giacomo Gentiomo. Gordon Scott, Jacques Sernas, Gianna Maria Canale. Cloak-and-sandal nonsense; spotty special effects add only color to film.

Gone are the Days (1963) 97m. *** D: Nicholas Webster. Ruby Dee, Alan Alda, Ossie Davis, Sorrell Booke, Godfrey Cambridge. Intelligent comedy-satire on racial problems, based on Ossie Davis play, PURLIE VICTORIOUS.

Goodbye Charlie (1964) C-117m. *½ D: Vincente Minnelli. Tony Curtis, Debbie Reynolds, Pat Boone, Walter Matthau, Martin Gabel. Tasteless, flat version of George Axelrod's play; crude gangster dies and comes back to earth as Reynolds.

Good-bye, My Lady (1956) 95m. **½ D: William Wellman. Walter Brennan, Phil Harris, Brandon de Wilde, Sidney Poitier. James Street novel of small boy (De Wilde), an elderly man (Brennan), and the dog that brings joy into their lives is easygoing, poignant film, set in the South.

Good Dame (1934) 74m. **½ D: Marion Gering. Sylvia Sidney, Fredric March, Jack LaRue, Helene Chadwick, Noel Francis. Lively little film of carnival sharpster March attracting wide-eyed Sidney.

Good Day for a Hanging (1958) C-85m. **½ D: Nathan Juran. Fred MacMurray, Maggie Hayes, Robert Vaughn, Denver Pyle. Straightforward account of MacMurray taking over for slain sheriff and bringing in killer, only to find townspeople don't care if murderer is sentenced.

Good Die Young, The (1955-British) 100m. ** D: Lewis Gilbert. Laurence Harvey, Gloria Grahame, Richard Basehart, Stanley Baker, Margaret Leighton. Good cast in standard robbery tale, concentrating on escape attempt.

Good Earth, The (1937) 138m. **** D: Sidney Franklin. Paul Muni, Luise Rainer, Walter Connolly, Charley Grapewin, Jessie Ralph, Tilly Losch, Keye Luke, Harold Huber. Mammoth Pearl Buck Chinese novel recreated in detail, telling story of greed ruining lives of simple farming couple. Rainer won Oscar as the ever-patient wife of Muni; special effects outstanding.

Good Fairy, The (1935) 90m. **½ D: William Wyler. Margaret Sullavan, Herbert Marshall, Frank Morgan, Reginald Owen, Alan Hale, Beulah Bondi, Cesar Romero. Pat romance of Sullavan dreaming of being Marshall's wife, then working to arrange it for real. Fine cast buoys film.

Good Girls Go to Paris (1939) 75m. **½ D: Alexander Hall. Melvyn Douglas, Joan Blondell, Walter Connoly, Alan Curtis, Isabel Jeans, Clarence Kolb. Spunky waitress Blondell will do anything to visit France; she sees a good prospect in millionaire Douglas.

Good Humor Man, The (1950) 79m. **½ D: Lloyd Bacon. Jack Carson, Lola Albright, Jean Wallace, George Reeves, Richard Egan. Rambunctious antics with Carson in title role, getting involved in murder plot, aided by gang of "Captain Marvel Kids."

Good Morning, Miss Dove (1955) C-107m. *** D: Henry Koster. Jennifer Jones, Robert Stack, Marshall Thompson, Chuck Connors, Jerry Paris, Mary Wickes, Robert Douglas. Spinster schoolteacher Jones goes to hospital for operation; flashbacks reveal her romantic past, while she solves everyone's problems in the present.

Good Neighbor Sam (1964) C-130m. *** D: David Swift. Jack Lemmon, Romy Schneider, Edward G. Robinson, Michael Connors, Dorothy Provine, Neil Hamilton, Joyce Jameson. Good comedy of Lemmon's adventures pretending he's not married to his real wife but to luscious neighbor Schneider. Plenty of sight gags and good chase scenes make this a lot of fun.

Good News (1947) C-95m. **½ D: Charles Walters. June Allyson, Peter Lawford, Patricia Marshall, Joan McCracken, Ray McDonald, Mel Torme. Average 1920's college campus musical with last-minute touchdowns and complicated subplots all nearly coming together at the end. Bright score includes "The French Lesson."

Good Sam (1948) 113m. ** D: Leo McCarey. Gary Cooper, Ann Sheridan, Ray Collins, Edmund Lowe, Joan Lorring, Ruth Roman. Almost complete misfire, despite cast and director. Cooper is incurable good Samaritan in this lifeless comedy.

Good Time Girl (1950-British) 81m. *½ D: David MacDonald. Jean Kent, Dennis Price, Herbert Lom, Flora Robson. Inoffensive trivia about young girl prevented from wayward life by a judge's telling of tragic fate of another teen-ager.

Goodbye Again (1961) 120m. *** D: Anatole Litvak. Ingrid Bergman, Tony Perkins, Yves Montand, Jessie Royce Landis, Diahann Carroll. Françoise Sagan's chic soaper becomes teary Bergman vehicle of middle-aged woman having affair with Perkins, still craving playboy Montand. Set in Paris.

Goodbye, My Fancy (1951) 107m. *** D: Vincent Sherman. Joan Crawford, Robert Young, Frank Lovejoy, Eve Arden. Congresswoman Crawford returns to her old college, more to see former boyfriend Young than to receive honorary degree. Lovejoy is callous newsman.

Goose and the Gander, The (1935) 65m. ** D: Alfred E. Green. Kay Francis, George Brent, Genevieve Tobin, John Eldrege, Claire Dodd. Woman's story of high-living Francis keeping an eye on ex-husband Brent.

Gorgeous Hussy, The (1936) 102m. **½ D: Clarence Brown. Lionel Barrymore, Joan Crawford, Robert Taylor, Franchot Tone, Melvyn Douglas, James Stewart. Star-studded cast in strained historical drama of Andrew Jackson's belle, who disgraces herself and those connected with her. Crawford et al are beautifully costumed in well-appointed settings.

Gorgo (1961-British) C-78m. **½ D: Eugene Lourie. Bill Travers, William Sylvester Vincent Winter, Bruce Seton. Special effects heighten sci-fi of baby monster put into London sideshow. Gigantic parent rescues it, destroying much of the city.

Gorgon, The (1964-British) C-83m. **½ D: Terence Fisher. Christopher Lee, Richard Pasco, Barbara Shelley, Michael Goodliffe. Ancient legend of stone monster coming to life is basis of this complex plot of killing spree in Middle European village. Atmospheric.

Gorilla SEE: Nabonga

Gorilla at Large (1954) C-84m. *** D: Harmon Jones. Cameron Mitchell, Anne Bancroft, Lee J. Cobb, Raymond Burr. Offbeat murder mystery at amusement park, with exceptionally able cast.

Gorilla Man, The (1942) 64m. ** D: D. Ross Lederman, John Loder, Ruth Ford, Marian Hall, Richard Fraser, Creighton Hale. Title is misleading. Pro-Nazis try to discredit RAF pilot by linking him with series of brutal murders. Grade-B material with adequate acting.

Government Girl (1943) 94m. **½ D: Dudley Nichols. Olivia de Havilland, Sonny Tufts, Anne Shirley, Jess Barker, James Dunn, Paul Stewart, Agnes Moorehead. Tufts has clear field in wartime Washington, but De Havilland gets him; that's about it for this breezy comedy.

Gracie Allen Murder Case, The (1939) 74m. D: Alfred E. Green. Warren William, Gracie Allen, Ellen Drew, Kent Taylor, Jerome Cowan, Judith Barrett. SEE: **Philo Vance** series.

Grand Hotel (1932) 105m. **** D: Edmund Goulding. Greta Garbo, Joan Crawford, John Barrymore, Wallace Beery, Lionel Barrymore, Lewis Stone, Jean Hersholt, Rafaela Ottiano, Ferdinand Gottschalk. Vicki Baum's novel of plush Berlin hotel where "nothing ever happens"; stars prove the contrary: Garbo as lonely ballerina, John B. her jewel-thief lover, Lionel B. a dying man, Crawford an ambitious stenographer, Beery a hardened businessman, Stone the observer. Another must.

Grand Illusion (1938-French, dubbed) **** D: Jean Renoir. Jean Gabin, Erich von Stroheim, Dita Parlo, Pierre Fresnay, Dalio. Renoir's WW1 classic of French prisoners (beautifully played by Gabin, Fresnay, Dalio) and stern German officer Von Stroheim coming to realize the human aspect of war.

Grapes of Wrath, The (1940) 129m. **** D: John Ford. Henry Fonda, Jane Darwell, John Carradine, Charley Grapewin, Dorris Bowden, Russell Simpson, John Qualen. Steinbeck Americana of Okies moving from dust bowl to California during Depression, lovingly brought to screen. Darwell won an Oscar as determined family head; Fonda plays her ex-con son. Don't miss this one.

Grass Is Greener, The (1960) C-105m. *** D: Stanley Donen. Cary Grant, Deborah Kerr, Robert Mitchum, Jean Simmons. Chic drawing-room fare that suffers from staginess. Grant-Kerr marriage is threatened by Simmons and Mitchum romancing the two, respectively.

Grave Robbers from Outer Space SEE: **Plan 9 from Outer Space.**

Great American Broadcast, The (1941) 92m. **½ D: Archie Mayo. Alice Faye, John Payne, Jack Oakie, Cesar Romero, The Four Ink Spots, James Newill, Mary Beth Hughes. Fictional fun of development of radio industry, with such musical guests as zany Wiere Brothers. Entertaining; bright cast.

Great American Pastime, The (1956) 89m. ** D: Herman Hoffman. Tom Ewell, Anne Francis, Ann Miller, Dean Jones, Ruby Dee. Ewell manages to work some enthusiasm into this programmer about Little League baseball and its effect on suburban families.

Great Caruso, The (1951) C-109m. *** D: Richard Thorpe. Mario Lanza, Ann Blyth, Jarmila Novotna, Dorothy Kirsten. Outstanding mixture of biographical fiction about the great singer. Fine music, and Lanza's voice, overcome some creaky dialogue.

Great Chase, The (1963) 77m. ***½ Narrated by Frank Gallop. Buster Keaton, Douglas Fairbanks, Sr., Pearl White, Richard Barthelmess, Lillian Gish. Entertaining silent-film compilation of great chase scenes from THE MARK OF ZORRO, WAY DOWN EAST, etc., with most of film devoted to Keaton's classic, THE GENERAL.

Great Dan Patch, The (1949) 94m. **½ D: Joseph M. Newman. Dennis O'Keefe, Gail Russell, Ruth Warrick, Charlotte Greenwood. Acceptable horseracing yarn.

Great Day (1946-British) 94m. **½ D: Lance Comfort. Eric Portman, Flora Robson, Sheila Sim, Walter Fitzgerald. Somber, effective study of the courageous women who helped Britain win WW2.

Great Day in the Morning (1956) C-92m. ** D: Jacques Tourneur. Virginia Mayo, Robert Stack, Ruth Roman, Alex Nicol, Raymond Burr. Excellent cast for hackneyed Western set in pre-Civil War Colorado, when the gold-rush fever was high.

Great Diamond Robbery, The (1953) 69m. ** D: Robert Z. Leonard. Red Skelton, Cara Williams, James Whitmore, Dorothy Stickney, Steven Geray. Limp vehicle buoyed by Skelton. Red is hoodwinked by jewel thief who wants him to recut huge diamond.

Great Escape, The (1963) C-168m. ***½ D: John Sturges. Steve McQueen, James Garner, Richard Attenborough, Charles Bronson, James Coburn, David McCallum, Donald Pleasence. Terrific actioner with marvelous cast. Allied POW's plot to tear free from German prison camp. Action holds up despite length of film.

Great Expectations (1934) 100m. **½ D: Stuart Walker. Jane Wyatt, Phillips Holmes, George Breakston, Henry Hull, Florence Reed, Alan Hale, Francis L. Sullivan. Not bad version of Dickens tale of young boy and mysterious benefactor, but dwarfed by '47 classic. Sullivan plays Jaggers in both films.

Great Expectations (1947-British) 115m. **** D: David Lean. John Mills, Valerie Hobson, Anthony Wager, Martita Hunt, Bernard Miles, Francis L. Sullivan, Finlay Currie, Jean Simmons, Alec Guinness. Stirring adaptation of Dickens; cast faithfully realizes tale of 19th-century England in story of unknown benefactor making poor boy a gentleman of means. Currie's graveyard sequence is standout.

Great Flamarion, The (1945) 78m. **½ D: Anthony Mann. Erich von Stroheim, Mary Beth Hughes, Dan Duryea, Stephen Barclay, Lester Allen, Esther Howard. Better than most of Stroheim's cheapies, this one has him double-crossed by circus star Hughes to make way for Duryea.

Great Gambini, The (1937) 70m. **½ D: Charles Vidor. Akim Tamiroff, Marian Marsh, Genevieve Tobin, William Demarest, Reginald Denny, Roland Drew. Engaging low-budget film, with Tamiroff starring as magico who predicts deaths, becomes his own victim.

Great Garrick, The (1937) 89m. **½ D: James Whale. Brian Aherne, Olivia de Havilland, Edward Everett Horton, Melville Cooper, Lionel Atwill, Lana Turner, Marie Wilson, Dorothy Tree, Trevor Bardette. Life of famed 18th-century British stage actor David Garrick makes fairly interesting film, with cast enhancing formula material.

Great Gatsby, The (1949) 92m. *** D: Elliott Nugent. Alan Ladd, Betty Field, Macdonald Carey, Barry Sullivan, Ruth Hussey, Shelley Winters. Valiant attempt to reproduce 1920's atmosphere of F. Scott Fitzgerald novel, with Ladd the gangster out to recapture his lost love.

Great Gilbert and Sullivan, The (1953-British) C-105m. ***½ D: Sidney Gilliat. Robert Morley, Maurice Evans, Eileen Herlie, Peter Finch, Martyn Green. Highly flavorful biography of operetta composers with many highlights from their works.

Great Guns (1941) 74m. ** D: Monty Banks. Stan Laurel, Oliver Hardy, Sheila Ryan, Dick Nelson, Edmund MacDonald. Later L&H army comedy is weak, not as bad as some but far below their classic films.

Great Guy (1936) 75m. ** D: John G. Blystone. James Cagney, Mae Clarke, James Burke, Edward Brophy, Henry Kolker, Bernardine Hayes, Edward McNamara. Second-rate Cagney in low-budget production about inspector crusading against corruption in meat business.

Great Imposter, The (1960) 112m. *** D: Robert Mulligan. Tony Curtis, Edmond O'Brien, Arthur O'Connell, Gary Merrill. Incredible story of Ferdinand Demara, who succeeded in a variety of professional guises. Film is episodic and pat.

Great Jesse James Raid, The (1953) C-74m. **½ D: Reginald Le Borg. Willard Parker, Barbara Payton, Tom Neal, Wallace Ford. Generally action-packed tale blending fact and legend about the notorious outlaw and his last big robbery caper.

Great Jewel Robber, The (1950) 91m. ** D: Peter Godfrey. David Brian, Marjorie Reynolds, John Archer, Warren Douglas. Brian chomps through title role; film recounts his many criminal capers.

Great John L., The (1945) 96m. **½ D: Frank Tuttle. Greg McClure, Linda Darnell, Barbara Britton, Lee Sullivan, Otto Kruger, Wallace Ford, George Matthews. Not bad little biography of famous boxer's rise and fall, his two loves and unhappy end.

Great Lie, The (1941) 107m. *** D: Edmund Goulding. Bette Davis, Mary Astor, George Brent, Lucile Watson, Hattie McDaniel, Grant Mitchell. Brent marries Davis when alliance with Astor is annulled. He is lost in plane crash, leaving Davis and pregnant Astor to battle each other and the elements. Well-mounted soaper won Astor an Oscar as fiery concert pianist.

Great Lover, The (1949) 80m. *** D: Alexander Hall. Bob Hope, Rhonda Fleming, Roland Young, Roland

Culver, George Reeves, Jim Backus. Vintage Hope; Bob's a boy scout leader on ship filled with his troop, luscious Fleming, and murderer Young.

Great McGinty, The (1940) 81m. *** D: Preston Sturges. Brian Donlevy, Muriel Angelus, Akim Tamiroff, Louis Jean Heydt, Harry Rosenthal, Arthur Hoyt, Libby Taylor. Sturges' first directing effort is A-1 satire on politics, with genial Donlevy rising from bum to influential statesman in no time at all.

Great Man, The (1956) 92m. ***1/2 D: Jose Ferrer. Jose Ferrer, Dean Jagger, Keenan Wynn, Julie London, Jim Backus, Ed Wynn. Well-loved TV star dies and Ferrer prepares memorial show, only to discover star was a despicable phony. Hard-bitten look at TV industry; top performances by senior and junior Wynns.

Great Man Votes, The (1939) 70m. ***1/2 D: Garson Kanin. John Barrymore, Peter Holden, Virginia Weidler, Donald MacBride, William Demarest. Outstanding film of souse Barrymore attempting to straighten out in order to keep his two children; kids Weidler and Holden are first-rate.

Great Manhunt, The (1950) 97m. *** D: Sidney Gilliat. Douglas Fairbanks, Jr., Glynis Johns, Jack Hawkins, Herbert Lom. Genuine suspenser; American doctor tries to flee Middle European country with valuable information. Retitled: STATE SECRET.

Great Man's Lady, The (1942) 90m. **1/2 D: William Wellman. Barbara Stanwyck, Joel McCrea, Brian Donlevy, Thurston Hall, K. T. Stevens, Lucien Littlefield. Saga of the West is no great shakes as McCrea dreams of oil wells, Donlevy takes his girl. Stanwyck ages to 100 years to frame story.

Great Mike, The (1944) 70m. ** D: Wallace Fox. Stuart Erwin, Robert Henry, Marion Martin, Carl Switzer, Pierre Watkins, Lane Chandler. Sloppy comedy-drama of horseracing, with Erwin as lovable rogue who trains unlikely horse to win big race.

Great Missouri Raid, The (1950) C-83m. ** D: Gordon Douglas. Wendell Corey, Macdonald Carey, Ellen Drew, Ward Bond, Anne Revere. Another account of the infamous outlaws, James brothers and Younger brothers.

Great Moment, The (1944) 83m. ** D: Preston Sturges. Joel McCrea, Betty Field, Harry Carey, William Demarest, Franklin Pangborn, Grady Sutton, Louis Jean Heydt, Jimmy Conlin. Confused biography of anasthesia inventor wavers from comedy to drama; ineffectual, filled with frustrating flashbacks. Very offbeat for writer-director Sturges.

Great O'Malley, The (1937) 71m. *1/2 D: William Dieterle. Pat O'Brien, Humphrey Bogart, Ann Sheridan, Donald Crisp, Mary Gordon, Frieda Inescort, Sybil Jason. Syrupy film of ruthless cop O'Brien and poor man Bogart who has lame daughter and turns to crime to support her. Pretty sticky stuff.

Great Profile, The (1940) 82m. **1/2 D: Walter Lang. John Barrymore, Mary Beth Hughes, Gregory Ratoff, John Payne, Anne Baxter, Lionel Atwill, Edward Brophy. Barrymore on downslide provides some laughs in self-parodying tale of aging, conceited actor.

Great Race, The (1965) C-150m. **1/2 D: Blake Edwards. Tony Curtis, Natalie Wood, Jack Lemmon, Peter Falk, Keenan Wynn, Larry Storch, Dorothy Provine, Arthur O'Connell, Vivian Vance, Ross Martin, George Macready. Long, sometimes funny, often labored comedy, not the greatest ever made, as advertised. Duel sequence and barroom brawl are highlights, but pie fight falls flat, other gimmicks don't work. Definitely a mixed bag; one good song, "The Sweetheart Tree."

Great Rupert, The (1950) 86m. **1/2 D: Irving Pichel. Jimmy Durante, Terry Moore, Queenie Smith, Chick Chandler. Agreeable comedy of a trained squirrel who discovers a cache of money.

Great St. Louis Bank Robbery, The (1959) 86m. *1/2 D: Charles Guggenheim, John Stix. Steve McQueen, David Clarke, Crahan Denton, Molly McCarthy, James Dukas. Modest robbery caper with virtue of McQueen in cast.

Great Sinner, The (1949) 110m. **1/2 D: Robert Siodmak. Gregory Peck, Ava Gardner, Melvyn Douglas, Walter Huston, Ethel Barrymore. Murky romance lavishly produced, meandering along with tale of Peck saving Gard-

ner from drowning in gambling fever.
Great Sioux Massacre, The (1965) C-91m. **½ D: Sidney Salkow. Joseph Cotten, Darren McGavin, Philip Carey, Julie Sommars, Nancy Kovack, John Matthews, Frank Ferguson. Good acting enhances this version of Custer's last stand.
Great Sioux Uprising, The (1953) C-80m. **½ D: Lloyd Bacon. Jeff Chandler, Faith Domergue, Lyle Bettger, Glenn Strange. Chandler as ex-Yankee officer is adequate in formula Western about threatened Indian war.
Great Victor Herbert, The (1939) 84m. **½ D: Andrew L. Stone. Allan Jones, Mary Martin, Walter Connolly, Lee Bowman, Susanna Foster, Jerome Cowan. Music overshadows plot in this fanciful biography of composer in turn-of-the-century N.Y.C. "March Of The Toys," "Ah Sweet Mystery Of Life," etc. are included.
Great Waltz, The (1938) 102m. **½ D: Julien Duvivier. Luise Rainer, Fernand Gravet, Miliza Korjus, Hugh Herbert, Lionel Atwill, Curt Bois. Music outdoes drama in this elaborately produced biography of composer Johann Strauss, with plenty of waltzes covering up a standard triangle tale.
Great War, The (1961-Italian, dubbed) 118m. ** D: Mario Monicelli. Vittorio Gassman, Silvana Mangano, Alberto Sordi, Folco Lulli. Gassman does his best to stay out of WW1 but once in combat proves his worth.
Great Ziegfeld, The (1936) 180m. ***½ D: Robert Z. Leonard. William Powell, Myrna Loy, Luise Rainer, Frank Morgan, Fannie Brice, Virginia Bruce, Reginald Owen, Ray Bolger, Dennis Morgan. Spectacular biography of great 20th-century showman, with extravagant musical numbers, stunning Oscar-winning performance by Rainer as Anna Held.
Greatest Love, The (1951-Italian) 116m. *½ D: Roberto Rossellini. Ingrid Bergman, Alexander Knox, Giulietta Masina, Teresa Pellati, Sandro Frachina. Slow-moving, dull account of life and fickle meaning of romance; waste of everyone's efforts. Retitled: EUROPA '51.
Greatest Show on Earth, The (1952) C-153m. ***½ D: Cecil B. de Mille. Betty Hutton, Charlton Heston, Cornel Wilde, Dorothy Lamour, Gloria Grahame, James Stewart, Henry Wilcoxon, Lawrence Tierney, Lyle Bettger. Big package of fun from De Mille, complete with hokey performances, many clichés. Stewart well cast as circus clown, tops rest of cast. Some funny surprise guests appear.
Greeks Had a Word for Them, The (1932) 79m. *** D: Lowell Sherman. Joan Blondell, Ina Claire, Madge Evans, David Manners, Lowell Sherman. Retitled: THREE BROADWAY GIRLS. Vintage comedy of three gold-digging girls looking for husbands; still most entertaining although redone several times since.
Green Archer, The (1961-German, dubbed) 95m. **½ D: Jurgen Roland. Gert Frobe, Karin Dor, Klausjurgen Wussow, Edith Teichman. Nicely paced actioner with plenty of excitement as masked archer eliminates his victims, baffles police; from Edgar Wallace novel.
Green Dolphin Street (1947) 141m. **½ D: Victor Saville. Lana Turner, Van Heflin, Donna Reed, Richard Hart, Frank Morgan, Edmund Gwenn. If only for its glossy production values, this plodding costumer has merit. Story of two sisters (Turner, Reed) after the same man in New Zealand is tedious; set in 19th century.
Green-Eyed Blonde, The (1957) 76m. ** D: Bernard Girard. Susan Oliver, Tommie Moore, Juanita Moore, Evelyn Scott, Roy Glenn. Oliver in title role is properly rebellious as teenager involved in homicide and her own tragic end.
Green Fire (1954) C-100m. **½ D: Andrew Marton. Grace Kelly, Stewart Granger, Paul Douglas, John Ericson, Murvyn Vye. Hokum of conflict between owners of emerald mines and tobacco fields, set in South America; attractive stars, slimy villain (Vye).
Green for Danger (1947-British) 93m. *** D: Sidney Gilliat. Sally Gray, Trevor Howard, Rosamund John, Alastair Sim. Neatly handled murder yarn, as Sim investigates a mysterious homicide at a hospital filled with potential suspects; good characterizations.
Green Glove, The (1952) 88m. **½ D: Rudolph Mate. Glenn Ford, Ger-

aldine Brooks, Cedric Hardwicke, George Macready. Occasionally interesting tale of Ford returning to France to find cache of gems he hid during WW2, becoming involved in murder.

Green Goddess, The (1930) 80m. ** D: Alfred E. Green. George Arliss, Alice Joyce, H. B. Warner, Ralph Forbes, Reginald Sheffield, Nigel de Brulier, Ivan Simpson. Stagy early talkie, with Arliss a self-righteous potentate who holds innocent Britishers prisoners.

Green Grass of Wyoming (1948) C-89m. **½ D: Louis King. Peggy Cummins, Robert Arthur, Charles Coburn, Lloyd Nolan. Atmospheric tale of rival horse-breeding families; the usual, but nicely done.

Green Grow the Rushes (1951-British) 77m. *** D: Derek Twist. Richard Burton, Honor Blackman, Roger Livesey. Droll English comedy involving villagers trying to hide their whiskey-brewing from interfering government agent; flavorful account.

Green Hell (1940) 87m. **½ D: James Whale. Douglas Fairbanks, Jr., Joan Bennett, Alan Hale, John Howard, George Bancroft, Vincent Price, George Sanders. Standard jungle-expedition film worthwhile for fine cast.

Green Light (1937) 85m. **½ D: Frank Borzage. Errol Flynn, Anita Louise, Margaret Lindsay, Cedric Hardwicke, Erin O'Brien-Moore, Henry Kolker, Spring Byington, Russell Simpson, Pierre Watkin. Dedicated doctor gives up practice when man dies on his operating table; offbeat casting for Flynn, but interesting film. Based on Lloyd C. Douglas novel.

Green Man, The (1957-British) 80m. *** D: Robert Day. Alastair Sim, George Cole, Jill Adams, Avril Angers. Droll comedy of a seemingly timid clockmaker who prefers his part-time job as paid assassin.

Green Mansions (1959) C-101m. **½ D: Mel Ferrer. Audrey Hepburn, Anthony Perkins, Lee J. Cobb, Sessue Hayakawa, Henry Silva, Nehemiah Persoff. W. H. Hudson's romance set in South America suffers from miscast Hepburn as Rima the Bird Girl, whom fate decrees shall not leave her sanctuary. Perkins properly puzzled as male lead.

Green Pastures, The (1936) 90m. ***½ D: William Keighley, Marc Connelly. Rex Ingram, Oscar Polk, Eddie Anderson, Frank Wilson, George Reed, Abraham Gleaves, Myrtle Anderson. All-Negro cast in Marc Connelly fable of life in heaven, and biblical stories which give more meaning to Adam, Noah, and Moses than many so-called biblical films. Ingram is fine as "de Lawd."

Green Promise, The (1949) 93m. **½ D: William D. Russell. Marguerite Chapman, Walter Brennan, Robert Paige, Natalie Wood. Grim little film of Brennan and his four children trying to eke out a living on their farm; unpretentious and engaging.

Green Scarf, The (1955-British) 96m. *** D: George More O'Ferrall. Michael Redgrave, Ann Todd, Kieron Moore, Leo Genn. Imaginative handling of blind man accused of homicide, defended by aging attorney; set in Paris.

Green Years, The (1946) 127m. *** D: Victor Saville. Charles Coburn, Tom Drake, Hume Cronyn, Gladys Cooper, Dean Stockwell. Touching story of young boy brought up in Ireland under domineering parentage, loved only by grandfather.

Greene Murder Case, The (1929) 69m. D: Frank Tuttle. William Powell, Florence Eldridge, Ulrich Haupt, Jean Arthur, Eugene Pallette. SEE: Philo Vance series.

Greenwich Village (1944) C-82m. ** D: Walter Lang. Carmen Miranda, Don Ameche, William Bendix, Vivian Blaine, Felix Bressart, Tony and Sally De Marco, Step Brothers. Limp musical with dubious casting, routine score.

Grisbi (1953-French; dubbed) 94m. **½ D: Jacques Becker. Jean Gabin, Jeanne Moreau, Rene Dary, Lino Ventura, Dora Doll. Gabin is tough in unorthodox tale of Parisian underground, involving gold heist and its mysterious disappearance. Retitled: DON'T TOUCH THE LOOT.

Grissly's Millions (1944) 54m. **½ D: John English. Paul Kelly, Virginia Grey, Don Douglas, Elisabeth Risdon. Programmer involving murder of wealthy man and the typical manhunt for the killer; smoothly done.

Groom Wore Spurs, The (1951) 80m.

**　** D: Richard Whorf. Ginger Rogers, Jack Carson, Joan Davis, Stanley Ridges. Occasionally zesty comedy of attorney Rogers marrying cowboy actor Carson, divorcing him, but coming to his defense in criminal case.

Grounds for Marriage (1950) 91m. ****½** D: Robert Z. Leonard. Van Johnson, Kathryn Grayson, Paula Raymond, Barry Sullivan, Lewis Stone. Cutesy musicomedy of opera star Grayson and her ex-husband, physician Johnson.

Guadalcanal Diary (1943) 93m. ***½ D: Lewis Seiler. Preston Foster, Lloyd Nolan, William Bendix, Richard Conte, Anthony Quinn, Richard Jaeckel. Richard Tregaskis' hot-off-the-wire account of marines fighting for vital Pacific base becomes one of best WW2 actioners; large, competent cast.

Guerrillas in Pink Lace (1964) 96m. *½ D: George Montgomery. George Montgomery, Valerie Varda, Roby Grace, Joan Shawlee. Poorly produced yarn filmed in Philippines about Montgomery and group of showgirls on the lam from Manila and the Japs.

Guest in the House (1944) 121m. **½ D: John Brahm. Anne Baxter, Ralph Bellamy, Aline MacMahon, Ruth Warrick, Jerome Cowan, Margaret Hamilton, Marie McDonald. Baxter is disturbed girl who turns a happy household into one of chaos in this grim melodrama.

Guest Wife (1945) 90m. **½ D: Sam Wood. Claudette Colbert, Don Ameche, Dick Foran, Charles Dingle, Grant Mitchell, Wilma Francis. Breezy comedy depends on stars for flair; they do just fine, with Claudette posing as Ameche's wife to husband Foran's chagrin.

Guide for the Married Man, A (1967) C-89m. ***½ D: Gene Kelly. Walter Matthau, Inger Stevens, Robert Morse, Sue Anne Langdon, Claire Kelly, Elaine Devry; Guest stars Lucille Ball, Jack Benny, Polly Bergen, Joey Bishop, Sid Caesar, Art Carney, Wally Cox, Jayne Mansfield, Hal March, Louis Nye, Carl Reiner, Phil Silvers, Terry-Thomas, Ben Blue, Ann Morgan Guilbert, Jeffrey Hunter, Marty Ingels, Sam Jaffe. Consistently funny, imaginative adult comedy of Morse trying to teach faithful husband Matthau the ABC's of adultery, with the aid of many guest stars who demonstrate Morse's theories. Joke of it all is that Matthau is married to gorgeous Inger Stevens!

Guilt of Janet Ames, The (1947) 83m. *** D: Henry Levin. Rosalind Russell, Melvyn Douglas, Sid Caesar, Betsy Blair, Nina Foch, Charles Cane, Harry Von Zell. Good casting highlights well-done film of Russell at the end of her rope when husband dies and she seeks the cause.

Guilty, The (1947) 70m. **½ D: John Reinhardt. Bonita Granville, Don Castle, Wally Cassell, Regis Toomey. At times engaging murder yarn; twin sisters clash over their love for Castle.

Guilty Bystander (1950) 92m. **½ D: Joseph Lerner. Zachary Scott, Faye Emerson, Mary Boland, Sam Levene, Kay Medford. Down-and-out ex-house detective finds new zest for life when estranged wife reports their child kidnapped.

Guilty of Treason (1949) 86m. **½ D: Felix E. Feist. Charles Bickford, Paul Kelly, Bonita Granville, Richard Derr. Splendidly acted account of the famed Cardinal Mindszenty trial in Hungary, marred by low production values.

Gulliver's Travels (1939) C-74m. **½ D: Dave Fleischer. Singing voices of Jessica Dragonette, Lanny Ross. Perhaps not as Jonathan Swift wanted, but enjoyable cartoon version of his novel aimed at child audience.

Gun Battle at Monterey (1957) 67m. *½ D: Carl G. Hittleman, Sidney A. Franklin, Jr. Sterling Hayden, Pamela Duncan, Mary Beth Hughes, Lee Van Cleef, Byron Foulger, Ted de Corsia. Unremarkable oater with stern Hayden the gunslinger out for revenge against former friend.

Gun Belt (1953) C-77m. **½ D: Ray Nazarro. George Montgomery, Tab Hunter, Helen Westcott, Jack Elam. Notorious outlaw trying to go straight is implicated in crime by his old gang.

Gun Brothers (1956) 79m. ** D: Sidney Salkow. Buster Crabbe, Ann Robinson, Neville Brand, Michael Ansara. Innocuous Western of two brothers, one who becomes a rancher, the other an outlaw who wants to go straight.

Gun Duel in Durango (1957) 73m. ** D: Sidney Salkow. George Montgomery, Steve Brodie, Bobby Clark, Mary Treen. Montgomery must wipe out his outlaw gang before he can reform. Retitled: DUEL IN DURANGO.

Gun for a Coward (1957) 73m. **1/2 D: Abner Biberman. Fred MacMurray, Jeffrey Hunter, Janice Rule, Chill Wills, Josephine Hutchinson. MacMurray is rancher with two younger brothers, each with contrasting personalities, leading to predictable results.

Gun Fury (1953) C-83m. *1/2 D: Raoul Walsh. Rock Hudson, Donna Reed, Phil Carey, Lee Marvin, Neville Brand. Innocuous oater with Hudson gunning for kidnapper of fiancee Reed.

Gun Glory (1957) C-89m. ** D: Roy Rowland. Stewart Granger, Rhonda Fleming, Chill Wills, James Gregory. Granger is reformed gunslinger rejected by his community until outlaw rampage allows him to redeem himself.

Gun Hawk, The (1963) C-92m. **1/2 D: Edward Ludwig. Rory Calhoun, Rod Cameron, Ruta Lee, John Litel, Lane Bradford. Outlaw Cameron attempts to reform Calhoun, who's heading for criminal life.

Gun Runners, The (1958) 83m. ** D: Don Siegel. Audie Murphy, Eddie Albert, Patricia Owens, Everett Sloane, Jack Elam. Murphy is involved with gun-smuggling to Cuba; standard plot stolen from TO HAVE AND HAVE NOT.

Gun That Won the West, The (1955) C-71m. ** D: William Castle. Dennis Morgan, Paula Raymond, Richard Denning, Robert Bice. Harmless Grade-B Western of cavalry's use of Springfield rifles to put down Indian uprising.

Gun the Man Down (1956) 78m. ** D: Andrew V. McLaglen. James Arness, Angie Dickinson, Robert Wilke, Emile Meyer. Wounded outlaw swears vengeance on cohorts who left him during hold-up. Retitled: ARIZONA MISSION.

Gunfight at Dodge City, The (1959) C-81m. ** D: Joseph M. Newman. Joel McCrea, Julie Adams, John McIntire, Nancy Gates, Richard Anderson, James Westerfield. McCrea plays Bat Masterson, who cleans up gangster-ridden town with ironic results.

Gunfight at Indian Gap (1957) 70m. *1/2 D: Joseph Kane. Vera Ralston, Anthony George, George Macready, Glenn Strange. Exactly what the title implies, with lovely Ralston to boot.

Gunfight at the O.K. Corral (1957) C-122m. *** D: John Sturges. Burt Lancaster, Kirk Douglas, Rhonda Fleming, Jo Van Fleet, John Ireland, Lee Van Cleef. Stimulating Western filled with tense action sequences in recreating of Doc Holliday-Wyatt Earp battle with Clanton gang.

Gunfight in Abilene (1967) C-86m. **1/2 D: William Hale. Bobby Darin, Emily Banks, Leslie Nielsen, Michael Sarrazin. Undistinguished post-Civil War account of gun-shy Darin, town sheriff, taking up arms against outlaws.

Gunfighter, The (1950) 84m. ***1/2 D: Henry King. Gregory Peck, Helen Westcott, Jean Parker, Karl Malden, Richard Jaeckel. Peck is most impressive as gunslinger trying to overcome his bloody past. A top-notch Western.

Gunfighters (1947) C-87m. **1/2 D: George Waggner. Randolph Scott, Barbara Britton, Dorothy Hart, Bruce Cabot, Charles Grapewin, Forrest Tucker. Strictly average story of gunfighter who vows never again to spill blood. Good cast, but there must be fifty like this one.

Gunfire (1950) 60m. *1/2 D: William Berke. Don Barry, Robert Lowery, Wally Vernon, Pamela Blake. Flabby Western cashing in on the Jesse James legend, as a man resembling Frank James creates a series of robberies.

Gung Ho! (1943) 88m. *** D: Ray Enright. Randolph Scott, Grace McDonald, Alan Curtis, Noah Beery, Jr., J. Carrol Naish, David Bruce, Peter Coe, Robert Mitchum. Good WW2 action film of marines taking Japanese-held island has routine plot with fine battle scenes.

Gunga Din (1939) 117m. **** D: George Stevens. Cary Grant, Victor McLaglen, Douglas Fairbanks, Jr., Joan Fontaine, Sam Jaffe, Eduardo Ciannelli, Montagu Love, Abner Biberman, Robert Coote. THE Hollywood action-adventure yarn, somehow based on Kipling, with three soldier-comrades in 19th-century India battling savage punjabs. Water-boy Jaffe saves the day; splendid work by everyone. Remade as SERGEANTS THREE and SOLDIERS THREE.

Gunman's Walk (1958) C-97m. *** D: Phil Karlson. Van Heflin, Tab Hunter, Kathryn Grant, James Darren. Rancher Heflin tries to train sons Hunter and Darren to be respectable citizens, but clashing personalities cause outburst of violence. Tight-knit Western.

Gunmen from Laredo (1959) C-67m. Bomb D: Wallace MacDonald. Robert Knapp, Jana Davi, Walter Coy, Paul Birch, Don C. Harvey. Hackneyed hunt-the-real-killer Western.

Gunmen of the Rio Grande (1965-Italian, dubbed) C-86m. ** D: Tulio Demicheli. Guy Madison, Madeleine LeBeau, Carolyn Davys, Massimo Serato. Madison portrays Wyatt Earp, who helps heroine ward off schemes of grasping mine owner.

Gunpoint (1966) C-86m. ** D: Earl Bellamy. Audie Murphy, Joan Staley, Warren Stevens, Edgar Buchanan. Murphy as sheriff gathers a posse to catch outlaw gang who have kidnapped saloon girl.

Guns at Batasi (1964-British) 103m. **½ D: John Guillermin. Richard Attenborough, Jack Hawkins, Mia Farrow, Flora Robson, John Leyton. Acting is all in this intelligent if predictable account of British military life in present-day Africa.

Guns of Darkness (1962) 95m. **½ D: Anthony Asquith. David Niven, Leslie Caron, David Opatoshu, James Robertson Justice, Eleanor Summerfield, Ian Hunter. Civilized drama of Niven searching for life's meaning, set in South America.

Guns of Fort Petticoat, The (1957) C-82m. *** D: George Marshall. Audie Murphy, Kathryn Grant, Hope Emerson, Jeff Donnell, Isobel Elsom. Most enjoyable Western, with army deserter Murphy supervising a group of Texan women in the art of warfare against pending Indian attack.

Guns of Navarone, The (1961) C-157m. ***½ D: J. Lee Thompson. Gregory Peck, David Niven, Anthony Quinn, Stanley Baker, Anthony Quayle, James Darren, Irene Papas, Gia Scala, James Robertson Justice, Richard Harris. Explosive action film of three allied commandos during WW2 plotting to destroy German boats and munitions; high-powered adventure throughout in this first-rate production.

Guns of the Black Witch (1961-Italian, dubbed) C-83m. ** D: Domenico Paolella. Don Megowan, Silvana Pampanini, Emma Daniell, Livio Lorenzon. Tepid account of pirate leader Megowan out to avenge his father's death; Pampanini his love interest. Set in 17th-century Caribbean.

Guns of the Timberland (1960) C-91m. **½ D: Robert D. Webb. Alan Ladd, Jeanne Crain, Gilbert Roland, Frankie Avalon. Pat telling of loggers vs. townpeople.

Gunsight Ridge (1957) 85m. ** D: Francis D. Lyon. Joel McCrea, Mark Stevens, Joan Weldon, Addison Richards, Slim Pickens. Townsfolk finally band together to rid themselves of outlaws; OK Western.

Gunslinger, The (1956) C-83m. *½ D: Roger Corman. John Ireland, Beverly Garland, Allison Hayes, Martin Kingsley. Strange little Western of female marshal trying to maintain law and order in outlaw-ridden town.

Gunsmoke (1953) C-79m. **½ D: Nathan Juran. Audie Murphy, Susan Cabot, Paul Kelly, Charles Drake, Jack Kelly. Compact Western with Murphy reforming to run a ranch and marry his employer's daughter.

Gunsmoke in Tucson (1958) C-80m. **½ D: Thomas Carr. Mark Stevens, Forrest Tucker, Gale Robbins, Gail Kobe, Bill Henry. Sheriff vs. outlaw brother in Arizona territory; not bad.

Guy Called Caesar, A (1962-British) 62m. *½ D: Frank Marshall. Conrad Phillips, George Moon, Phillip O'Flynn, Maureen Toal. Sloppy account of gangsters on the loose in England, with the inevitable showdown with cops.

Guy Named Joe, A (1943) 120m. **½ D: Victor Fleming. Spencer Tracy, Irene Dunne, Van Johnson, Ward Bond, James Gleason, Lionel Barrymore, Barry Nelson, Esther Williams. Good cast flounders in meandering fantasy about heavenly Tracy coming to earth to lend a hand to WW2 serviceman Johnson.

Guy Who Came Back, The (1951) 91m. ** D: Joseph M. Newman. Paul

Douglas, Linda Darnell, Joan Bennett, Don DeFore, Zero Mostel. Cast is above such material but does well by it. Navy reject during WW2 manages to prove his worth.

Guys and Dolls (1955) C-150m. *** D: Joseph L. Mankiewicz. Frank Sinatra, Marlon Brando, Jean Simmons, Vivian Blaine, Stubby Kaye, Veda Ann Borg, Sheldon Leonard. Despite widespread criticism of Brando, lavish musical comedy is most enjoyable. Damon Runyon characters sing fine Frank Loesser score in story of New York gamblers and their gals. Songs: "Guys And Dolls," "Luck Be A Lady," and Kaye's unforgettable "Sit Down, You're Rocking The Boat."

Gypsy (1962) C-149m. **½ D: Mervyn LeRoy. Rosalind Russell, Natalie Wood, Karl Malden, Paul Wallace, Betty Bruce, Parley Baer, Harry Shannon. Fair adaptation of Broadway show with a fine score, including "Everything's Coming Up Roses," "Small World," "Let Me Entertain You." Russell is a good stage mother, but Natalie is no Gypsy Rose Lee.

Gypsy and the Gentleman, The (1958-British) C-89m. **½ D: Joseph Losey. Melina Mercouri, Keith Michell, Patrick McGoohan, Flora Robson. Mercouri as fiery gypsy makes a spicy drama of her love affair with a member of the nobility.

Gypsy Colt (1954) C-72m. **½ D: Andrew Marton. Donna Corcoran, Ward Bond, Frances Dee, Larry Keating. Tender little film of faithful horse who returns to its mistress (Corcoran) after parents have sold horse to racing stable.

Gypsy Fury (1951) 63m. ** D: Christian-Jaque. Viveca Lindfors, Christopher Kent, Romney Brent, Johnny Chabot, Lauritz Falk. Fable about gypsy Lindfors and her aristocratic lover, who gives up all to marry her.

Gypsy Girl (1966-British) C-102m. **½ D: John Mills. Hayley Mills, Ian McShane, Laurence Naismith, Geoffrey Bayldon. Brooding account of backward Hayley Mills finding her first romance with McShane; atmospheric but meandering.

Gypsy Wildcat (1944) C-75m. ** D: Roy William Neill. Maria Montez, Jon Hall, Nigel Bruce, Leo Carrillo, Gale Sondergaard, Douglass Dumbrille. Lowbrow saga of princess raised by gypsies; colorful, splashy, but routine.

H. M. Pulham, Esq. (1941) 120m. ***½ D: King Vidor. Hedy Lamarr, Robert Young, Ruth Hussey, Charles Coburn, Van Heflin, Fay Holden, Bonita Granville. Upper-class Bostonian Young has fling in N.Y.C. before returning to family duties; Lamarr gives one of her best performances in this John P. Marquand story.

H-Man, The (1958-Japanese; dubbed) C-79m. ** D: Inoshiro Honda. Kenji Sahara, Yumi Shirakawa, Akihiko Hirata, Koreye Senda. Good special effects marred by dumb script involving radioactive liquid causing havoc in Tokyo, subplot of cops vs. underworld.

Hail the Conquering Hero (1944) 101m. **** D: Preston Sturges. Eddie Bracken, Ella Raines, Raymond Walburn, William Demarest, Elizabeth Patterson, Jimmy Conlin, Franklin Pangborn, Jack Norton, Paul Porcasi. Frail Bracken, rejected by army, is mistaken for war hero by home town. Satirical Sturges at his best, with Demarest and Pangborn stealing much of the proceedings.

Hairy Ape, The (1944) 90m. *** D: Alfred Santell. William Bendix, Susan Hayward, John Loder, Alan Napier, Dorothy Comingore, Eddie Kane. Well-acted film of O'Neill's play of bestial ship stoker in love with socialite passenger Hayward; unpleasant, thought-provoking film.

Hal Roach Comedy Carnival SEE: Curley

Hal Roach Comedy Carnival, The SEE: Fabulous Joe, The

Half a Hero (1953) 71m. **½ D: Don Weis. Red Skelton, Jean Hagen, Mary Wickes, Willard Waterman, Polly Bergen. Tame Skelton hijinks, with Red a magazine writer who moves to the suburbs and causes trouble with controversial article on his town.

Half Angel (1951) C-77m. **½ D: Richard Sale. Loretta Young, Joseph Cotten, Cecil Kellaway, Jim Backus. Pleasant comedy of Young blessed with sleepwalking troubles, leading to romantic complications.

Half-Breed, The (1952) C-81m. ** D:

Lewis D. Collins. Robert Young, Janis Carter, Jack Buetel, Barton MacLane, Porter Hall. Unstimulating Western about Indian attacks on the whites.

Half-Human (1955-Japanese, dubbed) 70m. *½ D: Inoshiro Honda, Kenneth Crane. John Carradine, Morris Ankrum, Russ Thorson, Robert Karnes. Low-budget horror yarn slopped together, involving a most unconvincing prehistoric zombie monster.

Halfway House, The (1944-British) 94m. **½ D: Basil Dearden. Glynis Johns, Mervyn Johns, Françoise Rosay, Tom Wallis. Effective little yarn of people meeting at a house, discovering that they are reliving events from the prior year.

Hallelujah Trail, The (1965) C-165m. **½ D: John Sturges. Burt Lancaster, Lee Remick, Jim Hutton, Brian Keith, Martin Landau, Donald Pleasence. Remick is rambunctious temperance leader out to reform Lancaster et al in the old West; lumbering satire goes on and on.

Halliday Brand, The (1957) 77m. **½ D: Joseph H. Lewis. Joseph Cotten, Viveca Lindfors, Betsy Blair, Ward Bond. Brooding account of rancher Cotten whose domination of family and workers leads to gunplay.

Halls of Montezuma (1950) C-113m. **½ D: Lewis Milestone. Richard Widmark, Jack Palance, Robert Wagner, Jack Webb, Reginald Gardiner, Karl Malden, Philip Ahn. Grim WW2 actioner dealing with marine action in the Pacific. Good cast makes stereotypes acceptable.

Hamlet (1948-British) C-153m. **** D: Laurence Olivier. Laurence Olivier, Eileen Herlie, Basil Sydney, Felix Aylmer, Jean Simmons. Olivier's brilliant adaptation of the Shakespearean drama of a man "who just couldn't make up his mind" is stimulating drama, with haunting atmosphere.

Hand, The (1960-British) 60m. *½ D: Henry Cass. Derek Bond, Ronald Leigh Hunt, Reed De Rouen, Ray Cooney. Slowly paced murder caper, with Scotland Yard tracking down one-armed killer; a few gruesome scenes.

Hand in Hand (1960-British) 75m. **½ D: Philip Leacock. Loretta Parry, Philip Needs, John Gregson, Sybil Thorndike. Good film with a moral for children, about a Jewish girl and a Catholic boy who become friends and learn about each other. Adults may find it hard to take at times.

Hand of the Gallows SEE: **Terrible People**

Handle with Care (1958) 82m. **½ D: David Friedkin. Dean Jones, Joan O'Brien, Thomas Mitchell, John Smith, Walter Abel. Earnest minor film about law student Jones investigating crime within the town where classmates are assigned mock grand-jury work.

Hands Across the Table (1935) 80m. *** D: Mitchell Leisen. Carole Lombard, Fred MacMurray, Ralph Bellamy, Astrid Allwyn, Marie Prevost. Lombard sparkles as fortune-hunting manicurist who has to choose between MacMurray and Bellamy.

Hands of a Stranger (1962) 86m. **½ D: Newton Arnold. Paul Lukather, Joan Harvey, Irish McCalla, Barry Gordon, Michael Rye. Another version of THE HANDS OF ORLAC, with a pianist receiving a hand-transplant from a criminal, causing him to go berserk.

Hanged Man, The (1964) 120m. **½ D: Don Siegel. Robert Culp, Edmond O'Brien, Vera Miles, J. Carrol Naish, Brenda Scott, Gene Raymond. Modest mystery telefeature set in New Orleans during Mardi Gras, with Culp digging up data to prove that his friend was really murdered.

Hanging Tree, The (1959) 106m. *** D: Delmer Daves. Gary Cooper, Maria Schell, Karl Malden, George C. Scott, Karl Swenson, Ben Piazza, Virginia Gregg. Literate, low-key Western with outstanding performance by Schell as a blind girl nursed by Cooper, a frontier doctor with a past. Not for all tastes.

Hangman, The (1959) 86m. ** D: Michael Curtiz. Robert Taylor, Tina Louise, Fess Parker, Jack Lord, Mickey Shaughnessy, Shirley Harmer. Rugged Taylor is the lawman who must buck the entire Western town defending a man wanted for murder.

Hangman's Knot (1952) C-81m. ** D: Roy Huggins. Randolph Scott, Donna Reed, Claude Jarman, Jr., Richard Denning, Lee Marvin. Above-par Scott Western involving Rebs robbing gold shipment and Captain Scott deciding they should return it.

Hangmen Also Die (1943) 131m. **½ D: Fritz Lang. Brian Donlevy, Walter Brennan, Anna Lee, Gene Lockhart, Dennis O'Keefe. OK WW2 drama written by Bertolt Brecht; lethargic Donlevy performance as assassin of notorious Nazi leader; exciting climax including frame-up of poor Lockhart.

Hangover Square (1945) 77m. *** D: John Brahm. Laird Cregar, Linda Darnell, George Sanders, Glenn Langan, Faye Marlowe, Alan Napier, Frederic Worlock. Unbalanced pianist-composer experiences periods of insanity, goes on murder sprees. Good cast, script, and music.

Hannah Lee SEE: **Outlaw Territory**

Hannibal (1960) 103m. ** D: Edgar G. Ulmer. Victor Mature, Rita Gam, Gabriele Ferzetti, Milly Vitale. Lowbrow production makes famed foe of Rome a cardboard figure.

Hans Christian Andersen (1952) C-120m. **½ D: Charles Vidor. Danny Kaye, Farley Granger, Jeanmaire, Roland Petit, John Qualen. Melodic Frank Loesser score ("Inchworm," "Ugly Duckling," "Thumbelina," etc.) can't save glossy musical biography of vagabond tale-teller.

Happiest Days of Your Life, The (1950-British) 81m. *** D: Frank Launder. Alastair Sim, Margaret Rutherford, Richard Wattis, Joyce Grenfell. Unsung comedy involving a boys school sharing quarters with a displaced girls academy, frantic resulting situations.

Happy Anniversary (1959) 81m. **½ D: David Miller. David Niven, Mitzi Gaynor, Carl Reiner, Loring Smith, Monique Van Vooren, Patty Duke, Elizabeth Wilson. Funny but strained comedy of married couple Niven-Gaynor being embarrassed by daughter Duke telling the nation on TV show that father was indiscreet in his younger days.

Happy Go Lovely (1951-British) C-87m. ** D: H. Bruce Humberstone. David Niven, Vera-Ellen, Cesar Romero, Bobby Howes, Diane Hart. Minor musical about producer who hires a chorus girl hoping that her boyfriend has money to invest in the show.

Happy Go Lucky (1943) C-81m. **½ D: Curtis Bernhardt. Mary Martin, Dick Powell, Eddie Bracken, Betty Hutton, Rudy Vallee, Mabel Paige. Happy little musical with flighty plot, no great songs, but spirited cast to keep it moving.

Happy is the Bride (1959-British) 84m. ** D: Roy Boulting. Ian Carmichael, Janette Scott, Cecil Parker, Terry-Thomas, Joyce Grenfell, Eric Barker, Virginia Maskell. Restrained slapstick revolving around couple trying desperately to get through their wedding day.

Happy Land (1943) 73m. **½ D: Irving Pichel. Don Ameche, Frances Dee, Harry Carey, Ann Rutherford, Cara Williams, Richard Crane, Henry Morgan, Dickie Moore. Sincere but not always successful Americana of grieving father Ameche learning meaning of war as he questions his son's death in WW2 combat.

Happy Landing (1938) 102m. **½ D: Roy Del Ruth. Sonja Henie, Don Ameche, Cesar Romero, Ethel Merman, Jean Hersholt, Billy Gilbert. Predictable Henie vehicle is not up to her other musicals. Pilot Ameche lands near her home; romance blossoms instantly.

Happy Thieves, The (1962) 88m. **½ D: George Marshall. Rex Harrison, Rita Hayworth, Joseph Wiseman, Gregoire Aslan, Alida Valli. Sad pairing of star duo, out of place in museum theft caper, set in Spain.

Happy Time, The (1952) 94m. **½ D: Richard Fleischer. Charles Boyer, Louis Jourdan, Marsha Hunt, Linda Christian, Bobby Driscoll. Pleasant nostalgia dealing with everyday events in life of a typical family, set in 1920's Canada.

Happy Years, The (1950) C-110m. *** D: William Wellman. Dean Stockwell, Scotty Beckett, Darryl Hickman, Leo G. Carroll, Margola Gillmore. Owen Johnson's LAWRENCEVILLE STORIES served as basis for this account of high-spirited youth who finds new values at prep school.

Harbor Lights (1963) 68m. Bomb D: Maury Dexter. Kent Taylor, Jeff Morrow, Miriam Colon, Allan Sague. Cheap film of intrigue, with B-picture perennial Taylor. Congratulations to anyone who can find some relation between title and what goes on in film.

Harbor of Missing Men (1950) 60m.

**½ D: R. G. Springsteen. Richard Denning, Barbara Fuller, Steven Geray, George Zucco, Ray Teal, Percy Helton. Unsparkling Republic Picture programmer with Denning innocently involved with jewel smuggling.

Hard Boiled Mahoney (1947) 63m. D: William Beaudine. Leo Gorcey, Huntz Hall, Betty Compson, Bobby Jordan, Gabriel Dell, Billy Benedict, David Gorcey. SEE: **Bowery Boys** series.

Hard Day's Night, A (1964-British) C-85m. **** D: Richard Lester. John Lennon, Paul McCartney, George Harrison, Ringo Starr, Wilfred Brambell, Victor Spinetti, Anna Quayle. First Beatles film is director Lester's idea of a typical day in the group's life. He lets his imagination run wild; result is a visual delight, with many Beatles songs on the soundtrack.

Hard, Fast and Beautiful (1951) 79m. ** D: Ida Lupino. Claire Trevor, Sally Forrest, Carleton Young, Robert Clarke. Satisfactory drama: tennis player is driven by social-climbing mother, almost costing the girl her boyfriend.

Hard Man, The (1957) C-80m. ** D: George Sherman. Guy Madison, Lorne Green, Valerie French, Trevor Bardette. Madison is earnest sheriff who falls in love with murdered rancher's widow.

Hard to Get (1938) 80m. **½ D: Ray Enright. Dick Powell, Olivia de Havilland, Charles Winninger, Allen Jenkins, Bonita Granville. Spoiled rich girl De Havilland is tamed by nononsense Powell; it's fun, but you've seen it all before. Song: "You Must Have Been A Beautiful Baby."

Hard to Handle (1933) 75m. **½ D: Mervyn LeRoy. James Cagney, Mary Brian, Ruth Donnelly, Allen Jenkins, Emma Dunn. It's all Cagney, and he's fine as sharper who arranges marathon dance as publicity stunt; Donnelly helps out as Brian's mother.

Hard Way, The (1942) 109m. *** D: Vincent Sherman. Ida Lupino, Dennis Morgan, Joan Leslie, Jack Carson, Gladys George, Julie Bishop, Ann Doran. Powerful script of Leslie being pushed into show biz by older sister Lupino is equaled by Lupino's virtuoso performance.

Harder They Fall, The (1956) 109m. *** D: Mark Robson. Humphrey Bogart, Rod Steiger, Jan Sterling, Mike Lane. Bogart's last feature. He plays a cynical sports-reporter-turned-fight-promoter tied in with crime ring, who has a change of heart.

Hardys Ride High, The (1939) 80m. D: George B. Seitz. Lewis Stone, Mickey Rooney, Cecilia Parker, Fay Holden, Ann Rutherford, Sara Haden, Virginia Grey, Marsha Hunt, William T. Orr. SEE: **Andy Hardy** series.

Harem Girl (1952) 70m. ** D: Edward Bernds. Joan Davis, Peggie Castle, Arthur Blake, Minerva Urecal. Wacky Davis does her best to enliven slim vehicle about her substituting for a princess.

Harlem Globetrotters, The (1951) 80m. ** D: Phil Brown. Thomas Gomez, Dorothy Dandridge, Bill Walker, Angela Clarke. Vehicle built around famed basketball team, with a few romantic interludes.

Harlow (1965) C-125m. **½ D: Gordon Douglas. Carroll Baker, Peter Lawford, Red Buttons, Michael Connors, Raf Vallone, Angela Lansbury, Martin Balsam, Leslie Nielsen. Slick, colorful garbage will hold your interest, but doesn't ring true. Baker could never match the real Harlow, but Vallone and Lansbury are good as her parents.

Harlow (1965) 109m. ** D: Alex Segal. Carol Lynley, Efrem Zimbalist, Jr., Barry Sullivan, Hurd Hatfield, Ginger Rogers, Hermione Baddeley, Lloyd Bochner, Audrey Totter, John Williams, Robert Strauss. Amateurish off-the-cuff tedium loosely based on screen star of the 1930's. Rogers as Mama Harlow is best.

Harold Lloyd's World of Comedy (1962) 94m. **** Compiled by Harold Lloyd. Harold Lloyd, Bebe Daniels, Mildred Smith. Delightful comedy scenes not shown in a long time, including Lloyd's classic building-climbing episode and other great sight gags. A real gem.

Harper (1966) C-121m. ***½ D: Jack Smight. Paul Newman, Lauren Bacall, Julie Harris, Shelley Winters, Robert Wagner, Janet Leigh, Arthur Hill. High-grade actioner: Newman is private eye hired by Bacall to investigate disappearance of her husband; blowsy Winters, frustrated

Harris are involved in fast-paced, sophisticated yarn.

Harriet Craig (1950) 94m. *** D: Vincent Sherman. Joan Crawford, Wendell Corey, Lucile Watson, Allyn Joslyn, Ellen Corby. Remake of CRAIG'S WIFE is well cast, with Crawford in title role of perfectionist wife who'll stop at nothing to have her house and life run as she wishes.

Harry Black and the Tiger (1958) C-107m. Bomb D: Hugo Fregonese. Stewart Granger, Barbara Rush, Anthony Steel, I. S. Johar. Moldy jungle film tangled in the underbrush, with flashbacks causing confusion. Sorry, Harry.

Harum Scarum (1965) C-95m. **½ D: Gene Nelson. Elvis Presley, Mary Ann Mobley, Fran Jeffries, Michael Ansara, Jay Novello, Philip Reed, Theo Marcuse, Billy Barty. Visiting the Middle East gives usual Presley musical formula a change of scenery albeit back-lot desert locations.

Harvey (1950) 104m. ***½ D: Henry Koster. James Stewart, Josephine Hull, Cecil Kellaway, Peggy Dow, Jesse White, Ida Moore. Stewart gives one of his best performancese as tippler Elwood P. Dowd, whose companion is a six-foot rabbit named Harvey. Hull won Oscar as distraught relative. From Mary Chase's play.

Harvey Girls, The (1946) C-101m. ***½ D: George Sidney. Judy Garland, Ray Bolger, John Hodiak, Angela Lansbury, Preston Foster, Virginia O'Brien, Marjorie Main, Kenny Baker, Cyd Charisse. Western musical is one of Garland's best. Small Western town boasts girls trying to attain regional standards and local men. Score and songs won Oscar ("Atchison, Topeka, and the Santa Fe").

Has Anybody Seen My Gal? (1952) C-89m. ** D: Douglas Sirk. Charles Coburn, Piper Laurie, Rock Hudson, Gigi Perreau, Lynn Bari. Pleasant lightweight musical about family inheriting big sum of money, and wacky repercussions.

Hasty Heart, The (1949) 99m. ***½ D: Vincent Sherman. Ronald Reagan, Patricia Neal, Richard Todd, Anthony Nicholls, Howard Crawford. Sensitive film version of John Patrick's play, focusing on proud Scottish soldier who discovers he has short time to live, and friendships he finally makes among his hospital mates.

Hatari! (1962) C-159m. ***½ D: Howard Hawks. John Wayne, Elsa Martinelli, Red Buttons, Hardy Kruger, Gerard Blain, Bruce Cabot. Marvelous lighthearted action film of wild-animal hunters in Africa, with just-right mixture of adventure and comedy. Wayne at his best, rest of the cast fine. Notable Henry Mancini score.

Hatchet Man, The (1932) 74m. *½ D: William Wellman. Edward G. Robinson, Loretta Young, Dudley Digges, Blanche Frederici, J. Carrol Naish, Willie Fung. Interesting contra-type casting about San Francisco's Tong wars and Robinson's affair with Young.

Hatful of Rain, A (1957) 109m. *** D: Fred Zinnemann. Eva Marie Saint, Don Murray, Anthony Franciosa, Lloyd Nolan, Henry Silva. Realistic melodrama of the living hell dope addict Murray undergoes, and the effects on those around him; fine performances.

Hatter's Castle (1948-British) 90m. **½ D: Lance Comfort. Deborah Kerr, James Mason, Robert Newton, Emlyn Williams. Fine cast must support fair material in tale of poor man who relentlessly pursues his dream of social acceptance; from A. J. Cronin's novel.

Haunted Honeymoon (1940-British) 83m. **½ D: Arthur B. Woods. Robert Montgomery, Leslie Banks, Constance Cummings, Seymour Hicks, Robert Newton, Googie Withers. Average mystery of investigator and mystery-writer wife combining efforts to solve murder during honeymoon.

Haunted Strangler, The (1958) 81m. **½ D: Robert Day. Boris Karloff, Anthony Dawson, Elizabeth Allan, Derek Birch, Jean Kent, Dorothy Gordon. Offbeat yarn of mystery-writer Karloff investigating case of murderer hung twenty years ago, with dismaying results.

Haunting, The (1963) 112m. *** D: Robert Wise. Julie Harris, Claire Bloom, Richard Johnson, Russ Tamblyn, Lois Maxwell, Fay Compton. Shirley Jackson's novel is given careful handling, producing psychological tale of fright; slowly paced, well acted.

Have Rocket, Will Travel (1959) 76m.
** D: David Lowell Rich. The Three
Stooges, Jerome Cowan, Anna Lisa,
Bob Colbert. Good slapstick with the
Stooges accidentally launched into
space, where they meet a unicorn
and become national heroes.

Having Wonderful Crime (1945) 70m.
*** D: A. Edward Sutherland. Pat
O'Brien, George Murphy, Carole
Landis, Lenore Aubert, George Zucco. Lighthearted mystery of trio of
friends investigating magic act which
ended in murder; O'Brien a lot of
fun.

Having Wonderful Time (1938) 71m.
**½ D: Alfred Santell. Ginger
Rogers, Douglas Fairbanks, Jr., Peggy Conklin, Lucille Ball, Lee Bowman, Eve Arden, Red Skelton. Big
cast in OK film about Catskills resort hotel; Ginger wants culture on
summer vacation but gets Doug instead. Skelton does well in feature
film debut.

Hawk of the Wilderness SEE: **Lost Island of Kioga**

Hawkeye and the Last of the Mohicans SEE: **Long Rifle and the Tomahawk**.

Hazard (1948) 95m. ** D: George
Marshall. Paulette Goddard, Macdonald Carey, Fred Clark, Stanley Clements. Routine comedy of privateeye Carey following Goddard, falling
in love in the process.

He Married His Wife (1940) 83m. **
D: Roy Del Ruth. Joel McCrea, Nancy
Kelly, Roland Young, Mary Boland,
Cesar Romero. McCrea doesn't want
to bear the expense of divorce; solution is obvious, and so is most of the
film.

He Ran All the Way (1951) 77m. **½
D: John Berry. John Garfield, Shelley
Winters, Wallace Ford, Selena Royle,
Gladys George. Garfield is criminal
on the lam hiding out at Winters'
home, with predictable results.

He Rides Tall (1964) 84m. **½ D:
R. G. Springsteen. Tony Young, Dan
Duryea, Madlyn Rhue, George Petrie.
Stark Western about the sheriff forced
to shoot it out with foster-father's
son.

He Stayed for Breakfast (1940) 89m.
** D: Alexander Hall. Loretta Young,
Melvyn Douglas, Una O'Connor, Eugene Pallette, Alan Marshal. NINOTCHKA and COMRADE X in reverse,
as Russian Douglas is Americanized
by beautiful Young; trivial.

He Walked by Night (1948) 79m. ***
D: Alfred L. Werker. Richard Basehart, Scott Brady, Roy Roberts,
Whit Bissell. Grade-A drama of killer
hunted by police; told in semi-documentary style. Effective performances
by all.

He Was Her Man (1934) 70m. ** D:
Lloyd Bacon, James Cagney, Joan
Blondell, Victor Jory, Frank Craven,
Sarah Padden. Most disappointing
for Cagney as con-man who snatches
Blondell away from Jory, who tries
to get even.

Head, The (1959-German, dubbed)
92m. ** D: Victor Trivas. Horst
Frank, Karin Kernke, Michel Simon,
Helmut Schmid, Dieter Eppler. Oldfashioned chiller involving headtransplants, with obligatory murders
and blood-drenched revenge; not very
convincing.

Head of a Tyrant (1958-Italian,
dubbed) C-83m. ** D: Fernando
Cerchio. Massimo Girotti, Isabelle
Corey, Renato Baldini, Yvette Masson. Humdrum spectacle involving
seige of Bethulia by Assyrians, with
Corey playing the legendary Judith.

Heading for Heaven (1947) 71m. *½
D: Lewis D. Collins. Stuart Erwin,
Glenda Farrell, Irene Ryan, Milburn
Stone, Selmer Jackson, Janis Wilson.
Soggy account of well-meaning Erwin
trying to build model middle-incomebracket community, being fleeced by
racketeers.

Headless Ghost, The (1958-British)
63m. ** D: Peter Graham Scott. Richard Lyon, Liliane Sottane, David
Rose, Clive Revill, Carl Bernard,
Trevor Barnett. Offbeat fantasyhorror film with strange doings in a
haunted castle; not bad, with younger audiences sure to enjoy special
effects.

Headline Hunters (1955) 70m. ** D:
William Witney. Rod Cameron, Julie
Bishop, Ben Cooper, Raymond Greenleaf. Uninspired tale of fledgling reporter tracking down big-city racketeers.

Headlines of Destruction (1955-French, dubbed) ** D: John Berry.
Eddie Constantine, Bella Darvi, Paul
Frankeur, Walter Chiari. Interesting
concept poorly executed: Darvi is defense attorney involved with Con-

stantine in trial of man accused of murder.

Hear Me Good (1957) 80m. *½ D: Don McGuire. Hal March, Joe E. Ross, Merry Anders, Jean Willes. Trivia concerning a fixed beauty contest.

Heart of the Matter, The (1954-British) 100m. *** D: George More O'Ferrall. Trevor Howard, Elizabeth Allan, Maria Schell, Denholm Elliott. Grahame Greene's novel of inner and outward conflict set in South Africa, with Howard as police officer on verge of mental collapse.

Heartbeat (1946) 102m. ** D: Sam Wood. Ginger Rogers, Jean-Pierre Aumont, Adolphe Menjou, Basil Rathbone, Melville Cooper. So-so drama of lady pickpocket and diplomat who eventually fall for each other; benefits from good cast.

Hearts Divided (1936) 87m. ** D: Frank Borzage. Marion Davies, Dick Powell, Charlie Ruggles, Claude Rains, Edward Everett Horton, Arthur Treacher. Davies is French girl and Powell is Napoleon's brother in OK musical romance.

Heat Wave (1954-British) 68m. *½ D: Ken Hughes. Alex Nicol, Hillary Brooke, Paul Carpenter, Sidney James. Tame murder yarn, with Brooke the sultry dame involved in homicide.

Heat's On, The (1943) 80m. ** D: Gregory Ratoff. Mae West, Victor Moore, William Gaxton, Lester Allen, Mary Roche, Xavier Cugat. The heat's off in West's only flat comedy. Mae is submerged by this low-budget nightclub musical, her last starring vehicle.

Heaven Can Wait (1943) C-112m. ***½ D: Ernst Lubitsch. Gene Tierney, Don Ameche, Charles Coburn, Marjorie Main, Laird Cregar, Spring Byington, Allyn Joslyn, Eugene Pallette, Signe Hasso, Louis Calhern. Excellent comedy-fantasy with Lubitsch touch, of sinner Ameche, circa 1890, requesting admission to Hades.

Heaven Knows, Mr. Allison (1957) C-107m. *** D: John Huston. Deborah Kerr, Robert Mitchum. Marvelous duo of nun Kerr stranded on WW2 Jap-infested Pacific island and soldier Mitchum.

Heaven Only Knows (1947) 95m. **½ D: Albert S. Rogell. Robert Cummings, Brian Donlevy, Jorja Curtright, Marjorie Reynolds, Bill Goodwin, John Litel, Stuart Erwin. Strictly standard Western with fantasy touches as angel Cummings descends to earth to help soulless gambler. Good cast but nothing new. Retitled: MONTANA MIKE.

Heaven With a Barbed Wire Fence (1940) 62m. **½ D: Ricardo Cortez. Jean Rogers, Glenn Ford, Raymond Walburn, Marjorie Rambeau, Richard Conte. Good little romance with down-and-out Rogers and Ford deciding to marry despite many obstacles.

Heavenly Body, The (1943) 95m. ** D: Alexander Hall. Hedy Lamarr, William Powell, James Craig, Fay Bainter, Henry O'Neill, Spring Byington. Hedy is heavenly, but script is silly; astrologer Powell suspects neglected wife Lamarr of being unfaithful.

Heavenly Days (1944) 71m. ** D: Howard Estabrook. Fibber McGee and Molly, Barbara Hale, Eugene Pallette, Gordon Oliver. Mild entry in famed radio comedians' series, with the battling married couple off to Washington to help run the Senate.

Heavens Above! (1963-British) 105m. *** D: John and Roy Boulting. Peter Sellers, Cecil Parker, Isabel Jeans, Eric Sykes. Wry satire on British clergy life, with Sellers generally top-notch as the reverend who becomes bishop of outer space.

Heidi (1937) 88m. **½ D: Allan Dwan. Shirley Temple, Jean Hersholt, Arthur Treacher, Helen Westley, Mady Christians, Sidney Blackmer, Sig Ruman, Marcia Mae Jones. Classic children's story set in 19th-century Switzerland is good vehicle for Shirley, playing girl taken from father (Hersholt) to live with cruel Westley. Nice tear-jerker for children.

Heidi (1952-Swiss, dubbed) *** D: Luigi Comencini. Elsbeth Sigmund, Heinrich Gretler, Thomas Klameth, Elsie Attenoff. Faithful, flavorful retelling of Johanna Spyri's children's classic.

Heidi and Peter (1955-Swiss, dubbed) C-89m. **½ D: Franz Schnyder. Heinrich Gretler, Elsbeth Sigmund, Thomas Klameth, Anita Mey. Further adventures of Johanna Spyri's characters, involving flood threatening Heidi's village.

Heiress, The (1949) 115m. **** D: William Wyler. Olivia de Havilland, Ralph Richardson, Montgomery Clift, Miriam Hopkins, Vanessa Brown. Henry James' novel WASHINGTON SQUARE receives plush screen treatment with Oscar-winning De Havilland as spinster wooed by fortune-hunter Clift in early 20th-century N.Y.C.

Helen Morgan Story, The (1957) 118m. **½ D: Michael Curtiz. Ann Blyth, Paul Newman, Richard Carlson, Gene Evans, Cara Williams. Fiction about dynamic 1920-30's torch singer, overfocusing on her romances and alcoholism; Blyth never captures the star's pathos or greatness. She's dubbed by Gogi Grant.

Helen of Troy (1955) C-118m. ** D: Robert Wise. Stanley Baker, Rossana Podesta, Brigitte Bardot, Jaques Sernas, Cedric Hardwicke, Harry Andrews. Sweeping pageantry, but empty script spoils this version of story about the woman who caused the Trojan War.

Hell and High Water (1954) C-103m. **½ D: Samuel Fuller. Richard Widmark, Bella Darvi, Victor Francen, Cameron Mitchell, Gene Evans, David Wayne. Uneven mixture of romance, espionage, and a demolition caper, stemming from U.S. sub's mission to Arctic; originally released in Cinemascope, which gave tame film some novelty.

Hell Below (1933) 105m. **½ D: Jack Conway. Robert Montgomery, Walter Huston, Madge Evans, Jimmy Durante, Robert Young, Sterling Holloway, Eugene Pallette. Vintage submarine drama surpasses many more elaborate efforts; Huston is captain, Montgomery his seaman nemesis.

Hell Below Zero (1954) C-91m. ** D: Mark Robson. Alan Ladd, Joan Tetzel, Basil Sydney, Stanley Baker. Tepid adventure yarn casting Ladd as helper of Tetzel, who commands a whaling vessel while searching for her dad's killer.

Hell Bent for Leather (1960) C-82m. **½ D: George Sherman. Audie Murphy, Felicia Farr, Stephen McNally, Robert Middleton. Western focuses on battle of power between reward-hungry sheriff and innocent man mistaken for killer.

Hell Canyon Outlaws (1957) 72m. ** D: Paul Landres. Dale Robertson, Brian Keith, Rossana Rory, Dick Kallman, Buddy Baer. Triumph against outlaw forces in the old West; that's it.

Hell Drivers (1958-British) 91m. **½ D: Cy Endfield. Stanley Baker, Herbert Lom, Peggy Cummins, Patrick McGoohan. Taut account of truck drivers carrying explosive cargoes over rugged roads.

Hell Is for Heroes (1962) 90m. *** D: Don Siegel. Steve McQueen, Bobby Darin, Fess Parker, Harry Guardino, James Coburn, Mike Kellin, Nick Adams, Bob Newhart. Action-packed war film that minimizes clichés; rugged cast put through grueling paces.

Hell on Devil's Island (1957) 74m. *½ D: Christian Nyby. Helmut Dantine, William Talman, Donna Martell, Rex Ingram, Alan Lee. Unlurid exposé of unsavory working conditions in prison mining operations.

Hell on Frisco Bay (1955) C-98m. **½ D: Frank Tuttle. Alan Ladd, Edward G. Robinson, Joanne Dru, William Demarest, Fay Wray. Thirties-style gangster film recounting the exposure of crime syndicate and its head; actionful, with good cast.

Hell Ship Mutiny (1957) 66m. *½ D: Lee Sholem and Elmo Williams. Jon Hall, John Carradine, Peter Lorre, Roberta Haynes, Mike Mazurki, Stanley Adams. Hall looks bored in rehash of South Seas tale of ship captain overcoming sinister forces exploiting the natives.

Hell to Eternity (1960) 132m. **½ D: Phil Karlson. Jeffrey Hunter, David Janssen, Vic Damone, Patricia Owens. Hunter gives credence to role of American raised in Japanese household in L.A. who finds his background valuable when WW2 starts.

Hell with Heroes, The (1968) C-102m. **½ D: Joseph Sargent. Rod Taylor, Claudia Cardinale, Harry Guardino, Kevin McCarthy, Peter Deuel, William Marshall. Engrossing tale of post-WW2 espionage just misses the mark, but Miss Cardinale is gorgeous, and the cast is quite good. Young Deuel shines in a supporting role.

Hellcats of the Navy (1957) 82m. **½ D: Nathan Juran. Ronald Reagan, Nancy Davis, Arthur Franz, Harry Lauter, Selmer Jackson. Satisfactory actioner of WW2 exploits of U.S. submarine and its crew.

Heller in Pink Tights (1960) C-100m. **½ D: George Cukor. Sophia Loren, Anthony Quinn, Margaret O'Brien, Steve Forrest, Edmund Lowe. Oddball Western involving traveling show troupe and their encounters with belligerent townsfolk and Indians; colorful production.

Hellgate (1953) 87m. **½ D: Charles Marquis Warren. Sterling Hayden, Joan Leslie, James Arness, Ward Bond. Offbeat account of Hayden falsely sent to prison, and strange manner in which he redeems himself during convict breakout.

Hellions, The (1962-British) C-87m. **½ D: Ken Annakin. Richard Todd, Anne Aubrey, Lionel Jeffries, Zena Walker, Jamie Uys, Marty Wilde. Western revenge plot transferred to 19th-century South Africa; inevitable shoot-out intact.

Hello Elephant (1954-Italian, dubbed) 78m. *½ D: Gianni Franciolini. Vittorio DeSica, Sabu, Maria Mercader, Nando Bruno. Misfire of comedy-satire involving royalty who bestows an elephant on one of his subjects as a fitting reward. Retitled: PARDON MY TRUNK.

Hello, Frisco, Hello (1943) C-98m. ** D: H. Bruce Humberstone. Alice Faye, John Payne, Jack Oakie, Lynn Bari, Laird Cregar, June Havoc, Ward Bond. Hackneyed musicomedy of Faye aiming for stardom; periodpiece, with Oscar-winning song: "You'll Never Know." Big comedown from earlier musicals with star trio.

Hello Sucker (1941) 60m. *½ D: Edward Cline. Peggy Moran, Tom Brown, Walter Catlett, Hugh Herbert. Dingy little film of Moran and Brown acquiring vaudeville booking agency, making it a success and finding love with one another.

Hell's Crossroads (1957) 73m. ** D: Franklin Adreon. Stephen McNally, Peggie Castle, Robert Vaughn, Barton MacLane. Oater involving members of the James Brothers outlaw gang.

Hell's Five Hours (1958) 73m. ** D: Jack L. Copeland. Stephen McNally, Coleen Gray, Vic Morrow, Maurice Manson. Several people are held prisoners at missile fuel depot by McNally, bent on blowing the place sky-high.

Hell's Half Acre (1954) 91m. *½ D: John H. Auer. Wendell Corey, Evelyn Keyes, Elsa Lanchester, Marie Windsor. Strange little film of wife who goes to Hawaii in search of missing husband.

Hell's Horizon (1955) 80m. ** D: Tom Gries. John Ireland, Marla English, Bill Williams, Hugh Beaumont, Jerry Paris, Kenneth Duncan. Interaction among men of bombing squad in the Korean War.

Hell's Island (1955) C-84m. *½ D: Phil Karlson. John Payne, Mary Murphy, Francis L. Sullivan, Jose Oliveira. Payne accepts assignment to track down gem thief, hoping to locate his former girlfriend.

Hell's Kitchen (1939) 81m. **½ D: Lewis Seiler, E. A. Dupont. Ronald Reagan, Stanley Fields, Grant Mitchell, Margaret Lindsay, Dead End Kids. Ex-con Reagan goes straight, tries to bail Dead End Kids out of their usual trouble, sets them on the right road.

Hell's Long Road (1963-Italian, dubbed) C-89m. **½ D: Charles Roberti. Elena Brazzi, Kay Nolandi, Berto Frankis, Bela Kaivi, Marcello Charli. Offbeat costume sudser set in ancient Rome during rule of Nero (Frankis), focusing on personal life of arch senator (Charli) and romance with splendiforous Brazzi; vivid settings.

Hell's Outpost (1954) 90m. ** D: Joseph Kane. Rod Cameron, Joan Leslie, Chill Wills, John Russell. Cameron is ambitious miner in this sturdy little film; Leslie is the fetching love interest.

Hellzapoppin (1941) 84m. *** D: H. C. Potter. Ole Olsen, Chic Johnson, Martha Raye, Mischa Auer, Jane Frazee, Hugh Herbert. Can't capture madness of Broadway show, but makes good try with some funny gimmicks and wacky supporting cast.

Help! (1965) C-90m. ***½ D: Richard Lester. John Lennon, Paul McCartney, George Harrison, Ringo Starr, Leo McKern, Eleanor Bron, Victor Spinetti, Roy Kinnear, Patrick Cargill. Crazy, funny film, the Beatles' second. Lots of wild gags, many songs, some really far-out sequences involving some sort of spying.

Hemingway's Adventures of a Young Man (1962) C-145m. ** D: Martin Ritt. Richard Beymer, Diane Baker, Paul Newman, Eli Wallach, Arthur Kennedy, Ricardo Montalban, Dan Dailey, Susan Strasberg, Fred Clark, Corinne Calvet. Overblown, cornball, embarrassing the memory of famed American writer; pretentious in thought and drawnout plot, loosely based on autobiographical data in author's stories.

Henry, the Rainmaker (1949) 64m. *½ D: Jean Yarbrough. Raymond Walburn, Walter Catlett, William Tracy, Mary Stuart. Mild little comedy of homey Walburn who develops a "scientific" way to make rain.

Her Adventurous Night (1946) 76m. **½ D: John Rawlins. Dennis O'Keefe, Helen Walker, Tom Powers, Fuzzy Knight. Youngster with wild imagination fabricates tale of murder and crime, causing parents to go to jail and the youth's life put in peril.

Her Cardboard Lover (1942) 93m. *½ D: George Cukor. Norma Shearer, Robert Taylor, George Sanders, Frank McHugh, Elizabeth Patterson. Tired comedy that chic Shearer couldn't salvage. Her last film to date.

Her First Romance (1951) 73m. *½ D: Seymour Friedman. Margaret O'Brien, Allen Martin, Jr., Jimmy Hunt, Sharyn Moffett. O'Brien's first grown-up role and her first screen kiss are only assets of this plodding summer camp story.

Her Highness and the Bellboy (1945) 112m. **½ D: Richard Thorpe. Hedy Lamarr, Robert Walker, June Allyson, Carl Esmond, Agnes Moorehead, Rags Ragland. Sentimental fluff of N.Y.C. bellboy Walker, crippled girlfriend Allyson, captivating Princess (Lamarr) he escorts; a bit creaky.

Her Husband's Affairs (1947) 83m. *½ D: S. Sylvan Simon. Lucille Ball, Franchot Tone, Edward Everett Horton, Mikhail Rasumny, Gene Lockhart, Nana Bryant. Pretty sterile comedy about Ball learning not to poke into husband's business affairs.

Her Jungle Love (1938) C-81m. **½ D: George Archainbaud. Dorothy Lamour, Ray Milland, Lynne Overman, J. Carrol Naish, Dorothy Howe. Flyers Milland and Overman stranded on tropical isle with Lamour; Ray teaches her how to kiss, Naish tries to destroy everyone in this escapist fare.

Her Kind of Man (1946) 78m. ** D: Frederick de Cordova. Dane Clark, Janis Paige, Zachary Scott, Faye Emerson, George Tobias. Lukewarm drama of young singer with gangster background making good in Big City and falling in love with gossip columnist. Fair cast.

Her Lucky Night (1945) 63m. ** D: Edward Lilley. Andrews Sisters, Martha O'Driscoll, Noah Beery, Jr., George Barbier, Grady Sutton, Ida Moore. Minor comedy with singing trio seeking romance at any cost.

Her Majesty, Love (1931) 75m. *½ D: William Dieterle. Marilyn Miller, W. C. Fields, Leon Errol, Ford Sterling, Chester Conklin, Ben Lyon, Virginia Sale. Unbearable musical with sweet Miller in love with Lyon in old Berlin. Errol as persistent suitor, Fields as juggling father, provide only uplifting moments.

Her Man Gilbey (1948-British) 89m. **½ D: Harold French. Albert Lieven, Margaret Rutherford, Peggy Cummins, Martin Miller. Capable cast nicely handles contrived yarn of quartet of people whose lives intertwine in Geneva.

Her Panelled Door (1951-British) 84m. *** D: Ladislas Vajda. Phyllis Calvert, Edward Underdown, Helen Cherry, Richard Burton. During an air raid Calvert is shellshocked, forgetting her past, leading to dramatic results. Thoughtful study.

Her Primitive Man (1944) 79m. *½ D: Charles Lamont. Robert Paige, Louise Allbritton, Robert Benchley, Edward Everett Horton. Grade-C flick with Paige pretending to be a savage to win love of anthropologist Allbritton.

Her Sister's Secret (1946) 86m. **½ D: Edgar G. Ulmer. Nancy Coleman, Margaret Lindsay, Felix Bressart, Regis Toomey, Henry Stephenson. Young woman discovers she's pregnant after brief affair. Fair weeper with competent cast.

Her 12 Men (1954) C-91m. ** D:

Robert Z. Leonard. Greer Garson, Robert Ryan, Barry Sullivan, Richard Haydn. Maudlin script has Greer as dedicated teacher in boys' school; tries unsuccessfully to repeat success of MR. CHIPS and MISS DOVE.

Hercules (1959-Italian, dubbed) C-107m. **½ D: Pietro Francisci. Steve Reeves, Sylva Koscina, Fabrizio Mioni, Ivo Garrani, Gina Rovere. Prototype of all cloak-and-sandal pictures to come: Reeves as musclebound mythical hero who undergoes myriad of ordeals for woman he loves.

Hercules Against Rome (1960-Italian, dubbed) C-87m. ** D: Piero Pierott. Alan Steel, Wandisa Gulda, Livio Lorenzon, Daniele Vargas. Steel fights a series of unconvincing villains to protect the late emperor's daughter.

Hercules Against the Moon Men (1964-Italian, dubbed) C-88m. ** D: Giacomo Gentilomo. Alan Steel, Jany Clair, Anna-Maria Polani, Nando Tamberlani. Steel is muscular hero who frees people of Samar from control of magical lunar people holding them in bondage; potential action never occurs.

Hercules Against the Sons of the Sun (1963-Italian, dubbed) C-91m. ** D: Osvaldo Civirani. Mark Forrest, Anna Pace, Giuliano Gemma, Andrea Rhu. Forrest helps Romans defend themselves against Peruvian-type invaders; nothing exceptional.

Hercules and the Captive Women (1963-Italian, dubbed) C-87m. ** D: Vittorio Cottafavi. Reg Park, Fay Spain, Ettore Manni, Marlo Petri. Cardboard costumer with Park vs. Spain, the despotic ruler of Atlantis.

Hercules in the Haunted World (1961-Italian, dubbed) C-83m. ** D: Mario Bava. Reg Park, Christopher Lee, Leonora Ruffo, Giorgio Ardisson, Ida Galli. Occasionally sparked by atmospheric settings, this sword-and-sandal epic narrates adventures of Park in the devil's kingdom.

Hercules, Samson and Ulysses (1965-Italian, dubbed) C-85m. ** D: Pietro Francisci. Kirk Morris, Richard Lloyd, Liana Orfei, Enzo Cerusico. Title alerts one for gymnastics of trio of legendary musclemen.

Hercules Unchained (1960-Italian, dubbed) C-101m. ** D: Pietro Francisci. Steve Reeves, Sylva Koscina, Primo Carnera, Sylvia Lopez. Par for the muscleman hero entry, dealing with rescue of his bride-to-be.

Here Come the Co-eds (1945) 87m. **½ D: Jean Yarbrough. Bud Abbott, Lou Costello, Peggy Ryan, Martha O'Driscoll, June Vincent, Lon Chaney, Donald Cook. Pretty zany Abbott and Costello comedy of two wacky caretakers turning formerly staid girls' school on its ear.

Here Come the Girls (1953) C-78m. **½ D: Claude Binyon. Bob Hope, Arlene Dahl, Rosemary Clooney, Tony Martin, Fred Clark. At times amusing romp with Hope a naive show biz-ite who becomes involved with killer on the loose.

Here Come the Nelsons (1952) 76m. ** D: Frederick de Cordova. Ozzie, Harriet, David, Ricky Nelson, Rock Hudson, Ann Doran, Jim Backus. Expanded version of typical radio-TV Nelson family fare, dealing with gangsters.

Here Come the Waves (1944) 99m. *** D: Mark Sandrich. Bing Crosby, Betty Hutton, Sonny Tufts, Ann Doran, Catherine Craig. Zippy wartime musicomedy of singer Crosby joining the navy. Hit song "Ac-cent-u-ate the Positive."

Here Comes Mr. Jordan (1941) 93m. ***½ D: Alexander Hall. Robert Montgomery, Evelyn Keyes, Claude Rains, Rita Johnson, Edward Everett Horton, James Gleason. Fantasy of prizefighter Montgomery who is accidentally sent to heaven before his time, forced to find new body to occupy. Most enjoyable, with good cast.

Here Comes the Groom (1951) 113m. *** D: Frank Capra. Bing Crosby, Jane Wyman, Franchot Tone, Alexis Smith, Anna Maria Alberghetti, Alan Reed, Louis Armstrong, Cass Daley. Crosby is relaxed news reporter in love with Wyman. Tone and Smith secondary love interests. Song "In the Cool, Cool, Cool of the Evening" won an Oscar in this lightweight outing.

Here Come the Marines (1952) 66m. D: William Beaudine. Leo Gorcey, Huntz Hall, Bernard Gorcey, Gil Stratton, Jr., Arthur Space, Tim Ryan. SEE: Bowery Boys series.

Here Comes the Navy (1934) 86m. **½ D: Lloyd Bacon. James Cagney, Pat O'Brien, Gloria Stuart, Dorothy Tree, Frank McHugh. Enjoyable but standard tale of cocky Cagney who becomes navy hero; nothing new, but well done.

Here Is My Heart (1934) 77m. **½
D: Frank Tuttle. Bing Crosby, Kitty Carlisle, Roland Young, Alison Skipworth, Reginald Owen. Bing's a radio star in love with princess Carlisle in this filmsy little musical. Songs include "Love Is Just Around the Corner."

Herod the Great (1960-Italian, dubbed) C-93m. *½ D: Arnaldo Genoino. Edmund Purdom, Sylvia Lopez, Sandra Milo, Alberto Lupo. Juvenile account of ruler of ancient Judea, his warring and his jealousy of wife's admirers.

Heroes for Sale (1933) 73m. **½ D: William Wellman. Loretta Young, Aline MacMahon, Richard Barthelmess, Grant Mitchell, Ward Bond, Douglass Dumbrille. Low-keyed Depression story of ex-soldier Barthelmess trying to make something of himself, thwarted at every turn.

Heroes of Telemark, The (1965) C-131m. **½ D: Anthony Mann. Kirk Douglas, Richard Harris, Michael Redgrave, Mervyn Johns, Eric Porter. Douglas and Harris spend more time battling each other than the Nazis overriding Norway in this pictorially gorgeous, predictable blow-up-the-German-factory yarn.

Hero's Island (1962) C-94m. **½ D: Leslie Stevens. James Mason, Kate Manx, Neville Brand, Rip Torn, Warren Oates, Brendan Dillon. Peculiar mixture of adventure and soap opera set on 18th-century island near North Carolina, involving pirates and homesteaders.

Hers to Hold (1943) 94m. ** D: Frank Ryan. Deanna Durbin, Joseph Cotten, Charles Winninger, Nella Walker, Gus Schilling, Ludwig Stossel, Irving Bacon. Grown-up Durbin is in love with serviceman Cotten in undistinguished romance, brightened by Deanna's singing. Songs: "Begin The Beguine," etc.

He's a Cockeyed Wonder (1950) 77m. *½ D: Peter Godfrey. Mickey Rooney, Terry Moore, William Demarest, Ross Ford, Mike Mazurki. Bland Rooney film has him as energetic young man who captures a gang of robbers and gets to marry his boss' daughter.

Hey Boy! Hey Girl! (1959) 81m. *½
D: David Lowell Rich. Louis Prima, Keely Smith, James Gregory, Henry Slate, Asa Maynor, Sam Butera and the Witnesses. Low-budget film helped only by music of Prima, Keely Smith, and their musicians.

Hey, Let's Twist! (1961) 80m. Bomb D: Greg Garrison. Joey Dee, The Starliters, Peppermint Loungers, Jo Ann Campbell. Let's not. This minor film came out at the height of the Twist dance rage and wasn't very good then . . . now it's just a bad way to kill 80 minutes.

Hey, Rookie (1944) 77m. **½ D: Charles Barton. Larry Parks, Ann Miller, Condos Brothers, Joe Sawyer, Jack Gilford, Selmer Jackson. Typical let's-put-on-a-show-for-the-servicemen, allowing for Miller's versatility to shine through.

Hey There It's Yogi Bear (1964) C-89m. ** D: William Hanna, Joseph Barbera. Voices of: Mel Blanc, J. Pat O'Malley, Julie Bennett, Daws Butler, Don Messick. First full-length cartoon from Hanna-Barbera studio stars Yogi Bear in amusing musical tale for younger folk.

Hi Diddle Diddle (1943) 72m. **½ D: Andrew L. Stone. Adolphe Menjou, Martha Scott, Pola Negri, Dennis O'Keefe, Billie Burke, June Havoc, Walter Kingsford. OK screwball comedy of young lovers and wacky con-artist parents, notable for appearance of silent-screen vamp Negri.

Hi, Nellie (1934) 75m. **½ D: Mervyn LeRoy. Paul Muni, Glenda Farrell, Berton Churchill, Donald Meek, Marjorie Gateson. Minor but enjoyable Muni as ex-editor who now writes advice to lovelorn, gets involved in citywide racket as well.

Hiawatha (1952) C-80m. *½ D: Kurt Neumann. Vincent Edwards, Keith Larsen, Michael Tolan, Yvette Dugay. Juvenile low-budget version of the Longfellow classic.

Hidden Eye, The (1945) 69m. **½ D: Richard Whorf. Edward Arnold, Frances Rafferty, Ray Collins, Paul Langton, Raymond Largay, William Phillips. Follow-up to EYES IN THE NIGHT, with blind detective Arnold making good use of other senses to solve murder mystery; fast-moving, entertaining mystery.

Hidden Fear (1957) 83m. *½ D: Andre de Toth. John Payne, Alexander

Knox, Conrad Nagel, Natalie Norwick. On-location filming in Copenhagen is chief virtue of mild huntdown-the-murderer plot.

Hidden Homicide (1959-British) 70m. *½ D: Tony Young. Griffith Jones, James Kenney, Patricia Laffan, Bruce Seton, Charles Farrell. Circumstantial evidence makes writer think he's a murderer.

Hidden Room, The (1949-British) 98m. *** D: Edward Dmytryk. Robert Newton, Sally Gray, Naunton Wayne, Phil Brown, Michael Balfour, Olga Lindo. Very effective suspenser involving Newton's plan to eliminate a man threatening his marriage; nifty climax. Retitled: OBSESSION.

Hideout, The (1961-French, dubbed) 80m. **½ D: Raoul Andre. Marcel Mouloudji, Yves Vincent, Francis Blanche, Louise Garletti. Diverting account of Mouloudji seeking refuge in an insane asylum during WW2, kept there as a patient.

High and Dry (1951-British) 93m. **½ D: Alexander Mackendrick. Paul Douglas, Alex Mackenzie, James Copeland, Abe Barker. Satisfactory, minor yarn about U.S. financier Douglas in conflict with the captain of broken-down ship carrying valuable cargo; static at times. Retitled: THE MAGGIE.

High and Low (1962-Japanese, dubbed) 142m. *** D: Akira Kurosawa. Toshiro Mifune, Kyoko Kagawa. Carefully paced study of Mifune, business executive who is financially ruined when he nobly pays ransom money to kidnappers who mistakenly stole his chauffeur's son.

High and the Mighty, The (1954) C-147m. *** D: William Wellman. John Wayne, Claire Trevor, Laraine Day, Robert Stack, Jan Sterling, Phil Harris. Grand Hotel takes wings in lengthy movie of disabled airplane and passengers who meditate about their lives. Big John whistles title tune.

High Barbaree (1947) 91m. *½ D: Jack Conway. Van Johnson, June Allyson, Thomas Mitchell, Marilyn Maxwell, Cameron Mitchell. Navy flier's life story told in flashback as he awaits rescue in plane in ocean. Good cast in inferior story.

High Flight (1958-British) 89m. *½ D: John Gilling. Ray Milland, Bernard Lee, Kenneth Haigh, Anthony Newley. Stale British drama of recruits in training for the RAF—not as good as I WANTED WINGS. Last reel, in the air, only exciting scene.

High Fury (1948) 71m. ** D: Harold French. Madeleine Carroll, Ian Hunter, Michael Rennie, Anne Marie Blanc. Standard film of couple quarreling over adopting war orphan. Nice locations in Switzerland.

High Hell (1958) 87m. **½ D: Burt Balaban. John Derek, Elaine Stewart, Rodney Burke, Patrick Allen. Mine owner's wife has an affair with husband's partner; trio snowbound for winter fight about it.

High Lonesome (1950) 81m. ** D: Alan LeMay. John Barrymore, Jr., Chill Wills, Lois Butler, Jack Elam. Moody little drama set in the West with Barrymore a brooding youth involved with killers.

High Noon (1952) 85m. **** D: Fred Zinnemann. Gary Cooper, Grace Kelly, Lloyd Bridges, Thomas Mitchell, Katy Jurado, Otto Kruger, Lon Chaney. Retiring sheriff Cooper feels responsibility to ungrateful town when challenged by gunfighter. Oscar-winning Western with Dimitri Tiomkin theme, memorable cameos by character actors. Cooper awarded Oscar for his role.

High School Confidential! (1958) 85m. *½ D: Jack Arnold. Russ Tamblyn, Jan Sterling, John Drew Barrymore, Mamie Van Doren. Amateurish mishmash involving young undercover agent infiltrating school dope-pushing gang to get evidence. Retitled: YOUNG HELLIONS.

High Sierra (1941) 100m. *** D: Raoul Walsh. Humphrey Bogart, Ida Lupino, Alan Curtis, Arthur Kennedy, Joan Leslie, Henry Hull, Henry Travers, Cornel Wilde. Bogie is Mad Dog Earle, killer with a soft heart on the lam from police, in rousing gangster caper. Lupino as the moll and Leslie as the lame innocent Bogart befriends offer interesting contrast. Not always convincing. Remade as I DIED A THOUSAND TIMES.

High Society (1956) C-107m. *** D: Charles Walters. Bing Crosby, Grace Kelly, Frank Sinatra, Celeste Holm, Louis Calhern, Louis Armstrong. Fluffy remake of PHILADELPHIA STORY is enjoyable, but has lost all the bite of the original. Kelly is about to marry John Lund when ex-hubby Crosby arrives, along with reporters Sinatra and Holm. Cole Porter songs include "True Love," "Did You Evah?" "You're Sensational."

High Society (1955) 61m. D: William Beaudine. Leo Gorcey, Huntz Hall, Bernard Gorcey, Amanda Blake, David Condon, Addison Richards, Paul Harvey, Bennie Bartlett. See: Bowery Boys series.

High Terrace (1956-British) 77m. ** D: Henry Cass. Dale Robertson, Lois Maxwell, Derek Bond, Eric Pohlmann. Fledgling actress is implicated in murder in minor drama.

High Tide (1947) 72m. **½ D: John Reinhardt. Lee Tracy, Don Castle, Julie Bishop, Regis Toomey, Anabel Shaw, Francis Ford. Low-budget gets lots of good mileage from players convincingly relating story of racketeers running small town.

High Time (1960) C-130m. **½ D: Blake Edwards. Bing Crosby, Fabian, Tuesday Weld, Nicole Maurey. Middling Crosby vehicle has Bing a widower resuming college career and trying to be one of the boys; forced comedy.

High Treason (1952-British) 93m. **½ D: Roy Boulting. Andre Morell, Liam Redmond, Mary Morris. Well-handled drama involving complex caper to instigate chaos in English industrial life via high-explosive bomb.

High Wall (1947) 99m. *** D: Curtis Bernhardt. Robert Taylor, Audrey Totter, Herbert Marshall, Dorothy Patrick, H. B. Warner, Warner Anderson. Well-paced mystery of former air force bomber pilot who attempts to establish innocence in murder case by working with psychiatrist.

High, Wide, and Handsome (1937) 112m. **½ D: Rouben Mamoulian. Irene Dunne, Randolph Scott, Dorothy Lamour, Elizabeth Patterson, Charles Bickford, Raymond Walburn, Alan Hale, Akim Tamiroff, William Frawley. Jerome Kern-Oscar Hammerstein old-time musical of determined Scott drilling for oil in 19th-century Pennsylvania, fighting corrupt Hale. Corny plot put over by energetic cast; result is entertaining. Songs include "The Folks Who Live On The Hill."

High Wind in Jamaica, A (1965-British) C-104m. *** D: Alexander Mackendrick. Anthony Quinn, James Coburn, Dennis Price, Gert Frobe, Lila Kedrova, Nigel Davenport, Kenneth J. Warren. Excellent cast and intelligent script about group of children who reveal their basic natures when left adrift aboard a pirate vessel.

Higher and Higher (1943) 90m. *** D: Tim Whelan. Michele Morgan, Jack Haley, Frank Sinatra, Leon Errol, Marcy McGuire, Victor Borge, Mary Wickes, Mel Torme. Sprightly musical of penniless Errol joining forces with servants to raise money; Sinatra's first lead role is good showcase for him.

Highly Dangerous (1951-British) 88m. **½ D: Roy Baker. Dane Clark, Marius Goring, Margaret Lockwood, Wilfrid Hyde-White, Olaf Pooley, Eric Pohlmann. Clark is American reporter accompanying scientist (Lockwood) on secret mission; well paced.

Highway Dragnet (1954) 71m. ** D: Nathan Juran. Richard Conte, Joan Bennett, Wanda Hendrix, Reed Hadley, Mary Beth Hughes. Tawdry caper of Conte trying to prove his innocence of a murder rap.

Highway 301 (1950) 83m. ** D: Andrew L. Stone. Steve Cochran, Virginia Grey, Robert Webber, Richard Egan. Good little gangster film relating robbery capers in straightforward manner.

Highway to Battle (1960-British) 71m. ** D: Ernest Morris. Gerard Heinz, Margaret Tyzack, Peter Reynolds, Richard Shaw. Trim little film set in 1935 England involving Nazi diplomats who try to defect, chased by Gestapo agents.

Highwayman, The (1951) C-82m. **½ D: Lesley Selander. Charles Coburn, Wanda Hendrix, Philip Friend, Cecil Kellaway, Victor Jory. Filmization of famous poem, involving innkeeper's daughter in love with nobleman who masquerades as bandit to help the oppressed; set in 1760's England.

Hilda Crane (1956) C-87m. **½ D: Philip Dunne. Jean Simmons, Guy Madison, Jean-Pierre Aumont, Judith Evelyn, Evelyn Varden. Florid melodrama of Simmons, two-time divorcee, who returns home to learn what life means.

Hill, The (1965) 122m. *** D: Sidney Lumet. Sean Connery, Harry Andrews, Ian Bannen, Ossie Davis, Michael Redgrave, Alfred Lynch, Roy Kinnear. Powerful drama of military prison camp, with fine performances by all. One problem: British actors bark at each other and much dialogue is unintelligible to American ears. Good luck.

Hill 24 Doesn't Answer (1955-Israeli) 100m. *** D: Thorold Dickinson. Edward Mulhare, Haya Harareet, Michael Wagner, Arieh Lavi. Events in the life of various participants in the Israeli-Arab War of 1948.

Hills of Home (1948) C-97m. *** D: Fred M. Wilcox. Edmund Gwenn, Donald Crisp, Tom Drake, Janet Leigh. Gwenn stars in Lassie movie about doctor convincing Scottish father to urge son to study medicine.

Hippodrome (1961-German, dubbed) C-96m. **½ D: Herbert Gruber. Gerhard Reidmann, Margit Nunke, Willy Birgel, Mady Rahl, Walter Giller. Atmospheric circus mystery yarn, integrating varied circus acts with tale of murder and lust under big top.

Hired Gun, The (1957) 63m. **½ D: Ray Nazarro. Rory Calhoun, Anne Francis, Vince Edwards, John Litel, Chuck Connors. Francis is fetching as condemned killer Calhoun determines to prove innocent.

Hired Wife (1940) 93m. *** D: William A. Seiter. Rosalind Russell, Brian Aherne, Virginia Bruce, Robert Benchley, John Carroll. Secretary Russell marries boss Aherne for business reasons; then the fun begins. Hilarious trifle with cast of comedy experts.

Hiroshima, Mon Amour (1960-French, dubbed) 88m. ***½ D: Alain Resnais. Emmanuele Riva, Eiji Okada, Stella Dassas, Pierre Barband. Thoughtful study of French movie actress and Japanese architect whose sensual love affair in 1950 Hiroshima evokes strange memories of the past and thoughts of the future.

His Brother's Wife (1936) 90m. ** D: W. S. Van Dyke, II. Barbara Stanwyck, Robert Taylor, Jean Hersholt, Joseph Calleia, John Eldredge, Samuel S. Hinds. Glossy soaper of dedicated scientist Taylor scorning Stanwyck, who marries his brother Eldredge for spite.

His Butler's Sister (1943) 94m. **½ D: Frank Borzage. Deanna Durbin, Pat O'Brien, Franchot Tone, Evelyn Ankers, Else Janssen, Walter Catlett, Iris Adrian, Akim Tamiroff, Alan Mowbray. Entertaining romantic comedy of maid Durbin in love with boss Tone; musical scenes not too exciting, but film is spry.

His Girl Friday (1940) 92m. **** D: Howard Hawks. Cary Grant, Rosalind Russell, Ralph Bellamy, Gene Lockhart, Porter Hall, Roscoe Karns, John Qualen, Frank Jenks, Billy Gilbert. Frantic comedy remake of THE FRONT PAGE with Grant as conniving editor, Russell as star reporter, Bellamy as hayseed she's trying to marry amid hot murder story. Terrific character actors add sparkle to this must-see comedy.

His Kind of Woman (1951) 120m. **½ D: John Farrow. Robert Mitchum, Jane Russell, Vincent Price, Tim Holt. Coy little film involving deported racketeer trying to sneak back into U.S., and Mitchum, who helps prevent it.

His Majesty O'Keefe (1953) C-92m. **½ D: Byron Haskin. Burt Lancaster, Joan Rice, Benson Fong, Philip Ahn, Grant Taylor. Another athletic Lancaster buccaneer romp, set in the South Seas.

His Woman (1931) 80m. ** D: Edward Sloman. Gary Cooper, Claudette Colbert, Douglass Dumbrille, Harry Davenport. Stiff, early-talkie romance between skipper Cooper and passenger, nurse Colbert.

History Is Made at Night (1937) 97m. ***½ D: Frank Borzage. Charles Boyer, Jean Arthur, Leo Carrillo, Colin Clive, Andre St. Maur. Excellent tragicomedy of despicable husband Clive divorcing Arthur, who falls for suave Boyer.

History of Mr. Polly, The (1949-British) 96m. *** D: Anthony Pelissier. John Mills, Sally Ann Howes, Finlay Currie, Megs Jenkins, Diana Churchill. H. G. Wells' yarn of romantic idler who goes on a bicycle tour, hoping to find new values in life; admirably acted.

Hit and Run (1957) 84m. Bomb D: Hugo Haas. Hugo Haas, Cleo Moore, Vince Edwards. Trash involving

Haas' efforts to rid himself of wife's young boyfriend.

Hit the Ice (1943) 82m. ** D: Charles Lamont. Bud Abbott, Lou Costello, Ginny Simms, Patric Knowles, Elyse Knox, Sheldon Leonard, Marc Lawrence, Joseph Sawyer. Bud and Lou are newspaper photographers involved with gang of thugs in zany comedy with good gags on skating rink.

Hitch-Hiker, The (1953) 71m. *** D: Ida Lupino. Edmond O'Brien, Frank Lovejoy, William Talman, Jose Torvay. Tense account of two vacationing businessmen held captive by a psychopath.

Hitler (1962) 107m. **1/2 D: Stuart Heisler. Richard Basehart, Cordula Trantow, Maria Emo, Martin Kosleck, John Banner, Carl Esmond. Basehart gives a cerebral interpretation to the career of the leader of the Third Reich.

Hitler—Dead or Alive (1943) 70m. ** D: Nick Grinde. Ward Bond, Dorothy Tree, Warren Hymer, Paul Fix, Russell Hicks, Felix Basch, Bobs Watson. Low-budget epic of con-men shooting for high stakes by attempting to kill the Fuehrer.

Hitler Gang, The (1944) 101m. **1/2 D: John Farrow. Robert Watson, Martin Kosleck, Victor Varconi, Luis Van Rooten, Sig Ruman, Tonio Selwart, Ludwig Donath. Historical drama of Hitler's rise to power had greatest impact on WW2 audiences but is still fairly interesting, though dwarfed by recent documentaries.

Hitler's Children (1943) 83m. *** D: Edward Dmytryk. Irving Reis, Tim Holt, Bonita Granville, Kent Smith, Otto Kruger, H. B. Warner, Lloyd Corrigan. Engrossing exploitation film of young people forced to live life of horror in Nazi Germany.

Hitler's Madman (1943) 84m. **1/2 D: Douglas Sirk. Patricia Morison, John Carradine, Alan Curtis, Ralph Morgan, Howard Freeman, Ludwig Stossel, Edgar Kennedy. Exciting saga based on true story of small Czech village destroyed by Nazis, and commander Heydrich, assassinated by determined Czechs. Look for Ava Gardner in a small part.

Hitting a New High (1937) 60m. **1/2 D: Raoul Walsh. Lily Pons, Jack Oakie, Edward Everett Horton, Lucille Ball, Eric Blore, Eduardo Ciannelli. Title refers to Pons' voice, not the film per se; fluffy musical romance relies on supporting cast for entertainment.

Hobson's Choice (1954-British) 107m. *** D: David Lean. Charles Laughton, John Mills, Brenda De Banzie, Daphne Anderson. Laughton is delightful as bootshop owner in the 1890's who has decided whom his two daughters will marry despite their complaints.

Hold Back the Dawn (1941) 115m. ***1/2 D: Mitchell Leisen. Charles Boyer, Olivia de Havilland, Paulette Goddard, Victor Francen, Walter Abel, Rosemary DeCamp. First-rate soaper with Billy Wilder-Charles Brackett script of gigolo Boyer marrying spinsterish Olivia to get into U.S.

Hold Back the Night (1956) 80m. **1/2 D: Allan Dwan. John Payne, Mona Freeman, Peter Graves, Chuck Connors. Korean War officer Payne recounts facts about bottle of liquor he always has with him.

Hold Back Tomorrow (1955) 75m. *1/2 D: Hugo Haas. Cleo Moore, John Agar, Frank de Kova, Harry Guardino, Jan Englund. Strange B-film concerning condemned murderer who marries a girl on the night before his execution.

Hold On! (1966) C-85m. **1/2 D: Arthur Lubin. Peter Noone, Herman's Hermits, Sue Anne Langdon, Karl Green, Shelley Fabares. U.S. tour by rock 'n' roll group is thin plot on which to hinge a display of Herman's Hermits musical talents, with pretty girls thrown into story for diversion.

Hold That Baby (1949) 64m. D: Reginald Le Borg. Leo Gorcey, Huntz Hall, Gabriel Dell, Frankie Darro, Billy Benedict, John Kellog, Anabel Shaw, Bernard Gorcey. SEE: **Bowery Boys** series.

Hold That Blonde (1945) 76m. ** D: George Marshall. Eddie Bracken, Veronica Lake, Albert Dekker, Frank Fenton, George Zucco, Donald MacBride. OK comedy, sometimes strained, of kleptomaniac Bracken tangling with sultry thief Lake.

Hold That Co-ed (1938) 80m. *** D: George Marshall. John Barrymore, George Murphy, Marjorie Weaver, Joan Davis, Jack Haley, George Barbier. Good musicomedy supercharged by Barrymore as windy politician; he makes the whole film.

Hold That Ghost (1941) 86m. *** D: Arthur Lubin. Bud Abbott, Lou Costello, Richard Carlson, Joan Davis, Mischa Auer, Evelyn Ankers. Prime A&C, with the boys loose in haunted house. Fine cast includes hilarious Davis as professional radio screamer.

Hold That Hypnotist (1957) 61m. D: Austin Jewell. Huntz Hall, Stanley Clements, Jane Nigh, David Condon. SEE: Bowery Boys series.

Hold That Line (1952) 64m D: William Beaudine. Leo Gorcey, Huntz Hall, John Bromfield, Veda Ann Borg, Pierre Watkin. SEE: Bowery Boys series.

Hold Your Man (1933) 89m. *** D: Sam Wood. Jean Harlow, Clark Gable, Stuart Erwin, Elizabeth Patterson, Blanche Frederici. Gable and Harlow are flawless lovers in this delightful comedy-drama; the two stars really sparkle here.

Hole in the Head, A (1959) C-120m. ** D: Frank Capra. Frank Sinatra, Edward G. Robinson, Eleanor Parker, Carolyn Jones, Thelma Ritter, Eddie Hodges, Keenan Wynn, Joi Lansing. Sticky story of Sinatra and his son (Hodges) doesn't seem sincere. Only distinction is Oscar-winning song, "High Hopes."

Holiday (1938) 93m. ***½ D: George Cukor. Katharine Hepburn, Cary Grant, Doris Nolan, Lew Ayres, Edward Everett Horton, Binnie Barnes, Henry Daniell. Fine, literate filming of Philip Barry's play about nonconformist Grant confronting stuffy N.Y.C. society family, finding his match in Hepburn. A delight.

Holiday Affair (1949) 87m. *** D: Don Hartman. Robert Mitchum, Janet Leigh, Wendell Corey, Gordon Gebert. Well-done Christmas season story about widow Leigh, her small son, and two contrasting men courting her.

Holiday Camp (1948-British) 97m. **½ D: Ken Annakin. Dennis Price, Flora Robson, Jack Warner. Pleasantly handled account of life and love at British summer resort; atmospheric, with good characterizations.

Holiday for Lovers (1959) C-103m. **½ D: Henry Levin. Clifton Webb, Jane Wyman, Jill St. John, Carol Lynley, Paul Henreid, Gary Crosby, Jose Greco. Arch Dr. Webb and Wyman escort attractive daughters on South American vacation, with predictable mating.

Holiday for Sinners (1952) 72m. **½ D: Gerald Mayer. Gig Young, Janice Rule, Keenan Wynn, William Campbell. Strange goings-on at Mardi Gras as several people try to forget their troublesome lives and have a good time.

Holiday in Mexico (1946) C-127m. *** D: George Sidney. Walter Pidgeon, Ilona Massey, Roddy McDowall, Jose Iturbi, Xavier Cugat, Jane Powell. Engaging, well cast musical comedy of daughter of ambassador falling for noted musician.

Holiday Inn (1942) 101m. *** D: Mark Sandrich. Bing Crosby, Fred Astaire, Marjorie Reynolds, Virginia Dale, Walter Abel, Louise Beavers. Perky musical with great Irving Berlin songs. Bing introduces "White Christmas," Fred dances . . . who needs much of a plot? Better than partial remake, WHITE CHRISTMAS.

Hollow Triumph (1948) 83m. *** D: Steve Sekely. Paul Henreid, Joan Bennett, Eduard Franz, Leslie Brooks. Tense melodrama of killer assuming identity of lookalike doctor. Retitled: THE SCAR.

Holly and the Ivy, The (1953-British) 80m. *** D: George More O'Ferrall. Ralph Richardson, Celia Johnson, Margaret Leighton, Denholm Elliott, Hugh Williams, Roland Culver. Straightforward adaptation of Wynyard Browne play revolving around Christmas holiday with Richardson, the smalltown cleric learning about his three grown-up children; nicely acted.

Hollywood Canteen (1944) 124m. **½ D: Delmer Daves. Joan Crawford, Bette Davis, John Garfield, Sydney Greenstreet, Peter Lorre, Ida Lupino, Eleanor Parker, Alexis Smith, Barbara Stanwyck, S. Z. Sakall, Joan Leslie, Andrews Sisters, Jack Benny, Eddie Cantor, Jack Carson, Faye Emerson, Irene Manning, Janis Paige. A bevy of Warner Bros. stars make token appearances in this all-star movie, which offers some fun. Loosely hinged tale of GI wanting to date Leslie; Davis, who founded the Canteen, explains its function.

Hollywood Cavalcade (1939) C-96m.

*** D: Irving Cummings. Alice Faye, Don Ameche, Al Jolson, Mack Sennett, Stuart Erwin, Buster Keaton, Mary Forbes, Chester Conklin, Rin-Tin-Tin, Jr. First half a delight, with Don bringing Alice to Hollywood in silent days with flavorful recreation of old-time comedies; remainder of film bogs down in phony dramatics.

Hollywood Hotel (1937) 109m. **½ D: Busby Berkeley. Dick Powell, Rosemary and Lola Lane, Hugh Herbert, Glenda Farrell, Johnnie Davis, Louella Parsons, Frances Langford, Fritz Feld, Allyn Joslyn, Alan Mowbray. Title sums it up, with plenty of guests, music, and songs like "I'm Like a Fish Out of Water" and "Hooray for Hollywood."

Hollywood or Bust (1956) C-95m. **½ D: Frank Tashlin. Dean Martin, Jerry Lewis, Anita Ekberg, Pat Crowley. Star-struck Lewis teams up with gambler Martin on trek to crash the movie capital; typical comedy by the frantic team.

Hollywood Story (1951) 77m. **½ D: William Castle. Richard Conte, Julia Adams, Richard Egan, Henry Hull. Trying to solve an old murder, producer makes a picture on the subject, hoping to uncover culprit.

Holy Matrimony (1943) 87m. *** D: John M. Stahl. Monty Woolley, Gracie Fields, Laird Cregar, Una O'Connor, Alan Mowbray, Melville Cooper, Franklin Pangborn. Delightful tale of artist Woolley assuming late butler's identity to avoid publicity, finding many complications.

Hombre (1967) C-111m. *** D: Martin Ritt. Paul Newman, Fredric March, Richard Boone, Diane Cilento, Cameron Mitchell, Barbara Rush, Martin Balsam. Interesting story of Indian-raised Newman trying to survive in white man's world in Arizona circa 1880. Encounters with various characters on a stagecoach provide basis for film's action and drama; well acted, entertaining.

Home at Seven (1953-British) 85m. *** D: Vincente Minnelli. Robert Richardson, Margaret Leighton, Jack Hawkins, Campbell Singer. Taut thriller involving bank clerk who can't account for a day in his life when a murder and a bank robbery occurred. Retitled: MURDER ON MONDAY.

Home Before Dark (1958) 136m. *** D: Mervyn LeRoy. Jean Simmons, Dan O'Herlihy, Rhonda Fleming, Efrem Zimbalist, Jr. Shiny but poignant telling of Simmons readjustment to life after nervous breakdown; on-location shooting in Massachusetts.

Home from the Hill (1960) C-150m. *** D: Vincente Minnelli. Robert Mitchum, Eleanor Parker, George Peppard, George Hamilton. Despite MGM sheen, film glows with fine performances in turgid study of Southern landowner and his relationship with wife, son, and illegitimate offspring.

Home In Indiana (1944) C-103m. *** D: Henry Hathaway. Walter Brennan, Jeanne Crain, June Haver, Charlotte Greenwood, Lon McCallister, Ward Bond, Willie Best, George Cleveland. Typical horseracing saga gets a good rehashing here with colorful production and sincere performances; climactic race is well-handled.

Home Is the Hero (1959-Irish) 83m. **½ D: Fielder Cook. Walter Macken, Eileen Crowe, Arthur Kennedy, Joan O'Hara. Modest yarn with Abbey Theatre group, telling story of excon (Macken) trying to pick up pieces of home-life.

Home of the Brave (1949) 85m. *** D: Mark Robson. James Edwards, Douglas Dick, Steve Brodie, Jeff Corey, Lloyd Bridges. More daring when made than now, but still hard-hitting WW2 account of Negro soldier who suffers more abuse from fellow-GI's than from missions against the enemy. From Arthur Laurents' play.

Home, Sweet Homicide (1946) 90m. ** D: Lloyd Bacon. Peggy Ann Garner, Randolph Scott, Lynn Bari, Dean Stockwell. Nothing-special comedy-mystery, as children of mystery writer solve local murder and find husband for their mother.

Homecoming (1948) 113m. ** D: Mervyn LeRoy. Clark Gable, Lana Turner, Anne Baxter, John Hodiak, Ray Collins, Cameron Mitchell. Gable and Turner have exciting WW2 romance in the trenches, but that can't support 113 minutes of dreary drama; one of Gable's lesser efforts.

Homestretch, The (1947) C-96m ** D: H. Bruce Humberstone. Cornel Wilde, Maureen O'Hara, Glenn Langan, Helen Walker, James Gleason. Harmless film of romance between young girl and horse-owner suffers from uneven acting and script.

Homicidal (1961) 87m. ****½** D: William Castle. Glenn Corbett, Patricia Breslin, Jean Arless, Eugenie Leontovich. Film almost makes it as genuine shocker, filled with terrifying occurences; set in spooky old house.

Hondo (1953) C-84m. ******* D: John Farrow. John Wayne, Geraldine Page, Ward Bond, James Arness, Lee Aaker. Well-done Western, with Wayne the army soldier who comes across a widow and her son living in a farmhouse in a deserted area of southwest Texas, unalarmed about pending Indian uprising. Page won an Oscar nomination.

Honeychile (1951) C-90m. ***½** D: R. G. Springsteen. Judy Canova, Eddie Foy, Jr., Alan Hale, Jr., Walter Catlett. Cornball stuff involving Canova in the music-publishing business.

Honeymoon (1947) 74m. ****** D: William Keighley. Shirley Temple, Franchot Tone, Guy Madison, Lina Romay, Gene Lockhart, Grant Mitchell. Unmemorable mixture of romance and comedy in story of GI who longs for fiancée in Mexico during three-day pass. Good cast fails to make film click.

Honeymoon (1959-Spanish, dubbed) 90m. ****** D: Michael Powell. Anthony Steel, Ludmilla Tcherina, Antonio, Rosita Segovia. Muddled romancer intertwined with ballet sequences. Steel on wedding trip with Tcherina, encounters Antonio who tries to court the ex-ballerina. Excerpts from ballets LOS AMANTES DE TERUEL and EL AMOR BRUJO.

Honeymoon Ahead (1945) 60m. ****** D: Reginald Le Borg. Allan Jones, Raymond Walburn, Grace McDonald, Vivian Austin. Nonsensical musical trivia involving kindly prisoner (head of convicts' choir) and his involvement with the world outside the big walls.

Honeymoon for Three (1941) 77m. ****½** D: Lloyd Bacon. Ann Sheridan, George Brent, Charlie Ruggles, Osa Massen, Walter Catlett, Jane Wyman. Breezy comedy of novelist Brent warding off female admirers by pretending to be married; Sheridan is his witty, amorous secretary.

Honeymoon Hotel (1964) C-89m. ***½** D: Henry Levin. Robert Goulet, Jill St. John, Nancy Kwan, Robert Morse, Elsa Lanchester, Keenan Wynn. Asinine shenanigans with bachelors Goulet and Morse arriving at resort for newlyweds. Lanchester is fun despite all.

Honeymoon in Bali (1939) 95m. ******* D: Edward H. Griffith. Fred MacMurray, Madeleine Carroll, Allan Jones, Osa Massen, Helen Broderick, Akim Tamiroff. Funny romantic boy-chases-girl film, with MacMurray after beautiful Carroll with interference from aristocratic Jones.

Honeymoon Machine, The (1961) C-87m. ****½** D: Richard Thorpe. Steve McQueen, Jim Hutton, Paula Prentiss, Brigid Bazlen, Dean Jagger, Jack Weston. Pleasant comedy with a spirited cast about two sailors who find a way to beat the roulette table in Monte Carlo. Easy to take, easy to forget.

Hong Kong (1951) C-92m. ****** D: Lewis R. Foster. Ronald Reagan, Rhonda Fleming, Nigel Bruce, Marvin Miller. Mediocre account of Reagan trying to heist a valuable antique from orphaned girl but going straight before finale. Strictly back-lot Hong Kong.

Hong Kong Affair (1958) 79m. ***½** D: Paul F. Heard. Jack Kelly, May Wynn, Richard Loo, Lo Lita Shek. Kelly is the Yank who comes to the Orient to investigate his property holdings, getting more than he bargained for.

Hong Kong Confidential (1958) 67m. ****½** D: Edward L. Cahn. Gene Barry, Beverly Tyler, Allison Hayes, Noel Drayton. Harmless B-film about Anglo-American agents rescuing a kidnapped Arabian prince.

Honky Tonk (1941) 105m. ****½** D: Jack Conway. Clark Gable, Lana Turner, Frank Morgan, Claire Trevor, Marjorie Main, Albert Dekker, Chill Wills. Good gal Lana loves gambler Gable in romantic Western that's fun for a spell, then drags into talky marathon. Morgan and Wills offer fine character performances.

Honolulu (1939) 83m. ****½** D: Edward Buzzell. Eleanor Powell, Robert Young, George Burns, Gracie Allen, Rita Johnson, Willie Fung, Sig Ruman, Ruth Hussey. Standard musical about mistaken identities.

Screen idol changes places with plantation owner.

Hoodlum, The (1951) 61m. ** D: Max Nosseck. Lawrence Tierney, Allene Roberts, Marjorie Riordan, Lisa Golm. Once a crook, always a crook is plot of this caper about ex-con planning bank robbery.

Hoodlum Empire (1952) 98m. **½ D: Joseph Kane. Brian Donlevy, Claire Trevor, Forrest Tucker, Vera Ralston, Luther Adler. Cast is sufficiently versed in format to make this exposé of a crime syndicate better than average.

Hoodlum Priest, The (1961) 101m. *** D: Irvin Kershner. Don Murray, Larry Gates, Keir Dullea, Logan Ramsey, Cindi Wood. Based on real-life clergyman who devoted himself to trying to help would-be criminals, focusing on Murray's efforts to rehabilitate delinquent Dullea; splendidly acted.

Hoodlum Saint, The (1946) 91m. **½ D: Norman Taurog. William Powell, Esther Williams, Angela Lansbury, James Gleason, Rags Ragland, Lewis Stone, Emma Dunn. Modest film benefits from good Powell performance as cynic who sees The Light.

Hook, The (1963) 98m. **½ D: George Seaton. Kirk Douglas, Robert Walker, Nick Adams, Nehemiah Persoff. Professional cast baited with age-old problem of war, the guilt associated with killing the enemy.

Horizons West (1952) C-81m. **½ D: Budd Boetticher. Robert Ryan, Julia Adams, Rock Hudson, Raymond Burr, James Arness. Standard Western of two brothers on the opposite sides of the law.

Horizontal Lieutenant, The (1962) C-90m. **½ D: Richard Thorpe. Jim Hutton, Paula Prentiss, Miyoshi Umeki, Jim Backus, Jack Carter, Marty Ingels, Charles McGraw. Artificial service comedy set on WW2 Pacific island involving army officer Hutton's capture of innocuous supply thief.

Horn Blows at Midnight, The (1945) 78m. **½ D: Raoul Walsh. Jack Benny, Alexis Smith, Dolores Moran, Allyn Joslyn, Reginald Gardiner, Guy Kibbee. Enjoyable fantasy of angel (Benny) sent to destroy earth with Gabriel's horn; Franklin Pangborn standout as flustered hotel detective. Not as bad as Benny pretends it is.

Horrible Dr. Hichcock, The (1962-Italian, dubbed) C-76m. **½ D: Robert Hampton. Robert Flemyng, Barbara Steele, Teresa Fitzgerald, Maria Teresa Vianello. Flavorful Gothic horror yarn, with Flemyng the deranged doctor trying to revive his long-dead first wife; Steele is hysterical second bride.

Horror Chamber of Dr. Faustus (1960-French, dubbed) 84m. ** D: Georges Franju. Pierre Brasseur, Alida Valli, Edith Scob. Gory chiller of demented physician seeking facial transplants for his disfigured daughter, with tragic results. Original title: EYES WITHOUT A FACE.

Horror Hotel (1963-British) 76m. **½ D: John Moxey. Dennis Lotis, Christopher Lee, Betta St. John, Patricia Jessel. Seventeenth-century witch burned at the stake maintains an inn to lure victims for blood sacrifice to the devil.

Horror of Dracula (1958-British) C-82m. *** D: Terence Fisher. Peter Cushing, Michael Gough, Melissa Stribling, Christopher Lee. Vivid retelling of the vampire classic, well handled.

Horrors of the Black Museum (1959-British) C-95m. **½ D: Arthur Crabtree. Michael Gough, June Cunningham, Graham Curnow, Shirley Ann Field, Geoffrey Keen. Gruesome sequences highlight chiller about writer who uses his hypnotized helper to commit a series of killings.

Horse Feathers (1932) 70m. ***½ D: Norman Z. McLeod. Groucho, Harpo, Chico and Zeppo Marx, Thelma Todd, Nat Pendleton. Groucho is head of Darwin College, building up football team to play rival Huxley U. in crazy Marx nonsense. The password is "swordfish."

Horse Soldiers, The (1959) C-119m. *** D: John Ford. John Wayne, William Holden, Constance Towers, Althea Gibson, Hoot Gibson, Anna Lee, Russell Simpson. Large-scale oater about Yankees' drive through the South to help speed Civil War victory. Typical Wayne actioner.

Horse's Mouth, The (1958-British) C-93m. ***½ D: Ronald Neame.

Alec Guinness, Kay Walsh, Renee Houston, Mike Morgan. Joyce Cary's wry novel is admirably handled, with Guinness as the eccentric painter living on the cuff, seeking oddball surfaces to use for his more ambitious paintings.

Hostages (1943) 88m. ** D: Frank Tuttle. Luise Rainer, William Bendix, Roland Varno, Oscar Homolka, Katina Paxinou, Paul Lukas. Routine tale of underground movement in WW2; Bendix outshines Rainer acting-wise.

Hot Blood (1956) C-85m. **½ D: Nicholas Ray. Jane Russell, Cornel Wilde, Luther Adler, Joseph Calleia. Strange film about gypsy Russell living by her beauty, meeting her match in gypsy Wilde.

Hot News (1953) 68m. *½ D: Edward Bernds. Stanley Clements, Gloria Henry, Ted de Corsia, Veda Ann Borg. Programmer tale of dedicated newspaperman cleaning up crime syndicate involved in sporting events.

Hot Rod Gang (1958) 72m. *½ D: Lew Landers. John Ashley, Gene Vincent, Jody Fair, Steve Drexel. Cheap little flick about hot-rod-happy youth with yearning to enter the big race, using his singing talents to get the cash.

Hot Rod Girl (1956) 75m. Bomb D: Leslie Martinson. Lori Nelson, Chuck Connors, John Smith, Frank Gorshin, Roxanne Arlen, Dabbs Greer. Tedious trash, with Nelson in title role as "hip" gal who helps crack down on city hot-car racing.

Hot Rod Rumble (1957) 79m. *½ D: Leslie Martinson. Brett Halsey, Richard Hartunian, Joey Forman, Leigh Snowden. Title tells all in this formula programmer of juvenile delinquents.

Hot Rods to Hell (1967) C-92m. **½ D: John Brahm. Dana Andrews, Jeanne Crain, Mimsy Farmer, Laurie Mock. Sluggish yarn of Andrews and family tormented by hot-rod-happy juvenile delinquents. Original title: 52 MILES TO MIDNIGHT.

Hot Shots (1956) 61m. D: Jean Yarbrough. Huntz Hall, Stanley Clements, Joi Lansing, Phil Phillips. SEE: Bowery Boys series.

Hot Spell (1958) 86m. *** D: Daniel Mann. Shirley Booth, Anthony Quinn, Shirley MacLaine, Earl Holliman. Booth makes soaper worthwhile; she's middle-aged housewife trying to conceal misery at husband Quinn's philandering while seeking to solve her children's problems.

Hot Summer Night (1957) 86m. **½ D: David Friedkin. Leslie Nielsen, Colleen Miller, Edward Andrews, Claude Akins, Paul Richards. Offbeat story about reporter seeking an interview with leader of robbery gang.

Hotel Berlin (1945) 98m. **½ D: Peter Godfrey. Helmut Dantine, Andrea King, Raymond Massey, Faye Emerson, Peter Lorre, Alan Hale. GRAND HOTEL author Baum tries again with sundry characters based in hotel during decline of Nazi Germany; good cast makes it generally interesting.

Hotel for Women (1939) 83m. ** D: Gregory Ratoff. Linda Darnell, Ann Sothern, Elsa Maxwell, Lynn Bari, Sidney Blackmer, Alan Dinehart. Weak film about group of man-hunting girls, noteworthy only as Darnell's film debut.

Hotel Imperial (1939) 67m. ** D: Robert Florey. Isa Miranda, Ray Milland, Reginald Owen, Gene Lockhart, Albert Dekker. Miranda encounters intrigue while searching for man responsible for her sister's death; fairly entertaining drama.

Hotel Paradiso (1966-British) C-96m. **½ D: Peter Glenville. Alec Guinness, Gina Lollobrigida, Robert Morley, Akim Tamiroff. Pretentious farce of manners is only fitfully amusing; meek Guinness tries to carry on his rendezvous with gorgeous neighbor Gina, but everything interferes.

Hotel Reserve (1944-British) 79m. *** D: Lance Comfort, Max Greene. James Mason, Lucie Mannheim, Herbert Lom, Patricia Medina, Anthony Shaw, David Ward. Suspenseful, moody film about visitor at French resort during WW2 accused of being Nazi spy, trying to prove innocence. Based on Eric Ambler novel.

Hotel Sahara (1951-British) 87m. ** D: Ken Annakin. Yvonne de Carlo, David Tomlinson, Peter Ustinov, Roland Culver. Adequate WW2 actioner dealing with a hotel situated in the back-and-forth contest between Allies-Axis.

Houdini (1953) C-106m. **½ D: George Marshall. Tony Curtis, Janet

Leigh, Torin Thatcher, Ian Wolfe, Sig Ruman. Fanciful biography of famed escape artist; more fiction than fact, perhaps better this way.

Hound of the Baskervilles, The (1939) 80m. D: Sidney Lanfield. Basil Rathbone, Nigel Bruce, Richard Greene, Wendy Barrie, Lionel Atwill, John Carradine, Beryl Mercer, Mary Gordon, E. E. Clive, Ralph Forbes, Ivan Simpson. SEE: Sherlock Holmes series.

Hound of the Baskervilles, The (1959-British) C-84m. *** D: Terence Fisher. Peter Cushing, Andrea Morell, Christopher Lee, Marla Landi, Miles Malleson, John LeMesurier. Sherlock Holmes mystery well produced with proper eerie atmosphere—excellent telling of the Conan Doyle novel.

Hour Before the Dawn, The (1944) 75m. ** D: Frank Tuttle. Franchot Tone, Veronica Lake, John Sutton, Binnie Barnes, Henry Stephenson, Mary Gordon, Nils Asther. Polished, empty WW2 romance-espionage, with Tone falling for Nazi spy Lake; unlikely casting doesn't help.

Hour of Decision (1955-British) 74m. ** D: Pennington Richards. Jeff Morrow, Hazel Court, Anthony Dawson, Lionel Jeffries, Carl Bernard, Robert Sansom. Morrow is newspaperman who tracks down murderer of fellow columnist, discovering his wife was involved with the man.

Hour of Glory SEE: Small Back Room.

Hour of 13, The (1952) 79m. **½ D: Harold French. Peter Lawford, Dawn Addams, Roland Culver, Colin Gordon. Mystery yarn set in 1890's London, with Lawford a ritzy thief who develops a heart of gold in order to do a good deed for society.

Hours of Love, The (1965-Italian, dubbed) 89m. **½ D: Luciano Salce. Ugo Tognazzi, Emmanuele Riva, Barbara Steele, Umberto D'Orsi, Mara Berni. Pleasant little sex farce proving the adage that illicit love is sweeter than blessed marriage.

House Across the Bay, The (1940) 72m. **½ D: Archie Mayo. George Raft, Joan Bennett, Lloyd Nolan, Gladys George, Walter Pidgeon, June Knight. Raft's out to get Pidgeon, who has taken wife Bennett from him while he's been in jail. Familiar but exciting film.

House Across the Street, The (1949) 69m. ** D: Richard Bare. Wayne Morris, Janis Paige, James Mitchell, Alan Hale, Bruce Bennett. Pleasant little comedy of newspaperman who hunts down murderer. Paige is peppery as always.

House by the River (1950) 88m. ** D: Fritz Lang. Louis Hayward, Jane Wyatt, Lee Bowman, Ann Shoemaker, Kathleen Freeman. Murky historical melodrama involving murder and romance; low-grade Lang.

House of Bamboo (1955) C-102m. **½ D: Samuel Fuller. Robert Ryan, Robert Stack, Shirley Yamaguchi, Cameron Mitchell, Sessue Hayakawa. Picturesque if not credible story of army officers and Japanese police tracking down a gang of former soldiers working for a well-organized syndicate.

House of Dracula (1945) 67m. ** D: Erle C. Kenton. Lon Chaney, John Carradine, Martha O'Driscoll, Lionel Atwill, Jane Adams, Onslow Stevens. Scientist Stevens treats Dracula, Wolfman, and Frankenstein; eventually turns into vampire. Good cast but script fluctuates.

House of Fear, The (1945) 69m. D: Roy William Neill. Basil Rathbone, Nigel Bruce, Dennis Hoey, Aubrey Mather, Paul Cavanagh, Holmes Herbert, Gavin Muir. SEE: Sherlock Holmes series.

House of Frankenstein (1945) 71m. **½ D: Erle C. Kenton. Boris Karloff, Lon Chaney, J. Carrol Naish, John Carradine, Anne Gwynne, Peter Coe, Lionel Atwill, George Zucco. Traveling freak show exhibitor sidelines as mad scientist seeking revenge from past enemies. Good cast makes script bearable.

House of Horrors (1946) 65m. ** D: Jean Yarbrough. Bill Goodwin, Robert Lowery, Virginia Grey, Rondo Hatton, Martin Kosleck. Slightly below average horror meller. Frustrated artist uses fiend The Creeper to knock off critics. Laughable script, adequate acting.

House of Intrigue, The (1959-Italian, dubbed) 94m. **½ D: Duilio Coletti, Curt Jurgens, Dawn Addams, Folco Lulli, Dario Michaelis, Philippe Hersent. WW2 espionage caper with pleasing on-location European backgrounds.

House of Mystery (1961-British) 56m. **½ D: Vernon Sewell. Jane Hylton, Peter Dyneley, Nanette Newman, Maurice Kaufman, John Merivale. Nifty little story of haunted house, with its new owners learning the mysterious history of the premises; supernatural played up well.

House of Numbers (1957) 92m. **½ D: Russell Rouse. Jack Palance, Barbara Lang, Harold J. Stone, Edward Platt. Palance plays dual role as man seeking to spring gangster brother from prison and take his place.

House of Ricordi (1956-Italian, dubbed) C-117m. ** D: Carmine Gallone. Paolo Stoppa, Roland Alexandre, Marta Toren, Roldano Lupi. Passable biography of well-known music-publishing house, set in the 18th century, with many musical interludes. Retitled: CASA RICORDI.

House of Rothschild (1934) 88m. *** D: Alfred L. Werker. George Arliss, Boris Karloff, Loretta Young, Robert Young, Florence Arliss, C. Aubrey Smith. Elaborate but stagy production. Famed financial family is chronicled, with Arliss as Nathan Rothschild at time of Napoleonic Wars, Loretta his daughter, R. Young her suitor, Karloff as civilized villain.

House of Strangers (1949) 101m. *** D: Joseph L. Mankiewicz. Edward G. Robinson, Susan Hayward, Richard Conte, Luther Adler. Dynamic drama of ruthless financier Robinson who uses his four sons to suit his own schemes. Unique plot-line has been utilized for many subsequent films in various disguises.

House of the Seven Gables, The (1940) 89m. *** D: Joe May. George Sanders, Margaret Lindsay, Vincent Price, Nan Gray, Alan Napier. Fine acting in adaptation of Hawthorne story of jealous brother sending sister's fiancée to prison; intriguing drama set in 17th-century New England.

House of the Seven Hawks, The (1959) 92m. **½ D: Richard Thorpe. Robert Taylor, Nicole Maurey, Linda Christian, Donald Wolfit, David Kossoff, Eric Pohlmann. Diverting account of skipper Taylor involved in shipboard murder and hunt for long-lost Nazi loot.

House of Wax (1953) C-88m. *** D: Andre de Toth. Vincent Price, Frank Lovejoy, Phyllis Kirk, Carolyn Jones, Philip Tonge, Paul Cavanagh. Price romps through this horror tale as a deranged museum owner who utilizes human bodies for his wax displays. Originally released in 3-D, it still throws jolts at viewer.

House of Women (1962) 85m. **½ D: Walter Doniger. Shirley Knight, Andrew Duggan, Constance Ford, Barbara Nichols, Margaret Hayes, Virginia Gregg. Trite rendition of conditions in a women's prison elevated by good cast and fast pacing

House on Haunted Hill (1958) 75m. ** D: William Castle. Vincent Price, Carol Ohmart, Richard Long, Alan Marshal, Elisha Cook, Jr. Updating of the old dark house theme isn't bad; Price as the spooky proprietor and the others his wary guests. Cook has a great closing line.

House on Marsh Road, The SEE: **Invisible Creature, The**

House on 92nd St., The (1945) 88m. *** D: Henry Hathaway. William Eythe, Lloyd Nolan, Signe Hasso, Gene Lockhart, Leo G. Carroll, Lydia St. Clair. Trend-setting documentary-style spy film of WW2 activity in N.Y.C., with realism the true star.

House on Telegraph Hill (1951) 93m. **½ D: Robert Wise. Richard Basehart, Valentina Cortesa, William Lundigan, Fay Baker. Good cast in intriguing tale of WW2 refugee assuming dead man's identity so that he can come to San Francisco where wealthy relatives reside.

Houseboat (1958) C-110m. *** D: Melville Shavelson. Cary Grant, Sophia Loren, Martha Hyer, Charles Herbert, Eduardo Ciannelli. Loren becomes Grant's housekeeper, taking his three kids in hand, with predictable romance occurring; still diverting comedy.

Housekeeper's Daughter, The (1939) 79m. ** D: Hal Roach. Joan Bennett, Victor Mature, Adolphe Menjou, William Gargan. Pleasant murder mystery enhanced by chic Bennett, who helps crack a homicide case.

Housewife (1934) 69m. ** D: Alfred E. Green. Bette Davis, George Brent,

Ann Dvorak, John Halliday, Ruth Donnelly. Little punch in story of struggling copywriter Brent deserting wife Dvorak for old-flame Davis (playing unsubtle vamp).

Houston Story, The (1956) 79m. **½ D: William Castle. Gene Barry, Barbara Hale, Edward Arnold, Paul Richards, Jeanne Cooper. Barry portrays greedy oil worker who plans to take over crime syndicate involved in stealing oil.

How Green Was My Valley (1941) 118m. **** D: John Ford. Walter Pidgeon, Maureen O'Hara, Donald Crisp, Anna Lee, Roddy McDowall, John Loder, Sara Allgood, Barry Fitzgerald. Warm drama of Welsh coal miners, centering on Crisp's large, close-knit family. Beautifully filmed, lovingly directed, winner of many Academy Awards.

How I Spent My Summer Vacation (1967) C-120m. ** D: William Hale. Robert Wagner, Peter Lawford, Walter Pidgeon, Jill St. John. Weird mixture of unreality and spy spoof don't mix well in this telefeature, with Wagner attempting to unravel the mysterious events surrounding Lawford's death, set in Europe.

How to Be Very, Very Popular (1955) C-89m. **½ D: Nunnally Johnson. Betty Grable, Robert Cummings, Charles Coburn, Sheree North, Fred Clark, Alice Pearce, Orson Bean. Grable and North on the lam hide in a college fraternity in this semi-remake of SHE LOVES ME NOT. Sheree does wild "Shake, Rattle and Roll" number, stealing Grable's spotlight.

How to Make a Monster (1958) C-74m. Bomb D: Herbert L. Strock. Robert Harris, Walter Reed, Gary Clarke, Paul Brinegar. Dismal chiller involving studio make-up artist who goes berserk and turns his creations into zombie killers.

How to Marry a Millionaire (1953) C-95m. *** D: Jean Negulesco. Marilyn Monroe, Betty Grable, Lauren Bacall, William Powell, Rory Calhoun, David Wayne, Fred Clark. Terrific ensemble work in dandy comedy of three man-hunting females pooling their resources to trap eligible bachelors.

How to Murder a Rich Uncle (1957-British) 80m. ** D: Nigel Patrick. Charles Coburn, Nigel Patrick, Wendy Hiller, Anthony Newley, Michael Caine. Coburn is wry as American returning home to England only to find his relatives want to kill him for his money.

How to Murder Your Wife (1965) C-118m. *** D: Richard Quine. Jack Lemmon, Virna Lisi, Terry-Thomas, Eddie Mayehoff, Claire Trevor, Sidney Blackmer, Max Showalter, Jack Albertson, Mary Wickes. Engaging comedy that almost holds up to finale. Cartoonist Lemmon marries Lisi by error and she thinks he's going to kill her.

How to Steal a Million (1966) C-127m. *** D: William Wyler. Audrey Hepburn, Peter O'Toole, Charles Boyer, Eli Wallach, Hugh Griffith. Hepburn and O'Toole are a delightful match in this sophisticated comedy about a million-dollar theft in a Paris art museum. Boyer, O'Toole's boss, and Griffith, Hepburn's father, are equally good.

How to Stuff a Wild Bikini (1965) C-90m. ** D: William Asher. Annette Funicello, Dwayne Hickman, Brian Donlevy, Harvey Lembeck, Beverly Adams, Jody McCrea, John Ashley, Buster Keaton, Mickey Rooney. Beach party romp time. Training manual one can do without, although Keaton and Rooney appear.

Howards of Virginia, The (1940) 122m. **½ D: Frank Lloyd. Cary Grant, Martha Scott, Cedric Hardwicke, Alan Marshal, Richard Carlson, Paul Kelly, Irving Bacon. Historical account of Revolutionary War is OK, but too long for such standard retelling.

Hucksters, The (1947) 115m. *** D: Jack Conway. Clark Gable, Deborah Kerr, Sydney Greenstreet, Adolphe Menjou, Ava Gardner, Keenan Wynn, Edward Arnold. Glossy dig at advertising and radio industries, with Gable battling for integrity among yes-men. Greenstreet memorable as despotic head of soap company; Kerr's first American movie.

Hud (1963) 112m. **** D: Martin Ritt. Paul Newman, Patricia Neal, Melvyn Douglas, Brandon de Wilde, John Ashley. Excellent story of moral degradation set in modern West, with impeccable performances by all concerned. Miss Neal won an Oscar for her performance as family housekeeper who doesn't want to get involved with no-account Newman.

Hudson's Bay (1940) 95m. **½ D: Irving Pichel. Paul Muni, Gene Tierney, Laird Cregar, John Sutton, Virginia Field, Vincent Price, Nigel Bruce. Muni's good, but life of founder of Hudson Bay fur-trading company lacks punch. Expansive production.

Hue and Cry (1950-British) 82m. *** D: Charles Crichton. Alastair Sim, Jack Warner, Frederick Piper, Jack Lambert, Joan Dowling. Outrageous romp with wry Sim having field-day involved with youngsters and rambunctious youths.

Huk (1956) C-84m. *½ D: John Barnwell. George Montgomery, Mona Freeman, John Baer, James Bell. Philippine-made hokum about Montgomery returning to the Islands to revenge his dad's murder.

Human Comedy, The (1943) 118m. ***½ D: Clarence Brown. Mickey Rooney, Frank Morgan, James Craig, Marsha Hunt, Fay Bainter, Ray Collins. Filmization of Saroyan novel is long but generally excellent tale of Rooney supporting family during WW2; memorable Americana.

Human Desire (1954) 90m. *** D: Fritz Lang. Glenn Ford, Gloria Grahame, Broderick Crawford, Edgar Buchanan, Kathleen Case. Sultry Grahame as Crawford's man-hungry wife hopes to get Ford to do away with her undesirable spouse; a minor classic.

Human Duplicators, The (1965) C-82m. ** D: Hugo Grimaldi. George Nader, Barbara Nichols, George Macready, Dolores Faith, Hugh Beaumont, Richard Arlen. Quickie production mars gimmick of outer-space aliens coming to earth to establish human-like agents.

Human Jungle, The (1954) 82m. **½ D: Joseph M. Newman. Gary Merrill, Jan Sterling, Paula Raymond, Emile Meyer, Regis Toomey, Chuck Connors. Documentary-style account of a typical day at a busy police precinct house; nicely done.

Human Monster, The (1939-British) 73m. **½ D: Walter Summers. Bela Lugosi, Hugh Williams, Greta Gynt, Edmon Ryan, Wilfred Walter, Alexander Field. British filmization of Edgar Wallace tale of maniac Lugosi who drowns his victims; intriguing melodrama. Remade as DARK EYES OF LONDON.

Humoresque (1946) 125m. *** D: Jean Negulesco. Joan Crawford, John Garfield, Oscar Levant, J. Carrol Naish, Craig Stevens, Tom D'Andrea, Peggy Knudsen. Plush woman's picture, with patroness Crawford in love with violinist Garfield. Smoothly presented, Crawford at her loveliest.

Hunchback of Notre Dame, The (1923) 60m. *** D: Wallace Worsley. Lon Chaney, Patsy Ruth Miller, Ernest Torrence, Tully Marshall, Norman Kerry. Lavish filming of Hugo classic, capturing flair of medieval Paris and strange attraction of outcast Chaney for dancing girl (Miller). Silent classic holds up well, with Chaney's make-up still incredible.

Hunchback of Notre Dame, The (1939) 117m. *** D: William Dieterle. Charles Laughton, Maureen O'Hara, Cedric Hardwicke, Thomas Mitchell, Edmond O'Brien, Walter Hampden, George Zucco. Fine remake of Lon Chaney silent with Laughton as hunchback bell-ringer in Paris of the Middle Ages.

Hunchback of Notre Dame, The (1957-French, dubbed) C-104m. **½ D: Jean Delannoy. Gina Lollobrigida, Anthony Quinn, Jean Danet, Alain Cuny. Quinn makes a valiant try in lead role, but film misses scope and flavor of Victor Hugo novel.

Hungry Hill (1947-British) 92m. ** D: Brian Desmond Hurst. Margaret Lockwood, Dennis Price, Cecil Parker, Jean Simmons, Eileen Herlie, Siobhan McKenna. Based on Daphne DuMaurier's book focusing on 19th-century Irish family with their vices and virtues highlighted; capable cast.

Hunt the Man Down (1950) 68m. ** D: George Archainbaud. Gig Young, Lynn Roberts, Willard Parker, Gerald Mohr. Adequate courtroomer involving public defender whose key witness is presently in a mental institution.

Hunted, The (1948) 67m. **½ D: Jack Bernhard. Preston Foster, Belita, Pierre Watkin, Edna Holland. Trim minor film with Foster a cop out to reform girlfriend Belita; efficiently produced.

Hunters, The (1958) C-108m. **½ D: Dick Powell. Robert Mitchum, Robert Wagner, Richard Egan, Mai Britt. Story of Korean War pilots with their associated personal and career problems.

Hurricane, The (1937) C-102m. ***½ D: John Ford. Jon Hall, Dorothy Lamour, Mary Astor, C. Aubrey Smith, Raymond Massey, Thomas Mitchell, John Carradine, Jerome Cowan. Firstrate escapism on isle of Manikoora, where idyllic native life of Hall and Lamour is disrupted by vindictive governor Massey. Climactic hurricane effects have never been equaled.

Hurricane Island (1951) C-70m. *½ D: Lew Landers. Jon Hall, Marie Windsor, Marc Lawrence, Edgar Barrier. Low-budget nonsense involving the fountain of youth and female buccaneer.

Hurricane Smith (1952) C-90m. ** D: Jerry Hopper. Yvonne de Carlo, John Ireland, James Craig, Forrest Tucker. Romance and a search for gold are the substance of this tale involving a ship beached on a South Sea island.

Hush . . . Hush, Sweet Charlotte (1965) 133m. *** D: Robert Aldrich. Bette Davis, Olivia de Havilland, Joseph Cotten, Agnes Moorehead, Cecil Kellaway, Victor Buono, Mary Astor. Macabre story of a family with a skeleton in its closet, confusing at times but worth watching for its cast. Bette is Olivia's victimized sister; Cotten is Olivia's boyfriend.

Hustler, The (1961) 135m. **** D: Robert Rossen. Paul Newman, Jackie Gleason, Piper Laurie, George C. Scott, Myron McCormick. Realistic study of pool hustler Newman, outstanding as disenchanted drifter. Memorable performances by Scott and Gleason (Minnesota Fats). Dingy N.Y.C. pool-hall atmosphere vividly realized.

Hypnotic Eye, The (1960) 79m. ** D: George Blair. Jacques Bergerac, Merry Anders, Marcia Henderson, Allison Hayes. Partially successful chiller of theatrical mesmerizer with penchant for having female victims disfigure themselves.

I Accuse! (1958) 99m. **½ D: Jose Ferrer. Jose Ferrer, Anton Walbrook, Viveca Lindfors, Leo Genn. Sincere but pretentious narrative of the trial of French officer Alfred Dreyfus; he is sent to Devil's Island, causing great repercussions.

I Aim at the Stars (1960) 107m. *** D: J. Lee Thompson. Curt Jurgens, Victoria Shaw, Herbert Lom, Gia Scala. Low-keyed fictional history of Nazi missile scientist Werner Von Braun and his problems adjusting to life in America.

I am a Camera (1955-British) 98m. ***½ D: Henry Cornelius. Julie Harris, Laurence Harvey, Shelley Winters, Ron Randell, Patrick McGoohan, Peter Prowse. John Van Druten's play of prewar Berlin is recaptured, with Harris most vivid as fun-loving gal who'll accept anything from anyone. Made into Broadway musical CABARET.

I am a Fugitive from a Chain Gang (1932) 76m. ***½ D: Mervyn LeRoy. Paul Muni, Glenda Farrell, Helen Vinson, Preston Foster, Roscoe Karns, Robert Warwick, Berton Churchill. Vintage social document chronicles life of WW1 veteran (Muni) who becomes victim of Southern chain gang, experiencing hell on earth. As with most classics of the 30's, story told compactly, realistically, with solid acting from all.

I am a Thief (1935) 64m. ** D: Robert Florey. Mary Astor, Ricardo Cortez, Dudley Digges, Robert Barrat, Irving Pichel. Stilted adventure of jewel thieves and insurance fraud in Orient. Good cast can't save indifferent script.

I am the Law (1938) 83m. **½ D: Alexander Hall. Edward G. Robinson, Otto Kruger, Wendy Barrie, John Beal, Louis Jean Heydt, Fay Helm, Barbara O'Neil. No surprises in this story of D.A. Robinson fighting corrupt city government, but it's done so smoothly you forget you've seen it before. Don't miss E.G. dancing the Big Apple at the beginning.

I Became a Criminal (1948-British) 80m. **½ D: Alberto Cavalcanti. Trevor Howard, Sally Gray, Rene Ray, Griffith Jones, Mary Merrall, Vida Hope, Eve Ashley. Often entertaining study of black market syndicate and its operations; sturdy cast. Retitled: THEY MADE ME A CRIMINAL.

I Believe In You (1952-British) 93m. **½ D: Michael Relph, Basil Dearden. Cecil Parker, Celia Johnson, Harry Fowler, Godfrey Tearle, Laurence Harvey. Intelligent study of methods used by probation officers to reform their charges; tight editing.

I Bury the Living (1958) 76m. ** D: Albert Band. Richard Boone, Theodore Bikel, Peggy Maurer, Herbert Anderson. Lugubrious goings-on involving a cemetery caretaker who plots victims' deaths.

I Can Get it for You Wholesale (1951) 90m. *** D: Michael Gordon. Susan Hayward, Dan Dailey, Sam Jaffe, George Sanders. Jerome Weidman's flavorful novel about New York garment industry, with Hayward the fiery designer who'll cheat anybody to get ahead. Retitled: ONLY THE BEST.

I Confess (1953) 95m. ** D: Alfred Hitchcock. Montgomery Clift, Anne Baxter, Karl Malden, Brian Aherne, Dolly Haas. Plodding yarn of priest's plight when a murderer confesses and priest (Clift) cannot reveal info to police; second-rate Hitchcock.

I Could Go on Singing (1963) C-99m. **½ D: Ronald Neame. Judy Garland, Dirk Bogarde, Jack Klugman, Aline MacMahon, Gregory Phillips. Garland is famed singer returning to England to claim illegitimate son living with real father (Bogarde). Garland is exceptional in singing sequences revealing the true Judy.

I Cover Big Town (1947) 63m. ** D: William C. Thomas. Philip Reed, Hillary Brooke, Robert Lowery, Robert Shayne, Louis Jean Heydt. Uninspired mystery has female reporter solving complicated murder case. Uneven cast. Retitled: I COVER THE UNDERWORLD.

I Cover the Underworld (1955) 70m. *½ D: R. G. Springsteen. Sean McClory, Ray Middleton, Lee Van Cleef, Joanne Jordan. Republic programmer of clergyman whose twin brother is an about-to-be-released gangster.

I Cover the Underworld (1947) SEE: I Cover Big Town

I Cover the War (1937) 68m. ** D: Arthur Lubin. John Wayne, Gwen Gaze, Major Sam Harris, James Bush, Earl Hodgins, Frank Lackteen. Second-rate pulp fiction about correspondent Wayne tangling with Arab rebel leader.

I Cover the Waterfront (1933) 70m. *** D: James Cruze. Claudette Colbert, Ernest Torrence, Ben Lyon, Wilfred Lucas, George Humbert. Hard-hitting account of dockside reporter falling in love with daughter (Colbert) of seafaring smuggler Torrence.

I Deal in Danger (1966) C-89m. **½ D: Walter Grauman. Robert Goulet, Christine Carere, Donald Harron, Werner Peters. Feature version of TV series BLUE LIGHT involves adventures of Goulet pretending to be Nazi convert in order to help Allies.

I Died a Thousand Times (1955) 109m. ** D: Stuart Heisler. Jack Palance, Shelley Winters, Lori Nelson, Lee Marvin, Lon Chaney. Overblown remake of Bogart's HIGH SIERRA with Palance as mad killer with soft spot for crippled girl (Nelson). Winters is his moll in this gangster runthrough.

I Don't Care Girl, The (1953) C-78m. **½ D: Lloyd Bacon. Mitzi Gaynor, David Wayne, Oscar Levant, Warren Stevens. Premise of George Jessel preparing film biography of Eva Tanguay is vehicle to recreate facets in life of the vaudeville star.

I Dood It (1943) 102m. **½ D: Vincente Minnelli. Red Skelton, Eleanor Powell, Richard Ainley, Patricia Dane, Sam Levene, Thurston Hall, Lena Horne, Hazel Scott, John Hodiak. Overlong Skelton vehicle of tailor and movie-star sweetheart Powell; obvious comedy spiced by good songs like "Taking A Chance On Love."

I Dream of Jeannie (1952) C-90m. ** D: Allan Dwan. Ray Middleton, Bill Shirley, Muriel Lawrence, Lynn Bari, Louise Beavers, James Kirkwood. Fictional biog of Stephen Foster, 19th-century American composer, suffers from low-budget Republic production.

I Dream Too Much (1935) 95m. **½ D: John Cromwell. Lily Pons, Henry Fonda, Eric Blore, Lucille Ball, Osgood Perkins. One of Pons' typical operatic vehicles; she and Fonda are married couple with career problems.

I Escaped from the Gestapo (1943) 75m. ** D: Harold Young. Dean Jagger, John Carradine, Mary Brian, William Henry, Sidney Blackmer, Ian Keith. Low-budget WW2 thriller; title tells the story. Retitled: NO ESCAPE.

I Found Stella Parish (1935) 84m. ** D: Mervyn LeRoy. Kay Francis, Ian Hunter, Paul Lukas, Sybil Jason, Jessie Ralph, Barton MacLane. Shady actress with a past (Francis) comes to U.S. with her daughter (Jason) hoping for a quiet future; mild soaper.

I Have Seven Daughters SEE: **My Seven Little Sins**

I, Jane Doe (1948) 85m. *½ D: John H. Auer. Ruth Hussey, John Carroll, Vera Ralston, Gene Lockhart, John Howard, John Litel. Ludicrous courtroom "drama" of murderess Ralston, with the victim's wife (Hussey) defending her.

I Know Where I'm Going (1947-British) 91m. **** D: Michael Powell, Emeric Pressburger. Wendy Hiller, Roger Livesey, Finlay Currie, Pamela Brown, Valentine Dyall, Petula Clark. Sensitive yet restrained account of wealthy Hiller discovering true love means more than money; story set on isle near Scotland. Hiller's performance is noteworthy; film is a little gem.

I Like Money (1962-British) C-97m. **½ D: Peter Sellers. Peter Sellers, Nadia Gray, Herbert Lom, Leo McKern, Martita Hunt, John Neville, Michael Gough, Billie Whitelaw. Subdued satirical remake of TOPAZE, with Sellers the timid schoolteacher who becomes an unscrupulous businessman.

I Live My Life (1935) 81m. ** D: W. S. Van Dyke II. Joan Crawford, Brian Aherne, Frank Morgan, Aline MacMahon, Eric Blore. Crawford and Aherne are in love, but she's flighty and he's an archaeologist. Glossy and empty.

I Love a Bandleader (1945) 70m. ** D: Del Lord. Phil Harris, Leslie Brooks, Walter Catlett, Eddie Anderson, Frank Sully, Pierre Watkin. Formula claptrap about meek Harris who becomes swinging bandleader; actors' natural abilities rise above material.

I Love a Mystery (1945) 70m. ** D: Henry Levin. Jim Bannon, Nina Foch, George Macready, Barton Yarborough, Carole Mathews, Lester Matthews. Film based on popular radio show is just ordinary murder yarn with series of murders springing from actions of cruel wife.

I Love a Soldier (1944) 106m. ** D: Mark Sandrich. Paulette Goddard, Sonny Tufts, Beulah Bondi, Mary Treen, Barry Fitzgerald. Reteaming of Goddard and Tufts after their hit in SO PROUDLY WE HAIL doesn't match original; story examines problems of wartime marriages.

I Love Melvin (1953) C-76m. **½ D: Don Weis. Donald O'Connor, Debbie Reynolds, Una Merkel, Allyn Joslyn, Jim Backus. Pleasant musicomedy of magazine photographer O'Connor and would-be cinema star Reynolds. Guest appearances by Robert Taylor, Howard Keel.

I Love Trouble (1948) 94m. *** D: S. Sylvan Simon. Franchot Tone, Janet Blair, Janis Carter, Adele Jergens, Glenda Farrell. Flippant mystery with private-eye Tone romancing Blair while searching for her missing sister-in-law.

I Love You Again (1940) 99m. *** D: W. S. Van Dyke II. William Powell, Myrna Loy, Frank McHugh, Edmund Lowe, Don Douglas. Screwball comedy of amnesiac Powell changed from quiet, reserved husband to fast-talking con-artist.

I Love, You Love (1961-Italian, dubbed) C-84m. **½ D: Alessandro Blasetti. Marny Trio, Fattini and Cairoli, Don Yada's Japanese Dance Troupe, The Benitez Sisters. Documentary-styled survey of love in various capitals of the worlds, occasionally spiced by imaginative use of footage.

I Married a Communist (1949) 73m. **½ D: Robert Stevenson. Laraine Day, Robert Ryan, John Agar, Thomas Gomez. Minor propaganda classic of Red party member who wants to become good American again. Retitled: WOMAN ON PIER 13.

I Married a Monster from Outer Space (1958) 78m. ** D: Gene Fowler, Jr. Tom Tryon, Gloria Talbott, Ken Lynch, John Eldredge. Wife discovers what she thought was her husband is an alien monster with sinister plans; promised action never delivered.

I Married a Witch (1942) 76m. **½

D: René Clair. Fredric March, Veronica Lake, Robert Benchley, Susan Hayward, Cecil Kellaway, Elizabeth Patterson. Witch burned in Salem centuries ago (Lake) comes back to haunt descendants of Puritan (March) who sent her to her death. Special effects heighten amusing comedy-fantasy.

I Married a Woman (1958) 84m. ** D: Hal Kanter. George Gobel, Diana Dors, Adolphe Menjou, Jessie Royce Landis, Mona Maris, Janis Carter, Anne Jeffreys. Lackluster events concerning harrassed ad man Gobel who'd rather spend time with his gorgeous wife than overtime at office.

I Married an Angel (1942) 84m. ** D: W. S. Van Dyke II. Jeanette MacDonald, Nelson Eddy, Edward Everett Horton, Binnie Barnes, Reginald Owen, Douglass Dumbrille. Rodgers and Hart musical fantasy was last MacDonald-Eddy film, not a great success. Nice songs like "Spring Is Here," title tune.

I Met Him in Paris (1937) 86m. *** D: Wesley Ruggles. Claudette Colbert, Melvyn Douglas, Robert Young, Lee Bowman, Mona Barrie, Fritz Feld. Love triangle on the ski slopes in bubbly romantic comedy; slick, entertaining.

I Met My Love Again (1938) 77m. **½ D: Arthur Ripley, Joshua Logan. Joan Bennett, Henry Fonda, Dame May Whitty, Alan Marshal, Louise Platt, Alan Baxter, Tim Holt. Familiar soaper of young girl Bennett running off with amorous author, with tragic consequences; acting surpasses script.

I, Mobster (1958) 80m. **½ D: Roger Corman. Steve Cochran, Lita Milan, Robert Strauss, Celia Lovsky. Rugged account of Cochran's life as gangster and events in his crime-filled life.

I Passed for White (1960) 93m. ** D: Fred M. Wilcox. Sonya Wilde, James Franciscus, Pat Michon, Elizabeth Council, Griffin Crafts, Isabelle Cooley. Exploitation film handled with slight dignity involving light-skinned Negress and her rich white boyfriend.

I Remember Mama (1948) 134m. ***½ D: George Stevens. Irene Dunne, Barbara Bel Geddes, Oscar Homolka, Philip Dorn. Grade-A sentimental drama with Dunne as Mama raising her Norwegian family in San Francisco; not for the hardboiled, a delight for others. From John Van Druten's play. Supporting actress Ellen Corby was nominated for an Academy Award.

I Saw What You Did (1965) 82m. *** D: William Castle. Joan Crawford, John Ireland, Leif Erickson, Pat Breslin, Andi Garrett. Taut chiller of two youths who accidentally become involved with a vicious murderer.

I Shot Jesse James (1949) 81m. **½ D: Samuel Fuller. Preston Foster, Barbara Britton, John Ireland, Reed Hadley, J. Edward Bromberg. Modest account of man who killed the notorious 19th-century outlaw.

I Take This Woman (1940) 97m. ** D: W. S. Van Dyke II. Spencer Tracy, Hedy Lamarr, Verree Teasdale, Kent Taylor, Laraine Day, Mona Barrie, Jack Carson. Disappointing soaper with dedicated doctor Tracy sacrificing all for Lamarr, who at first isn't grateful. Not up to stars' talents.

I, the Jury (1953) 87m. ** D: Harry Essex. Biff Elliott, Preston Foster, Peggie Castle, Elisha Cook, Jr., John Qualen. Unsadistic Mickey Spillane caper with Mike Hammer seeking the one who killed his friend.

I Wake Up Screaming (1941) 82m. *** D: H. Bruce Humberstone. Betty Grable, Victor Mature, Carole Landis, Laird Cregar, William Gargan, Alan Mowbray. Entertaining whodunit with Grable and Mature implicated in Betty's sister's (Landis') murder, pursued by determined cop Cregar. Twist finish to good mystery.

I Walk Alone (1948) 98m. ** D: Byron Haskin. Burt Lancaster, Lizabeth Scott, Kirk Douglas, Wendell Corey, Kristine Miller, George Rigauld, Marc Lawrence. A prison term changes Lancaster's outlook on life, and return to outside world makes him bitter. Good cast, weak film.

I Walked with a Zombie (1943) 69m. *** D: Jacques Tourneur. James Ellison, Frances Dee, Tom Conway, Edith Barrett, James Bell. Suspenseful horror film of nurse treating patients on Caribbean island where voodoo runs wild. Starless cast gives very fine performances.

I Want a Divorce (1940) 75m. **½ D: Ralph Murphy. Joan Blondell,

Dick Powell, Gloria Dickson, Frank Fay, Dorothy Burgess, Jessie Ralph, Harry Davenport, Conrad Nagel. Powell and Blondell have just gotten married but already they're beginning to wonder.

I Want to Live! (1958) 120m. ***½ D: Robert Wise. Susan Hayward, Simon Oakland, Virginia Vincent, Theodore Bikel. Hayward won an Oscar for her gutsy performance as the prostitute-crook who (according to the film) is framed for murder and goes to gas chamber. Smart presentation, fine acting.

I Want You (1951) 102m. *** D: Mark Robson. Dana Andrews, Dorothy McGuire, Farley Granger, Peggy Dow. Perhaps-pretentious soaper, but emotional account of Korean War's effect on an American family.

I Wanted Wings (1941) 131m. ** D: Mitchell Leisen. Ray Milland, William Holden, Wayne Morris, Brian Donlevy, Constance Moore, Veronica Lake, Hedda Hopper. Stale plot of three men undergoing air force training served to introduce Lake as star material; that remains only real point of interest.

I Was a Communist for the FBI (1951) 83m. **½ D: Gordon Douglas. Frank Lovejoy, Dorothy Hart, Philip Carey, James Millican. Documentary-style counterspy caper, low-keyed and effective.

I Was a Male War Bride (1949) 105m. **½ D: Howard Hawks. Cary Grant, Ann Sheridan, Marion Marshall, Randy Stuart. Forced, predictable comedy of errors, with military man Grant traveling through Europe with WAC Sheridan.

I Was a Shoplifter (1950) 82m. **½ D: Charles Lamont. Scott Brady, Mona Freeman, Charles Drake, Andrea King. Interesting study of crime syndicate blackmailing compulsive stealers into joining their gang, and police break-up of crooked dealings. One of Tony Curtis' early films.

I Was a Teen-age Frankenstein (1957) 72m. *½ D: Herbert L. Strock. Whit Bissell, Gary Conway, Phyllis Coats, Robert Burton. Programmer-type horror film aimed at the teen-age market. Pretty bad.

I Was a Teen-age Werewolf (1957) 70m. ** D: Gene Fowler, Jr. Michael Landon, Yvonne Lime, Whit Bissell, Vladimir Sokoloff, Guy Williams. Interesting mixture of juvenile delinquency and horror monster; marred by low production values.

I Was an Adventuress (1940) 81m. **½ D: Gregory Ratoff. Vera Zorina, Erich von Stroheim, Richard Greene, Peter Lorre, Sig Ruman. Jewel-thief Zorina goes straight, marries Greene, but can't shake off former associates Von Stroheim, Lorre, et al. With that cast, it should have been better.

I Was an American Spy (1951) 85m. **½ D: Lesley Selander. Ann Dvorak, Gene Evans, Douglas Kennedy, Richard Loo, Philip Ahn, Lisa Ferraday. Dvorak is chanteuse in Manila who helps combat Japanese attack in WW2 spy story, elevated by veteran star. Song: "Because of You."

I Was Monty's Double (1959-British) 100m. ** D: John Guillermin. Clifton James, John Mills, Cecil Parker, Patrick Allen, Patrick Holt, Leslie Philips, Michael Hordern. Lukewarm actioner with lookalike for famed WW2 general used to divert German Intelligence. Retitled: MONTY'S DOUBLE.

I Wonder Who's Kissing Her Now (1947) C-104m. **½ D: Lloyd Bacon. June Haver, Mark Stevens, Martha Stewart, Reginald Gardiner, Lenore Aubert, William Frawley. Engrossing recreation of life and loves of 1890's songwriter, Joseph E. Howard. As usual, music is better than script.

Ice Cold in Alex SEE: **Desert Attack**

Ice Palace (1960) C-113m. **½ D: Vincent Sherman. Richard Burton, Robert Ryan, Carolyn Jones, Martha Hyer, Jim Backus, Ray Danton, Shirley Knight, Diane McBain. Filmization of Edna Ferber novel about development of Alaska's statehood, focusing on incredibly hokey lifelong battle between Burton and Ryan.

Iceland (1942) 79m. ** D: H. Bruce Humberstone. Sonja Henie, John Payne, Jack Oakie, Felix Bressart, Osa Massen, Joan Merrill. Labored love story defeats this Henie musical, although skating and singing interludes are pleasant; song standard, "There Will Never Be Another You."

I'd Climb the Highest Mountain (1951) C-88m. *** D: Henry King. Susan Hayward, William Lundigan, Rory Calhoun, Barbara Bates, Gene Lockhart. Touching story of 1900's family life in Georgia, reflecting Americana at its best.

I'd Rather Be Rich (1964) C-96m. **½ D: Jack Smight. Sandra Dee, Maurice Chevalier, Andy Williams, Robert Goulet, Gene Raymond, Charles Ruggles, Hermione Gingold, Airy remake of IT STARTED WITH EVE. Dee finds substitute fiance to please dying grandfather who wants to see her happy. Only Chevalier-Gingold scenes have spice.

Ideal Husband, An (1948-British) C-96m. **½ D: Alexander Korda. Paulette Goddard, Michael Wilding, Diana Wynyard, Constance Collier, Glynis Johns, Roland Young. Oscar Wilde's drawing-room comedy receives classy presentation but is slow-moving.

Identity Unknown (1945) 71m. ** D: Walter Colmes. Richard Arlen, Cheryl Walker, Roger Pryor, Bobby Driscoll, Lola Lane, Ian Keith. Amnesiac soldier Arlen returning from WW2 tries to learn his identity in minor but fairly interesting drama.

Idiot, The (1960-Russian, dubbed) C-122m. **½ D: Ivan Pyriev. Julia Borisova, Yuri Yakovlev, N. Podgorny, L. Parkhomenko, R. Maximova, N. Pazhitnov. Faithful if not inspired adaptation of Dostoyevsky novel of tormented soul and his peculiar interactions with others.

Idiot's Delight (1939) 105m. ***½ D: Clarence Brown. Norma Shearer, Clark Gable, Edward Arnold, Charles Coburn, Joseph Schildkraut, Virginia Grey, Burgess Meredith. Gable's a song-and-dance man stranded at frontier hotel near Italian border. There he encounters Shearer, an old romance, in thoughtful adaptation of Robert Sherwood's pre-WW2 pacifist play.

If a Man Answers (1962) C-102m. **½ D: Henry Levin. Sandra Dee, Bobby Darin, Stefanie Powers, Cesar Romero, Micheline Presle, John Lund. Trite pap of Dee and Darin trying to outdo each other with jealousy-baiting antics.

If I Had a Million (1932) 88m. ***½ D: James Cruze, H. Bruce Humberstone, Stephen Roberts, William A. Seiter, Ernst Lubitsch, Norman Taurog. Gary Cooper, George Raft, Mary Boland, Charles Laughton, W. C. Fields, Wynne Gibson, Gene Raymond, Charlie Ruggles, Alison Skipworth, Jack Oakie, Frances Dee. Wealthy Richard Bennett gives that sum to various people to see their reactions; all of them interesting in star-studded episodes.

If I Had My Way (1940) 94m. **½ D: David Butler. Bing Crosby, Gloria Jean, Charles Winninger, El Brendel, Allyn Joslyn, Claire Dodd. Title tune is chief asset of pleasant but standard Crosby vehicle in which he helps little Gloria find her guardian, vaudevillian Winninger.

If I Were King (1938) 100m. *** D: Frank Lloyd. Ronald Colman, Frances Dee, Basil Rathbone, Ellen Drew, C. V. France, Henry Wilcoxon, Heather Thatcher, Sidney Toler. Preston Sturges script of roguish poet François Villon (Colman) in battle of wits with King Louis XI (Rathbone) plays with facts but makes good entertainment.

If I'm Lucky (1946) 79m. ** D: Lewis Seiler. Perry Como, Carmen Miranda, Phil Silvers, Vivian Blaine. Lukewarm musical with Harry James' band involved in political campaign; Miranda is good as always.

If This Be Sin (1950-British) 72m. ** D: Gregory Ratoff. Myrna Loy, Peggy Cummins, Richard Greene, Elizabeth Allan. Maudlin multi-love-affair story set on isle of Capri.

If Winter Comes (1947) 97m. ** D: Victor Saville. Walter Pidgeon, Deborah Kerr, Angela Lansbury, Binnie Barnes, Janet Leigh, Dame May Whitty, Reginald Owen. Good cast fails to enliven wooden drama of young man who finds happiness by following code of honor; set in England.

If You Could Only Cook (1935) 70m. *** D: William A. Seiter. Herbert Marshall, Jean Arthur, Leo Carrillo, Lionel Stander, Alan Edwards. Arthur and Marshall are superb team in comedy of wealthy couple pretending to be mobster Carrillo's maid and butler.

If You Knew Susie (1948) 90m. ** D: Gordon Douglas. Eddie Cantor, Joan Davis, Allyn Joslyn, Charles Dingle. Weak film of show biz couple is a delight for Cantor-Davis fans but pointless for others.

I'll Be Seeing You (1944) 85m. **½ D: William Dieterle. Ginger Rogers, Joseph Cotten, Shirley Temple, Spring

Byington, Tom Tully. Overblown David Selznick schmaltz. Rogers, convict home on leave, meets disturbed soldier Cotten; they fall in love.

I'll Be Yours (1947) 93m. ** D: William A. Seiter. Deanna Durbin, Tom Drake, Adolphe Menjou, William Bendix, Franklin Pangborn. Below-average comedy of complications when innocent girl tells white lie to meet baron. Good cast.

I'll Cry Tomorrow (1955) 117m. ***½ D: Daniel Mann. Susan Hayward, Richard Conte, Jo Van Fleet, Ray Danton, Eddie Albert, Margo. Superlative portrayal by Hayward of star Lillian Roth, her assorted marriages and alcoholic problems. Everything a movie biography should be.

I'll Get By (1950) C-83m. **½ D: Richard Sale. June Haver, William Lundigan, Gloria De Haven, Dennis Day, Thelma Ritter. Remake of TIN PAN ALLEY, involving songwriter and his gal; Jeanne Crain, Victor Mature, Dan Dailey make guest appearances.

I'll Get You (1953-British) 79m. ** D: Seymour Friedman. George Raft, Sally Gray. OK gangster yarn of Raft (FBI man) and Gray (British Intelligence) cracking a kidnapping syndicate.

I'll Give a Million (1938) 72m. ** D: Walter Lang. Warner Baxter, Lynn Bari, Jean Hersholt, John Carradine, Peter Lorre. Amusing little idyll of rumor that an eccentric millionaire is posing as a hobo, causing droll results.

Ill Met By Moonlight SEE: **Night Ambush**

I'll Never Forget You (1951) C-90m. **½ D: Roy Baker. Tyrone Power, Ann Blyth, Michael Rennie, Dennis Price, Beatrice Campbell. Remake of BERKELEY SQUARE never captures flavor of original; Power is man who finds himself back in 18th-century London, in love with Blyth.

I'll Remember April (1945) 63m. *½ D: Harold Young. Gloria Jean, Kirby Grant, Samuel S. Hinds, Milburn Stone, Addison Richards, Mary Forbes. Jean lacks verve as goodie-goodie vocalist out to solve crime for which Dad was blamed.

I'll See You In My Dreams (1951) 110m. **½ D: Michael Curtiz. Doris Day, Danny Thomas, Frank Lovejoy, Patrice Wymore, James Gleason. Warner Bros. formula musical biography at its hokiest: trite telling of Gus Kahn's life and times; Day is bouncy.

I'll Take Romance (1937) 85m. **½ D: Edward H. Griffith. Grace Moore, Melvyn Douglas, Stuart Erwin, Helen Westley, Margaret Hamilton. Silly story of opera star Moore kidnapped by agent Douglas has lovely title tune, operatic arias to keep it moving along.

I'll Take Sweden (1965) C-96m. ** D: Frederick de Cordova. Bob Hope, Dina Merrill, Tuesday Weld, Frankie Avalon, Jeremy Slate. Pseudo-sexy Hope vehicle, with everyone frantic over life and love; witless proceedings, lacking usual Hope humor.

I'll Tell the World (1945) 61m. ** D: Leslie Goodwins. Lee Tracy, Brenda Joyce, Raymond Walburn, June Preisser, Thomas Gomez, Howard Freeman, Lorin Raker. Minor comedy with idea-man Tracy saving Walburn's failing radio station.

Illegal (1955) 88m. **½ D: Lewis Allen. Edward G. Robinson, Nina Foch, Hugh Marlowe, Jayne Mansfield, Albert Dekker. Ex-D.A. Robinson becomes mixed up with gangsters, leading to his wife's implication in a crime.

Illegal Entry (1949) 84m. **½ D: Frederick de Cordova. Howard Duff, Marta Toren, George Brent, Gar Moore. Harsh narrative of federal agent assigned to uncover smuggling racket.

Illicit Interlude (1951-Swedish) 90m. **½ D: Ingmar Bergman. Maj-Britt Nilsson, Alf Kjellin, Birger Malmsten, Georg Funkquist. Moody film using flashback retells Britt-Nilsson's romance with now-dead lover, and its relationship to her present frame of mind. Original title: SUMMERPLAY; also known as SUMMER INTERLUDE.

I'm All Right, Jack (1960-British) 104m. *** D: John and Roy Boulting. Ian Carmichael, Peter Sellers, Terry-Thomas, Richard Attenborough, Dennis Price, Margaret Rutherford. Amusing Sellers romp, with him working in a factory, sidetracking his uncle's crooked scheme; well-paced nonsense.

I'm No Angel (1933) 87m. ***½ D: Wesley Ruggles. Mae West, Cary Grant, Edward Arnold, Gertrude Michael, Kent Taylor. West in rare form as star of Arnold's sideshow who chases after playboy Grant; highlight is Mae's courtroom plea.

Imitation General (1958) 120m. **½ D: George Marshall. Glenn Ford, Red Buttons, Taina Elg, Dean Jones. Travesty of what WW2 was all about has Ford taking place of killed superior officer, saving day and winning Elg.

Imitation of Life (1934) 106m. **½ D: John M. Stahl. Claudette Colbert, Warren William, Rochelle Hudson, Louise Beavers, Fredi Washington, Ned Sparks, Alan Hale, Henry Armetta. Believable but dated first version of Fannie Hurst's soaper of working-girl Colbert who makes good with Beavers' pancake recipe; Washington is fine as latter's daughter who passes for white. Ultra-sentimental.

Imitation of Life (1959) C-124m. *** D: Douglas Sirk. Lana Turner, John Gavin, Sandra Dee, Dan O'Herlihy, Susan Kohner, Robert Alda, Juanita Moore, Mahalia Jackson, Troy Donahue, John Vivyan. Plush Ross Hunter updated version of Fannie Hurst soaper. Turner is gal who becomes glamorous actress with an empty life. Racial element is low-keyed; focus on sumptuous settings and platitudes on the good life.

Immortal Battalion, The (1944-British)91m. *** D: Carol Reed. David Niven, Raymond Huntley, Stanley Holloway, Leo Genn, Hugh Burden. Rugged WW2 actioner set during North African campaign. Retitled: THE WAY AHEAD.

Immortal Monster, The (1959-Italian, dubbed) 76m. ** D: Robert Hampton. John Merivale, Didi Sullivan, Gerard Herter, Daniela Rocca. Set in Mexico, sci-fi has blob-ish fiend pursuing members of scientific expedition; poorly conceived but amusing.

Immortal Sergeant, The (1943) 91m. **½ D: John M. Stahl. Henry Fonda, Maureen O'Hara, Thomas Mitchell, Allyn Joslyn, Reginald Gardiner, Melville Cooper. OK wartime drama of inexperienced Fonda forced to take command of his battalion in Africa.

Impact (1949) 111m. **½ D: Arthur Lubin. Brian Donlevy, Ella Raines, Helen Walker, Charles Coburn, Anna May Wong. Deftly told yarn of woman and boyfriend planning to murder her husband, with ironic results.

Impatient Years, The (1944) 91m. **½ D: Irving Cummings. Jean Arthur, Lee Bowman, Charles Coburn, Edgar Buchanan, Harry Davenport, Grant Mitchell, Jane Darwell. Thin comedy of soldier Bowman returning to civilian life with wife Arthur, finding trouble readjusting.

Imperfect Lady, The (1947) 97m. ** D: Lewis Allen. Teresa Wright, Ray Milland, Cedric Hardwicke, Virginia Field, Anthony Quinn, Reginald Owen. Undistinguished drama of Parliament member falling in love with ballerina in London during 1890's.

Impersonator, The (1961-British) 64m. ** D: Alfred Shaughnessy. John Crawford, Jane Griffiths, Patricia Burke, John Salew, Yvonne Ball. Satisfactory chiller programmer of murder in a small village, with Crawford trying to clear himself; offbeat climax.

Importance of Being Earnest, The (1952-British) C-95m. *** D: Anthony Asquith. Michael Redgrave, Michael Dennison, Richard Wattis, Edith Evans, Margaret Rutherford, Joan Greenwood, Dorothy Tutin. Oscar Wilde's peerless comedy of manners set in Victorian England is given admirable treatment by most able cast.

Imposter, The (1944) 95m. **½ D: Julien Duvivier. Jean Gabin, Richard Whorf, Allyn Joslyn, Ellen Drew, Peter Van Eyck, Ralph Morgan. Well-acted but ordinary story of patriotic Frenchman who escapes prison, assumes new identity to join WW2 fight again. Retitled: STRANGE CONFESSION.

In a Lonely Place (1950) 91m. *** D: Nicholas Ray. Humphrey Bogart, Gloria Grahame, Frank Lovejoy, Robert Warwick, Jeff Donnell, Martha Stewart. Offbeat drama of screenwriter Bogart falling for Grahame, who helps clear him when he's accused of murder.

In Caliente (1935) 84m. **½ D: Lloyd Bacon. Dolores Del Rio, Pat O'Brien, Leo Carrillo, Glenda Farrell, Wini Shaw, Judy Canova, Edward Everett Horton. Enjoyable nonsense, spiced by Busby Berkeley geometric dance numbers, including "The Lady In Red."

In Enemy Country (1968) C-107m. ** D: Harry Keller. Tony Franciosa,

Anjanette Comer, Guy Stockwell, Paul Hubschmid, Tom Bell, Emile Genest. So-so programmer of WW2 intrigue, set in France and England, filmed on Universal Pictures' back lot. Not very convincing.

In Fast Company (1947) 61m. D: Del Lord. Leo Gorcey, Huntz Hall, Jane Randolph, Judy Clark, Bobby Jordan. SEE: Bowery Boys series.

In Love and War (1958) C-111m. **½ D: Philip Dunne. Robert Wagner, Dana Wynter, Jeffrey Hunter, Hope Lange. WW2 film in 1940's style, tracing the effects of war on three soldiers; handsome cast uplifts soaper.

In Name Only (1939) 102m. *** D: John Cromwell. Carole Lombard, Cary Grant, Kay Francis, Charles Coburn, Helen Vinson, Peggy Ann Garner. High-grade soaper of married Grant in love with Lombard, trying desperately to obtain a divorce. Francis gives good performance as selfish socialite wife.

In Old California (1942) 88m. ** D: William McGann. John Wayne, Binnie Barnes, Albert Dekker, Helen Parrish, Patsy Kelly, Edgar Kennedy, Dick Purcell, Harry Shannon. Wayne moves into Western town controlled by shifty Dekker, with inevitable confrontation.

In Old Chicago (1938) 115m. ***½ D: Henry King. Tyrone Power, Alice Faye, Don Ameche, Alice Brady, Andy Devine, Brian Donlevy, Phyllis Brooks, Tom Brown. Lavish periodpiece building up to Chicago fire of 1871; Oscar-winning Brady is Mrs. O'Leary, whose sons Power, Ameche, and Brown find their own adventures in the Windy City.

In Old Kentucky (1935) 86m. **½ D: George Marshall. Will Rogers, Dorothy Wilson, Bill "Bojangles" Robinson, Russell Hardie, Louise Henry, Charles Sellon. Story is as old as the hills—a family feud—but Rogers' natural charm and Bojangles' fantastic footwork make it most enjoyable.

In Old Oklahoma SEE: **War of the Wildcats, The**

In Our Time (1944) 110m. **½ D: Vincent Sherman. Ida Lupino, Paul Henreid, Nazimova, Nancy Coleman, Mary Boland, Victor Francen, Michael Chekhov. Lupino and Henreid try to save Poland from Nazi takeover in plush soaper that seeks to be meaningful propaganda; Nazimova is touching as Henreid's aristocratic mother. Never quite hits the mark.

In Society (1944) 75m. ** D: Jean Yarbrough. Bud Abbott, Lou Costello, Marion Hutton, Arthur Treacher, Thomas Gomez, Thurston Hall, Kirby Grant. Minor A&C, with the boys as plumbers mistaken for members of society; hectic slapstick finale.

In the Cool of the Day (1963) C-89m. **½ D: Robert Stevens. Jane Fonda, Peter Finch, Angela Lansbury, Arthur Hill, Constance Cummings. Finch loves Fonda although he's married to Lansbury. Turgid soaper filmed largely in Greece.

In the French Style (1963) 105m. **½ D: Robert Parrish. Jean Seberg, Stanley Baker, Addison Powell, James Leo Herlihy, Philippe Forquet, Claudine Auger. Two short stories by Irwin Shaw are basis for this overlong account of American girl who discovers transient affairs are marring her life.

In the Good Old Summertime (1949) C-102m. *** D: Robert Z. Leonard. Judy Garland, Van Johnson, S. Z. Sakall, Spring Byington, Buster Keaton. Musical remake of THE SHOP AROUND THE CORNER, with Garland and Johnson the pen pals who fall in love. Not up to most MGM Garland vehicles, but pleasant.

In the Meantime, Darling (1944) 72m. ** D: Otto Preminger. Jeanne Crain, Eugene Pallette, Mary Nash, Cara Williams, Reed Hadley, Frank Latimore, Blake Edwards. Whimsical comedy of rich-girl Crain "roughing it" when she marries soldier Latimore.

In the Money (1958) 61m. D: William Beaudine. Huntz Hall, Stanley Clements, Patricia Donahue, Paul Cavanagh. SEE Bowery Boys series.

In the Navy (1941) 85m. **½ D: Arthur Lubin. Bud Abbott, Lou Costello, Dick Powell, The Andrews Sisters, Claire Dodd, Dick Foran. Bud and Lou are somehow in the navy; Lou has hallucinations and nearly wrecks the entire fleet by playing captain. Powell and Andrews Sisters provide songs.

In the Wake of a Stranger (1958-British) 69m. ** D: David Eady.

Tony Wright, Shirley Eaton, Danny Green, Harry H. Corbett, Willoughby Goddard, Barbara Archer. Sailor implicated in murder tries to clear himself; just fair.

In This Our Life (1942) 97m. *** D: John Huston. Bette Davis, Olivia de Havilland, George Brent, Dennis Morgan, Charles Coburn, Frank Craven, Billie Burke. Fine drama of neurotic family with husband-stealing Davis ruining sister's (De Havilland's) life, and eventually her own; Davis at histrionic height. Based on Ellen Glasgow novel. Walter Huston has cameo role as bartender in one scene.

In Which We Serve (1942-British) 115m. **** D: Noel Coward, David Lean. Noel Coward, John Mills, Bernard Miles, Celia Johnson, Kay Walsh, Michael Wilding. Practically one-man show by Coward—directing, writing, acting, scoring music. Saga of crew of British fighting ship during WW2 is superb.

Incendiary Blonde (1945) C-113m. *** D: George Marshall. Betty Hutton, Arturo de Cordova, Charlie Ruggles, Albert Dekker, Barry Fitzgerald, Mary Phillips, Bill Goodwin. Hollywoodized biography of 1920's nightclub queen Texas Guinan is Hutton all over. Plenty of old-time songs.

Incident at Midnight (1963-British) 58m. ** D: Norman Harrison. Anton Diffring, William Sylvester, Tony Garnett, Martin Miller. Based on Edgar Wallace short story, film deals with drugstore hangout of dope addicts and gangsters who ply their trade there; trim yarn.

Incident at Phantom Hill (1966) C-88m. **½ D: Earl Bellamy. Robert Fuller, Dan Duryea, Jocelyn Lane, Claude Akins. Solid little Western about greedy trio chasing after horde of gold, combating Indians, the elements, and each other.

Incredible Mr. Limpet, The (1964) C-102m. ** D: Arthur Lubin. Don Knotts, Jack Weston, Elizabeth MacRae, Andrew Duggan. Cornball, preposterous vehicle for Knotts as timid soul who becomes dolphin aiding U.S. navy during WW2 and finding true love with a fish. Strictly for fans, and for kids.

Incredible Petrified World, The (1958-British) 78m. ** D: Jerry Warren. John Carradine, Allen Windsor, Phyllis Coates, Lloyd Nelson, George Skaff. Potentially exciting sci-fi marred by low budget; group of scientists explore ocean's depths, discovering underwater civilization.

Incredible Shrinking Man, The (1957) 81m. *** D: Jack Arnold. Grant Williams, Randy Stuart, April Kent, Paul Langton. Masterful special effects make this Tom Thumb believable and frightening.

Indestructible Man, The (1956) 70m. ** D: Jack Pollexfen. Lon Chaney, Jr., Marian Carr, Casey Adams, Ross Elliott, Stuart Randall. Man returns from the dead seeking revenge on robbery cohorts who betrayed him; OK science-fiction.

Indian Fighter, The (1955) C-88m. *** D: Andre de Toth. Kirk Douglas, Walter Matthau, Elsa Martinelli, Walter Abel, Lon Chaney. Exciting account of Douglas leading wagon train through rampaging Indian country.

Indian Love Call SEE: Rose Marie

Indian Scarf, The (1963-German, dubbed) 85m. ** D: Alfred Vohrer. Heinz Drache, Gisela Uhlen, Corny Collins, Klaus Kinski. Edgar Wallace suspenser, with heirs to an estate being strangled one by one during sojourn at benefactor's country home.

Indian Uprising (1952) C-75m. ** D: Ray Nazarro. George Montgomery, Audrey Long, Carl Benton Reid, Robert Shayne. Geronimo on the warpath again.

Indiscreet (1958) C-100m. *** D: Stanley Donen. Cary Grant, Ingrid Bergman, Cecil Parker, Phyllis Calvert. Bergman is renowned actress whom American playboy Grant romances and can't forget. Delightful social comedy based on Norman Krasna play KIND SIR.

Indiscretion of an American Wife (1954) 63m. **½ D: Vittorio DeSica. Jennifer Jones, Montgomery Clift, Gino Cervi, Richard Beymer. Turgid melodrama set in Rome's railway station, with Jones the adulterous wife meeting lover Clift for one more clinch.

Inferno (1953) C-83m. **½ D: Roy Baker. Robert Ryan, Rhonda Fleming, William Lundigan, Henry Hull, Carl Betz. Fleming plots rich husband's (Ryan's) demise, with surprising results. Good desert sequences.

Information Received (1962-British) 77m. ** D: Robert Lynn. Sabina Sesselman, William Sylvester, Hermione Baddeley, Edward Underdown. Potentially effective seesaw cat-and-mouse account of criminals Sesselman and Sylvester each trying to kill the other.

Informer, The (1935) 91m. **** D: John Ford. Victor McLaglen, Heather Angel, Preston Foster, Margot Grahame, Wallace Ford, Una O'Connor, Joseph Sawyer. Masterpiece study of human nature tells of hard-drinking McLaglen, who informs on buddy to collect reward during Irish Rebellion. Powerful drama, memorable Max Steiner score.

Informers, The SEE: **Underworld Informers**

Inherit the Wind (1960) 127m. ***½ D: Stanley Kramer. Spencer Tracy, Fredric March, Gene Kelly, Florence Eldridge, Dick York, Donna Anderson. Jerome Lawrence and Robert E. Lee's play brought to movies with two pros in leads: March and Tracy as the prototypes of blustery William Jennings Bryan and Clarence Darrow, battling theory of evolution in famous Monkey Trial. Kelly not perfectly suited for his role, but York as the teacher, Elliott Reid as lawyer, and Harry Morgan as judge are all fine.

Inheritance, The (1947-British) 90m. *** D: Charles Frank. Jean Simmons, Derrick DeMarney, Derek Bond, Katina Paxinou. Well-appointed chiller, with Simmons as innocent preyed upon by corrupt uncle; situated in Victorian London and Paris. Retitled: DON'T TRUST UNCLE SILAS.

Inn of the Sixth Happiness, The (1958) C-158m. *** D: Mark Robson. Ingrid Bergman, Curt Jurgens, Robert Donat, Michael David. Bergman is beautiful as a stoic missionary in pre-WW2 China. Especially notable for Donat's last screen appearance as Mandarin. Combines war scenes with soaper love affair between Bergman and Jurgens. Exciting musical score.

Inn on the River, The (1962-German, dubbed) 95m. **½ D: Alfred Vohrer. Joachim Fuchsberger, Klaus Kinski, Brigitte Grothum, Richard Much. Remake of THE RETURN OF THE FROG (1939), this Edgar Wallace yarn involves series of brutal murders on the waterfront by the "Shark's" gang.

Inner Sanctum (1948) 62m. ** D: Lew Landers. Charles Russell, Mary Beth Hughes, Lee Patrick, Nana Bryant. Satisfactory low-budgeter based on famous radio show, with fortuneteller predicting tragedy for a young girl on a train.

Innocent Affair, An (1948) 90m. ** D: Lloyd Bacon. Fred MacMurray, Madeleine Carroll, Buddy Rogers, Rita Johnson, Alan Mowbray, Louise Allbritton, Anne Nagel. Outmoded marital sex comedy of love and jealousy, bolstered by pros MacMurray-Carroll. Retitled: DON'T TRUST YOUR HUSBAND.

Innocent and the Damned SEE: **Girls Town**

Innocents in Paris (1955-British) 93m. *** D: Gordon Parry. Alastair Sim, Claude Dauphin, Claire Bloom, Laurence Harvey, Margaret Rutherford. Most engaging comedy about seven diverse types crossing the channel to France, each having wacky adventures.

Inside Daisy Clover (1965) C-128m. **½ D: Robert Mulligan. Natalie Wood, Robert Redford, Christopher Plummer, Roddy McDowall, Ruth Gordon, Katherine Bard. Potentially biting account of Wood's rise as Hollywood star in 1930's misfires; pat situations with caricatures instead of people.

Inside Detroit (1955) 82m. ** D: Fred F. Sears. Dennis O'Keefe, Pat O'Brien, Margaret Field, Mark Damon. Ordinary exposé-style narrative of corruption in automobile industry.

Inside Job (1946) 65m. ** D: Jean Yarbrough. Preston Foster, Ann Rutherford, Alan Curtis, Jimmy Moss. Sensible minor film of struggling young marrieds tempted to enter life of crime to solve their financial problems.

Inside Story, The (1948) 87m. ** D: Allan Dwan. Marsha Hunt, William Lundigan, Charles Winninger, Gail Patrick. Warm, minor film set in Depression days in Vermont, involving sudden circulation of large amount of money.

Inside Straight (1951) 89m. **½ D: Gerald Mayer. David Brian, Arlene Dahl, Barry Sullivan, Mercedes McCambridge. Study of greed and corruption as ambitious man rises to fortune in 1870's San Francisco only to find life empty.

Inside the Mafia (1959) 72m. **½ D: Edward L. Cahn. Cameron Mitchell, Elaine Edwards, Robert Strauss, Jim L. Brown, Ted de Corsia, Grant Richards. Gun-blasting account of the Black Hand organization, with cast having field-day.

Inside the Walls of Folsom Prison (1951) 87m. ** D: Crane Wilbur. Steve Cochran, David Brian, Philip Carey, Ted de Corsia. Moderately successful account of crusade to improve harsh penitentiary conditions.

Inspector Calls, An (1954-British) 80m. *** D: Guy Hamilton. Alastair Sim, Arthur Young, Olga Lindo, Eileen Moore. J. B. Priestley's play detailing British police detective's (Sim's) investigation of girl's murder. Via flashbacks he learns a family's responsibility for her fate. Clever plot finale.

Inspector General, The (1949) C-102m. *** D: Henry Koster. Danny Kaye, Walter Slezak, Barbara Bates, Elsa Lanchester, Gene Lockhart, Alan Hale, Walter Catlett. Kaye has nice vehicle as town buffoon who pretends to be visiting bureaucrat; set in 1800's France.

Inspector Maigret (1958-French, dubbed) 110m. **½ D: Jean Delannoy. Jean Gabin, Annie Girardot, Oliver Hussenot, Jeanne Boitel. Famed French detective must track down notorious woman-killer. Retitled: WOMAN-BAIT.

Inspiration (1931) 74m. **½ D: Clarence Brown. Greta Garbo, Robert Montgomery, Lewis Stone, Marjorie Rambeau, Beryl Mercer, Oscar Apfel. Lesser Garbo about beautiful Parisian woman whose past makes her decide to leave Montgomery, even though she still loves him. Garbo has had much better material than this modern version of Alphonse Daudet's SAPPHO.

Intent to Kill (1958-British) 89m. **½ D: Jack Cardiff. Richard Todd, Betsy Drake, Herbert Lom, Warren Stevens. Potboiler about attempted assassination of Latin American dictator who has gone north for brain surgery.

Interlude (1957) C-90m. **½ D: Douglas Sirk. June Allyson, Rossano Brazzi, Marianne Cook, Jane Wyatt, Françoise Rosay. Adequate tear-jerker of Allyson falling in love with Continental composer Brazzi, whose wife refuses to accept the situation. Remade in 1968 under same title.

Intermezzo (1939) 66m. ***½ D: Gregory Ratoff. Ingrid Bergman, Leslie Howard, Edna Best, Cecil Kellaway, John Halliday. Vintage romance of world-famous violinist Howard, a married man, and musical protegee Bergman (in first English-speaking film). Sensitive portrayals backed by Robert Henning-Heinz Provost love themes.

International House (1933) 70m. ***½ D: A. Edward Sutherland. W. C. Fields, Peggy Hopkins Joyce, Stuart Erwin, George Burns, Gracie Allen, Bela Lugosi, Franklin Pangborn, Rudy Vallee, Sterling Holloway, Cab Calloway. Offbeat, delightful film with early television experiment bringing people from all over the world to large Oriental hotel. Spotlight alternates between Fields and Burns and Allen, all in rare form, with guest spots by various radio entertainers. Short and sweet, a must-see film.

International Lady (1941) 102m. **½ D: Tim Whelan. Ilona Massey, George Brent, Basil Rathbone, Gene Lockhart. Really fun flick: Massey a femme fatale spy, Brent the U.S. government agent involved in cracking espionage ring. Superficial but entertaining.

International Settlement (1938) 75m. **½ D: Eugene Forde. Dolores Del Rio, George Sanders, June Lang, Dick Baldwin, Ruth Terry. Sanders gets involved in Shanghai intrigue, with beautiful Del Rio assigned to kill him.

International Squadron (1941) 87m. **½ D: Lothar Mendes. Ronald Reagan, James Stephenson, Julie Bishop, Cliff Edwards, Reginald Denny. Air force straightens out no-account Reagan and turns him into fighting ace. Standard war story.

Internes Can't Take Money (1937) 77m. D: Alfred Santell. Barbara Stanwyck, Joel McCrea, Lloyd Nolan, Stanley Ridges, Lee Bowman, Irving Bacon, Pierre Watkin, Charles Lane, Fay Holden. SEE: Dr. Kildare series.

Interns, The (1962) 129m. *** D: David Swift. Michael Callan, Cliff Robertson, James MacArthur, Nick Adams, Suzy Parker, Haya Harareet, Stefanie Powers, Buddy Ebsen, Telly Savalas, Kaye Stevens. Glossy, renovated DR. KILDARE soap opera, kept afloat by interesting young cast.

Interrupted Journey (1949-British) 80m. **½ D: Daniel Birt. Richard Todd, Valerie Hobson. Eerie film about Todd involved in bizarre dream concerning his marital life and its present complexities.

Interrupted Melody (1955) C-106m. ***½ D: Curtis Bernhardt. Eleanor Parker, Glenn Ford, Roger Moore, Cecil Kellaway. Exceedingly fine biography of Marjorie Lawrence, Australian opera star who made a comeback after being crippled by polio.

Intrigue (1947) 90m. ** D: Edwin L. Marin. George Raft, June Havoc, Helena Carter, Tom Tully, Marvin Miller, Dan Seymour, Philip Ahn. Predictable Raft vehicle of ex-military man with mar on his record turning Shanghai crime ring over to cops to clear himself.

Intruder, The (1955-British) 84m. **½ D: Guy Hamilton. Jack Hawkins, Hugh Williams, Michael Medwin, Dennis Price, Dora Bryan. Hawkins is resolute army veteran who digs into past to discover why one of his old military group went astray.

Intruder in the Dust (1949) 87m. *** D: Clarence Brown. David Brian, Claude Jarman, Jr., Juano Hernandez, Porter Hall, Elizabeth Patterson. William Faulkner novel holds up well in screen version. Negro in Southern town is accused of murder, and gathering mob wants to lynch him.

Invaders, The SEE: **Forty-Ninth Parallel**

Invaders from Mars (1953) C-78m. ** D: William Cameron Menzies. Helena Carter, Arthur Franz, Jimmy Hunt, Leif Erickson, Hillary Brooke. Title reveals all of standard sci-fi epic.

Invasion (1966-British) 82m. **½ D: Alan Bridges. Edward Judd, Yoko Tani, Lyndon Brook, Eric Young, Anthony Shark, Stephanie Bidmead. Entertaining little sci-fi flick involving interplanetary travelers forced to land on earth, and their conflict with humans.

Invasion Earth 2150 A.D. SEE: **Daleks—Invasion Earth 2150 A.D.**

Invasion of the Body Snatchers (1956) 80m. *** D: Don Siegel. Kevin McCarthy, Dana Wynter, Larry Gates, King Donovan, Carolyn Jones. Intelligent sci-fi of threatened takeover by alien monsters who transplant themselves into human bodies.

Invasion of the Saucer-Men (1957) 69m. *½ D: Edward L. Cahn. Steve Terrell, Gloria Castillo, Frank Gorshin, Raymond Hatton, Ed Nelson. Minor sci-fi of title monsters being outdone by the ingenuity of teenagers.

Invasion, U.S.A. (1952) 74m. *½ D: Alfred E. Green. Gerald Mohr, Peggie Castle, Dan O'Herlihy, Phyllis Coates. Unspecified enemy invades Alaska; mild science-fiction.

Invincible Gladiator (1962-Italian, dubbed) 96m. **½ D: Anthony Momplet. Richard Harrison, Isabelle Corey, Joseph Marco. Above-average spectacle with good battle sequences, set typically in ancient Rome, with Harrison as Rezius, who helps the oppressed peasants.

Invisible Agent (1942) 81m. ** D: Edwin L. Marin. Ilona Massey, Jon Hall, Peter Lorre, Cedric Hardwicke, J. Edward Bromberg, John Litel. Hall plays agent fighting Nazis with invisibility. Fun for the kids; dialogue is witless.

Invisible Boy, The (1957) 85m. **½ D: Herman Hoffman. Richard Eyer, Diane Brewster, Philip Abbott, Harold J. Stone. One of the earlier sci-fi flicks to deal with the unwieldy computers gone berserk and power-happy; not bad.

Invisible Creature, The (1959-British) 70m. ** D: Montgomery Tully. Sandra Dorne, Patricia Dainton, Tony Wright. Oddball little film of ghost that interferes with homicide plot in eerie English mansion. Retitled: **THE HOUSE ON MARSH ROAD**.

Invisible Dr. Mabuse, The (1961-German, dubbed) 89m. **½ D: Harald Reinl. Lex Barker, Karin Dor, Siegfried Lowitz, Wolfgang Preiss, Rudolf Fernau. Well-paced entry in archvillain series, with U. S. detective Barker in Germany to track down killer, involved with Mabuse (Preiss); offbeat setting enhances film.

Invisible Ghost, The (1941) 64m. ** D: Joseph H. Lewis. Bela Lugosi, Polly Ann Young, John McGuire, Clarence Muse, Terry Walker, Betty Compson. Low-grade horror about domineering wife who hypnotizes her husband into murder plot.

Invisible Invaders (1959) 67m. *1/2 D: Edward L. Cahn. John Agar, Jean Byron, Robert Hutton, Philip Tonge, John Carradine, Hal Torey. Low-grade thriller with few surprises.

Invisible Man, The (1933) 71m. ***1/2 D: James Whale. Claude Rains, Gloria Stuart, Una O'Connor, William Harrigan, E. E. Clive, Dudley Digges. H. G. Wells' fantasy brilliantly materializes on screen in spooker of mad scientist who makes himself invisible, wreaking havoc on British country village. Rains' first film.

Invisible Man Returns, The (1940) 81m. *** D: Joe May. Cedric Hardwicke, Vincent Price, John Sutton, Nan Grey, Cecil Kellaway, Alan Napier. Fine follow-up to exciting original, with Price going invisible to clear himself of murder charge.

Invisible Man's Revenge, The (1944) 77m. **1/2 D: Ford Beebe. Jon Hall, Alan Curtis, Evelyn Ankers, Leon Errol, John Carradine, Gale Sondergaard, Ian Wolfe, Billy Bevan. Hall made invisible by doctor to obtain estate; he then kills doctor after being refused visibility. Better-than-average cast saves rather innocuous script.

Invisible Monster, The SEE: Slaves of the Invisible Monster

Invisible Ray, The (1936) 81m. **1/2 D: Lambert Hillyer. Boris Karloff, Bela Lugosi, Frances Drake, Frank Lawton, Walter Kingsford, Beulah Bondi. Fellow-scientists Bela and Boris are torn apart when Karloff contracts strange radiation which gives him touch of death.

Invisible Stripes (1940) 82m. *** D: Lloyd Bacon. George Raft, Jane Bryan, William Holden, Flora Robson, Humphrey Bogart, Paul Kelly, Moroni Olsen, Tully Marshall. Earnest account of parolee Raft trying to go straight, protecting brother Holden from gangster Bogart; subdued acting is effective.

Invisible Woman, The (1941) 72m. **1/2 D: A. Edward Sutherland. Virginia Bruce, John Barrymore, John Howard, Charlie Ruggles, Oscar Homolka, Edward Brophy. Gimmick film about screwy professor Barrymore making model Bruce invisible; hardly a classic, but enjoyable.

Invitation (1952) 84m. **1/2 D: Gottfried Reinhardt. Van Johnson, Dorothy McGuire, Louis Calhern, Ray Collins, Ruth Roman. Society tearjerker decked out in MGM gloss about invalid McGuire; her father (Calhern) tries to buy Johnson to romance dying daughter.

Invitation to a Gunfighter (1964) C-92m. **1/2 D: Richard Wilson. Yul Brynner, George Segal, Janice Rule, Pat Hingle, Brad Dexter. Cast surpasses turgid script about town that hires gunslinger to kill an outcast, with surprising results; overly talky.

Invitation to Happiness (1939) 95m. **1/2 D: Wesley Ruggles. Irene Dunne, Fred MacMurray, Charles Ruggles, William Collier, Sr., Eddie Hogan. Ordinary story, well acted: society girl marries fighter, but marriage can't survive because of his driving ambition in boxing ring.

Ipcress File, The (1965-British) C-108m. ***1/2 D: Sidney J. Furie. Michael Caine, Nigel Green, Guy Doleman, Sue Lloyd, Gordon Jackson. First and best of Len Deighton's Harry Palmer series, with Caine unemotional cockney crook turned secret agent, involved in grueling mental torture caper.

Irene (1940) 104m. *** D: Herbert Wilcox. Anna Neagle, Ray Milland, Roland Young, Alan Marshal, May Robson, Billie Burke, Arthur Treacher. Entertaining musicomedy of playboy Milland romancing working girl Neagle. Bright cast, good songs in one of British star Neagle's few American-made films.

Irish Eyes are Smiling (1944) C-90m. **1/2 D: Gregory Ratoff. June Haver, Monty Woolley, Dick Haymes, Anthony Quinn, Maxie Rosenbloom, Veda Ann Borg. Colorful corn about composer of famous Irish songs, with pleasant cast and familiar tunes.

Irish In Us, The (1935) 84m. ** D: Lloyd Bacon. James Cagney, Pat O'Brien, Olivia de Havilland, Frank McHugh, Allen Jenkins. Pretty stale comedy about rivalry between policemen and prizefighters, with good cast to hold one's interest.

Irma la Douce (1963) C-142m. **½
D: Billy Wilder. Shirley MacLaine, Jack Lemmon, Lou Jacobi, Herschel Bernardi, Hope Holiday. Wilder's straight-comedy adaptation of Broadway musical is quite raw, definitely not for the tiny tots, as gendarme Lemmon becomes involved with prostitute MacLaine. Reteaming of stars and director can't equal THE APARTMENT.

Iron Curtain, The (1948) 87m. ***
D: William Wellman. Dana Andrews, Gene Tierney, June Havoc, Berry Kroeger, Edna Best. Excellent cast and intelligent direction make this Cold War espionage story set in Canada of superior caliber. Retitled: BEHIND THE IRON CURTAIN.

Iron Glove, The (1954) C-77m. **½
D: William Castle. Robert Stack, Ursula Thiess, Richard Stapley, Charles Irwin, Alan Hale, Jr. Typical swashbuckler about 18th-century England and Prince James, pretender to the throne.

Iron Major, The (1943) 85m. **½ D: Ray Enright. Pat O'Brien, Ruth Warrick, Robert Ryan, Leon Ames, Russell Wade, Bruce Edwards. Good biography of Frank Cavanaugh, who in civilian life was famous football coach, in WWI became a military hero; O'Brien is convincing in lead.

Iron Man (1931) 73m. ** D: Tod Browning. Lew Ayres, Jean Harlow, Robert Armstrong, John Miljan, Eddie Dillon. Routine early talkie of prizefighter Ayres and gold-digging wife Harlow (who hadn't clicked yet in films). Manager-pal Armstrong is only one who sees through her.

Iron Man (1951) 82m. **½ D: Joseph Pevney. Jeff Chandler, Evelyn Keyes, Stephen McNally, Joyce Holden, Rock Hudson. Remake of Harlow film focuses more on boxer (Chandler) and his unhappy rise in the boxing world.

Iron Mistress, The (1952) C-110m. **½ D: Gordon Douglas. Alan Ladd, Virginia Mayo, Joseph Calleia, Phyllis Kirk. Spotty Western adventure of Jim Bowie (Ladd), who invented the famed two-edged knife.

Iron Sheriff, The (1957) 73m. *½ D: Sidney Salkow. Sterling Hayden, Constance Ford, John Dehner, Kent Taylor, Darryl Hickman. Marshal Hayden sets out to prove son is not guilty of murder.

Ironside (1967) C-120m. *** D: Michael Caffey. Raymond Burr, James Gregory, Gene Evans, Don Mitchell. Telefeature served as pilot for current TV series. Burr is wheelchair-bound chief on San Francisco detective force, engaged in solving a racetrack robbery; well-paced, engrossing drama.

Iroquois Trail, The (1950) 85m. **
D: Phil Karlson. George Montgomery, Brenda Marshall, Dan O'Herlihy, Glenn Langan. Too often flabby account of French and Indian War, lacking sufficient plot motivation and action sequences.

Is Paris Burning? (1966) 173m. **
D: René Clement. Jean-Paul Belmondo, Charles Boyer, Leslie Caron, Alain Delon, Kirk Douglas, Glenn Ford, Gert Frobe, Simone Signoret, Orson Welles, Claude Dauphin. Rambling pseudo-documentary-style recreation of WW2 France, showing liberation of Paris and Nazis' attempt to burn the city. Cameos by international players confuse blotchy film made in Europe.

Island, The (1962-Japanese, dubbed) 96m. *** D: Kaneto Shindo. Nobuko Otowa, Taiji Tonoyama, Shinji Tanaka, Masanori Horimoto. Engrossing documentary study of peasant family living on rocky island near Japan, struggling to survive.

Island in the Sky (1953) 109m. **½
D: William Wellman. John Wayne, Lloyd Nolan, James Arness, Andy Devine. Sometimes actionful search for downed troop plane set in WW2 off Greenland coast.

Island in the Sun (1957) C-119m. **
D: Robert Rossen. James Mason, Joan Fontaine, Dorothy Dandridge, Joan Collins, Michael Rennie, Diana Wynyard, John Williams, Stephen Boyd, Harry Belafonte. Misfire adaptation of Alec Waugh's book about idyllic West Indies island torn by racial struggle. Good cast can't do much with unconvincing script.

Island of Desire (1952) C-103m. **½
D: Gordon Douglas. Linda Darnell, Tab Hunter, Donald Gray, Sheila Chong. Humdrum script of nurse Darnell, marine Hunter, and injured flier Gray on lovely desert isle; torrid romance scenes almost materialize.

Island of Doomed Men (1940) 67m.
** D: Charles Barton. Peter Lorre,

Robert Wilcox, Rochelle Hudson, George E. Stone, Don Beddoe, Kenneth MacDonald. Low-grade melodrama even Lorre can't save as man who traps unsuspecting victims on island, turns them into his slaves.

Island of Lost Men (1939) 63m. *½ D: Kurt Neumann. Anna May Wong, J. Carrol Naish, Eric Blore, Ernest Truex, Anthony Quinn, Broderick Crawford. Generally dull mystery of Wong searching for Oriental general along the waterfront. A few atmospheric scenes, but stilted dialogue throughout.

Island of Lost Souls (1933) 70m. *** D: Erle C. Kenton. Charles Laughton, Bela Lugosi, Richard Arlen, Stanley Fields, Kathleen Burke, Joe Bonomo, Leila Hyams. Renowned horror film of mad scientist Laughton changing jungle beasts into "mansters," human savages. Laughton overplays, but it is worth seeing.

Island of Lost Women (1959) 71m. ** D: Frank Tuttle. Jeff Richards, Venetia Stevenson, John Smith, Diane Jergens, Alan Napier, June Blair. Plane forced down on remote island leads to complications with scientist and daughters who inhabit the jungle isle.

Island of Love (1963) C-101m. **½ D: Morton Da Costa. Robert Preston, Tony Randall, Giorgia Moll, Walter Matthau, Betty Bruce. Dud attempt to make bubbly romantic comedy. Filmed in Greece.

Island Princess, The (1955-Italian, dubbed) C-98m. ** D: Paolo Moffa. Marcello Mastroianni, Silvana Pampanini, Gustavo Rojo. Rather hackneyed yarn set in 1500's, with Mastroianni a Spanish captain falling in love with princess of the Canary Islands.

Island Rescue (1952-British) 87m. ** D: Ralph Thomas. David Niven, Glynis Johns, George Coulouris, Barry Jones, Noel Purcell. Lukewarm comedy involving rescue of cows from German-occupied island during WW2. Retitled: APPOINTMENT WITH VENUS.

Isle of Fury (1936) 60m. ** D: Frank McDonald. Humphrey Bogart, Margaret Lindsay, Donald Woods, Paul Graetz, Gordon Hart, E. E. Clive. Mild remake of Somerset Maugham novel NARROW CORNER (1933), involving love triangle on South Sea island; early Bogart.

Isle of Sin (1960-German, dubbed) 63m. *½ D: Johannes Kai. Christiane Nielsen, Erwin Strahl, Jan Hendriks, Slavo Schwaiger. Trite tale of passengers on plane which crashed on deserted island, with expected friction between types.

Isle of the Dead (1945) 72m. *** D: Mark Robson. Boris Karloff, Ellen Drew, Marc Cramer, Katherine Emery, Helene Thimig, Jason Robards. Eerie horror tale of assorted characters stranded on Greek island during quarantine. Good Val Lewton production.

Isn't It Romantic? (1948) 87m. ** D: Norman Z. McLeod. Veronica Lake, Mary Hatcher, Mona Freeman, Billy DeWolfe, Roland Culver, Pearl Bailey. No.

Istanbul (1957) 84m. ** D: Joseph Pevney. Errol Flynn, Cornell Borchers, John Bentley, Torin Thatcher, Nat King Cole. Unsatisfying drama of adventurer Flynn returning to title city to find cache of gems, discovering his old girlfriend still alive.

It Ain't Hay (1943) 80m. **½ D: Erle C. Kenton. Bud Abbott, Lou Costello, Patsy O'Connor, Grace McDonald, Leighton Noble, Cecil Kellaway, Eugene Pallette, Eddie Quillan. Pretty good Abbott and Costello from Damon Runyon story of racehorse Teabiscuit; good supporting cast helps.

It All Came True (1940) 97m. **½ D: Lewis Seiler. Ann Sheridan, Humphrey Bogart, Jeffrey Lynn, Zasu Pitts, Jessie Busley, Una O'Connor, John Litel, Grant Mitchell. Improbable but amusing: gangster Bogart hides out in theatrical boarding house and is won over by assorted characters there.

It Always Rains on Sunday (1948-British) 92m. **½ D: Robert Hamer. Googie Withers, Edward Chapman, Sydney Tafler, Jane Hylton, Alfie Bass, Hermione Baddeley. Sordid, realistic yarn of grimy slum life in London and its effects on families living there.

It Came from Beneath the Sea (1955) 80m. ** D: Robert Gordon. Kenneth Tobey, Faith Domergue, Donald Curtis, Ian Keith, Harry Lauter.

Oversized sea monster threatens the world's safety; eh!

It Came from Outer Space (1953) 81m. **½ D: Jack Arnold. Richard Carlson, Barbara Rush, Charles Drake, Kathleen Hughes. Slow-paced sci-fi promising much but delivering little real suspense as townsfolk react to invasion of unknown monsters from beyond.

It Conquered the World (1956) 68m. ** D: Roger Corman. Peter Graves, Beverly Garland, Lee Van Cleef, Sally Fraser. Low-budget sci-fi which intelligently attempts to create atmospheric excitement in yarn of superego power from another world.

It Grows on Trees (1952) 84m. ** D: Arthur Lubin. Irene Dunne, Dean Jagger, Richard Crenna, Les Tremayne. Dunne's last feature to date is slim vehicle of wife who discovers backyard foliage is blossoming crisp money.

It Had to Be You (1947) 98m. **½ D: Don Hartman, Rudolph Maté. Ginger Rogers, Cornel Wilde, Percy Waram, Spring Byington, Ron Randell. Rogers has severe indecision before every scheduled marriage, until Wilde (as a fireman) appears. Airy, fanciful comedy.

It Had to Happen (1936) 79m. ** D: Roy Del Ruth. George Raft, Rosalind Russell, Leo Carrillo, Arline Judge, Alan Dinehart. Raft's rise from penniless immigrant to corrupt political leader is OK but predictable, as is his romance with Russell.

It Happened at the World's Fair (1963) C-105m. *** D: Norman Taurog. Elvis Presley, Joan O'Brien, Gary Lockwood, Yvonne Craig. Entertaining Presley vehicle set at Seattle World's Fair, with Elvis and O'Brien brought together by little Ginny Tiu. Listenable tunes help make this most enjoyable.

It Happened in Brooklyn (1947) 105m. ** D: Richard Whorf. Frank Sinatra, Kathryn Grayson, Jimmy Durante, Peter Lawford, Gloria Grahame. Hokey musical of group of Brooklynites trying to make it big in show biz; all coating, no substance. One good song, "Time After Time."

It Happened on 5th Avenue (1947) 115m. ** D: Roy Del Ruth. Don DeFore, Ann Harding, Charlie Ruggles, Victor Moore, Gale Storm, Grant Mitchell. Overlong comedy about elegant N.Y.C. mansion taken over by thoughtful bum, who invites horde of friends and real owner in disguise to be his guests.

It Happened One Night (1934) 105m. **** D: Frank Capra. Clark Gable, Claudette Colbert, Walter Connolly, Roscoe Karns, Alan Hale, Ward Bond. Oscar-studded screwball comedy doesn't age a bit. Still as enchanting as ever, with reporter Gable and runaway heiress Colbert falling in love on rural bus trip. Hitch-hiking scene, the Walls of Jericho, other memorable scenes remain fresh and delightful. Remade as musical YOU CAN'T RUN AWAY FROM IT.

It Happened One Summer SEE: State Fair

It Happened to Jane (1959) C-98m. **½ D: Richard Quine. Doris Day, Jack Lemmon, Ernie Kovacs, Steve Forrest, Teddy Rooney, Russ Brown, Mary Wickes, Parker Fennelly. Funny little comedy with Doris and Lemmon running Maine lobstery, tangling with villain Kovacs (who hams mercilessly). Breezy and likable. Also known as TWINKLE AND SHINE.

It Happened Tomorrow (1944) 84m. ***½ D: René Clair. Dick Powell, Linda Darnell, Jack Oakie, Edgar Kennedy, Edward Brophy, George Cleveland, Sig Ruman. Nifty fantasy-comedy of reporter Powell receiving news 24 hours before it occurs; set at turn of the century. Fine cast.

It Happens Every Spring (1949) 80m. ***½ D: Lloyd Bacon. Ray Milland, Jean Peters, Paul Douglas, Ed Begley. Clever little film of chemistry professor (Milland) discovering serum that makes baseballs jump over bats; most enjoyable and unpretentious.

It Happens Every Thursday (1953) 80m. *** D: Joseph Pevney. Loretta Young, John Forsythe, Frank McHugh, Edgar Buchanan. Warm comedy about married couple who buy small-town newspaper and try every method conceivable to make it click.

It Should Happen to You (1954) 81m. *** D: George Cukor. Judy Holliday, Peter Lawford, Jack Lemmon, Michael O'Shea, Vaughn Taylor. Raucous comedy about publicity-seeking actress (Holliday) who has her name plastered on billboards in N.Y.C. with deft results.

It Shouldn't Happen to a Dog (1946) 70m. **½ D: Herbert I. Leeds. Carole Landis, Allyn Joslyn, Margo Woode, Henry Morgan, Reed Hadley, Jean Wallace. Fluff of fast-talking reporter Joslyn, policewoman Landis, and a troublesome dog.

It Started in Naples (1960) C-100m. **½ D: Melville Shavelson. Clark Gable, Sophia Loren, Vittorio DeSica, Marietto, Paolo Carlini, Claudio Ermelli. Gable is American lawyer, in Italy to bring nephew back to America; only Aunt Sophia won't agree. Star duo never clicks as love match, but they do their best.

It Started with a Kiss (1959) C-104m. **½ D: George Marshall. Glenn Ford, Debbie Reynolds, Eva Gabor, Fred Clark, Edgar Buchanan, Harry Morgan. Airy comedy about wacky Reynolds and her army officer husband Ford, trying to make a go of marriage, set in Spain.

It Started with Eve (1941) 90m. *** D: Henry Koster. Deanna Durbin, Charles Laughton, Robert Cummings, Guy Kibbee, Margaret Tallichet. Conniving Laughton matches son Cummings with Deanna in this bright comedy, one of Durbin's best films. Remade as I'D RATHER BE RICH.

It Takes a Thief (1960-British) 90m. ** D: John Gilling. Jayne Mansfield, Anthony Quayle, Carl Mohner, Edward Judd. Mansfield is gangland leader with big heist in the workings; supporting cast uplifts flick. Original title: THE CHALLENGE.

It! The Terror from Beyond Space (1958) 69m. *½ D: Edward L. Cahn. Marshall Thompson, Shawn Smith, Kim Spalding, Ann Doran. Mild scifi of space ship returning to earth with a most unwelcome creature stowed away on it.

Italiano Brava Gente (1965-Italian, dubbed) 156m. *** D: Giuseppe De Santis. Arthur Kennedy, Peter Falk, Tatyana Samoilova, Rafaelle Pisu, Andrea Checchi. Expansive chronicle of Italian-Russian warfront during WW2, focusing on a variety of strata of soldiers and civilians. Much edited since European opening. Retitled: ATTACK AND RETREAT.

It's a Big Country (1951) 89m. *** D: Charles Vidor, Richard Thorpe, John Sturges, Don Hartman, Don Weis, Clarence Brown, William Wellman. Ethel Barrymore, Keefe Brasselle, Gary Cooper, Nancy Davis, Gene Kelly, Keenan Wynn, Fredric March, Van Johnson, James Whitmore. Dore Schary's plug for America uses several pointless episodes about the variety of people and places in U.S. Other segments make up for it in very uneven film.

It's a Dog's Life (1955) C-88m. **½ D: Herman Hoffman. Jeff Richards, Edmund Gwenn, Dean Jagger, Sally Fraser. Film uses gimmick of having the canine star tell his life story from slums to luxury. Retitled: BAR SINISTER.

It's a Gift (1934) 73m. **** D: Norman Z. McLeod. W. C. Fields, Baby LeRoy, Kathleen Howard, Tommy Bupp, Morgan Wallace. Fields is grocery store owner who goes West with his family. Beautiful comedy routines in one of the Great Man's unforgettable films. Charles Sellon as a blind man, T. Roy Barnes as a salesman looking for Carl La Fong, contribute some hilarious moments.

It's a Great Feeling (1949) C-85m. *** D: David Butler. Dennis Morgan, Doris Day, Jack Carson, Bill Goodwin. Temperamental film-worker Carson and starlet Day involved in filmmaking are vehicle for back-lot look at Warner Bros. Guest appearances by Bacall, Bogart, Crawford, Flynn, et al.

It's a Great Life (1943) 75m. D: Frank Strayer. Penny Singleton, Arthur Lake, Larry Simms, Hugh Herbert, Jonathan Hale, Danny Mummert, Alan Dinehart. SEE: Blondie series.

It's a Joke, Son (1947) 63m. ** D: Ben Stoloff. Kenny Delmar, Una Merkel, June Lockhart, Kenneth Farrell, Douglass Dumbrille. Folksy comedy featuring further exploits of Senator Claghorn (Delmar) from the Fred Allen radio show.

It's a Pleasure! (1945) C-90m. ** D: William A. Seiter. Sonja Henie, Michael O'Shea, Bill Johnson, Marie McDonald, Gus Schilling, Iris Adrian. Skater Henie and hockey player O'Shea get married but can't seem to break the ice; pretty weak.

It's a Wonderful Life (1946) 129m. ***½ D: Frank Capra. James Stewart,

Donna Reed, Lionel Barrymore, Henry Travers, Beulah Bondi, Gloria Grahame. Sentimental comedy-drama of dejected Stewart being shown the great things in life by an angel. Most enjoyable.

It's a Wonderful World (1939) 86m. *** D: W. S. Van Dyke II. Claudette Colbert, James Stewart, Guy Kibbee, Nat Pendleton, Edgar Kennedy, Sidney Blackmer, Hans Conried. Screwball comedy with Colbert a runaway poetess, Stewart a fugitive chased by cops Pendleton and Kennedy. Very, very funny, with Stewart having a field-day.

It's Always Fair Weather (1955) C-102m. *** D: Gene Kelly, Stanley Donen. Gene Kelly, Dolores Gray, Dan Dailey, Cyd Charisse, Michael Kidd, David Burns. Fine dancing and singing hampered by plot. Three WW2 buddies aren't overjoyed that their tenth reunion is being exploited as TV special.

It's in the Air (1935) 80m. ** D: Charles Reisner. Jack Benny, Una Merkel, Ted Healy, Nat Pendleton, Mary Carlisle, Grant Mitchell. Uncharacteristic Benny as con-artist who goes to ex-wife Merkel for help. Fair comedy; mainly a curiosity item.

It's In the Bag (1945) 87m. *** D: Richard Wallace. Fred Allen, Jack Benny, William Bendix, Binnie Barnes, Robert Benchley, Jerry Colonna, Don Ameche, Victor Moore, Rudy Vallee. Allen stars in farce of flea-circus showman entitled to large sum of money; many guest stars in this entertaining comedy.

It's Love I'm After (1937) 90m. *** D: Archie Mayo. Bette Davis, Leslie Howard, Olivia de Havilland, Patric Knowles, Eric Blore, Bonita Granville, Spring Byington, Veda Ann Borg. Sprightly comedy with Davis and Howard as perfect onstage lovers, constantly battling when curtain goes down. Cast puts over witty script.

It's Never Too Late (1956-British) C-95m. **½ D: Michael McCarthy. Phyllis Calvert, Guy Rolfe, Sarah Lawson, Peter Illing, Patrick Barr. Pleasant frou-frou about Calvert becoming famed writer, caught between choice of being good mother or living a celebrity's life.

It's Only Money (1962) 84m. *** D: Frank Tashlin. Jerry Lewis, Zachary Scott, Joan O'Brien, Mae Questel, Jesse White, Jack Weston. Jerry, a TV repairman turned detective, in a wacky comedy, one of his better later films. Slapstick and sight gags blend perfectly.

Ivanhoe (1952) C-106m. *** D: Richard Thorpe. Robert Taylor, Elizabeth Taylor, Joan Fontaine, George Sanders, Finlay Currie, Sebastian Cabot. Almost a classic spectacular, marred by draggy scripting of Walter Scott's epic of England in Middle Ages, in days of chivalrous knights; beautifully photographed on location in Great Britain.

I've Always Loved You (1946) C-117m. *** D: Frank Borzage. Philip Dorn, Catherine McLeod, William Carter, Maria Ouspenskaya, Felix Bressart. Lavish romancer with classical music background; Ouspenskaya stands out in cast.

I've Lived Before (1956) 82m. **½ D: Richard Bartlett. Jock Mahoney, Leigh Snowden, Ann Harding, John McIntire, Raymond Bailey. Strange small-budget film about pilot who thinks he is an aviator who died in WW1.

Ivory Hunter (1951-British) C-97m. **½ D: Harry Watt. Anthony Steel, Dinah Sheridan, Harold Warrender, William Simons. Documentary-ish account of establishment of Mount Kilimanjaro Game Preserve Park in Africa. Retitled: WHERE NO VULTURES FLY.

Ivy (1947) 99m. **½ D: Sam Wood. Joan Fontaine, Patric Knowles, Herbert Marshall, Richard Ney, Cedric Hardwicke, Lucile Watson. Average drama of murderess snared in her own seemingly faultless plans. Good cast gives film added boost.

Jack and the Beanstalk (1952) C-87m. **½ D: Jean Yarbrough. Bud Abbott, Lou Costello, Dorothy Ford, Barbara Brown, Buddy Baer. A&C version of fairy tale OK for kids; not as amusing as their earlier films.

Jack London (1943) 94m. *** D: Albert Santell. Michael O'Shea, Susan Hayward, Osa Massen, Harry Davenport, Frank Craven, Virginia Mayo, Ralph Morgan. At times vivid biography of globetrotting writer London: sailing ships, fighting wars, leading

fascinating life; unpretentious, effective film.
Jack McCall, Desperado (1953) C-76m. ** D: Sidney Salkow. George Montgomery, Angela Stevens, Jay Silverheels, Douglas Kennedy. Civil War yarn of Southerner Montgomery capturing man who framed him as spy.
Jack Slade (1953) 90m. ** D: Harold Schuster. Mark Stevens, Dorothy Malone, Barton MacLane, John Litel. Oater programmer of Stevens turning criminal with tragic results; Malone is wasted.
Jack the Giant Killer (1962) C-94m. *** D: Nathan Juran. Kerwin Matthews, Judi Meredith, Torin Thatcher, Walter Burke. Marvelous special effects make this costume adventure yarn a joy to watch.
Jack the Ripper (1960-British) 88m. ** D: Robert Baker, Monty Berman. Lee Patterson, Eddie Byrne, George Rose, Betty McDowall. Middling retelling of notorious knife-wielder, with alternating scenes of Scotland Yard and fiend at work in London. Sometimes hits the mark with gory sensationalism.
Jackass Mail (1942) 80m. ** D: Norman Z. McLeod. Wallace Beery, Marjorie Main, J. Carrol Naish, Darryl Hickman, William Haade, Dick Curtis. Easygoing Beery vehicle about fugitive who accidentally becomes a hero. Take it or leave it; no harm done either way.
Jackie Robinson Story, The (1950) 76m. *** D: Alfred E. Green. Jackie Robinson, Ruby Dee, Louise Beavers, Minor Watson, Richard Lane. Straightforward account of baseball star, with effective telling of racial issues involved.
Jackpot, The (1950) 85m. **½ D: Walter Lang. James Stewart, Barbara Hale, James Gleason, Fred Clark, Natalie Wood. Dated, minor comedy, uplifted by stars; Stewart is winner of radio contest but can't pay taxes on winnings.
Jacqueline (1957-British) 92m. ** D: Roy Baker. John Gregson, Kathleen Ryan, Noel Purcell, Cyril Cusack. Low-keyed family fare of small girl and her everyday adventures with the world.
Jade Mask, The (1945) 66m. D: Phil Rosen. Sidney Toler, Mantan Moreland, Edwin Luke, Janet Warren, Edith Evanson, Alan Bridge, Ralph Lewis. SEE: **Charlie Chan** series.
Jaguar (1956) 66m. *½ D: George Blair. Sabu, Chiquita, Barton MacLane, Jonathan Hale, Mike Connors. Presence of former elephant-boy Sabu is only virtue of ridiculous programmer about mysterious murders on an oilfield.
Jail Busters (1955) 61m. D: William Beaudine. Leo Gorcey, Huntz Hall, Percy Helton, Lyle Talbot, Fritz Feld, Barton MacLane. SEE: **Bowery Boys** series.
Jailhouse Rock (1957) 96m. *** D: Richard Thorpe. Elvis Presley, Judy Tyler, Vaughn Taylor, Dean Jones. Presley is more energetic than usual in yarn of ex-con with talent for guitar-playing who becomes famous.
Jalopy (1953) 62m. D: William Beaudine. Leo Gorcey, Huntz Hall, Bernard Gorcey, Robert Lowrey, Murray Alper. SEE: **Bowery Boys** series.
Jam Session (1944) 77m. ** D: Charles Barton. Ann Miller, Jess Barker, Charles Brown, Eddie Kane, Louis Armstrong, Charlie Barnet Orchestra, Nan Wynn, Pied Pipers. Mild musical of showgirl Miller trying to crash Hollywood; notable for many musical guests doing enjoyable specialty numbers.
Jamaica Inn (1939-British) 98m. ** D: Alfred Hitchcock. Charles Laughton, Maureen O'Hara, Leslie Banks, Robert Newton, Emlyn Williams, Mervyn Johns. Stodgy Victorian costumer of cutthroat band headed by nobleman Laughton; O'Hara is lovely in film debut, but plodding Hitchcock film is disappointing.
Jamaica Run (1953) C-92m. ** D: Lewis R. Foster. Ray Milland, Arlene Dahl, Wendell Corey, Patric Knowles. Ray goes salvage-diving in the Caribbean for Dahl's nutty family. Unexciting production.
James Dean Story, The (1957) 82m. ** D: George W. George, Robert Altman. Narrated by Martin Gabel. Uninspired use of available material makes this a slow-moving documentary on life of 1950's movie star.
Jane Eyre (1944) 96m. *** D: Robert Stevenson. Orson Welles, Joan Fontaine, Margaret O'Brien, Peggy Ann Garner, John Sutton. Artistically successful if slow-moving version of

Charlotte Brontë novel about orphan girl who grows up to become a governess in mysterious household. One of Elizabeth Taylor's early films.

Janie (1944) 106m. **½ D: Michael Curtiz. Joyce Reynolds, Edward Arnold, Ann Harding, Robert Benchley, Robert Hutton, Alan Hale, Hattie McDaniel. Naive (now) but pleasant comedy about small-town girl falling in love with serviceman despite father's objections to love-hungry soldiers.

Janie Gets Married (1946) 89m. **½ D: Vincent Sherman. Joan Leslie, Robert Hutton, Edward Arnold, Ann Harding, Robert Benchley, Dorothy Malone. Pleasant follow-up to JANIE, with bright-eyed Leslie helping soldier-hubby Hutton readjust to civilian life.

Japanese War Bride (1952) 91m. **½ D: King Vidor. Don Taylor, Shirley Yamaguchi, Cameron Mitchell, Marie Windsor, Philip Ahn. Penetrating study of WW2 veterans who return to life in U.S.A. with Oriental brides.

Jason and the Argonauts (1963) C-104m. **½ D: Don Chaffey. Todd Armstrong, Gary Raymond, Nancy Kovack, Honor Blackman, Nigel Green. Good special effects and colorful backgrounds uplift fable about Jason's search for golden fleece.

Jassy (1944-British) 96m. **½ D: Bernard Knowles. Margaret Lockwood, Patricia Roc, Dermot Walsh, Dennis Price. Brooding drama of gypsy girl accused of causing her husband's death.

Java Head (1935-British) 70m. ** D: J. Walter Ruben. Anna May Wong, Elizabeth Allan, Edmund Gwenn, John Loder, Ralph Richardson, Herbert Lomas. Nothing-special drama about two sons given shipping business by aging father. One, of course, attempts to take over. Good cast in very uneven film.

Jayhawkers, The (1959) C-100m. **½ D: Melvin Frank. Jeff Chandler, Fess Parker, Nicole Maurey, Henry Silva, Herbert Rudley. Turgid Western set in 1850's, with Chandler and Parker battling for power, Maurey the love interest.

Jazz Boat (1960-British) 90m. **½ D: Ken Hughes. Anthony Newley, Anne Aubrey, Lionel Jeffries, David Lodge, Bernie Winters, James Booth. Energetic caper of handyman Newley pretending to be a crook and then having to carry through, with dire results.

Jazz Singer, The (1927) 89m. **½ D: Alan Crosland. Al Jolson, May McAvoy, Warner Oland, Eugenie Besserer, Otto Lederer. Legendary first talkie is actually silent with several sound musical sequences. Story of Cantor Oland's son (Jolson) going into show business is creaky, but this movie milestone should be seen once. Songs: "Mammy," "Toot Toot Tootsie," etc. Look fast for Myrna Loy as a chorus girl.

Jazz Singer, The (1953) C-107m. *** D: Michael Curtiz. Danny Thomas, Peggy Lee, Mildred Dunnock, Eduard Franz. Well-done remake of famous first talkie of young man who dares to make it as singer rather than cantor. Score nominated for Oscar. Some big names in cast may make this one interesting.

Jealousy (1945) 71m. ** D: Gustav Machaty. John Loder, Nils Asther, Jane Randolph, Karen Morley. Obvious plot-line of renowned writer being murdered and wrong person accused; well served by capable cast.

Jeanne Eagels (1957) 109m. **½ D: George Sidney. Kim Novak, Jeff Chandler, Agnes Moorehead, Gene Lockhart, Virginia Grey. Novak tries but can't rise to demands of portraying famed actress of 1920's. Chandler is her virile love interest.

Jennie Gerhardt (1933) 85m. *** D: Marion Gering. Sylvia Sidney, Donald Cook, Mary Astor, Edward Arnold, Louise Carver, Cora Sue Collins, H. B. Warner. Meticulously produced version of Theodore Dreiser saga of poor-girl Sidney finding kind benefactor Arnold, losing him, and living as Cook's back-street lover. Actors and elaborate production lend credibility to episodic soaper set at turn of the century.

Jennifer (1953) 73m. **½ D: Joel Newton. Ida Lupino, Howard Duff, Robert Nichols, Mary Shipp. Turgid programmer of Lupino working at eerie old mansion where she discovers a murder.

Jeopardy (1953) 69m. **½ D: John Sturges. Barbara Stanwyck, Barry Sullivan, Ralph Meeker, Lee Aaker.

Taut but superficial account of Stanwyck trying to save husband from drowning.

Jesse James (1939) C-105m. *** D: Henry King. Tyrone Power, Henry Fonda, Nancy Kelly, Randolph Scott, Henry Hull, Brian Donlevy, Jane Darwell. Sprawling, glamorous Western with Power and Fonda as Jesse and Frank James; movie builds for audience acceptance that Jesse was misguided; sturdy presentation.

Jesse James Meets Frankenstein's Daughter (1966) C-88m. *½ D: William Beaudine. John Lupton, Estelita, Cal Bolder, Steven Geray, Jim Davis. Low-budget nonsense mixture of horror and Western genres, with title monster practicing weird experiments, conflicting with noted outlaw.

Jesse James vs. the Daltons (1954) C-65m. ** D: William Castle. Brett King, Barbara Lawrence, James Griffith, Bill Phipps, John Cliff. Bland shoot-out between alleged son of Jesse James and the other notorious outlaw gang.

Jesse James' Women (1954) C-83m. *½ D: Donald Barry. Don Barry, Jack Buetel, Peggie Castle, Lita Baron. Romancing a variety of women leaves James little time for outlaw activities; cute premise doesn't work out.

Jessica (1962) C-112m. **½ D: Jean Negulesco. Angie Dickinson, Maurice Chevalier, Noel-Noel, Gabriele Ferzetti, Sylva Koscina, Agnes Moorehead. Dickinson is an Italian midwife who has men in her village lusting for her, with Chevalier as the local priest. Malarkey.

Jet Attack (1958) 68m. Bomb D: Edward L. Cahn. John Agar, Audrey Totter, Gregory Walcott, James Dobson. Sloppy Korean War programmer about rescue of U.S. scientist caught behind North Korean lines.

Jet Over the Atlantic (1960) 95m. ** D: Byron Haskin. Guy Madison, Virginia Mayo, George Raft, Ilona Massey. Capable cast in clichéd situation of plane with engine trouble. Madison's the former air force pilot saving the day; predictable plot-line.

Jewel Robbery (1932) 70m. **½ D: William Dieterle. Kay Francis, William Powell, Hardie Albright, C. Henry Gordon, Helen Vinson, Herman Bing. Pleasing fluff of noblewoman (Francis) falling in love with debonair burglar (Powell) during well-executed theft; everyone très chic.

Jezebel (1938) 103m. ***½ D: William Wyler. Bette Davis, Henry Fonda, George Brent, Margaret Lindsay, Donald Crisp, Fay Bainter, Spring Byington, Richard Cromwell. Davis won her second Oscar as tempestuous Southern belle who goes too far to make fiancé Fonda jealous; Bainter also received Oscar as Davis' sympathetic aunt. Fine production, entire cast excellent.

Jigsaw (1949) 70m. ** D: Fletcher Markle. Franchot Tone, Jean Wallace, Myron McCormick, Marc Lawrence, Betty Harper (Doe Avedon). Pedestrian caper of assistant D.A. solving murder, spiked by guest appearances of Marlene Dietrich, Henry Fonda, John Garfield, Burgess Meredith, Marsha Hunt. Retitled: GUN MOLL.

Jigsaw (1968) 97m. **½ D: James Goldstone. Harry Guardino, Bradford Dillman, Hope Lange, Pat Hingle, Diana Hyland, Victor Jory. Fast-paced, utterly confusing yarn about amnesiac Dillman trying to figure out his past, and unravel murder caper he was involved in. Frantic editing and music don't help viewer.

Jim Thorpe—All American (1951) 107m. *** D: Michael Curtiz. Burt Lancaster, Charles Bickford, Steve Cochran, Phyllis Thaxter. Lancaster pushes hard to make clichéd script detailing life of famed athlete rise to some meaning.

Jimmy the Gent (1934) 67m. **½ D: Michael Curtiz. James Cagney, Bette Davis, Alice White, Allen Jenkins, Philip Reed, Mayo Methot. Crooked businessman Cagney pretends to refine himself to impress Davis in this bouncy comedy.

Jinx Money (1948) 61m. D: William Beaudine. Leo Gorcey, Huntz Hall, Billy Benedict, David Gorcey, Bennie Bartlett, Sheldon Leonard, Donald MacBride, Wanda McKay, John Eldredge. SEE: **Bowery Boys** series.

Jitterbugs (1943) 74m. ** D: Mal St. Clair. Stan Laurel, Oliver Hardy, Vivian Blaine, Robert Bailey, Douglas Fowley, Noel Madison. One of the team's better later efforts, with Blaine sharing the spotlight and doing quite nicely. Ollie's scene with Southern belle Lee Patrick is a gem.

Jivaro (1954) **C**-91m. ** D: Edward Ludwig. Fernando Lamas, Rhonda Fleming, Brian Keith, Lon Chaney, Richard Denning. Cornball adventure in wild head-hunting country, with gold-hungry group seeking valuable ore.

Joan of Arc (1948) C-145m. **½ D: Victor Fleming. Ingrid Bergman, Jose Ferrer, Francis L. Sullivan, J. Carrol Naish, Ward Bond. Bergman is staunchly sincere in this overlong, faithful adaptation of Maxwell Anderson's play. Not enough spectacle to balance talky sequences.

Joan of Ozark (1942) 80m. ** D: Joseph Santley. Judy Canova, Joe E Brown, Eddie Foy, Jr., Jerome Cowan, Alexander Granach, Anne Jeffreys. Hillbilly Canova hunts down Nazi underground ring in U.S.

Joan of Paris (1942) 95m. ***½ D: Robert Stevenson. Michele Morgan, Paul Henreid, Thomas Mitchell, Laird Cregar, May Robson, Alexander Granach, Alan Ladd. Excellent WW2 tale of dedicated Morgan giving herself up so Henreid and fellow-pilots can return to Allied lines.

Joe Butterfly (1957) 90m. **½ D: Jesse Hibbs. Audie Murphy, Burgess Meredith, George Nader, Keenan Wynn, Fred Clark. Another variation on TEAHOUSE OF THE AUGUST MOON, set in post-WW2 Japan. American soldiers at mercy of wily Jap Meredith to get needed supplies.

Joe Dakota (1957) C-79m. **½ D: Richard Bartlett. Jock Mahoney, Luana Patten, Charles McGraw, Lee Van Cleef. Folksy oater of Mahoney renewing a town's pride in itself.

Joe Louis Story, The (1953) 88m. ** D: Robert Gordon. Coley Wallace, Paul Stewart, Hilda Simms, James Edwards. Tame biography of famed boxer.

Joe Macbeth (1956-British) 90m. **½ D: Ken Hughes. Paul Douglas, Ruth Roman, Bonar Colleano, Gregoire Aslan, Sidney James. Interesting variation on Shakespeare's MACBETH, adaptated to gangland life.

Joe Smith, American (1942) 63m. ** D: Richard Thorpe. Robert Young, Marsha Hunt, Harvey Stephens, Darryl Hickman. Dated WW2 morale-booster about kidnapped muntions worker Young who refuses to divulge secrets to Nazis.

John Goldfarb, Please Come Home (1964) C-96m. *½ D: J. Lee Thompson. Shirley MacLaine, Peter Ustinov, Richard Crenna, Jim Backus, Fred Clark. Trapped in desert kingdom, two Americans (pilot, gal reporter) conspire to help Arabian chief Ustinov's football team beat Notre Dame. Notre Dame University found this spoof so offensive it sued in court; the viewer has an easier alternative.

John Loves Mary (1949) 96m. **½ D: David Butler. Ronald Reagan, Patricia Neal, Jack Carson, Wayne Morris, Edward Arnold. Bright WW2 comedy of Reagan marrying British gal so she can come to U.S.; seems naive now.

John Meade's Woman (1937) 87m. ** D: Richard Wallace. Edward Arnold, Gail Patrick, Francine Larrimore, George Bancroft, Aileen Pringle, Sidney Blackmer. Arnold plays another Great American Businessman, marrying one girl to spite another. Idea backfires; so does film.

John Paul Jones (1959) C-126m. **½ D: John Farrow. Robert Stack, Marisa Pavan, Charles Coburn, Erin O'Brien, Macdonald Carey, Jean-Pierre Aumont, Peter Cushing, Bruce Cabot, Bette Davis. Empty spectacle of 18th-century American hero, with cameo by Davis as Russian empress.

Johnny Allegro (1949) 81m. **½ D: Ted Tetzlaff. Nina Foch, George Raft, George Macready, Will Geer. Seamy gangster melodrama of ex-racketeer Raft helping federal agents capture counterfeiting gang.

Johnny Angel (1945) 79m. *** D: Edwin L. Marin. George Raft, Claire Trevor, Signe Hasso, Lowell Gilmore, Hoagy Carmichael, Marvin Miller. Tough, well-done melodrama, with Raft cleaning up notorious mob, solving mystery of father's murder. Trevor lends good support.

Johnny Apollo (1940) 93m. *** D: Henry Hathaway. Tyrone Power, Lloyd Nolan, Dorothy Lamour, Edward Arnold, Charles Grapewin, Lionel Atwill, Marc Lawrence. Good-natured Power turns crook, resentful of father Arnold, white-collar thief. Good acting, especially by Lamour as girlfriend, improves film.

Johnny Belinda (1948) 103m. ***½

D: Jean Negulesco. Jane Wyman, Lew Ayres, Charles Bickford, Jan Sterling, Agnes Moorehead, Stephen McNally. Sensitively acted, atmospheric drama of young deaf-mute girl (Wyman) and doctor (Ayres) who works with her. Setting of provincial fishing-farming community vividly realized. Wyman won an Oscar for her fine performance.

Johnny Come Lately (1943) 97m. **½ **D**: William K. Howard. James Cagney, Grace George, Marjorie Main, Marjorie Lord, Hattie McDaniel, Ed McNamara. Tame but amusing Cagney vehicle, with Jimmy as wandering newspaperman who helps elderly editor George in small-town political battle.

Johnny Concho (1956) 84m. **½ **D**: Don McGuire. Frank Sinatra, Keenan Wynn, William Conrad, Phyllis Kirk, Wallace Ford, Dorothy Adams. Plodding Western with novelty of Sinatra as cowardly soul who must build courage for inevitable shoot-out.

Johnny Cool (1963) 101m. *** **D**: William Asher. Henry Silva, Elizabeth Montgomery, Sammy Davis, Jr., Wanda Hendrix, Telly Savalas, Jim Backus, Joey Bishop. Sadistic study of Silva, vicious gangster seeking revenge. Brutal account, realistically told.

Johnny Dark (1954) C-85m. **½ **D**: George Sherman. Tony Curtis, Piper Laurie, Don Taylor, Paul Kelly, Ilka Chase, Sidney Blackmer. Curtis is energetic as auto designer who enters big sports-car race.

Johnny Doesn't Live Here Any More (1944) 77m. **½ **D**: Joe May. Simone Simon, James Ellison, Minna Gombell, Alan Dinehart, Robert Mitchum, Grady Sutton. WW2 ancestor of THE APARTMENT, with Simon's flat becoming a madhouse, all ending happily with marriage. Retitled: AND SO THEY WERE MARRIED.

Johnny Eager (1941) 107m. **½ **D**: Mervyn LeRoy. Robert Taylor, Lana Turner, Edward Arnold, Van Heflin, Robert Sterling, Patricia Dane, Glenda Farrell. Slick gangster tale with Taylor as heel, Turner his society girl, Arnold her father, with Heflin in Academy Award role as alcoholic.

Johnny Guitar (1954) C-110m. *** **D**: Nicholas Ray. Joan Crawford, Sterling Hayden, Scott Brady, Mercedes McCambridge, Ward Bond, Ben Cooper, Ernest Borgnine, John Carradine. Offbeat Western, with tough gambling-house owner Crawford discovering money won't buy everything.

Johnny Holiday (1949) 92m. *** **D**: Willis Goldbeck. William Bendix, Allen Martin, Jr., Stanley Clements, Jack Hagen. Remarkably sincere study of juvenile delinquent torn between friends from dishonest past and those trying to help him at reform farm.

Johnny in the Clouds (1945-British) 87m. ***½ **D**: Anthony Asquith. Michael Redgrave, John Mills, Rosamond John, Douglass Montgomery, Renee Asherson, Joyce Carey, Stanley Holloway. Excellent British wartime drama of young man who must choose between love and devotion to military service; fine cast, script, production. Jean Simmons' first film. Original title: THE WAY TO THE STARS.

Johnny Nobody (1960-British) 88m. **½ **D**: Nigel Patrick. Nigel Patrick, Yvonne Mitchell, Aldo Ray, William Bendix. Involved, miscast murder yarn, with Bendix a murdered author, Patrick a priest trying to sort out the supposed "miracle" killing.

Johnny O'Clock (1947) 95m. **½ **D**: Robert Rossen. Dick Powell, Evelyn Keyes, Lee J. Cobb, Ellen Drew, Nina Foch. Cast and director make script about high-class gambler in trouble with the law seem better than it is; Powell is fine in lead role.

Johnny One Eye (1950) 78m. ** **D**: Robert Florey. Pat O'Brien, Wayne Morris, Dolores Moran, Gayle Reed. Schmaltzy Damon Runyon yarn of O'Brien, a gangster with proverbial heart of gold on the lam.

Johnny Rocco (1958) 84m. ** **D**: Paul Landres. Richard Eyer, Stephen McNally, Coleen Gray, Russ Conway. Gangster's son (Eyer) is focal point of gangland hunt because he witnessed a killing; OK drama.

Johnny Stool Pigeon (1949) 76m. **½ **D**: William Castle. Howard Duff, Shelley Winters, Dan Duryea, Anthony Curtis. Turgid drama of convict being sprung from prison so he can lead federal agents to former gang members.

Johnny Tiger (1966) C-102m. **½

D: Paul Wendkos. Robert Taylor, Geraldine Brooks, Chad Everett, Brenda Scott. Set in Florida, tame tale of teacher Taylor, doctor Brooks, and half-breed Seminole Everett trying to come to conclusions about Indians' role in modern world.

Johnny Trouble (1957) 80m. **½ D: John H. Auer. Ethel Barrymore, Cecil Kellaway, Carolyn Jones, Stuart Whitman. Tender tale of elderly Barrymore convinced that her long-missing son will still turn up, and that he wasn't a bad person.

Joker Is Wild, The (1957) 123m. *** D: Charles Vidor. Frank Sinatra, Mitzi Gaynor, Jeanne Crain, Eddie Albert, Beverly Garland, Jackie Coogan. Sinatra is fine in biography of nightclub performer Joe E. Lewis, with Crain and Gaynor diverting as his two loves. Song "All The Way" won an Oscar.

Jokers, The (1966-British) 94m. *** D: Michael Winner. Michael Crawford, Oliver Reed, Gabriella Licudi, Harry Andrews, James Donald, Daniel Massey. Droll satire on the Establishment with Reed and Crawford two brothers from upper classes, putting everyone on and carrying out perfect caper; ironic results.

Jolly Bad Fellow, A (1964-British) 94m. ** D: Don Chaffey. Leo McKern, Janet Munro, Maxine Audley, Duncan MacRae. Peculiar yarn of college professor who plays God by trying to kill those people whom he feels are evil parasites; strange blend of drama-satire. Retitled: THEY ALL DIED LAUGHING.

Jolson Sings Again (1949) C-96m. ** D: Henry Levin. Larry Parks, Barbara Hale, William Demarest, Ludwig Donath. Attempt to continue THE JOLSON STORY is pointless, especially when Parks (playing Jolson) meets Parks (playing Parks). Jolson standards are still good to hear.

Jolson Story, The (1946) C-128m. ***½ D: Alfred E. Green. Larry Parks, Evelyn Keyes, William Demarest, Bill Goodwin, Ludwig Donath. Smooth biography of all-time great Al Jolson, with Parks giving his all in story of brash vaudeville performer's rise in the show biz world. Songs: "Swanee," "April Showers," "Mammy," etc. dubbed by Jolson.

Joseph and His Brethren (1962) C-103m. ** D: Irving Rapper. Marietto, Geoffrey Horne, Belinda Lee, Finlay Currie, Antonio Segurini, Charles Borromel, Carlo Giustini. Juvenile biblical tale, lavishly produced but empty-headed.

Josette (1938) 73m. **½ D: Allan Dwan. Don Ameche, Simone Simon, Robert Young, Bert Lahr, Joan Davis, Tala Birell, Paul Hurst, William Collier, Sr. Above-par musicomedy of mistaken identity, with sturdy cast and such forgettable songs as "May I Drop A Petal In Your Glass of Wine."

Journey, The (1959) C-125m. *** D: Anatole Litvak. Deborah Kerr, Yul Brynner, Jason Robards, Jr., Robert Morley, E. G. Marshall, Anne Jackson, Ronny Howard, Kurt Kasznar, Anouk Aimee. Heady melodrama set in 1956 Budapest, with assorted types seeking to leave. Offbeat romance between Kerr and Communist officer Brynner.

Journey for Margaret (1942) 81m. *** D: W. S. Van Dyke II. Robert Young, Laraine Day, Fay Bainter, Nigel Bruce, Margaret O'Brien, William Severn. Stirring WW2 drama of children left homeless by British bombing. O'Brien is very appealing scene-stealer, Young her adopted father.

Journey Into Fear (1942) 69m. *** D: Norman Foster. Orson Welles, Joseph Cotten, Dolores Del Rio, Ruth Warrick, Agnes Moorehead. Often baffling WW2 spy drama started by Welles, taken out of his hands. Much of tale of smuggling munitions into Turkey still exciting.

Journey Into Light (1951) 87m. **½ D: Stuart Heisler. Sterling Hayden, Viveca Lindfors, Thomas Mitchell, H. B. Warner, Ludwig Donath. Thought-provoking theme, poorly paced; Hayden is clergyman who finds his belief in God again with aid of blind Lindfors.

Journey to Freedom (1957-British) 60m. *½ D: Robert C. Dertano. Jacques Scott, Genevieve Aumont, Morgan Lane, Fred Kohler, Don Marlowe. Lukewarm spy hunt, with Communist agents tracking down pro-American refugee now in the U.S.

Journey to Shiloh (1968) C-101m. *½ D: William Hale. James Caan,

Michael Sarrazin, Brenda Scott, Don Stroud, Paul Petersen. Limp Civil War programmer about young Texans anxious to engage in battle. Veterans Rex Ingram, John Doucette, and Noah Beery are lost in this jumble.

Journey to the Center of the Earth (1959) C-132m. *** D: Henry Levin. James Mason, Pat Boone, Arlene Dahl, Diane Baker, Thayer David, Peter Ronson, Alan Napier. Stunning version of Jules Verne's yarn, muddled script-wise but high on special effects. Boone even sings.

Journey to the Lost City (1960-German, dubbed) C-94m. **½ D: Fritz Lang. Debra Paget, Paul Christian, Walter Reyer, Claus Holm, Vladimir Inkijinoff, Sabina Bettmann. On-location filming in India enhances story of Britisher Christian's romance with native dancing girl Paget, but it's slow going most of the way.

Journey to the Seventh Planet (1962) C-83m. ** D: Sidney Pink. John Agar, Greta Thyssen, Ann Smyrner, Mimi Heinrich, Carl Ottosen. Passable sci-fi of exploratory trip to foreign planet and attempt to destroy alien forces there.

Journey Together (1946-British) 80m. ** D: John Boulting. Richard Attenborough, Jack Watling, Edward G. Robinson, Bessie Love. More of a documentary than a feature story, this film retraces lives of U.S. fliers in England during WW2.

Joy House (1964-French, dubbed) C-98m. **½ René Clement. Jane Fonda, Alain Delon, Lola Albright, Sorrell Booke. Living on his looks, a playboy on the run seeks refuge in a gloomy French mansion run by two American women. Fate and quicker wits than his control this brooding tale of irony. Original title: LOVE CAGE.

Joy in the Morning (1965) C-103m. ** D: Alex Segal. Richard Chamberlain, Yvette Mimieux, Arthur Kennedy, Sidney Blackmer. Betty Smith's gentle novel of struggling law student and his marital problems becomes mild vehicle for Chamberlain, who crusades for human dignity amid stereotypes of a college town.

Joy of Living (1938) 90m. *** D: Tay Garnett. Irene Dunne, Douglas Fairbanks, Jr., Alice Brady, Guy Kibbee, Jean Dixon, Eric Blore, Lucille Ball. Delightful screwball musicomedy with gay-blade Fairbanks wooing singing star Dunne.

Joy of Loving SEE: School for Love

Joy Ride (1958) 60m. *½ D: Edward Bernds. Rad Fulton, Ann Doran, Regis Toomey, Nicholas King. Minor account of middle-aged man trying to reform hot-rod gang members; occasionally bristling.

Juarez (1939) 132m. *** D: William Dieterle. Paul Muni, Bette Davis, Brian Aherne, Claude Rains, John Garfield, Gale Sondergaard, Donald Crisp, Gilbert Roland, Louis Calhern, Grant Mitchell. Interesting biography of Mexican leader (Muni), with unforgettable performance by Rains as Napoleon III; also notable is Garfield's offbeat casting as Mexican gunman. Elaborately done, but never as inspiring as it's intended to be.

Jubal (1956) C-101m. **½ D: Delmer Daves. Glenn Ford, Ernest Borgnine, Rod Steiger, Valerie French, Felicia Farr, Noah Beery, Jr. Smoldering Western involving tense interaction on Borgnine's ranch; cast gives appropriately brooding performances.

Jubilee Trail (1954) C-103m. **½ D: Joseph Kane. Vera Ralston, Joan Leslie, Forrest Tucker, John Russell, Ray Middleton, Pat O'Brien. Expansive Republic Western vehicle for Ralston as heart-of-gold chanteuse sorting out rancher's life in old California.

Judge, The (1949) 69m. *½ D: Elmer Clifton. Milburn Stone, Katherine de Mille, Paul Guilfoyle, Jonathan Hale, Norman Budd. Cheapie flick vaguely detailing man's moral disintegration from respected attorney to fugitive criminal.

Judge Hardy & Son (1939) 87m. D: George B. Seitz. Lewis Stone, Mickey Rooney, Cecilia Parker, Fay Holden, Sara Haden, Ann Rutherford, June Preisser, Maria Ouspenskaya, Henry Hull, Martha O'Driscoll. SEE: Andy Hardy series.

Judge Hardy's Children (1938) 78m. D: George B. Seitz. Lewis Stone, Mickey Rooney, Cecilia Parker, Fay Holden, Betty Ross Clark, Ann Rutherford, Robert Whitney, Ruth Hussey. SEE: Andy Hardy series.

Judge Steps Out, The (1949) 91m.

**½ D: Boris Ingster. Alexander Knox, Ann Sothern, George Tobias, Shyran Moffett. Mild froth as prim judge Knox finds refuge in being short-order cook on days off from bench.

Judgment at Nuremberg (1961) 178m. **** D: Stanley Kramer. Spencer Tracy, Burt Lancaster, Richard Widmark, Marlene Dietrich, Judy Garland, Maximilian Schell, Montgomery Clift, William Shatner. Superior production revolving around U.S. judge Tracy presiding over German war-criminal trials. Schell won Oscar as defense attorney. Fine performances by Dietrich as widow of German officer, Garland as hausfrau, Clift as unbalanced war camp victim.

Juggler, The (1953) 86m. **½ D: Edward Dmytryk. Kirk Douglas, Milly Vitale, Paul Stewart, Alf Kjellin. Sentimental account of Jewish refugee Douglas going to Israel to rebuild his life, overcoming bitterness from life in a concentration camp.

Juke Box Rhythm (1959) 81m. *½ D: Arthur Dreifuss. Jo Morrow, Jack Jones, Brian Donlevy, George Jessel, Hans Conried, Karin Booth, Marjorie Reynolds, Fritz Feld. Minor songfest musical worthwhile only for veteran cast and young Jones on his way up.

Juke Girl (1942) 90m. **½ D: Curtis Bernhardt. Ann Sheridan, Ronald Reagan, Richard Whorf, Gene Lockhart, Faye Emerson, George Tobias. Saga of fruit-workers' troubles in Florida never really hits the mark, but Sheridan and Reagan are good as laborers who get involved in murder.

Julia Misbehaves (1948) 99m. *** D: Jack Conway. Greer Garson, Walter Pidgeon, Peter Lawford, Elizabeth Taylor, Cesar Romero, Mary Boland, Nigel Bruce. Bouncy account of showgal Garson returning to dignified husband Pidgeon when daughter Taylor is about to marry; Romero is fun as bragging acrobat. Stars seem right at home with slapstick situations.

Julie (1956) 99m. **½ D: Andrew L. Stone. Doris Day, Louis Jourdan, Barry Sullivan, Frank Lovejoy, Mae Marsh. Shrill melodrama of Day being chased by psychopathic husband who murdered his first spouse; tense till preposterous climax.

Juliet of the Spirits (1965-Italian, dubbed) C-148m. *** D: Federico Fellini. Giulietta Masina, Sandra Milo, Mario Pisu, Valentina Cortesa, Lou Gilbert, Sylva Koscina. Surrealistic fantasy triggered by wife's fears that her well-to-do husband is cheating on her. A film requiring viewer to delve into woman's psyche via a rash of symbolism; counterbalanced with rich visual delights.

Julietta (1957-French, dubbed) 96m. **½ D: Marc Chamarat. Jean Marais, Jeanne Moreau, Dany Robin, Denise Grey. Frilly comedy with sturdy cast. Heroine journeys to marry a prince, misses her train and dallies with handsome lawyer.

Julius Caesar (1953) 120m. ***½ D: Joseph L. Mankiewicz. Marlon Brando, James Mason, John Gielgud, Louis Calhern, Edmond O'Brien, Greer Garson, Deborah Kerr. Superior adaptation of William Shakespeare's play of political power and honor in ancient Rome, lavishly produced with excellent cast.

Jump Into Hell (1955) 93m. **½ D: David Butler. Jacques Sernas, Kurt Kasznar, Peter Van Eyck, Pat Blake. Neatly paced actioner of paratroopers involved in Indo-China War.

Jumping Jacks (1952) 96m. **½ D: Norman Taurog. Dean Martin, Jerry Lewis, Mona Freeman, Don DeFore, Robert Strauss. Daffy duo has good opportunity for plenty of sight gags when they join military paratroop squad.

June Bride (1948) 97m. *** D: Bretaigne Windust. Bette Davis, Robert Montgomery, Fay Bainter, Tom Tully, Barbara Bates, Jerome Cowan. Flippant comedy of magazine writers Davis and Montgomery inspired by feature story they are doing on June brides.

Jungle, The (1952) 74m. *½ D: William Berke. Rod Cameron, Cesar Romero, Marie Windsor, Sulchana. Low-grade chiller with too many backlot sets and stock shots; story centers on journey into India Jungle, prehistoric monsters romping about.

Jungle Book, The (1942) C-109m. *** D: Zoltan Korda. Sabu, Joseph Calleia, John Qualen, Frank Puglia, Rosemary DeCamp. Colorful Kipling fantasy of boy (Sabu) raised by wolves. Exciting family fare, showing great imagination.

Jungle Captive (1945) 63m. Bomb D: Harold Young. Otto Kruger, Amelita Ward, Phil Brown, Vicky Lane, Jerome Cowan, Rondo Hatton. Sloppy Universal quickie dealing with mad scientists and woman transformed into ape creature.

Jungle Drums of Africa SEE: U-238 and the Witch Doctor

Jungle Fighters SEE: Long, the Short and the Tall, The

Jungle Gents (1954) 64m. D: Edward Bernds, Austen Jewell. Leo Gorcey, Huntz Hall, Laurette Luez, Bernard Gorcey, David Condon. SEE: Bowery Boys series.

Jungle Girl SEE: Bomba and the Jungle Girl

Jungle Goddess (1949) 65m. *½ D: Lewis D. Collins. Ralph Byrd, George Reeves, Wanda McKay, Armida. Very low-budget swamp saga is good only for laughs.

Jungle Gold (1944) 100m. ** D: Spencer Bennet, Wallace Grissell. Allan Lane, Linda Stirling, Duncan Renaldo, George J. Lewis. Republic cliffhanger vehicle for the Queen of the serials. Stirling (Tiger Woman) romps through innumerable adventures to prevent wrong parties from uncovering gold treasure. Re-edited movie serial: THE TIGER WOMAN, reissued under title PERILS OF THE DARKEST JUNGLE.

Jungle Jim When athletic Johnny Weissmuller left the Tarzan series after sixteen years in the role, enterprising producer Sam Katzman proposed a new series that would enable the more mature but still rugged star to cavort in familiar surroundings. It was Jungle Jim, presold to an anxious audience via a successful comic strip and radio show. One critic accurately summed it up as "Tarzan with clothes on." The series was sure-fire and performed well at the box office for seven years, despite a conspicuous absence of commendation by the critics. From the first film, JUNGLE JIM, to the last, CANNIBAL ATTACK, the series was noted for its incredible plots and rousing action scenes, aimed primarily at juvenile audiences. Most efforts had Jungle Jim helping some Columbia Pictures heroine in distress (a lady scientist seeking a rare drug, a WAC captain lost in the jungle, etc.) and getting tangled up with hostile natives, voodoo curses, and nefarious villains (often all three at once). In the last three films of the series (JUNGLE MOON MEN, DEVIL GODDESS, CANNIBAL ATTACK) the name Jungle Jim was dropped and Weissmuller played himself, but the format remained the same, with Johnny's ever-faithful chimpanzee friend Timba at his side. Perhaps the highlight of the series was CAPTIVE GIRL, an average entry which had the distinction of Buster Crabbe, whose career paralleled Weissmuller's in many ways, as the villain.

Jungle Jim (1948) 73m. D: William Berke. Johnny Weissmuller, Virginia Grey, George Reeves, Lita Baron.

Jungle Jim in the Forbidden Land (1952) 65m. D: Lew Landers. Johnny Weissmuller, Angela Greene, Jean Willes, William Fawcett.

Jungle Man-Eaters (1954) 68m. D: Lee Sholem. Johnny Weissmuller, Karin Booth, Richard Stapley, Bernard Hamilton. SEE: Jungle Jim series.

Jungle Manhunt (1951) 66m. D: Lew Landers. Johnny Weissmuller, Bob Waterfield, Sheila Ryan, Rick Vallin, Lyle Talbot. SEE: Jungle Jim series.

Jungle Moon Men (1955) 70m. D: Charles S. Gould. Johnny Weissmuller, Jean Byron, Helene Stanton, Myron Healy. SEE: Jungle Jim series.

Jungle Princess, The (1936) 85m. *** D: William Thiele. Dorothy Lamour, Ray Milland, Akim Tamiroff, Lynne Overman, Molly Lamont, Mala, Hugh Buckler. Lamour's first sarong film is quite unpretentious and pleasant; Milland is explorer who brings her back to civilization.

Jungle Woman (1944) 54m. *½ D: Reginald LeBorg. Acquanetta, Evelyn Ankers, J. Carrol Naish, Samuel S. Hinds. Silly horror quickie set in back-lot jungle; transformation of ape into native woman.

Junior Miss (1945) 94m. **½ D: George Seaton. Peggy Ann Garner, Allyn Joslyn, Michael Dunne, Faye Marlowe, Mona Freeman, Sylvia Field, Barbara Whiting. Naive but entertaining comedy of teen-ager

Garner and harried father Joslyn, based on Broadway play.

Jupiter's Darling (1955) C-96m. **½ D: George Sidney. Esther Williams, Howard Keel, George Sanders, Marge and Gower Champion, Norma Varden. Lavish musical of Robert Sherwood's ROAD TO ROME, which bogs down in tedium: Williams is temptress who dallies with Hannibal (Keel) to prevent attack on Rome.

Just Across the Street (1952) 78m. ** D: Joseph Pevney. Ann Sheridan, John Lund, Cecil Kellaway, Natalie Schafer, Harvey Lembeck. Mild shenanigans with working-gal Sheridan being mistaken for wealthy estate owner.

Just Around the Corner (1938) 70m. ** D: Irving Cummings. Shirley Temple, Joan Davis, Charles Farrell, Amanda Duff, Bill Robinson, Bert Lahr. A good place to be for most of this film, one of Shirley's lesser efforts. Musical numbers with Robinson still a delight, though.

Just Before Dawn (1946) 65m. D: William Castle. Warner Baxter, Adele Roberts, Charles D. Brown, Martin Kosleck, Mona Barrie, Marvin Miller. SEE: Crime Doctor series.

Just for You (1952) C-104m. *** D: Elliott Nugent. Bing Crosby, Jane Wyman, Ethel Barrymore, Natalie Wood, Cora Witherspoon. Zesty musical of producer Crosby who can't be bothered with his growing children, till Wyman shows him the way.

Just This Once (1952) 90m. **½ D: Don Weis. Janet Leigh, Peter Lawford, Lewis Stone, Marilyn Erskine, Richard Anderson. Cute little comedy of stern Leigh in charge of playboy Lawford's dwindling fortunes, and their inevitable romance.

Just Off Broadway (1942) 66m. ** D: Herbert I. Leeds. Lloyd Nolan, Marjorie Weaver, Phil Silvers, Janis Carter. Acceptable Michael Shayne caper, with swanky dame on trial for murder; outcome is easy for mystery fans.

Kanal (1956-Polish, dubbed) 90m. *** D: Andrezej Wajda. Teresa Izewska, Tadeusz Janczar, Wienczylaw Glinski, Wladyslaw Sheybal. Intense, stark study of partisans involved in Warsaw rebellion during 1944 when Nazis occupied country. Retitled: THEY LOVED LIFE.

Kangaroo (1952) C-84m. ** D: Lewis Milestone. Maureen O'Hara, Peter Lawford, Finlay Currie, Richard Boone. Uninspired blend of romance and adventure, salvaged by good on-location Australian landscapes and fetching O'Hara.

Kansan, The (1943) 79m. **½ D: George Archainbaud. Richard Dix, Jane Wyatt, Victor Jory, Albert Dekker, Eugene Pallette, Robert Armstrong. Zippy Western, with Dix becoming town hero, taming gangsters, but facing more trouble with corrupt town official.

Kansas City Confidential (1952) 98m. ** D: Phil Karlson. John Payne, Coleen Gray, Preston Foster, Neville Brand, Lee Van Cleef. Another routine exposé-type film, with veteran cast.

Kansas City Kitty (1944) 63m. ** D: Del Lord. Joan Davis, Bob Crosby, Jane Frazee, Erik Rolf. Programmer sparked by Davis, involved in purchase of song-publishing company on the skids.

Kansas Pacific (1953) C-73m. ** D: Ray Nazarro. Sterling Hayden, Eve Miller, Barton MacLane, Reed Hadley, Irving Bacon. Inoffensive account of building of title railway during 1860's, with Reb soldiers trying to prevent its completion.

Kansas Raiders (1950) C-80m. *½ D: Ray Enright. Audie Murphy, Brian Donlevy, Marguerite Chapman, Tony Curtis, Richard Arlen. Murphy plays Jesse James, involved with myriad of distinguished outlaws in post-Civil War West, all leading up to same old Western formula.

Kathleen (1941) 88m. ** D: Harold S. Bucquet. Shirley Temple, Herbert Marshall, Laraine Day, Gail Patrick, Felix Bressart. Predictable story of neglected daughter Temple bringing widower father Marshall and Day together.

Kathy O' (1958) C-99m. **½ D: Jack Sher. Dan Duryea, Jan Sterling, Patty McCormack, Mary Fickett. Sluggish frolic of temperamental child star McCormack and her desperate public relations agent Duryea.

Katie Did It (1951) 81m. **½ D: Frederick de Cordova. Ann Blyth, Mark Stevens, Cecil Kellaway, Jesse

White. Blyth is perkier than usual as square New England librarian who becomes hep when romanced by swinging New Yorker Stevens.

Keep 'em Flying (1941) 86m. *** D: Arthur Lubin. Bud Abbott, Lou Costello, Carol Bruce, Martha Raye, William Gargan, Dick Foran. Top A&C, with duo in air force; great sight gags involving planes; Raye is double-barreled fun playing twins.

Keep 'em Slugging (1943) 60m. D: Christy Cabanne. Bobby Jordan, Huntz Hall, Gabriel Dell, Norman Abbott, Evelyn Ankers. SEE: Bowery Boys series.

Keep Your Powder Dry (1945) 93m. ** D: Edward Buzzell. Lana Turner, Laraine Day, Susan Peters, Agnes Moorehead, Bill Johnson, Natalie Schafer, Lee Patrick. Hackneyed tale of WW2 WACs, glossy on the outside, empty on the inside.

Keeper of the Flame (1942) 100m. *** D: George Cukor. Spencer Tracy, Katharine Hepburn, Richard Whorf, Margaret Wycherly, Forrest Tucker, Frank Craven. Excellent drama of reporter Tracy exposing unsavory background of late American hero; Hepburn is man's widow. Engrossing idea.

Kelly and Me (1957) C-86m. ** D: Robert Z. Leonard. Van Johnson, Piper Laurie, Martha Hyer, Onslow Stevens. Johnson is unsuccessful hoofer who hits movie big-time with talented dog for partner. Mild musical.

Kennel Murder Case (1933) 73m. D: Michael Curtiz. William Powell, Mary Astor, Eugene Pallette, Ralph Morgan, Helen Vinson, Jack LaRue, Robert Barrat, Robert McWade, Frank Conroy, Henry O'Neill. SEE: Philo Vance series.

Kentuckian, The (1955) C-104m. **½ D: Burt Lancaster. Burt Lancaster, Diana Lynn, Walter Matthau, John Carradine, Una Merkel. Spirited Western set in 1820's has Lancaster battling all odds to reach Texas and begin new life.

Kentucky (1938) C-95m. *** D: David Butler. Loretta Young, Richard Greene, Walter Brennan, Douglass Dumbrille, Karen Morley, Moroni Olsen, Russell Hicks. Lushly filmed story of rival horsebreeding families in blue-grass country, with lovers Young and Greene clinching at finale. Brennan won Best Supporting Actor Oscar.

Kentucky Moonshine (1938) 85m. ** D: David Butler. Tony Martin, Marjorie Weaver, Ritz Brothers, Slim Summerville, John Carradine. Slim little vehicle with Ritz Brothers causing chaos amidst feuding hillbillies in Kentucky; Martin and Weaver are the love/musical interest.

Kettles in the Ozarks, The (1956) 81m. D: Charles Lamont. Marjorie Main, Arthur Hunnicutt, Una Merkel, Ted de Corsia, Olive Sturgess. SEE: Ma and Pa Kettle series.

Kettles on Old Macdonald's Farm, The (1957) 80m. D: Virgil Vogel. Marjorie Main, Parker Fennelly, Gloria Talbott, John Smith, Pat Morrow. SEE: Ma and Pa Kettle series.

Key, The (1958-British) 125m. **½ D: Carol Reed. William Holden, Sophia Loren, Trevor Howard, Oscar Homolka. Jan de Hartog novel becomes pointless romance tale. Loren is disillusioned woman passing out key to her room to series of naval captains during WW2, hoping to make their dangerous lives a little happier.

Key Largo (1948) 101mm. ***½ D: John Huston. Humphrey Bogart, Edward G. Robinson, Lauren Bacall, Lionel Barrymore, Claire Trevor, Thomas Gomez. Dandy cast in adaptation of Maxwell Anderson's play of tough gangster (Robinson) holding people captive in Key West hotel during rough storm. Trevor as E. G.'s moll won Best Supporting Actress Oscar.

Key Man (1954-British) 78m. **½ D: Montgomery Tully. Angela Lansbury, Keith Andes, Brian Keith. Competent little picture about illicit love affair leading to mysterious accidents involving Lansbury's architect husband. Retitled: A LIFE AT STAKE.

Key to the City (1950) 99m. **½ D: George Sidney. Clark Gable, Loretta Young, Frank Morgan, Marilyn Maxwell, Raymond Burr, James Gleason. Bland romance between Gable and Young, two mayors who meet at convention in San Francisco.

Key Witness (1960) 82m. **½ D: Phil Karlson. Jeffrey Hunter, Pat Crowley, Dennis Hopper, Joby Baker, Susan Harrison, Johnny Nash, Corey Allen. Overlong but effective narrative of pressures from street gang on

Hunter's family to prevent his wife from testifying in criminal case.

Keys of the Kingdom (1944) 137m. *** D: John M. Stahl. Gregory Peck, Thomas Mitchell, Vincent Price, Edmund Gwenn, Roddy McDowall, Cedric Hardwicke, Peggy Ann Garner. Peck is fine in this long but generally good film about missionary's life (played as boy by McDowall); from A. J. Cronin novel.

Khyber Patrol (1954) C-71m. ** D: Seymour Friedman. Richard Egan, Dawn Addams, Patric Knowles, Raymond Burr. Cast is above pedestrian film of British officers fighting in India, with usual love conflicts.

Kid Dynamite (1943) 73m. D: Wallace Fox. Leo Gorcey, Huntz Hall, Bobby Jordan, Gabriel Dell, Pamela Blake, Bennie Bartlett, Sammy Morrison. SEE: Bowery Boys series.

Kid for Two Farthings, A (1956-British) C-91m. *** D: Carol Reed. Celia Johnson, Diana Dors, David Kossoff, Joe Robinson, Jonathan Ashmore, Brenda De Banzie, Primo Carnera, Lou Jacobi. Imaginative fable of London youth who buys a little lamb thinking him a unicorn, leading to some delightful vignettes on human nature.

Kid from Brooklyn, The (1946) C-113m. *** D: Norman Z. McLeod. Danny Kaye, Virginia Mayo, Vera-Ellen, Steve Cochran, Eve Arden, Walter Abel, Lionel Stander, Fay Bainter. Comedy of milkman accidentally turned into prizefighter is often overdone but still a funny Kaye vehicle; remake of Harold Lloyd's MILKY WAY.

Kid from Cleveland, The (1949) 89m. ** D: Herbert Kline. George Brent, Lynn Bari, Rusty Tamblyn, Tommy Cook, Ann Doran. Brent is a sports reporter involved with a disturbed youth; Cleveland Indians ball team play themselves. A bit sticky at times.

Kid from Kansas, The (1941) 66m. *½ D: William Nigh. Leo Carrillo, Andy Devine, Dick Foran, Ann Doran. When a fruit buyer offers ridiculously low prices for planters' crops, competitors take drastic measures; low budget, low quality.

Kid from Left Field, The (1951) 80m. ** D: Harmon Jones. Dan Dailey, Anne Bancroft, Billy Chapin, Lloyd Bridges, Ray Collins, Richard Egan. Homey little film about baseball, with Dailey as ex-star turned coach.

Kid from Spain, The (1932) 90m. *** D: Leo McCarey. Eddie Cantor, Lyda Roberti, Robert Young, Ruth Hall, John Miljan, Stanley Fields. Lavish Cantor musical with Eddie mistaken for famed bullfighter; Roberti is his vivacious leading lady. Striking Busby Berkeley musical numbers; look for Paulette Goddard and Betty Grable in the chorus line.

Kid from Texas, The (1950) C-78m. ** D: Kurt Neumann. Audie Murphy, Gale Storm, Albert Dekker, Shepperd Strudwick. Another version of life of Billy the Kid, with Murphy in title role, Storm the romantic interest.

Kid Galahad (1937) 101m. *** D: Michael Curtiz. Edward G. Robinson, Bette Davis, Humphrey Bogart, Wayne Morris, Jane Bryan, Harry Carey, Veda Ann Borg. Well-paced actioner of promoter Robinson making naive Morris boxing star, losing his girl Davis to him at same time. Retitled: BATTLING BELLHOP. Remade as THE WAGONS ROLL AT NIGHT.

Kid Galahad (1962) C-95m. **½ D: Phil Karlson. Elvis Presley, Gig Young, Lola Albright, Joan Blackman, Charles Bronson, Ned Glass. Remake lacks wallop of original. Presley is boxer who wins championship fight but prefers quieter life of garage mechanic.

Kid Millions (1934) 90m. *** D: Roy Del Ruth. Eddie Cantor, Ethel Merman, Ann Sothern, George Murphy, Warren Hymer. Elaborate Cantor musical about Eddie inheriting a fortune, having the time of his life; color segment in ice-cream factory a delight. Songs include "When My Ship Comes In." Lucille Ball is one of the Goldwyn Girls in this one.

Kidnapped (1938) 90m. **½ D: Alfred L. Werker. Warner Baxter, Freddie Bartholomew, Arleen Whelan, C. Aubrey Smith, Reginald Owen, John Carradine, Nigel Bruce. Good adventure yarn of 1750's Scotland and England but not Robert Louis Stevenson; fine cast in generally entertaining script.

Kidnapped (1948) 80m. ** D: William Beaudine. Roddy McDowall, Sue

England, Dan O'Herlihy, Roland Winters, Jeff Corey. Disappointing low-budget adaptation of Robert Louis Stevenson novel.

Kill Her Gently (1957-British) 73m. ** D: Charles Saunders. Marc Lawrence, Maureen Connell, George Mikell, Griffith Jones, John Gayford. Brutal B-film of supposedly cured mental patient hiring two convicts-at-large to kill his wife.

Kill Me Tomorrow (1958-British) 80m. ** D: Terence Fisher. Pat O'Brien, Lois Maxwell, George Coulouris, Robert Brown. Adequate B-film about newspaperman cracking murder case leading to arrest of diamond-smuggling syndicate.

Kill or Be Killed (1950) 67m. *1/2 D: Max Nosseck. Lawrence Tierney, George Coulouris, Marissa O'Brien, Rudolph Anders. Pedestrian account of man on lam hunted down in jungle by law enforcers.

Kill the Umpire (1950) 78m. *** D: Lloyd Bacon. William Bendix, Una Merkel, Ray Collins, Gloria Henry, William Frawley. Amusing film pointing up foibles of the great American pastime, with Bendix a baseball lover who becomes an umpire.

Killer Ape (1953) 68m. D: Spencer Bennet. Johnny Weismuller, Carol Thurston, Max Palmer, Nestor Palva, Nick Stuart. SEE: **Jungle Jim** series.

Killer Is Loose, The (1956) 73m. **1/2 D: Budd Boetticher. Joseph Cotten, Rhonda Fleming, Wendell Corey, Alan Hale, Michael Pate. Fairly tense vengeance tale of ex-con swearing to get even with detective who nabbed him.

Killer Leopard (1954) 70m. D: Ford Beebe, Edward Morey, Jr. Johnny Sheffield, Beverly Garland, Barry Bernard, Donald Murphy. SEE: **Bomba, the Jungle Boy** series.

Killer McCoy (1947) 104m. *** D: Roy Rowland. Mickey Rooney, Brian Donlevy, Ann Blyth, James Dunn, Tom Tully, Sam Levene. Good drama of fighter Rooney accidentally involved in murder, with fine supporting cast of promoters and racketeers.

Killer Shark (1950) 76m. *1/2 D: Budd Boetticher. Roddy McDowall, Laurette Luez, Roland Winters, Edward Norris, Douglas Fowley, Dick Moore. Back Bay-ite McDowall learns new values as skipper of shark-hunting vessel; cheapie film.

Killer Spy (1958-French, dubbed) 82m. ** D: Georges Lampin. Jean Marais, Nadja Tiller, Andre Luguet, Bernadette Lafont. Capable cast tries to instill life into this spy-and-murder yarn; scenery outshines script.

Killer that Stalked New York, The (1950) 79m. **1/2 D: Earl McEvory. Evelyn Keyes, Charles Korvin, William Bishop, Dorothy Malone. Interesting B-film of diamond-smuggling couple sought by police because they contracted contagious disease while abroad.

Killers, The (1946) 105m. **** D: Robert Siodmak. Burt Lancaster, Ava Gardner, Edmond O'Brien, Albert Dekker, Sam Levene, Charles D. Brown. Compelling crime story of ex-fighter found murdered, subsequent investigation. Film provides fireworks, early success of Lancaster, Gardner.

Killers, The (1964) C-95m. **1/2 D: Don Siegel. Lee Marvin, Angie Dickinson, Ronald Reagan, John Cassavetes, Claude Akins. Shot for TV but thought too violent, this was released in theaters—now it's back on TV. Loosely based on Hemingway short story, violent film tells of teacher's involvement in robbery plot, eventual murder.

Killers are Challenged SEE: **Secret Agent Fireball.**

Killers from Space (1954) 71m. ** D: W. Lee Wilder. Peter Graves, James Seay, Barbara Bestar, Frank Gerstle, Steve Pendleton. Graves is captured by alien space invaders who want vital information. Nothing special here.

Killer's Kiss (1955) 67m. ** D: Stanley Kubrick. Frank Silvers, Jamie Smith, Irene Kane, Jerry Jarret. Meandering account of revenge when boxer's courting of working girl causes her boss to commit murder.

Killers of Kilimanjaro (1960) C-91m. ** D: Richard Thorpe. Robert Taylor, Anne Aubrey, John Dimech, Gregoire Aslan, Anthony Newley, Martin Boddey. Spotty adventure yarn of railroad-building in East Africa.

Killing, The (1956) 83m. ***1/2 D: Stanley Kubrick. Sterling Hayden, Coleen Gray, Vince Edwards, Jay C.

Flippen, Marie Windsor, Ted de Corsia, Elisha Cook, Timothy Carey. Slowly becoming a classic of sorts is this early Kubrick film of elaborate gangland plot involving crucial horserace. Memorable sequences include Carey's cool killer role, and Windsor-Cook marriage, doomed at the outset.

Kilroy Was Here (1947) 68m. *½ D: Phil Karlson. Jackie Cooper, Jackie Coogan, Wanda McKay, Frank Jenks. Supposedly topical comedy (then) is pretty limp now, with innocent victim of "Kilroy Was Here" joke trying to lead normal life despite his name.

Kim (1950) C-113m. ***½ D: Victor Saville. Errol Flynn, Dean Stockwell, Paul Lukas, Thomas Gomez, Cecil Kellaway. Rousing actioner based on Kipling classic, set in 1880's India, with British soldiers combatting rebellious natives. Flavorful production.

Kimberley Jim (1965) C-82m. ** D: Emil Nofal. Jim Reeves, Madeleine Usher, Clive Parnell, Arthur Swemmer, Mike Holt. Minor actioner of two carefree gamblers who win a diamond mine from miner and his daughter but have a change of heart.

Kind Hearts and Coronets (1950-British) 104m. *** D: Robert Hamer. Dennis Price, Valerie Hobson, Joan Greenwood, Alec Guinness. Peerless black comedy of cast-off member of titled family setting out to eliminate them all. Guinness plays nine roles.

Kind Lady (1951) 78m. *** D: John Sturges. Ethel Barrymore, Maurice Evans, Angela Lansbury, Betsy Blair. Bleak drama, excellently acted, of con-man Evans ingratiating himself into Barrymore's home and fleecing her.

Kind of Loving, A (1962-British) 112m. *** D: John Schlesinger. Alan Bates, June Ritchie, Thora Hird, Bert Palmer, Gwen Nelson, Malcolm Patton. Intelligent account of young couple forced to marry when girl becomes pregnant, detailing their home life; well acted.

King and Country (1964-British) 90m. *** D: Joseph Losey. Dirk Bogarde, Tom Courtenay, Leo McKern, Barry Foster, James Villiers, Peter Copley. Vivid antiwar treatise, played subtly. Bogarde is detached army lawyer assigned to defend deserter Courtenay during WW1.

King and Four Queens, The (1956) C-86m. **½ D: Raoul Walsh. Clark Gable, Eleanor Parker, Jo Van Fleet, Jean Willes, Barbara Nichols, Sara Shane, Jay C. Flippen. Static misfire with Gable on the search for money hidden by husbands of four women he encounters.

King and I, The (1956) C-133m. ***½ D: Walter Lang. Deborah Kerr, Yul Brynner, Rita Moreno, Martin Benson, Terry Saunders, Rex Thompson, Alan Mowbray. Excellent Rodgers and Hammerstein musicalization of ANNA AND THE KING OF SIAM: Kerr is widowed teacher who runs head-on into the stubborn King (Brynner), gradually falling in love with him; beautifully acted. Songs: "Hello Young Lovers," "Getting to Know You," "Shall We Dance," "Something Wonderful." Kerr's singing voice was dubbed by Marni Nixon.

King and the Chorus Girl, The (1937) 94m. **½ D: Mervyn LeRoy. Joan Blondell, Fernand Gravet, Edward Everett Horton, Jane Wyman. Gravet is nobleman on a lark, finding true love with beautiful chorine Blondell. Lively production.

King Creole (1958) 116m. **½ D: Michael Curtiz. Elvis Presley, Carolyn Jones, Dolores Hart, Dean Jagger. Harold Robbins' seamy book A STONE FOR DANNY FISHER is toned down considerably to make a musical-drama vehicle for Presley.

King in Shadow (1956-German, dubbed) 87m. ** D: Harald Braun. O. W. Fischer, Horst Buchholz, Odile Versois, Gunther Hadank. Buchholz is mentally disturbed young King of Sweden in 1760's; court intrigue encouraged by his domineering mother (Versois) makes only occasionally interesting costume tale.

King Kong (1933) 100m. **** D: Merian C. Cooper, Ernest B. Schoedsack. Fay Wray, Bruce Cabot, Robert Armstrong, Noble Johnson, James Flavin, Victor Long, Frank Reicher. Classic version of beauty-and-beast theme is a moviegoing must, with special effects and animation of monster Kong still unsurpassed. Final sequence atop Empire State Building is now folklore; Max Steiner music score also memorable.

King Kong vs. Godzilla (1963-Japanese, dubbed) C-90m. **½ D: Thomas Montgomery. Michael Keith, James Yagi, Tadao Takashima, Mie Hama. Good special effects make hokey plot worthwhile; two famed monsters clash.

King of Alcatraz (1938) 56m. **½ D: Robert Florey. Gail Patrick, Lloyd Nolan, Harry Carey, J. Carrol Naish, Robert Preston, Anthony Quinn. Racketeer Naish engineers Alcatraz prison break in B-actioner; Preston made screen debut as Nolan's navy buddy.

King of Burlesque (1935) 83m. *** D: Sidney Lanfield. Warner Baxter, Jack Oakie, Alice Faye, Mona Barrie, Herbert Mundin, Dixie Dunbar, Arline Judge. First-rate backstage musical with intelligent script. Faye sings "I'm Shooting High," other good songs. "Fats" Waller has very enjoyable scene.

King of Chinatown (1939) 60m. **½ D: Nick Grinde. Anna May Wong, Sidney Toler, Akim Tamiroff, J. Carrol Naish, Anthony Quinn, Roscoe Karns, Philip Ahn. Interesting little B-movie with good cast, about underworld racketeers trying to gain power in Chinatown.

King of Kings (1961) C-168m. *** D: Nicholas Ray. Jeffrey Hunter, Siobhan McKenna, Robert Ryan, Hurd Hatfield, Viveca Lindfors, Rita Gam, Rip Torn. Ornate but empty spectacle based on the life of Jesus, with Hunter earnest in lead role. Banal script.

King of the Coral Sea (1956-Australian) 74m. **½ D: Lee Robinson. Chips Rafferty, Charles Tingwell, Ilma Adey, Rod Taylor, Lloyd Berrell, Reginald Lye. On-location filming in Australia aids this account of wetback smuggling into the mainland.

King of the Jungle (1933) 65m. **½ D: H. Bruce Humberstone, Max Marcin. Buster Crabbe, Frances Dee, Douglass Dumbrille, Sidney Toler, Nydia Westman. Imitation Tarzan comes off well, with Crabbe being dragged into civilization against his will.

King of the Khyber Rifles (1953) C-100m. **½ D: Henry King. Tyrone Power, Terry Moore, Michael Rennie, John Justin. Power is half-caste British officer involved in native skirmishes, Moore the general's daughter he loves. Film lacks finesse or any sense of Kipling reality-fantasy.

King of the Roaring 20's—The Story of Arnold Rothstein (1961) 106m. **½ D: Joseph M. Newman. David Janssen, Dianne Foster, Jack Carson, Diana Dors, Mickey Rooney. Gun-roaring narrative of notorious gangster's life and crimes.

King of the Rocket Men SEE: **Lost Planet Airmen.**

King of the Underworld (1939) 69m. **½ D: Lewis Seiler. Humphrey Bogart, Kay Francis, James Stephenson, John Eldredge, Jessie Busley. Hard-hitting tale of dedicated doctor Francis involved with gangland chieftain Bogart; well acted, if a bit familiar. Remake of DR. SOCRATES.

King of the Wild Horses (1947) 79m. *½ D: George Archainbaud. Preston Foster, Gail Patrick, Bill Sheffield, Guinn Williams. Youth's companionship with fierce stallion is focus of this mild Western.

King of the Wild Stallions (1959) C-75m. ** D: R. G. Springsteen. George Montgomery, Diane Brewster, Edgar Buchanan, Emile Meyer, Byron Foulger. Horse is the hero of this oater, protecting a widow and her son.

King of the Zombies (1941) 67m. *½ D: Jean Yarbrough. Dick Purcell, Joan Woodbury, Mantan Moreland, Henry Victor, Joan Archer. Scientist develops corps of zombies to use in WW2 missions; ridiculous.

King Rat (1965) 133m. *** D: Bryan Forbes. George Segal, Tom Courtenay, James Fox, Patrick O'Neal, Denholm Elliott, James Donald, John Mills, Alan Webb. James Clavell novel of WW2 Japanese POW camp, focusing on effect of captivity on Allied prisoners. Thoughtful presentation rises above clichés; many exciting scenes.

King Richard and the Crusaders (1954) C-114m. **½ D: David Butler. Rex Harrison, Virginia Mayo, George Sanders, Laurence Harvey, Robert Douglas. Cardboard costumer of Middle Ages, with laughable script.

King Solomon's Mines (1950) C-102m. ***½ D: Compton Bennett, Andrew Marton. Deborah Kerr, Stewart Granger, Richard Carlson, Hugo Haas. Thin on H. Rider Haggard plot, but large on sweeping spectacle of

African hunt for missing explorer, with Granger-Kerr-Carlson trio leading safari on search for famed diamond mines.

King Steps Out, The (1936) 85m. *** D: Josef von Sternberg. Grace Moore, Franchot Tone, Walter Connolly, Raymond Walburn, Elizabeth Risdon, Nana Bryant, Victor Jory. Fanciful musical romance with fine cast supporting Moore's lovely voice; direction big asset to otherwise average musical.

Kings Go Forth (1958) 109m. *** D: Delmer Daves. Frank Sinatra, Tony Curtis, Natalie Wood, Leora Dana. Soapy yet telling account of two contrasting GI's in WW2 France involved with part-Negro Wood, their three-cornered romance.

Kings of the Sun (1963) C-108m. **½ D: J. Lee Thompson. Yul Brynner, George Chakiris, Shirley Anne Field, Richard Basehart, Brad Dexter. Skin-deep spectacle, badly cast, telling of Mayan leader who comes to America with surviving tribesmen and encounters savage Indians.

King's Pirate, The (1967) C-100m. **½ D: Don Weis. Doug McClure, Jill St. John, Guy Stockwell, Mary Ann Mobley. Cardboard, juvenile swashbuckler set in 18th century, with McClure the nominal hero.

King's Row (1941) 127m. ***½ D: Sam Wood. Ann Sheridan, Robert Cummings, Ronald Reagan, Betty Field, Charles Coburn, Claude Rains, Judith Anderson, Maria Ouspenskaya. Forerunner of PEYTON PLACE still retains its sweep of life in pre-WW1 Midwestern town, with the fates of many townsfolk intertwined. Erich Wolfgang Korngold music score backs up plush production, fine characterizations.

King's Thief, The (1955) C-78m. *** D: Robert Z. Leonard. David Niven, Ann Blyth, George Sanders, Edmund Purdom, Roger Moore, Alan Mowbray. Ornately produced costumer of 17th-century court intrigue involving England's King Charles II.

King's Vacation (1933) 60m. **½ D: John G. Adolfi. George Arliss, Dudley Digges, Dick Powell, Patricia Ellis, Florence Arliss. Refreshing story of monarch's experiences before he realizes that marriage of state holds love and true values.

Kismet (1944) C-100m. *** D: William Dieterle. Ronald Colman, Marlene Dietrich, Edward Arnold, Florence Bates, James Craig, Joy Ann Page, Harry Davenport. Unremarkable but entertaining color fable of Arabian Nights, hokey but worthwhile if only for Dietrich's dancing scene with her body painted gold. Remade as Broadway musical, filmed in 1955. Retitled: ORIENTAL DREAM.

Kismet (1955) C-113m. **½ D: Vincente Minnelli. Howard Keel, Ann Blyth, Dolores Gray, Monty Woolley, Sebastian Cabot, Vic Damone. Opulent but static filming of Robert Wright-George Forrest musical. Songs: "Stranger In Paradise," "Baubles, Bangles, and Beads."

Kiss and Tell (1945) 90m. **½ D: Richard Wallace. Shirley Temple, Jerome Courtland, Walter Abel, Katharine Alexander, Robert Benchley, Porter Hall. Film of successful Broadway play about wacky teenager Corliss Archer is a bit forced but generally funny; one of Temple's better grown-up roles.

Kiss Before Dying, A (1956) C-94m. *** D: Gerd Oswald. Robert Wagner, Jeffrey Hunter, Virginia Leith, Joanne Woodward, Mary Astor, George Macready. Black adventure tale with Wagner superb as psychopathic killer and Astor his devoted mother; well paced.

Kiss for Corliss, A (1949) 88m. ** D: Richard Wallace. Shirley Temple, David Niven, Tom Tully, Virginia Welles. Puffed-up comedy of teenager Temple convincing all that she and playboy Niven are going together; naïve fluff. Limp follow-up to KISS AND TELL with Shirley as Corliss Archer. Retitled: ALMOST A BRIDE.

Kiss in the Dark, A (1949) 87m. ** D: Delmer Daves. David Niven, Jane Wyman, Victor Moore, Wayne Morris, Broderick Crawford. Drab comedy effort involving pianist Niven, who gets more than he bargained for when he inherits an apartment building.

Kiss Kiss-Bang Bang (1966-Spanish, dubbed) C-90m. **½ D: Duccio Tessari. Giuliano Gemma, George Martin, Antonio Casas, Daniel Vargas. Routine spy yarn of British Secret Service efforts to prevent sale of secret formula to foreign powers.

Kiss Me Deadly (1955) 105m. ** D: Robert Aldrich. Ralph Meeker, Albert Dekker, Paul Stewart, Cloris Leachman, Maxine Cooper, Gaby Rodgers. Low-keyed Mickey Spillane murder caper with occasional brutality.

Kiss Me Kate (1953) C-109m. *** D: George Sidney. Kathryn Grayson, Howard Keel, Ann Miller, Bobby Van, Keenan Wynn. Cole Porter's bouncy musical of Shakespeare's TAMING OF THE SHREW combines backstage shenanigans with onstage dramatics. Songs: "Always True To You In My Fashion," "So In Love." Miller is in peak form.

Kiss of Death (1947) 98m. ***½ D: Henry Hathaway. Victor Mature, Brian Donlevy, Coleen Gray, Richard Widmark, Karl Malden, Taylor Holmes. Grim melodrama of captured thief who informs on his own gang. Terrific suspense; one of Mature's best performances.

Kiss of Evil SEE: Kiss of the Vampire.

Kiss of Fire (1955) C-87m. **½ D: Joseph M. Newman. Barbara Rush, Jack Palance, Rex Reason, Martha Hyer. Run-of-the-mill costumer. Rush gives up Spanish throne to remain in America with true love.

Kiss of the Vampire (1963-British) C-88m. **½ D: Don Sharp. Clifford Evans, Edward DeSouza, Noel Willman, Jennifer Daniel. Almost gruesome enough to be good. Tale set in eerie Bavarian castle where vampire lures victim with violent results. Retitled: KISS OF EVIL.

Kiss the Blood Off My Hands (1948) 79m. ** D: Norman Foster. Joan Fontaine, Burt Lancaster, Robert Newton, Lewis Russell. Title suggests film's unlikely combination of love and murder, which doesn't mix well.

Kiss the Boys Goodbye (1941) 85m. **½ D: Victor Schertzinger. Mary Martin, Don Ameche, Oscar Levant, Virginia Dale, Barbara Jo Allen, Raymond Walburn, Elizabeth Patterson, Connee Boswell. Enjoyable backstage musical of aspiring actress Martin and director Ameche, with good support from Levant and bright score.

Kiss Them for Me (1957) C-105m. **½ D: Stanley Donen. Cary Grant, Jayne Mansfield, Leif Erickson, Suzy Parker, Larry Blyden, Ray Walston. Forced comedy about romantic entanglements of navy officers on shore leave.

Kiss Tomorrow Goodbye (1950) 102m. *** D: Gordon Douglas. James Cagney, Barbara Payton, Helena Carter, Luther Adler, William Frawley. Turgid gangster caper with Cagney in rare form as convict-at-large who marries but still has itchy trigger finger.

Kisses for My President (1964) 113m. **½ D: Curtis Bernhardt. Fred MacMurray, Polly Bergen, Arlene Dahl, Edward Andrews, Eli Wallach. Thirties-style comedy of Bergen becoming President of the U.S., with MacMurray her husband caught in unprecedented protocol. Sometimes funny, often witless.

Kissin' Cousins (1964) C-96m. **½ D: Gene Nelson. Elvis Presley, Arthur O'Connell, Glenda Farrell, Pamela Austin, Yvonne Craig. Presley is military officer trying to convince yokel relative to allow missile site to be built on homestead; usual amount of singing.

Kissing Bandit, The (1948) C-102m. ** D: Laslo Benedek. Frank Sinatra, Kathryn Grayson, Ann Miller, J. Carrol Naish, Ricardo Montalban, Mildred Natwick, Cyd Charisse, Billy Gilbert. Frail Sinatra vehicle about son of Western kissing bandit who picks up where Dad left off; song "Siesta" sums it up.

Kit Carson (1940) 97m. *** D: George B. Seitz. Jon Hall, Lynn Bari, Dana Andrews, Harold Huber, Ward Bond, Renie Riano, Clayton Moore. Sturdy Western with Hall in title role, Andrews as cavalry officer, Bari the woman they fight over; plenty of action in Indian territory.

Kitten with a Whip (1964) 83m. ** D: Douglas Heyes. Ann-Margret, John Forsythe, Patricia Barry, Peter Brown, Ann Doran. Uninspired account of delinquent (Ann-Margret) and friends forcing businessman Forsythe to drive them to Mexico.

Kitty (1945) 104m. *** D: Mitchell Leisen. Paulette Goddard, Ray Milland, Patric Knowles, Reginald Owen, Cecil Kellaway, Constance Collier. Overlong costumer of girl's rise from guttersnipe to lady in 18th-century England with help of impoverished artist Milland; one of Goddard's best roles.

Kitty Foyle (1940) 107m. ***½ D: Sam Wood. Ginger Rogers, Dennis Morgan, James Craig, Eduardo Ciannelli, Ernest Cossart, Gladys Cooper. Tender love story won Rogers an Oscar as Christopher Morley's working-girl heroine; Ciannelli memorable as speakeasy waiter.

Klondike Annie (1936) 80m. *** D: Raoul Walsh. Mae West, Victor McLaglen, Philip Reed, Harold Huber, Soo Yong, Lucile Webster Gleason. West and McLaglen are rugged team, with Mae on the lam from police, going to the Yukon and masquerading as Salvation Army worker. West chants: "I'm An Occidental Woman in An Oriental Mood For Love," and other hits.

Klondike Kate (1943) 64m. *½ D: William Castle. Ann Savage, Tom Neal, Glenda Farrell, Constance Worth, Sheldon Leonard, Lester Allen. Low-budget humdrum of innocent Neal accused of murder in Alaska, fighting for his life and his girl.

Knickerbocker Holiday (1944) 85m. ** D: Harry Brown. Nelson Eddy, Charles Coburn, Constance Dowling, Shelley Winters, Percy Kilbride, Chester Conklin. Plodding film of Kurt Weill-Maxwell Anderson musical of New York's early days, with score including "September Song."

Knife in the Water (1963-Polish, dubbed) 95m. ***½ D: Roman Polanski. Leon Niemczyk, Jolanta Umecka, Zygmunt Malanowicz. Slowly paced yet absorbing account of three-cornered romance aboard a small boat; expertly directed by Polanski.

Knight Without Armour (1937-British) 107m. *** D: Jacques Feyder. Marlene Dietrich, Robert Donat, Irene Vanbrugh, Herbert Lomas, Miles Malleson, David Tree. Secret agent Donat helps Czarina Dietrich flee Russian revolutionaries. Sumptuous production merely backdrop for two stars.

Knights of the Round Table (1953) C-115m. **½ D: Richard Thorpe. Robert Taylor, Ava Gardner, Mel Ferrer, Stanley Baker, Felix Aylmer. MGM's first wide-screen film was excuse for this pretty but empty mini-spectacle of King Arthur's Court, revealing famous love triangle.

Knock on Any Door (1949) 100m. *** D: Nicholas Ray. Humphrey Bogart, John Derek, George Macready, Allene Roberts. Earnest attorney Bogart defends family friend Derek accused of murder; frank murder mystery with good courtroom interaction.

Knock on Wood (1954) C-103m. *** D: Norman Panama, Melvin Frank. Danny Kaye, Mai Zetterling, Torin Thatcher, David Burns, Leon Askin, Abner Biberman. Superior Kaye vehicle involved with beautiful Zetterling and international spies; good Kaye routines.

Knockout (1941) 73m. **½ D: William Clemens. Arthur Kennedy, Virginia Field, Anthony Quinn, Olympe Bradna. Slick little programmer of a prizefighter seesawing between fame and folly.

Knute Rockne—All American (1940) 98m. *** D: Lloyd Bacon. Pat O'Brien, Gale Page, Donald Crisp, Ronald Reagan, Albert Basserman, John Qualen. Lots of standard football stuff, but O'Brien as Notre Dame coach and Reagan as star player Gipper make this one memorable.

Konga (1961-British) C-90m. ** D: John Lemont. Michael Gough, Margo Johns, Jess Conrad, Claire Gordon. Small monkey grows into huge beast threatening the people of London; adequate sci-fi.

Kongo (1932) 85m. **½ D: William Cowan. Walter Huston, Lupe Velez, Conrad Nagel, Virginia Bruce, C. Henry Gordon. No literary classic, but heap big fun in the dark jungle, with helpless expedition at mercy of savage Huston. Remake of Lon Chaney's WEST OF ZANZIBAR.

Kon-Tiki (1951) 73m. *** Narrated by Ben Grauer. This documentary won an Oscar in 1951; it traces Thor Heyerdahl's raft trip from Peru to Tahiti, substantiating his theory that sailing boats in ancient times crossed the Pacific Ocean.

Kronos (1957) 78m. ** D: Kurt Neumann. Jeff Morrow, Barbara Lawrence, John Emery, Morris Ankrum. Potentially good sci-fi lacks the imaginative special effects to carry the vehicle of rampaging monster.

L-Shaped Room, The (1963-British) 125m. *** D: Bryan Forbes. Leslie Caron, Tom Bell, Brock Peters, Avis Bunnage, Emlyn Williams, Cicely Courtneidge. Adult love story sensibly handled. Caron is convincing as unwed pregnant girl jilted by lover, left to face life in her squalid surroundings.

La Dolce Vita (1961-Italian, dubbed) 175m. ***½ D: Federico Fellini. Marcello Mastroianni, Anita Ekberg Anouk Aimee, Lex Barker, Nadia Gray, Alain Cuny. Lengthy trendsetting film, not as ambiguous as other Fellini works—much more entertaining, with strong cast. Mastroianni stars as gossip columnist who sees his life in shallow Rome society as worthless but can't change.

La Parisienne (1958-French, dubbed) C-85m. **½ D: Michel Boisrond. Brigitte Bardot, Charles Boyer, Henri Vidal, Andre Luguet, Nadia Gray. At times spicy account of plucky Bardot involved with visiting royalty, much to her diplomat father's dismay.

La Strada (1956-Italian, dubbed) 115m. **** D: Federico Fellini. Anthony Quinn, Giulietta Masina, Richard Basehart, Aldo Silvani, Marcella Rovere, Livia Venturini. Quinn is crude strongman, Masina the wispish girl, and Basehart the philosopher in entourage of traveling circus, focusing on man's values in life, forcefully told, one of Fellini's greatest films. Don't miss it.

La Viaccia (1962-Italian, dubbed) 103m. **½ D: Mauro Bolognini. Jean-Paul Belmondo, Claudia Cardinale, Pietro Germi, Romolo Valli, Gabriella Pallotta, Gina Sammarco. Zesty yarn of country youth finding romance in the city with prostitute. Retitled: THE LOVEMAKERS.

Lad: A Dog (1962) C-98m. **½ D: Aram Avakian, Leslie H. Martinson. Peter Breck, Peggy McCay, Carroll O'Connor, Angela Cartwright, Maurice Dallimore. Genuine if schmaltzy version of Albert Payson Terhune novel of dog who brings new zest for life to lame child.

Ladies Courageous (1944) 88m. ** D: John Rawlins. Loretta Young, Geraldine Fitzgerald, Diana Barrymore, Evelyn Ankers, Frank Jenks, Ruth Roman, Anne Gwynne, Philip Terry, Lois Collier, Kane Richmond. Well-meant idea fails because of hackneyed script and situations; saga of the WAFs during WW2 who played a vital part in air warfare.

Ladies First SEE: **Your Turn, Darling.**

Ladies in Love (1936) 97m. **½ D: Edward Griffith. Janet Gaynor, Loretta Young, Constance Bennett, Simone Simon. Don Ameche, Paul Lukas, Tyrone Power. Man-hunting girls in Budapest stick together to find likely victims; large cast makes it entertaining; young Power seen to good advantage.

Ladies in Retirement (1941) 92m. ***½ D: Charles Vidor. Ida Lupino, Louis Hayward, Evelyn Keyes, Elsa Lanchester, Edith Barrett, Isobel Elsom, Emma Dunn. First-rate melodrama about housekeeper going to great lengths to protect retarded family she lives with. Acting is superb, with Lupino a standout.

Ladies' Man (1931) 70m. ** D: Lothar Mendes. William Powell, Kay Francis, Carole Lombard, Gilbert Emery, John Holland. Lifeless romance with young Lombard infatuated with playboy Powell, who once loved her mother.

Ladies' Man (1947) 91m. ** D: William D. Russell. Eddie Bracken, Cass Daley, Virginia Welles, Spike Jones and His City Slickers. Brassy comedy of hayseed inheriting a fortune, coming to New York to paint the town.

Ladies' Man, The (1961) C-106m. *** D: Jerry Lewis. Jerry Lewis, Helen Traubel, Jack Kruschen, Doodles Weaver. Pretty funny comedy with Jerry the handyman in a girls' school run by Helen Traubel (Mrs. Wellenmelon). Jerry Lester and George Raft have amusing cameo appearances.

Ladies of the Big House (1932) 76m. **½ D: Marion Gering. Sylvia Sidney, Gene Raymond, Wynne Gibson, Purnell Pratt, Louise Beavers, Jane Darwell, Noel Francis. Sidney is framed and imprisoned; a tearful, well-acted prison drama.

Ladies of the Chorus (1949) 61m. ** D: Phil Karlson. Adele Jergens, Rand Brooks, Marilyn Monroe, Nana Bryant. Cheapie about burlesque chorines and their offstage romances. Primary interest is young, beautiful Monroe as one of the ladies.

Ladies Should Listen (1934) 62m. **

GARBO

COMEDY TEAMS

Laurel and Hardy

The Marx Brothers

Abbott and Costello

The Three Stooges

Bing Crosby and Bob Hope

Martin and Lewis

GLAMOUR GIRLS

Raquel Welch (with Marcello Mastroianni)

Rita Hayworth

Betty Grable (with Dan Dailey)

Jane Russell and Marilyn Monroe

Brigitte Bardot (with Billy Mumy)

Jean Harlow

CLARK GABLE

MOVIE GANGSTERS

Edward G. Robinson

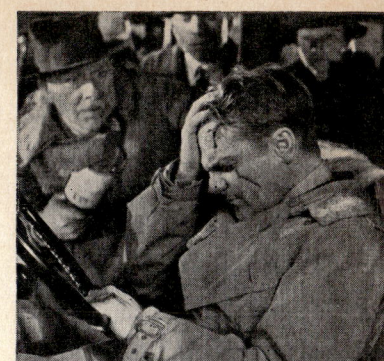

James Cagney

George Raft

Humphrey Bogart
(with Lauren Bacall)

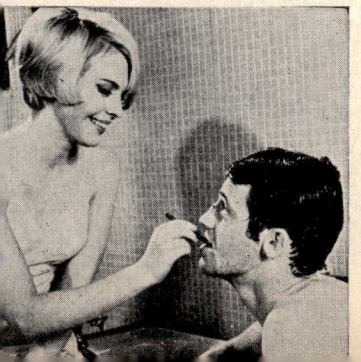

Jean-Paul Belmondo
(with Jean Seberg)

Warren Beatty
and Faye Dunaway

JOHNNY WEISSMULLER AS TARZAN

SERIES FILMS

Blondie (Arthur Lake, Penny Singleton)

Dr. Kildare (Lew Ayres, Lionel Barrymore)

Andy Hardy (Lewis Stone, Mickey Rooney)

Dead End Kids (Huntz Hall, Billy Halop, Gabriel Dell)

Ma and Pa Kettle (Percy Kilbride, Marjorie Main)

Francis the Talking Mule (with Donald O'Connor)

W. C. FIELDS

MARLENE DIETRICH

Cleopatra (1934)—Claudette Colbert

Cleopatra (1963)—Elizabeth Taylor

CHILD STARS

Shirley Temple
(with Lois Wilson)

Jane Withers
(with John Qualen)

Jackie Cooper

Freddie Bartholomew
(with Billy Gilbert)

Margaret O'Brien
(with Laraine Day)

Hayley Mills
(with James MacArthur)

GARY COOPER

MUSICAL TEAMS

Jeanette MacDonald
and Maurice Chevalier

Ginger Rogers
and Fred Astaire

Ruby Keeler
and Dick Powell

Nelson Eddy
and Jeanette MacDonald

Judy Garland
and Mickey Rooney

Frankie Avalon and
Annette Funicello

JOAN CRAWFORD

EDWARD G. ROBINSON

MAE WEST

HUMPHREY BOGART

MONSTERS AND MADMEN

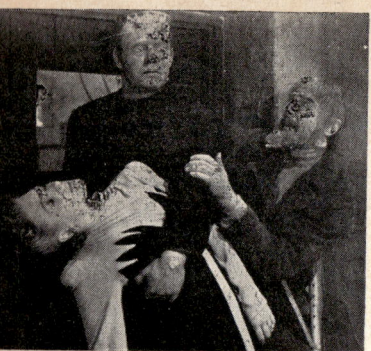

Frankenstein (Lon Chaney, Jr., with Evelyn Ankers and Bela Lugosi)

Dracula (Bela Lugosi with Dwight Frye)

The Mummy (Boris Karloff)

The Wolfman (Lon Chaney, Jr.)

The Invisible Man (Vincent Price with Nan Gray)

Fu Manchu (Christopher Lee)

Frank Sinatra Shirley MacLaine

Tony Curtis Jack Lemmon

BETTE DAVIS

CARY GRANT

SCREEN TEAMS

Clark Gable
and Joan Crawford

Wallace Beery
and Marie Dressler

Fred MacMurray
and Claudette Colbert

Boris Karloff
and Bela Lugosi

Olivia de Havilland
and Errol Flynn

Greer Garson
and Walter Pidgeon

SCREEN TEAMS

Spencer Tracy
and Katharine Hepburn

Humphrey Bogart
and Lauren Bacall

Sydney Greenstreet and
Peter Lorre
(with Geraldine Fitzgerald)

Joanne Woodward
and Paul Newman

Doris Day
and Rock Hudson

Richard Burton
and Elizabeth Taylor

BARBARA STANWYCK

SPENCER TRACY AND KATHARINE HEPBURN

WESTERN STARS

John Wayne

Randolph Scott
(with Joan Bennett)

Gary Cooper
(with Loretta Young)

Joel McCrea
(with Vera Miles)

Audie Murphy

The Lone Ranger
(Clayton Moore)

Elvis Presley

Sophia Loren

Charlton Heston

Sidney Poitier

HENRY FONDA

JAMES STEWART

SCREEN DETECTIVES

Philo Vance
(William Powell)

Nick and Nora Charles
(William Powell and Myrna Loy)

Charlie Chan and No. 1 Son
(Warner Oland and Keye Luke)

The Saint
(Louis Hayward with
Jack Carson and Paul Guilfoyle)

Mr. Moto (Peter Lorre
with Harold Huber)

Bulldog Drummond
(John Howard with
John Barrymore)

SCREEN DETECTIVES

Sherlock Holmes (Basil Rathbone with Nigel Bruce)

Boston Blackie (Chester Morris with Lynn Merrick)

The Falcon (Tom Conway with Rita Corday)

The Crime Doctor (Warner Baxter)

Inspector Clouseau (Peter Sellers with Elke Sommer)

Ellery Queen (Ralph Bellamy with Margaret Lindsay)

JOHN WAYNE

D: Frank Tuttle. Cary Grant, Frances Drake, Edward Everett Horton, Nydia Westman, Ann Sheridan. Grant's life is manipulated by telephone operator Drake in flimsy comedy, no great shakes.

Ladies Who Do (1963-British) 85m. **½ D: C. M. Pennington-Richards. Peggy Mount, Robert Morley, Harry H. Corbett, Nigel Davenport, Carol White, Miriam Karlin. When a charwoman discovers that waste paper scraps contain valuable stock market tips, a mild satire on British financial world unfolds.

Lady and the Bandit, The (1951) 79m. ** D: Ralph Murphy. Louis Hayward, Patricia Medina, Suzanne Dalbert, Tom Tully. Harmless costumer about career and love of highwayman Dick Turpin.

Lady and the Mob, The (1939) 66m. **½ D: Ben Stoloff. Fay Bainter, Lee Bowman, Ida Lupino, Henry Armetta. Bainter gives dignity to this mini-tale of eccentric rich lady involved with gangster mob.

Lady and the Monster, The (1944) 86m. ** D: George Sherman. Vera Ralston, Erich von Stroheim, Richard Arlen, Sidney Blackmer. Pretty good chiller of mysterious brain taking over man's life. Remade as DONOVAN'S BRAIN.

Lady Be Good (1941) 111m. *** D: Norman Z. McLeod. Eleanor Powell, Ann Sothern, Robert Young, Lionel Barrymore, John Carroll, Red Skelton, Virginia O'Brien. Spunky musical of married songwriters Sothern and Young, with dancer Powell and comic Skelton for good measure. Fine score: title tune, "Fascinating Rhythm," "You'll Never Know," "Last Time I Saw Paris."

Lady by Choice (1934) 78m. **½ D: David Burton. Carole Lombard, May Robson, Roger Pryor, Walter Connolly, Arthur Hohl. Enjoyable followup to LADY FOR A DAY; dancer Lombard takes in scraggly Robson, makes her proper lady.

Lady Confesses, The (1945) 66m. *½ D: Sam Newfeld. Mary Beth Hughes, Hugh Beaumont, Edmund McDonald, Claudia Drake, Emmett Vogan. Quickie independent flick enhanced by Hughes in title role as gal willing to take murder rap to protect boyfriend.

Lady Consents, The (1936) 75m. **½ D: Stephen Roberts. Ann Harding, Herbert Marshall, Margaret Lindsay, Walter Abel. Pat triangle with married Marshall discovering that he still loves his ex-wife.

Lady Dances, The SEE: **Merry Widow, The** (1934).

Lady Doctor (1956-Italian, dubbed) 90m. **½ D: Camillo Mastrocinque. Abbe Lane, Vittorio DeSica, Toto, Titina De Filippo, German Cobos, Teddy Reno. Pungent nonsense as Toto and DeSica try to con doctor Lane out of a fortune hidden in her house.

Lady Eve, The (1941) 97m. **** D: Preston Sturges. Barbara Stanwyck, Henry Fonda, Charles Coburn, Eugene Pallette, William Demarest. Beautifully funny treatment of standard plot of nice boy who falls for pretty girl working for cardshark father. Remade as THE BIRDS AND THE BEES, which didn't capture Sturges' beguiling lunacy.

Lady for a Day (1933) 88m. *** D: Frank Capra. Warren William, May Robson, Guy Kibbee, Glenda Farrell, Jean Parker, Nat Pendleton. Sentimental Damon Runyon fable of seedy apple vendor Robson transformed into perfect lady by producer William. Remade as POCKETFUL OF MIRACLES.

Lady for a Night (1941) 87m. ** D: Leigh Jason. Joan Blondell, John Wayne, Ray Middleton, Philip Merivale, Blanche Yurka, Edith Barrett. Plodding costume drama of woman gambling-boat owner marrying wealthy man for position, then implicated in murder. Good cast out of place.

Lady from Cheyenne (1941) 87m. **½ D: Frank Lloyd. Loretta Young, Robert Preston, Edward Arnold, Frank Craven, Gladys George. Average fare of Young et al conspiring to get themselves on jury, with both political parties becoming involved.

Lady from Chungking (1942) 66m. ** D: William Nigh. Anna May Wong, Harold Huber, Mae Clarke, Rick Vallin, Paul Bryar. Middling account of Wong heading band of Chinese partisans against Japs during WW2.

Lady from Louisiana (1941) 82m. **½ D: Bernard Vorhaus. John

Wayne, Ona Munson, Ray Middleton, Henry Stephenson, Helen Westley, Jack Pennick. OK costume drama of lovers who separate because of meddling parents Poor script mars production.

Lady from Shanghai, The (1948) 87m. *** D: Orson Welles. Rita Hayworth, Orson Welles, Everett Sloane, Glenn Anders, Ted de Corsia, Gus Schilling. The camera's the star of this Welles thriller, with the cast incidental in bizarre murder-mystery plot; hall of mirrors scene is fascinating.

Lady from Texas, The (1951) C-77m. ** D: Joseph Pevney. Howard Duff, Mona Freeman, Josephine Hull, Gene Lockhart, Craig Stevens. Strange minor film of eccentric old lady Hull; Duff and Freeman come to her rescue.

Lady Gambles, The (1949) 99m. *** D: Michael Gordon. Barbara Stanwyck, Robert Preston, Stephen McNally, Edith Barrett. Dynamic acting by Stanwyck as compulsive gambler buoys this bland tale of a woman who almost wrecks her marriage.

Lady Godiva (1955) C-89m. **½ D: Arthur Lubin. Maureen O'Hara, George Nader, Victor McLaglen, Torin Thatcher, Robert Warwick. Cardboard costumer involving famed lady and her horseback ride set in Middle Ages England . . . and what a dull ride!

Lady Has Plans, The (1942) 77m. ** D: Sidney Lanfield. Paulette Goddard, Ray Milland, Roland Young, Albert Dekker, Margaret Hayes, Cecil Kellaway. Jumbled spy drama, with innocent Goddard suspected of being agent and Milland tailing her in Lisbon.

Lady in a Cage (1964) 93m. **½ D: Walter Grauman. Olivia de Havilland, Ann Sothern, Jeff Corey, James Caan, Rafael Campos. What seems like another imitation of PSYCHO is actually a serious and well-acted thriller that can stand on its own merits.

Lady in a Jam (1942) 78m. **½ D: Gregory La Cava. Irene Dunne, Patric Knowles, Ralph Bellamy, Eugene Pallette, Queenie Vassar, Jane Garland. Thirties-type screwball comedy doesn't really hit bull's-eye, with wacky Dunne convincing psychiatrist Knowles to marry her to cure her ills.

Lady in Distress (1942-British) 76m. **½ D: Herbert Mason. Paul Lukas, Sally Gray, Michael Redgrave, Patricia Roc, Hartley Power, Alf Goodard. Nifty suspenser with fake magico involved in real murder plot; most capable cast.

Lady in Question, The (1940) 81m. **½ D: Charles Vidor. Brian Aherne, Rita Hayworth, Glenn Ford, Irene Rich, George Coulouris, Lloyd Corrigan. Aherne plays a juror interested in defendant Hayworth. He manages to save her, but later falls prey to jealousy.

Lady in the Dark (1944) C-100m. **½ D: Mitchell Leisen. Ginger Rogers, Ray Milland, Jon Hall, Warner Baxter, Barry Sullivan, Gail Russell, Billy Daniels. Unremarkable, lavish version of Kurt Weill musical minus most of the songs. Then-novel subject of psychoanalysis is now mundane, undoing effect of story about fashion magazine editor in mental turmoil.

Lady in the Iron Mask (1952) C-78m. ** D: Ralph Murphy. Louis Hayward, Patricia Medina, Alan Hale, John Sutton. Variation of Dumas tale, with Three Musketeers still about; moderate costumer.

Lady in the Lake (1946) 103m. *** D: Robert Montgomery. Robert Montgomery, Audrey Totter, Lloyd Nolan, Tom Tully, Leon Ames, Jayne Meadows. Camera is first-person in offbeat film featuring Raymond Chandler's private eye Philip Marlowe involved in whodunit.

Lady in the Morgue (1938) 67m. ** D: Otis Garrett. Preston Foster, Patricia Ellis, Frank Jenks, Barbara Pepper. When a girl's body is stolen from city morgue, law enforcers set out to solve snowballing mystery; acceptable programmer.

Lady is Willing, The (1942) 92m. *** D: Mitchell Leisen. Marlene Dietrich, Fred MacMurray, Aline MacMahon, Arline Judge, Stanley Ridges, Roger Clark. Agreeable comedy; glamorous Dietrich wants to adopt a baby, so she marries pediatrician MacMurray. Dramatic segment near the end spoils lively mood.

Lady Killer (1933) 76m. *** D: Roy Del Ruth. James Cagney, Mae Clarke, Leslie Fenton, Margaret Lindsay, Henry O'Neill, Raymond Hatton, George Chandler. Vintage Cagney, with tangy tale of mobster becoming Hollywood actor, torn between two professions; Cagney repeats his Clarke slapfest.

Lady L (1966) C-107m. **½ D: Peter Ustinov. Sophia Loren, Paul Newman, David Niven, Claude Dauphin, Philippe Noiret, Michel Piccoli. Stars and sets are elegant, but this wacky comedy set in early 20th-century London and Paris fizzles, despite Ustinov's writing, directing, and cameo appearance.

Lady Luck (1946) 97m. *** D: Edwin L. Marin. Robert Young, Barbara Hale, Frank Morgan, James Gleason. Hale marries gambler Young with hopes of reforming him but meets more problems than she bargained for.

Lady of Burlesque (1943) 91m. *** D: William Wellman. Barbara Stanwyck, Michael O'Shea, J. Edward Bromberg, Iris Adrian, Marion Martin, Pinky Lee, Frank Conroy, Gloria Dickson. Gypsy Rose Lee's G-STRING MURDERS makes amusing film. Series of murders of burlesque dolls sets Stanwyck's mind working to solve mystery.

Lady of Secrets (1936) 73m. **½ D: Marion Gering. Ruth Chatterton, Otto Kruger, Lionel Atwill, Marian Marsh, Lloyd Nolan, Robert Allen. Amorous heel tries to get to Chatterton by romancing her daughter Marsh; smooth soaper.

Lady of the Tropics (1939) 92m. ** D: Jack Conway. Hedy Lamarr, Robert Taylor, Joseph Schildkraut, Frederick Worlock, Natalie Moorhead. Sad love affair between playboy Taylor and halfbreed Lamarr in exotic setting; slow-moving.

Lady of Vengeance (1957-British) 73m. ** D: Burt Balaban. Dennis O'Keefe, Ann Sears, Patrick Barr, Vernon Greeves. Tedious account of man hiring killer to avenge a girl's death, becoming embroiled in further murder.

Lady on a Train (1945) 93m. *** D: Charles David. Deanna Durbin, Ralph Bellamy, Edward Everett Horton, George Coulouris, Allen Jenkins, David Bruce, Patricia Morison, Dan Duryea. Engrossing murder mystery with inquisitive Durbin getting tangled up in shady doings; film has good sense of humor, several good songs by Deanna.

Lady Pays Off, The (1951) 80m. **½ D: Douglas Sirk. Linda Darnell, Stephen McNally, Gigi Perreau, Virginia Field. Fanciful drama of schoolteacher Darnell who must pay off gambling debts in Reno by tutoring casino owner's daughter.

Lady Possessed (1952) 87m. ** D: William Spier, Roy Kellino. James Mason, June Havoc, Pamela Kellino, Fay Compton, Odette Myrtil. Bizarre film of ill woman thinking she is controlled by will of Mason's dead wife.

Lady Says No, The (1951) 80m. ** D: Frank Ross. David Niven, Joan Caulfield, Lenore Lonergan, James Robertson Justice. Lightweight comedy of fickle Caulfield, who won't decide if marriage is for her.

Lady Scarface (1941) 69m. ** D: Frank Woodruff. Dennis O'Keefe, Judith Anderson, Frances Neal, Mildred Coles, Eric Blore, Marc Lawrence. Anderson tries to elevate this episodic yarn of police hunting for dangerous gunwoman and her gang.

Lady Takes a Chance, A (1943) 86m. *** D: William A. Seiter. Jean Arthur, John Wayne, Charles Winninger, Phil Silvers, Mary Field, Don Costello. Wayne and Arthur make fine comedy team as burly rodeo star and wide-eyed city girl who falls for him; Silvers adds zip as bus-tour guide.

Lady Takes a Flyer, The (1958) C-94m. **½ D: Jack Arnold. Lana Turner, Jeff Chandler, Richard Denning, Andra Martin. Different-type Turner fare. Lana is lady flier who marries pilot Chandler, each finds it hard to settle down to married life.

Lady Takes a Sailor, The (1949) 99m. ** D: Michael Curtiz. Jane Wyman, Dennis Morgan, Eve Arden, Robert Douglas, Allyn Joslyn. Featherweight comedy fully described by title tag.

Lady Vanishes, The (1938-British) 97m. ***½ D: Alfred Hitchcock. Margaret Lockwood, Michael Redgrave, Paul Lukas, Dame May Whitty, Cecil Parker. Vintage mystery, with Lockwood and Redgrave looking for kidnapped Whitty on train ride through Europe; atmospheric and taut.

Lady Wants Mink, The (1953) C-

92m. *** D: William A. Seiter. Eve Arden, Ruth Hussey, Dennis O'Keefe, William Demarest, Gene Lockhart. Most diverting little film of wife Hussey breeding mink to get the coat she's always wanted.

Lady with a Dog (1959-Russian, dubbed) 90m. **½ D: Josif Heifits. Ya Savvina, Alexei Batalov, Ala Chostakova, N. Alisova. Intelligent tale of adulterous love, sensibly handled, with no contrived ending.

Lady with a Lamp, The (1951-British) 85m. *** D: Herbert Wilcox. Anna Neagle, Michael Wilding, Felix Aylmer, Maureen Pryor, Gladys Young, Julian D'Albie. Methodical recreation of 19th-century nurse-crusader Florence Nightingale, tastefully enacted by Neagle.

Lady with Red Hair (1940) 81m. ** D: Curtis Bernhardt. Miriam Hopkins, Claude Rains, Richard Ainley, Laura Hope Crews, Helen Westley, John Litel. Rains is producer David Belasco, Hopkins his star Leslie Carter, in fiction that's pretty dull despite elaborate settings.

Lady Without a Passport, A (1950) 72m. **½ D: Joseph H. Lewis. Hedy Lamarr, John Hodiak, James Craig, George Macready. Turgid melodrama as Lamarr seeks to leave Havana, former romantic and business associations behind her.

Ladykillers, The (1955-British) C-94m. *** D: Alexander Mackendrick. Alec Guinness, Cecil Parker, Herbert Lom, Peter Sellers, Danny Green, Katie Johnson. Droll comedy of not-so-bright crooks involved with seemingly harmless old lady.

Lady's from Kentucky, The (1939) 67m. **½ D: Alexander Hall. George Raft, Ellen Drew, Hugh Herbert, Zasu Pitts, Louise Beavers, Stanley Andrews. Regardless of title, Raft's horse takes precedence over his lady in this usual but well-done horse-racing saga.

Lady's Morals, A (1930) 75m. ** D: Sidney Franklin. Grace Moore, Reginald Denny, Wallace Beery, Jobyna Howland. First attempt to make star of opera singer Moore doesn't click. She plays Jenny Lind, who learns value of love from devoted Denny.

Lafayette (1963-French, dubbed) C-110m. **½ D: Jean Dreville. Jack Hawkins, Orson Welles, Howard St. John, Edmund Purdom, Vittorio DeSica, Liselotte Pulver. Overblown, badly scripted costumer of famed 18th-century Frenchman, resulting in episodic minor spectacle film.

Lafayette Escadrille (1958) 93m. **½ D: William Wellman. Tab Hunter, Etchika Choureau, Marcel Dalio, David Janssen. Attempted epic of famous French flying legion of WW1 becomes pat actioner with typical romantic interlude, featuring wholesome Hunter.

Lake Placid Serenade (1944) 85m. ** D: Steve Sekely. Vera Ralston, Vera Vague, Eugene Pallette, Stephanie Bachelor, Walter Catlett, John Litel, Roy Rogers, Twinkle Watts. Ice-skater's rise to fame, featuring lovely Ralston . . . ugh!

Lancer Spy (1937) 84m. *** D: Gregory Ratoff. Dolores Del Rio, George Sanders, Peter Lorre, Joseph Schildkraut, Virginia Field, Sig Ruman, Fritz Feld. Sanders disguises himself as Nazi officer to get information in this taut thriller; Del Rio has to choose between love and loyalty to her country.

Land of the Pharaohs (1955) C-106m. ** D: Howard Hawks. Jack Hawkins, Joan Collins, Dewey Martin, Alexis Minotis. Well-intentioned, literate spectacle that bogs down for lack of action; set in ancient Egypt.

Land Unknown, The (1957) 78m. ** D: Virgil Vogel. Jock Mahoney, Shawn Smith, Henry Brandon, Douglas Kennedy. Mahoney leads expedition in search of missing husband and stumbles upon prehistoric monsters. Adequate special effects.

Landru SEE: **Bluebeard.**

Larceny (1948) 89m. **½ D: George Sherman. John Payne, Joan Caulfield, Dan Duryea, Shelley Winters, Dorothy Hart. Slick but ordinary underworld tale, with roguish Payne deciding to help lovely Caulfield; Duryea is slimy villain.

Larceny, Inc. (1942) 95m. ***½ D: Lloyd Bacon. Edward G. Robinson, Jane Wyman, Broderick Crawford, Jack Carson, Anthony Quinn, Edward Brophy. Hilarious little comedy of ex-cons Robinson, Crawford, and Brophy using luggage store as front for shady activities; villain Quinn tries to horn in. Look for Jackie Gleason in a small role as a soda jerk.

Las Vegas Shakedown (1955) 79m. **
D: Sidney Salkow. Dennis O'Keefe, Coleen Gray, Charles Winninger, Thomas Gomez, Elizabeth Patterson, Robert Armstrong. Improbable yet diverting account of O'Keefe's effort to run an honest gambling house, with on-location filming in Las Vegas.

Las Vegas Story, The (1952) 88m. **
D: Robert Stevenson. Jane Russell, Victor Mature, Vincent Price, Hoagy Carmichael, Brad Dexter. Synthetic murder yarn supposedly set in gambling capital, sparked by Russell's vitality.

Lassie Come Home (1943) C-88m. ***
D: Fred M. Wilcox. Roddy McDowall, Donald Crisp, Dame May Whitty, Edmund Gwenn, Nigel Bruce, Elsa Lanchester, Elizabeth Taylor. Winning family film of poor family forced to sell their beloved dog, who undertakes torturous journey to return to them.

Last Angry Man, The (1959) 100m. ***
D: Daniel Mann. Paul Muni, David Wayne, Betsy Palmer, Luther Adler, Joby Baker, Joanna Moore, Godfrey Cambridge. Low-key filming of Gerald Green's pensive account of aged N.Y.C. slum doctor Muni, whose life story is going to be shown on TV. Muni is superb as idealistic but practical physician.

Last Blitzkrieg, The (1958) 84m. **
D: Arthur Dreifuss. Van Johnson, Kerwin Matthews, Dick York, Larry Storch. WW2 actioner trying to focus on German point of view.

Last Bridge, The (1957-Austrian, dubbed) 90m. ***½ D: Helmut Kautner. Maria Schell, Bernhard Wicki, Barbara Rutting, Carl Mohner. Schell gives well-modulated performance as German doctor captured by Yugoslavian partisans during WW2, first administering medical aid reluctantly, then realizing all people deserve equal attention.

Last Command, The (1955) C-110m. **½ D: Frank Lloyd. Sterling Hayden, Anna Maria Aberghetti, Richard Carlson, Ernest Borgnine, J. Carrol Naish, Virginia Grey, Ben Cooper. Elaborate, sweeping account of the battle of the Alamo, hampered by tedious script.

Last Days of Dolwyn, The SEE: Dolwyn.

Last Days of Pompeii, The (1935) 96m. *** D: Ernest B. Schoedsack. Preston Foster, Basil Rathbone, Dorothy Wilson, David Holt, Alan Hale, John Wood, Louis Calhern. Blacksmith Foster aspires to wealth and power as gladiator; climactic spectacle scenes are thrilling and expertly done.

Last Days of Pompeii, The (1960-Italian, dubbed) C-105m. **½ D: Mario Bonnard. Steve Reeves, Christine Kaufmann, Barbara Carroll, Anne Marie Baumann, Mimmo Palmara. New version of venerable tale focuses on muscleman Reeves and synthetic account of Christian martyrs. Very little spectacle.

Last Frontier, The (1955) C-98m. **½ D: Anthony Mann. Victor Mature, Guy Madison, Robert Preston, James Whitmore, Anne Bancroft. Usual happenings involving stupid cavalry commander who incites Indian attack. Retitled SAVAGE WILDERNESS.

Last Gangster, The (1937) 81m. *** D: Edward Ludwig. Edward G. Robinson, Rose Stradner, James Stewart, John Carradine, Sidney Blackmer, Louise Beavers, Edward Brophy. Thoughtful gangster film has Robinson released from jail, trying to reinstate himself as powerful mobster; side-action involves ex-wife now remarried and not wanting anything to do with him.

Last Holiday (1950-British) 89m. *** D: Henry Cass. Alec Guinness, Kay Walsh, Bernard Lee, Beatrice Campbell, Wilfrid Hyde-White. Droll, biting account of Guinness thinking he is dying, living it up at ritzy resort; twist ending adds strength to film.

Last Hunt, The (1956) C-108m. **½ D: Richard Brooks. Robert Taylor, Stewart Granger, Lloyd Nolan, Debra Paget, Russ Tamblyn, Constance Ford. Rampaging buffalo herd is primary excitement of Taylor-Granger feuding partnership in 1880's West.

Last Hurrah, The (1958) 121m. *** D: John Ford. Spencer Tracy, Jeffrey Hunter, Dianne Foster, Basil Rathbone, Pat O'Brien, Donald Crisp, James Gleason, Ed Brophy, John Carradine, Ricardo Cortez, Frank McHugh, Jane Darwell. Leisurely paced version of Edwin O'Connor novel of politics, loosely based on life of Boston's Mayor Curley. Top-notch veteran cast makes film sparkle.

Last Man on Earth, The (1964) 86m. ** D: Sidney Salkow. Vincent Price, Franca Bettoia, Emma Danieli, Giacomo Rossi, Tony Cerevi, Rossi Stuart. Often crude chiller with Price the sole survivor of plague, besieged by victims who arise at night thirsting for his blood; erratic production.

Last Man to Hang, The (1956-British) 75m. ** D: Terence Fisher. Tom Conway, Elizabeth Sellars, Eunice Gayson, Freda Jackson, Raymond Huntley, Anthony Newley. Forthright courtroom film of man on trial for alleged murder of wife.

Last Mile, The (1959) 81m. **½ D: Howard W. Koch. Mickey Rooney, Clifford David, Harry Millard, John McCurry, Ford Rainey, Leon Janney. Above-par account of attempted breakout from big house by those on death row. Rooney is excellent.

Last Musketeer, The (1954-French, dubbed) C-95m. ** D: Fernando Cerchio. Georges Marchal, Dawn Addams, Jacques Dumesnil. Another variation on the THREE MUSKETEERS, with Marchal as D'Artagnan combating corruption in Louis XIV's court; adequate swashbuckler. Retitled: THE COUNT OF BRAGELONNE.

Last of the Badmen (1957) C-79m. ** D: Paul Landres. George Montgomery, Meg Randall, James Best, Michael Ansara, Keith Larsen. Western about Chicago detectives in 1880's chasing after killers of their fellow-worker.

Last of the Buccaneers (1950) C-79m. *½ D: Lew Landers. Paul Henreid, Jack Oakie, Mary Anderson, John Dehner. Quickie costumer tainting the legendary name of Jean Lafitte with plodding account of his post-War of 1812 exploits.

Last of the Comanches (1952) C-85m. ** D: Andre de Toth. Broderick Crawford, Barbara Hale, Lloyd Bridges, Martin Milner, John War Eagles. Trite rehash of cavalrymen fighting off Indian attack.

Last of the Fast Guns, The (1958) C-82m. ** D: George Sherman. Jock Mahoney, Gilbert Roland, Linda Cristal, Eduard Franz. Adequately told Western of search for missing man, and obstacles the hired gunslinger must overcome.

Last of the Mohicans, The (1936) 91m. *** D: George B. Seitz. Randolph Scott, Binnie Barnes, Heather Angel, Hugh Buckler, Henry Wilcoxon, Bruce Cabot. Big-scale action based on James Fenimore Cooper tale of the French-Indian War in colonial America. Cabot makes good villainous Indian.

Last of the Redmen (1947) C-77m. **½ D: George Sherman. Jon Hall, Michael O'Shea, Evelyn Ankers, Julie Bishop, Buster Crabbe. OK color Western with thoughtful Indian (Hall) facing decision involving group of ambushed white men; loosely based on James Fenimore Cooper's LAST OF THE MOHICANS.

Last of the Secret Agents?, The (1966) C-90m. ** D: Norman Abbott. Marty Allen, Steve Rossi, John Williams, Nancy Sinatra, Lou Jacobi. Tiring spoof on spy movies ends up unintentional self-mockery. Strictly for Allen and Rossi fans.

Last of the Vikings, The (1960-Italian, dubbed) C-102m. ** D: Giacomo Gentilomo. Cameron Mitchell, Edmund Purdom, Isabelle Corey, Helene Remy. Filmed with gusto, elaborate epic deals with Mitchell out to punish the Norse for devastating his homelands; poorly acted.

Last Outpost, The (1935) 70m. *** D: Louis Gasnier, Charles Barton. Cary Grant, Claude Rains, Gertrude Michael, Kathleen Burke, Colin Tapley, Akim Tamiroff. Exciting action-adventure with British troops in Africa, along lines of LOST PATROL, BENGAL LANCERS, etc.

Last Outpost, The (1951) C-88m. **½ D: Lewis R. Foster. Ronald Reagan, Rhonda Fleming, Bruce Bennett, Bill Williams. Burst of action saves worn-out yarn of two brothers on opposite sides of Civil War, teaming up to fight off Indian attack.

Last Posse, The (1953) 73m. ** D: Alfred L. Werker. Broderick Crawford, John Derek, Charles Bickford, Wanda Hendrix, Warner Anderson. Sheriff's men track down robbers, not without surprising results.

Last Ride, The (1944) 56m. ** D: D. Ross Lederman. Richard Travis, Eleanor Parker, Charles Lang, Jack LaRue. Smooth programmer involving a series of "accidental" deaths and the detective who tracks down the "murderer."

Last Stagecoach West (1957) 67m. *½ D: Joseph Kane. Jim Davis, Victor Jory, Mary Castle, Lee Van Cleef. Fair cast cannot save bland Western about stage-driver who loses government contracts and goes out of business.

Last Sunset, The (1961) C-112m. **½ D: Robert Aldrich. Rock Hudson, Kirk Douglas, Dorothy Malone, Joseph Cotten, Carol Lynley. Curious film of three men pursuing the same woman (Malone). Amid a cattle roundup, there is much meditation by all.

Last Ten Days, The (1956-German, dubbed) 113m. *** D: G. W. Pabst. Albin Skoda, Oskar Werner, Lotte Tobisch, Willy Krause, Helga Kennedy-Dohrn. Finely etched study of downfall of leader of Third Reich. Retitled: LAST TEN DAYS OF ADOLPH HITLER.

Last Time I Saw Archie, The (1961) 98m. *½ D: Jack Webb. Robert Mitchum, Jack Webb, Martha Hyer, France Nuyen. Off-duty from DRAGNET, Webb directed and co-starred in this dull army comedy about conman Mitchum.

Last Time I Saw Paris, The (1954) 116m. *** D: Richard Brooks. Elizabeth Taylor, Van Johnson, Donna Reed, Walter Pidgeon, Eva Gabor. Updated version of F. Scott Fitzgerald story, set in post-WW2 Paris, of ruined marriages and disillusioned people. MGM gloss helps.

Last Train from Bombay (1952) 72m. *½ D: Fred F. Sears. Jon Hall, Christine Larson, Lisa Ferraday, Douglas Kennedy. Hall single-handedly attempts to prevent a train wreck; set in India.

Last Train from Gun Hill (1959) C-94m. *** D: John Sturges. Kirk Douglas, Anthony Quinn, Carolyn Jones, Earl Holliman, Brad Dexter, Brian Hutton, Ziva Rodann. Superior Western of staunch sheriff determined to leave Gun Hill with murder suspect, despite necessity for shoot-out.

Last Train from Madrid, The (1937) 77m. ** D: James Hogan. Lew Ayres, Dorothy Lamour, Gilbert Roland, Anthony Quinn, Lee Bowman, Karen Morley, Helen Mack, Evelyn Brent, Robert Cummings, Lionel Atwill, Olympe Bradna. Love, mystery, suspense in group of people caught in war-ravaged Spain. Nothing new to offer; fairly well done on small scale, with large cast of young stars-to-be.

Last Voyage, The (1960) C-91m. *** D: Andrew L. Stone. Robert Stack, Dorothy Malone, George Sanders, Edmond O'Brien, Woody Strode. Engrossing drama of luxury ship that goes down at sea, and the ways the crew and passengers are affected. Sanders is ill-fated captain, Stack and Malone a married couple in jeopardy.

Last Wagon, The (1956) C-99m. *** D: Delmer Daves. Richard Widmark, Felicia Farr, Susan Kohner, Tommy Rettig, Stephanie Griffin, Ray Stricklyn, Nick Adams. Widmark is condemned killer who saves remnants of wagon train after Indian attack, leading them to safety. Clichéd plot well handled.

Last Woman on Earth, The (1961) C-71m. Bomb D: Roger Corman. Anthony Carbone, Edward Wain, Betsy Jones-Moreland. Dull three-cornered romance involving last survivors on earth after radioactive blast.

Last Year at Marienbad (1962-French, dubbed) 93m. *** D: Alain Resnais. Delphine Seyrig, Giorgio Albertazzi, Sacha Pitoeff, Françoise Bertin, Luce Garcia-Ville. Beautifully photographed but murky, bewildering story of young man attempting to lure a woman to run away with him.

Late George Apley, The (1947) 98m. *** D: Joseph L. Mankiewicz. Ronald Colman, Peggy Cummins, Vanessa Brown, Richard Haydn, Charles Russell. Film of J. P. Marquand's satire on blue-blooded Boston families lacks punch of Mankiewicz's other films, but is still entertaining.

Latin Lovers (1953) C-104m. **½ D: Mervyn LeRoy. Lana Turner, Ricardo Montalban, John Lund, Jean Hagen, Louis Calhern. Hokey romance yarn set in South America, with Turner ambling about seeking true love; pointless script.

Latin Lovers (1961-Italian, dubbed) 80m. ** D: Lorenza Mazzetti, et al.

Maria di Giuseppe, Mariella Zanetti, Jose Creci, Renza Volpi. Eight episodes dealing with love in Italy; most tales superficial and strained.

Laughter (1930) 81m. **½ D: Harry D'Arrast. Nancy Carroll, Fredric March, Frank Morgan, Leonard Carey. Fair combination of romance and drama in story of affair of former Follies girl and admirer, leading to murder.

Laughter in Paradise (1951-British) 95m. **½ D: Mario Zampi. Alastair Sim, Fay Compton, Audrey Hepburn, Beatrice Campbell. Witty study of human nature, as four recipients of large bequests must carry out peculiar tasks to get inheritance.

Laura (1944) 88m. **** D: Otto Preminger. Gene Tierney, Dana Andrews, Clifton Webb, Vincent Price, Judith Anderson, Grant Mitchell, Lane Chandler, Dorothy Adams. Classic mystery with lovely Tierney supposedly killed, detective Andrews trying to assemble murder puzzle. Fascinating, witty, a classic, with Webb a standout as cynical columnist.

Laurel and Hardy's Laughing 20's (1965) 90m. ***½ Compiled by Robert Youngson. Stan Laurel, Oliver Hardy, Charley Chase, Edgar Kennedy, James Finlayson, Anita Garvin. Some of L&H's best moments on film are included, with everything from pie-throwing to pants-ripping. Also some excellent sequences of Charley Chase, adding to the fun.

Lavender Hill Mob, The (1950-British) 82m. ***½ D: Charles Crichton. Alec Guinness, Stanley Holloway, Sidney James, Alfie Bass. Excellent comedy with droll Guinness a timid bank clerk who has perfect scheme for robbing the safe, with a madcap chase climax.

Law, The SEE: **Where the Hot Wind Blows**.

Law and Disorder (1958-British) 76m. **½ D: Charles Crichton. Michael Redgrave, Robert Morley, Ronald Squire, Elizabeth Sellars. Brisk comedy of con-man who gives up life of crime to avoid embarrassing situation of making up stories to tell prim son.

Law and Jake Wade, The (1958) C-86m. *** D: John Sturges. Robert Taylor, Richard Widmark, Patricia Owens, Robert Middleton. Robust Western of outlaw forcing his cohort-turned-good to lead him to buried loot. Taylor and Widmark make good adversaries.

Law and Order (1932) 70m. *** D: Edward L. Cahn. Walter Huston, Harry Carey, Ralph Ince, Andy Devine, Russell Simpson. Western holds no surprises, but it's well done, with an exceptional cast for this kind of film; scripted by John Huston, the star's son.

Law is the Law, The (1959-French, dubbed) 103m. **½ D: Christian-Jaque. Fernandel, Toto, Mario Besozzi, René Genin. Two top Continental comedians work well together in yarn of French customs official and his crooked pal smuggling items over the border.

Law of the Lawless (1964) C-88m. **½ D: William F. Claxton. Dale Robertson, Yvonne de Carlo, William Bendix, Bruce Cabot, Richard Arlen, John Agar, Lon Chaney, Kent Taylor. Veteran cast is chief interest of this programmer, with Robertson an ex-gunman turned judge, saving the town from outlaws.

Law of the Tropics (1941) 76m. ** D: Ray Enright. Constance Bennett, Jeffrey Lynn, Regis Toomey, Mona Maris, Hobart Bosworth. Fair cast in routine drama of man discovering his wife is accused murderess.

Law vs. Billy the Kid, The (1954) C-73m. ** D: William Castle. Scott Brady, Betta St. John, James Griffith, Alan Hale, Jr., Paul Cavanagh. Title gives away plot-line of unmemorable Western.

Lawless, The (1950) 83m. ** D: Joseph Losey. Gail Russell, Macdonald Carey, Lalo Rios, Lee Patrick, John Sands, Martha Hyer. Vaguely interesting study of Mexican-American fruit-pickers in Southern California, with facets of racial discrimination pointed out.

Lawless Breed, The (1952) 83m. **½ D: Raoul Walsh. Rock Hudson, Julia Adams, Hugh O'Brian, Michael Ansara, Dennis Weaver. Neatly turned Western involving ex-con who's determined that his son will lead a clean life.

Lawless Eighties, The (1957) 70m. ** D: Joseph Kane. Buster Crabbe, John Smith, Ted de Corsia, Marilyn Saris.

Crabbe and solid back-up cast provide average story of gunfighter who protects circuit rider beaten up by thugs.

Lawless Street, A (1955) C-78m. **½ D: Joseph H. Lewis. Randolph Scott, Angela Lansbury, Warner Anderson, Jean Parker, Wallace Ford, Ruth Donnelly. Lansbury as dance-hall singer adds pep to usual Scott formula Western of marshal cleaning up the town.

Lawyer Man (1932) 72m. **½ D: William Dieterle. William Powell, Joan Blondell, Claire Dodd, Sheila Terry, Alan Dinehart. Lawyer working his way up gets involved with gangsters; Powell and Blondell bring this one up to par.

Lay That Rifle Down (1955) 71m. *½ D: Charles Lamont. Judy Canova, Robert Lowery, Jacqueline DeWitt, Richard Deacon, Tweeny Canova. Mild Canova musicomedy, with Judy an overworked drudge in Southern town with hopes of being chic.

League of Gentlemen, The (1960-British) 114m. *** D: Basil Dearden. Jack Hawkins, Nigel Patrick, Bryan Forbes, Kieron Moore, Patrick Wymark, Richard Attenborough. Engrossing study of former service officer utilizing ex-army demolition specialists to aid him in big bank heist.

Lease of Life (1955-British) C-93m. **½ D: Charles French. Robert Donat, Kay Walsh, Denholm Elliott, Adrienne Corri, Cyril Raymond. Mild Donat yarn of timid priest with short time to live, struggling to maintain integrity.

Leather Boys, The (1966-British) 105m. *** D: Sidney J. Furie. Rita Tushingham, Colin Campbell, Dudley Sutton, Gladys Henson. Uncompromising study of impulsive Tushingham's incompatible marriage to motorcycle-loving mechanic, focusing on their opposing viewpoints and sleazy environment.

Leather Gloves (1948) 75m. ** D: Richard Quine, William Asher. Cameron Mitchell, Virginia Grey, Sam Levene, Jane Nigh, Henry O'Neill, Blake Edwards. Fight flick about on-the-skids boxer Mitchell lacks sufficient punch to push over clichés.

Leather Saint, The (1956) 86m. **½ D: Alvin Ganzer. Paul Douglas, John Derek, Jody Lawrance, Cesar Romero, Ernest Truex. Forthright account of clergyman who becomes a boxer to earn money to help congregation.

Leave Her to Heaven (1945) C-110m. *** D: John M. Stahl. Gene Tierney, Cornel Wilde, Jeanne Crain, Vincent Price, Mary Phillips, Ray Collins, Darryl Hickman, Gene Lockhart. Tierney is fiery as wife possessive of husband's attention, willing to commit murder to have her way; handsomely mounted production.

Leave It To Blondie (1945) 75m. D: Abby Berlin. Penny Singleton, Arthur Lake, Larry Simms, Marjorie Kent, Jonathan Hale, Chick Chandler, Danny Mummert, Arthur Space. SEE: Blondie series.

Leave It to Henry (1949) 57m. *½ D: Jean Yarbrough. Raymond Walburn, Walter Catlett, Gary Gray, Mary Stuart. Quickie film has Walburn destroying the town bridge when son is fired as toll-booth collector.

Leda SEE: Web of Passion.

Leech Woman, The (1960) 77m. *½ D: Edward Dein. Coleen Gray, Grant Williams, Philip Terry, Gloria Talbott, John Van Dreelen. Sloppy production about woman who finds youth-giving formula with unspectacular results.

Left Hand of God, The (1955) C-87m. *** D: Edward Dmytryk. Humphrey Bogart, Gene Tierney, Lee J. Cobb, Agnes Moorehead, E. G. Marshall, Benson Fong. Bogart manages to be convincing as American caught in post-WW2 China, posing as clergyman with diverting results.

Left-Handed Gun, The (1958) 102m. **½ D: Arthur Penn. Paul Newman, Lita Milan, John Dehner, Hurd Hatfield. Faltering psychological Western dealing with Billy the Kid's career, method-acted by Newman.

Left, Right and Center (1961-British) 95m. ** D: Sidney Gilliat, Frank Launder. Patricia Bredin, Ian Carmichael, Alastair Sim, Eric Barker. Frenzied little film involving two opponents in political campaign falling in love with Sim, the bemused campaign manager.

Legend of the Lost (1957) C-109m. ** D: Henry Hathaway. John Wayne, Sophia Loren, Rossano Brazzi, Kurt Kasznar, Sonia Moser. Incredibly insipid hodgepodge interesting as curio: Wayne and Brazzi on treasure hunt in Sahara battle over rights to Loren.

Legend of Tom Dooley, The (1959) 79m. ** D: Ted Post. Michael Landon, Jo Morrow, Jack Hogan, Richard Rust, Dee Pollock, Ken Lynch. Landon is pleasing in title role of Rebel soldier who robs a stage for the cause, only to discover war is over and he's now an outlaw.

Legion of the Doomed (1958) 75m. */2 D: Thor Brooks. Bill Williams, Dawn Richard, Anthony Caruso, Kurt Kreuger. Minor actioner about French Foreign Legion and its perennial battle with the natives.

Lemon Drop Kid, The (1951) 91m. **1/2 D: Sidney Lanfield. Bob Hope, Marilyn Maxwell, Lloyd Nolan, Jane Darwell. Hope is flavorful as Damon Runyonesque racetrack tout who is in dutch with gangster for big sum and must pay up or else.

Leopard, The (1963-Italian, dubbed) *** C-165m. D: Luchino Visconti. Burt Lancaster, Alain Delon, Claudia Cardinale, Rina Morelli, Paolo Stoppa. Meticulously produced version of famed novel of 19th-century life in Sicily, with revolution crumbling social structure. Slow pacing and dubbing make atmospheric account tough going.

Leopard Man, The (1943) 66m. ***1/2 D: Jacques Tourneur. Dennis O'Keefe, Margo, Jean Brooks, Isabel Jewell, James Bell, Margaret Landry, Abner Biberman. Superb suspense tale of series of murders in small New Mexico town blamed on leopard which escaped from traveling show.

Les Girls (1957) C-114m. ***1/2 D: George Cukor. Gene Kelly, Kay Kendall, Mitzi Gaynor, Taina Elg, Jacques Bergerac. Charming, sprightly musical involving three show girls who (via flashback) reveal their relationship to hoofer Kelly; chicly handled in all departments, with Cole Porter tunes.

Les Miserables (1935) 108m. ***1/2 D: Richard Boleslawski. Fredric March, Charles Laughton, Cedric Hardwicke, Rochelle Hudson, Frances Drake, John Beal, Florence Eldridge. Ornate production of Victor Hugo novel; minor culprit March escapes prison, relentlessly pursued by detective Javert, played with gusto by Laughton; good vignettes of 19th-century French life.

Les Miserables (1952) 104m. *** D: Lewis Milestone. Michael Rennie, Robert Newton, Sylvia Sidney, Edmund Gwenn, Cameron Mitchell, Elsa Lanchester, Florence Bates. Glossy but thoughtful remake of the venerable Victor Hugo classic.

Let Freedom Ring (1939) 100m. **1/2 D: Jack Conway. Nelson Eddy, Virginia Bruce, Victor McLaglen, Lionel Barrymore, Edward Arnold, Guy Kibbee, Raymond Walburn. Hokey but enjoyable pap of crusading Eddy righting wrongs in home town, combating crooked bosses.

Let No Man Write My Epitaph (1960) 106m. *** D: Philip Leacock. Burl Ives, Shelley Winters, James Darren, Jean Seberg, Ricardo Montalban, Ella Fitzgerald. Bizarre account of slum life, focusing on Darren and his dope-addicted mother involved with a variety of corrupt individuals.

Let Us Live (1939) 68m. **1/2 D: John Brahm. Maureen O'Sullivan, Henry Fonda, Ralph Bellamy, Alan Baxter, Stanley Ridges. Weepy melodrama about innocent man Fonda convicted of murder and his girl O'Sullivan trying to clear him.

Let's Be Happy (1957-British) C-93m. **1/2 D: Henry Levin. Tony Martin, Vera-Ellen, Zena Marshall, Guy Middleton. Featherweight musical of girl going to Scotland to claim a castle she's inherited.

Let's Dance (1950) C-112m. **1/2 D: Norman Z. McLeod. Betty Hutton, Fred Astaire, Roland Young, Ruth Warrick, Shepperd Strudwick. Slim plot-line of Hutton's efforts to win her son back from Back Bay in-laws. Astaire's dancing is film's highlight.

Let's Do It Again (1953) C-95m. *** D: Alexander Hall. Jane Wyman, Ray Milland, Aldo Ray, Leon Ames. Musical remake of AWFUL TRUTH with Milland in Cary Grant's role, Wyman in Irene Dunne's, and Ray in Ralph Bellamy's. Songs add to spicy plot, but no classic like original '37 film.

Let's Face It (1943) 76m. ** D: Sidney Lanfield. Bob Hope, Betty Hutton, Zasu Pitts, Phyllis Povah, Dave

Willock, Eve Arden. Brassy comedy with loud Hutton competing with Hope for laughs in forced wartime comedy of soldiers hired as male companions.

Let's Get Tough! (1942) 62m. D: Wallace Fox. Leo Gorcey, Bobby Jordan, Huntz Hall, Gabriel Dell, Tom Brown, Florence Rice. SEE Bowery Boys series.

Let's Go Navy (1951) 68m. D: William Beaudine. Leo Gorcey, Huntz Hall, Allen Jenkins, Charlita, Dorothy Ford, Tom Neal. SEE Bowery Boys series.

Let's Live a Little (1948) 85m. **½ D: Richard Wallace, Hedy Lamarr, Robert Cummings, Anna Sten, Robert Shayne, Mary Treen. Amusing but unspectacular romantic comedy, with Lamarr and Cummings falling in love.

Let's Make It Legal (1951) 77m. **½ D: Richard Sale. Claudette Colbert, Macdonald Carey, Zachary Scott, Robert Wagner, Marilyn Monroe. OK comedy of couple planning divorce but parting as friends. Good cast is main asset.

Let's Make Love (1960) C-118m. *** D: George Cukor. Marilyn Monroe, Yves Montand, Tony Randall, Frankie Vaughan, Wilfrid Hyde-White, David Burns. Millionaire Montand hears of show spoofing him, wants to stop it, then meets cast member Monroe. To join cast, he hires Bing Crosby to teach him to sing, Milton Berle to coach on comedy, Gene Kelly to make him dance. Bubbly cast.

Let's Make Up (1955-British) C-94m. ** D: Herbert Wilcox. Errol Flynn, Anna Neagle, David Farrar, Kathleen Harrison, Peter Graves. Froth about overimaginative Neagle trying to decide between suitors Flynn and Farrar. Original title: LILACS IN THE SPRING.

Letter, The (1940) 95m. ***½ D: William Wyler. Bette Davis, Herbert Marshall, James Stephenson, Frieda Inescort, Gale Sondergaard. Lushly photographed Somerset Maugham drama set in Malaya, tells of murderess (Davis) who tries to cover up her deed by pleading self-defense. Davis quite appealing in her unsympathetic role. Previously filmed in 1929 (also with Herbert Marshall in cast).

Letter for Evie, A (1945) 89m. ** D: Jules Dassin. Marsha Hunt, John Carroll, Spring Byington, Hume Cronyn, Pamela Britton, Norman Lloyd. Inconsequential romancer; Hunt is torn between pen-pal Cronyn and his buddy Carroll.

Letter from an Unknown Woman (1948) 90m. ***½ D: Max Ophuls. Joan Fontaine, Louis Jourdan, Mady Christians, Marcel Journet. Lavish, well-acted romance of beautiful Fontaine and insincere musician Jourdan who "uses" her.

Letter of Introduction (1938) 104m. **½ D: John M. Stahl. Adolphe Menjou, Andrea Leeds, Edgar Bergen (and Charlie McCarthy), George Murphy, Rita Johnson, Eve Arden, Ann Sheridan. Smoothly done account of aspiring actress Leeds trying to make it without famous father's (Menjou's) help; personality-plus cast.

Letter to Three Wives, A (1948) 103m. **** D: Joseph L. Mankiewicz. Jeanne Crain, Linda Darnell, Ann Sothern, Kirk Douglas, Paul Douglas, Jeffrey Lynn, Thelma Ritter. Delicious Americana showing reactions of three women who receive a letter from town flirt who has run off with one of their husbands. Celeste Holm does the voice of the letter's authoress.

Libel (1959-British) 100m. **½ D: Anthony Asquith. Dirk Bogarde, Olivia de Havilland, Robert Morley, Paul Massie, Wilfrid Hyde-White. Good cast sidetracked by muddled script about upper-class man suing for claim that he is an impostor, with his wife not so sure he isn't.

Libeled Lady (1936) 98m. *** D: Jack Conway. Jean Harlow, William Powell, Myrna Loy, Spencer Tracy, Walter Connolly, Charley Grapewin, Cora Witherspoon. Everyone is in love with someone else's spouse in this bright marital mix-up with top-notch cast. Remade as EASY TO WED.

License to Kill (1964-French, dubbed) 95m. ** D: Henri Decoin. Eddie Constantine, Yvonne Monlaur, Daphne Dayle, Paul Frankeur, Vladimir Inkijinoff, Charles Belmont. Constantine is modern-day Nick Carter involved with Oriental spies and superduper guided missile weapon wanted by Allies; elaborate nonsense.

Lieutenant Wore Skirts, The (1956) C-99m. **½ D: Frank Tashlin. Tom

Ewell, Sheree North, Rita Moreno, Rick Jason, Les Tremayne, Jean Willes, Alice Reinhart. Ewell makes nonsense acceptable as he chases after wife who reenlisted in service thinking he'd been drafted again.

Life and Death of Colonel Blimp SEE: Colonel Blimp.

Life at Stake, A SEE: Key Man.

Life at the Top (1965-British) 117m. **½ D: Ted Kotcheff. Laurence Harvey, Jean Simmons, Honor Blackman, Michael Craig, Donald Wolfit, Robert Morley, Margaret Johnston, Nigel Davenport. Follow-up to ROOM AT THE TOP picks up the account a decade later; film lacks flavor or life—best moments are flashbacks to Signoret-Harvey romance.

Life Begins (1932) 71m. *** D: James Flood, Elliott Nugent. Loretta Young, Aline MacMahon, Glenda Farrell, Vivienne Osborne, Eric Linden, Preston Foster, Elizabeth Patterson, Dorothy Tree. Offbeat film of maternity ward, with fine Warner Bros. cast depicting nurses, mothers, and others involved in life-giving process. Remade as A CHILD IS BORN.

Life Begins at College SEE: Life Begins In College.

Life Begins at Eight-Thirty (1942) 85m. *** D: Irving Pichel. Monty Woolley, Ida Lupino, Cornel Wilde, Sara Allgood, Melville Cooper, J. Edward Bromberg. Drunken washed-up actor Woolley disrupts daughter Lupino's life. Highlight is scene of Woolley as intoxicated Santa Claus.

Life Begins at Forty (1935) 85m. *** D: George Marshall. Will Rogers, Rochelle Hudson, Richard Cromwell, Jane Darwell, Slim Summerville, George Barbier, Thomas Beck, Sterling Holloway. Delightful Americana, with newspaper editor Rogers trying to clear name of Cromwell, who was framed for bank robbery years ago. Rogers' comments on American life are surprisingly contemporary.

Life Begins for Andy Hardy (1941) 100m. D: George B. Seitz. Lewis Stone, Mickey Rooney, Judy Garland, Fay Holden, Ann Rutherford, Sara Haden. SEE: Andy Hardy series.

Life Begins In College (1937) 94m. **½ D: William A. Seiter. Joan Davis, Tony Martin, Ritz Brothers, Gloria Stuart, Nat Pendleton, Fred Stone. Sis-boom-bah college nonsense with zany Ritz trio helping the school team win the big game. Pendleton is fun as an Indian who comes to college.

Life in the Balance, A (1955) 74m. ** D: Harry Horner. Ricardo Montalban, Anne Bancroft, Lee Marvin, Jose Perez. Lukewarm narrative set in a Latin American city, about a series of woman-killings; the police hunt for guilty person.

Life of Emile Zola, The (1937) 116m. **** D: William Dieterle. Paul Muni, Gale Sondergaard, Joseph Schildkraut, Gloria Holden, Donald Crisp, Erin O'Brien-Moore, Morris Carnovsky, Louis Calhern, Henry Davenport, Marcia Mae Jones, Dickie Moore, Ralph Morgan. Sincere biography of famed 19th-century French writer who rose to cause of wrongly accused Captain Dreyfus (Schildkraut); detailed production filled with fine vignettes.

Life of Her Own, A (1950) 108m. **½ D: George Cukor. Lana Turner, Ray Milland, Tom Ewell, Louis Calhern, Ann Dvorak, Margaret Phillips, Jean Hagen, Barry Sullivan, Phyllis Kirk. Turner is at the center of three-cornered romance leading to heartbreak for all. MGM fluff; Dvorak wraps it up with her expert portrayal of an aging model.

Life of Vergie Winters, The (1934) 82m. **½ D: Alfred Santell. Ann Harding, John Boles, Helen Vinson, Betty Furness, Lon Chaney, Jr., Bonita Granville. Successful adaption of Louis Bromfield weeper chronicling life of Harding, who defies small-town gossip, following her own instincts.

Life Upside Down (1965-French, dubbed) 93m. **½ D: Alain Jessua. Charles Denner, Anna Gaylor, Guy Saint-Jean, Nicole Gueden, Jean Yanne. Somber account of Denner, whose retreat from reality becomes so absorbing that he no longer cares about everyday life.

Life with Blondie (1946) 64m. D: Abby Berlin. Jonathan Hale, Ernest Truex, Marc Lawrence, Veda Ann Borg, Jack Rice, Penny Singleton, Arthur Lake, Larry Simms, Marjorie Kent. SEE: Blondie series.

Life with Father (1947) C-116m. *** D: Michael Curtiz. Irene Dunne, William Powell, Edmund Gwenn, Zasu

Pitts. Richly done adaptation of Howard Lindsay-Russell Crouse play of 1800's N.Y.C., with Powell in title role as irascible head of the household.

Lifeboat (1944) 96m. ***½ D: Alfred Hitchcock. Tallulah Bankhead, William Bendix, John Hodiak, Mary Anderson, Walter Slezak, Canada Lee, Hume Cronyn, Heather Angel, Henry Hull. Penetrating revelations about shipwreck survivors adrift in lonely lifeboat during WW2. Bankhead remarkable as spoiled rich girl, Slezak fine as Nazi taken aboard.

Light Across the Street, The (1957-French, dubbed) 76m. **½ D: George Lacombe. Brigitte Bardot, Raymond Pellegrin, Berval, Roger Pigaut. Above-par Bardot fare, involving three-cornered romance leading to murder. Retitled: FEMALE AND THE FLESH.

Light Fingers (1957-British) 90m. ** D: Terry Bishop. Guy Rolfe, Eunice Gayson, Roland Culver, Lonnie Donegan, Hy Hazell, Ronald Howard. Miserly husband (Culver) thinks wife is kleptomaniac; hires bodyguard butler who is really a thief. Adequate production.

Light in the Piazza (1962) C-101m. ***½ D: Guy Green. Olivia de Havilland, Rossano Brazzi, Yvette Mimieux, George Hamilton, Barry Sullivan. Splendid soaper that moves smoothly. De Havilland is anxious to marry off retarded daughter Mimieux, but isn't sure if she's being fair to suitor Hamilton.

Light That Failed, The (1939) 97m. *** D: William Wellman. Ronald Colman, Walter Huston, Ida Lupino, Dudley Digges, Muriel Angelus, Fay Helm, Francis McDonald. Fine cast in Kipling melodrama of London artist Colman going blind, determined to finish portrait of Lupino, whose florid cockney performance steals film.

Light Touch, The (1951) 110m. **½ D: Richard Brooks. Stewart Granger, Pier Angeli, George Sanders, Kurt Kasznar. On-location shooting in Europe perks up lukewarm drama of art thief Granger and his innocent girlfriend Angeli.

Lightning Strikes Twice (1951) 91m. **½ D: King Vidor. Richard Todd, Ruth Roman, Mercedes McCambridge, Zachary Scott. Muddled yet engaging yarn of ex-con returning home to start new life, finding actual killer of his wife.

Likely Story, A (1947) 88m. **½ D: H. C. Potter. Bill Williams, Barbara Hale, Sam Levene, Lanny Rees. OK comedy about veterinarian mistakenly thinking he's about to die, taking a last fling, finding romance with Hale and misadventures with crooks.

Li'l Abner (1959) C-113m. **½ D: Melvin Frank. Leslie Parrish, Peter Palmer, Stubby Kaye, Howard St. John, Julie Newmar, Stella Stevens, Billie Hayes, Robert Strauss. Lively Gene DePaul-Johnny Mercer musical is loud and brassy, with corny comedy, some good songs. Stubby Kaye is fine as Marryin' Sam; other Dogpatch characters vividly enacted.

Lilacs in the Spring SEE: **Let's Make Up.**

Lili (1953) C-81m. **** D: Charles Walters. Leslie Caron, Mel Ferrer, Zsa Zsa Gabor, Jean-Pierre Aumont, Amanda Blake, Kurt Kasznar. Enchanting musical with Leslie as French orphan who attaches herself to carnival and self-pitying puppeteer Ferrer. Award-winning song "Hi Lili Hi Lo."

Lili Marlene (1950-British) 75m. ** D: Arthur Crabtree. Hugh McDermott, Lisa Daniely, John Blythe, Stanley Baker. Potentially exciting film is middling fare, with Daniely the girl used by the Nazis to broadcast pessimistic news to British army.

Lilies of the Field (1963) 94m. *** D: Ralph Nelson. Sidney Poitier, Lilia Skala, Lisa Mann, Isa Crino, Stanley Adams. A "little" film that made good, won Poitier an Oscar. Poitier is a handyman who helps build a chapel for Lilia Skala and her French-speaking nuns. Quiet, well acted, enjoyable.

Lilith (1964) 114m. **½ D: Robert Rossen. Warren Beatty, Jean Seberg, Peter Fonda, Kim Hunter, Jessica Walter, Anne Meachem, Gene Hackman. Fairly faithful version of controversial novel is generally underrated. Benefits from performances of now well-known actors.

Lillian Russell (1940) 127m. ** D: Irving Cummings. Alice Faye, Don Ameche, Henry Fonda, Edward Arnold, Warren William, Leo Carrillo, Nigel Bruce. Strained biog of early 20th-century star; lavish backgrounds and weak plot-line diminish Faye's vehicle; Arnold repeats his Diamond Jim Brady role with gusto.

Limehouse Blues (1934) 65m. ** D: Alexander Hall. George Raft, Jean Parker, Anna May Wong, Kent Taylor, Billy Bevan. Good atmosphere but no script to match. Parker has shady past, tries to start fresh with roustabout Oriental Raft who has jealous mistress Wong. Retitled: EAST END CHANT.

Limping Man, The (1953-British) 76m. ** D: Charles De Latour. Lloyd Bridges, Moira Lister, Leslie Phillips, Helene Cordet, Alan Wheatley. Bridges is ex-GI returning to England to renew romance with Lister, discovering she's involved with racketeers. Nothing special.

Lineup, The (1958) 86m. **½ D: Don Siegel. Eli Wallach, Robert Keith, Warner Anderson, Richard Jaeckel. Expanded version of TV series set in San Francisco, focusing on gun-happy hoodlum after a cache of dope and the cops who track him down.

Lion, The (1962) C-96m. **½ D: Jack Cardiff. William Holden, Trevor Howard, Capucine, Pamela Franklin, Samuel Romboh, Christopher Agunda, Paulo Oduiori. Turgid melodrama set in Africa. Young girl Franklin is attached to pet lion, with running debate among family whether she is civilizing animal or lion is turning her into a savage.

Lion and the Horse, The (1952) C-83m. ** D: Louis King. Steve Cochran, Bob Steele, Sherry Jackson, Ray Teal. Warm B-film of valiant horse who combats a fierce mountain lion; geared for children.

Lion Hunters, The (1951) 75m. D: Ford Beebe. Johnny Sheffield, Morris Ankrum, Ann B. Todd, Douglas Kennedy. SEE Bomba, the Jungle Boy series.

Lion of St. Mark, The (1963-Italian, dubbed) C-87m. ** D: Luigi Capuano. Gordon Scott, Gianna Maria Canale, Rik Battaglia, Alberto Farnese. Canale is pirate girl who wins the love of Scott, heir to the throne of Venice, in this routine period yarn.

Liquidator, The (1966-British) C-105m. **½ D: Jack Cardiff. Rod Taylor, Trevor Howard, Jill St. John, Wilfrid Hyde-White. Nice location photography and adequate acting add up to a rather limp Bondian imitation. Even Taylor can't save this one.

Lisa (1962) C-112m. ** D: Philip Dunne. Stephen Boyd, Dolores Hart, Hugh Griffith, Donald Pleasence, Harry Andrews. Jan De Hartog novel of smuggling Jewish girl out of WW2 Europe into Israel becomes specious travelogue-love yarn.

Lisbon (1956) C-90m. **½ D: R. Milland. Ray Milland, Maureen O'Hara, Claude Rains, Yvonne Furneaux, Francis Lederer, Percy Marmont, Jay Novello. On-location tale of international thief Rains hiring skipper Milland to rescue Maureen's husband from Communist imprisonment. Nice scenery, nothing special.

List of Adrian Messenger, The (1963) 98m. *** D: John Huston. George C. Scott, Clive Brook, Dana Wynter, Herbert Marshall, Tony Curtis, Kirk Douglas, Burt Lancaster, Robert Mitchum, Frank Sinatra. Good murder mystery has a gimmick: Curtis, Douglas, Lancaster, Mitchum, and Sinatra are disguised in character roles. All that trouble wasn't necessary; the mystery is good on its own.

Listen, Darling (1938) 70m. **½ D: Edwin L. Marin. Judy Garland, Freddie Bartholomew, Mary Astor, Walter Pidgeon, Alan Hale, Scotty Beckett. Judy and Freddie try to land mother (Astor) a husband; Garland sings "Zing Went The Strings Of My Heart."

Little Big Horn (1951) 86m. **½ D: Charles Marquis Warren. Lloyd Bridges, John Ireland, Marie Windsor, Reed Hadley. Small-budget film manages to generate excitement in its account of Custer's last stand.

Little Bit of Heaven, A (1940) 87m. ** D: Andrew Marton. Gloria Jean, Robert Stack, Hugh Herbert, C. Aubrey Smith, Stuart Erwin, Nan Gray. Jean has vocal outing as 12-year-old singer supporting family; OK vehicle.

Little Boy Lost (1953) 95m. *** D: George Seaton. Bing Crosby, Claude Dauphin, Nicole Maurey, Gabrielle Dorziat. Synthetic tear-jerker set in post-WW2 France, where newspaperman Crosby is trying to locate his son, not knowing which boy at orphanage is his.

Little Caesar (1931) 80m. ***½ D: Mervyn LeRoy. Edward G. Robinson, Douglas Fairbanks, Jr., Glenda Farrell, Stanley Fields, Sidney Blackmer, Ralph Ince, George E. Stone. Smalltime hood becomes underworld bigshot; Robinson as Caesar Enrico Bandello gives memorable performance in classic gangster film, still exciting.

Little Colonel, The (1935) 80m. *** D: David Butler. Shirley Temple, Lionel Barrymore, Evelyn Venable, John Lodge, Sidney Blackmer, Alden Chase. Even non-fans will like this. One of Shirley's best films, as she mends broken ties between Grandpa Barrymore and Mama Venable.

Little Egypt (1951) C-82m. **½ D: Frederick de Cordova. Mark Stevens, Rhonda Fleming, Nancy Guild, Charles Drake. Chicago Fair in the 1890's is setting for tale of entrepreneurs who popularized the later-famous belly dancer.

Little Foxes, The (1941) 116m. ***½ D: William Wyler. Bette Davis, Herbert Marshall, Teresa Wright, Richard Carlson, Patricia Collinge, Dan Duryea, Charles Dingle. Outstanding filmization of Lillian Hellman's play of greed and corruption within a Southern family on the financial outs, headed by majestic Davis as ruthless Regina.

Little Fugitive, The (1953) 75m. *** D: Ray Ashley. Richie Andrusco, Rickie Brewster, Winifred Cushing, Will Lee. Minor classic based on adventures of little boy wandering around Coney Island who thinks he killed his brother.

Little Giant (1946) 91m. ** D: William A. Seiter. Bud Abbott, Lou Costello, Brenda Joyce, Jacqueline De Wit, George Cleveland, Elena Verdugo, Mary Gordon. Fairly good A&C with Lou becoming a vacuum cleaner salesman in series of familiar but amusing routines.

Little Hut, The (1957) C-78m. **½ D: Mark Robson. Ava Gardner, Stewart Granger, David Niven, Finlay Currie. Smutty Andre Roussin play becomes static comedy of innuendoes, with Gardner stranded on desert isle with husband and boyfriend.

Little Kidnappers, The (1954-British) 93m. *** D: Philip Leacock. Jon Whiteley, Vincent Winter, Adrienne Corri, Duncan Macrae, Jean Anderson. Offbeat account of youngsters who take care of a deserted baby, not telling anyone of its existence.

Little Lord Fauntleroy (1936) 98m. *** D: John Cromwell. Freddie Bartholomew, C. Aubrey Smith, Guy Kibbee, Dolores Costello, Mickey Rooney, Jessie Ralph. Young New Yorker Bartholomew suddenly finds himself a British lord in this charming film from classic story. Story and acting are often dated, but high production values make one forget dull spots.

Little Men (1940) 84m. ** D: Norman Z. McLeod. Kay Francis, Jack Oakie, George Bancroft, Jimmy Lydon, Ann Gillis. Louisa May Alcott tale is updated and revised, becoming routine adolescent tale.

Little Minister, The (1934) 110m. ***½ D: Richard Wallace. Katharine Hepburn, John Beal, Donald Crisp, Andy Clyde, Beryl Mercer. Charming film of James M. Barrie story of Scottish pastor falling in love, with Hepburn radiant in period romance tale.

Little Miss Broadway (1938) 70m. ** D: Irving Cummings. Shirley Temple, George Murphy, Jimmy Durante, Phyllis Brooks, Edna May Oliver, George Barbier. Not bad Temple, with Shirley bringing Oliver's theatrical boarding house to life; Shirley and Durante are good together. Songs: "Be Optimistic," "If All the World Were Paper," "Hop Skip and Jump."

Little Miss Marker (1934) 80m. *** D: Alexander Hall. Adolphe Menjou, Shirley Temple, Dorothy Dell, Charles Bickford, Lynne Overman. Flavorful Damon Runyon tale of bookie Menjou reformed by Shirley, who wins over N.Y.C. gambling colony. Remade as SORROWFUL JONES.

Little Nellie Kelly (1940) 100m. **½ D: Norman Taurog. Judy Garland, George Murphy, Charles Winninger, Douglas McPhail. Lightweight musical based on George M. Cohan play about Judy patching up differences between father Murphy and grandfather Winninger. Garland sings "It's A Great Day For The Irish," "Singin' In The Rain," others.

Little Nuns, The (1965-Italian, dubbed) 101m. **½ D: Luciano Salce. Catherine Spaak, Sylva Koscina, Amedeo Nazzari, Didi Perego, Umberto D'Orsi. Innocent little film of nuns trying to persuade airline to reroute their jets, which disturb the convent.

Little Old New York (1940) 100m. **½ D: Henry King. Alice Faye, Brenda Joyce, Fred MacMurray, Richard Greene, Henry Stephenson. Claims to be story of Fulton and his steamboat; merely serves as framework for standard romance.

Little Princess, The (1939) 91m. *** D: Walter Lang. Shirley Temple, Richard Greene, Anita Louise, Ian Hunter, Cesar Romero, Arthur Treacher, Marcia Mae Jones. One of Temple's best-mounted productions; not too cloying tale of poor Victorian waif who makes good.

Little Shepherd of Kingdom Come, The (1961) C-108m. **½ D: Andrew V. McLaglen. Jimmie Rodgers, Luana Patten, Chill Wills, Neil Hamilton. Bland family-type film of boy who fought for the North during Civil War and his return to rural life.

Little Women (1933) 115m. **** D: George Cukor. Katharine Hepburn, Joan Bennett, Paul Lukas, Frances Dee, Jean Parker, Edna May Oliver, Douglass Montgomery, Spring Byington. Film offers endless pleasure no matter how many times you've seen it; a faithful, beautiful adaptation of Alcott's book, with uniformly superb cast.

Little Women (1949) C-121m. **½ D: Mervyn LeRoy. June Allyson, Peter Lawford, Margaret O'Brien, Elizabeth Taylor, Janet Leigh, Mary Astor. Glossy remake of Louisa May Alcott's gentle account of teen-age girls finding maturity and romance—patly cast.

Little World of Don Camillo (1951-Franco-Italian, dubbed) 96m. **½ D: Julien Duvivier. Fernandel, Sylvie, Gino Cervi. Fernandel romps through role of small-town priest who can't keep out of mischief; here he combats Communist threat to his village.

Littlest Hobo, The (1958) 77m. **½ D: Charles Rondeau. Buddy Hart, Wendy Stuart, Carlyle Mitchell, Howard Hoffman. Aimed at child audience, film recounts tale of dog who saves his master's pet lamb from being killed.

Littlest Rebel, The (1935) 70m. *** D: David Butler. Shirley Temple, John Boles, Jack Holt, Karen Morley, Bill Robinson. Top-notch Temple as Shirley saves soldier-daddy Boles from Civil War imprisonment by seeing President Lincoln; dances with Robinson are always a treat.

Live Fast, Die Young (1958) 82m. ** D: Paul Henreid. Mary Murphy, Norma Eberhardt, Michael Connors. Turgid B-film of runaway girl and her sister who prevents her from starting a life of crime.

Live, Love and Learn (1937) 78m. **½ D: George Fitzmaurice. Robert Montgomery, Rosalind Russell, Mickey Rooney, Helen Vinson, Monty Woolley, E. E. Clive, Al Shean, Billy Gilbert. Contract stars glide through this formula MGM fluff, with ritzy Russell marrying nonconformist artist Montgomery.

Live Wires (1946) 64m. D: Phil Karlson. Leo Gorcey, Huntz Hall, Bobby Jordan, Billy Benedict, William Frambes, Pamela Blake. SEE: Bowery Boys series.

Lively Set, The (1964) C-95m. **½ D: Jack Arnold. James Darren, Pamela Tiffin, Doug McClure, Marilyn Maxwell, Charles Drake, Greg Morris. Empty-headed account of the swinging crowd at college, especially those involved in sports-car racing.

Lives of a Bengal Lancer (1935) 109m. **** D: Henry Hathaway. Gary Cooper, Franchot Tone. Richard Cromwell, Sir Guy Standing, C. Aubrey Smith, Monte Blue, Kathleen Burke. Terrific actioner set in 19th-century India, with Cooper and Tone well cast; snake-charming sequence is classic.

Living in a Big Way (1947) 103m. ** D: Gregory La Cava. Gene Kelly, Marie McDonald, Charles Winninger, Phyllis Thaxter, Spring Byington. Soldier Kelly finds his wartime marriage a disappointment.

Living It Up (1954) C-95m. *** D: Norman Taurog. Dean Martin, Jerry Lewis, Janet Leigh, Edward Arnold, Fred Clark, Sheree North. Bright remake of NOTHING SACRED. Jerry has Lombard's role as supposed radiation victim brought to N.Y.C. as publicity stunt by reporter Leigh. Martin is Jerry's doctor.

Living on Velvet (1935) 80m. ** D: Frank Borzage. Kay Francis, George Brent, Warren William, Russell Hicks, Maude Turner Gordon, Samuel S. Hinds. Romance between Brent, in state of shock, and upper-class Francis, who vanishes when he gains senses. Chic fluff.

Lizzie (1957) 81m. **½ D: Hugo Haas. Eleanor Parker, Richard Boone, Joan Blondell, Hugo Haas, Ric Roman. Shirley Jackson's THE BIRD'S NEST is basis for sensibly acted melodrama of Parker discovering she has split personality.

Lloyds of London (1936) 115m. ***½ D: Henry King. Freddie Bartholomew, Madeleine Carroll, Sir Guy Standing, Tyrone Power, C. Aubrey Smith, Virginia Field, George Sanders. Handsomely mounted fiction of rise of British insurance company; young messenger boy Bartholomew grows up to be Power, who competes with Sanders for affection of Carroll.

Loan Shark (1952) 74m. ** D: Seymour Friedman. George Raft, Dorothy Hart, Paul Stewart, John Hoyt. Raft tries hard to instill life into flabby yarn about ex-convict smashing a loan-shark racket.

Local Boy Makes Good (1931) 67m. **½ D: Mervyn LeRoy. Joe E. Brown, Dorothy Lee, Ruth Hall, Robert Bennett, Edward Woods. Entertaining Brown vehicle, with shy botanist Joe afraid to tell perky Lee that he loves her.

Locker Sixty-Nine (1962-British) 56m. ** D: Norman Harrison. Eddie Byrne, Paul Daneman, Walter Brown, Penelope Horner. Byrne is the private eye framed for his boss' murder in this typically gimmicky Edgar Wallace mystery tale.

Locket, The (1946) 86m. ** D: John Brahm. Laraine Day, Brian Aherne, Robert Mitchum, Gene Raymond, Sharyn Moffet, Ricardo Cortez. Weak drama of psychopathic Day has confusing construction in unconvincing tale of girl who destroys men. Film has distinction of the most flashbacks within flashbacks of any picture we've seen.

Lodger, The (1944) 84m. *** D: John Brahm. Merle Oberon, George Sanders, Laird Cregar, Cedric Hardwicke, Sara Allgood, Doris Lloyd, Olaf Hytten, Billy Bevan. That new lodger at a turn-of-the-century London boarding house is Jack the Ripper. Good, atmospheric chiller with fine performances.

Lolita (1962) 152m. *** D: Stanley Kubrick. James Mason, Shelley Winters, Peter Sellers, Sue Lyon, Marianne Stone, Diana Decker. Strange film from Vladimir Nabokov's provocative novel. Sexually precocious Lyon becomes involved with stolid professor Mason, and bizarre Sellers provides peculiar romance leading to murder and lust. Winters outstanding as Lyon's sex-starved mother.

London Belongs to Me SEE: **Dulcimer Street.**

Lone Gun, The (1954) C-78m. ** D: Ray Nazarro. George Montgomery, Dorothy Malone, Frank Faylen, Neville Brand. Standard Western of valiant hero shooting it out with outlaws, winning hand of rancher's daughter, nicely played by Malone.

Lone Hand (1953) C-80m. **½ D: George Sherman. Joel McCrea, Barbara Hale, James Arness, Charles Drake. Sturdy McCrea is undercover agent posing as outlaw to get the goods on a gang.

Lone Ranger, The (1956) C-86m. **½ D: Stuart Heisler. Clayton Moore, Jay Silverheels, Lyle Bettger, Bonita Granville, Perry Lopez, Robert Wilke. Based on radio and TV series, film focuses on Masked Man and Tonto trying to pacify war-minded Indians.

Lone Ranger and the Lost City of Gold, The (1958) C-80m. ** D: Lesley Selander. Clayton Moore, Jay Silverheels, Douglas Kennedy, Charles Watts. Typical Lone Ranger fiction for younger audiences, involving hooded killers and mysterious clues to a hidden treasure city.

Lone Star (1952) 94m. **½ D: Vincent Sherman. Clark Gable, Ava Gardner, Lionel Barrymore, Beulah Bondi, Broderick Crawford, Ed Begley. Texas fights for independence, with good guy Gable vs. badman Crawford, Ava the woman in between. OK oater.

Lone Texan (1959) 70m. *½ D: Paul Landres. Willard Parker, Grant Williams, Audrey Dalton, Douglas Kennedy, June Blair. Oater's potential never realized. Civil War veteran returns home to find brother a corrupt sheriff.

Lone Wolf, The Michael Lanyard, better known as the Lone Wolf, figured as the leading character in about a dozen films from 1935 to 1949. Louis Joseph Vance's character was a jewel thief who would always sacrifice his own ambitions to help a lady in distress; after the first two films he turned to the right side of the law. Melvyn Douglas played the dapper character in 1935's LONE WOLF RETURNS, with Gail Patrick as leading lady, and Francis Lederer essayed the role in 1938's LONE WOLF IN PARIS with Frances Drake as a rival thief. In 1939 Warren William took over the role and played Lanyard in eight low-budget, fast-moving, enjoyable films which lacked the class of the first two entries but had a certain charm of their own. There was a heavy accent on comedy, and Eric Blore was added to the cast as Lanyard's valet Jamison, who not only served as comic relief but usually got tangled up in the plot as well. William's best effort by far was his first, THE LONE WOLF SPY HUNT, in which he was aided by a delightfully screwball Ida Lupino as his girlfriend, an alluring Rita Hayworth as a slinky spy, Ralph Morgan as the spy leader, and Virginia Weidler as his curious daughter. Unfortunately the other films in the series lacked the same impressive casts, but William carried them quite well, and the plots, usually involving jewels of some kind, were harmless enough. After a respite of a few years, Gerald Mohr took up the role for several fairly good efforts like LONE WOLF IN LONDON, which brought back valet Eric Blore. Ron Randell played Lanyard in the final entry, THE LONE WOLF AND HIS LADY. An enjoyable if not compelling series was the LONE WOLF, with THE LONE WOLF SPY HUNT measuring up as an excellent, chic, entertaining film by any standards.

Lone Wolf and His Lady, The (1949) 60m. D: John Hoffman. Ron Randell, June Vincent, Alan Mowbray, William Frawley.

Lone Wolf in London, The (1947) 68m. D: Leslie Goodwins. Gerald Mohr, Nancy Saunders, Eric Blore, Evelyn Ankers.

Lone Wolf in Mexico, The (1947) 69m. D: D. Ross Lederman. Gerald Mohr, Sheila Ryan, Jacqueline DeWit, Eric Blore, Nestor Paiva, John Gallaudet.

Lone Wolf in Paris, The (1938) 66m. D: Albert S. Rogell. Francis Lederer, Frances Drake, Walter Kingsford, Leona Maricle, Olaf Hytten, Albert Van Dekker.

Lone Wolf Keeps a Date, The (1941) 65m. D: Sidney Salkow. Warren William, Frances Robinson, Bruce Bennett, Eric Blore, Thurston Hall, Jed Prouty.

Lone Wolf Meets a Lady, The (1940) 71m. D: Sidney Salkow. Warren William, Eric Blore, Jean Muir, Warren Hull, Thurston Hall, Victor Jory, Roger Pryor.

Lone Wolf Returns, The (1936) 69m. D: Roy William Neill. Melvyn Douglas, Gail Patrick, Tala Birell, Arthur Hohl, Thurston Hall.

Lone Wolf Spy Hunt, The (1939) 67m. D: Peter Godfrey. Warren William, Ida Lupino, Rita Hayworth, Virginia Weidler, Ralph Morgan, Don Beddoe.

Lone Wolf Strikes, The (1940) 57m. D: Sidney Salkow. Warren William, Joan Perry, Alan Baxter, Astrid Allwyn, Eric Blore, Montagu Love, Robert Wilcox.

Lone Wolf Takes a Chance, The (1941) 76m. D: Sidney Salkow. Warren William, June Storey, Henry Wilcoxson, Eric Blore, Thurston Hall, Don Beddoe, Evalyn Knapp.

Loneliness of the Long Distance Runner, The (1962-British) 103m. **** D: Tony Richardson. Michael Redgrave, Tom Courtenay, Avis Bunnage, Peter Madden, James Bolam, James Fox, Julia Foster. Excellently acted story of a confused young man in prison chosen to represent institution in a race. Tight direction makes for convincing atmosphere.

Lonely are the Brave (1962) 107m. *** D: David Miller. Kirk Douglas, Gena Rowlands, Walter Matthau, Michael Kane, Carroll O'Connor, William Schallert. Penetrating study of rebellious cowboy Douglas escaping from jail, pursued by posse utilizing modern means of communications and transportation.

Lonely Man, The (1957) 87m. *** D: Henry Levin. Anthony Perkins, Jack Palance, Elaine Aiken, Neville Brand, Claude Akins. Solid acting and taut direction remove sting of hackneyed gunslinger-trying-to-reform plot.

Lonelyhearts (1958) 108m. **½ D: Vincent J. Donehue. Montgomery Clift, Robert Ryan, Myrna Loy, Dolores Hart, Maureen Stapleton. Unsuccessful attempt to make meaningful film about assorted emotionally unhappy people, tied together by gimmick of Clift being assigned the lonely hearts column on his newspaper.

Lonesome Trail, The (1955) 73m. ** D: Richard Bartlett. John Agar, Wayne Morris, Edgar Buchanan, Adele Jergens. Offbeat oater with ranch owner fighting off land-grabbers, using bow and arrow instead of conventional six-shooter.

Long, The Short and the Tall, The (1961-British) 105m. *** D: Leslie Norman. Richard Todd, Laurence Harvey, Richard Harris, Ronald Fraser. Well-delineated account of British patrol unit during WW2, focusing on their conflicting personalities and raids on Japs. Retitled: JUNGLE FIGHTERS.

Long Dark Hall, The (1951-British) 86m. **½ D: Anthony Bushell, Reginald Beck. Rex Harrison, Lilli Palmer, Tania Held, Henrietta Barry. Sturdy melodrama of man accused of killing girlfriend, with wife remaining loyal to him.

Long Day's Journey Into Night (1962) 108m. **** D: Sidney Lumet. Katharine Hepburn, Ralph Richardson, Jason Robards, Jr., Dean Stockwell, Jeanne Barr. Faithful, stagy adaptation of Eugene O'Neill's detailed study of family in the 1910's. Hepburn his dope-addicted wife, Richardson her pompous actor husband, Stockwell the son dying of TB, and Robards the alcoholic son.

Long Gray Line, The (1955) C-138m. *** D: John Ford. Tyrone Power, Maureen O'Hara, Robert Francis, Ward Bond, Donald Crisp, Betsy Palmer. Lengthy sentimental melodrama of West Point athletic trainer Power and his many years at the Academy. O'Hara is radiant as his wife.

Long Haul, The (1957-British) 88m. ** D: Ken Hughes. Victor Mature, Diana Dors, Patrick Allen, Gene Anderson. Mature is truck driver whose turbulent marriage paves way for his becoming involved with crooks. Minor fare.

Long, Hot Summer, The (1958) C-117m. *** D: Martin Ritt. Paul Newman, Joanne Woodward, Anthony Franciosa, Orson Welles, Lee Remick, Angela Lansbury. Well-blended William Faulkner short stories make a flavorful, brooding drama of domineering Southerner (Welles) and a wandering handyman (Newman), who decides to stick around and marry Woodward. Excellent Alex North score, weak finish to strong film.

Long John Silver (1954) C-109m. **½ Byron Haskin. Robert Newton, Connie Gilchrist, Kit Taylor, Grant Taylor. Roughly derived from Robert Louis Stevenson's TREASURE ISLAND. Film is a romp for Newton in title role as lusty buccaneer out for the gold. Filmed on location in Australia. One of Rod Taylor's early films.

Long, Long Trailer, The (1954) C-103m. **½ D: Vincente Minnelli. Lucille Ball, Desi Arnaz, Marjorie Main, Keenan Wynn, Gladys Hurlbut. Vibrant vehicle for Lucy and Desi, on honeymoon with cumbersome trailer that creates havoc for the duo.

Long Memory, The (1952-British) 91m. ** D: Robert Hamer. John Mills, John McCallum, Elizabeth Sellars, Geoffrey Keen, John Chandos, Vida Hope. Mills is framed for murder by girlfriend Sellers; when he's released from prison twelve years later, he sets out to prove his innocence. Film often strains for offbeat reality; characterizations wooden.

Long Night, The (1947) 101m. ** D: Anatole Litvak. Henry Fonda, Barbara Bel Geddes, Vincent Price, Ann Dvorak, Queenie Smith. Plodding drama of killer hiding out overnight with girl who tries to get him to confess; pretty tired drama. Remake of Jean Gabin film DAYBREAK.

Long Rope, The (1961) 61m. ** D: William Witney. Hugh Marlowe, Robert Wilke, Alan Hale, John Alonzo. Lumbering minor oater about circuit judge seeking aid of gunslinger to prevent injustice done to Mexican youth on trial for murder.

Long Shadow, The (1961-British) 64m. *½ D: Peter Maxwell. John Crawford, Susan Hampshire, Bill Nagy, Humphrey Lestocq. Flabby espionage caper set in 1950's Vienna, with Crawford an American foreign correspondent caught up in it all.

Long Ships, The (1964) C-125m. **½ D: Jack Cardiff. Richard Widmark, Sidney Poitier, Rosanna Schiaffino, Russ Tamblyn, Oscar Homolka, Colin Blakely. Fairly elaborate costume adventure of Vikings battling Moors for fabled treasure has better-than-average cast to recommend it.

Long Voyage Home, The (1940) 105m. **** D: John Ford. John Wayne, Thomas Mitchell, Ian Hunter, Barry Fitzgerald, Wilfrid Lawson, Mildred Natwick, John Qualen. Beautiful Ford film of Eugene O'Neill short plays about seafaring friends who share same thoughts, ambitions. One of Wayne's outstanding performances.

Long Wait, The (1954) 93m. ** D: Victor Saville. Anthony Quinn, Charles Coburn, Gene Evans, Peggie Castle, Dolores Donlan, Mary Ellen Kay. Meandering, actionless account of man with loss of memory discovering he's been framed for several crimes.

Longest Hundred Miles, The (1966) C-120m. ** D: Don Weis. Doug McClure, Ricardo Montalban, Katharine Ross, Ronald Remy. Clichéd WW2 telefeature, with McClure an army man driving a busload of refugees to escape Jap-controlled Philippines. Only virtue is Franz Waxman music score.

Look Back in Anger (1958-British) 99m. ***½ D: Tony Richardson. Richard Burton, Claire Bloom, Edith Evans, Mary Ure, Gary Raymond, Glen Byam Shaw, Donald Pleasence. John Osborne's trend-setting angry-young-man play, with Burton rebelling against life and wife, realistically filmed and acted; dialogue bristles.

Look for the Silver Lining (1949) C-100m. **½ D: David Butler. June Haver, Ray Bolger, Gordon MacRae, Charles Ruggles, Rosemary DeCamp. Superficial biography of Marilyn Miller's career in show business, with vintage vaudeville numbers bolstering trivial plot-line.

Look In Any Window (1961) 87m. ** D: William Alland. Paul Anka, Ruth Roman, Alex Nicol, Gigi Perreau, Jack Cassidy. Attempted lurid account of young man turned to crime by unhappy home life; tame film.

Looking for Danger (1957) 62m. D: Austen Jewell. Huntz Hall, Stanley Clements, Eddie LeRoy, Otto Reichow. SEE: Bowery Boys series.

Looking for Love (1964) C-83m. Bomb D: Don Weis. Connie Francis, Susan Oliver, Jim Hutton, Barbara Nichols, Danny Thomas, Johnny Carson, George Hamilton, Paula Prentiss. They should have looked for a script instead. Very weak, with "guest stars" thrown in. Susan Oliver tries, as Connie's best friend.

Loophole (1954) 80m. **½ D: Harold D. Schuster. Barry Sullivan, Charles McGraw, Dorothy Malone, Don Haggerty, Mary Beth Hughes, Don Beddoe. Imaginative handling of oft-told tale of bank employee accused of theft, catching actual crooks.

Loose in London (1953) 63m. D: Edward Bernds. Leo Gorcey, Huntz Hall, Bernard Gorcey, Norma Varden, Angela Greene. SEE: Bowery Boys series.

Looters, The (1955) 87m. **½ D: Abner Biberman. Rory Calhoun, Julie Adams, Ray Danton, Thomas Gomez. OK drama of survivors of plane crash fighting amongst themselves for money aboard wreckage.

Lord Jeff (1938) 78m. ** D: Sam Wood. Freddie Bartholomew, Mickey Rooney, Charles Coburn, Herbert Mundin, Terry Kilburn, Gale Sondergaard, Peter Lawford. Acceptable family film about good-boy Bartholomew led astray, sent to straighten out at naval school.

Lord Jim (1965) C-154m. **½ D: Richard Brooks. Peter O'Toole, James Mason, Curt Jurgens, Eli Wallach, Jack Hawkins, Paul Lukas, Daliah Lavi, Akim Tamiroff. Overlong, uneven adaptation of Joseph Conrad's story about idealistic young man in British Merchant Marine in the 19th century who is discredited as a coward and lives with that scar for the rest of his life. Film's great moments provided by outstanding supporting cast.

Lord of the Flies (1963-British) 90m. *** D: Peter Brook. James Aubrey,

Tom Chapin, Hugh Edwards, Roger Elwin, Tom Gaman. Strange, suspenseful story of a group of British boys stranded on remote island. Their gradual degeneration into a savage horde is compelling. Adapted from William Golding's novel.

Lord of the Jungle (1955) 69m. D: Ford Beebe. Johnny Sheffield, Wayne Morris, Nancy Hale, Smoki Whitfield, Paul Picerni. SEE: **Bomba, The Jungle Boy** series.

Lorna Doone (1951) C-88m. **½ D: Phil Karlson. Barbara Hale, Richard Greene, Carl Benton Reid, William Bishop. Middling screen version of Richard D. Blackmore's novel of 1680's England, with farmers rebelling against oppressive landlords. Done on small budget, but not bad.

Los Tarantos (1964-Spanish, dubbed) C-81m. *** D: Rovira-Beleta. Carmen Amaya, Sara Lezana, Daniel Martin, Antonio Prieto. Sentimental yet touching account of two young people from rival gypsy families falling in love, with tragic results.

Loser Takes All (1956-British) C-88m. ** D: Ken Annakin. Rossano Brazzi, Glynis Johns, Robert Morley, Tony Britton, Geoffrey Keen, Peter Illing. Brazzi and Johns celebrate their honeymoon in Monte Carlo and try out their "perfect system" for winning at roulette, with unusual effect on their marriage. On-location filming helps.

Loss of Innocence (1961-British) C-99m. **½ D: Lewis Gilbert. Kenneth More, Danielle Darrieux, Susannah York, Maurice Denham. York gives poignant performance as teen-ager who, through love affair, becomes a woman; events leave her and younger sisters and brother stranded on the Continent. Original title: THE GREENGAGE SUMMER.

Lost (1955-British) C-89m. **½ D: Guy Green. David Farrar, David Knight, Julia Arnall, Anthony Oliver, Marjorie Rhodes. Offbeat account of effects of a child kidnapping on parents, police, press, and crooks.

Lost Angel (1943) 91m. **½ D: Roy Rowland. Margaret O'Brien, James Craig, Marsha Hunt, Philip Merivale, Henry O'Neill, Donald Meek, Keenan Wynn. Cutesy film of little O'Brien lost, taken in by reporter Craig, who grows to love her.

Lost Boundaries (1949) 99m. *** D: Alfred L. Werker. Beatrice Pearson, Mel Ferrer, Richard Hylton, Carleton Carpenter, Susan Douglas, Canada Lee. Negro family passes for white in New England town, till their heritage is discovered. One of the first racially conscious films; not bad.

Lost Command (1966) C-130m. *** D: Mark Robson. Anthony Quinn, Alain Delon, George Segal, Michele Morgan, Maurice Ronet, Claudia Cardinale, Gregoire Aslan, Jean Servais. Taut, well-made story of French-Algerian guerrilla warfare in North Africa, with Quinn as the peasant who has risen to a position of command. Fine international cast, good direction, and some top-notch action sequences blend very well.

Lost Continent, The (1951) 86m. **½ D: Samuel Newfield. Cesar Romero, Hillary Brooke, John Hoyt, Acquanetta. Lavish production values are obviously lacking as Romero leads expedition to prehistoric mountaintop to recover missing rocket.

Lost Honeymoon (1947) 71m. ** D: Leigh Jason. Franchot Tone, Ann Richards, Frances Rafferty, Una O'Connor, Winston Severn. Trivial comedy of amnesiac Tone discovering he's the father of two children.

Lost Horizon (1937) 118m. **** D: Frank Capra. Ronald Colman, Edward Everett Horton, Jane Wyatt, Sam Jaffe, Margo, H. B. Warner, John Howard, Thomas Mitchell, Isabel Jewell. James Hilton's optimistic escapism of five people kidnapped to strange Tibetan monastery where all are immortal. Memorable in all respects, with haunting ending.

Lost in a Harem (1944) 89m. **½ D: Charles Riesner. Bud Abbott, Lou Costello, Marilyn Maxwell, John Conte, Douglass Dumbrille, Lottie Harrison, Jimmy Dorsey Orchestra. Slicker-than-usual Abbott and Costello (made on infrequent trip to MGM), but strictly routine. Some good scenes here and there with sultan Dumbrille; Maxwell is perfect harem girl.

Lost in Alaska (1952) 76m. ** D: Jean Yarbrough. Bud Abbott, Lou Costello, Mitzi Green, Tom Ewell, Bruce Cabot. Unremarkable slapstick set in 1890's, with A&C off to the wilds to help a friend but doing more hindering.

Lost Island of Kioga (1938) 100m. ** D: William Witney, John English. Bruce Bennett, Mala, Monte Blue, Jill Martin, Noble Johnson. Acceptable Republic cliff-hanger with white native muscleman (Bennett) saving shipwrecked survivors from a variety of near-disasters; better than usual settings. Re-edited movie serial: HAWK OF THE WILDERNESS.

Lost Lagoon (1958) 79m. *½ D: John Rawlins. Jeffrey Lynn, Peter Donat, Leila Barry, Don Gibson. Bland account of Lynn starting life anew on South Sea island. His sense of responsibility to family spoils idyll.

Lost Missile, The (1958) 70m. ** D: Lester Berke. Robert Loggia, Ellen Parker, Larry Kerr, Philip Pine. Unexciting narrative of race-against-time to destroy a rocket before it explodes in N.Y.C.

Lost Moment, The (1947) 88m. *** D: Martin Gabel. Robert Cummings, Susan Hayward, Agnes Moorehead, Joan Lorring, Eduardo Ciannelli. Henry James' ASPERN PAPERS becomes offbeat drama. Publisher Cummings in Italy seeking lost love letters of famous writer, comes across neurotic Hayward who claims to have access to them.

Lost Patrol, The (1934) 74m. **** D: John Ford. Victor McLaglen, Boris Karloff, Wallace Ford, Reginald Denny, Alan Hale, J. M. Kerrigan, Billy Bevan. McLaglen's small British military group lost in Mesopotamian desert, as Arabs repeatedly attack the dwindling unit. Classic, delightful actioner filled with slice-of-life stereotypes, headed by religious fanatic Karloff. Fast-moving, great fun.

Lost Planet Airmen (1949) 65m. *½ D: Fred Brannon. Tristram Coffin, Mae Clarke, Dale Van Sickel, Tom Steele, Buddy Roosevelt, House Peters, Jr. Feature version of Republic Pictures' twelve-chapter serial KING OF THE ROCKET MEN. This condensation poorly highlights the scheme of mad scientist trying to rule the world. Special effects are main virtue.

Lost Squadron, The (1932) 72m. **½ D: George Archainbaud. Richard Dix, Mary Astor, Erich von Stroheim, Joel McCrea, Dorothy Jordan, Robert Armstrong. WW1 pilots forced to find work as stunt flyers for movies; interesting idea boosted by Von Stroheim's overacting as director "Erich von Furst."

Lost Tribe, The (1949) 72m. D: William Berke. Johnny Weissmuller, Myrna Dell, Elena Verdugo, Joseph Vitale. SEE: Jungle Jim series.

Lost Volcano, The (1950) 67m. D: Ford Beebe. Johnny Sheffield, Donald Woods, Marjorie Lord, John Ridgely, Elena Verdugo. SEE: **Bomba, The Jungle Boy** series.

Lost Weekend, The (1945) 101m. **** D: Billy Wilder. Ray Milland, Jane Wyman, Philip Terry, Howard da Silva, Doris Dowling, Frank Faylen, Mary Young. Unrelenting drama of alcoholism with superb Wilder script, powerhouse performance by Milland which won him an Oscar. Fine support from bartender Da Silva, sanitarium worker Faylen.

Lost World, The (1925) 60m. **½ D: Harry Hoyt. Bessie Love, Wallace Beery, Lewis Stone, Lloyd Hughes. Silent film version of A. Conan Doyle adventure yarn is remarkable for special effects recreating prehistoric beasts encountered on scientific trip to deserted island. Monsters make film worthwhile.

Lost World, The (1960) C-98m. ** D: Irwin Allen. Michael Rennie, Jill St. John, David Hedison, Claude Rains, Fernando Lamas, Richard Haydn. Despite cinematic advances, this remake of the 1925 film doesn't match original's special effects. OK juvenile entry of an expedition into remote territory hopefully inhabited by prehistoric monsters.

Louisa (1950) 90m. *** D: Alexander Hall. Spring Byington, Charles Coburn, Edmund Gwenn, Ronald Reagan, Piper Laurie, Ruth Hussey. Delightful romantic yarn of Byington seeking to become a December bride, undecided between Coburn and Gwenn; most disarming.

Louisiana Hayride (1944) 67m. ** D: Charles Barton. Judy Canova, Ross Hunter, Minerva Urecal, Lloyd Bridges, Russell Hicks. Hillbilly Canova goes Hollywood in this typical cornball vehicle.

Louisiana Purchase (1941) C-98m. **½ D: Irving Cummings. Bob Hope,

Vera Zorina, Victor Moore, Irene Bordoni, Donna Drake. Brassy Irving Berlin musicomedy, with Hope's comedy very funny, especially famous filibuster scene in Congress. Opening scene of chorus girls singing lines about characters being fictitious is probably a movie first . . . and last.

Love and Kisses (1965) C-87m. **½ D: Ozzie Nelson. Rick Nelson, Kristin Nelson, Jack Kelly, Jerry Van Dyke, Pert Kelton, Madelyn Hines. Harmless fare; Rick gets married, disrupting his family's life.

Love and Larceny (1963-Italian, dubbed) 94m. **½ D: Dino Risi. Vittorio Gassman, Anna Maria Ferrero, Dorian Gray, Peppino de Filippo. Saucy comedy of exuberant con-man Gassman making no pretense about his carefree life and pleasures.

Love and Learn (1947) 83m. ** D: Frederick de Cordova. Jack Carson, Robert Hutton, Martha Vickers, Janis Paige, Otto Kruger. Overdone idea of songwriters Carson and Hutton waiting for their big break; young girl comes to their aid, but she doesn't save film.

Love and the Frenchwoman (1961-French, dubbed) 143m. *** D: Jean Delannoy, Michel Boisrond, René Clair, Christian-Jaque, Jean-Paul Lechannois. Martine Lambert, Claude Rich, Dany Robin, Jean-Paul Belmondo, Annie Girardot, Martine Carol. Savory account of the seven ages of love in a woman's life, sensitively acted.

Love at Twenty (1963-International, dubbed) 113m. **½ D: François Truffaut, Renzo Rossellini, Shintaro Ishihara, Max Ophuls, Andrezej Wajda. Jean-Pierre Leaud, Eleonora Rossi-Drago, Zbigniew Cybulski, Nami Tamara. Quintet of middling stories produced in France, Germany, Italy, Japan, Poland; variations on theme of love among younger generation.

Love Before Breakfast (1936) 70m. **½ D: Walter Lang. Carole Lombard, Preston Foster, Cesar Romero, Janet Beecher, Betty Lawford, Douglas Blackley. Fast-starting comedy slows down to obvious ending, but Lombard as object of Foster's and Romero's attention is worth viewing.

Love Crazy (1941) 100m. *** D: Jack Conway. William Powell, Myrna Loy, Gail Patrick, Jack Carson, Florence Bates, Sidney Blackmer, Sig Ruman. Chicly done comedy about third wedding anniversary celebration taking sudden turn for the worse.

Love Finds Andy Hardy (1938) 90m. D: George B. Seitz. Mickey Rooney, Lewis Stone, Judy Garland, Cecilia Parker, Fay Holden, Lana Turner, Ann Rutherford, Betty Ross Clark, Marie Blake. SEE: **Andy Hardy** series.

Love from a Stranger (1947) 81m. **½ D: Richard Whorf. Sylvia Sidney, John Hodiak, John Howard, Isobel Elsom, Ernest Cossart. Along the lines of SUSPICION, Sidney marries and learns her husband's a psychopathic killer.

Love Goddesses, The (1965) 87m. **½ Compiled by Saul J. Turell and Graeme Ferguson. Marilyn Monroe, Mae West, Jean Harlow, Theda Bara, Rita Hayworth, Claudette Colbert, Dorothy Lamour. Compilation covers a lot of ground, featuring many major female stars from silents to the present. Not always best clips, but glimpses of the cinema beauties are worthwhile.

Love Happy (1949) 91m. **½ D: David Miller. Harpo, Chico, and Groucho Marx, Ilona Massey, Vera-Ellen, Marion Hutton, Raymond Burr. No NIGHT AT THE OPERA, but even diluted Marx Brothers are better than none. Putting on a musical forms background for Harpo's antics, with Chico in support, Groucho in a few unrelated scenes. Marilyn Monroe has a brief bit.

Love Has Many Faces (1965) C-105m. **½ D: Alexander Singer. Lana Turner, Cliff Robertson, Hugh O'Brian, Ruth Roman, Stefanie Powers, Virginia Grey. Timid attempt at lurid soaper; playgirl Turner's costume changes are the highlights. O'Brian and Robertson are gigolos. Filmed in Acapulco.

Love, Honor and Goodbye (1945) 87m. ** D: Albert S. Rogell. Virginia Bruce, Nils Asther, Victor McLaglen, Helen Broderick, Veda Ann Borg, Edward Ashley. Bruce is actress in Broadway show, spending more time at rehearsals than with hubby. Mild frou-frou.

Love in a Goldfish Bowl (1961) C-

88m. Bomb D: Jack Sher. Tommy Sands, Fabian, Jan Sterling, Edward Andrews. Film is as bad as its title, a worthless, boring trifle about teenagers taking over a beach house. Forget it.

Love in Bloom (1935) 75m. ** D: Elliott Nugent. George Burns, Gracie Allen, Joe Morrison, Dixie Lee, J. C. Nugent, Lee Kohlmar, Richard Carle, Mary Foy. Minor musical of down-and-out troupers forced to travel in a calliope; mainly for Burns and Allen fans.

Love in the Afternoon (1957) 130m. ***1/2 D: Billy Wilder. Gary Cooper, Audrey Hepburn, Maurice Chevalier, John McGiver. Forget age difference between Cooper and Hepburn and enjoy sparkling romantic comedy, with Chevalier as Audrey's private-eye dad. McGiver lends good support in witty Wilder comedy set in Paris.

Love in the City (1953-Italian, dubbed) 90m. ** D: Michelangelo Antonioni, Federico Fellini, Dino Risi, Carlo Lizzani, Alberto Lattuada, Maselli Zavattini. Ugo Tognazzi, Maresa Gallo, Caterina Rigoglioso, Silvio Lillo, Angela Pierro. Six-part film using a hidden-camera technique to give production seeming reality as it relates various aspects of romance in Rome.

Love is a Ball (1963) C-111m. **1/2 D: David Swift. Glenn Ford, Hope Lange, Charles Boyer, Ricardo Montalban, Telly Savalas. Forced froth trying hard to be chic; gold-digging and romance on the Riviera.

Love is a Many-Splendored Thing (1955) C-102m. *** D: Henry King. Jennifer Jones, William Holden, Isobel Elsom, Jorja Cutright, Virginia Gregg, Torin Thatcher, Richard Loo. Well-mounted soaper set in Hong Kong at time of Korean War. Eurasian doctor Jones falls in love with war correspondent Holden. Trite plot, beautifully executed.

Love is Better Than Ever (1952) 81m. **1/2 D: Stanley Donen. Elizabeth Taylor, Larry Parks, Josephine Hutchinson, Tom Tully, Ann Doran. Froth involving talent agent Parks' decision to marry Taylor. Mild music, luscious Liz.

Love Is News (1937) 78m. ** D: Tay Garnett. Tyrone Power, Loretta Young, Don Ameche, Slim Summerville, George Sanders, Jane Darwell, Stepin Fetchit, Pauline Moore, Elisha Cook, Jr., Dudley Digges, Walter Catlett. Comedy misfire of heiress Young marrying reporter Power to get even for his stories about her. Better in remake THAT WONDERFUL URGE.

Love Laughs at Andy Hardy (1946) 93m. D: Willis Goldbeck. Mickey Rooney, Lewis Stone, Sara Haden, Bonita Granville, Lina Romay, Fay Holden, Dorothy Ford. SEE: Andy Hardy series.

Love Letters (1945) 101m. ** D: William Dieterle. Jennifer Jones, Joseph Cotten, Ann Richards, Anita Louise, Cecil Kellaway, Gladys Cooper. Artificial soaper of amnesiac Jones cured by Cotten's love; only real asset is Victor Young's lovely title song.

Love Lottery, The (1953-British) 89m. ** D: Charles Crichton. David Niven, Peggy Cummins, Anne Vernon, Herbert Lom, Hugh McDermott. Niven is famed movie star involved in international lottery; the winner gets him! Vernon is the girl he really loves. Potential satire never comes off. Humphrey Bogart has guest bit at finale.

Love Me Forever (1935) 90m. **1/2 D: Victor Schertzinger. Grace Moore, Leo Carrillo, Robert Allen, Spring Byington, Douglass Dumbrille. Entertaining musical of down-and-out singer who miraculously rises to top and becomes star. Good cast helped make Moore become star in real life too.

Love Me or Leave Me (1955) C-122m. ***1/2 D: Charles Vidor. Doris Day, James Cagney, Cameron Mitchell, Robert Keith, Tom Tully. Doris is singer Ruth Etting, Cagney her gangster boyfriend, the Gimp. Fine musical biography has great songs of 1920's: "Ten Cents A Dance," "Never Look Back," title tune, etc.

Love Me Tender (1956) 89m. **1/2 D: Robert D. Webb. Richard Egan, Debra Paget, Elvis Presley, Robert Middleton, William Campbell, Neville Brand, Mildred Dunnock. Presley's film debut is Civil War yarn of conflicting politics among sons in a Southern family, and their mutual love for Paget.

Love Me Tonight (1932) 104m. ***1/2 D: Rouben Mamoulian. Maurice Chevalier, Jeanette MacDonald, Charlie Ruggles, Myrna Loy, C. Aubrey

Smith, Elizabeth Patterson, Blanche Frederici, Ethel Griffies. Fine Rodgers-Hart musical, well directed, with obligatory story of French tailor romancing royalty flowing smoothly. Songs: "Mimi," title tune, "Isn't It Romantic?" "Lover."

Love Nest (1951) 84m. ** D: Joseph M. Newman. June Haver, William Lundigan, Frank Fay, Marilyn Monroe, Jack Paar, Leatrice Joy. Tepid comedy based on premise that wacky goings-on in apartment building can carry a film.

Love on a Pillow (1963-French, dubbed) C-102m. ** D: Roger Vadim. Brigitte Bardot, Robert Hossein, James Robertson Justice, Jean-Marc Bory. Charitable Bardot bestows her pleasures on young man, hoping to divert his intended suicide; saucy little comedy.

Love on the Dole (1941-British) 89m. *** D: John Baxter. Deborah Kerr, Clifford Evans, Mary Merrall, George Carney, Geoffrey Hibbert, Joyce O'Neill. Serious, well-acted study of struggling London family during Depression. From Walter Greenwood novel.

Love on the Run (1936) 80m. **½ D: W. S. Van Dyke II. Joan Crawford, Clark Gable, Franchot Tone, Reginald Owen, Mona Barrie, Ivan Lebedeff, Charles Judels. Another film that's all stars and no plot to support them. If you like Gable or Crawford, you'll enjoy this globetrotting romance involving foreign correspondents and Continental spies.

Love Parade, The (1930) 110m. **½ D: Ernst Lubitsch. Maurice Chevalier, Jeanette MacDonald, Lillian Roth, Lionel Belmore, Lupino Lane, Ben Turpin. Initial teaming of Chevalier and MacDonald is enjoyable operetta with chic Lubitsch touch, about love among French royalty. Virginia Bruce is one of Jeanette's ladies-in-waiting. "Dream Lover" is film's best song.

Love Slaves of the Amazon (1957) C-81m. ** D: Curt Siodmak. Don Taylor, Eduardo Ciannelli, Gianna Segale, Harvey Chalk. Title tag removes all surprises about this programmer.

Love Story (1944-British) 110m. *** D: Maurice Ostrer. Stewart Granger, Margaret Lockwood, Patricia Roc. Granger, ill with a fatal disease, finds true romance at summer resort; touching romance, thoughtful musical interludes.

Love That Brute (1950) 85m. **½ D: Alexander Hall. Paul Douglas, Jean Peters, Cesar Romero, Joan Davis, Arthur Treacher. Douglas comes off well as loud-talking, good-natured prohibition racketeer with a yen for innocent Peters. Remake of GENTLEMAN AT HEART.

Love Thy Neighbor (1940) 82m. **½ D: Mark Sandrich. Jack Benny, Fred Allen, Mary Martin, Verree Teasdale, Eddie Anderson, Virginia Dale, Theresa Harris. Film based on famous Benny-Allen radio feud is vintage fun, with Martin providing musical interludes.

Love Under Fire (1937) 75m. **½ D: George Marshall. Loretta Young, Don Ameche, Frances Drake, Walter Catlett, Sig Ruman, John Carradine, Holmes Herbert. Romance and adventure as detective Ameche has to arrest alleged thief Young in Madrid amid Spanish Civil War. Disjointed but enjoyable.

Love with the Proper Stranger (1963) 100m. *** D: Robert Mulligan. Natalie Wood, Steve McQueen, Edie Adams, Herschel Bernardi, Tom Bosley. Nifty, cynical romance tale of working-girl Wood and trumpet-player McQueen. Much N.Y.C. on-location filming, good support from Adams.

Lovemakers, The SEE: La Viaccia.

Lover Boy SEE: Lovers, Happy Lovers!

Lover Come Back (1946) 90m. **½ D: William A. Seiter. Lucille Ball, George Brent, Vera Zorina, Carl Esmond, William Wright, Charles Winninger. Bright little comedy of Lucy suing Brent for divorce when she sees his companion during war, photographer Zorina.

Lover Come Back (1961) C-107m. ***½ D: Delbert Mann. Rock Hudson, Doris Day, Tony Randall, Edie Adams, Jack Oakie. Early Day-Hudson vehicle is one of the best. Funny, fast-moving comedy, with Doris' honor at stake until the last reel. Edie Adams stands out in a supporting role.

Lovers, The (1959-French, dubbed) 90m. *** D: Louis Malle. Jeanne Moreau, Alain Cuny, Jose-Luis de Villalonga, Jean-Marc Bory. Sensational, chic love tale of Moreau bored with husband and home, having a most sensual romance with an overnight guest.

Lovers and Lollipops (1956) 80m. **½ D: Morris Engel, Ruth Orkin. Lori March, Gerald O'Loughlin, Cathy Dunn, William Ward. Pleasing minor film of romance between widow and professional man, disrupted by her daughter's jealousy of their happiness.

Lovers, Happy Lovers! (1954-British) 105m. **½ D: René Clement. Gerard Philippe, Valerie Hobson, Joan Greenwood, Margaret Johnston, Natasha Parry. Philippe is footloose playboy in London who finally meets his match and is marriage-bound. Retitled: LOVER BOY.

Lovers of Montparnasse, The (1957-French, dubbed) 103m. **½ D: Jacques Becker. Gerard Philippe, Lilli Palmer, Anouk Aimee, Lea Padovani, Lino Ventura, Gerard Sety. Fictionalized biog of 1900's painter Modigliani, his romances and escapades; cast is forced into stereotyped performances. Original title: MONTPARNASSE 19.

Lovers of Paris (1957-French, dubbed) 115m. **½ D: Julien Duvivier. Gerard Philippe, Danielle Darrieux, Dany Carrel. Spirited drama of Philippe coming to Paris bent on success and marriage; Darrieux is his perfect choice. Original title: POT-BOUILLE.

Loves of a Blonde, The (1966-Czech, dubbed) 88m. *** D: Milos Forman. Hana Brejchova, Vladimir Pucholt, Antonin Blazejovsky, Joseph Sebanek. Exuberant, free-flowing account of young generation, focusing on Brejchova in title role, with her many involvements.

Loves of Carmen, The (1948) C-99m. **½ D: Charles Vidor. Rita Hayworth, Glenn Ford, Ron Randell, Victor Jory, Luther Adler. Hayworth's beauty is all there is in this colorful but routine retelling of the story of a gypsy man-killer, minus Bizet's music.

Loves of Edgar Allan Poe, The (1942) 67m. ** D: Harry Lachman. Linda Darnell, John (Shepperd Strudwick) Shepperd, Virginia Gilmore, Jane Darwell, Mary Howard. Plodding biography of 19th-century writer and women who influenced him.

Loves of Salammbo, The (1962-Italian, dubbed) C-72m. ** D: Sergio Grieco. Jeanne Valerie, Jacques Sernas, Edmund Purdom, Arnold Foa, Riccardo Garrone. Spectacle features Purdom in an uneven tale of Carthaginians battling the Mercenaries. Filmed on location.

Loves of Three Queens (1953-Italian, dubbed) 90m. ** D: Marc Allegret. Hedy Lamarr, Massimo Serato, Cathy O'Donnell, Luigi Tosi, Guido Celano, Robert Beatty. Three-part film involving lives and loves of Genevieve of Brabant, Empress Josephine, and Helen of Troy (Lamarr). Originally three-hour meandering epic, now chopped down; still lacks continuity or interest. Retitled: THE FACE THAT LAUNCHED A THOUSAND SHIPS.

Loving You (1957) C-101m. **½ D: Hal Kanter. Elvis Presley, Lizabeth Scott, Wendell Corey, Dolores Hart, James Gleason. Scott discovers Presley and he becomes singing idol; formula musical.

Luck of Ginger Coffey, The (1964-Canadian) 100m. ***½ D: Irvin Kershner. Robert Shaw, Mary Ure, Liam Redmond, Tom Harvey, Libby McClintock. Shaw is superb as Irish-born dreamer moved to Montreal with wife and child, unwilling to face realities of workaday life.

Luck of the Irish, The (1948) 99m. **½ D: Henry Koster. Tyrone Power, Anne Baxter, Cecil Kellaway, Lee J. Cobb, Jayne Meadows. Leprechaun Kellaway becomes reporter Power's conscience in this "cute" but unremarkable romance.

Lucky Jordan (1942) 84m. **½ D: Frank Tuttle. Alan Ladd, Helen Walker, Marie McDonald, Mabel Paige, Sheldon Leonard, Lloyd Corrigan. Far-fetched story of army conman Ladd involved with Nazi agents with USO worker Walker (her feature-film debut).

Lucky Me (1954) C-100m. ** D: Jack Donohue. Doris Day, Robert Cummings, Phil Silvers, Eddie Foy, Nancy Walker, Martha Hyer. Unemployed chorus girl in Florida finds love instead of work. Lackluster musical with then-widescreen-novelty lost to viewers. Angie Dickinson's first film.

Lucky Nick Cain (1951) 87m. **½ D: Joseph M. Newman. George Raft, Coleen Gray, Charles Goldner, Walter

Rilla. Acceptable gangster yarn of Raft involved with counterfeiting gang, accused of murder; filmed in Italy.

Lucky Night (1939) 90m. *½ D: Norman Taurog. Myrna Loy, Robert Taylor, Henry O'Neill, Marjorie Main, Irving Bacon. Fizzle with Loy and Taylor as struggling young marrieds.

Lucky Partners (1940) 102m. **½ D: Lewis Milestone. Ronald Colman, Ginger Rogers, Jack Carson, Spring Byington, Cecilia Loftus, Harry Davenport. Far-fetched comedy about Colman-Rogers winning sweepstakes together, then taking "imaginary" honeymoon. Stars support fair script.

Lucky Stiff, The (1949) 99m. ** D: Lewis R. Foster. Dorothy Lamour, Brian Donlevy, Claire Trevor, Irene Hervey, Marjorie Rambeau. Sturdy cast in slim vehicle of lawyer setting trap for actual killer after girl suspect has death sentence reprieved.

Lucky to Be a Woman (1958-Italian, dubbed) 95m. **½ D: Alessandro Blasetti. Charles Boyer, Sophia Loren, Marcello Mastroianni, Nino Besozzi, Titina de Filippo. Boyer is lecherous count who helps make peasant gal Loren a cultured movie star; Mastroianni is her photographer boyfriend; charmingly acted.

Lucy Gallant (1955) C-104m. **½ D: Robert Parrish. Charlton Heston, Jane Wyman, Thelma Ritter, Claire Trevor, William Demarest, Wallace Ford. Spiritless soaper of success-bent Wyman rejecting suitors Heston et al, wanting to get ahead instead; set in Western oil town.

Lullaby of Broadway, The (1951) C-92m. **½ D: David Butler. Doris Day, Gene Nelson, S. Z. Sakall, Billy De Wolfe, Gladys George. Another Doris Day-Warner Bros. vehicle, with Doris a singer returning to N.Y.C. to discover mother (George) is down-and-out chanteuse.

Lulu Belle (1948) 87m. ** D: Leslie Fenton. Dorothy Lamour, George Montgomery, Albert Dekker, Otto Kruger, Glenda Farrell. Hackneyed drama of singer Lamour stepping on anyone and everyone to achieve fame.

Lure of the Swamp (1957) 74m. *½ D: Hubert Cornfield. Marshall Thompson, Willard Parker, Joan Vohs, Jack Elam. Tawdry B-film of man's lust for wealth, leading to destruction of group hunting loot in murky swamp.

Lure of the Wilderness (1952) C-92m. **½ D: Jean Negulesco. Jeffrey Hunter, Jean Peters, Constance Smith, Walter Brennan, Jack Elam. Remake of SWAMP WATER doesn't match earlier version's atmosphere of Southern swamps where murderer holds young man hostage to keep his whereabouts secret.

Lured (1947) 102m. **½ D: Douglas Sirk. George Sanders, Lucille Ball, Charles Coburn, Alan Mowbray, Cedric Hardwicke, Boris Karloff. Ball turns detective in this melodrama, encounters strange characters and harrowing experiences while tracking murderer; pretty good, with top cast.

Lust for Gold (1949) 90m. **½ D: S. Sylvan Simon. Ida Lupino, Glenn Ford, Jay Silverheels, Eddy Waller. Lupino gets overly dramatic as grasping woman stopping at nothing to obtain riches of gold-laden mine.

Lust for Life (1956) C-122m. **** D: Vincente Minnelli. Kirk Douglas, Anthony Quinn, James Donald, Pamela Brown, Everett Sloane. Brilliant adaptation of Irving Stone's biography of painter Van Gogh (Douglas), highlighting his life of personal anguish. Quinn plays his mentor Gauguin in this beautiful color production.

Lusty Men, The (1952) 113m. *** D: Nicholas Ray. Susan Hayward, Robert Mitchum, Arthur Kennedy, Arthur Hunnicutt. Atmospheric rodeo tale, solidly acted by all.

Luxury Liner (1948) C-98m. ** D: Richard Whorf. George Brent, Jane Powell, Lauritz Melchior, Frances Gifford, Xavier Cugat. MGM fluff aboard a cruise ship, with Powell singing her heart out.

Lydia (1941) 144m. *** D: Julien Duvivier. Merle Oberon, Edna May Oliver, Alan Marshal, Joseph Cotten, Hans Yaray, George Reeves. Sentimental tale of elderly woman (Oberon) meeting her former beaus and recalling their courtship. Adapted from famous French film CARNET DU BAL.

Lydia Bailey (1952) C-89m. **½ D: Jean Negulesco. Dale Robertson, Anne Francis, Luis Van Rooten, Juanita Moore, William Marshall. Handsome but empty version of Kenneth Roberts actioner of 1800's Haiti and revolt against French rulers.

M (1951) 88m. **½ D: Joseph Losey. David Wayne, Howard da Silva, Luther Adler, Karen Morley, Jorja Cutright, Martin Gabel. Tepid remake of famed Peter Lorre German classic, concerning child-killer hunted down by fellow-criminals not wanting police investigation of underworld.

Ma and Pa Kettle Betty MacDonald's best-selling book THE EGG AND I told of the hardships a city girl faced moving with her husband to a rural chicken farm. Among the problems were the incredible local characters, two of whom, Ma and Pa Kettle, were given prime footage in the screen version of THE EGG AND I. Played by veterans Marjorie Main and Percy Kilbride, the hillbilly duo created a hit and became the stars of their own series, which was extremely popular through the 1950's. Rambunctious Ma and hesitant Pa's adventures were not exactly out of Noel Coward, but they scored a hit and the two stars were naturals for the roles. In fact, the role of Ma was not so different from the stereotyped character Marjorie Main had become associated with in scores of other films. Meg Randall and Lori Nelson took turns playing the eldest daughter in the Kettle's tremendous brood (at least a dozen kids), as the Kettles battled with neighbors and local authorities, visited Paris, Hawaii, and New York, and engaged in predictable but amusing situations for eight years. In 1955 Percy Kilbride left the series; Arthur Hunnicutt took the role in THE KETTLES IN THE OZARKS and Parker Fennelly took his turn in THE KETTLES ON OLD MACDONALD'S FARM, but neither one caught on and the series came to an end in 1957. Intellectuals liked to assume that the cornball humor had lost its audience, but then several years later a TV show called THE BEVERLY HILLBILLIES came along to prove them wrong.

Ma and Pa Kettle (1949) 75m. D: Charles Lamont. Marjorie Main, Percy Kilbride, Richard Long, Meg Randall, Patricia Alphin, Esther Dale.

Ma and Pa Kettle at Home (1954) 81m. D: Charles Lamont. Marjorie Main, Percy Kilbride, Alice Kelley, Brett Halsey, Alan Mowbray, Oliver Blake, Stan Ross.

Ma and Pa Kettle at the Fair (1952) 78m. D: Charles Barton. Marjorie Main, Percy Kilbride, Lori Nelson, James Best, Esther Dale.

Ma and Pa Kettle at Waikiki (1955) 79m. D: Lee Sholem. Marjorie Main, Percy Kilbride, Lori Nelson, Lowell Gilmore, Mabel Albertson, Ida Moore.

Ma and Pa Kettle Back on the Farm (1951) 80m. D: Edward Sedgwick. Marjorie Main, Percy Kilbride, Richard Long, Barbara Brown, Meg Randall.

Ma and Pa Kettle Go to Town (1950) 79m. D: Charles Lamont. Percy Kilbride, Marjorie Main, Richard Long, Jim Backus, Hal March, Meg Randall.

Ma and Pa Kettle on Vacation (1953) 75m. D: Charles Lamont. Percy Kilbride, Marjorie Main, Ray Collins, Sig Ruman, Jack Kruschen, Teddy Hart.

Ma Barker's Killer Brood (1960) 82m. ** D: Bill Karn. Lurene Tuttle, Tris Coffin, Paul Dubov, Nelson Leigh. Energetic performance by Tuttle in lead role and occasional bursts of gunplay hoist this programmer gangster yarn above tedium.

Macabre (1958) 73m. ** D: William Castle. William Prince, Jim Backus, Christine White, Jacqueline Scott. Weird goings-on in small town when doctor's wife and her sister are murdered. Film promises much, delivers little.

Macao (1952) 80m. ** D: Josef von Sternberg. Robert Mitchum, Jane Russell, William Bendix, Gloria Grahame, Thomas Gomez, Philip Ahn. Flat yarn supposedly set in murky title port, with Russell a singer and Mitchum the action-seeking man she loves.

Macbeth (1948) 105m. *** D: Orson Welles. Orson Welles, Jeanette Nolan, Dan O'Herlihy, Edgar Barrier, Roddy McDowall, Robert Coote. Strange Welles version of Shakespeare, made quickly on old Western sets; worth seeing once but not a definitive version of the classic.

McConnell Story, The (1955) C-107m. *** D: Gordon Douglas. Alan Ladd, June Allyson, James Whitmore, Frank Faylen. Weepy yet effective fictional biography of jet test pilot, with Allyson as his understanding wife.

McGuire, Go Home! (1966-British) C-101m. **½ D: Ralph Thomas. Dirk

Bogarde, George Chakiris, Susan Strasberg, Denholm Elliott. Set in 1954 Cyprus; peppy account of terrorist campaign against British occupation, with side-plot of officer Bogarde in love with American girl Strasberg.

McHale's Navy (1964) C-93m. ** D: Edward J. Montagne. Ernest Borgnine, Joe Flynn, Tim Conway, Claudine Longet, Jean Willes, George Kennedy. Usual shenanigans from PT 73 in the Pacific during WW2, expanded from TV series, of same title. Show was half hour, so feature comes off weak.

McHale's Navy Joins the Air Force (1965) C-90m. ** D: Edward J. Montagne. Joe Flynn, Tim Conway, Bob Hastings, Gary Vinson, Billy Sands, Jean Hale, Susan Silo, Edson Stroll, John Wright, Cliff Norton. Generally uninspired comedy with familiar crew from TV series, unimpressive due to television look.

Machine Gun Kelly (1958) 80m. **½ D: Roger Corman. Charles Bronson, Susan Cabot, Barboura Morris, Morey Amsterdam, Wally Campo, Jack Lambert, Connie Gilchrist. With typical efficiency, Corman gives this gangster chronicle pacing and more than passing interest. Bronson is fine in title role.

Maciste—The Mighty (1960-Italian, dubbed) C-87m. ** D: Carlo Campogalliani. Mark Forrest, Chelo Alonso, Angelo Zanolli, Federica Ranchi. Forrest in title role tries to instill some animation in wooden tale of old Egypt and the barbaric Persians.

McLintock! (1963) C-127m. *** D: Andrew V. McLaglen. John Wayne, Maureen O'Hara, Patrick Wayne, Stefanie Powers, Yvonne de Carlo, Chill Wills, Bruce Cabot, Jack Kruschen, Jerry Van Dyke. Rowdy, lively Western-comedy with Wayne encountering his refined wife O'Hara, who wants a divorce, and his grown-up daughter Powers, caught between father and mother. Plenty of slapstick to keep things moving; entertaining.

Macomber Affair, The (1947) 89m. ***½ D: Zoltan Korda. Gregory Peck, Joan Bennett, Robert Preston, Reginald Denny, Carl Harbord. Action and romance combine in Hemingway story of love triangle on African expedition, with sparkling performances by all.

Macumba Love (1960) C-86m. *½ D: Douglas Fowley. Walter Reed, Ziva Rodann, William Wellman, Jr., June Wilkinson. Trivia of author delving into voodoo practices in South America. -

Mad About Music (1938) 98m. *** D: Norman Taurog. Deanna Durbin, Herbert Marshall, Gail Patrick, Arthur Treacher, Helen Parrish, Marcia Mae Jones, William Frawley. Excellent Durbin vehicle; busy mother Patrick leaves Deanna in Swiss girls' school, where she pretends Marshall is her father. Holds up better than remake TOY TIGER.

Mad at the World (1955) 72m. *½ D: Harry Essex. Frank Lovejoy, Keefe Brasselle, Cathy O'Donnell, Karen Sharpe. Pointless study of Brasselle seeking vengeance on teen-age slum gang who harmed his baby; Lovejoy the detective in the case.

Mad Doctor, The (1941) 90m. ** D: Tim Whelan. Basil Rathbone, Ellen Drew, John Howard, Barbara Jo Allen, Ralph Morgan, Martin Kosleck. Standard B-film has Rathbone as doctor who marries pretty women and then does away with them.

Mad Doctor of Market Street, The (1942) 61m. *½ D: Joseph H. Lewis. Una Merkel, Claire Dodd, Lionel Atwill. Mini-chiller from Universal Pictures about insane scientist on Pacific Isle using natives for strange experiments.

Mad Dog Coll (1961) 86m. *½ D: Burt Balaban. John Davis Chandler, Brooke Hayward, Kay Doubleday, Jerry Orbach, Telly Savalas. Minor account of gangster who rises to top of heap and gets just deserts.

Mad Executioners, The (1963-German, dubbed) 94m. ** D: Edwin Zbonek. Wolfgang Preiss, Harry Riebauer, Rudolph Fernau, Chris Howland. Muddled Edgar Wallace-ish suspenser about Scotland Yard inspector setting up his own court of justice to execute criminals.

Mad Genius, The (1931) 81m. **½ D: Michael Curtiz. John Barrymore, Marian Marsh, Donald Cook, Carmel Myers, Boris Karloff. Reworking of SVENGALI has dance coach Barrymore thwarting romance of Marsh and Cook so he can have girl for himself.

Mad Ghoul, The (1943) 65m. **½ D:

James Hogan. David Bruce, Evelyn Ankers, George Zucco, Turhan Bey, Charles McGraw, Robert Armstrong, Milburn Stone, Rose Hobart. Strong cast buoys grim story of scientist and his strange life-preserving methods.

Mad Little Island (1957-British) C-94m. ** D: Michael Relph. Jeannie Carson, Donald Sinden, Roland Culver, Catherine Lacey. Tame goings-on as island dwellers join together to prevent their land becoming missile base.

Mad Love (1935) 83m. *** D: Karl Freund. Peter Lorre, Frances Drake, Colin Clive, Isabel Jewell, Ted Healy, Sara Haden, Edward Brophy, Keye Luke. Famous Hands-of-Orlac story refitted for Lorre as mad doctor in love with married Drake. He agrees to operate on her husband's hands with disastrous results. Lavishly done, good chiller.

Mad Magician, The (1954) 72m. **½ D: John Brahm. Vincent Price, Mary Murphy, Eva Gabor, Patrick O'Neal, John Emery. Far-fetched hokum of demented magico whose gimmicks eventually backfire and destroy him. Shot in 3-D; most effects retain excitement on small screen.

Mad Miss Manton, The (1938) 65m. **½ D: Leigh Jason. Barbara Stanwyck, Henry Fonda, Sam Levene, Frances Mercer, Stanley Ridges, Vicki Lester, Whitney Bourne, Hattie McDaniel, Penny Singleton, Grady Sutton. Socialite Stanwyck involves her friends in murder mystery; trivial but very enjoyable film, with sleuthing and slapstick combined.

Madam Satan (1930) 80m. **½ D: Cecil B. de Mille. Lillian Roth, Kay Johnson, Reginald Denny, Roland Young, Martha Sleeper, Mary Carlisle. Ornate early De Mille talkie about woman trying to make her husband jealous; climax on party-going zeppelin still exciting.

Mad Wednesday (1947) 89m. **½ D: Preston Sturges. Harold Lloyd, Frances Ramsden, Jimmy Conlin, Edgar Kennedy, Rudy Vallee. Reworking of old footage (from Lloyd's silent THE FRESHMAN) along with a twenty-years-later episode of madcap frenzy leaves one wistful for the young, inventive Lloyd.

Madame (1962-French, dubbed) C-104m. **½ D: Christian-Jaque. Sophia Loren, Robert Hossein, Julien Bertheau, Marina Berti. Uninspired remake of MADAME SANS-GENE with Loren, who uses looks and wits to rise from laundress to nobility in Napoleonic France.

Madame Bovary (1949) 115m. **½ D: Vincente Minnelli. Jennifer Jones, James Mason, Van Heflin, Louis Jourdan, Gene Lockhart, Gladys Cooper, George Zucco. Static remake of Gustave Flaubert's 19th-century novel of sensual French woman who sacrifices everyone for her love whims. Jones is too sedate in lead role.

Madame Butterfly (1932) 86m. **½ D: Marion Gering. Sylvia Sidney, Cary Grant, Charlie Ruggles, Irving Pichel, Helen Jerome Eddy. Puccini opera (minus music) of Oriental woman in love with American (Grant) is sensitive, tragic romance, dated but well handled.

Madame Curie (1943) 124m. *** D: Mervyn LeRoy. Greer Garson, Walter Pidgeon, Henry Travers, Albert Basserman, Robert Walker, C. Aubrey Smith. Despite stretches of plodding footage, biography of famed female scientist is generally excellent. Garson and Pidgeon team well, as usual.

Madame X (1966) C-100m. **½ D: David Lowell Rich. Lana Turner, John Forsythe, Constance Bennett, Ricardo Montalban, Burgess Meredith, Keir Dullea, Virginia Grey. Plush remake of perennial soaper of attorney defending a woman accused of murder, not knowing it's his mother. Fine cast and varied backgrounds bolster Turner's pivotal performance. Constance Bennett's last film.

Made For Each Other (1939) 85m. *** D: John Cromwell. Carole Lombard, James Stewart, Charles Coburn, Lucile Watson, Alma Kruger, Esther Dale, Ward Bond, Louise Beavers. First-rate soaper of struggling young marrieds Stewart and Lombard, battling meddling in-laws, poverty, illness, etc. Fine acting makes this all work.

Made in Paris (1966) C-101m. **½ D: Boris Sagal. Ann-Margret, Louis Jourdan, Richard Crenna, Edie Adams, Chad Everett. Witless, unpolished shenanigans of Ann-Margret, fashion designer in France, falling for Jourdan.

Madeleine (1949-British) 101m. **½ D: David Lean. Ann Todd, Leslie Banks, Elizabeth Sellars, Ivor Barnard. Superior cast improves oft-told drama of woman accused of murdering her lover. Retitled: STRANGE CASE OF MADELEINE.

Madeleine (1958-German, dubbed) 86m. *½ D: Kurt Meisel. Eva Bartok, Sabina Sesselmann, Ilse Steppat, Alexander Kerst. Unsensational study of prostitutes, with a witless plot of Bartok trying to shed her shady past.

Mademoiselle Fifi (1944) 69m. ** D: Robert Wise. Simone Simon, John Emery, Alan Napier, Kurt Kreuger, Jason Robards, Sr., Fay Helm, Helen Freeman. Simon is French working girl involved with partisan action in 1870's when Prussians invade France.

Mademoiselle Striptease SEE: Please! Mr. Balzac.

Madigan (1968) C-101m. ***½ D: Donald Siegel. Richard Widmark, Henry Fonda, Harry Guardino, Inger Stevens, James Whitmore, Michael Dunn, Steve Inhat, Sheree North. Excellent, unpretentious film which blends the day-to-day problems of detective Madigan (Widmark) with the endless dilemmas facing police commissioner Fonda. Shot largely on location in N.Y.C., film benefits from fine work by Guardino, Whitmore, and others in supporting roles.

Madison Avenue (1962) 94m. **½ D: H. Bruce Humberstone. Dana Andrews, Eleanor Parker, Jeanne Crain, Eddie Albert, Howard St. John, Henry Daniell, Kathleen Freeman. Tightly produced programmer centering on machinations in N.Y.C.'s advertising jungle.

Madmen of Mandoras (1964) 74m. ** D: David Bradley. Carlos Rivas, Marshall Reed, Nestor Paiva, Scott Peters. Weird minor chiller of bloblike monster seeking to destroy the world.

Madonna of the Seven Moons (1946-British) 88m. *** D: Arthur Crabtree. Phyllis Calvert, Stewart Granger, Patricia Roc, Jean Kent, John Stuart, Peter Glenville. Calvert is pushed in two directions because of strange gypsy curse; she is wife, mother, and mistress at same time. Taut melodrama, may be considered "camp" in some circles.

Madonna's Secret, The (1946) 79m. ** D: William Thiele. Francis Lederer, Gail Patrick, Ann Rutherford, Linda Stirling, John Litel, Pierre Watkin. OK whodunit involving hunt for killer of murdered artist's model.

Maedchen in Uniform (1965-German, dubbed) 91m. **½ D: Geza Radvanyi. Lilli Palmer, Romy Schneider, Christine Kaufmann, Therese Giehse. Rather talky story of girls' school and one particularly sensitive youngster (Schneider) who is attracted to her teacher (Palmer). Remake of famous early German sound movie is shade above average.

Magic Bow, The (1947) 105m. **½ D: Bernard Knowles. Stewart Granger, Phyllis Calvert, Jean Kent, Dennis Price, Cecil Parker. As usual, music overshadows weak plot in biography of violinist Paganini.

Magic Box, The (1951-British) C-103m. **** D: John Boulting. Robert Donat, Maria Schell, Margaret Johnston, Robert Beatty; guests Laurence Olivier, Michael Redgrave, Eric Portman, Glynis Johns, Emlyn Williams, Richard Attenborough, Stanley Holloway, Margaret Rutherford, Peter Ustinov, Bessie Love, Cecil Parker, etc. Practically every British star appears in this superb biography of William Friese-Greene, the forgotten inventor of movies. Beautifully done; one scene where Donat perfects the invention, pulling in a cop off the street (Olivier) to see it, is superb.

Magic Carpet, The (1951) C-84m. ** D: Lew Landers. Lucille Ball, John Agar, Patricia Medina, Raymond Burr, George Tobias. Mild costumer that has virtue of Ball as heroine, and little else.

Magic Face, The (1951) 89m. ** D: Frank Tuttle. Luther Adler, Patricia Knight, William L. Shirer, Ilka Windish. Low-keyed study of impersonator who murders Hitler and assumes his place; Adler rises above material.

Magic Fire (1956) C-95m. ** D: William Dieterle. Yvonne de Carlo, Carlos Thompson, Rita Gam, Valentina Cortesa, Alan Badel. Low-budget musical biography of 19th-century German composer Richard Wagner.

Magic Sword, The (1962) C-80m. **½ D: Bert I. Gordon. Basil Rathbone, Estelle Winwood, Gary Lockwood, Anne Helm, Liam Sullivan, Jacques

Gallo. Fanciful juvenile costumer with fine special effects, pleasing cast.

Magic Town (1947) 103m. **½ D: William Wellman. James Stewart, Jane Wyman, Kent Smith, Ned Sparks, Regis Toomey. Satire doesn't hit bull's-eye as pollster Stewart declares small town "average" but sees it change when people become conscious of it.

Magic World of Topo Gigio, The (1965-Italian, dubbed) C-75m. *½ D: Luca de Rico. Ermanno Roveri, Ignazio Colnaghi, Frederica Milani, Topo Gigio. Cash-in on the popular puppet act from Ed Sullivan show. Poorly done animation, but children might enjoy it.

Magician, The (1959-Swedish, dubbed) 102m. *** D: Ingmar Bergman. Max von Sydow, Ingrid Thulin, Gunnar Bjornstrand, Naima Wifstrand, Bibi Andersson. Brooding, complex account set in 19th-century Sweden involving mesmerizer and magician who becomes involved in murder and after-life; revealing parable of life's realities.

Maggie, The SEE: **High and Dry.**

Magnet, The (1951-British) 78m. *** D: Charles Frend. William Fox, Kay Walsh, Stephen Murray, Meredith Edwards. Disarming study of fun-loving children at play, told intelligently from their own point of view; no phony psychology thrown in. Young William Fox is known today as James Fox.

Magnetic Monster, The (1953) 76m. **½ D: Curt Siodmak. Richard Carlson, King Donovan, Jean Byron, Byron Fougler. Engaging premise of unknown force pulling earth off its gravity belt.

Magnificent Ambersons, The (1942) 88m. **** D: Orson Welles. Joseph Cotten, Dolores Costello, Anne Baxter, Tim Holt, Agnes Moorehead, Ray Collins. Brilliant drama from Booth Tarkington novel of family unwilling to change its way of life with the times; mother and son conflict over her lover. Welles' follow-up to CITIZEN KANE is equally exciting.

Magnificent Brute, The (1936) 80m. ** D: John G. Blystone. Victor McLaglen, Binnie Barnes, William Hall, Jean Dixon. Pertly acted love triangle, with McLaglen the roughneck blast furnace boss, involved in romance and stolen money.

Magnificent Cuckold, The (1966-Italian, dubbed) 111m. **½ D: Antonio Pietrangeli. Claudia Cardinale, Ugo Tognazzi, Michele Girardon, Bernard Blier. Saucy sex comedy of marital infidelity, with Tognazzi, the businessman husband of Cardinale, outwitted by his curvaceous wife.

Magnificent Doll (1946) 95m. ** D: Frank Borzage. Ginger Rogers, Burgess Meredith, David Niven, Horace McNally, Peggy Wood. Rogers just isn't right as Dolly Madison, and historical drama with Meredith as President Madison and Niven as Aaron Burr falls flat.

Magnificent Dope, The (1942) 83m. *** D: Walter Lang. Henry Fonda, Lynn Bari, Don Ameche, Edward Everett Horton, Hobart Cavanaugh, Pierre Watkin. Entertaining comedy of hopeless hayseed Fonda who shows up sharper Ameche in big city; Bari is the girl between them.

Magnificent Fraud, The (1939) 78m. ** D: Robert Florey. Akim Tamiroff, Lloyd Nolan, Mary Boland, Patricia Morison. Spry Paramount B-film involving South American republic and its phony dictator.

Magnificent Matador, The (1955) C-94m. **½ D: Budd Boetticher. Maureen O'Hara, Anthony Quinn, Thomas Gomez, Richard Denning, Lola Albright. Pulsating account of bullfighter seeking glory and O'Hara, not necessarily in that order.

Magnificent Obsession (1954) C-108m. **½ D: Douglas Sirk. Jane Wyman, Rock Hudson, Barbara Rush, Otto Kruger, Agnes Moorehead. Overblown theatrics almost obscure Lloyd Douglas poignant account of playboy Hudson who becomes a doctor to restore Wyman's eyesight.

Magnificent Roughnecks (1956) 73m. Bomb D: Sherman A. Rose. Jack Carson, Mickey Rooney, Nancy Gates, Jeff Donnell. Allied Artists disaster with two "comics" as partners trying to wildcat oilfields.

Magnificent Seven, The (1954-Japanese, dubbed) 158m. *** D: Akira Kurosawa. Toshiro Mifune, Takashi Shimura, Yoshio Inaba, Isao Kimura, Seiji Miyaguchi, Minoru Chiaki. Battle-weary 16th-century Japanese village hires professional warriors to end bloody warfare. Remade as an American Western in 1960. Retitled: SEVEN SAMURAI.

Magnificent Seven, The (1960) C-126m. *** D: John Sturges. Yul Brynner, Eli Wallach, Steve McQueen, Horst Buchholz, James Coburn, Charles Bronson, Robert Vaughn. Rousing Western actioner derived from prior Japanese film. Paid gunslingers blast away at bandits, devastating small Mexican town.

Magnificent Sinner (1963-French, dubbed) C-91m. ** D: Robert Siodmak. Romy Schneider, Curt Jurgens, Pierre Blanchar, Monique Melinand. Lackluster proceedings of Schneider as mistress to Russian Czar, involved in court intrigue.

Magnificent Yankee, The (1950) 80m. *** D: John Sturges. Louis Calhern, Ann Harding, Eduard Franz, James Lydon, Philip Ober. Calhern as Oliver Wendell Holmes, Supreme Court Justice, and Harding his patient wife, give poignancy to this sensitive biographical study.

Maid in Paris (1957-French, dubbed) 84m. ** D: Gaspard-Huit. Dany Robin, Daniel Gelin, Marie Daems, Tilda Thamar. Bland story of girl going to the big city seeking romance.

Maid of Salem (1937) 86m. *** D: Frank Lloyd. Claudette Colbert, Fred MacMurray, Louise Dresser, Gale Sondergaard, Beulah Bondi, Bonita Granville, Virginia Weidler, Donald Meek, Harvey Stephens, Edward Ellis, Mme. Sul-te-wan. Colonial witch-hunting era is backdrop for fine drama with many similarities to Arthur Miller's CRUCIBLE (minus the philosophy).

Maid's Night Out (1938) 64m. ** D: Ben Holmes. Joan Fontaine, Allan Lane, Hedda Hopper, George Irving, William Brisbane, Billy Gilbert, Cecil Kellaway. Fontaine is one of those heiresses of the 1930's, mistaken for housemaid, in mild low-budget comedy.

Mailbag Robbery (1958-British) 70m. ** D: Compton Bennett. Lee Patterson, Kay Callard, Alan Gifford, Kerry Jordan. Title explains full contents of programmer.

Main Chance, The (1966-British) 60m. **½ D: John Knight. Gregoire Aslan, Tracy Reed, Edward De Souza, Stanley Meadows. Offbeat account of diamond robbery.

Main Street After Dark (1944) 57m. **½ D: Edward L. Cahn. Edward Arnold, Audrey Totter, Dan Duryea, Hume Cronyn, Selena Royle. Offbeat drama of family pickpocket gang put out of business by civic clean-up campaign.

Main Street to Broadway (1953) 102m. **½ D: Tay Garnett. Tom Morton, Mary Murphy; guest stars Tallulah Bankhead, Ethel and Lionel Barrymore, Gertrude Berg, Rex Harrison, Lilli Palmer, Mary Martin, Agnes Moorehead, Herb Shriner. Thin tale of girl deciding between would-be playwright and successful N.Y.C. businessman. Vehicle allows for interesting cameos by host of theatrical luminaries.

Maisie Maisie was a middling series of ten MGM features made between 1939 and 1947, starring lively Ann Sothern as a brassy showgirl involved in a progression of topical if trivial situations encompassing the changing role of American women during WW2 America. The series never rose above the B category; all were filmed in black and white and ran about 85 minutes. Production values were too often static, utilizing rear projection and indoor sets to establish the varied locales of the episodes. The Maisie series relied almost exclusively on Miss Sothern's vivacious personality to carry the slight tales of the conventional tough-girl-with-a-heart-of-gold. Her co-stars were competent contract players such as Lew Ayres, John Hodiak, Robert Sterling, and George Murphy. Unlike the Andy Hardy series, few fledgling starlets appeared in these features, although guests like Red Skelton helped out from time to time. In general the series lacked a basic continuity and flavor; the earlier entries such as MAISIE and CONGO MAISIE, while no classics, had more punch than later efforts such as UNDERCOVER MAISIE.

Maisie (1939) 74m. D: Edwin L. Marin. Ann Sothern, Robert Young, Ruth Hussey, Ian Hunter, George Tobias.

Maisie Gets Her Man (1942) 85m. D: Roy Del Ruth. Ann Sothern, Red

Skelton, Leo Gorcey, Pamela Blake, Allen Jenkins, Donald Meek, Walter Catlett, Fritz Feld, Rags Ragland, Frank Jenks.

Maisie Goes to Reno (1944) 90m. D: Harry Beaumont. Ann Sothern, John Hodiak, Tom Drake, Ava Gardner, Donald Meek.

Maisie Was a Lady (1941) 79m. D: Edwin L. Marin. Ann Sothern, Lew Ayres, Maureen O'Sullivan, C. Aubrey Smith, Joan Perry, Paul Cavanagh.

Major and the Minor, The (1942) 100m. ***½ D: Billy Wilder. Ginger Rogers, Ray Milland, Rita Johnson, Robert Benchley, Diana Lynn, Norma Varden. Memorable comedy of working-girl Rogers disguised as 12-year-old to save train fare, becoming involved with Milland's military school. Wilder's first directorial effort is still amusing.

Major Barbara (1941-British) 115m. **** D: Gabriel Pascal. Wendy Hiller, Rex Harrison, Robert Morley, Robert Newton, Emlyn Williams, Sybil Thorndike, Deborah Kerr. Top-notch adaptation of Shaw play about wealthy girl who joins Salvation Army. Excellent cast in intelligent comedy.

Major Dundee (1965) C-134m. **½ D: Sam Peckinpah. Charlton Heston, Richard Harris, Jim Hutton, James Coburn, Michael Anderson, Jr., Senta Berger, Warren Oates, Slim Pickens. Very fine cast and lavish production make up for overlong, confused story of cavalry officer (Heston) who leads assorted misfits against Apaches.

Majority of One, A (1961) C-153m. **½ D: Mervyn LeRoy. Rosalind Russell, Alec Guinness, Ray Danton, Madlyn Rhue, Mae Questel. Compared to Broadway play, this is overblown, overacted account of Jewish matron Russell falling in love with Japanese widower Guinness.

Make Haste to Live (1954) 90m. **½ D: William A. Seiter. Dorothy McGuire, Stephen McNally, Mary Murphy, Edgar Buchanan, John Howard. McGuire gives believable performance as woman faced with criminal husband returned to seek vengeance.

Make Me an Offer (1955-British) C-88m. **½ D: Cyril Frankel. Peter Finch, Adrienne Corri, Rosalie Crutchley, Finlay Currie. Satisfactory highbrow shenanigans in the antique-buying field, with Finch after priceless vase.

Make Mine Laughs (1949) 64m. *½ D: Richard Fleischer. Frances Langford, Joan Davis, Leon Errol, Ray Bolger, Gil Lamb. RKO mini-musical, no more than uninspired footage lumped together à la vaudeville.

Make Way For a Lady (1936) 65m. ** D: David Burton. Herbert Marshall, Anne Shirley, Gertrude Michael, Margot Grahame, Clara Blandick, Frank Coghlan, Jr. Routine comedy of Shirley playing matchmaker for her widowed father Marshall; pleasant enough, but just average.

Make Way For Tomorrow (1937) 92m. ***½ D: Leo McCarey. Victor Moore, Beulah Bondi, Fay Bainter, Thomas Mitchell, Porter Hall, Barbara Reed, Louise Beavers. Sensitive film of elderly couple in financial difficulty, shunted by their children, unwanted and unloved; shatteringly true, beautifully done.

Make Your Own Bed (1944) 82m. *½ D: Peter Godfrey. Jack Carson, Jane Wyman, Alan Hale, Irene Manning, George Tobias, Ricardo Cortez. Forced comedy of detective Carson disguised as butler, Wyman as maid, to get lowdown on racketeer.

Malaga (1962-British) 97m. **½ D: Laslo Benedek. Trevor Howard, Dorothy Dandridge, Edmund Purdom, Michael Hordern. Bizarre casting in routine robbery tale is primary diversion.

Malaya (1949) 98m. **½ D: Richard Thorpe. Spencer Tracy, James Stewart, Valentina Cortesa, Sydney Greenstreet. Routine WW2 melodrama set in the Pacific, about Allies' efforts to smuggle out rubber. Good cast let down by so-so script.

Male Animal, The (1942) 101m. ***½ D: Elliott Nugent. Henry Fonda, Olivia de Havilland, Jack Carson, Joan Leslie, Herbert Anderson, Don DeFore, Hattie McDaniel, Eugene Pallette. Intelligent, entertaining Elliott Nugent-James Thurber comedy of college professor Fonda defending his rights, while losing wife De Havilland to old-flame Carson. Fine performances in this fine, contemporary film, with spoof on typical football rallies a highlight. Remade as SHE'S WORKING HER WAY THROUGH COLLEGE.

Male Hunt (1965-French, dubbed) 92m. *** D: Edouard Molinaro. Jean-Paul Belmondo, Jean-Claude Brialy, Catherine Deneuve, Françoise Dorleac, Marie Laforet. Spicy romp about trio of Frenchmen avoiding the clutches of marriage-minded women.

Malta Story, The (1953-British) 98m. **½ D: Brian Desmond Hurst. Alec Guinness, Jack Hawkins, Anthony Steele, Muriel Pavlow. On-location filming of this WW2 British-air-force-in-action yarn is sparked by underplayed acting.

Maltese Falcon, The (1941) 100m. **** D: John Huston. Humphrey Bogart, Mary Astor, Peter Lorre, Sydney Greenstreet, Gladys George, Barton MacLane, Elisha Cook, Jr., Lee Patrick, Jerome Cowan. Outstanding detective drama improves with each viewing; Bogie is Dashiell Hammett's "hero" Sam Spade, Astor his client, Lorre the evasive Joel Cairo, Greenstreet the Fat Man, and Cook the neurotic gunsel Wilmer. Huston's first directorial attempt moves at lightning pace, with cameo by his father Walter Huston as Captain Jacoby. Previously filmed in 1931 and in 1936 as SATAN MET A LADY.

Maltese Falcon (1931) SEE: Dangerous Female.

Mambo (1955-Italian, dubbed) 94m. **½ D: Robert Rossen. Shelley Winters, Silvana Mangano, Michael Rennie, Katherine Dunham, Vittorio Gassman, Eduardo Ciannelli. Muddled yet unusual account of working gal becoming famed dancer; offbeat entertainment.

Mammy (1930) 84m. ** D: Michael Curtiz. Al Jolson, Lois Moran, Louise Dresser, Lowell Sherman, Hobart Bosworth. Jolson sings "Let Me Sing and I'm Happy." Story of backstage murder is only tolerable during musical numbers.

Mam'zelle Pigalle (1958-French, dubbed) C-77m. **½ D: Michel Boisrond. Brigitte Bardot, Jean Bretonniere, Françoise Fabian, Bernard Lancret. Not as saucy as most BB flicks; here she's a songstress mixed up with counterfeiters. Retitled: NAUGHTY GIRL.

Man About the House, A (1947-British) 83m. **½ D: Leslie Arliss. Kieron Moore, Margaret Johnston, Dulcie Gray, Guy Middleton. Murky drama of British girls almost outmaneuvered by Italian con-artist.

Man About Town (1939) 85m. *** D: Mark Sandrich. Jack Benny, Dorothy Lamour, Edward Arnold, Binnie Barnes, Phil Harris, Betty Grable, Monty Woolley, Eddie Anderson. Enjoyable musicomedy with big cast. Jack tries to crash London society; lively and entertaining.

Man About Town (1947-French, dubbed) 89m. *** D: René Clair. Maurice Chevalier, François Perier, Marcelle Derrien, Dany Robin. Chevalier in a quaint musical, doing what he knows best: a boulevardier with an eye for les femmes.

Man Afraid (1957) 84m. **½ D: Harry Keller. George Nader, Phyllis Thaxter, Tim Hovey, Reta Shaw, Martin Milner. Well-acted story of clergyman Nader protecting family against father of boy he killed in self-defense.

Man Alive (1945) 70m. **½ D: Ray Enright. Pat O'Brien, Adolphe Menjou, Ellen Drew, Rudy Vallee, Fortunio Bonanova, Joseph Crehan, Jonathan Hale, Minna Gombell, Jason Robards, Sr. Amusing comedy of O'Brien, supposedly dead, playing ghost to scare away wife's new love interest; not overdone, moves along at brisk pace.

Man Alone, A (1955) C-96m. **½ D: Ray Milland. Ray Milland, Mary Murphy, Ward Bond, Raymond Burr, Lee Van Cleef. Intelligent oater of fugitive from lynch mob (Milland) hiding with sheriff's daughter (Murphy) in small town. Milland's first directorial attempt isn't bad.

Man and a Woman, A (1966-French, dubbed) C-102m. ***½ D: Claude Lelouch. Anouk Aimee, Jean-Louis Trintignant, Pierre Barouh, Valerie Lagrange. Sensitive story of young French widow and widower falling in love is genuinely told, gracefully photographed. Intriguing moviemaking and racing car sequences; haunting score.

Man at the Carlton Tower (1961-British) 57m. ** D: Robert Tronson. Maxine Audley, Lee Montague, Allan

Cuthbertson, Terence Alexander. Routine Edgar Wallace thriller churned out against backdrop of plush London hotel involving jewel robbery and murder.

Man Bait (1952-British) 80m. ** D: Terence Fisher. George Brent, Marguerite Chapman, Diana Dors, Raymond Huntley. Standard murder yarn with Brent suspected of committing homicide.

Man Behind the Gun, The (1952) C-82m. ** D: Felix E. Feist. Randolph Scott, Patrice Wymore, Philip Carey, Alan Hale. Tepid fiction of Scott helping to found city of Los Angeles.

Man Betrayed, A (1941) 83m. ** D: John H. Auer. John Wayne, Frances Dee, Edward Ellis, Wallace Ford, Ward Bond, Harold Huber, Alexander Granach. Country lawyer crusades against father of girlfriend to prove that he's crooked politician. Minor mystery-romance. Retitled: WHEEL OF FORTUNE.

Man Between, The (1953-British) 100m. *** D: Carol Reed. James Mason, Claire Bloom, Hildegarde Neff, Geoffrey Toone. Well-handled suspenser set in post-WW2 Berlin, with Mason pulled by conflicting political loyalties.

Man Called Adam, A (1966) 102m. **½ D: Leo Penn. Sammy Davis, Jr., Ossie Davis, Cicely Tyson, Louis Armstrong, Frank Sinatra, Jr., Peter Lawford, Mel Torme. Pretentious melodrama of trumpet-player Davis trying to find some purpose in life; amateurishly produced.

Man Called Flintstone, The (1966) C-87m. **½ D: Joseph Barbera, William Hanna. The voices of: Alan Reed, Mel Blanc, Jean Vander Pyl, June Foray. Feature-length cartoon based on TV series of Stone Age characters; satirizes superspy films. Mainly for kids.

Man Called Peter, A (1955) C-119m. *** D: Henry Koster. Richard Todd, Jean Peters, Marjorie Rambeau, Doris Lloyd, Emmett Lynn. Moving account of Scotsman Peter Marshall who became clergyman and U.S. Senate chaplain; sensitively played by Todd, with fine supporting cast.

Man Could Get Killed, A (1966) C-99m. **½ D: Ronald Neame, Cliff Owen. James Garner, Melina Mercouri, Sandra Dee, Tony Franciosa, Robert Coote, Roland Young. Mix-up involving businessman Garner, thought to be international spy; sparkling Mercouri buoys spoof.

Man Detained (1961-British) 59m. **½ D: Robert Tronson. Bernard Archard, Elvi Hale, Paul Stassino, Michael Coles. Trim Edgar Wallace yarn, enhanced by Hale's performance as secretary involved with counterfeiting gang and murder.

Man-Eater of Kumaon (1948) 79m. **½ D: Byron Haskin. Sabu, Wendell Corey, Joy Ann Page, Morris Carnovsky, Argentina Brunetti. Good adventure tale of hunter determined to kill deadly tiger on the loose.

Man From Bitter Ridge, The (1955) C-80m. **½ D: Jack Arnold. Lex Barker, Mara Corday, Stephen McNally, Trevor Bardette. Peppy oater of Barker tracking down outlaws by tying in with local banker.

Man From Cairo (1954-Italian, dubbed) 81m. ** D: Edoardo Anton. George Raft, Gianna Maria Canale, Massimo Serato. Disappointing mishmash of intrigue set in Africa, with everyone scurrying about for gold.

Man From Colorado, The (1948) C-99m. *** D: Henry Levin. Glenn Ford, William Holden, Ellen Drew, Ray Collins, Edgar Buchanan. Unusual Western of brutal Ford appointed Federal judge, taking tyrannical hold of the territory.

Man From Dakota, The (1940) 75m. **½ D: Leslie Fenton. Wallace Beery, John Howard, Dolores Del Rio, Donald Meek, Robert Barrat. Above-average Beery vehicle set in Civil War times, with glamorous Del Rio helping him and Howard, Union spies, cross Confederate lines.

Man From Del Rio (1956) 82m. ** D: Harry Horner. Anthony Quinn, Katy Jurado, Peter Whitney, Douglas Fowley, John Larch, Whit Bissell. Dank Western of Mexican gunslinger Quinn saving a town from outlaws.

Man From Down Under, The (1943) 103m. **½ D: Robert Z. Leonard. Charles Laughton, Binnie Barnes, Richard Carlson, Donna Reed, Christopher Severn, Clyde Cook. Well-meaning Laughton claims two orphan waifs as his own children, raising them in

Australia. Entertaining, trivial little comedy.

Man From God's Country (1958) C-72m. ** D: Paul Landres. George Montgomery, Randy Stuart, Gregg Barton, Kim Charney, Susan Cummings. Quiet oater involving land-hungry ranchers trying to outfox the railroad.

Man From Laramie, The (1955) C-104m. *** D: Anthony Mann. James Stewart, Arthur Kennedy, Donald Crisp, Cathy O'Donnell, Alex Nicol, Aline MacMahon, Wallace Ford. Taut action tale of revenge, with Stewart seeking those who killed his brother.

Man From Planet X, The (1951) 70m. *½ D: Edgar G. Ulmer. Robert Clarke, Margaret Field, Raymond Bond, William Schallert. Tame sci-fi of alien visitors from outer space getting outdone by crafty newspaperman.

Man From the Alamo, The (1953) C-79m. **½ D: Budd Boetticher. Glenn Ford, Julia Adams, Victor Jory, Hugh O'Brian. Fictional historical sidelight with Ford surviving Alamo massacre and helping General Houston fight the Mexicans. More action sequences would have helped.

Man From the Diner's Club, The (1963) 96m. **½ D: Frank Tashlin. Danny Kaye, Martha Hyer, Cara Williams, Telly Savalas, Everett Sloane, George Kennedy. Silly shenanigans of Diner's Club employee Kaye involved with Damon Runyon-ish gangsters. Danny has certainly had more inspired antics than these.

Man From Yesterday, The (1932) 71m. ** D: Berthold Viertel. Claudette Colbert, Clive Brook, Charles Boyer, Andy Devine, Alan Mowbray. Stuffy tale of Colbert marrying Boyer thinking husband Brook has died. Unexciting despite fine cast.

Man Hunt (1941) 105m. ***½ D: Fritz Lang. Walter Pidgeon, Joan Bennett, George Sanders, John Carradine, Roddy McDowall. Far-fetched yet absorbing drama of man attempting to kill Hitler, getting into more trouble than he bargained for. Tense, well-done.

Man I Killed, The SEE: Broken Lullaby.

Man I Love, The (1946) 96m. **½ D: Raoul Walsh. Ida Lupino, Robert Alda, Bruce Bennett, Andrea King, Dolores Moran, Martha Vickers, Alan Hale. Offbeat casting of Lupino as slinky nightclub singer involved in murder and suspense with mobster Alda doesn't always work, but film is slick and Ida gets to sing.

Man I Married, The (1940) 77m. *** D: Irving Pichel. Joan Bennett, Francis Lederer, Lloyd Nolan, Anna Sten, Otto Kruger. Strong story of German Lederer taken in by Nazi propaganda while American wife Bennett tries to stop him. Taut, exciting story.

Man In a Cocked Hat (1960-British) 88m. **½ D: Jeffrey Dell, Roy Boulting. Terry-Thomas, Peter Sellers, Luciana Paluzzi, Thorley Walters. OK satire on British politics involving undiplomatic clerk in foreign office who can't stay out of mischief.

Man In Grey, The (1945-British) 116m. *** D: Leslie Arliss. Margaret Lockwood, James Mason, Phyllis Calvert, Stewart Granger, Martita Hunt. Elaborate costumer with good performances but trite script of criss-cross love affair among royalty.

Man In Half Moon Street, The (1944) 92m. ** D: Ralph Murphy. Nils Asther, Helen Walker, Brandon Hurst, Reginald Sheffield. Not-bad horror tale of scientist Asther experimenting with rejuvenation; done on better scale than many of these little epics.

Man In Hiding (1953-British) 79m. *½ D: Terence Fisher. Paul Henreid, Lois Maxwell, Kieron Moore, Hugh Sinclair. Tame detective-capturing-elusive-killer plot.

Man In the Attic (1954) 82m. **½ D: Hugo Fregonese. Jack Palance, Constance Smith, Byron Palmer, Frances Bavier, Rhys Williams, Sean McClory, Isabel Jewell, Leslie Bradley. Flavorful account of notorious Jack the Ripper, with Palance going full-blast.

Man In the Dark (1953) 70m. **½ D: Lew Landers. Edmond O'Brien, Audrey Totter, Horace McMahon, Ted de Corsia. Diverting mystery of blind songwriter combating wife's scheme to murder him.

Man In the Gray Flannel Suit, The (1956) C-153m. ***½ D: Nunnally Johnson. Gregory Peck, Jennifer Jones, Fredric March, Marisa Pavan,

Lee J. Cobb, Ann Harding, Keenan Wynn. Sloan Wilson's slick novel of Madison Avenue executive struggling to get ahead and to find meaning to his home life. Nice cameo by Harding as March's wife.

Man in the Iron Mask, The (1939) 110m. *** D: James Whale. Louis Hayward, Joan Bennett, Warren William, Joseph Schildkraut, Alan Hale, Montagu Love, Doris Kenyon. Topnotch adventure from Dumas novel, filmed before with Douglas Fairbanks. This time Hayward is imprisoned twin brother of King Louis XIV of France, with plenty of action, romance, and swordplay.

Man in the Middle (1964) 94m. ** D: Guy Hamilton. Robert Mitchum, France Nuyen, Barry Sullivan, Keenan Wynn, Alexander Knox, Trevor Howard. Unconvincing, confusing film of Howard Fast novel THE WINSTON AFFAIR, about American military officer accused of homicide; static courtroom sequences.

Man in the Moon (1961-British) 98m. *** D: Basil Dearden. Kenneth More, Shirley Anne Field, Norman Bird, Michael Hordern, John Phillips. Top comedy satirizing space race. Government recruits man unaffected by cold, heat, speed, etc., to be perfect astronaut.

Man in the Net, The (1959) 97m. **½ D: Michael Curtiz. Alan Ladd, Carolyn Jones, Diane Brewster, Charles McGraw, John Lupton, Tom Helmore. Fair drama of Ladd trying to clear himself of murder charge for wife's death.

Man in the Road, The (1957-British) 83m. *½ D: Lance Comfort. Derek Farr, Ella Raines, Donald Wolfit, Karel Stepanek. Despite sturdy cast, humdrum telling of Communists trying to get scientist to divulge secret formula.

Man in the Saddle (1951) C-87m. ** D: Andre de Toth. Randolph Scott, Joan Leslie, Ellen Drew, Alexander Knox. Scott is involved in romantic triangle causing death on the range; justice triumphs.

Man in the Shadow (1957) 80m. **½ D: Jack Arnold. Orson Welles, Jeff Chandler, Colleen Miller, James Gleason. Welles chomps his way through role of rancher responsible for helper's death. Chandler is the earnest sheriff.

Man in the Vault (1956) 73m. *½ D: Andrew V. McLaglen. William Campbell, Karen Sharpe, Anita Ekberg, Berry Kroeger, Paul Fix. Programmer of drab locksmith involved in robbery; nothing special.

Man in the White Suit, The (1952-British) 84m. ***½ D: Alexander Mackendrick. Alec Guinness, Joan Greenwood, Cecil Parker, Michael Gough, Ernest Thesiger. Guinness is inventor who discovers a fabric that can't wear out or soil; dismayed garment manufacturers set out to buy his formula. Most engaging comedy.

Man Inside, The (1958-British) 90m. *½ D: John Gilling. Jack Palance, Anita Ekberg, Nigel Patrick, Anthony Newley. Shoddy robbery caper with private investigator hunting jewel thieves throughout Europe.

Man is Armed, The (1956) 70m. *½ D: Franklin Adreon. Dane Clark, William Talman, May Wynn, Robert Horton, Barton MacLane. Lowjinks about robbery; competent cast stifled by incompetent production.

Man-Made Monster (1941) 59m. ** D: George Waggner. Lionel Atwill, Lon Chaney, Jr., Anne Nagel, Frank Albertson, Samuel S. Hinds, William B. Davidson, Ben Taggart, Connie Bergen. Sci-fi yarn of scientist Atwill making Chaney invulnerable to electricity; fairly well done. Mainly for fans of the genre.

Man of a Thousand Faces (1957) 122m. ***½ D: Joseph Pevney. James Cagney, Dorothy Malone, Jane Greer, Marjorie Rambeau, Jim Backus, Snub Pollard, Jeanne Cagney. Surprisingly dedicated, well-acted biography of silent star Lon Chaney. Cagney as Chaney, Malone as disturbed first wife, Greer as wife who brings him happiness, are all fine. Chaney's life and screen career are recreated with taste; touching portrayal of movie extra by Rambeau.

Man of Conflict (1953) 72m. ** D: Hal Makelim. Edward Arnold, John Agar, Susan Morrow, Russell Hicks. Lukewarm drama of generation clash between father Arnold and son Agar over business and philosophy of life.

Man of Conquest (1939) 105m. **½ D: George Nichols, Jr. Richard Dix,

Gail Patrick, Edward Ellis, Joan Fontaine. Republic Pictures tried to give this biography of Texas' Sam Houston good production values, but script slows down action.

Man of Evil (1948-British) 90m. ** D: Anthony Asquith. Phyllis Calvert, James Mason, Stewart Granger, Wilfrid Lawson, Jean Kent. Elaborate but ponderous costumer of maniac who tries to run people's lives to suit his fancy; overdone and not effective.

Man of Iron (1956-Italian, dubbed) 116m. *** D: Pietro Germi. Pietro Germi, Luisa Della Noce, Sylva Koscina, Carlo Giuffre. Somber account of Germi, railroad engineer, whose life takes a tragic turn, affecting his whole family; realistically presented. Original title: THE RAILROAD MAN.

Man of the West (1958) C-100m. **½ D: Anthony Mann. Gary Cooper, Julie London, Lee J. Cobb, Arthur O'Connell, Jack Lord. Pensive Western that picks up at end for shoot-out climax, with Cooper vs. Cobb.

Man of the World (1931) 71m. ** D: Richard Wallace. William Powell, Carole Lombard, Wynne Gibson, Guy Kibbee, George Chandler. Routine tale of good-girl Lombard in love with con-man Powell.

Man on a String (1960) 92m. *** D: Andre de Toth. Ernest Borgnine, Kerwin Matthews, Colleen Dewhurst, Alexander Scourby, Glenn Corbett. Fictionalized account of counterspy Boris Morros, involved in Russian-U.S. Cold War conflict. Taut action sequences.

Man on a Tightrope (1953) 105m. *** D: Elia Kazan. Fredric March, Gloria Grahame, Terry Moore, Cameron Mitchell, Adolphe Menjou. Atmospheric circus drama of troupe planning to escape from behind the Iron Curtain; sturdy cast.

Man on Fire (1957) 95m. **½ D: Ranald MacDougall. Bing Crosby, Inger Stevens, Mary Fickett, E. G. Marshall. Middling soaper. Crosby and Stevens, a divorced couple, reunite to give their son a proper home.

Man on the Eiffel Tower, The (1949) C-97m. *** D: Burgess Meredith. Charles Laughton, Franchot Tone, Burgess Meredith, Robert Hutton, Jean Wallace, Patricia Roc, Wilfrid Hyde-White, Belita. Taut psychological drama filmed in Paris involving cat-and-mouse game between police investigator and suspected murderer. Meredith's first try at directing a feature film.

Man on the Flying Trapeze, The (1935) 65m. ***½ D: Clyde Bruckman. W. C. Fields, Mary Brian, Kathleen Howard, Grady Sutton, Vera Lewis. Hilarious Fieldsian study in frustration, with able assistance from hard boiled wife Howard, good-for-nothing Sutton. Best sequence has W. C. receiving four traffic tickets in a row!

Man or Gun (1958) 79m. ** D: Albert Gannaway. Macdonald Carey, Audrey Totter, James Craig, James Gleason. Bland Western with Carey cleaning up the town.

Man-Proof (1938) 74m. ** D: Richard Thorpe. Myrna Loy, Franchot Tone, Rosalind Russell, Walter Pidgeon, Nana Bryant, Rita Johnson, Ruth Hussey. Flimsy plot with bright stars: Loy and Russell both love Pidgeon, but Tone is ready to step in any time.

Man They Could Not Hang, The (1939) 72m. **½ D: Nick Grinde. Boris Karloff, Lorna Gray, Robert Wilcox, Roger Pryor, Ann Doran. Karloff's done the same plot before, but it's still good; hanged man brought back to life seeks revenge on his killers.

Man to Man Talk (1958-French, dubbed) 89m. ** D: Luis Saslavski. Yves Montand, Nicole Berger, Yves Noel. Trite little tale of father forced to explain facts of life to youngster when mother is having a baby. Retitled: PREMIER MAY.

Man-Trap (1961) 93m. **½ D: Edmond O'Brien. Jeffrey Hunter, David Janssen, Stella Stevens, Hugh Sanders. Capable cast involved in adultery, robbery, and disaster; unusual fling at directing by O'Brien.

Man Upstairs, The (1958-British) 88m. *** D: Don Chaffey. Richard Attenborough, Bernard Lee, Donald Houston, Virginia Maskell. Compact study, excellently acted, of Attenborough, a man gone berserk much to everyone's amazement.

Man Who Broke the Bank at Monte Carlo, The (1935) 70m. **½ D: Stephen Roberts. Ronald Colman, Joan Bennett, Colin Clive, Nigel Bruce, Montagu Love, Ferdinand Gottschalk, Charles Coleman. Flimsy film carried by Colman charm, which translates the famous title song into story of man who calculates to clean the treasury at Riviera gambling establishment.

Man Who Came to Dinner, The (1941) 112m. ***½ D: William Keighley. Monty Woolley, Bette Davis, Ann Sheridan, Billie Burke, Richard Travis, Grant Mitchell, Mary Wickes, Elizabeth Fraser, Reginald Gardiner. Pompous author Woolley is forced to stay with Burke's family for the winter, driving them crazy with assorted wacky friends passing through. Davis has thankless role, but oomphgirl Sheridan is in peak form.

Man Who Changed His Mind SEE: Man Who Lived Again, The

Man Who Cheated Himself, The (1950) 81m. **½ D: Felix E. Feist. Lee J. Cobb, Jane Wyatt, John Dall, Terry Frost. Good cast uplifts typical murder film.

Man Who Could Cheat Death, The (1959-British) C-83m. ** D: Terence Fisher. Anton Diffring, Hazel Court, Christopher Lee, Arnold Marle, Delphi Lawrence. Turgid remake of THE MAN IN HALF MOON STREET, about man trying to rekindle romance with former girlfriend; typical Hammer production.

Man Who Could Work Miracles, The (1937-British) 82m. ***½ D: Lothar Mendes. Roland Young, Ralph Richardson, Joan Gardner, Ernest Thesiger, Wallace Lupino, George Zucco, Bernard Nedell. H. G. Wells' fantasy of timid British department store clerk (Young) endowed with power to do anything he wants. Special effects are marvelous, supported by good cast, in charming film.

Man Who Died Twice, The (1958) 70m. ** D: Joseph Kane. Rod Cameron, Vera Ralston, Mike Mazurki, Gerald Milton. Ralston's last film to date is mild account of chanteuse involved in murder.

Man Who Knew Too Much, The (1956) C-120m. **½ D: Alfred Hitchcock. James Stewart, Doris Day, Brenda De Banzie, Bernard Miles, Ralph Truman, Alan Mowbray, Carolyn Jones, Hillary Brooke. Hitchcock's remake of his 1935 film is disappointing. Even famous Albert Hall murder sequence rings flat in tale of American couple accidentally involved in international intrigue. Doris' song "Que Sera, Sera" grows tiresome after several performances.

Man Who Lived Again, The (1936-British) 61m. ** D: Robert Stevenson. Boris Karloff, Anna Lee, John Loder, Frank Cellier, Lyn Harding, Cecil Parker. Mad doctor plot X-22 again, with Karloff transplanting brains from one human to another; not bad. Retitled: MAN WHO CHANGED HIS MIND.

Man Who Lived Twice, The (1936) 73m. ** D: Harry Lachman. Ralph Bellamy, Marian Marsh, Thurston Hall, Isabel Jewell, Nana Bryant, Ward Bond. Routine story of Bellamy's personality being changed by mad doctor so he can elude police.

Man Who Never Was, The (1956) C-103m. *** D: Ronald Neame. Clifton Webb, Gloria Grahame, Robert Flemying, Josephine Griffin, Stephen Boyd. Diverting WW2 spy yarn with unique plot-line, well handled by Webb and Grahame, of Allies trying to out-bluff Axis forces.

Man Who Played God, The (1932) 81m. **½ D: John G. Adolfi. George Arliss, Bette Davis, Violet Heming, Louise Closser Hale, Donald Cook, Ray Milland. Well-acted tale of musician Arliss going deaf, infatuated student Davis sticking by him. Not as stagy as other Arliss films, with Bette getting her first break and young Milland in a small role. Remade as SINCERELY YOURS.

Man Who Shot Liberty Valance, The (1962) 122m. **½ D: John Ford. James Stewart, John Wayne, Vera Miles, Lee Marvin, Edmond O'Brien, Andy Devine, Woody Strode, Ken Murray, John Qualen. Fine cast, directed by Western master Ford, produces a passable film. Marvin stands out as a despicable villain; Wayne and Stewart fight over Miles. O'Brien doesn't bother with subtlety in role of boozing newspaperman.

Man Who Talked Too Much, The (1940) 75m. **½ D: Vincent Sherman. George Brent, Virginia Bruce, Brenda Marshall, Richard Barthelmess, William Lundigan, George Tobias. Good courtroom drama with D.A. Brent and lawyer Lundigan, brothers fighting same case.

Man Who Turned to Stone, The (1957) 80m. Bomb D: Leslie Kardos. Victory Jory, Ann Doran, Charlotte Austin, William Hudson, Paul Cavanagh, Jean Willes, Victor Varconi. Weirdos find life-restoring formula. Hokum!

Man Who Understood Women, The (1959) C-105m. **½ D: Nunnally Johnson. Leslie Caron, Henry Fonda, Cesare Danova, Myron McCormick, Marcel Dalio, Conrad Nagel. Unsatisfactory narrative of moviemaker genius Fonda who hasn't slightest notion of how to treat wife Caron.

Man Who Wouldn't Die, The (1942) 65m. ** D: Herbert I. Leeds. Lloyd Nolan, Marjorie Weaver, Helene Reynolds, Henry Wilcoxon. Nolan is efficient as wisecracking detective Mike Shayne with a tougher caper than usual.

Man Who Wouldn't Talk, The (1940) 72m. ** D: David Burton. Lloyd Nolan, Jean Rogers, Onslow Stevens, Eric Blore, Mae Marsh. Routine courtroom drama with intriguing idea of man who won't defend himself of accused crime. Bogs down and ruins potential.

Man With a Cloak, The (1951) 81m. **½ D: Fletcher Markle. Joseph Cotten, Barbara Stanwyck, Louis Calhern, Leslie Caron. Period melodrama of Stanwyck's love for Cotten, revealed in climax to be famous American writer.

Man With a Million (1954-British) C-90m. **½ D: Ronald Neame. Gregory Peck, Jane Griffith, Ronald Squire, A. E. Matthews, Wilfrid Hyde-White, Reginald Beckwith. Often tedious telling of Mark Twain story of American Peck given million-pound note, and the havoc it causes.

Man With My Face, The (1951) 86m. ** D: Edward Montagne. Barry Nelson, Lynn Ainley, John Harvey, Carole Mathews. Good plot idea not handled too well: predicament of businessman who discovers lookalike has taken over his life completely.

Man With Nine Lives, The (1940) 73m. **½ D: Nick Grinde. Boris Karloff, Roger Pryor, Jo Ann Sayers, Stanley Brown, John Dilson, Hal Taliaferro. Boris gets his as mad scientist whose device for restoring life to the deceased causes him many problems. Hokey but fun.

Man With the Golden Arm, The (1955) 119m. *** D: Otto Preminger. Frank Sinatra, Eleanor Parker, Kim Novak, Darren McGavin, Arnold Stang, Doro Merande. Then-daring film of drug addiction is now dated, but still powerful; Sinatra as addict, Parker the crippled wife. Memorable Elmer Bernstein jazz score.

Man With the Gun (1955) 83m. **½ D: Richard Wilson. Robert Mitchum, Jan Sterling, Angie Dickinson, Barbara Lawrence, Karen Sharpe, Henry Hull. Mitchum as lawman who brings peace to a Western town is the whole show.

Man With Two Faces, The (1934) 72m. ** D: Archie Mayo. Edward G. Robinson, Mary Astor, Ricardo Cortez, Mae Clarke, Louis Calhern. So-so murder yarn of death of cruel husband investigated by police.

Man Without a Star (1955) C-89m. **½ D: King Vidor. Kirk Douglas, Jeanne Crain, Claire Trevor, Richard Boone. Rugged Western with individualist Douglas helping Crain keep her ranch land, dallying with saloon gal Trevor.

Manchurian Candidate, The (1962) 126m. ***½ D: John Frankenheimer. Frank Sinatra, Laurence Harvey, Janet Leigh, Angela Lansbury, Henry Silva, James Gregory. Topical drama of political assassination, brilliantly directed, with cast filling their roles admirably; set in Korea and U.S. Lansbury stands out in fine cast.

Mandalay (1934) 65m. **½ D: Michael Curtiz. Kay Francis, Lyle Talbot, Warner Oland, Rafaela Ottiano, Ruth Donnelly, Shirley Temple. Exotic Rangoon is setting for yarn about shady girl Francis in love with alcoholic medico Talbot.

Manfish (1956) C-76m. ** D: W. Lee Wilder. John Bromfield, Lon Chaney, Victor Jory, Barbara Nichols. Variation of Edgar Allen Poe's GOLD BUG story. Film is timid account of treasure hunt in Jamaica.

Manhandled (1949) 97m. ** D: Lewis R. Foster. Dan Duryea, Dorothy

Lamour, Sterling Hayden, Irene Hervey. Turgid murder drama that reliable cast can't salvage; incredibly slow.

Manhattan Melodrama (1934) 93m. *** D: W. S. Van Dyke, II. Clark Gable, William Powell, Myrna Loy, Leo Carrillo, Isabel Jewell, Mickey Rooney, Nat Pendleton. Boyhood chums Gable and Powell become gangster and D. A., respectively; friendship and love for Loy conflict in interesting drama. Story reused many times, seldom topped this version.

Manhunt in the Jungle (1958) C-79m. Bomb D: Tom McGowan. Robin Hughes, Luis Alvarez, James Wilson, Jorge Montoro, John B. Symmes. Hackneyed safari set in Brazil.

Maniac (1962-British) 86m. **1/2 D: Michael Carreras. Kerwin Matthews, Nadia Gray, Donald Houston, Justine Lord. One of the better British thrillers made in wake of PSYCHO, with Matthews as vacationing artist in France arousing hatred of girlfriend's sick father. Good plot twists.

Manila Calling (1942) 81m. ** D: Herbert I. Leeds. Lloyd Nolan, Carole Landis, Cornel Wilde, James Gleason, Martin Kosleck, Ralph Byrd, Elisha Cook, Jr., Louis Jean Heydt. Pat WW2 film of one guy taking 'em all on with his small but dedicated outfit.

Mannequin (1937) 95m. **1/2 D: Frank Borzage. Joan Crawford, Spencer Tracy, Alan Curtis, Ralph Morgan, Leo Gorcey, Elizabeth Risdon, Mary Philips. Prototype rags-to-riches soaper, with working-girl Crawford getting ahead via wealthy Tracy; predictable script, but nice job by stars, usual MGM gloss (even in the tenements).

Manpower (1941) 105m. *** D: Raoul Walsh. Edward G. Robinson, Marlene Dietrich, George Raft, Alan Hale, Walter Catlett, Frank McHugh, Eve Arden. Lively, lusty entertainment, with Robinson and Raft as power linemen both after Dietrich, an alluring cafe hostess.

Man's Castle, A (1933) 75m. ***1/2 D: Frank Borzage. Spencer Tracy, Loretta Young, Glenda Farrell, Arthur Hohl, Walter Connolly, Marjorie Rambeau. Lovely little Depression film of young couple struggling for happiness despite poverty.

Man's Favorite Sport? (1964) C-120m. **1/2 D: Howard Hawks. Rock Hudson, Paula Prentiss, John McGiver, Maria Perschy, Roscoe Karns. Labored comedy of author Hudson trying to live up to his book on outdoor life, with predictable sight gags about fishing.

Many Rivers to Cross (1955) C-92m. **1/2 D: Roy Rowland. Robert Taylor, Eleanor Parker, Victor McLaglen, James Arness, Josephine Hutchinson, Rosemary DeCamp. Parker shows more vim and vigor than Taylor in this 1800's Western, centering on her yen for him.

Mara Maru (1952) 98m. **1/2 D: Gordon Douglas. Errol Flynn, Ruth Roman, Raymond Burr, Richard Webb, Nestor Paiva. Turgid flick of Flynn vs. Burr for sunken treasure, with Roman the love interest.

Mara of the Wilderness (1965) C-90m. **1/2 D: Frank McDonald. Adam West, Linda Saunders, Theo Marcuse, Denver Pyle, Sean McClory. Sometimes diverting account of Saunders, who grew up in the wild north country, with West trying to rehabilitate her.

Maracaibo (1958) C-88m. **1/2 D: Cornel Wilde. Cornel Wilde, Jean Wallace, Abbe Lane, Francis Lederer, Michael Landon. Wilde is expert firefighter who goes to Venezuela to combat oil blaze, romancing ex-girlfriend between action scenes.

Marauders, The (1955) C-81m. ** D: Gerald Mayer. Dan Duryea, Jeff Richards, Keenan Wynn, Jarma Lewis. OK story of rancher fighting against greedy cattle ranchers.

March of the Wooden Soldiers SEE: Babes in Toyland.

Marco Polo (1962-Italian, dubbed) C-90m. **1/2 D: Hugo Fregonese. Rory Calhoun, Yoko Tani, Robert Hundar, Camillo Pilotto, Pierre Cressoy, Michael Chow. Unspectacular epic about medieval adventurer and his journey to China. Calhoun and film lack needed vigor.

Marco the Magnificent (1966) C-100m. **1/2 D: Denys De La Patelliere, Noel Howard. Horst Buchholz, Anthony Quinn, Omar Sharif, Elsa Martinelli, Akim Tamiroff, Orson

Welles. Laughable mini-epic, extremely choppy, with episodic sequences pretending to recount events in life of medieval adventurer.

Mardi Gras (1958) C-107m. **½ D: Edmund Goulding. Pat Boone, Christine Carere, Tommy Sands, Sheree North, Gary Crosby. Perky, unpretentious musical with energetic cast. Boone wins military school raffle date with movie star Carere.

Margie (1946) C-94m. *** D: Henry King. Jeanne Crain, Glenn Langan, Lynn Bari, Esther Dale, Hobart Cavanaugh, Ann B. Todd. Occasionally cloying but entertaining tale of teenagers during the roaring 20's; good song "3:00 in the Morning," title tune.

Margin for Error (1943) 74m. ** D: Otto Preminger. Joan Bennett, Milton Berle, Otto Preminger, Carl Esmond, Howard Freeman, Ed McNamara. Dated, awkward "comedy" of Jewish cop Berle assigned to guard German consul in N.Y.C. during WW2. Director Preminger should have told actor Preminger to stop overacting.

Marie Antoinette (1938) 160m. **½ D: W. S. Van Dyke II. Norma Shearer, Tyrone Power, John Barrymore, Robert Morley, Gladys George, Anita Louise, Joseph Schildkraut. Opulent MGM production of life of 18th-century French queen lacks pace but has good acting, with great performance by Morley as Louis XVI. Shearer captures essence of title role as costumer retells her life from Austrian princess to doomed queen of crumbling empire.

Marie Antoinette (1955-French, dubbed) C-108m. **½ D: Jean Delannoy. Michele Morgan, Richard Todd, Jean Morel. Epic on life of famed 18th-century French queen has marvelous Morgan in title role but lacks perspective and scope.

Marine Raiders (1944) 91m. ** D: Harold D. Schuster. Pat O'Brien, Robert Ryan, Ruth Hussey, Frank McHugh, Barton MacLane. Typical RKO WW2 film, this time focusing on marines training for warfare.

Marines, Let's Go (1961) C-104m. *½ D: Raoul Walsh. Tom Tryon, David Hedison, Barbara Stuart, William Tyler. Tedium of four GI's on leave in Tokyo.

Marjorie Morningstar (1958) C-123m. **½ D: Irving Rapper. Gene Kelly, Natalie Wood, Claire Trevor, Ed Wynn, Everett Sloane, Carolyn Jones, Martin Milner. Wood is only adequate as Herman Wouk's heroine in tale of N.Y.C. gal aspiring to greatness but ending up a suburban housewife, with Kelly her summer romance.

Mark, The (1961-British) 127m. **** D: Guy Green. Stuart Whitman, Maria Schell, Rod Steiger, Brenda De Banzie. Whitman received Oscar nomination for portrayal of emotionally broken sex criminal who has served time, now wants to make new start. Excellent cast and direction.

Mark of the Gorilla (1950) 68m. D: William Berke. Johnny Weissmuller, Trudy Marshall, Onslow Stevens, Selmer Jackson. SEE: **Jungle Jim** series.

Mark of the Hawk, The (1958) C-83m. *** D: Michael Audley. Eartha Kitt, Sidney Poitier, Juano Hernandez, John McIntire. Unusual tale intelligently acted, set in contemporary Africa, with peaceful vs. violent means for Negro equality the main theme.

Mark of the Renegade (1951) C-81m. **½ D: Hugo Fregonese. Ricardo Montalban, Cyd Charisse, J. Carrol Naish, Gilbert Roland. Peculiar Western tale of 1820's, with Montalban an outlaw who romances Charisse.

Mark of the Vampire (1935) 85m. *** D: Tod Browning. Lionel Barrymore, Elizabeth Allan, Bela Lugosi, Lionel Atwill, Carol Borland, Jean Hersholt, Henry Wadsworth. Classy horror tale with Lugosi terrorizing small Czech town under influence of far-out Barrymore. Remake of LONDON AFTER MIDNIGHT.

Mark of the Vampire (1957) SEE: **Vampire, The.**

Mark of the Whistler, The (1944) 61m. D: William Castle. Richard Dix, Janis Carter, Porter Hall, Paul Guilfoyle, John Calvert. SEE: **The Whistler** series.

Mark of Zorro, The (1920) 60m. ***½ D: Fred Niblo. Douglas Fairbanks, Sr., Marguerite de la Motte, Noah Beery, Robert McKim, Charles Mailes. A don't-miss silent classic.

The hero of old California is enthusiastically played by Fairbanks. Silent swashbuckler is still effective, probably Fairbanks' best film.

Mark of Zorro, The (1940) 93m. ***½ D: Rouben Mamoulian. Tyrone Power, Linda Darnell, Basil Rathbone, Gale Sondergaard, Eugene Pallette, J. Edward Bromberg. Lavish swashbuckler with Power as foppish son of California aristocrat in 1800's, masquerading as dashing avenger of evil: climactic duel with Rathbone a cinematic gem.

Marked Woman (1937) 96m. *** D: Lloyd Bacon. Bette Davis, Humphrey Bogart, Lola Lane, Isabel Jewell, Jane Bryan, Eduardo Ciannelli, Allen Jenkins, Mayo Methot, Rosalind Marquis, John Litel, Robert Strange. Bristling gangster drama of D.A. Bogart convincing Bette and four girlfriends to testify against their boss, underworld king Ciannelli.

Marksman, The (1953) 62m. *½ D: Lewis D. Collins. Wayne Morris, Elena Verdugo, Frank Ferguson, Rick Vallin. Flabby little tale of Morris, a law enforcer with a telescopic gun, chasing after outlaws.

Marnie (1964) C-129m. **½ D: Alfred Hitchcock. Sean Connery, Tippi Hedren, Diane Baker, Martin Gabel, Louise Latham, Alan Napier. Glossy melodrama full of loopholes, with Hedren a compulsive burglar, Connery her husband determined to make their marriage work. Not top-notch Hitchcock.

Marriage-Go-Round, The (1960) C-98m. **½ D: Walter Lang. Susan Hayward, James Mason, Julie Newmar, Robert Paige, June Clayworth. Film version of Leslie Stevens' saucy play about marriage: Mason is professor attracted to free-love-oriented Newmar. Amusing, but lacks real bite.

Marriage is a Private Affair (1944) 116m. ** D: Robert Z. Leonard. Lana Turner, James Craig, John Hodiak, Frances Gifford, Hugh Marlowe, Keenan Wynn. Somewhat dated, glossy MGM yarn of man-chasing Turner, not about to be stopped just because she's married.

Marriage Italian-Style (1964-Italian, dubbed) C-102m. *** D: Vittorio DeSica. Sophia Loren, Marcello Mastroianni, Aldo Puglisi, Pia Lindstrom, Vito Moriconi. Spicy account of Loren's efforts to get long-time lover Mastroianni to marry her and stay her husband.

Married Woman, The (1965-French, dubbed) 94m. **½ D: Jean-Luc Godard. Macha Meril, Philippe Leroy, Bernard Noel. Turgid three-cornered romance, with Meril involved with husband and lover; often pretentious film.

Marry Me Again (1953) 73m. ** D: Frank Tashlin. Robert Cummings, Marie Wilson, Mary Costa, Jess Barker. Mild shenanigans of aviator Cummings and beauty contest winner Wilson's on-again, off-again romance.

Marrying Kind, The (1952) 93m. *** D: George Cukor. Judy Holliday, Aldo Ray, Madge Kennedy, Mickey Shaughnessy, Griff Barnett. Pungent comedy of Holliday and Ray on verge of divorce, recounting events in their marriage.

Marshal's Daughter, The (1953) 71m. *½ D: William Berke. Ken Murray, Laurie Anders, Preston Foster, Hoot Gibson. Cornpone oater with Murray and Anders ridding their town of outlaws: Tex Ritter even sings a song, with veteran Gibson in supporting role.

Marty (1955) 91m. ***½ D: Delbert Mann. Ernest Borgnine, Betsy Blair, Joe De Santis, Esther Minciotti, Jerry Paris, Karen Steele. Oscar for Borgnine as Bronx butcher who doesn't hope to find love, but does, in this incisive Paddy Chayefsky script, originally a TV play.

Marx Brothers at the Circus SEE: At the Circus.

Marx Brothers Go West SEE: Go West.

Mary Burns, Fugitive (1935) 84m. *** D: William K. Howard. Sylvia Sidney, Melvyn Douglas, Pert Kelton, Alan Baxter, Wallace Ford, Brian Donlevy. Fine gangster melodrama. Sidney is dragged into underworld, valiantly tries to escape her gangster lover (Baxter).

Mary, Mary (1963) C-126m. **½ D: Mervyn LeRoy. Debbie Reynolds, Barry Nelson, Michael Rennie, Diane McBain. Unremarkable, stagy adaptation of Jean Kerr's sex comedy.

Mary of Scotland (1936) 123m. ***½ D: John Ford. Katharine Hepburn,

Fredric March, Florence Eldridge, Douglas Walton, John Carradine, Robert Barrat. Lavish, excellent historical drama, with Hepburn playing Scottish queen sentenced to death by jealous English rival Elizabeth.

Maryland (1940) C-92m. **½ D: Henry King. Walter Brennan, Fay Bainter, Brenda Joyce, John Payne, Charles Ruggles, Marjorie Weaver. Predictable story given elaborate treatment. Bainter refuses to let son Payne ride horses since his father was killed that way. Beautiful color scenery.

Mask of Diijon, The (1946) 73m. ** D: Lewis Landers. Erich von Stroheim, Jeanne Bates, Denise Vernac, William Wright, Edward Van Sloan. Stroheim is hypnotist who has delusions of grandeur, and schemes in murder attempts; exciting finish.

Mask of Dimitrios, The (1944) 95m. *** D: Jean Negulesco. Peter Lorre, Sydney Greenstreet, Zachary Scott, Faye Emerson, Victor Francen, Eduardo Ciannelli, Florence Bates. Fine, offbeat mystery-melodrama with mild-mannered mystery writer Lorre reviewing life of notorious scoundrel Scott. As always, Lorre and Greenstreet make a marvelous team.

Mask of Fu Manchu, The (1932) 72m. **½ D: Charles Brabin. Boris Karloff, Lewis Stone, Karen Morley, Myrna Loy, Charles Starrett, Jean Hersholt. Elaborate chiller of Chinese madman Karloff menacing expedition in tomb of Ghengis Khan; ornate and hokey, but fun. Loy has exotic role in one of her pre-Thin Man ventures.

Mask of the Avenger (1951) C-83m. ** D: Phil Karlson. John Derek, Anthony Quinn, Jody Lawrance, Arnold Moss. Not up to snuff; man posing as count of Monte Cristo is involved in swordplay.

Masked Marvel, The SEE: **Captain Mephisto and the Transformation Machine.**

Masquerade (1965-British) C-101m. **½ D: Basil Dearden. Cliff Robertson, Jack Hawkins, Marisa Mell, Michel Piccoli, Bill Fraser, John Le-Mesurier. Above-average spy satire saved by Robertson's portrayal of recruited agent. Good support casting with good location shooting to give Arabic atmosphere.

Masquerade in Mexico (1945) 96m. ** D: Mitchell Leisen. Dorothy Lamour, Arturo de Cordova, Patric Knowles, Ann Dvorak, George Rigaud, Natalie Schafer, Billy Daniels. Frivolous plot, forgettable songs combine in this limp musicomedy of bullfighters, romance, and Mexican intrigue. Remake of MIDNIGHT (1939).

Masquerader, The (1933) 78m. **½ D: Richard Wallace. Ronald Colman, Elissa Landi, Halliwell Hobbes, Helen Jerome Eddy. Dated but enjoyable film goes on theory that two Colmans are better than one; journalist pretends he is member of Parliament; both roles played by Colman.

Massacre (1956) C-76m. ** D: Louis King. Dane Clark, James Craig, Marta Roth, Miguel Torruco, Jaime Fernandez. Uninspired account of greedy Indian gun-sellers.

Massacre River (1949) 75m. *½ D: John Rawlins. Guy Madison, Rory Calhoun, Johnny Sands, Carole Mathews, Cathy Downs. Minor Western of trio of soldiers fighting over gals.

Master Minds (1949) 64m. D: Jean Yarbrough. Leo Gorcey, Huntz Hall, Glenn Strange, Gabriel Dell, Alan Napier, Jane Adams, Billy Benedict, Bernard Gorcey, Bennie Bartlett, David Gorcey. SEE: **Bowery Boys** series.

Master of Ballantrae, The (1953) C-89m. **½ D: William Keighley. Errol Flynn, Roger Livesey, Anthony Steel, Yvonne Fulneaux. Robert Louis Stevenson's historical yarn. Flynn involved in plot to make Bonnie Prince Charles king of England; on-location filming in Great Britain adds scope to costumer.

Master of the World (1961) C-104m. *** D: William Witney. Vincent Price, Charles Bronson, Mary Webster, Henry Hull, Richard Harrison. Good science-fiction based on Jules Verne's stories about a man (Price) who sees himself as the world's ruler, operating from a futuristic zeppelin. Very well done.

Master Race, The (1944) 96m. *** D: Herbert J. Biberman. George Couloris, Stanley Ridges, Osa Massen, Nancy Gates, Lloyd Bridges. Engrossing account of German officer who escapes when Nazi empire is destroyed, continuing to plot even afterward.

Master Spy (1964-British) 71m. **½ D: Montgomery Tully. Stephen Murray, June Thorburn, Alan Wheatley, John Carson. OK drama of Allied counter-agent escaping from Communist prison.

Masterson of Kansas (1954) C-73m. ** D: William Castle. George Montgomery, Nancy Gates, James Griffith, Jean Willes, Benny Rubin. Despite presence of trio of famed gunmen, Doc Holliday, Wyatt Earp and Bat Masterson, film is still standard oater.

Mata Hari (1932) 90m. *** D: George Fitzmaurice. Greta Garbo, Ramon Novarro, Lionel Barrymore, Lewis Stone, C. Henry Gordon, Karen Morley. Garbo is the alluring spy of WW1, beguiling everyone from Novarro to Barrymore. Highlights: Garbo's exotic dance sequence, Morley stalked by gang executioner.

Mata Hari's Daughter (1954-Italian, dubbed) C-102m. ** D: Renzo Meruis. Frank Latimore, Ludmilla Tcherina, Erno Crisa. Humdrum account of alleged daughter of famed WW1 spy in 1940 Java involved in espionage; sterile dubbing. Retitled: DAUGHTER OF MATA HARA.

Matchmaker, The (1958) 101m. *** D: Joseph Anthony. Shirley Booth, Anthony Perkins, Shirley MacLaine, Paul Ford, Robert Morse. Thornton Wilder's comedy (pre-HELLO DOLLY) of turn-of-the century Yonkers matchmaker (Booth) seeking a wife for cantankerous shopowner. Good period-piece; Booth is bright.

Mating Game, The (1959) C-96m. *** D: George Marshall. Debbie Reynolds, Tony Randall, Paul Douglas, Fred Clark, Una Merkel, Philip Ober, Charles Lane. Zippy comedy romp of tax agent Randall falling in love with farm girl Reynolds, with Douglas rambunctious as Debbie's father.

Mating of Millie, The (1948) 87m. **½ D: Henry Levin. Glenn Ford, Evelyn Keyes, Ron Randell, Willard Parker, Virginia Hunter. Ford and Keyes marry so she can adopt a child, but love blossoms. That's it.

Mating Season, The (1951) 101m. **½ D: Mitchell Leisen. Gene Tierney, John Lund, Miriam Hopkins, Thelma Ritter, Jan Sterling. Bubbly froth when society gal Tierney marries Lund and his mother (Ritter) comes to live with them, posing as servant.

Matter of Innocence, A (1968-British) C-102m. **½ D: Guy Green. Hayley Mills, Trevor Howard, Sashi Kapoor, Brenda De Banzie. Plain Jane (Mills) travels to Singapore with aunt, has an affair with Eurasian Kapoor and becomes woman. Trite soaper with unusual role for suave Howard.

Matter of Who, A (1962-British) 90m. *** D: Don Chaffey. Terry-Thomas, Alex Nicol, Sonja Ziemann, Guy Deghy, Richard Briers, Carol White, Honor Blackman. Thomas goes through madcap antics involving World Health Organization's tracking down of disease-carrier.

Maverick Queen, The (1956) C-92m. **½ D: Joseph Kane. Barbara Stanwyck, Barry Sullivan, Scott Brady, Mary Murphy, Wallace Ford. Stanwyck is peppy as outlaw who's willing to go straight for lawman Sullivan.

Maxime (1958-French, dubbed) 93m. **½ D: Henri Verneuil. Michele Morgan, Charles Boyer, Arletty, Felix Marten. Morgan is good match for Parisian scoundrel Boyer in this love tale set in 1910's.

Maytime (1937) 132m. *** D: Robert Z. Leonard. Jeanette MacDonald, Nelson Eddy, John Barrymore, Herman Bing, Rafaela Ottiano, Porcasi, Sig Ruman, Guy Bates Post, Frank Puglia. One of them singers falling in love in Paris; Barrymore, her mentor, interferes. Songs: "Will You Remember," "Sweetheart," "Ouvre Ton Coeur," "Shortnin' Bread."

Maytime in Mayfair (1952-British) 94m. **½ D: Herbert Wilcox. Anna Neagle, Michael Wilding, Peter Graves, Nicholas Phipps. Guided tour through chic London with its society folks, enhanced by Neagle and Wilding.

Maze, The (1953) 81m. ** D: William Cameron Menzies. Richard Carlson, Veronica Hurst, Hillary Brooke, Michael Pate. Spotty chiller, with eerie British castle inherited by Carlson the focal point.

Me and the Colonel (1958) 109m. **½ D: Peter Glenville. Danny Kaye, Curt Jurgens, Nicole Maurey, Françoise Rosay. Franz Werfel's JACOBOWSKY AND THE COLONEL is source for spotty satire; Jacobowsky is played by Kaye, and Jurgens is the anti-Semitic military officer, both brought together during crisis in WW2.

Meanest Man in the World, The (1943) 57m. ** Sidney Lanfield. Jack Benny, Priscilla Lane, Edmund Gwenn, Matt Briggs, Anne Revere, Eddie "Rochester" Anderson. Lawyer Benny is too kind, decides success will come only if he's nasty. Minor effort which may please Benny fans.

Medal for Benny, A (1945) 77m. ***½ D: Irving Pichel. Dorothy Lamour, Arturo de Cordova, J. Carrol Naish, Mikhail Rasumny, Fernando Alvarado, Charles Dingle, Frank McHugh. Small town hypocritically honoring one of its war dead; Steinbeck script is sharp, excellent comedy-drama.

Medium, The (1951) 84m. **½ D: Gian-Carlo Menotti. Marie Powers, Anna Maria Alberghetti, Leo Coleman, Belva Kibler. Murky filmization of Gian-Carlo Menotti opera about eccentric spiritualist, the girl living in her seedy apartment, the outcast mute boy in love with gal.

Meet Boston Blackie (1941) 61m. D: Robert Florey. Chester Morris, Rochelle Hudson, Richard Lane, Charles Wagenheim, Constance Worth. See Boston Blackie series.

Meet Danny Wilson (1952) 86m. **½ D: Joseph Pevney. Frank Sinatra, Shelley Winters, Alex Nicol, Raymond Burr. Sinatra gives solid performance as entertainer involved with racketeers; script wavers.

Meet Dr. Christian (1939) 63m. ** D: Bernard Vorhaus. Jean Hersholt, Dorothy Lovett, Robert Baldwin, Enid Bennett, Paul Harvey, Marcia Mae Jones, Jackie Moran. Overly folksy entry in film series of small-town doctor who solves everyone's difficulties.

Meet John Doe (1941) 123m. *** D: Frank Capra. Gary Cooper, Barbara Stanwyck, Edward Arnold, Walter Brennan, Spring Byington, James Gleason, Gene Lockhart. Overlong but interesting social commentary, with naive Cooper hired to spearhead national goodwill drive benefiting corrupt politician Arnold. Wordy idealism can't bury good characterizations, usual Capra touches.

Meet Me After the Show (1951) C-86m. **½ D: Richard Sale. Betty Grable, Macdonald Carey, Rory Calhoun, Eddie Albert, Lois Andrews, Irene Ryan. Undistinguished Grable musical lacking bounce of her other vehicles, with usual show biz storyline.

Meet Me at the Fair (1952) 87m. **½ D: Douglas Sirk. Dan Dailey, Diana Lynn, Hugh O'Brian, Carole Mathews, Rhys Williams. Dailey is good as a sideshow medicine man who helps a young orphan and courts Lynn; pleasant musical.

Meet Me in Las Vegas (1956) C-112m. **½ D: Douglas Sirk. Dan Dailey, Cyd Charisse, Agnes Moorehead, Lili Darvas, Jim Backus. Charisse's dancing is highlight of mild musical involving rancher Dailey and ballet star Cyd in gambling capital.

Meet Me in St. Louis (1944) C-113m. **** D: Vincente Minnelli. Judy Garland, Margaret O'Brien, Mary Astor, Lucille Bremer, Marjorie Main, June Lockhart, Harry Davenport, Leon Ames, Tom Drake. Captivating musical of St. Louis during 1903 World's Fair. Judy lilts "The Boy Next Door" (Drake), "Trolley Song," title tune, "Have Yourself A Merry Little Christmas" in beautiful pastel settings. Ames and Astor are heads of a wholesome American family, O'Brien an appealing little sister.

Meet Me Tonight SEE: Tonight at 8:30.

Meet Mr. Lucifer (1953-British) 83m. ** D: Anthony Pelissier. Stanley Holloway, Peggy Cummins, Jack Watling, Barbara Murray. Meek little satire on the evils of television, with Holloway in dual role as Devil and his earthly helper.

Meet the People (1944) 100m. **½ D: Charles Riesner. Lucille Ball, Dick Powell, Virginia O'Brien, Bert Lahr, Rags Ragland, June Allyson, Mata and Hari. OK musicomedy of ex-stage star Ball trying to revive career; so-so score, many guests (Spike Jones, Vaughn Monroe, etc.).

Meet the Stewarts (1942) 73m. **½ D: Alfred E. Green. William Holden, Frances Dee, Grant Mitchell, Anne Revere, Mary Gordon, Marjorie Gateson, Margaret Hamilton, Don Beddoe. Wealthy girl marries hard-working Holden, can't adjust to new financial

Mein Kampf (1961-Swedish) 121m. *** Narrated by Claude Stephenson. Technically smooth documentary on horrors of Nazi Germany. Restrained narration lets the visual speak for itself.

Melba (1953) C-113m. **½ D: Lewis Milestone. Patrice Munsel, Robert Morley, Sybil Thorndike, Martita Hunt, John McCallum. Occasionally interesting biography of Australian opera star Nellie Melba.

Melody for Three (1941) 67m. ** D: Erle C. Kenton. Jean Hersholt, Fay Wray, Walter Woolf King, Astrid Allwyn, Schuyler Standish. Another Dr. Christian saga, enhanced only by presence of lovely Wray, stuck with sagging script.

Member of the Wedding, (1952) 91m. *** D: Fred Zinnemann. Ethel Waters, Julie Harris, Brandon de Wilde, Arthur Franz, Nancy Gates, James Edwards. Carson McCullers' sensitive account of child Harris prodded into growing up by her brother's forthcoming marriage. Cast makes slow-moving film worthwhile.

Men, The (1950) 85m. ***½ D: Fred Zinnemann. Marlon Brando, Teresa Wright, Jack Webb, Everett Sloane, Howard St. John. Brando excels in film debut as ex-GI trying to readjust to life after wartime injury; low-keyed acting is most effective. Retitled: BATTLE STRIPE.

Men Against the Sky (1940) 75m. *½ D: Leslie Goodwins. Richard Dix, Wendy Barrie, Kent Taylor, Edmund Lowe, Granville Bates, Grant Withers. Veteran cast in RKO programmer about personnel at aircraft-building plant.

Men Are Not Gods (1937-British) 82m. **½ D: Walter Reisch. Miriam Hopkins, Gertrude Lawrence, Sebastian Shaw, Rex Harrison, A. E. Matthews. Talky predecessor to A DOUBLE LIFE, with Harrison et al almost making their play-acting OTHELLO come true.

Men in Her Diary (1945) 73m. **½ D: Charles Barton. Peggy Ryan, Jon Hall, Louise Allbritton, Ernest Truex, Virginia Grey, William Terry, Alan Mowbray, Eric Blore, Maxie Rosenbloom. Zesty comedy of jealous wife, helpless husband, and knockout secretary; vivacious Allbritton never really got her due in films, is seen to good advantage here.

Men In Her Life, The (1941) 90m. **½ D: Gregory Ratoff. Loretta Young, Conrad Veidt, Dean Jagger, Eugenie Leontovich, John Shepperd, Otto Kruger. Ballerina Young marries her dancing teacher but recalls many suitors she's known in the past. Fairly interesting love-life saga. Remake of BALLERINA.

Men in War (1957) 104m. **½ D: Anthony Mann. Robert Ryan, Aldo Ray, Robert Keith, Vic Morrow, James Edwards, Scott Marlowe, Victor Sen Yung. Standard war film set in Korea in 1950's, with good action scenes distinguishing usual story.

Men in White (1934) 80m. **½ D: Richarl Boleslawski. Clark Gable, Myrna Loy, Jean Hersholt, Elizabeth Allan, Otto Kruger, Wallace Ford, Henry B. Walthall, Samuel S. Hinds. Sterling cast in sterile filming of Sidney Kingsley's play; Gable is doctor torn between study with Hersholt and marriage to society girl Loy.

Men of Boys Town (1941) 106m. **½ D: Norman Taurog. Spencer Tracy, Mickey Rooney, Bobs Watson, Larry Nunn, Darryl Hickman, Henry O'Neill, Lee J. Cobb. If you liked BOYS TOWN . . .

Men of Brazil (1960-Brazil, dubbed) C-68m. ** D: Nelson Marcellino de Carvalho, Otto Lopes Barbosa, Carlos Anselmo. Damasio Cardoso, Nair Cardoso, Nelson Marcellino de Carvalho, Odette de Carvalho. Strained diatribe on labor unions, mixed with farfetched human-interest dramatics.

Men of Sherwood Forest (1954-British) C-77m. ** D: Val Guest. Don Taylor, Reginald Beckwith, Eileen Moore, David King Wood. Yet another Robin Hood yarn, with Taylor properly sword-wielding and cavalier.

Men of the Fighting Lady (1954) C-80m. *** D: Andrew Marton. Van Johnson, Walter Pidgeon, Louis Calhern, Dewey Martin, Keenan Wynn, Frank Lovejoy, Robert Horton, Bert Freed. Above-par Korean War actioner, focusing on lives of men on U. S. aircraft carrier.

Men of Two Worlds (1946-British) C-107m. ** D: Thorould Dickinson. Phyllis Calvert, Eric Portman, Robert

Adams, Cathleen Nesbitt, Orlando Martins, Cyril Raymond. Unhappy conglomeration of clichés about well-meaning British officials trying to protect natives in Africa. Retitled: WITCH DOCTOR.

Men With Wings (1938) C-105m. **½ D: William Wellman. Fred MacMurray, Louise Campbell, Ray Milland, Andy Devine, Walter Abel, Virginia Weidler. Fictional tale of the epic of flight, with usual love triangle. After good start, it drags on. Donald O'Connor is one of the kids in the opening scenes.

Men Without Souls (1940) 62m. ** D: Nick Grinde. Barton MacLane, John Litel, Rochelle Hudson, Glenn Ford, Don Beddoe, Cy Kendall. Strictly standard prison film, with young Ford caught up in prison scandal. MacLane repeats role from dozens of other bighouse epics.

Menace In the Night (1958-British) 78m. *½ D: Lance Comfort. Griffith Jones, Lisa Gastoni, Vincent Ball, Eddie Byrne. Tired tale of murder being pressured by gang not to testify.

Merrill's Marauders (1962) C-98m. **½ D: Samuel Fuller. Jeff Chandler, Ty Hardin, Peter Brown, Andrew Duggan, Will Hutchins. Rugged action scenes spark this typical WW2 actioner set in Burma.

Merrily We Go to Hell (1932) 78m. **½ D: Dorothy Arzner. Sylvia Sidney, Fredric March, Adrianne Allen, Skeets Gallagher, Kent Taylor, Cary Grant. Stars are vibrant in tale of rich girl marrying irresponsible reporter, facing tragedy. Sidney is her fine, tearful self.

Merrily We Live (1938) 90m. *** D: Norman Z. McLeod. Constance Bennett, Brian Aherne, Alan Mowbray, Billie Burke, Bonita Granville, Tom Brown, Ann Dvorak, Patsy Kelly. It's all been done before, but fluttery Burke hiring suave Aherne as butler who tames spoiled Bennett is still engaging fun.

Merry Andrew (1958) C-103m. **½ D: Michael Kidd. Danny Kaye, Pier Angeli, Baccaloni, Robert Coote. Danny is a British teacher-archeologist with a yen for the circus and one of its performers (Angeli) in this bright musicomedy. Not as wacky as earlier Kaye efforts, but good.

Merry Monahans, The (1944) 91m. *** D: Charles Lamont. Donald O'Connor, Peggy Ryan, Jack Oakie, Ann Blyth, Rosemary DeCamp, Isabel Jewell, Marion Martin, John Miljan. Spirited cast breathes life into bland vaudeville tale, doing old song favorites like "When You Wore A Tulip."

Merry Widow, The (1934) 99m *** D: Ernst Lubitsch. Maurice Chevalier, Jeanette MacDonald, Una Merkel, Edward Everett Horton, George Barbier, Herman Bing. Lavish, delightful filming of Lehar operetta, with usual Lubitsch charm and handpicked cast. Infectious score is still first-rate. Retitled: THE LADY DANCES.

Merry Widow, The (1952) C-105m. **½ D: Curtis Bernhardt. Lana Turner, Fernando Lamas, Una Merkel, Richard Haydn. Franz Lehar's operetta seems dated and trite in plush but unenthusiastic remake.

Message to Garcia, A (1936) 77m. *** D: George Marshall. Wallace Beery, Barbara Stanwyck, John Boles, Alan Hale, Mona Barrie, Herbert Mundin. Historical fiction about agent Boles trying to reach General Garcia during Spanish-American war, with dubious help of roguish Beery and well-bred Stanwyck. Very entertaining.

Mexican Hayride (1948) 77m. ** D: Charles Barton. Bud Abbott, Lou Costello, Virginia Grey, Luba Malina, John Hubbard, Pedro de Cordoba, Fritz Feld. Typical A&C nonsense, with the boys on a wild goose chase with a mine deed in Mexico.

Mexican Manhunt (1953) 71m. *½ D: Rex Bailey. George Brent, Hillary Brooke, Morris Ankrum, Karen Sharpe. Actors walk through thin script about solving of old crime.

MGM's Big Parade of Comedy (1964) 100m. **½ Compiled by Robert Youngson. Fifty of the greatest stars of all time appear in this compilation, but too briefly. Harlow's scenes are seconds long; you can miss others if you blink. Still worthwhile for many priceless sequences with Garbo, Laurel and Hardy, Keaton, Gable, Robert Benchley, Marion Davies, Marx Brothers, et al.

Miami Expose (1956) 73m. *½ D: Fred F. Sears. Lee J. Cobb, Patricia Medina, Edward Arnold, Michael

Granger. Boring round-up of criminal syndicate in Sunshine State.

Miami Story, The (1954) 75m. ** D: Fred F. Sears. Barry Sullivan, Luther Adler, John Baer, Adele Jergens, Beverly Garland. Stern ex-con Sullivan redeems himself in Florida resort city.

Michael Shayne, Private Detective (1940) 77m. **½ D: Eugene Forde. Lloyd Nolan, Marjorie Weaver, Joan Valerie, Walter Abel, Elizabeth Patterson, Donald MacBride. Nolan gives vivid portrayal of detective Shayne, keeping an eye on heavy gambler Weaver in average private-eye thriller.

Michigan Kid, The (1947) C-69m. ** D: Ray Taylor. Jon Hall, Victor McLaglen, Rita Johnson, Andy Devine, Byron Foulger. Colorful but routine refilming of Rex Beach story of female ranch-owner Johnson falling victim to corrupt town government.

Mickey (1948) C-87m. ** D: Ralph Murphy. Lois Butler, Bill Goodwin, Irene Hervey, Hattie McDaniel, John Sutton, Rose Hobart. Naive yarn about rambunctious teen-ager (Butler) who turns matchmaker for father (Goodwin).

Mickey One (1965) 93m. *** D: Arthur Penn. Warren Beatty, Hurd Hatfield, Alexandra Stewart, Teddy Hart, Jeff Corey, Franchot Tone. Beatty stars as confused nightclub comedian looking for new life and some worthwhile values. Will disturb some because of hero's offbeat character. Highly underrated, quite good.

Middle of the Night (1959) 118m. **½ D: Delbert Mann. Kim Novak, Fredric March, Glenda Farrell, Jan Norris, Lee Grant, Effie Afton, Martin Balsam, Joan Copeland. Slow-moving screen version of Paddy Chayefsky play, with March a middle-aged man about to marry much younger Novak.

Midnight (1939) 94m. *** D: Mitchell Leisen. Claudette Colbert, Don Ameche, Francis Lederer, John Barrymore, Mary Astor, Hedda Hopper. Stars glide through Parisian marital mix-up in amusing comedy with Billy Wilder script. Barrymore shines in supporting role.

Midnight Lace (1960) C-108m. *** D: David Miller. Doris Day, Rex Harrison, John Gavin, Myrna Loy, Roddy McDowall, Herbert Marshall, Natasha Parry. Shrill murder mystery; unbelievable plot-line, but star cast and decor smooth over rough spots. Set in London.

Midnight Story, The (1957) 89m. **½ D: Joseph Pevney. Tony Curtis, Marisa Pavan, Gilbert Roland, Ted de Corsia, Kathleen Freeman. Atmospheric murder yarn with Curtis an ex-cop seeking the culprit who killed neighborhood priest.

Midsummer Night's Dream, A (1935) 132m. *** D: Max Reinhardt, William Dieterle. James Cagney, Dick Powell, Olivia de Havilland, Joe E. Brown, Jean Muir, Mickey Rooney, Verree Teasdale, Ian Hunter, Hugh Herbert, Victoy Jory, Ross Alexander. Hollywood-Shakespeare has good and bad points; Cagney as Bottom and the Mendelssohn music are among good parts; Hugh Herbert and other incongruous cast members make up the latter. After a while Rooney (as Puck) gets to be a bit too much.

Mighty Barnum, The (1934) 87m. *** D: Walter Lang. Wallace Beery, Adolphe Menjou, Virginia Bruce, Rochelle Hudson, Janet Beecher, Herman Bing. Fanciful biography of world-famous showman, with Menjou as his reluctant partner Bailey. More Beery than Barnum.

Mighty Crusaders, The (1957-Italian, dubbed) C-87m. ** D: Carlo Ludovico Bragaglia. Francisco Rabal, Sylva Koscina, Gianna Maria Canale, Rik Battaglia. Sloppy picturization of Tasso's epic poem, with contrived love tale between Saracen and Christian backdrop to siege of Jerusalem; amateurish production values.

Mighty Joe Young (1949) 94m. *** D: Ernest B. Schoedsack. Terry Moore, Ben Johnson, Robert Armstrong, Mr. Joseph Young, Frank McHugh. Updating of KING KONG theme has comparable special effects, but no matching story-line, and Moore is no Fay Wray. Mr. Young is good, though.

Mighty McGurk, The (1946) 85m. *½ D: John Waters. Wallace Beery, Dean Stockwell, Dorothy Patrick, Edward Arnold, Aline McMahon, Cameron Mitchell. Formula Beery vehicle with the star a punchy prizefighter and Stockwell as adorable boy he adopts.

Mighty Ursus, The (1962-Italian, dubbed) C-92m. ** D: Carlo Campogalliani. Ed Fury, Christina Gajoni, Maria Orfei, Mario Scaccia, Mary Marlon, Luis Prendez. In title role Fury goes through expected gymnastics, rescuing his woman from marauding natives.

Mikado, The (1939) C-90m. *** D: Victor Schertzinger. Kenny Baker, John Barclay, Martyn Green, Jean Colin, Constance Wills. Baker may not be the ideal Nanki-Poo, but this color film of Gilbert and Sullivan's operetta is still worthwhile, with the marvelous G&S songs intact.

Mildred Pierce (1945) 111m. ***½ D: Michael Curtiz. Joan Crawford, Jack Carson, Zachary Scott, Eve Arden, Bruce Bennett, Ann Blyth, Veda Ann Borg, Butterfly McQueen, Jo Ann Marlowe. Crawford's Oscar-winning performance as housewife-turned-waitress who finds business success but loses control of ungrateful daughter Blyth, amidst romantic competition for same lover. Able support by smooth Carson, playboy Scott, friend Arden. Blyth is excellent as the bitchy daughter.

Milkman, The (1950) 87m. ** D: Charles Barton. Donald O'Connor, Jimmy Durante, Joyce Holden, Piper Laurie, Henry O'Neill. Trivia of O'Connor working for dairy company, with Durante doing his best to liven up the proceedings.

Millerson Case, The (1947) 72m. D: George Archainbaud. Warner Baxter, Nancy Saunders, Barbara Pepper, Clem Bevans, Griff Barnett, Paul Guilfoyle. SEE: Crime Doctor series.

Million Dollar Baby (1941) 100m. ** D: Curtis Bernhardt. Priscilla Lane, Ronald Reagan, Jeffrey Lynn, May Robson, Lee Patrick, Helen Westley, John Qualen. Timeworn Warner Bros. entry of spankingly naive Lane who inherits lots of money, getting lots of headaches.

Million Dollar Kid (1944) 65m. D: Wallace Fox. Leo Gorcey, Huntz Hall, Gabriel Dell, Louise Currie, Noah Beery, Sr., Iris Adrian, Mary Gordon. SEE: Bowery Boys series.

Million Dollar Legs (1932) 64m. ***½ D: Edward Cline. W. C. Fields, Jack Oakie, Andy Clyde, Ben Turpin, Dickie Moore, Billy Gilbert, Lyda Roberti. Wacky nonsense with Fields as King of Klopstokia, a nutty country entering the Olympics. Oakie is a young American pursuing W. C.'s daughter, Susan Fleming. Many fine comics appear in cameos.

Million Dollar Legs (1939) 59m. **½ D: Nick Grinde. Betty Grable, Jackie Coogan, Donald O'Connor, Buster Crabbe, Richard Denning. Title supposedly refers to winning horse, but Grable is star so draw your own assumptions. Pleasant college comedy of school trying to keep on its feet has nothing to do with W. C. Fields film of same name.

Million Dollar Mermaid (1952) C-115m. **½ D: Mervyn LeRoy. Esther Williams, Victor Mature, Walter Pidgeon, David Brian, Jesse White. Williams does OK as aquatic star Annette Kellerman, alternating her swimming with romancing Mature.

Million Dollar Weekend (1948) 72m. ** D: Gene Raymond. Gene Raymond, Francis Lederer, Stephanie Paull (Osa Massen), Robert Warwick, James Craven. Average mystery yarn with veteran cast. Stockbroker steals firm's money and heads for Hawaii, where complications snowball. Star Raymond also directed.

Millionaire for Christy, A (1951) 91m. **½ D: George Marshall. Fred MacMurray, Eleanor Parker, Richard Carlson, Una Merkel. Satisfactory frolic of Parker deciding MacMurray is the man for her.

Millionairess, The (1960-British) C-90m. **½ D: Anthony Asquith. Sophia Loren, Peter Sellers, Alastair Sim, Vittorio DeSica, Dennis Price. Sometimes diverting comedy of manners, oddly cast, with Loren in title role seeking to comply with father's will to gain inheritance. Based on Shaw play.

Min and Bill (1930) 70m. **½ D: George Hill. Marie Dressler, Wallace Beery, Dorothy Jordan, Marjorie Rambeau, Frank McGlynn. Sentimental early talkie with unforgettable team of Beery and Dressler as waterfront characters trying to protect Marie's daughter (Jordan) from being taken to "proper" home. Dressler won an Academy Award for her performance.

Mind Benders, The (1963-British) 101m. *** D: Basil Dearden. Dirk Bogarde, Mary Ure, John Clements, Michael Bryant, Wendy Craig. Top cast in slow-moving but compelling account of experiments testing man's will power and senses, with espionage theme weaved into plot.

Mine Own Executioner (1948) 103m. *** D: Anthony Kimmins. Burgess Meredith, Dulcie Gray, Kieron Moore, Christine Norden, Michael Shepley. Realistic drama of quack psychiatrist Meredith encountering trouble of his own; some fine suspenseful sequences.

Ministry of Fear (1944) 85m. ***½ D: Fritz Lang. Ray Milland, Marjorie Reynolds, Carl Esmond, Dan Duryea, Hillary Brooke, Alan Napier, Percy Waram. Beautifully atmospheric thriller of wartime London, with Milland framed in complicated espionage plot; good cast, fine touches by director Lang.

Miniver Story, The (1950) 104m. **½ D: H. C. Potter. Greer Garson, Walter Pidgeon, John Hodiak, Leo Genn, Cathy O'Donnell, Henry Wilcoxon, Reginald Owen, Peter Finch. Sequel to MRS. MINIVER doesn't work as well, but Garson and Pidgeon have some poignant sequences as family reunites in post-WW2 England.

Minotaur, The (1961-Italian, dubbed) C-92m. *½ D: Silvio Amadio. Bob Mathias, Rosanna Schiaffino, Alberto Lupo, Rik Battaglia. Occasional atmosphere and Schiaffino's appearance still cannot elevate story of mythological hero thwarting attempt of evil queen to subjugate city-dwellers with hideous monster.

Miracle, The (1959) C-121m. **½ D: Irving Rapper. Carroll Baker, Roger Moore, Walter Slezak, Vittorio Gassman, Katina Paxinou, Dennis King, Isobel Elsom. Claptrap vehicle resurrected as glossy, empty spectacle of 1810's Spain, with Baker the would-be nun unsure of her decision, Moore the soldier she romances.

Miracle in the Rain (1956) 107m. **½ D: Rudolph Mate. Jane Wyman, Van Johnson, Peggie Castle, Fred Clark, Eileen Heckart, Josephine Hutchinson, Barbara Nichols, William Gargan. Above-par soaper of two lost souls, Wyman and Johnson, falling in love in N.Y.C. LAUGH-IN's Arte Johnson has a featured role.

Miracle of Fatima SEE: **Miracle of Our Lady of Fatima, The.**

Miracle of Morgan's Creek, The (1944) 99m. **** D: Preston Sturges. Eddie Bracken, Betty Hutton, Diana Lynn, Brian Donlevy, William Demarest, Porter Hall, Almira Sessions, Jimmy Conlin. Frantic, hilarious comedy of Betty attending all-night party, forgetting who's the father of her offspring nine months later. Bracken and Demarest have never been better than in this gem.

Miracle of Our Lady of Fatima, The (1952) C-102m. *** D: John Brahm. Gilbert Roland, Angela Clarke, Frank Silvera, Jay Novello, Sherry Jackson. Tastefully handled account of religious miracle witnessed by farm children in 1910's; intelligent script. Retitled: MIRACLE OF FATIMA.

Miracle of the Bells, The (1948) 120m. *½ D: Irving Pichel. Fred MacMurray, Valli, Frank Sinatra, Lee J. Cobb, Charles Meredith. Contrived story of miracle occurring when movie star is laid to rest in coalmining home town; often ludicrous, despite sincere cast.

Miracle of the Hills (1959) 73m. *½ D: Paul Landres. Rex Reason, Theona Bryant, Jay North, Gilbert Smith, Tracy Stratford, Gene Roth. Timid little Western of town-running gal who bucks new clergyman.

Miracle on 34th Street (1947) 96m. ***½ D: George Seaton. Maureen O'Hara, John Payne, Edmund Gwenn, Gene Lockhart, Natalie Wood, Porter Hall, William Frawley, Thelma Ritter. Classic Valentine Davies fable of "Kris Kringle" (Gwenn) working in Macy's, encountering unbelieving child (Wood), going on trial to prove he's Santa. Delightful comedy-fantasy.

Miracle Worker, The (1962) 107m. ***½ D: Arthur Penn. Anne Bancroft, Patty Duke, Victor Jory, Inga Swenson, Andrew Prine, Kathleen Comegys. Broadway play is filmized with few changes. Duke and Bancroft unforgettable as Helen Keller and her devoted teacher. Worthwhile; the fight-for-authority sequence especially memorable.

Miraculous Journey (1948) C-83m. *½ D: Peter Stewart. Rory Calhoun, Audrey Long, Virginia Grey, George Cleveland. Substandard psychological study of victims of plane crash in jungle.

Mirage (1965) C-109m. *** D: Edward Dmytryk. Gregory Peck, Diane

Baker, Walter Matthau, Kevin McCarthy, Jack Weston, Leif Erickson, Walter Abel, George Kennedy. Fine Hitchcock-like thriller, with Peck the victim of amnesia and everyone else out to get him. Walter Matthau steals the film as an easygoing private eye; some interesting on-location footage in N.Y.C.

Miranda (1948-British) 80m. **½ D: Ken Annakin. Glynis Johns, Griffith Jones, Googie Withers, John McCallum, Margaret Rutherford. Droll frou-frou of mermaid preferring sophisticated land-life to the sea; capably played by all. Johns is a very fetching mermaid.

Mirror Has Two Faces, The (1959-French, dubbed) 98m. **½ D: Andre Cayatte. Michele Morgan, Bourvil, Gerard Oury, Ivan Desny, Elizabeth Manet, Sylvie, Sandra Milo. Morgan is quite good as woman who begins life anew after plastic surgery.

Misfits, The (1961) 124m. *** D: John Huston. Clark Gable, Marilyn Monroe, Montgomery Clift, Thelma Ritter, Eli Wallach, James Barton, Estelle Winwood. Unsatisfying but engrossing parable authored by Arthur Miller, involving disillusioned divorcee Monroe and her brooding cowboy friends. Both Monroe's and Gable's last film.

Miss Annie Rooney (1942) 84m. ** D: Edwin L. Marin. Shirley Temple, William Gargan, Guy Kibbee, Dickie Moore, Peggy Ryan, Gloria Holden, Selmer Jackson, June Lockhart, Virginia Sale. Moore gives Shirley her first screen kiss in slight tale of girl from wrong side of tracks in love with rich boy.

Miss Grant Takes Richmond (1949) 87m. **½ D: Lloyd Bacon. Lucille Ball, William Holden, Janis Carter, James Gleason, Frank McHugh. Ball is wacky secretary innocently involved with crooks; she's the whole show.

Miss Pinkerton (1932) 66m. ** D: Lloyd Bacon. Joan Blondell, George Brent, John Wray, Ruth Hall, C. Henry Gordon, Elizabeth Patterson, Holmes Herbert. Nurse Blondell has sixth sense for mysteries, decides to go after one in easy-to-take story.

Miss Robin Crusoe (1954) C-75m. *½ D: Eugene Frenke. Amanda Blake, George Nader, Rosalind Hayes. Female version of Robinson Crusoe; nothing added, a lot to be desired.

Miss Robin Hood (1952-British) 78m. ** D: John Guillermin. Margaret Rutherford, Richard Hearne, Edward Lexy, Frances Rowe. OK mixture of fantasy and farce, with Rutherford an elderly nut seeking retrieval of family whiskey formula; Hearne is meek girl's-magazine writer who aids her.

Miss Sadie Thompson (1953) C-91m. *** D: Curtis Bernhardt. Rita Hayworth, Jose Ferrer, Aldo Ray, Russell Collins, Charles Bronson. Rita Hayworth gives a provocative performance in remake of Somerset Maugham's RAIN.

Miss Susie Slagle's (1945) 88m. **½ D: John Berry. Veronica Lake, Sonny Tufts, Joan Caulfield, Lillian Gish, Ray Collins, Billy DeWolfe, Lloyd Bridges. Mild tale of turn-of-the-century boarding house for aspiring doctors and nurses.

Miss Tatlock's Millions (1948) 101m. *** D: Richard Haydn. John Lund, Wanda Hendrix, Barry Fitzgerald, Monty Woolley, Robert Stack, Ilka Chase, Dorothy Stickney. Original comedy of Hollywood stunt-man who must masquerade as a nitwit to help young heiress; several guest stars appear.

Missile Base at Taniak (1953) 100m. *½ D: Franklin Adreon. William Henry, Susan Morrow, Arthur Space, Dale Van Sickel. Uninspired Republic cliff-hanger concerning Canadian mounties' efforts to track down foreign agents setting up rocket centers to launch projectiles and destroy key American cities. Re-edited movie serial: CANADIAN MOUNTIES VS. ATOMIC INVADERS.

Missile Monsters (1958) 75m. *½ D: Fred C. Brannon. Walter Reed, Lois Collier, Gregory Gay, James Craven. Tedious sci-fi about Martian attempt to take over the earth via guided missiles.

Missile to the Moon (1959) 78m. Bomb D: Richard Cunha. Richard Travis, Cathy Downs, K. T. Stevens, Tommy Cook. Low-grade junk about rocket trip to lunar planet.

Missiles From Hell (1958-British) 72m. ** D: Vernon Sewell. Michael Rennie, Patricia Medina, Milly Vitale, David Knight. British work with

**Polish partisans during WW2 to obtain projectile weapon held by Nazis; choppy editing.

Missing Corpse, The (1945) 62m. *½ D: Albert Herman. J. Edward Bromberg, Eric Sinclair, Frank Jenks, Isabel Randolph, Paul Guilfoyle, John Shay, Lorell Sheldon. Cheaply made chiller of harried newspaperman Bromberg involved in murder mystery.

Missing Juror, The (1945) 66m. *** D: Budd Boetticher. Jim Bannon, Janis Carter, George Macready, Jean Stevens, Joseph Crehan, Carole Mathews. Brisk, engrossing drama of unknown killer taking revenge on jury that sent innocent man to his death; low budget, but quite good.

Mission Over Korea (1953) 85m. *½ D: Fred F. Sears. John Hodiak, John Derek, Maureen O'Sullivan, Audrey Totter. Substandard Korean War tale.

Mission to Moscow (1943) 123m. ***½ D: Michael Curtiz. Walter Huston, Ann Harding, Oscar Homolka, George Tobias, Gene Lockhart, Frieda Inescort, Eleanor Parker, Richard Travis. Excellent, important film of real-life ambassador Joseph Davies in then-peaceful Russia. Well-done, giving interesting insights to American concepts of USSR at the time.

Mississippi (1935) 73m. ***½ D: A. Edward Sutherland. Bing Crosby, W. C. Fields, Joan Bennett, Queenie Smith, Gail Patrick, Claude Gillingwater. Fine cast in musicomedy of riverboat captain Fields and singer Crosby, with Rodgers-Hart score including "It's Easy To Remember But So Hard To Forget." Unforgettable poker game with W. C. Look quickly for Ann Sheridan.

Mississippi Gambler (1953) C-98m. **½ D: Rudolph Mate. Tyrone Power, Piper Laurie, Julia Adams, John McIntire, Dennis Weaver. Power is title figure with ambitions of establishing a gambling business in New Orleans.

Missouri Traveller, The (1958) C-104m. **½ D: Jerry Hopper. Brandon de Wilde, Lee Marvin, Gary Merrill, Mary Hosford, Paul Ford. Folksy, minor account of orphaned youth (De Wilde) finding new roots in Southern country town in 1910's; earnest but predictable.

Mr. Ace (1946) 84m. **½ D: Edwin L. Marin. George Raft, Sylvia Sidney, Stanley Ridges, Sara Haden, Jerome Cowan. Ordinary dirty-politics drama of office-seeking Sidney using Raft to achieve her goals.

Mr. and Mrs. North (1941) 67m. **½ D: Robert B. Sinclair. Gracie Allen, William Post, Jr., Paul Kelly, Rose Hobart, Virginia Grey, Tom Conway. Radio characters come to screen in comedy involving dead bodies being discovered; sometimes funny, sometimes forced.

Mr. and Mrs. Smith (1941) 95m. *** D: Alfred Hitchcock. Carole Lombard, Robert Montgomery, Gene Raymond, Jack Carson, Philip Merivale, Betty Compson, Lucile Watson. Madcap comedy of Lombard and Montgomery discovering their marriage wasn't legal. Not many Hitchcock touches, but bouncy.

Mr. Arkadin (1955-British) 99m. **½ D: Orson Welles. Orson Welles, Michael Redgrave, Patricia Medina, Akim Tamiroff, Mischa Auer. Brooding, rambling drama about oddball financier. Retitled: CONFIDENTIAL REPORT.

Mr. Belvedere Goes to College (1949) 83m. ** D: Elliott Nugent. Clifton Webb, Shirley Temple, Tom Drake, Alan Young, Jessie Royce Landis, Kathleen Hughes. Weary script and flat supporting players give Webb, in title role, nothing to thrust his wry archness at, alas.

Mr. Belvedere Rings the Bell (1951) 87m. **½ D: Henry Koster. Clifton Webb, Joanne Dru, Hugh Marlowe, Zero Mostel, Doro Merande, Billy Lynn. Another follow-up to SITTING PRETTY isn't as witty. Webb enters old folks' home to prove his theory that age has nothing to do with leading a full life.

Mr. Blandings Builds His Dream House (1948) 94m. *** D: H. C. Potter. Cary Grant, Myrna Loy, Melvyn Douglas, Sharyn Moffet, Connie Marshall, Louise Beavers. Slick comedy of city couple attempting to build a house in the country; expertly handled.

Mister Buddwing (1966) 100m. **½ D: Delbert Mann. James Garner, Jean Simmons, Suzanne Pleshette, Angela Lansbury, Katharine Ross, Raymond St. Jacques, Nichelle Nichols. Misfire; over-familiar amnesia plot with Garner trying to fill in his past, meeting assorted women who might have been part of his prior life.

Mister Cory (1957) C-92m. **½ D: Blake Edwards. Tony Curtis, Charles Bickford, Martha Hyer, Kathryn Grant. Curtis does OK as poor-boy-turned-rich-gambler who returns to home town to show off his wealth.

Mr. Deeds Goes to Town (1936) 115m. ***½ D: Frank Capra. Gary Cooper, Jean Arthur, George Bancroft, Lionel Stander, Douglass Dumbrille, Mayo Methot, Raymond Walburn. Cooper is Longfellow Deeds, who inherits a million dollars and wants to spend it on people during Depression; Arthur is appealing as city reporter captivated by the naive Deeds.

Mr. Denning Drives North (1953-British) 93m. **½ D: Anthony Kimmins. John Mills, Phyllis Calvert, Eileen Moore, Sam Wanamaker. Cast's sincerity makes this murder yarn palatable, the biggest hunt being for the corpus delicti.

Mister Drake's Duck (1950-British) 76m. *** D: Val Guest. Douglas Fairbanks, Jr., Yolande Donlan, Howard Marion-Crawford, Reginald Beckwith. Droll comedy of Fairbanks on honeymoon getting more publicity than he bargained for when pet duck lays radioactive eggs.

Mister 880 (1950) 90m. *** D: Edmund Goulding. Dorothy McGuire, Burt Lancaster, Edmund Gwenn, Millard Mitchell. Easygoing comedy, with Gwenn an elderly counterfeiter tracked down by federal agent Lancaster.

Mr. Hex (1946) 63m. D: William Beaudine. Leo Gorcey, Huntz Hall, Bobby Jordan, Gabriel Dell, Gale Robbins, Billy Benedict, David Gorcey, Ian Keith. SEE: Bowery Boys series.

Mr. Hobbs Takes a Vacation (1962) C-116m. **½ D: Henry Koster. James Stewart, Maureen O'Hara, Fabian, John Saxon, Marie Wilson, Reginald Gardiner, Laurie Peters. Ultra-wholesome family fare. Stewart and O'Hara, taking brood to seaside summer house, try to meet family problems.

Mr. Hulot's Holiday (1954-French, dubbed) 85m. *** D: Jacques Tati. Jacques Tati, Nathalie Pascaud, Michelle Rolla, Valentine Camax, Louis Perrault. Wry Tati recreating his fun-loving character on vacation at seaside resort. Through pantomime he conveys more meaning than most do with words.

Mr. Imperium (1951) C-87m. **½ D: Don Hartman. Lana Turner, Ezio Pinza, Marjorie Main, Barry Sullivan, Cedric Hardwicke, Debbie Reynolds. Threadbare romance between Turner and Pinza, now a monarch; colorful but paper-thin.

Mr. Lucky (1943) 100m. *** D: H. C. Potter. Cary Grant, Laraine Day, Charles Bickford, Gladys Cooper, Alan Carney, Henry Stephenson, Paul Stewart, Kay Johnson, Florence Bates. Gambling-ship-owner Grant intends to fleece virtuous Day, instead falls in love and goes straight. Basis for later TV series has spirited cast, engaging script.

Mister Moses (1965) C-113m **½ D: Ronald Neame. Robert Mitchum, Carroll Baker, Ian Bannen, Alexander Knox, Raymond St. Jacques, Reginald Beckwith. Malarkey of rugged Mitchum and virtuous Baker leading African native tribe to their new homeland.

Mr. Moto With the Charlie Chan films going strong, John P. Marquand's character of a seemingly timid but cunning and intelligent sleuth named Mr. Moto seemed a natural for the movies. Twentieth Century-Fox, the same studio that was making the Chans, inaugurated the series in 1937 with THINK FAST, MR. MOTO, with the offbeat casting of Peter Lorre in the lead. Lorre fell into the role of the crafty, lighthearted Moto quite well, and played the character in all eight Moto films, through 1939. The series was entertaining, but somehow lacked the heart of the Chan films. Fortunately, they were endowed with slick productions and fine casts of character actors, which tended to overshadow the films' shortcomings. Moto globetrotted from country to country, solving various mysteries with and without the help of police authorities, and confronted such formidable villains as Sig Ruman, Sidney Blackmer, John Carradine, Leon Ames, Ricardo Cortez, Jean Hersholt and Lionel Atwill. Needless to say, the diminutive Lorre was victorious in every encounter, with the negligible help of such "assistants" as dimwitted Warren Hymer in MR. MOTO IN DANGER ISLAND. Many consider THANK YOU MR. MOTO (1938) the best of the series, with our hero hunting for a valuable map leading to an ancient treasure. In 1965 Fox decided to revive the long-dormant Moto character in a very low-budget second feature called appropriately enough, THE RETURN OF MR. MOTO. Movie villain Henry Silva starred as Moto, but the film was cheaply done and completely unfaithful to the original conception of the character. Hopefully, future movie historians will ignore the recent failure and realize that for everyone Peter Lorre was the Mr. Moto.

Mr. Moto in Danger Island (1939) 63m. D: Herbert I. Leeds. Peter Lorre, Jean Hersholt, Amanda Duff, Warren Hymer, Richard Lane, Leon Ames, Douglass Dumbrille, Robert Lowery.

Mr. Moto Takes a Chance (1938) 63m. D: Norman Foster. Peter Lorre, Rochelle Hudson, Robert Kent, J. Edward Bromberg, Chick Chandler, George Regas, Fredrik Vogeding.

Mr. Moto Takes a Vacation (1939) 61m. D: Norman Foster. Peter Lorre, Joseph Schildkraut, Lionel Atwill, Virginia Field, Iva Stewart, Victor Varconi, John Davidson.

Mr. Moto's Gamble (1938) 71m. D: James Tinling. Peter Lorre, Keye Luke, Dick Baldwin, Lynn Bari, Douglas Fowley, Jayne Regan, Harold Huber, Maxie Rosenbloom.

Mr. Moto's Last Warning (1939) 71m. D: Norman Foster. Peter Lorre, Ricardo Cortez, Virginia Field, John Carradine, George Sanders, Robert Coote, John Davidson.

Mr. Muggs Rides Again (1945) 63m. D: Wallace Fox. Leo Gorcey, Huntz Hall, Billy Benedict, Nancy Brinckman, George Meeker, Pierre Watkin, Bernard Thomas. SEE: Bowery Boys series.

Mr. Music (1950) 113m. **½ D: Richard Haydn. Bing Crosby, Nancy Olson, Charles Coburn, Ruth Hussey, Marge and Gower Champion, Peggy Lee, Groucho Marx. Easygoing vehicle for crooner Crosby as Broadway producer who wants to live the easy life.

Mr. Peabody and the Mermaid (1948) 89m. **½ D: Irving Pichel. William Powell, Ann Blyth, Irene Hervey, Andrea King, Clinton Sundberg. Comedy-fantasy has its moments, with unsuspecting Powell coming across a lovely mermaid while fishing. Powell makes anything look good.

Mr. Perrin and Mr. Traill (1948-British) 90m. ** D: Lawrence Huntington. Marius Goring, David Farrar, Greta Gynt, Raymond Huntley. Lukewarm study of progressive vs. conservative schoolteaching.

Mister Roberts (1955) C-123m. *** D: John Ford, Mervyn LeRoy. Henry Fonda, James Cagney, William Powell, Jack Lemmon, Betsy Palmer, Ward Bond, Nick Adams. Superb comedy-drama of WW2 cargo ship and its restless officer (Fonda) yearning for combat. Cagney as eccentric captain, Powell as philosophical doctor, Lemmon in Academy Award-winning performance as Ensign Pulver, all great.

Mr. Sardonicus (1961) 89m. ** D: William Castle. Oscar Homolka, Ronald Lewis, Audrey Dalton, Guy Rolfe. Recluse count with hideous grin pasted on face lures wife's boyfriend/ doctor to castle to cure him. Minor fare despite good ending.

Mister Scoutmaster (1953) 87m. *** D: Henry Levin. Clifton Webb, Edmund Gwenn, George Winslow, Frances Dee, Veda Ann Borg. Child-hater Webb becomes scoutmaster in this airy film which will appeal mainly to kids.

Mr. Skeffington (1944) 146m. *** D: Vincent Sherman. Bette Davis, Claude Rains, Walter Abel, Richard Waring, Jerome Cowan, Gigi Perreau, Charles Drake, Marjorie Riordan, George Coulouris. Grand soap opera spanning several decades of N.Y.C. life from 1900's onward. Davis is vain society girl who marries stockbroker Rains for convenience, discovering his true love of her only after many years. Lavish settings, virtuoso Davis performance.

Mr. Smith Goes to Washington (1939) 125m. **** D: Frank Capra. Jean Arthur, James Stewart, Claude Rains, Edward Arnold, Guy Kibbee, Thomas

Mitchell, Eugene Pallette, Beulah Bondi, Harry Carey, Pierre Watkin, Jack Carson. Stewart is young idealist who finds nothing but corruption (Rains, Arnold, et al) in U. S. Senate; fine Capra Americana, with Stewart's top performance, bolstered by Arthur as hard-boiled dame won over by earnest Mr. Smith.

Mr. Soft Touch (1949) 93m. ** D: Henry Levin, Gordon Douglas. Glenn Ford, Evelyn Keyes, John Ireland, Beulah Bondi, Percy Kilbride, Ted de Corsia. Ford and Keyes are mild romantic duo in unimportant story of ex-GI involved with social worker and gangster-run nightclub.

Mr. Universe (1951) 79m. *½ D: Joseph Lerner. Jack Carson, Janis Paige, Vincent Edwards, Bert Lahr, Robert Alda. Quickie film trying to milk all laughs possible from premise of Carson being a wrestler, with tired sight gags.

Mister V SEE: **Pimpernel Smith**.

Mr. Winkle Goes to War (1944) 80m. **½ D: Alfred E. Green. Edward G. Robinson, Ruth Warrick, Ted Donaldson, Robert Armstrong, Ann Shoemaker. Minor yarn of aging henpecked man accidentally drafted during WW2, who becomes military hero. Spirited Robinson is enjoyable.

Mr. Wise Guy (1942) 70m. D: William Nigh. Leo Gorcey, Huntz Hall, Bobby Jordan, Guinn Williams, Billy Gilbert, Benny Rubin, Douglas Fowley, Ann Doran, Jack Mulhall, Warren Hymer, David Gorcey. SEE: Bowery Boys series.

Mrs. Mike (1949) 99m. **½ D: Louis King. Dick Powell, Evelyn Keyes, J. M. Kerrigan, Angela Clarke. Powell and Keyes are pleasing duo, as Canadian mountie indoctrinates his urban wife to rural life.

Mrs. Miniver (1942) 134m. ***½ D: William Wyler. Greer Garson, Walter Pidgeon, Dame May Whitty, Teresa Wright, Reginald Owen, Henry Travers, Richard Ney, Tom Conway, Henry Wilcoxon. Garson, Wright and director Wyler were among Oscar-winners in emotional story of family struggling through German Blitz of England. Still good.

Mrs. O'Malley and Mr. Malone (1950) 69m. ** D: Norman Taurog. Marjorie Main, James Whitmore, Ann Dvorak, Fred Clark, Dorothy Malone, Phyllis Kirk. Main is rambunctious but can't elevate film about small-towner winning prize contest, involved with murder on a New York-bound train. Whitmore is most enjoyable.

Mrs. Parkington (1944) 124m. *** D: Tay Garnett. Greer Garson, Walter Pidgeon, Edward Arnold, Gladys Cooper, Agnes Moorehead, Peter Lawford, Dan Duryea, Selena Royle, Lee Patrick. Determined Garson has lofty ambitions, marries wealthy but homespun Pidgeon, and pushes her way into society; overlong, well-mounted soaper.

Mrs. Wiggs of the Cabbage Patch (1934) 80m. *** D: Norman Taurog. W. C. Fields, Pauline Lord, ZaSu Pitts, Evelyn Venable, Kent Taylor, Donald Meek, Virginia Weidler. More story than Fields in this one, a melodrama of poor woman about to be evicted; the domestic scenes with W. C. and Pitts are priceless.

Mrs. Wiggs of the Cabbage Patch (1942) 80m. **½ D: Ralph Murphy. Fay Bainter, Hugh Herbert, Vera Vague, Barbara Britton, Carolyn Lee, Billy Lee, Carl Switzer, Moroni Olsen. Abandoned wife with large family waits patiently for husband to return. A notch above average.

Mob, The (1951) 87m. ** D: Robert Parrish. Broderick Crawford, Betty Buehler, Richard Kiley, Otto Hulett, Neville Brand, Ernest Borgnine, Charles Bronson. Study of lawman cracking waterfront gang syndicate; Crawford is good but script is second-rate. Interesting cast, however.

Mob Town (1941) 70m. D: William Nigh. Billy Halop, Huntz Hall, Gabriel Dell, Bernard Punsley, Dick Foran, Anne Gwynne, Samuel S. Hinds. SEE: Bowery Boys series.

Moby Dick (1956) C-116m. *** D: Lloyd Bacon. John Barrymore, Joan Bennett, Walter Long, Nigel de Brulier, Nobel Johnson, Virginia Sale. Not Melville but good, with dashing Barrymore as Captain Ahab; good special effects too. Pointless love story added to original narrative.

Moby Dick (1956) C-116m. *** D: John Huston. Gregory Peck, Richard Basehart, Leo Genn, Orson Welles, James Robertson Justice. Moody, spotty version of Herman Melville sea classic, with Peck miscast as

Captain Ahab. Some fine scenes scattered about.

Model and the Marriage Broker, The (1951) 103m. *** D: George Cukor. Jeanne Crain, Scott Brady, Thelma Ritter, Zero Mostel, Michael O'Shea, Frank Fontaine, Nancy Kulp. The title tells all as fast-talking Ritter pairs up Crain and Brady.

Model For Murder (1958-British) 75m. ** D: Terry Bishop. Keith Andes, Hazel Court, Jean Aubrey, Michael Gough. Andes is American in England seeking late brother's girlfriend, becoming involved in jewel robbery. Adequate yarn.

Model Wife (1941) 78m. **½ D: Leigh Jason. Joan Blondell, Dick Powell, Lee Bowman, Charlie Ruggles, Lucile Watson, Ruth Donnelly, Billy Gilbert. Joan's boss won't let her get married, but she does, to Powell, and has to keep it a secret. Fairly amusing comedy.

Modesty Blaise (1966-British) C-119m. ** D: Joseph Losey. Monica Vitti, Dirk Bogarde, Terence Stamp, Harry Andrews, Michael Craig, Scilla Gabel, Tina Marquand, Clive Revill, Alexander Knox. Director Losey ate watermelon, pickles, and ice cream, went to sleep, woke up, and made this film. Made at the height of the pop-art craze, it tries to be a spoof at times, doesn't know what it's supposed to be at other moments.

Mogambo (1953) C-115m. ***½ D: John Ford. Clark Gable, Ava Gardner, Grace Kelly, Laurence Naismith, Donald Sinden. Lusty remake of RED DUST. Gable repeats his role, Ava replaces Harlow, Kelly has Mary Astor's part. Romantic triangle in Africa combines love and action; beautifully filmed in color.

Mohawk (1956) C-79m. **½ D: Kurt Neumann. Scott Brady, Rita Gam, Neville Brand, Lori Nelson, Allison Hayes. Bouncy Western of Indian uprising thwarted by peace-loving Brady and squaw Gam.

Mokey (1942) 88m. ** D: Wells Root. Dan Dailey, Donna Reed, Bobby Blake, William "Buckwheat" Thomas, Cordell Hickman, Matt Moore, Etta McDaniel. Reed has problems with her stepson, who almost winds up in reform school. Typical of genre.

Mole People, The (1956) 78m. ** D: Virgil Vogel. John Agar, Cynthia Patrick, Hugh Beaumont, Alan Napier. Dank horror tale set in Asia involving underground people with warped thoughts.

Molly SEE: **Goldbergs, The**.

Molly and Me (1945) 76m. *** D: Lewis Seiler. Gracie Fields, Monty Woolley, Roddy McDowall, Reginald Gardiner, Natalie Schafer, Edith Barrett, Clifford Brooke. Entertaining little comedy of Fields becoming Woolley's housekeeper, taking over his life as well. Well played by fine cast.

Moment of Truth, The (1952-French, dubbed) 90m. ** D: Jean Delannoy. Michele Morgan, Jean Gabin, Daniel Gelin, Simone Paris. Effective playing of trite yarn of married couple realizing how little they know each other.

Moment to Moment (1966) C-108m. **½ D: Mervyn LeRoy. Jean Seberg, Honor Blackman, Sean Garrison, Arthur Hill. Unconvincing, confused murder mystery set on the Riviera, but filmed largely on Universal's sound stage.

Mondo Cane (1963-Italian, dubbed) C-105m. **½ Producer: Gualtiero Jacopetti. First and best of Italian shockumentaries, with dubbed American narration; focuses on peculiarities of man in various parts of the world. Features song "More."

Money From Home (1953) C-100m. *** D: George Marshall. Dean Martin, Jerry Lewis, Pat Crowley, Robert Strauss, Jack Kruschen. Above average hijinks of duo involved with gangsters, steeplechase racing, Arab ruler and his harem.

Money Trap, The (1966) 92m. **½ D: Burt Kennedy. Glenn Ford, Rita Hayworth, Elke Sommer, Joseph Cotten, Ricardo Montalban. Ford is detective turned crook in pedestrian murder yarn. Hayworth most convincing as middle-aged woman no longer self-sufficient.

Money, Women and Guns (1958) C-80m. ** D: Richard Bartlett. Jock Mahoney, Kim Hunter, Tim Hovey, Gene Evans. Modest Western about lawman sent to track down killers and to find heirs to victim's will.

Mongols, The (1960-Italian, dubbed) C-102m. ** D: Andre de Toth, Leopoldo Savona. Jack Palance, Anita Ekberg, Antonella Lualdi, Franco

314

Silva. Unimaginative spectacle set in 19th century, with Palance the son of Genghis Khan on the rampage in Europe, Ekberg his girl.

Monkey Business (1931) 77m. ***½ D: Norman Z. McLeod. Groucho, Harpo, Chico, Zeppo Marx, Thelma Todd, Ruth Hall, Harry Woods. Four brothers stow away on luxury liner; Groucho goes after Thelma, all four pretend to be Maurice Chevalier to get off ship. Full quota of sight gags and puns in typically wacky comedy.

Monkey Business (1952) 97m. *** D: Howard Hawks. Ginger Rogers, Cary Grant, Charles Coburn, Marilyn Monroe, Hugh Marlowe. Grant discovers rejuvenation serum which affects him, his wife Rogers, boss Coburn, and secretary Monroe in this wacky comedy. Coburn's classic line to MM: "Get someone to type this."

Monkey on My Back (1957) 93m. **½ D: Andre de Toth. Cameron Mitchell, Paul Richards, Dianne Foster, Jack Albertson, Kathy Garver. Mitchell as fighter Barney Ross who became a dope addict turns in sincere performance. Well-meant, engrossing little film.

Monolith Monsters, The (1957) 77m. ** D: John Sherwood. Lola Albright, Grant Williams, Les Tremayne, Trevor Bardette. For a change of pace, the title villains are slabs of rocks sucking out human energy.

Monsieur Beaucaire (1946) 93m. *** D: George Marshall. Bob Hope, Joan Caulfield, Patric Knowles, Marjorie Reynolds, Cecil Kellaway, Joseph Schildkraut, Reginald Owen, Constance Collier. Pleasing Hope vehicle with Bob in costume as barber sent on mission as dead duck sure to be murdered. Plush settings, funny gags.

Monsoon (1953) C-79m. *½ D: Rodney Amateau. Ursula Thiess, Diana Douglas, George Nader, Ellen Corby. Trite drama of several people destroyed by their passions; set in India.

Monster of Piedras Blancas, The (1958) 71m. ** D: Irvin Berwick. Les Tremayne, Forrest Lewis, John Harmon, Frank Arvidson, Wayne Berwick. Sluggish chiller with crustacean terror thirsting for blood on a deserted seacoast; obvious and amateurish.

Monster Maker, The (1944) 62m. ** D: Sam Newfield. J. Carrol Naish, Ralph Morgan, Wanda McKay, Terry Frost. For horror buffs, a low-budget yarn of mad-scientist Naish transplanting something-or-other to create his strange beings.

Monster on the Campus (1958) 76m. **½ D: Jack Arnold. Arthur Franz, Joanna Moore, Judson Pratt, Nancy Walters, Troy Donahue. Above-par chiller involving blood formula that turns a college professor into rampaging beast.

Monster That Challenged the World, The (1957) 83m. **½ D: Arnold Laven. Tim Holt, Audrey Dalton, Hans Conried, Casey Adams. Imaginative special effects improve this chiller about oversized water monster.

Monstrosity (1964) 72m. *½ D: Joseph Mascelli. Frank Gerstle, Erika Peters, Judy Bamber, Frank Fowler, Marjorie Eaton. Eaton is wealthy matron who hires doctor (Gerstle) to perform brain transplant on her; lumbering mess. Retitled: ATOMIC BRAIN, THE.

Montana (1950) C-76m. **½ D: Ray Enright. Errol Flynn, Alexis Smith, S. Z. Sakall, Monte Blue, Douglas Kennedy. Slick yet unexciting Western with formula Warner Bros. plotline and type casting; minor Flynn vehicle.

Montana Belle (1952) C-81m. ** D: Allan Dwan. Jane Russell, George Brent, Scott Brady, Andy Devine, Forrest Tucker. Mildly interesting Western with Russell as Belle Starr, involved with fellow-outlaws, the Dalton brothers.

Montana Mike SEE: **Heaven Only Knows.**

Montana Territory (1952) C-64m. ** D: Ray Nazarro. Lon McCallister, Wanda Hendrix, Preston Foster, Jack Elam, Clayton Moore. McCallister is deputized cowboy who's out to bring in the outlaws.

Monte Carlo (1930) 90m. **½ D: Ernst Lubitsch. Jeanette MacDonald, ZaSu Pitts, Jack Buchanan, Lionel Belmore. Lavish early musical of penniless countess MacDonald who's romanced by royal Buchanan, incognito. "Beyond the Blue Horizon" is major song.

Monte Carlo Story, The (1957) C-99m. ** D: Samuel Taylor. Marlene

Dietrich, Vittorio DeSica, Arthur O'Connell, Natalie Trundy. Lackluster Dietrich vehicle, as Marlene and DeSica each try to out-con the other.

Monty's Double SEE: **I Was Monty's Double.**

Moon and Sixpence, The (1942) 89m. *** D: Albert Lewin. George Sanders, Herbert Marshall, Doris Dudley, Eric Blore, Elena Verdugo, Florence Bates, Albert Basserman, Heather Thatcher. Faithful film of Maugham's tale of man who decides to fulfill lifelong ambition to paint, moving to Tahitian island. Superb acting by Sanders in lead, Marshall as the author.

Moon is Blue, The (1953) 95m. **½ D: Otto Preminger. William Holden, David Niven, Maggie McNamara, Tom Tully. Once-saucy sex comedy now seems tame, too much a filmed stage play, with most innuendoes lacking punch.

Moon is Down, The (1943) 90m. *** D: Irving Pichel. Cedric Hardwicke, Henry Travers, Lee J. Cobb, Dorris Bowden, Margaret Wycherly, Peter Van Eyck, William Post, Jr. Fine drama from Steinbeck novel of Norway's invasion by Nazis, tracing local effect and reactions.

Moon Over Burma (1940) 76m. ** D: Louis King. Dorothy Lamour, Preston Foster, Robert Preston, Doris Nolan, Albert Basserman, Frederick Worlock. Island setting tries to cover up for same old triangle with Foster and Preston fighting over Lamour.

Moon Over Miami (1941) C-91m. **½ D: Walter Lang. Don Ameche, Betty Grable, Robert Cummings, Charlotte Greenwood, Jack Haley, Carole Landis. Sisters Grable and Landis go fortune-hunting in Miami, finding Ameche and Cummings. Good title song. Remake of THREE BLIND MICE, remade as THREE LITTLE GIRLS IN BLUE.

Moonfleet (1955) C-89m. **½ D: Fritz Lang. Stewart Granger, John Whitely, George Sanders, Viveca Lindfors, Joan Greenwood, Ian Wolfe. Tepid 18th-century story of Britisher Granger becoming a buccaneer.

Moonlight and Cactus (1944) 60m. *½ D: Edward Cline. Andrews Sisters, Elyse Knox, Leo Carrillo, Eddie Quillan, Shemp Howard, Minerva Urecal. Singing trio find themselves out West running a ranch and chasing romance. Lightweight production.

Moonlighter, The (1953) 75m. ** D: Roy Rowland. Barbara Stanwyck, Fred MacMurray, Ward Bond, William Ching, John Dierkes, Jack Elam. Dull Western with its 3-D virtue lost to TV viewers; MacMurray is a rustler and Stanwyck his ex-girlfriend.

Moonraker, The (1958-British) C-82m. *** D: David MacDonald. George Baker, Sylvia Syms, Peter Arne, Marius Goring. Well-mounted costumer set in 1650's England, involving followers of Charles Stuart.

Moonrise (1948) 90m. **½ D: Frank Borzage. Dane Clark, Gail Russell, Ethel Barrymore, Allyn Joslyn, Henry Morgan, Lloyd Bridges, Selena Royle, Rex Ingram. Low-keyed drama of man unwittingly murdering someone, on the run from the law with his devoted girl; good cast helps so-so material.

Moontide (1942) 94m. **½ D: Archie Mayo. Jean Gabin, Ida Lupino, Thomas Mitchell, Claude Rains, Jerome Cowan, Helene Reynolds, Ralph Byrd, Sen Yung, Tully Marshall. Jean Gabin's portrayal of rough seaman who cares for potential suicide (Lupino) saves an otherwise average "realistic" movie.

Moon's Our Home, The (1936) 80m. ** D: William A. Seiter. Margaret Sullavan, Henry Fonda, Charles Butterworth, Beulah Bondi. Bubbly comedy is perhaps too superficial; actress Sullavan and novelist Fonda try to work out a marriage.

More Than a Secretary (1936) 77m. ** D: Alfred E. Green. Jean Arthur, George Brent, Lionel Stander, Ruth Donnelly, Reginald Denny, Dorothea Kent. Arthur's charm gives distinction to routine comedy of secretary in love with handsome boss Brent.

More the Merrier, The (1943) 104m. *** D: George Stevens. Jean Arthur, Joel McCrea, Charles Coburn, Richard Gaines, Bruce Bennett, Ann Savage, Ann Doran, Frank Sully, Grady Sutton. Working-girl Arthur finds herself sharing small apartment in WW2 Washington with McCrea and Coburn (who won an Oscar for this). Later remade as WALK DON'T RUN, but peerless Arthur can't be beat.

Morgan! (1966-British) 97m. ***½ D: Karel Reisz. Vanessa Redgrave, David Warner, Robert Stephens, Irene

Handl. Decidedly offbeat gem. Artist Warner verges on insanity, keyed off by wife Redgrave's divorcing him, and goes on eccentric escapades.

Morgan the Pirate (1961-Italian, dubbed) C-95m. ** D: Andre de Toth. Steve Reeves, Valerie Lagrange, Lydia Alfonsi, Chelo Alonso. Considering cast and Reeves career, fairly lively and interesting swashbuckler based on life of illustrious pirate.

Morning Glory (1933) 74m. ***½ D: Lowell Sherman. Katharine Hepburn, Douglas Fairbanks, Jr., Adolphe Menjou, C. Aubrey Smith, Mary Duncan. Hepburn won an Oscar as young girl determined to become stage star; sharp adaptation of Zoë Akins play. Remade as STAGE STRUCK.

Morocco (1930) 90m. *** D: Josef von Sternberg. Gary Cooper, Marlene Dietrich, Adolphe Menjou, Francis MacDonald, Eve Southern, Paul Porcasi. Dietrich is alluring cafe performer who gives up wealthy Menjou to follow legionnaire lover Cooper across the desert. Marlene sings "Give Me The Man," "What Am I Bid?"

Mortal Storm, The (1940) 100m. ***½ D: Frank Borzage. Margaret Sullavan, James Stewart, Robert Young, Frank Morgan, Robert Stack, Bonita Granville, Irene Rich, Maria Ouspenskaya. Nazi takeover in Germany splits family, ruins life of father, professor Morgan; Stewart tries to leave country with professor's daughter (Sullavan). Sincere filming of Phyllis Bottome's novel is beautifully acted, with one of Morgan's finest performances.

Moss Rose (1947) 82m. **½ D: Gregory Ratoff. Peggy Cummins, Victor Mature, Ethel Barrymore, Vincent Price, Margo Woode. OK period-piece of ambitious chorus girl who blackmails her way into high society; scheme nearly backfires on her.

Most Dangerous Man Alive (1961) 82m. ** D: Allan Dwan. Ron Randell, Debra Paget, Elaine Stewart, Anthony Caruso, Gregg Palmer. Inventive premise adequately handled; escaped convict involved in chemical explosion is transformed into "iron man" and seeks revenge on enemies.

Most Dangerous Sin, The SEE: Crime and Punishment (1958).

Most Wanted Man SEE: Most Wanted Man in the World, The

Most Wanted Man in the World, The (1953-French, dubbed) 85m. ** D: Henri Verneuil. Fernandel, Zsa Zsa Gabor, Nicole Maurey, Alfred Adam. Fernandel vehicle is heavy-handed buffoonery, with bucolic comic mistaken for arch-criminal. Retitled: MOST WANTED MAN, THE.

Most Wonderful Moment, The (1959-Italian, dubbed) 94m. ** D: Luciano Emmer. Marcello Mastroianni, Giovanna Ralli, Marisa Merlini, Ernesto Calindri. Lackluster account of doctor Mastroianni and nurse Ralli, involved in new method of childbirth.

Mother Carey's Chickens (1938) 82m. ** D: Rowland V. Lee. Fay Bainter, Anne Shirley, Ruby Keeler, James Ellison, Walter Brennan, Frank Albertson, Virginia Weidler, Ralph Morgan. Bainter is mother, Keeler and Shirley her "chickens" in ordinary tear-jerker romance based on Kate Douglas Wiggin's novel.

Mother Didn't Tell Me (1950) 88m. **½ D: Claude Binyon. Dorothy McGuire, William Lundigan, June Havoc, Gary Merrill, Jessie Royce Landis. McGuire brightens this lightweight comedy. Naive young woman marries a doctor, not contemplating demands of being a professional man's wife.

Mother is a Freshman (1949) C-81m. **½ D: Lloyd Bacon. Loretta Young, Van Johnson, Rudy Vallee, Barbara Lawrence, Robert Arthur, Betty Lynn. Refreshing, wholesome confection; Young and daughter Lynn both attend college, vying for Van's affection.

Mother Wore Tights (1947) C-107m. *** D: Walter Lang. Betty Grable, Dan Dailey, Mona Freeman, Connie Marshall, Vanessa Brown, Veda Ann Borg. One of Grable's most popular films. About a vaudeville couple, with colorful production, costumes, and nostalgic songs, plus specialty act by Señor Wences.

Mothra (1962-Japanese, dubbed) C-100m. ** D: Inoshiro Honda, Lee Kresel. Franky Sakai, Hiroshi Koizumi, Kyoko Kagawa, Emi Itoh, Yumi Itoh, Jelly Itoh, Ken Uehara. Satisfactory Japanese science-fiction of flying monster who disrupts Tokyo, submitting only to the control of twin girls with supernatural powers.

Motorcycle Gang (1957) 78m. *½ D: Edward L. Cahn. Anne Neyland,

John Ashley, Carl Switzer, Raymond Hatton, Edmund Cobb. Cheap production dealing with crackdown on rampaging cycle gang.

Moulin Rouge (1952) C-123m. ***1/2 D: John Huston. Jose Ferrer, Zsa Zsa Gabor, Suzanne Flon, Eric Pohlmann, Colette Marchand, Christopher Lee, Michael Balfour. Picturesque story of 1900's Parisian artist Toulouse-Lautrec, whose stunted growth affects his work and relationships. Masterfully acted by Ferrer, with zesty cast, memorable theme song.

Mountain, The (1956) C-105m. **1/2 D: Edward Dymtryk. Spencer Tracy, Robert Wagner, Claire Trevor, William Demarest, Richard Arlen, E. G. Marshall. Turgid tale of brothers Tracy and Wagner climbing peak to reach wreckage, for different reasons.

Mountain Road, The (1960) 102m. *** D: Daniel Mann. James Stewart, Lisa Lu, Glenn Corbett, Henry Morgan, Frank Silvera, James Best. Well-paced WW2 actioner, with Stewart staunch as squadron leader.

Mourning Becomes Electra (1947) 173m. *** D: Dudley Nichols. Rosalind Russell, Michael Redgrave, Raymond Massey, Katina Paxinou, Nancy Coleman, Leo Genn, Kirk Douglas. Eugene O'Neill's play, an adaptation of classic Greek tragedy; children drive mother insane to avenge her murder of their father. Epic drama is long on talk.

Mouse on the Moon, The (1963-British) C-82m. ***1/2 D: Richard Lester. Margaret Rutherford, Bernard Cribbins, Ron Moody, Terry-Thomas, Michael Crawford. Hilarious sequel to THE MOUSE THAT ROARED, about Duchy of Grand Fenwick. Tiny country enters space race, with little help from its befuddled Grand Duchess, Margaret Rutherford.

Mouse That Roared, The (1959-British) C-83m. ***1/2 D: Jack Arnold. Peter Sellers, Jean Seberg, David Kossoff, William Hartnell, Monty Landis, Leo McKern. Hilarious satire about the Duchy of Grand Fenwick declaring war on the U. S. Sellers stars in three roles, equally amusing. Gag before opening titles is a masterpiece.

Mouthpiece, The (1932) 90m. **1/2 D: James Flood, Elliott Nugent. Warren William, Sidney Fox, Mae Madison, Aline MacMahon. Diverting pseudo-biography of noted lawyer William Fallon (William), renowned for exaggeration in order to prove a point. Look for young, blonde Paulette Goddard in a bit part.

Move Over, Darling (1963) C-103m. **1/2 D: Michael Gordon. Doris Day, James Garner, Polly Bergen, Thelma Ritter, Fred Clark, Chuck Connors. Day, Garner, and Bergen redo the Irene Dunne, Cary Grant, and Gail Patrick roles from MY FAVORITE WIFE in this amusing film. Edgar Buchanan stands out as a judge confused by the wife-brought-back-to-life situation.

Mudlark, The (1950) 99m. **1/2 D: Jean Negulesco. Irene Dunne, Alec Guinness, Finlay Currie, Anthony Steele, Andrew Ray, Beatrice Campbell, Wilfrid Hyde-White. Offbeat drama of Queen Victoria (Dunne), a recluse since her husband's death, coming back to reality after meeting a waif who stole into her castle. Dunne does quite well as Queen, with Guinness a joy as Disraeli.

Mug Town (1943) 60m. D: Ray Taylor. Billy Halop, Huntz Hall, Bernard Punsley, Gabriel Dell, Tommy Kelly, Grace McDonald, Edward Norris. SEE: Bowery Boys series.

Mummy, The (1932) 72m. ***1/2 D: Karl Freund. Boris Karloff, Zita Johann, David Manners, Bramwell Fletcher, Noble Johnson. Horror classic. Egyptian mummy, revived after thousands of years, believes Johann is reincarnation of ancient mate. Remarkable makeup and atmosphere make it chills ahead of many sequels.

Mummy's Curse, The (1944) 62m. ** D: Leslie Goodwins. Lon Chaney, Martin Kosleck, Virginia Christine, Kurt Katch, Addison Richards, Kay Harding. Double trouble when two mummies come alive in Egypt and turn on the local citizenry.

Mummy's Ghost, The (1944) 60m. ** D: Reginald Le Borg. John Carradine, Lon Chaney, Robert Lowery, Ramsay Ames, George Zucco. Above-average cast can't do much with far-fetched tale of mummy searching America for ancient heart-throb, reborn as American girl.

Mummy's Hand, The (1940) 67m. ** D: Christy Cabanne. Dick Foran,

**Peggy Moran, Wallace Ford, Eduardo Ciannelli, George Zucco, Cecil Kellaway. Absurd story of ancient mummy coming to life to protect lover's tomb from scientist's interference. Cowboy star Foran is no match for Karloff, who created the role.

Mummy's Tomb, The (1942) 61m. *½ D: Harold Young. Lon Chaney, Dick Foran, John Hubbard, Elyse Knox, George Zucco, Wallace Ford, Turhan Bey, Mary Gordon. One of the weakest in Mummy series. Colorful cast struggles through B-plot of Egyptian finding remains of mummy and reviving it.

Munster, Go Home (1966) C-96m. **½ D: Earl Bellamy. Fred Gwynne, Yvonne de Carlo, Terry-Thomas, Hermione Gingold, John Carradine, Debby Watson, Butch Patrick. Based on TV series. Monster family goes to England to claim a castle they've inherited; juvenile production.

Murder at 45 R.P.M. (1960-French, dubbed) 105m. **½ D: Etienne Perier. Danielle Darrieux, Michel Auclair, Jean Servais, Henri Guisol. Darrieux is an engaging songstress, whose husband seemingly returns from the grave to haunt her and lover (Auclair) ; neat plot twists, but slow-moving.

Murder at the Vanities (1934) 70m. **½ D: Mitchell Leisen. Jack Oakie, Kitty Carlisle, Gertrude Michael, Donald Meek, Gail Patrick, Toby Wing, Victor McLaglen, Jessie Ralph, Ann Sheridan, Dorothy Stickney. Offbeat murder mystery set backstage at Broadway show; Oakie's the detective. Songs include "Cocktails For Two." Duke Ellington's orchestra is featured.

Murder By Contract (1958) 81m. ** D: Irving Lerner. Vince Edwards, Philip Pine, Herschel Bernardi, Caprice Toriel. Agreeable yarn of professional killer Edwards who muffs his job and is now gangland target.

Murder, He Says (1945) 91m. *** D: George Marshall. Fred MacMurray, Helen Walker, Marjorie Main, Jean Heather, Porter Hall, Peter Whitney, Barbara Pepper, Mabel Paige. Zany slapstick of insurance salesman MacMurray encountering Main's family of hayseed murderers. Too strong at times, but generally funny.

Murder in the Air (1940) 55m. *½ D: Lewis Seiler. Ronald Reagan, John Litel, Lya Lys, James Stephenson, Eddie Foy, Jr., Robert Warwick. Juvenile secret agent yarn, with Reagan assigned to stop enemy agents from stealing secret plans.

Murder in the Music Hall (1946) 84m. ** D: John English. Vera Hruba Ralston, William Marshall, Helen Walker, Nancy Kelly, William Gargan, Ann Rutherford, Julie Bishop. Not-bad whodunit, a backstage murder with above-average cast for low-grade Republic Pictures.

Murder, Inc. (1960) 103m. *** D: Burt Balaban, Stuart Rosenberg. Stuart Whitman, May Britt, Henry Morgan, Peter Falk, David J. Stewart, Simon Oakland. Blasting gun action, taut direction, and fierce performances make this gangster saga well above par.

Murder is My Beat (1955) 77m. ** D: Edgar G. Ulmer. Paul Langton, Barbara Payton, Robert Shayne, Selena Royle. Standard B-treatment of alleged killer Payton discovering actual criminal.

Murder is My Business (1946) 64m. ** D: Sam Newfield. Hugh Beaumont, Cheryl Walker, Lyle Talbot, George Meeker, Pierre Watkin. Programmer Mike Shayne caper, with Beaumont a tame shamus on prowl for killer.

Murder Man, The (1935) 70m. **½ D: Tim Whelan. Spencer Tracy, Virginia Bruce, Lionel Atwill, Harvey Stephens, Robert Barrat, James Stewart. Reporter Tracy convinces cops someone else is guilty of murder he actually committed. Good melodrama is also Stewart's first film.

Murder My Sweet (1944) 95m. **½ D: Edward Dmytryk. Dick Powell, Claire Trevor, Anne Shirley, Otto Kruger, Mike Mazurki. Based on Raymond Chandler's book FAREWELL MY LOVELY, this remake of THE FALCON TAKES OVER gave Powell new image as hardboiled detective Philip Marlowe, involved in homicide and blackmail.

Murder on Approval (1956-British) 90m. ** D: Bernard Knowles. Tom Conway, Delphi Lawrence, Brian Worth, Michael Balfour. Veteran detective-player Conway can't save humdrum treasure-hunt caper. Retitled: BARBADOS QUEST.

Murder on Monday SEE: **Home at Seven**

Murder Over New York (1940) 65m.

D: Harry Lachman. Sidney Toler, Marjorie Weaver, Robert Lowery, Ricardo Cortez, Donald MacBride, Melville Cooper, Sen Yung. SEE: Charlie Chan series.

Murder Will Out (1952-British) 83m. *** D: John Gilling. Valerie Hobson, Edward Underdown, James Robertson Justice, Henry Kendall. Underplayed suspenser with creditable red herrings to engage the viewer. Retitled: THE VOICE OF MERRILL.

Murders in the Rue Morgue (1932) 75m. ** D: Robert Florey. Bela Lugosi, Sidney Fox, Leon Ames, Brandon Hurst, Arlene Francis. Very mild horror film based on Poe story, with Lugosi as fiendish Dr. Mirakle, with eyes on lovely Fox as the bride of his pet ape.

Muriel (1963-French, dubbed) C-115m. **½ D: Alain Resnais. Delphine Seyrig, Jean-Pierre Kerien, Nita Klein, Claude Sainval. Confusing/depressing/brilliant film (take your choice). Not for all tastes, this French film of people who lead empty lives isn't an evening of fun. Cinema students may find interest in Resnais' direction.

Muscle Beach Party (1964) C-94m. ** D: William Asher. Frankie Avalon, Annette Funicello, Morey Amsterdam, Buddy Hackett, Luciana Paluzzi. Here they are again, dancing on the shores of sunny California. Hackett and Amsterdam try to liven it up.

Music for Millions (1944) 120m. **½ D: Henry Koster. Margaret O'Brien, Jimmy Durante, June Allyson, Marsha Hunt, Hugh Herbert, Jose Iturbi, Connie Gilchrist, Harry Davenport. Teary tale of sisters joining the great Iturbi's orchestra is overly long; Durante steals film with "Umbriago."

Music in My Heart (1940) 70m. ** D: Joseph Stanley. Tony Martin, Rita Hayworth, Edith Fellows, Alan Mowbray, Eric Blore, George Tobias. Routine musical of Continental Martin cast in show where he meets lovely Hayworth. One good song, "It's a Blue World."

Music is Magic (1935) 65m. ** D: George Marshall. Alice Faye, Ray Walker, Bebe Daniels, Frank Mitchell, Jack Durant. Limp musical of fading star Daniels and rising Faye, with no great songs and not much else either.

Music Man, The (1962) C-151m. ***½ D: Morton DaCosta. Robert Preston, Shirley Jones, Buddy Hackett, Hermione Gingold, Paul Ford, Pert Kelton. Exuberant musical with Preston dynamic as Professor Harold Hill, the traveling music man stranded in turn-of-the-century River City. Jones is Marian the librarian, Gingold the mayor's wife. Score includes "76 Trombones," "Till There Was You."

Musketeers of the Sea (1960-Italian, dubbed) C-116m. ** D: Massimo Patrizi. Robert Alda, Pier Angeli, Aldo Ray. Anonymous sea yarn, standard in all departments, involving search for gold on Maracaibo.

Mutineers, The (1949) 60m. *½ D: Jean Yarbrough. Jon Hall, Adele Jergens, George Reeves, Noel Cravat. Hastily-thrown-together flick of Hall and mates combating rebellion aboard ship. Retitled: PIRATE SHIP.

Mutiny (1952) 77m. *½ D: Edward Dmytryk. Mark Stevens, Angela Lansbury, Patric Knowles, Gene Evans. Sloppy flick of Stevens et al trying to capture gold to help cause against British during War of 1812.

Mutiny on the Bounty (1935) 132m. **** D: Frank Lloyd. Charles Laughton, Clark Gable, Franchot Tone, Herbert Mundin, Eddie Quillan, Dudley Digges, Donald Crisp, Movita. Vivid Nordhoff-Hall account of mutiny against tyrannical Captain Bligh (Laughton) on worldwide sea voyage, with all the horrors of 18th-century British sea life portrayed. Won Oscar as Best Picture; knots ahead of recent remake.

Mutiny on the Bounty (1962) C-179m. **½ D: Lewis Milestone. Marlon Brando, Trevor Howard, Richard Harris, Hugh Griffith, Richard Haydn, Tim Seely, Percy Herbert, Tarita. Lavish remake of the 1935 classic can't come near it, although it's visually beautiful; Howard is good as Captain Bligh, but Brando is all wrong as Fletcher Christian. Where are you, Clark Gable?

My Bill (1938) 64m. **½ D: John Farrow. Kay Francis, Bonita Granville, Anita Louise, Bobby Jordan, Dickie Moore. Francis is poverty-stricken widow with four children, involved in scandal; OK soaper.

My Blue Heaven (1950) C-96m. **½
D: Henry Koster. Betty Grable, Dan Dailey, David Wayne, Jane Wyatt, Mitzi Gaynor, Una Merkel. Pleasing musicomedy with Grable and Dailey as radio stars who try to adopt a child.

My Brother Talks to Horses (1946) 93m. ** D: Fred Zinnemann. "Butch" Jenkins, Peter Lawford, Beverly Tyler, Edward Arnold, Charlie Ruggles, Spring Byington. Gimmick comedy that's fun at the start but drags to slow finish.

My Brother's Keeper (1949) 96m. ** D: Alfred Roome. Jack Warner, Jane Hylton, George Cole, Bill Owen, David Tomlinson. Hunt-the-escaped-convicts film has gimmick of the two escaped prisoners being handcuffed together.

My Cousin Rachel (1952) 98m. *** D: Henry Koster. Olivia de Havilland, Richard Burton, Audrey Dalton, John Sutton, Ronald Squire. Successful filmization of Daphne du Maurier mystery, with Burton trying to discover if De Havilland is guilty or innocent of murder and intrigue.

My Darling Clementine (1946) 97m. ***½ D: John Ford. Henry Fonda, Linda Darnell, Victor Mature, Walter Brennan, Tim Holt, Ward Bond, Alan Mowbray, John Ireland. Sturdy Western about Wyatt Earp (Fonda) and Doc Holliday (Mature), with fine direction; one of Mature's best roles.

My Dear Secretary (1948) 94m. **½ D: Charles Martin. Laraine Day, Kirk Douglas, Keenan Wynn, Helen Walker, Rudy Vallee, Florence Bates, Alan Mowbray. Bright, trivial comedy of writer Douglas and best-seller authoress Day; Wynn steals the show. Douglas is a bit too earnest at times.

My Dream is Yours (1949) C-101m. **½ D: Michael Curtiz. Jack Carson, Doris Day, Lee Bowman, Adolphe Menjou, Eve Arden. Carson makes Doris a radio star in standard musicomedy; highlights are Bugs Bunny dream sequence, Edgar Kennedy's role as Day's uncle.

My Favorite Blonde (1942) 78m. *** D: Sidney Lanfield. Bob Hope, Madeleine Carroll, Gale Sondergaard, George Zucco, Victor Varconi. Bob and his trained penguin become sitting ducks when spy Madeleine uses them to help deliver secret orders; very funny Hope vehicle.

My Favorite Brunette (1947) 87m. *** D: Elliott Nugent. Bob Hope, Dorothy Lamour, Peter Lorre, Lon Chaney, John Hoyt. Better-than-usual Hope nonsense with Bob as a photographer mixed up with mobsters; Lorre and Chaney add authenticity.

My Favorite Spy (1942) 86m. ** D: Tay Garnett. Kay Kyser, Ellen Drew, Jane Wyman, Robert Armstrong, William Demarest, Una O'Connor, Helen Westley, George Cleveland, Ish Kabibble. How did we win WW2 with bandleader Kyser as spy? Nonsensical musicomedy tries to explain.

My Favorite Spy (1951) 93m. *** D: Norman Z. McLeod. Bob Hope, Hedy Lamarr, Francis L. Sullivan, John Archer, Iris Adrian, Arnold Moss. Bob resembles murdered spy, finds himself thrust into international intrigue. Fast-moving fun, with glamorous Hedy aiding Bob on all counts.

My Favorite Wife (1940) 88m. *** D: Garson Kanin. Cary Grant, Irene Dunne, Gail Patrick, Randolph Scott, Ann Shoemaker, Scotty Beckett, Donald MacBride. Dunne, supposedly dead, returns to U.S. to find hubby Grant remarried to Patrick, in familiar but witty marital mix-up, remade as MOVE OVER, DARLING.

My Foolish Heart (1949) 98m. *** D: Mark Robson. Dana Andrews, Susan Hayward, Kent Smith, Lois Wheeler, Jessie Royce Landis, Robert Keith, Gigi Perreau. Deftly handled sentimental WW2 romance tale between soldier Andrews and Hayward; Victor Young's lovely theme helps, too.

My Forbidden Past (1951) 81m. **½ D: Robert Stevenson. Robert Mitchum, Ava Gardner, Melvyn Douglas, Janis Carter. Period drama of shady girl Gardner coming into money, but unable to buy affection of doctor Mitchum.

My Friend Flicka (1943) C-89m. *** D: Harold Schuster. Roddy MacDowall, Preston Foster, Rita Johnson, James Bell, Jeff Corey, Diana Hale. Sentimental story of boy who loves rebellious horse, nicely done, with colorful scenery.

My Friend Irma (1949) 103m. ** D: George Marshall. John Lund, Diana Lynn, Don DeFore, Marie Wilson, Dean Martin, Jerry Lewis. Based on radio series, movie concerns Wilson in title role as dumb blonde, encountering wacky Martin and Lewis in their film debut.

My Friend Irma Goes West (1950) 90m. **½ D: Hal Walker. Marie Wilson, Diana Lynn, Dean Martin, Jerry Lewis, Corinne Calvet, John Lund. Daffy Irma (Wilson) and pals join Martin and Lewis on their trek to Hollywood.

My Gal Sal (1942) C-103m. *** D: Irving Cummings. Rita Hayworth, Victor Mature, John Sutton, Carole Landis, James Gleason, Phil Silvers, Mona Maris, Hermes Pan, Walter Catlett. Nostalgic gay 90's musical about songwriter Paul Dresser (Mature) in love with beautiful singer Hayworth. Includes Dresser's songs, such as title tune and other old-time numbers.

My Geisha (1962) C-120m. **½ D: Jack Cardiff. Shirley MacLaine, Yves Montand, Edward G. Robinson, Robert Cummings, Yoko Tani. Occasionally amusing comedy. MacLaine is movie star who tries the hard way to convince husband-director that she's right for his movie. Filmed in Japan.

My Girl Tisa (1948) 95m. **½ D: Elliott Nugent. Lilli Palmer, Sam Wanamaker, Akim Tamiroff, Gale Robbins, Stella Adler. Sincere but uninspiring tale of devoted immigrant girl Palmer working to bring her father to the U. S. Palmer is fine as usual in lead.

My Gun is Quick (1957) 88m. *½ D: George White, Phil Victor. Robert Bray, Whitney Blake, Pamela Duncan, Donald Randolph. Drab Mickey Spillane yarn about detective Mike Hammer tracking down a murderer.

My Life With Caroline (1941) 81m. **½ D: Lewis Milestone. Ronald Colman, Anna Lee, Charles Winninger, Reginald Gardiner, Gilbert Roland. Colman's charm sustains this frothy comedy of man suspecting his wife of having a lover.

My Little Chickadee (1940) 83m. **½ D: Edward Cline. Mae West, W. C. Fields, Joseph Calleia, Dick Foran, Ruth Donnelly, Margaret Hamilton, Donald Meek. Team of West and Fields out West is good, but should have been funnier; W. C.'s saloon scenes are notable.

My Love Came Back (1940) 81m. **½ D: Curtis Bernhardt. Olivia de Havilland, Jeffrey Lynn, Eddie Albert, Jane Wyman, Charles Winninger, Spring Byington, Grant Mitchell. Entertaining little romance of violinist De Havilland looking for husband.

My Lucky Star (1938) 84m. **½ D: Roy Del Ruth. Sonja Henie, Richard Greene, Cesar Romero, Buddy Ebsen, Joan Davis, Arthur Treacher. Henie as attractive co-ed; an excuse for her ice-skating and such songs as "This May Be The Night," "The All-American Swing," "I've Got A Date With A Dream."

My Man and I (1952) 99m. **½ D: William Wellman. Shelley Winters, Ricardo Montalban, Wendell Corey, Claire Trevor. Trials and tribulations of kindly Mexican worker Montalban; good cast helps OK script.

My Man Godfrey (1936) 95m. ***½ D: Gregory La Cava. William Powell, Carole Lombard, Gail Patrick, Alice Brady, Eugene Pallette, Alan Mowbray, Mischa Auer. Delightful romp with Lombard and crazy household hiring Powell as butler. Mischa Auer is impressive as starving artist, sheltered by patroness Brady. Less dated comedy of manners than 1957 remake.

My Man Godfrey (1957) C-92m. **½ D: Henry Koster. June Allyson, David Niven, Martha Hyer, Eva Gabor, Jeff Donnell. Shallow compared to original, but on its own a harmless comedy of rich gal Allyson finding life's truths from butler Niven.

My Name is Ivan (1963-Russian, dubbed) 94m. *** D: Andrei Tarkovsky. Kolya Burlaiev, Valentin Zubkov, Ye Zharikov. Taut account of Russian youth sent as spy into Nazi territory. Retitled: THE YOUNGEST SPY.

My Name is Julia Ross (1945) 65m. ***½ D: Joseph H. Lewis. Nina Foch, Dame May Whitty, George Macready, Roland Varno, Anita Bolster, Doris Lloyd. Little gem of unsuspecting girl given new identity by madman Macready. First-rate thriller.

My Outlaw Brother (1951) 82m. ** D: Elliott Nugent. Mickey Rooney, Wanda Hendrix, Robert Preston, Robert Stack. Dude Rooney discovers brother is outlaw, joins with Texas Rangers to fight crime.

My Own True Love (1948) 84m. ** D: Compton Bennett. Melvyn Douglas, Phyllis Calvert, Wanda Hendrix, Philip Friend, Binnie Barnes. Calvert is placed in the awkward position of choosing between two suitors, a father and son; drama lacks ring of truth.

My Pal Gus (1952) 83m. **½ D: Robert Parrish. Richard Widmark, Joanne Dru, Audrey Totter, George Winslow, Regis Toomey. Wholesome film of Widmark coming to realize importance of son Winslow, finding romance with teacher Dru.

My Reputation (1946) 94m. *** D: Curtis Bernhardt. Barbara Stanwyck, George Brent, Warner Anderson, Lucile Watson, John Ridgely, Eve Arden. Well-mounted Warner Bros. soaper; widow Stanwyck is center of scandal when she dates Brent soon after her husband's death.

My Seven Little Sins (1954-French, dubbed) C-98m. ** D: Jean Boyer. Maurice Chevalier, Collette Ripert, Paolo Stoppa, Delia Scala. Pleasant, inconsequential musicomedy, with Chevalier an old roué "adopting" group of Riviera chorines. Retitled: I HAVE SEVEN DAUGHTERS.

My Sister Eileen (1942) 96m. **½ D: Alexander Hall. Rosalind Russell, Brian Aherne, Janet Blair, George Tobias, Allyn Joslyn, Elizabeth Patterson, June Havoc. Amusing tale of two Ohio girls trying to survive in Greenwich Village apartment; strained at times. Belongs mainly to Russell as older sister of knockout Blair.

My Sister Eileen (1955) C-108m. ***½ D: Richard Quine. Betty Garrett, Janet Leigh, Jack Lemmon, Kurt Kasznar, Dick York, Horace MacMahon, Bob Fosse, Tommy Rall. Delightful, unpretentious musical version of 1942 comedy of Ohio girls seeking success while living in nutty Greenwich Village apartment. Lemmon even sings in this one.

My Six Convicts (1952) 104m. *** D: Hugo Fregonese. Millard Mitchell, Gilbert Roland, John Beal, Marshall Thompson, Regis Toomey. Unusual comedy of prison life centering on title group who manage to make jail routine tolerable, egged on by prison psychiatrist.

My Six Loves (1963) C-101m. **½ D: Gower Champion. Debbie Reynolds, Cliff Robertson, David Janssen, Eileen Heckart, Hans Conried, Alice Pearce, Jim Backus. Syrupy fluff of theater star Reynolds "adopting" six waifs; courted by clergyman Robertson among others.

My Son John (1952) 122m. **½ D: Leo McCarey. Helen Hayes, Robert Walker, Van Heflin, Dean Jagger, Frank McHugh. Turgid anti-Communist melodrama, with Walker a Red party member. Despite fine cast, a misfire; Walker's last film.

My Son, My Son (1940) 115m. *** D: Charles Vidor. Madeleine Carroll, Brian Aherne, Louis Hayward, Laraine Day, Henry Hull, Josephine Hutchinson, Sophie Stewart. Fine cast in bristling drama of no-account son who takes advantage of soft-hearted father but comes through in the end.

My Son, The Hero (1963-Italian, dubbed) C-111m. ** D: Duccio Tessari. Pedro Armendariz, Jacqueline Sassard, Antonella Lualdi, Tanya Lopert. Italian spectacle with good twist. Instead of typical, ludicrous dialogue, U. S. firm dubbed Jewish accents onto the track.

My Uncle (1958-French, dubbed) C-110m. **** D: Jacques Tati. Jacques Tati, Jean-Pierre Zola, Adrienne Servantie, Alain Becourt. Tati revives silent comedy in this French gem reminiscent of Keaton's pantomime films of yore. Refreshing change of pace, wonderful fun.

My Wife's Best Friend (1952) 87m. ** D: Richard Sale. Anne Baxter, Macdonald Carey, Cecil Kellaway, Leif Erickson, Frances Bavier. Unexceptional film of married couple Baxter-Carey confessing their past indiscretions when their plane seems about to crash.

My Wild Irish Rose (1947) C-101m. ** D: David Butler. Dennis Morgan, Andrea King, Arlene Dahl, Alan Hale, George Tobias. Irish songs galore support limp biography of songwriter Chauncey Olcott.

Mysterians, The (1959-Japanese, dubbed) C-85m. **½ D: Inoshiro Honda. Kenji Sahara, Yumi Shirakawa, Momoko Kochi, Akihiko Hirata. When their planet is destroyed, highly intellectual aliens try to invade earth to carry on their civilization; above average.

Mysterious Doctor, The (1943) 57m. **½ D: Ben Stoloff. John Loder, Eleanor Parker, Bruce Lester, Lester Matthews, Forrester Harvey. Average story of a doctor who murders people to keep secret of his being Nazi. Moor locations interesting; cast adequate.

Mysterious Dr. Satan SEE: **Doctor Satan's Robot.**

Mysterious Intruder, The (1946) 61m. D: William Castle. Richard Dix, Nina Vale, Regis Toomey, Pamela Blake, Charles Lane, Helen Mowery, Mike Mazurki. SEE: **The Whistler** series.

Mysterious Island (1961-British) C-101m. *** D: Cy Endfield. Michael Craig, Joan Greenwood, Michael Callan, Gary Merrill, Herbert Lom. Exciting, solid story, based freely on several Verne stories. Confederate prison escapees, blown off course, find uncharted island with gigantic animals. Great special effects.

Mysterious Magician, The (1965-German, dubbed) 95m. **½ D: Alfred Vohrer. Joachim Fuchsberger, Eddi Arent, Sophie Hardy, Karl John, Heinz Drache. Mysterious murder-wave in London causes Scotland Yard to suspect that the "Wizard," arch-fiend, is still alive; enjoyable suspenser from Edgar Wallace story.

Mysterious Mr. Moto (1938) 62m. D: Norman Foster. Peter Lorre, Henry Wilcoxon, Mary Maguire, Erik Rhodes, Harold Huber, Leon Ames, Forrester Harvey. SEE: **Mr. Moto** series.

Mystery of Edwin Drood, The (1935) 86m. *** D: Stuart Walker. Claude Rains, Douglass Montgomery, Heather Angel, David Manners, E. E. Clive, Valerie Hobson. Seemingly respectable Rains is responsible for series of horrible murders. Fine thriller adapted from Dickens' unfinished novel.

Mystery of Marie Roget, The (1942) 91m. **½ D: Phil Rosen. Maria Montez, Maria Ouspenskaya, John Litel, Patric Knowles, Charles Middleton. Poe story provides basis for fairly good murder mystery. Detective tries to unravel mystery of actress' strange disappearance.

Mystery of the Black Jungle (1955) 72m. *½ D: Ralph Murphy. Lex Barker, Jane Maxwell, Luigi Tosi, Paul Muller. Embarrassing lowjinks set in India involving idol-worshiping natives. Retitled: THE BLACK DEVILS OF DALI.

Mystery Street (1950) 93m. **½ D: John Sturges. Ricardo Montalban, Sally Forrest, Bruce Bennett, Elsa Lanchester, Marshall Thompson, Jan Sterling. Trim murder caper set in Boston, nicely done, with fine cast.

Mystery Submarine (1950) 78m. **½ D: Douglas Sirk. Macdonald Carey, Marta Toren, Carl Esmond, Ludwig Donath. Involved plot of military officer Carey being instrumental in destruction of Nazi sub in South America.

Mystery Submarine (1963-British) 90m. *½ D: C. M. Pennington-Richards. Edward Judd, James Robertson Justice, Laurence Payne, Arthur O'Sullivan, Albert Lieven. A tame WW2 espionage tale of German submarine manned by British crew, only to be recaptured by English fleet. Alternate title: DECOY.

Nabonga (1944) 75m. *½ D: Sam Newfield. Buster Crabbe, Julie London, Fifi D'Orsay, Barton MacLane, Bryant Washburn. Incredible cheapie of plane-crash survivor (London) making friends with local gorilla. Good for laughs, anyway. Retitled: GORILLA.

Naked Alibi (1954) 86m. **½ D: Jerry Hopper. Sterling Hayden, Gloria Grahame, Gene Barry, Marcia Henderson, Casey Adams. Hayden is persistent ex-cop hunting down actual killer to prove his innocence.

Naked and the Dead, The (1958) C-131m. *** D: Raoul Walsh. Aldo Ray, Cliff Robertson, Raymond Massey, Lili St. Cyr, Barbara Nichols. Norman Mailer's intensive novel of WW2 soldiers in action gets a superficial but rugged filmization.

Naked Brigade, The (1965) 99m. ** D: Maury Dexter. Shirley Eaton, Ken Scott, Mary Chronopoulou, John Holland, Sonia Zoidou. Mild WW2 actioner of Eaton hiding from Nazi invasion of Crete.

Naked City, The (1948) 96m. ***½ D: Jules Dassin. Barry Fitzgerald, Howard Duff, Dorothy Hart, Don Taylor, Ted de Corsia. Realistic police drama shot on location with New York settings overshadowing actual story of young girl brutally murdered, subsequent manhunt.

Naked Dawn, The (1955) 82m. **½ D: Edgar G. Ulmer. Arthur Kennedy, Betta St. John, Roy Engel, Eugene

Iglesias, Charita. Acceptable robbery caper of initial act snowballing into series of crimes.

Naked Earth (1958) 96m. */½ D: Vincent Sherman. Juliette Greco, Richard Todd, John Kitzmiller, Finlay Currie. Misguided soap opera set in 1890's Africa, trying to build up aspiring star Greco.

Naked Edge, The (1961) 99m. **½ D: Michael Anderson. Gary Cooper, Deborah Kerr, Eric Portman, Diane Cilento, Hermione Gingold, Michael Wilding. Uneven suspenser of Kerr thinking husband Cooper is guilty of murder. Cooper's last film, made in London.

Naked Heart, The (1949-Canadian) 96m. ** D: Marc Allegret. Michele Morgan, Kieron Moore, Françoise Rosay, Jack Watling. Little of consequence happens in this sad story based on book MARIA CHAPDELAINE by Louis Hermon.

Naked Hills, The (1956) C-73m. */½ D: Josef Shaftel. David Wayne, Keenan Wynn, James Barton, Marcia Henderson, Jim Backus. Raggedy account of Wayne who has gold fever and spends life searching for ore, ignoring wife and family.

Naked In the Sun (1957) C-79m. ** D: R. John Hugh. James Craig, Lita Milan, Barton MacLane, Tony Hunter. Somewhat sluggish account of Indian tribes involved with slave traders.

Naked Jungle, The (1954) C-95m. *** D: Byron Haskin. Eleanor Parker, Charlton Heston, Abraham Sofaer, William Conrad. High-class South American jungle adventure, with Heston and wife Parker surrounded by their plantation by advancing army of red ants.

Naked Kiss, The (1964) 93m. **½ D: Samuel Fuller. Constance Towers, Anthony Eisley, Virginia Grey, Betty Bronson, Patsy Kelly, Michael Dante. Girl arrested for murder reveals her shady past; moderately interesting account.

Naked Maja, The (1959) C-111m. ** D: Henry Koster. Ava Gardner, Anthony Franciosa, Amedeo Nazzari, Gino Cervi, Massimo Serato, Lea Padovani, Carlo Rizzo. Mishmash involving 18th-century Spanish painter Goya and famed model for title painting.

Naked Paradise (1956) C-68m. Bomb D: Roger Corman. Richard Denning, Beverly Garland, Lisa Montell, Richard Miller, Leslie Bradley. On-location filming in Hawaii can't salvage this balderdash about crooks using cruise boat to rob local plantations. Retitled: THUNDER OVER HAWAII.

Naked Prey, The (1966) C-94m.*** D: Cornel Wilde. Cornel Wilde, Gert Van Den Bergh, Ken Gampu. Harrowing, well-done safari movie. African natives give prisoner Wilde headstart before they close in on him for kill, forcing Wilde to combat them with savage tactics; memorable brutal sequences.

Naked Spur, The (1953) C-91m. **½ D: Anthony Mann. James Stewart, Janet Leigh, Ralph Meeker, Robert Ryan. Diverse group of people weatherbound in the Rockies, setting stage for character study of the quartet.

Naked Street, The (1955) 84m. ** D: Maxwell Shane. Farley Granger, Anthony Quinn, Anne Bancroft, Peter Graves, Jerry Paris, Jeanne Cooper. Capable cast wasted in bland yarn of reporter exposing crime syndicate.

Namu the Killer Whale (1966) C-88m. **½ D: Laslo Benedek. Robert Lansing, John Anderson, Lee Meriwether, Richard Erdman, Robin Mattson. Intriguing tale, based on true story of naturalist Lansing capturing and training a killer whale. Nicely done, good family fare.

Nana (1934) 89m. **½ D: Dorothy Arzner. Anna Sten, Phillips Holmes, Lionel Atwill, Muriel Kirkland, Richard Bennett, Mae Clarke. Initially interesting adaptation of Emile Zola story of luxury-loving woman in tragic love affair runs out of steam towards the middle. Producer Samuel Goldwyn's attempt to make a new Garbo out of exotic Sten.

Nancy Drew and the Hidden Staircase (1939) 60m. */½ D: William Clemens. Bonita Granville, Frankie Thomas, John Litel, Frank Orth, Vera Lewis. Formula happenings as Granville et al aid elderly spinsters being victimized by crooks.

Nancy Drew, Detective (1938) 60m. */½ D: William Clemens. Bonita Granville, John Litel, James Stephenson, Frankie Thomas. Timid entry in girl-detective series, as amateur sleuth tries to help rich woman involved with gangsters.

Nancy Drew—Reporter (1939) 68m. *½ D: William Clemens. Bonita Granville, John Litel, Frankie Thomas. Granville come to rescue of another elderly victim of crooked schemes.

Nancy Drew—Trouble Shooter (1939) 69m. *½ D: William Clemens. Bonita Granville, John Litel, Frankie Thomas, Aldrich Bowker, Renie Riano. Warner Bros. mystery programmer loosely based on famed girls' story heroine, with Granville tracking down crooks.

Nancy Goes to Rio (1950) C-99m. **½ D: Robert Z. Leonard. Ann Sothern, Jane Powell, Barry Sullivan, Carmen Miranda, Louis Calhern, Fortunio Bonanova, Hans Conried. Snappy MGM musical with Powell and mother (Sothern) both actresses in South American resort, competing for juicy stage roles and rich men.

Nancy Steel is Missing (1937) 85m. **½ D: George Marshall. Victor McLaglen, Walter Connolly, Peter Lorre, June Lang, Jane Darwell, John Carradine. Story of ex-con McLaglen passing off Lang as long-ago kidnapped child is pat but smooth-going.

Nanny, The (1965-British) 93m. *** D: Seth Holt. Bette Davis, Wendy Craig, Jill Bennett, James Villiers, Pamela Franklin, William Dix, Maurice Denham. Twisting, scary plot plus fine direction reap results. Suspects of child murder narrowed to governess Davis and disturbed youngster Dix.

Narrow Corner, The (1933) 71m. ** D: Alfred E. Green. Douglas Fairbanks, Jr., Patricia Ellis, Ralph Bellamy, Dudley Digges, Sidney Toler, Willie Fung. Fairbanks is kidnapped by crooks to avoid his talking; he is taken to East Indies where romance and intrigue blossom. OK drama of Somerset Maugham novel. Remade as ISLE OF FURY.

Narrow Margin, The (1952) 70m. **½ D: Richard Fleischer. Charles McGraw, Marie Windsor, Jacqueline White, Queenie Leonard. Effective yarn of jury witness on train, suspect for variety of happenings. One of Windsor's best roles.

Nasty Rabbit, The (1964) 85m. ** D: James Landis. Arch Hall, Jr., Micha Terr, Melissa Morgan, John Akana. Weak spoof with serious overtones involving Russian attempt to set loose a disease-infected rabbit in the U. S. Retitled: SPIES A GO GO.

National Velvet (1944) C-125m. ***½ D: Clarence Brown. Mickey Rooney, Elizabeth Taylor, Donald Crisp, Anne Revere, Angela Lansbury, Reginald Owen, Norma Varden. Excellent family film of determined kids training horse to win famed Grand National race; Revere won Best Supporting Actress Oscar.

Naughty But Nice (1939) 90m. **½ D: Ray Enright. Ann Sheridan, Dick Powell, Gale Page, Helen Broderick, Ronald Reagan, Allen Jenkins, ZaSu Pitts, Jerry Colonna. Breezy Warner Bros. musical with Powell a songwriter-professor with a yen for Broadway.

Naughty Girl SEE: Mam'zelle Pigalle.

Naughty Marietta (1935) 80m. **½ D: W. S. Van Dyke II. Jeanette MacDonald, Nelson Eddy, Frank Morgan, Elsa Lanchester, Douglass Dumbrille, Cecilia Parker. First teaming of Eddy and MacDonald has her a French princess running off to America, falling in love with Indian Scout Eddy. Victor Herbert songs: "Tramp, Tramp, Tramp," and "Ah Sweet Mystery of Life."

Naughty Nineties, The (1945) 76m. ** D: Jean Yarbrough. Bub Abbott, Lou Costello, Alan Curtis, Rita Johnson, Henry Travers, Lois Collier, Joe Sawyer, Joe Kirk. Ordinary Abbott and Costello comedy of riverboat gamblers, sparked by duo's verbal exchanges and slapstick finale.

Navy Blue and Gold (1937) 94m. **½ D: Sam Wood. Robert Young, James Stewart, Tom Brown, Florence Rice, Billie Burke, Lionel Barrymore, Paul Kelly, Samuel S. Hinds. Hackneyed but entertaining saga of three pals (one rich and bored, one young and earnest, one mysterious "with a past") going to Annapolis. Predictable football-game climax is fun.

Navy Blues (1941) 108m. *** D: Lloyd Bacon. Ann Sheridan, Jack Oakie, Martha Raye, Jack Haley, Herbert Anderson, Jack Carson. Brassy musical with fine cast (including young Jackie Gleason), with Raye stealing most of the film.

Navy Comes Through, The (1942) 82m. ** D: A. Edward Sutherland. Pat O'Brien, George Murphy, Jane Wyatt, Jackie Cooper, Carl Esmond, Max Baer, Desi Arnaz. RKO programmer dealing with merchant marines in action during WW2.

Navy Wife (1956) 83m. *½ D: Edward Bernds. Joan Bennett, Gary Merrill, Shirley Yamaguchi, Maurice Manson, Judy Nugent. Trivial tale of Japanese women revolting to obtain equal treatment from their men as they observe American military and their wives.

Neanderthal Man, The (1953) 78m. *½ D: E. A. Dupont. Robert Shayne, Richard Crane, Robert Long, Doris Merrick. Typical horror film from fifties. Scientist Shayne experiments with animals and himself, with new serum. Cast fails to save film.

Nearly a Nasty Accident (1962-British) 86m. ** D: Don Chaffey. Jimmy Edwards, Kenneth Connor, Shirley Eaton, Richard Wattis, Ronnie Stevens, Jon Pertwee, Eric Barker. Strange minor drama of mechanic who innocently puts the touch of disaster on everyone.

'Neath Brooklyn Bridge (1942) 61m. D: Wallace Fox. Leo Gorcey, Huntz Hall, Bobby Jordan, Gabriel Dell, Noah Beery, Jr., Sunshine Sammy Morrison, Jack Mulhall, Dave O'Brien, Ann Gillis. SEE: Bowery Boys series.

Nebraskan, The (1953) C-68m. ** D: Fred F. Sears. Phil Carey, Roberta Haynes, Wallace Ford, Richard Webb, Lee Van Cleef, Jay Silverheels. Tame Western of white man justice preventing Indian uprising.

Neptune's Daughter (1949) C-93m. *** D: Edward Buzzell. Esther Williams, Red Skelton, Keenan Wynn, Betty Garrett, Ricardo Montalban, Mel Blanc. South American romance with Esther a bathing-suit designer, Skelton a no-account mistaken for polo star by Garrett. Bubbly fun, with Award-winning song: "Baby It's Cold Outside."

Nevada (1944) 62m. ** D: Edward Killy. Robert Mitchum, Anne Jeffreys, Guinn "Big Boy" Williams, Nancy Gates, Harry Woods. Standard Zane Grey Western of good-guy Mitchum mopping up gang of outlaws.

Nevadan, The (1950) C-81m. ** D: Gordon Douglas. Randolph Scott, Dorothy Malone, Forrest Tucker, George Macready, Jock Mahoney. Stern Scott is the lawman who tracks down crooks, still finding time to court Malone.

Never a Dull Moment (1950) 89m. **½ D: George Marshall. Irene Dunne, Fred MacMurray, William Demarest, Natalie Wood, Andy Devine, Ann Doran, Gigi Perreau. Middling froth of chic Dunne marrying rancher MacMurray, adjusting to country life and his two daughters.

Never Fear (1950) 82m. ** D: Ida Lupino. Sally Forrest, Keefe Brasselle, Hugh O'Brien, Eve Miller, Larry Dobkin. Low-budget flick; Forrest is gal who overcomes polio and its disastrous effects on her dancing career.

Never Give a Sucker an Even Break (1941) 71m. **½ D: Edward Cline. W. C. Fields, Gloria Jean, Leon Errol, Susan Miller, Franklin Pangborn, Charles Lang, Anne Nagel, Margaret Dumont. The great man with even less plot than usual, with Fields' verbal and sight antics for amusement. Dumont plays "Mrs. Hemoglobin" with her usual finesse.

Never Let Go (1963-British) 90m. **½ D: John Guillermin. Richard Todd, Peter Sellers, Elizabeth Sellars, Carol White, Mervyn Johns. Lukewarm comedy snowballing from theft of salesman's car.

Never Let Me Go (1953) 69m. **½ D: Delmer Daves. Clark Gable, Gene Tierney, Bernard Miles, Kenneth More, Belita. Unconvincing yet smooth account of Gable trying to smuggle ballet dancer wife Tierney out of Russia.

Never Love a Stranger (1958) 91m. **½ D: Robert Stevens. John Drew Barrymore, Lita Milan, Peg Murray, Robert Bray, Steve McQueen. Chronicle of hoodlum's life, more interesting for its cast than story.

Never on Sunday (1960-Greek, dubbed) 91m. ***½ D: Jules Dassin. Melina Mercouri, Jules Dassin, Georges Foundas, Titos Vandis, Mitsos Liguisos, Despo Diamantidou. Charming idyll of intellectual boob coming to Greece, trying to make earthy prostitute Mercouri cultured. Grand entertainment, with memorable title song.

Never Say Die (1939) 80m. **½ D: Elliott Nugent. Martha Raye, Bob Hope, Andy Devine, Gale Sondergaard, Sig Ruman, Alan Mowbray, Monty Woolley. Bob marries Martha at Swiss spa of Bad Gaswasser, thinking he has only two weeks to live. Good cast in lively, trivial romp.

Never Say Goodbye (1946) 97m. **½ D: James V. Kern. Errol Flynn, Eleanor Parker, Lucile Watson, S. Z. Sakall, Hattie McDaniel, Forrest Tucker, Donald Woods. Flynn tries hard in routine comedy of husband rewinning his divorce-bound wife.

Never Say Goodbye (1956) C-96m. **½ D: Jerry Hopper. Rock Hudson, Cornell Borchers, George Sanders, Ray Collins, David Janssen, Shelley Fabares. Spotty tear-jerker of Hudson and Borchers, long separated, discovering one another again and creating fit home for their child.

Never So Few (1959) C-124m. **½ D: John Sturges. Frank Sinatra, Gina Lollobrigida, Peter Lawford, Steve McQueen, Richard Johnson, Paul Henreid, Brian Donlevy, Dean Jones, Charles Bronson. WW2 action and romance tale filled with salty performances which make one forget the clichés and improbabilities.

Never Steal Anything Small (1959) C-94m. **½ D: Charles Lederer. James Cagney, Shirley Jones, Roger Smith, Cara Williams, Nehemiah Persoff, Royal Dano, Horace MacMahon. Oddball musical drama, with Cagney a waterfront union racketeer who eventually changes his ways. From Maxwell Anderson-Rouben Mamoulian play THE DEVIL'S HORNPIPE.

Never to Love SEE: Bill of Divorcement.

Never Trust a Gambler (1951) 79m. *½ D: Ralph Murphy. Dane Clark, Cathy O'Donnell, Tom Drake, Jeff Corey, Myrna Dell. Hackneyed account of man on the run, seeking shelter from ex-wife who has fallen in love with detective seeking him.

Never Wave at a WAC (1952) 87m. **½ D: Norman Z. McLeod. Rosalind Russell, Marie Wilson, Paul Douglas, Arleen Whelan, Hillary Brooke, Louise Beavers, Frieda Inescort. Expanded from a TV play, this farce involves socialite Russell joining the WACs, forced to buckle down to hard work; Wilson as dumb comrade-at-arms is most diverting.

New Adventures of Tarzan (1935) 75m. D: Edward Kull. Herman Brix (Bruce Bennett), Ula Holt, Don Costello, Frank Baker, Louis Sargent, Dale Walsh. SEE: Tarzan series.

New Faces (1954) C-99m. **½ D: Harry Horner. Ronny Graham, Robert Clary, Eartha Kitt, Alice Ghostley, Paul Lynde. Vaudeville hodgepodge of variety numbers, without enhancement of wide screen. Based on Leonard Sillman's popular Broadway revue, which was springboard for much new talent.

New Interns, The (1964) 123m. **½ D: John Rich. Michael Callan, Dean Jones, Telly Savalas, Inger Stevens, George Segal, Greg Morris, Stefanie Powers, Lee Patrick, Barbara Eden. Follow-up to THE INTERNS contains usual hospital soap opera with better than average cast and a nifty party sequence.

New Kind of Love, A (1963) C-110m. **½ D: Melville Shavelson. Paul Newman, Joanne Woodward, Thelma Ritter, Eva Gabor, Maurice Chevalier, George Tobias. Newman as reporter and Woodward as fashion buyer on the loose in Paris fall in love; lacks oomph to make fluff worthwhile.

New Mexico (1951) C-76m. **½ D: Irving Reis. Lew Ayres, Marilyn Maxwell, Robert Hutton, Andy Devine, Raymond Burr. Moderately exciting Western of cavalry vs. Indians.

New Moon (1940) 105m. **½ D: Robert Z. Leonard. Jeanette MacDonald, Nelson Eddy, Mary Boland, George Zucco, H. B. Warner, Grant Mitchell, Stanley Fields. Nelson and Jeanette in old Louisiana, falling in love, singing: "One Kiss," "Softly as In A Morning Sunrise," "Lover Come Back To Me," and "Stout-Hearted Men."

New Orleans After Dark (1958) 69m. *½ D: John Sledge. Stacy Harris, Louis Sirgo, Ellen Moore, Tommy Pelle. Programmer about capture of dope smugglers.

New Orleans Uncensored (1955) 76m. *½ D: William Castle. Arthur Franz, Beverly Garland, Helene Stanton,

Michael Ansara. Weak exposé account of racketeer-busting in Louisiana, with competent cast trying to overcome script.

New York Confidential (1955) 87m. **½ D: Russell Rouse. Broderick Crawford, Richard Conte, Marilyn Maxwell, Anne Bancroft, J. Carrol Naish. Energetic cast perks up formula exposé of racketeer narrative.

New York Town (1941) 94m. **½ D: Charles Vidor. Fred MacMurray, Mary Martin, Robert Preston, Akim Tamiroff, Lynne Overman, Eric Blore, Fuzzy Knight. Bright little comedy of wide-eyed Martin man-hunting in N.Y.C., assisted by photographer MacMurray. Songs include "Love In Bloom."

News Hounds (1947) 68m. D: William Beaudine. Leo Gorcey, Huntz Hall, Bobby Jordan, Christine McIntyre, Gabriel Dell, Billy Benedict. SEE: Bowery Boys series.

Next Time We Love (1936) 87m. *** D: Edward H. Griffith. Margaret Sullavan, James Stewart, Ray Milland, Grant Mitchell, Robert McWade, Anna Demetrio. Trim romantic soaper with Milland in love with actress Sullavan, who is married to struggling reporter Stewart.

Next to No Time (1960-British) C-93m. ** D: Henry Cornelius. Kenneth More, Betsy Drake, Roland Culver, Bessie Love, Harry Green, Patrick Barr. Standard narrative of meek factory worker who conceives a method to automate his plant.

Next Voice You Hear, The (1950) 82m. **½ D: William Wellman. James Whitmore, Nancy Davis, Lillian Bronson, Jeff Corey. Cast manages to keep story of hearing the voice of God on radio somewhat believable. Not as convincing as intended.

Niagara (1953) C-89m. *** D: Henry Hathaway. Marilyn Monroe, Joseph Cotten, Jean Peters, Don Wilson, Richard Allan, Casey Adams. Black murder tale of honeymoon couple staying at Niagara Falls, the wife planning to kill husband.

Nice Girl? (1941) 95m. *** D: William A. Seiter. Deanna Durbin, Franchot Tone, Walter Brennan, Robert Stack, Robert Benchley. Little Deanna grows up in this cute comedy, with Tone and Stack developing amorous ideas about her. Songs: "Love At Last," "Thank You America."

Nice Little Bank That Should be Robbed, A (1958) 87m. ** D: Henry Levin. Tom Ewell, Mickey Rooney, Mickey Shaughnessy, Dina Merrill. Cast is game, but story is pure cornball about goofy crooks using their gains to buy a racehorse.

Nicholas Nickleby (1947-British) 95m. *** D: Alberto Cavalcanti. Derek Bond, Cedric Hardwicke, Mary Merrall, Sally Ann Howes, Bernard Miles. Dandy British film of Dickens' story of young boy's attempts to shield family from cruel uncle; worthwhile viewing.

Nick Carter—Master Detective (1939) 60m. **½ D: Jacques Tourneur. Walter Pidgeon, Rita Johnson, Henry Hull, Donald Meek, Milburn Stone, Addison Richards, Sterling Holloway. Pidgeon is good, tracking down industrial spy in slickly done detective film.

Night After Night (1932) 70m. **½ D: Archie Mayo. Mae West, George Raft, Constance Cummings, Wynne Gibson, Roscoe Karns, Louis Calhern, Alison Skipworth. Raft stars as a saloon-owner in this film, but whenever Mae steps in (it's her film debut) he takes a back seat. Enjoyable period-piece.

Night Ambush (1958-British) 93m. *** D: Michael Powell, Emeric Pressburger. Dirk Bogarde, Marius Goring, David Oxley, Cyril Cusack. Taut WW2 actioner set in Crete, with fine British cast. Retitled: ILL MET BY MOONLIGHT.

Night and Day (1946) C-128m. ** D: Michael Curtiz. Cary Grant, Alexis Smith, Monty Woolley, Ginny Simms, Jane Wyman, Eve Arden, Mary Martin, Victor Francen, Alan Hale, Dorothy Malone. Music only worthy aspect of fabricated biography of songwriter Cole Porter, stiffly played by Grant, who even sings "You're The Top." Martin recreates "My Heart Belongs To Daddy" in film's highlight.

Night and the City (1950) 95m. **½ D: Jules Dassin. Richard Widmark, Gene Tierney, Googie Withers, Hugh Marlowe, Herbert Lom. Slowly paced yet effective account of Widmark on the lam from gangland reprisal; filmed in England.

Night at the Opera, A (1935) 90m. **** D: Sam Wood. Groucho, Chico, Harpo Marx, Kitty Carlisle, Allan Jones, Walter King, Margaret Dumont, Sig Ruman. Captivating lunacy of comedy trio blends perfectly with nice score sung by Jones and Carlisle, as the brothers destroy Ruman's opera with the greatest of ease.

Night Club Scandal (1937) 70m. **½ D: Ralph Murphy. John Barrymore, Lynne Overman, Louise Campbell, Charles Bickford, Evelyn Brent, Elizabeth Patterson, J. Carrol Naish. Enjoyable B-mystery with detectives seeking murderer who tried to frame innocent man. Barrymore is the guilty party.

Night Creatures (1962-British) C-81m. ** D: Peter Graham Scott. Peter Cushing, Yvonne Romain, Patrick Allen, Oliver Reed, Michael Ripper, Martin Benson, David Lodge. British creeper takes patience to watch, will only be enjoyed by horror buffs. Cushing as a sober minister is appropriately dour.

Night Editor (1946) 68m. ** D: Henry Levin. William Gargan, Janis Carter, Jeff Donnell, Coulter Irwin. Minor yarn about Gargan, a law enforcer gone wrong, trying to redeem himself.

Night Fighters, The (1960) 85m. **½ D: Tay Garnett. Robert Mitchum, Anne Heywood, Dan O'Herlihy, Cyril Cusack, Richard Harris, Marianne Benet. Sporadically actionful tale of the Irish Revolution, with Mitchum joining the cause against his will.

Night Freight (1955) 79m. **½ D: Jean Yarbrough. Forrest Tucker, Barbara Britton, Keith Larsen, Thomas Gomez. Straightforward tale about railroad competing with trucking line for survival.

Night Has a Thousand Eyes (1948) 80m. **½ D: John Farrow. Edward G. Robinson, Gail Russell, John Lund, Virginia Bruce, William Demarest. Intriguing story of magician who has uncanny power to predict the future; script is corny at times.

Night Heaven Fell, The (1958-French, dubbed) C-90m. **½ D: Roger Vadim. Brigitte Bardot, Alida Valli, Stephen Boyd, Pepe Nieto. Turgid drama of Bardot dallying with Boyd, who's planning to kill her uncle.

Night Holds Terror, The (1955) 86m. ** D: Andrew L. Stone. Jack Kelly, Hildy Parks, Vince Edwards, John Cassavetes, Jack Kruschen, Joel Marston, Jonathan Hale. Somber little film of family being held captive for ransom.

Night in Casablanca, A (1946) 85m. **½ D: Archie Mayo. Groucho, Harpo, Chico Marx, Lisette Verea, Charles Drake, Lois Collier, Dan Seymour, Sig Ruman. Disappointing Marx Brothers comedy of spies, jewel thieves, assorted others in mysterious Casablanca; lacks the old spirit and lunacy.

Night in New Orleans, A (1942) 75m. *½ D: William Clemens. Preston Foster, Patricia Morison, Albert Dekker, Charles Butterworth, Dooley Wilson, Cecil Kellaway. Thin yarn of Foster and family trying to clear him of murder charge.

Night in Paradise, A (1946) C-84m. **½ D: Arthur Lubin. Merle Oberon, Turhan Bey, Thomas Gomez, Gale Sondergaard, Ray Collins, Ernest Truex. Tongue-in-cheek costumer of Aesop wooing lovely princess Oberon in ancient times; colorful, pleasant at best.

Night Into Morning (1951) 86m. *** D: Fletcher Markle. Ray Milland, John Hodiak, Nancy Davis, Lewis Stone, Jean Hagen, Rosemary DeCamp. Small-town professor loses family in fire, almost ruins own life through drink and self-pity. Realistic settings in modest production, with fine performance by Milland.

Night Is My Future (1947-Swedish, dubbed) 87m. **½ D: Ingmar Bergman. Mai Zetterling, Birger Malmsten, Olof Winnerstrand, Naima Wifstrand, Hilda Borgstrom. Somber, brooding tale of blind young man finding happiness with Zetterling.

Night Key (1937) 67m. *½ D: Lloyd Corrigan. Boris Karloff, Warren Hull, Jean Rogers, Hobart Cavanaugh. Unimaginative yarn about crooks forcing inventor to help them with their crimes.

Night Monster (1942) 73m. ** D: Ford Beebe. Irene Hervey, Don Porter, Nils Asther, Lionel Atwill, Leif

Erickson, Bela Lugosi, Ralph Morgan, Elyse Knox. Incredible plot-line, but amusing histrionics by cast, involving cripple who prowls the land at night on murdering spree.

Night Must Fall (1937) 117m. ***½ D: Richard Thorpe. Robert Montgomery, Rosalind Russell, Dame May Whitty, Alan Marshal, Kathleen Harrison, E. E. Clive, Merle Tottenham. Famous film of Emlyn Williams' suspenseful play of girl (Russell) slowly learning identity of mysterious brutal killer terrorizing the countryside. Montgomery has showy role in sometimes stagy but generally effective film, with outstanding aid from Russell and Whitty.

Night Must Fall (1964-British) 105m. **½ D: Karel Reisz. Albert Finney, Susan Hampshire, Mona Washbourne, Sheila Hancock. Cerebral attempt to match flair of original, this remake is too obvious and theatrical for any credibility.

Night My Number Came Up, The (1955-British) 94m. * D: Leslie Norman. Michael Redgrave, Sheila Sim, Alexander Knox, Denholm Elliott. Well told drama of British air force officer finding his nightmare dreams coming true.

Night Nurse (1931) 72m. **½ D: William Wellman. Barbara Stanwyck, Ben Lyon, Joan Blondell, Clark Gable, Charlotte Merriam, Charles Winninger, Marcia Mae Jones. Devoted nurse Stanwyck interferes with cruel mother's treatment of her children. Worth seeing for early Gable as gangster.

Night of January 16th, The (1941) 79m. *½ D: William Clemens. Robert Preston, Ellen Drew, Nils Asther, Donald Douglas, Rod Cameron, Alice White, Cecil Kellaway. Threadbare Broadway murder mystery play becomes tame movie.

Night of the Generals (1967-British) C-148m. * D: Anatole Litvak. Peter O'Toole, Omar Sharif, Tom Courtenay, Donald Pleasence, Joanna Pettet, Christopher Plummer, John Gregson, Philippe Noiret. Essentially a WW2 whodunit, film has potential but gets lost in murky script, lifeless performances. A dud.

Night of the Grizzly, The (1966) C-102m. **½ D: Joseph Pevney. Clint Walker, Martha Hyer, Keenan Wynn, Nancy Kulp, Ron Ely, Regis Toomey, Jack Elam. Acceptable Western of rancher Walker overcoming all obstacles, even a persistent vicious bear, to Western life.

Night of the Hunter, The (1955) 90m. ** D: Charles Laughton. Robert Mitchum, Shelley Winters, Lillian Gish, Evelyn Varden, Peter Graves, James Gleason. Brooding tale of psychopathic killer Mitchum hunting for cache of stolen money, menacing everyone who stands in his way. Laughton's only fling at directing is quite good.

Night of the Iguana, The (1964) 125m. * D: John Huston. Richard Burton, Deborah Kerr, Ava Gardner, Sue Lyon, Skip Ward, Grayson Hall, Cyril Delevanti. More interesting for its cast than for plodding tale based on Tennessee Williams play; former clergyman Burton, a bus-tour guide in Mexico, is involved with Kerr, Gardner, and Lyon.

Night of the Quarter Moon (1959) 96m. *½ D: Hugo Haas. Julie London, John Drew Barrymore, Nat King Cole, Dean Jones, James Edwards, Anna Kashfi, Agnes Moorehead, Jackie Coogan. Trite handling of miscegenation theme; good cast wasted. Retitled: FLESH AND FLAME.

Night Passage (1957) C-90m. * D: James Neilson. James Stewart, Audie Murphy, Dan Duryea, Brandon de Wilde, Dianne Foster. Soundly handled Western of Stewart working for railroad and brother Murphy belonging to gang planning to rob train payroll; exciting climactic shoot-out.

Night People (1954) C-93m. * D: Nunnally Johnson. Gregory Peck, Broderick Crawford, Anita Bjork, Rita Gam, Walter Abel, Buddy Ebsen. Sensibly told, intertwining plots of Cold War espionage; filmed on location in Berlin.

Night Runner, The (1957) 79m. * D: Abner Biberman. Ray Danton, Colleen Miller, Merry Anders, Eddy Waller. Violent B-film of insane Danton on killing spree, about to gun down his girlfriend.

Night Song (1947) 101m. * D: John Cromwell. Dana Andrews, Merle Oberon, Ethel Barrymore, Hoagy Carmichael, Jacqueline White. Overlong, soapy drama of socialite Oberon falling in love with blind pianist Andrews.

Night the World Exploded, The (1957) 94m. ** D: Fred F. Sears. Kathryn Grant, William Leslie, Tris Coffin, Raymond Greenleaf, Marshall Reed. Lack of visual excitement weakens this sci-fi of scientists fighting to prevent the title catastrophe.

Night to Remember, A (1943) 91m. ***½ D: Richard Wallace. Loretta Young, Brian Aherne, Jeff Donnell, William Wright, Sidney Toler, Gale Sondergaard, Donald MacBride, Blanche Yurka. Sparkling comedy-mystery of whodunit author Aherne and wife Young trying to solve murder.

Night to Remember, A (1958-British) 123m. **** D: Roy Baker. Kenneth More, Ronald Allen, Robert Ayres, Honor Blackman. Meticulously produced documentary-style account of sinking of the passenger liner Titanic. Vivid enacting of Walter Lord's book.

Night Train (1959-Polish, dubbed) 90m. ** D: Jerzy Kawalerowicz. Lucyna Winnicka, Leon Niemczyk, Teresa Szmigielowna, Zbigniew Cybulski. Murky account of young woman on a train, forced to share compartment with a doctor; their lack of communication and presence of killer on train are film's focal points.

Night Unto Night (1949) 92m. **½ D: Don Siegel. Ronald Reagan, Viveca Lindfors, Broderick Crawford, Osa Massen, Craig Stevens, Rosemary De-Camp. Somber romance story of dying scientist and mentally ill widow who find love together.

Night Walker, The (1964) 86m. *** D: William Castle. Barbara Stanwyck, Robert Taylor, Lloyd Bochner, Rochelle Hudson, Judi Meredith. One of better Castle horror films has Stanwyck as wealthy widow discovering cause of recurring dreams about lost husband. Effective psychological thriller with good cast.

Night Without Sleep (1952) 77m. ** D: Roy Baker. Linda Darnell, Gary Merrill, Hildegarde Neff, Hugh Beaumont, Mae Marsh. Pat treatment of man thinking he's committed murder.

Nightfall (1956) 78m. **½ D: Jacques Tourneur. Aldo Ray, Brian Keith, Anne Bancroft, Jocelyn Brando, James Gregory, Frank Albertson. Capable cast in fast-moving account of innocent man wanted by police for killing of friend, chased by actual killers for stolen money he found.

Nightmare (1956) 89m. **½ D: Maxwell Shane. Edward G. Robinson, Kevin McCarthy, Connie Russell, Virginia Christine. McCarthy is musician involved in bizarre murder set in New Orleans; OK mystery, with Robinson sparking proceedings.

Nightmare (1964-British) 82m. *** D: Freddie Francis. David Knight, Moira Redmond, Brenda Bruce, John Welsh. Well-directed thriller with enough subplots to keep any viewer busy. Girl is blackmailed into committing murder by scheming gardener.

Nightmare Alley (1947) 111m. ***½ D: Edmund Goulding. Tyrone Power, Joan Blondell, Coleen Gray, Helen Walker, Mike Mazurki. Morbid story of carnival heel Power entangled with mind-reading Blondell, blackmailing psychiatrist Walker, other assorted weirdos in original, fascinating melodrama.

Nightmare Castle (1966-Italian, dubbed) 90m. ** D: Allan Grunewald. Barbara Steele, Paul Miller, Helga Line, Lawrence Clift. Typically atmospheric European horror film about doctor experimenting in regeneration of human blood through electrical impulses. Good photography.

Nightmare in the Sun (1965) C-80m. *½ D: Marc Lawrence. John Derek, Aldo Ray, Arthur O'Connell, Ursula Andress. Lackluster account of innocent man hunted for crime by people who know he was framed; contrived production.

Nights of Cabiria (1957-Italian, dubbed) 110m. **½ D: Federico Fellini. Giulietta Masina, François Perier, Amedeo Nazzari, Franca Marzi, Dorian Gray. Masina is a joy as waifish prostitute dreaming a rich wonderful life but always finding sorrow. Basis for Broadway musical SWEET CHARITY.

Nights of Rasputin (1960-Italian, dubbed) C-95m. ** D: Pierre Chenal. Edmund Purdom, Gianna Maria Canale, John Drew Barrymore, Jany Clair. Purdom is miscast as Rasputin in this plodding retelling of the conniving quack who gained power in Czarina Alexandra's court.

Nine Girls (1944) 78m. **½ D: Leigh Jason. Ann Harding, Evelyn Keyes, Jinx Falkenburg, Anita Louise, Jeff Donnell, Nina Foch, Marcia Mae Jones, Leslie Jones, Lynn Merrick, Shirley Mills. Atmospheric murder whodunit set in girls sorority; low-budgeter isn't bad, with attractive cast.

Nine Hours to Rama (1963) C-125m. **½ D: Mark Robson. Horst Buchholz, Jose Ferrer, Robert Morley, Diane Baker, Harry Andrews. Ambitious attempt to make a meaningful story of events leading up to assassination of Mahatma Ghandi; bogs down in trite script and predictable happenings.

1984 (1956-British) 91m. *** D: Michael Anderson. Edmond O'Brien, Michael Redgrave, Jan Sterling, David Kossoff, Mervyn Johns, Donald Pleasence. Thought-provoking version of George Orwell's futuristic novel. Lovers O'Brien and Sterling are trapped in all-powerful state, try valiantly to rebel against "Big Brother."

Ninety Degrees in the Shade (1964-Czech) 90m. **½ D: Jiri Weiss. Anne Heywood, James Booth, Donald Wolfit, Ann Todd. Turgid account of Heywood, who works in food store, accused of theft; intertwined with passionate love episodes. Czech-made with British stars.

99 River Street (1953) 83m. *** D: Phil Karlson. John Payne, Evelyn Keyes, Brad Dexter, Peggie Castle, Ian Wolfe, Frank Faylen. Rugged crime caper with Payne caught up in tawdry surroundings, trying to prove himself innocent of murder charge. Unpretentious film really packs a punch.

Ninotchka (1939) 110m. ***½ D: Ernst Lubitsch. Greta Garbo, Melvyn Douglas, Ina Claire, Bela Lugosi, Sig Ruman, Felix Bressart, Richard Carle. Amid much outdated sociological banter, a lighthearted Garbo still shines. Lubitsch's comedy pegged on tale of cold Russian agent Garbo coming to Paris, falling in love with gay-blade Douglas. Supporting cast shows fine comedy flair. Basis for Broadway musical and film SILK STOCKINGS.

Nitwits, The (1935) 81m. *** D: George Stevens. Bert Wheeler, Robert Woolsey, Betty Grable, Evelyn Brent, Hale Hamilton. Above-average nonsense from vaudeville duo of W&W, this time involved with a murder caper and pert young Grable.

No Down Payment (1957) 105m. *** D: Martin Ritt. Joanne Woodward, Jeffrey Hunter, Sheree North, Tony Randall, Cameron Mitchell, Patricia Owens, Barbara Rush, Pat Hingle. Turgid suburban soaper of intertwining problems of several young married couples; very capable cast.

No Escape (1953) 76m. *½ D: Charles Bennett. Lew Ayres, Marjorie Steele, Sonny Tufts, Gertrude Michael. Modest narrative about married couple seeking actual killer to clear themselves of homicide charge. Retitled: CITY ON A HUNT.

No Escape (1956) SEE: I Escaped From the Gestapo.

No Highway in the Sky (1951) 98m. *** D: Henry Koster. James Stewart, Marlene Dietrich, Glynis Johns, Jack Hawkins, Elizabeth Allan, Kenneth More. Excellent drama of Stewart's discovery of metal fatigue causing plane crashes; Dietrich a glamorous passenger on crash-bound plane; Johns a girl in love with Stewart.

No Holds Barred (1952) 65m. D: William Beaudine. Leo Gorcey, Huntz Hall, Marjorie Reynolds, Bernard Gorcey, Tim Ryan, Leonard Penn. SEE: Bowery Boys series.

No Leave, No Love (1946) 119m. ** D: Charles Martin. Van Johnson, Keenan Wynn, Pat Kirkwood, Guy Lombardo, Edward Arnold, Marie Wilson. No script, no laughs; Johnson and Wynn are sailors on the town in this overlong romantic comedy.

No Love for Johnnie (1961-British) 110m. *** D: Ralph Thomas. Peter Finch, Stanley Holloway, Mary Peach, Mervyn Johns, Donald Pleasence, Dennis Price. Civilized study of politician who cares only about winning the election.

No Man Is an Island (1962) C-114m. **½ D: John Monks, Jr., Richard Goldstone. Jeffrey Hunter, Marshall Thompson, Barbara Perez, Ronald Remy, Paul Edwards, Jr., Rolf Bayer, Vicente Liwanag. Spotty production values mar true story of serviceman Hunter trapped on Guam during the three years Japanese controlled area.

No Man of Her Own (1932) 85m. **½ D: Wesley Ruggles. Clark Gable, Carole Lombard, Dorothy Mackaill, Grant Mitchell, Elizabeth Patterson, Lillian Harmer. Usual story of heel reformed by good girl, noteworthy for only co-starring of Gable-Lombard.

No Man of Her Own (1950) 98m. **½ D: Mitchell Leisen. Barbara Stanwyck, John Lund, Jane Cowl, Phyllis Thaxter, Richard Denning, Milburn Stone. Turgid drama based on Cornell Woolrich tale of Stanwyck assuming another's identity, later being blackmailed by ex-boyfriend.

No Man's Woman (1955) 70m. ** D: Franklin Adreon. Marie Windsor, John Archer, Patric Knowles, Nancy Gates, Louis Jean Heydt. OK whodunit about finding murderer of strongwilled woman.

No Minor Vices (1948) 96m. ** D: Lewis Milestone. Dana Andrews, Lilli Palmer, Louis Jourdan, Jane Wyatt, Norman Loyd. Comedy of mooching house guest Jourdan winning over Andrew's wife Palmer; starts out well but bogs down.

No More Ladies (1935) 81m. **½ D: Edward H. Griffith. Joan Crawford, Robert Montgomery, Charlie Ruggles, Franchot Tone, Edna May Oliver, Gail Patrick. Crawford marries playboy Montgomery, but to settle him down, makes him jealous by seeing Tone. Cast glides through airy romantic comedy. Joan Burfield (later Fontaine) makes her film debut here.

No My Darling Daughter (1964-British) 97m. **½ D: Betty Box. Michael Redgrave, Michael Craig, Juliet Mills, Roger Livesy. Generally funny film with Mills, rich industrialist's daughter, torn between two suitors, playboy and hard-working businessman.

No Name on the Bullet (1959) C-77m. **½ D: Jack Arnold. Audie Murphy, Charles Drake, Joan Evans, Virginia Grey, Warren Stevens, R. G. Armstrong. Different-type Western; psychological study of townfolk's reaction when hired gunslinger arrives.

No One Man (1932) 73m. ** D: Lloyd Corrigan. Carole Lombard, Ricardo Cortez, Paul Lukas, George Barbier. Naive rich-girl Lombard is victimized by gigolo Cortez and returns to hubby Lukas.

No Place for Jennifer (1951-British) 89m. ** D: Henry Cass. Leo Genn, Rosamund John, Beatrice Campbell, Guy Middleton. Low-keyed sob story of little girl with bleak future when parents divorce.

No Place Like Homicide! (1962-British) 87m. ** D: Pat Jackson. Kenneth Connor, Sidney James, Shirley Eaton, Donald Pleasence, Dennis Price, Michael Gough. At times strained satire about group of people gathered at haunted house for the reading of a will.

No Place to Hide (1956) C-71m. **½ D: D: Josef Shaftel. David Brian, Marsha Hunt, Hugh Corcoran, Ike Jariego, Jr., Celia Flor. Tense account of search for two children who accidently have disease-spreading pellets in their possession; filmed in Philippines.

No Place to Land (1958) 78m. *½ D: Albert Gannaway. John Ireland, Mari Blanchard, Gail Russell, Jackie Coogan. Sleazy little film of three-cornered romance, leading nowhere.

No Questions Asked (1951) 81m. **½ D: Harold F. Kress. Barry Sullivan, Arlene Dahl, Jean Hagen, George Murphy, William Reynolds, Mari Blanchard. Snappy little film of Sullivan seeking easy road to success via crime rackets.

No Room for the Groom (1952) 82m. **½ D: Douglas Sirk. Tony Curtis, Piper Laurie, Spring Byington, Don DeFore, Jack Kelly. Harmless shenanigans of ex-GI Curtis returning home to find it filled with in-laws.

No Sad Songs for Me (1950) 89m. *** D: Rudolph Mate. Margaret Sullavan, Wendell Corey, Viveca Lindfors, Natalie Wood, Ann Doran. Moving account of dying mother Sullavan preparing her family to go on without her; sensibly enacted.

No Time for Comedy (1940) 93m. *** D: William Keighley. James Stewart, Rosalind Russell, Genevieve Tobin, Charles Ruggles, Allyn Joslyn. Fine filmization of S. N. Behrman play about playwright Stewart and the influence his wife Russell has on his career. Two pros click in leads.

No Time for Flowers (1952) 83m. ** D: Don Siegel. Viveca Lindfors, Paul Christian, Ludwig Stossel, Manfred Ingor. Low-grade version of Ninotchka theme, a pale shadow of its ancestor.

No Time for Love (1943) 83m. *** D: Mitchell Leisen. Claudette Colbert, Fred MacMurray, Ilka Chase, Richard Haydn, Paul McGrath, June Havoc. Sophisticated romance between photographer Colbert and illiterate MacMurray, who becomes her un-chic assistant. Duo are always bouncy together, in good form here.

No Time for Sergeants (1958) 111m. ***½ D: Mervyn LeRoy. Andy Griffith, Myron McCormick, Nick Adams, Murray Hamilton, Don Knotts. Funny army comedy based on Broadway play. Griffith and McCormick repeat roles as hayseed inducted into service and his harried sergeant. Griffith's best film, with good support from Adams, and in a small role, Don Knotts.

No Time to be Young (1957) 82m. ** D: David Lowell Rich. Robert Vaughn, Roger Smith, Merry Anders, Kathy Nolan. Programmer of supermarket robbery and repercussions thereafter to those involved. Early effort of four cast members who fared better on TV.

No Trees in the Street (1958-British) 108m. ** D: J. Lee Thompson. Sylvia Syms, Stanley Holloway, Herbert Lom, Ronald Howard, Joan Miller. Lower-class British life examined for its strengths and weaknesses; too sterile a human document.

No Way Out (1950) 106m. **½ D: Joseph L. Mankiewicz. Richard Widmark, Linda Darnell, Stephen McNally, Sidney Poitier, Ruby Dee, Ossie Davis, Bill Walker. Violent tale of racial hatred involving bigot Widmark, who has gangster pals avenge his brother's death by creating race riots. Film was far ahead of its time; still engrossing today. Poitier's first film.

Noah's Ark (1929) 75m. **½ D: Michael Curtiz. Dolores Costello, George O'Brien, Noah Beery, Louise Fazenda, Guinn Williams, Paul McAllister, Myrna Loy. Bible story with modern-day allegory allows for spectacular silent film, with added music and sound effects. Flood sequence is still impressive.

Nob Hill (1945) C-95m. *½ D: Henry Hathaway. George Raft, Joan Bennett, Vivian Blaine, Peggy Ann Garner, Alan Reed, B. S. Pully, Emil Coleman. Glossy trash of saloon-owner Raft stepping up in society to win high-class Bennett.

Nobody Lives Forever (1946) 100m. *** D: Jean Negulesco. John Garfield, Geraldine Fitzgerald, Water Brennan, Faye Emerson, George Coulouris, George Tobias. Well-done but familiar yarn of con-man Garfield fleecing rich widow Fitzgerald, then falling in love for real.

Nobody Waved Goodbye (1965-Canadian) 80m. *** D: Don Owen. Peter Kastner, Julie Biggs, Claude Rae, Toby Tarnow, Charmion King, Ron Taylor. Straightforward account of teen-ager fed up with the generation gap, leaving home for anywhere or nowhere.

Nobody's Perfect (1968) C-103m. **½ D: Alan Rafkin. Doug McClure, Nancy Kwan, James Whitmore, David Hartmann, Gary Vinson. Witless military service comedy involving pat shenanigans of U.S. submarine based in Japan, with every predictable gimmick thrown in.

Nocturne (1946) 88m. *** D: Edwin L. Marin. George Raft, Lynn Bari, Virginia Huston, Joseph Pevney, Myrna Dell. Detective Raft is convinced supposed suicide was murder; police force suspends him, but he continues investigation on his own; taut private-eye thriller.

None but the Lonely Heart (1944) 113m. ***½ D: Clifford Odets. Cary Grant, Ethel Barrymore, Barry Fitzgerald, Jane Wyatt, Dan Duryea, George Coulouris, June Duprez. Moody, well-acted drama of cockney drifter trying to find himself before outbreak of WW2; Grant is fine in rare dramatic role.

None Shall Escape (1944) 85m. *** D: Andre de Toth. Marsha Hunt, Alexander Knox, Henry Travers, Richard Crane, Dorothy Morris, Trevor Bardette. Trial of Nazi officer reviews his savage career, in taut drama that retains quite a punch.

Noose Hangs High, The (1948) 77m. ** D: Charles Barton. Bud Abbott, Lou Costello, Joseph Calleia, Leon Errol, Cathy Downs, Mike Mazurki, Fritz Feld. Mistaken identity leads to complications with the boys robbed

Nora Prentiss (1947) 111m. **½
D: Vincent Sherman. Ann Sheridan, Kent Smith, Robert Alda, Bruce Bennett, Rosemary DeCamp. Chanteuse Sheridan ruins doctor Smith's life; contrived but glossy melodrama.

North By Northwest (1959) C-136m. ***½ D: Alfred Hitchcock. Cary Grant, Eva Marie Saint, James Mason, Jessie Royce Landis, Martin Landau, Leo G. Carroll, Philip Ober. Lively Hitchcock thriller with Grant mistaken for a spy by secret agent Mason and accomplice Saint. Good cast helps maintain excitement. Mount Rushmore climax and crop-dusting scenes are now classics.

North Star, The (1943) 105m. **½ D: Lewis Milestone. Anne Baxter, Dana Andrews, Walter Huston, Ann Harding, Erich von Stroheim, Jane Withers, Farley Granger, Walter Brennan. Dramatic battle sequences in WW2 Russia marred by uninteresting stretches until German Von Stroheim matches wits with village leader Huston. Harding a joy as his gentle peasant wife, who undergoes torture stoically; Withers unusually good in her scenes. Political changes of events during film's shooting caused studio to reedit plot, leaving viewer emotionally confused. Retitled: ARMORED ATTACK.

North to Alaska (1960) C-122m. *** D: Henry Hathaway. John Wayne, Stewart Granger, Ernie Kovacs, Fabian, Capucine, Mickey Shaughnessy. Fast-moving actioner with delightful tongue-in-cheek approach; set in the north country. Two-fisted Wayne is the whole show.

North West Mounted Police (1940) C-125m. **½ D: Cecil B. de Mille. Gary Cooper, Madeleine Carroll, Paulette Goddard, Preston Foster, Robert Preston, George Bancroft, Akim Tamiroff, Lon Chaney, Jr. De Mille at his most ridiculous, with Cooper as "Dusty Rivers," Goddard a stereotyped half-breed in love with Preston, Lynne Overman as Scottish philosopher in superficial tale of Texas ranger searching for fugitive in Canada. Much of outdoor action filmed on obvious indoor sets.

Northern Pursuit (1943) 94m. **½ D: Raoul Walsh. Errol Flynn, Julie Bishop, Helmut Dantine, John Ridgely, Gene Lockhart, Tom Tully. Mountie Flynn tracks his man, a downed Nazi pilot, throughout Canada in this standard but slickly done drama, aided by Warner Bros. stock cast.

Northwest Outpost (1947) 91m. *½ D: Allan Dwan. Nelson Eddy, Ilona Massey, Hugo Haas, Elsa Lanchester, Lenore Ulric. Rudolf Friml operetta of California cavalrymen lumbers along pretty lamely.

Northwest Passage (1940) C-125m. ***½ D: King Vidor. Spencer Tracy, Robert Young, Walter Brennan, Ruth Hussey, Nat Pendleton, Louis Hector, Isabel Jewell, Robert Barrat. Kenneth Roberts' rousing Americana comes vividly alive in MGM's glossy account of colonial rangers battling redskins as they seek to open seaway north of America.

Northwest Stampede (1948) C-79m. **½ D: Albert S. Rogell. Joan Leslie, James Craig, Jack Oakie, Chill Wills, Victor Kilian, Stanley Andrews. Lightweight oater about lady rancher Leslie competing with cowboy Craig for prize horses.

Not as a Stranger (1955) 125m. *** D: Stanley Kramer. Olivia de Havilland, Frank Sinatra, Robert Mitchum, Charles Bickford, Gloria Grahame, Broderick Crawford, Lee Marvin, Lon Chaney. Morton Thompson novel of Mitchum marrying nurse De Havilland who supports him through medical school despite oft-strained relationship. Glossy tribute to medical profession contains excellent performances by all.

Not for Each Other SEE: Bill of Divorcement.

Not of This Earth (1957) 67m. ** D: Roger Corman. Paul Birch, Beverly Garland, Morgan Jones, William Roerick. Low-budget Corman film of advance scout for interplanetary force. Fair cast enables one to bear defects.

Not Wanted (1949) 94m. **½ D: Elmer Clifton. Sally Forrest, Keefe Brasselle, Leo Penn, Dorothy Adams. Well-intentioned account of unwed mother seeking affection and understanding; produced and co-scripted by Ida Lupino.

Not With My Wife You Don't!

(1966) C-118m. **½ D: Norman Panama. Tony Curtis, Virna Lisi, George C. Scott, Carroll O'Connor, Richard Eastham. Trivial fluff about air force officer Curtis and bored wife Lisi; pointless and aimless, but attractive to the eye.

Nothing but a Man (1964) 92m. *** D: Michael Roemer. Ivan Dixon, Abbey Lincoln, Gloria Foster, Julius Harris, Martin Priest. Sincere study of Negro worker Dixon deciding that his family should not suffer from his frustrations over racial inequality.

Nothing but the Best (1964-British) 99m. ***½ D: Clive Donner. Alan Bates, Denholm Elliott, Harry Andrews, Millicent Martin, Pauline Delany. Biting look at social-climbing playboy Bates who commits murder to get ahead in the world.

Nothing but Trouble (1944) 69m. ** D: Sam Taylor. Stan Laurel, Oliver Hardy, Mary Boland, Philip Merivale, Henry O'Neill. Lesser L&H vehicle with duo hired as servants, meeting young boy-king whose life is in danger. Boland is amusing as usual.

Notorious (1946) 101m. ***½ D: Alfred Hitchcock. Cary Grant, Ingrid Bergman, Claude Rains, Louis Calhern, Reinhold Schunzel, Moroni Olsen. Top-notch espionage tale set in WW2 South America, with Ingrid marrying spy Rains to aid U.S. and agent Grant. Frank, tense, well acted, with amazingly suspenseful climax.

Notorious Gentleman (1945-British) 108m. *** D: Frank Launder, Sidney Gilliat. Rex Harrison, Lilli Palmer, Godfrey Tearle, Griffith Jones, Margaret Johnston. Well-mounted telling of playboy Harrison's moral disintegration, leading dissolute life. Original title: THE RAKE'S PROGRESS.

Notorious Landlady, The (1962) 123m. **½ D: Richard Quine. Kim Novak, Jack Lemmon, Fred Astaire, Lionel Jeffries, Estelle Winwood, Maxwell Reed. Lemmon entranced by house-woman Novak, decides to find out if she really did kill her husband; set in London. Offbeat comedy-mystery.

Notorious Lone Wolf, The (1946) 64m. D: D. Ross Lederman. Gerald Mohr, Janis Carter, Eric Blore, John Abbott, William B. Davidson, Don Beddoe, Adele Roberts. SEE: **Lone Wolf** series.

Notorious Mr. Monks, The (1958) 70m. ** D: Joseph Kane. Vera Ralston, Don Kelly, Paul Fix, Leo Gordon. Tame Ralston vehicle involving a hitchhiker and murder.

Notorious Sophie Lang (1934) 64m. **½ D: Ralph Murphy. Gertrude Michael, Paul Cavanagh, Alison Skipworth, Leon Errol, Arthur Hoyt. Tightly knit yarn of police using title character (Michael) to lead them to international crime ring.

Novel Affair, A (1958-British) C-83m. *** D: Muriel Box. Ralph Richardson, Margaret Leighton, Patricia Dainton, Carlo Justini. Amusing tale of Leighton who writes a sexy novel, finding the fantasy come true.

Now and Forever (1934) 81m. **½ D: Henry Hathaway. Gary Cooper, Carole Lombard, Shirley Temple, Sir Guy Standing, Charlotte Granville, Harry Stubbs. Standard jewel-thief-going-straight yarn; Lombard overshadowed by Cooper and Temple.

Now, Voyager (1942) 117m. ***½ D: Irving Rapper. Bette Davis, Claude Rains, Paul Henreid, Gladys Cooper, Bonita Granville, Janis Wilson, Ilka Chase, John Loder, Lee Patrick. Vintage, first-class soaper with Bette as sheltered spinster brought out of her shell by psychiatrist Rains, falling in love with suave Henreid, helping shy girl Wilson. All this set to beautiful Max Steiner music makes top entertainment of this kind.

Nude in a White Car (1960-French, dubbed) 87m. **½ D: Robert Hossein. Marina Vlady, Robert Hossein, Odile Versois, Helena Manson, Henri Cremieux. Hossein's only clue to a crime is title person; suspenser set on French Riviera. Retitled: BLONDE IN A WHITE CAR.

Number Six (1962-British) 59m. ** D: Robert Tronson. Nadja Regin, Ivan Desny, Brian Bedford, Michael Goodliffe. Regin is heiress mixed up in espionage and murder; OK Edgar Wallace suspenser.

Nun and the Sergeant, The (1962) 73m. ** D: Franklin Adreon. Robert Webber, Anna Sten, Leo Gordon. Hari Rhodes, Robert Easton, Dale Ishimoto, Linda Wong. Set in Korea during the war; title tells rest.

Nun's Story, The (1959) **C-149m.** ***½ D: Fred Zinnemann. Audrey Hepburn, Peter Finch, Edith Evans, Peggy Ashcroft, Dean Jagger, Mildred Dunnock. Tasteful filming of Kathryn Hulme book, with Hepburn the nun who serves in Belgian Congo and later leaves convent. Colleen Dewhurst, as a homicidal patient, is electrifying.

Nurse Edith Cavell (1939) 95m. *** D: Herbert Wilcox. Anna Neagle, Edna May Oliver, George Sanders, ZaSu Pitts, May Robson, H. B. Warner, Robert Coote. Neagle is fine as dedicated WW1 nurse who worked on battlefield to aid wounded soldiers. Sturdy production.

Nutty, Naughty Chateau (1964-French, dubbed) **C-100m.** **½ D: Roger Vadim. Monica Vitti, Curt Jurgens, Jean-Claude Brialy, Sylvie, Jean-Louis Trintignant, Françoise Hardy. Bizarre minor comedy involving the strange inhabitants of a castle romping about in 1750's styles; most diverting cast. Based on a Françoise Sagan play.

Nutty Professor, The (1963) **C-107m.** *** D: Jerry Lewis. Jerry Lewis, Stella Stevens, Howard Morris, Kathleen Freeman, Skip Ward. Lewis romp has inventive sight gags. He is meek college teacher who becomes idol of females on campus through strange experiments.

Nyoka and the Lost Secrets of Hippocrates (1942) 100m. **½ D: William Witney. Kay Aldridge, Clayton Moore, William Benedict, Lorna Gray, Charles Middleton. Enjoyable, campy cliff-hanger set in Africa with Kay Aldridge (Nyoka) pitted against Lorna Gray (Vultura) in search for mystical beliefs. Re-edited movie serial: PERILS OF NYOKA. Re-issued under title: NYOKA AND THE TIGERMEN.

Nyoka and the Tigermen SEE: **Nyoka and the Lost Secrets of Hippocrates.**

O.S.S. (1946) 107m. *** D: Irving Pichel. Alan Ladd, Geraldine Fitzgerald, Patric Knowles, Richard Benedict, Richard Webb, Don Beddoe, Onslow Stevens. Brisk WW2 espionage film with Ladd and company on important mission in France unaware that D-Day is rapidly approaching.

O. S. S. 117—Mission for a Killer (1966-French, dubbed) **C-84m.** **½ D: Andre Hunebelle. Frederick Stafford, Mylene Demongeot, Raymond Pellegrin. At times interesting malarkey about super spy trying to combat a world-hungry political organization.

Oasis (1956-French, dubbed) **C-84m.** ** D: Yves Allegret. Michele Morgan, Pierre Brasseur, Cornell Borchers, Carl Raddatz. Morgan's radiance brightens this oft-told story of gold-smuggling in Africa.

Objective, Burma! (1945) 142m. ***½ D: Raoul Walsh. Errol Flynn, William Prince, James Brown, George Tobias, Henry Hull, Warner Anderson. Zestful WW2 action film with Flynn and company as paratroopers invading Burma to wipe out important Japanese post; top excitement.

Obliging Young Lady (1941) 80m. **½ D: Richard Wallace. Eve Arden, Edmond O'Brien, Ruth Warrick, Joan Carroll, Franklin Pangborn, George Cleveland. Agreeable comedy about youngster, center of custody fight, finding herself the focal point at a country resort.

Obsessed, The (1951-British) 77m. ** D: Maurice Elvey. David Farrar, Geraldine Fitzgerald, Roland Culver, Jean Cadell. Lackluster story of Farrar suspected of homicide.

Obsession SEE: **Hidden Room, The**

Ocean's Eleven (1960) **C-127m.** **½ D: Lewis Milestone. Frank Sinatra, Dean Martin, Sammy Davis, Jr., Peter Lawford, Angie Dickinson, Richard Conte, Cesar Romero, Patrice Wymore, Joey Bishop, Akim Tamiroff. Fanciful crime comedy about eleven-man team headed by Danny Ocean (Sinatra) attempting a "caper" in Las Vegas. Everyone's in it, but no one does much; including some surprise guests. There is a clever twist ending, though.

October Man, The (1947-British) 89m. *** D: Roy Baker. John Mills, Kay Walsh, Joan Greenwood, Felix Aylmer, John Boxer. Intelligently presented study of Mills trying to prove he's innocent of homicide, not always sure of it himself.

October Moth (1959-British) 54m. *½ D: John Kruse. Lee Patterson,

Lana Morris, Peter Dyneley, Robert Crawdon. Turgid melodrama set on lonely farm, with Morris trying to cope with dim-witted brother (Patterson) who has injured a passerby.

Odd Man Out (1947-British) 113m. **** D: Carol Reed. James Mason, Kathleen Ryan, Robert Newton, Dan O'Herlihy, Robert Beatty, Fay Compton, Cyril Cusack. Incredibly suspenseful tale of Irish rebel leader hunted by police after daring robbery. Watch this one!

Odds Against Tomorrow (1959) 95m. *** D: Robert Wise. Harry Belafonte, Robert Ryan, Shelley Winters, Ed Begley, Gloria Grahame. Brutal robbery story with entire cast pulling out all stops; taut, exciting drama.

Odette (1951-British) 100m. **½ D: Herbert Wilcox. Anna Neagle, Trevor Howard, Marius Goring, Peter Ustinov. Neagle is the whole show as Winston Churchill's relative, held by Nazis as hostage.

Odongo (1956-British) C-85m. Bomb D: John Gilling. Rhonda Fleming, Macdonald Carey, Juma, Eleanor Summerfield, Francis De Wolff. Juvenile jungle flick about search for missing native boy.

Oedipus Rex (1957-Canadian) C-87m. **½ D: Tyrone Guthrie. Douglas Rain, Douglas Campbell, Eric House, Eleanor Stuart. Restrained, professional rendering of Sophocles' Greek tragedy.

Of Flesh and Blood (1962-French, dubbed) C-92m. **½ D: Christian Marquand. Robert Hossein, Renato Salvatori, Anouk Aimee, André Bervil, Jean Lefevre. Murky account of passerby Salvatori having an affair with Aimee, involved with card-cheat-turned-murderer Hossein.

Of Human Bondage (1964-British) 98m. **½ D: Ken Hughes. Kim Novak, Laurence Harvey, Siobhan McKenna, Robert Morley, Roger Livesey, Nanette Newman. Third and least successful filming of Maugham novel of early 20th-century doctor, Harvey, and his passion for lowbrow waitress Novak; miscast, superficial account.

Of Human Hearts (1938) 100m. ***½ D: Clarence Brown. Walter Huston, James Stewart, Gene Reynolds, Beulah Bondi, Guy Kibbee, Charles Coburn, John Carradine, Ann Rutherford, Leatrice Joy Gilbert. Straying son Stewart is reunited with parents Huston and Bondi because of Abraham Lincoln (Carradine) in this sentimental, well-acted film. Nineteenth-century rural America is well depicted.

Of Life and Love (1957-Italian, dubbed) 103m. **½ D: Aldo Fabrizi, Luchino Visconti, Mario Soldati, Giorgio Pastina. Anna Magnani, Walter Chiari, Natale Cirino, Turi Pandolfini, Myriam Bru, Lucia Bose. Four satisfactory episodes, three of which are based on Pirandello tales; fourth is actual event in Magnani's life (THE LAPDOG).

Of Mice and Men (1939) 107m. **** D: Lewis Milestone. Lon Chaney, Jr., Burgess Meredith, Betty Field, Charles Bickford, Bob Steele, Noah Beery, Jr. Chaney gives best performance of his career as feeble-brained Lenny who, with migrant-worker Meredith, tries to live peacefully on Bickford's farm. Steinbeck's morality tale remains intact in sensitive screen version.

Off Limits (1953) 89m. *** D: George Marshall. Bob Hope, Mickey Rooney, Marilyn Maxwell, Marvin Miller. Peppy shenanigans with Hope and Rooney in the army, Maxwell a night-club singer.

Oh, Men! Oh, Women! (1957) C-90m. **½ D: Nunnally Johnson. Ginger Rogers, David Niven, Dan Dailey, Barbara Rush, Tony Randall. Often bouncy sex farce revolving around psychiatrist and his assorted patients.

Oh, Susanna (1951) C-90m. ** D: Joseph Kane. Rod Cameron, Forrest Tucker, Adrian Booth, Chill Wills. Too much feuding between cavalry officers and too little real action mar this Western.

Oh! Those Most Secret Agents (1966-Italian, dubbed) 83m. *½ D: Lucio Fulci. Franco Franchi, Cicci Ingrassia, Ingrid Schoeller, Arnoldo Tieri. Pathetic superspy spoof. Retitled: WORST SECRET AGENTS.

Oh, You Beautiful Doll (1949) C-93m. **½ D: John M. Stahl. June Haver, Mark Stevens, S. Z. Sakall, Charlotte Greenwood, Gale Robbins, Jay C. Flippen. Chipper period musical, with wispy career biog of serious composer whose works become popular hits.

O'Henry's Full House (1952) 117m. **½ D: Henry Hathaway, Howard Hawks, Henry King, Henry Koster, Jean Negulesco. Fred Allen, Anne Baxter, Charles Laughton, Marilyn Monroe, Gregory Ratoff, Jeanne Crain, Oscar Levant, Jean Peters, Richard Widmark, Farley Granger. Five varying stories by O'Henry; cast better than script. THE CLARION CALL, LAST LEAF, RANSOM OF RED CHIEF, GIFT OF THE MAGI, and COP AND THE ANTHEM.

Oil for the Lamps of China (1935) 110m. *** D: Mervyn LeRoy. Pat O'Brien, Josephine Hutchinson, Jean Muir, Lyle Talbot, Arthur Byron, John Eldredge, Henry O'Neill, Donald Crisp. Tear-jerker drama of American oil-company representative in China, dedicating his life to his work, finding sympathetic wife, beset by myriad problems. Well-produced drama.

Okinawa (1952) 67m. ** D: George Brooks. Pat O'Brien, Cameron Mitchell, James Dobson, Richard Denning, Richard Benedict, Alvy Moore. Adequate programmer about the men on a warship during the Pacific campaign of WW2.

Oklahoma! (1955) C-145m. *** D: Fred Zinnemann. Gordon MacRae, Shirley Jones, Charlotte Greenwood, Rod Steiger, Gloria Grahame, Eddie Albert, James Whitmore, Gene Nelson. Rodgers and Hammerstein's trend-setting 1945 musical comes to screen in tremendous, generally entertaining form. Too long, but songs like "People Will Say We're In Love" and the many other hits, plus Greenwood's comedy and Grahame's offbeat casting, keep film alive.

Oklahoma Annie (1952) C-90m. *½ D: R. G. Springsteen. Judy Canova, John Russell, Grant Withers, Allen Jenkins, Almira Sessions, Minerva Urecal. Rambunctious Canova is involved with mopping up corruption in her Western town.

Oklahoma Kid, The (1939) 85m. *** D: Lloyd Bacon. James Cagney, Humphrey Bogart, Rosemary Lane, Donald Crisp, Ward Bond. Cagney's the hero, Bogie's the villain in this sturdy Western. Classic scene has Cagney singing "I Don't Want to Play in Your Yard."

Oklahoma Territory (1960) 67m. ** D: Edward L. Cahn. Bill Williams, Gloria Talbott, Ted de Corsia, Grant Richards, Walter Sande. Western concentrating on Williams' effort to find actual killer of local Indian agent.

Oklahoma Woman, The (1956) 72m. Bomb D: Roger Corman. Richard Denning, Peggie Castle, Cathy Downs, Mike Connors, Tudor Owen. Denning is ex-con trying to do right back on the farm, but fate intervenes. A nothing film.

Oklahoman, The (1957) C-80m. ** D: Francis D. Lyon. Joel McCrea, Barbara Hale, Brad Dexter, Gloria Talbott, Verna Felton, Douglas Dick. Restrained Western with McCrea helping an outcast Indian protect his rights.

Old Acquaintance (1943) 110m. *** D: Vincent Sherman. Bette Davis, Miriam Hopkins, Gig Young, John Loder, Dolores Moran. Sizzling stars of OLD MAID reunited in well-played tale of two girlhood pals finding each other increasingly nasty as years go by; Loder is the man who comes between them.

Old Dark House, The (1963-British) 86m. **½ D: William Castle. Tom Poston, Robert Morley, Peter Bull, Joyce Grenfell, Janette Scott. Uneven blend of comedy and chiller, with Poston at loose ends in eerie old mansion.

Old-Fashioned Way, The (1934) 66m. ***½ D: William Beaudine. W. C. Fields, Judith Allen, Joe Morrison, Baby LeRoy, Jack Mulhall, Oscar Apfel. Fields is in fine form managing troupe of old-time melodrama THE DRUNKARD, encountering various troubles as they travel from town to town. Baby LeRoy has memorable scene throwing W.C.'s watch into a jar of molasses.

Old Hutch (1936) 80m. ** D: J. Walter Ruben. Wallace Beery, Eric Linden, Cecilia Parker, Elizabeth Patterson, Robert McWade. Cute story of shiftless bum discovering $1000, trying to use it without arousing suspicion.

Old Maid, The (1939) 95m. ***½ D: Edmund Goulding. Bette Davis, Miriam Hopkins, George Brent, Jane Bryan, Donald Crisp, Louise Fazenda, Jerome Cowan. Soap opera par excellence based on Zoe Akins play about unwed mother (Davis), whose unsuspecting daughter Bryan grows up ignoring her, loving Bette's scheming cousin Hopkins. The two female stars create fireworks as they enact this chronicle of love and hate in the 1860's.

Old Man and the Sea, The (1958) C-86m. *** D: John Sturges. Spencer Tracy, Felipe Pazos, Harry Bellaver. Well-intentioned but uneven parable of aging fisherman's daily battle with the elements. Tracy is the whole film, making the most of Hemingway's un-filmic story.

Oliver Twist (1948-British) 105m. **** D: David Lean. Alec Guinness, Robert Newton, John Howard Davies, Kay Walsh, Francis L. Sullivan, Anthony Newley, Henry Stephenson. Superlative realization of Dickens tale of ill-treated London waif involved with arch-fiend Fagin (Guinness) and his youthful gang, headed by the Artful Dodger (Newley). Later musicalized as OLIVER.

Omar Khayyam (1957) C-101m. **½ D: William Dieterle. Cornel Wilde, Debra Paget, John Derek, Raymond Massey, Michael Rennie, Yma Sumac, Sebastian Cabot. Childish but spirited costumer set in medieval Persia; cast defeated by juvenile script.

On an Island With You (1948) 107m. **½ D: Richard Thorpe. Esther Williams, Peter Lawford, Ricardo Montalban, Jimmy Durante, Cyd Charisse, Xavier Cugat, Leon Ames. Splashy, colorful Williams vehicle of movie star who finds offscreen romance on location in Hawaii.

On Approval (1944-British) 80m. *** D: Clive Brook. Beatrice Lillie, Clive Brook, Googie Withers, Roland Culver. Minor British gem showcasing the hilarious Bea Lillie as woman who exchanges boyfriends with her companion. Drawing-room comedy par excellence.

On Borrowed Time (1939) 99m. *** D: Harold S. Bucquet. Lionel Barrymore, Cedric Hardwicke, Beulah Bondi, Una Merkel, Ian Wolfe, Philip Terry, Eily Malyon. Engrossing fable of Death, Mr. Brink (Hardwicke), coming for grandpa Barrymore, finding himself trapped in tree by Lionel and grandson Bobs Watson.

On Dangerous Ground (1951) 82m. **½ D: Nicholas Ray. Ida Lupino, Robert Ryan, Ward Bond, Ed Begley, Cleo Moore, Charles Kemper. Lupino gives an overly dramatic performance as blind girl courted by detective hunting her brother, a murder suspect.

On Dress Parade (1939) 62m. D: William Clemens. Billy Halop, Bobby Jordan, Huntz Hall, Gabriel Dell, Leo Gorcey, Selmer Jackson, John Litel, Bernard Punsley, Don Douglas, Alrich Bowker. SEE: Bowery Boys series.

On Moonlight Bay (1951) C-95m. **½ D: Roy Del Ruth. Doris Day, Gordon MacRae, Billy Gray, Mary Wickes, Leon Ames, Rosemary DeCamp. Folksy musical based on Booth Tarkington tale, with Day and MacRae the wholesome love interest.

On Our Merry Way (1948) 107m. **½ D: King Vidor, Leslie Fenton. Burgess Meredith, Paulette Goddard, Fred MacMurray, Hugh Herbert, James Stewart, Henry Fonda, Dorothy Lamour, Victor Moore. Episodic film has good Stewart-Fonda segment, but flock of stars can't overcome mediocre stretches as reporter Meredith asks various people about their relationship to children.

On Stage Everybody (1945) 65m. ** D: Jean Yarbrough. Jack Oakie, Peggy Ryan, Otto Kruger, Julie London, Wallace Ford, King Sisters. Run-of-the-mill Universal musical, with frantic Oakie helping to put on the big radio variety program.

On the Avenue (1937) 89m. *** D: Roy Del Ruth. Dick Powell, Madeleine Carroll, Alice Faye, Ritz Brothers, Alan Mowbray, Billy Gilbert, Cora Witherspoon, Joan Davis, Sig Ruman. Tasteful, intelligent musical of socialite Carroll getting involved with stage star Powell. One good Irving Berlin song after another: "I've Got My Love To Keep Me Warm," "This Year's Kisses," "Let's Go Slumming," "The Girl on the Police Gazette."

On the Beach (1959) 133m. **** D: Stanley Kramer. Gregory Peck, Ava Gardner, Fred Astaire, Anthony Perkins, Donna Anderson, John Tate, Guy Doleman. Thoughtful version of Nevil Shute's novel about Australians awaiting effects of explosion that has destroyed the rest of the world. Good performances by all, including Astaire in a straight role.

On the Beat (1962-British) 105m. **½ D: Robert Asher. Norman Wisdom, Jennifer Jayne, Raymond Huntley, David Lodge. Overly cute comedy with Wisdom a dumb-bunny helping Scotland Yard round up a criminal gang; too many pat routines and stereotyped performances.

On The Double (1961) C-92m. *** D: Melville Shavelson. Danny Kaye, Dana Wynter, Wilfrid Hyde-White, Margaret Rutherford, Diana Dors. Danny's resemblance to German officer makes him valuable as a WW2 spy. At one point he does a Dietrich imitation! Similar to early Kaye vehicle ON THE RIVIERA, but just as enjoyable.

On the Isle of Samoa (1950) 65m. *½ D: William Berke. Jon Hall, Susan Cabot, Raymond Greenleaf, Henry Marco. Sloppy little story of Hall finding love with native girl, inspiring him to clear up his shady past.

On the Loose (1951) 78m. *½ D: Charles Lederer. Joan Evans, Melvyn Douglas, Lynn Bari, Robert Arthur, Hugh O'Brian. Lukewarm drama of overindulgent parents and their wayward daughter.

On the Riviera (1951) C-90m. *** D: Walter Lang. Danny Kaye, Gene Tierney, Corinne Calvet, Marcel Dalio, Jean Murat. Bouncy musi-comedy with Danny in dual role as entertainer and French military hero. "Ballin' the Jack," other songs in lively film. Gwen Verdon is one of chorus girls. Remake of Maurice Chevalier's FOLIES BERGERE.

On the Threshold of Space (1956) C-98m. **½ D: Robert D. Webb. Guy Madison, Virginia Leith, John Hodiak, Dean Jagger, Warren Stevens. Capable cast merely bridges the span between sequences of astronaut endurance tests and other space-flight maneuvers.

On the Town (1949) C-98m. **** D: Gene Kelly, Stanley Donen. Gene Kelly, Frank Sinatra, Vera-Ellen, Betty Garrett, Ann Miller, Jules Munshin, Alice Pearce. Sparkling Comden-Green musical of three sailors and their gals in N.Y.C. for a day. "New York, New York" heads good score. Fluid choreography, with dandy comedy relief by Garrett and Pearce.

On the Waterfront (1954) 108m. **** D: Elia Kazan. Marlon Brando, Eva Marie Saint, Karl Malden, Lee J. Cobb, Rod Steiger, Pat Henning, Leif Erickson, James Westerfield. Budd Schulberg's unflinching report on N.Y.C. harbor unions, with Brando fine as misfit, Steiger his crafty brother, Cobb his waterfront boss, and Saint the girl he loves.

On Trial (1953-French, dubbed) 70m. ** D: Julien Duvivier. Madeleine Robinson, Daniel Gelin, Eleonora Rossi-Drago, Charles Vanel, Anton Walbrook, Jacques Chabassol. Chabassol, son of D.A. Vanel, investigates conviction of Gelin, discovering disparity between justice and truth; well-intentioned film gone astray.

On Your Toes (1939) 94m. **½ D: Ray Enright. Vera Zorina, Eddie Albert, Frank McHugh, Alan Hale, James Gleason. Long-winded account of backstage jealousy and attempted murder, highlighted by Zorina's footwork in ballet numbers.

Once a Thief (1950) 88m. ** D: W. Lee Wilder. June Havoc, Cesar Romero, Marie McDonald, Lon Chaney, Iris Adrian. Solid little film of shoplifter Havoc and her tawdry romance with Romero.

Once Before I Die (1965) C-97m. **½ D: John Derek. Ursula Andress, John Derek, Rod Lauren, Richard Jaeckel, Ron Ely. Brutal, offbeat story of band of American soldiers in Philippines during WW2, trying to survive Japanese attack. Andress is only woman in group, and you can guess the rest.

Once More My Darling (1949) 94m. **½ D: Robert Montgomery. Robert Montgomery, Ann Blyth, Jane Cowl, Taylor Holmes, Charles McGraw. Satisfying comedy of young girl infatuated with middle-aged movie star.

Once More, With Feeling (1960) C-92m. **½ D: Stanley Donen. Yul Brynner, Kay Kendall, Maxwell Shaw, Mervyn Johns. Despite sparkling Kendall (her last film) as musical conductor Brynner's dissatisfied wife, this marital sex comedy fizzles.

Once Upon a Honeymoon (1942) 117m. **½ D: Leo McCarey. Ginger Rogers, Cary Grant, Walter Slezak, Albert Dekker, Albert Basserman. Slightly dated adventure comedy of innocent Ginger marrying Nazi officer, with Cary rescuing her. Slezak is perfect as Rogers' Hitlerite spouse.

Once Upon a Horse (1958) 85m. *½ D: Hal Kanter. Dan Rowan, Dick Martin, Martha Hyer, Leif Erickson. Silly Western spoof with pre-TV Rowan and Martin as zany heroes. Old-time western stars Tom Keene, Bob Livingston, Kermit Mayhard, and Bob Steele are in the cast.

Once Upon a Time (1944) 89m. **½ D: Alexander Hall. Cary Grant, Janet Blair, James Gleason, Ted Donaldson, Art Baker. Amusing comedy-fantasy of entrepreneur Grant promoting a dancing caterpillar; trivial fun.

One Big Affair (1952) 80m. ** D: Peter Godfrey. Evelyn Keyes, Dennis O'Keefe, Mary Anderson, Connie Gilchrist. On-location filming in Mexico highlights this lightweight romance yarn of Keyes and O'Keefe.

One Body Too Many (1944) 75m. ** D: Frank McDonald. Bela Lugosi, Jack Haley, Jean Parker, Blanche Yurka, Lyle Talbot, Douglas Fowley. Detective comedy-spoof with Lugosi tossed in for good measure; Haley is carefree salesman mistaken for private eye, forced to solve caper.

One Dangerous Night (1943) 77m. D: Michael Gordon. Warren William, Marguerite Chapman, Eric Blore, Mona Barrie, Tala Birell, Margaret Hayes, Ann Savage. SEE: Lone Wolf series.

One Desire (1955) 94m. **½ D: Jerry Hopper. Anne Baxter, Rock Hudson, Julie Adams, Natalie Wood, Betty Garde. Baxter's strong performance as woman in love with gambler Hudson elevates standard soaper.

One-Eyed Jacks (1961) C-141m. **½ D: Marlon Brando. Marlon Brando, Karl Malden, Pina Pellicer, Katy Jurado, Ben Johnson, Slim Pickens. Pensive, meandering Western mishmash, dominated by Brando as the outlaw combating ex-friend Malden. Intriguing at times but overlong.

One Fatal Hour SEE: Two Against the World.

One Foot in Heaven (1941) 108m. ***½ D: Irving Rapper. Fredric March, Martha Scott, Beulah Bondi, Gene Lockhart, Elisabeth Fraser, Harry Davenport, Laura Hope Crews, Grant Mitchell. Chronicle of devoted minister (March) and wife (Scott) facing the problems of life; beautifully told, good characterizations.

One Foot in Hell (1960) C-90m. **½ D: James B. Clark. Alan Ladd, Don Murray, Dan O'Herlihy, Dolores Michaels, Barry Coe, Larry Gates, Karl Swenson. Ambitious in intent but peculiar production of sheriff seeking retribution for death of his wife.

One for the Book SEE: Voice of the Turtle.

One Girl's Confession (1953) 74m. Bomb D: Hugo Haas. Cleo Moore, Hugo Haas, Glenn Langan, Russ Conway. Moore is gal gone wrong, serving her time and starting new life. Another gem from Hugo Haas.

One Good Turn (1954-British) 78m. ** D: John Paddy Carstairs. Norman Wisdom, Joan Rice, Shirley Abicair, William Russell, Thora Hird. Minor musical vehicle for man-on-the-street comedian Wisdom, putting forth such homey tunes as "Take Step In The Right Direction."

One Horse Town SEE: Small Town Girl

One Hour With You (1932) 80m. ***½ D: Ernst Lubitsch. Maurice Chevalier, Jeanette MacDonald, Genevieve Tobin, Roland Young, Charles Ruggles. Singing duo in chic romance of happily married couple upset by arrival of flirtatious Tobin. Remake of Lubitsch's 1924 MARRIAGE CIRCLE. Songs: "What Would You Do?" title tune, "We Will Always Be Sweethearts."

100 Men and a Girl (1937) 84m. *** D: Henry Koster. Deanna Durbin, Leopold Stokowski, Adolphe Menjou, Alice Brady, Eugene Pallette, Mischa Auer, Billy Gilbert. Menjou's a starving violinist, but daughter Deanna fixes everything up with Stokowski for happy ending. Deanna's lovely voice and personality make vehicle more than acceptable.

One in a Million (1936) 95m. *** D: Sidney Lanfield. Sonja Henie, Adolphe Menjou, Don Ameche, Ned Sparks, Jean Hersholt, The Ritz Brothers, Arline Judge. Henie in film debut is surrounded by fine cast. Skating scenes are most enjoyable, lively music helping, too. The Ritz Brothers are in fine form, with amusing horror-film spoof.

One Last Fling (1949) 74m. ** D: Peter Godfrey. Alexis Smith, Zachary

Scott, Douglas Kennedy, Ann Doran, Veda Ann Borg, Helen Westcott. Limp tale of overly suspicious wife checking up on her husband by going to work for him.

One Man's Way (1964) 105m. *** D: Denis Sanders. Don Murray, Diana Hyland, Veronica Cartwright, Ian Wolfe, Virginia Christine, Carol Ohmart, William Windom. Tasteful fictionalized biography of Norman Vincent Peale, his religious convictions and preaching; Murray is earnest in lead role.

One Million B. C. (1940) 80m. **½ D: Hal Roach, Hal Roach, Jr. Victor Mature, Carole Landis, Lon Chaney, Jr., John Hubbard, Mamo Clarke, Jean Porter. Bizarre caveman saga told in flashback is real curio, part of it supposedly directed by silent film pioneer D. W. Griffith. Excellent special effects.

One Million Years B. C. (1966-British) C-100m. ** D: Don Chaffey. John Richardson, Raquel Welch, Percy Herbert, Robert Brown, Martine Beswick, Jean Wladon, Lisa Thomas. Silly prehistoric saga which capitalized on Miss Welch's anatomy in its advertising; that remains its only real virtue.

One Minute to Zero (1952) 105m. **½ D: Tay Garnett. Robert Mitchum, Ann Blyth, William Talman, Richard Egan, Charles McGraw. Mitchum adds guts to generally bloodless tale about Korean War.

One More Tomorrow (1946) 88m. ** D: Peter Godfrey. Ann Sheridan, Dennis Morgan, Alexis Smith, John Loder, Jane Wyman, Reginald Gardiner. Light-comedy players flounder in overambitious reworking of Philip Barry's THE ANIMAL KINGDOM.

One Mysterious Night (1944) 61m. D: Budd Boetticher. Chester Morris, Janis Carter, Richard Lane, William Wright, George E. Stone, Dorothy Malone, Joseph Crehan. SEE: Boston Blackie series.

One Night in Lisbon (1941) 97m. **½ D: Edward H. Griffith. Fred MacMurray, Madeleine Carroll, Patricia Morison, Billie Burke, John Loder. Mild screwball comedy with gorgeous Carroll falling in love with flier MacMurray despite interference from his ex (Morison).

One Night of Love (1934) 80m. ***½ D: Victor Schertzinger. Grace Moore, Tullio Carminati, Lyle Talbot, Mona Barrie, Luis Alberni, Jessie Ralph. Classic musical of aspiring opera star Moore and her demanding teacher Carminati, a delight from start to finish with Miss Moore performing several operatic excerpts. A must for music-lovers, film remains remarkably fresh.

One Night With You (1948-British) 90m. ** D: Terence Young. Nino Martini, Patricia Roc, Bonar Colleano, Guy Middleton, Stanley Holloway, Miles Malleson. Diluted musical with socialite Roc intrigued by singer Martini.

One of Our Aircraft Is Missing (1941-British) 106m. ***½ D: Michael Powell and Emeric Pressburger. Godfrey Tearle, Eric Portman, Hugh Williams, Pamela Brown, Googie Withers, Peter Ustinov, Roland Culver. Thoughtful study of RAF pilots who crash-land in Netherlands, seek to return to England.

One Potato, Two Potato (1964) 92m. ***½ D: Larry Peerce. Barbara Barrie, Bernie Hamilton, Richard Mulligan, Robert Earl Jones, Harry Bellaver, Faith Burwell, Tom Ligon. Frank study of interracial marriage, beautifully acted, with intelligent script.

One Spy Too Many (1966) C-102m. D: Joseph Sargent. Robert Vaughn, David McCallum, Rip Torn, Dorothy Provine, Leo G. Carroll. Feature edited from MAN FROM UNCLE TV-er, has Torn trying to take over the world, while putting wife Provine out of the way.

One Step to Eternity (1955-French, dubbed) 94m. ** D: Henri Decoin. Danielle Darrieux, Michel Auclair, Corinne Calvet, Gil Delamare. Capable cast led astray by meandering production about unknown persons trying to kill four women.

One Sunday Afternoon (1948) C-90m. **½ D: Raoul Walsh. Dennis Morgan, Janis Paige, Don DeFore, Dorothy Malone, Ben Blue. Musical remake of STRAWBERRY BLONDE is pleasant but nothing more, with attractive cast and unmemorable songs.

One That Got Away, The (1958-British) 106m. **½ D: Roy Baker. Hardy Kruger, Colin Gordon, Michael Goodliffe, Terence Alexander. Kruger gives sincere performance as Nazi prisoner in England who escapes back to homeland.

One Third of a Nation (1939) 79m. **½ D: Dudley Murphy. Sylvia Sidney, Leif Erickson, Myron McCormick, Hiram Sherman, Sidney Lumet, Iris Adrian, Byron Russell. Sidney is poor girl yearning for escape from tenements, meeting man who could make the change for her. Still timely social document.

1001 Arabian Nights (1959) C-75m. **½ D: Jack Kinney. Voices of Jim Backus, Kathryn Grant, Dwayne Hickman, Hans Conried, Herschel Bernardi, Alan Reed. Elaborate updating of Arabian Nights tales featuring nearsighted Mr. Magoo has a nice score, pleasing animation, especially in color.

One Touch of Venus (1948) 81m. **½ D: William A. Seiter. Ava Gardner, Robert Walker, Dick Haymes, Eve Arden, Olga San Juan, Tom Conway. Broadway success of young man in love with store-window statue of Venus which suddenly comes to life; not great, but amusing, with good cast.

One, Two, Three (1961) C-108m. **** D: Billy Wilder. James Cagney, Arlene Francis, Horst Buchholz, Pamela Tiffin, Lilo Pulver, Red Buttons. Hilarious Wilder comedy about Coke executive (Cagney) in contemporary West Berlin. Cagney is a marvel to watch in this fast-paced comedy; brisk Andre Previn score helps.

One Way Passage (1932) 69m. ***½ D: Tay Garnett. Kay Francis, William Powell, Aline MacMahon, Warren Hymer, Frank McHugh, Herbert Mundin. Tender shipboard romance of con-man Powell and fatally ill Francis, splendidly acted, with good support by MacMahon and McHugh as two other con-artists playing Cupid. Remade as TILL WE MEET AGAIN.

One-Way Street (1950) 79m. **½ D: Hugo Fregonese. James Mason, Marta Toren, Dan Duryea, William Conrad, Jack Elam. Turgid crime story of doctor (Mason) involved with gangland robberies, trying to reform.

One Way to Love (1946) 83m. ** D: Ray Enright. Chester Morris, Janis Carter, Marguerite Chapman, Willard Parker. Pleasant programmer about two radio writers finding romance and new program ideas on cross-country train trip.

One Woman's Story (1949) 86m. ***½ D: David Lean. Ann Todd, Claude Rains, Trevor Howard, Isabel Dean, Arthur Howard, Wilfrid Hyde-White. Intelligent romancer of married woman encountering former lover, finding herself involved with him again.

Onionhead (1958) 110m. **½ D: Norman Taurog. Andy Griffith, Felicia Farr, Walter Matthau, Erin O'Brien, Joey Bishop. Film tries to capture flavor of NO TIME FOR SERGEANTS but is pat imitation of life in the Coast Guard.

Only Angels Have Wings (1939) 121m. ***½ D: Howard Hawks. Cary Grant, Jean Arthur, Richard Barthelmess, Rita Hayworth, Thomas Mitchell, Sig Ruman, John Carroll, Allyn Joslyn. Mail fliers in South America provide background for interesting story: showgirl Arthur falls in love with Grant; Rita is bored with husband Barthelmess.

Only the French Can (1955-French, dubbed) C-93m. **½ D: Jean Renoir. Jean Gabin, Françoise Arnoul, Maria Felix, Edith Piaf. Pictorially flattering but static musical about nightclub owner Gabin discovering the cancan dance. Retitled: FRENCH CANCAN.

Only the Valiant (1951) 105m. ** D: Gordon Douglas. Gregory Peck, Barbara Payton, Ward Bond, Gig Young, Lon Chaney, Neville Brand, Jeff Corey. Unmemorable oater of army officer Peck showing his courage by holding off the rampaging Indians.

Only Two Can Play (1962-British) 106m. *** D: Sidney Gilliat. Peter Sellers, Mai Zetterling, Virginia Maskell, Richard Attenborough, Kenneth Griffith. Well-intentioned filming of Kingsley Amis novel, striving for quick laughs rather than satire. Sellers is librarian flirting with society woman Zetterling.

Open City (1946-Italian, dubbed) 105m. **** D: Roberto Rossellini. Aldo Fabrizi, Anna Magnani, Marcello Pagliero, Maria Michi, Vito Annicchiarico, Nando Bruno, Harry Feist. Classic Rossellini account of Italian underground movement during Nazi occupation of Rome; powerful moviemaking gem.

Open the Door and See All the Peo-

ple (1964) 82m. **½ D: Jerome Hill. Maybelle Nash, Alec Wilder, Charles Rydell, Ellen Martin. Weird little comedy of elderly twin sisters, their contrasting personalities and rivalry.

Operation Bikini (1963) 83m. ** D: Anthony Carras. Tab Hunter, Frankie Avalon, Eva Six, Scott Brady, Gary Crosby, Jim Backus. Occasionally perky cast livens tame WW2 narrative of attempt to destroy sunken treasure before enemy grabs it.

Operation Bottleneck (1961) 78m. *½ D: Edward L. Cahn. Ron Foster, Miiko Taka, Norman Alden, John Clarke, Ben Wright. Mini-actioner of WW2 Burma; not much to offer.

Operation CIA (1965) 90m. **½ D: Christian Nyby. Burt Reynolds, Kieu Chinh, Danielle Aubry, John Hoyt, Cyril Collack. Diverting drama set in Saigon; federal agent Reynolds uncovers a misplaced secret message meant for Allies.

Operation Conspiracy (1957-British) 69m. *½ D: Joseph Sterling. Philip Friend, Mary Mackenzie, Leslie Dwyer, Allan Cuthbertson. Timid little espionage film. Retitled: CLOAK WITHOUT DAGGER.

Operation Disaster (1951-British) 102m. *** D: Roy Baker. John Mills, Helen Cherry, Richard Attenborough, Lana Morris. Vivid actioner of submarine warfare during WW2, tautly presented.

Operation Eichmann (1961) 93m. **½ D: R. G. Springsteen. Werner Klemperer, Ruta Lee, Donald Buka, Barbara Turner, John Banner. Fairly intriguing account of the Nazi leader's postwar life and his capture by Israelis.

Operation Haylift (1950) 75m. ** D: William Berke. Bill Williams, Ann Rutherford, Jane Nigh, Tom Brown. Minor account of air force assisting farmers to save stranded cattle during snowstorm.

Operation Mad Ball (1957) 105m. ** D: Richard Quine. Jack Lemmon, Kathryn Grant, Mickey Rooney, Ernie Kovacs, Arthur O'Connell, James Darren, Roger Smith. Weak service comedy about crafty soldiers planning wild party on base. Dull stretches, few gags. O'Connell comes off better than supposed comedians in film.

Operation Mermaid SEE: Bay of Saint Michel.

Operation Pacific (1951) 111m. *** D: George Waggner. John Wayne, Patricia Neal, Ward Bond, Scott Forbes. Overzealous Wayne is ultradedicated to his navy command; the few WW2 action scenes are taut, and Neal makes a believable love interest.

Operation Petticoat (1959) C-124m. **½ D: Blake Edwards. Cary Grant, Tony Curtis, Dina Merrill, Gene Evans, Arthur O'Connell, Richard Sargent, Virginia Gregg. Slapstick comedy aboard a sub runs hot and cold; when it's hot, it's very funny, but there are plenty of cold spots in between. Grant and Curtis team well.

Operation Secret (1952) 108m. ** D: Lewis Seiler. Cornel Wilde, Steve Cochran, Phyllis Thaxter, Karl Malden, Dan O'Herlihy. Tame WW2 actioner involving a traitor in midst of Allied division.

Operation Snafu (1965-British) 97m. **½ D: Cyril Frankel. Alfred Lynch, Sean Connery, Cecil Parker, Stanley Holloway, Alan King, Wilfrid Hyde-White, Eric Barker, Kathleen Harrison. Sluggish WW2 account of two buddies becoming heroes unintentionally; most capable cast. Retitled: OPERATION WARHEAD.

Operation Snatch (1962-British) 83m. ** D: Robert Day. Terry-Thomas, George Sanders, Lionel Jeffries, Jackie Lane, Lee Montague, Michael Trubshawe. Fitfully funny satire involving British attempt to keep "their flag flying" on Gibraltar during WW2.

Operation Warhead SEE: Operation Snafu.

Operation X (1951-British) 79m. ** D: Gregory Ratoff. Edward G. Robinson, Peggy Cummins, Richard Greene, Nora Swinburn. Heady yarn with Robinson overly ambitious businessman forgetting his scruples.

Opposite Sex, The (1956) C-117m. *** D: David Miller. June Allyson, Joan Collins, Dolores Gray, Ann Sheridan, Joan Blondell, Ann Miller, Agnes Moorehead, Carolyn Jones, Charlotte Greenwood. Well-heeled musical remake of Clare Booth Luce's THE WOMEN has stellar cast, but still pales next to brittle original (Shearer, Crawford, Russell, etc.).

Major difference: music and men appear in this expanded version.

Orchestra Wives (1942) 98m. *** D: Archie Mayo. George Montgomery, Glenn Miller, Lynn Bari, Carole Landis, Cesar Romero, Ann Rutherford, Virginia Gilmore, Mary Beth Hughes, Jackie Gleason. Story woven around Glenn Miller band and the musicians' neglected wives. Vintage music is chief asset of film: "I've Got A Gal In Kalamazoo," "At Last," "Serenade In Blue."

Ordered to Love (1960-German, dubbed) 82m. **½ D: Werner Klinger. Maria Perschy, Marisa Mell, Rosemarie Kirstein, Birgitt Bergen. Potentially explosive film gets tame treatment; account of Nazi "breeding" camps for new generation of master race soldiers.

Orders are Orders (1954-British) ** D: David Paltenghi. Margot Grahame, Maureen Swanson, Peter Sellers, Tony Hancock, Sidney James. Hancock as befuddled lieutenant is best item in this slapstick yarn of movie company using an army barracks for headquarters. Based on a 1932 play, filmed once before.

Orders to Kill (1958-British) 93m. **½ D: Anthony Asquith. Eddie Albert, Paul Massie, Lillian Gish, James Robertson Justice. Low-keyed account of American agent sent into France to kill a traitor.

Oregon Passage (1957) C-82m. *½ D: Paul Landres. John Ericson, Lola Albright, Edward Platt, Jon Shepodd. Bland fare about army officer trying to do good, but interfering with Indian way of life.

Oregon Trail, The (1959) C-86m. ** D: Gene Fowler, Jr. Fred MacMurray, William Bishop, Nina Shipman, Gloria Talbott, Henry Hull, John Carradine. Uneventful Western with MacMurray a reporter investigating Indian attacks on settlers; set in 19th-century Oregon.

Organizer, The (1964-Italian, dubbed) 126m. *** D: Mario Monicelli. Marcello Mastroianni, Annie Girardot, Renato Salvatori, Bernard Blier. Serious look at labor union efforts in Italy, with Mastroianni giving low-keyed performance in title role.

Oriental Dream SEE: **Kismet.**

Oscar, The (1966) C-119m. **½ D: Russell Rouse. Stephen Boyd, Elke Sommer, Eleanor Parker, Milton Berle, Joseph Cotten, Jill St. John, Ernest Borgnine, Edie Adams, Tony Bennett, Jean Hale. Shiny tinsel view of Hollywood and those competing for Academy Awards; Parker as love-hungry talent agent comes off best. Loosely based on Richard Sale novel, with many guest stars thrown in. Some of the dialogue is so bad it's laughable.

Oscar Wilde (1960-British) 96m. **½ D: Gregory Ratoff. Robert Morley, Phyllis Calvert, John Neville, Ralph Richardson, Dennis Price, Alexander Knox, Edward Chapman. Ironical biography of famed 19th-century wit and playwright; lacks essential satirical humor. Morley does his best in title role.

O'Shaughnessy's Boy (1935) 88m. **½ D: Richard Boleslawski. Wallace Beery, Jackie Cooper, Spanky McFarland, Henry Stephenson, Leona Maricle, Sara Haden. Sentimental tale of Beery searching for his son, taken from him by cruel wife.

Othello (1955-Italian) 92m. **½ D: Orson Welles. Orson Welles, Suzanne Cloutier, Robert Coote, Michael Lawrence, Fay Compton. Welles gives an intelligent but overdramatic interpretation to Shakespeare's tale of the Moor jealous of wife Desdemona.

Other Love, The (1947) 95m. **½ D: Andre de Toth. Barbara Stanwyck, David Niven, Richard Conte, Maria Palmer, Joan Lorring, Gilbert Roland, Richard Hale, Lenore Aubert. Dying Stanwyck decides to live wild life with gambler Conte, unaware that doctor Niven loves her. Not convincing, but enjoyable.

Other Woman, The (1954) 81m. Bomb D: Hugo Haas. Hugo Haas, Cleo Moore, Lance Fuller, Lucille Barkley, Jack Macy, John Qualen. Nonsense involving a girl's plot for revenge on her former boss.

Our Betters (1933) 78m. **½ D: George Cukor. Constance Bennett, Gilbert Roland, Charles Starrett, Anita Louise, Alan Mowbray, Minor Watson, Violet Kemble-Cooper. Dated but enjoyable film of Somerset Maugham drawing-room comedy about British lord marrying rich American girl.

Our Blushing Brides (1930) 79m. ** D: Harry Beaumont. Joan Crawford,

Anita Page, Dorothy Sebastian, Robert Montgomery, Hedda Hopper, John Miljan. Cast would blush to see this antiquated soaper of three husband-hunting salesgirls involved with trio of brothers. Campy fun today.

Our Daily Bread (1934) 74m. *** D: King Vidor. Karen Morley, John Qualen, Tom Keene, Barbara Pepper, Addison Richards, Harry Holman. Simple yet powerful Depression story of destitute couple trying to survive; now considered a classic in many circles, with memorable direction by Vidor.

Our Hearts Were Growing Up (1946) 83m. **½ D: William D. Russell. Gail Russell, Diana Lynn, Brian Donlevy, James Brown, Bill Edwards, William Demarest. Follow-up to OUR HEARTS WERE YOUNG AND GAY doesn't match it, with girls on their own at Princeton.

Our Hearts Were Young and Gay (1944) 81m. *** D: Lewis Allen. Gail Russell, Diana Lynn, Charlie Ruggles, Dorothy Gish, Beulah Bondi, Alma Kruger. Nostalgic comedy of young girls Cornelia Otis Skinner and Emily Kimbrough sailing to Europe in the 1920's; fine cast sparkles.

Our Little Girl (1935) 63m. **½ D: John Robertson. Shirley Temple, Rosemary Ames, Joel McCrea, Lyle Talbot, Erin O'Brien-Moore. Usual Temple plot of Shirley bringing separated parents McCrea and Ames together again.

Our Man Flint (1966) C-107m. **½ D: Daniel Mann. James Coburn, Lee J. Cobb, Gila Golan, Edward Mulhare, Benson Fong, Gianna Serra. One of the countless James Bond spoofs, this saga of the man from Z.O.W.I.E. starts briskly, becomes forced after a while. Coburn makes a zesty hero, Golan an attractive decoration.

Our Man in Havana (1960) 107m. **½ D: Carol Reed. Alec Guinness, Burl Ives, Maureen O'Hara, Ernie Kovacs, Noel Coward, Ralph Richardson, Jo Morrow. Weak satirical spy spoof, claiming origin from Graham Greene novel. Guinness is vacuum cleaner salesman who becomes British agent.

Our Miss Brooks (1956) 85m. **½ D: Al Lewis. Eve Arden, Gale Gordon, Don Porter, Robert Rockwell, Jane Morgan, Richard Crenna. Feature version of TV series, with Arden as Connie Brooks, Gordon as Principal Osgood Conklin, Rockwell as Mr. Boynton, and young Crenna as student Walter Denton. OK entry for series fans.

Our Relations (1936) 65m. **½ D: Harry Lachman. Stan Laurel, Oliver Hardy, Alan Hale, Sidney Toler, Daphne Pollard, Betty Healy, James Finlayson, Arthur Housman, Iris Adrian, Lona Andre. Duo in amusing comedy of errors with their twin brothers; best scenes in Hale's beer garden.

Our Town (1940) 90m. ***½ D: Sam Wood. William Holden, Martha Scott, Fay Bainter, Beulah Bondi, Thomas Mitchell, Guy Kibbee. Sensitive adaptation of Thornton Wilder play about small New England town with human drama and conflict in every family.

Our Very Own (1950) 93m. **½ D: David Miller. Ann Blyth, Farley Granger, Jane Wyatt, Donald Cook, Ann Dvorak, Natalie Wood, Martin Milner. Melodramatic account of Blyth's shock upon discovering she's an adopted child.

Our Vines Have Tender Grapes (1945) 105m. ***½ D: Roy Rowland. Edward G. Robinson, Margaret O'Brien, James Craig, Frances Gifford, Agnes Moorehead, Morris Carnovsky. Excellent view of American life in Wisconsin town with uncharacteristic Robinson as O'Brien's kind, understanding father.

Our Wife (1941) 95m. **½ D: John M. Stahl. Melvyn Douglas, Ruth Hussey, Ellen Drew, Charles Coburn, John Hubbard. Douglas adds dignity to this OK marital comedy involving musician seeking divorce to marry another.

Out of Sight (1966) C-87m. *½ D: Lennie Weinrib. Jonathan Daly, Karen Jensen, Robert Pine, Carole Shelyne, Gary Lewis and The Playboys. Silly combination of beach and spy formulas doesn't succeed in either department.

Out of the Blue (1947) 84m. **½ D: Leigh Jason. Virginia Mayo, George Brent, Turhan Bey, Ann Dvorak, Carole Landis, Hadda Brooks. Naive Brent is in trouble when far from innocent young woman is discovered unconscious in his apartment; fluffy fun. Dvorak is a delight in an offbeat role.

Out of the Clouds (1957-British) C-80m. ** D: Michael Relph, Basil Dearden. Anthony Steel, James Robertson Justice, Gordon Harker, Bernard Lee, Megs Jenkins. Work and play among commercial pilots; nothing special.

Out of the Fog (1941) 93m. *** D: Anatole Litvak. Ida Lupino, John Garfield, Thomas Mitchell, Eddie Albert, George Tobias, Leo Gorcey. Fine filmization of Irwin Shaw's THE GENTLE PEOPLE, about gangster terrorizing innocent Brooklyn family.

Out of the Frying Pan SEE: Young and Willing.

Out of the Past (1947) 97m. *** D: Jacques Tourneur. Robert Mitchum, Jane Greer, Kirk Douglas, Richard Webb, Rhonda Fleming, Dickie Moore, Steve Brodie. Grim melodrama of cool detective Mitchum, moll Greer, and shady employer Douglas; excellent film of Geoffrey Homes' BUILD MY GALLOWS HIGH.

Out of this World (1945) 96m. **½ D: Hal Walker. Eddie Bracken, Veronica Lake, Diana Lynn, Cass Daley, Parkyakarkus, Donald MacBride, Florence Bates, Gary, Philip, Dennis and Lindsay Crosby. Bracken becomes pop crooner; a cute idea mercilessly padded with loud musical specialties by Daley, Lynn, and guest stars.

Out West with the Hardys (1938) 90m. D: George B. Seitz. Lewis Stone, Mickey Rooney, Cecilia Parker, Fay Holden, Ann Rutherford, Sara Haden, Don Castle, Virginia Weidler, Gordon Jones, Ralph Morgan. SEE: Andy Hardy series.

Outcast, The (1954) C-90m. **½ D: William Witney. John Derek, Joan Evans, Jim Davis, Catherine McLeod, Ben Cooper. Simply told Western of Derek battling to win his rightful inheritance.

Outcasts of the City (1958) 61m *½ D: Boris Petroff. Osa Massen, Robert Hutton, Maria Palmer, Nestor Paiva, George Neise. Junky flick of pilot Hutton involved with German doll Palmer.

Outcast of the Islands (1952-British) 93m. *** D: Carol Reed. Ralph Richardson, Wendy Hiller, Trevor Howard, Robert Morley, Kerima. Joseph Conrad's character study of a manhunt on Malayan Island is given sturdy treatment by sound cast.

Outcasts of Poker Flat, The (1952) 81m. **½ D: Joseph M. Newman. Anne Baxter, Miriam Hopkins, Dale Robertson, Cameron Mitchell, John Ridgely. Obvious, uninspired version of Bret Harte tale of social rejects trapped together in cabin during snowstorm.

Outcry (1957-Italian, dubbed) 115m. **½ D: Michelangelo Antonioni. Steve Cochran, Alida Valli, Dorian Gray, Betsy Blair, Lyn Shaw. Leisurely paced yet compelling study of Cochran's mental disintegration due to lack of communication with those he loves; Cochran is quite good. Original title: IL GRIDO.

Outlaw, The (1943) 123m. ** D: Howard Hughes. Jack Buetel, Jane Russell, Thomas Mitchell, Walter Huston. Notorious sex-Western has been tamed by recent films, but still has plenty of suggestiveness. Russell is alluring, film only fair.

Outlaw Stallion, The (1954) C-64m. *½ D: Fred F. Sears. Phil Carey, Dorothy Patrick, Billy Gray, Roy Roberts, Gordon Jones. Programmer of horse thieves conning ranch woman and her son to get their herd.

Outlaw's Daughter, The (1954) C-75m. *½ D: Wesley Barry. Bill Williams, Kelly Ryan, Jim Davis, George Cleveland, Elisha Cook. Weak oater of stagecoach robbery and girl implicated because her elderly father used to be an outlaw.

Outlaws Is Coming, The (1965) 89m. ** D: Norman Maurer. The Three Stooges, Adam West, Nancy Kovack, Mort Mills, Don Lamond, Emil Sitka, Joe Bolton. Mild comedy pitting the Stooges against gang of outlaws. West (Batman) is on their side, so they have a good chance. Typical slapstick, but they've had better material.

Outlaw's Son (1957) 89m. ** D: Lesley Selander. Dane Clark, Ben Cooper, Lori Nelson, Ellen Drew, Eddie Foy III. Clark is most earnest in modest Western about outlaw and the son he deserted years before.

Outpost in Malaya (1952-British) 88m. **½ D: Ken Annakin. Claudette Colbert, Jack Hawkins, Anthony

Steel, Jeremy Spencer. Mostly about marital disharmony on a rubber plantation. Original title: PLANTER'S WIFE.

Outpost In Morocco (1949) 92m. ** D: Robert Florey. George Raft, Marie Windsor, Akim Tamiroff, John Litel, Eduard Franz. Cardboard adventure saga of good-guy Raft battling desert foes while romancing enemy-girl Windsor.

Outrage, The (1964) 97m. **½ D: Martin Ritt. Paul Newman, Edward G. Robinson, Claire Bloom, Laurence Harvey, William Shatner, Albert Salmi. Pretentious fizzle, based on Japanese film RASHOMON, with Newman hamming it as Mexican bandit who allegedly rapes Bloom while husband Harvey stands by. Robinson as philosophical narrator is best thing about film.

Outriders, The (1950) C-93m. ** D: Roy Rowland. Joel McCrea, Arlene Dahl, Barry Sullivan, Claude Jarman, Jr., Ramon Novarro. Standard account of Reb soldiers trying to capture gold shipment for Confederate cause.

Outside the Law (1956) 81m. *½ D: Jack Arnold. Ray Danton, Leigh Snowden, Grant Williams, Onslow Stevens. Half-baked yarn of Danton proving his worth by snaring counterfeiters.

Outside the Wall (1950) 80m. **½ D: Crane Wilbur. Richard Basehart, Dorothy Hart, Marilyn Maxwell, Signe Hasso, Henry Morgan. Excellent cast carries off this tale of former convict snafuing a robbery syndicate.

Outsider, The (1961) 108m. **½ D: Delbert Mann. Tony Curtis, James Franciscus, Bruce Bennett, Gregory Walcott, Vivian Nathan. Potentially gutsy account of American Indian Ira Hayes who was one of the marines to raise U.S. flag at Iwo Jima, becomes timid formula biography.

Outsider, The (1967) C-120m. **½ D: Michael Ritchie. Darren McGavin, Sean Garrison, Shirley Knight, Nancy Malone, Edmond O'Brien, Ann Sothern. Private eye telefeature set in L.A., with McGavin the detective hired by O'Brien to solve mystery behind death of an office worker; formula plot served as pilot for new TV series.

Over-Exposed (1956) 80m. *½ D: Lewis Seiler. Cleo Moore, Richard Crenna, Isobel Elsom, Raymond Greenleaf, Shirley Thomas. Flabby study of blackmail, with Cleo Moore vacationing from Hugo Haas spectacles . . . some vacation!

Over My Dead Body (1942) 68m. **½ D: Malcolm St. Clair. Milton Berle, Mary Beth Hughes, Reginald Denny, Frank Orth, William Davidson. Berle gives peppery performance in farfetched yarn about amateur sleuth who accidentally frames himself for murder.

Over the Moon (1937-British) 78m. *½ D: Thornton Freeland. Merle Oberon, Rex Harrison, Robert Douglas, Louis Borell. Disappointingly bad comedy of country girl squandering inherited fortune. Interesting cast cast cannot save clinker.

Over 21 (1945) 102m. *** D: Charles Vidor. Irene Dunne, Alexander Knox, Charles Coburn, Jeff Donnell, Lee Patrick, Phil Brown, Cora Witherspoon. Zesty comedy of middle-aged Knox trying to survive in officer's training for WW2 service, with help of wife Dunne; from Ruth Gordon's play.

Overland Pacific (1954) C-73m. ** D: Fred F. Sears. Jock Mahoney, Peggie Castle, Adele Jergens, William Bishop. Mahoney is staunch railroad investigator trying to get at crux of Indian attacks on the trains.

Ox-Bow Incident, The (1943) 75m. **** D: William Welman. Henry Fonda, Dana Andrews, Mary Beth Hughes, Anthony Quinn, William Eythe, Henry Morgan, Jane Darwell. Grim account of mob rule in Western town, lynching of suspected rustlers Andrews and Quinn. Fonda and Morgan are lone pacifists, Harry Davenport the level-headed doc, Frank Conroy the stubborn general. Superb in every respect.

PT 109 (1963) C-140m. ** D: Leslie Martinson. Cliff Robertson, Robert Culp, Ty Hardin, James Gregory, Robert Blake. Standard action film based on true story of PT-boat and commander John F. Kennedy; neither here nor there; for younger audiences.

PT Raiders SEE: **Ship That Died of Shame, The.**

Pacific Liner (1939) 75m. ** D: Lew Landers. Chester Morris, Wendy Barrie, Victor McLaglen, Barry Fitzgerald. Formula programmer focusing on breakout of epidemic and mutiny aboard a ship; cast is better than the material.

Pack Up Your Troubles (1932) 68m. **½ D: George Marshall, Ray McCarey. Stan Laurel, Oliver Hardy, Mary Carr, James Finlayson, Charles Middleton, Grady Sutton, Billy Gilbert. Daffy duo are drafted during WW1; after some army shenanigans they try to locate relatives of late pal's daughter. Good fun.

Pack Up Your Troubles (1939) 75m. ** D: H. Bruce Humberstone. Ritz Brothers, Jane Withers, Lynn Bari, Joseph Schildkraut, Stanley Fields, Leon Ames. Watch the Ritz Brothers' opening routine, then forget the rest of this WW1 hodgepodge, especially when Jane is focus of the film.

Pad and How to Use It, The (1966) C-86m. **½ D: Brian Hutton. Brian Bedford, Julie Sommars, James Farentino, Edy Williams. Peter Shaffer play THE PRIVATE EAR is basis for sex romp involving Bedford's attempt to become Sommars' lover.

Pagan Love Song (1950) C-76m. ** D: Robert Alton. Esther Williams, Howard Keel, Minna Gombell, Rita Moreno. Stale MGM musical; Keel goes to Tahiti, romances Williams.

Pagans, The (1958-Italian, dubbed) 80m. *½ D: Ferrucio Cereo. Pierre Cressoy, Helen Remy, Vittorio Sanipoli, Luigi Tosi, Franco Fabrizi. Uninspired costumer set in Rome, with the Spanish invaders ramming the city walls.

Page Miss Glory (1935) 90m. **½ D: Mervyn LeRoy. Marion Davies, Pat O'Brien, Dick Powell, Mary Astor, Frank McHugh, Lyle Talbot, Patsy Kelly, Allen Jenkins, Barton MacLane. Amiable spoof of beauty contests, with Davies chosen through mishap as the winner. Fine cast provides a lot of fun.

Paid (1931) 80m. **½ D: Sam Wood. Joan Crawford, Kent Douglass (Douglass Montgomery), Robert Armstrong, Marie Prevost, John Miljan, Polly Moran. Not-bad early Crawford. Innocent girl sent to prison; she hardens and seeks revenge. Remade as WITHIN THE LAW.

Paid in Full (1950) 105m. **½ D: William Dieterle. Robert Cummings, Lizabeth Scott, Diana Lynn, Eve Arden. Turgid soaper involving sisters Scott and Lynn both in love with Cummings.

Paid to Kill (1954-British) 70m. ** D: Montgomery Tully. Dane Clark, Paul Carpenter, Thea Gregory, Anthony Forwood. Oft-told premise of man who hires hood to kill him for insurance and changes his mind.

Painted Hills, The (1951) C-65m. **½ D: Harold F. Kress. Paul Kelly, Bruce Cowling, Gary Gray, Art Smith. Nicely photographed Lassie tale set in 1870's West.

Painted Veil, The (1934) 83m. **½ D: Richard Boleslawsky. Greta Garbo, Herbert Marshall, George Brent, Warner Oland, Jean Hersholt. Set in mysterious Orient, film tells Maugham's story of unfaithful wife mending her ways. Mundane script uplifted by Garbo's personality, supported by Marshall as her husband, Brent as her lover. Remade as THE SEVENTH SIN.

Painting the Clouds with Sunshine (1951) C-87m. ** D: David Butler. Dennis Morgan, Virginia Mayo, Gene Nelson, Lucille Norman, Virginia Gibson, Tom Conway. Lukewarm musical of trio of gold-diggers in Las Vegas searching for rich husbands, a mild reworking of an old musical formula.

Paisan (1947-Italian, dubbed) 90m. ***½ D: Roberto Rossellini. Carmela Sazio, Gar Moore, Robert van Loon, Maria Michi, Bill Tubbs, Carlo Pisacane, Harriet White. Stark realism via six vignettes of effect of Allied soldiers in WW2 Italy, largely unprofessional cast.

Pajama Game, The (1957) C-101m. *** D: George Abbott and Stanley Donen. Doris Day, John Raitt, Carol Haney, Eddie Foy, Jr., Barbara Nichols, Reta Shaw. Rousing movie version of Broadway musical, with Day a joy as the head of factory grievance's committee and Raitt the foreman.

Pajama Party (1964) C-85m. **½ D: Don Weis. Tommy Kirk, Annette Funicello, Elsa Lanchester, Buster Keaton, Dorothy Lamour, Harvey Lembeck. Mild mixture of sci-fi and beach party shenanigans; notable only for supporting veteran cast.

Pal Joey (1957) C-111m. *** D:

George Sidney. Rita Hayworth, Frank Sinatra, Kim Novak, Barbara Nichols, Elizabeth Patterson, Bobby Sherwood. Heel-hero of Rodgers and Hart's musical becomes a flippant nice guy who seeks to build a sleek nightclub in Frisco. Hayworth and Novak battle over Frank with diverting results. Songs: "Bewitched, Bothered, and Bewildered," "Small Hotel," "My Funny Valentine," "The Lady Is a Tramp," etc.

Paleface, The (1948) C-91m. *** D: Norman Z. McLeod. Bob Hope, Jane Russell, Robert Armstrong, Iris Adrian, Robert Watson, Jack Searle. Enjoyable Western-comedy with timid Bob backed up by sharpshooting Russell in gunfighting encounters; Oscar-winning song "Buttons and Bows." Remade as **The Shakiest Gun In The West.**

Palm Beach Story, The (1942) 90m. ***1/2 D: Preston Sturges. Claudette Colbert, Joel McCrea, Mary Astor, Rudy Vallee, William Demarest, Jack Norton, Franklin Pangborn, Jimmy Conlin. Hilarious screwball comedy with Claudette running away from hubby McCrea, landing in Palm Beach with nutty millionairess Astor and her bumbling brother Vallee, who steals the film from everyone.

Palm Springs Weekend (1963) C-100m. **1/2 D: Norman Taurog. Troy Donahue, Connie Stevens, Stefanie Powers, Robert Conrad, Ty Hardin, Jack Weston, Andrew Duggan. Cast tries to play teen-agers; yarn of group on a spree in resort town is mostly predictable.

Palmy Days (1931) 77m. **1/2 D: A. Edward Sutherland. Eddie Cantor, Charlotte Greenwood, Charles Middleton, George Raft, Walter Catlett. Elaborate early musical. Cantor romps through story of patsy for shady fortune-telling gang.

Pan Americana (1945) 84m. ** D: John H. Auer. Philip Terry, Eve Arden, Robert Benchley, Audrey Long, Jane Greer. Another 40's gesture toward Latin American goodwill. Romantic trivia of magazine writers visiting South American country.

Panama Hattie (1942) 79m.**1/2 D: Norman Z. McLeod. Ann Sothern, Red Skelton, Rags Ragland, Ben Blue, Marsha Hunt, Virginia O'Brien, Alan Mowbray, Lena Horne, Dan Dailey, Carl Esmond. Successful Cole Porter musical (starring Ethel Merman) about nightclub owner in Panama, falls flat on screen. Porter's score mostly absent.

Panama Sal (1957) 70m. Bomb D: William Witney. Elena Verdugo, Carlos Rivas, Joe Flynn, Edward Kemmer. Lowjinks blend of poor comedy and flat songs.

Pandora and the Flying Dutchman (1951) C-123m. **1/2 D: Albert Lewin. James Mason, Ava Gardner, Nigel Patrick, Sheila Sim, Harold Warrender. Slowly paced fantasy romance with Gardner encountering mysterious Mason who seems to have no future, just an endless past.

Panic Button (1964) 90m. **1/2 D: George Sherman. Maurice Chevalier, Eleanor Parker, Jayne Mansfield, Michael Connors, Akim Tamiroff. Good cast wasted in amateurish production involving the making of a TV pilot in Italy that's supposed to flop so gangster producers will have legitimate tax loss.

Panic in the Parlor (1957-British) 81m. **1/2 D: Gordon Parry. Peggy Mount, Shirley Eaton, Gordon Jackson, Ronald Lewis. Broad but diverting humor about a sailor coming home to get married, and the chaos it causes all concerned.

Panic in the Streets (1950) 93m. *** D: Elia Kazan. Richard Widmark, Paul Douglas, Barbara Bel Geddes, Jack Palance, Zero Mostel. Taut drama involving gun-happy gangsters, one of whom is carrier of disease, and the police-hunt to find him.

Panic in the Year Zero (1962) 95m. **1/2 D: Ray Milland. Ray Milland, Jean Hagen, Frankie Avalon, Mary Mitchel, Joan Freeman, Richard Garland. Intriguing film about family that escapes atomic bomb explosion to find a situation of every-man-for-himself. Milland doubles as actor-director. Good cast, but loud, tinny music spoils much of film's effect.

Pantaloons (1957-French, dubbed) C-93m. **1/2 D: John Berry. Fernandel, Carmen Sevilla, Christine Carrere, Fernando Rey. Fernandel stars in this brisk little period-piece as a phony gay-blade intent on female conquests.

Panther Girl of the Kongo SEE: **Claw Monsters, The.**

Panther Island SEE: **Bomba on Panther Island.**

Papa, Mama, the Maid and I (1956-French, dubbed) 94m. **½ D: Jean-Paul Le Chanois. Fernand Ledoux, Gaby Morlay, Nicole Courcel, Robert Lamoureux. Sometimes saucy sex comedy, fully explained by title tag.

Papa's Delicate Condition (1963) C-98m. ***½ D: George Marshall. Jackie Gleason, Glynis Johns, Charlie Ruggles, Laurel Goodwin, Elisha Cook, Juanita Moore, Murray Hamilton. Amusing nostalgia of Corinne Griffith's childhood; Gleason dominates everything as tipsy railroad inspector father; set in 1900's. Oscar-winning song "Call Me Irresponsible."

Parachute Battalion (1941) 75m. ** D: Leslie Goodwins. Edmond O'Brien, Nancy Kelly, Robert Preston, Harry Carey, Buddy Ebsen, Paul Kelly. Efficient WW2 programmer which gets a bit sticky with flag-waving.

Paradine Case, The (1948) 125m. **½ D: Alfred Hitchcock. Gregory Peck, Ann Todd, Charles Laughton, Charles Coburn, Ethel Barrymore, Louis Jourdan, Valli. Talk, talk, talk in complicated, stagy courtroom drama, set in England. Below par for Hitchcock.

Paradise Alley (1961) 85m. *½ D: Hugo Haas. Marie Windsor, Hugo Haas, Billy Gilbert, Carol Morris, Chester Conklin, Margaret Hamilton, Corinne Griffith. Grade-D mishmash about elderly moviemaker involved in amateur film production. Interesting only for veteran cast. Original title: STARS IN THE BACK YARD.

Paradise for Three (1938) 75m. ** D: Edward Buzzell. Frank Morgan, Robert Young, Mary Astor, Edna May Oliver, Florence Rice, Reginald Owen, Henry Hull. Strange story of American businessman trying to mingle with German people to discover how they live. Good cast helps fair script.

Paradise, Hawaiian Style (1966) C-91m. **½ D: Michael Moore. Elvis Presley, Suzanna Leigh, James Shigeta, Donna Butterworth. Rehash of Presley's earlier BLUE HAWAII, with Elvis a pilot who runs a charter service while romancing local dolls. Attractive fluff.

Paradise Lagoon SEE: **Admirable Crichton, The.**

Paramount on Parade (1930) 75m. **½ D: Dorothy Arzner, Otto Brower, Edmund Goulding, Victor Heerman, Edwin Knopf, Rowland V. Lee, Ernst Lubitsch, Lothar Mendes, Victor Schertzinger, A. Edward Sutherland, Frank Tuttle. Jean Arthur, Clara Bow, Maurice Chevalier, Kay Francis, Helen Kane, Fredric March, Jack Oakie, Warner Oland, Lillian Roth, Fay Wray. Variety format with all of Paramount Pictures' stars at the time in songs, dances, sketches. Interesting early talkie, with Chevalier sequence a highlight.

Paranoiac (1963-British) 80m. **½ D: Freddie Francis, Janette Scott, Oliver Reed, Liliane Brousse, Alexander Davion, Sheila Burrell, Maurice Denham. Murder, impersonation, insanity all part of thriller set in large English country estate.

Paratrooper, The (1954-British) C-87m. ** D: Terence Young. Alan Ladd, Leo Genn, Susan Stephen, Harry Andrews. Minor Ladd vehicle involving special tactical forces and Ladd's guilt-ridden past.

Pardners (1956) C-90m. **½ D: Norman Taurog. Jerry Lewis, Dean Martin, Lori Nelson, Jackie Loughery, John Baragrey, Jeff Morrow, Agnes Moorehead, Lon Chaney, Jr. Vehicle is good excuse for above-par hijinks of Martin and Lewis on Western farm.

Pardon My French (1951) 81m. **½ D: Bernard Vorhaus. Paul Henreid, Merle Oberon, Paul Bonifas, Maximillienne, Jim Gerald. Fluff of Oberon inheriting a mansion in France occupied by charming composer Henreid.

Pardon My Past (1945) 88m. *** D: Leslie Fenton. Fred MacMurray, Marguerite Chapman, Akim Tamiroff, William Demarest, Rita Johnson, Harry Davenport. Excellent tale of unsuspecting MacMurray, lookalike for famous playboy, incurring his debts and many enemies; fine comedy-drama.

Pardon My Rhythm (1944) 62m. ** D: Felix E. Feist. Gloria Jean, Evelyn Ankers, Patric Knowles, Bob Crosby. Naive minor musical set in ultra-wholesome high school, with Gloria the singing belle of the ball.

Pardon My Sarong (1942) 84m. *** D: Erle C. Kenton. Lou Costello, Bud

Abbott, Lionel Atwill, Nan Wynn, Four Ink Spots, Virginia Bruce, Tip, Tap, Toe. A&C in good form as bus drivers who end up on tropical island, getting involved with notorious jewel thieves.

Pardon My Trunk SEE: **Hello Elephant.**

Pardon Us (1931) 55m. **½ D: James Parrott. Stan Laurel, Oliver Hardy, Wilfred Lucas, Walter Long, James Finlayson, June Marlowe. First L&H feature is spoof of BIG HOUSE prison movies; very funny, with great mess hall scene, among many others.

Paris After Dark (1943) 85m. ** D: Leonide Moguy. George Sanders, Philip Dorn, Brenda Marshall, Madeleine LeBeau, Marcel Dalio. Tame anti-Nazi film with husband and wife on opposite sides of fence.

Paris Blues (1961) 98m. *** D: Martin Ritt. Paul Newman, Joanne Woodward, Diahann Carroll, Sidney Poitier, Louis Armstrong. Film improves with each viewing; offbeat account of musicians Newman-Poitier in Left Bank Paris, romancing tourists Woodward-Carroll.

Paris Calling (1941) 95m. *** D: Edwin L. Marin. Elizabeth Bergner, Randolph Scott, Basil Rathbone, Gale Sondergaard, Eduardo Ciannelli, Lee J. Cobb. Exciting story of underground movement in Paris to destroy Nazis occupying France, with top-notch cast.

Paris Does Strange Things (1957-French, dubbed) C-86m. ** D: Jean Renoir. Ingrid Bergman, Mel Ferrer, Jean Marais, Elina Labourdette, Juliette Greco, Magali Noel. Beautifully photographed costume romance, with empty script and lifeless performances.

Paris Express, The (1953) C-83m. **½ D: Harold French. Claude Rains, Marta Toren, Marius Goring, Herbert Lom. Sturdy cast intertwined in tales of embezzlement, murder, and adultery aboard train heading for Paris.

Paris Follies of 1956 SEE: **Fresh From Paris.**

Paris Holiday (1958) C-100m. **½ D: Gerd Oswald. Bob Hope, Fernandel, Anita Ekberg, Martha Hyer, Preston Sturges. Mixture of French and American farce humor makes for uneven entertainment, with Hope in France to buy a new screenplay.

Paris Honeymoon (1939) 92m. **½ D: Frank Tuttle. Bing Crosby, Shirley Ross, Edward Everett Horton, Akim Tamiroff, Ben Blue, Rafaela Ottiano, Raymond Hatton. Texan Crosby visits France planning to marry Ross, but meets native Franciska Gaal and falls in love with her.

Paris Model (1953) 81m. *½ D: Alfred E. Green. Eva Gabor, Tom Conway, Paulette Goddard, Marilyn Maxwell, Cecil Kellaway, Barbara Lawrence, Florence Bates. Lackluster vehicle for veteran actors, revolving around a dress and four women who purchase copies of same.

Paris Playboys (1954) 62m. D: William Beaudine. Leo Gorcey, Huntz Hall, Bernard Gorcey, Veola Vonn, Steven Geray. SEE: **Bowery Boys** series.

Paris-Underground (1945) 97m. **½ D: Gregory Ratoff. Constance Bennett, Gracie Fields, George Rigaud, Kurt Kreuger, Leslie Vincent, Charles Andre. Well-acted story of American Bennett and Britisher Fields working in underground movement even while imprisoned in Nazi POW camp.

Paris When It Sizzles (1964) C-110m. ** D: Richard Quine. William Holden, Audrey Hepburn, Noel Coward, Tony Curtis, Marlene Dietrich. Thud of a romance story, ambling nowhere, barely interesting for its cast; a real disappointment.

Park Row (1952) 83m. **½ D: Samuel Fuller. Gene Evans, Mary Welch, Herbert Hayes, Tina Rome, Forrest Taylor. Engaging account of N.Y.C. newspaperman in 19th-century trying to be an energetic reporter. Good, unpretentious saga.

Parole, Inc. (1949) 71m. ** D: Alfred Zeisler. Michael O'Shea, Evelyn Ankers, Turhan Bey, Lyle Talbot. Turgid independent cheapie with low-budget class, about crackdown on gangster infiltration of parole system.

Parrish (1961) C-140m. *½ D: Delmer Daves. Claudette Colbert, Troy Donahue, Karl Malden, Dean Jagger, Connie Stevens, Diane McBain, Sharon Hugueny, Madeleine Sherwood. Slurpy soaper has so bad that at times it's funny; emotionless Donahue lives with his mother (Colbert) on Jagger's tobacco plantation and falls in love with three girls there. Malden overplays tyrannical tobacco czar to the nth degree.

Parson and the Outlaw, The (1957) C-71m. *½ D: Oliver Drake. Anthony Dexter, Sonny Tufts, Marie Windsor, Buddy Rogers, Jean Parker, Bob Steele. Minor version of life and times of Billy the Kid.

Parson of Panamint, The (1941) 84m. **½ D: William McGann. Charlie Ruggles, Ellen Drew, Philip Terry, Joseph Schildkraut, Porter Hall. Minor, offbeat Western with Ruggles as preacher in untamed mining town, involved in murder while reforming the community.

Part-Time Wife (1961-British) 70m. *½ D: Max Varnel. Anton Rodgers, Nyree Dawn Porter, Kenneth J. Warren, Henry McCarthy. Lumbering account of Rodgers loaning wife Porter to scoundrel friend Warren, who wants to make an impression; wooden farce.

Party Crashers, The (1958) 78m. *½ D: Bernard Girard. Mark Damon, Bobby Driscoll, Connie Stevens, Frances Farmer. Sleazy goings-on of teen-age gangs who become involved in reckless mayhem.

Party Girl (1958) C-99m. **½ D: Nicholas Ray. Robert Taylor, Cyd Charisse, Lee J. Cobb, John Ireland. Chicago-gangster-vs.-cop caper, in the 1920's; old-fashioned in concept and tritely handled.

Party's Over, The (1966-British) 94m. ** D: Guy Hamilton. Oliver Reed, Catherine Woodville, Clifford David, Ann Lynn. Sordid drama of wealthy American girl becoming involved with a group of London donothing youths.

Passage to Marseilles (1944) 110m. **½ D: Michael Curtiz. Humphrey Bogart, Michele Morgan, Claude Rains, Philip Dorn, Sydney Greenstreet, Peter Lorre, George Tobias, Helmut Dantine, John Loder, Eduardo Ciannelli. WW2 Devil's Island escape film marred by flashback-within-flashback confusion. Disappointing for such a fine cast, but still good.

Passage West (1951) C-80m. *½ D: Lewis R. Foster. John Payne, Dennis O'Keefe, Arleen Whelan, Mary Beth Hughes, Frank Faylen, Dooley Wilson. Outlaws join up with wagon train with predictable results.

Passion (1954) C-84m. **½ D: Allan Dwan. Cornel Wilde, Yvonne de Carlo, Raymond Burr, Lon Chaney, John Qualen. Picturesque tale of old California, with Wilde the outlaw seeking revenge for wrongs done to his family.

Passionate Sentry, The (1952-British) 84m. ** D: Anthony Kimmins. Nigel Patrick, Peggy Cummins, Valerie Hobson, George Cole, A. E. Matthews, Anthony Bushell. Wispy romantic comedy about madcap gal who falls in love with a guard at Buckingham Palace. Retitled: WHO GOES THERE?

Passionate Thief, The (1960-Italian, dubbed) 105m. **½ D: Mario Monicelli. Anna Magnani, Peggy Cummins, Toto, Ben Gazzara, Fred Clark, Edy Vessel. Offbeat serio-comedy with Magnani a film extra, Gazzara a pickpocket, Toto an unemployed actor—all meshed together in a minor tale of love and larceny.

Passport to Adventure SEE: **Passport to Destiny**

Passport to China (1961-British) 75m. ** D: Michael Carreras. Richard Basehart, Alan Gifford, Athene Seyler, Bert Kwouk, Eric Pohlmann. Uninspired help-the-refugee-out-of-Red-China caper.

Passport to Destiny (1944) 64m. ** D: Ray McCarey. Elsa Lanchester, Gordon Oliver, Lloyd Corrigan, Gavin Muir, Lenore Aubert, Fritz Feld. Tidy programmer with Elsa a patriotic scrubwoman determined to eliminate the Fuehrer. Retitled: PASSPORT TO ADVENTURE.

Passport to Pimlico (1948-British) 72m. ***½ D: Henry Cornelius. Stanley Holloway, Margaret Rutherford, Betty Warren, Hermione Baddeley, Barbara Murray, Paul Dupuis. Salty farce of ancient treaty enabling small group of people to form their own bounded territory in the middle of London.

Passport to Treason (1955-British) 70m. *½ D: Robert S. Baker. Rod Cameron, Lois Maxwell, Clifford Evans. Minor drama, with Cameron trying to solve homicide case for sake of friend.

Password is Courage, The (1963-British) 116m. *** D: Andrew L. Stone. Dirk Bogarde, Maria Perschy, Alfred Lynch, Nigel Stock, Reginald Beckwith, Richard Marner. Bogarde tops a fine cast in droll account of British soldier's plot to escape from WW2 prison camp.

Pat and Mike (1952) 95m. *** D: George Cukor. Spencer Tracy, Katharine Hepburn, Aldo Ray, William Ching, Jim Backus, Shelley Winters, Carl Switzer, Charles Buchinski (Bronson), William Self. Hepburn is Pat, top female athlete; Tracy is Mike, her manager, in pleasing comedy, not up to duo's other films. Ray is good as thickwitted sports star.

Patch of Blue, A (1965) 105m. *** D: Guy Green. Sidney Poitier, Elizabeth Hartman, Shelley Winters, Wallace Ford, Ivan Dixon, John Qualen, Elizabeth Fraser. Sensitive drama of a blind girl (Hartman) falling in love with a Negro (Poitier) is well acted, not too sticky. Winters won an Oscar for her bad-girl role as Hartman's guardian.

Pather Panchali (1958-Indian, dubbed) 112m. *** D: Satyajit Ray. Kanu Banerjii, Karuna Barnerjii, Subir Banerjii, Runki Banerjii. Unrelenting study of life in povertystricken Indian village; gripping, realistic. Music by Ravi Shankar.

Pathfinder, The (1952) C-78m. *½ D: Sidney Salkow. George Montgomery, Helena Carter, Jay Silverheels, Elena Verdugo, Chief Yowlachie. Low-budget version of James Fenimore Cooper tale of 1750's Great Lakes area, with Indian and French attacks on Americans.

Paths of Glory (1957) 86m. **** D: Stanley Kubrick. Kirk Douglas, Ralph Meeker, Adolphe Menjou, George Macready, Wayne Morris, Timothy Carey. One of the finest indictments of war ever produced. Superb acting by all. Forceful direction in powerful story of army politics in WW1 France.

Patsy, The (1964) C-101m. ** D: Jerry Lewis. Jerry Lewis, Ina Balin, Everett Sloane, Keenan Wynn, Peter Lorre, John Carradine, Neil Hamilton, Nancy Kulp. Forced, unfunny combination of humor and pathos, much inferior to somewhat similar ERRAND BOY. Even first-rate supporting cast can't bail itself out.

Patterns (1956) 83m. ***½ D: Fielder Cook. Van Heflin, Everett Sloane, Ed Begley, Beatrice Straight, Elizabeth Wilson. Trenchant Rod Serling drama of company power struggle, with bravura performance by Begley. Executive psychology of mid-50's is dated, but much better than similar EXECUTIVE SUITE.

Paula (1952) 80m. **½ D: Rudolph Mate. Loretta Young, Kent Smith, Alexander Knox, Tommy Rettig. Young gives credibility to role of woman who repents for hit-and-run accident by helping injured child regain his speech.

Pawnbroker, The (1965) 116m. **** D: Sidney Lumet. Rod Steiger, Geraldine Fitzgerald, Brock Peters, Jaime Sanchez, Thelma Oliver, Juano Hernandez. Important, engrossing film, realistically directed by Sidney Lumet in New York. Steiger has never been better than as Sol Nazerman, a Jewish pawnbroker in Harlem who lives in a sheltered world with haunting memories of Nazi prison camps.

Pawnee (1957) C-80m. ** D: George Waggner. George Montgomery, Bill Williams, Lola Albright, Francis J. McDonald, Raymond Hatton. Pat Western about Indian-raised white man with conflicting loyalties.

Pay or Die (1960) 110m. **½ D: Richard Wilson. Ernest Borgnine, Zohra Lampert, Al Austin, John Duke, Robert Ellenstein, Franco Corsaro, Mario Siletti. Above-par, flavorful account of Mafia activities in 1910's N.Y.C.; sturdy performances.

Payment Deferred (1932) 75m. *** D: Lothar Mendes. Charles Laughton, Maureen O'Sullivan, Dorothy Peterson, Verree Teasdale, Neil Hamilton, Ray Milland, Billy Bevan. Laughton is memorable as meek man who inadvertently gets involved in murder. Excellent melodrama with fine supporting cast.

Payment on Demand (1951) 90m. *** D: Curtis Bernhardt. Bette Davis, Barry Sullivan, Peggie Castle, Jane Cowl, Kent Taylor, Betty Lynn, John Sutton, Frances Dee, Otto Kruger. Well-handled chronicle of Davis-Sullivan marriage, highlighting events which lead to divorce.

Payroll (1961-British) 94m. **½ D: Sidney Hayers. Michael Craig, Françoise Prevost, Billie Whitelaw, William Lucas, Kenneth Griffith, Tom Bell. Well-handled account involving widow of payroll guard tracking down culprits.

Peacemaker, The (1956) 82m. ** D: Ted Post. James Mitchell, Rosemarie Bowe, Robert Armstrong, Jan Merlin, Dorothy Patrick, Jess Barker, Hugh Sanders. Ex-gunslinger, now clergyman, tries to clean up the town.

Pearl, The (1948) 77m. ***½ D: Emilio Fernandez. Pedro Armendariz, Maria Elena Marques. Mexican-filmed John Steinbeck tale of poor fisherman whose life is unhappily altered by finding valuable pearl; subtle and poignant.

Pearl of Death, The (1944) 69m. D: Roy William Neill. Basil Rathbone, Nigel Bruce, Evelyn Ankers, Miles Mander, Dennis Hoey, Rondo Hatton, Richard Nugent, Mary Gordon, Holmes Herbert. SEE: **Sherlock Holmes** series.

Pearl of the South Pacific (1955) C-86m. *½ D: Allan Dwan. Virginia Mayo, Dennis Morgan, David Farrar, Murvyn Vye. Dud of a film trying to be exotic, intriguing; just a boring murder tale.

Peck's Bad Boy (1934) 70m. **½ D: Edward Cline. Jackie Cooper, Thomas Meighan, Jackie Searle, O. P. Heggie. Cooper is ideally cast in familiar tale of troublesome brat causing his parents endless problems.

Peck's Bad Boy With the Circus (1938) 78m. ** D: Edward Cline. Tommy Kelly, Ann Gillis, Edgar Kennedy, Billy Gilbert, Benita Hume, Spanky MacFarland, Grant Mitchell. Standard circus story slanted for kiddies. Kennedy and Gilbert wrap this one up.

Peggy (1950) C-77m. **½ D: Frederick de Cordova. Diana Lynn, Charles Coburn, Charlotte Greenwood, Rock Hudson, Jerome Cowan, Barbara Lawrence. Lightweight comedy of sisters Lynn and Lawrence entered in Rose Bowl Parade beauty contest.

Peking Express (1951) 95m. **½ D: William Dieterle. Joseph Cotten, Corinne Calvet, Edmund Gwenn, Marvin Miller. Remake of SHANGHAI EXPRESS lacks flavor or distinction. Cotten is the doctor and Calvet the shady lady he encounters on train.

Penalty, The (1941) 81m. ** D: Harold S. Bucquet. Edward Arnold, Lionel Barrymore, Marsha Hunt, Robert Sterling, Gene Reynolds, Emma Dunn, Veda Ann Borg. Unengrossing mystery-drama of FBI agent's scheme to catch gangster by using his son for bait. Good cast in dull script.

Penguin Pool Murder, The (1932) 70m. **½ D: George Archainbaud. Edna May Oliver, James Gleason, Mae Clarke, Robert Armstrong, Donald Cook. Cop Gleason and schoolteacher Oliver team up to solve unusual murder in entertaining film with two veteran stars.

Pennies From Heaven (1936) 90m. ** D: Norman Z. McLeod. Bing Crosby, Madge Evans, Edith Fellows, Louis Armstrong, Donald Meek. Title song is chief asset of syrupy plot about orphan Fellows and grandfather Meek left alone when her convict father is executed.

Penny Princess (1951-British) C-91m. *** D: Val Guest. Dirk Bogarde, Yolande Donlan, Fletcher Lightfoot, Kynaston Reeves. Charming frou-frou of American Donlan going to Europe to collect inheritance of small principality, and Bogarde who courts her.

Penny Serenade (1941) 125m. ***½ D: George Stevens. Irene Dunne, Cary Grant, Beulah Bondi, Edgar Buchanan, Ann Doran, Eva Lee Kuney. Couple adopts child after their baby dies in attempt to find happiness. Soapy drama extremely well acted.

Penrod and His Twin Brother (1938) 63m. ** D: William McGann. Billy Mauch, Bobby Mauch, Frank Craven, Spring Byington, Charles Halton, Claudia Coleman. Penrod gets blamed for something he didn't do; answer is his lookalike who's really guilty. Vaguely captures 1900's Midwest America.

Penrod and Sam (1937) 64m. **½ D: William McGann. Billy Mauch, Frank Craven, Spring Byington, Craig Reynolds, Bernice Pilot. Based on Booth Tarkington characters, family-style film relates tale of Mauch getting involved with bank robbers.

Penrod's Double Trouble (1938) 61m. ** D: Lewis Seiler. Billy Mauch, Bobby Mauch, Dick Purcell, Gene Lockhart, Kathleen Lockhart, Hugh O'Connell. There's a reward up for Penrod's return, but a lookalike is turned in instead. Satisfactory for younger audiences; based on Booth Tarkington characters.

People vs. Dr. Kildare, The (1941) 78m. D: Harold S. Bucquet. Lew Ayres, Lionel Barrymore, Laraine Day, Bonita Granville, Alma Kruger, Red Skelton, Paul Stanton, Diana Lewis. SEE: **Dr. Kildare** series.

People Against O'Hara, The (1951) 102m. **1/2 D: John Sturges. Spencer Tracy, Pat O'Brien, Diana Lynn, John Hodiak, Eduardo Ciannelli, Jay C. Flippen. Middling drama, with Tracy a noted criminal lawyer who repents for unethical behavior during a case.

People Will Talk (1935) 67m. **1/2 D: Alfred Santell. Mary Boland, Charles Ruggles, Leila Hyams, Dean Jagger, Ruthelma Stevens, Hans Steinke. Slim plot about married couple pretending to fight to teach daughter a lesson. Boland and Ruggles could read a newspaper and make it funny.

People Will Talk (1951) 110m. ***1/2 D: Joseph L. Mankiewicz. Cary Grant, Jeanne Crain, Finlay Currie, Walter Slezak, Hume Cronyn, Sidney Blackmer. Genuinely offbeat, absorbing comedy-drama of philosophic doctor Grant and patient Crain who becomes his wife. Fine cast in talky but most worthwhile film.

Pepe (1960) C-195m. Bomb D: George Sidney. Cantinflas, Dan Dailey, Shirley Jones, 35 guest stars. Incredibly long, pointless film wastes talents of Cantinflas and many, many others (Edward G. Robinson, Maurice Chevalier, etc.) This one's only if you're desperate.

Perfect Furlough, The (1958) C-93m. **1/2 D: Blake Edwards. Tony Curtis, Janet Leigh, Keenan Wynn, Linda Cristal, Elaine Stritch, Troy Donahue. Diverting comedy of soldier Curtis winning trip to France, romancing military psychiatrist Leigh.

Perfect Marriage, The (1946) 87m. ** D: Lewis Allen. Loretta Young, David Niven, Eddie Albert, Charles Ruggles, Virginia Field, Rita Johnson, ZaSu Pitts. Niven's tired of wife Young; Young's tired of husband Niven; tired comedy-drama.

Perfect Strangers (1945) SEE: **Vacation From Marriage.**

Perfect Strangers (1950) 88m. **1/2 D: Bretaigne Windust. Ginger Rogers, Dennis Morgan, Thelma Ritter, Margalo Gillmore, Paul Ford, Alan Reed. Rogers and Morgan are jury members who fall in love; engaging romance story.

Perfect Woman, The (1949-British) 72m. **1/2 D: Bernard Knowles. Patricia Roc, Stanley Holloway, Nigel Patrick, Irene Handl, Patti Morgan. Mild satire on well-meaning professor who decides to show up society by showing them a woman with no social flaws.

Perilous Holiday (1946) 89m. *** D: Edward H. Griffith. Pat O'Brien, Ruth Warrick, Alan Hale, Edgar Buchanan, Audrey Long. Another good O'Brien vehicle, with troubleshooter encountering dangerous counterfeiting gang south of the border.

Perilous Journey, A (1953) 90m. ** D: R. G. Springsteen. Vera Ralston, David Brian, Scott Brady, Virginia Grey, Ben Cooper, Hope Emerson, Veda Ann Borg, Leif Erickson. Predictable but diverting Western of several wagons manned by women heading to California to find husbands.

Perils of Nyoka SEE: **Nyoka and the Lost Secrets of Hippocrates.**

Perils of Pauline, The (1967) C-99m. ** D: Herbert Leonard, Joshua Shelley. Pat Boone, Terry-Thomas, Pamela Austin, Edward Everett Horton, Hamilton Camp. Cutesy expanded TV pilot, with Boone traveling around the globe seeking childhood sweetheart Austin; overlong, mainly for kids.

Perils of the Darkest Jungle SEE: **Jungle Gold.**

Period of Adjustment (1962) 112m. **1/2 D: George Roy Hill. Tony Franciosa, Jane Fonda, Jim Hutton, Lois Nettleton, John McGiver, Mabel Anderson, Jack Albertson. Fonda tries hard to perk up this bleak Tennessee Williams comedy of young newlyweds visiting with troubled married man Franciosa.

Personal Affair (1954-British) 82m. ** D: Anthony Pelissier. Gene Tierney, Leo Genn, Glynis Johns, Walter Fitzgerald, Pamela Brown. Timid murder story involving suspected schoolteacher.

Personal Property (1937) 84m. **½ D: W. S. Van Dyke, II. Jean Harlow, Robert Taylor, Una O'Connor, Reginald Owen, Cora Witherspoon. Taylor stiffly maneuvers through a series of masquerades, and finally courts Harlow in this MGM fluff.

Persuader, The (1957) 72m. ** D: Dick Ross. William Talman, James Craig, Kristine Miller, Darryl Hickman. Another Western involved with clergyman taking up arms to combat outlaws.

Pete Kelly's Blues (1955) C-95m. **½ D: Jack Webb. Jack Webb, Janet Leigh, Edmond O'Brien, Peggy Lee, Andy Devine, Lee Marvin, Jayne Mansfield, Ella Fitzgerald, Martin Milner. Realistic to the point of tedium, this film recreates the jazz age of the 1920's and musicians involved. Cast perks goings-on, despite Webb. Peggy Lee, in a rare dramatic role, was nominated for an Academy Award.

Peter Ibbetson (1935) 88m. **½ D: Henry Hathaway. Gary Cooper, Ann Harding, John Halliday, Ida Lupino, Douglass Dumbrille, Virginia Weidler, Dickie Moore, Doris Lloyd. Elaborate romantic drama of man who kills ex-sweetheart's husband, pays for it for the rest of his life.

Petrified Forest, The (1936) 83m. ***½ D: Archie Mayo. Leslie Howard, Bette Davis, Dick Foran, Humphrey Bogart, Genevieve Tobin, Charley Grapewin, Porter Hall. Robert Sherwood play, focusing on ironic survival of the physically fit in civilized world. Bogart is Duke Mantee, escaped gangster, who holds writer Howard, dreamer Davis, and others hostage at roadside restaurant in Arizona. Stagy, but extremely well acted.

Petticoat Fever (1936) 81m. **½ D: George Fitzmaurice. Robert Montgomery, Myrna Loy, Reginald Owen, Irving Bacon. Professionally handled comedy with lonely Montgomery (working for U.S. in northlands) romancing pilot Loy, whose plane crashes nearby.

Petty Girl, The (1950) C-87m. **½ D: Henry Levin. Robert Cummings, Joan Caulfield, Elsa Lanchester, Melville Cooper, Mary Wickes, Tippi Hedren. Mild comedy of artist Cummings falling for prudish Caulfield, with Lanchester stealing every scene she's in.

Peyton Place (1957) C-162m. ***½ D: Mark Robson. Lana Turner, Hope Lange, Arthur Kennedy, Lloyd Nolan, Lee Philips, Terry Moore, Russ Tamblyn, Betty Field, David Nelson, Mildred Dunnock, Diane Varsi. Grace Metalious' sexsational novel receives Grade-A filming. Soaper story of small New England town life has virtue of strong cast, gorgeous photography, and Franz Waxman's score. Won many Academy Award nominations.

Phantom From Space (1953) 72m. *½ D: W. Lee Wilder. Ted Cooper, Rudolph Anders, Noreen Nash, Harry Landers. Not very action-packed sci-fi, dealing with deadly particles causing widespread death on earth.

Phantom Lady (1944) 87m. ***½ D: Robert Siodmak. Ella Raines, Franchot Tone, Fay Helm, Alan Curtis, Thomas Gomez, Aurora Miranda, Elisha Cook, Jr. Siodmak's direction of story of innocent man in prison well handled. Friends investigate on their own to find real murderer.

Phantom of the Opera, The (1943) C-92m. *** D: Arthur Lubin. Nelson Eddy, Susanna Foster, Claude Rains, Edgar Barrier, Jane Farrar, J. Edward Bromberg, Hume Cronyn. Not up to 1925 silent, but far ahead of 1962 remake. Too much emphasis on Eddy, but Rains is fine and film is colorful depiction of crazed inhabitant of Paris Opera catacombs.

Phantom of the Opera, The (1962-British) C-84m. ** D: Terence Fisher. Herbert Lom, Heather Sears, Thorley Walters, Edward De Souza, Michael Gough, Martin Miller. Third version of horror classic, too slow-moving to be effective. There are occasional moments of terror, but generally it's a plodding film, not up to first two.

Phantom of the Rue Morgue (1954) C-84m. ** D: Roy Del Ruth. Karl Malden, Claude Dauphin, Patricia Medina, Steve Forrest, Merv Griffin, Erin O'Brien-Moore. Chiller lacks flavor of Poe story, and Malden hams it up too much.

Phantom Planet, The (1961) 82m. *½ D: William Marshall. Dean Fredericks, Coleen Gray, Tony Dexter, Dolores Faith, Francis X. Bushman. Dull low-budget sci-fi, distinguished only by Bushman's appearance as alien leader.

Phantom President, The (1932) 80m. ** D: Norman Taurog. George M. Cohan, Claudette Colbert, Jimmy Durante, Sidney Toler. Musical antique about presidential candidate, with lookalike entertainer (Cohan) falling in love with former's girl (Colbert). Interesting only as a curio, with forgettable Rodgers-Hart score.

Phantom Stagecoach, The (1957) 69m. *½ D: Ray Nazarro. William Bishop, Kathleen Crowley, Richard Webb, Frank Ferguson. Programmer Western about clashing stagecoach lines competing for business.

Phantom Thief, The (1946) 65m. D: D. Ross Lederman. Chester Morris, Jeff Donnell, Richard Lane, Dusty Anderson, George E. Stone, Marvin Miller, Murray Alper. SEE: Boston Blackie series.

Pharaoh's Curse (1957) 66m. ** D: Lee Sholem. Mark Dana, Ziva Rodann, Diane Brewster. Standard story of Egyptian expedition finding centuries-old monster guarding tomb.

Pharaoh's Woman, The (1960-Italian, dubbed) C-87m. ** D: Giorgio Rivalta. Linda Cristal, Pierre Brice, Armando Francioli, John Drew Barrymore. Senseless epic set in Egypt, with Francioli combating Barrymore, pretender to the throne; ornate settings.

Phffft (1954) 91m. *** D: Mark Robson. Judy Holliday, Jack Lemmon, Jack Carson, Kim Novak, Donald Curtis. Saucy sex romp, with Holliday and Lemmon discovering that they were better off before they divorced.

Philadelphia Story, The (1940) 112m. **** D: George Cukor. Cary Grant, Katharine Hepburn, James Stewart, Ruth Hussey, John Howard, Roland Young, Henry Daniell, Virginia Weidler. Talky but brilliant adaptation of Philip Barry play about society girl who yearns for down-to-earth romance; Grant is her ex-husband, Stewart a reporter who falls in love with her. Entire cast is excellent, but Stewart really shines in his offbeat, Academy Award-winning role. Remade as HIGH SOCIETY.

Philo Vance Based on the enormously successful series of ingenious detective novels by S. S. Van Dine (real name Willard Wright) begun in 1926, Philo Vance had a long film career, with various actors and studios participating in the series. The first three entries were made by Paramount, with William Powell initially portraying the suave sleuth solving bizarre murder capers in New York. THE CANARY MURDER CASE, THE GREENE MURDER CASE, and THE BENSON MURDER CASE kept viewers guessing the identity of the murderer until the last reel; they remain A-1 whodunits today. Powell continued in THE KENNEL MURDER CASE for Warner Bros., then Basil Rathbone took over in MGM's BISHOP MURDER CASE, a clever but slow-moving Vance film, with the villain matching his crimes to Mother Goose rhymes. Generally Eugene Pallette portrayed Sgt. Heath of the homicide squad, with E. H. Calvert as the New York D.A. Production values were high in these early talkie films, which featured such leading ladies as Jean Arthur, Louise Brooks, and Virginia Bruce. Warren William was the debonair detective in THE DRAGON MURDER CASE and Paul Lukas took a turn in THE CASINO MURDER CASE, with Rosalind Russell as co-star. Edmund Lowe was Vance in THE GARDEN MURDER CASE, surrounded by an outstanding supporting cast, and newcomer Grant Richards played Vance in NIGHT OF MYSTERY (a remake of THE GREENE MURDER CASE). Warren William returned to the role for THE GRACIE ALLEN MURDER CASE, which author Van Dine tailored for the comedienne just before his death. In CALLING PHILO VANCE (a remake of THE KENNEL MURDER CASE) James Stephenson took the role, but by this time producers lavished little attention or money on the Vance films. In 1947 PRC picked up the series with a trio of low-budget quickies with William

Wright in the first, PHILO VANCE RETURNS, and Alan Curtis in the last two. The location of these was switched from New York to Los Angeles. The series didn't catch on again, and no further Vance films were made. The early 1930's entries set a high standard for the series with lavish sets, fine casts, witty repartee, and devious red herrings to baffle the police and viewers alike.

Philo Vance Returns (1947) 64m. D: William Beaudine. William Wright, Terry Austin, Leon Belasco, Clara Blandick, Iris Adrian, Frank Wilcox.

Philo Vance's Gamble (1947) 62m. D: Basil Wrangell. Alan Curtis, Terry Austin, Frank Jenks, Tala Birell, Gavin Gordon.

Philo Vance's Secret Mission (1947) 58m. D: Reginald Le Borg. Alan Curtis, Shelia Ryan, Tala Birell, Frank Jenks, James Bell.

Phoenix City Story, The (1955) 100m. **½ D: Phil Karlson. John McIntire, Richard Kiley, Kathryn Grant, Edward Andrews. Fast-paced exposé film, compactly told, with realistic production, fine performances.

Phone Call From a Stranger (1952) 96m. *** D: Jean Negulesco. Bette Davis, Shelley Winters, Gary Merrill, Michael Rennie, Keenan Wynn, Evelyn Varden, Warren Stevens. Engrossing narrative of Merrill, survivor of a plane crash, visiting families of various victims.

Phony American, The (1962-German) 72m. **½ D: Akos Rathony. William Bendix, Christine Kaufmann, Michael Hinz, Ron Randell. Strange casting is more interesting than tale of a German WW2 orphan, now grown up, wishing to become an American, and a U.S. air force pilot.

Photo Finish (1957-French, dubbed) 110m. ** D: Norbert Carbonnaux. Fernand Gravet, Jean Richard, Micheline, Louis de Funes. Strained comedy about con-men at work at the race track.

Piccadilly Incident (1946-British) 88m. *** D: Herbert Wilcox. Anna Neagle, Michael Wilding, Michael Laurence, Reginald Owen, Frances Mercer. Familiar Enoch Arden theme of supposedly dead wife appearing after husband has remarried. Good British cast gives life to oft-filmed plot.

Piccadilly Jim (1936) 100m. *** D: Robert Z. Leonard. Robert Montgomery, Frank Morgan, Madge Evans, Eric Blore, Aileen Pringle, Billie Burke, Robert Benchley. Fine comedy with father and son Morgan and Montgomery, the former causing constant trouble for the latter.

Pick a Star (1937) 70m. **½ D: Edward Sedgwick. Patsy Kelly, Jack Haley, Mischa Auer, Russell Hicks, Tom Dugan, James Finlayson, Wesley Barry. Mistaken as Laurel and Hardy vehicle, actually story of small-town girl Kelly coming to Hollywood, touring studio. L&H have brief, amusing bit.

Pickup (1951) 78m. *½ D: Hugo Haas. Beverly Michaels, Allan Nixon, Howard Chamberlin, Jo Carroll Dennison, Hugo Haas. Drab little account of older man marrying Michaels, who plans to have him killed.

Pickup Alley (1957-British) 92m. *½ D: John Gilling. Victor Mature, Anita Ekberg, Trevor Howard, Eric Pohlmann. Lackluster account of federal agent's tracking down of dope-smuggling syndicate.

Pickup on South Street (1953) 80m. **½ D: Samuel Fuller. Richard Widmark, Jean Peters, Thelma Ritter, Richard Kiley. Nifty suspenser involving federal agents tracking down Communist agents in U.S.

Pickwick Papers (1954-British) 109m. *** D: Noel Langley. James Hayter, James Donald, Hermione Baddeley, Kathleen Harrison, Hermione Gingold, Joyce Grenfell, Alexander Gauge, Lionel Morton, Nigel Patrick. Flavorful, episodic version of Dickens' classic of sly actor whose underhanded enterprises pay off.

Picnic (1955) C-115m. ***½ D: Joshua Logan. William Holden, Rosalind Russell, Kim Novak, Betty Field, Cliff Robertson, Arthur O'Connell, Verna Felton, Susan Strasberg, Nick Adams, Phyllis Newman. Excellent film of William Inge play about drifter (Holden) who stops over in Kansas, stealing alluring Novak from his old buddy Robertson. Russell and O'Connell almost steal film in second leads, and supporting roles are expertly filled by Field, Felton, and the others.

Picture of Dorian Gray, The (1945) 110m. ***½ D: Albert Lewin. George Sanders, Hurd Hatfield, Donna Reed, Angela Lansbury, Peter Lawford. Haunting Oscar Wilde story of man whose painting ages while he retains youth; young Lansbury chirps "Little Yellow Bird," Sanders elegant as sophisticated heavy.

Picture Mommy Dead (1966) C-88m. **½ D: Bert I. Gordon. Don Ameche, Martha Hyer, Zsa Zsa Gabor, Signe Hasso, Susan Gordon. Hokey melodrama with Hyer newly married to Ameche, battling stepdaughter Gordon, possessed by late mother's spirit.

Pied Piper, The (1942) 86m. *** D: Irving Pichel. Monty Woolley, Roddy McDowall, Otto Preminger, Anne Baxter, Peggy Ann Garner. Woolley, not very fond of children, finds himself leading a swarm of them on chase from the Nazis. Entertaining wartime film.

Pied Piper of Hamelin (1957) C-87m. **½ D: Bretaigne Windust. Van Johnson, Kay Starr, Claude Rains, Jim Backus, Doodles Weaver. TV special of famed children's tale, musicalized, with Johnson in title role; uses haunting Edvard Grieg music for effective results.

Pier 13 (1940) 66m. *½ D: Eugene Forde. Lynn Bari, Lloyd Nolan, Joan Valerie, Douglas Fowley. Nolan is a cop trailing waterfront crooks in this 20th Century-Fox programmer.

Pigeon That Took Rome, The (1962) 101m. **½ D: Melville Shavelson. Charlton Heston, Elsa Martinelli, Harry Guardino, Baccaloni, Marietto, Gabriella Pallotta, Debbie Price, Brian Donlevy. Sometimes amusing WW2 comedy of Heston, behind enemy lines, using pigeons to send messages to Allies, romancing local girl.

Pigskin Parade (1936) 95m. *** D: David Butler. Stuart Erwin, Judy Garland, Patsy Kelly, Jack Haley, Johnny Downs, Betty Grable. Entertaining football musicomedy with fine cast; songs include: "It's Love I'm After," "You Say the Darndest Things." Garland's first feature film.

Pillars of the Sky (1956) C-95m. **½ D: George Marshall. Jeff Chandler, Dorothy Malone, Ward Bond, Keith Andes, Lee Marvin, Sydney Chaplin. Chandler is apt as swaggering army officer fighting Indians, courting Malone.

Pillow of Death (1945) 55m. ** D: Wallace Fox. Lon Chaney, Brenda Joyce, J. Edward Bromberg, Rosalind Ivan, Clara Blandick. Another Chaney murder vehicle with lawyer Lon turning to murder to clear the way for his true love.

Pillow Talk (1959) C-105m. ***½ D: Michael Gordon. Doris Day, Rock Hudson, Tony Randall, Thelma Ritter, Nick Adams, Julia Meade, Allen Jenkins, Lee Patrick. This one started them all. Rock pursues Doris, with interference from Randall and sideline witticisms from Ritter. Imaginative sex comedy has two stars sharing a party line without knowing each other's identity. Fast-moving; plush sets, gorgeous fashions.

Pillow to Post (1946) 92m. ** D: Vincent Sherman. Ida Lupino, Sydney Greenstreet, William Prince, Stuart Erwin, Ruth Donnelly, Barbara Brown. Obvious WW2 comedy of salesgirl Lupino having soldier Prince pose as her husband so she can get a room; good cast saddled with predictable script.

Pilot No. 5 (1943) 70m. ** D. George Sidney. Franchot Tone, Marsha Hunt, Gene Kelly, Van Johnson, Alan Baxter, Dick Simmons. Sad waste of fine cast, as Tone takes on suicide mission and others recall his jumbled life.

Pimpernel Smith (1941-British) 122m. *** D: Leslie Howard. Leslie Howard, Mary Morris, Francis L. Sullivan, Hugh McDermott. Zesty updating of THE SCARLET PIMPERNEL to WW2, with Howard replaying the role of the savior of Nazi-hounded individuals. Retitled: MISTER V.

Pin-Up Girl (1944) C-83m. **½ D: H. Bruce Humberstone. Betty Grable, Martha Raye, John Harvey, Joe E. Brown, Eugene Pallette, Mantan Moreland, Charlie Spivak Orchestra. One of Grable's weaker vehicles, despite support from Raye and Brown; songs are nil, so is plot.

Pink Jungle, The (1968) C-104m.

**½ D: Delbert Mann. James Garner, Eva Renzi, George Kennedy, Nigel Green, Michael Ansara, George Rose. Offbeat blend of comedy and adventure with photographer Garner and model Renzi involved in diamond smuggling while on-location in Africa. Film shifts gears too often, but provides lighthearted entertainment.

Pink Panther, The (1964) C-113m. **½ D: Blake Edwards. Peter Sellers, David Niven, Robert Wagner, Claudia Cardinale, Capucine, Fran Jeffries. Almost everything is overdone in this slick slapstick comedy with Sellers as bumbling Inspector Clouseau. There are funny moments, but too much is just silly. Niven and Cardinale are best.

Pinky (1949) 102m. *** D: Elia Kazan. Jeanne Crain, Ethel Barrymore, Ethel Waters, Nina Mae McKinney, William Lundigan. Pioneer racial drama of Negro girl passing for white, returning to Southern home; still has impact, with fine support from Mmes. Waters and Barrymore.

Pirate, The (1948) C-102m. *** D: Vincente Minnelli. Judy Garland, Gene Kelly, Walter Slezak, Gladys Cooper, Reginald Owen. Judy thinks circus clown Kelly is really Caribbean buccaneer; lavish costuming, dancing, and Cole Porter songs bolster stagy plot.

Pirate and the Slave Girl (1961-Italian, dubbed) C-87m. ** D: Piero Pierotti. Lex Barker, Massimo Serato, Chelo Alonso, Michele Malaspina, Enzo Maggio. Formula costumer with Barker the hero who sees the light of the true cause, helping benevolent pirates vs. wicked governor.

Pirate Ship SEE: **Mutineers, The**.

Pirates of Blood River, The (1962-British) C-87m. ** D: John Gilling. Kerwin Matthews, Glenn Corbett, Christopher Lee, Marla Landi, Oliver Reed, Andrew Keir, Peter Arne. Earnest but hackneyed account of Huguenots fighting off buccaneers.

Pirates of Capri, The (1949) 94m. ** D: Edgar G. Ulmer. Louis Hayward, Binnie Barnes, Alan Curtis, Rudolph Serato. Below-average adventure film has Neapolitan natives revolting against tyrant. Lots of action but not much else. Retitled: CAPTAIN SIROCCO.

Pirates of Monterey (1947) C-77m. ** D: Alfred L. Werker. Maria Montez, Rod Cameron, Mikhail Rasumny, Philip Reed, Gilbert Roland, Gale Sondergaard. Dull film of exciting period in history, the fight against Mexican control of California in the 1800's.

Pirates of Tortuga (1961) C-97m. ** D: Robert D. Webb. Ken Scott, John Richardson, Leticia Roman, Dave King, Rafer Johnson. Lumbering costumer involving buccaneer Sir Henry Morgan.

Pirates of Tripoli (1955) C-72m. ** D: Felix E. Feist. Paul Henreid, Patricia Medina, Paul Newland, John Miljan, William Fawcett. Veteran cast tries to be lively in tired costumer, with colorful scenery the only virtue.

Pistol for Ringo, A (1966-Italian, dubbed) C-97m. **½ D: Duccio Tessari. Montgomery Wood, Fernando Sancho, Hally Hammond, Nieves Navarro. Wood is the gun-shooting hero in Texas where he combats marauding Mexicans hiding out at a ranch.

Pitfall, The (1948) 84m. ***½ D: Andre de Toth. Dick Powell, Lizabeth Scott, Jane Wyatt, Raymond Burr, Ann Doran. Taut melodrama of happily married Powell regretting brief fling with shady Scott.

Pittsburgh (1942) 90m. ** D: Lewis Seiler. Marlene Dietrich, John Wayne, Randolph Scott, Louise Allbritton, Thomas Gomez, Shemp Howard. Big John loves the coal and steel business more than he does Marlene, which leaves field open for rival Scott. Slow-moving despite cast.

Place Called Glory, A (1966-German, dubbed) C-92m. ** D: Ralph Gideon. Lex Barker, Pierre Brice, Marianne Koch, Jorge Rigaud. German-made Western with Karl May, recurring characters Winnetou and Old Satterhand. Plot killed by dubbing.

Place in the Sun, A (1951) 122m. **** D: George Stevens. Montgomery Clift, Elizabeth Taylor, Shelley Winters, Keefe Brasselle, Raymond Burr, Anne Revere. Thoughtful version of Theodore Dreiser's AMERICAN TRAGEDY, extremely well cast. Clift is confused young man seeking social success via girlfriend Taylor, trying to get rid of mistress Winters.

Place of One's Own, A (1944-British) 91m. **½ D: Bernard Knowles. James Mason, Margaret Lockwood, Dennis Price, Dulcie Gray, Edie Martin. Pleasant trivia involving a haunted home and its effect on new owners.

Plague of the Zombies, The (1966-British) C-90m. **½ D: John Gilling. Andre Morell, Diane Clare, Brook Williams, Jacqueline Pearce. Beautiful low-key photography and direction in fairly tense story of voodoo cult in Cornish Village.

Plainsman, The (1936) 115m. *** D: Cecile B. DeMille. Gary Cooper, Jean Arthur, Charles Bickford, James Ellison, Porter Hall, Victor Varconi, Anthony Quinn. Big Western with Cooper as Wild Bill Hickok, Arthur as Calamity Jane, plenty of well-paced action, with offbeat romance tossed in.

Plainsman, The (1966) C-92m. *½ D: David Lowell Rich. Don Murray, Guy Stockwell, Abby Dalton, Bradford Dillman, Leslie Nielsen. Static remake of the Cooper-Arthur vehicle, that is dull even on its own.

Plainsman and the Lady, The (1946) 87m. ** D: Joseph Kane. William Elliott, Vera Ralston, Gail Patrick, Joseph Schildkraut, Andy Clyde. Wild Bill Elliott is tame in uninspiring saga of pony express pioneer battling slimy villains and winning lovely Ralston.

Plan 9 From Outer Space (1956-British) 79m. BOMB D: Edward Wood, Jr. Gregory Walcott, Mona McKinnon, Bela Lugosi, Lyle Talbot, Joanna Lee. Wacked-out sci-fi that isn't much of anything. Alien forces seek aid of human zombies. Retitled: GRAVE ROBBERS FROM OUTER SPACE. Lugosi died during production, and it shows.

Planet of the Vampires (1965-Italian, dubbed) C-86m. **½ D: Mario Bava. Barry Sullivan, Norma Bengell, Angel Aranda, Evi Marandi, Fernando Villena. Eerily photographed, atmospheric science-fantasy of spaceship looking for missing comrades on misty planet where strange power controls their minds. Alternate title: PLANET OF BLOOD.

Platinum High School (1960) 93m. ** D: Charles Haas. Mickey Rooney, Terry Moore, Dan Duryea, Yvette Mimieux, Conway Twitty, Jimmy Boyd. Limp attempt at sensationalism, with Rooney a father discovering that his son's death at school wasn't accidental. Retitled: TROUBLE AT 16.

Play Girl (1940) 75m. **½ D: Frank Woodruff. Kay Francis, Nigel Bruce, James Ellison, Margaret Hamilton, Mildred Coles. Francis is hip gold-digger who teaches younger women how to fleece clients; offbeat programmer.

Play it Cool (1963-British) 82m. *½ D: Michael Winner. Billy Fury, Michael Anderson, Jr., Dennis Price, Richard Wattis, Anna Palk, Keith Hamshere, Ray Brooks. Mild rock 'n' roll entry, with thin plot-line of groovy group preventing a rich girl from going wrong.

Playgirl (1954) 85m. **½ D: Joseph Pevney. Shelley Winters, Barry Sullivan, Gregg Palmer, Richard Long, Kent Taylor. Winters is most comfortable in drama about girl involved with gangsters.

Playmates (1941) 94m. *½ D: David Butler. Kay Kyser, Lupe Velez, John Barrymore, May Robson, Patsy Kelly, Peter Lind Hayes. Poor musical "comedy" of Shakespearean actor teaming up with bandleader to pay back taxes. Film is unbelievably bad at times, only worth seeing for poor John Barrymore.

Please Believe Me (1950) 87m. **½ D: Norman Taurog. Deborah Kerr, Robert Walker, James Whitmore, Peter Lawford, Mark Stevens, Spring Byington. Pleasant fluff of Britisher Kerr aboard liner headed for America, wooed by assorted bachelors aboard, who think she's an heiress.

Please Don't Eat the Daisies (1960) C-111m. *** D: Charles Walters. Doris Day, David Niven, Janis Paige, Spring Byington, Richard Haydn, Patsy Kelly. Bright film based on Jean Kerr's play about a drama critic and his family. Doris sings title song; her kids are very amusing, as are Byington (the mother-in-law), Kelly (housekeeper), and especially

Janis Paige as a temperamental star.

Please! Mr. Balzac (1957-French, dubbed) 99m. *** D: Marc Allegret. Daniel Gelin, Brigitte Bardot, Robert Hirsch, Darry Cowl. Engaging BB romp of girl involved in theft of rare book and her shenanigans to become disinvolved. Retitled: MADEMOISELLE STRIPTEASE.

Please Murder Me (1956) 78m. **½ D: Peter Godfrey. Angela Lansbury, Raymond Burr, Dick Foran, John Dehner, Lamont Johnson. Lansbury and Burr's energetic performances elevate this homicide yarn.

Please Turn Over (1960-British) 86m. **½ D: Gerald Thomas. Ted Ray, Jean Kent, Leslie Phillips, Joan Sims, Julia Lockwood, Tim Seely. OK froth about wife's lurid novel-writing and the repercussions it causes.

Pleasure of His Company, The (1961) C-115m. ***½ D: George Seaton. Fred Astaire, Lilli Palmer, Debbie Reynolds, Tab Hunter, Charlie Ruggles. Delightful piece of fluff with Astaire and Palmer at their best. He is her ex-husband who comes to visit and enchant his daughter (Reynolds) and hound Lilli's new spouse (Gary Merrill). Entire cast is in rare form.

Pleasure Seekers, The (1964) C-107m. **½ D: Jean Negulesco. Ann-Margret, Tony Franciosa, Carol Lynley, Gene Tierney, Brian Keith, Gardner McKay, Isobel Elsom. Glossy romance à la THREE COINS IN THE FOUNTAIN of three girls seeking fun in Spain.

Plot Thickens, The (1936) 69m. ** D: Ben Holmes. James Gleason, ZaSu Pitts, Oscar Apfel, Owen Davis, Jr., Louise Latimer. Offbeat RKO programmer with Pitts the schoolmarm who helps solve robbery and murder with inspector Gleason.

Plunder of the Sun (1953) 81m. **½ D: John Farrow. Glenn Ford, Diana Lynn, Patricia Medina, Francis L. Sullivan. Competent cast in above-average goings-on. Ford is involved with treasure hunt and murder in Mexico.

Plunder Road (1957) 71m. **½ D: Hubert Cornfield. Gene Raymond, Jeanne Cooper, Wayne Morris, Elisha Cook, Jr., Stafford Repp. A little "sleeper" about robbery caper, with competent cast giving life to intriguing story.

Plunderers, The (1948) 87m. ** D: Joseph Kane. Rod Cameron, Ilona Massey, Adrian Booth, Forrest Tucker. OK Republic Pictures Western involving outlaws and army joining forces against rampaging redskins; clichés are there.

Plunderers, The (1960) 93m. **½ D: Joseph Pevney. Jeff Chandler, John Saxon, Dolores Hart, Marsha Hunt, Jay C. Flippen, Ray Stricklyn, James Westerfield. Above-par study of outlaws interacting with honest townsfolk.

Plunderers of Painted Flats (1959) 77m. *½ D: Albert C. Gannaway. Corinne Calvet, John Carroll, Skip Homeier, George Macready, Edmund Lowe, Bea Benadaret, Madge Kennedy, Joe Besser. Flabby Western of cowpoke seeking his father's killer.

Plymouth Adventure (1952) C-105m. *** D: Clarence Brown. Spencer Tracy, Gene Tierney, Van Johnson, Leo Genn, Dawn Addams. Superficial soap opera, glossily done, of the 17th-century settlers who came to Massachusetts.

Poacher's Daughter, The (1960-Irish) 74m. **½ D: George Pollock. Julie Harris, Harry Brogan, Tim Seeley, Marie Keen, Brid Lynch, Noel Magee, Paul Farrell. Harris lends authenticity in title role as simple girl who straightens out her philandering boyfriend.

Pocketful of Miracles (1961) C-136m. **½ D: Frank Capra. Bette Davis, Glenn Ford, Hope Lange, Thomas Mitchell, Peter Falk, Edward Everett Horton, Ann-Margret, Jack Elam. Capra's remake of his 1933 LADY FOR A DAY is just as sentimental, but doesn't work as well. Bette is Apple Annie, a Damon Runyan character; Ford is the producer who turns her into a lady. Ann-Margret is appealing in her first film.

Poison Ivy (1953-French, dubbed) 90m. ** D: Bernard Borderie. Eddie Constantine, Dominique Wilms, Howard Vernon, Dario Moreno, Gaston Modot. Constantine is again FBI agent Lemmy Caution, involved in stolen gold shipment in North Africa; grade-B actioner.

Polly of the Circus (1932) 72m. **
D: Alfred Santell. Marion Davies, Clark Gable, C. Aubrey Smith, Ray Milland, Raymond Hatton. Strange Davies vehicle of beautiful acrobat in love with minister Gable, over objections of priest Smith.

Polo Joe (1936) 62m. ** D: William McGann. Joe E. Brown, Carol Hughes, Skeets Gallagher, Joseph King, Gordon Elliott, George E. Stone. Typical Brown comedy in which Joe's got to learn polo fast to impress his girl.

Pony Express (1953) C-101m. *** D: Jerry Hopper. Charlton Heston, Rhonda Fleming, Jan Sterling, Forrest Tucker. Exuberant action Western (set in 1860's) of the founding of mail routes westward, involving historical figures Buffalo Bill and Wild Bill Hickok.

Pony Soldier (1952) 82m. **½ D: Joseph M. Newman. Tyrone Power, Cameron Mitchell, Robert Horton, Thomas Gomez, Penny Edwards. Power is sturdy in actioner about Canadian mounties and their efforts to stave off Indian war.

Poor Little Rich Girl, The (1939) 72m. *** D: Irving Cummings. Shirley Temple, Alice Faye, Gloria Stuart, Jack Haley, Michael Whalen. Shirley manipulates her father Whalen into romance, and vaudeville act Haley and Faye into stardom in this enjoyable musicomedy.

Poppy (1936) 75m. **½ D: A. Edward Sutherland. W. C. Fields, Rochelle Hudson, Richard Cromwell, Catherine Doucet, Lynne Overman. Mild Fields, recreating his stage role as Hudson's ever-conniving dad. Too much romantic subplot, not enough of W. C.'s antics.

Poppy is Also a Flower, The (1966) C-100m. Bomb D: Terence Young. Senta Berger, Stephen Boyd, E. G. Marshall, Trevor Howard, Eli Wallach, Marcello Mastroianni, Angie Dickinson, Rita Hayworth, Yul Brynner, Trini Lopez, Gilbert Roland, Bessie Love. Incredibly bad feature from story by Ian Fleming, originally produced as United Nations project for TV. Acting is downright poor at times.

Porgy and Bess (1959) C-138m. **½ D: Otto Preminger. Sidney Poitier, Dorothy Dandridge, Pearl Bailey, Sammy Davis, Jr., Brock Peters, Diahann Carroll, Ivan Dixon. Classic Gershwin folk opera is a bit stiff, but contains unforgettable melodies: "Summertime," "It Ain't Necessarily So," "I Got Plenty Of Nothin." Davis top-drawer as Sportin' Life.

Pork Chop Hill (1959) 97m. *** D: Lewis Milestone. Gregory Peck, Harry Guardino, Rip Torn, George Peppard, James Edwards, Bob Steele, Woody Strode. Grim Korean War actioner with Peck et al rugged and believable.

Port Afrique (1956) C-92m. ** D: Rudolph Mate. Pier Angeli, Anthony Newley, Christopher Lee, Dennis Price, Eugene Deckers, Pat O'Mera, Maureen Connell, James Hayter, Phil Carey. Bernard Dryer's picaresque actioner gets middling screen version; adulterous wife's past comes to light when husband investigates her death.

Port of Hell (1954) 80m. ** D: Harold Schuster. Wayne Morris, Dane Clark, Carole Mathews, Otto Waldis, Marshall Thompson, Marjorie Lord, Tom Hubbard. Poor production values detract from tense situation of skipper et al trying to take an A-bomb out to sea before it explodes.

Port of New York (1949) 96m. ** D: Laslo Benedek. Scott Brady, Richard Rober, K. T. Stevens, Yul Brynner. Gloomy tale of customs agents cracking down on narcotics smuggling; Brynner's film debut.

Port of Seven Seas (1938) 81m. ** D: James Whale. Wallace Beery, Frank Morgan, Maureen O'Sullivan, John Beal, Jessie Ralph, Cora Witherspoon. Marcel Pagnol's FANNY isn't quite suitable Beery material, but he and good cast try their best as O'Sullivan falls in love with adventuresome sailor.

Portrait From Life SEE: **Girl in the Painting**.

Portrait in Black (1960) C-112m. **½ D: Michael Gordon. Lana Turner, Anthony Quinn, Sandra Dee, John Saxon, Richard Basehart, Lloyd Nolan, Ray Walston, Anna May Wong. Average murder mystery filled with gaping holes that producer Ross Hunter tried to hide with glamorous decor and offbeat casting.

Portrait of a Mobster (1961) 108m. **½ D: Joseph Pevney. Vic Morrow, Leslie Parrish, Peter Breck, Ray Danton, Norman Alden, Ken Lynch. Better-than-usual chronicle of a gangster's rise in the underworld.

Portrait of a Sinner (1959-British) 96m. **½ D: Robert Siodmak. William Bendix, Nadja Tiller, Tony Britton, Donald Wolfit, Adrienne Corri, Joyce Carey. Tiller is effective in leading role as corrupting female who taints all in her path. Based on Robin Maugham story. Alternate title: THE ROUGH AND THE SMOOTH.

Portrait of Clare (1951-British) 94m. ** D: Lance Comfort. Margaret Johnston, Richard Todd, Robin Bailey, Ronald Howard. Unpretentious little film, pegged on gimmick of woman telling granddaughter about her past romances.

Portrait of Jennie (1948) 86m. ***½ D: William Dieterle. Jennifer Jones, Joseph Cotten, Ethel Barrymore, Lillian Gish, David Wayne, Henry Hull. Atmospheric film from Robert Nathan's story of strange other-worldly girl who inspires artist Cotten. Haunting, beautifully acted.

Posse From Hell (1961) C-89m. ** D: Herbert Coleman. Audie Murphy, John Saxon, Zohra Lampert, Vic Morrow, Lee Van Cleef. Murphy is tight-lipped gunslinger hunting outlaws who killed his sheriff pal. The usual.

Possessed (1931) 72m. **½ D: Clarence Brown. Joan Crawford, Clark Gable, Wallace Ford, Skeets Gallagher, John Miljan. Better-than-usual soaper with Crawford sacrificing her happiness for Gable's career. Good performances put this one above most of its kind.

Possessed (1947) 108m. **½ D: Curtis Bernhardt. Joan Crawford, Van Heflin, Raymond Massey, Geraldine Brooks, Stanley Ridges. Interesting soaper of schizophrenic Crawford and the two men in her life.

Possessors, The (1958-French, dubbed) 94m. **½ D: Denys De La Patelliere. Jean Gabin, Jean Desailly, Pierre Brasseur Emmanuelle Riva, Bernard Blier. Diffuse yet forceful study of patriarch Gabin forcing issues to make his family self-sufficient.

Postman Always Rings Twice, The (1946) 113m. **** D: Tay Garnett. Lana Turner, John Garfield, Cecil Kellaway, Hume Cronyn, Audrey Totter, Leon Ames. Garfield and Turner sparkle in bristling drama of lovers who get her husband (Kellaway) out of the way; A-1 James Cain story.

Postmark for Danger (1956-British) 84m. ** D: Guy Green. Terry Moore, Robert Beatty, William Sylvester, Josephine Griffin. Mild Scotland Yard investigation story.

Pot O' Gold (1941) 86m. ** D: George Marshall. James Stewart, Paulette Goddard, Horace Heidt, Charles Winninger, Mary Gordon, Frank Melton, Jed Prouty. Harmless musical of girl who manages to get Heidt band on father's radio program.

Powder River (1953) C-78m. ** D: Louis King. Rory Calhoun, Corinne Calvet, Cameron Mitchell, Carl Betz. Straightforward minor Western, with Calhoun becoming town sheriff and clearing up a friend's murder.

Power and the Prize, The (1956) 98m. **½ D: Henry Koster. Robert Taylor, Elisabeth Mueller, Burl Ives, Charles Coburn, Cedric Hardwicke, Mary Astor. Sporadically effective study of big men in corporation and their private lives; lacks necessary gloss.

Power of the Whistler, The (1945) 66m. D: Lew Landers. Richard Dix, Janis Carter, Jeff Donnell, Loren Tindall, Tala Birell, John Abbott. SEE: Whistler series.

Powers Girl, The (1942) 93m. ** D: Norman Z. McLeod. George Murphy, Anne Shirley, Dennis Day, Benny Goodman, Carole Landis. Trifling plot revolving about Shirley's attempt to become member of famed modeling school, with musical numbers tossed in.

Practically Yours (1944) 90m. ** D: Mitchell Leisen. Claudette Colbert, Fred MacMurray, Gil Lamb, Robert Benchley, Rosemary DeCamp, Cecil Kellaway. Stars' expertise redeems contrived story of girl intercepting pilot's message to his dog.

Prehistoric Women (1951) C-74m. Bomb D: Gregg Tallas. Laurette Luez, Allan Nixon, John Shawlee, Judy Landon. Ludicrous account of cavewomen hunting for their mates, only good for laughs.

Premier May SEE Man to Man Talk.

Prescription Murder (1968) C-120m. **½ D: Richard Irving. Peter Falk, Gene Barry, Katherine Justice, Nina Foch, Andrea King. Telefeature from abortive pre-Broadway play by William Link-Richard Levinson. Falk is stereotyped wily detective trying to catch Barry for killing wife Foch. Nothing new, but slickly done.

Presenting Lily Mars (1943) 104m. ** D: Norman Taurog. Judy Garland, Van Heflin, Fay Bainter, Richard Carlson, Spring Byington, Marta Eggerth, Marilyn Maxwell. Well, there she is, and there lies the script. Stale story of determined girl getting big chance on Broadway only comes alive when Judy sings.

President's Lady, The (1953) 96m. *** D: Henry Levin. Charlton Heston, Susan Hayward, John McIntire, Fay Bainter, Carl Betz. Heston as Andrew Jackson and Hayward as the lady with a past he marries work well together in this fictional history of 1800's America.

Pressure Point (1962) 91m. *** D: Hubert Cornfield. Sidney Poitier, Bobby Darin, Peter Falk, Carl Benton Reid, Mary Munday, Barry Gordon, Howard Caine. Intelligent drama, with Poitier the prison psychiatrist trying to ferret out the problems of his Nazi patient (Darin).

Pretender, The (1947) 69m. **½ D: W. Lee Wilder. Albert Dekker, Catherine Craig, Linda Stirling, Charles Drake, Charles Middleton, Alan Carney. Dekker gives sharply etched performance as N.Y.C. financier trying to do in a competitor, discovering he may be the victim instead.

Pretty Baby (1950) 92m. ** D: Bretaigne Windust. Dennis Morgan, Betsy Drake, Zachary Scott, Edmund Gwenn, Barbara Billingsley. Coy minor comedy involving working-girl Drake, who snowballs a gimmick to a get a subway seat on the morning train into a good job and romance.

Pretty Boy Floyd (1960) 96m. ** D: Herbert J. Leder. John Ericson, Barry Newman, Joan Harvey, Herb Evers, Carl York, Roy Fant, Shirley Smith. Average chronicle of infamous 1930's gangster, played energetically by Ericson.

Price of Fear, The (1956) 79m. **½ D: Abner Biberman. Merle Oberon, Lex Barker, Charles Drake, Gia Scala, Warren Stevens. Middling account of Oberon involved in hit-and-run accident which snowballs her life into disaster.

Pride and Prejudice (1940) 118m. *** D: Robert Z. Leonard. Greer Garson, Laurence Olivier, Edna May Oliver, Edmund Gwenn, Mary Boland, Maureen O'Sullivan, Karen Morley, Ann Rutherford, Marsha Hunt. Jane Austen's novel of four sisters in 18th-century England hunting for husbands is good drawing-room comedy; O'Sullivan stands out in supporting cast.

Pride and the Passion, The (1957) C-132m. **½ D: Stanley Kramer. Cary Grant, Frank Sinatra, Sophia Loren, Theodore Bikel. Miscast actioner involving the capture of huge cannon by partisans from France, set in 1800's Spain. Spectacle scenes are impressive, but much of film is ridiculous.

Pride of St. Louis, The (1952) 93m. **½ D: Harmon Jones. Dan Dailey, Joanne Dru, Richard Crenna, Hugh Sanders. Pleasing if fanciful biography of baseball player Dizzy Dean.

Pride of the Blue Grass (1954) C-71m. ** D: William Beaudine. Lloyd Bridges, Vera Miles, Margaret Sheridan, Arthur Shields. Familiar racetrack story; competent production.

Pride of the Bowery (1941) 63m. D: Joseph H. Lewis. Leo Gorcey, Bobby Jordan, Donald Haines, Carlton Young, Kenneth Howell, David Gorcey. SEE: Bowery Boys series.

Pride of the Marines (1945) 119m. ***½ D: Delmer Daves. John Garfield, Eleanor Parker, Dane Clark, John Ridgely, Rosemary DeCamp, Ann Doran, Ann Todd, Warren Douglas. Ensemble acting by Warner Bros. stock company enhances true account of marine blinded during Japanese attack, with Garfield as injured Al Schmid, Clark as sympathetic buddy.

Pride of the Yankees, The (1942) 127m. **** D: Sam Wood. Gary Cooper, Teresa Wright, Babe Ruth, Walter Brennan, Dan Duryea, Ludwig Stossel, Addison Richards, Hardie Albright. Superb biography of baseball star Lou Gehrig, with Cooper giving excellent performance; fine support from Wright as devoted wife. Final sequence is truly memorable.

Primrose Path, The (1940) 93m. **½ D: Gregory La Cava. Ginger Rogers, Joel McCrea, Marjorie Rambeau, Miles Mander, Henry Travers, John Carroll. Rambeau is sheer delight as virtue-less mom of Rogers, who wants wholesome marriage to square McCrea.

Prince and the Pauper, The (1937) 120m. ***½ D: William Keighley. Errol Flynn, Billy and Bobby Mauch, Claude Rains, Alan Hale, Eric Portman, Ivan Simpson, Fritz Lieber, Holmes Herbert. Elaborate costume picture of 16th-century England, based on Mark Twain's tale of young prince's poor lookalike who trades places with him.

Prince and the Showgirl, The (1957-British) C-117m. **½ D: Laurence Olivier. Marilyn Monroe, Laurence Olivier, Sybil Thorndike, Jeremy Spencer. Thoughtful but slow-moving account of saucy American showgirl (Monroe) being romanced in London by foreign nobleman (Olivier), heir to his country's throne.

Prince of Foxes (1949) 107m. ** D: Henry King. Tyrone Power, Wanda Hendrix, Orson Welles, Marina Berti, Everett Sloane, Katina Paxinou. Meandering costumer set in medieval Italy, with adventurer Power defying all-powerful Cesare Borgia.

Prince of Pirates (1953) C-80m. **½ D: Sidney Salkow. John Derek, Barbara Rush, Whitfield Connor, Edgar Barrier. Enjoyable little costumer involving French-Spanish wars.

Prince of Players (1955) C-102m. **½ D: Philip Dunne. Richard Burton, Maggie McNamara, Raymond Massey, Charles Bickford, John Derek, Eva Le Gallienne, Mae Marsh, Sarah Padden. Burton is 19th-century actor Edwin Booth, embroiled in more offstage drama than on. Shakespearean excerpts thrown in; well performed by earnest cast.

Prince of Thieves, The (1948) C-72m. ** D: Howard Bretherton. Jon Hall, Patricia Morison, Adele Jergens, Alan Mowbray, Michael Duane. Colorful swashbuckler of Robin Hood and Maid Marian, aimed at juvenile audiences.

Prince Valiant (1954) C-100m. **½ D: Henry Hathaway. James Mason, Janet Leigh, Robert Wagner, Debra Paget, Sterling Hayden. Famed cartoon character becomes cardboard costumer decked out in 20th Century-Fox splendor, battling and loving in Middle Ages England.

Prince Who Was a Thief, The (1951) 88m. **½ D: Rudolph Maté. Tony Curtis, Piper Laurie, Everett Sloane, Jeff Corey, Betty Garde. Juvenile costumer sparked by enthusiastic performances.

Princess and the Pirate, The (1944) C-94m. *** D: David Butler. Bob Hope, Virginia Mayo, Walter Brennan, Walter Slezak, Victor McLaglen. One of Bob's wackiest; he and glamorous Virginia are on the lam from pirate McLaglen, trapped by potentate Slezak. Brennan is hilarious in truly offbeat pirate role.

Princess Comes Across, The (1936) 76m. *** D: William K. Howard. Carole Lombard, Fred MacMurray, Douglass Dumbrille, Alison Skipworth, William Frawley, Porter Hall. Lombard, posing as royalty on ocean voyage, meets romantic MacMurray; together they are involved in murder mystery. Delightful blend of comedy and mystery.

Princess of the Nile (1954) C-71m. **½ D: Harmon Jones. Debra Paget, Jeffrey Hunter, Michael Rennie, Dona Drake, Wally Cassell. Hokey script diverts any potential this costumer may have had.

Princess O'Rourke (1943) 94m. ***½ D: Norman Krasna. Olivia de Havilland, Robert Cummings, Charles Coburn, Jack Carson, Jane Wyman, Harry Davenport, Gladys Cooper. Princess Olivia falls in love with American Cummings, doesn't tell him about her title. Director-writer Krasna won Best Screenplay Oscar for this delightful comedy.

Prisoner, The (1955-British) 91m. *** D: Peter Glenville. Alec Guinness, Jack Hawkins, Raymond Huntley, Wilfrid Lawson. Grim account of cardinal in iron curtain country undergoing grueling interrogation. Guinness-Hawkins interplay is superb.

Prisoner of Shark Island, The (1936) 95m. *** D: John Ford. Warner Baxter, Gloria Stuart, Claude Gillingwater, Arthur Byron, Harry Carey, John Carradine. Excellent film with intriguing true story of doctor exiled to Shark Island for innocently treating John Wilkes Booth after Lincoln assassination; vivid period production.

Prisoner of the Iron Mask, The (1962-Italian, dubbed) C-80m. **½ D: Francesco De Feo. Michel Lemoine, Wandisa Guida, Andrea Bosic, Jany Clair, Giovanni Materassi. Typical costumer; title tells all.

Prisoner of the Volga, (1960-Yugoslavian dubbed) C-102m. **½ D: W. Tourjansky. John Derek, Elsa Martinelli, Dawn Addams, Wolfgang Preiss, Gert Frobe, Igmar Zeisberg. Slightly above-par costumer, with title telling all.

Prisoner of War (1954) 80m. ** D: Andrew Marton. Ronald Reagan, Steve Forrest, Dewey Martin, Stephen Bekassy. Bland account of POW's in Korean War camp.

Prisoner of Zenda, The (1937) 101m. ***½ D: John Cromwell. Ronald Colman, Madeleine Carroll, Mary Astor, Douglas Fairbanks, Jr., C. Aubrey Smith, Raymond Massey, Montagu Love, Alexander D'Arcy. Lavish costumer with excellent casting; Colman is forced to substitute for lookalike cousin, the King of Ruritanian country, but commoner Colman falls in love with regal Carroll. Fairbanks is outstanding as Rupert of Hentzau.

Prisoner of Zenda, The (1952) C-101m. *** D: Richard Thorpe. Stewart Granger, Deborah Kerr, Jane Greer, Louis Calhern, Lewis Stone, James Mason. Plush remake of Colman classic with spirited cast. Traveler who is deadringer for small European country's king becomes involved in plot of murder.

Prisoners of the Casbah (1953) C-78m. *½ D: Richard Bare. Gloria Grahame, Turhan Bey, Cesar Romero, Nestor Paiva. Low-budget costumer with diverting cast.

Private Affairs of Bel Ami, The (1947) 112m. **½ D: Albert Lewin. George Sanders, Angela Lansbury, Ann Dvorak, Frances Dee, Susan Douglas, Marie Wilson. Sanders is well cast as 19th-century rogue who steps on people on way to top, from Guy de Maupassant stort story.

Private Buckaroo (1942) 68m. ** D: Edward Cline. The Andrews Sisters, Dick Foran, Joe E. Lewis, Jennifer Holt. Mini-musical from Universal Pictures is vehicle for 1940's favorite sister trio, accompanied by Harry James et al in army camp show.

Private Eyes (1953) 64m. D: Edward Bernds. Leo Gorcey, Huntz Hall, Bernard Gorcey, Chick Chandler, Myron Healey, Tim Ryan. SEE: Bowery Boys series.

Private Hell 36 (1954) 81m. **½ D: Don Siegel. Ida Lupino, Steve Cochran, Howard Duff, Dean Jagger, Dorothy Malone. Well-handled account of greed corrupting supposedly honest people.

Private Life of Don Juan, The (1934-British) 80m. ** D: Alexander Korda. Douglas Fairbanks, Merle Oberon, Binnie Barnes, Joan Gardner, Benita Hume, Athene Seyler, Melville Cooper. Lifeless costumer with aging Fairbanks in title role, pursuing a bevy of beauties.

Private Life of Henry VIII, The (1933-British) 97m. **** D: Alexander Korda. Charles Laughton, Binnie Barnes, Robert Donat, Elsa Lanchester, Merle Oberon, Miles Mander, Wendy Barrie, John Loder. Sweeping historical chronicle of 16th-century British monarch, magnificently captured by Laughton, revealing man and king; Lanchester fine as Anne of Cleves, with top supporting cast.

Private Lives of Adam and Eve, The (1960) C-87m. *½ D: Albert Zugsmith, Mickey Rooney. Mickey Rooney, Mamie Van Doren, Fay Spain, Mel Torme, Martin Milner, Tuesday Weld. Bizarre, crude attempt at mixing contemporary soap opera with parallels to the past via dream sequences.

Private Lives of Elizabeth and Essex, The (1939) C-106m. ***½ D: Michael Curtiz. Bette Davis, Errol Flynn, Olivia de Havilland, Donald Crisp, Vincent Price, Nanette Fabray, Henry Daniell, Robert Warwick, Henry Stephenson, Leo G. Carroll. Colorful, elaborate costume drama with outstanding performance by Davis as queen whose love for dashing Flynn is thwarted. Not authentic history, but good drama.

Private Number (1936) 80m. ** D:

Roy Del Ruth. Robert Taylor, Loretta Young, Patsy Kelly, Basil Rathbone, Marjorie Gateson, Paul Harvey, Joe E. Lewis. Not to disgrace family, wealthy Taylor must keep marriage to family housemaid Young a secret. Tearful soaper is OK.

Private War of Major Benson, The (1955) 100m. **½ D: Jerry Hopper. Charlton Heston, Julie Adams, William Demarest, Tim Hovey, Sal Mineo, David Janssen. Hovey is the little boy at military school who charms rugged commander Heston into sympathetic person; Adams is the love interest.

Private Worlds (1935) 84m. **½ D: Gregory La Cava. Claudette Colbert, Charles Boyer, Joan Bennett, Joel McCrea, Helen Vinson, Esther Dale, Jean Rouverol. Dated but engrossing tale of mental institution, with doctors Boyer and Colbert giving restrained performances; noteworthy support by Bennett.

Private's Affair, A (1959) C-92m. **½ D: Raoul Walsh. Sal Mineo, Christine Carere, Barry Coe, Barbara Eden, Gary Crosby, Terry Moore, Jim Backus, Jessie Royce Landis. Energetic young cast involved in putting on the "big army show" on TV.

Private's Progress (1956-British) 99m. *** D: John Boulting. Richard Attenborough, Jill Adams, Dennis Price, Terry-Thomas, Ian Carmichael, Peter Jones. Prize collection of funny men, splendidly played by cast, involved in shenanigans.

Privilege (1967-British) C-101m. *** D: Peter Watkins. Paul Jones, Jean Shrimpton, Marc London, Max Bacon, Jeremy Child. Overambitious yet effective account of 1970's England where all-powerful welfare state manipulates masses through such media as pop singers. Jones is good as disillusioned teen-age idol.

Prize, The (1963) C-136m. *** D: Mark Robson. Paul Newman, Edward G. Robinson, Elke Sommer, Diane Baker, Micheline Presle, Leo G. Carroll. Irving Wallace novel is mere stepping stone for glossy spy yarn set in Stockholm, involving participants in Nobel Prize ceremony. Newman and Sommer make handsome leads; Robinson has dual role. Fast-moving fun.

Prize of Arms, A (1961-British) 105m. **½ D: Cliff Owen. Stanley Baker, Tom Bell, Helmut Schmid, John Phillips. Effective yarn is hindered by heavy British accents ruining much dialogue. Tale unfolds methodical plan for big heist of army funds.

Prize of Gold, A (1955-British) C-98m. *** D: Mark Robson. Richard Widmark, Mai Zetterling, Nigel Patrick, Donald Wolfit, Eric Pohlmann. Taut caper in post-WW2 Berlin involving a planned heist of gold from the air lift circuit.

Prodigal, The (1955) C-114m. **½ D: Richard Thorpe. Lana Turner, Edmund Purdom, James Mitchell, Louis Calhern, Audrey Dalton, Neville Brand, Taina Elg, Cecil Kellaway, Henry Daniell, Walter Hampden, Joseph Wiseman. Juvenile biblical semi-spectacle, with Turner the evil goddess of love corrupting Purdom; glossy MGM production.

Professional Soldier (1935) 75m. **½ D: Tay Garnett. Victor McLaglen, Freddie Bartholomew, Gloria Stuart, Constance Collier, Michael Whalen. McLaglen is hired to kidnap prince Bartholomew, but mutual friendship gets in the way. Good teaming supports average script.

Professional Sweetheart (1933) 68m. ** D: William A. Seiter. Ginger Rogers, ZaSu Pitts, Norman Foster, Frank McHugh, Edgar Kennedy, Betty Furness, Gregory Ratoff. Good cast can't put over weak radio spoof, with Rogers as airwaves star who becomes engaged to hick Foster in publicity stunt.

Professionals, The (1966) C-117m. *** D: Richard Brooks. Burt Lancaster, Lee Marvin, Robert Ryan, Jack Palance, Claudia Cardinale, Woody Strode, Ralph Bellamy. Bellamy employs four soldiers-of-fortune to rescue his wife (Cardinale) from Mexican varmint Palance. Far-fetched story, but real action and taut excitement throughout.

Professor Beware (1938) 87m. **½ D: Elliott Nugent, Harold Lloyd, Phyllis Welch, William Frawley, Etienne Girardot, Raymond Walburn, Lionel Stander, Thurston Hall, Cora Witherspoon. One of Lloyd's last vehicles has good moments, but tale of archeologist searching for rare results is thin.

Promise Her Anything (1966) C-98m. **½ D: Arthur Hiller. Warren Beatty, Leslie Caron, Bob Cummings, Hermione Gingold. Limp premise of blue-moviemaker (Beatty) taking care of neighbor Caron's baby. Filmed in England but supposed to be Greenwich Village.

Promoter, The (1952-British) 88m. *** D: Ronald Neame. Alec Guinness, Glynis Johns, Valerie Hobson, Petula Clark, Michael Hordern. Amusing vehicle showing Guinness virtuosity with droll comedian in rags-to-riches chronicle of a con-artist.

Proud and the Beautiful, The (1956-French, dubbed) 94m. *** D: Yves Allegret. Michele Morgan, Gerard Philippe, Victor Manuel Mendoza, Michele Cordoue. Morgan and Philippe interact beautifully as widow in Mexico whose love for down-and-out doctor helps him regain sense of values.

Proud and the Profane, The (1956) 111m. **½ D: George Seaton. William Holden, Deborah Kerr, Thelma Ritter, Dewey Martin, William Redfield. Spotty WW2 romance story has many parallels to FROM HERE TO ETERNITY, but Kerr-Holden romance is never believable.

Proud Ones, The (1956) C-94m. **½ D: Robert D. Webb. Robert Ryan, Virginia Mayo, Jeffrey Hunter, Robert Middleton, Walter Brennan. Staunch acting involving the inevitable showdown between sheriff and outlaws perks up this Western.

Proud Rebel, The (1958) C-103m. *** D: Michael Curtiz. Alan Ladd, Olivia de Havilland, Dean Jagger, David Ladd, Cecil Kellaway, Henry Hull. Well-presented study of two-fisted Ladd seeking medical help for mute son; De Havilland is the woman who tames him.

Prowler, The (1951) 92m. *** D: Joseph Losey. Van Heflin, Evelyn Keyes, John Maxwell, Katharine Warren. Well-handled suspenser of Heflin in love with Keyes, planning to kill her rich husband.

Psyche '59 (1964-British) 94m. **½ D: Alexander Singer. Patricia Neal, Curt Jurgens, Samantha Eggar, Ian Bannen, Elspeth March. Turgid melodrama involving infidelity, with good cast doing their best.

Psycho (1960) 109m. ***½ D: Alfred Hitchcock. Anthony Perkins, Janet Leigh, Vera Miles, John Gavin, Martin Balsam, John McIntire, Patricia Hitchcock. Hitchcock's very black comedy is suspenseful and confusing, with the now-legendary shower scene to keep everyone awake. Beware of cuts in some violent scenes.

Psychomania (1964) 90m. **½ D: Richard Hilliard. Lee Philips, Shepperd Strudwick, Jean Hale, James Farentino, Richard Van Patten. Offbeat chiller of killer on the rampage at a college.

Psychopath, The (1966-British) 83m. *** D: Freddie Francis. Patrick Wymark, Margaret Johnston, John Standing, Judy Huxtable. Another demented killer on loose leaves dolls as calling card; effectively acted and directed by Britishers. They have a knack at this sort of thing.

Public Enemy (1931) 74m. ***½ D: William Wellman. James Cagney, Jean Harlow, Eddie Woods, Beryl Mercer, Donald Cook, Joan Blondell, Mae Clarke. Prohibition gangster's rise and fall is all Cagney, who makes up for the film's occasional faults. This one includes the now-legendary scene of Jimmy pushing a grapefruit into Clarke's face.

Public Hero Number One (1935) 81m. *** D: J. Walter Ruben. Lionel Barrymore, Jean Arthur, Chester Morris, Joseph Calleia, Paul Kelly, Lewis Stone, Sam Baker. Fine tale of G-man Morris tracking down mobster Calleia with help of Barrymore and complication of Calleia's sister Jean Arthur. Most enjoyable.

Public Pigeon No. One (1957) C-79m. ** D: Norman Z. McLeod. Red Skelton, Vivian Blaine, Janet Blair, Allyn Joslyn, Jay C. Flippen. Bland Skelton vehicle with Red accidentally exposing gang of crooks; typical slapstick.

Pumpkin Eater, The (1964-British) 110m. *** D: Jack Clayton. Anne Bancroft, Peter Finch, James Mason, Cedric Hardwicke, Alan Webb, Richard Johnson, Maggie Smith, Eric Porter. Intelligent soap opera, with top-notch acting by Bancroft as much-married woman who discovers husband has been unfaithful.

Pure Hell of St. Trinian's, The (1961-British) 94m. ** D: Frank Launder. Cecil Parker, Joyce Grenfell, George Cole, Thorley Walters. Absence of Alastair Sim from series lessens glow;

outrageous girls' school is visited by sheik seeking harem gals.
Purlie Victorious SEE: Gone Are the Days.
Purple Gang, The (1960) 85m. ** D: Frank McDonald. Barry Sullivan, Robert Blake, Elaine Edwards, Marc Cavell, Jody Lawrance, Suzy Marquette, Joseph Turkel. Capable cast, limpid police-vs.-gangster yarn.
Purple Heart, The (1944) 99m. *** D: Lewis Milestone. Dana Andrews, Farley Granger, Sam Levene, Richard Conte, Tala Birell, Nestor Paiva, Benson Fong, Marshall Thompson. Absorbing tale of U.S. air force crew shot down during Tokyo raid receives strong performances by good cast.
Purple Hills, The (1961) C-60m. *1/2 D: Maury Dexter. Gene Nelson, Joanna Barnes, Kent Taylor, Russ Bender. Cheapie oater, with ex-dancer Nelson unconvincing as cowpoke on the run from rampaging Indians.
Purple Mask, The (1955) C-82m. **1/2 D: H. Bruce Humberstone. Tony Curtis, Gene Barry, Angela Lansbury, Colleen Miller, Dan O'Herlihy. Set in the early 19th-century France; Curtis is sword-wielding nobleman out to champion the cause of justice.
Purple Monster Strikes, The SEE: D-Day on Mars.
Purple Noon (1961-French, dubbed) C-115m. *** D: René Clement. Alain Delon, Marie Laforet, Maurice Ronet, Frank Latimore, Ave Ninchi. Marvelously photographed, tautly edited study of playboy Delon who commits murders and thinks he has gotten away with it.
Purple Plain, The (1955-British) C-100m. *** D: Robert Parrish. Gregory Peck, Bernard Lee, Win Min Than, Maurice Denham, Brenda De Banzie. Set in WW2 Burma; Peck is neurotic pilot whose plane crashes, forcing him to fight his way to freedom and new sense of values.
Pursued (1947) 101m. *** D: Raoul Walsh. Teresa Wright, Robert Mitchum, Judith Anderson, Dean Jagger, John Rodney. Grim Western of determined Mitchum out to find father's killers; very well acted, suspenseful.
Pursuers, The (1961-British) 63m. ** D: Godfrey Grayson. Cyril Shaps, Francis Matthews, Susan Denny, Sheldon Lawrence. Trim programmer with Matthews tracking down Nazi war criminal Shaps in England; conventionally told.

Pursuit of the Graf Spee (1957-British) C-106m. **1/2 D: Michael Powell, Emeric Pressburger. John Gregson, Anthony Quayle, Peter Finch, Ian Hunter, Bernard Lee, Patrick MacNee, Christopher Lee. Taut documentary-style account of WW2 chase of German warship by British forces.
Pursuit to Algiers (1945) 65m. D: Roy William Neill. Basil Rathbone, Nigel Bruce, Marjorie Riordan, Rosalind Ivan, Martin Kosleck, John Abbott, Frederick K. Worlock. SEE: **Sherlock Holmes** series.
Pushover (1954) 88m. **1/2 D: Richard Quine. Fred MacMurray, Kim Novak, Phil Carey, Dorothy Malone, E. G. Marshall. MacMurray is cop who falls in love with gangster moll Novak; supporting cast reduced to stereotypes in moody actioner.
Puzzle of the Red Orchid, The (1962-German, dubbed) 94m. ** D: Helmut Ashley. Christopher Lee, Marisa Mell, Klaus Kinski, Fritz Rasp, Adrian Hoven. Moderate Edgar Wallace entry; Scotland Yard and FBI track down international crime syndicate. Retitled: THE SECRET OF THE RED ORCHID.
Pygmalion (1938-British) 85m. **** D: Anthony Asquith, Leslie Howard. Leslie Howard, Wendy Hiller, Wilfrid Lawson, Marie Lohr, David Tree. Superlative filmization of G. B. Shaw play which became MY FAIR LADY. Howard excels as the professor, with Hiller his cockney pupil.
Pygmy Island (1950) 69m. D: William Berke. Johnny Weissmuller, Ann Savage, David Bruce, Tristram Coffin, Steven Geray. SEE: **Jungle Jim** series.
Pyro (1964-Spanish) C-99m. **1/2 D: Julio Coll. Barry Sullivan, Martha Hyer, Sherry Moreland, Soledad Miranda. Strange chiller of man burned in fire seeking revenge on ex-girlfriend who started it.

Q Planes SEE: Clouds Over Europe.
Quality Street (1937) 84m. *** D: George Stevens. Katharine Hepburn, Fay Bainter, Franchot Tone, Eric Blore, Estelle Winwood, Joan Fontaine, Cora Witherspoon, Bonita Granville. Hepburn confounds Tone by enacting dual role; blend of comedy and drama is quietly effective in adaptation of James Barrie's play.
Quantez (1957) C-80m. **1/2 D:

Harry Keller. Fred MacMurray, Dorothy Malone, Sydney Chaplin, John Gavin. Above-par Western involving robbery gang heading for Mexican border, encountering stiff opposition along the way.

Quantrill's Raiders (1958) C-68m. ** D: Edward Bernds. Steve Cochran, Diane Brewster, Leo Gordon, Gale Robbins. Predictable Civil War account of the outlaw's planned attack on a Kansas arsenal.

Quare Fellow, The (1962-Irish) 85m. ***1/2 D: Arthur Dreifuss. Patrick McGoohan, Sylvia Syms, Walter Macken, Dermot Kelly, Jack Cunningham, Hilton Edwards. Irish-made adaptation of Behan play deals with new prison guard, well-played by McGoohan, who changes mind about views on capital punishment. Finely acted, excellent script.

Quartet (1949-British) 120m. **** D: Ken Annakin, Arthur Crabtree, Harold French, Ralph Smart. Basil Radford, Naunton Wayne, Mai Zetterling, Ian Fleming, Jack Raine, Dirk Bogarde. Superb movie with Somerset Maugham introducing four of his tales, each with different casts and moods.

Quebec (1951) C-85m. ** D: George Templeton. John Barrymore, Jr., Corinne Calvet, Barbara Rush, Patric Knowles. Historical nonsense set in 1830's Canada during revolt against England.

Queen Bee (1955) 95m. *** D: Ranald MacDougall. Joan Crawford, Barry Sullivan, Betsy Palmer, John Ireland, Fay Wray, Tim Hovey. Crawford in title role has field-day maneuvering the lives of all in her Southern mansion, with husband Sullivan providing the final ironic twist.

Queen Christina (1933) 97m. **** D: Rouben Mamoulian. Greta Garbo, John Gilbert, Ian Keith, Lewis Stone, C. Aubrey Smith, Gustav von Seyffertitz, Reginald Owen, Elizabeth Young. Probably Garbo's best film, with a haunting performance by the radiant star as 17th-century Swedish queen who relinquishes her throne for her lover, Gilbert. Garbo and Gilbert's love scenes together are truly memorable, as is the famous final shot. Don't miss this one.

Queen of Babylon, The (1956-Italian, dubbed) C-98m. *1/2 D: Carlo Bragaglia. Rhonda Fleming, Ricardo Montalban, Roldano Lupi, Carlo Ninchi. American stars can't elevate elephantine study of ancient Babylonia.

Queen of Burlesque (1946) 70m. *1/2 D: Sam Newfield. Evelyn Ankers, Carleton Young, Marion Martin, Rose La Rose, Alice Fleming, Craig Reynolds. Low-budget suspenser unstrung backstage at burlesque theater.

Queen of Outer Space (1958) C-80m. *1/2 D: Edward Bernds. Zsa Zsa Gabor, Eric Fleming, Laurie Mitchell, Paul Birch. Inane sci-fi about expedition that crash-lands on Venus, where planet is ruled entirely by women. Script is ridiculous; acting indifferent.

Queen of Spades (1960-Russian, dubbed) C-100m. **1/2 D: Roman Tikhomirov. Oleg Strizhenov, Zurab Anzhaparidze, Olga Krasina, Tamara Milashkina. Stark version of Tchaikovsky opera PIKOVAYA DAMA, performed by Bolshoi Theater company; deals with young man consumed by gambling urge, leading to his and girlfriend's destruction.

Queen of the Nile (1961-Italian, dubbed) C-85m. ** D: Fernando Cerchio. Jeanne Crain, Vincent Price, Edmund Purdom, Amedeo Nazzari. Dull account of court life in 2000 B.C. Egypt. Not even campy.

Queen of the Pirates (1960-Italian, dubbed) C-79m. ** D: Mario Costa. Gianna Maria Canale, Massimo Serato, Scilla Gabel, Paul Muller. Vivid setting can't salvage wooden account of Canale in title role overcoming tyrannical Duke of Doruzzo (Muller).

Queen's Guards, The (1960-British) C-110m. ** D: Michael Powell. Daniel Massey, Robert Stephens, Raymond Massey, Ursula Jeans. Tedious, patriotic chronicle of young Massey distinguishing himself in service, saving family name; humdrum film.

Question of Adultery, A (1959-British) 86m. **1/2 D: Don Chaffey. Julie London, Anthony Steel, Basil Sydney, Donald Houston, Anton Diffring, Andrew Cruickshank. Tepid drama involving pros and cons of artificial insemination. Retitled: THE CASE OF MRS. LORING.

Quick Before It Melts (1964) C-98m. **1/2 D: Delbert Mann. George Maharis, Robert Morse, Anjanette Comer, James Gregory, Yvonne Craig, Doodles Weaver. Trivia involving Maharis and Morse in the Antarctic; they have bright idea of bringing in a planeload of girls, with predictable results.

Quick Gun, The (1964) C-87m. ** D: Sidney Salkow. Audie Murphy, Merry Anders, James Best, Ted de Corsia, Frank Ferguson, Raymond Hatton. Formula Murphy Western, with Audie redeeming himself by combating town outlaws.

Quicksand (1950) 79m. **½ D: Irving Pichel. Mickey Rooney, Jeanne Cagney, Barbara Bates, Peter Lorre, Minerva Urecal. Earnest little film with Rooney a simple workingman whose first minor criminal act snowballs into tragedy.

Quiet American, The (1958) 120m. **½ D: Joseph L. Mankiewicz. Audie Murphy, Michael Redgrave, Claude Dauphin, Giorgia Moll. At-times effective account of Murphy, who comes to Saigon with his own plans for ending the warring there.

Quiet Man, The (1952) C-129m. **** D: John Ford. John Wayne, Maureen O'Hara, Barry Fitzgerald, Victor McLaglen, Mildred Natwick, Arthur Shields, Ward Bond. American boxer Wayne returns to native Ireland, wins over townsfolk, and tames strong-willed O'Hara. Boisterous location film with beautiful scenery and score. Academy Award-winner.

Quiet Please, Murder (1942) 70m. **½ D: John Larkin. George Sanders, Gail Patrick, Richard Denning, Sidney Blackmer, Lynne Roberts, Kurt Katch, Minerva Urecal, Theodore Von Eltz. Priceless Shakespeare manuscripts stolen, leads to murder in the library. Intriguing murder mystery with good cast.

Quincannon, Frontier Scout (1956) C-83m. *½ D: Lesley Selander. Tony Martin, Peggie Castle, John Bromfield, John Smith, Ron Randell. Martin is miscast in title role of programmer.

Quo Vadis (1951) C-171m. *** D: Mervyn LeRoy. Robert Taylor, Deborah Kerr, Leo Genn, Peter Ustinov, Patricia Laffan, Finlay Currie, Abraham Sofaer. Marathon epic based on Henryk Sienkiewicz novel of the persecution of Christians during reign of Emperor Nero in ancient Rome; lavish in every detail, most serviceable cast.

R.C.M.P. and the Treasure of Genghis Khan (1948) 100m. *½ D: Fred Brannon, Yakima Canutt. Jim Bannon, Virginia Belmont, Anthony Warde, Dorothy Granger. Spotty actioner with too few real cliff-hangers, dealing with Canadian mounties' efforts to combat criminal syndicate searching for fabled Oriental buried treasure. Re-edited movie serial: DANGERS OF THE CANADIAN MOUNTED.

RX Murder (1958-British) 85m. ** D: Derek Twist. Rick Jason, Marius Goring, Lisa Gastoni, Mary Merrall. Jason stars as American physician settling in British village to find strange murder. Fair mystery.

Rabbit Trap, The (1959) 72m. **½ D: Philip Leacock. Ernest Borgnine, David Brian, Bethel Leslie, Kevin Corcoran, June Blair, Jeanette Nolan, Don Rickles. Intelligent if slow-moving study of motivational factors behind Borgnine's compulsive work life and ignoring of his family.

Race Street (1948) 79m. ** D: Edwin L. Marin. George Raft, William Bendix, Marilyn Maxwell, Frank Faylen, Henry Morgan, Gale Robbins. San Francisco bookie Raft is up against an extortion ring in this well-acted but ordinary crime story.

Racers, The (1955) C-112m. **½ D: Henry Hathaway. Kirk Douglas, Bella Darvi, Gilbert Roland, Lee J. Cobb, Cesar Romero, Katy Jurado. Hackneyed sports-car racing yarn, not salvaged by Douglas' dynamics or European location shooting.

Rachel and the Stranger (1948) 93m. *** D: Norman Foster. Loretta Young, William Holden, Robert Mitchum, Tom Tully, Sara Haden. Star trio are fine in this Western of man whose love for his wife is first aroused when stranger Mitchum visits their home.

Racing Fever, (1964) C-80m. Bomb D: William Grefe. Joe Morrison, Charles Martin, Maxine Carroll, Barbara Biggart. Torrid trash of speedboat racing, an accidental killing, and revenge.

Rack, The (1956) 100m. *** D: Arnold Laven. Paul Newman, Wendell Corey, Walter Pidgeon, Edmond O'Brien, Anne Francis, Lee Marvin. Newman is pensively convincing as Korean War veteran on trial for treason, with Pidgeon as his father and Francis his friend. Slick production adapted from Rod Serling teleplay.

Racket, The (1951) 88m. **½ D:

John Cromwell. Robert Mitchum, Lizabeth Scott, Robert Ryan, William Talman. Taut melodrama of rugged police captain fighting corruption in the city; sensibly acted.

Racket Busters (1938) 71m. ** D: Lloyd Bacon. George Brent, Humphrey Bogart, Gloria Dickson, Allen Jenkins, Walter Abel, Henry O'Neill, Penny Singleton. Mobster Bogie's going to take over the trucking business, but Brent doesn't want to co-operate. Standard programmer moves along well.

Radar Men From the Moon SEE: Retik, The Moon Menace.

Raffles (1940) 72m. **½ D: Sam Wood. David Niven, Olivia de Havilland, Dudley Digges, Dame May Whitty, Douglas Walton, Lionel Pape. Mild remake of tale of famous British jewel thief. Niven not up to snuff as dapper thief (played by John Barrymore in 1917 silent version, by Ronald Colman in 1931).

Rage at Dawn (1955) C-87m. ** D: Tim Whelan. Randolph Scott, Forrest Tucker, Mala Powers, J. Carrol Naish, Edgar Buchanan. Routine Scott Western entry, with Randy et al involved in hunting down outlaw gang.

Rage in Heaven (1941) 83m. ** D: W. S. Van Dyke II. Robert Montgomery, Ingrid Bergman, George Sanders, Lucile Watson, Oscar Homolka, Philip Merivale, Matthew Boulton. Disappointing story of mentally disturbed steel mill owner who suggests double suicide scheme; set in England.

Rage of Paris, The (1938) 75m. **½ D: Henry Koster. Danielle Darrieux, Douglas Fairbanks, Jr., Mischa Auer, Louis Hayward, Helen Broderick. Zesty account of fast-talkers using Darrieux's beauty to snare wealthy men; set in N.Y.C.

Rage of the Buccaneers, The (1961-Italian, dubbed) C-88m. ** D: Mario Costa. Ricardo Montalban, Vincent Price, Giulia Rubini, Liana Orfei. Juvenile but bouncy yarn which is set more on land than at sea, with pirate Montalban vs. Price, villainous governor's secretary.

Raging Tide, The (1951) 93m. **½ D: George Sherman. Richard Conte, Shelley Winters, Stephen McNally, Charles Bickford. Stereotyped script and typecast acting make this murderer-on-the-run yarn tame.

Raid, The (1954) C-83m. *** D: Hugo Fregonese. Van Heflin, Anne Bancroft, Richard Boone, Lee Marvin, Tommy Rettig. Well-handled story of Confederate prisoners escaping from jail in upper New England, with Bancroft and Rettig trying to snafu their marauding.

Raiders, The (1952) C-80m. **½ D: Lesley Selander. Richard Conte, Viveca Lindfors, Barbara Britton, Hugh O'Brian, Richard Martin, William Reynolds. Sometimes with-it oater about judge during California gold rush days, leading a land-grabbing gang. Retitled: RIDERS OF VENGEANCE.

Raiders, The (1963) C-75m. **½ D: Herschel Daughtery. Robert Culp, Brian Keith, Judi Meredith, James McMullan, Alfred Ryder, Simon Oakland. Enthusiastic cast helps this story of cattle drives and the railroad expansion westward.

Raiders of Leyte Gulf, The (1963) 80m. **½ D: Eddie Romero. Michael Parsons, Leopold Salcedo, Jennings Sturgeon, Liza Moreno, Efren Reyes. Grisly account of WW2 battle against Japanese forces.

Raiders of Old California (1957) 72m. Bomb D: Albert Gannaway. Jim Davis, Arleen Whelan, Lee Van Cleef, Louis Jean Heydt. Minor Western set in the 1850's.

Raiders of the Seven Seas (1953) C-88m. **½ D: Sidney Salkow. John Payne, Donna Reed, Gerald Mohr, Lon Chaney. Pirate Barbarossa saves countess from marriage to cutthroat, eventually falls in love.

Railroad Man, The SEE: Man of Iron.

Rails Into Laramie (1954) C-81m. ** D: Jesse Hibbs. John Payne, Mari Blanchard, Dan Duryea, Joyce MacKenzie, Barton MacLane. Pat movie of Payne's efforts to clean up title town and keep railroad construction moving westward.

Rainbow Island (1944) C-97m. **½ D: Ralph Murphy. Dorothy Lamour, Eddie Bracken, Gil Lamb, Barry Sullivan, Anne Revere, Olga San Juan, Elena Verdugo, Yvonne De Carlo. Good cast main asset in musical comedy of merchant marines stranded on island with beautiful natives.

Rainbow Jacket, The (1954-British) C-99m. ** D: Basil Dearden. Kay Walsh, Bill Owen, Fella Edmonds, Robert Morley. Colorful racetrack sequences spark this predictable study of Owen, veteran jockey gone wrong, who teaches Edmonds' how to race properly.

Rainbow 'Round My Shoulder (1952) C-78m. *½ D: Richard Quine. Frankie Laine, Billy Daniels, Charlotte Austin, Arthur Franz, Barbara Whiting. Comedown from 1940's all-star musicals. Here Austin is gal thrust into movie career. "Musical" interludes are passé.

Rainmaker, The (1956) C-121m. *** D: Joseph Anthony. Burt Lancaster, Katharine Hepburn, Wendell Corey, Lloyd Bridges, Earl Holliman, Cameron Prud'homme, Wallace Ford. Hepburn brings conviction to story of spinster in Southwestern town romanced by glib con-man (Lancaster). N. Richard Nash play was later musicalized as 110 IN THE SHADE.

Rains Came, The (1939) 104m. **½ D: Clarence Brown. Myrna Loy, Tyrone Power, George Brent, Brenda Joyce, Nigel Bruce, Maria Ouspenskaya, Joseph Schildkraut, Laura Hope Crews. Louis Bromfield novel reduced to Hollywood terms. Indian Power loves socialite Loy. Good earthquake scenes. Remade as THE RAINS OF RANCHIPUR.

Rains of Ranchipur, The (1955) C-104m. **½ D: Jean Negulesco. Lana Turner, Richard Burton, Fred MacMurray, Joan Caulfield, Michael Rennie, Eugenie Leontovich. Superficial remake of THE RAINS CAME; story of wife of Englishman having affair with Hindu doctor. Attractive in color.

Raintree County (1957) C-187m. *** D: Edward Dmytryk. Montgomery Clift, Elizabeth Taylor, Eva Marie Saint, Lee Marvin, Rod Taylor, Agnes Moorehead, Walter Abel. Elaborate but confused Civil War romantic epic. Taylor has mild tour de force as Southern belle bent on having everything. Clift as her love interest is erratic.

Raisin in the Sun, A (1961) 128m. **** D: Daniel Petrie. Sidney Poitier, Claudia McNeil, Ruby Dee, Diana Sands. Ivan Dixon. Lorraine Hansberry play receives perceptive handling by outstanding cast in drama of Chicago Negro family and their attempts to find sense in their constrained existence.

Raising a Riot (1957-British) C-90m. ** D: Wendy Toye. Kenneth More, Shelagh Frazer, Ronald Squire, Bill Shine. Predictable situation comedy of More trying to cope with his rambunctious trio of children.

Raising the Wind (1961-British) 91m. **½ D: Gerald Thomas. James Robertson Justice, Leslie Phillips, Sidney James, Paul Massie, Kenneth Williams. Zany shenanigans of eccentric group of students at a London school of music; well paced.

Rally 'Round the Flag Boys! (1958) 106m. **½ D: Leo McCarey. Paul Newman, Joanne Woodward, Joan Collins, Jack Carson. Disappointing film of Max Shulman's book about small community in uproar over projected missile base. Wit is noticeably lacking.

Ramona (1936) C-90m. ** D: Henry King. Loretta Young, Don Ameche, Kent Taylor, Pauline Frederick, Jane Darwell, Katherine DeMille. Oft-told tale doesn't wear well, with Young and Ameche as Indians in love, shunned by American society. Settings are picturesque.

Rampage (1963) C-98m. **½ D: Phil Karlson. Robert Mitchum, Elsa Martinelli, Jack Hawkins, Sabu, Cely Carillo, Emile Genest. German game-hunter (Hawkins), his mistress (Martinelli), and hunting guide (Mitchum) form love triangle, with men battling for Elsa. Sabu's last movie; Elmer Bernstein's score is memorable.

Rampage at Apache Wells (1966-German, dubbed) C-90m ** D: Harold Philipps. Stewart Granger, Pierre Brice, Macha Meril, Harold Leipnitz. Granger stars as Old Shatterhand, who fights for rights of Indians taken in by crooked white men. Adequate acting cannot compete with atrocious dubbing.

Ramrod (1947) 94m. **½ D: Andre de Toth. Veronica Lake, Joel McCrea, Arleen Whelan, Don DeFore, Preston Foster, Charles Ruggles, Donald Crisp, Lloyd Bridges. Fairly good Western of territorial dispute between ranch-owner Lake and her father Foster; good supporting cast.

Rancho Notorious (1952) C-89m. ***½ D: Fritz Lang. Marlene Dietrich, Arthur Kennedy, Mel Ferrer, Frank Ferguson, Stuart Randall. Well-done Western of Kennedy looking for murderers of sweetheart. Good cast and direction, with Dietrich alluring as ever.

Random Harvest (1942) 124m. ***

D: Mervyn LeRoy. Greer Garson, Ronald Colman, Philip Dorn, Susan Peters, Reginald Owen, Bramwell Fletcher, Una O'Connor, Margaret Wycherly, Ann Richards. Colman stars in James Hilton story of amnesiac who forgets about woman he loves; she attempts to rekindle their love honestly. Memorable for Garson's kilt dance; won many Academy Award nominations.

Rangers of Fortune (1940) 80m. **½ **D:** Sam Wood. Fred MacMurray, Albert Dekker, Gilbert Roland, Patricia Morison, Dick Foran, Joseph Schildkraut. Smartly-whipped-together yarn of trio fleeing Mexicans, stopping off in Southwestern town to offer assistance.

Ransom (1956) 109m. **½ **D:** Alex Segal. Glenn Ford, Donna Reed, Leslie Nielsen, Juano Hernandez, Alexander Scourby, Juanita Moore, Robert Keith. Brooding narrative of Ford's efforts to rescue his son who's been kidnapped.

Rape of Malaya SEE: **Town Like Alice, A.**

Rapture (1965-French) 104m. *** **D:** John Guillermin. Melvyn Douglas, Dean Stockwell Patricia Gozzi, Gunnel Lindblom, Leslie Sands. Intensive, sensitive account of Gozzi's tragic romance with Stockwell, a man on the run.

Rare Breed, The (1966) C-108m. **½ **D:** Andrew V. McLaglen. James Stewart, Maureen O'Hara, Brian Keith, Juliet Mills. Wholesome oater, with fetching O'Hara as woman who brings Hereford bull to U.S. to be bred, and can't decide whether to marry ranch owner Keith or former associate Stewart.

Rashomon (1951-Japanese, dubbed) 90m. ***½ **D:** Akira Kurosawa. Toshiro Mifune, Machiko Kyo, Masayuki Mori, Takashi Shimura. Superlative study of truth and human nature as four people involved in a rape-murder tell varying accounts of what happened. Remade as THE OUTRAGE.

Rasputin and the Empress (1932) 123m. *** **D:** Richard Boleslawsky. John, Ethel and Lionel Barrymore, Ralph Morgan, Diana Wynyard, C. Henry Gordon. Good drama that should have been great, with all three Barrymores in colorful roles, unfolding story of mad monk's plotting against Russia.

Rasputin—the Mad Monk (1966-British) C-92m. ** **D:** Don Sharp. Christopher Lee, Barbara Shelley, Richard Pasco, Francis Matthews. Confused historical drama of "monk" who actually controlled Russia before Revolution. Script uncommonly bad; Lee's performance manages to redeem film.

Rat Race, The (1960) C-105m. *** **D:** Robert Mulligan. Tony Curtis, Debbie Reynolds, Jack Oakie, Kay Medford, Don Rickles, Joe Bushkin. Comedy-drama of would-be musician (Curtis) and dancer (Reynolds) coming to N.Y.C., platonically sharing an apartment, and falling in love. Nice comic cameos by Oakie and Medford. Based on Garson Kanin play.

Rationing (1944) 93m. **½ **D:** Willis Goldbeck. Wallace Beery, Marjorie Main, Donald Meek, Gloria Dickson, Henry O'Neill, Connie Gilchrist. Butcher in small town is main character in story of problems during WW2; typical Beery vehicle.

Raton Pass (1951) 84m. **½ **D:** Edwin L. Marin. Dennis Morgan, Patricia Neal, Steve Cochran, Scott Forbes, Dorothy Hart. Middling Warner Bros. Western, with Morgan and Neal married couple fighting each other for cattle empire.

Rattle of a Simple Man (1964-British) 96m. *** **D:** Muriel Box. Harry H. Corbett, Diane Cilento, Thora Hird, Michael Medwin. Pleasant saucy sex comedy of timid soul Corbett spending the night with Cilento to win a bet; set in London.

Ravagers, The (1965) 79m. *½ **D:** Eddie Romero. John Saxon, Fernando Poe, Jr., Bronwyn Fitzsimmons, Mike Parsons, Kristina Scott. Uninspired account of partisan fight against Japanese in WW2 Philippines.

Raven, The (1935) 62m. *** **D:** Louis Friedlander (Lew Landers). Boris Karloff, Bela Lugosi, Irene Ware, Lester Matthews, Samuel S. Hinds. Momentous teaming of horror greats with Lugosi as doctor with Poe-obsession, Karloff a victim of his wicked schemes. Hinds is subjected to torture from PIT AND THE PENDULUM in film's climax. Great fun throughout.

Raw Deal (1948) 79m. *** **D:** Anthony Mann. Dennis O'Keefe, Claire Trevor, Marsha Hunt, John Ireland, Raymond Burr. Story of man unjustly sent to prison, seeking revenge when he's released. Cast bristles in A-1 crime drama.

Raw Edge (1956) C-76m. **½ D: John Sherwood. Rory Calhoun, Yvonne De Carlo, Mara Corday, Rex Reason, Neville Brand. Bizarre premise routinely told; rancher's workers plan to kill him, with his widow to be the prize stake.

Raw Wind in Eden (1958) C-89m. **½ D: Richard Wilson. Esther Williams, Jeff Chandler, Rossana Podesta, Carlos Thompson. Melodramatic soaper of clash and romance on small isolated island when yacht is wrecked in a storm.

Rawhide (1951) 86m. **½ D: Henry Hathaway. Tyrone Power, Susan Hayward, Hugh Marlowe, Dean Jagger. Climactic shoot-out sparks this Western of outlaws hiding at stagecoach station, holding a group of people captive. Retitled: DESPERATE SIEGE.

Rawhide Trail, The (1958) 67m. *½ D: Robert Gordan. Rex Reason, Nancy Gates, Richard Erdman, Ann Doran. Humdrum tale of duo proving their innocence of helping the Indians attack settlers.

Rawhide Years, The (1956) C-85m. ** D: Rudolph Mate. Tony Curtis, Colleen Miller, Arthur Kennedy, William Demarest, William Gargan. Youthful Curtis perks this routine fare of gambler trying to clear himself of murder charge.

Raymie (1960) 72m. ** D: Frank McDonald. David Ladd, Julie Adams, John Agar, Charles Winninger, Richard Arlen, Frank Ferguson, Ray Kellogg. Quiet little film about youngster (Ladd) whose greatest ambition is to catch the big fish that always eludes him.

Razor's Edge, The (1946) 146m. ***½ D: Edmund Goulding. Tyrone Power, Gene Tierney, John Payne, Anne Baxter, Clifton Webb, Herbert Marshall. Maugham's philosophical novel, with Marshall as the author, Power as hero seeking goodness in life, Baxter in Oscar-winning role as a dipsomaniac, Elsa Lanchester sparkling in bit as social secretary. Long but engrossing.

Reach for Glory (1963-British) 89m. **½ D: Philip Leacock. Harry Andrews, Kay Walsh, Oliver Grimm, Michael Anderson, Jr., Martin Tomlinson, Alexis Kanner. Sensitive if minor tale about WW2 England, involving youths and their special code of ethics, leading to one member's death.

Reach for the Sky (1956-British) 123m. *½ D: Lewis Gilbert. Kenneth More, Muriel Pavlow, Alexander Knox, Sydney Tafler, Nigel Green. Sensibly told account of British pilot who overcame leg injury to continue his flying career.

Reaching for the Moon (1931) 90m. **½ D: Edmund Goulding. Douglas Fairbanks, Sr., Bebe Daniels, Edward Everett Horton, Jack Mulhall, Helen Jerome Eddy, Bing Crosby. Enjoyable Depression film of financier Fairbanks, with Horton as his valet, Bebe the girl, and Crosby singing one song.

Reaching for the Sun (1941) 90m. **½ D: William Wellman. Joel McCrea, Ellen Drew, Eddie Bracken, Albert Dekker, Billy Gilbert, George Chandler. OK comedy of North Woods clam-digger who journeys to Detroit to earn money for outboard motor.

Real Glory, The (1939) 95m. *** D: Henry Hathaway. Gary Cooper, David Niven, Andrea Leeds, Reginald Owen, Kay Johnson, Broderick Crawford, Vladimir Sokoloff, Henry Kolker. Cooper's fine as Army medic who solves all of Philippines' medical and military problems almost singlehandedly after destructive Spanish-American War. Excellent action scenes.

Reap the Wild Wind (1942) C-124m. *** D: Cecil B. de Mille. Ray Milland, John Wayne, Paulette Goddard, Raymond Massey, Robert Preston, Susan Hayward, Charles Bickford, Hedda Hopper, Louise Beavers, Martha O'Driscoll, Lynne Overman. Brawling De Mille hokum of 19th-century salvagers in Georgia, with Goddard as fiery Southern belle, Ray and John fighting for her, Massey as odious villain. Milland is good in offbeat characterization.

Rear Window (1954) C-122m. **** D: Alfred Hitchcock. James Stewart, Grace Kelly, Wendell Corey, Thelma Ritter, Raymond Burr, Judith Evelyn. Grade-A Hitchcock has Stewart confined to wheelchair, using binoculars to spy on courtyard neighbors, discovering murder. Kelly chic as society girlfriend, Ritter wry as housekeeper.

Rebecca (1940) 115m. **** D: Alfred Hitchcock. Laurence Olivier,

Joan Fontaine, George Sanders, Judith Anderson, Nigel Bruce, Reginald Denny. Oscar-winning adaptation of Daphne du Maurier tale of girl who marries British nobleman but lives in shadow of former wife. Stunning performances by Fontaine and Anderson.

Rebecca of Sunnybrook Farm (1938) 80m. **½ D: Allan Dwan. Shirley Temple, Randolph Scott, Jack Haley, Gloria Stuart, Phyllis Brooks, Helen Westley, Slim Summerville. Misleading title has nothing to do with famous story; this is story of Shirley becoming radio star while Scott and Stuart romance. Shirley also dances with "Bojangles" Robinson.

Rebel in Town (1956) 78m. ** D: Alfred L. Werker. John Payne, Ruth Roman, J. Carrol Naish, Ben Cooper, John Smith. Sensitive minor Western; cowpoke accidentally kills a child, and ironic events bring him into contact with boy's father.

Rebel Set, The (1959) 52m. *½ D: Gene Fowler, Jr. Gregg Palmer, Kathleen Crowley, Edward Platt, Ned Glass, John Lupton. Minor crime caper involving youths used by gangster to help carry out a robbery.

Rebel Without a Cause (1955) C-111m. ***½ D: Nicholas Ray. James Dean, Natalie Wood, Sal Mineo, Jim Backus, Ann Doran, Dennis Hopper, Nick Adams. Classic study of preconditioned juvenile delinquency, with gutsy telling of why Dean-Wood-Mineo became involved in tragic outcome.

Reckless (1935) 96m. **½ D: Victor Fleming. Jean Harlow, William Powell, Franchot Tone, May Robson, Ted Healy, Nat Pendleton, Robert Light, Rosalind Russell. Big production, big cast, musical numbers—all can't save mediocre script of chorus girl tangling up several people's lives. Stars provide only interest.

Reckless Moment, The (1949) 82m. ***½ D: Max Ophuls. James Mason, Joan Bennett, Geraldine Brooks, Henry O'Neill, Shepperd Strudwick, Roy Roberts. Bennett becomes a murderer, pursued by blackmailer Mason. First-rate suspenser.

Red Badge of Courage, The (1951) 69m. ***½ D: John Huston. Audie Murphy, Bill Mauldin, John Dierkes, Royal Dano, Andy Devine. Stephen Crane's human focus on Civil War, not treated as spectacle, resulting in realistic drama with natural performances.

Red Ball Express (1952) 83m. *** D: Budd Boetticher. Jeff Chandler, Alex Nicol, Judith Braun, Hugh O'Brien, Jack Kelly, Sidney Poitier, Jack Warden. Energetic cast and fast-paced action blend well in this account of supply unit working behind the German lines.

Red Canyon (1949) C-82m. ** D: George Sherman. Ann Blyth, Howard Duff, George Brent, Edgar Buchanan, Chill Wills, Jane Darwell, Lloyd Bridges. Routine Zane Grey Western of wild horses being tamed.

Red Circle, The (1960-German, dubbed) 94m. **½ D: Jurgen Roland. Fritz Rasp, Karl Saebisch, Renate Ewert, Klausjurgen Wussow. Scotland Yard investigates series of murders, with each victim having telltale circle mark on his neck; slickly paced.

Red Danube, The (1949) 119m. **½ D: George Sidney. Walter Pidgeon, Ethel Barrymore, Peter Lawford, Angela Lansbury, Janet Leigh, Louis Calhern, Francis L. Sullivan. Meandering drama of ballerina Leigh pursued by Russian agents, aided by amorous Lawford; heavy-handed at times.

Red Dragon, The (1945) 64m. D: Phil Rosen. Sidney Toler, Fortunio Bonanova, Benson Fong, Robert Emmett Keane, Willie Best, Carol Hughes. SEE: Charlie Chan series.

Red Dragon (1967-German, dubbed) C-88m. **½ D: Ernest Hofbauer. Stewart Granger, Rosanna Schiaffino, Horst Frank, Suzanne Roquette. Granger is FBI agent in Hong Kong chasing smuggling gang, Schiaffino another agent. Well paced, but predictable script.

Red Dust (1932) 83m. ***½ D: Victor Fleming. Clark Gable, Jean Harlow, Mary Astor, Donald Crisp, Gene Raymond, Tully Marshall, Willie Fung. Robust romance of African rubber worker Gable, his floozie gal Harlow, and visiting Astor, who is married to Raymond, but falls for Gable. Harlow has fine comic touch. Remade as MOGAMBO.

Red Garters (1954) C-91m. **½ D: George Marshall. Rosemary Clooney, Jack Carson, Guy Mitchell, Pat Crowley, Gene Barry. Offbeat casting spices this Western tale of revenge.

Red Headed Woman (1932) 74m. ***

D: Jack Conway. Jean Harlow, Chester Morris, Lewis Stone, Una Merkel, May Robson, Charles Boyer. Sparkling Harlow vehicle of secretary who has social aspirations and stops at nothing to attain them.

Red, Hot and Blue (1949) 84m. **½ D: John Farrow. Betty Hutton, Victor Mature, William Demarest, June Havoc, Frank Loesser, Raymond Walburn. Noisy Hutton vehicle of ambitious girl trying to make it big in show biz, mixed up with gangsters.

Red House, The (1947) 100m. *** D: Delmer Daves. Edward G. Robinson, Lon McCallister, Allene Roberts, Judith Anderson, Rory Calhoun, Julie London, Ona Munson. Title refers to strange old house containing many mysteries, providing constant fear for farmer Robinson. Exciting melodrama with fine cast.

Red Inn, The (1954-French, dubbed) 100m. **½ D: Claude Autant-Lara. Fernandel, Françoise Rosay, Carette, Marie-Claude Olivia, Lud Germain. Bizarre account of wayside inn run by woman who robs and murders guests.

Red Light (1949) 83m. ** D: Roy Del Ruth. George Raft, Virginia Mayo, Gene Lockhart, Barton MacLane, Henry Morgan, Raymond Burr. Turgid drama of innocent Raft seeking revenge when freed from prison, hunting brother's killer.

Red Mountain (1951) C-84m. **½ D: William Dieterle. Alan Ladd, Lizabeth Scott, John Ireland, Arthur Kennedy. Generally actionful Western dealing with the career of Quantrill, Yankee renegade officer during Civil War.

Red Planet Mars (1952) 87m. **½ D: Harry Horner. Peter Graves, Andrea King, Marvin Miller, Herbert Berghof, House Peters, Vince Barnett. Interesting sci-fi of scientist deciphering messages from Mars. Cast is made up of faces you remember but can't name.

Red Pony, The (1949) C-89m. *** D: Lewis Milestone. Myrna Loy, Robert Mitchum, Peter Miles, Louis Calhern, Shepperd Strudwick, Margaret Hamilton. Tasteful version of John Steinbeck book about boy attached to horse, seeking escape from bickering family; leisurely pacing.

Red River (1948) 125m. **** D: Howard Hawks. John Wayne, Montgomery Clift, Joanne Dru, Walter Brennan, Coleen Gray, John Ireland, Harry Carey, Jr., Noah Beery, Jr. One of the all-time great Westerns, with young Clift rebelling from cattle baron father Wayne during important roundup; beautifully filmed.

Red Shoes, The (1948) C-133m. *** D: Michael Powell, Emeric Pressburger. Anton Walbrook, Marius Goring, Moira Shearer, Robert Helpmann. Fine ballet sequences make up for lowbrow script of dancer who must choose between a career and marriage. A must for dance afficianados.

Red Skies of Montana (1952) C-89m. **½ D: Joseph M. Newman. Richard Widmark, Jeffrey Hunter, Constance Smith, Richard Boone, Richard Crenna. Trite account of forest-fire fighters, salvaged by spectacular fire sequences.

Red Stallion, The (1947) C-82m. *½ D: Lesley Selander. Robert Paige, Noreen Nash, Ted Donaldson, Jane Darwell, Daisy. Weak little film of ranch boy and his pet horse.

Red Stallion in the Rockies (1949) C-85m. ** D: Ralph Murphy. Arthur Franz, Wallace Ford, Ray Collins, Jean Heather. OK outdoor drama of two men rounding up herd of wild horses.

Red Sundown (1956) C-81m. **½ D: Jack Arnold. Rory Calhoun, Martha Hyer, Dean Jaggar, Robert Middleton, James Millican. Virile cast adds zest to standard yarn of bad-guy-gone-good (Calhoun), squeezing out the criminal elements in town.

Redhead and the Cowboy, The (1950) 82m. **½ D: Leslie Fenton. Glenn Ford, Rhonda Fleming, Edmond O'Brien, Morris Ankrum. Effective Western set in Civil War times, with Fleming a Reb spy trying to get message across Union lines.

Redhead From Wyoming, The (1952) C-80m. **½ D: Lee Sholem. Maureen O'Hara, Alexander Scourby, Alex Nicol, Jack Kelly, William Bishop, Dennis Weaver. Saucy Western pepped up by exuberant O'Hara as girl who falls in love with sheriff while protecting local cattle rustler.

Reform School Girl (1957) 71m. Bomb D: Edward Bernds. Gloria Catillo, Ross Ford, Edward Byrnes, Ralph Reed, Jack Kruschen, Sally Kellerman. Cheapie production about girl involved with hit-and-run murder.

Reformer and the Redhead, The (1950) 90m. **½ D: Norman Panama, Melvin Frank. June Allyson,

Dick Powell, David Wayne, Cecil Kellaway, Ray Collins. Sassy shenanigans with Allyson, a zoo-keeper's daughter, courted by lawyer Powell.

Reign of Terror (1949) 89m. *** D: Anthony Mann. Robert Cummings, Arlene Dahl, Richard Hart, Richard Basehart, Arnold Moss, Beulah Bondi. Vivid costume drama set during French Revolution, with valuable diary eluding both sides of battle; Retitled: BLACK BOOK.

Relentless (1948) C-93m. **½ D: George Sherman. Robert Young, Marguerite Chapman, Willard Parker, Akim Tamiroff. Satisfactory Western about cowpoke and his gal trying to prove him innocent of murder charge.

Reluctant Astronaut, The (1967) C-101m. ** D: Edward Montagne. Don Knotts, Leslie Nielsen, Joan Freeman, Arthur O'Connell, Jesse White. Featherweight comedy dealing with hicksville alumnus Knotts becoming title figure; predictable and often not even childishly humorous. For kids only.

Reluctant Debutante, The (1958) C-94m. **½ D: Vincente Minnelli. Rex Harrison, Kay Kendall, John Saxon, Sandra Dee, Angela Lansbury. Bright drawing-room comedy which Harrison, Kendall, and Lansbury make worthwhile: British parents must present their Americanized daughter to society.

Reluctant Spy, The (1963-French, dubbed) 93m. **½ D: Jean-Charles Dudrumet. Jean Marais, Genevieve Page, Maurice Teynac, Jean Gallar. Marais properly spoofs James Bond spy thrillers as secret agent chasing around the Continent.

Reluctant Widow, The (1951-British) 86m. *½ D: Bernard Knowles. Jean Kent, Guy Rolfe, Kathleen Byron, Paul Dupuis. Mild drama set in late 18th century, of governess Kent marrying rogue Rolfe.

Remains to be Seen (1953) 89m. *** D: Don Weis. Van Johnson, June Allyson, Angela Lansbury, Louis Calhern, Dorothy Dandridge. Disarming comedy based on Howard Lindsay-Russel Crouse play, with Allyson a singer and Johnson the apartment-house manager involved in swank East Side N.Y.C. murder.

Remarkable Andrew, The (1942) 80m. **½ D: Stuart Heisler. William Holden, Ellen Drew, Brian Donlevy, Rod Cameron, Porter Hall, Nydia Westman, Montagu Love, Jimmy Conlin. Donlevy is the ghost of Andrew Jackson, who comes back to help crusading Holden in small town. Farfetched fantasy, well played.

Remarkable Mr. Pennypacker, The (1959) C-87m. **½ D: Henry Levin. Clifton Webb, Dorothy McGuire, Charles Coburn, Ray Stricklyn, Jill St. John, Ron Ely, David Nelson. Prodded along by Webb's brittle manner, period tale unfolds of Pennsylvania businessman who leads dual life, with two families (17 kids in all).

Rembrandt (1936-British) 84m. ***½ D: Alexander Korda. Charles Laughton, Elsa Lanchester, Gertrude Lawrence, Marius Goring, Abraham Sofaer, John Bryning, Richard Gofe, Laughton is brilliant in realistic biography of Dutch painter, with Lawrence as his wife and Lanchester his true love, a servant.

Remedy for Riches (1940) 60m. ** D: Erle C. Kenton. Jean Hersholt, Dorothy Lovett, Edgar Kennedy, Jed Prouty, Walter Catlett. Hersholt is kindly Dr. Christian in minor account of coping with patient obsessed by money.

Remember? (1939) 83m. ** D: Norman Z. McLeod. Robert Taylor, Greer Garson, Lew Ayres, Billie Burke, Reginald Owen, Laura Hope Crews, Sig Ruman. Unbelievable tale of man romancing pal's bride-to-be; pleasant but muddled.

Remember the Day (1941) 85m. *** D: Henry King. Claudette Colbert, John Payne, John Shepperd (Shepperd Strudwick), Ann B. Todd, Douglas Croft, Jane Seymour, Anne Revere. Sentimental flashback story of pre-WW1 America, with fine performances by Colbert and Payne as schoolteachers who fall in love.

Remember the Night (1940) 86m *** D: Mitchell Leisen. Barbara Stanwyck, Fred MacMurray, Beulah Bondi, Elizabeth Patterson. Sterling Holloway. Good comedy-romance about prosecutor who falls in love with shoplifter during Xmas recess; written by Preston Sturges.

Rendezvous (1935) 91m. **½ D: William K. Howard. William Powell, Rosalind Russell, Binnie Barnes, Lionel Atwill, Cesar Romero. OK WW1 intrigue, with Powell assigned to office work instead of combat during war, running into notorious spy ring.

Repeat Performance (1947) 93m. **½

D: Alfred L. Werker. Louis Hayward, Joan Leslie, Tom Conway, Benay Venuta, Richard Basehart, Virginia Field, Natalie Schafer. Capably acted account of group of people who are able to relive the past dramatic year.

Reprieve SEE: **Convicts Four.**

Reprisal! (1956) C-74m. ****½** D: George Sherman. Guy Madison, Felicia Farr, Kathryn Grant, Michael Pate, Edward Platt. Pleasing cast enhances this tale of Madison blamed for death of rancher baron, with Grant and Farr the gals in love with him.

Repulsion (1965-British) 105m. ******** D: Roman Polanski. Catherine Deneuve, Ian Hendry, John Fraser, Patrick Wymark, Yvonne Furneaux. Excellent psychological horror film of mental deterioration of secluded girl. Not for children.

Reptile, The (1966-British) C-90m. ******* D: John Gilling. Noel Willman, Jennifer Daniels, Ray Barrett, Jacqueline Pearce. Average film story of girl with strange power to change into snake receives excellent direction and sympathetic characterizations.

Requiem for a Gunfighter (1965) C-91m. ***½** D: Spencer G. Bennet. Rod Cameron, Stephen McNally, Mike Mazurki, Olive Sturgess, Tim McCoy, John Mack Brown, Bob Steele, Lane Chandler, Raymond Hatton. Veteran cast is sole virtue of low-budget Western. Cameron impersonates a judge to insure that justice is done at murder trial.

Requiem for a Heavyweight (1962) 95m. ******* D: Ralph Nelson. Anthony Quinn, Jackie Gleason, Mickey Rooney, Julie Harris, Nancy Cushman, Madame Spivy. Grim account of fighter Quinn whose ring career is over, forcing him into degradation and corruption. Rooney as pathetic cohort and Harris as unrealistic social worker are fine. Based on Rod Serling teleplay.

Rest is Silence, The (1960-German, dubbed) 106m. ******* D: Helmut Kautner. Hardy Kruger, Peter Van Eyck, Ingrid Andree, Adelheid Seeck, Rudolf Forster, Boy Gobert. Updating of Hamlet, with young man trying to prove uncle killed his father.

Restless Breed, The (1957) C-81m. ****** D: Allan Dwan. Scott Brady, Anne Bancroft, Jim Davis, Scott Marlowe, Evelyn Rudie. Usual Western fare of Brady out to get his father's killer.

Restless Years, The (1958) 86m. ****½**

D: Helmut Kautner. John Saxon, Sandra Dee, Margaret Lindsay, Teresa Wright, James Whitmore. Capable cast in overblown melodramatics involving smalltown life, the generation gap, skeletons in family closets, etc.

Retik, the Moon Menace (1952) 100m. ***½** D: Fred C. Brannon. George Wallace, Aline Towne, Roy Barcroft, William Bakewell, Clayton Moore. Ludicrous low-grade cliffer from Republic Pictures, involving Commander Cody, who zooms through space with his jet pack, combating alien lunar powers trying to conquer earth. Re-edited movie serial: RADAR MEN FROM THE MOON.

Retreat, Hell! (1952) 95m. ****½** D: Joseph H. Lewis. Frank Lovejoy, Richard Carlson, Russ Tamblyn, Anita Louise. Occasional grim action enlivens this Korean War tale.

Return from the Ashes (1965-British) 105m. ******* D: J. Lee Thompson. Maximilian Schell, Samantha Eggar, Ingrid Thulin, Herbert Lom, Talitha Pol. Engrossing melodrama of a philandering husband taking up with his step-daughter when his wife is supposedly killed. Trio of stars lend credibility to the far-fetched proceedings.

Return From the Sea (1954) 80m. ****** D: Lesley Selander. Jan Sterling, Neville Brand, John Doucette, Paul Langton, John Pickard. Tepid story of Brand-Sterling romance, set in San Diego.

Return of a Stranger (1961-British) 63m. ****½** D: Max Varnel. John Ireland, Susan Stephen, Cyril Shaps, Timothy Beaton. Taut thriller of psychopath Shaps released from prison, terrorizing former victim Stephen and husband Ireland.

Return of Dr. X, The (1939) 62m. ****** D: Vincent Sherman. Humphrey Bogart, Rosemary Lane, Dennis Morgan, John Litel, Huntz Hall, Wayne Morris. Only Bogart as a zombie makes this low-grade sci-fi yarn worth viewing.

Return of Don Camillo, The (1965-Italian, dubbed) 115m. ****½** D: Julien Duvivier. Fernandel, Gino Cervi, Charles Vissieres, Edouard Delmont. Fernandel is again the irresponsible smalltown Italian priest involved in more projects of goodwill.

Return of Dracula, The (1958) 77m.****** D: Paul Landres. Francis Lederer, Norma Eberhardt, Ray Stricklyn, Jimmie Baird. Low-budget flick about the Count (Lederer) killing a man, taking his papers, and coming to U.S. Lederer thwarted by medium script.

Return of Frank James, The (1940) C-92m. *** D: Fritz Lang. Henry Fonda, Gene Tierney, Jackie Cooper, Henry Hull, John Carradine, J. Edward Bromberg, Donald Meek. Jesse James' brother (Fonda) goes out on his own to avenge brother's death; colorful Western with a choice cast.

Return of Jack Slade, The (1955) 79m. ** D: Harold Schuster. John Ericson, Mari Blanchard, Neville Brand, Angie Dickinson. To redeem his father's wrongdoings, Ericson joins the law to fight outlaws; adequate Western.

Return of Jesse James, The (1950) 75m. **½ D: Arthur Hilton. John Ireland, Ann Dvorak, Henry Hull, Hugh O'Brian, Reed Hadley. Compact budget Western dealing with rumors that lookalike for outlaws is notorious gunslinger.

Return of Mr. Moto, The (1965-British) 71m. D: Ernest Morris. Henry Silva, Terence Longdon, Suzanne Lloyd, Marne Maitland, Martin Wyldeck. SEE: Mr. Moto series.

Return of Monte Cristo, The (1946) 91m. ** D: Henry Levin. Louis Hayward, Barbara Britton, George Macready, Una O'Connor, Henry Stephenson. Rather ordinary swashbuckler of original count's young descendant, thwarted in attempt to claim inheritance by dastardly villain.

Return of October, The (1948) C-98m. ** D: Joseph H. Lewis. Glenn Ford, Terry Moore, Albert Sharpe, James Gleason, Steve Dunne. Moore is wholesome gal who is strongly attached to her horse (October), much to her relatives' consternation.

Return of Peter Grimm, The (1935) 83m. *** D: George Nichols, Jr. Lionel Barrymore, Helen Mack, Edward Ellis, Donald Meek, Lucien Littlefield. Entertaining fantasy of Barrymore returning from death to visit family, guiding them with their problems.

Return of Sophie Lang, The (1936) 65m. **½ D: George Archainbaud. Gertrude Michael, Sir Guy Standing, Ray Milland, Elizabeth Patterson, Colin Tapley, Paul Harvey. Jewel-thief-gone-straight Michael seeks Milland's help in staying out of public eye. OK low-budgeter.

Return of the Ape Man (1944) 60m. ** D: Philip Rosen. Bela Lugosi, John Carradine, Judith Gibson, Michael Ames, George Zucco, Mary Currier. Lugosi returns in same role of scientist who discovers serum enabling him to turn into ape with human mind. Cast is better here than in predecessor, but script isn't.

Return of the Bad Men (1948) 90m. **½ D: Ray Enright. Randolph Scott, Robert Ryan, Anne Jeffreys, George Hayes, Jacqueline White, Steve Brodie, Jason Robards. OK Western, with romance, outlaws, and early Western land rush combining; Ryan is despicable villain.

Return of the Fly, The (1959) 80m. **½ D: Edward L. Bernds. Vincent Price, Brett Halsey, David Frankham, John Sutton, Dan Seymour, Danielle De Metz. Adequate sequel to THE FLY proves "like father like son." Youth attempts to reconstruct his late father's disintegrator machine and is likewise transformed into an insect.

Return of the Frontiersman (1950) 74m. ** D: Richard Bare. Gordon MacRae, Rory Calhoun, Julie London, Jack Holt, Fred Clark. Easygoing yarn of sheriff's son falsely accused of murder.

Return of the Gunfighter (1967) C-120m. **½ D: James Neilson. Robert Taylor, Chad Everett, Ana Martin, Mort Mills, Lyle Bettger. OK Western telefeature, with Taylor the gunslinger aided by Everett in revenging the death of Martin's parents.

Return of the Scarlet Pimpernel, The (1938-British) 80m. ** D: Hans Schwartz. Barry K. Barnes, Sophie Stewart, Margaretta Scott, James Mason, Francis Lister, Anthony Bushell. Far below stunning original, with lower production values and less-than-stellar cast in costumer set in 1790's London and Paris.

Return of the Texan (1952) 88m. ** D: Delmer Daves. Dale Robertson, Joanne Dru, Walter Brennan, Richard Boone, Robert Horton. Flabby Western about Robertson et al fighting to save his ranch.

Return of the Vampire, The (1943) 69m. ** D: Lew Landers, Kurt Neumann. Bela Lugosi, Frieda Inescort, Nina Foch, Roland Varno, Miles Mander, Matt Willis. Lugosi returns in limp attempt to capitalize on previous success as Dracula. Final scene is memorable, though.

Return of the Whistler, The (1948) 63m. D: D. Ross Lederman. Michael Duane, Lenore Aubert, Richard Lane, James Cardwell, Ann Doran. SEE: Whistler series.

Return to Paradise (1953) 100m. ** D: Mark Robson. Gary Cooper, Roberta Haynes, Barry Jones, Moira MacDonald. Lackluster South Sea tale of beach bum Cooper in love with native girl; loosely based on James Michener's story.

Return to Peyton Place (1961) C-122m. ** D: Jose Ferrer. Jeff Chandler, Eleanor Parker, Carol Lynley, Mary Astor, Tuesday Weld, Robert Sterling. Muddled followup to PEYTON PLACE suffers from faulty direction, poor production, and, save for stalwarts Astor and Parker, bad casting.

Return to Sender (1963-British) 63m. ** D: Gordon Hales. Nigel Davenport, Yvonne Romain, Geoffrey Keen, William Russell, John Horsley. Programmer action tale of revenge, based on Edgar Wallace yarn of industralist's plot to ruin career and life of a D.A.

Return to Treasure Island (1954) C-75m. *1/2 D: E. A. Dupont. Tab Hunter, Dawn Addams, Porter Hall, James Seay, Harry Lauter. Poor updating of Stevenson novel, with student Hunter vying with crooks for buried treasure.

Return to Warbow (1958) C-67m. *1/2 D: Ray Nazarro. Phil Carey, Catherine McLeod, Andrew Duggan, William Leslie. Pedestrian narrative of outlaws backtracking to site of crime to collect loot left behind.

Reunion in France (1942) 104m. ** D: Jules Dassin. Joan Crawford, John Wayne, Philip Dorn, Reginald Owen, Albert Basserman, John Carradine, Henry Daniell. Glossy romance, with Crawford and Wayne trying to flee Nazi-occupied France; propaganda elements date the presentation badly.

Reunion in Reno (1951) 79m. **1/2 D: Kurt Neumann. Mark Stevens, Peggy Dow, Gigi Perreau, Frances Dee, Leif Erickson. Diverting comedy of Perreau deciding to divorce her parents so she won't be in the way.

Reunion in Vienna (1933) 100m. *** D: Sidney Franklin. John Barrymore, Diana Wynyard, Frank Morgan, May Robson, Eduardo Ciannelli, Una Merkel. Sparkling version of Robert Sherwood fluff about members of ousted royalty making their way to Austrian capital and rekindling their love.

Reveille With Beverly (1943) 78m. ** D: Charles Barton. Ann Miller, William Wright, Dick Purcell, Franklin Pangborn, Larry Parks. Columbia Pictures mini-musical, with Miller a versatile disk jockey throwing "big show" for servicemen.

Revenge of Frankenstein (1958-British) C-91m. *** D: Terence Fisher. Peter Cushing, Francis Matthews, Eunice Gayson, Michael Gwynn. Tight remake of Karloff classic is handled differently, but in its own way quite effective. Fine atmosphere, especially in color.

Revenge of the Creature (1955) 82m. ** D: Jack Arnold. John Agar, Lori Nelson, John Bromfield, Nestor Paiva. Further exploits of Creature from Black Lagoon falling for woman ichthyologist.

Revenge of the Gladiators (1965-Italian, dubbed) C-100m. *1/2 D: Michele Lupo. Roger Browne, Scilla Gabel, Giacomo Rossi Stuart, Daniele Vargas, Gordon Mitchell. Badly directed story of gladiator rescuing princess from barbarians.

Revenge of the Pirates (1951-Italian, dubbed) 95m. ** D: Primo Zeglio. Maria Montez, Milly Vitale, Jean-Pierre Aumont, Saro Urzi, Paul Muller, Roberto Risso. Aumont and Montez try to spark this trite swashbuckler of wicked governor hoarding stolen gold, with Robin Hood of the seas coming to rescue.

Revenge of the Zombies (1943) 61m. *1/2 D: Steve Sekely. John Carradine, Robert Lowery, Gale Storm, Veda Ann Borg, Mantan Moreland, Mauritz Hugo. Low-budget mad doctor saga, with Carradine experimenting on human guinea pigs.

Revolt at Fort Laramie (1957) C-73m. ** D: Lesley Selander. John Dehner, Frances Helm, Gregg Palmer, Don Gordon, Robert Keys. Grade-B Western of internal rivalries of North-South soldiers at government fort during Civil War.

Revolt in the Big House (1958) 79m. **1/2 D: R. G. Springsteen. Gene Evans, Robert Blake, Timothy Carey, John Qualen. Taut little programmer about convict life.

Revolt of Mamie Stover, The (1956) C-92m. **1/2 D: Raoul Walsh. Jane Russell, Richard Egan, Joan Leslie, Agnes Moorehead, Jorja Cutright,

Jean Willes, Michael Pate. Gorgeous Jane, in Technicolor, is Honolulu-based "saloon singer" in 1941. Weak plot; Jane sings "Keep Your Eyes On The Hands."

Revolt of the Tartars SEE: **Michael Strogoff.**

Revolt of the Zombies (1936) 65m. ** D: Victor Halperin. Dorothy Stone, Dean Jagger, Roy D'Arcy, Robert Noland, George Cleveland. Below average mixture of horror and mystery in story of strange series of murders. Liberal doses of Poe and Edgar Wallace.

Reward, The (1965) C-92m. **½ D: Serge Bourguignon. Max von Sydow, Yvette Mimieux, Efrem Zimbalist, Jr., Gilbert Roland, Emilio Fernandez, Henry Silva, Rodolfo Acosta. Promising premise and good cast led astray in static Western: group of bounty hunters turn on each other, as greed for larger share of reward money goads them into conflict.

Rhapsody (1954) C-115m. **½ D: Charles Vidor. Elizabeth Taylor, Vittorio Gassman, John Ericson, Louis Calhern, Michael Chekhov. Three-cornered romance among rich Taylor, violinist Gassman, and pianist Ericson: melodic interludes bolster soaper.

Rhapsody In Blue (1945) 139m. **½ D: Irving Rapper. Robert Alda, Joan Leslie, Alexis Smith, Charles Coburn, Julie Bishop, Albert Basserman, Morris Carnovsky, Rosemary De-Camp, Oscar Levant, Paul Whiteman. Stale formula biography about George Gershwin, saved only by music, some twenty-odd songs, plus Levant's rendition of title work.

Rhino! (1964) C-91m. **½ D: Ivan Tors. Robert Culp, Harry Guardino, Shirley Eaton, Harry Mekela. Diverting African game-hunting nonsense, with an enthusiastic cast, good action scenes.

Rhubarb (1951) 95m. **½ D: Arthur Lubin. Ray Milland, Jan Sterling, Gene Lockhart, Elsie Holmes. Frisky comedy of baseball team owned by a cat, from famous story by H. Allen Smith.

Rhythm on the Range (1936) 85m. **½ D: Norman Taurog. Bing Crosby, Frances Farmer, Bob Burns, Martha Raye, Lucile Gleason, Samuel S. Hinds. Film noteworthy as Raye's feature-film debut and pleasant excuse for musical nonsense. Remade as PARDNERS.

Rhythm on the River (1940) 92m. *** D: Victor Schertzinger. Bing Crosby, Mary Martin, Basil Rathbone, Oscar Levant, Oscar Shaw. Lots of fun, with Crosby and Martin ghost-writing songs for phony Rathbone, trying to break loose on their own.

Rhythm Romance SEE: **Some Like It Hot.**

Rice Girl (1963-Italian, dubbed) C-90m. **½ D: Raffaello Matarazzo. Elsa Martinelli, Folco Lulli, Michel Auclair, Rik Battaglia, Susanne Levesy, Liliana Gerace. Atmospheric account of seamy rice workers and Martinelli's past life catching up with her.

Rich Are Always With Us, The (1932) 73m. ** D: Alfred E. Green. Ruth Chatterton, Adrienne Dore, George Brent, Bette Davis, John Miljan, Robert Warwick, Berton Churchill. Chatterton and Miljan break up after long marriage, but she still loves him. Pat film sparked by Chatterton's personality.

Rich Man, Poor Girl (1938) 65m. ** D: Reinhold Schunzel. Robert Young, Lew Ayres, Ruth Hussey, Lana Turner, Rita Johnson, Don Castle, Guy Kibbee. Good cast, fair film. Title tells story; only noteworthy item is radiant young Turner.

Rich, Young and Pretty (1951) C-95m. **½ D: Norman Taurog. Jane Powell, Danielle Darrieux, Wendell Corey, Vic Damone, Fernando Lamas. Frivolous MGM musical, with Powell in Paris, sightseeing and romancing, meeting mother Darrieux.

Richard III (1956-British) C-158m. ***½ D: Laurence Olivier. Laurence Olivier, John Gielgud, Ralph Richardson, Claire Bloom, Alec Clunes, Cedric Hardwicke. Elaborate if stagy version of Shakespeare's chronicle of insane 15th-century British king and his court intrigues.

Richest Girl in the World, The (1960-Danish, dubbed) C-78m. *½ D: Lau Lauritzen. Nina, Frederik, Poul Reichhardt, Birgitte Bruun. Syrupy musical fluff with Nina out to marry singer Frederik; overly cute.

Ricochet Romance (1954) 80m. **½ D: Charles Lamont. Marjorie Main, Chill Wills, Pedro Gonzalez-Gonzalez, Rudy Vallee, Ruth Hampton. Another Main frolic, with the rambunctious gal hired as ranch cook but putting her two cents' worth into everything.

Ride a Crooked Trail (1958) C-87m. **½ D: Jesse Hibbs. Audie Murphy, Gia Scala, Walter Matthau, Henry

Silva. Trim Western with Murphy involved in bank robbery.

Ride a Violent Mile (1957) 80m. *½ D: Charles Marquis Warren. John Agar, Penny Edwards, John Pickard, Sheb Wooley, Eva Novak. Trivial Western set in Civil War times about Southern blockade runners.

Ride Back, The (1957) 79m. *** D: Allen H. Miner. Anthony Quinn, Lita Milan, William Conrad, Ellen Hope Monroe, Louis Towers. Well-handled account of sheriff and prisoner who find they need each other's help to survive elements and Indian attacks.

Ride Beyond Vengeance (1966) C-100m. **½ D: Bernard McEveety. Chuck Connors, Michael Rennie, Kathryn Hays, Joan Blondell, Gloria Grahame, Gary Merrill, Bill Bixby, James MacArthur. Good supporting cast makes the most of stereotyped roles in this flashback account of Connors' sundry encounters with outlaws.

Ride Clear of Diablo (1954) C-80m. **½ D: Jesse Hibbs. Audie Murphy, Dan Duryea, Susan Cabot, Abbe Lane, Russell Johnson. Above-par Murphy oater, with Audie swearing revenge for family's murder.

Ride 'Em Cowboy (1942) 86m. **½ D: Arthur Lubin. Bud Abbott, Lou Costello, Dick Foran, Anne Gwynne, Johnny Mack Brown, Ella Fitzgerald, Douglass Dumbrille. Good combination of Western, comedy, and musical in A&C vehicle, with Ella and the Merry Macs singing tunes including "A Tisket A Tasket."

Ride Lonesome (1959) C-73m. ** D: Budd Boetticher. Randolph Scott, Karen Steele, Pernell Roberts, James Coburn, Lee Van Cleef, James Best. Scott is his usual restrained self as sheriff gunning it out with energetic outlaws.

Ride Out for Revenge (1957) 79m. *½ D: Bernard Girard. Rory Calhoun, Gloria Grahame, Lloyd Bridges, Vince Edwards. Tiresome account of gold-hungry men trying to dispossess Indians from their lands.

Ride the High Country (1962) C-94m. ***½ D: Sam Peckinpah. Randolph Scott, Joel McCrea, Mariette Hartley, Ronald Starr, Warren Oates, Edgar Buchanan. Memorable Western of two aging gunfighters reunited after twenty years to deliver a gold shipment. Scott and McCrea have never been better; direction, action and scenery are first-rate. Buchanan unforgettable as drunken judge, Oates as rambunctious Indian.

Ride the High Iron (1956) 74m. *½ D: Don Weis. Don Taylor, Sally Forrest, Raymond Burr, Lisa Golm, Otto Waldis, Nestor Paiva, Mae Clarke. Programmer about P.R. man who makes his living keeping people's indiscretions out of the paper.

Ride the Man Down (1952) C-90m. ** D: Joseph Kane. Brian Donlevy, Rod Cameron, Ella Raines, Barbara Britton, Chill Wills, Jack LaRue. Lumbering account of ranchland feuding in old West.

Ride the Pink Horse (1947) 101m. ***½ D: Robert Montgomery. Robert Montgomery, Wanda Hendrix, Rita Conde, Andrea King, Fred Clark, Iris Flores, Grandon Rhodes. Top notch melodrama, with bad-guy Montgomery changing his outlook when he meets Hendrix; further complications draw him into suspense.

Ride the Wild Surf (1964) C-101m. **½ D: Don Taylor. Fabian, Tab Hunter, Barbara Eden, Anthony Hayes, James Mitchum, Shelley Fabares. Formula beach boys tale.

Ride to Hangman's Tree, The (1967) C-90m. **½ D: Al Rafkin. Jack Lord, James Farentino, Don Galloway, Melodie Johnson, Richard Anderson, Robert Yuro. Formula Universal Pictures back-lot Western, of outlaws in old West.

Ride, Vaquero (1953) C-90m. **½ D: John Farrow. Robert Taylor, Ava Gardner, Howard Keel, Anthony Quinn, Charlita. Oddball casting perks brooding Western set on Mexican border, with sultry Gardner responsible for most of the action.

Rider on a Dead Horse (1962) 72m. *½ D: Herbert L. Strock. John Vivyan, Bruce Gordon, Kevin Hagen, Lisa Lu, Charles Lampkin. Seedy account of trio of gold prospectors trying to do each other in.

Riders of Vengeance SEE: **Raiders, The.**

Riders to the Stars (1954) C-81m. **½ D: Richard Carlson. William Lundigan, Herbert Marshall, Richard Carlson, Martha Hyer. Labored programmer about early days of space missiles, quite outdated now.

Riding High (1950) 112m. **½ D: George Marshall. Dorothy Lamour, Dick Powell, Victor Moore, Gil Lamb, Cass Daley, Milt Britton and Band, Rod Cameron. Unmemorable songs, flat script, fair performances add up to dubious entertainment, with Powell obsessed with silver mine while wooing Lamour.

Riding High (1956) 112m. **½ D: Frank Capra. Bing Crosby, Coleen Gray, Charles Bickford, Margaret Hamilton, Frances Gifford, James Gleason, Raymond Walburn, Oliver Hardy. Musical remake of BROADWAY BILL features some "big" songs and occasionally engrossing plot of racehorse owner whose prize entry has had disappointing track record. Oliver Hardy is fun in a rare solo appearance.

Riding Shotgun (1954) C-74m. ** D: Andre de Toth. Randolph Scott, Wayne Morris, Joan Weldon, Joe Sawyer, James Millican. Typical, undemanding Scott Western of man seeking to clear his reputation.

Riff Raff Girls (1962-French, dubbed) 97m. **½ D: Alex Joffe. Nadja Tiller, Robert Hossein, Silvia Monfort, Roger Hanin, Pierre Blanchar. Tiller is quite convincing as club owner whose aim is to be self-sufficient; set on Brussels waterfront.

Riffraff (1935) 89m. **½ D: J. Walter Ruben. Jean Harlow, Spencer Tracy, Una Merkel, Joseph Calleia, Victor Kilian, Mickey Rooney. Comedy-drama doesn't always work, but worth viewing for stars playing married couple in fishing business who end up on wrong side of law.

Riffraff (1947) 80m. *** D: Ted Tetzlaff. Pat O'Brien, Anne Jeffreys, Walter Slezak, Percy Kilbride, Jerome Cowan, George Givot, Jason Robards. Fast-paced story of O'Brien foiling villains' attempts to take over oilfield in Panama.

Rififi (1954-French, dubbed) 115m. **** D: Jules Dassin. Jean Servais, Carl Mohner, Magali Noel, Robert Manuel, Perlo Vita. Most engaging Gallic study of quartet of jewel thieves, who find each other more dangerous than cops; tongue-in-cheek treatment throughout.

Rififi in Tokyo (1963-French, dubbed) 89m. ** D: Jacques Deray. Karl Boehm, Michel Vitold, Charles Vanel, Eiji Okada, Keiko Kishi, Barbara Lass, Yanagi. Aging European gangster recruits men for bank heist. Cast is so-so; strictly standard plot-line.

Right Approach, The (1961) 92m. **½ D: David Butler. Frankie Vaughan, Martha Hyer, Juliet Prowse, Gary Crosby, Jane Withers. Plucky minor film of Vaughan, a good-for-nothing who uses anyone to get ahead.

Right Cross (1950) 90m. **½ D: John Sturges. June Allyson, Dick Powell, Lionel Barrymore, Ricardo Montalban. Fairly compact account of boxing world, with sports-writer Powell and fighter Montalban in love with Allyson. One of Marilyn Monroe's early films.

Ring, The (1952) 79m. ** D: Kurt Neumann. Gerald Mohr, Rita Moreno, Lalo Rios, Robert Arthur. Typical boxing yarn with racial angle; Rios is determined to succeed to raise prestige of Mexican-Americans.

Ring of Fear (1954) C-93m. ** D: James Grant. Clyde Beatty, Pat O'Brien, Mickey Spillane, Sean McClory, Marian Carr, John Bromfield. Agreeable blend of Mickey Spillane and life under the big top.

Ring of Fire (1961) C-91m. **½ D: Andrew L. Stone. David Janssen, Joyce Taylor, Frank Gorshin, Joel Marston, Doodles Weaver. Assistant sheriff is held hostage by trio of escaping gangsters. Highlight of film is climactic forest holocaust.

Rings on Her Fingers (1942) 85m. **½ D: Rouben Mamoulian. Henry Fonda, Gene Tierney, Laird Cregar, Spring Byington, Marjorie Gateson, Iris Adrian, Clara Blandick, Mary Treen. Con-artist Tierney falls for Fonda instead of fleecing him; standard romance with good cast.

Ringside Maisie (1941) 96m. D: Edwin L. Marin. Ann Sothern, George Murphy, Robert Sterling, Virginia O'Brien, Natalie Thompson. SEE: Maisie series.

Rio (1939) 75m. **½ D: John Brahm. Basil Rathbone, Victor McLaglen, Sigrid Gurie, Robert Cummings, Leo Carrillo, Billy Gilbert. Crazed husband escapes from jail to get even with wife's new boyfriend. Good cast in predictable story, well photographed.

Rio Bravo (1959) C-141m. *** D: Howard Hawks. John Wayne, Dean Martin, Ricky Nelson, Angie Dickinson, Walter Brennan, Ward Bond, John Russell, Claude Akins, Bob Steele. Fairly good Western, with Wayne for action, Martin for laughs, Dickinson for the boys, and Nelson for the girls. Well directed, but overlong.

Rio Conchos (1964) **C-107m.** ***** D:** Gordon Douglas. Richard Boone, Stuart Whitman, Tony Franciosa, Edmond O'Brien. Post-Civil war Texas is setting for masculine adult Western, with Boone vs. Franciosa, and zesty characterization by O'Brien.

Rio Grande (1950) **105m.** ***** D:** John Ford. John Wayne, Maureen O'Hara, Ben Johnson, Harry Carey, Jr., Victor McLaglen, Claude Jarman, Jr. Post-Civil War friction between settlers and Apaches is focal point of rugged, taut Western, featuring Wayne as tough cavalry commander.

Rio Rita (1942) **91m.** ****1/2 D:** S. Sylvan Simon. Bud Abbott, Lou Costello, Kathryn Grayson, John Carroll, Tom Conway, Barry Nelson. Vintage Broadway musical brought up to date, with Nazis invading Western ranch where Bud and Lou work; some good music helps this one.

Riot in Cell Block II (1954) **80m.** ***** D:** Don Siegel. Neville Brand, Emile Meyer, Frank Faylen, Leo Gordon, Robert Osterloh. Forthright, grim account of prison rioting.

Riot in Juvenile Prison (1959) **71m.** Bomb **D:** Edward L. Cahn. Jerome Thor, Marcia Henderson, Scott Marlowe, John Hoyt, Dick Tyler, Dorothy Provine, Ann Doran. Programmer fully explained by title.

Riptide (1934) **90m.** ***** D:** Edmund Goulding. Norma Shearer, Robert Montgomery, Herbert Marshall, Lilyan Tashman, Mrs. Patrick Campbell, Skeets Gallagher, Ralph Forbes. Chic soaper about unhappily married Shearer taking up with young Montgomery, who's too honorable to ignore husband Marshall; MGM gloss works well in all departments.

Rise and Fall of Legs Diamond, The (1960) **101m.** ****1/2 D:** Budd Boetticher. Ray Danton, Karen Steele, Elaine Stewart, Jesse White, Simon Oakland, Robert Lowery. Snappy chronicle of Depression-days gangster, well balanced between action gun battles and Danton's romancing flashy dolls.

Rise and Shine (1941) **93m.** ****1/2 D:** Allan Dwan. Jack Oakie, Linda Darnell, George Murphy, Walter Brennan, Sheldon Leonard, Donald Meek, Ruth Donnelly. Oakie has field day as dumb football player abducted by crooks so team won't win big game. Film is often unconsciously funny.

Rising of the Moon, The (1957-Irish) **81m.** ****1/2 D:** John Ford. Introduced by Tyrone Power; Cyril Cusack, Maureen Connell, Noel Purcell, Frank Lawton, Jimmy O'Dea. Trio of flavorful stories about Irish life; MAJESTY OF THE LAW, A MINUTE'S WAIT, 1921.

Risk, The (1961-British) **81m.** ***** D:** Roy and John Boulting. Tony Britton, Peter Cushing, Ian Bannen, Virginia Maskell, Donald Pleasence. Tense drama of spies chasing scientist who has secret formula to combat plague. Good direction and cast.

River, The (1951-Indian, dubbed) **C-99m.** ****1/2 D:** Jean Renoir. Patricia Walters, Nora Swinburne, Arthur Shields, Radha, Adrienne Corri, Esmond Knight. Sharply photographed study of British family in India, trying to throw some new light on interracial marriage.

River Lady (1948) **C-78m.** **** D:** George Sherman. Yvonne de Carlo, Dan Duryea, Rod Cameron, Helena Carter, Lloyd Gough, Florence Bates. Typical De Carlo vehicle about riverboat queen trying to buy her man when she can't win him with love; colorful and empty.

River of No Return (1954) **C-91m.** ****1/2 D:** Otto Preminger. Robert Mitchum, Marilyn Monroe, Rory Calhoun, Tommy Rettig, Murvyn Vye. Monroe hires Mitchum to catch up to husband who deserted her. Name cast good, excellent photography.

River's Edge, The (1957) **C-87m.** ***** D:** Allan Dwan. Ray Milland, Anthony Quinn, Debra Paget, Byron Foulger. Melodrama about heel (Milland), his ex-girlfriend (Paget), and her husband (Quinn) trying to cross Mexican border with suitcase of money. Ray has never been nastier.

Road House (1948) **95m.** ***** D:** Jean Negulesco. Ida Lupino, Cornel Wilde, Celeste Holm, Richard Widmark, O.Z. Whitehead. Lupino comes between bitter enemies, roadhouse owner Widmark and parolee Wilde; Ida even sings in this engrossing melodrama.

Road Show (1941) **87m.** ****1/2 D:** Hal Roach, Gordon Douglas, Hal Roach, Jr. Adolphe Menjou, Carole Landis, John Hubbard, Charles Butterworth, Patsy Kelly, George E. Stone. Offbeat comedy of young man escaped from insane asylum arriving at traveling carnival; low budget mars efforts of veteran cast.

Road to Bali, The (1952) **C-90m.** ***** D:** Hal Walker. Bob Hope, Dorothy

Lamour, Bing Crosby, Murvyn Vye, Ralph Moody. Only color ROAD film has lush trappings, many guest stars, as Bob and Bing save Dorothy from evil princess and jungle perils. More laughs than usual.

Road to Denver, The (1955) C-90m. **½ D: Joseph Kane. John Payne, Lee J. Cobb, Skip Homeier, Mona Freeman, Ray Middleton, Lee Van Cleef, Andy Clyde, Glenn Strange. Fast pacing aids this narrative of Payne and brother Homeier on opposite sides of the law, involved in shoot-out.

Road to Glory, The (1936) 95m. *** D: Howard Hawks. Fredric March, Warner Baxter, Lionel Barrymore, June Lang, Gregory Ratoff, Victor Killan. Gripping WW1 tale of officer March who knows he's licked but must continue with a regiment including Barrymore, his father.

Road to Hong Kong, The (1962) 91m. **½ D: Norman Panama. Bing Crosby, Bob Hope, Joan Collins, Dorothy Lamour, Robert Morley, Walter Gotell, Roger Delgado, Peter Sellers. First ROAD picture in a decade is fun but lacks punch of original series. Lamour makes a token appearance; Sellers has hilarious guest role.

Road to Morocco, The (1942) 83m. *** D: David Butler. Bing Crosby, Dorothy Lamour, Bob Hope, Anthony Quinn, Vladimir Sokoloff, Monte Blue, Yvonne De Carlo, Dona Drake. Typically funny ROAD picture, with Bing selling Bob to slave-trader in mysterious Morocco, both going after princess Lamour. Songs include: "Moonlight Becomes You."

Road to Rio, The (1947) 100m. *** D: Norman Z. McLeod. Bing Crosby, Bob Hope, Dorothy Lamour, Gale Sondergaard, Frank Faylen, The Wiere Brothers. Bob and Bing are musicians trying to wrest Dorothy from sinister aunt Sondergaard. Songs: "But Beautiful," "You Don't Have To Know The Language," sung with guests, Andrews Sisters.

Road To Singapore, The (1940) 84m. **½ D: Victor Schertzinger. Bing Crosby, Dorothy Lamour, Bob Hope, Charles Coburn, Judith Barrett, Anthony Quinn. Bing and Bob swear off women, hiding out in Singapore; then they meet saronged Lamour. First ROAD film is not the best, but still fun.

Road to Utopia, The (1945) 90m. *** D: Hal Walker. Bing Crosby, Bob Hope, Dorothy Lamour, Hillary Brooke, Douglass Dumbrille, Jack LaRue. Bob and Bing in the Klondike with usual quota of gags, supplemented by talking animals, Dorothy's song "Personality," Robert Benchley's dry commentary.

Road to Zanzibar, The (1941) 92m. **½ D: Victor Schertzinger. Bing Crosby, Bob Hope, Dorothy Lamour, Una Merkel, Eric Blore. Weaker ROAD series entry, still amusing, with Bob and Bing circus performers traveling through jungle with Lamour and Merkel, looking for diamond mine.

Roar of the Crowd (1953) C-71m. *½ D: William Beaudine. Howard Duff, Helene Stanley, Louise Arthur, Harry Shannon, Minor Watson, Don Haggerty. Hackneyed auto-racing tale done on low budget.

Roaring Twenties, The (1939) 104m. ***½ D: Raoul Walsh. James Cagney, Priscilla Lane, Humphrey Bogart, Gladys George, Jeffrey Lynn, Frank McHugh, Joe Sawyer. Slick gangster saga recalling history of Prohibition days, with Cagney becoming notorious bootlegger, teaming with Bogart.

Robber's Roost (1955) C-82m. ** D: Sidney Salkow. George Montgomery, Richard Boone, Bruce Bennett, Warren Stevens, Peter Graves, Sylvia Findley. Rugged cast gives zip to this Western of outlaw gangs fighting for control of ranchland.

Robbery (1967-British) C-114m. *** D: Peter Yates. Stanley Baker, Joanna Pettet, James Booth, Frank Finlay, Barry Foster, William Marlowe. Another study of the British Royal Mail robbery; few surprises, but generally exciting, well-handled.

Robbery Under Arms (1958-British) C-83m. ** D: Jack Lee. Peter Finch, Ronald Lewis, Laurence Naismith, Maureen Swanson, David McCallum. Quiet account of romance and robbery set in 19th-century Australia.

Robe, The (1953) C-135m. *** D: Henry Koster. Richard Burton, Jean Simmons, Victor Mature, Michael Rennie, Richard Boone, Dawn Addams, Dean Jagger. Episodic spectacle taken from Lloyd C. Douglas novel features Burton in Award-nominated portrayal of Gallio, Roman put in charge of execution of Christ. Big cast does well with uneven script; first Cinemascope feature.

Robin and the Seven Hoods (1964) C-103m. **½ D: Gordon Douglas. Frank Sinatra, Dean Martin, Sammy Davis, Jr., Peter Falk, Barbara Rush, Bing Crosby, Victor Buono. The Rat Pack goes Chicago in musical gangster spoof that's no great shakes, but entertaining. Crosby has thankless character role. Good song, "My Kind Of Town."

Robin Hood of El Dorado (1936) 86m. **½ D: William Wellman. Warner Baxter, Ann Loring, Margo, Bruce Cabot, J. Carrol Naish. Good Western-drama of Baxter seeking revenge on gang who ruined his life. Well made, with good cast.

Robinson Crusoe of Clipper Island SEE: Robinson Crusoe of Mystery Island.

Robinson Crusoe of Mystery Island (1936) 100m. ** D: Mack V. Wright, Ray Taylor. Mala, Rex, Buck, Mamo Clark, Herbert Rawlinson. Overly simple plot is salvaged by spotty action in this cliff-hanger set on a South Sea island; federal agents hunt down foreign powers causing chaos. Re-edited movie serial: ROBINSON CRUSOE OF CLIPPER ISLAND.

Robinson Crusoe on Mars (1964) C-109m. **½ D: Byron Haskin. Paul Mantee, Vic Lundin, Adam West. Adventure film pegged on Daniel Defoe theme, with astronaut and chimp stranded on Mars, trying to eke out existence.

Rocambole (1962-French, dubbed) C-106m. **½ D: Bernard Borderie. Channing Pollock, Hedy Vessel, Nadia Gray, Guy Delorme, Lilla Brignone. Further adventures of Ponson du Terrail's carefree rogue, played tongue-in-cheek by Pollock, involved in Parisian nightlife.

Rocco and His Brothers (1961-Italian, dubbed) 95m. ***½ D: Luchino Visconti. Annie Girardot, Alain Delon, Katina Paxinou, Max Cartier, Roger Hanin, Spiros Folas, Claudia Cardinale, Renato Salvatori, Suzy Delair. Craftsman directorship makes overlong (film originally 165m) study of Paxinou and her sons involved in Milanese life forcefully effective.

Rock-A-Bye-Baby (1958) C-103m. *** D: Frank Tashlin. Jerry Lewis, Marilyn Maxwell, Connie Stevens, Baccaloni, Reginald Gardiner. Movie siren Maxwell leaves her triplets with Jerry. Well-paced comedy, with Baccaloni a great comedy foil as Connie's father. Good spoofing of Hollywood religious epics included in this fine Lewis vehicle.

Rock Around the Clock (1956) 77m. ** D: Fred F. Sears. Bill Haley and His Comets, The Platters, Tony Martinez and His Band, Freddie Bell and His Bellboys, Alan Freed, Johnny Johnston. Premise is slim (unknown band brought to N.Y.C. where they become famous) but picture is good social history of phase of American culture fast disappearing.

Rock Around the World (1957-British) 71m. *½ D: Gerard Bryant. Tommy Steele, Patrick Westwood, Dennis Price, Tom Littlewood. Humdrum account of Tommy Steele's rise in the singing profession.

Rock, Pretty Baby (1956) 89m. ** D: Richard Bartlett. Sal Mineo, John Saxon, Luana Patten, Edward C. Platt, Fay Wray, Rod McKuen. Prototype of rock 'n' roll entries of 1950's, revolving around high school rock group's effort to win big-time musical contest.

Rocket Man, The (1954) 79m. ** D: Oscar Rudolph. Charles Coburn, Spring Byington, Anne Francis, John Agar, George Winslow. OK fantasy of Winslow possessing a space gun that turns crooked people honest.

Rocket Ship X-M (1950) 77m. **½ D: Kurt Neumann. Lloyd Bridges, Osa Massen, Hugh O'Brien, John Emery. Slightly better than average production of spaceship to moon that is blown off-course to Mars. Nice photography, good acting.

Rocking Horse Winner, The (1950-British) 91m. ***½ D: Anthony Pelissier. Valerie Hobson, John Howard Davies, John Mills, Ronald Squire. Truly unique, fascinating drama; small boy has knack for picking racetrack winners, but complications set in before long. Beautifully done.

Rocky Mountain (1950) 83m. **½ D: William Keighley. Errol Flynn, Patrice Wymore, Scott Forbes, Slim Pickens, Sheb Wooley, Yakima Canutt. Lumbering Flynn vehicle set in Civil War times, with Rebs and Yankees fighting off an Indian attack.

Rodan (1957-Japanese, dubbed) C-70m. ** D: Inoshiro Honda. Kenji Sawara, Yumi Shirakawa, Akihiko Hirato, Ako Kobori. Special effects star in sci-fi of prehistoric flying monster and his efforts to destroy civilization.

Rodeo (1950) C-70m. *½ D: William Beaudine. Jane Nigh, John Archer, Wallace Ford, Frances Rafferty. Tame little account of girl managing a roping show.

Roger Touhy, Gangster (1944) 65m. **½ D: Robert Florey. Preston Foster, Victor McLaglen, Lois Andrews, Anthony Quinn, Kent Taylor, Trudy Marshall, Kane Richmond. Supposed biographical film of famous murderer is just another gangster film.

Rogue Cop (1954) 92m. *** D: Roy Rowland. Robert Taylor, Janet Leigh, George Raft, Steve Forrest, Anne Francis, Vince Edwards. Dynamic account of policeman Taylor on the underworld payroll, tracking down his brother's killer.

Rogue River (1950) C-81m. ** D: John Rawlins. Rory Calhoun, Peter Graves, Frank Fenton, Ralph Sanford. Talky study of family relationships; not much on Western action.

Rogue's March (1952) 84m. ** D: Allan Davis. Peter Lawford, Richard Greene, Janice Rule, Leo G. Carroll. Programmer-costumer set in India (via stock footage and rear projection scenes), with Lawford trying to redeem himself with regiment.

Rogues of Sherwood Forest (1950) 80m. ** D: Gordon Douglas. John Derek, Diana Lynn, George Macready, Alan Hale. Despite good production and fair cast, pretty limp rejuvenation of Robin Hood.

Rogue's Regiment (1948) 86m. ** D: Robert Florey. Dick Powell, Marta Toren, Vincent Price, Stephen McNally. Powell's in the foreign legion to track down a Nazi officer in hiding; ordinary drama.

Roman Holiday (1953) 119m. ***½ D: William Wyler. Audrey Hepburn, Gregory Peck, Eddie Albert, Tullio Carminati. Hepburn got first break and first Oscar as princess yearning for normal life; runs away from palace, has romance with reporter Peck.

Roman Scandals (1933) 85m. *** D: Frank Tuttle. Eddie Cantor, Ruth Etting, Gloria Stuart, David Manners, Verree Teasdale, Alan Mowbray, Edward Arnold. Old-fashioned, enjoyable musical vehicle for Cantor to romp through as dreamer who is transported back to ancient Rome. Big Busby Berkeley production numbers include young Lucille Ball.

Roman Spring of Mrs. Stone, The (1961) C-104m. *** D: Jose Quintero. Vivien Leigh, Warren Beatty, Lotte Lenya, Jill St. John, Jeremy Spenser. Middle-aged actress retreats to Rome, buying a fling at romance from gigolo Beatty. Lenya, as Leigh's waspish friend, comes off best. Adapted from Tennessee Williams novella.

Romance of Rosy Ridge, The (1947) 105m. *** D: Roy Rowland. Van Johnson, Thomas Mitchell, Janet Leigh, Marshall Thompson, Selena Royle. Set in post-Civil War days, Missouri farmer Mitchell casts suspicious eye on young Johnson, who is courting his daughter, Leigh (in her film debut).

Romance on the High Seas (1948) C-99m. *** D: Michael Curtiz. Jack Carson, Janis Paige, Don DeFore, Doris Day, Oscar Levant, S. Z. Sakall, Fortunio Bonanova, Eric Blore, Franklin Pangborn. Sparkling, trivial romantic musical on an ocean voyage, with Doris' film debut, singing "It's Magic."

Romanoff and Juliet (1961) C-103m. **½ D: Peter Ustinov. Peter Ustinov, Sandra Dee, John Gavin, Akim Tamiroff, John Phillips. Satire on East-West politics is pegged on Romeo-Juliet theme. Hollywood casting drains much of bubbliness, but Ustinov as wry president of small country is in fine form.

Rome Adventure (1962) C-119m. *** D: Delmer Daves. Troy Donahue, Angie Dickinson, Rossano Brazzi, Suzanne Pleshette, Constance Ford, Al Hirt, Hampton Fancher. Plush soaper with Pleshette as schoolteacher on Roman fling to find romance, torn between roué (Brazzi) and architect (Donahue). As Troy's mistress, Dickinson has some rare repartee. Lush Max Steiner score.

Romeo and Juliet (1936) 126m. **** D: George Cukor. Norma Shearer, Leslie Howard, John Barrymore, Edna May Oliver, Basil Rathbone, C. Aubrey Smith, Andy Devine. Cast gives its all in not always successful but very worthwhile adaptation of Shakespeare; Shearer and Howard are ill-fated lovers.

Romeo and Juliet (1954-British) C-140m. *** D: Renato Castellani. Laurence Harvey, Susan Shentall, Flora Robson, Mervyn Johns, Bill Travers. Sumptuously photographed in Italy, this pleasing version of Shakespeare's tragedy has the virtue of good casting.

Roof, The (1956-Italian, dubbed) 98m. **½ D: Vittorio De Sica. Gabriella Pallotta, Giorgio Listuzzi, Gastone Renzelli, Maria Di Rollo. Realistic if unexciting account of young couple trying to find a home in crowded postwar Rome; they find technicality in law to solve their problem.

Rookie, The (1959) 86m. Bomb D: George O'Hanlon. Tommy Noonan, Pete Marshall, Julie Newmar, Jerry Lester, Joe Besser, Vince Barnett, Peter Leeds. Feeble army comedy of draftee, tough sergeant, movie starlet, and other stereotypes set during 1940s.

Room at the Top (1959-British) 115m. **** D: Jack Clayton. Laurence Harvey, Simone Signoret, Heather Sears, Hermione Baddeley, Donald Wolfit, Ambrosine Philpotts, Donald Houston. Consistently brilliant atmospheric drama of Harvey sacrificing Signoret's love for jump to the financial top by marrying factory boss' daughter (Sears). Miss Signoret won a well-deserved Academy Award.

Room for One More (1952) 98m. *** D: Norman Taurog. Cary Grant, Betsy Drake, Lurene Tuttle, George Winslow, John Ridgely. Grant and Drake are softhearted couple who can't resist adopting needy kids. Sentimental comedy retitled THE EASY WAY, basis for later TV show.

Room Service (1938) 78m. *** D: William A. Seiter. Groucho, Chico and Harpo Marx, Lucille Ball, Ann Miller, Frank Albertson, Donald MacBride, Cliff Dunstan. The Brothers actually have a plot in this one, from a Broadway play about penniless producers doing their best to keep from being evicted from hotel room. Not as wacky as usual, but fun. Remade as STEP LIVELY.

Rooney (1958-British) 88m. ** D: George Pollock. John Gregson, Muriel Pavlow, Barry Fitzgerald, June Thorburn. Sprite tale of Irish sanitation worker Gregson with an eye for the girls, trying to avoid marriage; Fitzgerald is bedridden geezer whom Rooney helps.

Roots of Heaven, The (1958) C-131m. **½ D: John Huston. Errol Flynn, Juliette Greco, Trevor Howard, Eddie Albert, Orson Welles, Paul Lukas. Turgid melodramatics set in Africa, with conglomerate cast philosophizing over sanctity of elephants; loosely based on Romain Gary novel.

Rope (1948) C-80m. *** D: Alfred Hitchcock. James Stewart, John Dall, Farley Granger, Cedric Hardwicke. Grand Hitchcock chiller, with Granger and Dall college boys who unemotionally kill a friend for fun, and delight in confounding cops about same.

Rope of Sand (1949) 104m. *** D: William Dieterle. Burt Lancaster, Paul Henreid, Corinne Calvet, Claude Rains, Peter Lorre, Sam Jaffe, John Bromfield, Mike Mazurki. Sturdy cast in adventure tale of smooth thief trying to regain treasure he hid away, with various parties interfering.

Rose Bowl Story, The (1952) C-73m. ** D: William Beaudine. Marshall Thompson, Vera Miles, Natalie Wood, Ann Doran, Jim Backus. Clichéd hogwash about football players, their work and home life.

Rose for Everyone, A SEE: Every Man's Woman.

Rose Marie (1936) 110m. *** D: W. S. Van Dyke II. Jeanette MacDonald, Nelson Eddy, Reginald Owen, Allan Jones, James Stewart, Alan Mowbray, Gilda Gray. Singer Jeanette seeks fugitive brother Stewart in Canada; mountie Nelson also hunts him. They fall in love, and sing, among others, "Indian Love Call." Retitled, oddly enough, INDIAN LOVE CALL.

Rose Marie (1954) C-115m. **½ D: Mervyn LeRoy. Ann Blyth, Howard Keel, Fernando Lamas, Bert Lahr, Marjorie Main. Friml's operetta loses all its charm despite MGM gloss and wide screen. Main and Lahr supply much-needed comedy relief in threadbare tale of Canadian mountie and girl he loves.

Rose of Washington Square (1939) 86m. **½ D: Gregory Ratoff. Tyrone Power, Alice Faye, Al Jolson, William Frawley, Horace MacMahon, Moroni Olsen. Pleasant musical of thinly disguised Fanny Brice, with Alice singing her heart out as heel-husband Power hits the skids.

Rose Tattoo, The (1955) 117m. ***½ D: Daniel Mann. Anna Magnani, Burt Lancaster, Marisa Pavan, Ben Cooper, Virginia Grey, Jo Van Fleet. Magnani shines (she won an Oscar) as earthy widow in Gulf Coast city who puts aside her husband's memory when rambunctious truck driver Lancaster romances her. Flavorful adaptation of Tennessee Williams play.

Roseanna McCoy (1949) 100m. ** D: Irving Reis. Farley Granger, Joan Evans, Charles Bickford, Raymond Massey, Richard Basehart, Aline MacMahon. Witless drama of Hatfield-McCoy feud, with young lovers from opposite sides of the fence rekindling old wounds.

Rosie! (1968) 98m. *** D: David Lowell Rich. Rosalind Russell, Sandra Dee, Brian Aherne, Audrey Meadows, James Farentino, Vanessa Brown. One of Russell's best recent performances as madcap grandmother, whose children want her money now. Veteran supporting cast outshine "young" leads.

Rosemary (1958-German, dubbed) 99m. **½ D: Rolf Thiele. Nadja Tiller, Peter Van Eyck, Gert Frobe, Mario Adorf, Carl Raddatz. Convincing study of famed post-WW2 Frankfurt prostitute (Tiller) who blackmailed industrialist; satirically sensational.

Rotten to the Core (1965-British) 90m. *** D: John Boulting. Anton Rodgers, Eric Sykes, Charlotte Rampling, Ian Bannen, Avis Bunnage, Victor Maddern. Well-handled caper of ex-con trio joining forces with crook to carry off large-scale robbery.

Rouge et Noir (1958-French, dubbed) C-145m. *** D: Claude Autant-Lara. Gerard Philippe, Danielle Darrieux, Antonella Lualdi, Jean Martinelli. Flavorful handling of Stendhal novel of 1810 France, with Philippe and Darrieux a sparkling love team.

Roughly Speaking (1945) 117m. *** D: Michael Curtiz. Rosalind Russell, Jack Carson, Robert Hutton, Jean Sullivan, Alan Hale, Donald Woods. Generally good but long comedy-drama of Russell raising a family while hubby Carson embarks on wild moneymaking schemes; two stars are tops.

Roughshod (1949) 88m. **½ D: Mark Robson. Robert Sterling, Claude Jarman, Jr., Gloria Grahame, Jeff Donnell, John Ireland, Myrna Dell, Martha Hyer. Intriguing drama of three fugitives out West and the disturbed farmer who fears they are seeking revenge against him.

Roustabout (1964) C-101m. **½ D: John Rich. Elvis Presley, Barbara Stanwyck, Leif Erickson, Joan Freeman, Sue Anne Langdon. Elvis is a free-wheeling singer who joins Stanwyck's carnival, learns the meaning of hard work and true love. Stanwyck and supporting cast make this a pleasing Presley songer.

Roxie Hart (1942) 75m. **½ D: William Wellman. Ginger Rogers, Adolphe Menjou, George Montgomery, Lynne Overman, Nigel Bruce, Phil Silvers, Spring Byington, Iris Adrian. Fast-moving spoof of roaring 20's, with Ginger as publicity-seeking gal on trial for murder, Menjou her overdramatic lawyer. Hilarious antics make up for dry spells.

Royal Affairs in Versailles (1957-French, dubbed) C-152m. **½ D: Sacha Guitry. Claudette Colbert, Orson Welles, Jean-Pierre Aumont, Edith Piaf, Gerard Philippe, Jean Marais, Sacha Guitry. Overambitious, episodic approach to French history, with varying performances by host of guest stars. Retitled: AFFAIRS IN VERSAILLES.

Royal African Rifles, The (1953) C-75m. ** D: Lesley Selander. Louis Hayward, Veronica Hurst, Michael Pate, Angela Greene. Adequate actioner set in Africa in 1910, with Hayward the British officer leading mission to recover cache of arms.

Royal Scandal, A (1945) 94m. **½ D: Ernst Lubitsch, Otto Preminger. Tallulah Bankhead, Charles Coburn, Anne Baxter, William Eythe, Vincent Price, Mischa Auer. Comedy of manners about Catherine the Great of Russia promoting favored soldier Eythe to high rank; started by Lubitsch, "finished" by Preminger.

Royal Wedding (1951) C-93m. *** D: Stanley Donen. Fred Astaire, Jane Powell, Sarah Churchill, Keenan Wynn. Astaire's dancing overcomes bland plot-line of he and sister Powell performing in London at time of Queen Elizabeth II's marriage; each finds true love.

Ruby Gentry (1952) 82m. **½ D: King Vidor. Jennifer Jones, Charlton Heston, Karl Malden, Josephine Hutchinson. Turgid, meandering account of easy-virtue Jones marrying wealthy Malden to spite Heston, the man she loves.

Ruggles of Red Gap (1935) 76m. **** D: Leo McCarey. Charles Laughton, Mary Boland, Charlie Ruggles, ZaSu Pitts, Roland Young, Leila Hyams. Laughton is marvelous as butler hired by uncouth Westerner Ruggles and would-be chic wife Boland; Pitts is spinster he falls in love with. Remade as FANCY PANTS.

Rulers of the Sea (1939) 96m. **½

D: Frank Lloyd. Douglas Fairbanks, Jr., Will Fyffe, Margaret Lockwood, George Bancroft, Montagu Love, Alan Ladd, Mary Gordon, Neil Fitzgerald. Well-made drama of problems surrounding first steamship voyage across Atlantic.

Rumba (1935) 77m. ** D: Marion Gering. George Raft, Carole Lombard, Margo, Lynne Overman, Gail Patrick, Akim Tamiroff, Iris Adrian. Weak follow-up to BOLERO, with Raft and Lombard in and out of love; best scenes are those when the duo dances.

Rumble on the Docks (1956) 82m. ** D: Fred F. Sears. James Darren, Laurie Carroll, Michael Granger, Jerry Janger, Robert Blake, Edgar Barrier. Low-keyed waterfront corruption tale, with Darren the streetgang leader aiding racketeers.

Run for Cover (1955) C-93m. **½ D: Nicholas Ray. James Cagney, Viveca Lindfors, John Derek, Jean Hersholt, Ernest Borgnine. Cagney is pensive ex-con in 19th-century West who tries to do right by the woman he loves (Lindfors) and to teach a young friend (Derek) the value of honor. Hersholt in last film has nice cameo.

Run for the Sun (1956) C-99m. *** D: Roy Boulting. Richard Widmark, Trevor Howard, Jane Greer, Peter Van Eyck, Carlos Henning. Fine updating of MOST DANGEROUS GAME: Count Zaroff character traps writer Widmark in Mexican lair, and Greer comes to investigate. Previous version: GAME OF DEATH.

Run for Your Money (1949-British) 83m. *** D: Charles Frend. Donald Houston, Meredith Edwards, Moira Lister, Alec Guinness, Hugh Griffith, Joyce Grenfell. Way-above-par comic study of two Welsh miners having a spree in London.

Run of the Arrow (1957) C-86m. **½ D: Samuel Fuller. Rod Steiger, Brian Keith, Sarita Montiel, Ralph Meeker, Charles Bronson, Tim McCoy. Unusual Western dealing with cowpoke who discovers that despite gruesome Civil War, he belongs among white men, and not warring Indians.

Run Silent, Run Deep (1958) 93m. *** D: Robert Wise. Clark Gable, Burt Lancaster, Jack Warden, Brad Dexter, Don Rickles. Battle of wits between officers Gable and Lancaster on WW2 submarine is basis for interesting drama; little action, though.

Runaround, The (1946) 86m. ** D: Charles Lamont. Rod Cameron, Broderick Crawford, Ella Raines, Samuel S. Hinds. Raines is heiress whom detectives Cameron and Crawford must return to Gotham; tepid programmer.

Running Man, The (1963) C-103m. *** D: Carol Reed. Laurence Harvey, Lee Remick, Alan Bates, Felix Aylmer, Eleanor Summerfield, Allan Cuthbertson. Harvey fakes his death to collect insurance money, but pursuing insurance investigator Bates forces him and wife Remick to go on the lam in Spain. Entertaining but not suspenseful enough.

Running Target (1956) C-83m. *½ D: Marvin Weinstein. Doris Dowling, Arthur Franz, Richard Reeves, Myron Healey, James Parnell. Minor oater of sheriff forced to use gun-play against outlaws.

Running Wild (1955) 81m. **½ D: Abner Biberman. William Campbell, Mamie Van Doren, Keenan Wynn, Walter Coy. Tawdry, actionful account of young police officer getting the goods on car thief gangs.

Ruthless (1948) 104m. ** D: Edgar G. Ulmer. Zachary Scott, Louis Hayward, Diana Lynn, Sydney Greenstreet, Lucille Bremer, Martha Vickers, Raymond Burr. Scott steps on everyone to become big shot in this tired, predictable drama.

S.O.S. Pacific (1960-British) 92m. **½ D: Guy Green. Eddie Constantine, Pier Angeli, Richard Attenborough, John Gregson, Eva Bartok, Jean Anderson. Middling study of human nature when passengers on plane crash-land on nuclear-test island.

Saadia (1953) C-82m. *½ D: Albert Lewin. Cornel Wilde, Mel Ferrer, Rita Gam, Cyril Cusack, Richard Johnson. Misfire; intellectual story of modernistic Moroccan ruler and doctor vying for love of superstitious native dancing girl.

Sabaka (1955) C-81m. ** D: Frank Ferrin. Boris Karloff, Reginald Denny, Victor Jory, Lisa Howard, Jeanne Bates, Jay Novello, June Foray. Splashy trivia enhanced by veteran cast, about spooky religious cult in exotic India.

Saboteur (1942) 108m. **½ D: Alfred Hitchcock. Robert Cummings, Priscilla Lane, Norman Lloyd, Otto Kruger, Murray Alper, Alma Kruger,

Dorothy Peterson. Disappointing Hitchcock with intriguing Statue of Liberty climax, pegged on innocent Cummings accused of sabotage in munitions factory during WW2.

Saboteur, Code Name Morituri, The (1965) 123m. **½ D: Bernhard Wicki. Marlon Brando, Yul Brynner, Janet Margolin, Trevor Howard, Wally Cox, William Redfield, Carl Esmond. Brando highlights great cast in study of anti-Nazi German who helps British capture cargo ship. Cast is only asset; script degenerates.

Sabre Jet (1953) C-96m. **½ D: Louis King. Robert Stack, Coleen Gray, Richard Arlen, Julie Bishop. Routine Korean War story of lonely wives and fighting husbands.

Sabrina (1954) 113m. ***½ D: Billy Wilder. Humphrey Bogart, Audrey Hepburn, William Holden, John Williams, Francis X. Bushman, Martha Hyer. Samuel Taylor play is good vehicle for Hepburn as chauffeur's daughter romanced by aging tycoon Bogart to keep her from playboy Holden. Offbeat casting works in this fun film.

Sabu and the Magic Ring (1957) C-61m. *½ D: George Blair. Sabu, Darla Massey, Vladimir Sokoloff, Robin Moore. Low-budget back-lot jungle nonsense, with Sabu chasing thieves to regain girl and priceless gem.

Sad Horse, The (1959) C-78m. ** D: James B. Clark. David Ladd, Chill Wills, Rex Reason, Patrice Wymore. Tender, undemanding tale of a racehorse and a lonely boy (Ladd).

Sad Sack, The (1957) 98m. ** D: George Marshall. Jerry Lewis, Phyllis Kirk, David Wayne, Peter Lorre, Gene Evans, Mary Treen. Disjointed comedy vaguely based on George Baker comic strip of Army misfit. Not enough funny sequences to succeed. Lorre appears as Arab in last part of film.

Saddle the Wind (1958) C-84m. *** D: Robert Parrish. Robert Taylor, Julie London, John Cassavettes, Donald Crisp. Finely acted Western of turned-good rancher (Taylor) fated to shoot it out with brother (Cassavettes).

Saddle Tramp (1950) C-77m. **½ D: Hugo Eregonese. Joel McCrea, Wanda Hendrix, John McIntyre, John Russell, Ed Begley, Jeanette Nolan, Antonio Moreno. Homey Western with McCrea in title role "adopting" four kids and fighting the good cause.

Sadie McKee (1934) 90m. **½ D: Clarence Brown. Joan Crawford, Franchot Tone, Gene Raymond, Edward Arnold, Esther Ralston, Leo Carroll, Akim Tamiroff. Amusing romantic triangle with working-girl Crawford, wealthy Tone, fun-loving Raymond; prototype of the Crawford vehicle. Song: "All I Do Is Dream Of You."

Safari (1940) 80m. ** D: Edward H. Griffith. Douglas Fairbanks, Jr., Madeleine Carroll, Tullio Carminati, Lynne Overman, Muriel Angelus, Billy Gilbert. Standard jungle expedition story, with attractive stars.

Safari (1956) C-91m. **½ D: Terence Young. Victor Mature, Janet Leigh, John Justin, Roland Culver, Liam Redmond. Fierce jungle drama has Mature leading expedition against Mau Maus. Cast gives good performance.

Safari Drums (1953) 71m. D: Ford Beebe. Johnny Sheffield, Douglas Kennedy, Barbara Bestar, Emory Parnell, Smoki Whitfield. SEE: Bomba, the Jungle Boy series.

Safe at Home! (1962) 83m. ** D: Walter Doniger. Mickey Mantle, Roger Maris, William Frawley, Patricia Barry, Don Collier, Bryan Russell. Kid promises to produce Mantle and Maris for a Little League dinner; that's it.

Safecracker, The (1958) 96m. ** D: Ray Milland. Ray Milland, Barry Jones, Jeannette Sterke, Ernest Clark, Melissa Stribling, Victor Maddern. Contrived, OK story of burglar who almost goes straight, later forced to use his talents for war effort.

Saga of Hemp Brown, The (1958) C-80m. ** D: Richard Carlson. Rory Calhoun, Beverly Garland, John Larch, Russell Johnson. Calhoun is bounced from Army, and seeks to find real crooks in just another Western.

Sahara (1943) 97m. ***½ D: Zoltan Korda. Humphrey Bogart, Bruce Bennett, Lloyd Bridges, Rex Ingram, J. Carrol Naish, Dan Duryea. Excellent actioner of British-American unit stranded in Sahara desert; Bogie's the chief, of course, with fine support by Naish and Ingram.

Saigon (1948) 94m. ** D: Leslie Fenton. Alan Ladd, Veronica Lake, Luther Adler, Douglas Dick, Wally

Cassell, Morris Carnovsky. Glossy Paramount Pictures' espionage drama set in Saigon is only fair.

Sail a Crooked Ship (1961) 88m. **½ D: Irving S. Brecher. Robert Wagner, Ernie Kovacs, Dolores Hart, Carolyn Jones, Frankie Avalon, Harvey Lembeck. Bungled crime-caper comedy has hilarious moments, but not enough to make it a winner.

Sail into Danger (1957-British) 72m. ** D: Kenneth Hume. Dennis O'Keefe, Kathleen Ryan, James Hayter, Pedro de Cordoba, John Bull, Felix de Pommes. O'Keefe is ensnared into helping Ryan in smuggling plot; set in Barcelona. Meek actioner.

Sailor Beware (1951) 108m. **½ D: Hal Walker. Dean Martin, Jerry Lewis, Corinne Calvet, Marion Marshall. Joining the navy gives the comedy duo a chance to go through their usual paces. Dated, often funny outing.

Sailor of the King (1953) 83m. **½ D: Roy Boulting. Jeffrey Hunter, Michael Rennie, Wendy Hiller, Bernard Lee, Peter Van Eyck. Taut account of British navy during WW2, with interwoven account of Rennie-Hunter-Hiller family relationship.

Sailor Takes a Wife, The (1945) 91m. ** D: Richard Whorf. Robert Walker, June Allyson, Hume Cronyn, Audrey Totter, Eddie "Rochester" Anderson, Reginald Owen. Mild little comedy is summed up by title.

Sailor's Lady (1940) 66m. ** D: Allan Dwan. Nancy Kelly, Jon Hall, Joan Davis, Dana Andrews, Mary Nash, Larry "Buster" Crabbe, Katherine Aldridge. Witless comedy of Kelly pretending to have baby to see if sailor-fiancee Hall will still marry her.

St. Benny the Dip (1951) 80m. **½ D: Edgar G. Ulmer. Dick Haymes, Nina Foch, Roland Young, Lionel Stander, Freddie Bartholomew. Offbeat account of con-men posing as clergymen who predictably become reformed; filmed in N.Y.C.

Saint, The Leslie Charteris' literate, debonair detective has been the subject of an extremely popular British television show in recent years. But he never quite made it in the movies. From 1938 to 1942, RKO tried no less than three actors in the leading role, finding moderate success but nothing earth-shaking. Louis Hayward seemed at home in the role in THE SAINT IN NEW YORK, a smooth underworld saga with a bland leading lady (Kay Sutton) and a fine supporting cast (Sig Ruman as a ganglord, Jack Carson as a thug, etc.). Nevertheless, he didn't repeat the role; it went instead to suave George Sanders, who portrayed the Saint, usually with Wendy Barrie as leading lady, in four quickly-made, entertaining mysteries taking him from Palm Springs to London. The scripts were competent, but it was Sanders' usual offhand manner that kept them alive. In 1942 stage star Hugh Sinclair took a fling in THE SAINT MEETS THE TIGER but gave up after a second effort. Sanders left the series only to begin another, The Falcon, at the same studio, although without the main titles to inform viewers which series it was, one could hardly have told the difference. The Falcon continued through the 1940's, while the Saint came to a premature end in 1942. There was one revival attempt with Louis Hayward made in England in 1953, THE SAINT'S GIRL FRIDAY, which was average but no improvement over the original series. It took British television and an actor named Roger Moore to give life to The Saint at last in the 1960's.

Saint in London, The (1939) 72m. D: John Paddy Carstairs. George Sanders, David Burns, Sally Gray, Henry Oscar, Ralph Truman, Norah Howard, Carl Jaffe.

Saint in New York, The (1938) 71m. D: Ben Holmes. Louis Hayward, Kay Sutton, Sig Ruman, Jonathan Hale, Frederick Burton, Jack Carson.

Saint in Palm Springs, The (1941) 65m. D: Jack Hively. George Sanders, Wendy Barrie, Paul Guilfoyle, Jonathan Hale, Linda Hayes, Ferris Taylor.

Saint Joan (1957) 110m. ** D: Otto Preminger. Jean Seberg, Richard Widmark, Richard Todd, Anton Walbrook, John Gielgud, Felix Aylmer. Big-scale filming of Shaw's play sounded large thud when released; some good acting, but Seberg, not suited to film's tempo, throws production askew.

St. Louis Blues (1958) 93m. **½ D: Allen Reisner. Nat 'King' Cole, Eartha Kitt, Ruby Dee, Pearl Bailey, Cab Calloway. Rags-to-modest-acclaim biography of blues musician W. C. Handy, with personality cast interpreting many of his well-known tunes.

St. Louis Kid (1934) 67m. **½ D: Ray Enright. James Cagney, Patricia Ellis, Allen Jenkins, Robert Barrat, Addison Richards. Cagney is dynamic self as truck driver battling crooked officials in dairy business, to protect local farmers.

Saint Meets the Tiger, The (1943-British) 70m. D: Paul Stein. Hugh Sinclair, Jean Gillie, Clifford Evans, Wylie Watson, Dennis Arundell. SEE: The Saint series.

Saint Strikes Back, The (1939) 67m. D: John Farrow. George Sanders, Wendy Barrie, Jonathan Hale, Jerome Cowan, Neil Hamilton, Barry Fitzgerald, Edward Gargan, Robert Strange. SEE: The Saint series.

Saint Takes Over, The (1940) 69m. D: Jack Hively. George Sanders, Jonathan Hale, Wendy Barrie, Paul Guilfoyle, Morgan Conway, Robert Emmett Keane, Cyrus W. Kendall. SEE: The Saint series.

St. Valentine's Day Massacre, The (1967) C-100m. **½ D: Roger Corman. Jason Robards, Jr., George Segal, Ralph Meeker, Jean Hale, Clint Ritchie, Frank Silvera, Joseph Campanella. This had the makings of a good film, but they blew it, with Robards (as Al Capone) and Segal (doing a Jimmy Cagney imitation) overacting as they've never done before. So much shooting throughout film that final massacre seems tame by comparison. Many familiar faces appear throughout, like Harold Stone, Kurt Kreuger, Milton Frome, Mickey Deems, John Agar, Alex D'Arcy, Reed Hadley, etc.

Sainted Sisters, The (1948) 89m. **½ D: William Russell. Veronica Lake, Joan Caulfield, Barry Fitzgerald, William Demarest, George Reeves, Beulah Bondi. Fitzgerald's blarney is a bit overdone in this tale of two bad girls who go straight under his guidance.

Saint's Double Trouble, The (1940) 68m. D: Jack Hively. George Sanders, Helene Whitney, Jonathan Hale, Bela Lugosi, Donald MacBride, John F. Hamilton. SEE: The Saint series.

Saint's Girl Friday, The (1954-British) 68m. D: Seymour Friedman. Louis Hayward, Naomi Chance, Sydney Tafler, Charles Victor. SEE: The Saint series.

Saint's Vacation, The (1941-British) 60m. D: Leslie Fenton. Hugh Sinclair, Sally Gray, Arthur Macrae, Cecil Parker, Leueen McGrath, Gordon McLeod. SEE: The Saint series.

Sakima and the Masked Marvel (1943) 100m. **½ D: Spencer Bennet. William Forrest, Louise Currie, Johnny Arthur, Rod Bacon, Richard Clarke. Above-par Republic actioner set during WW2, with Japanese espionage in the U.S. combatted by heroic mysterious Masked Marvel. Re-edited movie serial: THE MASKED MARVEL.

Sally and Saint Anne (1952) 90m. **½ D: Rudolph Mate. Ann Blyth, Edmund Gwenn, Hugh O'Brian, Jack Kelly, King Donovan. Cutesy and a bit tasteless; Blyth is daughter in screwball family who believes St. Anne will help them in times of need.

Sally, Irene and Mary (1938) 72m. *** D: William A. Seiter. Alice Faye, Tony Martin, Fred Allen, Joan Davis, Marjorie Weaver, Gregory Ratoff, Jimmy Durante, Louise Hovick (Gypsy Rose Lee). Trio of girls puts on a Broadway show. No surprises, but top cast and songs "I Could Use a Dream," "This Is Where I Came In."

Salome (1953) C-103m. **½ D: William Dieterle. Rita Hayworth, Stewart Granger, Charles Laughton, Judith Anderson, Cedric Hardwicke, Maurice Schwartz. Great cast struggles with unintentionally funny script in biblical drama of illustrious dancer who offers herself to spare John the Baptist.

Salome, Where She Danced (1945) C-90m. Bomb D: Charles Lamont. Yvonne de Carlo, Rod Cameron, David Bruce, Walter Slezak, Albert Dekker, Marjorie Rambeau, J. Edward Bromberg. Ludicrous film provides some laughs while trying to spin tale of exotic dancer becoming Mata Hari-type spy.

Salty O'Rourke (1945) 97m. *** D: Raoul Walsh. Alan Ladd, Gail Russell, William Demarest, Bruce Cabot, Spring Byington, Darryl Hickman. Lively racetrack yarn of gambler Ladd fixing races to recoup big loss; Russell is girl who makes him go straight.

Salute to the Marines (1943) C-101m. **½ D: S. Sylvan Simon. Wallace Beery, Fay Bainter, Reginald Owen, Keye Luke, Ray Collins, Marilyn Maxwell. OK Beery vehicle of army veteran who reluctantly retires, finds himself caught in surprise attack on Philippines.

Samar (1962) C-89m. ** D: George Montgomery. George Montgomery,

**Gilbert Roland, Ziva Rodann, Joan O'Brien, Nico Minardos, Mario Barri. Average actioner has Montgomery as head of prison compound on a Philippine Island, who rejects inhumane treatment of prisoners and leads them on escape route.

Samson and Delilah (1949) C-128m. **½ D: Cecil B. DeMille. Victor Mature, Hedy Lamarr, George Sanders, Angela Lansbury, Henry Wilcoxon, Olive Deering, Fay Holden. Typical elaborate, ridiculous De Mille spectacle, with terrible special effects and overplaying actors. In other words, great fun in the De Mille tradition.

Samson and the Slave Queen (1963-Italian, dubbed) C-92m. *½ D: Umberto Lenzi. Pierre Brice, Alan Steel, Moira Orfei, Maria Grazia Spina. Juvenile musceman epic that is ludicrous in its approach to adventure.

San Antonio (1945) C-111m. *** D: David Butler. Errol Flynn, Alexis Smith, S. Z. Sakall, Victor Francen, Florence Bates, John Litel, Paul Kelly. Elaborate Western; predictable plot but good production as dance-hall girl Smith, working for villain Francen, falls for good-guy Flynn.

San Diego, I Love You (1944) 83m. *** D: Reginald Le Borg. Jon Hall, Louise Allbritton, Edward Everett Horton, Eric Blore, Buster Keaton, Irene Ryan. Whimsical comedy of unconventional family trying to promote father Horton's inventions in San Diego. Allbritton is perky, Keaton memorable in delightful sequence as bored bus-driver.

San Francisco (1936) 115m. ***½ D: W. S. Van Dyke II. Clark Gable, Jeanette MacDonald, Spencer Tracy, Jack Holt, Jessie Ralph, Ted Healy, Shirley Ross. Top-grade entertainment with extremely lavish production. Jeanette overdoes it a bit as the belle of San Francisco, but the music, Tracy's performance, and earthquake climax are still fine.

San Francisco Story, The (1952) 80m. ** D: Robert Parrish. Joel McCrea, Yvonne de Carlo, Sidney Blackmer, Florence Bates. Tame Western actioner set in gold-rush days, with clean-up of city's criminal elements.

San Quentin (1937) 70m. **½ D: Lloyd Bacon. Pat O'Brien, Humphrey Bogart, Ann Sheridan, Veda Ann Borg, Barton MacLane. Warner Bros. formula prison film; convict Bogart's sister (Sheridan) loves warden O'Brien. MacLane is memorable as tough prison guard.

San Quentin (1946) 66m. **½ D: Gordon Douglas. Lawrence Tierney, Barton MacLane, Marian Carr, Harry Shannon, Carol Forman, Richard Powers. Prison drama with different plot for a change, of organization for ex-cons not having intended results.

Sanctuary (1961) 100m. ** D: Tony Richardson. Lee Remick, Yves Montand, Bradford Dillman, Odetta, Reta Shaw. Faulkner's novel of Southern degradation, rape, and murder, filmed before as STORY OF TEMPLE DRAKE; much more explicit here.

Sand (1949) C-78m. ** D: Louis King. Mark Stevens, Rory Calhoun, Coleen Gray, Charley Grapewin. Visually picturesque but cinematically dull account of show horse who turns wild. Retitled: WILL JAMES' SAND.

Sand Castle, The (1960) C-67m. **½ D: Jerome Hill. Barry Cardwell, Laurie Cardwell, George Dunham, Alec Wilder. Imaginative little film of small boy building mud castles on the beach, dreaming of people living in his creation.

Sanders of the River SEE: **Coast of Skeletons.**

Sandokan Against the Leopard of Sarawak (1964-Italian, dubbed) C-94m. ** D: Luigi Capuano. Ray Danton, Guy Madison, Franca Bettoja, Mario Petri. Danton vs. Madison in this papier maché, run-of-the-mill epic.

Sandokan Fights Back (1964-Italian, dubbed) C-96m. ** D: Luigi Capuano. Ray Danton, Guy Madison, Franca Bettoja, Mino Doro. Unconvincing, juvenile narrative of princely ruler fighting to regain his throne.

Sandokan the Great (1965-Italian, dubbed) C-105m. ** D: Umberto Lenzi. Steve Reeves, Genevieve Grad, Rik Battaglia, Maurice Poli. Reeves is put through his gymnastic paces in this juvenile sword-and-cloak entry.

Sandpiper, The (1965) C-116m. **½ D: Vincente Minnelli. Elizabeth Taylor, Richard Burton, Eva Marie Saint, Charles Bronson, Robert Webber, Torin Thatcher. Ordinary triangle love affair. Beatnik Taylor in love with Burton, who is married to Saint. Nothing new, but beautiful California Big Sur settings help; so does theme, "Shadow Of Your Smile."

Sands of Beersheba (1966) 90m. **½ D: Alexander Ramati. Diane Baker, David Opatoshu, Tom Bell, Paul

Stassino. Pretentious retelling of Absalom (Bell) and David (Opatoshu) conflict, filmed in Israel, dabbling in philosophy on the Arab-vs.-Jew animosity.

Sands of Iwo Jima (1949) 110m. ***½ D: Allan Dwan. John Wayne, John Agar, Adele Mara, Forrest Tucker, Arthur Franz, Julie Bishop, Richard Jaeckel. Rousing war story of cocky young man straightened out by military life, with Wayne in peak form as tough sergeant; superb battle scenes.

Sands of the Desert (1960-British) 92m. ** D: John Paddy Carstairs. Charlie Drake, Peter Arne, Sarah Branch, Rebecca Dignam. Heavyhanded comedy set in Arabia, with Drake trying to uncover sabotage attempts at holiday camp.

Sands of the Kalahari (1965-British) C-119m. *** D: Cy Endfield. Stuart Whitman, Stanley Baker, Susannah York, Harry Andrews, Theodore Bikel, Nigel Davenport. Well-done story of plane crash survivors struggling through desert and battling simian inhabitants.

Sandy Gets Her Man (1940) 74m. *½ D: Otis Garrett, Paul Smith. Stuart Erwin, Una Merkel, Baby Sandy, Edgar Kennedy, William Frawley. Precocious Baby Sandy is final arbiter of mama's courters; naive little film kept alive by character actors in cast.

Sandy is a Lady (1940) 65m. *½ D: Charles Lamont. Nan Gray, Baby Sandy, Eugene Pallette, Tom Brown, Mischa Auer, Billy Gilbert, Edgar Kennedy, Anne Gwynne. Simplicitysaturated comedy as precocious child helps her family get ahead.

Sangaree (1953) C-94m. **½ D: Edward Ludwig. Fernando Lamas, Arlene Dahl, Patricia Medina, Francis L. Sullivan. Frank Slaughter's historical novel set in 1780's becomes an empty, handsome costumer.

Santa Claus Conquers the Martians (1964) C-80m. ** D: Nicholas Webster. John Call, Leonard Hicks, Vincent Beck, Donna Conforti. Absurd fantasy; low-budget film. Santa and two earth children abducted by Martians to solve home problems.

Santa Fe (1951) C-89m. ** D: Irving Pichel. Randolph Scott, Janis Carter, Jerome Courtland, Peter Thompson. Routine account of brothers in postCivil War days, on opposite sides of the law.

Santa Fe Passage (1955) C-70m. ** D: William Witney. John Payne, Faith Domergue, Rod Cameron, Slim Pickens. Routine wagon train westward; Indian attacks, love among the pioneers, etc.

Santa Fe Trail (1940) 110m. *** D: Michael Curtiz. Errol Flynn, Olivia de Havilland, Raymond Massey, Ronald Reagan, Alan Hale, Van Heflin, Gene Reynolds. Elaborate Western of pre-Civil War days, with Flynn as fighting Jeb Stuart, Massey as John Brown, Reagan as young Custer. Lots of action.

Santiago (1956) C-93m. **½ D: Gordon Douglas. Alan Ladd, Rossana Podesta, Lloyd Nolan, Chill Wills, Paul Fix. Ladd and Nolan are involved in gun-running to Cuba during fight with Spain. Ladd becomes humane when he encounters partisan Podesta.

Sapphire (1958-British) C-92m. *** D: Basil Dearden. Nigel Patrick, Yvonne Mitchell, Michael Craig, Paul Massie, Harry Baird, Bernard Miles. Unusual Scotland Yard solving-themurder yarn, with the murdered girl being Negro, passing for white; zesty characterizations.

Saps at Sea (1940) 57m. **½ D: Gordon Douglas. Stan Laurel, Oliver Hardy, James Finlayson, Ben Turpin, Dick Cramer, Harry Bernard, Eddie Conrad. L&H comedy is short and sweet; Ollie has breakdown working in horn factory, tries to relax on small boat with Stan . . . and that's impossible!

Saraband (1948-British) C-95m. *** D: Basil Dearden. Stewart Granger, Joan Greenwood, Flora Robson, Françoise Rosay, Peter Bull, Anthony Quayle, Michael Gough. Lavish, tearful romance with Greenwood torn between royal responsibility and love for young rogue.

Saracen Blade, The (1954) C-76m. *½ D: William Castle. Ricardo Montalban, Betta St. John, Rick Jason, Carolyn Jones, Whitfield Connor. Pretty bad 13th-century stuff, of young man avenging death of father. Unbelievable script traps cast.

Sarah and Son (1930) 76m. ** D: Dorothy Arzner. Ruth Chatterton, Fredric March, Doris Lloyd, Philippe de Lacy. Chatterton is obsessed with finding her long lost son, which alienates her from lover (March).

Saratoga (1937) 94m. **½ D: Jack Conway. Clark Gable, Jean Harlow,

Lionel Barrymore, Frank Morgan, Walter Pidgeon, Una Merkel. Harlow's last film has stand-in Mary Dees doing many scenes, but comes off pretty well, with Jean as daughter of horse-breeder Barrymore, Gable an influential bookie.

Saratoga Trunk (1945) 135m. *1/2 D: Sam Wood. Gary Cooper, Ingrid Bergman, Flora Robson, Jerry Austin, John Warburton, Florence Bates. Elaborate but miscast, over-long version of Edna Ferber's novel of New Orleans vixen Bergman and cowboy Cooper. Unbearable at times.

Saskatchewan (1954) C-87m. **1/2 D: Raoul Walsh. Alan Ladd, Shelley Winters, J. Carrol Naish, Hugh O'Brian, Robert Douglas. Cotton-candy Western about Ladd and fellow Canadian mounties trying to prevent Indian uprisings.

Satan Bug, The (1965) C-114m. *** D: John Sturges. George Maharis, Richard Basehart, Anne Francis, Dana Andrews, Edward Asner, Frank Sutton, John Larkin. Good Sturges direction in sci-fi adventure of disappearance of vial containing deadly virus and search for it.

Satan Met a Lady (1936) 75m. ** D: William Dieterle. Bette Davis, Warren William, Alison Skipworth, Arthur Treacher, Winifred Shaw, Marie Wilson, Porter Hall. Dashiell Hammett's MALTESE FALCON incognito; far below 1941 remake. William is private eye, Davis the mysterious client, Skipworth the strange woman searching for priceless artifact (ram's horn).

Satan Never Sleeps (1962) C-126m. ** D: Leo McCarey. William Holden, Clifton Webb, France Nuyen, Athene Seyler, Martin Benson, Edith Sharpe. Dreary goings-on of two priests holding fast when Communist China invades their territory. Bad production.

Satan's Satellites (1958) 70m. *1/2 D: Fred Brannon. Judd Holdren, Aline Towne, Wilson Wood, Lane Bradford. Condensation of serial ZOMBIES FROM THE STRATOSPHERE. Confused, juvenile adventure of aliens making trouble.

Satellite in the Sky (1956-British) C-85m. **1/2 D: Paul Dickson. Kieron Moore, Lois Maxwell, Donald Wolfit, Bryan Forbes, Jimmy Hanley. Good English cast gives typical sympathetic performances in story of first satellite launching.

Saturday Night and Sunday Morning (1960-British) 90m. ***1/2 D: Karel Reisz. Albert Finney, Shirley Anne Field, Rachel Roberts, Norman Rossington. Grim yet refreshing look at angry young man, who in a burst of nonconformity alters the lives of girlfriends Field and Roberts. Superbly enacted.

Saturday's Children (1940) 101m. **1/2 D: Vincent Sherman. John Garfield, Anne Shirley, Claude Rains, Lee Patrick, George Tobias. N.Y.C. based story of poor, hardworking young lovers. Rains steals film as Shirley's sacrificing father. Based on Maxwell Anderson play.

Saturday's Hero (1951) 111m. **1/2 D: David Miller. John Derek, Donna Reed, Sidney Blackmer, Alexander Knox. Nicely handled account of football player Derek trying to make meaningful life at college; Reed is fine as love interest. One of Aldo Ray's first films.

Savage, The (1952) C-95m. **1/2 D: George Marshall. Charlton Heston, Susan Morrow, Peter Hanson, Joan Taylor, Ted de Corsia. Heston is sincere and energetic as white man raised by the Indians and forced to choose sides when skirmishes break out.

Savage Drums (1951) 73m. ** D: William Berke. Sabu, Lita Baron, H. B. Warner, Sid Melton, Steven Geray. U. S.-educated Sabu returns to the islands to put down local warfare; fair low-budgeter.

Savage Eye, The (1960) 68m. *** D: Ben Maddow, Sidney Meyers, Joseph Strick. Barbara Baxley, Herschel Bernardi, Gary Merrill, Jean Hidey. Dramatic study of Baxley trying to start life anew in L.A.; contrived but intriguing.

Savage Hordes, The (1961-Italian, dubbed) C-82m. ** D: Remigio Del Grosso. Ettore Manni, Yoko, Akim Tamiroff, Joe Robinson, Roland Lesaffre. Routine adventure yarn set in 17th-century Poland under siege by Tartars.

Savage Innocents, The (1959) C-110m. **1/2 D: Nicholas Ray. Anthony Quinn, Yoko Tani, Peter O'Toole, Marie Yank. Lukewarm, confusing account of life among the Eskimos, interacting with various visitors up north.

Savage Mutiny (1953) 73m. D: Spencer Bennet. Johnny Weissmuller, Angela Stevens, Lester Matthews,

Paul Marion. SEE: Jungle Jim series.

Savage Pampas (1966-Spanish) C-100m. ** D: Hugo Fregonese. Robert Taylor, Ron Randell, Ty Hardin, Rosenda Monteros. Remake of 1946 Argentinian film PAMPA BARBARA. Taylor is rugged army captain combating outlaw Randell whose gang is made up of army deserters. Adequate actioner.

Savage Wilderness SEE: Last Frontier, The.

Saxon Charm, The (1948) 88m. *** D: Claude Binyon. Robert Montgomery, Susan Hayward, John Payne, Audrey Totter, Henry Morgan, Cara Williams, Harry Von Zell, Heather Angel. Well-acted but unconvincing study of ruthless producer, with Montgomery miscast in lead role. Still interesting, with fine work from playwright Payne, wife Hayward, and chanteuse Totter.

Say It in French (1938) 70m. ** D: Andrew L. Stone. Ray Milland, Olympe Bradna, Irene Hervey, Janet Beecher, Mary Carlisle, Holmes Herbert, Walter Kingsford. Milland goes to great extremes with wife Bradna and ex-fiancee Hervey to pull father out of the red.

Say One for Me (1959) C-119m. *½ D: Frank Tashlin. Debbie Reynolds, Bing Crosby, Robert Wagner, Ray Walston, Les Tremayne, Connie Gilchrist, Stella Stevens, Frank McHugh, Joe Besser, Sebastian Cabot. Bing plays a Broadway priest who gets mixed up with a chorus girl (Debbie) and a TV charity show. Terribly contrived; no memorable music.

Sayonara (1957) C-147m. ***½ D: Joshua Logan. Marlon Brando, Ricardo Montalban, Miiko Taka, Miyoshi Umeki, Red Buttons, Martha Scott, James Garner. Romantic James Michener tale of Korean War pilot Brando falling in love with Japanese entertainer Taka, extremely well acted, with Oscar-winning support from Buttons and Umeki. Theme song by Irving Berlin.

Scalplock (1966) C-100m. **½ D: James Goldstone. Dale Robertson, Diana Hyland, Lloyd Bochner. Telefeature pilot for TV series THE IRON HORSE; Robertson is gambler who wins railroad line in old West; too often stagy vehicle.

Scamp, The SEE: Strange Affection.
Scandal at Scourie (1953) C-90m. **½ D: Jean Negulesco. Greer Garson, Walter Pidgeon, Donna Corcoran, Agnes Moorehead, Arthur Shields. Tepid Garson-Pidgeon entry set in Canada, involving couple who adopt a Catholic girl, much to Protestant townsfolk's dismay.

Scandal in Paris SEE: Thieves Holiday.

Scandal in Sorrento (1957-Italian, dubbed) C-92m. *½ D: Dino Risi. Vittorio DeSica, Sophia Loren, Antonio Cifariello, Tina Pica. Listless sex romp of Loren romancing DeSica to make lover jealous.

Scandal, Inc. (1956) 79m. *½ D: Edward Mann. Robert Hutton, Patricia Wright, Paul Richards, Robert Knapp. Low-grade sensational-style account of scandal magazines.

Scandal Street (1931) 77m. **½ D: John Cromwell. George Bancroft, Kay Francis, Clive Brook, Lucien Littlefield, Jackie Searl. Usual triangle with good twist. Editor Bancroft has goods on Brook, the man his wife Francis plans to run off with.

Scandal Sheet (1952) 82m. **½ D: Phil Karlson. Broderick Crawford, Donna Reed, John Derek, Rosemary DeCamp, Henry O'Neill. OK melodrama of gruff newspaper editor who kills his wife and then finds his ace reporters are hot on his trail.

Scapegoat, The (1959-British) 92m. **½ D: Robert Hamer. Alec Guinness, Bette Davis, Nicole Maurey, Irene Worth, Peter Bull, Pamela Brown, Geoffrey Keen. Decent acting rescues a fuzzy script. French gentleman who murders his wife, tries to involve his British lookalike in scheme. Davis has small but impressive role as the guilty Guinness' dope-ridden mother.

Scar, The SEE: Hollow Triumph.

Scaramouche (1952) C-118m. ***½ D: George Sidney. Stewart Granger, Eleanor Parker, Janet Leigh, Mel Ferrer, Henry Wilcoxon, Lewis Stone, Nina Foch. Excellent cast in roaring adaptation of Sabatini novel of illustrious cynic who sets out to avenge brother's death, set in 18th-century France. Impeccably done.

Scared Stiff (1953) 108m. **½ D: George Marshall. Dean Martin, Jerry Lewis, Lizabeth Scott, Carmen Miranda, Dorothy Malone. Usual Martin and Lewis hijinks with duo on spooky island; Jerry and Carmen make a wild team.

Scared to Death (1947) 70m. *½ D: Walt Mattox. Bela Lugosi, Joyce Compton, Douglas Fowley, George Zucco. Cheapie independent chiller, loosely revolving around effects of those who confront a murderess with her crime.

Scarf, The (1951) 93m. **½ D: E. A. Dupont. John Ireland, Mercedes McCambridge, Emlyn Williams, James Barton. Capably handled drama of Ireland trying to prove his innocence of murder charge.

Scarface Mob, The (1962) 90m. **½ D: Phil Karlson. Robert Stack, Keenan Wynn, Barbara Nichols, Pat Crowley, Neville Brand. Two-part segment from THE UNTOUCHABLES TV series forms this film, with Elliot Ness closing in on Chicago's Al Capone mob. Narrated by Walter Winchell.

Scarlet Angel (1952) C-80m. **½ D: Sidney Salkow. Yvonne de Carlo, Rock Hudson, Richard Denning, Amanda Blake. Neat little drama set in 1860 New Orleans, with De Carlo the dance-hall girl who assumes a dead woman's identity and goes West to stay with wealthy in-laws.

Scarlet Claw, The (1944) 74m. D: Roy William Neill. Basil Rathbone, Nigel Bruce, Gerald Hamer, Arthur Hohl, Miles Mander, Ian Wolfe, Paul Cavanagh. SEE: **Sherlock Holmes** series.

Scarlet Clue, The (1945) 65m. D: Phil Rosen. Sidney Toler, Mantan Moreland, Ben Carter, Benson Fong, Virginia Brissac, Robert Homans, Jack Norton, Janet Shaw. SEE: **Charlie Chan** series.

Scarlet Coat, The (1955) C-101m. **½ D: John Sturges. Cornel Wilde, Michael Wilding, George Sanders, Anne Francis, Bobby Driscoll. Plucky costumer livened by cast and bright photography; set in colonial America, dealing with Benedict Arnold spy caper.

Scarlet Empress, The (1934) 110m. **½ D: Josef von Sternberg. Marlene Dietrich, John Lodge, Louise Dresser, Sam Jaffe, C. Aubrey Smith, Edward Van Sloan, Rothelma Stevens, Jane Darwell. Dietrich is exotic as Catherine the Great; lush settings are marred by misguided script and ludicrous handling of Jaffe as half-witted Grand Duke Peter.

Scarlet Hour, The (1956) 95m. ** D: Michael Curtiz. Carol Ohmart, Tom Tryon, Jody Lawrance, James Gregory, Elaine Stritch, E. G. Marshall, Edward Binns. Sluggish study of marital discord.

Scarlet Pimpernel, The (1934-British) 95m. ***½ D: Harold Young. Leslie Howard, Merle Oberon, Joan Gardner, O. B. Clarence, Walter Rilla, Anthony Bushell. Excellent costumer with Howard leading double life, aiding innocent victims of French Revolution while continuing as hero of British court.

Scarlet Spear, The (1954) C-78m. Bomb D: George Breakston, Ray Stahl. John Bentley, Martha Hyer, Morasi. Programmer nonsense of African tribe with sacrifice ceremony.

Scarlet Street (1945) 103m. *** D: Fritz Lang. Edward G. Robinson, Joan Bennett, Dan Duryea, Margaret Lindsay, Rosalind Ivan. Engrossing melodrama of unhappily married Robinson falling in love with shady Bennett, who doublecrosses him; not as good as WOMAN IN THE WINDOW, which had same director and stars.

Scene of the Crime (1949) 94m. ** D: Roy Rowland. Van Johnson, Arlene Dahl, Gloria De Haven, Tom Drake, Leon Ames. Bland detective whodunit, with Johnson a cop trying to solve police murder.

School for Love (1955-French, dubbed) 72m. ** D: Yves Allegret. Jean Marais, Brigitte Bardot, Isabelle Pia. Occasionally sensual flick with Bardot and Pia competing for Marais' affection. Retitled: JOY OF LOVING.

School for Scoundrels (1960-British) 94m. *** D: Robert Hamer. Alastair Sim, Terry-Thomas, Ian Carmichael. Superb comedy barb about training school for one-upmanship, giving the viewer complete course in coming out tops in any situation.

Scorpio Letters, The (1967) 120m. *** D: Richard Thorpe. Alex Cord, Shirley Eaton, Laurence Naismith, Oscar Beregi, Lester Matthews. Diverting espionage telefeature set in England, with Cord and Eaton competing military agents tracking down a blackmail ring.

Scotland Yard Inspector (1952-British) 73m. ** D: Sam Newfield. Cesar Romero, Lois Maxwell, Bernadette O'Farrell, Geoffrey Keen, Alistair Hunter, Peter Swanwick. Run-of-the-mill actioner with Romero assisting Maxwell in capturing her brother's killer.

Scotland Yard Investigator (1945) 68m. ** D: George Blair. C. Aubrey Smith, Erich von Stroheim, Stephanie Bachelor, Forrester Harvey, Doris Lloyd, Eva Moore. Low-budget mystery wastes two leading players in routine art-theft tale.

Scott of the Antarctic (1948-British) C-110m. **1/2 D: Charles Frend. John Mills, Derek Bond, James Robertson Justice, Kenneth More, Christopher Lee. Unrelenting drama of dynamic British 20th-century explorer who led expedition to frigid sub-continent.

Scream of Fear (1961-British) 81m. *** D: Seth Holt. Susan Strasberg, Christopher Lee, Ann Todd, Ronald Lewis. Good thriller about girl who thinks people are deliberately driving her insane.

Screaming Eagles (1956) 81m. ** D: Charles Haas. Tom Tryon, Jan Merlin, Alvy Moore, Martin Milner, Jacqueline Beer. Routine WW2 film focusing on D-Day.

Screaming Mimi (1958) 79m. ** D: Gerd Oswald. Anita Ekberg, Phil Carey, Gypsy Rose Lee, Harry Townes. Lurid caper in which energetic dancer Ekberg is convinced she's a murderess; Lee hasn't enough to do in proceedings.

Scudda Hoo! Scudda Hay! (1948) C-95m. ** D: F. Hugh Herbert. June Haver, Lon McCallister, Walter Brennan, Anne Revere, Natalie Wood. Any film with a title like that can't be all good, and it isn't; McCallister's life is devoted to two mules.

Sea Around Us, The (1953) C-61m. *** Produced by: Irwin Allen. Narrated by: Don Forbes. Academy Award-winning documentary based on Rachel Carson's study of the history of the ocean, its fauna and life.

Sea Chase, The (1955) C-117m. **1/2 D: John Farrow. John Wayne, Lana Turner, Tab Hunter, James Arness, Claude Akins. Strange WW2 film, with Wayne as German captain of fugitive ship with unusual cargo, assorted crew, plus passenger/girlfriend Turner.

Sea Devils (1953) C-91m. **1/2 D: Raoul Walsh. Yvonne de Carlo, Rock Hudson, Maxwell Reed, Denis O'Dea. Handsome pairing of De Carlo-Hudson elevates this standard sea yarn of smugglers.

Sea Hawk, The (1940) 127m. ***1/2 D: Michael Curtiz. Errol Flynn, Brenda Marshall, Claude Rains, Donald Crisp, Flora Robson, Alan Hale. Top-notch combination of classy Warner Bros. costumer and Flynn at his dashing best in adventure on the high seas; lively balance of piracy, romance, and swordplay.

Sea Hornet, The (1951) 84m. *1/2 D: Joseph Kane. Rod Cameron, Adele Mara, Adrian Booth, Chill Wills. Lowjinks about deep-water divers and their gals.

Sea of Grass, The (1947) 131m. **1/2 D: Elia Kazan. Katharine Hepburn, Spencer Tracy, Melvyn Douglas, Phyllis Thaxter, Robert Walker, Ed Buchanan, Harry Carey. Plodding drama from Conrad Richter story of farmer-rancher feud over New Mexico grasslands. Walker stands out in hardworking but unsuccessful cast.

Sea of Lost Ships (1953) 85m. ** D: Joseph Kane. John Derek, Wanda Hendrix, Walter Brennan, Richard Jaeckel. Standard fare of two coast guard men fighting over Hendrix.

Sea of Sand SEE: Desert Patrol.

Sea Shall Not Have Them, The (1954-British) 91m. ** D: Lewis Gilbert. Michael Redgrave, Dirk Bogarde, Anthony Steel, Nigel Patrick, Nigel Green, Rachel Kempson. British bomber plane is forced down in the ocean during WW2; a rescue attempt is made.

Sea Tiger (1952) 75m. *1/2 D: Frank McDonald. John Archer, Mara Corday, Marguerite Chapman, Lyle Talbot. Heavy-handed mini-actioner, with Archer entangled with homicide; set in New Guinea.

Sea Wife (1957) C-82m. *** D: Bob McNaught. Richard Burton, Joan Collins, Basil Sydney, Ronald Squire, Cy Grant. Disarming yarn of Burton and Collins surviving from a torpedoed ship. He falls in love with her, not knowing she's a nun. Set in WW2.

Sea Wolf, The (1941) 100m. ***1/2 D: Michael Curtiz. Edward G. Robinson, Ida Lupino, John Garfield, Alexander Knox, Gene Lockhart, Barry Fitzgerald, Stanley Ridges. Bristling Jack London tale of brutal but educated sea captain (Robinson) battling wits with accidental passenger Knox; meanwhile brash seaman Garfield and fugitive Lupino try to escape.

Sealed Cargo (1951) 90m. **1/2 D: Alfred L. Werker. Dana Andrews, Carla Balenda, Claude Rains, Philip

Dorn. Taut melodrama of Nazi submarines in coastal waters off Newfoundland.

Sealed Verdict (1948) 83m. ** D: Lewis Allen. Ray Milland, Florence Marly, Broderick Crawford, John Hoyt, John Ridgely. Far-fetched drama of army lawyer who falls in love with traitorous woman he is supposed to prosecute in court; pretty dismal.

Seance on a Wet Afternoon (1964-British) 115m. **** D: Bryan Forbes. Kim Stanley, Richard Attenborough, Patrick Magee, Nanette Newman, Maria Kazan, Margaret Lacey. Gripping drama of crazed medium Stanley involving husband Attenborough in shady project. Brilliant acting, direction in this must-see film.

Search, The (1948) 105m. **** D: Fred Zinnemann. Montgomery Clift, Ivan Jandl, Aline MacMahon, Jarmila Novotna, Wendell Corey. Moving drama of American soldier who cares for European war orphan after WW2; beautifully directed and acted. Clift's film debut.

Search for Bridey Murphy, The (1956) 84m. **1/2 D: Noel Langley. Teresa Wright, Louis Hayward, Nancy Gates, Kenneth Tobey, Richard Anderson. Strange account of woman under hypnosis with recollection of prior life; low-keyed telling to obtain realism makes it sluggish going.

Search for Danger (1949) 62m. D: Jack Bernhard. John Calvert, Albert Dekker, Myrna Dell, Douglas Fowley, Ben Welden. SEE: The Falcon series.

Searchers, The (1956) C-119m. *** D: John Ford. John Wayne, Jeffrey Hunter, Vera Miles, Ward Bond, Natalie Wood, John Qualen, Harry Carey, Olive Carey, Antonio Moreno, Dorothy Jordan. Well-turned account of Wayne and Hunter seeking Wood and Miles, kidnapped by Indians; convincing throughout and highly actionful.

Searching Wind, The (1946) 108m. **1/2 D: William Dieterle. Robert Young, Sylvia Sidney, Ann Richards, Dudley Digges, Douglas Dick, Albert Basserman. Lillian Hellman's play about over-diplomatic diplomat Young, about to forsake family when tragedy makes him realize mistake; talky drama.

Season of Passion (1961-Australian) 93m. **1/2 D: Leslie Norman. Anne Baxter, John Mills, Angela Lansbury, Ernest Borgnine, Janette Craig. Tasteful study of human relationships; Mills and Borgnine are country workers who each year come to the city for their fling with Baxter and Lansbury. Based on play SUMMER OF THE 17TH DOLL by Ray Lawler.

Second Best Secret Agent in the Whole Wide World (1966-British) C-96m. **1/2 D: Lindsay Shonteff. Tom Adams, Peter Bull, Karel Stepanek, John Arnatt. Snappy James Bondish entry, with virtue of satirical performance by Adams and good supporting cast.

Second Chance (1953) C-82m. **1/2 D: Rudolph Mate. Robert Mitchum, Linda Darnell, Jack Palance, Reginald Sheffield. Darnell seeks Mitchum's aid, leading to gun-play; set in South America.

Second Chorus (1940) 83m. ** D: H. C. Potter. Fred Astaire, Paulette Goddard, Artie Shaw and Orchestra, Charles Butterworth, Burgess Meredith. Routine musical of Astaire and Meredith, members of Shaw's band, both with designs on Goddard. Easy to take, but nothing special.

Second Face, The (1950) 77m. **1/2 D: Jack Bernhard. Ella Raines, Bruce Bennett, Rita Johnson, Jane Darwell, John Sutton. Concise study of the effects of plastic surgery on Raines, whose face has been scarred.

Second Fiddle (1939) 86m. **1/2 D: Sidney Lanfield. Sonja Henie, Tyrone Power, Rudy Vallee, Edna May Oliver, Lyle Talbot, Brian Sisters. Contrived Henie musical of Power promoting Hollywood romance for Henie, falling in love himself. Irving Berlin score.

Second Greatest Sex, The (1955) C-87m. *1/2 D: George Marshall. Jeanne Crain, George Nader, Bert Lahr, Mamie Van Doren, Kitty Kallen, Keith Andes, Tommy Rall, Paul Gilbert, Jimmy Boyd. Second-rate updating of LYSISTRATA, about women protesting men's violence by going on sex strike.

Second Honeymoon (1937) 79m. **1/2 D: Walter Lang. Tyrone Power, Loretta Young, Stuart Erwin, Claire Trevor, Lyle Talbot. Power tries to win back ex-wife Young in pat marital farce with attractive past.

Second Time Around, The (1961) C-99m. **1/2 D: Vincent Sherman. Debbie Reynolds, Andy Griffith, Steve Forrest, Juliet Prowse, Thelma Ritter, Isobel Elsom. Mild comic Western with widow Debbie moving to Arizona, becoming sheriff, tangling with suitors Griffith and Forrest.

Second Woman, The (1951) 91m. **½ D: James V. Kern. Robert Young, Betsy Drake, John Sutton, Henry O'Neill, Florence Bates. Brooding drama of architect Young who feels responsible for girlfriend's accidental death.

Seconds (1966) 106m. *** D: John Frankenheimer. Rock Hudson, Salome Jens, John Randolph, Will Geer, Jeff Corey. Frustrated middle-aged businessman is transformed into new identity (Hudson), but finds himself at odds with old and new life. Fine premise goes astray in middle portion of film.

Secret Agent Fireball (1966-Italian, dubbed) C-89m. ** D: Martin Donan. Richard Harrison, Dominique Boschero, Wandisa Guida. Harrison is American superspy substituted for U.S. scientist in gambit to protect coalition between U.S.-Germany-Russia on new petroleum mechanism project; standard treatment. Retitled: KILLERS ARE CHALLENGED.

Secret Agent of Japan (1942) 72m. ** D: Irving Pichel. Preston Foster, Lynn Bari, Noel Madison, Janis Carter, Sen Yung, Addison Richards, Frank Puglia, Ian Wolfe. Dated espionage film of soldier-of-fortune Foster working in the Pacific for England before Pearl Harbor.

Secret Agent Super Dragon (1966) C-95m. *½ D: Calvin Padgett. Ray Danton, Marisa Mell, Margaret Lee, Jess Hahn. Sloppy foreign spy meller has fair cast but sometimes silly script and atrocious dubbing. Danton repeats role from CODE NAME: JAGUAR.

Secret Beyond the Door (1948) 98m. ** D: Fritz Lang. Joan Bennett, Michael Redgrave, Anne Revere, Barbara O'Neil, Natalie Schafer. Tedious Lang misfire along lines of Hitchcock's SUSPICION, with Bennett realizing her husband is a demented murderer.

Secret Bride (1935) 76m. **½ D: William Dieterle. Barbara Stanwyck, Warren William, Glenda Farrell, Grant Mitchell, Arthur Byron. D.A. William is trying to expose governor Mitchell while he's secretly married to his daughter Stanwyck.

Secret Command (1944) 82m. *** D: A. Edward Sutherland. Pat O'Brien, Carole Landis, Chester Morris, Ruth Warrick, Wallace Ford. No-nonsense O'Brien tries to find source of waterfront corruption, tracks down shady mentor and cleans up the graft; good, fast-moving story.

Secret Door, The (1964-British) 72m. *½ D: Gilbert Kay. Robert Hutton, Sandra Dorne, Peter Illing, George Pastell. Uneven direction mars otherwise OK plot of U.S. safecrackers out to steal Japanese code secrets in Lisbon.

Secret Fury, The (1950) 86m. *** D: Mel Ferrer. Claudette Colbert, Robert Ryan, Jane Cowl, Paul Kelly, Vivian Vance, Philip Ober. Unknown person tries to drive Claudette crazy to prevent her marriage to Ryan. Exciting whodunit with twist ending.

Secret Garden, The (1949) C-92m. *** D: Fred M. Wilcox. Margaret O'Brien, Herbert Marshall, Dean Stockwell, Gladys Cooper, Elsa Lanchester. Fine fantasy of youth who live in "magic" garden of his mind.

Secret Heart, The (1946) 97m. **½ D: Robert Z. Leonard. Claudette Colbert, Walter Pidgeon, June Allyson, Lionel Barrymore, Robert Sterling, Patricia Medina, Marshall Thompson. This is Allyson's film, as young girl obsessed with dead father, unable to accept stepmother Colbert. Film creates eerie mood, and acting is good, but it's offbeat and not for all tastes.

Secret Invasion, The (1964) C-95m. *** D: Roger Corman. Stewart Granger, Mickey Rooney, Raf Vallone, Henry Silva, Edd Byrnes, Mia Massini. Good action, location photography, and direction in story of British Intelligence using criminals to work behind enemy lines in WW2 Yugoslavia.

Secret Land, The (1948) C-71m. *** Produced by: Orville O. Dull. Narrated by: Van Heflin, Robert Montgomery, Robert Taylor. Glossy but penetrating documentary study of Admiral Richard Byrd's exploratory missions to Antarctic.

Secret Life of Walter Mitty, The (1947) C-105m. *** D: Norman Z. McLeod. Danny Kaye, Virginia Mayo, Boris Karloff, Fay Bainter, Ann Rutherford. More Kaye than Thurber, but great fun with Danny as daydreaming Mitty; includes his classic routine "Anatole of Paris."

Secret Mark of D'Artagnan, The (1962-Italian, dubbed) C-91m. **½ D: Siro Marcellini. George Nader, Mario Petri, Magali Noel, Georges Marchal. Loosely based on Dumas' characters, Nader is D'Artagnan fighting for Louis XIII and Richelieu; plot is silly but moves along.

Secret Mission (1942-British) 82m. **½ D: Harold French. Hugh Williams, James Mason, Roland Culver, Carla Lehmann, Michael Wilding, Herbert Lom, Stewart Granger. Well-paced WW2 actioner of Anglo mission in occupied France.

Secret of Blood Island, The (1965-British) C-84m. **½ D: Quentin Lawrence. Barbara Shelley, Jack Hedley, Charles Tingwell, Patrick Wymark. Woman agent parachutes into Malayan prison behind enemy lines.

Secret of Convict Lake, The (1951) 83m. **½ D: Michael Gordon. Glenn Ford, Gene Tierney, Ethel Barrymore, Zachary Scott, Ann Dvorak. Set in 1870's California, escaped prisoners hide out at settlement comprised largely of women; fine cast makes the most of script.

Secret of Dr. Kildare (1939) 84m. D: Harold S. Bucquet. Lew Ayres, Lionel Barrymore, Lionel Atwill, Helen Gilbert, Laraine Day, Sara Haden, Samuel S. Hinds, Emma Dunn, Grant Mitchell, Martha O'Driscoll, Alma Kruger. SEE: Dr. Kildare series.

Secret of Dr. Mabuse, The (1961-German, dubbed) 90m. **½ D: Fritz Lang. Peter Van Eyck, Dawn Addams, Gert Frobe. Well-paced yarn bringing back famed arch-criminal of 1920's, with Lang again directing. Mabuse still trying to rule the world, with police inspector Frobe intervening. Retitled: THE DIABOLICAL DOCTOR MABUSE.

Secret of My Success, The (1965) C-112m. *½ D: Andrew L. Stone. Shirley Jones, Stella Stevens, Honor Blackman, James Booth, Lionel Jeffries. Film certainly doesn't succeed. Naive boy is taken in by several crafty females on his road to maturity. Picturesque settings, variety of characterizations by Jeffries.

Secret of the Black Trunk, The (1962-German, dubbed) 96m. **½ D: Werner Klingler. Joachim Hansen, Senta Berga, Hans Reiser, Leonard Steckel, Peter Carsten. Filmed in England, this Edgar Wallace-esque yarn involves a series of murders at a famed hotel; predictable but engaging.

Secret of the Incas (1954) C-101m. **½ D: Jerry Hopper. Charlton Heston, Robert Young, Nicole Maurey, Thomas Mitchell, Glenda Farrell, Yma Sumac. Good adventure of explorer finding map indicating location of fabled treasure. Adequate direction, good performances.

Secret of the Purple Reef, The (1960) C-80m. ** D: William Witney. Jeff Richards, Margia Dean, Peter Falk, Richard Chamberlain, Robert Earle, Terence DeMarney. Programmer whose capable cast bounces the story along; brothers seek clues to their father's killing in the Caribbean.

Secret of the Red Orchid, The SEE: Puzzle of the Red Orchid, The.

Secret of the Whistler (1946) 65m. D: George Sherman. Richard Dix, Leslie Brooks, Mary Currier, Michael Duane, Mona Barrie, Ray Walker. SEE: Whistler series.

Secret of Treasure Mountain (1956) 68m. *½ D: Seymour Friedman. Valerie French, Raymond Burr, William Prince, Lance Fuller, Susan Cummings. Junky trivia about hunt for buried wealth in Indian country.

Secret Partner, The (1961-British) 91m. *** D: Basil Dearden. Stewart Granger, Haya Harareet, Bernard Lee, Conrad Phillips. Fast-paced, atmospheric mystery about man trying to pull off ingenious scheme whereby he is accused of robbery.

Secret People, The (1951-British) 87m. ** D: Thorold Dickinson. Valentina Cortesa, Serge Reggiani, Audrey Hepburn, Megs Jenkins, Irene Worth, Sydney Tafler. Capable cast invigorates this standard tale of intrigue set in pre-WW2 London.

Secret Service in Darkest Africa SEE: Baron's African War, The.

Secret Seven, The (1966-Italian, dubbed) C-94m. Bomb D: Alberto de Martino. Tony Russel, Helga Line, Massimo Serato, Gerard Tichy. Adventurer enlists aid of six illustrious heroes to restore rightful queen to throne. Typically poor Italian "spectacle."

Secret Six, The (1931) 83m. *** D: George Hill. Wallace Beery, Lewis Stone, Clark Gable, Jean Harlow, Johnny Mack Brown, Ralph Bellamy, Frank McGlynn, Theodore Von Eltz. Vintage crime melodrama with powerhouse cast. Beery and Bellamy's bootlegging ring investigated by reporters Gable and Brown, who are thrown off by hireling Harlow. Stone is Beery's brain trust.

Secret Ways, The (1961) 112m. **½ D: Phil Karlson. Richard Widmark, Sonja Ziemann, Senta Berger, Charles Regnier. Much on-location shooting helps strengthen caper with Widmark as grim American sent into Communist Hungary to plan escape of pro-West refugee.

Secret Weapon SEE: **Sherlock Holmes and The Secret Weapon.**

Secrets of a Secretary (1931) 71m. ** D: George Abbott. Claudette Colbert, Herbert Marshall, George Metaxa, Mary Boland, Berton Churchill. Stiff drawing-room stuff, with Colbert finding ex-hubby Marshall blackmailing her new boss.

Secrets of an Actress (1938) 71m. **½ D: William Keighley. Kay Francis, George Brent, Ian Hunter, Gloria Dickson, Isabel Jeans. Chic woman's picture: Francis is glamorous actress who attracts distraught Brent, an unhappily married architect.

Security Risk (1954) 69m. ** D: Harold Schuster. John Ireland, Dorothy Malone, Keith Larsen, John Craven, Joe Bassett. Routine FBI-vs.-Communist-agent; even Malone isn't diverting in this B-film.

Seduced and Abandoned (1964-Italian, dubbed) 118m. ***½ D: Pietro Germi. Stefania Sandrelli, Saro Urzi, Lando Buzzanca, Leopoldo Trieste. Richly flavorful bed-room romp involving a sex-loving man who plays and runs, till his activities catch up with him.

See Here, Private Hargrove (1944) *** D: Wesley Ruggles. Robert Walker, Donna Reed, Keenan Wynn, Robert Benchley, Bob Crosby, Grant Mitchell. Marion Hargrove's anecdotes of army life make an amusing, episodic film; Benchley hilarious as Reed's garrulous dad.

Seekers, The (1954-British) C-90m. **½ D: Ken Annakin. Jack Hawkins, Glynis Johns, Noel Purcell, Laya Raki, Tony Erstich. Sincere but clichéd account of British colonization of New England in 1820's, with Hawkins and Johns a married couple emigrating there.

Sellout, The (1951) 83m. *½ D: Gerald Mayer. Walter Pidgeon, John Hodiak, Audrey Totter, Paula Raymond. Slick gangster exposé tale, headed by Pidgeon as newspaper editor determined to find out the facts.

Seminole (1953) C-87m. **½ D: Budd Boetticher. Rock Hudson, Barbara Hale, Anthony Quinn, Richard Carlson, Hugh O'Brian. Capable cast improves this account of the Indian tribe's effort to remain free of white man law.

Seminole Uprising (1955) C-74m. *½ D: Earl Bellamy. George Montgomery, Karin Booth, John Pickard, Ed Hinton. Trite handling of Indians vs. cavalry; too little action.

Senator Was Indiscreet, The (1947) 81m. ***½ D: George S. Kaufman. William Powell, Ella Raines, Peter Lind Hayes, Arleen Whelan. Witplaywright Kaufman's only directorial fling turns out quite well, with Powell as senator whose diary causes embarrassment. Hilarious.

Send Me No Flowers (1964) C-100m. *** D: Norman Jewison. Rock Hudson, Doris Day, Tony Randall, Clint Walker, Paul Lynde. One of the top Day-Hudson comedies. Rock, convinced he has a short time to live, has Randall find new husband for wife Doris.

Senechal the Magnificent (1958-French, dubbed) 78m. **½ D: Jacques Boyer. Fernandel, Nadia Gray, Georges Chamarat, Jeanne Aubert, Armontel, Robert Pizani. Fernandel is well cast as buffoon actor who, through mistaken identities and an ability to mimic, becomes a Parisian hit.

Senior Prom (1959) 82m. *½ D: David Lowell Rich. Jill Corey, Paul Hampton, Tom Laughlin, Barbara Bostock. Flimsy excuse for low-grade musical with procession of "guest stars" such as Louis Prima, Keely Smith, Mitch Miller, etc.

Sensations (1944) 86m. **½ D: Andrew L. Stone. W. C. Fields, Eleanor Powell, Dennis O'Keefe, C. Aubrey Smith, Eugene Pallette, Sophie Tucker. When W.C. isn't hilarious you know something's wrong; weak story of dancer Powell putting show together has guests, just a few good scenes. Original title: SENSATIONS OF 1945.

Senso (1954-Italian, dubbed) C-90m. **½ D: Luchino Visconti. Alida Valli, Farley Granger, Massimo Girotti, Heinz Moog. Carefully paced study of human emotions, lingering on each twisted impact in relationship between aristocrat Valli and earthy, materialistic Granger. Retitled: WANTON CONTESSA: WANTON COUNTESS.

Sensualita (1954-Italian, dubbed) 72m. ** D: Clemente Fracassi. Eleonora Rossi-Drago, Amedo Nazzari, Marcello Mastroianni, Francesco Liddi, Corrado Nardi. At-times spicy account of two men fighting over sensual Rossi-Drago. Retitled: BAREFOOT SAVAGE.

Sentimental Journey (1946) 94m. ** D: Walter Lang. John Payne, Maureen O'Hara, William Bendix, Cedric Hardwicke, Glenn Langan, Mischa Auer, Connie Marshall. Maudlin yarn of dying actress O'Hara adopting little girl to give husband Payne a companion when she is gone; no holds barred here. Remade as GIFT OF LOVE.

Separate Tables (1958) 98m. **** D: Delbert Mann. Rita Hayworth, Deborah Kerr, David Niven, Wendy Hiller, Burt Lancaster. Latter-day GRAND HOTEL, from Terence Rattigan play, with Oscar-winners Niven, as seemingly debonair colonel, and Hiller, as Lancaster's timid mistress. Hayworth effective as Lancaster's ex-wife begging him for another chance.

September Affair (1950) 104m. **½ D: William Dieterle. Joseph Cotten, Joan Fontaine, Françoise Rosay, Jessica Tandy. Trim romance tale of married man Cotten and pianist Fontaine who find that they're listed as dead in plane crash and now have chance to continue their affair.

September Storm (1960) 99m. Bomb D: Byron Haskin. Joanne Dru, Mark Stevens, Robert Strauss, Asher Dann, M. Jean-Pierre Kerien, Vera Valmont. Scheming fashion model joins a group of adventurers searching for buried treasure off the coast of Majorca. Film's only novelty is lost: it was shot in 3-D Cinemascope.

Serena (1962-British) 62m. **½ D: Peter Maxwell. Patrick Holt, Emrys Jones, Honor Blackman, Bruce Beeby. Neat mystery programmer with Holt the detective inspector ferreting out the killer of artist Jones' wife.

Serenade (1956) C-121m. **½ D: Anthony Mann. Mario Lanza, Joan Fontaine, Sarita Montiel, Vincent Price, Joseph Calleia, Vince Edwards. James N. Cain novel becomes surface-soaper of Lanza, the protegé of swank Fontaine, manipulated by manager Price and loved by earthy Montiel; spotty musical interludes.

Sergeant Deadhead (1965) C-89m. ** D: Norman Taurog. Frankie Avalon, Deborah Walley, Fred Clark, Cesar Romero, Gale Gordon, Harvey Lembeck, John Ashley, Buster Keaton, Eve Arden, Reginald Gardiner. Avalon's space flight transforms him from timid soul into arrogant astronaut. Average comedy with ordinary songs, saved by pros in cast.

Sergeant Madden (1939) 82m. ** D: Josef von Sternberg. Wallace Beery, Tom Brown, Alan Curtis, Laraine Day, Fay Holden, David Gorcey, Etta McDaniel, Horace MacMahon. Director Sternberg out of his element with standard Beery vehicle of policeman whose son alienates him, marries orphan girl he raised.

Sergeant Rutledge (1960) C-118m. **½ D: John Ford. Jeffrey Hunter, Constance Towers, Billie Burke, Woody Strode, Juano Hernandez, Willis Bouchey, Mae Marsh. Strode is on trial for rape and murder; in course of court-martial, standard Western tale evolves. Memorable for appearance of Burke.

Sergeant Ryker (1968) 85m. **½ D: Buzz Kulik. Lee Marvin, Bradford Dillman, Vera Miles, Peter Graves, Lloyd Nolan, Murray Hamilton. Adapted from TV film THE CASE AGAINST SERGEANT RYKER, story concerns court-martial of Marvin in title role, an army sergeant during Korean War suspected of being a traitor; Miles is his wife and Dillman the dynamic defense attorney.

Sergeant York (1941) 134m. ***½ D: Howard Hawks. Gary Cooper, Walter Brennan, Joan Leslie, George Tobias, Stanley Ridges, Margaret Wycherly, Ward Bond, Noah Beery, Jr., June Lockhart. Excellent story of pacifist York (Cooper) drafted during WWI, realizing purpose of fighting and becoming hero. Oscar-winning performance by Cooper in fine, intelligent film, balancing segments of rural America with battle scenes.

Sergeants 3 (1962) C-112m. **½ D: John Sturges. Frank Sinatra, Dean Martin, Sammy Davis, Jr., Peter Lawford, Joey Bishop. Second reworking of GUNGA DIN is amusing, but not up to 1939 original. This time it's out West with the rat pack as cavalry sergeants. Davis can't eclipse Sam Jaffe as Gunga Din.

Serpent of the Nile (1953) C-81m. *½ D: William Castle. Rhonda Fleming, William Lundigan, Raymond Burr, Michael Ansara, Julie Newmar. Hokey spectacle of Cleopatra and Anthony having good time against Romans. Acting very uneven, script worse. Unconsciously funny.

Servant, The (1963-British) 115m. ***½ D: Joseph Losey. Dirk Bogarde, James Fox, Sarah Miles, Wendy Craig, Catherine Lacey, Patrick Magee. Insidious study of moral degradation as corrupt manservant Bogarde becomes master of employer Fox; superb study of brooding decadence.

Set-Up, The (1949) 72m. ***½ D: Robert Wise. Robert Ryan, Audrey Totter, George Tobias, Alan Baxter, James Edwards, Wallace Ford. Gutsy account of washed-up fighter refusing to give up or go crooked; Ryan has never been better.

Seven Angry Men (1955) 90m. *** D: Charles Marquis Warren. Raymond Massey, Debra Paget, Jeffrey Hunter, James Best, Dennis Weaver, Dabbs Greer, Ann Tyrrell. Good historical drama of John Brown (Massey) and family fighting to free slaves during 1800's. Massey is fine in lead role.

Seven Brides for Seven Brothers (1954) C-103m. *** D: Stanley Donen. Howard Keel, Jane Powell, Jeff Richards, Russ Tamblyn, Tommy Rall, Julie Newmar, Ruta Lee, Matt Mattox. Lively musical romp transferring the RAPE OF THE SABINE WOMEN to the Oregon territory; bouncy songs and sprightly dancing.

7 Capital Sins (1961-French, dubbed) 113m. ** D: Jean-Luc Godard, Roger Vadim, Sylvaine Dhomme, Edouard Molinaro, Philippe De Broca, Claude Chabrol, Jacques Demy. Marie-Jose Nat, Dominique Paturel, Jean-Marc Tennberg, Perrette Pradier. Potpourri of directors and talents play out modern parables concerning anger, envy, glutony, greed, laziness, lust, and pride.

Seven Cities of Gold (1955) C-103m. **½ D: Robert D. Webb. Richard Egan, Anthony Quinn, Jeffrey Hunter, Rita Moreno, Michael Rennie. Average spectacle, adventure from 50's has good cast and fair direction. "Roughneck" learns ways of God in search for fabled Indian treasure in Western U.S.

Seven Daring Girls (1960-German, dubbed) 62m. *½ D: Otto Meyer. Jan Hendriks, Adrian Hoven, Ann Smyrner, Dorothee Glocklen. Poorly executed yarn of seven girls from Swiss finishing school marooned on isle inhabited by crooks seeking gold there.

Seven Days in May (1964) 118m. *** D: John Frankenheimer. Burt Lancaster, Kirk Douglas, Fredric March, Ava Gardner, Edmond O'Brien, Martin Balsam, George Macready. Absorbing story of military scheme to overthrow the government. Staunch cast including Lancaster and Douglas as military officials, March as the U.S. President. Gardner effective in her cameo.

Seven Days' Leave (1942) 87m. **½ D: Tim Whelan. Lucille Ball, Victor Mature, Harold Peary, Ginny Simms, Peter Lind Hayes, Arnold Stang, Ralph Edwards. Two sailors ashore is basis for sprightly musicomedy with Freddy Martin and Les Brown's bands; songs include: "Can't Get Out Of This Mood."

Seven Days to Noon (1950-British) 93m. **** D: John and Roy Boulting. Barry Jones, Olive Sloane, Andre Morell, Sheila Manahan. Excellently paced thriller about scientist threatening to explode bomb in London if his demands are not met.

Seven Deadly Sins (1952) 120m. **½ D: Eduardo de Filippo, Jean Dreville, Yves Allegret, Roberto Rossellini, Carlo Rim, Claude Autant-Lara. Michele Morgan, Françoise Rosay, Gerard Philippe, Isabella Miranda, Eduardo de Filippo. Episodic portpourri illustrating seven major vices; lack of internal continuity mars total effort.

711 Ocean Drive (1950) 102m. **½ D: Joseph M. Newman. Edmond O'Brien, Joanne Dru, Otto Kruger, Bert Freed. Tidy racketeer yarn of the bookie syndicate in the U.S.

Seven Keys to Baldpate (1947) 66m. **½ D: Lew Landers. Philip Terry, Jacqueline White, Eduardo Ciannelli, Margaret Lindsay, Arthur Shields. Oft-filmed tale of mystery writer involved in murder himself is pretty good; probably not up to first two versions.

Seven Little Foys, The (1955) C-95m. *** D: Melville Shavelson. Bob Hope, Milly Vitale, George Tobias, Billy

Gray, James Cagney. Pleasant biography of vaudevillian Eddie Foy and his performing family. Hope lively in lead role, Cagney guests as George M. Cohan; both men's footwork is admirable.

Seven Men From Now (1956) C-78m. ** D: Budd Boetticher. Randolph Scott, Gail Russell, Lee Marvin, Walter Reed. Tame dust-raiser about ex-marshal Scott seeking revenge on outlaws who killed his wife during a robbery.

Seven Samurai SEE: **Magnificent Seven, The**.

Seven Sinners (1940) 87m. *** D: Tay Garnett. Marlene Dietrich, John Wayne, Albert Dekker, Broderick Crawford, Anna Lee, Mischa Auer, Billy Gilbert. Alluring Dietrich almost makes Wayne forget about navy in this routine love-action story enhanced by excellent cast of supporting players.

Seven Slaves Against the World (1965-Italian, dubbed) C-96m. Bomb D: Michele Lupo. Roger Browne, Gordon Mitchell, Scilla Gabel, Germano Longo, Alfredo Rizzo. Terrible spectacle with nonexistent plot of swordsman freeing ancient city from tyrant.

Seven Surprizes (1963-Canadian) 77m. **½. Unusual program of shorts from National Film Board of Canada including delightful animated work by Norman McLaren and Evelyn Lambart. Offbeat, entertaining.

Seven Sweethearts (1942) 98m. **½ D: Frank Borzage. Kathryn Grayson, Van Heflin, Marsha Hunt, S. Z. Sakall, Cecilia Parker, Peggy Moran, Diana Lewis, Isobel Elsom, Donald Meek, Louise Beavers. Schmaltz about Sakall's brood of daughters, none of whom can marry until the eldest does. Song: "You and the Waltz and I."

Seven Thieves (1960) 102m. ***½ D: Henry Hathaway. Edward G. Robinson, Rod Steiger, Joan Collins, Eli Wallach, Alexander Scourby, Michael Dante, Berry Kroeger, Sebastian Cabot. Taut caper of well-planned Monte Carlo heist, with excellent cast giving credibility to far-fetched premise.

Seven Ways From Sundown (1960) C-87m. **½ D: Harry Keller. Audie Murphy, Barry Sullivan, Venetia Stevenson, John McIntire, Kenneth Tobey, Mary Field. Murphy is Texas ranger assigned to bring in seasoned killer Sullivan, with usual results.

Seven Women (1965) C-93m. ** D: John Ford. Anne Bancroft, Sue Lyon, Margaret Leighton, Flora Robson, Mildred Dunnock, Anna Lee, Betty Field, Eddie Albert, Mike Mazurki, Woody Strode. Flat soaper of dedicated missionaries in China in 1935, menaced by warrior cutthroats. Despite cast and director, a dull film.

Seven Women From Hell (1961) 88m. ** D: Robert D. Webb. Patricia Owens, Denise Darcel, Cesar Romero, John Kerr, Yvonne Craig. Able cast wasted on trite account of female prisoners in Japanese prison, set in WW2 New Guinea.

Seven Year Itch, The (1955) C-105m. *** D: Billy Wilder. Marilyn Monroe, Tom Ewell, Evelyn Keyes, Sonny Tufts, Victor Moore, Oscar Homolka, Carolyn Jones, Doro Merande. Ewell's wife summer vacations, Marilyn moves in upstairs, in this George Axelrod comedy set in N.Y.C. MM delightful as dumb blonde with more obvious assets than brains.

Seventeen (1940) 78m. **½ D: Louis King. Jackie Cooper, Betty Field, Otto Kruger, Richard Denning, Peter Lind Hayes, Betty Moran, Ann Shoemaker, Norma Nelson. Cooper is delightful as teen-ager facing adolescent problems, in adaptation of Booth Tarkington story.

Seventh Cavalry (1956) C-75m. **½ D: Joseph H. Lewis. Randolph Scott, Barbara Hale, Jay O. Flippen, Jeanette Nolan, Frank Faylen. Scott plays an officer who must prove that he didn't desert Custer at the Little Big Horn.

Seventh Cross, The (1944) 110m. *** D: Fred Zinnemann. Spencer Tracy, Signe Hasso, Hume Cronyn, Agnes Moorehead, Jessica Tandy, George Macready, Kaaren Verne, George Zucco, Felix Bressart. Tracy is one of seven Americans to escape Nazi camp; German officer Zucco wants him back and chase begins in smooth WW2 adventure.

7th Dawn, The (1964) C-123m. **½ D: Lewis Gilbert. William Holden, Susannah York, Capucine, Maurice Denham, Sydney Tafler. Unremarkable mishmash set in Malaya with Communist forces battling the pro-Western forces; a few actionful raid sequences on plantation households.

Seventh Heaven (1937) 102m. ** D:

Henry King. Simone Simon, James Stewart, Jean Hersholt, Gregory Ratoff, Gale Sondergaard, J. Edward Bomberg, John Qualen. Classic silent film of poignant lovers in France doesn't do as well this time, with Gallic Stewart and soggy script.

Seventh Sin, The (1957) 94m. **½ D: Ronald Neame. Eleanor Parker, Bill Travers, Françoise Rosay, George Sanders, Jean-Pierre Aumont, Ellen Corby. Remake of Maugham's THE PAINTED VEIL has virtue of Parker's earnest performance as adulterous wife of a doctor who redeems herself during an epidemic; set in Hong Kong and inner China.

Seventh Sword (1962-Italian, dubbed) C-84m. ** D: Riccardo Freda. Brett Halsey, Beatrice Altariba, Giulio Bosetti, Gabriele Antonini. Wooden costumer with Halsey trying to stamp out plot to overthrow Philip III of Spain.

Seventh Veil, The (1946-British) 95m. ***½ D: Compton Bennett. James Mason, Ann Todd, Herbert Lom, Hugh McDermott, Albert Lieven. Excellent British drama of harried Todd running away from family to become pianist, sharing life with many men. Mason's famous bravura performance is worth seeing.

Seventh Victim, The (1943) 71m. *** D: Mark Robson. Tom Conway, Kim Hunter, Jean Brooks, Evelyn Brent, Elizabeth Russell, Hugh Beaumont, Erford Gage, Isabel Jewell, Barbara Hale. Offbeat Val Lewton horror chiller of innocent Hunter stumbling onto N.Y.C. group of devil-worshippers. Genuinely eerie.

7th Voyage of Sinbad, The (1958) C-87m. **½ D: Nathan Juran. Kerwin Matthews, Kathryn Grant, Richard Eyer, Torin Thatcher. Sinbad (Matthews) vs. sorcerer (Thatcher), encountering variety of demons. First-rate visual effects elevate juvenile tale.

Sex and the Single Girl (1964) C-114m. **½ D: Richard Quine. Natalie Wood, Tony Curtis, Lauren Bacall, Henry Fonda, Mel Ferrer, Fran Jeffries, Edward Everett Horton, Larry Storch, Stubby Kaye, Count Basie and Orchestra. Helen Gurley Brown's book shoved aside, title used to exploit fairly amusing tale of smut-magazine editor Curtis wooing notorious female psychologist Wood. Bacall and Fonda wrap it up as a battling married couple.

Sex Kittens Go to College (1960) 94m. *½ D: Albert Zugsmith. Mamie Van Doren, Tuesday Weld, Mijanou Bardot, Mickey Shaughnessy, Louis Nye, Pamela Mason. Tasteless satire filled with innuendoes and pat situations. Van Doren is stripper accidentally put in charge of campus science department.

Shack Out on 101 (1955) 80m. **½ D: Edward Dein. Terry Moore, Frank Lovejoy, Lee Marvin, Keenan Wynn, Whit Bissell. Minor low-budget classic with capable cast sparking tale of espionage agent working at seaside hash-joint near scientific lab; very low-keyed production.

Shadows in the Night (1944) 67m. D: Eugene Forde. Warner Baxter, Nina Foch, George Zucco, Minor Watson, Ben Welden, Edward Norris, Charles Halton, Jeanne Bates. SEE: Crime Doctor series.

Shadow in the Sky (1951) 78m. **½ D: Fred M. Wilcox. Ralph Meeker, Nancy Davis, James Whitmore, Jean Hagen, Gladys Hurlbut. Meeker is quite believable as shellshocked ex-GI trying to regain his sanity.

Shadow Man, The (1953-British) 75m. ** D: Richard Vernon. Cesar Romero, Kay Kendall, Victor Maddern. Standard action-programmer with Romero a casino owner in love with Kendall, involved with homicide.

Shadow of a Doubt (1943) 108m. ***½ D: Alfred Hitchcock. Teresa Wright, Joseph Cotten, Macdonald Carey, Patricia Collinge, Henry Travers, Wallace Ford, Hume Cronyn. Perceptive Americana intertwined with homicidal story of Merry Widow murderer; Cronyn steals film as nosy pulp-story fan.

Shadow of Fear (1956-British) 76m. ** D: Albert S. Rogell. Mona Freeman, Jean Kent, Maxwell Reed, Hugh Miller, Gretchen Franklin. Flabby suspenser of Freeman realizing that her stepmother is planning to murder her as she did hubby; set in England.

Shadow of the Cat (1961-British) 79m. ** D: John Gilling. Barbara Shelley, Andre Morell, William Lucas, Richard Warner, Freda Jackson. Engaging horror yarn about feline who avenges her mistress' murder.

Shadow of the Thin Man (1941) 97m. D: W. S. Van Dyke II. William Powell, Myrna Loy, Barry Nelson,

Donna Reed, Sam Levene, Alan Baxter. SEE: Thin Man series.

Shadow of Zorro, The (1962-Italian, dubbed) 84m. *½ D: Joaquin Romero Marchent. Frank Latimore, Maria Luz Galicia, Mario Felciani, Marco Tulli. Clumsy film unaided by Latimore in title role of Don Jose who combats outlaws masked as Zorro.

Shadow on the Wall (1950) 84m. *** D: Patrick Jackson. Ann Sothern, Zachary Scott, Nancy Davis, Gigi Perreau, Barbara Billingsley, Kristine Miller. Slick mystery of Perreau going into shock when she sees mother murdered, and the eventual trapping of killer.

Shadow on the Window (1957) 73m. ** D: William Asher. Phil Carey, Betty Garrett, John Barrymore, Jr., Corey Allen, Jerry Mathers. Fair programmer; Garrett is held hostage by robber-killers.

Shadow Over Elveron (1968) C-120m. **½ D: James Goldstone. James Franciscus, Shirley Knight, Leslie Nielsen, Don Ameche, Franchot Tone, James Dunn. Quite violent telefeature with Franciscus a town doctor clashing with vicious sheriff Nielsen over the fate of a youth framed for murder; script is far less competent than cast.

Shadows Over Chinatown (1947) 61m. D: Terry Morse. Sidney Toler, Mantan Moreland, Victor Sen Young, Tanis Chandler, Bruce Kellogg, John Gallaudet. SEE: Charlie Chan series.

Shady Lady (1945) 94m. ** D: George Waggner. Charles Coburn, Robert Paige, Ginny Simms, Alan Curtis, Martha O'Driscoll, Kathleen Howard. Shaky mixture of music and drama in crime tale with genial Coburn saving the day for all in the end.

Shake Hands With the Devil (1959) 100m. *** D: Michael Anderson. James Cagney, Don Murray, Dana Wynter, Glynis Johns, Michael Redgrave, Cyril Cusack, Sybil Thorndike. Murray, visiting Ireland during Irish Rebellion, tries to avoid involvement despite encouragement of underground leader Cagney. Good cast elevates standard story.

Shakedown (1950) 80m. **½ D: Joseph Pevney. Howard Duff, Peggy Dow, Brian Donlevy, Bruce Bennett, Peggie Castle, Anne Vernon, Lawrence Tierney. Story of photographer involved with racketeers to get ahead at any price; moves at fast clip. Look for Rock Hudson in a bit part.

Shakedown, The (1959-British) 92m. *½ D: John Lemont. Terence Morgan, Hazel Court, Donald Pleasence, Bill Owen. Lackluster account of shakedown racket involving a photography school of nudes; good cast but no script.

Shakiest Gun in the West, The (1968) C-101m. **½ D: Alan Rafkin. Don Knotts, Barbara Rhoades, Jackie Coogan, Donald Barry, Ruth McDevitt, Frank McGrath. This remake of Bob Hope's PALEFACE provides Knotts with one of his better vehicles, as a Philadelphia dentist who finds himself out West, tangled up with gunslingers and beautiful Rhoades.

Shall We Dance (1937) 116m. ***½ D: Mark Sandrich. Fred Astaire, Ginger Rogers, Eric Blore, Edward Everett Horton, Ann Shoemaker. Lesser Astaire-Rogers is still top musical, with Gershwins' "Let's Call The Whole Thing Off," "They All Laughed," "They Can't Take That Away From Me" holding together flimsy plot about dance team pretending to be wed.

Shane (1953) C-118m. **** D: George Stevens. Alan Ladd, Jean Arthur, Van Heflin, Jack Palance, Brandon de Wilde, Edgar Buchanan, Elisha Cook, Jr. Sensitively told account of boy's (De Wilde) idolization of gunfighter Ladd, who tries to be peaceful till forced into action by villain Palance. Arthur and Heflin are restrained as boy's homesteader parents.

Shanghai (1935) 75m. **½ D: James Flood. Loretta Young, Charles Boyer, Warner Oland, Fred Keating, Charles Grapewin, Alison Skipworth. Romance and drama in the mysterious East with Boyer rebuffed because of mixed parentage, finding consolation in love of Young.

Shanghai Chest, The (1948) 56m. D: William Beaudine. Roland Winters, Mantan Moreland, Deannie Best, John Alvin, Victor Sen Yung. SEE Charlie Chan series.

Shanghai Cobra, The (1945) 64m. D: Phil Karlson. Sidney Toler, Benson Fong, Mantan Moreland, Joan Barclay, James Flavin, Addison Richards. SEE Charlie Chan series.

Shanghai Express (1932) 80m. *** D: Josef von Sternberg. Marlene Dietrich, Anna May Wong, Warner Oland, Clive Brook, Eugene Pallette,

Louise Closser Hale. Dated but prime Dietrich vehicle, grandly photographed. Marlene is Shanghai Lily, Brook her old flame, Oland a cruel war lord, Wong a spunky partisan, in yarn of train ride through China during civil warfare. Remade as PEKING EXPRESS.

Shanghai Gesture, The (1941) 106m. ** D: Josef von Sternberg. Gene Tierney, Walter Huston, Victor Mature, Ona Munson, Maria Ouspenskaya, Phyllis Brooks, Albert Basselman. Slow, overblown drama of Huston discovering daughter Tierney in Oriental gambling set-up. Intriguing direction somehow never makes it.

Shanghai Story, The (1954) 90m. ** D: Frank Lloyd. Ruth Roman, Edmond O'Brien, Richard Jaeckel, Barry Kelley, Whit Bissell. Tawdry yet intriguing little film about Americans trapped by Red Chinese.

Sharad of Atlantis (1936) 100m. *½ D: B. Reeves Eason, Joseph Kane. Ray "Crash" Corrigan, Lois Wilde, Monte Blue, William Farnum, Boothe Howard, Lon Chaney, Jr. Mediocre actioner involving finding of underwater kingdom; uninspired special effects don't help. Re-edited movie serial: UNDERSEA KINGDOM.

Share Out, The (1962-British) 62m. **½ D: Gerard Flaister. Bernard Lee, Patrick Cargill, Alexander Knox, Moira Redmond. Another Edgar Wallace actioner with Lee the Scotland Yard investigator determined to crack a blackmail ring.

Sharkfighters, The (1956) C-73m. *½ D: Jerry Hopper. Victor Mature, Karen Steele, James Olson, Philip Coolidge, Claude Akins. Bland account of Mature et al seeking some way to repel the man-killing fish.

She (1965-British) C-106m. **½ D: Robert Day. Ursula Andress, John Richardson, Peter Cushing, Bernard Cribbins, Christopher Lee, Andre Morell. Effective refilming of H. Rider Haggard's fantasy of love-starved eternal queen, seeking the reincarnation of her long-dead lover. There's Andress for the men, Richardson for the women.

She Couldn't Say No (1954) 89m. **½ D: Lloyd Bacon. Robert Mitchum, Jean Simmons, Arthur Hunnicutt, Edgar Buchanan, Wallace Ford, Raymond Walburn. Simmons is appealing as wealthy gal who gives money away to all the folks in her town with backfiring results.

She Demons (1958) 80m. Bomb D: Richard Cunha. Tod Griffin, Victor Sen Yung, Irish McCalla, Rudolph Anders. Dull cheapie about four people stranded on Pacific isle, involved with Fascist agents.

She Devil (1957) 77m. Bomb D: Kurt Neumann. Mari Blanchard, Jack Kelly, Albert Dekker, John Archer. Low-grade melodrama about homicidal girl immune to death.

She Done Him Wrong (1933) 66m. **** D: Lowell Sherman. Mae West, Cary Grant, Gilbert Roland, Noah Beery, Rochelle Hudson, Rafaela Ottiano, Louise Beavers. West repeats her stage role of Diamond Lil in gay 90's spoof. Grant is invited by Mae to come up and see her sometimes—he does, fireworks result.

She Gets Her Man (1945) 65m. *½ D: Erle C. Kenton. Joan Davis, William Gargan, Leon Errol, Vivian Austin, Russell Hicks. Davis is scatterbrained private eye thrust into a homicide caper; mild shenanigans.

She Loves Me Not (1934) 83m. *** D: Elliott Nugent. Bing Crosby, Miriam Hopkins, Kitty Carlisle, Henry Stephenson, George Barbier, Warren Hymer, Matt McHugh. Fine Crosby musicomedy with collegiate Bing hiding murder-witness Hopkins in his room. Songs: "Straight From The Shoulder," "Love In Bloom."

She Married Her Boss (1935) 85m. **½ D: Gregory La Cava. Claudette Colbert, Melvyn Douglas, Edith Fellows, Michael Bartlett, Raymond Walburn, Jean Dixon, Katherine Alexander. That's what she did, and nothing much happens until tipsy butler Walburn staggers in. Good stars with fair script.

She Played With Fire (1958-British) 95m. ** D: Sidney Gilliat. Jack Hawkins, Arlene Dahl, Dennis Price, Violet Farebrother, Ian Hunter. OK drama of Hawkins, insurance investigator, becoming involved with Dahl, an arsonist.

She Went to the Races (1945) 86m. ** D: Willis Goldbeck. James Craig, Frances Gifford, Ava Gardner, Edmund Gwenn, Sig Ruman, Reginald Owen. Gifford has developed scientific system for beating the horses, but falls in love with horsetrainer; mild comedy.

She-Wolf of London (1946) 61m. **

D: Jean Yarbrough. Don Porter, June Lockhart, Sara Haden, Jan Wiley, Lloyd Corrigan. Low-grade thriller with Lockhart in title role.

She Wore a Yellow Ribbon (1949) C-103m. ***½ D: John Ford. John Wayne, Joanne Dru, John Agar, Ben Johnson, Harry Carey, Jr., Victor McLaglen, Mildred Natwick, George O'Brien. Wayne is properly leathery as cavalry officer determined to ward off Indian attack despite tremendous odds. Fine Ford atmosphere.

She Wouldn't Say Yes (1945) 87m. **½ D: Alexander Hall. Rosalind Russell, Lee Bowman, Adele Jergens, Charles Winninger, Harry Davenport, Sara Haden, Percy Kilbride. Psychiatrist Russell tests theories on Bowman but finds herself involved with him romantically, too; predictable but amusing comedy.

Sheep Has Five Legs, The (1954-French, dubbed) 95m. *** D: Henri Verneuil. Fernandel, Delmont, Françoise Arnoul, Paulette Dubost. Fernandel's tour de force, playing an old wine-grower and each of his five sons who have gathered together for a family reunion.

Sheepman, The (1958) C-85m. *** D: George Marshall. Glenn Ford, Shirley MacLaine, Leslie Nielsen, Mickey Shaughnessy, Edgar Buchanan. Modest, entertaining comedy-Western with Ford battling Nielsen for sheep herds and MacLaine, though not always in that order. Shaughnessy is typically amusing.

Shenandoah (1965) C-105m. *** D: Andrew V. McLaglen. James Stewart, Doug McClure, Glenn Corbett, Patrick Wayne, Rosemary Forsyth, Katherine Ross, George Kennedy. Rousing, well-acted saga of complacent Virginia widower (Stewart) indifferent to Civil War until his family is involved. Personal drama captures poignancy of war. Sentimental production.

Shepherd of the Hills (1941) C-98m. **½ D: Henry Hathaway. John Wayne, Betty Field, Harry Carey, Beulah Bondi, James Barton, Samuel S. Hinds. Uneven film adaptation of Wright story of emotional flare-up between Ozark natives and outsiders trying to buy land. Good performances, beautifully filmed in color.

Sherlock Holmes In 1939, by some genius of casting, Basil Rathbone and Nigel Bruce were signed to play Sherlock Holmes and Dr. Watson in an adaptation of Sir Arthur Conan Doyle's HOUND OF THE BASKERVILLES; its immediate success prompted a follow-up, THE ADVENTURES OF SHERLOCK HOLMES, that same year. These were beautiful, atmospheric productions, faithful to Doyle's stories. Three years later, the series resumed with SHERLOCK HOLMES AND THE VOICE OF TERROR, updating the Doyle tales to have Holmes battling the Nazis. The twelve "modern" films never captured the flavor of the initial two (THE SCARLET CLAW came closest), but they were always worth seeing for the performances of the two stars: Rathbone—smooth, cunning, seldom caught by surprise; and Bruce—talkative, bumbling, never close to understanding the situation at hand. Mary Gordon made token appearances as Holmes' landlady Mrs. Hudson, and Dennis Hoey appeared in several films as Scotland Yard Inspector Lestrade, who always managed to get in the way. Holmes was at his best battling wits with Professor Moriarty, played in various episodes by George Zucco and Henry Daniell. Every episode ended with a stirring ode by Holmes to the glory of England, America, Canada, or some comparable topic, in keeping with the wartime flag-waving nature of Hollywood films. Seldom faithful to Doyle, later episodes like DRESSED TO KILL wearing thin, dialogue often awkward (S. H. IN WASHINGTON, for example), the Sherlock Holmes series relied on Rathbone and Bruce for enjoyment, and they never failed. In 1957 Peter Cushing and Christopher Lee, noted for their horror films, appeared in a color remake of HOUND OF THE BASKERVILLES which retained much of the original atmosphere and came off rather well; no further attempt at a series was made until 1966, when John Neville and Donald Houston starred as Holmes and Watson in A STUDY IN TERROR, a fine, compact little British thriller which pitted Holmes against Jack the Ripper. Any devotee of Shrlock Holmes needn't ask who won.

Sherlock Holmes and the Secret Weapon (1942) 68m. D: Roy William Neill. Basil Rathbone, Nigel Bruce, Lionel Atwill, Kaaren Verne, William

Post, Jr., Dennis Hoey, Mary Gordon, Holmes Herbert.

Sherlock Holmes and the Spider Woman (1944) 62m. D: Roy William Neill. Basil Rathbone, Nigel Bruce, Gale Sondergaard, Dennis Hoey, Mary Gordon, Arthur Hohl, Alec Craig.

Sherlock Holmes and the Voice of Terror (1942) 65m. D: John Rawlins. Basil Rathbone, Nigel Bruce, Evelyn Ankers, Reginald Denny, Thomas Gomez, Henry Daniell, Montagu Love.

Sherlock Holmes Faces Death (1943) 68m. D: Roy William Neill. Basil Rathbone, Nigel Bruce, Hillary Brooke, Milburn Stone, Arthur Margetson.

Sherlock Holmes in Washington (1943) 71m. D: Roy William Neill. Basil Rathbone, Nigel Bruce, Marjorie Lord, Henry Daniell, George Zucco, John Archer, Gavin Muir.

She's a Soldier Too (1944) 67m. ** D: William Castle. Beulah Bondi, Lloyd Bridges, Nina Foch, Percy Kilbride, Shelley Winters, Ida Moore. OK little B-film with cab-driver Bondi helping out soldier Bridges.

She's a Sweetheart (1944) 69m. *1/2 D: Del Lord. Larry Parks, Jane Frazee, Jane Darwell, Nina Foch, Ross Hunter, Carole Matthews. Musical programmer with GI Parks doubting the quality of vocalist Frazee's affection for him.

She's Back on Broadway (1953) C-95m. **1/2 D: Gordon Douglas. Virginia Mayo, Steve Cochran, Gene Nelson, Frank Lovejoy, Patrice Wymore. Standard musical of theater, heightened by some smoldering Cochran-Mayo scenes.

She's Working Her Way Through College (1952) C-101m. **1/2 D: H. Bruce Humberstone. Virginia Mayo, Ronald Reagan, Gene Nelson, Phyllis Thaxter, Roland Winter. OK musical remake of THE MALE ANIMAL, with Mayo the burlesque queen with a yen for a collegiate education.

Shield for Murder (1954) 80m. **1/2 D: Edmond O'Brien, Howard Koch. Edmond O'Brien, John Agar, Mara English, Carolyn Jones. Tidy murder yarn of lawman involved in theft-murder and trying to keep his loot, while avoiding capture.

Shine on Harvest Moon (1944) 112m. **1/2 D: David Butler. Ann Sheridan, Jack Carson, Dennis Morgan, Irene Manning, S. Z. Sakall, Marie Wilson, Step Brothers. Lives of great entertainers Nora Bayes and Jack Norworth merely provide starting point for fairly entertaining musical.

Shining Hour, The (1938) 80m. **1/2 D: Frank Borzage. Joan Crawford, Margaret Sullavan, Robert Young, Melvyn Douglas, Fay Bainter, Allyn Joslyn. Raging fire burns out all hatred and problems from tangled family in intelligent soap opera. Crawford and Sullavan a most interesting contrast.

Shining Victory (1941) 80m. ***1/2 D: Irving Rapper. James Stephenson, Geraldine Fitzgerald, Donald Crisp, Barbara O'Neil, Montagu Love, Sig Ruman. Thoughtful drama of psychiatrist who falls in love with assistant. Plot may be clichéd, but production overcomes all.

Ship Ahoy (1942) 95m. **1/2 D: Edward Buzzell. Eleanor Powell, Red Skelton, Virginia O'Brien, Bert Lahr, John Emery, Tommy Dorsey Orch. with Frank Sinatra and Jo Stafford. Nonsensical plot of Skelton thinking U.S. agent is working for Axis; shipboard yarn has some salty dancing and singing.

Ship of Fools (1965) 149m. **** D: Stanley Kramer. Vivien Leigh, Oskar Werner, Simone Signoret, Jose Ferrer, Lee Marvin, Jose Greco, George Segal, Elizabeth Ashley, Michael Dunn, Charles Korvin, Lilia Skala. GRAND HOTEL at sea in pre-WW2 days. Superb cast including Leigh as disillusioned divorcée Werner and Signoret as illicit lovers, Marvin as punchy baseball player. Penetrating drama, when not a soaper.

Ship That Died of Shame, The (1956-British) 91m. ** D: Michael Relph, Basil Dearden. Richard Attenborough, George Baker, Bill Owen, Virginia McKenna, Roland Culver. Waterlogged farce involving ex-army cohorts using a rusty old ship to get rich quick via smuggling, etc., with mild results. Retitled: PT RAIDERS.

Ship Was Loaded, The (1957-British) 81m. ** D: Val Guest. David Tomlinson, Peggy Cummins, Alfie Bass, Ronald Shiner. Inconsequential zaniness involving impersonations and shenanigans in Her Majesty's Navy. Retitled: CARRY ON ADMIRAL.

Shipmates Forever (1935) 109m. **1/2

D: Frank Borzage. Dick Powell, Ruby Keeler, Lewis Stone, Ross Alexander, Eddie Acuff, Dick Foran, John Arledge. Cocky Powell takes navy lightly until pressed into action. Usual plot, with songs and dances with Keeler.

Ships With Wings (1942-British) 89m. *** D: Sergei Nolbandov. John Clements, Ann Todd, Leslie Banks, Hugh Williams, Michael Wilding, Michael Rennie, Cecil Parker. Sterling, patriotic WW2 movie showing British soldiers at their finest, despite momentary lapses of discipline.

Shock (1946) 70m. *½ D: Alfred L. Werker. Vincent Price, Lynn Bari, Frank Latimore, Anabel Shaw, Michael Dunne, Reed Hadley. Trash, for staunch fans and no one else.

Shock Corridor (1963) 101m. *½ D: Samuel Fuller. Peter Breck, Constance Towers, Gene Evans, James Best. Journalist Breck gets admitted to mental institution to unmask murderer, winds up committed himself. Fairly seedy meller.

Shock Treatment (1964) 94m. ** D: Denis Sanders. Lauren Bacall, Stuart Whitman, Carol Lynley, Roddy McDowall, Ossie Davis, Douglass Dumbrille. Contrived thriller located at mental institution. Stereotyped performances.

Shocking Miss Pilgrim, The (1947) C-85m. ** D: George Seaton. Betty Grable, Dick Haymes, Anne Revere, Allyn Joslyn, Gene Lockhart, Elizabeth Patterson. Labored story of pioneer woman in business world. Fair Gershwin score includes "For You, For Me, For Evermore."

Shockproof (1949) 79m. *** D: Douglas Sirk. Cornel Wilde, Patricia Knight, John Baragrey, Esther Minciotti. Offbeat romance of parole officer Wilde and parolee Knight.

Shoe Shine (1946-Italian, dubbed) 93m. **** D: Vittorio DeSica Rinaldo Smerdoni, Franco Interlenghi, Anniele Mele, Bruno Ortensi, Pacifico Astrologo. Excellent postwar Italian film of two youngsters who become involved in sordid life and reform school.

Shoot First (1953) 88m. **½ D: Robert Parrish. Joel McCrea, Evelyn Keyes, Herbert Lom, Marius Goring. Capable cast helps this routine espionage tale.

Shoot the Piano Player (1962-French, dubbed) 85m. ***½ D: François Truffaut. Charles Aznavour, Marie Dubois, Nicole Berger, Michele Mercier. Aznavour is marvelous as anti-hero playing away in rundown Parisian cafe, pushed by ambitious girlfriend to resume once-prominent concert career.

Shooting High (1940) 65m. *½ D: Alfred E. Green. Jane Withers, Gene Autry, Marjorie Weaver, Robert Lowery, Jack Carson. Over-helpful Withers, aided by cowboy Autry tries to restore peaceful times to her rambunctious family.

Shop Around the Corner, The (1940) 97m. ***½ D: Ernst Lubitsch. Margaret Sullavan, James Stewart, Frank Morgan, Joseph Schildkraut, Sara Haden. Lubitsch touch brightens story of budding romance in turn-of-the-century Vienna notions shop; Sullavan and Stewart are perfect team. Remade as IN THE GOOD OLD SUMMERTIME, then musicalized as SHE LOVES ME.

Shopworn (1932) 72m. ** D: Nick Grinde. Barbara Stanwyck, Regis Toomey, ZaSu Pitts, Lucien Littlefield, Clara Blandick. Standard Depression soaper with Toomey's rich family rejecting working girl Stanwyck, who shows 'em all and becomes famous star.

Shopworn Angel, The (1938) 85m. **½ D: H. C. Potter. Margaret Sullavan, James Stewart, Walter Pidgeon, Hattie McDaniel, Nat Pendleton, Sam Levene. Weepy melodrama of girl-with-a-past Sullavan and husband Stewart, who goes off to WW1. Previously filmed with Nancy Carroll and Gary Cooper.

Short Cut to Hell (1957) 87m. **½ D: James Cagney. Robert Ivers, Georgann Johnson, William Bishop, Murvyn Vye, Yvette Vickers, Roscoe Ates. Generally taut, if uninspired remake of Grahame Greene's THIS GUN FOR HIRE, about killer re-evaluating his situation. Unusual fling at directing by Cagney.

Shot in the Dark, A (1964) C-101m. *** D: Blake Edwards. Peter Sellers, Elke Sommer, George Sanders, Herbert Lom, Tracy Reed. Hilarious comedy tops PINK PANTHER with Sellers bumbling again as Inspector Clouseau on the loose in Paris with Elke Sommer. Scene in nudist colony is a gem.

Shotgun (1955) C-81m. ** D: Lesley Selander. Sterling Hayden, Zachary

Scott, Yvonne de Carlo, Guy Prescott, Angela Greene. Unremarkable Western with sheriff Hayden vs. culprit Scott; De Carlo is the half-breed girl they love.

Show Boat (1951) C-107m. **½ D: George Sidney. Kathryn Grayson, Ava Gardner, Howard Keel, Joe E. Brown, Marge and Gower Champion, Agnes Moorehead, Robert Sterling, William Warfield. Empty musical version of Edna Ferber novel of life on the Mississippi in 1900's. Songs: "My Bill," "Can't Help Loving That Man," "Old Man River," "Make Believe."

Show Business (1944) 92m. **½ D: Edwin L. Marin. Eddie Cantor, Joan Davis, George Murphy, Nancy Kelly, Constance Moore. If you like Cantor or Davis you'll enjoy this vaudeville musical entirely supported by them; songs include "It Had To Be You."

Showdown (1963) 79m. ** D: R. G. Springsteen. Audie Murphy, Kathleen Crowley, Charles Drake, Harold Stone. Unremarkable Western with Murphy and Drake escaped convicts involved in a holdup.

Showdown at Abilene (1956) C-80m. ** D: Charles Haas. Jock Mahoney, Martha Hyer, Lyle Bettger, David Janssen, Grant Williams. Standard Western fare. Mahoney as sheriff returns from Civil War sick of bloodshed.

Showdown at Boot Hill (1958) 72m. ** D: Gene Fowler, Jr. Charles Bronson, Fintan Meyler, Robert Hutton, John Carradine, Carole Mathews. Unpretentious Western of bounty killer Bronson trying to collect reward money.

Shrike, The (1955) 88m. **½ D: Jose Ferrer. June Allyson, Jose Ferrer, Joy Page, Ed Platt, Mary Bell. Allyson almost succeeds in change of pace title role, playing ultra-nag who has driven her theater director husband (Ferrer) into a nervous breakdown. Based on Joseph Kramm play.

Shut My Big Mouth (1942) 71m. ** D: Charles Barton. Joe E. Brown, Adele Mara, Victor Jory, Fritz Feld, Lloyd Bridges, Forrest Tucker, Pedro de Cordoba. Meek Joe goes West and innocently gets mixed up with gang of outlaws.

Side Street (1949) 83m. *** D: Anthony Mann. Farley Granger, Cathy O'Donnell, James Craig, Paul Kelly, Jean Hagen, Paul Harvey. Grim drama of poor clerk Granger whose minor theft snowballs, affecting his whole life.

Sidewalks of London (1940-British) 84m. *** D: Tim Whelan. Charles Laughton, Vivien Leigh, Rex Harrison, Larry Adler, Tyrone Guthrie. Atmospheric froth of street entertainer Laughton, losing protegee Leigh to aristocratic songwriter Harrison. Stars are wonderful. Original title: ST. MARTIN'S LANE.

Siege at Red River, The (1954) C-81m. **½ D: Rudolph Mate. Van Johnson, Joanne Dru, Richard Boone, Milburn Stone, Jeff Morrow. Predictable Western set during Civil War days with an Indian attack finale.

Siege of Sidney Street, The (1960-British) 94m. ** D: Robert Baker, Monty Berman. Donald Sinden, Nicole Berger, Kieron Moore, Peter Wyngarde. Based on real incident, this film traces account of anarchists in 1910 London, with climactic confrontation between hundreds of cops and battling criminals.

Siege of Syracuse (1962-Italian, dubbed) C-97m. */2 D: Pietro Francisci. Rossano Brazzi, Tina Louise, Enrico Maria Salerno, Gino Cervi. Another costumer more notable for what it promises than delivers.

Sierra (1950) C-83m. **½ D: Alfred E. Green. Audie Murphy, Wanda Hendrix, Dean Jagger, Burl Ives, Sara Allgood, James Arness. Capable cast elevates story of son and father on the lam from the law, trying to prove dad's innocence of crime.

Sierra Baron (1958) C-80m. ** D: James B. Clark. Brian Keith, Rick Jason, Rita Gam, Mala Powers, Steve Brodie. Western set in 19th-century California and Mexico has virtue of pleasing scenery, marred by usual land-grabbing shoot-out plot.

Sierra Passage (1951) 81m. *½ D: Frank McDonald. Wayne Morris, Lola Albright, Alan Hale, Jr., Roland Winters. Quickie oater with Morris on manhunt for father's murderer.

Sierra Stranger (1957) 74m. *½ D: Lee Sholem. Howard Duff, Dick Foran, Barton MacLane, Gloria McGhee. Tame dust-raiser of Duff intervening in a lynching, romancing McGhee.

Sign of the Cross, The (1932) 120m. *** D: Cecil B. de Mille. Fredric March, Elissa Landi, Claudette Colbert, Charles Laughton, Ian Keith,

Vivian Tobin, Nat Pendleton, Joe Bonomo. Well-meaning but heavy-handed account of Christians seeking religious freedom in Rome under Emperor Nero. Very slow going, despite fine work by March as Marcus Superbus, Laughton as Nero, and especially Colbert as the alluring Poppea. Prologue added in 1945 is no help.

Sign of the Gladiator (1959-Italian, dubbed) C-84m. *½ D: Vittorio Musy Glori. Anita Ekberg, Georges Marchal, Folco Lulli, Chelo Alonso, Jacques Sernas. Gladiator allows himself to be captured by queen of Syria so he can win her confidence.

Sign of the Pagan (1954) 92m. ** D: Douglas Sirk. Jeff Chandler, Jack Palance, Ludmilla Tcherina, Rita Gam, Jeff Morrow, Alexander Scourby. Uneven script plus Palance's overacting keep this spectacle of Attila the Hun threatening Rome from better rating.

Sign of the Ram (1948) 84m. **½ D: John Sturges. Susan Peters, Alexander Knox, Peggy Ann Garner, Dame May Whitty, Phyllis Thaxter, Ron Randell. Well-wrought drama of crippled wife using ailment to hamstring husband and children.

Silence, The (1963-Swedish, dubbed) 95m. ***½ D: Ingmar Bergman. Ingrid Thulin, Gunnel Lindblom, Hakan Jahnberg, Birger Malmsten. Stark, forceful symbolic narrative of two sisters who stop at a hotel in a North European city. One sister (Thulin) is a frustrated lesbian with no future, the other (Lindblom) a free-loving mother of a 10-year-old boy.

Silent Call, The (1961) 63m. Bomb D: John Bushelman. Gail Russell, Roger Mobley. Very mild yarn of a dog traveling cross-country to find his master in L.A.

Silent Enemy, The (1958-British) 92m. **½ D: William Fairchild. Laurence Harvey, Dawn Addams, John Clements, Michael Craig. British naval frogmen, headed by Harvey, are assigned to combat enemy counterpart during WW2; underwater sequences well handled, with some pre-THUNDERBALL gimmicks.

Silent World, The (1956-French) C-86m. *** D: Jacques-Yves Cousteau. Frederic Duman, Albert Falco, Jacques-Yves Cousteau. Award-winning documentary of ocean exploration of fauna and flora of the deep.

Silk Stockings (1957) C-117m. *** D: Rouben Mamoulian. Fred Astaire, Cyd Charisse, Janis Paige, Peter Lorre, George Tobias. Words, music, dance blend perfectly in stylish remake of Garbo's NINOTCHKA. This time Charisse is cold Russian on Paris mission, Astaire the movie director man-about-town who warms her up.

Silken Affair, The (1957-British) 96m. **½ D: Roy Kellino. David Niven, Genevieve Page, Ronald Squire, Wilfrid Hyde-White. Droll little comedy of meek accountant Niven sparked by saucy Page into some fast bookkeeping manipulations.

Silver Chalice, The (1954) C-144m. ** D: Victor Saville. Virginia Mayo, Pier Angeli, Jack Palance, Paul Newman, Walter Hampden, Joseph Wiseman, Alexander Scourby, Lorne Greene, E. G. Marshall, Natalie Wood. Newman's screen debut is undistinguished in story of Greek who designs framework for cup used at Last Supper. From Costain novel.

Silver City (1951) C-90m. ** D: Byron Haskin. Edmond O'Brien, Yvonne De Carlo, Richard Arlen, Gladys George, Barry Fitzgerald. Capable cast is above this mishmash set in the mining area of the West, with usual rivalry over gals and ore.

Silver Dollar (1932) 84m. **½ D: Alfred E. Green. Edward G. Robinson, Bebe Daniels, Aline MacMahon, Robert Warwick, Herman Bing, Bonita Granville, Marjorie Gateson. Well-mounted biography of Senator whose fortune was in silver, involved in political dispute over that commodity in Congress. Well handled by Warner Bros. stock company.

Silver Lode (1954) C-80m. **½ D: Allan Dwan. John Payne, Lizabeth Scott, Dan Duryea, Dolores Moran. Dynamic cast boosts this story of man trying to clear himself of murder charge.

Silver Queen (1942) 80m. ** D: Lloyd Bacon. George Brent, Priscilla Lane, Bruce Cabot, Lynne Overman, Eugene Pallette, Guinn Williams. Post-Civil War tinsel of devoted girl raising money for father; hubby throws it away on "worthless" silver mine.

Silver River (1948) 110m. *½ D: Raoul Walsh. Errol Flynn, Ann Sheridan, Thomas Mitchell, Bruce Bennett, Tom D'Andrea. Mediocre Flynn vehicle: Ann and Errol marry out West, he becomes corrupt.

Silver Whip, The (1953) 73m. **½
D: Harmon Jones. Dale Robertson, Rory Calhoun, Robert Wagner, Kathleen Crowley, Lola Albright. Occasionally actionful Western of outlaws vs. stage line.

Simba (1955-British) C-99m. ***½
D: Brian Desmond Hurst. Dirk Bogarde, Virginia McKenna, Basil Sydney, Donald Sinden. Fine cast in story of young man arriving in Kenya only to find brother killed by Mau Maus. Some grisly scenes.

Simon and Laura (1956-British) C-91m. **½ D: Muriel Box. Peter Finch, Kay Kendall, Muriel Pavlow, Ian Carmichael, Maurice Denham. Spunky farce involving Finch and Kendall, a married acting couple whose TV image contradicts their violent off-screen battles.

Sin Town (1942) 75m. **½ D: Ray Enright. Constance Bennett, Broderick Crawford, Anne Gwynne, Ward Bond, Andy Devine, Leo Carrillo, Patric Knowles, Hobart Bosworth. Fast-moving actioner of town in uproar after newspaper editor is killed; good cast in above-average film.

Sinbad the Sailor (1947) C-117m. ***
D: Richard Wallace. Douglas Fairbanks, Jr., Maureen O'Hara, Anthony Quinn, Walter Slezak, George Tobias, Jane Greer. Tongue-in-cheek swashbuckler, with lavish color production. Great fun.

Since You Went Away (1944) 172m. ***½ D: John Cromwell. Claudette Colbert, Jennifer Jones, Joseph Cotten, Shirley Temple, Monty Woolley, Hattie McDaniel, Nazimova, Robert Walker, Lionel Barrymore. Tearjerker-supreme with Colbert at her valiant best. Story of family suffering through WW2 with many tragedies and complications dates a bit, but still is very smooth film.

Sincerely Yours (1955) C-115m. Bomb D: Gordon Douglas. Liberace, Joanne Dru, Dorothy Malone, William Demarest, Richard Eyer, Lurene Tuttle. Remake of George Arliss' MAN WHO PLAYED GOD becomes a tinny vehicle for Liberace.

Sing and Swing (1964-British) 75m. ** D: Lance Comfort. David Hemmings, Veronica Hurst, Jennifer Moss, John Pike. Virtue of modest musical is Hemmings in lead role of messenger boy who joins pals in combo; they record a song, and find their musical career in full sway.

Sing, Baby, Sing (1936) 87m. ***
D: Sidney Lanfield. Alice Faye, Adolphe Menjou, Gregory Ratoff, Ted Healy, Patsy Kelly, Tony Martin. Pleasant musicomedy stolen by Menjou as John Barrymore prototype involved with publicity-seeking Faye. Songs: "When Did You Leave Heaven?" "You Turned The Tables On Me," title tune. Ritz Brothers are quite good in their feature-film debut.

Sing, Boy, Sing (1958) 90m. ** D: Henry Ephron. Tommy Sands, Lili Gentle, Edmond O'Brien, John McIntire. Expanded TV drama of the trials and tribulations of rock'n'roll star; energetically played by cast.

Sing You Sinners (1938) 88m. *** D: Wesley Ruggles. Bing Crosby, Fred MacMurray, Donald O'Connor, Elizabeth Patterson, Ellen Drew, John Gallaudet. Gambling gayblade Crosby can't face responsibility, despite prodding of brother MacMurray. Fine film with "I've Got A Pocketful Of Dreams" and memorable "Small Fry" number featuring young O'Connor.

Sing Your Way Home (1945) 72m. *½ D: Anthony Mann. Jack Haley, Anne Jeffreys, Marcy McGuire, Glenn Vernon. RKO Pictures mini-musical set on the high seas with youthful entertainers providing modicum of singing talent.

Sing Your Worries Away (1942) 71m. ** D: A. Edward Sutherland. June Havoc, Bert Lahr, Buddy Ebsen, Patsy Kelly, Sam Levene, Margaret Dumont, King Sisters, Alvino Rey. Mild musical-comedy as the theatrical world and racketeers clash.

Singapore (1947) 79m. ** D: John Brahm. Fred MacMurray, Ava Gardner, Roland Culver, Richard Haydn, Spring Byington. Weak drama of amnesiac Gardner forgetting her true love MacMurray.

Singapore Woman (1941) 64m. ** D: Jean Negulesco. Brenda Marshall, David Bruce, Virginia Field, Jerome Cowan, Rose Hobart, Heather Angel. Sluggish account of young rubber planter set upon helping to remove oriental curse from Marshall. Remake of DANGEROUS.

Singer Not the Song, The (1961-British) C-129m. **½ D: Roy Baker. Dirk Bogarde, John Mills, Mylene Demongeot, Eric Pohlmann. Offbeat, sluggish yarn set in Mexico involving conflict of Catholic priest and local bandit to control the town, with Demongeot in love with the clergyman.

Singin' in the Rain (1952) C-103m. **** D: Gene Kelly, Stanley Donen. Gene Kelly, Debbie Reynolds, Donald O'Connor, Jean Hagen, Cyd Charisse, Madge Blake, Millard Mitchell. Great musical spoofing Hollywood at time of early talking pictures. O'Connor at his peak doing "Make 'em Laugh," Hagen marvelous as squeaky-voiced romantic star. Songs: title tune, "My Lucky Star," "Broadway Melody," "Good Morning."

Singing Guns (1950) C-91m. *½ D: R. G. Springsteen. Vaughn Monroe, Ella Raines, Walter Brennan, Ward Bond, Billy Gray. Minor happenings in the old West with singer Monroe in straight role.

Singing Nun, The (1966) C-98m. ** D: Henry Koster. Debbie Reynolds, Ricardo Montalban, Greer Garson, Agnes Moorehead, Chad Everett, Katharine Ross, Ed Sullivan. Syrupy comic-book stuff about Belgian nun whose devotion is split between religious work and making records.

Sink the Bismarck! (1960-British) 97m. *** D: Lewis Gilbert. Kenneth More, Dana Wynter, Carl Mohner, Laurence Naismith, Geoffrey Keen, Karel Stepanek, Michael Hordern. Good war film based on fact. Exciting sea battles as British navy starts deadly hunt for famed German war vessel.

Sinner, The SEE: Desert Desperadoes.

Sinner's Holiday SEE: Christmas Eve.

Sinners in the Sun (1932) 70m. ** D: Alexander Hall. Carole Lombard, Chester Morris, Adrienne Ames, Cary Grant, Walter Byron, Alison Skipworth, Rita La Roy, Ida Lewis. Lovely Lombard learns that money isn't all in this slick, typical triangle; Grant has a bit role.

Sins of Jezebel (1953) 74m. *½ D: Reginald Le Borg. Paulette Goddard, George Nader, John Hoyt, Eduard Franz. Embarrassing low-budget costumer with Goddard miscast in title role.

Sins of Rachel Cade, The (1961) C-124m. **½ D: Gordon Douglas. Angie Dickinson, Peter Finch, Roger Moore, Woody Strode, Rafer Johnson, Juano Hernandez. Turgid melodrama set in Belgian Congo with Dickinson a missionary nurse involved in romance and native conflicts.

Sins of Rome (1954-Italian, dubbed) 75m. ** D: Riccardo Freda. Ludmilla Tcherina, Massimo Girotti, Gianna Maria Canale, Yves Vincent. Rebel slave Spartacus incites fellow prisoners to fight Roman republic. Early Italian spectacle doesn't have cheaper look of later grinds.

Siren of Atlantis (1948) 75m. Bomb D: Gregg Tallas. Maria Montez, Jean-Pierre Aumont, Dennis O'Keefe, Henry Daniell, Morris Carnovsky. Ridiculous hokum of soldiers Aumont and O'Keefe stumbling upon famed Lost Continent; Montez is the sultry queen.

Siren of Bagdad (1953) C-77m. **½ D: Richard Quine. Paul Henreid, Patricia Medina, Hans Conried, Charlie Lung. Comedy-adventure of magician and friend trying to save dancing girls in slave market. Conried provides film's best moments.

Sirocco (1951) 98m. **½ D: Curtis Bernhardt. Humphrey Bogart, Marta Toren, Lee J. Cobb, Everett Sloane, Zero Mostel. Rugged Bogart perks this yarn of gunrunning set in 1920's Syria.

Sis Hopkins (1941) 98m. **½ D: Joseph Santley. Judy Canova, Bob Crosby, Charles Butterworth, Jerry Colonna, Susan Hayward, Katherine Alexander. Fairly amusing comedy of country girl who comes to live with social uncle and attends girls' school. Even Canova is restrained!

Sister Kenny (1946) 116m. ***½ D: Dudley Nichols. Rosalind Russell, Alexander Knox, Dean Jagger, Philip Merivale, Beulah Bondi, Dorothy Peterson. Russell gives memorable performance as nurse crusading for treatment of infantile paralysis; fine drama.

Sisters, The (1938) 98m. *** D: Anatole Litvak. Errol Flynn, Bette Davis, Anita Louise, Ian Hunter, Donald Crisp, Beulah Bondi, Jane Bryan, Lee Patrick, Mayo Methot, Laura Hope Crews, Alan Hale. Davis, Louise, and Bryan are sisters whose marital problems are traced in this lavish film; Bette's got the most trouble, of course, with unreliable husband Flynn in San Francisco, 1905.

Sitting Bull (1954) C-105m. ** D: Sidney Salkow. Dale Robertson, Mary Murphy, J. Carrol Naish, Iron Eyes Cody, John Litel. Sluggish nonsense about army officer Robertson's efforts to prove he wasn't being overly helpful to the Indians.

Sitting Pretty (1933) 85m. **½ D: Harry Joe Brown. Ginger Rogers, Jack Oakie, Jack Haley, Thelma Todd, Gregory Ratoff, Lew Cody. First half is bouncy yarn of songwriters Oakie and Haley going Hollywood, meeting homespun Rogers, vamp Todd; remainder bogs down, rescued by finale "Did You Ever See A Dream Walking."

Sitting Pretty (1948) 84m. ***½ D: Walter Lang. Robert Young, Maureen O'Hara, Clifton Webb, Richard Haydn, Louise Allbritton. Webb is perfect as Mr. Belvedere, a self-centered brain who becomes a baby-sitter; scenes with bratty baby are marvelous.

Situation Hopeless—But Not Serious (1965) 97m. ** D: Gottfried Reinhardt. Alec Guinness, Michael Connors, Robert Redford, Anita Hoefer, Mady Rahl, Paul Dahnlike. Odd little comedy about German clerk Guinness holding two Americans (Redford, Connors) prisoners for years after WW2 has ended. Interesting characterization by Guinness, but a flat film.

Six Black Horses (1962) C-80m. ** D: Harry Keller. Audie Murphy, Dan Duryea, Joan O'Brien, George Wallace. O'Brien pays two men to take her across Indian lands, intending to murder gunman of duo who killed her husband.

Six Bridges to Cross (1955) 96m. **½ D: Joseph Pevney. Tony Curtis, Julia Adams, George Nader, Sal Mineo, Jay C. Flippen. Entertaining account of the Brinks robbery, tracing the events leading up to the famous heist; on-location filming in Boston.

Six Day Bike Rider (1934) 69m. **½ D: Lloyd Bacon. Joe E. Brown, Maxine Doyle, Frank McHugh, Lottie Williams. Intriguing gimmick has Brown trying to impress girlfriend by entering marathon race; good little comedy.

Six of a Kind (1934) 62m. *** D: Leo McCarey. W. C. Fields, George Burns, Gracie Allen, Charlie Ruggles, Mary Boland, Alison Skipworth. George and Gracie drive Mary and Charlie crazy traveling westward on vacation; Fields as pool-playing sheriff adds to confusion. Zany, wonderful nonsense.

633 Squadron (1964) C-101m. **½ D: Walter Grauman. Cliff Robertson, George Chakiris, Maria Perschy, Harry Andrews. Pretentious WW2 aviation film about title group's air mission to bomb German-run factory in Norway. Robertson and Chakiris are stiff-lipped throughout.

Sixty Glorious Years (1938-British) 90m. *** D: Herbert Wilcox. Anna Neagle, Anton Walbrook, C. Aubrey Smith, Walter Rilla, Charles Carson. Neagle's follow-up to VICTORIA THE GREAT is a repeat of her fine performance as England's legendary queen; good production values.

Ski Party (1965) C-90m. ** D: Alan Rafkin. Frankie Avalon, Dwayne Hickman, Deborah Walley, Yvonne Craig, Robert Q. Lewis, Bobbi Shaw, Aron Kincaid. Beach party gang puts on some clothes in this one, but the shenanigans are the same.

Skipper Surprised His Wife, The (1950) 85m. *½ D: Elliott Nugent. Robert Walker, Joan Leslie, Edward Arnold, Spring Byington, Jan Sterling. Unsurprising comedy; weak material about sailor Walker running home like ship. Good cast wasted.

Skirts Ahoy! (1952) C-109m. **½ D: Sidney Lanfield. Esther Williams, Joan Evans, Vivian Blaine, Barry Sullivan, Keefe Brasselle. Chipper cast can't buoy this worn-out story of three WACs and their boyfriends.

Skull, The (1965-British) C-83m. **½ D: Freddie Francis. Peter Cushing, Patrick Wymark, Christopher Lee, Nigel Green, Jill Bennett, Michael Gough, George Coulouris, Patrick Magee. Good cast leads needed support to questionable script of skull of Marquis De Sade that has mysterious powers.

Sky Above, The Mud Below, The (1961-French) C-90m. *** D: Pierre-Dominique Gaisseau. Narrated by William Peacock. Academy Award-winning documentary showing variety of primitive life found within confines of Dutch New Guinea.

Sky Commando (1953) 69m. *½ D: Fred F. Sears. Dan Duryea, Frances Gifford, Michael Connors, Michael Fox. Limping account of the responsibilities of being an air force officer, with usual rash of hackneyed situations.

Sky Dragon (1949) 64m. D: Lesley Selander. Roland Winters, Keye Luke, Mantan Moreland, Tim Ryan, Milburn Stone, Joel Marston, Noel Neill, Iris Adrian, Elena Verdugo, Lyle Talbot. SEE: **Charlie Chan** series.

Sky Full of Moon (1952) 73m. **
D: Norman Foster. Carleton Carpenter, Jan Sterling, Keenan Wynn, Elaine Stewart. Unassuming comedy of naive cowpoke falling in love with a not-so-innocent in Las Vegas.

Sky Murder (1940) 72m. ** D: George B. Seitz. Walter Pidgeon, Donald Meek, Kaaren Verne, Edward Ashley, Joyce Compton, Tom Conway. Pidgeon as detective Nick Carter decides to help refugee Verne in above-average private-eye yarn.

Skylark (1941) 94m. ***½ D: Mark Sandrich. Claudette Colbert, Ray Milland, Brian Aherne, Binnie Barnes, Walter Abel, Ernest Cossart, Grant Mitchell. Sophisticated romance with Aherne trying to take Claudette away from business-minded husband Milland. Stars are at their peak.

Sky's the Limit, The (1943) 89m. *** D: Edward H. Griffith. Fred Astaire, Joan Leslie, Robert Benchley, Robert Ryan, Elizabeth Patterson, Marjorie Gateson. Fred's a flier on leave who meets photographer Leslie; Benchley's dinner speech, Astaire's "One For My Baby" and "My Shining Hour" make this worthwhile.

Skyscraper Wilderness SEE: **Big City, The.**

Slander (1956) 81m. **½ D: Roy Rowland. Van Johnson, Ann Blyth, Steve Cochran, Marjorie Rambeau, Richard Eyer. Slick, superficial "inside study" of the smut magazines, focusing on their exclusive on a TV personality.

Slattery's Hurricane (1949) 83m. **½ D: Andre de Toth. Richard Widmark, Linda Darnell, Veronica Lake, John Russell, Gary Merrill. Weather-pilot Widmark, in midst of storm, thinks back on his life; Darnell and Lake are his two loves. Interesting idea.

Slaughter on Tenth Avenue (1957) 103m. *** D: Arnold Laven. Richard Egan, Jan Sterling, Dan Duryea, Julie Adams, Walter Matthau, Sam Levene. Well-handled water-front racketeer exposé, set in N.Y.C. with good supporting cast.

Slaughter Trail (1951) C-78m. ** D: Irving Allen. Brian Donlevy, Gig Young, Virginia Grey, Andy Devine. Routine narrative of outlaws killing Indians and cavalry men to get what they want.

Slave, The (1963-Italian, dubbed) C-110m. *½ D: Sergio Corbucci. Steve Reeves, Jacques Sernas, Gianna Maria Canale, Claudio Gora. Interminable Italian spectacle. Son of Spartacus learns story of father, vows vengeance. Good photography only asset.

Slave Girl (1947) C-80m. **½ D: Charles Lamont. Yvonne De Carlo, George Brent, Broderick Crawford, Albert Dekker, Lois Collier, Andy Devine. Tale of adventure with evil potentate holding Americans prisoner; not to be taken seriously, enjoyable on that scale.

Slave Ship (1937) 92m. *** D: Tay Garnett. William Baxter, Wallace Beery, Elizabeth Allan, Mickey Rooney, George Sanders, Jane Darwell, Joseph Schildkraut. Rousing drama of slave ship with fine atmosphere, good Beery-Rooney teaming, plenty of action.

Slaves of Babylon (1953) C-82m. ** D: William Castle. Richard Conte, Linda Christian, Maurice Schwartz, Michael Ansara, Julie Newmar. Jumbled biblical adventure mixed with romance. Nebuchadnezzar faces army of Israelites led by shepherd. Good cast struggles with uneven script.

Slaves of the Invisible Monster (1950) 100m. Bomb D: Fred Brannon. Richard Webb, Aline Towne, Lane Bradford, Stanley Price, John Crawford, George Meeker. With the aid of secret formula arch-criminal makes himself transparent and carries out master plan; blah actioner. Re-edited movie serial: THE INVISIBLE MONSTER.

Sleep My Love (1948) 97m. *** D: Douglas Sirk. Claudette Colbert, Robert Cummings, Don Ameche, Hazel Brooks, Rita Johnson, Raymond Burr, Ralph Morgan. Familiar territory covered by excellent cast as Ameche tries to drive wife Claudette crazy; Cummings saves her.

Sleeping Car Murder, The (1966-French, dubbed) 90m. *** D: Costa Gavras. Simone Signoret, Yves Montand, Pierre Mondy, Jean-Louis Trintinnant, Jacques Perrin, Catherine Allegret. Quick-paced, atmospheric police-chasing-mad-killer movie. Nice photography; original action good but dubbing hurts.

Sleeping City, The (1950) 85m. **½ D: George Sherman. Richard Conte, Coleen Gray, Alex Nicol, Peggy Dow. OK mystery of private eye who seeks to uncover clues to homicide and dope smuggling at a large hospital.

Sleeping Tiger, The (1954-British) 89m. *** D: Joseph Losey. Alexis Smith, Alexander Knox, Dirk Bogarde, Hugh Griffith, Patricia McCarron. Tense triangular love tale of Smith, her psychiatrist husband Knox, and Bogarde, a crook on parole to Knox.

Slender Thread, The (1965) 98m. **½ D: Sydney Pollack. Sidney Poitier, Anne Bancroft, Telly Savalas, Steven Hill, Edward Asner. Interchange between stars is the whole film in an interesting idea that doesn't fulfill potential. Bancroft takes overdose of sleeping pills, calls L. A. suicide clinic for help; Poitier tries to keep her on phone while rescue is organized.

Slight Case of Larceny, A (1953) 71m. ** D: Don Weis. Mickey Rooney, Eddie Bracken, Elaine Stewart, Marilyn Erskine. Low hijinks from Rooney and Bracken as two buddies who open a gas station, siphoning supplies from oil company's pipelines.

Slight Case of Murder, A (1938) 85m. ***½ D: Lloyd Bacon. Edward G. Robinson, Jane Bryan, Allen Jenkins, Ruth Donnelly, Willard Parker, John Litel, Edward Brophy, Harold Huber. Robinson's in peak comedy form as gangster trying to go straight, discovering corpse in his home; from Damon Runyon story.

Slightly Dangerous (1943) 94m. ** D: Wesley Ruggles. Lana Turner, Robert Walker, Walter Brennan, Dame May Whitty, Eugene Pallette, Florence Bates, Alan Mowbray, Bobby Blake. Slightly ridiculous comedy of waitress Turner who claims to be daughter of wealthy industrialist. Good cast in trivial piece of fluff.

Slightly French (1949) 81m. **½ D: Douglas Sirk. Dorothy Lamour, Don Ameche, Janis Carter, Willard Parker, Adele Jergens. Sassy musical of con-artist director Ameche passing off Lamour as French star.

Slightly Honorable (1940) 83m. *** D: Tay Garnett. Pat O'Brien, Edward Arnold, Broderick Crawford, Ruth Terry, Alan Dinehart, Eve Arden, Claire Dodd, Evelyn Keyes, Phyllis Brooks, Janet Beecher. Fast-paced mystery with snappy detective O'Brien involved in strange murders with corrupt politician Arnold.

Slightly Scarlet (1956) C-99m. **½ D: Allan Dwan. John Payne, Arlene Dahl, Rhonda Fleming, Kent Taylor, Ted de Corsia, Lance Fuller. Effective study of corruption within city officialdom; Payne involved with dynamic sister duo (Fleming, Dahl). Arlene steals the show as tipsy ex-con sister.

Slim (1937) 80m. **½ D: Ray Enright. Pat O'Brien, Henry Fonda, Stuart Erwin, Margaret Lindsay, Dick Purcell, John Litel. Interesting little story of telephone linemen with novice Fonda admiring veteran O'Brien; danger and romance combine, with good performances.

Slim Carter (1957) C-82m. ** D: Richard Bartlett. Jock Mahoney, Julie Adams, Tim Hovey, William Hopper, Barbara Hale. Mild goings-on of Mahoney becoming popular western star, aided by Adams, who loves him, and Hovey, an orphan who enters their lives.

Slime People, The (1962) 76m. ** D: Robert Hutton. Robert Hutton, Les Tremayne, Robert Burton. Diverting chiller of grimy blob monsters seeking to take over the earth.

Small Back Room, The (1949-British) 106m. *** D: Michael Powell, Emeric Pressburger. David Farrar, Jack Hawkins, Kathleen Byron, Anthony Bushell, Michael Gough. Well-modulated account of mentally disturbed WW2 veteran groping to find himself again. Retitled: HOUR OF GLORY.

Small Town Girl (1936) 90m. *** D: William Wellman. Janet Gaynor, Robert Taylor, Binnie Barnes, Lewis Stone, Andy Devine, Elizabeth Patterson, Isabel Jewell, James Stewart. Breezy romance of Gaynor trapping Taylor into marriage while he's drunk, then working to win him over sober. Musicalized in 1953 with Jane Powell. Retitled: ONE HORSE TOWN.

Small Town Girl (1953) C-93m. ** D: Leslie Kardos. Jane Powell, Farley Granger, Ann Miller, S. Z. Sakall, Billie Burke. Bland musical remake of 1937 film with Powell setting her sites on Granger, who's passing through town.

Smallest Show on Earth, The (1957-British) 80m. *** D: Basil Dearden. Bill Travers, Virginia McKenna, Margaret Rutherford, Peter Sellers, Stringer Davis. Droll comedy about young couple inheriting archaic movie house and several strange attendants as well (Sellers, Rutherford).

Smart Alecks (1942) 88m. D: Wallace Fox. Leo Gorcey, Huntz Hall, Bobby Jordan, Gabriel Dell, Maxie Rosenbloom, Gale Storm, Walter Woolf King, David Gorcey, Sunshine Sammy Morrison, Roger Pryor. SEE: Bowery Boys series.

Smart Girls Don't Talk (1948) 81m. ** D: Richard Bare. Virginia Mayo, Bruce Bennett, Helen Westcott, Robert Hutton, Tom D'Andrea. Dull drama of socialite Mayo forced to join up with racketeer.

Smart Money (1931) 90m. **½ D: Alfred E. Green. Edward G. Robinson, James Cagney, Margaret Livingston, Evalyn Knapp, Noel Francis. Known as Cagney-Robinson co-starring film, Robinson really stars, as lucky barber who becomes big-time gambler. Cagney is fine in supporting role; Boris Karloff has small part.

Smart Woman (1948) 93m. *** D: Edward A. Blatt. Brian Aherne, Constance Bennett, Barry Sullivan, Michael O'Shea, James Gleason, Otto Kruger, Iris Adrian, Isobel Elsom, Selena Royle. Lawyer Bennett doesn't let love interfere with her determined attempt to prosecute crooked D.A. and other officials.

Smash-Up, the Story of a Woman (1947) 103m. *** D: Stuart Heisler. Susan Hayward, Lee Bowman, Marsha Hunt, Eddie Albert, Carl Esmond, Carleton Young. One of Hayward's best performances in showy role of alcoholic wife of songwriter Bowman.

Smiles of a Summer Night (1955-Swedish, dubbed) 108m. *** D: Ingmar Bergman. Ulla Jacobsson, Eva Dahlbeck, Harriet Andersson, Gunnar Bjornstrand, Naima Wifstrand, Ake Fridell. Zingy yet tasteful partner-swapping tale elevated by fine acting and a story with a point of view; set at a Swedish summer country home.

Smiley (1957-Australian) 97-m. **½ D: Anthony Kimmins. Ralph Richardson, John McCallum, Chips Rafferty, Reg Lye. Soft-treading narrative of young boy who wants a bicycle, becoming entangled with drug-smugglers.

Smiley Gets a Gun (1959-Australian) C-89m. ** D: Anthony Kimmins. Sybil Thorndike, Keith Calvert, Bruce Archer, Chips Rafferty, Margaret Christensen. Easy-going account of young boy trying to win the right to have a gun.

Smilin' Through (1941) C-100m. **½ D: Frank Borzage. Jeanette MacDonald, Brian Aherne, Gene Raymond, Ian Hunter, Frances Robinson, Patrick O'Moore. Overly sentimental remake of time-worn account of romance and drama. MacDonald is orphaned girl who falls in love with son of murderer.

Smoke Signal (1955) C-88m. **½ D: Jerry Hopper. Dana Andrews, Piper Laurie, Rex Reason, Milburn Stone, William Talman. At-times zesty Western involving Indian massacre and survivors' trek downstream to escape.

Smoky (1946) C-87m. *** D: Louis King. Fred MacMurray, Anne Baxter, Burl Ives, Bruce Cabot, Esther Dale, Roy Roberts. First-rate family film from famous story of man's devotion to his horse.

Smuggler's Cove (1948) 66m. D: William Beaudine. Leo Gorcey, Huntz Hall, Gabriel Dell, Billy Benedict, David Gorcey, Martin Kosleck, Paul Harvey, Amelita Ward. SEE: Bowery Boys series.

Smuggler's Gold (1951) 64m. ** D: William Berke. Cameron Mitchell, Amanda Blake, Carl Benton Reid, Peter Thompson. Adequate drama about deep-sea diver Mitchell coping with girlfriend's (Blake's) father who's in the smuggling game.

Smuggler's Island (1951) C-75m. ** D: Edward Ludwig. Jeff Chandler, Evelyn Keyes, Philip Friend, Marvin Miller. Undemanding adventure story of diver Chandler involved with Keyes and search for sunken gold.

Snafu (1945) 82m. ** D: Jack Moss. Robert Benchley, Vera Vague, Conrad Janis, Nanette Parks, Janis Wilson, Marcia Mae Jones, Kathleen Howard, Jimmy Lloyd, Enid Markey, Eva Puig. Young C. Janis is sent home by army because of his age, but he can't get used to civilian life again; mild comedy with fine Benchley as perplexed father.

Snake Pit, The (1948) 108m. ***½ D: Anatole Litvak. Olivia de Havilland, Mark Stevens, Leo Genn, Celeste Holm, Glenn Langan, Helen Craig, Leif Erickson, Beulah Bondi, Lee Patrick, Isabel Jewell, Ruth Donnelly. Gripping film of mistreatment in mental institution lacks its original shock value but still packs a good punch, with De Havilland superb.

Sniper, The (1952) 87m. *** D: Edward Dmytryk. Adolphe Menjou, Arthur Franz, Marie Windsor, Richard Kiley, Mabel Paige. Excellent, realistically filmed drama of mentally deranged sniper (Franz) who can't help himself from killing unsuspecting women. Fine performances by all.

Sniper's Ridge (1961) 61m. ** D: John Bushelman. Jack Ging, Stanley Clements, John Goddard, Douglas Henderson. Standard Korean War battle actioner.

Snorkel, The (1958-British) 74m. **½ D: Guy Green. Peter Van Eyck, Betta St. John, Mandy Miller, Gregoire Aslan. Van Eyck ingeniously murders wife and plots to do away with stepdaughter, when she discovers his gimmick.

Snow Creature, The (1954) 70m. *½ D: W. Lee Wilder. Paul Langton, Leslie Denison, Teru Shimada, Rollin Moriyana. Often ludicrous sci-fi about abominable monster who's on the loose in the U.S.

Snow Queen, The (1959) C-70m. ** D: Phil Patton. Art Linkletter, Tammy Marihugh, Jennie Lynn. Voices of Sandra Dee, Tommy Kirk, Patty McCormack, Paul Frees, June Foray. Animated cartoon with live prologue featuring Linkletter is aimed at younger set.

Snow White and the Three Stooges (1961) C-107m. BOMB D: Walter Lang. Three Stooges, Patricia Medina, Carol Heiss, Buddy Baer, Edgar Barrier. Big mistake with skating star Heiss as Snow White, Three Stooges as . . . the Three Stooges. Comics aren't given much to do, despite title; rest of film is rather stodgy. Even kids won't be thrilled with it.

Snowball (1960-British) 69m. ** D: Pat Jackson. Gordon Jackson, Zena Walker, Kenneth Griffith, Daphne Anderson. At times intriguing B-film involving small boy's lie which led to the death of a villager.

Snows of Kilimanjaro, The (1952) C-117m. *** D: Henry King. Gregory Peck, Susan Hayward, Ava Gardner, Hildegarde Neff, Leo G. Carroll. Peck finds his forte as renowned writer coming to the end of his life in Africa, trying to decide if he found any meaning to his past; based on Hemingway story.

So Big (1953) 101m. *** D: Robert Wise. Jane Wyman, Sterling Hayden, Nancy Olson, Steve Forrest, Martha Hyer, Tommy Rettig. Superficial yet engrossing remake of Edna Ferber soaper about Wyman who brings up son to be self-sufficient.

So Ends Our Night (1941) 117m. ***½ D: John Cromwell. Fredric March, Margaret Sullavan, Frances Dee, Glenn Ford, Anna Sten, Erich von Stroheim, Allan Brett. Superior filmization of Erich Maria Remarque novel of German (March) rejecting Nazi reign, fleeing his country with hot pursuit by Axis agents.

So Evil My Love (1948) 109m. *** D: Lewis Allen. Ray Milland, Ann Todd, Geraldine Fitzgerald, Leo G. Carroll, Raymond Huntley. Excellent study of corruption; scoundrel Milland drags innocent Todd into larceny at expense of Fitzgerald.

So Goes My Love (1946) 88m. **½ D: Frank Ryan. Myrna Loy, Don Ameche, Rhys Williams, Bobby Driscoll, Richard Gaines, Molly Lamont. Amusing period comedy of fortune-hunting Loy marrying oddball inventor Ameche.

So Long At the Fair (1950-British) 90m. *** D: Terence Fisher, Anthony Darnborough. Jean Simmons, Dirk Bogarde, David Tomlinson, Honor Blackman. Tense atmospheric yarn set at the 1899 French Exposition, with Simmons searching for her brother who mysteriously disappeared.

So Proudly We Hail! (1943) 126m. *** D: Mark Sandrich. Claudette Colbert, Paulette Goddard, Veronica Lake, George Reeves, Sonny Tufts, Barbara Britton, Walter Abel. Flag-waving soaper of nurses in WW2 Pacific, headed by Colbert. Versatile cast, action scenes and teary romancing, combine well in this woman's service story. Not as stirring now as it was in 1943, when Paulette Goddard copped an Academy Award nomination.

So Red the Rose (1935) 82m. **½ D: King Vidor. Margaret Sullavan, Walter Connolly, Randolph Scott, Elizabeth Patterson, Janet Beecher, Robert Cummings, Dickie Moore. Story of Sullavan patiently waiting for Scott to return from Civil War battlefield lacks punch, but is well acted and generally enjoyable.

So This is Love (1953) C-101m. ** D: Gordon Douglas. Kathryn Grayson, Merv Griffin, Walter Abel, Rosemary DeCamp, Jeff Donnell. Glossy, empty biography of opera star Grace Moore, antiseptically played by Kathryn Grayson.

So This is New York (1948) 79m. ** D: Richard A. Fleischer. Rudy Vallee, Henry Morgan, Virginia Grey, Dona Drake, Bill Goodwin, Hugh Herbert, Leo Gorcey. Passable comedy with Vallee and Morgan involved in the ins-and-outs of N.Y.C.'s way of life.

So This is Paris (1954) C-96m. **½ D: Richard Quine. Tony Curtis, Gloria DeHaven, Gene Nelson, Corinne Calvet, Paul Gilbert, Mara Corday. Perky stars enliven this unmemorable musical of gobs on leave in France.

So Well Remembered (1947-British) 114m. *** D: Edward Dmytryk. John Mills, Martha Scott, Patricia Roc, Trevor Howard, Richard Carlson, Ivor Barnard. Based on James Hilton work, this graphic chronicle portrays struggle of newspaper editor (Mills) to rehabilitate conditions in factory town.

So You Won't Talk (1940) 69m. ** D: Edward Sedgwick. Joe E. Brown, Frances Robinson, Vivienne Osborne, Bernard Nedell, Tom Dugan. Good, typical mistaken identity comedy with bookworm Brown, a dead ringer for notorious mobster.

So Young, So Bad (1950) 91m. ** D: Bernard Vorhaus. Paul Henreid, Anne Francis, Rita Moreno, Anne Jackson, Enid Pulver, Catherine McLeod. Inexpensively filmed in N.Y.C. but still an effective study of female juvenile delinquents.

Sodom and Gomorrah (1963-Italian, dubbed) C-154m. **½ D: Robert Aldrich. Stewart Granger, Pier Angeli, Stanley Baker, Anouk Aimee, Rossana Podesta. Lavish retelling of life in biblical twin cities of sin. Strong cast, vivid scenes of vice, gore, and God's wrath, make this overly long tale of ancient Hebrews fairly entertaining.

Sofia (1948) C-82m. ** D: John Reinhardt. Gene Raymond, Sigrid Gurie, Patricia Morison, Mischa Auer. Acceptable programmer with Raymond helping nuclear scientists escape grip of Russians in Turkey.

Soft Skin, The (1964-French, dubbed) 120m. *** D: François Truffaut. Françoise Dorleac, Jean Desailly, Nelly Benedetti. Moody tale of married businessman drawn into tragic affair with beautiful airline stewardess Dorleac; smooth direction uplifts basic plot.

Soldier in the Rain (1963) 88m. *** D: Ralph Nelson. Jackie Gleason, Steve McQueen, Tuesday Weld, Tony Bill, Tom Poston. Strange film wavers from sentimental drama to high comedy. Gleason is swinging sergeant, McQueen his fervent admirer.

Soldier of Fortune (1955) C-96m. *** D: Edward Dmytryk. Clark Gable, Susan Hayward, Michael Rennie, Gene Barry, Tom Tully. Gable is hired to find Susan's husband (Barry) held captive in Hong Kong. Rennie is good as police chief.

Soldier of Love SEE: Fan Fan the Tulip.

Soldiers Three (1951) 87m. *** D: Tay Garnett. Stewart Granger, Walter Pidgeon, David Niven, Cyril Cusack, Greta Gynt. Boisterous action-adventure with light touch; an unofficial remake of GUNGA DIN with three soldiering comrades in and out of spats with each other as they battle in 19th-century India.

Solid Gold Cadillac, The (1956) 99m. *** D: Richard Quine. Judy Holliday, Paul Douglas, Fred Clark, John Williams, Arthur O'Connell. Narrated by George Burns. Dazzling Judy in hilarious comedy of small stockholder in large company becoming corporate heroine by reforming crooked board of directors. George S. Kaufman-Howard Teichman play adapted by Abe Burrows.

Solomon and Sheba (1959) C-139m. *** D: King Vidor. Yul Brynner, Gina Lollobrigida, George Sanders, Marisa Pavan, John Crawford, Alejandro Rey, Harry Andrews. Splashy spectacle with alluring Gina and stoic Brynner frolicking in biblical days. Tyrone Power died during filming, was replaced by Brynner who refilmed his early scenes.

Sombra, the Spider Woman (1947) 100m. ** D: Spencer Bennet, Fred Brannon. Bruce Edwards, Virginia Lindley, Carol Forman, Anthony Warde, Ramsay Ames. Unremarkable cliff-hanger turned feature, with title figure, daughter of Oriental archfiend, seeking to conquer the world. Re-edited movie serial: THE BLACK WIDOW.

Sombrero (1953) C-103m. *½ D: Norman Foster. Ricardo Montalban, Pier Angeli, Vittorio Gassman, Yvonne De Carlo, Nina Foch, Cyd Charisse.

Mishmash of three intertwining love tales set in Mexico.

Some Came Running (1958) C-127m. **½ D: Vincente Minnelli. Frank Sinatra, Dean Martin, Shirley MacLaine, Martha Hyer, Arthur Kennedy. James Jones novel of disillusionment in a small Southern town post-WW2 is well done, with good performances, especially by MacLaine. Fine Elmer Bernstein score. Both MacLaine and Hyer won Oscar nominations.

Some Like It Hot (1939) 64m. **½ D: George Archainbaud. Bob Hope, Shirley Ross, Una Merkel, Gene Krupa, Richard Denning. Sideshow owner Hope takes advantage of Ross to raise money for show. Airy comedy includes song "The Lady's In Love With You." Retitled RHYTHM ROMANCE.

Some Like It Hot (1959) 120m. **** D: Billy Wilder. Marilyn Monroe, Tony Curtis, Jack Lemmon, George Raft, Pat O'Brien, Joe E. Brown, Nehemiah Persoff, Joan Shawlee, Mike Mazurki. Terrific Billy Wilder comedy. Two musicians fleeing gangsters join all-girl band heading for Miami in 1920's. Monroe croons "Running Wild" and courts Curtis, who is in rare form. Brown has film's now-classic closing line.

Some May Live (1967) 105m. ** D: Vernon Sewell. Joseph Cotten, Martha Hyer, Peter Cushing, John Ronane. Unexciting suspenser made for TV set in contemporary Saigon with Cotten a U.S. intelligence officer setting a trap for the espionage agent within his department. Retitled: IN SAIGON, SOME MAY LIVE.

Somebody Loves Me (1952) C-97m. ** D: Irving S. Brecher. Betty Hutton, Ralph Meeker, Adele Jergens, Robert Keith. Schmaltzy vaudeville biography of troupers Blossom Seely and Benny Fields with no originality and not much entertainment either.

Somebody Up There Likes Me (1956) 113m. ***½ D: Robert Wise. Paul Newman, Pier Angeli, Everett Sloane, Eileen Heckart, Sal Mineo, Steve McQueen. Top biography of Rocky Graziano's rise from N.Y.C. sidewalks to arena success with fine Newman performance.

Something for the Birds (1952) 81m. ** D: Robert Wise. Patricia Neal, Victor Mature, Edmund Gwenn, Larry Keating. Mild romantic froth, with Mature and Neal on opposite sides of issue in lobbying for bird sanctuary protection.

Something for the Boys (1944) C-85m. **½ D: Lewis Seiler. Perry Como, Carmen Miranda, Vivian Blaine, Michael O'Shea, Phil Silvers, Cara Williams, Sheila Ryan. Pleasant, slick 20th Century-Fox musical with diverting Cole Porter score, set in Southern plantation recruited as home for soldiers' wives.

Something in the Wind (1947) 89m. **½ D: Irving Pichel. Deanna Durbin, Donald O'Connor, Charles Winninger, Helena Carter. Mild comedy of errors with Durbin as female disk jockey who sings too. Easy to take, amusing.

Something of Value (1957) 113m. *** D: Richard Brooks. Rock Hudson, Dana Wynter, Sidney Poitier, Wendy Hiller, Frederick O'Neal. Robert Ruark novel transformed to screen, sharply detailing brutal Mau Mau warfare in Kenya. Hudson gives fine performance as British colonial farmer; Hiller is memorable as widow struggling to retain dignity and spirit.

Something to Live For (1952) 89m. **½ D: George Stevens. Joan Fontaine, Ray Milland, Teresa Wright, Douglas Dick, Rudy Lee. Turgid melodrama trying to be another LOST WEEKEND. Fontaine is alcoholic in love with Milland, but he's married.

Something to Shout About (1943) 93m. ** D: Gregory Ratoff. Don Ameche, Janet Blair, Jack Oakie, Hazel Scott, William Gaxton, Veda Ann Borg, Cobina Wright Jr. Another Broadway backstage show-biz tale, a wispy excuse for soft-pedaled ensemble and solo numbers.

Something Wild (1961) 112m. **½ D: Jack Garfein. Carroll Baker, Ralph Meeker, Mildred Dunnock, Martin Kosleck. Bizarre study of rape-victim Baker falling in love with would-be attacker Meeker, coming to rational understanding with mother Dunnock. N.Y.C. location scenes perk melodramatic soaper.

Somewhere I'll Find You (1942) 108m. **½ D: Wesley Ruggles. Lana Turner, Clark Gable, Robert Sterling, Reginald Owen, Lee Patrick, Rags Ragland, Patricia Dane. Turner and Gable are improbable as WW2 war correspondents, but their love scenes between battles are most convincing.

Somewhere In the Night (1946) 100m. **½ D: Joseph L. Mankiewicz. John

Hodiak, Nancy Guild, Lloyd Nolan, Richard Conte, Josephine Hutchinson, Fritz Kortner, Sheldon Leonard. Satisfactory drama of amnesiac Hodiak trying to discover his true identity; not up to later Mankiewicz efforts.

Son-Daughter, The (1932) 79m. **½ D: Clarence Brown. Ramon Novarro, Helen Hayes, Warner Oland, Lewis Stone, Ralph Morgan. Dated drama of pre-WW1 Chinatown, notable mainly for Hayes performance as Chinese girl sold as slave. Good cast, interesting characterizations.

Son of a Gunfighter (1966-Spanish, dubbed) C-92m. *½ D: Paul Landres. Russ Tamblyn, Kieron Moore, James Philbrook, Fernando Rey. Title tells all in oater peppered with Anglo-Saxon actors and bits of the Old West.

Son of a Sailor (1933) 73m. **½ D: Lloyd Bacon. Joe E. Brown, Jean Muir, Thelma Todd, Frank McHugh, Johnny Mack Brown, Sheila Terry. Joe blunders into espionage and recovers stolen Navy plans; always-vivacious Todd lends fine support.

Son of Ali Baba (1952) C-75m. ** D: Kurt Neumann. Tony Curtis, Piper Laurie, Susan Cabot, Victor Jory, Hugh O'Brian. Caliph uses princess Laurie to obtain treasure of Ali Baba. After father is captured, son appears and wins hand of princess. Good sets, fair acting.

Son of Belle Starr (1953) 70m. ** D: Frank McDonald. Keith Larsen, Dona Drake, Peggie Castle, Regis Toomey. Fictional Western history is excuse for another shootout tale.

Son of Captain Blood, The (1962-Italian, dubbed) 90m. **½ D: Tullio Demichelli. Sean Flynn, Ann Todd, Alessandra Panaro, Jose Nieto. Flynn is not quite at ease in title role, but film is rousing account of Blood's old crew helping to combat the evil governor of Port Royal.

Son of Dr. Jekyll, The (1951) 77m. *½ D: Seymour Friedman. Louis Hayward, Jody Lawrance, Alexander Knox, Lester Matthews. Son discovers formula father used to become Hyde. Poorly scripted, produced. Cast manages to save film from complete ruin.

Son of Dracula (1943) 78m. **½ D: Robert Siodmak. Robert Paige, Louise Allbritton, Lon Chaney, Evelyn Ankers, Frank Craven, J. Edward Bromberg. Following in the old man's footsteps, Count Alucard (spell backwards) terrorizes a community, mostly the female population. Above-average horror.

Son of Frankenstein (1939) 95m. *** D: Rowland V. Lee. Basil Rathbone, Boris Karloff, Bela Lugosi, Lionel Atwill, Emma Dunn, Josephine Hutchinson, Edgar Norton. Rathbone follows in father's footsteps, revives monster (Karloff) with help of gruesome Ygor (Lugosi). Elaborate, talky production, but first-rate horror vehicle.

Son of Fury (1942) 98m. *** D: John Cromwell. Tyrone Power, Gene Tierney, George Sanders, Frances Farmer, Roddy McDowall, Kay Johnson, John Carradine, Elsa Lanchester, Harry Davenport, Dudley Digges, Ethel Griffies. Good costumer about Sanders shunning nephew Power, who flees to desert isle to plot revenge. Tierney's on the island too.

Son of Kong (1933) 70m. **½ D: Ernest B. Schoedsack. Robert Armstrong, Helen Mack, Victor Wong, John Marston, Lee Kohlmar. Disappointing sequel to KING KONG. Special effects and variations on the giant ape scenes are interesting, though.

Son of Lassie (1945) C-102m. **½ D: S. Sylvan Simon. Peter Lawford, Donald Crisp, June Lockhart, Nigel Bruce, William Severn, Leon Ames, Fay Helm, Donald Curtis, Nils Asther, Helen Koford (Terry Moore). Fairly good follow-up to LASSIE COME HOME unfortunately gets the collie mixed up in war episodes.

Son of Monte Cristo, The (1940) 102m. *** D: Rowland V. Lee. Louis Hayward, Joan Bennett, George Sanders, Florence Bates, Lionel Royce, Montagu Love. Nothing new in big-scale swashbuckler, but very well done with Hayward battling Sanders and vying for Bennett's hand.

Son of Paleface (1952) C-95m. **½ D: Frank Tashlin. Bob Hope, Jane Russell, Roy Rogers, Bill Williams, Harry Von Zell, Iron Eyes Cody. Wisecracking follow-up to PALEFACE, with Hope playing title role in Western spoof; he gets to sally with shapely Russell again.

Son of Robin Hood, The (1959-British) C-81m. ** D: George Sherman. David Hedison, June Laverick, David Farrar, Marius Goring, George Coulouris. Bland forest tale continuing the legend of merry men led by Robin's descendant.

Son of Sinbad (1955) **C-88m.** ***½ D:** Ted Tetzlaff. Dale Robertson, Sally Forrest, Lili St. Cyr, Vincent Price. Limp Arabian Nights adventure. Sinbad, captured by caliph, forced to performed wonders to win freedom and save Baghdad from evil Tamerlane.

Son of Spartacus (1962-Italian, dubbed) **C-102m.** **** D:** Sergio Corbucci. Steve Reeves, Jacques Sernas, Gianna Maria Canale, Claudio Gora. Talky spectacle with Reeves in title role trying to right wrongs in ancient Rome.

Son of the Gods (1930) **82m.** **** D:** Frank Lloyd. Richard Barthelmess, Constance Bennett, Dorothy Matthews, Dickie Moore. Harmless drama. Barthelmess journeys to Europe for college education but finds it no better than home. Fair cast trapped in hokey material.

Son of the Sheik (1926) **60m.** ***** D:** George Fitzmaurice. Rudolph Valentino, Vilma Banky, Agnes Ayres, Karl Dane, Bull Montana. Sequel to THE SHEIK contains flavorful account of desert leader who falls in love with dancing girl Banky. Silent film is romantic classic if taken in proper spirit.

Song for Miss Julie, A (1945) **69m.** *½ D:** William Rowland. Shirley Ross, Barton Hepburn, Jane Farrar, Roger Clark, Cheryl Walker, Elisabeth Risdon. Low-budget tale of woman who exposes family's past, then tries to cover it up again.

Song Is Born, A (1948) **C-113m.** ***½ D:** Howard Hawks. Danny Kaye, Virginia Mayo, Steve Cochran, Benny Goodman, Louis Armstrong, Charlie Barnet, Lionel Hampton. Below par musical remake of BALL OF FIRE has Kaye and Mayo supported by jazz greats.

Song of Bernadette, The (1943) **156m.** ***** D:** Henry King. Jennifer Jones, William Eythe, Charles Bickford, Vincent Price, Lee J. Cobb, Anne Revere, Gladys Cooper. Overlong but excellent story of religious French girl in 1800's who sees great vision, incurs local wrath because of it. Winner of many Oscars including Best Actress for Jones in lead role.

Song of India (1949) **77m.** *** D:** Albert S. Rogell. Sabu, Gail Russell, Turhan Bey, Anthony Caruso, Aminta Dyne. Well-meaning Sabu releases jungle animals callously trapped by royal family; typical jungle escapist adventure.

Song of Love (1947) **119m.** ***½ D:** Clarence Brown. Katharine Hepburn, Paul Henreid, Robert Walker, Henry Daniell, Leo G. Carroll, Gigi Perreau, Tala Birell, Henry Stephenson, Else Janssen. Classy production but slow-moving story of Clara Schuman (Hepburn), her composer husband (Henreid) and good friend Brahms (Walker).

Song of Russia (1943) **107m.** ***½ D:** Gregory Ratoff. Robert Taylor, Susan Peters, John Hodiak, Robert Benchley, Felix Bressart, Joan Lorring, Darryl Hickman, Jacqueline White. Conductor Taylor visiting Russia falls in love with native girl Peters. Then-topical film overpraised Russia's WW2 efforts. Fine musical score.

Song of Scheherazade (1947) **C-106m.** *** D:** Walter Reisch. Yvonne De Carlo, Brian Donlevy, Jean-Pierre Aumont, Eve Arden, Philip Reed. Colorful tripe about Rimsky-Korsakov's true inspiration, a dancing girl (De Carlo).

Song of Songs (1933) **90m.** ***** D:** Rouben Mamoulian. Marlene Dietrich, Brian Aherne, Lionel Atwill, Alison Skipworth, Hardie Albright, Helen Freeman. Set in 19th-century Germany, improbable romance tells of country maid Dietrich falling in love with sculptor Aherne, but marrying villainous Count Atwill. Dietrich is all, whether sulking or singing: "Johnny," "You Are My Song Of Songs."

Song of Surrender (1949) **93m.** *** D:** Mitchell Leisen. Wanda Hendrix, Claude Rains, Macdonald Carey, Andrea King, Henry O'Neill, Elizabeth Patterson. Mild turn-of-the-century tale of young woman (Hendrix) and older husband Rains.

Song of the Islands (1942) **C-75m.** ***½ D:** Walter Lang. Betty Grable, Victor Mature, Jack Oakie, Thomas Mitchell, Billy Gilbert. Mature is new arrival to Pacific isle, Grable local girl he feuds with and romances. Slick musical fluff.

Song of the Open Road (1944) **93m.** ***½ D:** S. Sylvan Simon. Edgar Bergen, W. C. Fields, Jane Powell, Bonita Granville, Reginald Denny, Rose Hobart, Sammy Kaye Orchestra. Showcase for young Powell's vocal talents is fairly good, with token appearances by Fields and nemesis Charlie McCarthy (Bergen).

Song of the Sarong (1945) 65m. ** D: Harold Young. William Gargan, Nancy Kelly, Eddie Quillan. Gargan is involved in pearl-snatching for island natives; moderate production values.

Song of the Thin Man (1947) 86m. D: Edward Buzzell. William Powell, Myrna Loy, Keenan Wynn, Dean Stockwell, Philip Reed, Patricia Morison, Leon Ames, Gloria Grahame, Marie Windsor, Jayne Meadows. SEE: Thin Man series.

Song to Remember, A (1945) C-113m. **½ D: Charles Vidor. Paul Muni, Merle Oberon, Cornel Wilde, Stephen Bekassy, Nina Foch, George Coulouris, Sig Arno. Colorful but superficial biography of Chopin with exaggerated Muni as his mentor, lovely Oberon as Georges Sand; good music, frail plot. Wilde was nominated for an Oscar, though.

Song Without End (1960) C-141m. **½ D: Charles Vidor. Dirk Bogarde, Capucine, Genevieve Page, Patricia Morison, Ivan Desny, Martita Hunt, Lou Jacobi. Beautiful music (scoring won an Oscar) submerged by dramatics of composer's Franz Liszt's life. Bogarde tries; settings are well-appointed.

Sons and Lovers (1960) 103m. *** D: Jack Cardiff. Trevor Howard, Dean Stockwell, Wendy Hiller, Mary Ure, Heather Sears, William Lucas. Grim D. H. Lawrence story of sensitive youth Stockwell egged on by mother to make something of his life, away from coal-mining town and drunken father Howard. Both the film and Miss Ure were nominated for Oscars.

Sons O' Guns (1936) 82m. ** D: Lloyd Bacon. Joe E. Brown, Joan Blondell, Eric Blore, Winifred Shaw, Robert Barrat, Beverly Roberts, Craig Reynolds. Stars spark strained comedy of Brown joining the Army, sent to France where Blondell saves him from being shot as spy.

Sons of Katie Elder, The (1965) C-112m. *** D: Henry Hathaway. John Wayne, Dean Martin, Martha Hyer, Michael Anderson, Jr., Earl Holliman, Jeremy Slate, James Gregory, George Kennedy. Typical John Wayne action Western with Duke, Holliman, Anderson, and Martin the rowdy sons of frontier woman Katie Elder, who set out to avenge her death. Lively fun.

Sons of the Desert (1934) 69m. *** D: William A. Seiter. Stan Laurel, Oliver Hardy, Charley Chase, Mae Busch, Dorothy Christy, Lucien Littlefield. L&H's best feature-film; duo sneaks up to fraternal convention without telling the wives; then the fun begins, with Chase as hilariously obnoxious conventioneer.

Sooky (1931) 85m. **½ D: Norman Taurog. Jackie Cooper, Jackie Coogan, Jackie Searl, Enid Bennett, Helen Jerome Eddy, Oscar Apfel. Entertaining but dated film of two young boys who become fast friends and engage in various escapades. Cooper is delightful as always.

Sorceress, The (1955-French, dubbed) 97m. **½ D: Andre Michel. Maurice Ronet, Marina Vlady, Nicole Courcel, Michel Etcheverry. Bizarre yarn of femme fatale Vlady and her beguiling alliance with Ronet.

Sorority Girl (1957) 60m. *½ D: Roger Corman. Susan Cabot, Dick Miller, Barbara Crane, Fay Baker. Tawdry account of college gal involved in absurd shenanigans on the campus.

Sorrowful Jones (1949) 88m. **½ D: Sidney Lanfield. Bob Hope, Lucille Ball, William Demarest, Mary Jane Saunders, Bruce Cabot, Thomas Gomez. Average racetrack comedy, actually a remake of 1934 LITTLE MISS MARKER and hardly as good.

Sorry, Wrong Number (1948) 89m. *** D: Anatole Litvak. Barbara Stanwyck, Burt Lancaster, Ann Richards, Wendell Corey, Ed Begley, Leif Erikson. Not up to original radio thriller, movie adaptation is still tense study of woman overhearing murder plan on telephone, discovering she's to be the victim. Stanwyck won an Oscar nomination for her bravura performance.

Soul of a Monster, The (1944) 61m. Bomb D: Will Jason. Rose Hobart, George Macready, Jim Bannon, Jeanne Bates. Other-worldly Hobart has strange control over doctor Macready.

Souls at Sea (1937) 92m. *** D: Henry Hathaway. Gary Cooper, George Raft, Frances Dee, Olympe Bradna, Henry Wilcoxon, Harry Carey, Robert Cummings, Joseph Schildkraut, George Zucco. Fine actioner with Cooper and Raft struggling to save lives during ship tragedy; Cooper wrongly accused of irresponsibility. The stars make good team in entertaining tale.

Sound and the Fury, The (1959) C-115m. **½ D: Martin Ritt. Yul Brynner, Joanne Woodward, Margaret Leighton, Stuart Whitman, Ethel Waters, Jack Warden, Albert Dekker. Strange adaptation of Willian Faulkner novel becomes plodding tale of girl seeking independence from strict family rule in the South.

Sound of Fury, The (1951) 85m. **½ D: Cyril Endfield. Frank Lovejoy, Lloyd Bridges, Richard Carlson, Katherine Locke, Adele Jergens, Irene Vernon. Taut suspenser as manhunt closes in on kidnapper who killed his victim. Retitled: TRY AND GET ME.

Sound Off (1952) C-83m. ** D: Richard Quine. Mickey Rooney, Anne James, John Archer, Sammy White. Too-often unimaginative army comedy with Rooney a performer who's drafted and can't stop showing off.

South of Pago Pago (1940) 98m. ** D: Alfred E. Green. Victor McLaglen, Jon Hall, Frances Farmer, Olympe Bradna, Gene Lockhart. Juvenile actioner of pirates stealing natives' supply of pearls, encountering local hostility; Farmer is properly sultry.

South of St. Louis (1949) C-88m. **½ D: Ray Enright. Joel McCrea, Alexis Smith, Zachary Scott, Dorothy Malone, Alan Hale, Victor Jory, Bob Steele. Fairly good Western with rival ranchers Scott and McCrea fighting over land and for the same girl, Malone.

South Sea Sinner (1950) 88m. ** D: H. Bruce Humberstone. Macdonald Carey, Shelley Winters, Luther Adler, Frank Lovejoy, Liberace. Muddled melodrama involving fugitive from justice being intimidated by those on island who knew his past; Winters is blowsy cafe singer.

South Sea Woman (1953) 99m. **½ D: Arthur Lubin. Burt Lancaster, Virginia Mayo, Chuck Connors, Arthur Shields, Paul Burke. Murky tropical isle story of love and deceit with soldier Lancaster sparking with Mayo.

Southern Yankee, A (1948) 90m. *** D: Edward Sedgwick. Red Skelton, Brian Donlevy, Arlene Dahl, George Coulouris, Lloyd Gough, John Ireland, Charles Dingle, Joyce Compton. Hilarious Skelton comedy set during Civil War with Red a bumbling Yankee spy down South. Reminiscent of silent comedies, since Buster Keaton devised many of the film's gags.

Southerner, The (1945) 91m. **** D: Jean Renoir. Zachary Scott, Betty Field, Beulah Bondi, Bunny Sunshine, Jay Gilpin, Estelle Taylor, Percy Kilbride, Blanche Yurka. Superb drama of family struggling to make farmland self-supporting against serious odds.

Southside 1-1000 (1950) 73m. **½ D: Boris Ingster. Don DeFore, Andrea King, George Tobias, Barry Kelley. Straightforward narrative of federal agent capturing counterfeiters.

Southwest Passage (1954) C-82m. ** D: Ray Nazarro. Joanne Dru, Rod Cameron, John Ireland, John Dehner, Guinn Williams, Mark Hanna. Familiar tale of bank robber and gal joining up with settlers heading west, staving off Indian attack.

Space Children, The (1958) 69m. *½ D: Jack Arnold. Michel Ray, Adam Williams, Peggy Webber, Johnny Washbrook, Jackie Coogan. Pacifist-oriented sci-fi located at missile test center on Pacific Island; badly done.

Space Master X-7 (1958) 70m. ** D: Edward Bernds. Bill Williams, Lyn Thomas, Robert Ellis, Paul Frees. OK sci-fi: space missile returning to earth carries hidden fungus cargo, which could destroy civilization.

Spaceflight Ic-1 (1965-British) 65m. **½ D: Bernard Knowles. Bill Williams, Norma West, John Cairney, Linda Marlowe, Jeremy Longhurst. Fair sci-fi has a few imaginative touches.

Spaceways (1953-British) 76m. *½ D: Terence Fisher. Howard Duff, Eva Bartok, Andrew Osborn, Alan Wheatley. Cheapie sci-fi about space missile and man's flight into outer stratosphere.

Spanish Affair (1958-Spanish) C-95m. ** D. Don Siegel. Richard Kiley, Carmen Sevilla, Jose Guardiola, Jesus Tordesillas. Virtually a travelogue pegged on slight plot of Kiley, American architect, traveling in Iberia, falling in love with local gal; nice scenery.

Spanish Gardener, The (1956-British) C-95m. ** D: Philip Leacock. Dirk Bogarde, Maureen Swanson, Jon Whiteley, Cyril Cusack, Bernard

Lee. A. J. Cronin novel nicely filmed as title figure (Bogarde) tries to uplift ideals of his employer's young son.

Spanish Main, The (1945) C-100m. **½ D: Frank Borzage. Paul Henreid, Maureen O'Hara, Walter Slezak, Binnie Barnes, John Emery, Barton MacLane. Colorful escapism with swashbuckling pirate Henreid foiling villain Slezak, winning fair maiden O'Hara.

Spare The Rod (1961-British) 93m. **½ D: Leslie Norman. Max Bygraves, Donald Pleasence, Jean Anderson, Betty McDowall, Peter Reynolds, Geoffrey Keen. Bygraves is idealistic teacher in tough London school trying to communicate with pupils and cope with the system; OK drama.

Spartacus (1960) C-196m. ***½ D: Stanley Kubrick. Kirk Douglas, Laurence Olivier, Jean Simmons, Tony Curtis, Charles Laughton, Peter Ustinov, John Gavin, Nina Foch, Herbert Lom, John Ireland, Charles McGraw, Woody Strode. Great spectacle based on historical fact. Douglas heads huge cast as leader of slaves rebelling against Republican Rome. Beautiful Alex North score.

Spawn of the North (1938) 130m. *** D: Henry Hathaway. George Raft, Henry Fonda, Dorothy Lamour, Louise Platt, John Barrymore, Akim Tamiroff, Lynne Overman. Action-packed film of Canadian fisheries with good cast; Lamour surprisingly good, Barrymore amusing as talky newspaperman.

Speaking of Murder (1959-French, dubbed) 80m. **½ D: Gilles Grangier. Jean Gabin, Annie Girardot, Paul Frankeur, Lino Ventura. Sensibly handled drama of brothers involved with life of crime.

Special Agent (1935) 78m. **½ D: William Keighley. Bette Davis, George Brent, Ricardo Cortez, Jack LaRue, Henry O'Neill. Programmer about Brent using Davis to get low-down on racketeer Cortez.

Special Delivery (1955) 86m. ** D: John Brahm. Joseph Cotten, Eva Bartok, Niall MacGinnis, Rene Deltgen. Mild froth with Cotten on U.S. diplomatic staff posted in Iron Curtain country, dealing with an abandoned baby and curvaceous refugee Bartok.

Specter of the Rose (1946) 90m. *** D: Ben Hecht. Judith Anderson, Michael Chekhov, Ivan Kirov, Viola Essen, Lionel Stander, Charles "Red" Marshall. Stagy but truly unusual Hecht film of insane ballet dancer accused of murder and woman (Anderson) who loves him nevertheless.

Speed Crazy (1959) 75m. BOMB D: William Hole, Jr. Brett Halsey, Yvonne Lime, Charles Wilcox, Slick Slavin. Programmer sports car racing yarn, tied in with homicide and police hunt for killer.

Spellbound (1945) 111m. *** D: Alfred Hitchcock. Ingrid Bergman, Gregory Peck, Leo G. Carroll, John Emery, Michael Chekhov, Wallace Ford, Rhonda Fleming, Bill Goodwin, Regis Toomey. Engaging tale of psychiatrist Bergman trying to uncover Peck's hangups; Dali dream sequences, twist ending are highlights.

Spencer's Mountain (1963) C-119m. ** D: Delmer Daves. Henry Fonda, Maureen O'Hara, James MacArthur, Donald Crisp, Wally Cox. Mawkish sudser about Wyoming landowner Fonda who keeps promising to build another family house. Good cast stuck with inferior script.

Spider, The (1945) 62m. ** D: Robert D. Webb. Richard Conte, Faye Marlowe, Kurt Kreuger, John Harvey, Ann Savage, Cara Williams, Martin Kosleck. Programmer mystery yarn from 20th Century-Fox, not allowing Conte to be his violent best.

Spider and the Fly, The (1951-British) 87m. **½ D: Robert Hamer. Guy Rolfe, Nadia Gray, Eric Portman, Maurice Denham, James Hayter, Arthur Lowe. Effective drama of Gallic law enforcer and British crook teaming up to retrieve government document; good interplay between cast members.

Spider Woman SEE: **Sherlock Holmes and the Spider Woman.**

Spider Woman Strikes Back, The (1946) 59m. BOMB D: Arthur Lubin. Brenda Joyce, Gale Sondergaard, Kirby Grant, Rondo Hatton, Milburn Stone, Hobart Cavanaugh. Pitiful waste of fine actress Sondergaard in nonsense about evil Spider woman; very campy.

Spies A Go Go SEE: **Nasty Rabbit, The.**

Spin A Dark Web (1956-British) 76m. *½ D: Vernon Sewell. Faith Domergue, Lee Patterson, Rona Anderson, Martin Benson. Feeble sensationalism with Domergue queen of the racketeers.

Spiral Road, The (1962) C-145m. *** D: Robert Mulligan. Rock Hudson, Burl Ives, Gena Rowlands, Geoffrey Keen. Overlong but interesting story of dedicated jungle doctor Hudson curing leprosy outbreak in Batavia.

Spiral Staircase, The (1946) 83m. ***1/2 D: Robert Siodmak. Dorothy McGuire, George Brent, Ethel Barrymore, Kent Smith, Rhonda Fleming, Gordon Oliver, Elsa Lanchester, Sara Allgood. Superb Hitchcock-like thriller with unforgettable performance by McGuire as mute servant in eerie household which is harboring a killer.

Spirit of Culver (1939) 89m. ** D: Joseph Santley. Jackie Cooper, Freddie Bartholomew, Tim Holt, Andy Devine, Gene Reynolds, Jackie Moran. All the usual prep-academy clichés adapted for military school setting with Cooper and Bartholomew predictable.

Spirit of St. Louis, The (1957) C-138m. **** D: Billy Wilder. James Stewart, Patricia Smith, Murray Hamilton, Marc Connelly. Long but inventive presentation of Lindbergh's flight across the Atlantic is mainly a tour de force by Stewart, backed by good Franz Waxman music score.

Spirit of West Point, The (1947) 77m. **1/2 D: Ralph Murphy. Felix 'Doc' Blanchard, Glenn Davis, Tom Harmon, Robert Shayne, Anne Nagel, Alan Hale, Jr. Good saga of West Point's football heroes, played by themselves; realistically done.

Spiritualist, The SEE: Amazing Mr. X, The.

Spitfire (1934) 88m. *** D: John Cromwell. Katharine Hepburn, Robert Young, Ralph Bellamy, Martha Sleeper, Sara Haden, Sidney Toler. Hepburn as backwoods girl in love with married Young is effective. Bellamy in the background again.

Spitfire (1942-British) 90m. *** D: Leslie Howard. Leslie Howard, David Niven, Rosamund John, Roland Culver, Anne Firth, David Horne, J. H. Roberts. Howard is man who developed the ace fighting-plane Spitfire and saw it become one of the Allies' most valuable WW2 assets. Good biographical drama. Original title: FIRST OF THE FEW.

Splendor (1935) 77m. **1/2 D: Elliott Nugent. Miriam Hopkins, Joel McCrea, Paul Cavanagh, Helen Westley, Billie Burke, Katherine Alexander, David Niven. Familiar story of McCrea's family upset when he loves poor-girl Hopkins instead of an upper-class young lady; based on Rachel Crothers' story.

Splendor in the Grass (1961) C-124m. *** D: Elia Kazan. Natalie Wood, Warren Beatty, Pat Hingle, Audrey Christie, Sean Garrison, Sandy Dennis, Phyllis Diller, Barbara Loden, Zohra Lampert. Sentimental sudser by William Inge about emotionally broken girl (Wood) rebuilding her life; set in late 1920's Midwest.

Split Second (1953) 85m. **1/2 D: Dick Powell. Stephen McNally, Alexis Smith, Jan Sterling, Paul Kelly, Richard Egan. Most capable cast elevates contrived story of escaped convict McNally holding several people hostage at a bomb-testing site.

Spoilers, The (1942) 87m. **1/2 D: Ray Enright. Marlene Dietrich, Randolph Scott, John Wayne, Margaret Lindsay, Harry Carey, Richard Barthelmess. Retelling of famous Yukon tale has good cast but thuds out as average Western, with Dietrich as stereotyped saloon gal.

Spoilers, The (1955) C-84m. **1/2 D: Jesse Hibbs. Anne Baxter, Jeff Chandler, Rory Calhoun, Barbara Britton, Raymond Walburn. Fifth filming of Rex Beach's Klondike actioner; elaborate fight scene intact.

Spoilers of the Forest (1957) C-68m. ** D: Joseph Kane. Rod Cameron, Vera Ralston, Ray Collins, Hillary Brooke, Edgar Buchanan. Another timberland Western, with Cameron a tree-cutting foreman, romancing Ralston.

Spook Busters (1946) 68m. D: William Beaudine. Leo Gorcey, Huntz Hall, Douglass Dumbrille, Janis Chandler, Bobby Jordan, Gabriel Dell, Billy Benedict. SEE: Bowery Boys series.

Spook Chasers (1957) 62m. D: George Blair. Huntz Hall, Stanley Clements, Percy Helton, Darlene Fields, Bill Henry, Pierre Watkin. SEE: Bowery Boys series.

Spooks Run Wild (1941) 69m. D: Phil Rosen. Bela Lugosi, Ava Gardner, Huntz Hall, Leo Gorcey, Bobby Jordan, Sunshine Sammy Morrison, David O'Brien, Dennis Moore. SEE: Bowery Boys series.

Spring in Park Lane (1947-British)

100m. **½ D: Herbert Wilcox. Anna Neagle, Michael Wilding, Tom Wallis, Marjorie Fielding, Nicholas Phipps, Josephine Fitzgerald. Stylish romance story of Wilding courting Neagle, his employer's niece.

Spring Madness (1938) 80m. **½ D: S. Sylvan Simon. Maureen O'Sullivan, Lew Ayres, Ruth Hussey, Burgess Meredith, Ann Morriss, Joyce Compton, Jacqueline Wells, Frank Albertson. Collegiate romance between O'Sullivan and brainy Ayres, elevated by strong cast. Enjoyable fluff.

Spring Parade (1940) 89m. *** D: Henry Koster. Deanna Durbin, Robert Cummings, Mischa Auer, Henry Stephenson, Butch and Buddy, Anne Gwynne. Delightful Austrian fluff with Durbin romancing Cummings, working for baker S. Z. Sakall, dancing with wacky Auer, and singing, of course.

Spring Reunion (1957) 79m. ** D: Robert Pirosh. Betty Hutton, Dana Andrews, Jean Hagen, James Gleason, Laura LaPlante, George Chandler. Potentially good soaper marred by low-budget production: Andrews and Hutton revive old memories at high school reunion and try to plan new future together; Hagen has some fine comic moments. Silent star LaPlante plays Hutton's mother.

Springfield Rifle (1952) C-93m. **½ D: Andre de Toth. Gary Cooper, Phyllis Thaxter, David Brian, Lon Chaney, Paul Kelly. Unmemorable Cooper fare, with Gary joining up with outlaws to determine who's stealing government arms.

Springtime in the Rockies (1942) C-91m. **½ D: Irving Cummings. Betty Grable, Carmen Miranda, Cesar Romero, Charlotte Greenwood, Edward Everett Horton, Jackie Gleason. Attractive cast in show biz musical; Harry James and band provide music, including "I Had The Craziest Dream."

Sputnik (1958-French) 85m. ** D: Jean Dreville. Noel-Noel, Denise Gray, Noel Roquevert, Mischa Auer. Mild Cold War spoof involving Russian missile experiment which has backfired and naive Frenchman caught in the red trap. Retitled: A DOG, A MOUSE AND A SPUTNIK.

Spy Chasers (1955) 61m. D: Edward Bernds. Leo Gorcey, Huntz Hall, Bernard Gorcey, Leon Askin, Sig Ruman, Veola Vonn, Bennie Bartlett, Richard Benedict. SEE: **Bowery Boys** series.

Spy Hunt (1950) 75m. **½ D: George Sherman. Howard Duff, Marta Toren, Robert Douglas, Philip Dorn, Walter Slezak. Diverting yarn of espionage agent planting microfilmed secrets in panthers' collars; when they escape captivity various sides of the law seek the animals.

Spy in Your Eye (1966-Italian, dubbed) C-88m. ** D: Vittorio Sala. Brett Halsey, Dana Andrews, Pier Angeli, Gaston Moschin. Hokum has Andrews as scientist with tele-camera implanted in eye, Halsey as U.S. agent trying to rescue Andrews' daughter (Angeli) captured by the Russians.

Spy Smasher SEE: **Spy Smasher Returns**.

Spy Smasher Returns (1942) 100m. **½ D: William Witney. Kane Richmond, Sam Flint, Marguerite Chapman, Hans Schumm, Tristram Coffin. Above par actioner from Republic Pictures dealing with famed crusader for good causes fighting for Allies in France during WW2, aided by twin brother. Re-edited movie serial: SPY SMASHER.

Spy Who Came In from the Cold, The (1965) 112m. ***½ D: Martin Ritt. Richard Burton, Claire Bloom, Oskar Werner, Peter Van Eyck, George Voskovec, Sam Wanamaker, Cyril Cusack. Realistic account of Cold War spy in Europe minus usual gimmicks. Taut, professional production; Burton is excellent. From John Le Carre's book.

Spy with a Cold Nose, The (1966-British) C-93m. ** D: Daniel Petrie. Laurence Harvey, Daliah Lavi, Lionel Jeffries, Eric Portman, Denholm Elliott. Tame spoof on secret agent movies. British agents plant bug in bulldog Disraeli, gift to Russian ambassador. Cast tries to keep story afloat.

Spy With My Face, The (1966) C-88m. **½ D: John Newland. Robert Vaughn, Senta Berger, David McCallum, Leo G. Carroll. Another expanded MAN FROM U.N.C.L.E. TV series entry, with Vaughn matching wits with his double (working for foreign powers); Berger the enemy femme fatale.

Squad Car (1960) 60m. BOMB D: Ed Leftwich. Vici Raaf, Paul Bryar,

Don Marlowe, Lyn Moore. Grade-C narrative of police investigating homicide and counterfeiting.

Square Jungle, The (1955) 86m. **½ D: Jerry Hopper. Tony Curtis, Pat Crowley, Ernest Borgnine, Paul Kelly, Jim Backus. Overly-familiar boxing yarn with Curtis the fighter on the way up—Crowley his girl.

Square Ring, The (1955-British) 73m. ** D: Michael Relph. Basil Dearden, Jack Warner, Kay Kendall, Joan Collins, Robert Beatty, Bill Owen, Maxwell Reed. Uninspired intertwining of events in lives of people involved in the fight game.

Squeaker, The (1965-German, dubbed) 95m. **½ D: Alfred Vohrer. Heinz Drache, Eddie Arent, Klaus Kinski, Barbara Rutting. Over complex actioner with a variety of plots spinning from action of underworld selling off proceeds of diamond robbery.

Stablemates (1938) 89m. ** D: Sam Wood. Wallace Beery, Mickey Rooney, Arthur Hohl, Margaret Hamilton, Minor Watson, Marjorie Gateson. Sticky story of jockey Rooney and racetrack mentor Beery. All the stops out during the syrupy scenes.

Stage Door (1937) 92m. **** D: Gregory La Cava. Katharine Hepburn, Ginger Rogers, Adolphe Menjou, Andrea Leeds, Gail Patrick, Constance Collier, Lucille Ball, Eve Arden, Ann Miller, Ralph Forbes, Franklin Pangborn. Theatrical boarding house is setting for superb film of Edna Ferber-George S. Kaufman play with fine acting by Hepburn as rich girl trying to succeed on her own, Menjou as propositioning producer, Leeds as hypersensitive actress.

Stage Door Canteen (1943) 132m. **½ D: Frank Borzage. Cheryl Walker, William Terry, Marjorie Riordan, Lon McCallister, Margaret Early, Michael Harrison. Soldier falls in love with canteen hostess. Plot abetted by cameo bits by Tallulah Bankhead, Katharine Hepburn, Harpo Marx, George Raft, Paul Muni, Merle Oberon, Helen Hayes, Ed Wynn, many others.

Stage Fright (1950) 110m. **½ D: Alfred Hitchcock. Marlene Dietrich, Jane Wyman, Michael Wilding, Richard Todd, Kay Walsh, Alastair Sim, Joyce Grenfell, Sybil Thorndike. Not top-notch Hitchcock, but OK; Dietrich as the chic stage star is the whole show, singing "Laziest Gal In Town"; set in London.

Stage Struck (1936) 86m. ** D: Busby Berkeley. Dick Powell, Joan Blondell, Warren William, Frank McHugh, Jeanne Madden. Plot is getting weary by now; director Powell and dancer Blondell decide to produce a show. Little music, just "Fancy Meeting You."

Stage Struck (1958) C-95m. **½ D: Sidney Lumet. Henry Fonda, Susan Strasberg, Joan Greenwood, Christopher Plummer, Herbert Marshall. Faded remake of MORNING GLORY retelling the ascent of Broadway-bound actress. Supporting cast hampered by unconvincing Strasberg in lead role and by unreal theater world atmosphere.

Stagecoach (1939) 99m. ***½ D: John Ford. John Wayne, Claire Trevor, Thomas Mitchell, Louise Platt, Andy Devine, George Bancroft, John Carradine, Berton Churchill, Donald Meek. Classic Western focusing on relationships between assorted stagecoach passengers, under pressure from Indian attack. Fine acting by all; Mitchell as drunken doctor won Oscar. Pictorially beautiful, ineptly remade in 1966.

Stagecoach (1966) C-114m. **½ D: Gordon Douglas. Ann-Margret, Alex Cord, Red Buttons, Michael Connors, Bing Crosby, Bob Cummings, Van Heflin, Slim Pickens, Stefanie Powers, Keenan Wynn. Colorful, star-studded Western is OK, but can't hold a candle to the 1939 masterpiece. Overlong, with only occasional action scenes to liven it up.

Stagecoach to Dancers' Rock (1962) 72m. ** D: Earl Bellamy. Warren Stevens, Martin Landau, Jody Lawrance, Judy Dan. Modest production involves stage passengers left stranded in wastelands when driver discovers one of them has smallpox.

Stagecoach to Fury (1956) 114m. *½ D: William Claxton. Forrest Tucker, Mari Blanchard, Wallace Ford, Margia Dean. Flat outlaw holdup oater.

Stairway to Heaven (1945-British) C-104m. ***½ D: Michael Powell, Emeric Pressburger. David Niven, Kim Hunter, Raymond Massey, Robert Coote, Roger Livesey, Richard Attenborough. HERE COMES MR. JORDAN on a more elaborate scale. A gem about pilot Niven accidentally taken to Heaven where he must plead for return to life. Original title: A MATTER OF LIFE AND DEATH.

Stakeout on Dope Street (1958) 83m. *½ D: Irvin Kershner. Yale Wexler, Jonathan Haze, Morris Miller, Abby Dalton, Herschel Bernardi. Trio of youths discover cache of heroin, believing their futures will now be uncomplicated; good premise poorly executed.

Stalag 17 (1953) 120m. ***½ D: Billy Wilder. William Holden, Don Taylor, Otto Preminger, Robert Strauss, Peter Graves, Sig Ruman. Much-awarded story of POW camp during WW2 confinement, frustration, and hope for escape. Holden won Oscar for role as hard-bitten prisoner; Ruman and Preminger are vicious Nazis, Strauss a homesick G. I.

Stamboul Quest (1934) 88m. **½ D: Sam Wood. Myrna Loy, George Brent, Lionel Atwill, C. Henry Gordon, Mischa Auer. Exotic combination of romance and intrigue with German spy Loy falling in love with American student Brent in WW1 Turkey.

Stampede (1949) 78m. **½ D: Lesley Selander. Rod Cameron, Gale Storm, Johnny Mack Brown, Don Castle, John Miljan. Good Western of range war between cattle ranchers.

Stand at Apache River, The (1953) C-77m. ** D: Lee Sholem. Stephen McNally, Julia Adams, Hugh Marlowe, Jack Kelly, Hugh O'Brian. Title tells all.

Stand by for Action (1942) 109m. **½ D: Robert Z. Leonard. Robert Taylor, Brian Donlevy, Charles Laughton, Walter Brennan, Marilyn Maxwell, Henry O'Neill. We're still waiting. Good cast in standard WW2 Navy saga.

Stand-In (1937) 91m. **½ D: Tay Garnett. Leslie Howard, Humphrey Bogart, Joan Blondell, Alan Mowbray, C. Henry Gordon, Jack Carson. Minor but enjoyable spoof of Hollywood. Way-out yarn of banker Howard closing in on bankrupt studio; producer Bogart saves the day.

Stand Up and Cheer (1934) 80m. *** D: Hamilton McFadden. Warner Baxter, Madge Evans, James Dunn, John Boles, Shirley Temple. Enjoyable Depression film about presidential commission to lighten country's spirits; Shirley steals show singing "Baby Take A Bow."

Stand Up and Fight (1939) 105m. ** D: W. S. Van Dyke II. Wallace Beery, Robert Taylor, Florence Rice, Charles Bickford, Charles Grapewin, Selmer Jackson. OK Western with railroading pioneer Taylor meeting crisis after crisis, battling stubborn stage-rider Beery.

Standing Room Only (1944) 83m. ** D: Sidney Lanfield. Fred MacMurray, Paulette Goddard, Edward Arnold, Hillary Brooke, Roland Young, Anne Revere. Topical war-time comedy is now dated. MacMurray and Goddard can't find rooms, so they work as servants.

Stanley & Livingstone (1939) 101m. ***½ D: Henry King. Spencer Tracy, Richard Greene, Nancy Kelly, Walter Brennan, Charles Coburn. Elaborate production with Tracy as determined reporter who searches Africa for missing doctor at turn of century; excellent drama.

Star, The (1953) 89m. ***½ D: Stuart Heisler. Bette Davis, Sterling Hayden, Natalie Wood, Warner Anderson. Incisive study of Oscar-winning actress (Davis) trying to make a comeback, but finding love instead; film is filled with many true Hollywoodisms.

Star Dust (1940) 85m. ** D: Walter Lang. Linda Darnell, John Payne, Roland Young, William Gargan, Charlotte Greenwood, Mary Beth Hughes. Trivial film of talent scout discovering Darnell and Payne, helping them to become Hollywood stars.

Star in the Dust (1956) C-80m. ** D: Charles Haas. John Agar, Mamie Van Doren, Richard Boone, Leif Erickson, Coleen Gray, James Gleason. Intriguing cast put through tame paces of sheriff Agar forced to fight his townsfolk to retain law and order.

Star Is Born, A (1954) C-154m. ***½ D: George Cukor. Judy Garland, James Mason, Jack Carson, Charles Bickford, Tom Noonan. Lengthy but well-acted musical remake of Janet Gaynor-Fredric March 1937 film of girl's overnight Hollywood success and decline of star-husband. Judy at pinnacle singing "The Man That Got Away."

Star of India (1956) C-84m. **½ D: Arthur Lubin. Cornel Wilde, Jean Wallace, Herbert Lom. So-so costumer, overly earnest. Wilde is Gallic nobleman trying to reestablish his rightful inheritance.

Star Maker, The (1939) 94m. **½ D: Roy Del Ruth. Bing Crosby, Louise

Campbell, Laura Hope Crews, Ned Sparks, Ethel Griffies, Billy Gilbert. Crosby plays Gus Edwards, vaudeville impressario who turned talented youngsters into stars. Pleasant musical doesn't always stick to facts.

Star Spangled Rhythm (1942) 99m. *** D: George Marshall. Bing Crosby, Ray Milland, Bob Hope, Veronica Lake, Dorothy Lamour, Susan Hayward, Dick Powell, Alan Ladd, Paulette Goddard, Cecil B. DeMille, Arthur Treacher, Eddie Anderson, William Bendix. Paramount's star-packed WW2 extravaganza, filled with songs and sketches, no plot. Better numbers include: "That Old Black Magic," "Time To Hit The Road To Dreamland."

Starlift (1951) 103m. ** D: Roy Del Ruth. Janice Rule, Dick Wesson, Don Haggerty, Richard Webb. Flimsy account of GI romancing an actress, allowing for scenes of movie stars entertaining troops. Cameos by Warner Bros. people like Cagney, Virginia Mayo, Ruth Roman, Doris Day, Gordon MacRae, etc.

Stars and Stripes Forever (1952) C-89m. **½ D: Henry Koster. Clifton Webb, Robert Wagner, Ruth Hussey, Debra Paget, Finlay Currie. Diverting, fictionalized biography of John Philip Sousa, well-played by Webb, with standard march tunes worked into plot nicely.

Stars Are Singing, The (1953) C-99m. **½ D: Norman Taurog. Rosemary Clooney, Anna Maria Alberghetti, Lauritz Melchoir, Fred Clark. Frothy musical with ridiculous plotline of immigration authorities tracking down Alberghetti as contestant on TV talent show.

Stars In my Crown (1950) 89m. **½ D: Jacques Tourneur. Joel McCrea, Ellen Drew, Dean Stockwell, Alan Hale, Lewis Stone, Ed Begley. Good atmosphere in melodrama of 19th-century minister preaching with six-guns.

Stars Look Down, The (1939-British) 110m. **** D: Carol Reed. Michael Redgrave, Margaret Lockwood, Emlyn Williams, Nancy Price, Edward Rigby, Cecil Parker. Absorbing classic about Welsh miners trying to work despite unsafe mining conditions; most realistic atmosphere.

Start Cheering (1938) 78m. *** D: Albert S. Rogell. Jimmy Durante, Walter Connolly, Joan Perry, Charles Starrett, Craig E. Earle, Gertrude Niesen. Durante goes to college in entertaining musical with fine cast, some good songs including Jimmy's "When I Strut Away In My Cutaway."

State Department File—649 (1949) 87m. ** D: Peter Stewart. Virginia Bruce, William Lundigan, Raymond Bond, Nana Bryant. Minor espionage story of American agent involved in Oriental intrigue with a demoniac warlord.

State Fair (1945) C-100m. *** D: Walter Lang. Jeanne Crain, Dana Andrews, Dick Haymes, Vivian Blaine, Charles Winninger, Fay Bainter, Donald Meek, Frank McHugh. Bright, engaging musical of family's adventures at Iowa State Fair; colorful with fine songs: "Grand Night For Singing," "It Might As Well Be Spring." Retitled: IT HAPPENED ONE SUMMER.

State Fair (1962) C-118m. BOMB D: Jose Ferrer. Pat Boone, Bobby Darin, Pamela Tiffin, Ann-Margret, Alice Faye, Tom Ewell. Remake of sprightly 1945 musical is pretty bad. Faye came out of retirement to play Tiffin's mother—bad mistake. Ewell even sings to a cow!

State of the Union (1948) 124m. ***½ D: Frank Capra. Spencer Tracy, Katharine Hepburn, Angela Lansbury, Van Johnson, Adolphe Menjou, Lewis Stone. Howard Lindsay-Russel Crouse play becomes smooth film with Presidential candidate (Tracy) battling for integrity with his wife (Hepburn); good support from Lansbury as millionairess backing campaign, Johnson as campaign manager.

State Penitentiary (1950) 66m. ** D: Lew Landers. Warner Baxter, Karin Booth, Robert Shayne, Richard Benedict. Programmer with Baxter a prisoner seeking to escape.

State Secret SEE: **Great Manhunt, The**.

State's Attorney (1932) 73m. **½ D: George Archainbaud. John Barrymore, Helen Twelvetrees, William Boyd, Jill Esmond, Mary Duncan, Ralph Ince, C. Henry Gordon. Minor courtroom drama. Barrymore as drunken lawyer who reforms is worth seeing; crime and romance conflict with client Twelvetrees.

Station Six-Sahara (1964-British) 99m. *½ D: Seth Holt. Carroll Baker,

Peter Van Eyck, Ian Bannen, Denholm Elliott, Biff McGuire. Dreary yarn of five love-starved men who find something new to fight over when sexpot Baker and her estranged husband crash land at their desert oasis.

Stations West (1948) 92m. *** D: Sidney Lanfield. Dick Powell, Jane Greer, Agnes Moorehead, Burl Ives, Tom Powers, Gordon Oliver, Steve Brodie, Raymond Burr. Well-acted Western features Powell as distinguished army officer solving mystery of hi-jackers and murderers.

Steamboat 'Round the Bend (1935) 96m. **½ D: John Ford. Will Rogers, Anne Shirley, Irvin S. Cobb, Eugene Pallette, John McGuire, Stepin Fetchit. Enjoyable period-piece, but Rogers' usual witticisms are sorely missed. Shirley is particularly good as swamp-girl taken in by steamboat captain Rogers.

Steel Against the Sky (1941) 68m. ** D: A. Edward Sutherland. Lloyd Nolan, Alexis Smith, Craig Stevens, Gene Lockhart, Edward Ellis. Routine tale of brothers Nolan and Stevens, steel workers, both interested in Smith.

Steel Bayonet (1958-British) 84m. ** D: Michael Carreras. Leo Genn, Kieron Moore, Michael Medwin, Robert Brown. Military unit is ordered to defend deserted farmhouse/lookout base at all costs; tame WW film set in Africa.

Steel Cage, The (1954) 80m. ** D: Walter Doniger. Paul Kelly, Maureen O'Sullivan, Walter Slezak, John Ireland, Lawrence Tierney, Alan Mowbray, George E. Stone, Lyle Talbot. Pedestrian telling of life at San Quentin, despite good cast.

Steel Claw, The (1961) C-96m. **½ D: George Montgomery. George Montgomery, Charito Luna, Mario Barri, Paul Sorensen. Montgomery turns partisan leader when he loses hand in WW2, forcing his marine discharge; on-location filming in Philippines and sufficient combat action spark story along.

Steel Fist, The (1952) 73m. *½ D: Wesley Barry. Roddy McDowall, Kristine Miller, Harry Lauter, Rand Brooks. Quickie flick with McDowall involved in escape from Iron Curtain country; low production values.

Steel Helmet, The (1951) 84m. *½ D: Samuel Fuller. Robert Hutton, Steve Brodie, Gene Evans, James Edwards. Run-of-the-mill Korean War flick.

Steel Jungle, The (1956) 86m. *½ D: Walter Doniger. Perry Lopez, Beverly Garland, Allison Hayes, Walter Abel, Ted de Corsia, Kenneth Tobey. Lukewarm account of prison life.

Steel Key, The (1953-British) 74m. **½ D: Robert Baker. Terence Morgan, Joan Rice, Raymond Lovell, Dianne Foster, Esmond Knight. Espionage and homicide abound in this fast-clipping caper about stolen formulas for processing hardened steel.

Steel Lady, The (1953) 84m. **½ D: E. A. Dupont. Rod Cameron, Tab Hunter, John Dehner, Anthony Caruso. Fair adventure of four trapped men in desert who find old German tank.

Steel Town (1952) C-85m. ** D: George Sherman. Ann Sheridan, John Lund, Howard Duff, James Best, Nancy Kulp. Uninspired story of steel-making and the personal problems of nephew of steel plant owner; Sheridan tries, but can't perk up this programmer.

Steel Trap, The (1952) 85m. **½ D: Andrew L. Stone. Joseph Cotten, Teresa Wright, Jonathan Hale, Walter Sande. Trim caper of Cotten who steals money from his bank and over the weekend decides to replace it.

Stella (1950) 83m. **½ D: Claude Binyon. Ann Sheridan, Victor Mature, David Wayne, Frank Fontaine. Screwball comedy and murder doesn't blend well in tale of nutty family that tries to hide a most persistently visible corpse.

Stella Dallas (1937) 111m. *** D: King Vidor. Barbara Stanwyck, John Boles, Anne Shirley, Barbara O'Neil, Alan Hale, Tim Holt, Marjorie Main. Definitive soap opera of woman who sacrifices everything for her daughter, but is unable to enjoy any happiness for all her efforts. Stanwyck was nominated for an Oscar.

Step by Step (1946) 62m. ** D: Phil Rosen. Lawrence Tierney, Anne Jeffreys, Lowell Gilmore, George Cleveland. Patriotic programmer with Tierney a WW2 veteran uncovering Fascist agents in America.

Step Down to Terror (1958) 75m. ** D: Harry Keller. Colleen Miller, Charles Drake, Rod Taylor, Josephine Hutchinson. Washed-out remake of Hitchcock's SHADOW OF A

DOUBT, retells account of psycho-murderer returning to home town after long absence.

Step Lively (1944) 88m. *** D: Tim Whelan. Frank Sinatra, George Murphy, Adolphe Menjou, Gloria De Haven, Eugene Pallette, Anne Jeffreys. Brisk musical version of ROOM SERVICE, with scheming producer Menjou wheeling and dealing to get his show produced.

Steppin' in Society (1945) 72m. *½ D: Alexander Esway. Edward Everett Horton, Ruth Terry, Gladys George, Jack LaRue, Lola Lane, Iris Adrian, Isabel Jewell. Minor flick with vacationing judge Horton involved with rehabilitating jail birds.

Stolen Heaven (1938) 88m. *½ D: Andrew L. Stone. Gene Raymond, Olympe Bradna, Glenda Farrell, Lewis Stone, Porter Hall, Douglass Dumbrille, Joseph Sawyer. Despite name cast, pretty limp drama of robber-on-the-run sheltered by notorious woman.

Stolen Hours (1963) C-100m. **½ D: Daniel Petrie. Susan Hayward, Michael Craig, Diane Baker, Edward Judd, Paul Rogers. Hayward takes Bette Davis' DARK VICTORY, transplants it to contemporary England, in tale of woman with fatal illness trying to get as much out of life as she can. Original is far superior in all departments.

Stolen Life, A (1946) 107m. **½ D: Curtis Bernhardt. Bette Davis, Glenn Ford, Dane Clark, Walter Brennan, Charles Ruggles, Bruce Bennett, Peggy Knudsen. Davis plays twin sisters both in love with Ford; not as effective as intended; set in N.Y.C. and Cape Cod. Remade from earlier film with Elizabeth Bergner.

Stooge, The (1952) 100m. **½ D: Norman Taurog. Dean Martin, Jerry Lewis, Polly Bergen, Eddie Mayehoff. Interesting premise of singer Martin who discovers that without partner Lewis his act is a flop; usual antics and songs with team in good form.

Stop! Look! and Laugh! (1960) 78m. **½ D: Jules White. The Three Stooges, Paul Winchell, Jerry Mahoney, Kuncklehead Smiff, The Marquis Chimps, Officer Joe Bolton. Original 3 Stooges' funniest sequences strung together by Paul Winchell and dummies is aimed at children. Much of it is familiar, but still amusing.

Stop Me Before I Kill! (1961-British) 121m. ** D: Val Guest. Claude Dauphin, Diane Cilento, Roland Lewis, Françoise Rosay. Turgid dramatics: mentally unhinged man's new marriage is threatened by his illness and his psychiatrist's yen for his wife.

Stop Train 349 (1964-German, dubbed) 95m. ** D: Rolf Haedrich. Jose Ferrer, Sean Flynn, Nicole Courcel, Jess Hahn. Average thriller of Communist manhunt for East German refugee hidden aboard U.S. military train heading from Berlin to west zone.

Stop, You're Killing Me (1952) 86m. ** D: Roy Del Ruth. Broderick Crawford, Claire Trevor, Virginia Gibson, Sheldon Leonard, Margaret Dumont. Mild froth based on Damon Runyon story of racketeer Crawford going legitimate. Remake of A SLIGHT CASE OF LARCENY.

Stopover Tokyo (1957) C-100m. **½ D: Richard L. Breen. Robert Wagner, Joan Collins, Edmond O'Brien, Ken Scott. Lumbering spy tale, loosely based on John P. Marquand novel. On location filming in Japan makes a pretty background, but flat characters remain.

Stork Club, The (1945) 98m. *** D: Hal Walker. Betty Hutton, Barry Fitzgerald, Don DeFore, Andy Russell, Iris Adrian, Robert Benchley. Hat-check girl Hutton mysteriously becomes wealthy in fanciful musicomedy, mainly for Betty's fans. She sings "Doctor, Lawyer, Indian Chief."

Stork Talk (1961-British) 97m. ** D: Michael Forlong. Tony Britton, Anne Heywood, John Turner, Nicole Perroult. Harmless sex comedy involving married couples' indiscretions and the pat resolution of their problems.

Storm, The (1938) 75m. **½ D: Harold Young. Charles Bickford, Barton MacLane, Preston Foster, Tom Brown, Nan Grey, Andy Devine. Not-bad yarn of brothers Bickford and MacLane constantly arguing, mostly over women, reconciled during climactic storm.

Storm at Daybreak (1933) 80m. **½ D: Richard Boleslavsky. Kay Francis, Nils Asther, Jean Parker, Walter Huston, Phillips Holmes, Eugene Pallette. Lavishly mounted soaper set in Serbia. Francis is wife of mayor Huston, and having affair with convalescing soldier Asther.

Storm Center (1956) 85m. *½ D:

Daniel Taradash. Bette Davis, Brian Keith, Kim Hunter, Paul Kelly. Librarian becomes center of controversy over censorship and communism. Not even Davis can uplift clichés.

Storm Fear (1956) 88m. ** D: Cornel Wilde. Cornel Wilde, Jean Wallace, Dan Duryea, Lee Grant. Good cast elevates this yarn of wounded bank robber hiding out at brother's home, intimidating everyone.

Storm In A Teacup (1937-British) C-103m. *** D: Victor Saville, Ian Dalrymple. Vivien Leigh, Rex Harrison, Cecil Parker, Sara Allgood, Arthur Wontner, Ivor Barnard. Witty social comedy with Leigh and Harrison barbing over words, loves and politics.

Storm Over Lisbon (1944) 86m. ** D: George Sherman. Vera Ralston, Richard Arlen, Erich von Stroheim, Otto Kruger, Eduardo Ciannelli, Mona Barrie. WW2 intrigue in Lisbon with nightclub performer Ralston siding with Von Stroheim to get goods on American Arlen; low-grade rehash of typical WW2 material.

Storm Over the Nile (1956-British) C-113m. **½ D: Zoltan Korda, Terence Young. Anthony Steel, Laurence Harvey, James Robertson Justice, Mary Ure. Remake of FOUR FEATHERS lacks class and flair, but story is still good.

Storm Rider, The (1957) 70m. *½ D: Edward Bernds. Scott Brady, Mala Powers, Bill Williams, John Goddard. Sagebrush lowjinks of cattle owners vs. ranchers.

Storm Warning (1950) 93m. **½ D: Stuart Heisler. Ginger Rogers, Ronald Reagan, Doris Day, Steve Cochran. Neatly handled yarn of Rogers and Day as sisters involved with the Ku Klux Klan in the South.

Stormy Weather (1943) 77m. *** D: Andrew L. Stone. Lena Horne, Bill Robinson, Cab Calloway and Band, Katherine Dunham Dancers, Fats Waller. Routine backstage musical plot enhanced by top-notch all Negro cast doing specialities and songs like "Ain't Misbehavin'."

Story of Alexander Graham Bell, The (1939) 97m. *** D: Irving Cummings. Don Ameche, Loretta Young, Henry Fonda, Charles Coburn, Spring Byington, Gene Lockhart, Polly Ann Young. Ameche overacts at times in title role, but entertaining version of inventor is given plush 20th Century-Fox presentation.

Story of Dr. Wassell, The (1944) C-140m. **½ D: Cecil B. DeMille. Gary Cooper, Laraine Day, Signe Hasso, Dennis O'Keefe, Paul Kelly, Philip Ahn, Barbara Britton. Far from top-grade Cooper or DeMille is this story of dedicated Navy doctor who saved fighting men in Japan during WW2; slow-moving account.

Story of Esther Costello, The (1957-British) 103m. **½ D: David Miller. Joan Crawford, Rossano Brazzi, Heather Sears, Lee Paterson, Fay Compton, Bessie Love, Megs Jenkins. Effective account of ritzy Crawford encountering mute Sears, rehabilitating her, only to have girl's condition exploited by lover Brazzi. Low-keyed unmannered production marred by climax.

Story of G. I. Joe, The (1945) 109m. ***½ D: William Wellman. Burgess Meredith, Robert Mitchum, Freddie Steel, Wally Cassell, Jimmy Lloyd. Meredith is superb as war correspondent Ernie Pyle living with Yank soldiers on front lines to report their stories; Mitchum's first outstanding film role as soldier.

Story of Louis Pasteur (1935) 85m. ***½ D: William Dieterle. Paul Muni, Josephine Hutchinson, Anita Louise, Donald Woods, Fritz Leiber. Another in the series of Muni's Warner Bros. biographical productions; this time as dedicated French scientist who cures hoof-and-mouth disease despite wide-spread skepticism among colleagues. Extremely well done.

Story of Mankind, The (1957) C-100m. ** D: Irwin Allen. Ronald Colman, Hedy Lamarr, Groucho, Harpo, Chico Marx, Virginia Mayo, Agnes Moorehead, Vincent Price, Francis X. Bushman, Charles Coburn, Marie Windsor, John Carradine. Ambitious in concept, laughable in juvenile results. Hendrik Von Loon book of highlights of man's history becomes string of clichéd costume episodes, badly cast and poorly handled.

Story of Molly X, The (1950) 82m. **½ D: Crane Wilbur. June Havoc, John Russell, Dorothy Hart, Charles McGraw. Havoc is most earnest as gangster's widow who goes out to find her husband's killer.

Story of Ruth, The (1960) C-132m.

Story of Ruth, The (1960) 132m. **½ D: Henry Koster. Stuart Whitman, Tom Tryon, Peggy Wood, Viveca Lindfors, Jeff Morrow, Elana Eden. Static biblical nonepic retelling story of woman renouncing her "gods" when she discovers true faith.

Story of Seabiscuit, The (1949) 93m. **½ D: David Butler. Shirley Temple, Barry Fitzgerald, Lon McCallister, Rosemary DeCamp. Standard horseracing saga with Fitzgerald supporting most of the film as a dedicated trainer.

Story of the Count of Monte Cristo, The SEE: Count of Monte Cristo.

Story of Three Loves, The (1953) C-122m. *** D: Vincente Minnelli. Pier Angeli, Ethel Barrymore, Kirk Douglas, Farley Granger, Leslie Caron, James Mason, Agnes Moorehead, Zsa Zsa Gabor. Excellent cast in three varying stories of human relationships.

Story of Vernon & Irene Castle, The (1939) 93m. *** D: H. C. Potter. Fred Astaire, Ginger Rogers, Edna May Oliver, Walter Brennan, Lew Fields. Usual Astaire-Rogers breeziness suffers from slow handling of events in lives of famous early 20th-century dancing duo. Still good, with many fine period dance and song numbers.

Story of Will Rogers, The (1952) C-109m. *** D: Michael Curtiz. Will Rogers, Jr., Jane Wyman, Carl Benton Reid, James Gleason, Mary Wickes, Eddie Cantor. One of few show biz biographies that rings true, with Rogers Jr. faithfully portraying his father, rodeo star-turned humorist; Wyman as his loving wife.

Story on Page One, The (1959) 123m. *** D: Clifford Odets. Rita Hayworth, Anthony Franciosa, Gig Young, Mildred Dunnock, Hugh Griffith, Sanford Meisner, Robert Burton. Lovers Hayworth and Young dispose of Rita's husband, hire Franciosa to represent her in court. Odets' stark film has high tension and sincere performances. Dunnock's mama portrayal is a bit much.

Stowaway (1936) 86m. **½ D: William A. Seiter. Robert Young, Alice Faye, Shirley Temple, Eugene Pallette, Helen Westley, Arthur Treacher. Predictable yet engaging shipboard story with Faye and Young romancing, Temple the incurably curious child.

Stowaway Girl (1957-British) 87m. **½ D: Guy Hamilton. Trevor Howard, Elsa Martinelli, Pedro Armendariz, Donald Pleasence, Warren Mitchell. Trim, sensible romancer of middle-aged captain Howard's infatuation with Martinelli, who hid aboard his ship.

Strait-Jacket (1964) 89m. **½ D: William Castle. Joan Crawford, Diane Baker, Leif Erickson, Anthony Hayes, Howard St. John, Rochelle Hudson. Crawford served twenty years for axe murders; now, living peacefully with daughter Baker, murders start again and she's suspect. Crawford's strong portrayal makes this one of best in horror-star entries.

Stranded (1935) 76m. ** D: Frank Borzage. Kay Francis, George Brent, Patricia Ellis, Donald Woods, Robert Barrat, Barton MacLane. Francis is a traveler's aid worker solving everybody's problems, tangling with band of racketeers.

Strange Adventure, A (1956) *½ D: William Witney. Joan Evans, Ben Cooper, Marla English, Jan Merlin, Nick Adams. Murky little drama of speed-demon youths involved in hold-up.

Strange Affair of Uncle Harry, The (1946) 80m. *** D: Robert Siodmak. George Sanders, Geraldine Fitzgerald, Ella Raines, Sara Allgood, Moyna MacGill, Samuel S. Hinds. Nifty murder mystery with soggy finish about Sanders growing tired of sisterly interference, turning to murder as solution. Retitled: UNCLE HARRY.

Strange Affection (1957-British) 84m. ** D: Wolf Rilla. Richard Attenborough, Colin Petersen, Jill Adams, Terence Morgan. OK drama involving conflict between son and father, climaxing when former is arrested for latter's crime. Original title: THE SCAMP.

Strange Awakening (1958-British) 75m. *½ D: Montgomery Tully. Lex Barker, Carole Mathews, Nora Swinburne, Richard Molinos, Peter Dyneley. Barker is tourist in France involved in snowballing case of fraud; muddled drama.

Strange Bargain (1949) 68m. ** D: Will Price. Martha Scott, Jeffery Lynn, Henry Morgan, Katherine Emery, Henry O'Neill. Routine story of innocent young man who gets mixed up in underworld activities.

Strange Bedfellows (1964) C-98m.

***½ D:** Melvin Frank. Rock Hudson, Gina Lollobrigida, Gig Young, Terry-Thomas, Nancy Kulp. Hudson ambles through another marital mix-up comedy, this one with fiery Gina and lots of slapstick. Mild entertainment.

Strange Cargo (1940) 105m. ***** D:** Frank Borzage. Joan Crawford, Clark Gable, Ian Hunter, Peter Lorre, Albert Dekker, Paul Lukas, Eduardo Ciannelli. Intriguing allegorical film of prisoners escaping from Devil's Island with Christ-like presence of Hunter. Not for all tastes, but there are fine, realistic performances by Crawford, Gable, and supporting cast.

Strange Case of Madeleine SEE: **Madeleine.**

Strange Confession SEE: **Imposter, The.**

Strange Conquest (1946) 64m. **** D:** John Rawlins. Jane Wyatt, Lowell Gilmore, Julie Bishop, Samuel S. Hinds, Abner Biberman. Inauspicious programmer from Universal Pictures set in the deep jungles where dedicated men try to conquer native diseases.

Strange Countess, The (1961-German, dubbed) 96m. **** D:** Josef Von Baky. Joachim Fuchsberger, Lil Dagover, Marianne Hoppe, Brigitte Grothum. Dagover is in title role, involved with fortune-hunting killers; from Edgar Wallace yarn.

Strange Death of Adolf Hitler, The (1943) 72m. **** D:** James Hogan. Ludwig Donath, Fritz Kortner, Gale Sondergaard, George Dolenz, Fred Giermann, William Trent, Merrill Rodin. Interesting story of Hitler's double helping to set trap for Fuehrer's death.

Strange Door, The (1951) 81m. ***½ D:** Richard Pevney. Charles Laughton, Boris Karloff, Sally Forrest, Richard Stapley. Pretty bad adaptation of Stevenson story. Laughton overacts as cruel tyrant who gets back at dead sweetheart by imprisoning members of family. Intended horror film may seem comic.

Strange Fascination (1952) 80m. BOMB **D:** Hugo Haas. Cleo Moore, Hugo Haas, Mona Barrie, Karen Sharpe. Lurid nonsense with pianist Haas ensnared by vixen Moore.

Strange Holiday (1946) 54m. **** D:** Arch Oboler. Claude Rains, Bobbie Stebbins, David Bradford, Barbara Bates, Paul Hilton, Gloria Holden, Milton Kibbee, Helen Mack, Martin Kosleck. Strange post-war Nazi escapade with businessman Rains taken to task by the Germans; Rains has to support this one himself.

Strange Interlude (1932) 110m. ***** D:** Robert Z. Leonard. Norma Shearer, Clark Gable, May Robson, Maureen O'Sullivan, Robert Young, Ralph Morgan, Henry B. Walthall, Mary Alden. Eugene O'Neill talky play becomes marathon of inner thoughts revealed only to audience in chronicle of Gable, Shearer, et al growing old without resolving their problems. Engrossing film, with Shearer at her radiant best.

Strange Intruder (1956) 82m. **** D:** Irving Rapper. Edmund Purdom, Ida Lupino, Ann Harding, Jacques Bergerac. Peculiar tale of Purdom promising dying Korean War buddy that he'll visit the man's family; he does, with strange results.

Strange Journey (1946) 65m. ***½ D:** James Tinling. Paul Kelly, Osa Massen, Hillary Brooke, Bruce Lester. Low-budget adventure story with group of people on desert isle fighting over treasure map.

Strange Lady in Town (1955) C-112m. ****½ D:** Mervyn LeRoy. Greer Garson, Dana Andrews, Cameron Mitchell, Lois Smith, Walter Hampden. Unsuccessful grand-scale soaper-Western. Set in 1880's Texas, Garson is the doctor coming to Santa Fe, involved with Andrews, perplexed by outlaw brother Mitchell.

Strange Love of Martha Ivers (1946) 117m. ***** D:** Lewis Milestone. Barbara Stanwyck, Kirk Douglas, Lizabeth Scott, Van Heflin, Judith Anderson, Darryl Hickman. Gripping melodrama, with Stanwyck bound to her husband by crime she committed long ago.

Strange Mr. Gregory, The (1946) 63m. **** D:** Phil Rosen. Edmund Lowe, Jean Rogers, Don Douglas, Marjorie Hoshelle, Robert Emmett Keane. Low-budget drama of magician who goes to any length to win love of married woman.

Strange One, The (1957) 100m. ***** D:** Jack Garfein. Ben Gazzara, George Peppard, Pat Hingle, Mark Richman, Geoffrey Horne. Bizarre military school account of far-out Gazzara's peculiar hold over various underclassmen. Remarkably frank version of Calder Willingham's END AS A MAN.

Strange Triangle (1946) 65m. ** D: Ray McCarey. Preston Foster, Signe Hasso, John Shepperd, Roy Roberts. OK drama with Hasso the maneuvering dame who inspires murder and robbery.

Strange Woman, The (1946) 100m. ** D: Edgar G. Ulmer. Hedy Lamarr, George Sanders, Louis Hayward, Gene Lockhart, Hillary Brooke, June Storey. Lamarr's a legendary man-killer in this tedious costumer.

Stranger, The (1946) 95m. *** D: Orson Welles. Orson Welles, Loretta Young, Edward G. Robinson, Richard Long, Martha Wentworth. Fine study of escaped Nazi war criminal Welles sedately living in small town, about to marry unsuspecting Young. Robinson nicely understates role as federal agent out to get him.

Stranger at My Door (1956) 85m. **1/2 D: William Witney. Macdonald Carey, Patricia Medina, Skip Homeier, Stephen Wootton, Slim Pickens. Offbeat Western about clergyman jeopardizing his family's safety when he tries to reform an outlaw.

Stranger Came Home, A SEE: **Unholy Four.**

Stranger in Between, The (1952-British) 84m. *** D: Charles Chrichton. Dirk Bogarde, Elizabeth Sellars, Kay Walsh, Geoffrey Keen. Odd sort of film about orphan boy who grows to understand murderer as both flee police in England.

Stranger in My Arms (1959) 88m. **1/2 D: Helmut Kautner. June Allyson, Jeff Chandler, Sandra Dee, Charles Coburn, Mary Astor, Peter Graves, Conrad Nagel. Undemanding old-fashioned weeper, with a high-breed soaper cast, based on Robert Wilder novel. Allyson falls in love with Chandler, army buddy of her late husband. Astor is the domineering mother-in-law.

Stranger on Horseback (1955) C-66m. ** D: Jacques Tourneur. Joel McCrea, Kevin McCarthy, Jaclynne Greene, Miroslava, Nancy Gates, John Carradine. McCrea is tight-lipped judge who's forced to kill in order to set justice straight and bring a murderer to trial.

Stranger on the Prowl (1953-Italian, dubbed) 82m. **1/2 D: Joseph Losey. Paul Muni, Vittorio Manunta, Joan Lorring, Aldo Silvani. Murky drama of Muni a fugitive on the run who tries to set a young would-be-crook straight.

Stranger on the Run (1967) C-120m. **1/2 D: Don Siegel. Henry Fonda, Anne Baxter, Dan Duryea, Sal Mineo. Murky telefeature set in 1880's Southwest, focusing on revelations of human nature as assorted people hunt down accused murderer Fonda; Baxter is a lonely rancher.

Stranger on the Third Floor (1940) 64m. *** D: Boris Ingster. Peter Lorre, John McGuire, Margaret Tallichet, Charles Waldron, Elisha Cook, Jr. Lorre's at his maniacal best in little "sleeper" about mysterious crime wave blamed on innocent man.

Stranger Wore a Gun, The (1953) C-83m. ** D: Andre de Toth. Randolph Scott, Claire Trevor, Joan Weldon, George Macready, Lee Marvin. Oddball plot in this Scott Western; Randy is befriended by bandit and becomes involved in a holdup before he can return to normal living.

Strangers (1953-Italian) 97m. *1/2 D: Roberto Rossellini. Ingrid Bergman, George Sanders, Paul Muller, Maria Mauban, Natalia Ray. Tedious hokum of married couple Bergman and Sanders trying to reconcile their faltering relationship while on Italian holiday.

Stranger's Hand, The (1954-Italian, dubbed) 86m. *** D: Mario Soldati. Richard Basehart, Trevor Howard, Alida Valli, Eduardo Ciannelli. Brooding suspenser involving British espionage officer who disappears on his trip to Venice to see his young son. Based on Grahame Greene story.

Strangers in Love (1932) 76m. ** D: Lothar Mendes. Kay Francis, Fredric March, Stuart Erwin, Juliette Compton, Sidney Toler, George Barbier, Lucien Littlefield. Mild comedy; Francis is secretary who loves March, weakling playboy forced to impersonate twin brother to expose family fraud.

Strangers May Kiss (1931) 85m. ** D: George Fitzmaurice. Norma Shearer, Robert Montgomery, Neil Hamilton, Marjorie Rambeau, Jed Prouty, Henry Armetta. Nothing-special comedy about relationship between blasé newspaperman and woman infatuated with him. Occasional laughs, usually dull.

Strangers on a Train (1951) 101m. **** D: Alfred Hitchcock. Farley Granger, Robert Walker, Ruth Roman,

Leo G. Carroll, Patricia Hitchcock, Marion Lorne. Walker gives his finest performance as psychopath involved with tennis star Granger in "exchange murders." Lorne is unforgettable as doting mother. First-class Hitchcock.

Strangers When We Meet (1960) C-117m. **½ D: Richard Quine. Kirk Douglas, Kim Novak, Ernie Kovacs, Barbara Rush, Walter Matthau, Virginia Bruce, Kent Smith. Expensive soaper with attractive stars; both are married, but fall in love with each other. Based on Evan Hunter novel.

Strangler, The (1964) 89m. *** D: Burt Topper. Victor Buono, David McLean, Ellen Corby, Jeanne Bates, Wally Campo. Buono gives fine performance as mad killer who strangles women and pitches Boston into frenzy.

Stranglers of Bombay, The (1960-British) 81m. **½ D: Terence Fisher. Andrew Cruickshank, Marne Maitland, Guy Rolfe, Paul Stassine, Jan Holden, Tutte Lemkow. Grisly story of fanatical Indian cult attempting to drive British from trading station. Good cast helped by tense direction.

Strategic Air Command (1955) C-114m. **½ D: Anthony Mann. June Allyson, James Stewart, Frank Lovejoy, Barry Sullivan, Bruce Bennett, Rosemary DeCamp. Film only gets off the ground when Stewart does, as baseball player recalled to air force duty; Allyson is his sugary wife.

Stratton Story, The (1949) 106m. ***½ D: Sam Wood. James Stewart, June Allyson, Frank Morgan, Agnes Moorehead, Bill Williams. Stewart is fine as Monty Stratton, baseball player whose loss of one leg did not mark an end to his career; well-played by good cast.

Strawberry Blonde, The (1941) 97m. *** D: Raoul Walsh. James Cagney, Olivia de Havilland, Rita Hayworth, Alan Hale, Jack Carson, George Tobias, Una O'Connor, George Reeves. Cagney's dynamic in 1890's story of dentist infatuated with gold-digger Hayworth, and his subsequent marriage to De Havilland. Remade as ONE SUNDAY AFTERNOON, the title of the early Gary Cooper film of which this is a remake.

Street of Chance (1942) 74m. **½ D: Jack Hively. Burgess Meredith, Claire Trevor, Sheldon Leonard, Frieda Inescort. Effective Paramount B-flick with Meredith an amnesia victim seeking clues to his past.

Street Scene (1931) 80m. ***½ D: King Vidor. Sylvia Sidney, William Collier, Jr., Estelle Taylor, Beulah Bondi, John Qualen. Powerful drama from Elmer Rice play of life in N.Y.C. tenements. Sidney does usual fine tear-stained work.

Street With No Name, The (1948) 91m. *** D: William Keighley. Mark Stevens, Richard Widmark, Lloyd Nolan, Barbara Lawrence, Ed Begley, Donald Buka. Fine movie based on actual FBI case of agent uncovering head of city mob. Suspense well handled.

Streetcar Named Desire, A (1951) 122m. **** D: Elia Kazan. Marlon Brando, Vivien Leigh, Kim Hunter, Karl Malden. Multi-Oscar-winning film from Tennessee Williams play. Brando superb as animalistic human interacting with wistful, neurotic Leigh. Brooding production set in grim New Orleans tenement district.

Streets of Laredo (1949) 92m. **½ D: Leslie Fenton. Macdonald Carey, William Holden, William Bendix, Mona Freeman. Standard Western, remake of THE TEXAS RANGERS, but not as good. Three pals out West split when two turn to law and another becomes lawbreaker.

Strictly Dishonorable (1951) 86m. ** D: Melvin Frank, Norman Panama. Ezio Pinza, Janet Leigh, Millard Mitchell, Gale Robbins. Tame shenanigans of opera star Pinza marrying Leigh to save her reputation.

Strike Me Pink (1936) 104m. *** D: Norman Taurog. Eddie Cantor, Ethel Merman, Sally Eilers, William Frawley, Parkyakarkus, Helen Lowell. Breezy Cantor musical about underworld gang making trouble for innocent amusement-park owner. Cantor and Merman are lively singing Harold Arlen tunes.

Strike Up the Band (1940) 120m. **½ D: Busby Berkeley. Mickey Rooney, Judy Garland, Paul Whiteman, June Preisser, William Tracy, Larry Nunn. Rooney is leader of high school band competing in Whiteman's nationwide radio contest. Garland sings "Our Love Affair," performs "Nell of New Rochelle," "Do The Conga."

Strip, The (1951) 85m. ** D: Leslie Kardos. Mickey Rooney, Sally Forrest, William Demarest, James Craig. Rooney gives sincere, energetic performance as former drummer involved with gangsters, trying to help Forrest get a movie break.

Stromboli (1950-Italian, dubbed) 81m. *½ D: Roberto Rossellini. Ingrid Bergman, Mario Vitale, Renzo Cesano, Mario Sponza. Rambling dreariness with Bergman marrying a fisherman; even an erupting volcano doesn't jar this plodding film.

Stronghold (1951) 82m. *½ D: Steve Sekely. Veronica Lake, Zachary Scott, Arturo de Cordova, Rita Macedo. Pedestrian costumer set in 1860's, with Lake fleeing U.S. and becoming embroiled in Mexican revolution.

Student Prince, The (1954) C-107m. ** D: Richard Thorpe. Ann Blyth, Edmund Purdom, John Ericson, Louis Calhern, Edmund Gwenn. Romberg music and voice of Mario Lanza used in venerable operetta of heir to throne sent to Heidelberg to live it up, falling for barmaid Blyth.

Study in Terror, A (1965-British) C-94m. D: James Hill. John Neville, Donald Houston, Georgia Brown, John Fraser, Anthony Quayle, Barbara Windsor, Edina Ronay. SEE: Sherlock Holmes series.

Submarine Command (1951) 87m. **½ D: John Farrow. William Holden, Nancy Olson, William Bendix, Don Taylor. Predictable but acceptable post-WW2 account of naval military life; Olson is wholesome love interest.

Subterraneans, The (1960) C-89m. **½ D: Ranald MacDougall. Leslie Caron, George Peppard, Janice Rule, Roddy McDowall, Anne Seymour, Jim Hutton, Scott Marlowe. Glossy, superficial study of life and love among the beatniks, with pure cornball stereotype performances.

Subway in the Sky (1959-German) 85m. *½ D: Muriel Box. Van Johnson, Hildegarde Neff, Katherine Kath, Cece Linder, Albert Lieven, Edward Judd. Flabby caper of soldier Johnson in post-WW2 Berlin, involved in the black market; terrible waste of Neff's talents.

Success, The (1963-Italian) 103m. *** D: Dino Risi. Vittorio Gassman, Anouk Aimee, Jean-Louis Trintignant. Intelligent delineation by Gassman as businessman overwhelmed by success urge makes this drama worthy.

Sudan (1945) C-76m. ** D: John Rawlins. Maria Montez, Jon Hall, Turhan Bey, Andy Devine, George Zucco, Robert Warwick. Queen Montez escapes evil prime minister Zucco with help of Hall and Bey in colorful but empty adventure-romance.

Sudden Danger (1955) 85m. *½ D: Hubert Cornfield. Bill Elliott, Tom Drake, Beverly Garland, Lucien Littlefield, Minerva Urecal, Lyle Talbot, Frank Jenks. Bland hunt-the-murderer-tale.

Sudden Fear (1952) 110m. ***½ D: David Miller. Joan Crawford, Jack Palance, Gloria Grahame, Bruce Bennett, Michael Connors. Excellently handled murder yarn with Crawford a famous playwright who marries Palance, then discovers he's trying to kill her.

Suddenly (1954) 77m. ***½ D: Lewis Allen. Frank Sinatra, Sterling Hayden, James Gleason, Nancy Gates. Tense Presidential assassination story, with Sinatra a hired killer. Fine performance by Mr. S.

Suddenly, It's Spring (1947) 87m. ** D: Mitchell Leisen. Paulette Goddard, Fred MacMurray, Macdonald Carey, Arleen Whelan, Lillian Fontaine. Strained comedy about married couple Goddard and MacMurray refusing to divorce each other.

Suddenly, Last Summer (1959) 114m. ***½ D: Joseph L. Mankiewicz. Elizabeth Taylor, Katharine Hepburn, Montgomery Clift, Mercedes McCambridge, Albert Dekker. Fascinating if talky Tennessee Williams yarn about wealthy Southern matriarch (Hepburn), her supposedly mad daughter-in-law (Taylor) and a neurosurgeon (Clift) ; grandly acted.

Suez (1938) 104m. *** D: Allan Dwan. Tyrone Power, Loretta Young, Annabella, Henry R. Stephenson, Maurice Moscovitch, Joseph Schildkraut, Sidney Blackmer. Power is French architect sent to build Suez Canal; his real problem is choosing between aristocratic Loretta and down-to-earth Annabella. Elaborate Darryl Zanuck production surrounds good cast of 1850's France-Egypt.

Sugarfoot (1951) 80m. **½ D: Edwin L. Marin. Randolph Scott, Adele Jergens, Raymond Massey, S. Z. Sakall. Above-par Scott Western. Randy is ex-Rebel officer who encounters his old adversary in Arizona. Retitled: SWIRL OF GLORY.

Suicide Battalion (1958) 79m. BOMB D: Edward L. Cahn. Michael Connors, John Ashley, Jewell Lain, Russ Bender. Static WW2 non-actioner. Army duo goes on mission to destroy government records hidden in building basement at Pearl Harbor.

Suicide Mission (1956-British) 70m.

** D: Michael Forlong. Leif Larsen, Michael Aldridge, Atle Larsen, Per Christensen. Standard WW2 actioner, set in Norway.

Suicide Squadron SEE: Dangerous Moonlight.

Sullivans, The (1944) 111m. *** D: Lloyd Bacon. Anne Baxter, Thomas Mitchell, Selena Royle, Ward Bond, Bobby Driscoll, Addison Richards. Patriotic drama from true story of five brothers during WW2 whose devotion for each other took precedence over everything else. They are played by Edward Ryan, John Campbell, James Cardwell, John Alvin, and George Offerman Jr.

Sullivan's Empire (1967) C-91m. **½ D: Harvey Hart, Thomas Carr. Martin Milner, Clu Galager, Karen Jensen, Linden Chiles, Don Quine, Arch Johnson. Unconvincing adventure yarn of rich landowner's trio of sons searching for father, whose plane crashed in South American jungle.

Sullivan's Travels (1941) 91m. ***½ D: Preston Sturges. Joel McCrea, Veronica Lake, Robert Warwick, William Demarest, Franklin Pangborn, Porter Hall. Movie director McCrea is tired of making trivial films, sets out to bum around country to capture flavor for a meaningful movie project. Satirical comedy hits bullseye, punctuated by fine dramatic episodes.

Summer and Smoke (1961) C-118m. ***½ D: Peter Glenville. Laurence Harvey, Geraldine Page, Rita Moreno, Una Merkel, Earl Holliman, Pamela Tiffin. Vivid performance by Page as Southern spinster yearning for love of young doctor Harvey; he ignores her, and both their lives are ruined. Sober Tennessee Williams play remains stagy.

Summer Holiday (1948) C-92m. **½ D: Rouben Mamoulian. Mickey Rooney, Gloria De Haven, Walter Huston, Frank Morgan, Butch Jenkins, Marilyn Maxwell, Anne Francis. Average musical adaptation of O'Neill play AH, WILDERNESS, about sensitive young boy who falls in love. Pastel-colored scenery is most winning.

Summer Interlude SEE: Illicit Interlude.

Summer Love (1958) 85m. ** D: Charles Haas. John Saxon, Molly Bee, Rod McKuen, Judi Meredith, Jill St. John. Sequel to ROCK, PRETTY BABY has Saxon et al hired to perform at summer resort camp; perky performances.

Summer Place, A (1959) C-130m. *** D: Delmer Daves. Richard Egan, Dorothy McGuire, Sandra Dee, Arthur Kennedy, Troy Donahue, Constance Ford, Beulah Bondi. Lushly photographed soaper of adultery and teen-age love at resort house on Maine coast. Excellent Max Steiner score.

Summer Stock (1950) C-100m. *** D: Charles Walters. Judy Garland, Gene Kelly, Eddie Bracken, Marjorie Main, Gloria De Haven, Phil Silvers, Hans Conried. Kelly's theater troupe take over Judy's farm, she gets show biz bug. Thin plot, breezy Judy, frantic Silvers, chipper De Haven.

Summer Storm (1944) 106m. *** D: Douglas Sirk. George Sanders, Linda Darnell, Edward Everett Horton, Sig Ruman, Anna Lee, Sarah Padden, Frank Orth. Darnell has one of her best roles as beautiful woman who brings tragedy to all involved with her, including herself; from Chekhov's story.

Summertime (1955) C-99m. ***½ D: David Lean. Katharine Hepburn, Rossano Brazzi, Isa Miranda, Darren McGavin. Lilting film of spinster Hepburn vacationing in Venice, falling in love with married Brazzi. Hepburn's sensitive portrayal is one of her best. Based on Arthur Laurents' THE TIME OF THE CUCKOO.

Sun Also Rises, The (1957) C-129m. *** D: Henry King. Tyrone Power, Ava Gardner, Errol Flynn, Mel Ferrer, Gregory Ratoff, Robert Evans, Juliette Greco, Eddie Albert. Hemingway story of expatriates in Parisian 1920's has slow stretches; worthwhile for outstanding cast, especially Flynn as a souse. Mexico City locations add flavor to tale of search for self-identity.

Sun Comes Up, The (1949) C-93m. ** D: Richard Thorpe. Jeanette MacDonald, Lloyd Nolan, Claude Jarman, Jr., Lewis Stone. Colorful but overly sentimental story of embittered widow MacDonald who is humanized by young Jarman and his dog, Lassie. MacDonald's last film.

Sun Never Sets, The (1939) 98m. **½ D: Rowland V. Lee. Douglas Fairbanks, Jr., Basil Rathbone, Barbara O'Neil, Lionel Atwill, Virginia Field, C. Aubrey Smith. Enjoyable patriotic drama of British brothers trying to prevent outbreak of war in

Africa. Well done with top-notch cast.

Sun Shines Bright, The (1953) 92m. **½ D: John Ford. Charles Winninger, Arleen Whelan, John Russell, Stepin Fetchit. Set in Civil War days, this modest production manages to capture flavor of rural life in tale of political contest.

Sun Valley Serenade (1941) 86m. *** D: H. Bruce Humberstone. Sonja Henie, John Payne, Glenn Miller, Milton Berle, Lynn Bari, Joan Davis. Light musicomedy with Henie a war refugee, Payne her foster parent, traveling with the Miller band and manager Berle to Sun Valley. Songs: "It Happened In Sun Valley," "Chattanooga Choo-Choo."

Sunbonnet Sue (1945) 89m. ** D: Ralph Murphy. Gale Storm, Phil Regan, George Cleveland, Minna Gombell, Edna Holland, Raymond Hatton. Programmer musical of the gay 90's enhanced by bouncy Storm in title role, as songstress in father's lower N.Y.C. saloon.

Sunday Dinner for a Soldier (1944) 86m. *** D: Lloyd Bacon. Anne Baxter, John Hodiak, Charles Winninger, Anne Revere, Chill Wills, Bobby Driscoll, Jane Darwell. Winning film of family that invites soldier to dinner; they are repaid for their kindness; enjoyable comedy-drama.

Sunday in New York (1963) C-105m. *** D: Peter Tewksbury. Cliff Robertson, Jane Fonda, Rod Taylor, Robert Culp, Jim Backus. Entire cast bubbles in this sex romp of virginal Fonda discovering New York and love. Peter Nero's score is perky.

Sundays and Cybele (1962-French, dubbed) 110m. ***½ D: Serge Bourguignon. Hardy Kruger, Nicole Courcel, Patricia Gozzi, Daniel Ivernel. Intelligently told account of shellshocked Kruger finding source of communication with the world via orphaned waif Gozzi, with tragic results. Splendidly realized film.

Sundown (1941) 90m. **½ D: Henry Hathaway. Gene Tierney, Bruce Cabot, George Sanders, Harry Carey, Joseph Calleia, Dorothy Dandridge, Reginald Gardiner. Tierney is surprisingly cast as native girl who assists British troops in Africa during WW2; fairly interesting, lushly photographed, but never scores.

Sundowners, The (1950) 83m. **½ D: George Templeton. Robert Preston, Cathy Downs, Robert Sterling, John Barrymore, Jr., Jack Elam. Tightly edited Western about brothers fighting on opposite sides of the law.

Sundowners, The (1960) C-133m. **** D: Fred Zinnemann. Deborah Kerr, Robert Mitchum, Peter Ustinov, Glynis Johns, Dina Merrill, Chips Rafferty. First-rate film of Australian family whose lives are devoted to sheepherding. Entire cast excellent, Kerr especially fine.

Sunny (1941) 98m. **½ D: Herbert Wilcox. Anna Neagle, Ray Bolger, John Carroll, Edward Everett Horton, Grace Hartman, Paul Hartman, Frieda Inescort. Wealthy Carroll loves showgirl Neagle in this pleasant musicomedy with Neagle and Bolger dancing in the film's most enjoyable sequence.

Sunny Side of the Street (1951) C-71m. *½ D: Richard Quine. Frankie Laine, Terry Moore, Jerome Courtland, Audrey Long. Moore has fickle notions over aspiring Laine in this low-grade musical, with guest stars such as Billy Daniels, Toni Arden.

Sunrise at Campobello (1960) C-143m. *** D: Vincent J. Donehue. Ralph Bellamy, Greer Garson, Hume Cronyn, Jean Hagen, Ann Shoemaker, Alan Bunce, Tim Considine, Zina Bethune, Frank Ferguson, Lyle Talbot. Sincere story of President Franklin Delano Roosevelt, his battle in politics and valiant struggle against polio. Well acted; Bellamy and Garson ARE Mr. and Mrs. Roosevelt.

Sunset Boulevard (1950) 110m. **** D: Billy Wilder. Gloria Swanson, William Holden, Erich von Stroheim, Fred Clark, Jack Webb, Hedda Hopper, Buster Keaton, Cecil B. DeMille, Anna Q. Nilsson, Nancy Olson. Faded silent-film star Norma Desmond (Swanson), living in the past with butler (Von Stroheim) shelters hack screen writer (Holden) as boyfriend. Bitter, funny, fascinating; Gloria's tour de force.

Supernatural (1933) 60m. **½ D: Victor Halperin. Carole Lombard, Randolph Scott, Vivienne Osborne, H. B. Warner, Beryl Mercer, William Farnum. Eerie tale of spirits taking over innocent people is far-fetched; Lombard is film's highlight.

Surgeon's Knife, The (1957-British) 75m. ** D: Gordon Parry. Donald Houston, Adrienne Corri, Lyndon Brook. Tepid drama of doctor Houston implicated in criminal negligence, becoming involved in murder.

Surprise Package (1960) 100m. **½ D: Stanley Donen. Yul Brynner, Mitzi Gaynor, Barry Foster, Eric Pohlmann, Noel Coward, George Coulouris. Versatile Brynner tries screwball comedy, not doing too badly as devil-may-care gambler planning big-time robbery; Gaynor is sprightly leading lady.

Surrender (1950) 90m. **½ D: Allan Dwan. Vera Ralston, John Carroll, Walter Brennan, Francis Lederer, Jane Darwell, Jeff York. Ralston is exotic if overdramatic gal playing everyone against each other; Republic Pictures' nicely mounted costumer.

Surrender—Hell! (1959) 85m. ** D: John Barnwell. Keith Andes, Susan Cabot, Paraluman, Nestor de Villa. Predictable account of Andes rallying partisan forces to combat Jap control of Philippines.

Susan and God (1940) 115m. **½ D: George Cukor. Joan Crawford, Fredric March, Ruth Hussey, John Carroll, Rita Hayworth, Nigel Bruce, Bruce Cabot, Rose Hobart, Rita Quigley, Marjorie Main, Gloria De Haven. Crawford is satisfactory as woman whose religious devotion loses her the love of her family. Gertrude Lawrence fared better on stage.

Susan Slade (1961) C-116m. **½ D: Delmer Daves. Troy Donahue, Dorothy McGuire, Connie Stevens, Lloyd Nolan, Brian Aherne, Kent Smith. Slick soaper beautifully photographed. McGuire pretends to be mother of daughter's (Stevens) illegitimate child. Donahue is Connie's true love.

Susan Slept Here (1954) C-98m. **½ D: Frank Tashlin. Dick Powell, Debbie Reynolds, Anne Francis, Glenda Farrell, Alvy Moore. Cutesy sex comedy filled with innuendoes, but little action.

Susannah of the Mounties (1939) 78m. **½ D: William A. Seiter. Shirley Temple, Randolph Scott, Margaret Lockwood, J. Farrell MacDonald, Moroni Olsen, Victor Jory. Mountie Scott raises orphan Shirley in this predictable but entertaining Temple vehicle.

Suspect, The (1944) 85m. ***½ D: Robert Siodmak. Charles Laughton, Ella Raines, Dean Harens, Molly Lamont, Henry Daniell, Rosalind Ivan. Superb, Hitchcock-like thriller of henpecked Laughton planning to get his wife out of the way so he can pursue lovely Raines.

Suspected Alibi SEE: **Suspended Alibi.**

Suspended Alibi (1956-British) 64m. *½ D: Alfred Shaughnessy. Patrick Holt, Honor Blackman, Andrew Keir, Valentine Dyall. Holt becomes involved in homicide via circumstantial evidence in this coincidence-laden drama. Retitled: SUSPECTED ALIBI.

Suspense (1946) 101m. ** D: Frank Tuttle. Barry Sullivan, Belita, Bonita Granville, Albert Dekker. Cheapie mystery caper with flavorful unraveling of homicide at an ice show.

Suspicion (1941) 99m. ***½ D: Alfred Hitchcock. Cary Grant, Joan Fontaine, Cedric Hardwicke, Nigel Bruce, Dame May Whitty, Isabel Jeans, Heather Angel. Fontaine won Oscar for portraying wife who believes husband Grant is trying to kill her. Suspenser is helped by Bruce as Cary's pal, but leaves viewer flat with finale.

Sutter's Gold (1936) 94m. *** D: James Cruze. Edward Arnold, Lee Tracy, Binnie Barnes, Katherine Alexander, Addison Richards, Montagu Love. Lush production set in 19th-century California, when gold was discovered and Sutter (Arnold) lost his lands. Good cast, sluggish script.

Suzy (1936) 99m. ** D: George Fitzmaurice. Jean Harlow, Franchot Tone, Cary Grant, Lewis Stone, Benita Hume. Fine cast sinks in romantic WW1 spy drama with Cary as a French flyer, Tone as Harlow's husband. Intended as semi-tragedy.

Svengali (1931) 76m. *** D: Archie Mayo. John Barrymore, Marian Marsh, Donald Crisp, Carmel Myers, Bramwell Fletcher. Prime Barrymore as man obsessed with young girl (Marsh) whom he considers his creation, Trilby. Classic tale is vividly enacted.

Svengali (1955-British) C-82m. **½ D: Noel Langley. Hildegarde Neff, Donald Wolfit, Terence Morgan, Noel Purcell, Alfie Bass. Lacks flair of earlier version of du Maurier's novel about mesmerizing teacher and his beautiful actress-pupil Trilby.

Swamp Diamonds SEE: **Swamp Women.**

Swamp Fire (1946) 69m. ** D: William Pine. Johnny Weissmuller, Virginia Grey, Buster Crabbe, Carol Thurston, Pedro DeCordova, Marcelle Corday. Ex-navy man Weissmuller has lost his nerve; friends try to help him out.

Swamp Water (1941) 90m. **½ D: Jean Renoir. Walter Brennan, Walter Huston, Anne Baxter, Dana Andrews, Virginia Gilmore, John Carradine. Well-meant but muddled tale of fugitive Brennan hiding out in Georgia swamps, bogs down into talk-fest. Remade as LURE OF THE WILDERNESS.

Swamp Women (1955) C-73m. *½ D: Roger Corman. Michael Connors, Marie Windsor, Beverly Garland, Carole Mathews, Susan Cummings. Heavy-handed nonsense of four female convicts escaping jail, chasing after buried loot. Retitled: SWAMP DIAMONDS; CRUEL SWAMP.

Swan, The (1956) C-112m. *** D: Charles Vidor. Grace Kelly, Alec Guinness, Louis Jourdan, Agnes Moorehead, Jessie Royce Landis, Brian Aherne. Mild Molnar comedy of manners, attractive cast but not much sparkle. Jourdan good as Kelly's suitor, but she's promised to prince Guinness.

Swanee River (1939) C-84m. **½ D: Sidney Lanfield. Don Ameche, Al Jolson, Andrea Leeds, Felix Bressart, Russell Hicks. Ameche isn't convincing as composer Stephen Foster, but Jolson and wonderful Foster songs keep this one afloat.

Sweet Adeline (1935) 87m. **½ D: Mervyn LeRoy. Irene Dunne, Donald Woods, Hugh Herbert, Ned Sparks, Joseph Cawthorn, Louis Calhern, Winifred Shaw. Combination of spy chase and operetta isn't always smooth, but songs like "Why Was I Born" and Dunne's know-how make this enjoyable.

Sweet and Lowdown (1944) 75m. ** D: Archie Mayo. Linda Darnell, Jack Oakie, Lynn Bari, James Cardwell, Allyn Joslyn, Dickie Moore. Thin story-line of Benny Goodman giving poor musician the big break, causing a rift with girfriend Darnell.

Sweet Bird of Youth (1962) C-120m. ***½ D: Richard Brooks. Paul Newman, Geraldine Page, Shirley Knight, Ed Begley, Madeleine Sherwood, Mildred Dunnock. Tennessee Williams' play, cleaned up for the movies, still is powerful drama. Newman returns to Southern town in entourage of dissipated movie queen Page, causing corrupt town "boss" Begley (who won an Oscar) to have him fixed proper. Glossy production with cast on top of material.

Sweet Rosie O'Grady (1943) C-74m. **½ D: Irving Cummings. Betty Grable, Robert Young, Adolphe Menjou, Reginald Gardiner, Virginia Grey, Phil Regan. Pleasant musical of ex-burlesque star Grable and exposé-reporter Young. Menjou steals film as editor of Police Gazette.

Sweet Smell of Success (1957) 96m. *** D: Alexander Mackendrick. Burt Lancaster, Tony Curtis, Marty Milner, Sam Levene, Barbara Nichols, Susan Harrison. Brittle Clifford Odets-Ernest Lehman script of vicious N.Y.C. columnist (Lancaster) and scheming press agent (Curtis) pulls no punches. Vivid performances and fine jazz score.

Sweethearts (1938) C-120m. *** D: W. S. Van Dyke II. Jeanette MacDonald, Nelson Eddy, Frank Morgan, Ray Bolger, Florence Rice, Mischa Auer. One of MacDonald and Eddy's best, in color, about two operetta stars who never stop fighting offstage. Victor Herbert songs: "Mademoiselle On Parade," "Sweethearts."

Swindle, The (1962-Italian, dubbed) 92m. ** D: Federico Fellini. Broderick Crawford, Giulietta Masina, Richard Basehart, Franco Fabrizi. Cast is better than story: trio of crooks fleece people in Rome, each planning rich future life.

Swing Fever (1944) 80m. *½ D: Tim Whelan. Kay Kyser, Marilyn Maxwell, William Gargan, Lena Horne. Most uneven blend of music, boxing, and romance pegged on personality of Kyser.

Swing Shift Maisie (1943) 87m. D: Norman Z. McLeod. Ann Sothern, James Craig, Jean Rogers, Connie Gilchrist, John Qualen, Kay Medford. SEE: Maisie series.

Swing Time (1936) 105m. **** D: George Stevens. Fred Astaire, Ginger Rogers, Victor Moore, Helen Broderick, Eric Blore, Betty Furness. One of the best Astaire-Rogers films, with stars as dance team whose romance is hampered by Fred's engagement to girl back home (Furness). Fine support by Moore and Broderick, unforgettable Jerome Kern-Dorothy Fields songs "A Fine Romance," "Pick Yourself Up." Oscar-winning "The Way You Look Tonight." Astaire's Bojangles production number is a screen classic.

Swinger, The (1966) C-81m. ** D: George Sidney. Ann-Margret, Tony Franciosa, Robert Coote, Horace McMahon, Nydia Westman. Brassy, artificial yarn of good-girl Ann-Margret posing as swinger to impress girlie magazine editor Franciosa.

Swingtime Johnny (1944) 61m. *½ D: Edward Cline. Andrews Sisters, Harriet Hilliard, Peter Cookson, Tim Ryan. Show biz performers desert the theater for work in munitions factory; lowbrow entertainment.

Swirl of Glory SEE: Sugarfoot.

Swiss Family Robinson (1940) 93m. *** D: Edward Ludwig. Thomas Mitchell, Edna Best, Freddie Bartholomew, Tim Holt, Terry Kilburn. Mitchell leads family to remote island where they live idyllic existence. Fine adaptation of Johann Wyss book.

Swiss Miss (1938) 72m. ** D: John Blystone. Stan Laurel, Oliver Hardy, Della Lind, Walter Woolf King, Eric Blore, Adia Kuznetzof, Charles Judels. Contrived romantic story with music tries hard to submerge L&H, but Stan and Ollie's scenes save film, especially when Ollie serenades his true love with Stan playing tuba.

Sword in the Desert (1949) 100m. **½ D: George Sherman. Dana Andrews, Marta Toren, Stephen McNally, Jeff Chandler, Philip Friend. Interesting account of underground trail of European refugees during WW2; fairly good suspenser.

Sword of Ali Baba, The (1965) C-81m. ** D: Virgil Vogel. Peter Mann, Jocelyn Lane, Pete Whitney, Gavin MacLeod, Frank Puglia. Outrageous remake of Jon Hall Ali Baba film of 1940's, using much footage from original. Puglia repeats role from original film.

Sword of El Cid, The (1962-Spanish, dubbed) C-85m. ** D: Miguel Iglesias. Roland Carey, Sandro Moretti, Chantal Deberg, Daniela Bianchi. Sparse plot ruins this potentially good costumer with Moretti et al battling corrupt ruler of Catalonia.

Sword of Lancelot (1963) C-116m. **½ D: Cornel Wilde. Cornel Wilde, Jean Wallace, Brian Aherne, George Baker. Camelot comes alive, minus music, with profuse action and splendid scenery. Some may find Wilde's approach too juvenile, overly sincere, and Aherne a bit too cavalier.

Sword of Monte Cristo, The (1951) C-80m. ** D: Maurice Geraghty. George Montgomery, Paula Corday, Berry Kroeger, William Conrad, Steve Brodie. Uninspired adventure of woman who finds legendary sword of Count with key to treasure inscribed on it. Army officer joins her in fight against evil prime minister.

Sword of Sherwood Forest (1961-British) C-80m. **½ D: Terence Fisher. Richard Greene, Niall MacGinnis, Peter Cushing, Nigel Green. Fair British continuation of Robin Hood saga as Earl of Newark plots murder of Archbishop of Canterbury.

Sword of the Conqueror (1961-Italian, dubbed) C-85m. *½ D: Carlo Campogalliani. Jack Palance, Eleonora Rossi-Drago, Guy Madison, Carlo D'Angelo. Flabby epic not livened by cast or sets; set in 6th-century Byzantine empire days.

Swordsman, The (1948) C-81m. ** D: Joseph H. Lewis. Larry Parks, Ellen Drew, George Macready, Edgar Buchanan. Parks and Drew have Romeo-Juliet relationship in 18th-century Scotland; OK costumer.

Sylvia (1965) 115m. **½ D: Gordon Douglas. Carroll Baker, George Maharis, Joanne Dru, Peter Lawford, Viveca Lindfors, Edmond O'Brien, Aldo Ray, Ann Sothern. Baker's prelude to HARLOW is much better, despite overuse of flashbacks and rambling episodes. Baker plays a bad girl turned good; melodrama unfolds as detective Maharis investigates her life. Good cameos.

Sylvia Scarlett (1935) 97m. **½ D: George Cukor. Katharine Hepburn, Cary Grant, Brian Aherne, Edmund Gwenn, Natalie Paley. Odd comedy-drama with Hepburn dressed as a boy, involved with gangsters, falling in love with Grant; most offbeat.

Synanon (1965) 107m. **½ D: Richard Quine. Chuck Connors, Stella Stevens, Alex Cord, Richard Conte, Eartha Kitt, Edmond O'Brien, Chanin Hale, Alejandro Rey. Potentially powerful study of dope-addiction treatment via the Synanon House methods bogs down in pat romantic tale with stereotyped performances.

Syncopation (1942) 88m. ** D: William Dieterle. Adolph Menjou, Jackie Cooper, Bonita Granville, Todd Duncan, George Bancroft, Connee Boswell, Mona Barrie, Hall Johnson Choir. Retelling early days of jazz is out of whack, but has great music to pep it up, many jazz guest stars.

System, The (1953) 90m. ** D: Lewis Seiler. Frank Lovejoy, Joan Weldon, Bob Arthur, Jerome Cowan. Uneven scripting spoils this potentially good study of gambling syndicate in large metropolitan city.

Systems, The (1966) SEE: **Girl-Getters, The.**

T-Men (1947) 96m. **½ D: Anthony Mann. Dennis O'Keefe, June Lockhart, Alfred Ryder, Charles McGraw. Dragnet-style documentary drama involving Treasury Department at work on counterfeiting case.

Taffy and the Jungle Hunter (1965) C-87m. ** D: Terry O. Morse. Jacques Bergerac, Manuel Padilla, Shary Marshall, Hari Rhodes. Unassuming tale of son of big game hunter who takes off for jungle adventures with pet elephant and chimp.

Taggart (1964) C-85m. **½ D: R. G. Springsteen. Tony Young, Dan Duryea, Peter Duryea, David Carradine, Jean Hale, Harry Carey, Bob Steele. Neat little action Western with Young on a revenge hunt, pursued by gunslingers in Indian territory.

Tail Spin (1939) 84m. ** D: Roy Del Ruth. Alice Faye, Constance Bennett, Nancy Kelly, Joan Davis, Charles Farrell, Jane Wyman. Hackneyed saga of female flyers, with nonsinging Faye in charge, worrier Kelly, funny-girl Davis, etc.

Tailor's Maid, The (1959-Italian; dubbed) 92m. **½ D: Mario Monicelli. Vittorio DeSica, Marcello Mastroianni, Marisa Merlini, Fiorella Mari, Memmo Carotenuto, Raffaele Pisu. Saucy, inconsequential comedy about an amorous tailor.

Take a Letter, Darling (1942) 93m. *** D: Mitchell Leisen. Rosalind Russell, Fred MacMurray, Constance Moore, Robert Benchley, Dooley Wilson, Cecil Kellaway. Witty repartee as advertising exec Roz hires MacMurray as secretary; but relationship doesn't end there. Benchley is wry as Russell's game-playing business partner.

Take Care of my Little Girl (1951) C-93m. ** D: Jean Negulesco. Jeanne Crain, Dale Robertson, Mitzi Gaynor, Jean Peters, Jeffrey Hunter, George Nader, Helen Westcott. Overdramatic story of sorority life at college.

Take Her, She's Mine (1963) C-98m. ** D: Henry Koster. James Stewart, Sandra Dee, Audrey Meadows, Robert Morley, Philippe Forquet, John McGiver. Obvious family comedy with Stewart the harried father of wild teen-age daughter Dee. Predictable gags don't help.

Take It or Leave It (1944) 70m. *½ D: Benjamin Stoloff. Phil Baker, Edward Ryan, Marjorie Massow, Stanley Prager, Roy Gordon. Claptrap hinged on lives of contestants on popular quiz show; film uses clips from older pictures to liven proceedings.

Take Me Out to the Ball Game (1949) C-93m. **½ D: Busby Berkeley. Frank Sinatra, Esther Williams, Gene Kelly, Betty Garrett, Edward Arnold, William Frawley, Jules Munshin. Contrived but colorful turn-of-the-century musical, with Sinatra and Kelly joining Williams' baseball team; pleasant froth.

Take Me to Town (1953) C-81m. **½ D: Douglas Sirk. Ann Sheridan, Sterling Hayden, Philip Reed, Lee Patrick, Lane Chandler. Unpretentious Americana of saloon singer Sheridan on the lam, finding love with widowed preacher Hayden and his three children.

Take One False Step (1949) 94m. **½ D: Chester Erskine. William Powell, Shelley Winters, James Gleason, Marsha Hunt, Dorothy Hart, Sheldon Leonard. OK mystery-drama with innocent Powell hunted by police as he tries to clear himself of murder charge.

Take the High Ground (1953) C-101m. *** D: Richard Brooks. Richard Widmark, Karl Malden, Elaine Stewart, Steve Forrest, Carleton Carpenter. Taut account of infantry basic training with on-location filming at Fort Bliss, Texas helping.

Tale of Two Cities, A (1935) 120m. **** D: Jack Conway. Ronald Colman, Elizabeth Allan, Edna May Oliver, Reginald Owen, Basil Rathbone, Blanche Yurka, Isabel Jewell. Dickens' panorama of the 1790's French Revolution becomes an MGM blockbuster, with Colman as carefree lawyer awakened to responsibility, aiding victims of the Reign of Terror. Tremendous cast supports lavish production.

Tales of Adventure SEE: **Jack London's Tales of Adventure.**

Tales of Hoffman (1951-British) C-138m. **½ D: Michael Powell, Emeric Pressburger. Moira Shearer, Leonide Massine, Robert Helpmann, Pamela Brown. Jacques Offenbach's fantasy opera of student who engages in bizarre dreams, revealing three states of his life. Long, not for all tastes.

Tales of Manhattan (1942) 118m. *** D: Julien Duvivier. Henry Fonda, Rita Hayworth, Ginger Rogers, Charles Boyer, Edward G. Robinson, Charles Laughton, Ethel Waters, Eddie Anderson, Thomas Mitchell, Gail Patrick, Roland Young. Episodic film in five segments is extremely variable, but stars make it worthwhile.

Tales of Robin Hood (1951) 60m. *½ D: James Tinling. Robert Clarke, Mary Hatcher, Paul Cavanagh, Wade Crosby. Minor account of folklore hero.

Talk of the Town, The (1942) 118m. **** D: George Stevens. Jean Arthur, Ronald Colman, Cary Grant, Glenda Farrell, Edgar Buchanan, Charles Dingle, Rex Ingram. Intelligent comedy with brilliant cast; fugitive Grant hides out with unsuspecting professor Colman and landlady Arthur, and tries to convince legal-minded Colman there's a human side to all laws. Splendid.

Tall, Dark and Handsome (1941) 78m. ** D: H. Bruce Humberstone. Cesar Romero, Virginia Gilmore, Milton Berle, Charlotte Greenwood. Runyonesque comedy of 1920's gangsters with hearts of gold. Remade as LOVE THAT BRUTE.

Tall in the Saddle (1944) 87m. *** D: Edwin L. Marin. John Wayne, Ella Raines, Ward Bond, Gabby Hayes, Elizabeth Risdon, Emory Parnell, Raymond Hatton. Cowboy Wayne avoids women until he goes to work at Raines' ranch; good, enjoyable Western.

Tall Lie, The SEE: For Men Only.

Tall Man Riding (1955) C-83m. **½ D: Lesley Selander. Randolph Scott, Dorothy Malone, Peggie Castle, John Dehner, Lane Chandler. Sturdy Western with Scott involved in outmaneuvering greedy ranchers during territorial land granting in Montana.

Tall Men, The (1955) C-122m. BOMB D: Raoul Walsh. Clark Gable, Jane Russell, Robert Ryan, Cameron Mitchell, Mae Marsh. Dismal oater unsaved by Jane in bloomers. Gable and Mitchell as brothers fight snowstorm and Indians. Blah.

Tall Story (1960) 91m. **½ D: Joshua Logan. Anthony Perkins, Jane Fonda, Ray Walston, Marc Connelly, Anne Jackson, Murray Hamilton, Bob Wright, Bart Burns. Fast-moving froth about man-hungry collegiate Fonda (in film debut) falling in love with college football star Perkins. Based on Howard Lindsay-Russell Crouse play.

Tall Stranger, The (1957) C-81m. ** D: Thomas Carr. Joel McCrea, Virginia Mayo, Michael Ansara, Michael Pate. Standard fare of McCrea helping wagon convoy cross Colorado territory.

Tall T, The (1957) C-78m. ** D: Budd Boetticher. Randolph Scott, Richard Boone, Maureen O'Sullivan, Henry Silva. Adequate gun-play perks this oater with Scott a rancher in Arizona up against a gang of robbers.

Tall Target, The (1951) 78m. **½ D: Anthony Mann. Dick Powell, Paula Raymond, Adolphe Menjou, Marshall Thompson, Ruby Dee. Set in 1850's, film traces detective Powell's attempt to avert assassination plot against incumbent President Lincoln.

Tall Women, The (1966-Spanish, dubbed) C-101m. ** D: Sidney Pink. Anne Baxter, Maria Perschy, Rosella Como, John Clarke. Western about seven women making their way through Indian country. Foreign-made movie suffers from dubbing and mediocre acting.

Tamango (1957-French, dubbed) C-98m. ** D: John Berry. Dorothy Dandridge, Curt Jurgens, Jean Servais, Roger Hanin, Guy Mairesse. Offbeat misfire about Dutch captain Jurgens involved with slave trader, romancing native Dandridge and trying to quell slave mutiny aboard.

Taming Sutton's Gal (1957) 71m. *½ D: Lesley Selander. John Lupton, Gloria Talbott, Jack Kelly, May Wynn, Verna Felton. Tedious hokum involving moonshiner's amorous wife.

Tammy and the Bachelor (1957) C-89m. *** D: Joseph Pevney. Debbie Reynolds, Walter Brennan, Leslie Nielsen, Mala Powers, Fay Wray, Sidney Blackmer, Louise Beavers. Unpretentious if cutesy romantic corn of country gal Reynolds falling in love with pilot Nielsen whom she's nursed back to health after plane crash.

Tammy and the Doctor (1963) C-88m. ****½ D:** Harry Keller. Sandra Dee, Peter Fonda, Macdonald Carey, Beulah Bondi, Margaret Lindsay, Reginald Owen. Sugary fluff involving homespun Tammy (Dee) courted by doctor Fonda; supporting cast adds touching cameos.

Tammy and the Millionaire (1967) C-87m. **** D:** Sidney Miller. Ezra Stone, Leslie Goodwins. Debbie Watson, Frank McGrath, Denver Pyle, George Furth, Donald Woods, Dorothy Green. Low-grade TV pilot expanded to feature, diluting the fuzzy folksy charm of backwoods girl trying to better the world.

Tammy Tell Me True (1961) C-97m. **** D:** Harry Keller. Sandra Dee, John Gavin, Virginia Grey, Beulah Bondi, Cecil Kellaway. Tired romance of girl coming to college for first time, makes name for herself by helping dean of women. Script and acting very uneven.

Tampico (1944) 75m. **** D:** Lothar Mendes. Edward G. Robinson, Lynn Bari, Victor McLaglen, Marc Lawrence, Mona Maris. Merchant-marine skipper Robinson senses espionage on his boat, but suspects wrong party. Routine WW2 intrigue, partially salvaged by stars.

Tanganyika (1954) C-81m. **** D:** Andre de Toth. Van Heflin, Ruth Roman, Howard Duff, Jeff Morrow. OK adventure of explorer attempting land claim in East Africa with numerous perils along the way.

Tangier (1946) 76m. **** D:** George Waggner. Maria Montez, Preston Foster, Robert Paige, Louise Allbritton, Kent Taylor, Sabu, J. Edward Bromberg, Reginald Denny. Limp intrigue in Tangier with vengeful dancer Montez, isn't even in color.

Tangier Incident (1953) 77m. ***½ D:** Lew Landers. George Brent, Mari Aldon, Dorothy Patrick, Bert Freed. Tame actioner with Brent a federal agent hunting an espionage ring.

Tank Force (1958-British) C-81m. ***½ D:** Terence Young. Victor Mature, Leo Genn, Anthony Newley, Luciana Paluzzi. Clichéd dud of WW2 with assorted British prisoners escaping across Libyan desert.

Tanks Are Coming, The (1951) 90m. **** D:** Lewis Seiler. Steve Cochran, Philip Carey, James Dodson, Mari Aldon, Paul Picerni. Moderate WW2 actioner set during Allied capture of Berlin.

Tap Roots (1948) C-109m. ****½ D:** George Marshall. Van Heflin, Susan Hayward, Boris Karloff, Julie London. Average historical drama about two lovers in secessionist Mississippi. Uneven script and standard acting.

Tarantula (1955) 80m. ****½ D:** Jack Arnold. John Agar, Mara Corday, Leo G. Carroll, Nestor Paiva, Ross Elliott. Slightly better than average horror film. Laboratory freak breaks loose and runs rampant; fair special effects.

Taras Bulba (1962) C-122m. ****½ D:** J. Lee Thompson. Tony Curtis, Yul Brynner, Christine Kaufmann, Sam Wanamaker. Cardboard costumer of 16th-century Russia, centering on Cossack life and fighting. Nice photography and fine musical score.

Tarawa Beachhead (1958) 77m. ****½ D:** Paul Wendkos. Kerwin Matthews, Julie Adams, Ray Danton, Karen Sharpe. Standard account of WW2 military assault with usual focus on problems of troops.

Target Earth (1954) 75m. ****½ D:** Sherman Rose. Richard Denning, Virginia Grey, Kathleen Crowley, Richard Reeves, Robert Ruark, Steve Pendleton. People in deserted city trapped by invading robot force. Competently acted movie starts off beautifully but bogs down too soon.

Target, Sea of China (1954) 100m. ***½ D:** Franklin Adreon. Harry Lauter, Aline Towne, Lyle Talbot, Robert Shayne, Fred Graham. Sloppy cliff-hanger nonsense of conspirators from unnamed foreign power aiding the rebellious natives. Re-edited movie serial: TRADER TOM OF THE CHINA SEAS.

Target Unknown (1951) 90m. ****½ D:** George Sherman. Mark Stevens, Alex Nicol, Joyce Holden, Robert Douglas, Don Taylor, Gig Young. Imaginative handling of worn-out premise of group of Allied soldiers caught in Nazi-occupied France.

Target Zero (1955) 92m. **** D:** Harmon Jones. Richard Conte, Charles Bronson, Chuck Connors, Peggie Castle. Unrewarding Korean War film.

Tarnished Angels, The (1957) 91m. ****½ D:** Douglas Sirk. Dorothy Malone, Rock Hudson, Robert Stack,

Jack Carson, Robert Middleton. William Faulkner's PYLON becomes predictable soaper set in 1930's South, about problems of people who work in a traveling air circus show.

Tarnished Lady (1931) 83m. **½ D: George Cukor. Tallulah Bankhead, Clive Brook, Phoebe Foster, Osgood Perkins, Elizabeth Patterson. Bankhead marries Brook for his money but falls in love with him almost too late. Ornate triangle has good performances.

Tartars, The (1962-Italian, dubbed) C-83m. ** D: Richard Thorpe. Orson Welles, Victor Mature, Folco Lulli, Liana Orfei. Welles' performance of Burundil, head of Tartar invasion of Volga River, plus appearance of Mature, are only distinguishing features of otherwise routine spectacle.

Tartu SEE: **Adventures of Tartu.**

Tarzan Although Edgar Rice Burroughs' king of the jungle has been played by some fourteen people from 1918 to the present, most aficionados agree that Johnny Weissmuller, who essayed the role from 1932 to 1948, was the one and only Tarzan. His early MGM efforts such as TARZAN THE APE MAN and TARZAN AND HIS MATE, co-starred with lovely Maureen O'Sullivan as Jane, were "class" films with fine production values, plenty of action, and excitement. Later entries at MGM like TARZAN'S NEW YORK ADVENTURE became more standardized, like other series films, with comedy relief supplied by Cheetah, the Chimp, the family interest sparked by Johnny Sheffield as Boy. On the whole, however, the six Weissmuller-O'Sullivan efforts were quite enjoyable. In 1942 Maureen left the series, but Weissmuller continued in lesser but still entertaining episodes produced for RKO release. Lex Barker took over the role in 1949, and continued through 1955; these films lost much of the original sparkle as budgets and inventiveness diminished. Various people (Denny Miller, Gordon Scott, Mike Henry, Ron Ely) have played Tarzan since, with Scott faring best in his late 50's-early 60's entries in the series, one of which, TARZAN'S GREATEST ADVENTURE, is an excellent jungle-adventure film shot in color with the added curio interest of pre-James Bond Sean Connery in the cast. The latest Tarzan films have been thrown together sloppily, some of them having only marginal relation to the Burroughs character. The 1959 "remake" of Weissmuller's 1932 TARZAN THE APE MAN was comprised mostly of stock footage from other films and tinted scenes from the original, with expected low-grade results. Other Tarzans, from Buster Crabbe to Bruce Bennett, have popped up from time to time in various competent vehicles but none of them have ever come up to the plateau of the MGM-Johnny Weissmuller efforts of the 1930's, which even today retain their punch and impact for a new generation of youngsters.

Tarzan and His Mate (1934) 105m. D: Cedric Gibbons, Jack Conway. Johnny Weissmuller, Maureen O'Sullivan, Neil Hamilton, Paul Cavanagh, Forrester Harvey.

Tarzan and the Amazons (1945) 76m. D: Kurt Neumann. Johnny Weissmuller, Brenda Joyce, Johnny Sheffield, Henry Stephenson, Maria Ouspenskaya, Barton MacLane.

Tarzan and the Green Goddess (1938) 72m. D: Edward Kull. Herman Brix (Bruce Bennett), Ula Holt, Frank Baker, Don Castellano, Lew Sargent.

Tarzan and the Huntress (1947) 72m. D: Kurt Neumann. Johnny Weissmuller, Brenda Joyce, John Sheffield, Patricia Morison, Barton MacLane.

Tarzan and the Leopard Woman (1946) 72m. D: Kurt Neumann. Johnny Weissmuller, Brenda Joyce, Johnny Sheffield, Acquanetta, Edgar Barrier, Tommy Cook.

Tarzan and the Lost Safari (1957) C-84m. D: H. Bruce Humberstone. Gordon Scott, Yolande Donlan, Betta St. John, Wilfrid Hyde-White, George Coulouris.

Tarzan and the Mermaids (1948) 68m. D: Robert Florey. Johnny Weissmuller, Brenda Joyce, Linda Christian, John Laurenz, Fernando Wagner.

Tarzan and the She-Devil (1953) 76m. D: Kurt Neumann. Lex Barker, Joyce McKenzie, Raymond Burr, Monique Van Vooren, Tom Conway.

Tarzan and the Slave Girl (1950) 74m. D: Lee Sholem. Lex Barker,

Vanessa Brown, Robert Alda, Denise Darcel, Hurd Hatfield.

Tarzan and the Trappers (1958) 74m. H. Bruce Humberstone. Gordon Scott, Eve Brent, Rickie Sorenson, Lesley Bradley, Maurice Marsac.

Tarzan Escapes (1936) 95m. D: Richard Thorpe. Johnny Weissmuller, Maureen O'Sullivan, John Buckler, Benita Hume, William Henry.

Tarzan Finds a Son (1939) 90m. D: Richard Thorpe. Johnny Weissmuller, Maureen O'Sullivan, Johnny Sheffield, Ian Hunter, Frieda Inescort, Laraine Day, Henry Wilcoxon.

Tarzan Goes to India (1962) C-86m. D: John Guillermin. Jock Mahoney, Mark Dana, Simi, Leo Gordon.

Tarzan, The Ape Man (1932) 99m. D: W. S. Van Dyke. Johnny Weissmuller, Maureen O'Sullivan, C. Aubrey Smith, Neil Hamilton, Doris Lloyd.

Tarzan, The Ape Man (1959) C-82m. D: Joseph M. Newman. Dennis Miller, Joanna Barnes, Cesare Danova, Robert Douglas, Thomas Yangha.

Tarzan the Magnificent (1960) C-88m. D: Robert Day. Gordon Scott, Jock Mahoney, Betta St. John, John Carradine, Alexandra Stewart, Lionel Jeffries, Earl Cameron.

Tarzan Triumphs (1943) 78m. D: William Thiele. Johnny Weissmuller, Frances Gifford, Johnny Sheffield, Stanley Ridges, Sig Ruman.

Tarzan's Desert Mystery (1943) 70m. D: William Thiele. Johnny Weissmuller, Nancy Kelly, Johnny Sheffield, Otto Kruger, Joseph Sawyer, Lloyd Corrigan, Robert Lowery.

Tarzan's Fight for Life (1958) C-86m. D: H. Bruce Humberstone. Gordon Scott, Eve Brent, Rickie Sorensen, Jil Jarmyn.

Tarzan's Greatest Adventure (1959) C-88m. D: John Guillermin. Gordon Scott, Anthony Quayle, Sara Shane, Niall McGinnis, Scilla Gabel.

Tarzan's Hidden Jungle (1955) 73m. D: Harold Schuster. Gordon Scott, Vera Miles, Peter Van Eyck, Jack Elam, Rex Ingram.

Tarzan's Magic Fountain (1949) 73m. D: Lee Sholem. Lex Barker, Brenda Joyce, Evelyn Ankers, Albert Dekker, Alan Napier, Charles Drake, Henry Brandon.

Tarzan's New York Adventure (1942) 71m. D: Richard Thorpe. Johnny Weissmuller, Maureen O'Sullivan, Johnny Sheffield, Virginia Grey, Charles Bickford, Paul Kelly, Russell Hicks, Miles Mander.

Tarzan's Peril (1951) 79m. D: Byron Haskin. Lex Barker, Virginia Huston, George Macready, Douglas Fowley.

Tarzan's Revenge (1938) 70m. D: Ross Lederman. Glenn Morris, Eleanor Holm, George Barbier, C. Henry Gordon, Hedda Hopper, George Meeker.

Tarzan's Savage Fury (1952) 80m. D: Cyril Endfield. Lex Barker, Dorothy Hart, Patric Knowles, Charles Korvin.

Tarzan's Secret Treasure (1941) 81m. D: Richard Thorpe. Johnny Weissmuller, Maureen O'Sullivan, Johnny Sheffield, Reginald Owen, Barry Fitzgerald, Tom Conway.

Tarzan's Three Challenges (1963) C-92m. D: Robert Day. Jock Mahoney, Woody Strode, Ricky Der, Tsuruko Kobayashi.

Task Force (1949) 116m. **½ D: Delmer Daves. Gary Cooper, Jane Wyatt, Wayne Morris, Walter Brennan, Julie London. Engaging tale of navy officer's service life, tracing aircraft carrier development; otherwise standard production.

Taste of Honey, A (1962-British) 100m. ***½ D: Tony Richardson. Dora Bryan, Rita Tushingham, Robert Stephens, Murray Melvin. Uncompristing version of Shelagh Delaney's grim but lively drama. Tushingham has an affair with Negro sailor, becomes pregnant. Her fun-loving mother ignoring her, she turns to homosexual boy for help.

Tattered Dress, The (1957) 93m. **½ D: Jack Arnold. Jeff Chandler, Jeanne Crain, Jack Carson, Gail Russell, George Tobias. Slowly paced but engaging account of lawyer Chandler defending society couple accused of murder; Crain is his sympathetic wife.

Taxi (1932) 70m. **½ D: Roy Del Ruth. James Cagney, Loretta Young, George E. Stone, Dorothy Burgess, Guy Kibbee, Nat Pendleton. Cagney is fine in this actionful vehicle of war among cab drivers.

Taxi (1953) 77m. ** D: Gregory

Ratoff. Dan Dailey, Constance Smith, Neva Patterson, Blanche Yurka, Stubby Kaye. Mild little comedy of N.Y.C. cab driver Dailey trying to help an Irish girl find her hubby.

Taxi For Tobruk (1965, French dubbed) 90m. **½ D: Denys De La Patelliere. Lino Ventura, Hardy Kruger, Charles Aznavour, German Cobos. Engaging study of French soldiers and their German prisoner crossing the desert during WW2.

Taza, Son of Cochise (1954) C-79m. ** D: Douglas Sirk. Rock Hudson, Barbara Rush, Gregg Palmer, Bart Roberts, Morris Ankrum. Production cannot help clichéd story of Indians fighting among themselves and against settlers.

Tea and Sympathy (1956) C-122m. *** D: Vincente Minnelli. Deborah Kerr, John Kerr, Leif Erickson, Edward Andrews, Darryl Hickman, Dean Jones, Norma Crane. Glossy but well-acted version of Robert Anderson play about prep school boy's affair with a teacher's wife, skirting homosexual issues. Both Kerrs give sensitive portrayals.

Tea for Two (1950) C-98m. **½ D: David Butler. Doris Day, Gordon MacRae, Gene Nelson, Eve Arden, Billy DeWolfe. One of Day's better Warner Bros. musicals, with socialite Doris catching the show biz bug.

Teacher and the Miracle, The (1961-Italian, dubbed) 88m. **½ D: Aldo Fabrizi. Aldo Fabrizi, Eduardo Nevola, Marco Paolette, Mary Lamar, Jose Calvo. Good tear-jerker of man broken by death of son who had inspired him to start art school. Cast gives adequate performance.

Teacher's Pet (1958) 120m. *** D: George Seaton. Clark Gable, Doris Day, Gig Young, Mamie Van Doren, Nick Adams, Charles Lane. City editor Gable accidentally enrolls in Doris' journalism course, tries to pursue her after class. Airy, amusing, with Young memorable as Doris' intellectual boyfriend.

Teahouse of the August Moon, The (1956) C-123m. ***½ D: Daniel Mann. Marlon Brando, Glenn Ford, Machiko Kyo, Eddie Albert, Paul Ford. Outstanding service comedy based on John Patrick play of army officers in post-WW2 Okinawa involved with geisha girls.

Techman Mystery, The (1954-British) 89m. ** D: Wendy Toye. Margaret Leighton, John Justin, Meier Tzelniker, Roland Culver, George Coulouris, Michael Medwin. Justin is writer commissioned to do a biography of Medwin, presumably dead war hero, with surprising results. Capably acted.

Teenage Bad Girl SEE: Bad Girl.

Tennage Doll (1957) 68m. BOMB D: Roger Corman. June Kennedy, Fay Spain, Richard Devon, Dorothy Neumann. Sloppy juvenile delinquency street gang narrative.

Teen-age Millionaire (1961) 84m. BOMB D: Lawrence Doheny. Jimmy Clanton, Zasu Pitts, Rocky Graziano, Diane Jergens, Chubby Checker. Virtually witless musical of teen-ager with huge inheritance becoming recording star.

Teen-age Rebel (1956) 94m. **½ D: Edmund Goulding. Ginger Rogers, Michael Rennie, Betty Lou Keim, Mildred Natwick, Rusty Swope, Warren Berlinger, Lili Gentle, Louise Beavers, Irene Hervey. Pat yet provocative film of divorcee Rogers, now remarried, trying to reestablish understanding with her daughter.

Teen-agers From Outer Space (1959) 86m. BOMB D: Tom Graeff. David Love, Dawn Anderson, Harvey B. Dunn, Bryant Grant, Tom Lockyear. Ridiculous sci-fi about alien youths who bring monster to earth.

Tell It to the Judge (1949) 87m. **½ D: Norman Foster. Rosalind Russell, Robert Cummings, Gig Young, Marie McDonald, Harry Davenport, Douglass Dumbrille. Flyweight marital farce with Russell and Cummings in and out of love every ten minutes; enjoyable if you like the stars.

Tell-Tale Heart, The (1963-British) 81m. ** D: Ernest Morris. Laurence Payne, Adrienne Corri, Dermot Walsh, Selma Vaz Dias. Edgar Allan Poe yarn elaborated into tale of jealous love murder; not sufficiently atmospheric.

Tempest (1959-Italian, dubbed) C-125m. **½ D: Alberto Lattuada. Silvana Mangano, Van Heflin, Viveca Lindfors, Geoffrey Horne, Oscar Homolka, Robert Keith, Agnes Moorehead, Finlay Currie, Vittorio Gassman, Helmut Dantine. Turgid, disjointed costumer set in 18th-century Russia, loosely based on Pushkin novel about peasant uprising to dethrone Catherine the Great (Lindfors).

Temptation (1946) 92m. ** D: Irving Pichel. Merle Oberon, Paul Lukas, George Brent, Charles Korvin, Lenore Ulric. Costume marital drama is heavy-handed, saddling cast with clichéd lines and situation.

Ten Days to Tulara (1958) 77m. BOMB D: George Sherman. Sterling Hayden, Grace Raynor, Rodolfo Hoyos, Carlos Muzquiz. Dud adventure account of Hayden et al pursued across Mexico by police for the gold they carry.

Ten Gentlemen From West Point (1942) 102m. *** D: Henry Hathaway. George Montgomery, Maureen O'Hara, John Sutton, Laird Cregar, Victor Francen, Harry Davenport, Ward Bond, Tom Neal. Early years of West Point, with focus on vicious commander Cregar and other assorted military film clichés; somehow it's still entertaining.

Ten Little Indians (1965) 92m. **1/2 D: George Pollock. Hugh O'Brian, Shirley Eaton, Fabian, Leo Genn, Stanley Holloway, Wilfrid Hyde-White, Daliah Lavi. Fair remake of Agatha Christie's whodunit AND THEN THERE WERE NONE, with suspects trapped in remote Alpine village. Gimmick of murder-minute for audience to guess killer.

Ten North Frederick (1958) 102m. *** D: Philip Dunne. Gary Cooper, Diane Varsi, Suzy Parker, Geraldine Fitzgerald. Timid but still effective filming of John O'Hara novel about Cooper allowing romance with Parker to overshadow his political ambitions. Fitzgerald fine as grasping wife.

Ten Seconds to Hell (1959) 93m. **1/2 D: Robert Aldrich. Jeff Chandler, Jack Palance, Martine Carol, Robert Cornthwaite, Dave Willock, Wesley Addy. Chandler and Palance are almost believable as Germans involved in defusing mobs in Berlin, while competing for Carol's affection.

Ten Tall Men (1951) C-97m. **1/2 D: Willis Goldbeck. Burt Lancaster, Jody Lawrance, Gilbert Roland, Kieron Moore. Above-average Foreign Legion tale, with dynamic Lancaster pushing the action along.

Ten Thousand Bedrooms (1957) C-114m. ** D: Richard Thorpe. Dean Martin, Anna Maria Alberghetti, Eva Bartok, Walter Slezak, Paul Henreid. Martin's first effort without Jerry is pretty tired: he's a playboy loose in Rome who finds love.

Ten Wanted Men (1955) C-80m. ** D: H. Bruce Humberstone. Randolph Scott, Jocelyn Brando, Richard Boone, Minor Watson. Soaper set on the sagebrush, with Scott a cattle rancher involved in gun battle to protect his nephew's right to marry his true love.

Tender Comrade (1943) 102m. ** D: Edward Dmytryk. Ginger Rogers, Robert Ryan, Ruth Hussey, Patricia Collinge, Mady Christians, Kim Hunter, Jane Darwell. Saga of girls who worked in factories while husbands and sweethearts were at war. Too syrupy at times.

Tender is the Night (1962) C-146m. **1/2 D: Henry King. Jennifer Jones, Jason Robards, Jr., Joan Fontaine, Tom Ewell, Jill St. John. Sluggish, unflavorful version of F. Scott Fitzgerald novel with Jones unsatisfactory as mentally unstable wife of psychiatrist Robards; Fontaine is her chic sister; set in 1920's Europe.

Tender Trap, The (1955) C-111m. ***1/2 D: Charles Walters. Frank Sinatra, Debbie Reynolds, Celeste Holm, David Wayne, Carolyn Jones, Lola Albright, Tom Helmore. Delightful romp of swinging bachelor Sinatra who stumbles into marriage with determined Debbie in N.Y.C.; impeccable support from Holm and Wayne, plus a fine title tune help out.

Tender Years, The (1947) 81m. ** D: Harold Schuster. Joe E. Brown, Richard Lyon, Noreen Nash, Charles Drake, Josephine Hutchinson. Warm drama of minister trying to protect dog his son is attached to; notably mainly for rare dramatic performance by Brown.

Tenderfoot, The (1932) 70m. **1/2 D: Ray Enright. Joe E. Brown, Ginger Rogers, Lew Cody, George Chandler, Allan Lane, Vivien Oakland. Brown's a naive cowboy who gets mixed up with gangsters, then gets to back a Broadway show starring Rogers.

Tennessee Champ (1954) C-73m. **1/2 D: Fred M. Wilcox. Shelley Winters, Keenan Wynn, Dewey Martin, Earl

Holliman, Dave O'Brien. Good performances highlight average story of boxer who reforms crooked employer.

Tennessee Johnson (1942) 103m. ****½ D:** William Dieterle. Van Heflin, Lionel Barrymore, Ruth Hussey, Marjorie Main, Charles Dingle, Regis Toomey, Grant Withers, Lynne Carver, Noah Beery, Sr., Morris Ankrum. Sincere historical drama of President Andrew Johnson's rise and subsequent conflicts with Congress, given a glossy MGM production.

Tennessee's Partner (1955) C-87m. ****½ D:** Allan Dwan. John Payne, Rhonda Fleming, Ronald Reagan, Coleen Gray, Morris Ankrum. Offbeat little Western with Payne excellent in an unusual "heel" characterization, Reagan accidentally becoming his pal.

Tension (1949) 95m. ****½ D:** John Berry. Richard Basehart, Audrey Totter, Cyd Charisse, Barry Sullivan, Tom D'Andrea. Timid Basehart methodically seeks revenge on his conniving wife who walked out on him; quiet melodrama.

Tension at Table Rock (1956) C-93m. **** D:** Charles Marquis Warren. Richard Egan, Dorothy Malone, Cameron Mitchell, Billy Chapin, Angie Dickinson. Soaper Western with Egan on the lam for a murder committed in self-defense.

Tenth Avenue Angel (1948) 74m. **BOMB D:** Roy Rowland. Margaret O'Brien, Angela Lansbury, George Murphy, Phyllis Thaxter, Warner Anderson. Capable cast lost in terrible script about street urchin who prevents young man from becoming gangster.

Tenth Victim, The (1965-Italian, dubbed) C-92m. ***** D:** Elio Petri. Marcello Mastroianni, Ursula Andress, Elsa Martinelli, Salvo Randone, Massimo Serato. Sci-fi of futuristic society where violence is channeled into legalized murder hunts. Here, Ursula hunts Marcello. Intriguing idea, well done.

Teresa (1951) 102m. **** D:** Fred Zinnemann. John Ericson, Pier Angeli, Patricia Collinge, Richard Bishop, Peggy Ann Garner. Intriguing, but superficially told story of WW2 veteran Ericson who returns to U.S. with his Italian bride, encountering home-town prejudice.

Terrible People, The (1960-German, dubbed) 95m. **** D:** Harold Reinl. Eddi Arent, Karin Dor, Elizabeth Flickenschildt, Fritz Rasp, Joachim Fuchsberger. Moderate actioner of condemned bank crook vowing to return from the dead to punish those who prosecuted him. Retitled: HAND OF THE GALLOWS.

Terror, The (1963) C-81m. ****½ D:** Roger Corman. Boris Karloff, Jack Nicholson, Sandra Knight, Richard Miller. Engaging chiller nonsense with Karloff the mysterious owner of a castle where eerie deeds occur; set on Baltic coast in 1800's.

Terror at Midnight (1956) 70m. **** D:** Franklin Adreon. Scott Brady, Joan Vohs, Frank Faylen, John Dehner. Undynamic telling of Vohs being blackmailed and her law-enforcer boyfriend (Brady) helping out.

Terror by Night (1946) 60m. **D:** Roy William Neill. Basil Rathbone, Nigel Bruce, Alan Mowbray, Dennis Hoey, Renee Godfrey, Mary Forbes. SEE: Sherlock Holmes series.

Terror in a Texas Town (1958) 80m. ***½ D:** Joseph H. Lewis. Sterling Hayden, Sebastian Cabot, Carol Kelly, Eugene Martin. Flabby shoot-out yarn in an oil-rich town.

Terror in the Midnight Sun (1958-Swedish, dubbed) 73m. **** D:** Virgil Vogel. Barbara Wilson, Robert Burton, Sten Gester, Bengt Blomgren. Pedestrian account of alien monster on prowl in Lapland; good photography.

Terror is a Man (1959) 89m. **BOMB D:** Gerry DeLeon. Francis Lederer, Greta Thyssen, Richard Derr, Oscar Keesee. Stupidity about doctor experimenting with panther to turn him into a human; filmed in Philippines.

Terror of the Red Mask (1960-Italian, dubbed) C-90m. **** D:** Piero Pierotti. Lex Barker, Chelo Alonso, Massimo Serato. Costumer strains to have air of a chiller as hero Barker sword-fights his way through castle of horror.

Terror of the Tongs (1961-British) C-80m. ****½ D:** Anthony Bushell. Geoffrey Toone, Bert Kwouk, Brian Worth, Christopher Lee, Richard Leech. Atmospheric British thriller of captain searching for killers of daughter; eventually breaks entire Tong society in Hong Kong. Good acting but may be a little gruesome for some viewers.

Terror on a Train (1953-British) 72m. **½ D: Ted Tetzlaff. Glenn Ford, Anne Vernon, Maurice Denham, Victor Maddern. Tense little film of Ford defusing time bomb placed aboard train full of high explosives.

Tess of the Storm Country (1960) C-84m. **½ D: Paul Guilfoyle. Diane Baker, Jack Ging, Lee Philips, Wallace Ford, Robert F. Simon, Bert Remsen. Grace White's period novel of Scottish girl and uncle coming to America and adjusting to life in Pennsylvania Dutch country; leisurely paced, nicely done.

Test Pilot (1938) 118m. *** D: Victor Fleming. Clark Gable, Myrna Loy, Spencer Tracy, Lionel Barrymore, Samuel S. Hinds, Marjorie Main, Louis Jean Heydt. Blend of romantic comedy and drama doesn't always work; Tracy steals film as Gable's pal in story of daredevils who try out new aircraft.

Testament of Dr. Mabuse, The (1961-German, dubbed) 87m. **½ D: Werner Klinger. Gert Frobe, Senta Berger, Walter Rilla, Helmut Schmid, Charles Regnier. Engaging continuation of arch-crimial series with infamous Dr. M masterminding his schemes from within his mental institution cell; actionful drama.

Texan Meets Calamity Jane, The (1950) C-71m. BOMB D: Ande Lamb. Evelyn Ankers, James Ellison, Jack Ingram, Lee "Lasses" White. Ankers is too subdued as famed cowgirl of yesteryear, involved in fight to prove claim to prosperous saloon.

Texans, The (1938) 92m. ** D: James Hogan. Randolph Scott, Joan Bennett, May Robson, Walter Brennan, Robert Cummings, Robert Barrat. Texas, post-Civil War, is setting for routine Western with good cast.

Texas (1941) 93m. *** D: George Marshall. William Holden, Glenn Ford, Claire Trevor, George Bancroft, Edgar Buchanan. High-level Western of two friends, one a rustler, the other a cattleman, competing for Trevor's affection.

Texas Across the River (1966) C-101m. *** D: Michael Gordon. Dean Martin, Alain Delon, Joey Bishop, Rosemary Forsyth, Peter Graves, Tina Marquand. Diverting takeoff on cowboy-and-Indian films, with Bishop hilarious as a deadpan Indian and Marquand cute as a young squaw.

Texas, Brooklyn and Heaven (1948) 76m. ** D: William Castle. Guy Madison, Diana Lynn, James Dunn, Lionel Stander, Florence Bates, Roscoe Karns. Stale "comedy" of cowboy who falls in love with city girl who loves horses. B-cast.

Texas Carnival (1951) C-77m. ** D: Charles Walters. Esther Williams, Red Skelton, Keenan Wynn, Howard Keel. Emptier than usual, this flabby MGM vehicle with Williams, Skelton, and Keel leaves them high and dry with no fresh material.

Texas Lady (1955) C-86m. ** D: Tim Whelan. Claudette Colbert, Barry Sullivan, Greg Walcott, Horace McMahon, John Litel. Genteel oater; Colbert lovely as crusading newspaper editor in old West. Mediocre script.

Texas Rangers, The (1936) 95m. *** D: King Vidor. Fred MacMurray, Jack Oakie, Jean Parker, Lloyd Nolan, Edward Ellis. Fine, elaborate Western of three comrades who split up; MacMurray and Oakie become rangers, Nolan an outlaw. Remade as STREETS OF LAREDO.

Texas Rangers, The (1951) C-68m. *½ D: Phil Karlson. George Montgomery, Gale Storm, Jerome Courtland, Noah Beery, Jr. Aimless Western involving Texas law enforcers against gang of outlaws.

Texas Rangers Ride Again (1941) 68m. ** D: James Hogan. John Howard, Akim Tamiroff, Ellen Drew, May Robson. Standard Western fare of lawmen involved with cow rustlers.

Thank You Jeeves (1936) 68m. ** D: Arthur Collins. Arthur Treacher, Virginia Fields, David Niven, Lester Matthews. Treacher is at peak form playing impeccable butler whose love of decorum leads him on merry chase. Retitled: THANK YOU MR. JEEVES.

Thank You Mr. Jeeves SEE: **Thank You Jeeves.**

Thank You, Mr. Moto (1937) 67m. D: Norman Foster. Peter Lorre, Pauline Frederick, Sidney Blackmer, Sig

Ruman, John Carradine, Nedda Harrigan, Philip Ahn. SEE: **Mr. Moto** series.

Thank Your Lucky Stars (1943) 127m. *** D: David Butler. Eddie Cantor, Humphrey Bogart, Bette Davis, Olivia de Havilland, Errol Flynn, John Garfield, Joan Leslie, Ida Lupino, Dennis Morgan, Ann Sheridan. Very lame plot frames all-star Warner Bros. show, with Davis singing "They're Either Too Young Or Too Old," other staid stars breaking loose.

Thanks a Million (1935) 87m. *** D: Roy Del Ruth. Dick Powell, Ann Dvorak, Fred Allen, Patsy Kelly, Alan Dinehart, Margaret Irving, Paul Whiteman and Orchestra, Yacht Club Boys. Very entertaining musical of crooner Powell running for governor, with help of wisecracking manager Allen, sweetheart Dvorak, and blustery politician Raymond Walburn. Good fun, with several breezy tunes and specialties by Whiteman and Yacht Club Boys.

That Certain Age (1938) 95m. *** D: Edward Ludwig. Deanna Durbin, Melvyn Douglas, Jackie Cooper, Irene Rich, Nancy Carroll, John Halliday, Jack Searl, Grant Mitchell. Deanna's at the age where she's torn between boyfriend Cooper and mature Douglas; cozy little comedy with Durbin singing "You're As Pretty As a Picture, "My Own."

That Certain Feeling (1956) C-103m. BOMB D: Norman Panama, Melvin Frank. Bob Hope, Eva Marie Saint, George Sanders, Pearl Bailey. Incredibly bad Hope comedy with Bob as neurotic cartoonist; Sanders gives only life to stale film. Pearl sings title song.

That Certain Woman (1937) 93m. **1/2 D: Edmund Goulding. Bette Davis, Henry Fonda, Donald Crisp, Ian Hunter, Minor Watson, Sidney Toler, Anita Louise. Remake of Gloria Swanson's early talkie THE TRANSGRESSOR features Bette as a gangster's widow who's trying to start life fresh, falling in love for real with Fonda. Well-acted soaper.

That Forsyte Woman (1949) C-114m. **1/2 D: Compton Bennett. Errol Flynn, Greer Garson, Walter Pidgeon, Robert Young, Janet Leigh, Harry Davenport. Rather superficial adaptation of John Galsworthy novel of a faithless woman (Garson) who finds herself attracted by her niece's fiancee; well-appointed period sets.

That Funny Feeling (1965) C-93m. **1/2 D: Richard Thorpe. Sandra Dee, Bobby Darin, Donald O'Connor, Nita Talbot, Larry Storch, Leo G. Carroll, Robert Strauss. Funny only if you adore Darin and Dee, and even then story of footloose playboys wears thin.

That Gang of Mine (1940) 62m. D: Joseph H. Lewis. Bobby Jordan, Leo Gorcey, Clarence Muse, Dave O'Brien, Joyce Bryant, Donald Haines, David Gorcey. SEE: **Bowery Boys** series.

That Girl from Paris (1936) 110m. **1/2 D: Leigh Jason. Lily Pons, Jack Oakie, Gene Raymond, Herman Bing, Mischa Auer, Frank Jenks, Lucille Ball. Breezy Pons vehicle. She flees Continental wedding and runs to America. Tuneful songs, fine supporting cast.

That Hagen Girl (1947) 83m. BOMB D: Peter Godfrey. Shirley Temple, Ronald Reagan, Dorothy Peterson, Charles Kemper, Rory Calhoun. Atrocious "comedy" of Temple convinced she's Reagan's illegitimate daughter.

That Hamilton Woman (1941) 128m. *** D: Alexander Korda. Vivien Leigh, Laurence Olivier, Alan Mowbray, Sara Allgood, Gladys Cooper, Henry Wilcoxon, Heather Angel. History and romance combine in patriotic version of Lord Nelson and Lady Hamilton episode, with star duo impressive in their flashy portrayals.

That Kind of Woman (1959) 92m. ** D: Sidney Lumet. Sophia Loren, Tab Hunter, George Sanders, Jack Warden, Barbara Nichols, Keenan Wynn. Flat attempt to recreate WW2 romantic comedy with Loren and Hunter not a very dynamic combination.

That Lady (1955) C-100m. **1/2 D: Terence Young. Olivia de Havilland, Gilbert Roland, Paul Scofield, Dennis Price, Christopher Lee. Unemotional costumer set in 16th-century Spain, with De Havilland a widowed noblewoman involved in court intrigue.

That Lady In Ermine (1948) C-89m. *** D: Ernst Lubitsch, Otto Preminger. Betty Grable, Douglas Fairbanks,

Jr., Cesar Romero, Walter Abel, Reginald Gardiner, Harry Davenport. Entertaining if overblown musical of mythical kingdom where ancestors magically return.

That Man from Rio (1964-French, dubbed) C-114m. *** D: Philippe De Broca. Jean-Paul Belmondo, Françoise Dorleac, Jean Servais, Adolfo Celi, Simone Renant. Engaging spoof of Bond-type movies features Belmondo as hero, chasing double-crosser and thief in search for Brazilian treasure. Nice color photography complements fast-moving script.

That Man in Istanbul (1966) C-117m. **½ D: Anthony Isasi. Horst Buchholz, Sylva Koscina, Mario Adorf, Klaus Kinski. Fairly engaging spy romp featuring Koscina as FBI agent with Buchholz as playboy in search for missing scientist.

That Midnight Kiss (1949) C-96m. **½ D: Norman Taurog. Kathryn Grayson, Mario Lanza, Jose Iturbi, Ethel Barrymore, Keenan Wynn, J. Carrol Naish, Jules Munshin. Flimsy musical romance between Lanza and Grayson salvaged by pleasant musical interludes and glossy production.

That Night (1957) 88m. **½ D: John Newland. John Beal, Augusta Dabney, Malcolm Brodrick, Shepperd Strudwick, Rosemary Murphy. Straightforward account of man suffering a heart attack, and the effect it has on his family.

That Night in Rio (1941) C-90m. **½ D: Irving Cummings. Alice Faye, Don Ameche, Carmen Miranda, S. Z. Sakall, J. Carrol Naish, Curt Bois, Leonid Kinsky, Frank Puglia. Standard 20th Century Fox musical of mistaken identities, uses Miranda to best advantage.

That Night with You (1945) 84m. ** D: William A. Seiter. Franchot Tone, Susanna Foster, David Bruce, Louise Allbritton, Jacqueline de Wit, Buster Keaton. OK vehicle for soprano Foster who connives her way to a show biz break via producer Tone.

That Touch of Mink (1962) C-99m. **½ D. Delbert Mann. Cary Grant, Doris Day, Gig Young, Audrey Meadows, John Astin. Attractive cast in silly piece of fluff with Grant vs. Day. Amusing at times, but wears thin. Astin is memorable as a creep with designs on poor Doris.

That Uncertain Feeling (1941) 84m. *** D: Ernst Lubitsch. Merle Oberon, Melvyn Douglas, Burgess Meredith, Alan Mowbray, Olive Blakeney, Harry Davenport, Eve Arden. Chic little Lubitsch comedy about married couple with problems, and their absurd pianist friend. Stolen hands-down by Meredith as the musical malcontent.

That Way with Women (1947) 84m. ** D: Frederick de Cordova. Dane Clark, Martha Vickers, Sydney Greenstreet, Alan Hale, Craig Stevens. Tired reworking of George Arliss' MILLIONAIRE, with Greenstreet as wealthy man who plays Cupid for Clark and Vickers.

That Wonderful Urge (1948) 82m. **½ D: Robert B. Sinclair. Tyrone Power, Gene Tierney, Arleen Whelan, Reginald Gardiner, Lucile Watson, Gene Lockhart, Gertrude Michael, Porter Hall. Fairly entertaining remake of LOVE IS NEWS about heiress getting back at nasty reporter. Good cast.

That's My Boy (1951) 98m. *** D: Hal Walker. Jerry Lewis, Dean Martin, Ruth Hussey, Eddie Mayehoff, Polly Bergen. Above-par hijinks with Mayehoff coaxing collegiate athlete Martin to make a man of puny Lewis, and Jerry becoming a football star.

That's the Spirit (1945) 93m. ** D: Charles Lamont. Peggy Ryan, Jack Oakie, June Vincent, Gene Lockhart, Johnny Coy, Andy Devine, Arthur Treacher, Irene Ryan, Buster Keaton. Whimsy is too studied in this syrupy fantasy of Oakie returning from heaven to make explanations to wife on earth.

Thelma Jordan SEE: **File on Thelma Jordan.**

Them (1954) 94m. ***½ D: Gordon Douglas. James Whitmore, Edmund Gwenn, Joan Weldon, James Arness, Onslow Stevens. Good cast gives added boost to nail-biting story of giant ant mutations running wild in Los Angeles. Very good direction and intelligent script with some truly memorable scenes.

Then There Were Three (1961-Italian, dubbed) 82m. ** D: Alex Nicol. Frank Latimore, Alex Nicol, Barry Cahill, Sid Clute. Routine WW2 actioner concerning Nazi officer going behind Allied lines to hunt down Italian partisans.

Theodora, Slave Empress (1954-Italian, dubbed) 88m. ** D: Riccardo Freda. Gianna Maria Canale, Georges Marchal, Renata Paldini, Henri Guisol, Irene Papas. Better-than-average production values are only asset in standard plot of hero thwarting plan of Roman generals to overthrow empress.

There Goes My Heart (1938) 81m. *** D: Norman Z. McLeod. Fredric March, Virginia Bruce, Patsy Kelly, Alan Mowbray, Nancy Carroll, Eugene Pallette, Claude Gillingwater, Arthur Lake. Typical 30's fluff about runaway heiress Bruce spotted by reporter March; good cast makes one forget trite story-line.

There's Always a Price Tag (1958-French) 102m. **½ D: Denys de la Patiliere. Michele Morgan, Daniel Gelin, Peter Van Eyck, Bernard Blier. Morgan is effective as wife consorting with her servant to murder husband.

There's Always a Woman (1938) 82m. *** D: Alexander Hall. Joan Blondell, Melvyn Douglas, Mary Astor, Frances Drake, Jerome Cowan, Robert Paige, Thurston Hall. Fine blend of mystery and comedy as D.A. Douglas and detective-wife Blondell try to solve same crime.

There's Always Tomorrow (1956) 84m. **½ D: Douglas Sirk. Barbara Stanwyck, Fred MacMurray, Joan Bennett, Pat Crowley, Jane Darwell. Sensibly acted weeper of MacMurray renewing romance with Stanwyck, but realizing wife Bennett and family need him more.

There's No Business Like Show Business (1954) C-117m. *½ D: Walter Lang. Ethel Merman, Donald O'Connor, Marilyn Monroe, Dan Dailey, Johnny Ray, Mitzi Gaynor. Gaudy musicomedy of show biz family spawned by vaudevillians Merman and Dailey; loud and obnoxious, with Marilyn's moments the only good ones in the film.

These Are the Damned (1965-British) 100m. *** D: Joseph Losey. MacDonald Carey, Shirley Anne Field, Viveca Lindfors, Alexander Knox, Oliver Reed, James Villiers. Absorbing Losey film about struggling society after nuclear war. Moving plot, very good acting and direction.

These Glamour Girls (1939) 80m. **½ D: S. Sylvan Simon. Lew Ayres, Lana Turner, Richard Carlson, Anita Louise, Marsha Hunt, Ann Rutherford, Mary Beth Hughes, Jane Bryan, Tom Brown. Turner is effective as nonsocialite who turns the tables on sneering gals at swank college weekend; naive but polished gloss.

These Thousand Hills (1959) C-96m. *** D: Richard Fleischer. Don Murray, Richard Egan, Lee Remick, Patricia Owens, Stuart Whitman, Albert Dekker, Harold J. Stone. Adult Western with Murray a rancher who learns to accept responsibility and and maintain loyalty to dependent friends; sturdy cast.

These Three (1936) 93m. **** D: William Wyler. Miriam Hopkins, Merle Oberon, Joel McCrea, Catherine Doucet, Alma Kruger, Bonita Granville, Marcia Mae Jones. Penetrating drama of two young women (Oberon, Hopkins) running school, ruined by lies of malicious student Granville; loosely based on Lillian Hellman's CHILDREN'S HOUR. Superb acting by all, with Granville especially impressive. Remade in 1961 as THE CHILDREN'S HOUR.

These Wilder Years (1956) 91m. **½ D: Roy Rowland. James Cagney, Barbara Stanwyck, Walter Pidgeon, Betty Lou Keim, Don Dubbins. Oddball soaper with Cagney a dynamic tycoon trying to regain custody of long-ago adopted son; Stanwyck is staunch official at orphan's home.

They All Died Laughing SEE: **Jolly Bad Fellow, A.**

They All Kissed the Bride (1942) 85m. **½ D: Alexander Hall. Joan Crawford, Melvyn Douglas, Roland Young, Billie Burke, Allen Jenkins. Good stars in fairly amusing film of man being arrested for kissing bride at wedding.

They Call It Sin (1932) 75m. ** D: Thornton Freeland. Loretta Young, David Manners, George Brent, Louis Calhern, Una Merkel, Elizabeth Patterson. Typical, standard soaper of Young's unhappy love affair while silent suitor stands by.

They Came to Blow Up America (1943) 73m. ** D: Edward Ludwig. George Sanders, Anna Sten, Ward Bond, Dennis Hoey, Sig Ruman,

Ludwig Stossel, Robert Barrat. Overzealous espionage yarn designed for WW2 audiences, dated now. Good cast is only virtue.

They Came to Cordura (1959) C-123m. **½ D: Robert Rossen. Gary Cooper, Rita Hayworth, Van Heflin, Tab Hunter, Richard Conte, Michael Callan, Dick York. Soapy oater set in 1916 Mexico. Cooper is Army officer accused of cowardice, sent to find five men worthy of Medal of Honor. Hayworth is shady lady he meets on the way.

They Dare Not Love (1941) 76m. *½ D: James Whale. George Brent, Martha Scott, Paul Lukas, Egon Brecher, Roman Bohnen, Edgar Barrier. Dull drama of obstacles confronting newlyweds in Austria.

They Died With Their Boots On (1951) 138m. *** D: Raoul Walsh. Errol Flynn, Olivia de Havilland, Arthur Kennedy, Charley Grapewin, Gene Lockhart, Anthony Quinn, Stanley Ridges, Sydney Greenstreet. Sweeping Hollywood version of Little Big Horn with Flynn flamboyant as Custer. Fine vignettes amidst episodic buildup to lavish massacre sequence.

They Drive By Night (1940) 93m. ***½ D: Raoul Walsh. George Raft, Ann Sheridan, Ida Lupino, Humphrey Bogart, Gale Page, Alan Hale, Roscoe Karns. Marvelous melodrama of truck-driving brothers battling crooked bosses, with appealing Sheridan and bravura Lupino sparking cast. Unforgettable dialogue. Partial reworking of BORDERTOWN.

They Gave Him a Gun (1937) 94m. ** D: W. S. Van Dyke II. Spencer Tracy, Gladys George, Franchot Tone, Edgar Dearing, Charles Trowbridge. Fine cast does more than justice to weak psychological story of war-hardened Tone turning to crime, Tracy trying to stop him.

They Got Me Covered (1943) 95m. ** D: David Butler. Bob Hope, Dorothy Lamour, Lenore Aubert, Otto Preminger, Eduardo Ciannelli, Marion Martin, Donald Meek. Spy yarn set in Washington was topical at the time, awkward now; not up to Hope standards.

They Knew What They Wanted (1940) 96m. *** D: Garson Kanin. Carole Lombard, Charles Laughton, William Gargan, Harry Carey, Frank Fay, Joe Bernard. Well-acted version of Sidney Howard play of Italian immigrant Laughton marrying waitress Lombard. Later musicalized as THE MOST HAPPY FELLA.

They Loved Life SEE: Kanal.

They Made Me a Criminal (1939) 92m. **½ D: Busby Berkeley. John Garfield, Claude Rains, Gloria Dickson, May Robson, Billy Halop, Huntz Hall, Barbara Pepper, Ward Bond, Ann Sheridan. Garfield takes it on the lam when he thinks he's killed a boxing opponent, stays out West with Robson and Dead End Kids. Enjoyable, with Rains miscast as a Dick Tracy type. Remake of THE LIFE OF JIMMY DOLAN.

They Made Me a Criminal (1948-British) SEE: I Became a Criminal.

They Met in Argentina (1941) 77m. *½ D: Leslie Goodwins, Jack Hively. Maureen O'Hara, James Ellison, Alberto Vila, Buddy Ebsen. Limp musical of O'Hara, a Latin heiress caught between U. S. engineer and local sportsman. Skip it.

They Met In Bombay (1941) 86m. **½ D: Clarence Brown. Clark Gable, Rosalind Russell, Peter Lorre, Jessie Ralph, Reginald Owen. Two jewel thieves team up in ordinary romantic comedy-actioner, spiced by Lorre as money-hungry cargo-ship captain.

They Rode West (1954) C-84m. **½ D: Phil Karlson. Robert Francis, Donna Reed, May Wynn, Phil Carey, Onslow Stevens. Camp commander prevents army surgeon from attempting to treat Indian epidemic. Good cast highlights better than average Western.

They Were Expendable (1945) 135m. ***½ D: John Ford. Robert Montgomery, John Wayne, Donna Reed, Jack Holt, Ward Bond, Louis Jean Heydt, Marshall Thompson. Grade A WW2 action film of PT boat combat in the Pacific, well handled by fine cast and director Ford.

They Were Sisters (1945-British) 110m. **½ D: Arthur Crabtree. Phyllis Calvert, James Mason, Hugh Sinclair, Dulcie Gary, Pamela Mason. Fresh approach to stock drama of trio of sisters with contrasting marriages and lives.

They Were So Young (1955-German, dubbed) 80m. *** D: Kurt Neumann. Scott Brady, Raymond Burr, Johanna Matz, Ingrid Stenn. Nicely produced, grim melodrama of girls sent to South America to be used by crooks. Even without "names" in cast, film would be good.

They Who Dare (1953-British) C-101m. **1/2 D: Lewis Milestone. Dirk Bogarde, Denholm Elliott, Akim Tamiroff, Eric Pohlmann, David Peel. Effective WW2 actioner with good character delineation, tracing commando raid on German-controlled Aegean air fields.

They Won't Believe Me (1947) 95m. ***1/2 D: Irving Pichel. Robert Young, Susan Hayward, Jane Greer, Rita Johnson, Tom Powers, Don Beddoe. Offbeat melodrama of no-good Young cheating on wife Johnson, mistreating other women, but paying in the end. Top-notch cast.

They Won't Forget (1937) 95m. ***1/2 D: Mervyn LeRoy. Claude Rains, Gloria Dickson, Otto Kruger, Allyn Joslyn, Lana Turner, Elisha Cook, Jr., Edward Norris, Ann Shoemaker, Trevor Bardette. Rains gives bravura performance as lawyer defending man wanted by lynch mob. Turner makes first noticeable film appearance in this still-timely story.

Thief, The (1952) 85m. **1/2 D: Russell Rouse. Ray Milland, Rita Gam, Martin Gabel, Harry Bronson. Spy yarn set in N.Y.C. with a difference: no dialogue. Gimmick grows wearisome, script is tame.

Thief of Bagdad, The (1940) C-106m. **** D: Ludwig Berger, Tim Whelan, Michael Powell. Sabu, John Justin, June Duprez, Conrad Veidt, Rex Ingram, Miles Malleson, Mary Morris. Remarkable fantasy of native boy Sabu outdoing evil magician Veidt in Arabian Nights fable with incredible Technicolor special effects. Ingram gives splendid performance as a genie.

Thief of Baghdad (1961-Italian, dubbed) C-90m. ** D: Arthur Lubin. Steve Reeves, Giorgia Moll, Arturo Dominici, Edy Vessel. Reeves searches for enchanted blue rose so he can marry Sultan's daughter. Nothing like Sabu version but occasionally atmospheric.

Thief of Damascus (1952) C-78m. ** D: Will Jason. Paul Henreid, John Sutton, Jeff Donnell, Lon Chaney, Elena Verdugo. Jumbled costume spectacle featuring Aladdin, Sinbad and Ali Baba out to rescue princess.

Thieves Fall Out (1941) 72m. ** D: Ray Enright. Eddie Albert, Joan Leslie, Alan Hale, William T. Orr, John Litel, Anthony Quinn, Edward Brophy. Innocuous drama of rival mattress factory families and their problems. Good cast working with limited material.

Thieves' Highway (1949) 94m. *** D: Jules Dassin. Richard Conte, Valentina Cortesa, Lee J. Cobb, Barbara Lawrence, Jack Oakie, Millard Mitchell. Exciting drama of underworld mobsters moving in on the California trucking business; fast-moving film has Cortesa's American debut.

Thieves Holiday (1946) 100m. *** D: Douglas Sirk. George Sanders, Signe Hasso, Carole Landis, Akim Tamiroff, Gene Lockhart. Famous French thief and rogue, beautifully played by Sanders, works his way into position as prefect of police. Delightful romantic adventure. Retitled: SCANDAL IN PARIS.

Thin Ice (1937) 78m. *** D: Sidney Lanfield. Sonja Henie, Tyrone Power, Arthur Treacher, Joan Davis, Alan Hale. Early Sonja Henie, and very good, with dashing prince Power in love with commoner Henie.

Thin Man, The One series stands apart from the others: its episodes were filmed two and three years apart, its stars were those of the major rank, and the films were not looked down at as Grade-B efforts. This was **The Thin Man**, a highly successful series launched quite unexpectedly in 1934 with a delightfully unpretentious blend of screwball comedy and murder mystery, from a story by Dashiell Hammett. William Powell and Myrna Loy starred as Nick and Nora Charles, a perfectly happy, sophisticated couple whose marriage never stood in the way of their having fun and going off on detective capers. This blithe, carefree portrayal of a modern American couple was beautifully handled by Loy and Powell, and audiences loved it. Five Thin Man films followed, from 1936 to 1947. None of them fully captured the essence of the original, although they retained much of the charm and had the infallible byplay of the two stars, aided by their dog Asta, who soon became a star in his own right. AFTER THE THIN MAN featured an upcoming actor named James Stewart as a suspect, and Sam Levene in the detective role played in the original by Nat Pendleton (and repeated in ANOTHER THIN MAN). ANOTHER THIN MAN also introduced Nick Charles, Jr. as a baby, who grew up in each successive film. THE THIN MAN GOES HOME presented Nick's parents (Harry Davenport and Lucile Watson), who never wanted him to be a detective in the first place. The final film, SONG OF THE THIN MAN, had Nick and Nora frequenting many jazz hangouts (à la PETER GUNN) for some offbeat sequences. While the original THIN MAN rated above its followups, even the weakest entries in the series were fresh and enjoyable, thanks mainly to the two stars. By the way, the name "Thin Man" did not refer to William Powell; it was a character in the original film played by Edward Ellis.

Thin Man, The (1934) 93m. D: W. S. Van Dyke II. William Powell, Myrna Loy, Maureen O'Sullivan, Nat Pendleton, Minna Gombell, Cesar Romero, Natalie Moorhead, Edward Ellis, Porter Hall.

Thin Man Goes Home, The (1944) 100m. D: Richard Thorpe. William Powell, Myrna Loy, Lucile Watson, Gloria De Haven, Anne Revere, Helen Vinson, Harry Davenport, Leon Ames, Donald Meek, Edward Brophy.

Thin Red Line, The (1964) 99m. **½ D: Andrew Marton. Keir Dullea, Jack Warden, James Philbrook, Kieron Moore. James Jones' novel about relationship between sergeant Warden and private Dullea, who cannot come to terms, is focus of WW2 tale, set in Guadalcanal.

Thing, The (1951) 87m. ***½ D: Christian Nyby. Margaret Sheridan, Kenneth Tobey, Robert Cornthwaite, Douglas Spencer, James Arness. Top sci-fi flick. Scientists in Arctic station stumble upon humanoid creature from space. Tense direction (often credited to producer Howard Hawks); good acting.

Thing That Couldn't Die, The (1958) 69m. ** D: Will Cowan. Andra Martin, William Reynolds, Carolyn Kearney, Jeffrey Stone. Title monster is a century-old head seeking the rest of itself; fair.

Things To Come (1936-British) 113m. ***½ D: William Cameron Menzies. Raymond Massey, Ralph Richardson, Maurice Braddell, Edward Chapman, Sophie Stewart, Ann Todd, Margaretta Scott. H. G. Wells' predictions of futuristic earth is still intriguing; Massey portrays ruler of new world, supported by marvelous special effects and production design.

Think Fast, Mr. Moto (1937) 66m. D: Norman Foster. Peter Lorre, Virginia Field, Sig Ruman, Murray Kinnell, Lotus Long, J. Carrol Naish, Fredrick Vogeding, George Cooper, Jr. SEE: Mr. Moto series.

Third Finger, Left Hand (1940) 96m. ** D: Robert Z. Leonard. Myrna Loy, Melvyn Douglas, Raymond Walburn, Lee Bowman, Bonita Granville. Mediocre comedy with attractive stars swallowed up. Loy loves Douglas but gives him a hard time in his pursuit.

Third Key, The (1956-British) 96m. ** D: Charles Frend. Jack Hawkins, Sydney Tafler, Alec McCowen, Sam Kydd, Dorothy Alison, Ian Bannen, George Rose, Ursula Howells. Unexceptional Scotland Yard yarn; Hawkins does his best with ordinary material.

Third Man, The (1950-British) 104m. **** D: Carol Reed. Orson Welles, Joseph Cotten, Valli, Trevor Howard, Wilfrid Hyde-White. Grahame Greene's account of mysterious Harry Lime (Welles) in post-WW2 Vienna becomes screen classic, with pulpwriter Cotten on manhunt for Harry. "Third Man Theme" à la zither adds just the right touch.

3rd Voice, The (1960) 79m. *** D: Hubert Cornfield. Edmond O'Brien, Laraine Day, Julie London, Ralph Brooks, Roque Ybarra, Henry Delgado. Neat suspense film involving murder, impersonation and doublecrossing.

13 Fighting Men (1960) 69m. *½ D: Harry Gerstad. Grant Williams, Brad Dexter, Carole Mathews, Robert Dix, Richard Garland, Rayford Barnes, John Erwin. Minor film about Union soldiers fighting off Rebel troops to protect gold shipment.

13 Frightened Girls (1963) C-89m. ** D: William Castle. Murray Hamilton, Joyce Taylor, Hugh Marlowe, Khigh Dhiegh. Mishmash of espionage intrigue with Taylor a double agent using a string of associates to penetrate diplomatic secrets.

13 Ghosts (1960) 88m. ** D: William Castle. Charles Herbert, Jo Morrow, Martin Milner, Rosemary De Camp, Donald Woods, Margaret Hamilton, John Van Dreelen. Medium thriller loses main attraction on TV; device enabling viewers to see or screen out ghosts in certain scenes. Fairly interesting, but nothing special.

13 Hours by Air (1936) 80m. ** D: Mitchell Leisen. Fred MacMurray, Joan Bennett, Zasu Pitts, John Howard, Bennie Bartlett, Grace Bradley, Alan Baxter. Dated drama of transcontinental flight, with mingling of diverse passengers as plane is hijacked.

13 Rue Madeleine (1946) 95m. **½ D: Henry Hathaway. James Cagney, Annabella, Richard Conte, Frank Latimore, Walter Abel, Melville Cooper, Sam Jaffe, E. G. Marshall. Fairly interesting yarn of U. S. secret service station in WW2 Paris, with Cagney in offbeat casting as underground leader.

13 West Street (1962) 80m. **½ D: Philip Leacock. Alan Ladd, Rod Steiger, Jeanne Cooper, Michael Callan, Dolores Dorn. Taut actioner with Ladd out to get gang of hoodlums; most capable cast.

13th Hour, The (1947) 65m. D: William Clemens. Richard Dix, Karen Morley, Mark Dennis, John Kellogg, Bernardene Hayes, Jim Bannon, Regis Toomey. SEE: The Whistler series.

13th Letter, The (1951) 85m. **½ D: Otto Preminger. Linda Darnell, Charles Boyer, Michael Rennie, Constance Moore, Judith Evelyn. Interesting account of effect of series of poison pen letters on townsfolk, set in Canada. Remake of H. G. Clouzot's Le Corbeau.

—30— (1959) 96m. **½ D: Jack Webb. Jack Webb, William Conrad, David Nelson, Whitney Blake, Louise Lorimer, Joe Flynn, James Bell. Low-keyed documentary-style account of an evening's work at a L. A. newspaper. Trim, fairly interesting.

Thirty Day Princess (1934) 75m. **½ D: Marion Gering. Sylvia Sidney, Cary Grant, Edward Arnold, Lucien Littlefield. Pleasant minor account of Sidney substituting for an ill princess who must make a goodwill tour in U. S., with expected results.

30 Foot Bride of Candy Rock, The (1959) 75m. ** D: Sidney Miller. Lou Costello, Dorothy Provine, Gale Gordon, Charles Lane, Jimmy Conlin, Peter Leeds. Lou Costello's only starring film without Bud Abbott is nothing much, mildly entertaining, with Miss Provine enlarged to gigantic proportions.

39 Steps, The (1935-British) 81m. **** D: Alfred Hitchcock. Robert Donat, Madeleine Carroll, Godfrey Tearle, Helen Haye, Lucie Mannheim, Peggy Ashcroft. Masterpiece suspenser with Donat and Carroll handcuffed together, fleeing the police though innocent. Blend of comedy, mystery, and romance paced to perfection by Hitchcock.

39 Steps, The (1960-British) C-95m. **½ D: Ralph Thomas. Kenneth More, Taina Elg, Brenda de Banzie, Barry Jones, Reginald Beckwith, Faith Brook. More plays young man accidentally involved in murder and espionage; good British cast sparks OK remake of Hitchcock classic.

Thirty Seconds Over Tokyo (1944) 138m. *** D: Mervyn LeRoy. Van Johnson, Robert Walker, Spencer Tracy, Phyllis Thaxter, Scott McKay, Robert Mitchum, Stephen McNally, Louis Jean Heydt, Leon Ames, Paul Langton. Exciting WW2 actioner of first American attack on Japan with sturdy cast, guest appearance by Tracy as General Doolittle.

36 Hours (1964) 115m. **½ D: George Seaton. James Garner, Eva Marie Saint, Rod Taylor, Werner Peters, Celia Lovsky, Alan Napier. Intriguing WW2 yarn with Garner as captured spy begins well, but peters out fast. Taylor as German officer is interesting casting.

30 Years of Fun (1963) 85m. **** compiled by Robert Youngson. Charlie Chaplin, Buster Keaton, Laurel and Hardy, Harry Langdon, Sydney Chaplin, Charley Chase, etc. Without repeating from previous films, Youngson presents hilarious silent comedy footage. Included is rare sequence of Laurel and Hardy performing together for the first time in 1917.

This Above All (1942) 110m. *** D: Anatole Litvak. Tyrone Power, Joan Fontaine, Thomas Mitchell, Nigel Bruce, Gladys Cooper, Sara Allgood, Philip Merivale. Timely WW2 film shows its age; still good with strong cast in Eric Knight tale of embittered soldier Power finding courage and love with patriotic Britisher Fontaine.

This Angry Age (1958) C-111m. ** Rene Clement. Silvana Mangano, Anthony Perkins, Alida Valli, Richard Conte, Jo Van Fleet, Nehemiah Persoff. Ludicrous mishmash set in Indo-China with Van Fleet a stereotyped, dominating mother who's convinced that her children (Perkins and Mangano) can make their rice fields a going proposition.

This Could be the Night (1957) 103m. **½ D: Robert Wise. Jean Simmons, Paul Douglas, Anthony Franciosa, Joan Blondell, Neile Adams, Zasu Pitts, J. Carrol Naish. Forced, frantic comedy of prim teacher Simmons working as secretary to gangster Douglas who runs a nightclub; Franciosa is the young associate who romances her.

This Earth Is Mine (1959) C-125m. **½ D: Henry King. Rock Hudson, Jean Simmons, Dorothy McGuire, Claude Rains, Kent Smith, Anna Lee, Ken Scott. Disjointed soaper set in 1930's California vineyards about intertwining family romances, with Hudson-Simmons love story the focal point.

This Gun for Hire (1942) 80m. *** D: Frank Tuttle. Alan Ladd, Veronica Lake, Robert Preston, Laird Cregar, Tully Marshall, Pamela Blake. Ladd came into his own as paid gunman seeking revenge on man who double-crossed him, with Lake as a fetching vis à vis. Remade as **Short Cut to Hell**.

This Happy Breed (1947-British) 110m. ***½ D: David Lean. Robert Newton, Celia Johnson, John Mills, Kay Walsh, Stanley Holloway. Cavalcade of strong British family through several decades, from Noel Coward play, is brilliantly acted.

This Happy Feeling (1958) C-92m. *** D: Blake Edwards. Debbie Reynolds, Curt Jurgens, John Saxon, Alexis Smith, Estelle Winwood. Most engaging cast gives zip to simple yarn of Reynolds enthralled by actor Jurgens, but sparked by suitor Saxon; Winwood fine as eccentric housekeeper.

This Is My Affair (1937) 99m. *** D: William A. Seiter. Barbara Stanwyck, Robert Taylor, Victor McLaglen, Brian Donlevy, Sidney Blackmer, John Carradine, Sig Ruman. Exciting film of Taylor joining gang of back robbers on orders from President McKinley to expose powerful mob; Stanwyck is saloon singer who loves Taylor.

This Is My Love (1954) C-91m. ** D: Stuart Heisler. Linda Darnell, Rick Jason, Dan Duryea, Faith Domergue, Hal Baylor, Connie Russell. Woman, married to invalid, tries to compete with sister who has fallen in love with Duryea. Nothing special.

This Is the Life (1944) 87m. ** D: Felix E. Feist. Donald O'Connor, Peggy Ryan, Susanna Foster, Patric Knowles. Spunky cast of versatile performers with Foster torn between swank Knowles and performer O'Connor.

This Is the Night (1932) 78m **½ D: Frank Tuttle. Lily Damita, Charles Ruggles, Roland Young, Thelma Todd, Cary Grant. Grant's feature film debut isn't bad, with Young hiring Damita to pose as his wife so he can pursue Todd. Grant is Todd's husband.

This Island Earth (1955) C-87m. **½ D: Joseph M. Newman. Jeff Morrow, Faith Domergue, Rex Reason, Lance Fuller. Imaginative photography highlights average story of scientist shanghaied by aliens to help their war-torn planet.

This Land Is Mine (1943) 103m. *** D: Jean Renoir. Charles Laughton, Maureen O'Hara, George Sanders, Walter Slezak, Kent Smith, Una O'Connor, Philip Merivale. Meek

French teacher Laughton, aroused by Nazi occupation, becomes hero. Patriotic wartime film has heady performances.

This Love of Ours (1945) 90m. **½ D: William Dieterle. Merle Oberon, Charles Korvin, Claude Rains, Carl Esmond, Sue England, Jess Barker, Harry Davenport, Ralph Morgan. Sudsy soaper of Korvin leaving wife Oberon, meeting twelve years later, falling in love again. Rains steals show in supporting role.

This Man's Navy (1945) 100m. *** D: William Wellman. Wallace Beery, Tom Drake, James Gleason, Jan Clayton, Selena Royle, Noah Beery, Sr., Henry O'Neill, Steve Brodie. Usual Beery service-story nicely rehashed; Beery treats Drake as a son, gets vicarious pleasure out of his navy career.

This Modern Age (1931) 76m. ** D: Nick Grinde. Joan Crawford, Neil Hamilton, Marjorie Rambeau, Hobart Bosworth, Emma Dunn. Upper-class Hamilton loves Crawford, but his family doesn't take to the poor working-girl. Standard predictable plot.

This Rebel Age SEE: Beat Generation, The.

This Rebel Breed (1960) 90m. ** D: Richard L. Bare. Rita Moreno, Mark Damon, Dyan Cannon, Gerald Mohr, Jay Novello, Eugene Martin, Tom Gilson, Richard Rust. Above-average tale detailing the apprehension of teen-age gangs. Retitled: THREE SHADES OF LOVE.

This Side of the Law (1950) 74m. ** D: Richard L. Bare. Viveca Lindfors, Kent Smith, Janis Paige, Monte Blue. Hokey script has Smith hired by crooked lawyer to impersonate missing wealthy man.

This Sporting Life (1963-British) 129m. ***½ D: Lindsay Anderson. Richard Harris, Rachel Roberts, Alan Badel, William Hartnell. Grim, adult story of rugby star Harris having an affair with landlady Roberts, leading to his overwhelming disillusionment with success and life.

This Thing Called Love (1941) 98m. *** D: Alexander Hall. Rosalind Russell, Melvyn Douglas, Binnie Barnes, Allyn Joslyn, Gloria Dickson, Lee J. Cobb. Adult comedy of newlyweds who set up three-month trial run for their marriage. Stars' expertise puts it over.

This Time for Keeps (1947) C-105m. **½ D: Richard Thorpe. Esther Williams, Lauritz Melchior, Jimmy Durante, Johnnie Johnston, Xavier Cugat. Empty-headed, enjoyable Williams bathing-suit musical with Durante around to relieve tedium.

This Woman is Dangerous (1952) 100m. **½ D: Felix E. Feist. Joan Crawford, Dennis Morgan, David Brian, Richard Webb, Sherry Jackson. In typical tough-girl role, Crawford finds true love after countless mishaps, including an eye operation.

This Woman is Mine (1941) 91m. ** D: Frank Lloyd. Franchot Tone, John Carroll, Walter Brennan, Carol Bruce, Nigel Bruce, Leo G. Carroll. Standard love triangle on merchant boat in northern waters plying the fur trade.

Thoroughbreds Don't Cry (1937) 80m. **½ D: Alfred E. Green. Judy Garland, Mickey Rooney, Sophie Tucker, C. Aubrey Smith, Frankie Darro, Henry Kolker, Helen Troy. Fairly good racetrack story with jockey Rooney involved in crooked deals, young Garland adding some songs.

Those Endearing Young Charms (1945) 81m. ** D: Lewis Allen. Robert Young, Laraine Day, Ann Harding, Marc Cramer, Anne Jeffreys, Glenn Vernon, Lawrence Tierney. Limp comedy-romance with serviceman Young and waitress Day; waste of good talent.

Those Fantastic Flying Fools SEE: Blast-Off.

Those Magnificent Men in Their Flying Machines (1965) C-113m. *** D: Ken Annakin. Stuart Whitman, Sarah Miles, James Fox, Alberto Sordi, Robert Morley, Gert Forbe, Jean-Pierre Cassel, Terry-Thomas, Irina Demick, Flora Robson, Red Skelton. Long but enjoyable film of great airplane race involving international conflicts, cheating, and romance. Skelton does funny cameo in amusing prologue, tracing history of aviation.

Those Redheads from Seattle (1953) C-90m. ** D: Lewis R. Foster. Rhonda Fleming, Gene Barry, Agnes Moorehead, Teresa Brewer, Guy Mitchell. Modestly produced musical nonsense set in gold-rush era with

Moorehead the mother of four gals who takes her brood to Alaska

Those Were the Days (1940) 76m. ** D: Jay Reed. William Holden, Bonita Granville, Ezra Stone, Judith Barrett, Alan Ladd. Pat college campus yarn, making the most of wholesome romance among naïve students.

Thou Shalt Not Kill (1961-Italian, dubbed) 129m. **½ D: Claude Autant-Lara. Laurent Terzieff, Horst Frank, Suzanne Flon, Mica Orlovic. Too-often sterile narrative dealing with trial of French conscientious objector, with side-plot of German priest facing penalty for having killed Frenchman during WW2.

Thousand and One Nights, A (1945) C-93m. *** D: Alfred E. Green. Cornel Wilde, Evelyn Keyes, Phil Silvers, Adele Jergens, Dusty Anderson, Dennis Hoey, Rex Ingram. Good escapism based on Arabian Nights fables; colorful production with serviceable cast including Ingram repeating genie-ish role from THIEF OF BAGDAD.

Thousand Clowns, A (1965) 118m. ***½ D: Fred Coe. Jason Robards, Barbara Harris, Martin Balsam, Barry Gordon, Gene Saks, William Daniels. Thoughtful, funny adaptation of Broadway play about a nonconformist and his son. Robards and Gordon are perfect; Saks and Daniels are unforgettable; and Balsam won an Oscar for his supporting role.

Thousand Eyes of Dr. Mabuse, The (1960-German, dubbed) 103m. **½ D: Fritz Lang. Dawn Addams, Peter Van Eyck, Gert Frobe, Wolfgang Preiss. Fast-moving if unconvincing revival of arch-villain of 1920's, with Frobe the police agent tracking down the reincarnated Mabuse in Berlin; gimmicky, complex plotline.

Thousands Cheer (1943) C-126m. *** D: George Sidney. Mickey Rooney, Judy Garland, Red Skelton, Eleanor Powell, Ann Sothern, Lucille Ball, Virginia O'Brien, Frank Morgan, Kathryn Grayson, Lena Horne. Grayson lives with officer-father John Boles at army base, decides to prepare all-star show for soldiers. Filmy plot, great entertainment.

Threat, The (1960) 66m. ** D: Charles R. Rondeau. Robert Knapp, Linda Lawson, Lisabeth Hush, James Seay, Mary Castle, Barney Phillips. Standard find-the-real-murderer yarn.

Three Avengers, The (1964-Italian, dubbed) C-97m. *½ D: Gianfranco Parolini. Alan Steel, Mimmo Palmara, Lisa Gastoni, Rosalba Neri. Below par Ursus (Steel) adventure tale, dealing with evil ruler of Atra.

Three Bad Sisters (1956) 76m. *½ D: Gilbert L. Kay. Marla English, Kathleen Hughes, Sara Shane, John Bromfield, Jess Barker, Madge Kennedy. Aimless account of title figures fighting among themselves to outdo the others, fighting over their father's estate.

Three Blind Mice (1938) 75m. **½ D: William A. Seiter. Loretta Young, Joel McCrea, David Niven, Stuart Erwin, Marjorie Weaver, Pauline Moore, Binnie Barnes. Familiar idea of three fortune-hunting girls going after well-heeled male prospects; slickly done. Remade, reworked many times.

Three Blondes In His Life (1960) 81m. ** D: Leon Chooluck. Jock Mahoney, Gretta Thyssen, Anthony Dexter, Jesse White. Occasionally tangy rehash of romances and misconduct of now-deceased insurance investigator.

Three Brave Men (1957) 88m. **½ D: Philip Dunne. Ray Milland, Frank Lovejoy, Ernest Borgnine, Nina Foch, Andrew Duggan. Veteran navy employee (Borgnine) is accused of Communist affiliations. Film is well intentioned, but has too many clichés to be effective. From Pulitzer Prize-winning story.

Three Broadway Girls SEE: Greeks Had a Word for Them, The.

Three Came Home (1950) 106m. ***½ D: Jean Negulesco. Claudette Colbert, Patric Knowles, Florence Desmond, Sessue Hayakawa, Helen Westcott. Stunning performances by Colbert and Hayakawa make this a must. British families living on Borneo during WW2 are sent to prison camps by Japanese, but cultured officer Hayakawa takes an interest in authoress Colbert.

Three Cases of Murder (1954-British) 99m. **½ D: Wendy Toye. David Eady, George O'Ferrall, Alan Badel, Hugh Pryse, John Salew, Eddie Bryne, Ann Hanslip, Elizabeth Sellars, Orson Welles. As title implies, three separate episodes involving killings; cast consistently better than material.

Three Cheers for the Irish (1940) 100m. **½ D: Lloyd Bacon. Thomas Mitchell, Dennis Morgan, Priscilla Lane, Alan Hale, Virginia Grey, Irene Hervey. Breezy little comedy of family feud when Irish Mitchell's daughter Lane falls for Scottish Morgan.

Three Coins in the Fountain (1954) C-102m. *** D: Jean Negulesco. Clifton Webb, Dorothy McGuire, Jean Peters, Louis Jourdan, Maggie McNamara, Rossano Brazzi. Splashy romance yarn made ultra-pleasing by Rome locations. Three women make wishes for romance at Fountain of Trevi, spurring several amorous adventures.

Three Comrades (1938) 100m. ***½ D: Frank Borzage. Robert Taylor, Margaret Sullavan, Franchot Tone, Robert Young, Guy Kibbee, Lionel Atwill. Beautifully poignant film of Erich Maria Remarque's tale of post-WW1 Germany, and three life-long friends who share a love for Margaret Sullavan. Excellent performances all around.

Three-Cornered Moon (1933) 77m. *** D: Elliott Nugent. Claudette Colbert, Richard Arlen, Mary Boland, Wallace Ford, Hardie Albright, Lyda Roberti. Pedates golden age of screwball comedies, but tops many of them; Boland is head of wacky family combating Depression.

Three Daring Daughters (1948) C-115m. **½ D: Fred M. Wilcox. Jeanette MacDonald, Jose Iturbi, Elinor Donahue, Ann B. Todd, Jane Powell, Edward Arnold, Harry Davenport. Woman magazine editor tells her daughters that she's remarrying. Despite predictable results, well-acted MGM comedy succeeds.

Three Desperate Men (1951) 71m. *½ D: Sam Newfield. Preston Foster, Virginia Grey, Jim Davis, Ross Latimer. Flabby little oater about three brothers who become outlaws.

Three Faces of Eve, The (1957) 91m. ***½ D: Nunnally Johnson. Joanne Woodward, David Wayne, Lee J. Cobb, Nancy Kulp, Vince Edwards. Narration: Alistair Cooke. Academy Award tour de force by Woodward as schizophrenic with three contrasting personalities and three separate lives. Cobb is psychiatrist who tries to cure her.

Three Faces West (1940) 79m. **½ D: Bernard Vorhaus. John Wayne, Charles Coburn, Sigrid Gurie, Spencer Charters. Unusual group traveling West includes Westerner Wayne, refugee Gurie. Above-average Western with offbeat romantic duo.

Three for Bedroom C (1952) C-74m. ** D: Milton Bren. Gloria Swanson, Fred Clark, Steve Brodie, Hans Conried, Margaret Dumont. Sadly uneven comedy of romance between movie star and scientist aboard transcontinental train heading to L. A.

Three for Jamie Dawn (1956) 81m. ** D: Thomas Carr. Laraine Day, Ricardo Montalban, Richard Carlson, June Havoc. Diverting story poorly executed, about jury members being pressured to swing a not-guilty verdict for the defendant.

Three for the Show (1955) C-93m. ** D: H. C. Potter. Betty Grable, Marge and Gower Champion, Jack Lemmon, Myron McCormick. Music is only thing that holds slight plot together in this dud remake of TOO MANY HUSBANDS.

Three Girls About Town (1941) 73m. **½ D: Leigh Jason. Joan Blondell, Binnie Barnes, Janet Blair, John Howard, Robert Benchley, Eric Blore, Hugh O'Connell, Una O'Connor. Wacky but amusing comedy of three sisters encountering a corpse in N.Y.C. hotel and the frantic consequences.

Three Guns for Texas (1968) C-99m. ** D: David Lowell Rich, Paul Stanley, Earl Bellamy. Neville Brand, Peter Brown, William Smith, Martin Milner, Philip Carey, Shelley Morrison. Three episodes from LAREDO TV series strung together, with the trio of Texas rangers involved with outlaw gang headed by Indian squaw Morrison.

Three Guys Named Mike (1951) 90m. **½ D: Charles Walters. Jane Wyman, Van Johnson, Barry Sullivan, Howard Keel, Phyllis Kirk. Pleasant, undemanding fluff of Wyman being courted by three suitors.

Three Hearts for Julia (1943) 89m. ** D: Richard Thorpe. Ann Sothern, Melvyn Douglas, Lee Bowman, Richard Ainley, Felix Bressart, Marta Linden, Reginald Owen. Only debonair Douglas could seem right as husband romancing his wife (Sothern) who is divorcing him, but he can't support whole film.

Three Hours to Kill (1954) C-77m. *** D: Alfred L. Werker. Dana Andrews, Donna Reed, Dianne Foster, Stephen Elliott. Andrews plays stagecoach driver unjustly accused of killing fiance's brother; he returns to find real killer. Tight, well-done movie.

300 Spartans, The (1962) C-114m. *½ D: Rudolph Mate. Richard Egan, Sir Ralph Richardson, Diane Baker, Barry Coe. Terrible script of heroic Greek stand at Thermopylae against Persians. Fair cast names seem awkward in roles.

Three Husbands (1950) 78m. **½ D: Irving Reis. Eve Arden, Ruth Warrick, Vanessa Brown, Shepperd Strudwick, Billie Burke, Emlyn Williams, Jane Darwell. Pleasing comedy of three husbands trying to find out whether or not deceased playboy spent time with their wives.

Three Is a Family (1944) 81m. **½ D: Edward Ludwig. Fay Bainter, Marjorie Reynolds, Charlie Ruggles, Helen Broderick, Arthur Lake, Hattie McDaniel, Jeff Donnell, Walter Catlett, Cheryl Walker. Above-par fluff of hectic homelife in apartment filled with family, friends, and new babies.

Three Little Girls In Blue (1946) C-90m. *** D: H. Bruce Humberstone. June Haver, George Montgomery, Vivian Blaine, Celeste Holm, Vera-Ellen. Colorful tale of three sisters out to trap wealthy husbands; familiar plot with good tunes like "You Make Me Feel So Young."

Three Little Words (1950) C-102m. *** D: Richard Thorpe. Fred Astaire, Vera-Ellen, Red Skelton, Arlene Dahl, Keenan Wynn, Gloria De Haven, Debbie Reynolds, Carleton Carpenter. Standard MGM musical about famous songwriters Kalmar and Ruby and their climb to fame; bouncy cast, fine tunes.

Three Loves Has Nancy (1938) 69m. **½ D: Richard Thorpe. Janet Gaynor, Robert Montgomery, Franchot Tone, Guy Kibbee, Claire Dodd, Reginald Owen. Breezy little romantic triangle with stood-up bride Gaynor playing the field for a while.

Three Men In a Boat (1956-British) C-84m. ** D: Ken Annakin. Laurence Harvey, Jimmy Edwards, David Tomlinson, Shirley Eaton, Jill Ireland, Martita Hunt, Adrienne Corri. Diverting minor comedy about trio of fun-loving men who take a boat trip up the Thames and find romantic adventures.

Three Men In White (1944) 85m. D: Willis Goldbeck. Lionel Barrymore, Van Johnson, Marilyn Maxwell, Keye Luke, Ava Gardner, Alma Kruger, Rags Ragland. SEE: **Dr. Kildare** series.

Three Men on a Horse (1936) 88m. *** D: Mervyn LeRoy. Frank McHugh, Joan Blondell, Guy Kibbee, Carol Hughes, Allen Jenkins, Sam Levene, Teddy Hart, Edgar Kennedy. First-rate comedy of timid McHugh who always picks winning racehorses. Age hasn't dulled sharp edge of fine film with top cast.

3 Murderesses (1960-French, dubbed) C-96m. **½ D: Michael Boisrond. Alain Delon, Mylene Demongeot, Pascale Petit, Jacqueline Sassard, Anita Ruf, Simone Renant. Most diverting cast in standard playboy yarn with Delon romancing trio of contrasting females. Retitled: WOMEN ARE WEAK.

Three Musketeers, The (1935) 90m. ** D: Rowland V. Lee. Walter Abel, Paul Lukas, Ian Keith, Onslow Stevens, Ralph Forbes, Margot Grahame, Heather Angel. Dullest version of Dumas story, with Abel miscast as D'Artagnan.

Three Musketeers, The (1939) 73m. *** D: Allan Dwan. Don Ameche, Ritz Brothers, Lionel Atwill, Binnie Barnes, Gloria Stuart, Pauline Moore, John Carradine, Joseph Schildkraut. Spirited musical, generally faithful to Dumas story; Ameche flavorful as D'Artagnan, Barnes lovely as Lady DeWinter, Ritz Brothers funny substitutes for unsuspecting musketeers.

Three Musketeers, The (1948) C-125m. **½ D: George Sidney. Lana Turner, Gene Kelly, June Allyson, Van Heflin, Angela Lansbury, Frank Morgan, Vincent Price, Keenan Wynn, Gig Young. Good action-packed adaptation of immortal Dumas novel has excellent star cast but soggy script.

Three on a Match (1932) 64m. *** D: Mervyn LeRoy. Warren William, Joan Blondell, Bette Davis, Ann Dvorak, Humphrey Bogart, Lyle Talbot, Glenda Farrell, Anne Shirley. Fine, fast-moving melodrama of three girls who renew their childhood friendship, only to find suspense and tragedy. Dvorak is simply marvelous. Remade as BROADWAY MUSKETEERS.

Three on a Spree (1961-British) 83m. *½ D: Sidney J. Furie. Jack Watling, Carole Lesley, Renee Houston, John Slater. Disconcerting, poorly directed comedy of man forced to spend a million pounds in sixty days to inherit eight million, à la Brewster's Millions.

Three Ring Circus (1954) C-103m. ** D: Joseph Pevney. Dean Martin, Jerry Lewis, Joanne Dru, Zsa Zsa Gabor, Wallace Ford, Elsa Lanchester. So-so Martin and Lewis comedy has them as discharged servicemen up to trouble in a circus.

Three Sailors and a Girl (1953) C-95m. ** D: Roy Del Ruth. Jane Powell, Gordon MacRae, Gene Nelson, Sam Levene, Jack E. Leonard. Bland musical of three gobs who invest ship's surplus funds in a musical show, starring Powell.

Three Secrets (1950) 98m. *** D: Robert Wise. Eleanor Parker, Patricia Neal, Ruth Roman, Frank Lovejoy, Leif Erikson. Sturdy melodrama; three women wait anxiously for word of which one's child survived plane crash.

Three Shades of Love SEE: **This Rebel Breed**.

Three Sisters, The (1966) 168m. **½ D: Lee Strasberg. Kim Stanley, Geraldine Page, Shelly Winters, Kevin McCarthy, Sandy Dennis. Taped recreation of Actors Studio Broadway production of Chekhov's play of 19th-century Russia and relationships amidst a most unhappy family.

Three Smart Girls (1937) 84m. ***½ D: Henry Koster. Deanna Durbin, Binnie Barnes, Alice Brady, Ray Milland, Barbara Read, Mischa Auer, Nan Gray, Charles Winninger. Delightful musicomedy with Deanna's debut as matchmaking young girl who brings parents back together. Songs: "Someone To Care For Me," "My Heart Is Singing."

Three Smart Girls Grow Up (1939) 90m. *** D: Henry Koster. Deanna Durbin, Charles Winninger, Nan Gray, Helen Parrish, Robert Cummings, William Lundigan. Little Deanna is still matchmaking for sisters, warming up stern father, singing "Because" and winning over everyone in sight.

Three Stooges Go Around the World in a Daze, The (1963) 94m. **½ D: Norman Maurer. Three stooges, Jay Sheffield, Joan Freeman, Walter Burke, Peter Forster. Even those who dislike the Stooges may enjoy this funny updating of Jules Verne's tale, replete with sight gags and world travel.

Three Stooges in Orbit, The (1962) 87m. ** D: Edward Bernds. The Three Stooges, Carol Christensen, Edson Stroll, Emil Sitka. Nutty scientist Sitka invents contraption that flies and floats. The Stooges accidentally launch it and run headlong into the army, with usual slapstick results for younger audiences.

Three Stooges meet Hercules, The (1962) 89m. ** D: Edward Bernds. The Three Stooges, Vicki Trickett, Quinn Redeker, George N. Neise. Time machine takes the Stooges back to era of Roman legions: they are trapped on galley ship, battle cyclops, and wind up with chariot chase. Good slapstick for kids.

Three Strangers (1946) 92m. ***½ D: Jean Negulesco. Sydney Greenstreet, Geraldine Fitzgerald, Peter Lorre, Joan Lorring, Robert Shayne, Marjorie Riordan. Greenstreet and Lorre team up with Fitzgerald as partners holding winning sweepstakes ticket under unusual circumstances. Bizarre John Huston script makes fascinating viewing.

Three Stripes in the Sun (1955) 93m. **½ D: Richard Murphy. Aldo Ray, Phil Carey, Dick York, Chuck Connors, Mitsuko Kimura. Good film of American GI falling in love with Japanese orphanage worker after years of hating enemy.

3:10 to Yuma (1957) ***½ D: Delmer Daves. Glenn Ford, Van Heflin, Leora Dana, Felicia Farr, Henry Jones, Richard Jaeckel. Outstanding Western of farmer Heflin bringing in killer Ford to claim reward; suspenseful, well-handled oater.

Three Violent People (1956) C-100m. **½ D: Rudolph Mate. Charlton Heston, Anne Baxter, Gilbert Roland, Tom Tryon, Forrest Tucker, Elaine Stritch, Barton MacLane. Adequately paced Western set in post-Civil War Texas; Heston, returning home with bride Baxter, is forced to fight carpetbaggers and deal with wife's shady past.

Three Wise Fools (1946) 90m. ** D: Edward Buzzell. Margaret O'Brien, Lionel Barrymore, Lewis Stone, Edward Arnold, Thomas Mitchell, Cyd Charisse. Intended as fanciful, this turns out mawkish with adorable O'Brien winning over three crusty old men.

3 Worlds of Gulliver, The (1960) C-100m. *** D: Jack Sher. Kerwin Matthews, Jo Morrow, June Thorburn, Lee Patterson, Gregoire Aslan, Basil Sydney. Hero is washed overboard and finds himself in land of Lilliputs. Quick-moving "kiddie" movie with sympathetic acting, fine special effects.

Three Young Texans (1954) C-78m. ** D: Henry Levin. Mitzi Gaynor, Keefe Brasselle, Jeffrey Hunter, Harvey Stephens, Dan Riss. Standard Western movie has Hunter pulling railroad robbery to prevent crooks from forcing his father to do same job, expected complications.

Threepenny Opera (1963) C-83m. **½ D: Wolfgang Staudte. Curt Jurgens, Hildegarde Neff, Sammy Davis, Jr., Gert Frobe. Stylized rendition of Kurt Weill-Bertolt Brecht version of THE BEGGAR'S OPERA, set in London's Soho District, following exploits of Mack The Knife (Jurgens).

Thrill of a Romance (1945) C-105m. ** D: Richard Thorpe. Van Johnson, Esther Williams, Frances Gifford, Henry Travers, Spring Byington, Lauritz Melchoir. Typical Williams swim-romance vehicle with one good song, "I Should Care."

Thrill of Brazil, The (1946) 91m. **½ D: S. Sylvan Simon. Evelyn Keyes, Keenan Wynn, Ann Miller, Allyn Joslyn, Tito Guizar. Pleasant South-of-the-border romance with music and spirited cast giving life to ordinary script.

Thrill of It All, The (1963) C-108m. *** D: Norman Jewison. Doris Day, James Garner, Arlene Francis, Edward Andrews, Reginald Owen, Zasu Pitts. Enjoyable spoof of TV and commercials by Carl Reiner; good vehicle for Doris and Garner. Reiner has a particularly funny series of cameos.

Thunder Afloat (1939) 94m. **½ D: George B. Seitz. Wallace Beery, Chester Morris, Virginia Grey, Clem Bevans, John Qualen, Regis Toomey. Above-average Beery vehicle of old salt pitted against rival (Morris) when he joins the Navy.

Thunder Bay (1953) C-102m. *** D: Anthony Mann. James Stewart, Joanne Dru, Gilbert Roland, Dan Duryea, Jay C. Flippen. Action-packed account of oil-drillers vs. Louisiana shrimp fishermen, with a peppery cast.

Thunder Below (1932) 67m. **½ D: Richard Wallace. Tallulah Bankhead, Charles Bickford, Paul Lukas, Eugene Pallette, James Finlayson, Edward Van Sloan. Tallulah loves Lukas, but when husband Bickford goes blind, she can't bear to leave him. Melodramatic triangle story, well-acted by all.

Thunder Birds (1942) 78m. ** D: William Wellman. Gene Tierney, Preston Foster, John Sutton, Dame May Whitty, Reginald Denny, Iris Adrian. Tame adventure as two rival fliers romance Tierney between air exploits.

Thunder in Carolina (1960) C-92m. ** D: Paul Helmick. Rory Calhoun, Alan Hale, Connie Hines, John Gentry, Ed McGrath, Troyanne Ross. Programmer account of stockcar racing in the South.

Thunder in the East (1953) 98m. **½ D: Charles Vidor. Alan Ladd, Deborah Kerr, Charles Boyer, Corinne Calvet, Cecil Kellaway. Melodramatic hodgepodge with Ladd a gunrunner mercenary involved in India with local political upheavals.

Thunder in the Sun (1959) C-81m. **½ D: Russell Rouse. Susan Hayward, Jeff Chandler, Jacques Bergerac, Blance Yurka, Carl Esmond, Fortunio Bonanova. Hayward is romanced by wagon train scout Chandler and Bergerac, head of French Basque immigrants on way to California.

Thunder in the Valley (1947) C-103m. **½ D: Louise King. Lon McCallister, Peggy Ann Garner, Edmund Gwenn, Reginald Owen. Usual tale of boy in love with his dog, cruel father

Thunder of Drums, A (1961) C-97m.
**½ D: Joseph M. Newman. George
Hamilton, Luana Patten, Richard
Boone, Charles Bronson, Richard
Chamberlain, Slim Pickens. Better
than average cast saves average story
of new lieutenant having rough time
in cavalry.

Thunder on the Hill (1951) 84m. ***
D: Douglas Sirk. Claudette Colbert,
Ann Blyth, Robert Douglas, Anne
Crawford, Gladys Cooper. Nun Colbert can't believe visitor Blyth, about
to be hanged, is murderess, sets out
to prove her innocent; Cooper fine as
Mother Superior. Sincere, interesting
drama.

Thunder Over Arizona (1956) C-175m.
** D: Joseph Kane. Skip Homeier,
Kristine Miller, George Macready,
Wallace Ford. Undemanding minor
Western showing the corruption and
greed of people incited by a rich
silver ore discovery.

Thunder Over Hawaii SEE: Naked
Paradise.

Thunder Over Tangier (1957-British)
66m. *½ D: Lance Comfort. Robert
Hutton, Martin Benson, Derek Sydney, Lisa Gastoni. Flabby account of
refugees being conned with phony
passports.

Thunder Over the Plains (1953) C-82m. ** D: Andre de Toth. Randolph
Scott, Lex Barker, Phyllis Kirk,
Henry Hull, Elisha Cook, Jr. Routine
Western set in post- Civil War Texas,
with Scott as army officer sent to prevent carpetbaggers from harassing
all.

Thunder Pass (1954) 76m. ** D:
Frank McDonald. Dane Clark, Andy
Devine, Dorothy Patrick, Raymond
Burr. Usual story of resolute army
officer (Clark) pushing settlers onward in face of Indian attack.

Thunder Road (1958) 92m. **½ D:
Arthur Ripley. Robert Mitchum, Gene
Barry, Jacques Aubuchon, Keely
Smith. Fast-paced account of Mitchum returning home down South
after Korean War, becoming involved
in bootleg liquor running; minor slice
of Americana.

Thunder Rock (1942-British) 95m.
*** D: John and Roy Boulting. James
Mason, Michael Redgrave, Barbara
Mullen, Lilli Palmer. Allegorical
fable of discouraged newspaperman
given renewed faith by visions of various drowned people. Excellent cast
makes this most enjoyable.

Thunderball (1965-British) C-120m.
**½ D: Terence Young. Sean Connery, Claudine Auger, Adolfo Celi,
Luciana Paluzzi, Rick Van Nutter,
Bernard Lee, Roland Culver. Fourth
James Bond film isn't as lively as the
others. Plenty of gimmicks, but it
just doesn't move as well as the first
three. Adolfo Celi is a good villain,
though.

Thunderbirds (1958) 98m. **½ D:
John H. Auer. John Derek, John
Barrymore, Jr., Mona Freeman, Gene
Evans. Standard tale of training aviators for WW2, with typical romantic
interludes.

Thundercloud SEE: Colt .45.

Thunderhead—Son of Flicka (1945)
C-78m. **½ D: Louis King. Roddy
McDowall, Preston Foster, Rita Johnson, James Bell, Diana Hale, Carleton
Young. Good, colorful attempt to repeat MY FRIEND FLICKA's success;
doesn't match original, but it's enjoyable.

Thundering Jets (1958) 73m. *½ D:
Helmut Dantine. Rex Reason, Dick
Foran, Audrey Dalton, Robert Dix.
Still another WW2 account of flight
officer trying to reevaluate his handling of servicemen.

Thunderstorm (1956-Spanish, dubbed) 81m. BOMB D: John Guillermin. Carlos Thompson, Linda Christian, Charles Korvin, Gary Thorne.
Warmed-over trivia concerning Christian's provocative arrival in a small
fishing village on the Spanish coast.

Tiara Tahiti (1962-British) C-1000m.
** D: William Kotcheff. James Mason, John Mills, Claude Dauphin,
Herbert Lom. Mild happenings involving Mason and Mills as two former
Army officers who have an old grudge
to settle; establishment of a resort
hotel on Tahiti sets the wheels in motion.

Ticket to Tomahawk, A (1950) C-90m. **½ D: Richard Sale. Dan Dailey, Anne Baxter, Rory Calhoun, Walter Brennan, Marilyn Monroe, Chief
Yowlachie. Good musical Western
spoof. Drummer in theatrical troupe
involves himself in railroad fight;
Monroe has bit part.

Tickle Me (1965) C-90m. **½ D:

Norman Taurog. Elvis Presley, Jocelyn Lane, Julie Adams, Jack Mullaney, Merry Anders, Connie Gilchrist. That's the only way to get any laughs out of this one: Elvis works at all-girl dude ranch singing his usual quota of songs.

Ticklish Affair, A (1963) 89m. ** D: George Sidney. Shirley Jones, Gig Young, Red Buttons, Carolyn Jones, Edgar Buchanan. Amiable film of Navy commander Young falling in love with widow Jones; all it lacks is wit, sparkle and a fresh script.

Tiger and the Pussycat, The (1967-Italian-American, dubbed) C-105m. **½ D: Dino Risi. Ann-Margret, Vittorio Gassman, Eleanor Parker, Antonella Stani, Fiorenzo Fiorentini. Innocuous sex-comedy of middle-aged businessman Gassman unintentionally getting involved with promiscuous young Ann-Margret. Italian and American players work well together.

Tiger Bay (1959-British) 105m. *** D: J. Lee Thompson. Hayley Mills, Horst Buchholz, Yvonne Mitchell, John Mills. Film debut of Hayley Mills as youth who witnesses Buchholz killing his girlfriend; sensitive study of truth triumphing.

Tiger of the Seven Seas (1962-Italian, dubbed) C-90m. ** D: Luigi Capuano. Gianna Maria Canale, Anthony Steel, Grazia Maria Spina, Ernesto Calindri. Follow-up to QUEEN OF THE PIRATES, with Canale the center of romance and swordfighting in this OK pirate yarn.

The Tiger Woman SEE: **Jungle Gold.**

Tight Little (1948-British) 81m. **** D: Alexander Mackendrick. Basil Radford, Catherine Lacey, Bruce Seton, Joan Greenwood, Wylie Watson. Hilarious British comedy of sinking ship loaded with liquor providing problems for Scottish island thirsting for the cargo.

Tight Shoes (1941) 68m. ** D: Albert S. Rogell. Broderick Crawford, Binnie Barnes, John Howard, Anne Gwynne. Cast pushes hard to make this Damon Runyon yarn amusing at times: Crawford is big-shot crook who has big feet.

Tight Spot (1955) 97m. ***½ D: Phil Karlson. Ginger Rogers, Edward G. Robinson, Brian Keith, Lorne Greene. Spunky movie of police using ex-con Rogers as bait to trap crooked cop. Very good cast makes it enjoyable.

Tijuana Story, The (1957) 72m. BOMB D: Leslie Kardos. James Darren, Jean Willes, Robert McQueeney, Rodolfo Acosta, Robert Blake. Juvenile melodrama of Darren a victim of narcotic addiction, set in Mexico.

Till the Clouds Roll by (1946) C-120m. **½ D: Richard Whorf. Van Johnson, June Allyson, Lucille Bremer, Judy Garland, Kathryn Grayson, Van Heflin, Lena Horne, Tony Martin, Angela Lansbury, Dinah Shore, Frank Sinatra. Glossy biography of songwriter Jerome Kern (Robert Walker) has often unbearable plot interspersed with good numbers by guest stars.

Till the End of Time (1946) 105m. *** D: Edward Dmytryk. Dorothy McGuire, Guy Madison, Robert Mitchum, Bill Williams, Tom Tully, William Gargan, Jean Porter. Story similar to BEST YEARS OF OUR LIVES, of three returning WW2 veterans; married McGuire, disillusioned, engages in romance. Good drama.

'Til We Meet Again (1940) 99m. **½ D: Edmund Goulding. Merle Oberon, George Brent, Pat O'Brien, Geraldine Fitzgerald, Binnie Barnes, Frank McHugh. Overblown remake of ONE WAY PASSAGE recounts romance between suave crook Brent and fatally ill Oberon; McHugh repeats comedy-relief role from 1932 original.

Till We Meet Again (1944) 88m. ** D: Frank Borzage. Ray Milland, Barbara Britton, Walter Slezak, Lucile Watson, Mona Freeman. Fair wartime drama of nun Britton helping pilot Milland return to Allied lines; elements don't always click in this one.

Tillie and Gus (1933) 58m. ***½ D: Francis Martin. W. C. Fields, Alison Skipworth, Baby LeRoy, Edgar Kennedy. Fields vs. Baby LeRoy, plus riverboat spark, spark this W.C. romp, with comedian croaking "Bringing In The Sheaves" after each poker game.

Timber Queen (1943) 66m. *½ D: Frank McDonald. Richard Arlen, Mary Beth Hughes, June Havoc, Sheldon Leonard. Static programmer with pilot Arlen helping Hughes solve her business problems and romancing her.

Timberjack (1955) C-94m. ** D:

Joseph Kane. Vera Ralston, Sterling Hayden, David Brian, Adolphe Menjou, Hoagy Carmichael. Young man fights crooks taking over lumber mill who also killed his father. Harmless potboiler.

Timbuktu (1959) 91m. ** D: Jacques Tourneur. Victor Mature, Yvonne De Carlo, George Dolenz, John Dehner, Marcia Henderson, James Foxx. Mature plays adventurer involved in African story of plot to overthrow government. Script is below average; cast is uneven.

Time Bomb (1961-French, dubbed) 92m. ** D: Yves Ciampi. Curt Jurgens, Mylene Demongeot, Alain Saury, Robert Porte, Jean Durand. So-so story of captain plotting to collect insurance by planting bomb on ship. Fair cast.

Time Limit (1957) 96m. *** D: Karl Malden. Richard Widmark, Richard Basehart, June Lockhart, Rip Torn, James Douglas. Imaginative direction and acting spark this courtroomer concerning the trial of American military officer suspected of collaborating with enemy while P.O.W. in North Korea.

Time Lost and Time Remembered (1966-British) 91m. *** D: Desmond Davis. Sarah Miles, Cyril Cusack, Julian Glover, Sean Caffrey. Thoughtful study of Miles' unhappy marriage to older man, emphasized by visit home where she discovers new set of values.

Time Machine, The (1960) C-103m. ***½ D: George Pal. Rod Taylor, Alan Young, Yvette Mimieux, Sebastian Cabot, Tom Helmore, Whit Bissell, Doris Lloyd. H. G. Wells' novel vividly realized in entertaining fantasy of travel into the distant future. Taylor in the leading role.

Time of Indifference (1965) 84m. **½ D: Francesco Maselli. Rod Steiger, Shelley Winters, Claudia Cardinale, Paulette Goddard, Thomas Milian. Turgid melodrama of Steiger lusting for Cardinale; Goddard tried one-picture comeback in mother role.

Time of Their Lives, The (1946) 82m. *** D: Charles Barton. Bud Abbott, Lou Costello, Marjorie Reynolds, Binnie Barnes, John Shelton, Gale Sondergaard, Jess Barker. Most unusual film for A&C, and one of their best. Costello and Reynolds are killed during Revolutionary times, and their ghosts haunt a country estate where Abbott and friends come to live. Imaginative, funny, and well done.

Time of Your Life, The (1948) 109m. **** D: H. C. Potter. James Cagney, William Bendix, Wayne Morris, Jeanne Cagney, Broderick Crawford, Ward Bond, James Barton. Thoughtful film based on William Saroyan play about assorted customers of small saloon in Big City; superb performances.

Time Out for Love (1961-French) 91m. **½ D: Phillipe De Broca. Jean Seberg, Maurice Ronet, Micheline Presle, Françoise Prevost. Amusing adult study of Yank Seberg engulfed by seemingly immoral world of new acquaintances, with their own code of standards. Retitled: FIVE DAY LOVER.

Time Out of Mind (1947) 88m. ** D: Robert Siodmak. Phyllis Calvert, Robert Hutton, Ella Raines, Eddie Albert, Leo G. Carroll. Plodding period-piece of girl in love above her station, seeing her lover live unhappy life.

Time, the Place and the Girl, The (1946) C-105m. **½ D: David Butler. Dennis Morgan, Martha Vickers, Jack Carson, Janis Paige, S. Z. Sakall, Alan Hale, Donald Woods. Flimsy story of two go-getters trying to operate nightclub; lively cast and OK songs.

Time to Love and a Time to Die, A (1958) 133m. **½ D: Douglas Sirk. John Gavin, Lilo Pulver, Jock Mahoney, Don DeFore. Erich Maria Remarque's rehash of ALL QUIET ON THE WESTERN FRONT, updated to WW2, receives lackluster treatment in film form, becoming unemotional war story.

Time Travelers, The (1964) C-82m. *½ D: Ib Melchior. Preston Foster, Philip Carey, Merry Anders, John Hoyt. Flashes of imagination in story of pre-destined journey into past and future. Cast is uneven; script is worse.

Time Without Pity (1956-British) 88m. **½ D: Joseph Losey. Michael Redgrave, Ann Todd, Peter Cushing, Leo McKern. Tense little film of father's effort to prove son's innocence of murder charge; occasionally overly talky.

Timetable (1956) 79m. ** D: Mark Stevens. Mark Stevens, King Calder, Felicia Farr, Marianne Stewart. Small-scale account of insurance detective involved in investigation of robbery he engineered.

Tin Pan Alley (1940) C-94m. *** D: Walter Lang. Alice Faye, Betty Grable, Jack Oakie, John Payne, Esther Ralston, Allen Jenkins, Nicholas Brothers, John Loder. Predictable plot of struggling pre-WW1 songwriters enlivened by colorful numbers including "Sheik of Araby" production with Billy Gilbert as sultan. Oakie is in top form.

Tin Star, The (1957) 93m. *** D: Anthony Mann. Anthony Perkins, Henry Fonda, Betsy Palmer, Neville Brand, Lee Van Cleef. Adult Western, well acted, with Perkins the fledging sheriff who seeks assistance from bounty-hunter Fonda in combating town outlaws.

Tingler, The (1959) 80m. ** D: William Castle. Vincent Price, Judith Evelyn, Darryl Hickman, Patricia Cutts, Philip Coolidge. Juvenile horor-fantasy is fun on its own terms as Price discovers nerve in spine that controls fright emotion. Gimmicked up for theaters, but special shock sequences still come across on TV.

Tip on a dead Jockey (1957) 129m. *** D: Richard Thorpe. Dorothy Malone, Robert Taylor, Martin Gabel, Jack Lord. Neat account of Taylor tied in with smuggling syndicate in Madrid, romancing Malone. Good adaptation of Irwin Shaw story.

Titanic (1953) 98m. *** D: Jean Negulesco. Clifton Webb, Barbara Stanwyck, Robert Wagner, Audrey Dalton, Thelma Ritter, Brian Aherne. Hollywoodized version of sea tragedy centers on shipboard story. Not bad, but events better told in A NIGHT TO REMEMBER.

Titfield Thunderbolt, The (1953-British) C-84m. *** D: Charles Crichton. Stanley Holloway, George Relph, Naunton Wayne, Godfrey Tearle. Boisterous comedy about villagers who are attached to their antiquated railway line and run it themselves in competition with the local bus line.

To Be or Not To Be (1942) 99m. ***½ D: Ernst Lubitsch. Jack Benny, Carole Lombard, Robert Stack, Lionel Atwill, Felix Bressart, Sig Ruman, Helmut Dantine, Stanley Ridges. Excellent black comedy of wartime Poland about acting troupe which becomes involved in international affairs: Lombard's last film, Benny's best. His scene playing Hamlet is standout.

To Bed . . . Or Not To Bed (1963-Italian, dubbed) 103m. ** ½ Gian Luigi Polidoro. Alberto Sordi, Bernhard Tarschys, Inger Sjostrand, Ulf Palme. Saucy sex romp with Sordi expecting to find free love on business trip to Stockholm, discovering home sweet home is best. Retitled: THE DEVIL.

To Catch a Thief (1955) C-97m. *** D: Alfred Hitchcock. Grace Kelly, Cary Grant, Jessie Royce Landis, John Williams, Charles Vanel. Fluffy yarn of cat burglar on Riviera prowl; Kelly and Grant charming in entertaining color spree courtesy of Hitchcock.

To Each His Own (1946) 122m. *** D: Mitchell Leisen. Olivia de Havilland, John Lund, Mary Anderson, Roland Culver, Philip Terry, Griff Barnett. Well-turned soaper of unwed mother giving up baby, lavishing love on him as his "aunt" without revealing truth. Fine support by Culver as aging Olivia's beau.

To Have and Have Not (1944) 100m. ***½ D: Howard Hawks. Humphrey Bogart, Lauren Bacall, Walter Brennan, Dolores Moran, Hoagy Carmichael, Sheldon Leonard. Loosely based on Hemingway story of skipper-for-hire Bogart tangled up in WW2 intrigue; very good, but really comes to life in love scenes between Bogart and Bacall. Remade as THE BREAKING POINT.

To Hell and Back (1955) C-106m. *** D: Jesse Hibbs. Audie Murphy, Marshall Thompson, Susan Kohner, Charles Drake, Gregg Palmer, Jack Kelly, David Janssen. Very good war film based on Audie Murphy's autobiography, with excellent battle sequences making up for uneven script.

To Kill a Mockingbird (1962) 129m. ***½ D: Robert Mulligan. Gregory Peck, Mary Badham, Philip Alford, John Megna, Brock Peters. Leisurely-paced, flavorful filming of Harper Lee novel. Peck won Oscar as lawyer who defends Negro accused of murder.

Badham, Alford, and Megna superb as youngsters trying to understand life in their small Southern town.

To Mary—With Love (1936) 87m. ****½ D:** John Cromwell. Warner Baxter, Myrna Loy, Ian Hunter, Claire Trevor, Jean Dixon, Pat Somerset. Dated but good drama of Baxter and Loy having stormy period of marriage but ending up loving each other more than ever.

To Paris with Love (1955-British) 78m. ****½ D:** Robert Hamer. Alec Guinness, Austin Trevor, Odile Versois, Vernon Gray. Fair comedy of rich father taking son to Paris to learn facts of life. Guinness stands out in average British cast.

To Please a Lady (1950) 91m. ****½ D:** Clarence Brown. Clark Gable, Barbara Stanwyck, Adolphe Menjou, Roland Winters. Unremarkable love story of reporter Stanwyck and racecar driver-heel Gable.

To Sir, with Love (1967-British) C-105m. *****½ D:** James Clavell. Sidney Poitier, Judy Geeson, Christian Roberts, Suzy Kendall, Lulu, Faith Brook, Patricia Routledge. Excellent film of novice Poitier assigned to roughhouse London school, gradually earning respect from his students. Well acted, with nice work by young British newcomers.

To the Ends of the Earth (1948) 109m. *****½ D:** Robert Stevenson. Dick Powell, Signe Hasso, Ludwig Donath, Vladimir Sokoloff, Edgar Barrier. Fast-moving thriller of government agent tracking down narcotics smuggling ring has good acting and ironic ending.

To the Shores of Tripoli (1942) C-86m. ****½ D:** H. Bruce Humberstone. John Payne, Maureen O'Hara, Randolph Scott, Nancy Kelly, William Tracy, Maxie Rosenbloom, Iris Adrian. Spoiled rich-boy Payne joins Marines with off-handed attitude, doesn't wake up until film's end. Routine material.

To the Victor (1948) 100m. ****½ D:** Delmer Daves. Dennis Morgan, Viveca Lindfors, Victor Francen, Bruce Bennett, Dorothy Malone. Story of collaborators standing trial in France for war crimes sadly could have been much better.

To Trap a Spy (1966) 90m. ****½ D:** Don Medford. Robert Vaughn, David McCallum, Luciana Paluzzi, Patricia Crowley. Expanded from initial segment of MAN FROM U.N.C.L.E. TV series, reflects small budget and cast's newness at formula action-espionage type plot.

Toast of New Orleans, The (1950) C-97m. ****½ D:** Norman Taurog. Kathryn Grayson, Mario Lanza, David Niven, Rita Moreno, J. Carrol Naish. Lanza plays fisherman transformed into operatic star. Rest of cast good, and Lanza sings "Be My Love."

Toast of New York, The (1937) 109m. ***** D:** Rowland V. Lee. Edward Arnold, Cary Grant, Frances Farmer, Jack Oakie, Donald Meek, Clarence Kolb, Billy Gilbert, Stanley Fields. Arnold is in fine form as rags-toriches businessman Jim Fiske in late 19th century. Grant is his partner in good biographical drama, well staged.

Tobacco Road (1941) 84m. ****½ D:** John Ford. Charley Grapewin, Marjorie Rambeau, Gene Tierney, William Tracy, Elizabeth Patterson, Dana Andrews. Southern degradation is theme of filmization of Erskine Caldwell hit play, well directed by Ford with good cast; punch isn't always there, though.

Tobor the Great (1954) 77m. ***½ D:** Lee Sholem. Charles Drake, Karin Booth, Billy Chapin, Taylor Holmes, Steven Geray. Weak sci-fi adventure of enemy agents ploting to capture secret robot plans; terrible acting and dialog.

Tobruk (1967) C-110m. ****½ D:** Arthur Hiller. Rock Hudson, George Peppard, Nigel Green, Guy Stockwell, Jack Watson, Norman Rossington, Percy Herbert, Liam Redmond. WW2 actioner of Allies trying to destroy Rommel's fuel supply in the Sahara, bogs down in pretentiousness, much social comment, etc.

Today We Live (1933) 113m. **** D:** Howard Hawks. Joan Crawford, Gary Cooper, Robert Young, Franchot Tone, Roscoe Karns. Stilted Faulkner story of WW1 heroism, despite starstudded cast.

Together Again (1944) 93m. ***** D:** Charles Vidor. Irene Dunne, Charles Boyer, Charles Coburn, Mona Freeman, Elizabeth Patterson. Little bit of nothing carried off beautifully by Dunne, lady mayor of small town, and Boyer, suave New Yorker; charming comedy.

Tokyo After Dark (1959) 80m. ** D: Norman Herman. Michi Kobi, Richard Long, Lawrence Dobkin, Paul Dubov, Butch Yamaoto. Uninspired account of military cop Long on the lam in Tokyo from unintentional homicide.

Tokyo Joe (1949) 88m. **½ D: Stuart Heisler. Humphrey Bogart, Alexander Knox, Florence Marly, Sessue Hayakawa, Jerome Courtland. Lesser Bogart film about man determined to rescue wife from Japanese imprisonment.

Tokyo Rose (1945) 69m. ** D: Lew Landers. Byron Barr, Osa Massen, Don Douglas, Richard Loo, Keye Luke, Grace Lem, Leslie Fong, H. T. Tsiang. Timid drama of slinky female propagandist for Axis during WW2.

Tom Brown's School Days (1940) 86m. *** D: Robert Stevenson. Cedric Hardwicke, Freddie Bartholomew, Gale Storm, Jimmy Lydon, Josephine Hutchinson, Billy Halop, Polly Moran. Nostalgic accout of life at Victorian boys' school. Although most of cast is American, British flavor seeps thru. Retitled: ADVENTURE AT RUGBY.

Tom Brown's Schooldays (1951-British) 93m. *** D: Gordon Parry. John Howard Davies, Robert Newton, James Hayter, John Charlesworth. Well-acted film of Victorian England school life with exceptional British cast and good direction.

Tom, Dick and Harry (1941) 86m. ***½ D: Garson Kanin. Ginger Rogers, George Murphy, Alan Marshal, Burgess Meredith, Joe Cunningham, Jane Seymour, Phil Silvers. Spirited comic dilemma as wide-eyed Ginger chooses among three anxious suitors: sincere Murphy, wealthy Marshal, nonconformist Meredith. Silvers has hilarious role as obnoxious ice-cream man. Remade as THE GIRL MOST LIKELY.

Tom Jones (1963-British) C-131m. **** D: Tony Richardson. Albert Finney, Susannah York, Hugh Griffith, Joyce Redman, Edith Evans, Diane Cilento, Joan Greenwood, Peter Bull, David Warner. Excellent adaptation of Henry Fielding novel about wild exploits of rustic playboy in and about London. Beautiful cast and direction. Bawdy humor is not really for the kids in this vivid period piece.

Tomahawk (1951) C-82m. **½ D: George Sherman. Yvonne De Carlo, Van Heflin, Preston Foster, Jack Oakie, Alex Nicol. Colorful Western spiked with sufficient action to overcome bland account of friction between redskins and the army.

Tomboy and the Champ (1961) C-92m. ** D: Francis D. Lyon. Candy Moore, Ben Johnson, Jesse White, Jess Kirkpatrick, Rex Allen. Mild B-film about a young girl and her prize cow; strictly for children, who will probably enjoy it, despite standard plot devices.

Tomorrow at Ten (1964-British) 80m. **½ D: Lance Comfort. John Gregson, Robert Shaw, Alec Clunes, Alan Wheatley. Taut drama involving kidnapper of youth who dies leaving boy in house with time bomb set to explode.

Tomorrow Is Another Day (1951) 90m. **½ D: Felix E. Feist. Ruth Roman, Steve Cochran, Lurene Tuttle, Ray Teal, Morris Ankrum. Frank little film of ex-con Cochran marrying dime-a-dance girl Roman, heading for California, thinking he's killed her old boyfriend.

Tomorrow Is Forever (1946) 105m. *** D: Irving Pichel. Claudette Colbert, Orson Welles, George Brent, Lucile Watson, Richard Long, Natalie Wood. Weepy yarn of man (Welles) listed dead in war, returning with new face to find wife Colbert remarried to Brent. Bravura work by Welles with good support by Wood as his adopted daughter.

Tomorrow the World (1944) 86m. ***½ D: Leslie Fenton. Fredric March, Betty Field, Agnes Moorehead, Skippy Homeier, Joan Carroll, Boots Brown. Thoughtful drama of American couple adopting German boy, trying to undo rigid Nazi influence in him.

Tonight and Every Night (1945) C-92m. *** D: Victor Saville. Rita Hayworth, Janet Blair, Lee Bowman, Marc Platt, Leslie Brooks, Professor Lamberti, Dusty Anderson. Top-notch wartime musical of London musical troupe performing despite war hazards; good but unmemorable score, colorful production.

Tonight at 8:30 (1952-British) 81m. **½ D: Anthony Pelissier. Valerie Hobson, Stanley Holloway, Nigel Patrick. Three Noel Coward playlets comprise this satirical study of English life. Retitled: MEET ME TONIGHT.

Tonight We Raid Calais (1943) 70m. **½ D: John Brahm. Annabella, John Sutton, Lee J. Cobb, Beulah Bondi, Blanche Yurka, Howard da Silva, Marcel Dalio. Fast-paced WW2 tale of sabotage mission in France with good performances by entire cast.

Tonight We Sing (1953) C-109m. **½ D: Mitchell Leisen. David Wayne, Ezio Pinza, Roberta Peters, Anne Bancroft. Hodgepodge supposedly based on impresario Sol Hurok's life, allowing for disjointed string of operatic/musical interludes.

Tonight's the Night (1954) C-88m. *** D: Mario Zampi. David Niven, Yvonne De Carlo, Barry Fitzgerald, George Cole, Robert Urquhart. Good British cast bolsters appealing comedy about house in Ireland which natives claim is haunted.

Tony Draws a Horse (1951-British) 90m. **½ D: John Paddy Carstairs. Cecil Parker, Anne Crawford, Derek Bond, Barbara Murray. Witty little film about parents bickering over proper psychology in dealing with their undisciplined child.

Too Bad She's Bad (1955-Italian, dubbed) 95m. ** D: Alessandro Blasetti. Sophia Loren, Vittorio De Sica, Marcello Mastroianni, Lina Furia. Unremarkable little comedy about life and love among happy-go-lucky crooks, set in Rome.

Too Hot to Handle (1938) 105m. *** D: Jack Conway. Clark Gable, Myrna Loy, Walter Pidgeon, Leo Carrillo, Johnny Hines, Virginia Weidler. Gable & Pidgeon are rival newsreel photographers vying for aviatrix Loy in this fast-paced action-comedy; Gable's scene faking enemy attack on China is a gem.

Too Hot to Handle (1959-British) C-92m. ** D: Terence Young. Jayne Mansfield, Leo Genn, Carl Boehm. Seamy study of chanteuse Mansfield involved with one man too many in the nightclub circuit.

Too Late Blues (1962) 100m. ** D: John Cassavetes. Bobby Darin, Stella Stevens, Cliff Carnell, Seymour Cassel. Pretentious nonsense about jazz musician Darin involved with selfish dame Stevens.

Too Late for Tears (1949) 99m. **½ D: Byron Haskin. Lizabeth Scott, Don Defore, Dan Duryea, Arthur Kennedy, Kristine Miller. Scott goes after big money, but gets tangled with gangsters and murder; sturdy melodrama.

Too Many Crooks (1958-British) 85m. **½ D: Mario Zampi. Terry-Thomas, George Cole, Brenda De Banzie, Sydney Tafler. OK satire on racketeer films buoyed by Terry-Thomas' presence.

Too Many Husbands (1940) 84m. *** D: Wesley Ruggles. Jean Arthur, Fred MacMurray, Melvyn Douglas, Harry Davenport, Dorothy Peterson. Jean's about to marry Douglas when husband MacMurray, thought dead, turns up. Excellent comedy from Maugham's play HOME AND BEAUTY. Remade as THREE FOR THE SHOW.

Too Much Harmony (1933) 76m. D: **½ A. Edward Sutherland. Bing Crosby, Jack Oakie, Grace Bradley, Judith Allen, Lilyan Tashman, Ned Sparks, Kitty Kelley, Henry Armetta. Crosby & Oakie form a vaudeville team in this pleasant backstage musical; songs: "Thanks," "The Day You Came Along."

Too Much, Too Soon (1958) 121m. ** D: Art Napoleon. Dorothy Malone, Errol Flynn, Efrem Zimbalist, Jr., Ray Danton. But not enough, in sensationalistic tale of Diana Barrymore's decline. Flynn steals the show as John Barrymore.

Too Young to Kiss (1951) 91m. **½ D: Robert Z. Leonard. June Allyson, Van Johnson, Gig Young, Paula Corday. Allyson is fetching as pianist posing as child prodigy to get her big break falling in love with Johnson.

Too Young to Know (1945) 86m. ** D: Frederick De Cordova. Joan Leslie, Robert Hutton, Rosemary DeCamp, Dolores Moran. Slick, empty drama of career gal Leslie torn between husband and job.

Top Banana (1954) C-100m. *** D: Alfred E. Green. Phil Silvers, Rose Marie, Danny Scholl, Judy Lynn, Jack Albertson. Very funny comedy has Silvers as TV comic about to lose sponsor, his girl and peace of mind. Adapted from Broadway show.

Top Gun (1955) 73m. **½ D: Ray Nazarro. Sterling Hayden, William Bishop, Karin Booth, Regis Toomey, Rod Taylor, Denver Pyle. Fair movie with adequate-to-good cast of man cleared of murder charge and elected marshal.

Top Hat (1935) 105m. **** D: Mark Sandrich. Fred Astaire, Ginger Rogers, Edward Everett Horton, Helen Broderick, Eric Blore. What can we say? Merely a knockout of a musical with Astaire and Rogers at their brightest doing "Top Hat, White Tie and Tails," "Cheek to Cheek," "Isn't This A Lovely Day To Be Caught In The Rain" and other Irving Berlin songs, as Astaire determines to find the elusive Ginger and win her over.

Top Man (1943) 74m. ** D: Charles Lamont. Donald O'Connor, Susanna Foster, Peggy Ryan, Lillian Gish. O'Connor is earnest youth who steers his family right when father goes to war; slow pacing throughout.

Top O' the Morning (1949) 100m. **½ D: David Miller. Bing Crosby, Barry Fitzgerald, Ann Blyth, Hume Cronyn, Eileen Crowe. Crosby-Fitzgerald malarkey is wearing thin in this fanciful musical of Bing searching for thief hiding the blarney stone.

Top of the World (1955) 90m. ** D: Lewis R. Foster. Dale Robertson, Evelyn Keyes, Frank Lovejoy, Nancy Gates. Set in Alaska, movie revolves around jet pilot Robertson, his ex-wife Keyes and her new boyfriend Lovejoy.

Top Secret Affair (1957) 100m. **½ D: H. C. Potter. Susan Hayward, Kirk Douglas, Paul Stewart, Jim Backus, John Cromwell. John P. Marquand's MELVILLE GOODWIN, U.S.A. becomes fair comedy, with most credit going to Hayward as fiery publisher who knows all about Senate appointee's (Douglas) past.

Topaze (1933) 78m. *** D: Harry D'Arrast. John Barrymore, Myrna Loy, Reginald Mason, Jobyna Howland, Jackie Searl. Delightful film of Pagnol's play about naive schoolteacher who unwittingly is exploited by crooked official. Remade as I LIKE MONEY.

Topkapi (1964) C-120m. **** D: Jules Dassin. Melina Mercouri, Peter Ustinov, Maximilian Schell, Robert Morley, Akim Tamiroff, Despo Diamantidou. First-rate entertainment of would-be thieves who plan perfect crime in Constantinople museum. Ingenious robbery methods a highlight, along with sparkling Mercouri.

Topper (1937) 97m. ***½ D: Norman Z. McLeod. Constance Bennett, Cary Grant, Roland Young, Billie Burke, Alan Mowbray, Hedda Hopper, Eugene Pallette. Delightful gimmick comedy with ghosts Grant and Bennett dominating life of meek Young; sparkling cast in adaptation of Thorne Smith novel.

Topper Returns (1941) 85m. *** D: Roy Del Ruth. Joan Blondell, Roland Young, Carole Landis, Billie Burke, Dennis O'Keefe, Patsy Kelly. Neat blend of comedy-murder mystery with bewildered Young haunted again by amiable ghosts Blondell and O'Keefe.

Topper Takes a Trip (1939) 85m. *** D: Norman Z. McLeod. Constance Bennett, Roland Young, Billie Burke, Alan Mowbray, Verree Teasdale, Franklin Pangborn. Cary Grant is missing, but TOPPER cast returns for repeat success as Young is frustrated on Riviera vacation by ghostess Bennett.

Tops Is the Limit SEE: **Anything Goes** (1936).

Torch, The (1950) 90m. ** D: Emilio Fernandez. Paulette Goddard, Pedro Armendariz, Gilbert Roland, Walter Reed. Mexican revolutionary captures town and falls for daughter of nobility. Script very uneven; fine photography.

Torch Song (1953) C-90m. *** D: Charles Walters. Joan Crawford, Michael Wilding, Marjorie Rambeau, Gig Young. Save for Wilding's poorly-conceived role as blind pianist, an untarnished account of Broadway musical star Crawford clawing to stay on top; beautiful acting by Rambeau as Joan's salty mother.

Tormented (1960) 75m. Bomb D: Bert I. Gordon. Richard Carlson, Juli Reding, Susan Gordon, Lugene Sanders, Joe Turkel, Lillian Adams. Low-budget hog-wash of guilt-ridden pianist dubious over his forthcoming marriage to society gal.

Torn Curtain (1966) C-128m. **½ D: Alfred Hitchcock. Paul Newman, Julie Andrews, Lila Kedrova, David Opatoshu, Ludwig Donath. Oddly unmoving Hitchcock thriller about American scientist pretending to be defector. Slick but empty film.

Torpedo Alley (1953) 84m. ** D: Lew Landers. Dorothy Malone, Mark Stevens, Charles Winninger, Bill Williams. Typical Korean War actioner involving U.S. submarine offensives.

Torpedo Bay (1962) 91m. **½ D: Charles Frend. James Mason, Lilli Palmer, Gabriele Ferzetti. Taut study of human nature as British and Italian ships' captains struggle for survival against each other, set in WW2 North African waters.

Torpedo of Doom, The (1938) 100m. *** D: William Witney, John English. Lee Powell, Herman Brix, Eleanor Stewart, Montague Love, Hugh Sothern. Superior cliff-hanger from Republic's golden age of serials, involving dynamic duo of Marines undergoing innumerable obstacles to subdue a world-hungry scientist; quite actionful. Re-edited movie serial: FIGHTING DEVIL DOGS.

Torpedo Run (1958) C-98m. **½ D: Joseph Pevney. Glenn Ford, Ernest Borgnine, Diane Brewster, Dean Jones. Sluggish WW2 revenge narrative of sub-commander Ford whose family was aboard Jap prison ship he had to blow up.

Torrid Zone (1940) 88m. ***½ D: William Keighley. James Cagney, Ann Sheridan, Pat O'Brien, Andy Devine, Helen Vinson, Jerome Cowan, George Tobias. South-of-the-border action and romance with nightclub star Sheridan coming between rivals O'Brien and Cagney. Zesty dialogue in this one is memorable.

Tortilla Flat (1942) 105m. *** D: Victor Fleming. Spencer Tracy, Hedy Lamarr, John Garfield, Frank Morgan, Akim Tamiroff, Donald Meek, John Qualen, Allen Jenkins. Steinbeck's salty novel of California fishing community vividly portrayed by three top stars, stolen by Morgan as devoted dog-lover.

Touch and Go (1955-British) C-85m. **½ D: Michael Truman. Jack Hawkins, Margaret Johnston, Roland Culver, June Thorburn. Wry study of sturdy English family trying to overcome obstacles upsetting their planned emigration to Australia.

Touch of Evil (1958) 95m. *** D: Orson Welles. Charlton Heston, Janet Leigh, Orson Welles, Joseph Calleia, Akim Tamiroff, Marlene Dietrich, Mercedes McCambridge, Zsa Zsa Gabor. Intriguing, if too slowly-paced account of Mexican police official Heston and new wife Leigh involved in murder frame-up; Dietrich most effective as fortune-telling cafe hostess.

Touch of Larceny, A (1959-British) 93m. *** D: Guy Hamilton. James Mason, George Sanders, Vera Miles, Oliver Johnston, William Kendall, Duncan Lamont. Ingenious comedy of officer who uses availability of military secrets to his advantage in offbeat plan.

Tougher They Come, The (1950) 69m. *½ D: Ray Nazarro. Wayne Morris, Preston Foster, William Bishop, Kay Buckley. Trivial study of ruthless operators trying to take over lumber camp.

Toughest Gun in Tombstone (1958) 72m. *½ D: Earl Bellamy. George Montgomery, Beverly Tyler, Don Beddoe, Jim Davis. Weak shoot-out tale with Montgomery in the title role.

Toughest Man Alive, The (1955) 72m. ** D: Sidney Salkow. Dane Clark, Lita Milan, Ross Elliott, Myrna Dell, Syd Saylor, Anthony Caruso. Mild caper of tracking down gun-smuggling in South America.

Toughest Man in Arizona, The (1952) C-90m. **½ D: R. G. Springsteen. Vaughn Monroe, Joan Leslie, Edgar Buchanan, Victor Jory. While waging war on crime marshal Monroe falls for girl with expected results. Fairly well produced and acted.

Tovarich (1937) 98m. ***½ D: Anatole Litvak. Claudette Colbert, Charles Boyer, Basil Rathbone, Anita Louise, Isabel Jeans, Morris Carnovsky. Boyer and Colbert, royal Russians, flee the Revolution with court treasury but nothing for themselves. Top cast in lavish romantic comedy set in Paris.

Toward the Unknown (1956) C-115m. *** D: Mervyn LeRoy. William Holden, Lloyd Nolan, Virginia Leith, Charles McGraw. Intelligent narrative involving test pilots, focusing on air officer Holden eager to make his men respect him.

Tower of London (1939) 92m. *** D: Rowland V. Lee. Basil Rathbone, Boris Karloff, Barbara O'Neil, Ian Hunter, Vincent Price, Leo G. Carroll, Ralph Forbes. Classy horror film with fine cast. Historical drama of royal execution during reign of Queen Elizabeth I, with Karloff helming the chopping block.

Tower of London (1962) 79m. **½ D: Roger Corman. Vincent Price, Michael Pate, Joan Freeman, Robert Brown. Minor historical thriller bears small resemblance to Karloff vehicle. Fair script hampered by uneven acting.

Town Like Alice, A (1956-British) 107m. **½ D: Jack Lee. Virginia McKenna, Peter Finch, Maureen Swanson, Vincent Ball. Taut WW2 tale, well acted, about Japanese oppression of stranded group of British females. Retitled: RAPE OF MALAYA.

Town on Trial (1956-British) 95m. *½ D: John Guillermin. John Mills, Charles Coburn, Barbara Bates, Elizabeth Seal. Restrained murder-hunt story raking up the coals of a small British town, as the police hunt the girl's killer.

Town Without Pity (1961) 105m. ** D: Gottfried Reinhardt. Kirk Douglas, E. G. Marshall, Christine Kaufmann, Robert Blake, Richard Jaeckel, Frank Sutton, Barbara Rutting. Courtroom drama of G.I.'s accused of raping German girl. Decent cast, but could have been better handled.

Toy Tiger (1956) C-88m. **½ D: Jerry Hopper. Jeff Chandler, Laraine Day, Tim Hovey, Cecil Kellaway. Pleasant remake of MAD ABOUT MUSIC with Hovey "adopting" Chandler as his father to back up tales to school chums about a real dad. Day is Hovey's mother.

Toy Wife, The (1938) 95m. ** D: Richard Thorpe. Luise Rainer, Melvyn Douglas, Robert Young, Barbara O'Neil, H. B. Warner, Alma Kruger, Libby Taylor. Southern belle Rainer is pursued by Young and Douglas, can't decide which one to marry; inconsequential confection.

Toys in the Attic (1963) 90m. **½ D: George Roy Hill. Dean Martin, Geraldine Page, Yvette Mimieux, Wendy Hiller, Gene Tierney, Nan Martin. Timid adaptation of Hellman play about man returning home with childlike bride; Page and Hiller are Martin's over-protective sisters.

Track of the Cat (1954) C-102m. ** D: William Wellman. Robert Mitchum, Teresa Wright, Tab Hunter, Diana Lynn, Beulah Bondi. Slow-moving film of cougar hunt and family difficulties. Photography is main asset.

Track the Man Down (1953-British) 75m. ** D: R. G. Springsteen. Kent Taylor, Petula Clark, Renee Houston, George Rose. Dog-tracking background makes this standard Scotland Yard murder hunt above par.

Trade Winds (1938) 90m. *** D: Tay Garnett. Fredric March, Joan Bennett, Ralph Bellamy, Ann Sothern, Sidney Blackmer, Thomas Mitchell. Debonair detective March goes after murder-suspect Bennett; by the end of the around-the-world chase, they fall in love and solve mystery.

Trader Horn (1930) 120m. *** D: W. S. Van Dyke II. Harry Carey, Edwina Booth, Duncan Renaldo, Olive Golden, Muti Omoolu, C. Aubrey Smith. Early talkie classic filmed largely in African jungles still retains plenty of excitement in tale of veteran native dealer Carey encountering tribal hostility.

Trader Tom of the China Seas SEE: **Target, Sea of China.**

Trail of the Lonesome Pine (1936) C-102m. *** D: Henry Hathaway. Sylvia Sidney, Fred MacMurray, Henry Fonda, Fred Stone, Fuzzy Knight, Beulah Bondi, Spanky MacFarland, Nigel Bruce. Fine entertainment of feuding families in Virginia experiencing change and progress with coming of railroad. Noted as first outdoor film shot in Technicolor.

Trail of the Vigilantes (1940) 78m. **½ D: Allan Dwan. Franchot Tone, Broderick Crawford, Peggy Moran, Andy Devine. Tone is Eastern law enforcer out West to hunt down outlaw gang; good actioner.

Trail Street (1947) 84m. ** D: Ray Enright. Randolph Scott, Robert Ryan, Anne Jeffreys, George Hayes, Madge Meredith, Steve Brodie. Scott stars as Bat Masterson, saving local townspeople from corrupt rule; standard oater, nothing more.

Train, The (1965) 113m. **** D: John Frankenheimer. Burt Lancaster, Paul Scofield, Michel Simon, Jeanne Moreau, Albert Remy, Wolfgang Preiss. Gripping WW2 actioner of French Resistance trying to waylay

train carting French art treasures to Germany. High-powered excitement all the way.

Train Robbery Confidential (1962-Brazilian, dubbed) 102m. **½ D: Roberto Farias. Eliezer Gomes, Reginaldo Farias, Grande Otelo, Atila Iorio. Labored account of six men involved in railroad heist, with disintegration of friendship due to greed.

Traitors, The (1963-British) 71m. **½ D: Robert Tronson. Patrick Allen, James Maxwell, Zena Walker, Harold Goodwin, Sean Lynch. Fair spy meller of U.S. and British agent assigned to catch source of security leak in NATO.

Traitor's Gate (1955-British) 80m. **½ D: Freddie Francis. Gary Raymond, Albert Lieven, Margot Trooger, Catherina Von Schell. Two brothers are involved at sea in plot to steel crown jewels. Based on Edgar Wallace novel, film has fair acting, good direction.

Tramp, Tramp, Tramp (1942) 70m. *½ D: Charles Barton. Jackie Gleason, Florence Rice, Jack Durant, Bruce Bennett. Meager comedy as Gleason and Durant, 4-F rejects, protect the homefront, becoming involved in murder caper.

Tramplers, The (1966-Italian, dubbed) C-105m. ** D: Albert Band. Joseph Cotten, Gordon Scott, James Mitchum, Ilaria Occhini. Foreign-made Western set in post-Civil War South, with Cotten the domineering father; all just an excuse for gunplay.

Trap, The (1947) 68m. D: Howard Bretherton. Sidney Toler, Mantan Moreland, Victor Sen Yung, Tanis Chandler, Larry Blake, Kirk Alyn, Rita Quigley, Anne Nagel. SEE: **Charlie Chan** series.

Trap, The (1959) C-84m. **½ D: Norman Panama. Richard Widmark, Lee J. Cobb, Tina Louise, Earl Holliman, Carl Benton Reid, Lorne Greene. Turgid drama set in Southwest desert town, with gangsters on the run intimidating the few townsfolk.

Trapeze (1956) C-105m. *** D: Carol Reed. Burt Lancaster, Tony Curtis, Gina Lollobrigida, Katy Jurado. Moody love triangle with a European circus background; aerialists Lancaster and Curtis vie in the air and on the ground for Gina's attention.

Trapped (1949) 78m. **½ D: Richard Fleischer. Lloyd Bridges, Barbara Payton, John Hoyt, James Todd. Narrative-style of federal agent manhunt against counterfeit gang; tightly edited.

Trapped by Boston Blackie (1948) 67m. D: Seymour Friedman. Chester Morris, June Vincent, Richard Lane, Patricia White, Edward Norris, George E. Stone. SEE: **Boston Blackie** series.

Trapped in Tangiers (1960-Italian, dubbed) 74m. BOMB D: Antonio Cervi. Edmund Purdom, Genevieve Page, Gino Cervi, Jose Guadiola, Felix Bafauce, Antonio Molino. Dubbed dialog kills otherwise unsophisticated actioner of American uncovering dope ring in Tangiers.

Trauma (1962) 92m. ** D: Robert Malcolm Young. John Conte, Lynn Bari, Lorrie Richards, David Garner, Warren Kemmerling, William Bissell. Heavy-handed chiller involving Richards' attempt to recover lost memory of past horrors in spooky mansion.

Traveling Saleswoman (1950) 75m. ** D: Charles F. Riesner. Joan Davis, Andy Devine, Adele Jergens, Chief Thundercloud. Davis and Devine mug it up as soap saleswoman and fiance in stale Western comedy.

Treasure Island (1934) 105m. ***½ D: Victor Fleming. Wallace Beery, Jackie Cooper, Lewis Stone, Lionel Barrymore, Otto Kruger, Nigel Bruce, Douglass Dumbrille. Stirring adaptation of Robert Louis Stevenson pirate yarn of 18th-century England and journey to isle of hidden bounty; Beery is a boisterous Long John Silver in fine film with top production values. Only flaw is a stiff young Cooper as Jack Hawkins.

Treasure of Lost Canyon, The (1952) C-82m. ** D: Ted Tetzlaff. William Powell, Julia Adams, Rosemary DeCamp, Charles Drake. Mild Western uplifted by Powell as old prospector. Youth uncovers treasure which causes unhappiness to all.

Treasure of Monte Cristo, The (1960-British) C-95m. ** D: Robert S. Baker, Monty Berman. Rory Calhoun, Patricia Bredin, Peter Arne, Gianna Maria Canale. Uninspired variation on Dumas tale, with Calhoun aiding Bredin unearth buried treasure; slow-moving yarn.

Treasure of Pancho Villa, The (1955) C-96m. *½ D: George Sherman. Rory Calhoun, Shelley Winters, Gilbert Roland, Joseph Calleia. Good cast wasted in plodding account of famed 1910's Mexican bandit.

Treasure of Ruby Hills (1955) 71m. *½ D: Frank McDonald. Zachary Scott, Carole Mathews, Barton MacLane, Dick Foran, Lola Albright. Uninspired Western of land-grabbing ranchers.

Treasure of Silver Lake, The (1965-German, dubbed) C-88m. D: Harold Reinl. Lex Barker, Gotz George, Pierre Brice, Herbert Lom, Karin Dor, Marianne Hoppe. Dubbed dialogue almost ruins average Western based on Karl May novels with familiar characters Shatterhand and Winnetou.

Treasure of the Golden Condor (1953) C-93m. **½ D: Delmer Daves. Cornel Wilde, Constance Smith, Fay Wray, Anne Bancroft, Leo G. Carroll, Bobby Blake. Predictable costumer set in 18th-century Latin America, with noble-born Wilde out to seek his fortune.

Treasure of the Sierra Madre, The (1948) 126m. **** D: John Huston. Humphrey Bogart, Walter Huston, Tim Holt, Bruce Bennett, Barton MacLane, Alfonso Bedoya. Excellent film of gold-prospecting, greed, and human nature at its worst, with Bogart, Huston, and Holt as unlikely trio of prospectors. Won many Academy Awards, including Huston's for Best Supporting Actor. That's director Huston as an American tourist near the beginning.

Tree Grows in Brooklyn, A (1945) 128m. ***½ D: Elia Kazan. Dorothy McGuire, Joan Blondell, James Dunn, Lloyd Nolan, Peggy Ann Garner, Ted Donaldson, James Gleason, Ruth Nelson, John Alexander. Sensitive film of Betty Smith's novel of young girl Garner struggling in unhappy family atmosphere; Dunn won Oscar for performance as alcoholic father, Garner received a special Oscar for hers.

Trent's Last Case (1952-British) 90m. **½ D: Herbert Wilcox. Michael Wilding, Margaret Lockwood, Orson Welles, Hugh McDermott. Superior cast in lukewarm tale of the investigation of businessman's suicide.

Trial (1955) 105m. *** D: Mark Robson. Glenn Ford, Dorothy McGuire, John Hodiak, Arthur Kennedy, Katy Jurado, Rafael Campos. Intelligent filming of Don Mankiewicz novel. Courtroomer involves Mexican boy accused of murder, but actually tied in with pro vs anti-communist politics.

Trial, The (1963) 118m. ***½ D: Orson Welles. Anthony Perkins, Jeanne Moreau, Romy Schneider, Elsa Martinelli, Orson Welles, Akim Tamiroff. Gripping, if somewhat muddled, adaptation of Kafka novel of man in nameless country arrested for crime that is never explained to him. Not for all tastes.

Tribute to a Bad Man (1956) C-95m. *** D: Robert Wise. James Cagney, Don Dubbins, Stephen McNally, Irene Papas. Cagney is the whole show in this Western about a resourceful, ruthless land baron using any means possible to retain his vast possessions.

Trio (1950-British) 91m. ***½ D: Ken Annakin. Nigel Patrick, Jean Simmons, Wilfrid Hyde-White, Roland Culver, Michael Rennie, Felix Aylmer. Absorbing adaptation of three Somerset Maugham stories. Acting very fine throughout; last story weakest of three.

Triple Deception (1956-British) C-85m. ** D: Guy Green. Michael Craig, Julia Arnall, Brenda De Banzie, Geoffrey Keen, Eric Pohlmann, Patrick Westwood. On-location filming in France enhances murder tale with Craig the wily imposter caught in his own web.

Triple Trouble (1950) 66m. D: Jean Yarbrough. Leo Gorcey, Huntz Hall, Gabriel Dell, Lyn Thomas, George Chandler, Bernard Gorcey. SEE: Bowery Boys series.

Tripoli (1950) C-95m. ** D: Will Price. John Payne, Maureen O'Hara, Howard da Silva, Connie Gilchrist. Good cast cannot save average script of U.S. marines battling Barbary pirates in 1805; sole standout is Howard da Silva.

Triumph of Hercules, The (1964-Italian, dubbed) C-90m. ** D: Alberto De Martino. Dan Vadis, Moira Orfei, Pierre Cressoy, Marilu Tolo, Piero Lupi. Average gymnastic run-through with Vadis more resourceful than most Hercules.

Triumph of the Ten Gladiators (1964-Italian, dubbed) C-94m. ** D: Nick

Nostro. Dan Vadis, Helga Line, Stanley Kent, Gianni Rizzo, Halina Zalewska, John Heston. If not strong on plot, film allows for exuberances of swordplay and knockout brawls; set in ancient Rome.

Trojan Horse, The (1962-Italian, dubbed) C-105m. **½ D: Giorgio Ferroni. Steve Reeves, John Drew Barrymore, Hedy Vessel, Juliette Mayniel. Above-average production values and Barrymore's presence in role of Ulysses inflates rating of otherwise stale version of Homer's epic.

Trooper Hook (1957) 81m. **½ D: Charles Marquis Warren. Joel McCrea, Barbara Stanwyck, Earl Holliman, Susan Kohner, Sheb Wooley, Celia Lovsky. Woman scorned by whites for having lived with Indians and having child by the chief, begins anew with calvary officer.

Tropic Holiday (1938) 78m. **½ D: Theodore Reed. Dorothy Lamour, Ray Milland, Martha Raye, Bob Burns, Tito Guizar. Non-message fun musical set in Mexico, with perky performances by all.

Tropic Zone (1953) C-94m. *½ D: Lewis R. Foster. Ronald Reagan, Rhonda Fleming, Estelita, Noah Beery. Blah actioner set in South America with Reagan fighting the good cause to save a banana plantation from outlaws.

Trottie True SEE: **Gay Lady.**

Trouble Along the Way (1953) 110m. **½ D: Michael Curtiz. John Wayne, Donna Reed, Charles Coburn, Sherry Jackson, Marie Windsor. Schmaltzy Wayne vehicle. Duke leads football team to victory while romancing Reed; Windsor play Wayne's ex-wife.

Trouble at 16 SEE: **Platinum High School.**

Trouble for Two (1936) 75m. *** D: J. Walter Ruben. Robert Montgomery, Rosalind Russell, Frank Morgan, Reginald Owen, Louis Hayward, David Holt, Virginia Weidler. Unique, offbeat film of Montgomery and Russell joining London Suicide Club; based on chilling Robert Louis Stevenson story.

Trouble in Paradise (1932) 83m. **** D: Ernst Lubitsch. Kay Francis, Miriam Hopkins, Herbert Marshall, Charles Ruggles, Edward Everett Horton, C. Aubrey Smith. Sparkling Lubitsch froth about chic Francis mixed up with con-artist couple (Marshall and Hopkins) in Paris. A witty, delightful classic.

Trouble in Store (1953-British) 85m. **½ D: John Paddy Carstairs. Margaret Rutherford, Norman Wisdom, Moira Lister, Megs Jenkins. Full of fun sight gags and good character actors, film traces ups-and-downs of naive department store worker.

Trouble in the Glen (1953-British) C-91m. ** D: Herbert Wilcox. Margaret Lockwood, Orson Welles, Forrest Tucker, Victor McLaglen. Scottish-based drama of feud over closing of road that has been used for a long time. Average-to-poor script benefits from Welles. Original title: LAUGHING ANNE.

Trouble Makers (1948) 69m. D: Reginald LeBorg. Leo Gorcey, Huntz Hall, Gabriel Dell, Helen Parrish, Lionel Stander, Frankie Darro. SEE: Bowery Boys series.

Trouble with Angels, The (1966) C-112m. **½ D: Ida Lupino. Rosalind Russell, Hayley Mills, June Harding, Binnie Barnes, Mary Wickes, Gypsy Rose Lee. Cutesy study of Pennsylvania convent school, with students Mills and Harding driving mother superior Russell to distraction. Very episodic, occasionally touching.

Trouble with Harry, The (1955) C-99m. *** D: Alfred Hitchcock. Shirley MacLaine, John Forsythe, Edmund Gwenn, Mildred Natwick, Mildred Dunnock. Offbeat, often hilarious black comedy courtesy Mr. Hitchcock about murdered man causing all sorts of problems for peaceful neighbors in New England community. Gwenn is fine as usual, MacLaine appealing in her first film.

Trouble with Women, The (1947) 80m. ** D: Sidney Lanfield. Ray Milland, Teresa Wright, Brian Donlevy, Rose Hobart, Charles Smith, Lewis Russell. Professor Milland announces that women like to be treated rough; you can guess the rest of this tame comedy.

Troublemaker, The (1964) 80m. ***½ D: Theodore Flicker. Tom Aldredge, Joan Darling, Theodore Flicker, Buck Henry, Godfrey Cambridge, Al Freeman, Jr. Hilarious offbeat story of country boy trying to set up coffee house in Greenwich Village. Very fine performances, great direction. Catch this one.

True Confession (1937) 84m. *** D: Wesley Ruggles. Carole Lombard, Fred MacMurray, John Barrymore, Una Merkel, Edgar Kennedy, Toby Wing, Hattie McDaniel. Lombard is charming in wacky story of girl innocently involved in murder trial; Barrymore has memorable bit as lawyer.

True Story of Jesse James, The (1957) C-92m. **½ D: Nicholas Ray. Jeffrey Hunter, Robert Wagner, Hope Lange, Agnes Moorehead, John Carradine, Frank Gorshin. Glossy but sufficiently actionful fictionalized account of lives of famed outlaws.

True Story of Lynn Stuart, The (1958) 78m. **½ D: Lewis Seiler. Betsy Palmer, Jack Lord, Barry Atwater, Kim Spalding. Modest, straightforward account of housewife Palmer posing as gun moll to trap gang.

True to Life (1943) 94m. *** D: George Marshall. Mary Martin, Franchot Tone, Dick Powell, Victor Moore, Mabel Paige. Engaging comedy of radio writer Powell going to live with "typical" American family to get material for his soap-opera.

True to the Army (1942) 76m. ** D: Albert S. Rogell. Allan Jones, Ann Miller, Judy Canova, Jerry Colonna. Zany nonsense erupts when military life and romance clash; loud WW2 escapism.

True to the Navy (1930) 71m. **½ D: Frank Tuttle. Clara Bow, Fredric March, Sam Hardy, Eddie Featherstone, Jed Prouty. Enjoyable early-talkie with aggressive young sailor March wooing soda-fountain waitress Bow; the two make a good team.

Trunk, The (1960-British) 72m. *½ D: Donovan Winter. Phil Carey, Julia Arnall, Dermot Walsh, Vera Day. Programmer involving trumped-up murder charge and usual dose of red herrings; ill-conceived tale.

Truth about Spring, The (1965) C-102m. *** D: Richard Thorpe. Hayley Mills, John Mills, James MacArthur, Lionel Jeffries, Harry Andrews, Niall MacGinnis, David Tomlinson. Skipper Mills introduces daughter Hayley to first boyfriend, MacArthur, in enjoyable film geared for young viewers.

Truth about Women, The (1958-British) C-98m. **½ D: Muriel Box. Laurence Harvey, Julie Harris, Diane Cilento, Mai Zetterling, Eva Gabor. Multi-episode tale about playboy Harvey's flirtations; well mounted and cast, but slow-going.

Try and Get Me SEE: **Sound of Fury, The**.

Tugboat Annie (1933) 87m. *** D: Mervyn LeRoy. Marie Dressler, Wallace Beery, Robert Young, Maureen O'Sullivan, Frankie Darro. Dressler and Beery are rowdy riverboat rivals in funny, sentimental comedy; scene of Beery drinking hair tonic is classic.

Tugboat Annie Sails Again (1940) 77m. ** D: Lewis Seiler. Marjorie Rambeau, Alan Hale, Jane Wyman, Ronald Reagan, Clarence Kolb, Charles Halton. Airy comedy with predictable plot about Annie's job in jeodardy. Rambeau takes up where Marie Dressler left off; Reagan saves the day for her.

Tulsa (1949) C-90m. *** D: Stuart Heisler. Susan Hayward, Robert Preston, Pedro Armendariz, Lloyd Gough, Chill Wills, Ed Begley. Bouncy drama of oil-woman Hayward fighting for her property, forgetting about human values while involved in wildcat drilling.

Tumbleweed (1953) C-79m. ** D: Nathan Juran. Audie Murphy, Lori Nelson, Chill Wills, Lee Van Cleef. Bland oater with Murphy trying to prove he didn't desert wagon train under Indian attack.

Tuna Clipper (1949) 79m *½ D: William Beaudine. Roddy McDowall, Elena Verdugo, Roland Winters, Rick Vallin, Dickie Moore. Flabby tale of youth (McDowall) who pushes himself into rugged fishing life to prove his worth.

Tunes of Glory (1960-British) C-106m. **** D: Ronald Neame. Alec Guinness, John Mills, Susannah York, Kay Walsh, Dennis Price, John Fraser, Allan Cuthbertson. Superbly acted character drama of conflict between callous colonel and younger replacement; set in Scotland.

Tunnel of Love (1958) 98m. *** D: Gene Kelly. Doris Day, Richard Widmark, Gig Young, Gia Scala. Bright comedy of married couple Widmark and Day enduring endless red tape to adopt a child. Good cast spices adaptation of Joseph Fields-Peter de Vries play.

Turn the Key Softly (1953-British) 83m. ** D: Jack Lee. Yvonne Mitchell, Terence Morgan, Joan Collins, Kathleen Harrison, Thora Hird, Geoffrey Keen. Film recounts incidents in lives of three women ex-convicts upon leaving prison; contrived dramatics.

Turning Point, The (1952) 85m. **½ D: William Dieterle. William Holden, Alexis Smith, Edmond O'Brien, Ed Begley, Don Porter. Love and intrigue with Holden investigating internal corruption within crime-investigation committee.

Tuttles of Tahiti, The (1942) 91m. *** D: Charles Vidor. Charles Laughton, Jon Hall, Peggy Drake, Florence Bates, Mala, Alma Ross, Victor Francen. Laughton and family lead leisurely life on South Seas island, avoiding any sort of hard labor. That's it . . . but it's good.

12 Angry Men (1957) 95m. **** D: Sidney Lumet. Henry Fonda, Lee J. Cobb, Ed Begley, E. G. Marshall, Jack Klugman, Jack Warden, Martin Balsam. Brilliant courtroom film; Fonda does his best to convince 11 other jurors that their hasty conviction of boy on trial should be reconsidered.

Twelve Hours to Kill (1960) 83m. *½ D: Edward L. Cahn. Nico Minardos, Barbara Eden, Grant Richards, Russ Conway, Art Baker, Gavin MacLeod. Poor crime melodrama of gangland murder witnessed by Greek immigrant in New York.

Twelve O'Clock High (1949) 132m. **** D: Henry King. Gregory Peck, Hugh Marlowe, Gary Merrill, Millard Mitchell, Dean Jagger. Taut WW2 story of U.S. flyers in England, an officer replaced for getting too involved with his men (Merrill) and his successor who has same problem (Peck). Jagger won Oscar in supporting role; Peck has never been better.

12 to the Moon (1960) 74m. BOMB D: David Bradley. Ken Clark, Michi Kobi, Tom Conway, Tony Dexter, John Wengraf, Anna-Lisa. Aimless account about international exploration of moon.

Twentieth Century (1934) 91m. **** D: Howard Hawks. John Barrymore, Carole Lombard, Walter Connolly, Roscoe Karns, Ralph Forbes, Edgar Kennedy. Super screwball comedy based on Ben Hecht-Charles MacArthur play. Producer Barrymore makes Lombard a star, then tries to woo her back aboard cross-country train trip. Connolly and Karns add fine support as Barrymore's cronies.

Twenty-Four Hours to Kill (1965) C-92m. **½ D: Peter Bezencenet. Mickey Rooney, Lex Barker, Walter Slezak, Michael Medwin, Helga Somerfeld, Wolfegang Lukschy. OK suspenser with Rooney marked for execution by Slezak's smuggling ring when his plane is forced to land in Beirut for 24 hours.

20 Million Miles to Earth (1957) 82m. **½ D: Nathan Juran. William Hopper, Joan Taylor, Frank Puglia, Thomas B. Henry. Monster runs wild in Italy; intelligent script with good special effects and acting.

20 Million Sweethearts (1934) 89m. **½ D: Ray Enright. Dick Powell, Pat O'Brien, Ginger Rogers, Allen Jenkins, Henry O'Neill. Breezy 1930's musical with Powell a novice radio crooner who freezes before a microphone. Ginger helps him out, and they fall in love.

20 Mule Team (1940) 84m. ** D: Richard Thorpe. Wallace Beery, Leo Carrillo, Marjorie Rambeau, Anne Baxter, Douglas Fowley. Minor Western of borax-miners in Arizona with usual Beery mugging and standard plot. Baxter's first film.

21 Days Together (1938-British) 72m. **½ D: Basil Dean. Vivien Leigh, Laurence Olivier, Hay Petrie, Leslie Banks, Francis L. Sullivan. Galsworthy's play of lovers with three weeks together before man goes on trial for murder; Olivier and Leigh are fine in worthwhile, but not outstanding, film. Original title: 21 DAYS.

Twenty Plus Two (1961) 102m. ** D: Joseph N. Newman. David Janssen, Jeanne Crain, Dina Merrill, Agnes Moorehead, Brad Dexter. Poor production values detract from potential of yarn with private eye Janssen investigating a murder, encountering a neat assortment of people.

27th Day, The (1957) 75m. **½ D: William Asher. Gene Barry, Valerie French, Arnold Moss, George Voskovec. Imaginative sci-fi study of human nature with five people given pellets capable of destroying the world.

20,000 Eyes (1961) 60m. *½ D: Jack Leewood. Gene Nelson, Merry Anders, John Banner, James Brown. Flabby robbery caper done on shoestring budget.

20,000 Pound Kiss, The (1963-British) 57m. **½ D: John Moxey. Dawn Addams, Michael Goodliffe, Richard Thorp, Anthony Newlands. Edgar Wallace tale of blackmail, with a most intricate plot.

20,000 Years in Sing Sing (1933) 81m. *** D: Michael Curtiz. Spencer Tracy, Bette Davis, Lyle Talbot, Sheila Terry, Warren Hymer, Louis Calhern, Grant Mitchell. Still-powerful prison drama has only teaming of Tracy and Davis. He's a hardened criminal, she's his girl. Remade as CASTLE ON THE HUDSON.

23 Paces to Baker Street (1956) C-103m. *** D: Henry Hathaway. Van Johnson, Vera Miles, Cecil Parker, Patricia Laffan. Fast-moving murder mystery set in London has clever gimmick; detective Johnson is blind.

Twice Round the Daffodils (1962-British) 89m. ** D: Gerald Thomas. Juliet Mills, Donald Sinden, Donald Houston, Kenneth Williams. Mills is charming nurse in a male TB ward, trying to avoid romantic inclinations of her patients; expected sex jokes abound.

Twice-Told Tales (1963) C-119m. *** D: Sidney Salkow. Vincent Price, Sebastian Cabot, Mari Blanchard, Brett Halsey, Richard Denning. Episodic adaptation of Hawthorne stories has good cast, imaginative direction, and sufficient atmosphere to keep one's interest.

Twilight for the Gods (1958) C-120m. **½ D: Joseph Pevney. Rock Hudson, Cyd Charisse, Arthur Kennedy, Leif Erickson. Ernest K. Gann book becomes turgid soaper of people on run-down vessel heading for Mexico, their trials and tribulations to survive when ship goes down.

Twilight of Honor (1963) 115m. **½ D: Boris Sagal. Richard Chamberlain, Nick Adams, Joan Blackman, Claude Rains, Joey Heatherton, James Gregory. Average drama of struggling lawyer Chamberlain who wins murder case with assistance of elder expert Rains.

Twin Beds (1942) 85m. ** D: Tim Whelan. Joan Bennett, George Brent, Mischa Auer, Una Merkel, Glenda Farrell. Life of married couple Bennett and Brent is constantly interrupted by wacky neighbor Auer; and it's his film too.

Twinkle in God's Eye, The (1955) 73m. ** D: George Blair. Mickey Rooney, Coleen Gray, Hugh O'Brian, Joey Forman, Michael Connors. Simple yarn of clergyman Rooney trying to convert wrongdoers in Western town to God's faith via good humor.

Twist of Fate (1954-British) 89m. ** D: David Miller. Ginger Rogers, Herbert Lom, Stanley Baker, Jacques Bergerac, Margaret Rawlings. Lukewarm script benefits from good performances in story of Riviera-based actress who discovers that fiance is dangerous criminal.

Two Against the World (1936) 64m. ** D: William McGann. Humphrey Bogart, Beverly Roberts, Linda Perry, Carlyle Moore, Jr., Henry O'Neill, Helen MacKellar, Claire Dodd. Remake of FIVE STAR FINAL set in radio station is more contrived, not as effective. Retitled: ONE FATAL HOUR.

Two and Two Make Six (1961-British) 89m. ** D: Freddie Francis. George Chakiris, Janette Scott, Alfred Lynch, Jackie Lane. Mild romantic yarn of A.W.O.L. soldier Chakiris falling in love with Scott.

Two Dollar Bettor (1951) 73m. ** D: Edward L. Cahn. John Litel, Marie Windsor, Steve Brodie, Barbara Logan. Nifty little programmer showing the snowballing of businessman Litel's problems, once he gets racetrack fever.

Two-Faced Woman (1941) 94m. **½ D: George Cukor. Greta Garbo, Melvyn Douglas, Constance Bennett, Roland Young, Robert Sterling, Ruth Gordon, Frances Carson. Garbo's last film to date, in which MGM tried unsuccessfully to Americanize her personality. Attempted chic comedy of errors is OK, but not what viewer expects from the divine Garbo. Constance Bennett is much more at home in proceedings, stealing the film with her hilarious performance.

Two Flags West (1950) 92m. ** D: Robert Wise. Joseph Cotten, Linda Darnell, Jeff Chandler, Cornel Wilde, Dale Robertson. Very uneven Civil War Western. Battle scenes of good quality mixed with unappealing script and weak performances.

Two for the Road (1967-British) C-112m. *** D: Stanley Donen. Audrey Hepburn, Albert Finney, Eleanor Bron, William Daniels, Claude Dauphin, Nadia Grey. Beautifully acted film of bickering couple Hepburn and Finney stopping to reminisce about their twelve years of marriage, trying to work to save their happiness. Perceptive, winning film, well directed by Donen.

Two for The Seesaw (1962) 120m. *** D: Robert Wise. Robert Mitchum, Shirley MacLaine, Edmond Ryan, Elisabeth Fraser. Intelligent handling of William Gibson Play. Mitchum is Midwest lawyer trying to rebuild life in N.Y.C., involved with eccentric gal MacLaine.

Two for Tonight (1935) 61m. **½ D: Frank Tuttle. Bing Crosby, Joan Bennett, Mary Boland, Lynne Overman, Thelma Todd, James Blakeley. Songwriter Crosby is forced to write musical play in one week. Entertaining musical with Boland as his mother, Bennett his girl.

Two Gals and a Guy (1951) 71m. ** D: Alfred E. Green. Janis Paige, Robert Alda, James Gleason, Lionel Stander. Trials and tribulations of married vocal duo, caught up in the early days of TV performing; standard production.

Two Girls and a Sailor (1944) 124m. *** D: Richard Thorpe. Van Johnson, June Allyson, Gloria De Haven, Jose Iturbi, Jimmy Durante, Lena Horne, Donald Meek, Virginia O'Brien, Harry James, Xavier Cugat orchestras. Weak plot of Allyson-Johnson-De Haven triangle doesn't interfere with large cast and many fine musical numbers; breezy entertainment.

Two Girls on Broadway (1940) 71m. ** D: S. Sylvan Simon. Lana Turner, George Murphy, Joan Blondell, Kent Taylor, Wallace Ford. Sisters love same man (Murphy) but everything works out in this routine musical, sparked by snappy Blondell.

Two Gun Lady (1956) 75m. ** D: Richard Bartlett. Peggie Castle, Marie Windsor, William Talman. Simple oater of sure-shot gal and law enforcer tracking down her father's murderer.

Two Guns and a Badge (1954) 69m. *½ D: Lewis D. Collins. Wayne Morris, Morris Ankrum, Beverly Garland, Roy Barcroft. Poor script uplifted by competent cast in story of ex-convict who is mistakenly hired as deputy sheriff.

Two Guys from Milwaukee (1946) 90m. **½ D: David Butler. Dennis Morgan, Jack Carson, Joan Leslie, Janis Paige, S. Z. Sakall, Patti Brady. Silly story of European prince Morgan Americanized by cabdriver Carson; cast is so engaging it doesn't matter.

Two Guys from Texas (1948) C-86m. **½ D: David Butler. Dennis Morgan, Jack Carson, Dorothy Malone, Penny Edwards, Forrest Tucker. Average musical about two stranded vaudevillians who get involved with crooks and gals. Good cast succeeds.

Two Little Bears, The (1961) 81m. ** D: Randall Hood. Eddie Albert, Jane Wyatt, Soupy Sales, Nancy Kulp, Brenda Lee. Harmless fable-comedy of Albert confused to discover that his two children turn into bears at night, cavorting around the house.

Two Lost Worlds (1951) 61m. ** D: Norman Dawn. Laura Elliott, James Arness, Bill Kennedy, Gloria Petroff. Draggy story of shipwreck on uncharted island with prehistoric monsters. Cast doesn't reach it until last thirty minutes.

Two Loves (1961) C-100m. ** D: Charles Walters. Shirley MacLaine, Laurence Harvey, Jack Hawkins, Juano Hernandez, Nobu McCarthy. Plodding sudser set in New Zealand with spinster teacher MacLaine trying to decide between suitors Harvey and Hawkins.

Two Mrs. Carrolls, The (1947) 99m. **½ D: Peter Godfrey. Humphrey Bogart, Barbara Stanwyck, Alexis Smith, Nigel Bruce, Isobel Elsom. Shrill murder drama with Bogie as psychopathic artist who paints wives as Angels of Death, then kills them; Stanwyck registers all degrees of panic as the next marital victim.

Two of a Kind (1951) 75m. **½ D: Henry Levin. Edmond O'Brien, Lizabeth Scott, Terry Moore, Alexander Knox. Uninspired suspenser about con-artists plotting to dupe an elderly couple out of their inheritance fund.

Two on a Guillotine (1965) 107m. **½ D: William Conrad. Connie Stevens, Dean Jones, Cesar Romero, Parley Baer, Virginia Gregg, Connie Gilchrist. To receive inheritance from late father (Romero), Connie must spend night in haunted house. Familiar plot with some visual scares.

Two Rode Together (1961) C-109m. **½ D: John Ford. James Stewart, Richard Widmark, Linda Cristal, Shirley Jones, Andy Devine, Mae Marsh, Henry Brandon, Anna Lee. Fair Western with Stewart and Widmark rescuing innocent pioneers from Commanche clutches during 1880's.

Two Seconds (1932) 68m. ** D: Mervyn LeRoy. Edward G. Robinson, Vivienne Osborne, Preston Foster, J. Carrol Naish, Guy Kibbee, Berton Churchill. Fair drama with intriguing premise. Just before he is executed, Robinson's life passes before him in two seconds. Full potential of idea unrealized.

Two Sisters from Boston (1946) 112m. *** D: Henry Koster. Kathryn Grayson, June Allyson, Lauritz Melchior, Jimmy Durante, Peter Lawford, Ben Blue. Grayson and Allyson go to work in Durante's bowery saloon in this entertaining turn-of-the-century musical; bright score helps.

Two Smart People (1946) 93m. ** D: Jules Dassin. Lucille Ball, John Hodiak, Lloyd Nolan, Hugo Haas, Lenore Ulric, Elisha Cook, Jr. Conniving couple involved in art forgery; laughs don't come very often.

Two Tickets to Broadway (1951) C-106m. **½ D: James V. Kern. Tony Martin, Janet Leigh, Gloria De Haven, Eddie Bracken, Ann Miller, Smith and Dale, Barbara Lawrence. Modest musical involving Martin et al trying to get on Bob Crosby's TV show; some bright moments.

Two Tickets to London (1943) 79m. ** D: Edwin L. Marin. Michele Morgan, Alan Curtis, Barry Fitzgerald, C. Aubrey Smith. Passable drama of Curtis helped by Morgan in hunting down espionage agents.

Two Way Stretch (1960-British) 78m. *** D: Robert Day. Peter Sellers, Wilfrid Hyde-White, Lionel Jeffries, Liz Fraser, Maurice Denham. Wry shenanigans of Sellers et al as prisoners who devise a means of escaping to commit a robbery and then return to safety of their cells.

Two Weeks in Another Town (1962) C-107m. *** D: Vincente Minnelli. Kirk Douglas, Edward G. Robinson, Cyd Charisse, George Hamilton, Claire Trevor, Daliah Lavi, Rossana Schiaffino, Constance Ford. Overly ambitious attempt to intellectualize Irwin Shaw novel, revolving around problems of people involved in moviemaking in Rome.

Two Weeks With Love (1950) C-92m. **½ D: Roy Rowland. Jane Powell, Ricardo Montalban, Louis Calhern, Ann Harding, Debbie Reynolds, Carleton Carpenter. Reynolds fans will enjoy her role as daughter vacationing in Catskills proving to her parents that she's grown up, and singing "Abba Dabba Honeymoon."

Two Wives at One Wedding (1960-British) 66m. *½ D: Montgomery Tully. Gordon Jackson, Christina Gregg, Lisa Daniely, Andre Maranne. Trite minor film involving Jackson confronted by extortion gang charging him with bigamy.

Two Women (1961-Italian, dubbed) 99m. **** D: Vittorio DeSica. Sophia Loren, Raf Vallone, Eleanora Brown, Jean-Paul Belmondo. Loren won an Oscar as distraught mother who along with young daughter is raped by Allied soldiers; penetrating drama is based on Alberto Moravia novel; set in WW2 Italy.

Two Yanks in Trinidad (1942) 88m. ** D: Gregory Ratoff. Brian Donlevy, Pat O'Brien, Janet Blair, Donald MacBride. Donlevy and O'Brien are hoods who join the army, turning their talents to fighting the enemy; flat patriotism.

Two Years Before the Mast (1946) 98m. *½ D: John Farrow. Alan Ladd, Brian Donlevy, William Bendix, Esther Fernandez, Howard da Silva, Barry Fitzgerald. Badly scripted story of William Henry Dana's (Donlevy) crusade to expose mistreatment of men at sea. Da Silva is standout as tyrannical captain.

Twonky, The (1953) 72m. *½ D: Arch Oboler. Hans Conried, Gloria

**Blondell, Trilby Conried, Billy Lynn. Satirical sci-fi is misfire entertainment.

Tycoon (1947) C-128m. **½ D: Richard Wallace. John Wayne, Laraine Day, Cedric Hardwicke, Judith Anderson, James Gleason, Anthony Quinn, Grant Withers. Wayne plays determined young railroad pioneer in this overlong, but well-acted drama with fine cast; better than usual Wayne vehicles.

Typhoon (1940) C-70m. **½ D: Louis King. Dorothy Lamour, Robert Preston, Lynne Overman, J. Carrol Naish, Chief Thunder Cloud, Jack Carson. Another Lamour sarong epic, typically romantic; Overman provides good comedy support.

UFO (Unidentified Flying Objects) (1956) 92m. ** D: Winston Jones. Documentary-style account of unknown missiles, detailing various reports of unidentified flying objects being spotted. Film lacks excitement.

U-238 and the Witch Doctor (1953) 100m. *½ D: Fred C. Brannon. Clayton Moore, Phyllis Coates, Johnny Spencer, Roy Glenn, John Cason. Tedious cliff-hanger utilizing an abundance of stock footage and minimum of action in tame account of uranium hunt in Africa, involving battles with natives and animals. Re-edited movie serial: JUNGLE DRUMS OF AFRICA.

Ugetsu (1953-Japanese) 96m. *** D: Kenji Mizoguchi. Machiko Kyo, Masayuki Mori, Kinyo Tanaka, Sakae Ozawa. Forceful study of contrasting walks of life caught up in the clutches of city life; set in 16th-century Japan.

Ugly American, The (1963) C-120m. **½ D: George H. Englund. Marlon Brando, Sandra Church, Pat Hingle, Eiji Okada, Arthur Hill, Jocelyn Brando. Brando is American ambassador to Asian country; his arrival stirs up pro-communist elements, leading to havoc. Political revelations of U.S. power struggle isn't meat for exciting film. Based on Burdick-Lederer book.

Ulysses (1955) C-104m. *** D: Mario Camerini. Kirk Douglas, Silvana Mangano, Anthony Quinn, Sylvie, Rossana Podesta. Ambitious filming of Homerian epic of post-Trojan war adventures; done on a lavish scale, but starts to bog down after a while.

Ulysses Against Hercules (1961-Italian, dubbed) C-99m. *½ D: Mario Caiano. Georges Marchal, Michael Lane, Alessandra Panaro, Gianni Santuccio. Childish blend of myth and muscleman antics with Hercules (Lane) sent to punish Ulysses (Marchal); special effects of bird-men not up to snuff.

Umberto D (1955-Italian, dubbed) 89m. ***½ D: Vittorio DeSica. Carlo Battisti, Maria Pia Casillo, Lina Gennari. Remarkably realistic study of elderly man living alone on meager pension, determined to retain his dignity to the end.

Umbrellas of Cherbourg, The (1964-French, dubbed) C-91m. ***½ D: Jacques Demy. Catherine Deneuve, Nino Castelnuovo, Anne Vernon, Marc Michel, Ellen Farnen. Haunting music (score by Michel Legrand, lyrics by Demy) and gorgeous photography make this an outstanding romantic drama. Dubbing hurts original effect.

Uncertain Glory (1944) 102m. ** D: Raoul Walsh. Errol Flynn, Jean Sullivan, Paul Lukas, Lucile Watson, Faye Emerson, Douglass Dumbrille, Dennis Hoey, Sheldon Leonard. Wavering script about French philanderer Flynn deciding to give his life for his country.

Unchained (1955) 75m. ** D: Hall Bartlett. Elroy Hirsch, Barbara Hale, Chester Morris, Johnny Johnston, Peggy Knudsen, Jerry Paris. Fair drama of life at prison farm at Chino, California; highlighted by theme song: "Unchained Melody."

Uncle Harry SEE: **Strange Affair of Uncle Harry, The.**

Unconquered (1947) C-146m. **½ D: Cecil B. DeMille. Gary Cooper, Paulette Goddard, Howard da Silva, Boris Karloff, Cecil Kellaway, Ward Bond, Katherine de Mille. Gargantuan De Mille cowboys-and-Indians nonsense, one of his most ludicrous films but still fun.

Under Capricorn (1949) C-117m. ** D: Alfred Hitchcock. Ingrid Bergman, Joseph Cotten, Michael Wilding, Margaret Leighton, Cecil Parker. Stuffy costumer set in Australia; Bergman is frail wife of hardened husband Cotten; Wilding comes to visit, upsetting everything. Leighton excellent in supporting role.

Under-Cover Man (1932) 70m. ** D: James Flood. George Raft, Nancy Carroll, Roscoe Karns, Gregory Ratoff, Lew Cody. Good but familiar tale of Raft devoting his life to finding father's killer. Well acted.

Under Fire (1957) 78m. ** D: James B. Clark. Rex Reason, Steve Brodie, Jon Locke, Henry Morgan. Bland war tale about soldiers alleged to have deserted under enemy fire.

Under My Skin (1950) 86m. **½ D: George Blair. John Garfield, Micheline Prelle, Luther Adler, Steven Geray. Pensive study of once-crooked jockey, trying to reform for his son's sake. Based on Ernest Hemingway's MY OLD MAN.

Under Ten Flags (1960) 92m. **½ D: Duillo Coletti. Van Heflin, Charles Laughton, Mylene Demongeot, John Ericson, Liam Redmond, Alex Nicol. German attack-ship during WW2 uses a variety of dodges to elude British pursuers, in naval cat and mouse game, told from Axis point of view.

Under the Gun (1950) 83m. **½ D: Ted Tetzlaff. Richard Conte, Audrey Totter, Sam Jaffe, Royal Dano. Effective study of gangsters behind bars, played by competent cast.

Under the Red Robe (1936-British) 82m. **½ D: Victor Seastrom. Conrad Veidt, Raymond Massey, Annabella, Romney Brent, Sophie Stewart. Offbeat costumer with Veidt as hero, Annabella lovely heroine, and Massey the cruel villain in story of French Cardinal Richelieu's oppression of the Huguenots. Offbeat sense of humor adds to film's enjoyment.

Under the Yum Yum Tree (1963) C-110m. **½ D: David Swift. Jack Lemmon, Carol Lynley, Dean Jones, Edie Adams, Imogene Coca, Paul Lynde, Robert Lansing. Obvious sex comedy owes most of its enjoyment to Lemmon as love-hungry landlord trying to romance tenant Lynley who's living with her fiancé (Jones).

Under Two Flags (1936) 105m. *** D: Frank Lloyd. Ronald Colman, Claudette Colbert, Victor McLaglen, Rosalind Russell, Gregory Ratoff, Nigel Bruce. Rich girl Russell and cigarette girl Colbert both love soldier Colman at Indian outpost; jealous McLaglen vents anger on impeccable Colman in good rendering of Ouida's adventure story.

Under Western Skies (1945) 83m. *½ D: Jean Yarbrough. Martha O'Driscoll, Noah Beery, Jr., Leon Errol. Uninspired blend of shoot-em-up and musical, with scatterbrained jokes tossed in.

Undercover Girl (1950) 83m. ** D: Joseph Pevney. Alexis Smith, Scott Brady, Richard Egan, Gladys George, Regis Toomey. Smith in title role joins police to locate her father's killer; George in cameo is outstanding.

Undercover Maisie (1947) 90m. D: Harry Beaumont. Ann Sothern, Barry Nelson, Mark Daniels, Leon Ames, Clinton Sundberg. SEE: Maisie series.

Undercover Man, The (1949) 85m. *** D: Joseph H. Lewis. Glenn Ford, Nina Foch, James Whitmore, Barry Kelley, Howard St. John. Realistic drama of mob-leader being hunted down by secret service men who hope to nail him on tax-evasion charge.

Undercurrent (1946) 116m. **½ D: Vincente Minnelli. Katharine Hepburn, Robert Taylor, Robert Mitchum, Edmund Gwenn, Marjorie Main, Jayne Meadows. Stale melodramatics of woman realizing her husband is wicked, saved only by fine cast and usual high MGM production quality.

Underground (1941) 95m. *** D: Vincent Sherman. Jeffrey Lynn, Philip Dorn, Kaaren Verne, Mona Maris, Frank Reicher, Martin Kosleck. Good sturdy WW2 morale-booster of underground leader Lynn trying to send radio broadcasts out from under the noses of Nazis in Germany.

Undersea Girl (1957) 75m. BOMB. D: John Peyser. Mara Corday, Pat Conway, Dan Seymour, Florence Marly, Myron Healey. Flabby murder yarn with all sides of law hunting for loot buried on ocean bottom.

Undersea Kingdom SEE: Sharad of Atlantis.

Undertow (1949) 71m. **½ D: William Castle. Scott Brady, John Russell, Dorothy Hart, Peggy Dow, Bruce Bennett, Rock Hudson. Well done story of man accused of murder he didn't commit, trying to bail himself out without being caught first.

Underwater! (1955) C-99m. ** D: John Sturges. Jane Russell, Gilbert Roland, Richard Egan, Lori Nelson. Standard skin-diving fare devised to show off Russell in bathing suit.

Underwater Warrior (1958) 90m. **½ D: Andrew Marton. Dan Dailey, Claire Kelly, James Gregory, Ross Martin. On-location filming in the Philippines adds zest to narrative-style account of frogmen in action during closing days of WW2.

Underworld After Dark SEE: Big Town After Dark.

Underworld Informers (1965-British) 105m. *** D: Ken Annakin. Nigel Patrick, Catherine Woodville, Margaret Whiting, Colin Blakely, Harry Andrews, Frank Finlay. Tight, taut crime tale as Scotland Yard inspector Patrick must clear his name by bringing in notorious gangland leaders. Vivid atmosphere, fine acting by all.

Underworld Story, The (1950) 90m. *** D: Cy Endfield. Gale Storm, Dan Duryea, Herbert Marshall, Mary Anderson, Michael O'Shea. Surprisingly effective gangster yarn of reporter joining small town newspaper and uncovering corruption; cast is uniformly good.

Underworld, U.S.A. (1961) 99m. *** D: Samuel Fuller. Cliff Robertson, Dolores Dorn, Beatrice Kay, Robert Emhardt, Larry Gates. Taut vengeance tale of Robertson helping to undermine gangland empire responsible for his father's death; well-cast actioner.

Undying Monster, The (1942) 60m. ** D: John Brahm. James Ellison, John Howard, Heather Angel, Bramwell Fletcher. London is setting for OK chiller of a werewolf on the prowl; nothing new.

Unearthly, The (1957) 73m. *½ D. Brooke L. Peters. John Carradine, Allison Hayes, Myron Healey, Sally Todd. Unconvincing sci-fi about scientific experiments on human guinea pigs.

Unfaithful, The (1947) 109m. **½ D: Vincent Sherman. Ann Sheridan, Lew Ayres, Zachary Scott, Eve Arden, Steven Geray, John Hoyt. Title refers to Sheridan who gets tangled in murder while husband is out of town; good cast in fairly interesting drama. Remake of THE LETTER.

Unfaithfully Yours (1948) 105m. *** D: Preston Sturges. Rex Harrison, Linda Darnell, Barbara Lawrence, Rudy Vallee, Kurt Kreuger, Lionel Stander. Ingenious Sturges comedy of symphony conductor (Harrison) who suspects his wife of infidelity and plots her murder during a concerto. Offbeat, with many hilarious scenes.

Unfaithfuls, The (1960-Italian, dubbed) 89m. **½ D: Stefano Steno. Mai Britt, Gina Lollobrigida, Pierre Cressoy, Marina Vlady, Anna Maria Ferrero, Tina Lattanzi, Carlo Romano. Multi-faceted film of life among rich, corrupt society of Rome.

Unfinished Business (1941) 96m. ** D: Gregory LaCava. Irene Dunne, Robert Montgomery, Preston Foster, Eugene Pallette, Dick Foran, Esther Dale, Walter Catlett. Ordinary romance between aristocratic Montgomery and ambitious singer Dunne.

Unfinished Dance, The (1947) C-101m. **½ D: Henry Koster. Margaret O'Brien, Cyd Charisse, Karin Booth, Danny Thomas, Esther Dale. Sugar-sweet story of young dancer O'Brien whose idol is ballerina Charisse.

Unforgiven, The (1960) 125m. *** D: John Huston. Burt Lancaster, Audrey Hepburn, Audie Murphy, John Saxon, Charles Bickford, Lillian Gish. Western set in 1850's Texas tells of two families at odds with Indians over Hepburn, whom the savages claim as one of theirs. Gish and Bickford are outstanding in stellar-cast story, with rousing Indian attack climax.

Unguarded Moment, The (1956) C-95m. **½ D: Harry Keller. Esther Williams, George Nader, John Saxon, Edward Andrews, Les Tremayne, Jack Albertson. Mild drama of school teacher whose emotional stability is endangered by lusting pupil. Film noteworthy only for Williams' non-aquatic role; co-scripted by Rosalind Russell.

Unholy Four, The (1953-British) 80m. *½ D: Terence Fisher. Paulette Goddard, William Sylvester, Patrick Holt, Paul Carpenter, Jeremy Hawk. Muddled drama of amnesiac Sylvester caught up in a murder plot. Retitled: A STRANGER CAME HOME.

Unholy Garden, The (1931) 85m. ** D: George Fitzmaurice. Ronald Colman, Fay Wray, Estelle Taylor, Tully Marshall, Henry Armetta, Warren Hymer. Limp romance about adventurous Colman with taste for crime and little respect for lasting love.

Unholy Night, The (1929) 94m. ** D: Lionel Barrymore. Ernest Torrence, Dorothy Sebastian, Roland Young, Natalie Moorhead, Sidney Jarvis, Polly Moran. With the murder of several members of their regiment, veterans from the Indian war gather at Young's London home to ferret out the murderer. Stagy melodrama, much hamming, especially by Boris Karloff as Indian mystic.

Unholy Partners (1941) 94m. *** D: Mervyn LeRoy. Edward G. Robinson, Edward Arnold, Laraine Day, Marsha Hunt, William T. Orr, Don Beddoe, Walter Kingsford. Intriguing premise: Robinson starts sensationalistic newspaper after WW1, is forced to bargain with underworld king Arnold. Day gives fine performance as E.G.'s girl Friday; Hunt sings "After You've Gone."

Unholy Three, The (1930) 75m. ** D: Jack Conway. Lon Chaney, Sr., Lila Lee, Elliott Nugent, John Miljan, Ivan Linow, Harry Earles. The Man of a Thousand Faces' only talkie, a remake of his own 1925 vehicle, is pretty bad, interesting only as a curio. Story deals with ventriloquist, strongman, and midget from sideshow teaming up for underhanded activities.

Unholy Wife, The (1957) C-94m. *½ D: John Farrow. Rod Steiger, Diana Dors, Tom Tryon, Beulah Bondi, Marie Windsor. Muddled melodrama about farmer's wife attempting to kill husband.

Unidentified Flying Objects SEE: UFO.

Uninvited, The (1944) 98m. ***½ D: Lewis Allen. Ray Milland, Ruth Hussey, Donald Crisp, Cornelia Otis Skinner, Alan Napier, Gail Russell. Ghost suspenser about Russell haunted by dead mother's spectre; Milland and Hussey try to solve mystery. No trick ending in this ingenious film.

Union Depot (1932) 75m. **½ D: Alfred E. Green. Joan Blondell. Douglas Fairbanks, Jr., Guy Kibbee, Alan Hale, Dickie Moore, Junior Coghlan, Dorothy Christy. GRAND HOTEL at train station: Tramp finds money, young lovers meet, etc. Fast-paced and diverting film.

Union Pacific (1939) 135m. *** D: Cecil B. DeMille. Barbara Stanwyck, Joel McCrea, Robert Preston, Brian Donlevy, Anthony Quinn, Lynne Overman, Evelyn Keyes, Fuzzy Knight, J. M. Kerrigan, Akim Tamiroff. Brawling DeMille saga of nationwide railroad building with McCrea the hero, Preston the villain, Stanwyck (with Irish brogue!) in between. Action scenes, including spectacular train wreck, are highlights.

Union Station (1950) 80m. *** D: Rudolph Mate. William Holden, Nancy Olson, Barry Fitzgerald, Jan Sterling, Allene Roberts. Suspense drama that works; blind girl is kidnapped, which leads to exciting police hunt for victim and kidnapper.

Unknown Guest, The (1943) 64m. **½ D: Kurt Neumann. Victor Jory, Pamela Blake, Veda Ann Borg, Harry Hayden, Emory Parnell. Murder whodunit manages to create suspense and perk interest, largely due to Jory's performance in this programmer.

Unknown Island (1948) 76m. *½ D: Jack Bernhard. Virginia Grey, Philip Reed, Richard Denning, Barton MacLane. Boring story of scientists searching for prehistoric monsters on strange island has unimaginative special effects, little else.

Unknown Man, The (1951) 86m. **½ D: Richard Thorpe. Walter Pidgeon, Ann Harding, Barry Sullivan, Keefe Brasselle. Most capable cast enhances this yarn of lawyer discovering client in murder trial was guilty, and the strange triumph of justice he plots.

Unknown Terror, The (1957) 77m. ** D: Charles Marquis Warren. John Howard, Paul Richards, May Wynn, Mala Powers, Sir Lancelot. Unremarkable chiller supposedly set in South America, involving living molecular monsters.

Unseen, The (1945) 81m. ** D: Lewis Allen. Joel McCrea, Gail Russell, Herbert Marshall, Phyllis Brooks, Isobel Elsom, Norman Lloyd. Man who made THE UNINVITED tries similar venture but doesn't succeed, with governess Russell haunted again by strange mystery; very weak ending.

Unsuspected, The (1947) 103m. **½ D: Michael Curtiz. Claude Rains,

Joan Caulfield, Audrey Totter, Constance Bennett, Hurd Hatfield. Predictable melodrama with good cast; superficially charming. Rains has murder on his mind, with niece Caulfield the victim.

Untamed (1955) C-111m. *** D: Henry King. Tyrone Power, Susan Hayward, Agnes Moorehead, Richard Egan, Rita Moreno, John Justin. Quite vivid account of Boer trek through hostile South African country, with Power romancing Hayward.

Untamed Breed, The (1948) C-79m. ** D: Charles Lamont. Sonny Tufts, Barbara Britton, William Bishop, Edgar Buchanan. Routine trials and tribulations of breeding cattle in old Texas, amid romance and gun-play.

Untamed Frontier (1952) C-75m. **½ D: Hugo Fregonese. Joseph Cotten, Shelley Winters, Scott Brady, Suzan Ball, Antonio Moreno. Range war between Texan cattle owners is basis for this Western improved by good cast.

Untamed Heiress (1954) 70m. *½ D: Charles Lamont. Judy Canova, Donold Barry, Taylor Holmes, George Cleveland. Slight Canova shenanigans involving the search for daughter of woman who financed a now-wealthy man.

Untamed Youth (1957) 80m. *½ D: Howard W. Koch. Mamie Van Doren, Lori Nelson, John Russell, Lurene Tuttle. Mishmash of dramatics, sensationalism and music set on a reform school farm.

Until Hell Is Frozen (1960-German, dubbed) 87m. ** D: Leopold Lahola. Charles Millot, Gotz George, Anna Smolik, Pierre Parel. Rambling account of P.O.W.'s in Russian prison camp in 1950, detailing their vain efforts to escape; muddled drama.

Until They Sail (1957) 95m. **½ D: Robert Wise. Paul Newman, Joan Fontaine, Jean Simmons, Sandra Dee, Piper Laurie. Soaper court-room story set in WW2 New Zealand, with sisters (Fontaine, Simmons, Laurie and Dee) involved in love, misery and murder. From James Michener story.

Unwed Mother (1958) 74m. *½ D: Walter Doniger. Norma Moore, Robert Vaughn, Diana Darrin, Billie Bird. Title tells all in this unsensational programmer.

Up from the Beach (1965) 99m. **½ D: Robert Parrish. Cliff Robertson, Red Buttons, Irina Demick, Marius Goring, Slim Pickens, James Robertson Justice, Broderick Crawford. Static film of American sergeant Robertson involved with French civilians in love and war during Normandy invasion.

Up Front (1951) 92m. **½ D: Alexander Knox. David Wayne, Tom Ewell, Marina Berti, Jeffrey Lynn, Richard Egan. Sometimes amusing WW2 comedy based on Bill Mauldin's cartoon characters "Willie and Joe", involved in assorted shenanigans.

Up Goes Maisie (1946) 89m. D: Harry Beaumont. Ann Sothern, George Murphy, Hillary Brooke, Stephen McNally, Ray Collins, Jeff York, Gloria Grafton. See: MAISIE series.

Up In Arms (1944) C-106m. **½ D: Elliott Nugent. Danny Kaye, Dana Andrews, Constance Dowling, Dinah Shore, Louis Calhern, Lyle Talbot, Margaret Dumont, Elisha Cook, Jr. Danny's first feature film doesn't wear well, biggest asset being vivacious Dinah Shore; Virginia Mayo is one of chorus girls. Only those great patter songs hold up.

Up In Central Park (1948) 88m. ** D: William A. Seiter. Deanna Durbin, Dick Haymes, Vincent Price, Albert Sharpe, Tom Powers. Nothing-special musical features Durbin as Irish colleen in turn-of-century New York as she and reporter uncover "Boss Tweed".

Up In Mabel's Room (1944) 76m. *** D: Allan Dwan. Marjorie Reynolds, Dennis O'Keefe, Gail Patrick, Mischa Auer, Charlotte Greenwood, Lee Bowman. Engaging comedy of innocent O'Keefe embarrassed by presence of old flame Patrick in front of wife Reynolds.

Up In Smoke (1957) 64m. D: William Beaudine. Huntz Hall, Stanley Clements, Benny Rubin, Jack Mulhall, Judy Bamber. SEE: Bowery Boys series.

Up Periscope (1959) C-111m. **½ D: Gordon Douglas. James Garner, Edmond O'Brien, Andra Martin, Alan Hale, Carleton Carpenter, Frank Gifford. Garner is Navy Lieutenant transferred to submarine during WW2, with usual interaction among crew as they reconnoiter Jap-held island.

Up the Creek (1958-British) 83m. **½ D: Val Guest. David Tomlinson, Wilfrid Hyde-White, Peter Sellers, Vera Day, Michael Goodliffe. Broad naval spoof à la MR. ROBERTS, which leans too much on slapstick rather than barbs; White is best as non-plussed admiral.

Upper Hand, The (1967-French, dubbed) C-86m. **½ D: Denys de la Patelliere. Jean Gabin, George Raft, Gert Frobe, Nadja Tiller. Labored international underworld yarn, with wooden performances by cast involved in gold smuggling.

Upstairs and Downstairs (1961-British) 100m. **½ D: Ralph Thomas. Mylene Demongeot, Michael Craig, Anne Heywood, James Robertson Justice. Witty study of human nature: Craig married boss' daughter (Heywood) and they must entertain firm's clients. Film traces chaos of party-giving, and odd assortment of servants who come and go.

Uranium Boom (1956) 67m. *½ D: William Castle. Dennis Morgan, Patricia Medina, William Talman, Tina Carver. Dull account of two ore prospectors striking it rich, but more concerned with who will win Medina's love.

Ursus in the Land of Fire (1963-Italian, dubbed) 87m. *½ D: Giorgio Simonelli. Ed Fury, Claudia Mori, Adriano Micantoni, Luciana Gilli. Stupid muscleman mini-film, with Fury battling all odds to help Gilli regain her throne.

Ursus in the Valley of the Lions (1961-Italian, dubbed) C-82m. ** D: Carlo Ludovico Bragaglia. Ed Fury, Moira Orfei, Mary Marlon, Alberto Lupo, Gerard Herter. Routine costumer with Fury teaming with friendly lions to overcome the barbarians.

Us SEE: **Benefit of the Doubt, The**

Utah Blaine (1957) 75m. *½ D: Fred F. Sears. Rory Calhoun, Angela Stevens, Max Baer, Paul Langton. Undistinguished Western about Calhoun helping to overcome landgrabbing outlaws.

Utopia (1950-French, dubbed) 80m. *½ D: Leo Jannon. Stan Laurel, Oliver Hardy, Suzy Delair, Max Elloy. Aside from L&H's half-hearted performances as two partners who inherit island full of uranium, a poorly scripted and acted film. Their last farewell, also titled ATOLL K.

V. I. P.S, The (1963) C-119m. **½ D: Anthony Asquith. Elizabeth Taylor, Richard Burton, Louis Jourdan, Margaret Rutherford, Rod Taylor, Maggie Smith, Orson Welles, Linda Christian, Elsa Martinelli. Glossy Grand Hotel plot, set in London airport. Everyone is terribly rich and beautiful; if you like watching rich, beautiful people, fine. If not, it's all meaningless. Rutherford (who won an Oscar for this) is excellent.

Vacation from Marriage (1945-British) 111m. *** D: Alexander Korda. Robert Donat, Deborah Kerr, Glynis Johns, Ann Todd, Roland Culver, Elliot Mason, Henry Longhurst, Billy Shine. Donat and Kerr sparkle in story of dull couple separated by WW2; each rejuvenated by wartime romance. Johns is perky as Kerr's military friend. Original title: PERFECT STRANGERS.

Vagabond King, The (1956) C-86m. **½ D: Michael Curtiz. Kathryn Grayson, Oreste, Rita Moreno, Cedric Hardwicke, Walter Hampden, Leslie Nielsen. Static remake of thread-bare Rudolph Friml operetta of the 15th-century poet.

Valentino, (1951) C-102m. *½ D: Lewis Allen. Anthony Dexter, Eleanor Parker, Richard Carlson, Patricia Medina. Undistinguished, superficial biography of famed star of American silent films.

Valerie (1957) 84m. *½ D: Gerd Oswald. Sterling Hayden, Anita Ekberg, Anthony Steel, Malcolm Atterbury. Unmemorable account (via flashbacks) of facts leading up to the wounding of Hayden's wife, and death of her parents.

Valiant is the Word for Carrie (1936) 110m. **½ D: Wesley Ruggles. Gladys George, Arline Judge, John Howard, Dudley Digges, Harry Carey, Isabel Jewell, Jackie Moran. Get out your handkerchiefs for this one, the epitome of 1930's soapers as selfless Gladys George devotes herself to orphan children. She won an Oscar nomination for her performance.

Valley of Decision, The (1945) 111m. *** D: Tay Garnett. Greer Garson, Gregory Peck, Donald Crisp, Lionel Barrymore, Preston Foster, Marsha

Hunt. Not overpowering, as intended, but good film of housemaid Garson marrying master's son Peck, continuing life in same household; set in Pittsburgh.

Valley of Mystery (1967) C-94m. **½ D: Joseph Leytes. Richard Egan, Peter Graves, Harry Guardino, Joby Baker, Lois Nettleton. Competent cast wasted on trite account of stereotyped passengers struggling to survive when plane crashes in South American jungle.

Valley of the Dragons (1961) 79m. *½ D: Edward Bernds. Cesare Danova, Sean McClory, Joan Staley, Danielle De Metz, Roger Til. Sloppy low-budget sci-fi about two men's adventures on a prehistoric planet.

Valley of Eagles (1951-British) 85m. **½ D: Terence Young. Jack Warner, Nadia Gray, Christopher Lee, Anthony Dawson. Above-par chase tale of scientist tracking down his wife and assistant who stole his research data and headed for the north country.

Valley of the Giants (1938) C-79m. ** D: William Keighley. Wayne Morris, Claire Trevor, Frank McHugh, Alan Hale, Donald Crisp, Charles Bickford. Color is only asset of juvenile film about man whose love of redwoods surpasses everything else.

Valley of the Headhunters (1953) 67m. D: William Berke. Johnny Weissmuller, Christine Larson, Nelson Leigh, Vince Townsend, Steven Ritch. SEE: Jungle Jim series.

Valley of the Kings (1954) C-86m. ** D: Robert Pirosh. Robert Taylor, Eleanor Parker, Kurt Kasznar, Carlos Thompson. Despite stars, a meandering adventure yarn of excavations in Egypt for tombs of ancient pharoahs.

Valley of the Redwoods (1960) 63m. *½ D: William Witney. John Hudson, Lynn Bernay, Ed Nelson, Michael Forest, Robert Shayne, John Brinkley. Programmer involving payroll theft and escape of robbers to Canada.

Valley of the Sun (1942) 84m. *** D: George Marshall. Lucille Ball, Cedric Hardwicke, Dean Jagger, James Craig, Billy Gilbert, Antonio Moreno, Tom Tyler. Intrigue of the old West with crooked white man provoking Indian uprising as he is being hunted by colonial agent.

Valley of the Zombies (1946) 56m. *½ D: Philip Ford. Robert Livingston, Adrian Booth, Ian Keith, Thomas Jackson, LeRoy Mason. Witless horror epic of man-returned-from-dead.

Value for Money (1955-British) C-89m. *** D: Ken Annakin. John Gregson, Diana Dors, Derek Farr, Donald Pleasence, Cyril Smith. Funny little comedy about young man inheriting father's money and his enjoyment of same.

Vampire, The (1957) 74m. *½ D: Paul Landres. John Beal, Coleen Gray, Dabbs Greer, Raymond Greenleaf. Minor chiller with scientist turned into blood-seeker. Retitled: MARK OF THE VAMPIRE.

Vampire Bat, The (1933) 63m. **½ D: Frank Strayer. Lionel Atwill, Melvyn Douglas, Fay Wray, Dwight Frye, Lionel Belmore. Good cast helps average story along. Atwill stars as mad doctor forced to kill townsfolk in search of "blood substitute."

Vanessa, Her Love Story (1935) 74m. ** D: William K. Howard. Helen Hayes, Robert Montgomery, Otto Kruger, May Robson, Lewis Stone. Soapy story of gypsy love with Hayes attracted to roughish Montgomery. Dated romance doesn't come off too well today.

Vanishing American, The (1955) 90m. ** D: Joseph Kane. Scott Brady, Audrey Totter, Forrest Tucker, Gene Lockhart, Jim Davis, Jay Silverheels. Mild, minor film about landgrabbers trying to take Navajo territory.

Vanishing Virginian, The (1942) 97m. *½ D: Frank Borzage. Kathryn Grayson, Frank Morgan, Spring Byington, Natalie Thompson. Tepid drama about suffragette movement down South.

Vanquished, The (1953) C-84m. *½ D: Edward Ludwig. John Payne, Jan Sterling, Coleen Gray, Lyle Bettger, Ellen Corby. Bland little Western about corruption within a town's administration.

Variety Girl (1947) 83m. **½ D: George Marshall. Mary Hatcher, Olga San Juan, De Forest Kelley, William Demarest, Frank Faylen, Frank Ferguson. Hatcher and San Juan head for Hollywood with hopes of stardom; flimsy excuse for Paramount guest stars Bob Hope, Bing Crosby, Gary Cooper, Ray Milland, etc. Hope and Crosby come off best in amusing golfing scene.

Veils of Bagdad (1953) C-82m. **½ D: George Sharman. Victor Mature, Virginia Field, James Arness, Nick Cravat. Standard Arabian nights costumer, with Mature zestier than most such cardboard heroes.

Velvet Touch, The (1948) 97m. **½ D: John Gage. Rosalind Russell, Leo Genn, Claire Trevor, Sydney Greenstreet, Leon Ames, Frank McHugh. Satisfying murder mystery features Russell as stage actress who commits perfect crime, with a nifty ending.

Venetian Affair (1967) C-92m. ** D: Jerry Thorpe. Robert Vaughn, Elke Sommer, Felicia Farr, Karl Boehm, Luciana Paluzzi, Boris Karloff. Limp spy vehicle not far removed from Vaughn's "Man from UNCLE" TV series. International intrigue isn't too intriguing in this one; Karloff is good in a supporting role.

Vengeance Valley (1951) C-83m. ** D: Richard Thorpe. Burt Lancaster, Robert Walker, Joanne Dru, Sally Forrest, John Ireland, Carleton Carpenter. Hugh O'Brian. Sex in the West with Lancaster and Walker as battling brothers, Dru and Forrest their women. Walker plays slimy villain with gusto.

Vera Cruz (1954) C-94m. *** D: Robert Aldrich. Gary Cooper, Burt Lancaster, Denise Darcel, Cesar Romero. Lumbering yet exciting Western set in 1860's Mexico with Cooper and Lancaster involved in plot to overthrow Emperor Maximilian.

Verboten! (1959) 93m. *½ D: Samuel Fuller. James Best, Susan Cummings, Tom Pittman, Paul Dubov, Dick Kallman, Steven Geray. Tame story of U.S. soldier uncovering neo-Nazi youth movement in Berlin.

Verdict, The (1946) 86m. **½ D: Don Siegel. Peter Lorre, Sydney Greenstreet, Joan Lorring, George Coulouris, Arthur Shields, Rosalind Ivan, Holmes Herbert. Murder-mystery script of "perfect crime" is rather weak, worth seeing for the marvelous duo of Lorre and Greenstreet, who support entire film.

Vertigo (1958) C-120m. ***½ D: Alfred Hitchcock. James Stewart, Kim Novak, Barbara Bel Geddes, Tom Helmore. Fascinating Hitchcock tale set in Frisco that defies rational description. Stewart is police detective with fear of heights who finds himself in a baffling situation involving an unusual girl (Novak). To reveal many more details would spoil a great film. Fine musical score adds to atmosphere.

Very Honorable Guy, A (1934) 62m. ** D: Lloyd Bacon. Joe E. Brown, Alice White, Alan Dinehart, Hobart Cavanaugh, Al Dubin. Par-for-the-course Brown vehicle, with Joe involved in scientific experiments regarding life-rejuvenating forces.

Very Special Favor, A (1965) C-104m. **½ D: Michael Gordon. Rock Hudson, Leslie Caron, Charles Boyer, Walter Slezak, Dick Shawn, Larry Storch, Nita Talbot, Jay Novello. Too-often blah, forced comedy of Boyer asking Hudson to romance daughter Caron.

Very Thought of You, The (1944) 99m. ** D: Delmer Daves. Eleanor Parker, Dennis Morgan, Dane Clark, Faye Emerson, Beulah Bondi. Flat romance of couple marrying during WW2, encountering family wrath when they return home; unusual Daves backfire.

Vice Squad (1931) 80m. **½ D: John Cromwell. Paul Lukas, Kay Francis, Helen Johnson, Esther Howard. Exciting melodrama of foreign emissary Lukas forced to inform on notorious gang by Vice Squad of police. Francis is love interest.

Vice Squad (1953) 87m. **½ D: Arnold Laven. Edward G. Robinson, Paulette Goddard, K. T. Stevens, Lee Van Cleef. Well-paced account of events in typical day of police detective department.

Vicious Circle, The SEE: The Circle.

Vicki (1953) 85m. **½ D: Harry Horner. Jeanne Crain, Jean Peters, Elliott Reid, Casey Adams, Richard Boone, Carl Betz, Aaron Spelling. Remake of I WAKE UP SCREAMING, with Boone the resolute cop convinced agent Reid killed chanteuse girlfriend Peters. Dramatic flair isn't always evident.

Victors, The (1963) 175m. *** D: Carl Foreman. George Hamilton, George Peppard, Vince Edwards, Eli

Wallach, Melina Mercouri, Romy Schneider, Jeanne Moreau, Peter Fonda, Senta Berger, Elke Sommer, Albert Finney. Sprawling WW2 drama of Allied soldiers on the march through Europe, focusing on their loving and fighting. Good cast and direction overcomes ambling script.

Victory (1940) 78m. *** D: John Cromwell. Fredric March, Betty Field, Cedric Hardwicke, Jerome Cowan, Rafaela Ottiano, Sig Ruman. March is authentic in tale of loner whose idyllic island life is disrupted by band of cutthroats; flavorful adaptation of Joseph Conrad novel sags at the end.

Victory at Sea (1955) 108m. *** Produced by: Henry Salomon. Narrated by: Alexander Scourby. Briskly-edited version of popular TV documentary series, highlighting Allied fight during WW2. Excellent photography, rousing Richard Rodgers score.

View from Pompey's Head, The (1955) C-97m. **½ D: Philip Dunne. Richard Egan, Dana Wynter, Cameron Mitchell, Marjorie Rambeau, Sidney Blackmer, Bess Flowers. Superficial gloss from Hamilton Basso novel about social and racial prejudice in small Southern town; Blackmer as aging novelist and Rambeau his wife come off best.

View from the Bridge, A (1962) 110m. D: Sidney Lumet. Raf Vallone, Maureen Stapleton, Carol Lawrence, Jean Sorel. Effective adaptation of Arthur Miller drama set near Brooklyn waterfront, involving dock worker Vallone's rejection of wife Stapleton and suppressed love of niece Lawrence; Sorel is smuggled-in immigrant Lawrence loves.

Vigil in the Night (1940) 96m. *** D: George Stevens. Carole Lombard, Brian Aherne, Anne Shirley, Rhys Williams, Peter Cushing, Rafaela Ottiano, Ethel Griffies, Blanche Frederici. Melodrama about events in big English hospital; atmosphere rings true, with fine dramatic performance by Lombard.

Vigilantes Return, The (1947) 67m. ** D: Ray Taylor. Margaret Lindsay, Jon Hall, Paula Drew, Andy Devine, Robert Wilcox, Jack Lambert. Standard Western with marshal Hall sent to bring law and order to untamed town.

Viking Queen, The (1967-British) C-91m. ** D: Don Chaffey. Don Murray, Carita, Donald Houston, Andrew Keir, Adrienne Corri, Niall MacGinnis. Wilfrid Lawson. Empty-handed costumer of early England under Roman rule, with plenty of gore as anarchists incite a violent uprising among the people. Murray and fine British actors are lost.

Vikings, The (1958) C-114m. **½ D: Richard Fleischer. Kirk Douglas, Tony Curtis, Ernest Borgnine, Janet Leigh. Big name cast and nice photography only stand-outs in routine Viking adventure about conflict between two brothers.

Villa! (1958) C-72m. *½ D: James B. Clark. Brian Keith, Cesar Romero, Margia Dean, Rodolfo Hoyos. Dull recreation of events in life of Mexican bandit.

Village of the Damned, The (1960-British) 78m. *** D: Wolf Rilla. George Sanders, Barbara Shelley, Michael Gwynne, Laurence Naismith, John Phillips, Richard Vernon. Very good adaptation of Wyndham novel of mishap in English village followed by birth of strange, emotionless children. Thriller has good cast, direction.

Village of the Giants (1965) C-80m. ** D: Bert I. Gordon. Tommy Kirk, Johnny Crawford, Beau Bridges, Ronny Howard, Tisha Sterling, Tim Rooney. Generally silly adaptation of Wells novel with teenagers in small town suddenly growing to tremendous heights. So-so special effects.

Villain Still Pursued Her, The (1940) 66m. **½ D: Edward Cline. Anita Louise, Hugh Herbert, Alan Mowbray, Buster Keaton, Joyce Compton, Billy Gilbert, Margaret Hamilton. Elaborate spoof of old-time melodramas is innocuous fun, with good cast hamming it up.

Vintage, The (1957) C-92m. ** D: Jeffrey Hayden. Pier Angeli, Michele Morgan, John Kerr, Mel Ferrer, Theodore Bikel. Leif Erickson. Strangely cast melodrama set in vineyard of France involving two brothers on the lam.

Violent Men, The (1955) C-96m. **½ D: Rudolph Mate. Barbara Stanwyck, Glenn Ford, Edward G. Robinson, Dianne Foster, Brian Keith, Richard Jaeckel. Robinson is unscrupulous, wealthy rancher in conflict with good folk of the valley, Stanwyck his wife. Some good action sequences.

Violent Road (1958) 86m. **½ D: Howard W. Koch. Brian Keith, Dick Foran, Efrem Zimbalist, Jr., Merry Anders. Well-done programmer involving men driving explosives over bumpy road, allowing for each to re-examine his way of life.

Violent Saturday (1955) C-91m. *** D: Richard Fleischer. Victor Mature, Richard Egan, Lee Marvin, Sylvia Sidney, Ernest Borgnine, Tommy Noonan. Effective study of repercussion on small town when bank robbers carry out a bloody hold-up.

Violent Summer (1961-French, dubbed) 85m. ** D: Michel Boisrond. Martine Carol, Jean Desailly, Dahlia Lavi, Henri-Jacques Huet. Unconvincing tale of murder of a halfwit girl, with most of the guests at a Riviera resort home prime suspects; too many loose threads.

Virgin Island (1959-British) C-84m. **½ D: Pat Jackson. John Cassavettes, Virginia Maskell, Sidney Poitier, Colin Gordon. Leisurely study of author Cassavettes and bride Maskell moving to Caribbean isle; film lightly touches on racial issue.

Virgin Queen, The (1955) C-92m. *** D: Henry Koster. Bette Davis, Richard Todd, Joan Collins, Herbert Marshall, Dan O'Herlihy, Rod Taylor. Davis is in full authority in her second portrayal of Queen Elizabeth I, and her conflicts with Walter Raleigh.

Virgin Spring, The (1960-Swedish, dubbed) 88m. *** D: Ingmar Bergman. Max von Sydow, Brigitta Valberg, Gunnel Lindblom, Brigitta Pettersson, Avel Duberg. Brooding dramatic fable involving farmer's daughter raped and murdered by lusting visitors, with a magical spring bursting forth from her death spot.

Virginia (1941) C-110m. ** D: Edward H. Griffith. Madeleine Carroll, Fred MacMurray, Stirling Hayden, Helen Broderick, Marie Wilson, Carolyn Lee. Labored Western despite production values; Carroll is young woman who must sacrifice her Southern heritage in order to raise money.

Virginia City (1940) 121m. **½ D: Michael Curtiz. Errol Flynn, Miriam Hopkins, Randolph Scott, Humphrey Bogart, Frank McHugh, Alan Hale. Big cast in lush Civil War Western, doesn't live up to expectations; Bogart cast as slimy Mexican bandido.

Virginian, The (1929) 90m. **½ D: Victor Fleming. Gary Cooper, Richard Arlen, Walter Huston, Mary Brian, Chester Conklin, Eugene Pallette. Owen Wister's novel becomes stiff but interesting Western, salvaged by good climactic shoot-out; Huston is slimy villain, and Cooper has one of his better early roles.

Virginian, The (1946) C-90m. **½ D: Stuart Gilmore. Joel McCrea, Brian Donlevy, Sonny Tufts, Barbara Britton, Fay Bainter, Henry O'Neill, William Frawley, Vince Barnett, Paul Guilfoyle. Remake of '29 classic Western follows story closely. Good, not great, results due to story showing its age. McCrea is hero, Donlevy the villain. Tufts a good-guy-turned-bad.

Virtuous Sin, The (1930) 82m. **½ D: George Cukor, and Louis Gasnier. Kay Francis, Walter Huston, Kenneth MacKenna, Jobyna Howland. Slow-moving early talkie has good performances as Russian general Huston wins over alluring Francis by promising to set prisoner-husband free.

Visit, The (1964) C-100m. **½ D: Bernhard Wicki. Ingrid Bergman, Anthony Quinn, Irina Demick, Paolo Stoppa, Hans-Christian Blech, Romolo Valli, Valentina Cortesa, Eduardo Ciannelli. Intriguing but uneven film parable of greed and evil; wealthy Bergman returns to European home town, offering a fantastic sum to the people there if they will legitimately kill her first seducer (Quinn). Actors struggle with melodramatic script; results are interesting if not always successful.

Visit to a Small Planet (1960) 85m. **½ D: Norman Taurog. Jerry Lewis, Joan Blackman, Earl Holliman, Fred Clark, Lee Patrick, Gale Gordon. Gore Vidal satire becomes talky Lewis vehicle with Jerry the alien landed on earth to observe man's strange ways.

Viva Las Vegas (1964) C-86m. **½

D: George Sidney. Elvis Presley, Ann-Margret, Cesare Danova, William Demarest. Perky cast and colorful gambling city locale elevate this Presley vehicle, with Elvis a sports car racer.

Viva Villa! (1934) 115m. ***½ **D:** Jack Conway. Wallace Beery, Leo Carrillo, Fay Wray, Donald Cook, Stuart Erwin, Joseph Schildkraut, Katherine DeMille. Viva Beery, in one of his best films as the rowdy Mexican rebel who led the fight for Madera's Mexican Republic. Film plays with facts, but is entertaining.

Viva Zapata! (1952) 113m. *** **D:** Elia Kazan. Marlon Brando, Jean Peters, Anthony Quinn, Joseph Wiseman, Margo, Mildred Dunnock. Brooding, actionful account of Mexican peasant Brando who becomes political leader. Quinn won supporting actor Oscar as Brando's brother.

Vivacious Lady (1938) 90m. *** **D:** George Stevens. Ginger Rogers, James Stewart, James Ellison, Beulah Bondi, Charles Coburn, Frances Mercer. Professor Stewart marries showgirl Rogers in amusing vintage comedy with fine performances by all.

Vogues (1937) C-108m. ** **D:** Irving Cummings. Warner Baxter, Joan Bennett, Helen Vinson, Mischa Auer, Alan Mowbray, Jerome Cowan, Marjorie Gateson, Polly Rowles, Hedda Hopper. Minor musical with wealthy Bennett deciding to work as fashion model to chagrin of fiancé Baxter. One good song, "That Old Feeling." Original title: VOGUES OF 1938.

Voice in the Mirror (1958) 102m. **½ **D:** Harry Keller. Richard Egan, Julie London, Arthur O'Connell, Walter Matthau, Troy Donahue. Effective, unpretentious account of Egan trying to combat alcoholism, with help of wife London.

Voice in the Wind (1944) 85m. *** **D:** Arthur Ripley. Francis Lederer, Sigrid Gurie, J. Edward Bromberg, J. Carrol Naish. Low-key drama of pianist Lederer haunted by Nazi oppression, later rekindling old love affair; unusual film, well acted.

Voice of Bugle Ann, The (1936) 70m. **½ **D:** Richard Thorpe. Lionel Barrymore, Maureen O'Sullivan, Eric Linden, Dudley Digges, Spring Byington, Charles Grapewin. Sentimental tale of remarkable dog's owner taking revenge on person who kills the animal; not always convincing.

Voice of Merrill, The SEE: **Murder Will Out.**

Voice of Terror SEE: **Sherlock Holmes & the Voice of Terror.**

Voice of the Turtle (1947) 103m. ***½ **D:** Irving Rapper. Eleanor Parker, Ronald Reagan, Eve Arden, Kent Smith, Wayne Morris. Delightful comedy of wide-eyed Parker letting soldier Reagan share apartment with her; from Broadway hit play. Retitled: ONE FOR THE BOOK.

Voice of the Whistler (1946) 60m. **D:** William Castle. Richard Dix, Lynn Merrick, Rhys Williams, James Cardwell, Donald Woods, Gigi Perreau. SEE: Whistler series.

Volcano (1953-Italian, dubbed) 106m. ** **D:** William Dieterle. Anna Magnani, Rossano Brazzi, Geraldine Brooks, Eduardo Ciannelli. Slowly-paced dramatics involving two sisters involved with unprincipled diver.

Voltaire (1933) 72m. *** **D:** John G. Adolfi. George Arliss, Margaret Lindsay, Doris Kenyon, Reginald Owen, Alan Mowbray. Excellent if stagy recreation of life and wit of famous 18th-century French writer.

Von Ryan's Express (1965) C-117m. *** **D:** Mark Robson. Frank Sinatra, Trevor Howard, Raffaella Carra, Brad Dexter, Sergio Fantoni, Wolfgang Preiss, Adolfo Celi, Vito Scotti, Edward Mulhare. Sprawling WW2 Sinatra saga. Colonel assigned to commando raids on Germans in Italy winds up capturing entire train.

Voodoo Island (1957) 76m. ** **D:** Reginald Le Borg. Boris Karloff, Beverly Tyler, Murvyn Vye, Elisha Cook. Boring horror-thriller has Karloff asked by businessmen to investigate strange doings on potential motel-island resort.

Voodoo Man (1944) 62m. ** **D:** William Beaudine. Bela Lugosi, John Carradine, George Zucco, Michael Ames, Henry Hall, Wanda McKay, Louise Curry, Mary Currier. With touching devotion to zombie-wife, Lugosi performs harrowing experiments with unsuspecting girls to cure her.

Voodoo Tiger (1952) 67m. **D:** Spencer Bennett. Johnny Weissmuller,

Jean Byron, Jeanne Dean, Robert Bray, Tamba. SEE: Jungle Jim series.

Voodoo Woman (1957) 77m. *½ D: Edward L. Cahn. Marla English, Tom Conway, Michael Connors, Lance Fuller. Cheater-chiller with few scares in lowjinks about deranged scientist changing English into a zombie-ite.

Voyage to the Bottom of the Sea (1961) C-105m. *** D: Irwin Allen. Walter Pidgeon, Joan Fontaine, Robert Sterling, Barbara Eden, Michael Ansara, Peter Lorre, Frankie Avalon. Entertaining, colorful nonsense of conflicts aboard massive submarine, with Pidgeon the domineering captain. No deep thinking, just fun.

Wabash Avenue (1950) C-92m. *** D: Henry Koster. Betty Grable, Victor Mature, Phil Harris, Reginald Gardiner, Margaret Hamilton. Tpyical turn of the century musical. Good performances of song-and-dance routines provided by Grable, with Mature as the object of her affection and occasional vase-throwing target. Remake of CONEY ISLAND.

WAC from Walla Walla, The (1952) 83m. *½ D: William Witney. Judy Canova, Stephen Dunne, Allen Jenkins, Irene Ryan, George Cleveland. Lame-brained service adventure of perennial yokel Canova.

Wackiest Ship in the Army, The (1960) C-99m. *** D: Richard Murphy. Jack Lemmon, Ricky Nelson, John Lund, Chips Rafferty, Tom Tully, Joby Baker. Comedy-drama sometimes has you wondering if it's serious or not; it succeeds most of the time. Offbeat WW2 story doesn't make fun of the War, for a change, and is entertaining.

Wages of Fear, The (1955-French, dubbed) 105m. ***½ D: H. G. Clouzot. Yves Montand, Charles Vanel, Peter Van Eyck, Vera Clouzot. Marvelous, taut suspenser set in South America of men driving trucks filled with high explosives over bumpy roads.

Wagonmaster (1950) 86m. *** D: John Ford. Ben Johnson, Joanne Dru, Ward Bond, Alan Mowbray, Jane Darwell, James Arness. Good Ford Western about two roaming cowhands who join a Mormon wagontrain heading for Utah frontier. Dru is love interest.

Wagons Roll at Night, The (1941) 84m. **½ D: Ray Enright. Humphrey Bogart, Sylvia Sidney, Eddie Albert, Joan Leslie, Sig Ruman, Cliff Clark, Charley Foy, Frank Wilcox. KID GALAHAD in circus trappings is OK, thanks to cast: Bogie's the circus manager, Sidney his star, Albert the hayseed turned lion-tamer.

Waikiki Wedding (1937) 89m. *** D: Frank Tuttle. Bing Crosby, Martha Raye, Shirley Ross, Bob Burns, Leif Erickson, Grady Sutton, Anthony Quinn. Press-agent Crosby promotes Ross as Pineapple Queen, sings "Blue Hawaii" and "Sweet Leilani" in this above-average musicomedy.

Wait 'Til the Sun Shines, Nellie (1952) C-108m. *** D: Henry King. Jean Peters, David Wayne, Hugh Marlowe, Albert Dekker, Warren Stevens. Nostalgic film of the hopes and disappointments of small town barber Wayne in the early 1900's.

Wait Until Dark (1967) C-108m. *** D: Terence Young. Audrey Hepburn, Alan Arkin, Richard Crenna, Jack Weston, Samantha Jones, Julie Herrod, Efrem Zimbalist, Jr. Taut suspenser adapted from Frederick Knott play. Hepburn is blind wife of Zimbalist, tormented by criminals Arkin, Weston, and Crenna to reveal source of smuggled dope placed in her apartment.

Wake Island (1942) 78m. *** D: John Farrow. Brian Donlevy, Robert Preston, Macdonald Carey, Albert Dekker, Walter Abel, Barbara Britton, William Bendix. Stirring war film of U.S.'s fight to hold Pacific Island at outbreak of WW2. True facts realistically filmed make the movie worthwhile.

Wake Me When It's Over (1960) C-126m. *** D: Mervyn LeRoy. Dick Shawn, Ernie Kovacs, Margo Moore, Jack Warden. Entertaining comedy of hustling Shawn making the most of his army station in the Far East by building a fancy hotel with army supplies. Kovacs lends good support.

Wake of the Red Witch (1948) 106m. **½ D: Edward Ludwig. John Wayne, Gail Russell, Luther Adler, Gig Young. Rivalry between East Indies magnate and adventuresome ship's captain over pearls and women. Film is a bit confused, but nicely photographed.

Wake Up and Dream (1946) C-92m.

** D: Lloyd Bacon, June Haver, John Payne, Charlotte Greenwood, Connie Marshall, John Ireland, Clem Bevans, Lee Patrick. Moody film from Robert Nathan's story about girl determined to find brother missing from WW2.

Wake Up and Live (1937) 91m. *** D: Sidney Lanfield. Alice Faye, Walter Winchell, Ben Bernie, Jack Haley, Patsy Kelly, Joan Davis, Grace Bradley, Warren Hymer. Fast-moving spoof of radio with battling Winchell and Bernie, mike-frightened singer Haley, and Faye singing "There's A Lull In My Life."

Walk a Crooked Mile (1948) 91m. **½ D: Gordon Douglas. Louis Hayward, Dennis O'Keefe, Louise Allbritton, Carl Esmond, Onslow Stevens, Raymond Burr. Average melodrama about secret service agent who breaks up mob with help of Scotland Yard.

Walk, Don't Run (1966) C-114m. *** D: Charles Walters. Cary Grant, Samantha Eggar, Jim Hutton, John Standing, Miiko Taka, Ted Hartley. Enjoyable fluff about Eggar unwittingly agreeing to share her apartment with businessman Grant and athlete Hutton during the Tokyo Olympics. Stars are most agreeable in this remake of THE MORE THE MERRIER.

Walk East on Beacon (1952) 98m. **½ D: Alfred L. Werker. George Murphy, Finlay Currie, Virginia Gilmore, George Roy Hill. Good documentary-style drama of FBI investigation of espionage; on-location filming in Boston.

Walk in the Shadow (1966-British) 93m. *** D: Basil Dearden. Michael Craig, Patrick McGoohan, Janet Munro, Paul Rogers, Megs Jenkins. Fine courtroom melodrama, as emotions flare after boy's drowning.

Walk in the Sun, A (1945) 117m. ***½ D: Lewis Milestone. Dana Andrews, Richard Conte, Sterling Holloway, George Tyne, John Ireland, Herbert Rudley. Human aspect of war explored as American battalion attacks German hideout in Italy; sensitive direction is very effective.

Walk Into Hell (1957) C-93m. *½ D: Lee Robinson. Chips Rafferty, Françoise Christophe, Reginald Lye, Pierre Cressoy. Lumbering account of civilized Australians vs native customs, filmed on location in New Guinea.

Walk Like a Dragon (1960) 95m. **½ D: James Clavell. Jack Lord, Nobu McCarthy, James Shigeta, Mel Torme, Josephine Hutchinson, Rodolfo Acosta. Offbeat drama of Lord saving McCarthy from life of prostitution, taking her to his home town, overcoming expected obstacles.

Walk on the Wild Side (1962) 114m. **½ D: Edward Dmytryk. Laurence Harvey, Capucine, Jane Fonda, Anne Baxter, Barbara Stanwyck. Lurid hodgepodge set in 1930's New Orleans, loosely based on Nelson Algren novel of Harvey seeking lost love Capucine, now a member of bordello run by lesbian Stanwyck.

Walk Softly, Stranger (1950) 81m. **½ D: Robert Stevenson. Joseph Cotten, Valli, Spring Byington, Paul Stewart, Jack Paar. Small-time crook Cotten reforms because of the love and faith of crippled girl Valli.

Walk Tall (1960) C-60m. *½ D: Maury Dexter. Willard Parker, Joyce Meadows, Kent Taylor. Flabby oater about capture of outlaws who killed Indian squaws.

Walk the Dark Street (1956) 74m. *½ D: Wyott Ordung. Chuck Connors, Don Ross, Regina Gleason, Eddie Kafafian. Uninspired revenge hunt, set in a metropolitan city, of two men stalking each other with rifles.

Walk the Proud Land (1956) C-88m. *** D: Jesse Hibbs. Audie Murphy, Anne Bancroft, Pat Crowley, Charles Drake. Sturdy scripting makes this oater attractive; Murphy is Indian agent trying to quell strife between redskins and settlers, with the capture of Geronimo his major feat.

Walking Dead, The (1936) 66m. *** D: Michael Curtiz. Boris Karloff, Marguerite Churchill, Ricardo Cortez, Barton MacLane, Warren Hull. Karloff is framed and electrocuted, but professor brings his back to life; Boris swears vengeance on those who sent him to death. Good horror tale.

Walking Hills, The (1949) 78m. *** D: John Sturges. Randolph Scott, Ella Raines, William Bishop, Edgar Buchanan, Arthur Kennedy. Well-acted oater of Westerners searching for abandoned gold mine.

Walking My Baby Back Home (1953)

C-95m. **½ D: Lloyd Bacon. Donald O'Connor, Buddy Hackett, Janet Leigh, Lori Nelson. Confused musical comedy redeemed by Buddy Hackett's wacky humor.

Wall of Noise (1963) 112m. **½ D: Richard Wilson. Suzanne Pleshette, Ty Hardin, Dorothy Provine, Ralph Meeker. Turgid racetrack drama with adultery, not horses, the focal point.

Wallflower (1948) 77m. *** D: Frederick de Cordova. Joyce Reynolds, Robert Hutton, Janis Paige, Edward Arnold, Barbara Brown. Amusing comedy based on Broadway success; two stepsisters (Reynolds and Paige) vie for the same love.

Walls Came Tumbling Down, The (1946) 82m. *** D: Lothar Mendes. Lee Bowman, Marguerite Chapman, Edgar Buchanan, Lee Patrick, J. Edward Bromberg, Jonathan Hale, Elizabeth Risdon, Miles Mander, Moroni Olsen. Detective Bowman goes to work when priest is murdered, finds connection with series of art thefts; fast-moving private-eye film.

Walls of Hell, The (1964) 88m. ** D: Gerardo De Leon. Jock Mahoney, Fernando Poe, Jr., Mike Parsons, Paul Edwards, Jr. WW2 actioner set in Manila. Filmed in the Philippines, suffers from amateurish native casting.

Walls of Jericho, The (1948) 106m. ** D: John M. Stahl. Cornel Wilde, Linda Darnell, Anne Baxter, Kirk Douglas, Ann Dvorak, Marjorie Rambeau, Henry Hull, Colleen Townsend, Barton MacLane. Good cast tries to perk up story of ambitious lawyer in Jericho, Kansas, whose marital problems stand in the way of success; pretty dreary going most of the way.

Waltz of the Toreadors (1962-British) C-105m. *** D: John Guillermin. Peter Sellers, Dany Robin, Margaret Leighton, John Fraser. Jean Anouilh's saucy sex romp gets top notch handling with Sellers the retired military officer who still can't keep his eye off the girls.

Wanted for Murder (1946) C-95m. **½ D: Lawrence Huntington. Eric Portman, Dulcie Gray, Derek Farr, Roland Culver, Stanley Holloway. Engaging whodunit yarn, effectively underplayed by the cast.

Wanton Contessa SEE: Senso.

War Against Mrs. Hadley, The (1942) 86m. ** D: Harold Bucquet. Edward Arnold, Fay Bainter, Richard Ney, Sara Allgood, Spring Byington, Jean Rogers, Frances Rafferty, Dorothy Morris, Rags Ragland, Isobel Elsom, Van Johnson. Mild WW2 human-interest tale about matron Bainter who refuses to participate in war support.

War and Peace (1956) C-208m. ***½ D: King Vidor. Audrey Hepburn, Henry Fonda, Mel Ferrer, Vittorio Gassman, John Mills, Herbert Lom, Oscar Homolka, Anita Ekberg, May Britt. Huge cast and good direction highlight good spectacle fairly faithful to Tolstoy novel. Some exciting battle sequences, well done.

War Arrow (1953) C-78m. ** D: George Sherman. Maureen O'Hara, Jeff Chandler, Suzan Ball, Charles Drake, Jay Silverheels. Western story of U.S. Cavalry man Chandler coming to Texas to train Seminole Indians to subdue a Kiowa uprising. O'Hara is object of his love.

War Drums (1957) C-75m. **½ D: Reginald LeBorg. Lex Barker, Joan Taylor, Ben Johnson, Stuart Whitman. Sufficiently bloody Western set in Civil War days of Indian uprisings against onslaught of gold miners.

War Hunt (1962) 81m. **½ D: Denis Sanders. John Saxon, Robert Redford, Charles Aidman, Sydney Pollack. Well-done Korean War story focusing on kill-happy soldier Saxon who tries to help an orphan boy.

War Is Hell (1964) 81m. ** D: Burt Topper. Tony Russell, Bayne Barron, Tony Rich, Burt Topper. Korean War actioner with no new ideas to offer.

War Italian Style (1967-Italian, dubbed) C-84m. ** D: Luigi Scattini. Buster Keaton, Franco and Ciccio, Martha Hyer, Fred Clark. Sloppy meandering spy satire set in WW2 Italy, redeemed only by Keaton's appearance.

War Lord, The (1965) C-123m. *** D: Franklin Schaffner. Charlton Heston, Richard Boone, Rosemary Forsyth, Maurice Evans, Guy Stockwell, Niall MacGinnis, Henry Wilcoxon. Overambitious to be intelligent, would-be epic lacks scope and sweep needed for spectacle. Medieval tale of knight Heston demanding his feudal tribute, another man's bride Forsyth. Based on Leslie Stevens play THE LOVERS.

War Lover, The (1962-British) 105m. **½ D: Philip Leacock. Steve McQueen, Robert Wagner, Shirley Ann Field, Gary Cockrell. John Hersey's thoughtful novel becomes superficial account of McQueen and Wagner, two WW2 pilots in England, both in love with Field; aerial photography is above par.

War of the Satellites (1958) 66m. *½ D: Roger Corman. Dick Miller, Susan Cabot, Richard Devon, Eric Sinclair. Tedious sci-fi about missile expert whose mind is controlled by alien forces.

War of the Wildcats, The (1943) 102m. **½ Albert S. Rogell. John Wayne, Martha Scott, Albert Dekker, Gabby Hayes, Marjorie Rambeau, Sidney Blackmer, Dale Evans. Slugger Wayne brooks no nonsense in this oil-drilling yarn; good action slowed by obligatory love scenes. Retitled: IN OLD OKLAHOMA.

War of the Worlds, The (1953) C-85m. *** D: Byron Haskin. Gene Barry, Les Tremayne, Ann Robinson, Henry Brandon, Jack Kruschen. Fantastic trick photography and special effects make this science thriller about Earth battling a Martian invasion a fascinating film.

War Paint (1953) C-89m. **½ D: Lesley Selander. Robert Stack, Joan Taylor, Charles McGraw, Peter Graves. Action-packed film of U. S. cavalry detachment overcoming danger and villainous attempts to prevent delivery of peace treaty to an Indian Chief.

Warlock (1959) C-121m. *** D: Edward Dmytryk. Richard Widmark, Henry Fonda, Anthony Quinn, Dorothy Malone, Dolores Michaels, Wallace Ford, Tom Drake, Richard Arlen, Regis Toomey. Intelligent, well-paced Western giving new depth to usual cowboys-vs.-outlaws shootout.

Warpath (1951) C-95m. **½ D: Byron Haskin. Edmond O'Brien, Dean Jagger, Forrest Tucker, Polly Bergen. Nifty action Western with O'Brien hunting down outlaws who killed his girlfriend; an Indian attack is thrown in for good measure.

Warrior and the Slave Girl, The (1958-Italian, dubbed) C-84m. ** D: Vittorio Cottafavi. Ettore Manni, Georges Marchal, Gianna Maria Canale, Rafael Calvo. Unsubtle costumer set in ancient Armenia, with Canale the evil princess, subdued by Roman Manni; usual amount of swordplay.

Warrior Empress, The (1960-Italian, dubbed) C-87m. ** D: Pietro Francisci. Kerwin Matthews, Tina Louise, Riccardo Garrone, Antonio Batistella, Enrico Maria Salerno. Senseless mixture of fantasy and adventure with Phaon (Matthews) falling in love with Sappho (Louise), overcoming treacherous Salerno.

Warriors, The (1955) C-85m. **½ D: Henry Levin. Errol Flynn, Joanne Dru, Peter Finch, Jack Lambert, Vincent Winter. Lush sets and lavish costumes are setting for dashing Flynn who fights for Dru, killing many evil ones on the way.

Warriors Five (1962-Italian, dubbed) 84m. **½ D: Leopoldo Savona. Jack Palance, Giovanna Ralli, Serge Reggiani, Folco Lulli. Moderate actioner set in WW2 Italy with Palance behind enemy lines trying to combat the Germans.

Washington Story (1952) 81m. ** D: Robert Pirosh. Van Johnson, Patricia Neal, Louis Calhern, Sidney Blackmer, Elizabeth Patterson. Newspaperwoman Neal assigned to harrass Congress and selects young Congressman Johnson as her target; just fair.

Watch It Sailor! (1961-British) 81m. ** D: Wolf Rilla. Dennis Price, Liz Fraser, Irene Handl, Graham Stark, Marjorie Rhodes. Mildly amusing stage farce adapted to screen, with Price managing to outdo Fraser's mother (Rhodes), getting to the church on time.

Watch on the Rhine (1943) 114m. **** D: Herman Shumlin. Bette Davis, Paul Lukas, Geraldine Fitzgerald, Lucile Watson, Beulah Bondi, George Coulouris, Donald Woods. Superb filmization of Lillian Hellman's play of German Lukas and wife Davis pursued and harried by Nazi agents during WW2, set outside of Washington, D.C.

Watch the Birdie (1950) 70m. **½ D: Jack Donahue. Red Skelton, Arlene Dahl, Ann Miller, Leon Ames, Pamela Britton, Richard Rober, Mike Mazurki. Average, insane Skelton comedy features him as photographer, silly father and grandfather. Rest of cast is also good with routine material, reworking of Buster Keaton's CAMERAMAN.

Watch Your Stern (1960-British) 88m. ** D: Gerald Thomas. Kenneth Connor, Eric Barker, Leslie Phillips, Joan Sims, Hattie Jacques. Amusing, obvious shenanigans on the seas, with Connor impersonating a scientist sent to perfect a Naval torpedo weapon.

Waterloo Bridge (1940) 103m. ***½ D: Mervyn LeRoy. Vivien Leigh, Robert Taylor, Lucile Watson, Virginia Field, Maria Ouspenskaya, C. Aubrey Smith. Sentimental love story, well-acted, of soldier and ballet dancer meeting during air raid, falling in love instantly. Beautiful performance by lovely Leigh. Remade as GABY.

Waterloo Road (1944-British) 77m. ** D: Sidney Gilliat. John Mills, Stewart Granger, Alastair Sim, Joy Shelton, Vera Frances. Fair drama set in WW2 London. Playboy is stalked by soldier-husband of unfaithful woman.

Watusi (1959) C-85m. **½ D: Kurt Neumann. George Montgomery, Taina Elg, David Farrar, Rex Ingram, Dan Seymour. MGM fabricated a plot similar to KING SOLOMON'S MINES to utilize left-over footage from its 1950 version of H. Rider Haggard yarn.

Way Ahead, The SEE: **Immortal Battalion, The.**

Way Down East (1920) 60m. **½ D: D. W. Griffith. Lillian Gish, Richard Barthelmess, Lowell Sherman, Mary Hay. Heavy-handed melodrama which became silent classic, noted for Gish's performance as wronged waif, and dramatic climax on iceflow; set in New England.

Way Down East (1935) 80m. *½ D: Henry King. Rochelle Hudson, Henry Fonda, Russell Simpson, Slim Summerville, Spring Byington, Edward Trevor. Romantic melodrama set in New England was hokey as a 1920 silent; the remake hasn't improved with age. Ridiculous script conquers all.

Way for a Sailor (1930) 83m. ** D: Sam Wood. John Gilbert, Wallace Beery, Leila Hyams, Jim Tully, Polly Moran. Early talkie with silent-star Gilbert as devoted sailor who loses girl for the sea. Mostly a curio for film buffs.

Way of a Gaucho (1952) C-91m. ** D: Jacques Tourneur. Gene Tierney, Rory Calhoun, Richard Boone, Everett Sloane. Soaper set in 1870's Argentina of Tierney and Calhoun trying to make a go of life on the Pampas.

Way of All Flesh, The (1940) 86m. ** D: Louis King. Akim Tamiroff, Gladys George, William Henry, Muriel Angelus, Berton Churchill, Roger Imhof. Overly sentimental tale of poor immigrant who is "taken" and must pay for his error; George is superlative as always. Remake of Emil Jannings silent film.

Way of Youth, The (1959-French) 81m. ** D: Michel Boisrond. Françoise Arnoul, Lino Ventura, Bourvil, Alain Delon. Obvious sensuality fails to arouse sufficient interest in contrived story of adultery and ill-gotten gains.

Way Out, The (1956-British) 90m. ** D: Montgomery Tully. Gene Nelson, Mona Freeman, John Bentley, Michael Goodliffe, Sydney Tafler. Lumbering story of husband who committed a crime going on the lam with wife.

Way Out West (1936) 65m. *** D: James V. Horne. Stan Laurel, Oliver Hardy, Sharon Lynne, James Finlayson, Rosina Lawrence, Stanley Fields, Vivien Oakland. Stan and Ollie are sent to deliver deed for mine to daughter of late prospector, but they find the wrong girl; good framework for duo to show their masterful bag of tricks.

Way to Love, The (1933) 80m. *** D: Norman Taurog. Maurice Chevalier, Ann Dvorak, Edward Everett Horton, Minna Gombell, Nydia Westman, Douglass Dumbrille, John Miljan. Chevalier falls in love with lady knife-thrower (Dvorak) in bouncy musicomedy; songs include title tune, "I'm A Lover Of Paris."

Way to the Gold, The (1957) 94m. ** D: Robert D. Webb. Jeffrey Hunter, Sheree North, Barry Sullivan, Neville Brand. Meandering buried-loot-hunt story.

Wayward Bus, The (1957) 89m. ** D: Victor Vicas. Joan Collins, Jayne Mansfield, Dan Dailey, Rick Jason. Low-brow version of John Steinbeck novel about passengers on bus in

Wayward Girl, The (1957) 71m. *½ D: Lesley Selander. Marcia Henderson, Peter Walker, Whit Bissell, Ray Teal. Turgid nonsense about mother and stepdaughter vying for same lover, leading to murder.

Wayward Girl, The (1959-Norwegian, dubbed) 91m. **½ D: Edith Carlmar. Liv Ullmann, Atle Merton, Rolf Soder, Tore Foss, Nana Stenersen. Moralistic romance tale of young lovers who seek refuge on a deserted farm, becoming involved with the returning owner.

Wayward Wife, The (1955-Italian, dubbed) 91m. ** D: Mario Soldati. Gina Lollobrigida, Gabriele Ferzetti, Franco Interlenghi, Renato Baldini. Unimaginative, predictable film of blackmail. Lollobrigida, girl with a past, finds her marriage threatened.

We Are All Murderers (1957-French, dubbed) 113m. *** D: André Cayatte. Marcel Mouloudji, Raymond Pellegrin, Louis Seigner, Antoine Balpetre. Most effective social plea against capital punishment, focusing on youth bred to kill in war involved in murder after the armistice.

We Are In the Navy Now (1962-British) C-102m. ** D: Wendy Toye. Kenneth More, Lloyd Nolan, Joan O'Brien, Mischa Auer. Farcical service comedy put together without enough slapstick or wit.

We Are Not Alone (1939) 112m. ***½ D: Edmund Goulding. Paul Muni, Jane Bryan, Flora Robson, Una O'Connor, Henry Daniell, Cecil Kellaway, Alan Napier. Superb acting and overall production make tale of man in love with governess (Bryan), accused of murdering his wife (Robson) a must.

We Live Again (1934) 82m. ** D: Rouben Mamoulian. Fredric March, Anna Sten, Sam Jaffe, C. Aubrey Smith, Jane Baxter, Ethel Griffies. Cumbersome costumer with March the Russian nobleman in love with peasant girl Sten.

We Were Dancing (1942) 94m. ** D: Robert Z. Leonard. Norma Shearer, Melvyn Douglas, Gail Patrick, Marjorie Main, Reginald Owen, Connie Gilchrist, Sig Ruman. Hokey story of princess running off with another man at her engagement party. Shearer et al try, but material defeats them.

We Were Strangers (1949) 106m. **½ D: John Huston. Jennifer Jones, John Garfield, Pedro Armendariz, Gilbert Roland, Ramon Novarro. Slow-moving story of romance set against a Cuban intrigue background, with promising cast and director but disappointing results.

We Who Are Young (1940) 79m. ** D: Harold S. Bucquet. Lana Turner, John Shelton, Gene Lockhart, Grant Mitchell, Henry Armetta, Jonathan Hale, Clarence Wilson. Turner marries Shelton though his company's policy forbids it; aimless comedy-drama.

Weak and the Wicked, The (1953-British) 81m. **½ D: J. Lee Thompson. Glynis Johns, John Gregson, Diana Dors, Jane Hylton. Frank study of women's prison life, focusing on their rehabilitation.

Weaker Sex, The (1945-British) 89m. ** D: Roy Baker. Ursula Jeans, Cecil Parker, Joan Hopkins, Derek Bond, Thora Hird, Bill Owen. Jeans is staunch English housewife showing her patriotic zest during WW2; small-scale drama.

Weapon, The (1955-British) 80m. **½ D: Hal E. Chester. Steve Cochran, Lizabeth Scott, Herbert Marshall, Nicole Maurey. Minor, trim account of youngster who accidentally shoots his pal.

Web, The (1947) 87m. *** D: Michael Gordon. Ella Raines, Edmond O'Brien, William Bendix, Vincent Price, Maria Palmer. Tough bodyguard engages in murder, then finds himself a patsy for boss' schemes. Exciting melodrama, one of O'Brien's best early roles.

Web of Evidence (1959-British) 88m. **½ D: Jack Cardiff. Van Johnson, Vera Miles, Emlyn Williams, Bernard Lee, Jean Kent, Ralph Truman, Leo McKern. Sincere drama of Johnson in England finding clues to prove his father innocent of long-standing murder sentence. Original title: BEYOND THIS PLACE.

Web of Fear (1963-French, dubbed) 92m. **½ D: François Villiers. Michele Morgan, Dany Saval, Claude Rich, George Rigaud. Morgan is music teacher set up as patsy by Saval and Rich in this moody drama of passion and murder.

Web of Passion (1959-French) C-

101m. **½ D: Claude Chabrol. Madeleine Robinson, Antonella Lualdi, Jean Paul Belmondo, Jacques Dacqmine. Non-conformist Belmondo insinuates himself into a family's graces, delighting in breaking down their standards, with murders resulting. Talky but intriguing drama. Retitled: LEDA.

Wedding Night, The (1935) 84m. **½ D: King Vidor. Gary Cooper, Anna Sten, Ralph Bellamy, Walter Brennan, Helen Vinson, Sig Ruman. Study of romance and idealism; unbelievable love yarn but entertaining. Another attempt to make Anna Sten a new Garbo.

Wee Geordie (1956-British) C-93m. ***½ D: Frank Launder. Bill Travers, Alastair Sim, Norah Gorsen, Molly Urquhart, Francis De Wolff. Flavorful romp with Travers a Scottish shotputter who goes to the Olympics. Despite predictable sight gags and romance, film makes one relish each situation.

Wee Willie Winkie (1937) 99m. *** D: John Ford. Shirley Temple, Victor McLaglen, C. Aubrey Smith, Cesar Romero, Constance Collier, Mary Forbes, June Lang. Kipling tale adapted for Temple as heroine of British regiment in India. Good action scenes, nice teaming of Shirley and McLaglen.

Week-end in Havana (1941) C-80m. **½ D: Walter Lang. Alice Faye, Carmen Miranda, John Payne, Cesar Romero, Cobina Wright, Jr., George Barbier, Leonid Kinskey, Sheldon Leonard, Billy Gilbert. Colorful musical has Faye landing in Havana, torn between Payne and Romero; Miranda lends peppery support.

Week-end Marriage (1932) 66m. ** D: Thornton Freeland. Loretta Young, Aline MacMahon, George Brent, Vivienne Osborne, Roscoe Karns, Sheila Terry. OK early romance combines comedy courtship with drama of money-hungry husband after marriage.

Weekend at the Waldorf (1945) 130m. *** D: Robert Z. Leonard. Ginger Rogers, Lana Turner, Walter Pidgeon, Van Johnson, Edward Arnold, Phyllis Thaxter, Keenan Wynn, Robert Benchley. Glossy remake of GRAND HOTEL with Rogers and Pidgeon outshining others; very superficial but entertaining.

Weekend for Three (1941) 61m. ** D: Irving Reis. Dennis O'Keefe, Jane Wyatt, Philip Reed, Zasu Pitts. Conventional marital comedy too domesticated for zesty tastes.

Weekend with Father (1951) 83m. **½ D: Douglas Sirk. Van Heflin, Patricia Neal, Virginia Field, Gigi Perreau, Richard Denning. Pleasant frou-frou of widow and widower courting despite their childrens' interference.

Weird Woman (1944) 64m. **½ D: Reginald LeBorg. Lon Chaney, Jr., Anne Gwynne, Evelyn Ankers, Ralph Morgan, Lois Collier. Chaney's ex-girlfriend objects to his Tropic-Isle bride, connives to get even. Way-out chiller is good fun. Remade as BURN, WITCH, BURN.

Welcome Stranger (1947) 107m. *** D: Elliott Nugent. Bing Crosby, Barry Fitzgerald, Joan Caulfield, Wanda Hendrix, Frank Faylen, Elisabeth Patterson. Entertaining film of Crosby filling in for vacationing doctor in small community, getting involved with local girl and lovely little town.

Welcome to Hard Times (1967) C-105m. *** D: Burt Kennedy. Henry Fonda, Janice Rule, Keenan Wynn, Janis Paige, John Anderson, Aldo Ray. Intriguing, if not fast-moving account of run-down town plagued by destructive outlaws, with Fonda finally forced to shoot it out to save what's left.

Well, The (1951) 85m. *** D: Leo Popkin, Russell Rouse. Richard Rober, Henry Morgan, Barry Kelley, Christine Larson, Maidie Norman, Ernest Anderson. Incisive study of crowd psychology, focusing on effects of townfolk when Negro child becomes lodged in deep well.

Well-Groomed Bride, The (1946) 75m. ** D: Sidney Lanfield. Olivia de Havilland, Ray Milland, Sonny Tufts, James Gleason, Percy Kilbride. Two Oscar-winners suffer with ridiculous comedy of stubborn girl insisting on champagne for her wedding.

Wells Fargo (1937) 115m. *** D: Frank Lloyd. Joel McCrea, Frances Dee, Ralph Morgan, Johnny Mack Brown, Porter Hall, Robert Cummings, Harry Davenport. McCrea,

We're No Angels (1955) C-106m. **½ D: Michael Curtiz. Humphrey Bogart, Aldo Ray, Joan Bennett, Peter Ustinov, Basil Rathbone, Leo G. Carroll. Mild entertainment as three escapees from Devil's Island find refuge with French family and extricate them from predicament with nasty landlord.

We're Not Dressing (1934) 63m. *** D: Norman Taurog. Bing Crosby, Carole Lombard, George Burns, Gracie Allen, Ethel Merman, Leon Errol, Ray Milland. Musical "Admirable Crichton" with rich-girl Lombard falling in love with sailor Crosby when entourage is shipwrecked on desert isle. Merman is man-chasing second fiddle, with Burns and Allen on tap as local expeditionists. Great fun; Bing sings "Love Thy Neighbor."

We're Not Married (1952) 85m. *** D: Edmund Goulding. Ginger Rogers, Fred Allen, Victor Moore, Marilyn Monroe, Paul Douglas, David Wayne, Eddie Bracken, Mitzi Gaynor. Fine froth served up in several episodes as married couples discover their weddings weren't legalized; segments vary in quality but the top-notch cast generally delivers the goods.

Werewolf, The (1956) 83m. *½ D: Fred F. Sears. Steven Ritch, Don Megowan, Joyce Holden, Eleanore Tanin. Juvenile treatment of the human-turned-blood-seeker.

Werewolf in a Girl's Dormitory (1963-Italian, dubbed) 84m. BOMB D: Richard Benson. Carl Schell, Barbara Lass, Curt Lowens, Maurice Marsac. Title tells all in generally witless, plotless story of killer-beast on the loose.

Werewolf of London (1935) 75m. *** D: Stuart Walker. Henry Hull, Warner Oland, Valerie Hobson, Lester Matthews, Spring Byington. Classic chiller of scientist who is cursed by lycanthropy; good performances in atmospheric horror tale.

West 11 (1963-British) 93m. *½ D: Michael Winner. Alfred Lynch, Kathleen Breck, Eric Portman, Diana Dors, Kathleen Harrison. Lumbering account of out-of-work Lynch agreeing to murder Portman's aunt, with the crime bringing about a reformation of his character.

West of Zanzibar (1953) 84m. ** D: Harry Watt. Anthony Steel, Sheila Sim, Edric Connor, Orlando Martins. Ivory hunters meet up with jungle obstacles and native tribes; Steel and Sim share the adventures.

West Point of the Air (1935) 100m. **½ D: Richard Rosson. Wallace Beery, Robert Young, Maureen O'Sullivan, Lewis Stone, James Gleason, Rosalind Russell. Commander Beery pushes reluctant son Young through army air-training for his own satisfaction. Good cast enlivens standard drama.

West Point Story, The (1950) 107m. **½ D: Roy Del Ruth. James Cagney, Virginia Mayo, Doris Day, Gordon MacRae, Gene Nelson. Pat musical about Broadway director and hoofer Cagney staging a spectacular revue at West Point.

Westbound (1959) C-72m. **½ D: Budd Boetticher. Randolph Scott, Virginia Mayo, Karen Steele, Michael Dante, Andrew Duggan, Michael Pate. Trim sagebrush tale of Yankee officer Scott organizing a stage coach line to bring in gold from California.

Western Union (1941) 94m. *** D: Fritz Lang. Robert Young, Randolph Scott, Dean Jagger, Virginia Gilmore, John Carradine, Slim Summerville, Chill Wills, Barton MacLane. Elaborate Western of cross-country cables being established amid various conflicts. Standard plot devices don't spoil big-scale excitement.

Westerner, The (1940) 100m. ***½ D: William Wyler. Gary Cooper, Walter Brennan, Fred Stone, Doris Davenport, Forrest Tucker, Lillian Bond. Excellent tale of land disputes getting out of hand in the old West, with Brennan's Judge Bean winning him an Oscar.

Westward Passage (1932) 75m. ** D: Robert Milton. Ann Harding, Laurence Olivier, Irving Pichel, Zasu Pitts, Irene Purcell, Bonita Granville, Ethel Griffies. Acting uplifts clichéd tale of girl who divorces to marry for true love, despite sacrifices.

Westward the Women (1951) 118m. *** D: William Wellman. Robert Taylor, Denise Darcel, Beverly Dennis, John McIntire, Hope Emerson,

Lenore Lonergan, Julie Bishop, Marilyn Erskine. Intriguing Western with Taylor heading wagon train full of females bound for California to meet mail-order husbands.

Wetbacks (1956) C-89m. *½ D: Hank McCune. Lloyd Bridges, Nancy Gates, John Hoyt, Barton MacLane. Tawdry study of smuggling Mexicans across Texas border.

We've Never Been Licked (1943) 103m. ** D: John Rawlins. Richard Quine, Noah Beery, Jr., Robert Mitchum, Anne Gwynne, Martha O'Driscoll. Overly-patriotic and melodramatic account of American youth brought up in Japan, and his involvement in WW2.

What a Life (1939) 75m. *** D: Jay Reed. Jackie Cooper, Betty Field, Lionel Stander, Hedda Hopper, Lucien Littlefield, Sidney Miller. Cooper is fine in filmization of original play about teen-ager Henry Aldrich and his complicated love life. Springboard for Aldrich radio and film series.

What a Way to Go! (1964) C-124m. **½ D: J. Lee Thompson. Shirley MacLaine, Paul Newman, Dean Martin, Robert Mitchum, Gene Kelly, Bob Cummings, Dick Van Dyke, Reginald Gardner, Margaret Dumont, Fifi D'Orsay. Elaborate comedy of perennial widow MacLaine has few bright spots. Authors Comden and Green use gimmick of spoofing various movie-period styles, but it fails to utilize the talent-loaded cast. Kelly stars in the funniest sequence.

What a Woman! (1943) 94m. **½ D: Irving Cummings. Rosalind Russell, Brian Aherne, Willard Parker, Alan Dinehart. Casting director Russell avoids love while putting professor Aherne into a movie. Trite script aided by good acting.

What Ever Happened to Baby Jane? (1962) 132m. ***½ D: Robert Aldrich. Bette Davis, Joan Crawford, Victor Buono, Marjorie Bennett, Anna Lee. Far-fetched, thoroughly engaging black comedy of two former movie stars; Joan's a cripple at the mercy of demented sister Baby Jane Hudson (Davis). Bette has a field day in her macabre characterization, with Buono a perfect match.

What Every Woman Knows (1934) 92m. **½ D: Gregory LaCava. Helen Hayes, Brian Aherne, Madge Evans, Lucile Watson, Dudley Digges, Donald Crisp, David Torrence. Vintage filmization of James Barrie's play detailing woman's superiority over man; presentation is dated, but Hayes is worth viewing.

What Every Woman Wants (1962-British) 69m. *½ D: Ernest Morris. William Fox, Hy Hazell, Dennis Lotis, Elizabeth Shepherd. Dull marital comedy of wives trying to reform husbands.

What Next, Corporal Hargrove? (1945) 95m. **½ D: Richard Thorpe. Robert Walker, Keenan Wynn, Jean Porter, Chill Wills, Hugo Haas, William Phillips, Fred Essler, Cameron Mitchell. Hargrove (Walker) is in France with con-man buddy (Wynn) in OK sequel to SEE HERE, PRIVATE HARGROVE; trivial and episodic.

What Price Glory (1952) C-111m. **½ D: John Ford. James Cagney, Corinne Calvet, Dan Dailey, Robert Wagner, Marisa Pavan. Classic silent film becomes shallow Cagney-Dailey vehicle of battling Army men Flagg and Quirt in WW1 France.

What Price Murder (1958-French, dubbed) 105m. **½ D: Henri Verneuil. Henri Vidal, Mylene Demongeot, Isa Miranda, Alfred Adam. Well-turned murder mystery of hubby and secretary planning to do away with wife.

What's Up, Tiger Lily? (1966) C-80m. **½ Compiled by Woody Allen. Mie Hama, Akiko Wakabayashi, Woody Allen, Lovin' Spoonful. Dull Japanese spy picture re-edited with narrative and spotty appearances by Woody Allen, attempting to make hip spoof.

Wheel of Fortune SEE: **Man Betrayed.**

Wheeler Dealers, The (1963) C-106m. *** D: Arthur Hiller. Lee Remick, James Garner, Jim Backus, Phil Harris, Shelley Berman, Louis Nye. Funny, fast-moving spoof of Texas millionaires who play with investments just for fun. Garner also catches Lee Remick along the way.

When a Woman Loves (1959-Japanese, dubbed) C-97m. **½ D: Heinosuke Gosho. Ineko Arima, Shin Saburi, Yatsuko Tan-ami, Nobuko Otowa. Utilizing flashbacks, film recalls love affair between Saburi and older man Arima, a war correspondent; sentimental weeper with almost enough class.

When Comedy Was King (1960) 81m. **** Compiled by Robert Youngson. Charlie Chaplin, Buster Keaton, Laurel and Hardy, Ben Turpin, Fatty Arbuckle, Wallace Beery, Gloria Swanson. Second Youngson compilation of silent comedy clips has many old favorites in classic scenes. Chaplin, Keaton, Laurel & Hardy, Keystone Kops, Charley Chase and others shine in this outstanding film.

When Gangland Strikes (1956) 70m. ** D: R. G. Springsteen. Raymond Greenleaf, Marjie Millar, John Hudson, Anthony Caruso. Blasé handling of law enforcer's dilemma between duty and protecting family when he's blackmailed.

When Hell Broke Loose (1958) 78m. ** D: Kenneth Crane. Charles Bronson, Violet Rensing, Richard Jaeckel, Arvid Nelson. Low-keyed trim episode involving assassination attempt on General Eisenhower, set in WW2 Europe.

When I Grow Up (1951) 80m. *** D: Michael Kanin. Bobby Driscoll, Robert Preston, Martha Scott, Sherry Jackson. Effective low-keyed study of the generation gap, with Driscoll most appealing as the child who runs away from home.

When in Rome (1952) 78m. **½ D: Clarence Brown. Van Johnson, Paul Douglas, Joseph Calleia, Mimi Aguglia, Tudor Owen. Tasteful yet unrestrained tale of con-artist Douglas disguising himself as priest attending Holy Year pilgrimage in Italy; through American priest Johnson et al he finds new faith.

When Ladies Meet (1941) 108m. ** D: Robert Z. Leonard. Joan Crawford, Robert Taylor, Greer Garson, Herbert Marshall, Spring Byington. Attractive performers in plodding remake of '33 Ann Harding-Myrna Loy vehicle of Rachel Crothers' play. Authoress Crawford loves Marshall, who's married to Garson; Taylor loves Joan. Talk marathon on woman's rights is vastly outdated. Taylor and Garson try to bring life to film, but can't.

When My Baby Smiles at Me (1948) C-98m. **½ D: Walter Lang. Betty Grable, Dan Dailey, Jack Oakie, June Havoc, James Gleason, Richard Arlen. Strictly routine musical about burlesque team that breaks up when one member gets job on Broadway. Eventually they're re-teamed, of course. Based on famous play Burlesque.

When Strangers Marry (1944) 67m. ** D: William Castle. Robert Mitchum, Kim Hunter, Dean Jagger, Neil Hamilton. Hunter is caught in midst of murder plot involving husband and old boyfriend; programmer mystery flick. Retitled: BETRAYED.

When the Boys Meet the Girls (1965) C-110m. ** D: Alvin Ganzer. Connie Francis, Harve Presnell, Herman's Hermits, Louis Armstrong, Liberace, Sue Ane Langdon, Fred Clark, Frank Faylen, Sam the Sham. Rehash of GIRL CRAZY, turned into a dull guest-star showcase.

When the Daltons Rode (1940) 80m. *** D: George Marshall. Randolph Scott, Kay Francis, Brian Donlevy, George Bancroft, Andy Devine, Broderick Crawford, Stuart Erwin. Fine Western actioner with good cast, typical plot; Francis and Scott provide romantic relief.

When the Redskins Rode (1951) C-78m. *½ D: Lew Landers. Jon Hall, Mary Castle, James Seay, John Ridgley. Lame-brained Western set during French and Indian War of 1750's.

When Tomorrow Comes (1939) 90m. **½ D: John N. Stahl. Irene Dunne, Charles Boyer, Barbara O'Neil, Nydia Westman, Onslow Stevens. Standard soapy story enhanced by leading players; Boyer loves Dunne, although he's already married.

When Willie Comes Marching Home (1950) 82m. **½ D: John Ford. Dan Dailey, Corinne Calvet, Colleen Townsend, William Demarest, Mae Marsh. Schmaltzy WW2 adventures of West Virginia youth Dailey, including interlude with French underground leader Calvet.

When Worlds Collide (1951) C-81m. **½ D: Rudolph Mate. Richard Derr, Barbara Rush, Peter Hanson, John Hoyt, Judith Ames. Very interesting sci-fi story of Earth forced to select crew to survive collision with planetoid. Award-winning special effects balanced by uneven dialog.

When You're in Love (1937) 104m. **½ D: Robert Riskin. Grace Moore,

Cary Grant, Aline MacMahon, Thomas Mitchell, Emma Dunn. Overlong, enjoyable Moore vehicle; opera star "hires" Grant as husband. Miss Moore does "Minnie the Moocher" in this one!

When's Your Birthday? (1937) 77m. **½ D: Harry Beaumont. Joe E. Brown, Marian Marsh, Edgar Kennedy, Margaret Hamilton, Frank Jenks. Entertaining Brown vehicle of timid boxer whose prowess depends on position of stars; good supporting cast.

Where Angels Go, Trouble Follows (1968) C-95m. **½ D: James Neilson. Rosalind Russell, Stella Stevens, Binnie Barnes, Mary Wickes, Dolores Sutton, Susan Saint James, Barbara Hunter; guest stars Milton Berle, Arthur Godfrey, Van Johnson, William Lundigan, Robert Taylor. For "Flying Nun" fans only; contrived comedy follow-up to TROUBLE WITH ANGELS with Mother Superior Russell pitted against young, progressive nun Stevens.

Where Are Your Children (1944) 73m. *½ D: William Nigh. Jackie Cooper, Patricia Morison, Gale Storm, Gertrude Michael, John Litel, Evelynne Eaton. Thoughtless study of juvenile delinquency.

Where Danger Lives (1950) 84m. ** D: John Farrow. Robert Mitchum, Faith Domergue, Claude Rains, Maureen O'Sullivan. Young physician Mitchum becomes involved with woman (Domergue) who is bordering on insanity.

Where Do We Go From Here? (1945) 77m. *** D: Gregory Ratoff. Fred MacMurray, Joan Leslie, June Haver, Gene Sheldon, Anthony Quinn, Carlos Ramirez, Alan Mowbray. Cute idea of MacMurray granted wishes by genie, traveling through American history; falters at times but in general is fun.

Where Love Has Gone (1964) C-114m. **½ D: Edward Dmytryk. Bette Davis, Susan Hayward, Michael Connors, Jane Greer, Joey Heatherton, George Macready. Glossy drama of Heatherton killing her mother's (Hayward) lover; Davis is the domineering grandmother, Greer is a sympathetic probation officer. Based on Harold Robbins' novel.

Where the Boys Are (1960) C-99m. ** D: Henry Levin. Dolores Hart, George Hamilton, Yvette Mimieux, Jim Hutton, Barbara Nichols, Paula Prentiss, Connie Francis. Not-bad film about teenagers during Easter Vacation in Ft. Lauderdale. Connie Francis, in her first film, is pretty good; other young players seen to good advantage. Nichols is hilarious as usual as a flashy blonde.

Where the Bullets Fly (1966-British) C-88m. **½ D: John Gilling. Tom Adams, Dawn Addams, Tim Barrett, Michael Ripper. Well-paced super spy satire involving Adams tracking down special fuel formula.

Where the Hot Wind Blows (1960-Italian, dubbed) 120m. ** D: Jules Dassin. Gina Lollobrigida, Pierre Brasseur, Marcello Mastroianni, Melina Mercouri, Yves Montand, Paolo Stoppa. Artsy film that meanders around subject of legalized immorality in small Italian village. Retitled: THE LAW.

Where the Sidewalk Ends (1950) 95m. **½ D: Otto Preminger. Dana Andrews, Gene Tierney, Gary Merrill, Karl Malden, Ruth Donnelly, Craig Stevens. Polished gloss about cop Andrews who unintentionally commits homicide; Tierney is girl in the case.

Where the Spies Are (1965) C-110m. *** D: Val Guest. David Niven, Françoise Dorleac, John Le Mesurier, Cyril Cusack, Eric Pohlmann, Reginald Beckwith. Well made mixture of dry comedy and suspense in tale of doctor forced into spying. Good cast names enhance already fine movie.

Where There's Life (1947) 75m. *** D: Sidney Lanfield. Bob Hope, Signe Hasso, William Bendix, George Coulouris. Wacky comedy with radio star Hope taken to small European country and made King; lots of laughs in above-average Hope antics.

While the City Sleeps (1956) 100m. *** D: Fritz Lang. Dana Andrews, Ida Lupino, Rhonda Fleming, George Sanders, Vincent Price, Thomas Mitchell, Sally Forrest, Howard Duff. Veteran cast and intertwining storylines keep interest in account of newspaper reporters and police on the track of a berserk killer.

Whiplash (1948) 91m. ** D: Lewis Seiler. Dane Clark, Alexis Smith,

Zachary Scott, Eve Arden, Jeffrey Lynn. Unmoving melodrama about artist turning into grim prizefighter. Script is main defect; acting OK.

Whipsaw (1935) 83m. **½ D: Sam Wood. Myrna Loy, Spencer Tracy, Harvey Stephens, William Harrigan, Clay Clement. Tracy uses bad-girl Loy to lead him to band of thieves; predictable complications follow in familiar but well-done crime drama.

Whirlpool (1949) 97m. *** D: Otto Preminger. Gene Tierney, Richard Conte, Jose Ferrer, Charles Bickford, Eduard Franz, Fortunio Bonanova, Constance Collier. Tense melodrama of nefarious hypnotist Ferrer using innocent Tierney to carry out his evil schemes; ingenious melodrama.

Whispering Ghosts (1942) 75m. ** D: Alfred L. Werker. Brenda Joyce, Milton Berle, John Shelton, John Carradine. Berle is effective as bumbling performer trying to live up to radio role as crackerjack detective.

Whispering Smith (1948) C-88m. *** D: Leslie Fenton. Alan Ladd, Brenda Marshall, Robert Preston, Donald Crisp, William Demarest. Well-acted Western about soft-spoken special agent investigating robberies who finds friend involved with crooks.

Whispering Smith Vs. Scotland Yard (1952-British) 77m. ** D: Francis Searle. Richard Carlson, Greta Gynt, Rona Anderson, Herbert Lom, Dora Bryan. Famed detective proves conclusively that suicide was actually well-staged murder. Good cast in below-average mystery.

Whistle at Eaton Falls, The (1951) 96m. **½ D: Robert Siodmak. Lloyd Bridges, Dorothy Gish, Carleton Carpenter, Murray Hamilton, Anne Francis, Ernest Borgnine, Doro Merande, Arthur O'Connell. Set in New Hampshire, this documentary-style film deals with labor relation problems in a small town when new plant manager has to lay off workers. Gish is factory owner in interesting supporting role.

Whistle Down the Wind (1962-British) 98m. *** D: Bryan Forbes. Hayley Mills, Bernard Lee, Alan Bates, Norman Bird, Diane Clare. Poignant, if artificial, drama of murderer on the run (Bates) seeking refuge in a barn, with three country children thinking him to be Christ.

Whistle Stop (1946) 85m. ** D: Leonide Moguy. George Raft, Ava Gardner, Victor McLaglen, Tom Conway, Jorja Cutright, Florence Bates, Charles Drake. Minor drama of nicegirl Gardner caught between no-account playboy Raft and uncouth nightclub owner McLaglen.

Whistler, The One of the most unusual —and one of the best—mystery series of the 30's and 40's was based on a popular radio show called "The Whistler." The premise of the show, and at least one of the films, was a mysterious figure who walked along whistling a haunting tune. "I am the Whistler," he would say, "And I know many things." He would introduce the current mystery and reappear from time to time to bridge gaps from one setting to another. Veteran Richard Dix starred in all but one of the eight Whistler films, but in keeping with the series' flexibility in presenting a new story every time, he alternated from hero to villain in various entries in the series. In the initial film, THE WHISTLER, Dix was a victim of circumstances about to be killed; in THE POWER OF THE WHISTLER he was an amnesiac murderer; in THE MYSTERIOUS INTRUDER he was a private eye; and in THE 13TH HOUR an innocent man framed for a murder he didn't commit. The one non-Dix film, RETURN OF THE WHISTLER, followed the radio format of the mysterious narrator with excellent results. That entry, and several others, had stories written by Cornell Woolrich, while others were written by Eric Taylor; they were all tightly knit, engrossing little mysteries, competently acted by contract players and directed in several cases by William Castle. One of the few series to gain acceptance with the public and critics alike, the Whistler films hold up quite well today as examples of the kind of mystery film "they just don't make any more."

Whistler, The (1944) 59m. D: William Castle. Richard Dix, Gloria Stuart, Alan Dinehart, Joan Woodbury, J. Carrol Naish, Byron Foulger, Trevor Bardette.

Whistling in Brooklyn (1943) 87m. **½ D: S. Sylvan Simon. Red Skelton, Ann Rutherford, Jean Rogers,

'Rags' Ragland, Ray Collins, Henry O'Neill, William Frawley, Sam Levene. Skelton again, as radio sleuth "The Fox," mixed up in murder and pretending to be a member of the Dodgers ball team.

Whistling in Dixie (1942) 74m. *** D: S. Sylvan Simon. Red Skelton, Ann Rutherford, George Bancroft, Guy Kibbee. Red, as radio's "Fox" marries Ann, but their Southern honeymoon is interrupted by murder and mystery. Funny Skelton vehicle.

Whistling in the Dark (1941) 77m. *** D: S. Sylvan Simon. Red Skelton, Conrad Veidt, Ann Rutherford, Virginia Grey, 'Rags' Ragland, Henry O'Neill, Eve Arden. Skelton's first starring vehicle as radio's "Fox" who finds himself in real-life trouble with odd band of evildoers.

White Angel, The (1936) 75m. ** D: William Dieterle. Kay Francis, Ian Hunter, Donald Woods, Nigel Bruce, Donald Crisp, Henry O'Neill, Billy Mauch. Lavish but unsuccessful biography of Florence Nightingale with Francis miscast in reworked history of 19th-century British nursing pioneer.

White Banners (1938) 88m. *** D: Edmund Goulding. Claude Rains, Fay Bainter, Jackie Cooper, Bonita Granville, Henry O'Neill, Kay Johnson. Bainter moves in with troubled family, tries to solve their problems; moralistic filming of Lloyd C. Douglas novel is noteworthy for Bainter's fine performance.

White Cargo (1942) 90m. ** D: Richard Thorpe. Hedy Lamarr, Walter Pidgeon, Frank Morgan, Richard Carlson, Reginald Owen. Lamarr is the seductive Tondelayo who entrances all at British plantation post in Africa, Pidgeon the expeditionist who really falls for her. Exotic love scenes, corny plot.

White Christmas (1954) C-120m. ** D: Michael Curtiz. Bing Crosby, Danny Kaye, Rosemary Clooney, Vera-Ellen, Dean Jagger. Nice Irving Berlin score is unfortunately interrupted by limp plot of army buddies Crosby and Kaye boosting popularity of winter resort run by their ex-officer Jagger. "What Can You Do With A General" stands out as Berlin's least memorable tune. Partial re-working of HOLIDAY INN, not half as good.

White Cliffs of Dover, The (1944) 126m. *** D: Clarence Brown. Irene Dunne, Alan Marshal, Van Johnson, C. Aubrey Smith, Dame May Whitty, Roddy McDowall, Peter Lawford. American Dunne marries Britisher Marshal in patriotic WWI romancer. Slick but shallow.

White Feather (1955) C-102m. **½ D: Robert D. Webb. Robert Wagner, Jeffrey Hunter, Debra Paget, John Lund, Eduard Franz, Hugh O'Brian. Pat Western film with some good action scenes of government agent Wagner attempting to convince Indian tribe to move to reservation; Paget and Hunter are members of Cheyenne tribe who resist.

White Heat (1949) 114m. ***½ D: Raoul Walsh. James Cagney, Virginia Mayo, Edmond O'Brien, Margaret Wycherly, Steve Cochran. Cagney's back in gangster films, older but forceful as ever as psycopathic hood with mother-obsession; Mayo is his neglected girl, O'Brien the cop out to get him.

White Nights (1957-Italian, dubbed) 94m. *** D: Luchino Visconti. Maria Schell, Jean Marais, Marcello Mastroianni. Elaborately interwoven love tale arising from casual meeting; based on Dostoyevsky story.

White Savage (1943) 75m. **½ D: Arthur Lubin. Jon Hall, Maria Montez, Sabu, Don Terry, Turhan Bey, Thomas Gomez, Sidney Toler. Standard jungle adventure spiced by colorful cast. Shark-hunter and island princess can't agree on marriage.

White Slave Ship (1962-Italian, dubbed) C-92m. *½ D: Silvio Amadio. Pier Angeli, Edmund Purdom, Armand Mestral, Ivan Desny. Childish hokum, set in 18th century, of rebellion aboard vessel carrying women to the colonies.

White Squaw, The (1956) 75m. *½ D: Ray Nazarro. David Brian, May Wynn, William Bishop, Nancy Hale. Tedious narrative and a reverse situation; government taking away land from white rancher to give back to the Indians.

White Tie and Tails (1946) 81m. **½ D: Charles Barton. Dan Duryea, William Bendix, Ella Raines, Clarence Kolb, Frank Jenks, John Miljan, Scotty Beckett. Breezy film with usual-villain Duryea in good comedy form as butler who pretends to be master of house while boss is away.

White Tower, The (1950) C-98m. *** D: Ted Tetzlaff. Glenn Ford, Claude Rains, Valli, Oscar Homolka, Cedric Hardwicke. Mountain-climbing drama about people risking their lives to climb the Swiss Alps.

White Voices (1965-Italian, dubbed) C-93m. *** D: Pasquale Festa Campanile, Massimo Franciosa. Paolo Ferrari, Sandra Milo, Anouk Aimee, Graziella Granata, Barbara Steele, Jeanne Valerie. Good lusty adventure à la Tom Jones concerns exploits of castrati-singers who have retained high singing voices by means of operation.

White Warrior, The (1961-Italian, dubbed) C-86m. *½ D: Riccardo Freda. Steve Reeves, Giorgia Moll, Renato Baldini, Gerard Herter. Tiring spectacle about tribal chieftain leading rebellion against advancing troops of Czar, set in 19th century.

White Witch Doctor (1953) C-96m. **½ D: Henry Hathaway. Susan Hayward, Robert Mitchum, Walter Slezak, Timothy Carey. Bakuba territory is scene of diverse interests of nurse Hayward who wants to bring modern medicine to natives and adventurers Mitchum and Slezak bent on finding hidden treasure.

White Zombie (1932) 73m. *** D: Victor Halperin. Bela Lugosi, Madge Bellamy, Robert Frazer, Brandon Hurst. Eerily made film about army of zombies at sugar mill working for white leader; unique chiller.

Who Done It? (1942) 75m. **½ D: Erle C. Kenton. Bud Abbott, Lou Costello, Louise Allbritton, Mary Wickes, William Gargan, William Bendix. Murder at a radio station is setting for better than usual A&C horseplay, with Bendix a flustered detective.

Who Goes There SEE: **Passionate Sentry, The**.

Who Killed Gail Preston? (1938) 60m. **½ D: Leon Barsha. Don Terry, Rita Hayworth, Robert Paige, Wyn Cahoon, Gene Morgan, Marc Lawrence, Arthur Loft. Minor whodunit fairly well played; murder in a nightclub is the premise.

Who Stole the Body? (1962-French, dubbed) 92m. ** D: Jean Girault. Francis Blanche, Darry Cowl, Clement Harari, Daniel Ceccaldi, Mario David. Weak farce on horror films, with Blanche and Cowl two dimwits trying to solve a crime.

Who Was That Lady? (1960) 115m. *** D: George Sidney. Tony Curtis, Dean Martin, Janet Leigh, James Whitmore, John McIntire, Barbara Nichols, Joi Lansing. Spicy shenanigans move along at lively pace as Curtis and Martin pretend to be secret agents to confuse Tony's jealous wife Leigh; based on Norman Krasna play.

Whole Town's Talking, The (1935) 95m. *** D: John Ford. Edward G. Robinson, Jean Arthur, Wallace Ford, Arthur Byron, Donald Meek. Entertaining comedy with meek Robinson thought to be lookalike for notorious gangster; fine performances by E. G. and Arthur.

Whole Truth, The (1958-British) 84m. **½ D: John Guillermin. Stewart Granger, Donna Reed, George Sanders, Gianna Maria Canale. Good cast lends strength to fair plot of almost perfect attempt to pin murder of movie starlet on producer Granger.

Who's Been Sleeping in My Bed? (1963) C-103m. **½ D: Daniel Mann. Dean Martin, Elizabeth Montgomery, Carol Burnett, Martin Balsam, Jill St. John. Undemanding fluff of TV star Martin being urged altar-wise by fiancee Montgomery; Burnett is his psychiatrist's nurse.

Who's Got the Action? (1962) C-93m. **½ D: Daniel Mann. Dean Martin, Lana Turner, Eddie Albert, Nita Talbot, Walter Matthau. Strained froth of Turner combatting hubby Martin's horse-racing fever by turning bookie.

Who's Minding the Mint? (1967) C-97m. ***½ D: Howard Morris. Jim Hutton, Dorothy Provine, Milton Berle, Joey Bishop, Bob Denver, Walter Brennan, Victor Buono, Jack Gilford, Jamie Farr, Jackie Joseph. Hilarious comedy, neglected at time of release, is tremendous fun in the classic comedy tradition, with motley gang of thieves helping U.S. Mint worker Hutton recover money he accidentally destroyed. Buono is especially funny as pompous ex-skipper.

Why Bother to Knock (1964-British) 88m. *½ D: Cyril Frankel. Elke

Sommer, Richard Todd, Nicole Maurey, Scot Fitch. Trashy smut about Todd traipsing around Europe giving out keys to his pals, with the girls all turning up unexpectedly.

Why Must I Die (1960) 86m. ** D: Roy Del Ruth. Terry Moore, Debra Paget, Bert Freed, Julie Reding. Very similar to I WANT TO LIVE, except in quality. Moore is singer falsely convicted of murder, with expected histrionics.

Wichita (1955) C-81m. **½ D: Jacques Tourneur. Joel McCrea, Vera Miles, Lloyd Bridges, Wallace Ford, Peter Graves. Action-filled Western; good cast helps Wyatt Earp (McCrea) restore order to Western town overrun with outlaws.

Wicked as They Come (1957-British) 94m. ** D: Ken Hughes. Arlene Dahl, Phil Carey, Herbert Marshall, David Kossoff. Dahl cavorts nicely in this minor story of a girl from the poor part of town involved with the wrong people.

Wicked City, The (1950-French, dubbed) 76m. *½ D: François Villiers. Maria Montez, Jean-Pierre Aumont, Lilli Palmer, Marcel Dalio. Even exotic Montez can't spice lazy telling of unscrupulous gal and the gob she involves in her sordid life.

Wicked Lady, The (1945-British) 98m. **½ D: Leslie Arliss. Margaret Lockwood, James Mason, Patricia Roc, Michael Rennie, Martita Hunt, Felix Aylmer. Title refers to Lockwood, in this unconvincing costumer of female outlaw who teams with robber Mason in evil doings.

Wicked Woman (1954) 77m. *½ D: Russell Rouse. Richard Egan, Beverly Michaels, Percy Helton, Evelyn Scott. Lumbering drama about no-good waitress leading assorted men astray.

Wide Blue Road, The (1956-Italian, dubbed) 100m. **½ D: Gillo Pontecorvo. Yves Montand, Alida Valli, Francisco Rabal, Peter Carsten, Ronaldino. Montand is non-plussed playboy taking pleasure where he finds it until Valli comes into picture. Performers outshine dialogue.

Wide Open Faces (1938) 67m. **½ D: Kurt Neumann. Joe E. Brown, Jane Wyman, Alison Skipworth, Lyda Roberti, Alan Baxter, Lucien Littlefield, Sidney Toler. Enjoyable Brown vehicle with top-notch supporting cast; innocent soda jerk mixed up with gangster.

Widow, The (1955-Italian, dubbed) ** D: Lewis Milestone. Patricia Roc, Anna Maria Ferrero, Massimo Serrato, Akim Tamiroff. Uneven soaper with Roc involved with lover Serrato, a sports car racer, who falls for Ferrero; film meanders.

Wife, Doctor and Nurse (1937) 85m. **½ D: Walter Lang. Loretta Young, Warner Baxter, Virginia Bruce, Jane Darwell, Sidney Blackmer, Minna Gombell. Baxter is caught between two women, but seems disinterested in both. Bright comedy with expert cast.

Wife, Husband and Friend (1939) 80m. *** D: Gregory Ratoff. Loretta Young, Warner Baxter, Binnie Barnes, George Barbier, Cesar Romero, Renie Riano. Entertaining comedy about aspiring singer Young whose husband Baxter tries to show her up; fun, but better as EVERYBODY DOES IT.

Wife of Monte Cristo, The (1946) 80m. ** D: Edgar G. Ulmer. John Loder, Lenore Aubert, Charles Dingle, Eduardo Ciannelli, Eva Gabor, Martin Kosleck. Corruption in the medical profession proves a formidable match for the Count; standard low-budget swashbuckler.

Wife Takes a Flyer, The (1942) 86m. ** D: Richard Wallace. Joan Bennett, Franchot Tone, Allyn Joslyn, Cecil Cunningham, Chester Clute. Weak WW2 espionage of Tone pretending to be Bennett's husband to escape from Holland.

Wife Versus Secretary (1936) 88m. *** D: Clarence Brown. Clark Gable, Jean Harlow, Myrna Loy, May Robson, George Barbier, James Stewart, Hobart Cavanaugh. Ordinary sudser of Gable caught between wife Loy and secretary Harlow is noteworthy for Harlow's fine performance.

Wife Wanted (1946) 73m. ** D: Phil Karlson. Kay Francis, Paul Cavanagh, Robert Shayne, Veda Ann Borg. In her last film, Francis is film star innocently hooked up with lonely-heart crooks; low production values.

Wild and the Innocent, The (1959) C-84m. **½ D: Jack Sher. Audie Murphy, Joanne Dru, Gilbert Roland, Jim Backus, Sandra Dee, George Mitchell, Peter Breck. Murphy and

Dee make an engaging duo as trapper and untamed country girl involved in gunplay in town during July 4th holiday.

Wild and the Willing, The (1962-British) 112m. ****** D: Ralph Thomas. Virginia Maskell, Paul Rogers, Samantha Eggar, Ian McShane, Richard Warner. Life and love at a provencial university, with over-earnest attempt to be realistic and daring.

Wild and Wonderful (1964) C-88m. ****½** D: Michael Anderson. Tony Curtis, Christine Kaufmann, Larry Storch, Marty Ingels. Empty slapstick froth involving canine movie star with Curtis and Kaufmann romancing.

Wild Blue Yonder, The (1951) 98m. ****½** D: Allan Dwan. Wendell Corey, Vera Ralston, Forrest Tucker, Phil Harris, Walter Brennan. Via flashback, film recounts episodes of Corey et al as air force pilots during WW2; Ralston effective as love interest.

Wild Cats on the Beach (1959-Italian) C-96m. ****½** D: Vittorio Sala. Elsa Martinelli, Alberto Sordi, Georges Marchal, Antonio Cifariello. Quartet of love tales set at resort area of Cote D'Azur; varying in quality.

Wild for Kicks (1962-British) 92m. ****** D: Edmond T. Greville. David Farrar, Noelle Adam, Christopher Lee, Gillian Hills, Shirley Ann Field, Oliver Reed. Strange little drama of rebellious teenager involved in murder. Retitled: BEAT GIRL.

Wild Geese Calling (1941) 77m. ****** D: John Brahm. Henry Fonda, Joan Bennett, Warren William, Ona Munson, Barton MacLane, Russell Simpson. Action and romance in 1890's Oregon and Alaska, but not enough of either to push this one over the hump.

Wild Harvest (1947) 92m. ***½** D: Tay Garnett. Alan Ladd, Dorothy Lamour, Robert Preston, Lloyd Nolan, Richard Erdman, Allen Jenkins. Pretty dismal film of travelling grain-harvesters with Preston and Ladd rivaling for Lamour's love.

Wild Heart, The (1952) C-82m. ****** D: Michael Powell, Emeric Pressburger. Jennifer Jones, David Farrar, Cyril Cusack, Sybil Thorndike, Hugh Griffith. Muddled romance yarn of lusty country lass Jones who allows Farrar to court her; aimless tale set in Wales.

Wild Heritage (1958) C-78m. ****½** D: Charles Haas. Will Rogers, Jr., Maureen O'Sullivan, Rod McKuen, Casey Tibbs. Soaper involving events in the intertwining lives of two westward-bound pioneer families.

Wild in the Country (1961) C-114m. ****½** D: Philip Dunne. Elvis Presley, Hope Lange, John Ireland, Tuesday Weld, Gary Lockwood. Literate Presley vehicle with Elvis a back-country youth with potential writing talents; film is earnest but clichéd.

Wild Is the Wind (1957) 114m. ****½** D: George Cukor. Anna Magnani, Anthony Quinn, Anthony Franciosa, Dolores Hart. Turgid soaper set in the West, with Quinn marrying the sister of his dead wife, not able to separate the two. Good acting helps script along; both leads won Oscar nominations.

Wild Man of Borneo, The (1941) 78m. ****** D: Robert B. Sinclair. Frank Morgan, Mary Howard, Billie Burke, Donald Meek, Marjorie Main, Connie Gilchrist, Bonita Granville, Dan Dailey. Good cast in weak sideshow comedy; Morgan masquerades as title character in one of his less memorable roles.

Wild North, The (1952) C-97m. ****** D: Andrew Marton. Stewart Granger, Cyd Charisse, Wendell Corey, J. M. Kerrigan, Ray Teal. Undazzling account of accused murderer hunted by Mountie, with the expected proving of innocence before finale; Charisse is love interest.

Wild One, The (1954) 79m. *****½** D: Laslo Benedek. Marlon Brando, Mary Murphy, Robert Keith, Lee Marvin. Original motorcycle film with Brando's renowned performance as gangleader terrorizing small town; dated, but worth viewing for acting.

Wild Party, The (1956) 81m. ***½** D: Harry Horner. Anthony Quinn, Carol Ohmart, Arthur Franz, Jay Robinson, Kathryn Grant. Blah attempt at naturalistic drama with Quinn the has-been football star going mildly berserk at a sleazy roadside dance hall.

Wild River (1960) C-110m. ******* D: Elia Kazan. Montgomery Clift, Lee Remick, Jo Van Fleet, Albert Salmi, Jay C. Flippen, James Westerfield. Engrossing account of Clift, a Tennessee Valley Authority official trying to get elderly Van Fleet to sell her land for new projects; Remick is love interest.

Wild Seed, The (1965) 99m. *** D: Brian Hutton. Michael Parks, Celia Kaye, Ross Elliott, Woodrow Chambliss, Eva Novak. Arty yet gripping story of runaway Kaye traveling to California, guided by road bum Parks.

Wild Stallion (1952) C-72m. *½ D: Lewis D. Collins. Martha Hyer, Edgar Buchanan, Hugh Beaumont, Ben Johnson. Shoddy military academy saga interlaced with soapish romance, told via flashbacks.

Wild Westerners, The (1962) C-70m. *½ D: Oscar Rudolph. James Philbrook, Nancy Kovack, Duane Eddy, Guy Mitchell. Humdrum account of marshal and new wife overcoming obstacles to bring gold east for Yankee cause.

Wild Wild Winter (1966) C-80m. ** D: Lennie Weinrib. Gary Clarke, Chris Noel, Steve Franken, Don Edmonds. Light-headed ski-slope musical froth, for and by the teenage set.

Will James' Sand SEE: Sand.

Will Success Spoil Rock Hunter? (1957) C-94m. **½ D: Frank Tashlin. Jayne Mansfield, Tony Randall, Joan Blondell, John Williams, Betsy Drake. George Axelrod play becomes mild social satire with digs at TV, etc.; Randall tries to get Mansfield to endorse a product to save his ad agency job. Blondell is breezy cohort of not-so-dumb movie star Jayne.

Willie and Joe Back at the Front SEE: Back at the Front.

Wilson (1944) C-154m. ***½ D: Henry King. Alexander Knox, Charles Coburn, Geraldine Fitzgerald, Thomas Mitchell, Cedric Hardwicke, Vincent Price, Mary Anderson, Francis X. Bushman. Superb biography of WW1-era President whose League of Nations idea became an obsession; one of Hollywood's solid films . . . but beware of cutting.

Winchester 73 (1950) 92m. *** D: Anthony Mann. James Stewart, Shelley Winters, Dan Duryea, Rock Hudson, Tony Curtis. Above-average action Western with good acting by Stewart and Duryea as long-time enemies settling old grudge with gunplay.

Winchester 73 (1967) C-120m. **½ D: Herschel Daugherty. Tom Tryon, John Saxon, Dan Duryea, John Drew Barrymore, Joan Blondell. Static remake of 1950 western; this telefeature retraces events in lives of people possessing title gun, involving shoot-outs and aimless talk; nice cameo by Blondell as roadhouse hostess.

Wind Across the Everglades (1958) C-93m. **½ D: Nicholas Ray. Burl Ives, Christopher Plummer, Gypsy Rose Lee, George Voskovec, Tony Galento. Oddball film, strangely cast, of life in 1900's Florida, with focus on natural beauty preservation attempt by Plummer.

Wind Cannot Read, The (1960-British) C-107m. **½ D: Ralph Thomas. Dirk Bogarde, Yoko Tani, Ronald Lewis, John Fraser, Anthony Bushell, Michael Medwin. Tidy tale of Bogarde escaping from Japanese prison camp during WW2 to find his ailing wife Tani.

Windom's Way (1958-British) C-108m. **½ D: Ronald Neame. Peter Finch, Mary Ure, Natasha Perry, Robert Flemying. Using an Oriental locale, film recounts efforts of small town doctor Finch to keep out communist forces.

Window, The (1949) 73m. ***½ D: Ted Tetzlaff. Barbara Hale, Bobby Driscoll, Arthur Kennedy, Paul Stewart, Ruth Roman. Superb suspense melodrama; young boy is only witness to murder but his tale is not believed by anyone. Stewart's villainous portrayal is classic.

Wing and a Prayer (1944) 97m. *** D: Henry Hathaway. Don Ameche, Dana Andrews, Charles Bickford, Cedric Hardwicke, Richard Jaeckel, Henry Morgan. Fine WW2 actioner of brave pilots aboard aircraft carrier. Excellent cast does well in exciting story.

Winged Victory (1944) 130m. ***½ D: George Cukor. Lon McCallister, Jeanne Crain, Edmond O'Brien, Don Taylor, Judy Holliday, Lee J. Cobb, Peter Lind Hayes, Red Buttons, Barry Nelson, Gary Merrill, Martin Ritt. Moving drama of pilots' lives from induction through dangerous missions, and devoted wives at home; from Moss Hart's story.

Wings for the Eagle (1942) 85m. ** D: Lloyd Bacon. Ann Sheridan, Dennis Morgan, Jack Carson, George Tobias, Don DeFore. Sincere tribute to aircraft workers during WW2 has little meaning today, but Sheridan et al give good performances.

Wings in the Dark (1935) 75m. **½ D: James Flood. Myrna Loy, Cary Grant, Hobart Cavanaugh, Roscoe Karns, Dean Jagger. Strange film of two flyers, Loy and Grant, in love. She does stunts, he wants to fly Atlantic, but goes blind.

Wings of Chance (1961) C-76m. *½ D: Edward Dew. Frances Rafferty, Jim Brown, Richard Tretter, Patrick Whyte. Tame tale of plane crash in the northern woods and rescue attempts.

Wings of Eagles, The (1957) C-110m. **½ D: John Ford. John Wayne, Dan Dailey, Maureen O'Hara, Ward Bond, Edmund Lowe, Sig Ruman, Mae Marsh. Well-handled, but uneven biography of naval commander who turned from barnstorming to building up the naval air fleet in pre-WW2 days.

Wings of Fire (1967) C-120m. **½ D: David Lowell Rich. Suzanne Pleshette, James Farentino, Ralph Bellamy, Juliet Mills, Jeremy Slate, Lloyd Nolan. Hokey melodramatic telefeature of aviatrix Pleshette involved in international air derby; Farentino her pilot boyfriend, Nolan a mechanic.

Wings of the Hawk (1953) C-80m. ** D: Budd Boetticher. Van Heflin, Julia Adams, Abbe Lane, Antonio Moreno, Noah Beery. Heflin is hero of thwarted attempt of renegades to overthrow Mexican government; Adams and Lane help him.

Wings of the Morning (1937-British) C-89m. *** D: Harold Schuster. Henry Fonda, Annabella, John McCormack, Irene Vanbrugh, Philip Frost, Sam Livesey. Engaging musical romance with Fonda preparing Annabella's horse to win great Irish Derby. Famed tenor McCormack adds some lovely songs. This was England's first color feature.

Winner Take All (1932) 68m. **½ D: Roy Del Ruth. James Cagney, Virginia Bruce, Marian Nixon, Guy Kibbee, Alan Mowbray, Dickie Moore. Minor but engaging Cagney vehicle with Jimmy as a thick-witted, cocky prizefighter torn between good-girl Nixon and fickle society-girl Bruce.

Winning Team, The (1952) 98m. **½ D: Lewis Seiler. Doris Day, Ronald Reagan, Frank Lovejoy, Russ Tamblyn, Tom Brown. Pleasant Americana about career of baseball player Grover Cleveland Alexander.

Winslow Boy, The (1950-British) 97m. ***½ D: Anthony Asquith. Robert Donat, Margaret Leighton, Cedric Hardwicke, Francis L. Sullivan. Superior courtroom melodrama from Terence Rattigan's play, headed by Donat as barrister defending innocent boy (Neil North).

Winter a Go-Go (1965) C-88m. ** D: Richard Benedict. James Stacy, William Wellman, Jr., Beverly Adams, Jill Donohue, Julie Parrish. Lowbrow shenanigans at a ski resort run by Stacy for the young, affluent set.

Winter Carnival (1939) 105m. **½ D: Charles F. Riesner. Richard Carlson, Ann Sheridan, Helen Parrish, James Corner, Virginia Gilmore, Robert Walker, Joan Leslie, Peggy Moran. Contrived romance flick set at Dartmouth College during festive weekend; Sheridan is divorcee in love with professor Carlson.

Winter Meeting (1948) 104m. **½ D: Brentaigne Windust. Bette Davis, Janis Paige, James Davis, John Hoyt, Florence Bates. Sluggish script of disillusioned poetess who loves embittered war hero, prevents well-acted film from achieving greater heights.

Winterset (1936) 78m. **** D: Alfred S. Santell. Burgess Meredith, Margo, Eduardo Ciannelli, John Carradine, Edward Ellis, Mischa Auer. Striking filmization of Maxwell Anderson play with original Broadway cast repeating roles; Meredith determines to avenge father's death.

Wintertime (1943) C-82m. ** D: John Brahm. Sonja Henie, Jack Oakie, Cesar Romero, Carole Landis, Cornel Wilde. Henie gives her all to save uncle's hotel from bankruptcy. Innocuous, below par for her vehicles.

Wiretappers (1956) 80m. BOMB D: Dick Ross. Bill Williams, Georgia Lee, Douglas Kennedy, Phil Tead. Obnoxious little film blending crime and religion. Williams is seedy character working for two rival syndicates.

Wise Girl (1937) 70m. **½ D: Leigh Jason. Miriam Hopkins, Ray Milland,

Walter Abel, Margaret Dumont, Tom Kennedy. Good cast in hot-and-cold story of wealthy Hopkins trying to provide home for late sister's children.

Wistful Widow of Wagon Gap, The (1947) 78m. ** D: Charles Barton. Bud Abbott, Lou Costello, Marjorie Main, George Cleveland, Gordon Jones, William Ching, Peter Thompson. Raucous widow Main and A&C have to carry this one without much material. Best sequence comes when Lou becomes sheriff.

Witch Doctor SEE: Men of Two Worlds.

Witchcraft (1964-British) 79m. ** D: Don Sharp. Lon Chaney, Jack Hedley, Jill Dixon, Viola Keats. Standard plot of witch cult happenings in English village after grave of 300-year-old witch is unearthed.

With A Song In My Heart (1952) C-117m. *** D: Walter Lang. Susan Hayward, Rory Calhoun, David Wayne, Thelma Ritter, Robert Wagner, Una Merkel. Well-intentioned schamltz based loosely on events in life of singer Jane Froman with Hayward most earnest as the spunky songstress.

With Fire and Sword (1961-Italian) C-96m. *½ D: Fernando Cerchio. Jeanne Crain, John Drew Barrymore, Pierre Brice, Akim Tamiroff. Costume spaghetti about Cossacks vs. Poles; embarrassing minor epic. Retitled: DAGGERS OF BLOOD.

Within These Walls (1945) 71m. ** D: H. Bruce Humberstone. Thomas Mitchell, Mary Anderson, Edward Ryan, Mark Stevens, B. S. Pully, Roy Kelly, Harry Shannon. Fairly good but predictable prison drama with warden Mitchell faced with his own son as a prisoner.

Without Honor (1949) 69m. ** D: Irving Pichel. Laraine Day, Dane Clark, Franchot Tone, Agnes Moorehead, Bruce Bennett. Good cast talks endlessly in melodrama of woman who thinks she's killed a man.

Without Love (1945) 111m. *** D: Harold S. Bucquet. Spencer Tracy, Katharine Hepburn, Lucille Ball, Keenan Wynn, Carl Esmond, Patricia Morison. Tracy and Hepburn have never been livelier, but script lets them down in story of inventor and widow who marry for convenience, later fall in love. Wynn and Ball are excellent second leads.

Without Reservations (1946) 107m. *** D: Mervyn LeRoy. Claudette Colbert, John Wayne, Don DeFore, Thurston Hall, Louella Parsons. Marine Wayne and novelist Colbert meet on a cross-country railroad trip, rapidly fall in love. Engaging comedy with several guest stars.

Witness Chair, The (1936) 64m. **½ D: George Nicholls, Jr. Ann Harding, Walter Abel, Douglass Dumbrille, Frances Sage, Moroni Olsen, Margaret Hamilton. Above-average courtroom drama of murderess Harding covering up her act, letting innocent man take the blame.

Witness for the Prosecution (1957) **** D: Billy Wilder. Marlene Dietrich, Tyrone Power, Charles Laughton, Elsa Lanchester, John Williams, Henry Daniell, Una O'Connor. Fantastically effective London courtroom suspenser from Agatha Christie story. Dietrich is peerless as alleged killer's (Power) wife; Laughton the defense attorney, and Lanchester, the amusing nurse.

Witness in the Dark (1959-British) 62m. *½ D: Wolf Rilla. Patricia Dainton, Conrad Phillips, Madge Ryan, Nigel Green, Enid Lorimer. Uncommonly obvious suspenser with murderer seeking to kill blind girl who was present when crime was committed.

Witness to Murder (1954) 83m. *** D: Roy Rowland. Barbara Stanwyck, George Sanders, Gary Merrill, Jesse White. Shrill suspenser of Stanwyck witnessing act of murder and trying to convince police of what she saw.

Wives and Lovers (1963) 103m. **½ D: John Rich. Janet Leigh, Van Johnson, Shelley Winters, Martha Hyer, Ray Walston. Surface, slick entertainment; newly famous writer Johnson, wife Leigh and child move to surburbia. Literary agent Hyer on the make almost causes divorce; Winters is wise-cracking neighbor.

Wives Never Know (1936) 75m. **½ D: Elliott Nugent. Charlie Ruggles, Mary Boland, Adolphe Menjou, Vivienne Osborne, Claude Gillingwater, Fay Holden, Louise Beavers. Flimsy tale of couple trying to awaken each other's love. Boland and Ruggles are marvelous, though, with them and Menjou making this worth seeing.

Wives Under Suspicion (1938) 75m. **½ D: James Whale. Warren William, Gail Patrick, Constance Moore, William Lundigan, Ralph Morgan. Minor but interesting drama of callous D.A. William waking up to love when he thinks his wife Patrick is seeing another man. Remake of THE KISS BEFORE THE MIRROR.

Wizard of Baghdad, The (1960) C-92m. ** D: George Sherman. Dick Shawn, Diane Baker, Barry Coe, John Van Dreelen, Robert F. Simon, Vaughn Taylor. Blah satire on costumers, with Shawn a lazy genie.

Wizard of Oz, The (1939) C-101m. **** D: Victor Fleming. Judy Garland, Frank Morgan, Bert Lahr, Jack Haley, Ray Bolger, Billie Burke, Margaret Hamilton, Charley Grapewin, Clara Blandick, Singer Midgets. American classic from Frank Baum tale of Kansas girl sailing "Over The Rainbow" to land of Oz with assorted unusual friends. Fine Harold Arlen-E. Y. Harburg songs. Just as good the fifth time as it is the first.

Wolf Dog (1958) 61m. *½ D: Sam Newfield. Jim Davis, Allison Hayes, Tony Brown, Austin Willis. Lowjinks about farm life in the north country involving land-hungry ranchers.

Wolf Larsen (1958) 83m. **½ D: Harmon Jones. Barry Sullivan, Peter Graves, Gita Hall, Thayer David. Nicely-done version of Jack London's THE SEA WOLF with Sullivan effective as the tyrannical captain of the eerie ship.

Wolf Man, The (1941) 71m. ***½ D: George Waggner. Claude Rains, Ralph Bellamy, Warren William, Patric Knowles, Bela Lugosi, Lon Chaney, Jr., Evelyn Ankers. One of the finest horror films ever made, with sturdy cast; Chaney is Larry Talbot, cursed by lycanthropy, Rains his unknowing father, Lugosi and Ouspenskaya local gypsies who foretell his doom, Bellamy and William helpless inspectors. Literate, very engrossing.

Woman and the Hunter, The (1957) 79m. *½ D: George Breakston. Ann Sheridan, David Farrar, John Loder. Tedious love triangle set in the jungles of Kenya; Sheridan tries hard but material defeats all.

Woman-Bait SEE: **Inspector Maigret**.

Woman Chases Man (1937) 71m. **½ D: John G. Blystone. Miriam Hopkins, Joel McCrea, Charles Winninger, Ella Logan, Broderick Crawford. Sometime hilarious, often strained screwball comedy of architect Hopkins going after her boss, McCrea.

Woman Eater (1959-British) 70m. *½ D: Charles Saunders. George Coulouris, Robert MacKenzie, Norman Claridge, Marpessa Dawn, Jimmy Vaughan. Hokey chiller about flesheating tree with preference for females.

Woman Hater (1949-British) 70m. ** D: Terence Young. Stewart Granger, Edwige Feuillere, Ronald Squire, Mary Jerrold. Contrived battle of wits between confirmed bachelor and single girl leads to predictable romance.

Woman in a Dressing Gown (1957-British) 93m. **½ D: J. Lee Thompson, Yvonne Mitchell, Anthony Quayle, Sylvia Syms, Michael Ripper. Unpretentious, "small" drama about marital discord.

Women in Bondage (1943) 70m. ** D: Steve Sekely. Gail Patrick, Nancy Kelly, Gertrude Michael, Anne Nagel, Tala Birell, Alan Baxter, H. B. Warner. Exploitation patriotism hammering away at Nazi maltreatment of conquered people. Dates badly.

Woman in Green, The (1945) 68m. D: Roy William Neill. Basil Rathbone, Nigel Bruce, Hillary Brooke, Henry Daniell, Paul Cavanagh, Matthew Boulton, Eve Amber. SEE: Sherlock Holmes series.

Woman in Hiding (1949) 92m. ** D: Michael Gordon. Ida Lupino, Howard Duff, Stephen McNally, Peggy Dow, John Litel. Overdone dramatics of wife discovering husband is killer, fleeing before it's too late; some restraint would have been most helpful.

Woman in Question (1952-British) 82m. *** D: Anthony Asquith. Dirk Bogarde, Jean Kent, Susan Shaw, Hermione Baddeley. Police inspector, investigating murder of a fortune teller, turns up with questions of character and mystery surrounding her life. Retitled: FIVE ANGLES ON MURDER.

Woman in Red (1935) 68m. ** D: Robert Florey. Barbara Stanwyck,

Gene Raymond, Genevieve Tobin, John Eldredge, Philip Reed, Dorothy Tree. Routine courtroom drama of Stanwyck and Raymond marriage interrupted by charge that she's been seeing Eldredge.

Woman in the Window, The (1944) 99m. ***½ D: Fritz Lang. Joan Bennett, Edward G. Robinson, Dan Duryea, Raymond Massey, Bobby Blake, Dorothy Peterson. High-grade melodrama about Robinson meeting subject of alluring painting (Bennett), becoming involved in murder and witnessing his own investigation. Surprise ending tops exciting film.

Woman in White, The (1948) 109m. ** D: Peter Godfrey. Eleanor Parker, Alexis Smith, Sydney Greenstreet, Gig Young, Agnes Moorehead. Although based on classic Wilkie Collins gothic mystery, story of tormented woman is far-fetched and often ludicrous.

Woman Obsessed (1959) C-102m. **½ D: Henry Hathaway. Susan Hayward, Stephen Boyd, Barbara Nichols, Dennis Holmes, Theodore Bikel, Ken Scott. Energetic stars try hard in Canadian ranch-life soaper of widow Hayward who marries Boyd, with predictable clashing and making up.

Woman of Devil's Island (1961-Italian, dubbed) C-95m. *½ D: Domenesco Paolella. Guy Madison, Michele Mercier, Fredrica Ranchi. Humdrum mini-epic with Madison helping aristocratic woman held prisoner on swamp-surrounded island.

Woman of Distinction, A (1950) 85m. *** D: Edward Buzzell. Rosalind Russell, Ray Milland, Edmund Gwenn, Janis Carter, Francis Lederer. Minor but very enjoyable slackstick, as visiting professor Milland causes scandal involving college dean Russell. Energetic cast puts this over; brief guest appearance by Lucille Ball.

Woman of Dolwyn, The SEE: Dolwyn.

Woman of Rome (1956-Italian, dubbed) 93m. ** D: Luigi Zampa. Gina Lollobrigida, Daniel Gelin, Franco Fabrizi, Raymond Pellegrin. Old stuff of girl of easy virtue with Lollobrigida for scenery.

Woman of Straw (1964) C-117m. **½ D: Basil Dearden. Sean Connery, Gina Lollobrigida, Ralph Richardson, Alexander Knox. Muddled suspenser of Connery and Lollobrigida plotting the "perfect murder" of old Richardson with ironic results.

Woman of the North Country (1952) C-90m. ** D: Joseph Kane. Gale Storm, Ruth Hussey, Rod Cameron, John Agar, J. Carrol Naish. Predictable love and fight tale set in the mining lands; Storm's last film to date.

Woman of the River (1957-Italian, dubbed) C-92m. ** D: Mario Soldati. Sophia Loren, Gerard Oury, Lise Bourdin, Rik Battaglia. Seamy, gloomy account of Loren involved with passion and criminals.

Woman of the Town, The (1943) 90m. *** D: George Archainbaud. Claire Trevor, Albert Dekker, Barry Sullivan, Henry Hull, Marion Martin. First class Western with Dekker as Bat Masterson who must choose between love for dance-hall Trevor or law and order.

Woman of the Year (1942) 112m. ***½ D: George Stevens. Spencer Tracy, Katharine Hepburn, Fay Bainter, Reginald Owen, Roscoe Karns, William Bendix. First teaming of Tracy and Hepburn is a joy: he's a sports reporter, she's a world-famed political commentator, he brings her down to earth. Bainter as Hepburn's mother is fine as marital referee.

Woman on the Beach, The (1947) 71m. *** D: Jean Renoir. Joan Bennett, Robert Ryan, Charles Bickford, Nan Leslie, Walter Sande. Ryan falls in love with Bennett but becomes wary of her blind husband Bickford; taut melodrama with fine performances all around.

Woman on the Run (1950) 77m. *** D: Norman Foster. Ann Sheridan, Dennis O'Keefe, Robert Keith, Frank Jenks. Sheridan is most convincing as wife trying to find her husband, witness to gangland murder, before the underworld does.

Woman Rebels, A (1936) 88m. *** D: Mark Sandrich. Katharine Hepburn, Herbert Marshall, Elizabeth Allan, Donald Crisp, Doris Dudley, Van Heflin. Fine costumer with Hepburn trying to break loose from strict shackles imposed by father Crisp; Victorian drama has excellent cast.

Woman They Almost Lynched (1953) 90m. ** D: Allan Dwan. John Lund, Joan Leslie, Audrey Totter, Brian Donlevy, Ellen Corby, Minerva Urecal, Jim Davis. Civil War period film about refined young woman Leslie who comes to Western town and learns to tote gun.

Woman Times Seven (1967) C-99m. *** D: Vittorio De Sica. Shirley MacLaine, Peter Sellers, Rossano Brazzi, Vittorio Gassman, Lex Barker, Elsa Martinelli, Robert Morley, Patrick Wymark, Adrienne Corri, Alan Arkin, Michael Caine, Anita Ekberg, Philippe Noiret. A seven-episode film with MacLaine showing seven types of women; some funny moments, some perceptive comments, but with that cast and director, it should have been much better.

Woman Who Came Back, The (1945) 68m. ** D: Walter Colmes. John Loder, Nancy Kelly, Otto Kruger, Ruth Ford, Harry Tyler. Fair yarn of woman (Kelly) who is convinced she has received witches' curse from ancient descendant.

Woman's Devotion, A (1956) C-88m. ** D: Paul Henreid. Ralph Meeker, Janice Rule, Paul Henreid, Rosenda Monteros. Choppy mystery of artist Meeker and wife Rule, involved in a murder while in Mexico.

Woman's Face, A (1941) 105m. *** D: George Cukor. Joan Crawford, Melvyn Douglas, Conrad Veidt, Osa Massen, Reginald Owen, Albert Basserman, Marjorie Main. One of Crawford's most substantial roles in exciting yarn of low-living girl whose life changes when she undergoes plastic surgery. Taut climax spotlights villain Veidt.

Woman's Secret, A (1949) 85m. *** D: Nicholas Ray. Maureen O'Hara, Melvyn Douglas, Gloria Grahame, Bill Williams, Victor Jory. Intriguing flashback drama of woman killing singer she built up to success; good performances by two female stars.

Woman's Vengeance, A (1947) 96m. ***½ D: Zoltan Korda. Charles Boyer, Ann Blyth, Jessica Tandy, Cedric Hardwicke, Mildred Natwick. Outstanding drama of philandering Boyer put on trial when his wife is found dead; brilliant cast gives vivid realistic performances. Based on an Aldous Huxley story.

Woman's World (1954) C-94m. *** D: Jean Negulesco. Clifton Webb, June Allyson, Van Heflin, Arlene Dahl, Lauren Bacall, Fred MacMurray. Sophisticated look at big business, the men and women involved, with arch Webb the corporation boss choosing a new successor.

Women, The (1939) 132m. **** D: George Cukor. Joan Crawford, Norma Shearer, Paulette Goddard, Rosalind Russell, Joan Fontaine, Hedda Hopper, Marjorie Main, Virginia Weidler, Mary Boland, Ruth Hussey, Mary Beth Hughes, Virginia Grey. Delicious adaptation of Clare Booth Luce play with all star cast. Men are taken to task in this brittle comedy, remade as THE OPPOSITE SEX. Don't miss this once-in-a-lifetime cast.

Women Are Like That (1938) 78m. **½ D: Stanley Logan. Kay Francis, Pat O'Brien, Ralph Forbes, Melville Cooper. Smooth fluff: Francis is daughter of ad executive in love with copywriter O'Brien.

Women Are Weak SEE **3 Murderesses**.

Women of Pitcairn Island, The (1956) 72m. *½ D: Jean Yarbrough. James Craig, Lynn Bari, John Smith, Arleen Whelan, Sue England, Carol Thurston, Charlita. Low-budget garbage about families developing from people who remained on island after MUTINY ON THE BOUNTY.

Women's Prison (1955) 80m. ** D: Lewis Seiler. Ida Lupino, Jan Sterling, Audrey Totter, Phyllis Thaxter, Howard Duff, Mae Clarke, Gertrude Michael, Juanita Moore. Film depicts deplorable prison conditions, and cruelty of superintendent Lupino. Totter and Thaxter are the victims whom Duff tries to help.

Wonder Bar (1934) 84m. **½ D: Lloyd Bacon. Al Jolson, Kay Francis, Dolores Del Rio, Dick Powell, Ricardo Cortez, Louise Fazenda, Guy Kibbee. Brisk musical set at Paris nightclub: chic Francis is fleeced by gigolo Cortez; dancer Del Rio romanced by crooner Powell; club owner Jolson solves everyone's woes. Busby Berkeley number: "Goin' To Heaven On A Mule."

Wonder Man (1945) C-98m. ***½ D: H. Bruce Humberstone. Danny Kaye,

Virginia Mayo, Vera-Ellen, Donald Woods, S. Z. Sakall, Allen Jenkins, Ed Brophy, Steve Cochran, Otto Kruger. Kaye's delightful as twins, the serious one forced to imitate his brash entertainer brother when the latter is killed; big, colorful production.

Wonderful Country, The (1959) C-96m. **½ D: Robert Parrish. Robert Mitchum, Julie London, Gary Merrill, Pedro Armandariz, Jack Oakie, Albert Dekker. Brooding Western involving Mitchum running guns along Mexico-Texas line, romancing London.

Wonders of Aladdin, The (1961) C-93m. ** D: Henry Levin. Donald O'Connor, Noelle Adam, Vittorio De Sica, Aldo Fabrizi. Few wonders to behold in this mild children's fantasy which the kids might enjoy.

Words and Music (1948) C-119m. **½ D: Norman Taurog. June Allyson, Perry Como, Judy Garland, Lena Horne, Gene Kelly, Mickey Rooney, Tom Drake, Ann Sothern, Cyd Charisse, Betty Garrett, Janet Leigh. Excellent score only highlight in badly scripted fiction about composers Rodgers and Hart. Big MGM name cast does their best.

Working Man, The (1933) 75m. **½ D: John G. Adolfi. George Arliss, Bette Davis, Hardie Albright, Theodore Newton, Gordon Westcott. Lukewarm drama, uplighted by cast, of shoe manufacturer gradually taking over rival factory.

World and the Flesh (1932) 75m. ** D: John Cromwell. George Bancroft, Miriam Hopkins, Alan Mowbray, George E. Stone. Labored drama of soldier-of-fortune Bancroft asking price of Hopkins to save her wealthy friends from Russian Revolution; moves very slowly.

World Changes, The (1933) 90m. **½ D: Mervyn LeRoy. Paul Muni, Mary Astor, Aline MacMahon, Donald Cook, Guy Kibbee, Margaret Lindsay, Anna Q. Nilsson, Patricia Ellis. Tale of ambitious farm-boy Muni whose life falls apart as he becomes wealthy businessman. Astor is excellent as crazed wife.

World for Ransom (1954) 82m. ** D: Robert Aldrich. Dan Duryea, Gene Lockhart, Patric Knowles, Reginald Denny. The unexpected helps this yarn about an adventurer Duryea who finds himself matching wits with a crime gang.

World In His Arms, The (1952) C-104m. **½ D: Raoul Walsh. Gregory Peck, Ann Blyth, Anthony Quinn, Andrea King, Eugenie Leontovich, Sig Ruman. Unlikely but entertaining tale of skipper Peck romancing Russian Blyth, set in 1850's San Francisco.

World In My Corner (1956) 82m. **½ D: Jesse Hibbs. Audie Murphy, Barbara Rush, Jeff Morrow, John McIntire, Tommy Rall. Murphy is poor boy who rises to fame via boxing, almost ruined by rich life with Rush standing by.

World of Abbott and Costello, The (1965) 75m. **½ Narrated by Jack E. Leonard. Bud Abbott, Lou Costello, Marjorie Main, Boris Karloff, Tom Ewell. Good compilation of scenes from some of the team's best films. Bud and Lou do "Who's on First?", have dinner with Marjorie Main, meet Frankenstein, and get lost in Alaska with Ewell.

World of Henry Orient, The (1964) C-106m. ***½ D: George Roy Hill. Peter Sellers, Paula Prentiss, Angela Lansbury, Phyllis Thaxter, Tom Bosley, Tippy Walker, Merrie Spaeth. Marvelous comedy of two teenage girls who idolize eccentric pianist (Sellers) and follow him around NY. Bosley and Lansbury are superb as Walker's parents, with Thaxter appealing as Spaeth's understanding mother.

World of Suzie Wong, The (1960) C-129m. **½ D: Richard Quine. William Holden, Nancy Kwan, Sylvia Syms, Michael Wilding, Laurence Naismith. Holden's sluggish performance as American artist in love with B-girl Kwan doesn't help this soaper, lavishly filmed in Hong Kong.

World Premiere (1941) 70m. **½ D: Ted Tetzlaff. John Barrymore, Frances Farmer, Eugene Pallette, Virginia Dale, Ricardo Cortez, Sig Ruman, Don Castle. Ridiculous comedy of Hollywood premiere held up by Nazis; worth seeing for Barrymore who even in declining years gave a good show.

World, the Flesh, and the Devil, The (1959) 95m. ** D: Ranald MacDougall. Harry Belafonte, Inger Stevens, Mel Ferrer. Hogwash soaper hidden beneath guise of sci-fi. Trio of stars are last people on earth after nuclear destruction; they form a happy relationship.

World Was His Jury, The (1958) 82m. *½ D: Fred F. Sears. Edmond O'Brien, Mona Freeman, Karin Booth, Robert McQueeney. Routine account of ship's captain proven innocent of negligence in sea disaster.

World Without End (1956) C-80m. **½ D: Edward Bernds. Hugh Marlowe, Nancy Gates, Nelson Leigh, Rod Taylor. Space flight headed for Mars breaks the time barrier and ends up on Earth in the 26th century. Pretty good sci-fi.

Worst Secret Agents SEE: **Oh! Those Most Secret Agents.**

Wreck of the Hesperus, The (1948) 70m. ** D: John Hoffman. Willard Parker, Edgar Buchanan, Patricia White. Loosely based on Longfellow poem, this low-budget flick suffers from lack of production values to enhance special effects of storms at sea.

Wreck of the Mary Deare, The (1959) C-105m. **½ D: Michael Anderson. Gary Cooper, Charlton Heston, Michael Redgrave, Emlyn Williams, Cecil Parker, Alexander Knox, Virginia McKenna, Richard Harris. Sticky going: Skipper of sunken ship accused of negligence, cleared at inquest by testimony of salvage boat captain. Special effects are real star.

Written on the Wind (1956) C-99m. *** D: Douglas Sirk. Rock Hudson, Lauren Bacall, Robert Stack, Dorothy Malone, Robert Keith, Grant Williams. Large-scale melodrama of family life revolving about spoiled heiress Malone who almost destroys her brother Stack and the man she sets out to get. Malone won Oscar as nymphomaniac.

Wrong Arm of the Law, The (1963-British) 91m. *** D: Cliff Owen. Peter Sellers, Lionel Jeffries, Bernard Cribbins, Irene Browne. Nifty hi-jinks; cockney trio have police and crooks after them because they've been dressing as cops and confiscating loot from apprehended robbers.

Wrong Kind of Girl SEE: **Bus Stop.**

Wrong Man, The (1957) 105m. *** D: Alfred Hitchcock. Henry Fonda, Vera Miles, Anthony Quayle, Nehemiah Persoff. Strange Hitchcock film done as semi-documentary, using true story of NY musician (Fonda) falsely accused of murder. Miles is excellent as wife who cracks under strain; Offbeat.

Wuthering Heights (1939) 103m. **** D: William Wyler. Merle Oberon, Laurence Olivier, David Niven, Flora Robson, Donald Crisp, Geraldine Fitzgerald, Leo G. Carroll, Cecil Kellaway, Hugh Williams. Stirring adaptation of Emily Bronte's novel stops at chapter 17, but viewers won't argue: sensitive direction with sweeping performances of downbeat story of strange love in pre-Victorian England. Haunting, a must-see film.

Wyoming (1940) 89m. ** D: Richard Thorpe. Wallace Beery, Leo Carrillo, Ann Rutherford, Lee Bowman, Joseph Calleia, Bobs Watson. OK oater with Beery and Carrillo fun as on-again, off-again comrades.

Wyoming (1947) 84m. **½ D: Joseph Kane. William Elliott, Vera Ralston, John Carroll, "Gabby" Hayes, Albert Dekker, Virginia Grey. Not-bad Wild Bill Elliott Western of ranchers vs. homesteaders in Wyoming territory.

Wyoming Kid, The SEE: **Cheyenne.**

Wyoming Mail (1950) C-87m. **½ D: Reginald LeBorg. Stephen Mcnally, Alexis Smith, Ed Begley, Richard Egan, James Arness, Frankie Darro. Postal robbery in old West, with capable cast shining up script's dull spots.

Wyoming Renegades (1955) C-73m. *½ D: Fred F. Sears. Phil Carey, Gene Evans, Martha Hyer, William Bishop, Aaron Spelling. Confused Western portraying the story of ex-bandit Carey who wants to go straight. Hyer helps him.

X-15 (1961) C-106m. ** D: Richard Donner. David McLean, Charles Bronson, Ralph Taeger, Brad Dexter, Mary Tyler Moore, Patricia Owens. Narrated by James Stewart. Mild narrative about life and loves of researchers at a California missile base.

X—the Man with the X-Ray Eyes (1963) 80m. **½ D: Roger Corman. Ray Milland, Diana Van Der Vlis, Harold J. Stone, John Hoyt, Don Rickles. Not-bad little film about mad scientist Milland developing serum that enables him to see through things.

X the Unknown (1957-British) 80m. ** D: Leslie Norman. Dean Jagger,

Leo McKern, William Lucas, Edward Chapman, Anthony Newley. Someone, or something, is trying to take over our planet; that's the basis for this weak sci-fi story set in Scotland.

Yank at Eton, A (1942) 88m. ** D: Norman Taurog. Mickey Rooney, Freddie Bartholomew, Tina Thayer, Ian Hunter, Edmund Gwenn, Alan Mowbray, Peter Lawford, Terry Kilburn. Rooney goes to school in England and it's a wonder he's not ejected immediately.

Yank at Oxford, A (1938) 100m. *** D: Jack Conway. Robert Taylor, Lionel Barrymore, Maureen O'Sullivan, Vivien Leigh, Edmund Gwenn. Attractive cast, including young Leigh, in familiar premise of American studying in England.

Yank in Indo-China, A (1952) 67m. *½ D: Wallace Grissell. John Archer, Douglas Dick, Jean Wiles, Don Harvey. Just adequate yarn of American pilots involved in guerilla warfare.

Yank in Korea, A (1951) 73m. *½ D: Lew Landers. Lon McCallister, William Phillips, Brett King, Larry Stewart. Corny war actioner.

Yank in the RAF, A (1941) 98m. *** D: Henry King. Tyrone Power, Betty Grable, John Sutton, Reginald Gardiner, Donald Stuart, Richard Fraser. Power's only there so he can see London-based chorine Grable; they make a nice team. Songs: "Another Little Dream Won't Do Us Any Harm," "Hi-Ya Love."

Yank in Viet-Nam, A (1964) 80m. ** D: Marshall Thompson. Marshall Thompson, Enrique Magalona, Mario Barri. Urban Drew. Low-budget topical actioner set in Saigon, with marine Thompson attempting to help the South Vietnamese. Retitled: YEAR OF THE TIGER.

Yankee Buccaneer (1952) C-86m. **½ D: Frederick de Cordova. Jeff Chandler, Scott Brady, Suzan Ball, David Janssen. Standard pirate tale, invigorated by healthy cast.

Yankee Doodle Dandy (1942) 126m. ***½ D: Michael Curtiz. James Cagney, Joan Leslie, Walter Huston, Irene Manning, Rosemary DeCamp, Jeanne Cagney, S. Z. Sakall, Walter Catlett, Frances Langford, George Tobias. Cagney wraps up film in neat little package all his own with dynamic recreation of George M. Cohan's life, backed by fine cast and period flavor.

Yankee Pasha (1954) 84m. **½ D: Joseph Pevney. Jeff Chandler, Rhonda Fleming, Mamie Van Doren, Bart Roberts. Nicely-paced costumer set in 1800's with Chandler crossing the ocean to France and beyond to find his true love, captured by pirates.

Yaqui Drums (1956) 71m. *½ D: Jean Yarbrough. Rod Cameron, J. Carrol Naish, Mary Castle, Robert Hutton. Soggy account of rancher vs. criminal saloon owner in old West.

Year of the Tiger SEE: **Yank in Viet-Nam, A.**

Yearling, The (1946) C-134m. ***½ D: Clarence Brown. Gregory Peck, Jane Wyman, Claude Jarman, Jr., Chill Wills, Margaret Wycherly, Henry Travers, Jeff York, June Lockhart. Marjorie Kinnan Rawlings' sensitive tale of young boy attached to a young deer is exquisitely done in lovely color, with memorable performances.

Years Between, The (1946-British) 88m. **½ D: Compton Bennett. Michael Redgrave, Valerie Hobson, Flora Robson, James McKechnie. Sensitively handled story of oft-told tale of man returning from war to discover wife thought him dead and is now about to remarry.

Yellow Balloon, The (1952-British) 80m. **½ D: J. Lee Thompson. Andrew Ray, Kenneth More, Veronica Hurst, William Sylvester, Bernard Lee. Sensible suspenser of small boy who witnesses chum's murder and is exploited by cheap crook.

Yellow Cab Man, The (1950) 85m. *** D: Jack Donahue. Red Skelton, Gloria De Haven, Walter Slezak, Edward Arnold, Polly Moran. Fine Skelton romp with Red as would be inventor of unbreakable glass, involved with gangsters and crooked businessman; Slezak is perfect as bad-guy.

Yellow Canary, The (1943-British) 84m. **½ D: Herbert Wilcox. Anna Neagle, Richard Greene, Albert Lieven, Margaret Rutherford, Valentine Dyall. Above average WW2 spy drama with Neagle feigning Nazi loyalty to obtain secrets for the Allies.

Yellow Jack (1938) 83m. ***½ D: George B. Seitz. Robert Montgomery, Virginia Bruce, Lewis Stone, Stanley

Ridges, Henry Hull, Andy Devine. Stirring tribute to dedicated man searching for yellow fever cure in 1890's Panama, from Sidney Howard play.

Yellow Mountain, The (1954) C-78m. *½ D: Jesse Hibbs. Lex Barker, Mala Powers, Howard Duff, William Demarest. Unremarkable tale of Barker rivaling Duff for gold and love of Powers.

Yellow Rolls-Royce, The (1965) C-122m. *** D: Anthony Asquith. Rex Harrison, Shirley MacLaine, Ingrid Bergman, Jeanne Moreau, Edmund Purdom, George C. Scott, Omar Sharif, Art Carney, Alain Delon, Roland Culver, Wally Cox. Slick drama involving trio of owners of title car, focusing on how romance plays a part in each of their lives; contrived but ever-so-smoothly handled.

Yellow Sky (1948) 98m. *** D: William Wellman. Gregory Peck, Anne Baxter, Richard Widmark, Robert Arthur, John Russell, Henry Morgan, James Barton. Exciting Western with exceptional cast in story of confrontation in Arizona ghost town.

Yellow Tomahawk, The (1954) C-82m. ** D: Lesley Selander. Rory Calhoun, Peggie Castle, Noah Beery, Warner Anderson. Calhoun is Indian guide who goes to any length to prevent redskin attack on settlers.

Yellowstone Kelly (1959) C-91m. **½ D: Gordon Douglas. Clint Walker, Edward Byrnes, John Russell, Ray Danton, Claude Akins, Rhodes Reason, Warren Oates. Rugged Western involving Indian uprising, with Walker the burly hero.

Yes, My Darling Daughter (1939) 86m. **½ D: William Keighley. Priscilla Lane, Fay Bainter, Roland Young, May Robson, Jeffrey Lynn, Ian Hunter. Everybody is enthused about young lovers running off together except young man in question (Lynn). Mildly amusing comedy.

Yes, Sir, That's My Baby (1949) C-82m. **½ D: George Sherman. Donald O'Connor, Charles Coburn, Gloria De Haven, Joshua Shelley, Barbara Brown. Flimsy musical of football-crazy O'Connor on college campus, rescued by spirit and verve of cast.

Yesterday, Today and Tomorrow (1964-Italian, dubbed) 119m. **** D: Vittorio de Sica. Sophia Loren, Marcello Mastroianni, Tina Pica, Giovanni Ridolfi. Spicy trio of tales giving insight into Italian morals; flavorfully acted by all.

Yesterday's Enemy (1959-British) 95m. *½ D: Val Guest. Stanley Baker, Guy Rolfe, Leo McKern, Gordon Jackson, David Oxley, Philip Ahn. Mild WW2 actioner set in Burma.

Yojimbo (1961-Japanese, dubbed) 110m. **** D: Akira Kurosawa. Toshiro Mifune, Eijiro Tono, Seizaburo Kawazu, Isuzu Yamada. Shattering samurai picture whose plot resembles Western; Samuari up for hire in town with two warring factors. Beautiful on all accounts.

Yokel Boy (1942) 69m. *½ D: Joseph Santley. Albert Dekker, Joan Davis, Eddie Foy, Jr., Alan Mowbray. Silly slapstick satire on movie gangster movies.

Yolanda and the Thief (1945) C-108m. **½ D: Vincente Minnelli. Fred Astaire, Lucille Bremer, Frank Morgan, Mildred Natwick, Mary Nash. Colorful thud of a film. Labored fantasy of con-artist Astaire trying to move in on princess Bremer's fortune.

You and Me (1938) 90m. *** D: Fritz Lang. Sylvia Sidney, George Raft, Robert Cummings, Roscoe Karns, Barton MacLane, Harry Carey, George E. Stone. Fine film of girl with a past (Sidney) marrying ex-con Raft, facing various problems together. Perceptive social commentary, well-played.

You Belong to Me (1941) 94m. **½ D: Wesley Ruggles. Barbara Stanwyck, Henry Fonda, Edgar Buchanan, Roger Clark, Ruth Donnelly, Melville Cooper. Brisk yarn of doctor Stanwyck and hubby Fonda who's wary of her male patients. Remade as EMERGENCY WEDDING.

You Came Along (1945) 103m. **½ D: John Farrow. Robert Cummings, Lizabeth Scott, Don DeFore, Charles Drake, Kim Hunter, Julie Bishop. Effective drama of three army buddies on bond-selling tours, their romantic involvements.

You Can't Cheat an Honest Man (1939) 76m. ***½ D: George Marshall. W. C. Fields, Edgar Bergen,

Constance Moore, James Bush, Mary Forbes, Thurston Hall. Fields (as Larson E. Whipsnade) runs circus, with interference from Bergen and Charlie McCarthy in frantic nonsense comedy, notch below other Fields romps but still hilarious.

You Can't Get Away With Murder (1939) 78m. **½ D: Lewis Seiler. Humphrey Bogart, Billy Halop, Gale Page, John Litel, Henry Travers, Joe Sawyer. Average but well-acted crime tale of young Halop teaming with gangster Bogart, taking rap with him in Sing Sing.

You Can't Have Everything (1937) 99m. *** D: Norman Taurog. Alice Faye, Ritz Bros., Don Ameche, Charles Winninger, Tony Martin, Louisé Hovick (Gypsy Rose Lee). Good show-biz musical as Faye writes drama which only succeeds as musical. Ritz Bros. have good material, Louis Prima adds music.

You Can't Run Away from It (1956) C-95m. ** D: Dick Powell. June Allyson, Jack Lemmon, Charles Bickford, Paul Gilbert, Jim Backus, Stubby Kaye, Henny Youngman. Slight musical remake of IT HAPPENED ONE NIGHT. Lemmon as reporter, Allyson a madcap heiress.

You Can't Take It with You (1938) 120m. ***½ D: Frank Capra. Jean Arthur, Lionel Barrymore, James Stewart, Edward Arnold, Mischa Auer, Ann Miller, Spring Byington. Engaging film of George Kaufman-Moss Hart play about eccentric family unable to conform to normal life when confronted by it.

You for Me (1952) 71m. **½ D: Don Weis. Peter Lawford, Jane Greer, Gig Young, Paula Corday, Elaine Stewart. Unpretentious romantic comedy with Greer as the well-intentioned nurse involved with a variety of suitors.

You Gotta Stay Happy (1948) 100m. **½ D: H. C. Potter. Joan Fontaine, James Stewart, Eddie Albert, Roland Young, Willard Parker. OK comedy about millionairess who runs off on wedding night to find new marriage. Could have been much better.

You Know What Sailors Are (1953-British) 89m. ** D: Ken Annakin. Akim Tamiroff, Donald Sinden, Sarah Lawson, Naunton Wayne. Attempted cold-war spoof of British navy officer, jokingly tell cohorts that salvaged scrap is a new secret weapon.

You Never Can Tell (1951) 78m. **½ D: Lou Breslow. Dick Powell, Peggy Dow, Charles Drake, Joyce Holden. Sometimes amusing fantasy of a murdered dog returning to earth in form of a human (Powell) to find his killer.

You Only Live Once (1937) 86m. *** D: Fritz Lang. Sylvia Sidney, Henry Fonda, William Gargan, Barton MacLane, Jean Dixon, Jerome Cowan, Margaret Hamilton, Ward Bond, Guinn Williams. Dated, but beautiful, sensitive film of escaped convict Fonda and devoted girl Sidney fleeing from police; superb direction and acting.

You Said a Mouthful (1932) 75m. *** D: Lloyd Bacon. Joe E. Brown, Ginger Rogers, Preston Foster, Guinn Williams, Sheila Terry, Selmer Jackson. One of Brown's best vehicles, about inventor of unsinkable bathing suit; Rogers is his vivacious leading lady.

You Were Meant for Me (1948) 92m. *** D: Lloyd Bacon. Jeanne Crain, Dan Dailey, Oscar Levant, Barbara Lawrence, Selena Royle. Nice combination of musical score and script of girl who marries band leader; their experiences in Depression are basis of film.

You Were Never Lovelier (1942) 97m. ***½ D: William A. Seiter. Fred Astaire, Rita Hayworth, Adolphe Menjou, Leslie Brooks, Adele Mara, Xavier Cugat. Astaire pursuing Hayworth via matchmaking father Menjou becomes lilting musical with such songs as title tune, "Dearly Beloved," "I'm Old-Fashioned."

You'll Never Get Rich (1941) 88m. ***½ D: Sidney Lanfield. Fred Astaire, Rita Hayworth, John Hubbard, Robert Benchley, Osa Massen, Frieda Inescort, Guinn Williams. Delicious musicomedy has Astaire drafted at inconvenient time, but show he's doing still goes on, and he manages to get Hayworth too. Cole Porter score includes "So Near and Yet So Far."

Young and Dangerous (1957) 78m. ** D: William Claxton. Mark Damon, Edward Binns, Lili Gentle, Ann Doran, Connie Stevens. Damon, a footloose youth, turns respectable for love of a nice girl. The usual.

Young and Wild (1958) 69m. *½ D: William Witney. Gene Evans, Scott Marlowe, Carolyn Kearney, Robert Arthur. Trashy account of thrill-seeking teenagers on the loose with a stolen car.

Young and Willing (1943) 82m. **½ D: Edward H. Griffith. William Holden, Eddie Bracken, Barbara Britton, James Brown, Martha O'Driscoll, Robert Benchley, Susan Hayward. Perennial summer-stock comedy OUT OF THE FRYING PAN becomes naive but zany comedy of show biz hopefuls trying to make good.

Young at Heart (1954) C-117m. *** D: Gordon Douglas. Doris Day, Frank Sinatra, Gig Young, Ethel Barrymore, Dorothy Malone. Musical remake of FOUR DAUGHTERS with Sinatra romancing Day amid much tear-shedding. Slickly done.

Young Bess (1953) C-112m. *** D: George Sidney. Jean Simmons, Charles Laughton, Deborah Kerr, Stewart Granger, Cecil Kellaway, Leo G. Carroll. Splashy costumer with Simmons as Elizabeth I; Laughton repeating role of Henry VIII. Fine cast does quite well in historical setting.

Young Captives, The (1959) 61m. ** D: Irvin Kershner. Steven Marlo, Tom Selden, Luana Patten, Ed Nelson, Joan Granville. Lurid melodrama of newly-weds involved with psychopathic killer.

Young Cassidy (1965) C-110m. *** D: Jack Cardiff, John Ford. Rod Taylor, Julie Christie, Maggie Smith, Flora Robson, Michael Redgrave, Edith Evans, Jack MacGowran. Taylor's best role to date as the earthy intellect Sean O'Casey, set in 1910 Dublin, filled with atmosphere and fine supporting players.

Young Daniel Boone (1950) 71m. *½ D: Reginald LeBorg. David Bruce, Kristine Miller, Mary Treen, Don Beddoe. Programmer adventure involving historical figure in conflict with Indians and settlers.

Young Dillinger (1965) 102m. **½ D: Terry O. Morse. Nick Adams, Mary Ann Mobley, Robert Conrad, John Ashley, Victor Buono, John Hoyt, Reed Hadley. Adams gives force to chronicle of gangster John Dillinger, his rise and seemingly inevitable fall; sufficient gunplay.

Young Dr. Kildare (1938) 81m. D: Harold S. Bucquet. Lew Ayres, Lionel Barrymore, Lynne Carver, Nat Pendleton, Jo Ann Sayers, Samuel S. Hinds. SEE: Dr. Kildare series.

Young Doctors, The (1961) 100m. *** D: Phil Karlson. Fredric March, Ben Gazzara, Dick Clark, Eddie Albert, Ina Balin, Aline MacMahon. Sturdy cast uplifts soaper set in large city hospital.

Young Don't Cry, The (1957) 89m. ** D: Alfred L. Werker. Sal Mineo, James Whitmore, J. Carrol Naish, Paul Carr. OK drama of loner youth Mineo who takes pity on an escaped murderer.

Young Guns, The (1956) 84m. ** D: Albert Band. Russ Tamblyn, Gloria Talbott, Perry Lopez, Scott Marlowe. Routine account of Tamblyn trying to erase everyone's memory of gunslinger father so he can live peaceful life.

Young Guns of Texas (1962) C-78m. **½ D: Maury Dexter. James Mitchum, Alan Ladd, Jody McCrea, Chill Wills. Second generation of movie stars perform satisfactorily in account of gold and girl hunt in old West, tied in with Indian raid.

Young Hellions SEE: **High School Confidential**.

Young Ideas (1943) 77m. *½ D: Jules Dassin. Susan Peters, Herbert Marshall, Mary Astor, Elliott Reid, Richard Carlson. Dismal comedy about writer who disappears and shows up later at resort spot, married to man her family considers unsuitable.

Young In Heart, The (1938) 90m. ***½ D: Richard Wallace. Janet Gaynor, Douglas Fairbanks, Jr., Paulette Goddard, Roland Young, Billie Burke, Minnie Dupree, Richard Carlson. Refreshing comedy about wacky family of con-artists going straight under influence of unsuspecting Dupree.

Young Jesse James (1960) 73m. *½ D: William Claxton. Ray Stricklyn, Willard Parker, Merry Anders, Robert Dix, Emile Meyer, Jacklyn O'Donnell. Title tells all in this routine oater.

Young Land, The (1959) C-89m. **½

D: Ted Tetzlaff. Pat Wayne, Yvonne Craig, Dennis Hopper, Dan O'Herlihy, Cliff Ketchum. Sincere Western of pre-Mexican war Texas.

Young Lions, The (1958) 167m. ***½ D: Edward Dmytryk. Marlon Brando, Montgomery Clift, Dean Martin, Hope Lange, Barbara Rush, Maximilian Schell, May Britt. One of all-time best WW2 studies, based on Irvin Shaw novel. Martin and Clift, U.S. soldiers, Brando a confused Nazi officer; effectively photographed, with Hugo Friedhofer's fine score.

Young Lovers, The (1964) 105m. ** D: Samuel Goldwyn, Jr. Peter Fonda, Nick Adams, Sharon Hugueny, Deborah Walley, Kent Smith. Amateurish, meandering drama of college youths involved in romance.

Young Man with a Horn (1950) 112m. *** D: Michael Curtiz. Kirk Douglas, Lauren Bacall, Doris Day, Juano Hernandez, Hoagy Carmichael, Mary Beth Hughes. Effective drama of trumpet-player Douglas compulsively drawn to music, with Bacall the bad girl, Day the wholesome one.

Young Man with Ideas (1952) 84m. **½ D: Mitchell Leisen. Glenn Ford, Ruth Roman, Denise Darcel, Nina Foch, Mary Wickes. Idealistic lawyer Ford overcomes all temptations in quest to move his family to California.

Young Mr. Lincoln (1939) 100m. ***½ D: John Ford. Henry Fonda, Alice Brady, Marjorie Weaver, Donald Meek, Richard Cromwell, Eddie Quillan, Milburn Stone, Ward Bond, Francis Ford. Fine Ford Americana with Abraham Lincoln (Fonda) facing years of struggle as a beginning lawyer in the 1800s. Brady lends fine support.

Young Mr. Pitt, The (1941-British) 103m. **½ D: Carol Reed. Robert Donat, Robert Morley, Phyllis Calvert, John Mills, Max Adrian. Long, only occasionally moving historical drama of young British prime minister during Napoleonic era; thinly veiled WW2 morale-booster.

Young One, The (1960-Mexican, dubbed) 96m. *½ D: Luis Bunuel. Zachary Scott, Bernie Hamilton, Key Meersman, Crahan Denton. Turgid melodramatics with Scott keeping Meersman, conflicting with a Negro musician on the run who comes to their deserted island.

Young People (1940) 78m. ** D: Alan Dwan. Shirley Temple, Jack Oakie, Charlotte Greenwood, Arleen Whelan, George Montgomery, Kathleen Howard. Show-biz team Oakie and Greenwood raise orphaned Shirley in this weak musical, a later and lesser Temple vehicle. Songs: "Fifth Avenue."

Young Philadelphians, The (1959) 136m. *** D: Vincent Sherman. Paul Newman, Barbara Rush, Alexis Smith, Brian Keith, Diane Brewster, Billie Burke, John Williams, Robert Vaughn, Otto Kruger, Adam West. Newman and Rush have memorable roles as poor lawyer who schemes to the top, and society girl he hopes to win; Vaughn is army buddy Newman defends on murder charge, Smith quite good as frustrated wife of attorney Kruger.

Young Racers, The (1963) C-87m. ** D: Roger Corman. Mark Damon, William Campbell, Patrick Magee, Luana Anders, Robert Campbell. Juvenile nonsense about sports car racing involving ex-racer turned expose writer, trying to do a book on the sport.

Young Savages, The (1961) 110m. *** D: John Frankenheimer. Burt Lancaster, Dina Merrill, Shelley Winters, Telly Savalas, Chris Robinson, Pilar Seurat, Milton Selzer. Lancaster is idealistic D.A. battling all odds to see justice done in streetgang slaying; at times brutal, too often pat. Based on Evan Hunter novel A MATTER OF CONVICTION.

Young Stranger, The (1957) 84m. *** D: John Frankenheimer. James MacArthur, Kim Hunter, James Daly, James Gregory, Marian Seldes. Evenly-paced, thoughtful study of juvenile delinquency among respected upper class; sincerely acted by all.

Young Tom Edison (1940) 82m. *** D: Norman Taurog. Mickey Rooney, Fay Bainter, George Bancroft, Virginia Weidler, Eugene Pallette, Victor Kilian. Inventor's early life depicted with flair by effective Rooney, who could tone down when he had to; followed by Spencer Tracy's EDISON THE MAN.

Young Warriors, The (1967) C-93m. ** D: John Peyser. James Drury,

Steve Carlson, Jonathan Daly, Robert Pine, Michael Stanwood. Cliched WW2 yarn filled with Universal Pictures contract players; loosely derived from Richard Matheson novel.

Young Widow (1946) 100m. ** D: Edwin L. Marin. Jane Russell, Marie Wilson, Louis Hayward, Faith Domergue, Kent Taylor, Penny Singleton, Cora Witherspoon. Soap-opera is not Russell's forte and she can't support teary WW2 tale of woman who can't forget her late husband.

Young Wives Tale (1951-British) 78m. **1/2 D: Henry Cass. Joan Greenwood, Nigel Patrick, Audrey Hepburn, Derek Farr. Comedy of situations deriving from post-war housing shortage and fabricated mistaken relationships.

Youngblood Hawke (1964) 137m. **1/2 D: Delmer Daves. James Franciscus, Suzanne Pleshette, Mary Astor, Eva Gabor, Genevieve Page, Kent Smith, Mildred Dunnock, Lee Bowman. Trivial but somehow engrossing account of southern writer who becomes N.Y.C. success, confronted by a myriad of loves; Astor comes off well as the Broadway star. Edward Andrews has fine role as acid literary critic.

Younger Brothers, The (1949) C-77m. **1/2 D: Edin L. Marin. Wayne Morris, Janis Paige, Bruce Bennett, Geraldine Brooks, Robert Hutton, Alan Hale, Fred Clark. OK Western of notorious Younger brothers and the incident that drives them to renewed violence and terror.

Youngest Profession, The (1943) 82m. **1/2 D: Edward Buzzell. Lana Turner, Greer Garson, Walter Pidgeon, Robert Taylor, William Powell, Virginia Weidler, Edward Arnold, Jean Porter. Weidler and Porter are incurable autograph hounds in innocent little film with many MGM guest stars puffing up slight vehicle.

Youngest Spy, The SEE: **My Name is Ivan.**

Your Cheatin' Heart (1964) 99m. *** D: Gene Nelson. George Hamilton, Susan Oliver, Red Buttons, Arthur O'Connell, Rex Ingram. Hamilton's best role to date, as the country-western singer Hank Williams who couldn't cope with fame on the ole opry circuit; songs dubbed by Hank Williams, Jr. Oliver most effective as Hank's wife.

Your Past is Showing (1958-British) 87m. **1/2 D: Mario Zampi. Terry-Thomas, Peter Sellers, Peggy Mount, Shirley Eaton. Droll hi-jinks of a strange grouping of folks brought together to rid themselves of the editor of a smut-expose magazine.

Your Turn, Darling (1963-French; dubbed) 93m. ** D: Bernard Borderie. Eddie Constantine, Henri Cogan, Gaia Germani, Elga Andersen. Constantine is Lemmy Caution, U.S. secret agent involved with gang of spies; lumbering account.

You're a Big Boy Now (1966) C-96m. ***1/2 D: Francis Ford Coppola. Elizabeth Hartman, Peter Kastner, Geraldine Page, Julie Harris, Rip Torn, Michael Dunn, Tony Bill, Karen Black. Beguiling, way-out film of young man with over-protective parents learning about life from callous young actress Hartman. Far-out film will not appeal to everyone, but acting is marvelous with Dolph Sweet hilarious as tough cop. Location filming in NY adds to film too.

You're a Sweetheart (1937) 96m. ** D: David Butler. Alice Faye, George Murphy, Ken Murray, Andy Devine, Charles Winninger, Donald Meek, Bobby Watson. Routine musical with go-getter Murphy dreaming up publicity stunt for show which stars Faye. Title song became a standard.

You're in the Army Now (1941) 79m. ** D: Lewis Seiler. Jimmy Durante, Phil Silvers, Jane Wyman, Regis Toomey, Donald MacBride, George Meeker, Joe Sawyer. Rather obvious service comedy with Durante and Silvers trying hard to rise above their material. Some funny scenes, with finale lifted from Chaplin's THE GOLD RUSH.

You're in the Navy Now (1951) 93m. ** D: Henry Hathaway. Gary Cooper, Jane Greer, Millard Mitchell, Eddie Albert, Lee Marvin, Jack Webb. Flat naval comedy set in WW2 with Cooper commanding a dumb crew on the U.S.S. Teakettle (the ship is outfitted with a steam engine).

You're my Everything (1949) C-94m. *** D: Walter Lang. Dan Dailey, Anne Baxter, Anne Revere, Stanley Ridges, Buster Keaton, Alan Mowbray, Selena Royle. Musical runs hot and cold, spoofing Hollywood of the 20s and 30s, but bogging down in slurpy romance; worthwhile for first half.

You're Never Too Young (1955) C-102m. **½ D: Norman Taurog. Dean Martin, Jerry Lewis, Diana Lynn, Raymond Burr, Nina Foch, Veda Ann Borg. OK remake of MAJOR & THE MINOR with Jerry disguised as 12-year old, involved in jewel robbery.

You're Not so Tough (1940) 71m. D: Joe May. Nan Gray, Henry Armetta, Rosina Galli, Billy Halop, Huntz Hall, Gabriel Dell. See: BOWERY BOYS series.

You're Only Young Once (1938) 78m. D: George B. Seitz. Lewis Stone, Cecilia Parker, Mickey Rooney, Fay Holden, Frank Craven, Ann Rutherford, Eleanor Lynn. See: ANDY HARDY series.

You're Telling Me (1934) 66m. *** D: Erle C. Kenton. W. C. Fields, Joan Marsh, Buster Crabbe, Adrienne Ames, Kathleen Howard. Despite a worthless romantic subplot and some "serious" moments, this comedy of would-be inventor Fields has many hilarious scenes (wait till you see his key-hole finder for helpless drunks). Not top-drawer W.C., but even a little of him is worth seeing.

Zamba (1949) 75m. *½ D: William Berke. Jon Hall, June Vincent, George Cooper, Jane Nigh, George O'Hanlon. Juvenile adventure story of boy raised by gorillas; rough going.

Zarak (1957-British) C-99m. **½ D: Terence Young. Victor Mature, Michael Wilding, Anita Ekberg, Bernard Miles, Finlay Currie. Hokum set in India with Mature the head of native outlaws, Wilding the British officer sent to get him.

Zebra in the Kitchen (1965) C-93m. **½ D: Ivan Tors. Jay North, Martin Milner, Andy Devine, Joyce Meadows, Jim Davis, Dorothy Green. Wholesome family fare of young North involved with wild pets and the city zoo's attempt to keep its inmates locked up.

Zero Hour! (1957) 81m. **½ D: Hall Bartlett. Dana Andrews, Linda Darnell, Sterling Hayden, Elroy Hirsch. Effective suspenser of passenger plane and effect of potential disaster when pilots are felled by ptomaine poisoning.

Ziegfeld Follies (1946) C-110m. **½ D: Vincente Minnelli. William Powell, Judy Garland, Lucille Ball, Fred Astaire, Fanny Brice, Lena Horne, Red Skelton, Victor Moore, Virginia O'Brien, Cyd Charisse, Gene Kelly, Edward Arnold, Esther Williams. Variable all-star film introduced by Powell as Ziegfeld in heaven. Highlights are Brice-Cronyn sketch, Astaire-Kelly dance, Moore-Arnold comedy routine, Skelton and Horne's solos, Garland's "The Interview."

Ziegfeld Girl (1941) 131m. *** D: Robert Z. Leonard. James Stewart, Judy Garland, Hedy Lamarr, Lana Turner, Tony Martin, Jackie Cooper, Ian Hunter. Thin but entertaining musical of showman Stewart and glamorous showgirls. Songs: "I'm Always Chasing Rainbows," "Whispering," and Busby Berkeley number "You Stepped Out Of A Dream."

Zombies of Mora-Tau (1957) 70m. *½ D: Edward L. Cahn. Gregg Palmer, Allison Hayes, Autumn Russell, Joel Ashley. Juvenile hodge-podge about zombie guardianship over diamond mine.

Zombies on Broadway (1945) 68m. ** D: Albert D'Agostino. Walter Keller, Wally Brown, Alan Carney, Bela Lugosi, Anne Jeffreys. RKO Pictures programmer with asset of Lugosi, low-jinks of Carney-Brown as debit. P.R. men palm off Bela as genuine voodoo victim.

Zorba the Greek (1964) 146m. ***½ D: Michael Cacoyannis. Anthony Quinn, Alan Bates, Irene Papas, Lila Kedrova, George Foundas. Brooding, flavorful rendering of Kazantzakis novel. Quinn is zesty in title role of earthy peasant, Bates his intellectual British cohort. Kedrova won Oscar as dying protitute.

Zorro (1961-Spanish, dubbed) C-90m. **½ D: Joaquin Luis Romero Marchent. Frank Latimore, Mary Anderson, Ralph Marsch, Howard Vernon. Foreign-made Western with salty flavor of old California; Latimore is appropriately zealous as Zorro.

Zorro Rides Again (1937) 68m. ** D: William Witney, John English. John Carroll, Helen Christian, Reed Howes, Duncan Renaldo, Noah Beery. Edited from vintage Republic serial, recounting adventures of Carroll in old West to help railroad; just so-so.

Zotz! (1962) 87m. ** D: William Castle. Tom Poston, Julia Meade, Jim Backus, Fred Clark. Goofy attempt at humorous chiller with Poston a teacher who gains mystical power over others.

Zulu (1964-British) C-138m. *** D: Cy Endfield. Stanley Baker, Jack Hawkins, Ulla Jacobsson, Michael Caine, Nigel Green, James Booth. Based on fact, story of handful of British soldiers fighting thousands of African warriors. Good stiff upper-lip adventure.

LEONARD MALTIN

A native New Yorker who now resides in suburban Teaneck, New Jersey, Leonard Maltin has been editing and publishing *Film Fan Monthly*, a magazine for film buffs, since May of 1966. In addition to his editorial duties, he has authored over twenty detailed career articles for the publication.

Having acquired an interest in old movies at an early age, Leonard first started submitting articles to *Film Fan Monthly* when it was published in Canada in 1964, and became a regular columnist before assuming editorship two years later. In the meantime, his stories and research articles on films of the past appeared in *The Classic Film Collector* and other film-oriented publications. An annotated index of the Walt Disney films appeared in *Films in Review,* and several articles on music in the movies were published in *Record World.*

A major article on the best and worst movies on late-night television appeared in the December, 1968, issue of *Esquire.* Most recently, Leonard prepared and co-hosted a series of programs on the silent film for New York's educational television station, WNDT. He is currently a film critic for *Washington Square Journal* and news editor of *Greater Amusements,* and is preparing a book on movie comedy teams over the years.